Employment Class and Collective Actions

Proceedings of the New York University
56th Annual Conference on Labor

KLUWER LAW INTERNATIONAL

EMPLOYMENT CLASS AND COLLECTIVE ACTIONS

Proceedings of the New York University 56th Annual Conference on Labor

Edited by:
David Sherwyn

Series Editor:
Samuel Estreicher

Wolters Kluwer
Law & Business

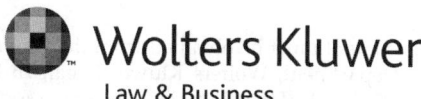

AUSTIN BOSTON CHICAGO NEW YORK THE NETHERLANDS

Published by:
Kluwer Law International
P.O. Box 316
2400 AH Alphen aan den Rijn
The Netherlands
Website: www.kluwerlaw.com

Sold and distributed in North, Central and South America by:
Aspen Publishers, Inc.
7201 McKinney Circle
Frederick, MD 21704
United States of America
Email: customer.care@aspenpubl.com

Sold and distributed in all other countries by:
Turpin Distribution Services Ltd.
Stratton Business Park
Pegasus Drive, Biggleswade
Bedfordshire SG18 8TQ
United Kingdom
Email: kluwerlaw@turpin-distribution.com

Printed on acid-free paper.

ISBN 978-90-411-2505-7

© 2009 Kluwer Law International BV, The Netherlands (Except chapters: 2-9, 13-14, 19, 21)

All rights reserved. No part of this publication may be reproduced, stored in a retrieval system, or transmitted in any form or by any means, electronic, mechanical, photocopying, recording or otherwise, without written permission from the publisher.

Permission to use this content must be obtained from the copyright owner. Please apply to Permissions Department, Wolters Kluwer Legal, 76 Ninth Avenue, 7th floor, New York, NY 10011-5201, USA. E-mail: permissions@kluwerlaw.com.

Printed in Great Britain.

Summary of Contents

Center for Labor and Employment Law at
New York University School of Law ... xxxi
Editor's Preface ... xxxiii

Chapter 1
The Price of Discrimination: The Nature of Class Action Employment Discrimination Litigation and Its Effects ... 1
Michael Selmi

Chapter 2
Measuring the Value of Class and Collective Action Employment Settlements: A Preliminary Assessment ... 107
Samuel Estreicher and Kristina Yost

Chapter 3
Class and Representative Actions ... 139
Richard T. Seymour and John F. Aslin

Chapter 4
Fighting to Keep Employment Discrimination Class Actions Alive: How *Allison v. Citgo*'s Predomination Requirement Threatens to Undermine Title VII Enforcement ... 203
Suzette M. Malveaux

Chapter 5
The Uncertain Future of Title VII Class Actions after the Civil Rights Act of 1991 ... 241
Daniel F. Piar

Chapter 6
**A Classless Act: The Ninth Circuit's Erroneous Class
Certification in *Dukes v. Wal-Mart, Inc.*** 287
Aaron B. Lauchheimer

Chapter 7
**Too Many Riches? *Dukes v. Wal-Mart* and the Efficacy
of Monolithic Class Actions** 329
Rachel M. Pickens

Chapter 8
**The Possibility of Avoiding Discrimination:
Considering Compliance and Liability** 353
Melissa Hart

Chapter 9
Preclusion in Class Action Litigation 383
Tobias Barrington Wolff

Chapter 10
**Opt-In Class Actions: Collective Litigation under
the FLSA, ADEA, and EPA** 499
Mark S. Dichter

Chapter 11
**Not without Class: Test Cases in Lieu of Class
Certification as a Paradigm for Litigating Multi-plaintiff
Harassment Cases** 549
Steven Arenson and Craig J. Ackermann

Chapter 12
'Pattern or Practice' Discrimination Litigation 581
Michael Delikat

Chapter 13
Disability, Disparate Impact, and Class Actions 593
Michael Ashley Stein and Michael E. Waterstone

SUMMARY OF CONTENTS

Chapter 14
Collective and Class Action Issues under the Fair
Labor Standards Act and State-Based Wages Statutes   663
Adam T. Klein, Nantiya Ruan, and Sean Farhang

Chapter 15
Working with the Equal Employment Opportunity
Commission   679
Wayne N. Outten and Piper Hoffman

Chapter 16
Green Tree v. Bazzle in the Supreme Court: 'How to
Succeed in Blocking Class Actions in Arbitration
without Really Saying So'   687
Daniel B. Edelman

Chapter 17
Arbitration Agreements, Unconscionability, and Bans
on Class Actions: Dueling Magic Wands? The California
Experience   713
Henry D. Lederman

Chapter 18
When Is Cost an Unlawful Barrier to Alternative
Dispute Resolution? The Ever Green Tree of Mandatory
Employment Arbitration   731
Michael H. LeRoy and Peter Feuille

Chapter 19
Arbitration and the Individuation Critique   807
W. Mark C. Weidemaier

Chapter 20
Building an Internal Defense Against Class
Action Lawsuits: Human Resources Practices Audits   867
*G. Roger King, Jeffrey D. Winchester, Lori A. Clary,
and Kimberly J. Potter*

EMPLOYMENT CLASS AND COLLECTIVE ACTIONS

Chapter 21
'Statistical Dueling' with Unconventional Weapons:
What Courts Should Know about Experts in Employment
Discrimination Class Actions 893
William T. Bielby and Pamela Coukos

Chapter 22
Symposium: Emerging Issues in Class Action Law:
Backdoor Federalization 941
Samuel Issacharoff and Catherine M. Sharkey

Chapter 23
From 'Predominance' to 'Resolvability': A New
Approach to Regulating Class Actions 1041
Allan Erbsen

Table of Contents

Center for Labor and Employment Law at New York University
School of Law   xxxi
Editor's Preface   xxxiii

Chapter 1
The Price of Discrimination: The Nature of Class Action
Employment Discrimination Litigation and Its Effects   1
Michael Selmi

1.1	Introduction		1
1.2	The Empirical Study		6
	1.2.1	The Hypothesis	6
	1.2.2	The Data	8
	1.2.3	The Statistical Analysis	13
		1.2.3.1 The Results	15
		1.2.3.2 Explaining the Statistical Analysis	19
1.3	Do the Lawsuits Produce Meaningful Change? Three Case Studies		25
	1.3.1	*Texaco*: The Public Relations Model	26
		1.3.1.1 The Lawsuit and the Tapes	26
		1.3.1.2 Texaco's Progress	34
	1.3.2	*Home Depot*: The Recalcitrance Model	40
		1.3.2.1 The Case	41
		1.3.2.2 The Aftermath	47
		1.3.2.3 Denny's: The Reform Model	51
		1.3.2.3.1 The Cases	51
		1.3.2.3.2 Denny's Reform Efforts	57
1.4	The Benefits and Effects of Class Action Litigation		61
	1.4.1	The Plaintiffs: Do They Come out Ahead?	63

		1.4.1.1	Structural Reforms after the Civil Rights Act of 1991	64
		1.4.1.2	Monetary Relief	66
		1.4.1.3	Diversity Initiatives	71
	1.4.2	Corporations and Class Action Litigation		73
		1.4.2.1	The Nature of Discrimination and its Reform	74
		1.4.2.2	The Deterrence Hypothesis: Do the Lawsuits Deter Discrimination?	80
		1.4.2.3	Will the Market Drive out Discrimination?	87
	1.4.3	Reforming the Process		91
		1.4.3.1	Higher Damages Should Be Available	92
		1.4.3.2	Restoring Public Accountability to Class Action Litigation	95
1.5	Conclusion			105

Chapter 2
Measuring the Value of Class and Collective Action Employment Settlements: A Preliminary Assessment   107
Samuel Estreicher and Kristina Yost

2.1	Introduction		107
2.2	Procedure for Settlement		110
2.3	Methodology		111
2.4	Findings		114
	2.4.1	General Findings	114
	2.4.2	Findings by Type of Claim	122
		2.4.2.1 Discrimination Claims	122
		2.4.2.2 FLSA and State Wage-Hour Claims	124
		2.4.2.3 ERISA Claims	128
		2.4.2.4 Other Claims	129
	2.4.3	Observations about Attorney Fees	130
	2.4.4	Findings by State of Settlement	134
	2.4.5	A Brief Comparison of Our Results to Recent Studies of Individual Recoveries in Arbitration	136
2.5	Conclusion		136

Chapter 3
Class and Representative Actions 139
Richard T. Seymour and John F. Aslin

3.1	Introduction	139
3.2	Necessity of Following Class Procedures before Granting Class Relief	140
3.3	Rule 23 Class Actions	141
	3.3.1 Suitability of the Issues for Class Treatment	141
	3.3.2 Suitability of the Class Representative	142
	3.3.3 Discretion to Consider Factors Not Specified in Rule 23	143
	3.3.4 Numerosity under Rule 23(a)(1)	145
	3.3.5 Commonality under Rule 23(a)(2)	145
	3.3.6 Typicality under Rule 23(a)(3)	149
	3.3.7 Adequacy of Representation under Rule 23(a)(4)	150
	3.3.8 Acting and Refusing to Act on Common Grounds under Rule 23(b)(2)	153
	3.3.9 Predominance of Class Questions and Superiority of Class Treatment under Rule 23(b)(3)	154
	3.3.10 'Hybrid' Class Actions under Rules 23(b)(2) and 23(b)(3)	156
	3.3.11 Adequacy of Notice under Rule 23(e)	156
3.4	Settlement Classes	157
3.5	Changes in Class Certification and Definition	158
3.6	Individualized Relief for Class Members	158
3.7	Class Actions Seeking Common-Law Damages	162
3.8	Opt-Outs from Rule 23 Class Actions	173
3.9	Representative Actions	173
3.10	Rule 23(f) Appeals of Decisions Granting or Denying Class Certification	176
3.11	Appealability of Class Determination	179
3.12	Judicial Approval of Class Settlements	179
3.13	Conclusiveness of Class Settlements, Decrees, and Decisions on the Merits	181
3.14	Changes in the Class Action Rules	182

EMPLOYMENT CLASS AND COLLECTIVE ACTIONS

Chapter 4
Fighting to Keep Employment Discrimination Class Actions Alive: How *Allison v. Citgo*'s Predomination Requirement Threatens to Undermine Title VII Enforcement   203
Suzette M. Malveaux

4.1	Introduction	203
4.2	The Development of the Circuit Conflict over the Interpretation of Rule 23's Predomination Requirement after the Enactment of the Civil Rights Act of 1991	206
	4.2.1 The Central Role of Rule 23(b)(2) Certification in Civil Rights Enforcement	206
	4.2.2 The Impact of the Civil Rights Act of 1991	209
	4.2.3 *Allison v. Citgo*	209
	4.2.4 *Robinson v. Metro-North*	213
	4.2.5 Hybrid Approaches to Class Certification	214
	4.2.6 The Supreme Court's Due Process Concerns	216
4.3	The Restrictive Interpretation of the Predomination Requirement Threatens to Undermine Civil Rights Enforcement	217
	4.3.1 Fewer Employment Discrimination Class Actions Will Be Certified	218
	4.3.2 Fewer Monetary Damages Will Be Awarded to Those Who Deserve Them	219
	4.3.3 Plaintiffs Will Have to Meet the More Rigorous and Costly Certification Standards of Rule 23(b)(3)	228
4.4	The *Robinson* Ad Hoc Balancing Test Is a Superior Predomination Test for the Enforcement of Title VII	231
4.5	The Impact of Recent Legislation on Preventing Potential Judicial Abuse of Class Certification	234
	4.5.1 Amended Rule 23	235
	4.5.2 The Class Action Fairness Act of 2005	237
4.6	Conclusion	238

TABLE OF CONTENTS

Chapter 5
The Uncertain Future of Title VII Class Actions after the Civil Rights Act of 1991 241
Daniel F. Piar

5.1	Introduction		241
5.2	Title VII and the Civil Rights Act of 1991		242
5.3	The Rule 23 Requirements for Class Actions		245
5.4	Title VII Class Actions before the Civil Rights Act of 1991		249
5.5	Title VII Class Actions after the Civil Rights Act of 1991		250
	5.5.1	The 23(b)(2) Class: The Problems of Predominance and Opt-Out Rights	252
		5.5.1.1 Rule 23(b)(2) and Money Damages	252
		5.5.1.2 The *Allison v. Citgo* Approach	252
		5.5.1.3 The Allison Dissent and the Issue of Back Pay	254
		5.5.1.4 Other Appellate Views: *Jefferson v. Ingersoll International, Inc.* and *Lemon v. International Union of Operating Engineers*	256
		5.5.1.5 Other Post-1991 Cases Restricting 23(b)(2) Certification	258
		5.5.1.6 Post-1991 Cases Granting 23(b)(2) Certification	259
		5.5.1.7 Forgoing Money Damages: *Zachery v. Texaco*	261
		5.5.1.8 The End of the 23(b)(2) Title VII Class?	262
	5.5.2	23(b)(3) Classes – Commonality, Manageability, and Negative Value	263
		5.5.2.1 Commonality	263
		5.5.2.2 Manageability	267
		5.5.2.3 Negative Value	269
	5.5.3	Procedural and Constitutional Problems of Bifurcation and Partial Certification	270
		5.5.3.1 Procedural Issues	270
		5.5.3.2 The Integrity of Rule 23	274
		5.5.3.3 Constitutional Issues	275
		5.5.3.4 The Allison Denial of Rehearing	279

		5.5.4 The Problem of the Blackmail Class	281
5.6	For Better or for Worse?		283
5.7	Conclusion		285

Chapter 6
A Classless Act: The Ninth Circuit's Erroneous Class Certification in *Dukes v. Wal-Mart, Inc.* 287
Aaron B. Lauchheimer

6.1	Introduction		287
6.2	*Dukes v. Wal-Mart*: An In-Depth Overview		292
6.3	Rule 23		295
	6.3.1	An Overview	295
	6.3.2	Commonality	297
	6.3.3	Typicality	299
6.4	The Court's Decision in *Dukes v. Wal-Mart*		302
	6.4.1	The Finding of Commonality	302
	6.4.2	The Typicality Finding	309
6.5	The Court's Use of Expert Witnesses and the Lack of a *Daubert* Analysis		313
6.6	The Court's Decision Regarding Title VII Issues		317
6.7	Blackmail Settlements		320
6.8	A Proposed Guide for Certifying Employment Class Actions		323
6.9	Conclusion		326

Chapter 7
Too Many Riches? *Dukes v. Wal-Mart* and the Efficacy of Monolithic Class Actions 329
Rachel M. Pickens

7.1	Introduction		329
	7.1.1	Addendum	331
7.2	Class Actions Generally		331
	7.2.1	Rule 23	334
	7.2.2	Class Action Manageability	337
	7.2.3	Certification Decisions	339
7.3	The Case at Bar: *Dukes v. Wal-Mart*		341
7.4	The Sheer Size of the Proposed Class Is Not Determinative of the Efficacy of the Action		347

7.5	*Dukes v. Wal-Mart* Should Be Maintained under Rule 23	348
7.6	Conclusion	352

Chapter 8
The Possibility of Avoiding Discrimination: Considering Compliance and Liability 353
Melissa Hart

8.1	Introduction		353
8.2	Litigation Trends: *Dukes* and Other Challenges to Entrenched Stereotypes		355
	8.2.1	Statistical Disparities, Centralized Policies, and Stories of Bias at Wal-Mart	356
	8.2.2	Potential for Challenging Culturally Entrenched Stereotypes	362
8.3	Avoiding Litigation Liability: What Should Employers Do?		365
	8.3.1	Quotas and Objective Testing: The Defendants' Parade of Horribles	367
	8.3.2	Best Practices?: Workplace Policies that May Reduce the Negative Effects of Stereotype and Bias and Limit the Risk of Liability	369
		8.3.2.1 Advertising and Posting Positions	371
		8.3.2.2 Establishing Written Standards	372
	8.3.3	Establishing Antidiscrimination Policies and Education	374
		8.3.3.1 Monitoring and Ensuring Accountability	375
	8.3.4	What if Compliance Does Not Work?	377
8.4	Conclusion		381

Chapter 9
Preclusion in Class Action Litigation 383
Tobias Barrington Wolff

9.1	Introduction		383
9.2	Defining the Problem		390
	9.2.1	The *Cooper* Case	391
	9.2.2	Conflicts of Interest	399

		9.2.2.1	Title VII and the Civil Rights Act of 1991	401
		9.2.2.2	Tort Class Actions	408
	9.2.3	Representation and Strategic Litigation Choices		418
		9.2.3.1	Stay-in-State-Court Suits	418
		9.2.3.2	Unpled Equitable Claims	423
9.3	The Structure of Preclusion Analysis			425
	9.3.1	A Positive Law Account of Preclusion Doctrine		426
		9.3.1.1	Preclusion as a Rule of Decision	427
		9.3.1.2	The Components of Preclusion Analysis	434
		9.3.1.3	Settlement and Preclusion	442
	9.3.2	Tools of Limitation in Class Action Proceedings		446
		9.3.2.1	Constraining a Judgment's Preclusive Effect	449
			9.3.2.1.1 Constraints Relating to a Parallel Proceeding	450
			9.3.2.1.2 Constraints Relating to a Specific Cause of Action	452
			9.3.2.1.3 Constraints Relating to the Entire Action	453
		9.3.2.2	The Seventh Amendment and Reexamination	456
		9.3.2.3	Alternative Mechanisms for Addressing Preclusion Problems	464
			9.3.2.3.1 Subclasses	465
			9.3.2.3.2 Notice and Opt-Out	468
		9.3.2.4	The Incentives of Counsel and the Need for Judicial Supervision	471
9.4	Harmonizing Joinder and Preclusion Policies			473
	9.4.1	Preclusion Policies		474
	9.4.2	Sources of Law and the Rules Enabling Act		481
9.5	The Role of the Recognizing Forum			490
9.6	Conclusion			496

Chapter 10
Opt-In Class Actions: Collective Litigation under the FLSA, ADEA, and EPA 499
Mark S. Dichter

10.1 Collective Litigation under the FLSA, ADEA, and EPA 499
    10.1.1 Similarities and Differences between Class Actions and Collective Actions 500
        10.1.1.1 Class Actions under Rule 23 500
        10.1.1.2 Collective Actions under 29 U.S.C. § 216(b) 500
        10.1.1.3 The Applicability of Rule 23 to Collective Actions 501
        10.1.1.4 The Legal Differences between Rule 23 Class Actions and § 216(b) Collective Actions 502
            10.1.1.4.1 The Need to Opt-In 502
            10.1.1.4.2 Notice to Class or Collective Action Members of Dismissal of Claims 503
            10.1.1.4.3 Tolling the Statute of Limitations 504
        10.1.1.5 The Legal Similarities between Rule 23 Class Actions and § 216(b) Collective Actions 505
    10.1.2 The Three-Step Process through Which Nationwide Collective Actions Are Born 505
        10.1.2.1 The Supreme Court's Treatment of Notice in § 216(b) Actions 507
        10.1.2.2 The 'Similarly Situated' Requirement of § 216(b) 507
            10.1.2.2.1 Initially Determining 'Similarly Situated' Is a Minimal Burden 507
            10.1.2.2.2 The 'Two-Tiered' System of Similarly Situated 508
            10.1.2.2.3 A Minimal Burden, but a Burden Nonetheless 509

		10.1.2.2.4 District Courts Have Broad Discretion	511
	10.1.2.3	Discovery Permitted to Assist in the Notice Process	511
		10.1.2.3.1 Allowing Plaintiffs to Discover Names, Addresses, and Other Information about Defendant's Current and Former Employees to Support Allegations that Potential Plaintiffs Are Similarly Situated and that Notice Is Warranted	511
		10.1.2.3.2 Types of Information Found to Be Discoverable	513
		10.1.2.3.3 Discovery of Names and Addresses	513
	10.1.2.4	Approaches to Arguing in Favor of Notice	515
		10.1.2.4.1 Notice Permitted Based Solely on Class-Wide Allegations of Illegality	515
		10.1.2.4.2 Notice Permitted Based upon Allegations and Supporting Proof	516
	10.1.2.5	Arguments that Can Be Used to Oppose the Sending of Notice	516
		10.1.2.5.1 Challenges to Allegations Made without Supporting Evidence that a Potential Class Exists	517
		10.1.2.5.2 Challenges Based upon the Argument that a Representative Plaintiff is Not Similarly Situated to Putative Class Members, or because Individualized Facts Would Apply to Each Plaintiff	518

	10.1.2.5.3	Challenges Based on Geographic Factors, Such as No Evidence of Nationwide, Statewide, or Class-Wide Wrongdoing	519
	10.1.2.5.4	Challenges Based upon Factual Differences in Pay Status, Job Requirements, Duties, Departments, Etc.	522
		10.1.2.5.4.1 Limits Based upon Different Job Requirements or Duties	523
		10.1.2.5.4.2 Limits Based upon Different Pay Provisions	524
	10.1.2.5.5	Other Bases for Challenges	524
	10.1.2.5.6	Temporal Limits (Statute of Limitations) upon the Scope of Discovery or Notice	525
10.1.2.6	Other Miscellaneous Points about Notice		526
	10.1.2.6.1	Nondisclosure Agreements and the Attorney-Client Privilege	526
	10.1.2.6.2	Potentially Applicable Local Rules of Civil Procedure	527
10.1.3 Communication with Class Plaintiffs			527
10.1.3.1	Generally		527
10.1.3.2	Special Considerations Regarding Communication with Managerial Employees		530
10.1.4 FLSA Statute of Limitations			533
10.1.4.1	Two-Year Statute of Limitations for Non-willful Violations; Three-Year Statute of Limitations for Willful Violations		533
10.1.4.2	When the Statute of Limitations Runs		534
	10.1.4.2.1	Generally	534
	10.1.4.2.2	No Relation Back	534

		10.1.4.2.3	Continuing Violations	534
	10.1.4.3	Tolling the Statute of Limitations		535
		10.1.4.3.1	Tolling, Generally	535
			10.1.4.3.1.1 Conduct that May Toll the Statute	535
			10.1.4.3.1.2 Employer Conduct that Has Been Held Not to Give Rise to Tolling	536
		10.1.4.3.2	Plaintiffs' Burden	536
	10.1.4.4	Attorneys' Fees		537
		10.1.4.4.1	The General Rule	537
		10.1.4.4.2	Method(s) of Calculating Fees Generally; What Is a 'Reasonable' Fee?	537
			10.1.4.4.2.1 The 'Lodestar' Approach	537
			10.1.4.4.2.2 The 'Common Fund' Approach	537
		10.1.4.4.3	What Is Reasonable?	538
		10.1.4.4.4	Is a Settlement in an FLSA Collective Action a Common Fund?	540
10.2	Overview of FLSA Cases: An Increasing Favorite of the Plaintiffs' Bar			541
	10.2.1	Enterprise Rent-A-Car		541
	10.2.2	Chapter Albertson's		541
	10.2.3	Longs Drug Stores		542
	10.2.4	Wal-Mart		543
	10.2.5	Prudential		543
	10.2.6	Sbarro		544
	10.2.7	Paine Webber		544
	10.2.8	Dean Witter		545
	10.2.9	Saipan Class Action		545
	10.2.10	Hooters Restaurants		546
	10.2.11	Perdue Farms, Inc.		546
	10.2.12	Aetna Services, Inc.		547

Chapter 11
Not without Class: Test Cases in Lieu of Class
Certification as a Paradigm for Litigating Multi-plaintiff
Harassment Cases 549
Steven Arenson and Craig J. Ackermann

11.1	Introduction	549
11.2	Defining the Terms 'Test Cases' and 'Bellwether Trials'	553
	11.2.1 Test Case	553
	11.2.2 Bellwether Trial	554
11.3	Legal Authority Supporting Test Cases	555
11.4	Putting the Test Case Approach to Work	559
11.5	Collateral Estoppel and the Test Case Model	569
11.6	Punitive Damages and the Test Case Model	577
11.7	Enhanced Settlement Prospects under the Test Case Model	579
11.8	Conclusion	580

Chapter 12
'Pattern or Practice' Discrimination Litigation 581
Michael Delikat

12.1	Introduction	581
12.2	Origins of Pattern or Practice Theory	583
12.3	Pattern or Practice Litigation by the EEOC and Private Plaintiffs	585
12.4	Can a Pattern or Practice Theory be Asserted in Discriminatory Harassment Claims?	587

Chapter 13
Disability, Disparate Impact, and Class Actions 593
Michael Ashley Stein and Michael E. Waterstone

13.1	Introduction	593
13.2	Title VII Group-Based Discrimination Theories	598
	13.2.1 Disparate Impact Theory	599
	13.2.2 Panethnicity and Class Actions	601
	13.2.3 Judicial Erosion of Collective Action	606
13.3	The Ordinary Course of ADA Claims	611
	13.3.1 Failure to Accommodate	612

	13.3.2 Missed Potential	619
13.4	The ADA as Group-Based Discrimination	628
	13.4.1 Pandisability Theory	629
	13.4.2 The Class Action Device	638
	13.4.3 Challenging Workplace Norms	647
13.5	Conclusion	660

Chapter 14
Collective and Class Action Issues under the Fair Labor Standards Act and State-Based Wages Statutes — 663
Adam T. Klein, Nantiya Ruan, and Sean Farhang

14.1	Litigation Issues	663
	14.1.1 Representational Evidence or Sampling	663
	14.1.2 Administrative Exemption	665
	14.1.3 Class and Collective Action Certification of Wage-Hour Claims	666
	14.1.3.1 FLSA Collective Action Certification	667
	14.1.3.2 State-Law-Based Class Action Certification	667
	14.1.4 Seventh Amendment Considerations	669
14.2	Regulatory Issues	671
	14.2.1 Introduction	671
	14.2.2 Minimum Salary Bar Raised	672
	14.2.3 'Duties' Tests Loosened for White-Collar Exemptions	672
	14.2.3.1 Administrative Employees	673
	14.2.3.2 Professional Employees	674
	14.2.3.3 Executive Employees	674
	14.2.3.4 Outside-Sales People	675
	14.2.4 New USD 65,000 Rule for 'Highly Compensated Employees'	675
	14.2.5 Salary Deductions and the Salary Basis Test	676
	14.2.6 Changes in Size of Covered Populations	677
	14.2.7 Conclusion	677

TABLE OF CONTENTS

Chapter 15
Working with the Equal Employment Opportunity Commission 679
Wayne N. Outten and Piper Hoffman

15.1	Introduction	679
15.2	The EEOC's Case Selection	679
15.3	Advantages of Litigating with the EEOC	680
	15.3.1 Avoid Rule 23	680
	15.3.2 Expand the Scope of the Case	681
	15.3.3 Avoid Confidentiality Provisions	681
	15.3.4 Increase Credibility	682
	15.3.5 Invoke Fear of Uncle Sam	682
	15.3.6 Negotiate Systemic Changes	682
	15.3.7 Gain Expertise	683
	15.3.8 Increase Media Interest	683
	15.3.9 Get More Hands at No Cost	683
15.4	Disadvantages of Litigating with the EEOC	684
	15.4.1 Too Many Chefs in the Kitchen	684
	15.4.2 Government Bureaucracy	684
	15.4.3 Culture Clash	684
	15.4.4 Different Goals and Rewards	685
	15.4.5 Consensus on Settlement	685
	15.4.6 Perception of the EEOC	686
15.5	Conclusion	686

Chapter 16
***Green Tree v. Bazzle* in the Supreme Court: 'How to Succeed in Blocking Class Actions in Arbitration without Really Saying So'** 687
Daniel B. Edelman

16.1	Introduction and Summary	687
16.2	The Debate over Class Arbitration	690
16.3	The State Court Proceedings	694
16.4	The South Carolina Supreme Court Decision	697
16.5	Does the FAA Preempt Application of State Class Action Procedures to a Silent Arbitration Agreement? Does the FAA Federalize Interpretation of Arbitration Agreements?	699

EMPLOYMENT CLASS AND COLLECTIVE ACTIONS

    16.5.1 Does the FAA Preempt Disapproval of
Express Class-Action Bans Based on State
Unconscionability Law?   702
    16.5.2 Class Action Procedures Are Not Incompatible
with Arbitration   703
16.6 Conclusion   710

Chapter 17
Arbitration Agreements, Unconscionability, and Bans on Class Actions: Dueling Magic Wands? The California Experience   713
Henry D. Lederman

17.1 Introduction   713
17.2 *Green Tree Financial Corp. v. Bazzle*   714
17.3 The California Approach: Where the Agreement Is Silent   715
17.4 Where Class Action Arbitrations Are Expressly Forbidden – The Two *Discover Bank* Cases   718
17.5 The Future   728

Chapter 18
When Is Cost an Unlawful Barrier to Alternative Dispute Resolution? The Ever Green Tree of Mandatory Employment Arbitration   731
Michael H. LeRoy and Peter Feuille

18.1 Introduction   731
    18.1.1 Statement of Research Question   732
    18.1.2 Organization of This Article   736
18.2 The Growth of Mandatory Employment Arbitration   738
    18.2.1 Some Courts Refuse to Enforce Mandatory Arbitration Agreements that Impose Unfair Procedures on Employees   745
    18.2.2 Some Courts Reject or Revise Mandatory Agreements that Shift Forum Costs to Employees   747
    18.2.3 Some Courts Reject or Revise Mandatory Agreements because They View the ADR System as Flawed by Comparison to Voluntary Labor Arbitration   748

18.3	The Allocation of Costs in Arbitration		750
	18.3.1 Elements of Cost in Arbitrating Employment Disputes		750
	18.3.2 The Supreme Court's Regulation of Arbitration Costs		757
18.4	Research Literature and Methods		764
	18.4.1 Research Literature		764
	18.4.2 Research Methods		767
18.5	Empirical Results: How Federal Courts Rule on Cost-Allocation Challenges to Mandatory Employment Arbitration		770
18.6	Appellate Decisions Adopt Divergent Theories: Forum Substitution Versus Comparative Cost of Litigation		773
	18.6.1 What Is a Cost Case?		773
	18.6.2 Appeals Courts that Accept Cost Arguments: Forum Substitution Theory and Lower-Wage Workers		775
		18.6.2.1 The U.S. Court of Appeals for the D.C. Circuit: *Cole v. Burns International Security Services*	776
		18.6.2.2 The U.S. Court of Appeals for the Tenth Circuit: *Shankle v. B-G Maintenance Management of Colorado, Inc.*	779
		18.6.2.3 The U.S. Court of Appeals for the Eleventh Circuit: *Perez v. Globe Airport Security Services, Inc.*	781
	18.6.3 Appeals Courts that Reject Cost Arguments: Comparative Cost of Litigation Theory and Higher-Wage Employees		783
		18.6.3.1 The U.S. Court of Appeals for the First Circuit: *Rosenberg v. Merrill Lynch, Pierce, Fenner & Smith, Inc.*	783
		18.6.3.2 The U.S. Court of Appeals for the Seventh Circuit: *Koveleskie v. SBC Capital Markets, Inc.*	786
	18.6.4 Appeals Courts that Use a Case-by-Case Approach to Cost Arguments		787
		18.6.4.1 The U.S. Court of Appeals for the Fourth Circuit: *Bradford v. Rockwell Semiconductor Systems, Inc.*	787

	18.6.4.2	The U.S. Court of Appeals for the Third Circuit: *Blair v. Scott Specialty Gases*	788
18.7	Conclusions		789

Chapter 19
Arbitration and the Individuation Critique   807
W. Mark C. Weidemaier

19.1	Introduction		807
19.2	The Individuation Critique		810
	19.2.1	Automatic Claims Aggregation and the Presumed Repeat-Player Advantage	810
	19.2.2	Repeat-Player Lawyers and the Benefits of Aggregation	814
	19.2.3	Aggregation of Consumer Claims	818
	19.2.4	The Individuation Critique	823
		19.2.4.1 Does Arbitration Individuate Claiming?	823
		19.2.4.2 The Potential Moderating Effect of ADR Provider Rules	830
		19.2.4.2.1 Reasoned versus Summary Awards	833
		19.2.4.2.2 Remedies Available in Arbitration	835
		19.2.4.2.3 Limits on the Right to Bring or Participate in a Class Action	835
		19.2.4.3 Summary	837
19.3	Rethinking the Ability to Aggregate Disputes in Arbitration		840
	19.3.1	Class Arbitration as a Laboratory for Innovation in Formal Aggregation	840
	19.3.2	Aggregation in Individual Disputes	850
		19.3.2.1 Reduced Cost	851
		19.3.2.2 Development of Precedent	852
		19.3.2.3 Facilitating Award Collection	856
		19.3.2.4 Punitive Damages and Other Remedies	857
		19.3.2.5 Summary	858

	19.3.3 The Effect and Evolution of Provider Rules	859
19.4	Conclusion	863

Chapter 20
Building an Internal Defense Against Class Action Lawsuits: Human Resources Practices Audits 867
G. Roger King, Jeffrey D. Winchester, Lori A. Clary, and Kimberly J. Potter

20.1	Introduction	867
20.2	Class Actions and Specific Federal Statutory Claims	868
	20.2.1 The Civil Rights Act of 1964, Title VII	868
	20.2.2 The Americans with Disabilities Act and the Rehabilitation Act	869
	20.2.3 The Fair Labor Standards Act	869
	20.2.4 The Age Discrimination in Employment Act of 1967	870
	20.2.5 The Equal Pay Act	870
	20.2.6 The Employee Retirement Income Security Act	871
20.3	Avoiding Disparate Impact Class Action Lawsuits	871
	20.3.1 The Nature and Danger of Disparate Impact Suits	871
	20.3.1.1 The Under-Utilization Analysis	873
	20.3.1.2 The 80% Benchmark Rule	873
	20.3.2 Preventing Disparate Impact Suits: How to Uncover Unseen Potential Disparate Impact Liability in an Organization	875
	20.3.2.1 Restriction of Job Advertising to Local Newspapers	875
	20.3.2.2 Requirement that Applicants Meet Certain Minimum Educational Requirements	875
	20.3.2.3 Reliance upon Subjective Personal or Family Ties as Hiring Criteria	876
	20.3.2.4 Some Tips on Avoiding Disparate Impact Discrimination Claims	877
20.4	Avoiding Wage and Hour, Sexual Harassment, and ERISA Class Action Liability	877
	20.4.1 Wage and Hour Claims under the FLSA	877
	20.4.2 Sexual and Other Workplace Harassment Claims	879

	20.4.3 ERISA Claims	882
20.5	Human Resources Audits	884
20.6	Conclusion	891

Chapter 21
'Statistical Dueling' with Unconventional Weapons: What Courts Should Know about Experts in Employment Discrimination Class Actions
William T. Bielby and Pamela Coukos

893

21.1	Introduction	893
21.2	Statistical Evidence in Second-Generation Class Actions	900
	21.2.1 The Historical Doctrinal Approach to Discrimination Class Actions	901
	21.2.2 The Current Conflict over Decentralization and Discretion	905
	21.2.3 Second-Generation Classes and Shifting Fact Patterns	908
21.3	The Meaning of Statistical 'Patterns': A Demonstration of the Statistical Power Problem	917
	21.3.1 *Smith, et al. v. UFS*: A Hypothetical Gender Discrimination Class Action	918
	21.3.2 Who's Got the Power: A Simulation Exercise	928
21.4	Conclusion: Recommendations for Courts	936

Chapter 22
Symposium: Emerging Issues in Class Action Law: Backdoor Federalization
Samuel Issacharoff and Catherine M. Sharkey

941

22.1	Introduction	941
22.2	Matrix: 'Substantive Law' by 'Procedural Forum'	946
	22.2.1 Historical Evolution: National Law for a National Market	948
	22.2.2 Disequilibrium: Federal Courts' Role in Facilitating Transition	954
22.3	Preemption and Federalism	955
	22.3.1 The Systemic Effects of Preemption	965
	22.3.2 Federal Regulatory Regimes	967
	22.3.2.1 Vertical Preemption	967

		22.3.2.2 Horizontal Preemption	975
	22.3.3	Products Liability	977
		22.3.3.1 The Need for National Regulation	981
		22.3.3.2 Horizontal Preemption	986
22.4	Forum Selection and Federalism		998
	22.4.1	From *Swift* to *Erie*: Federal Power and the Common Law	1000
	22.4.2	The Expanding Federal Interest	1010
	22.4.3	The Federal Ingredient in State Law	1012
22.5	Unstable Hybrids: Partial Federalization		1017
	22.5.1	The Class Action Fairness Act	1018
	22.5.2	Punitive Damages	1024
	22.5.3	Further Implications	1034
22.6	Conclusion: The Risk of Predation		1038
22.7	Preemption Cases in Sample (chronological listing)		1039

Chapter 23
From 'Predominance' to 'Resolvability': A New Approach to Regulating Class Actions — 1041
Allan Erbsen

23.1	Introduction		1041
23.2	The Implications of Dissimilarity for the Litigated and Negotiated Valuation of Class Members' Claims		1053
	23.2.1	A Thought Experiment Confirming the Distorting Effect of Dissimilarity	1053
	23.2.2	Trial Distortions: Cherry-Picking, Claim Fusion and Ad Hoc Lawmaking	1056
	23.2.3	The Distorting Effects of Dissimilarity on Valuation of Class Action Settlements	1062
		23.2.3.1 Ineffective Monitoring	1063
		23.2.3.2 Tainted Bargaining	1064
23.3	Principles that Should Shape Rules Governing the Effect of Individualized Issues on Class Certification Decisions		1072
	23.3.1	The Finality Principle: A Certified Class Action Seeking Damages Should Eventually Result in a Judgment Resolving the Claims of All Class Members	1073

  23.3.2 The Fidelity Principle: A Class Member Should Not Receive a Favorable Judgment Unless He or She Can Prove the Substantive Elements for a Cause of Action and Survive Any Applicable Defenses 1085
  23.3.3 The Feasibility Principle: Attempts to Adjudicate Class Actions Should Occur within Resource and Management Constraints 1099
  23.3.4 Synthesis of the Three Principles 1102
23.4 Inconsistencies between Class Certification Principles and Existing Class Certification Rules and Doctrine 1103
  23.4.1 The Origins and Role of the Predominance Test 1104
  23.4.2 Defects in the Predominance Concept 1113
  23.4.3 The Failure of Additional Rule 23 Certification Criteria to Cure Defects in the Predominance Standard 1126
    23.4.3.1 Typicality 1126
    23.4.3.2 Manageability 1129
  23.4.4 Doctrinal Consequences of Judicial Reliance on Predominance 1130
    23.4.4.1 Doctrine De-emphasizing Individualized Damages 1130
    23.4.4.2 Doctrine Under-Weighting Individualized Defenses 1133
    23.4.4.3 Doctrine Postponing Conflict of Laws Analysis 1136
23.5 Proposed Revision to Rule (23)(B)(3) and Implications 1140
  23.5.1 The 'Resolvability' Test 1140
  23.5.2 Avenues for Further Scholarship 1146

Center for Labor and Employment Law at New York University School of Law

The Center for Labor and Employment Law is a program established at New York University School of Law. Samuel Estreicher, Professor of Law at New York University and an internationally recognized expert on labor and employment law, serves as the Center's Director. The objectives of the Center are:

(a) to promote workplace efficiency and productivity, while at the same time recognizing the need for justice and safety in the workplace and respecting the dignity of work and employees;
(b) to promote independent, non-partisan research that would improve understanding of employment issues generally, with particular emphasis on the connections between human resources decisions and organizational performance;
(c) to sponsor a graduate program for the next generation of law teachers and leading practitioners in the fields; and
(d) to provide a forum for bringing together leaders from unions, employees and companies, as well as representatives of plaintiff and defense perspectives, for informal discussion exploring new frameworks for labor-management relations, workplace justice, fair and efficient resolution of employment disputes and representation in the workplace.

For information, contact Ben Eisenman:
Telephone: (212) 998-6242
Fax: (212) 995-4036
Email: ben.eisenman@nyu.edu

<www.law.nyu.edu/centers/labor>

Editor's Preface

Initially intended to be an efficient litigation procedure for dealing by a group of complainants based on the commonality of a discrimination practice, the class action has become a staple of the US litigation system. Reflecting presentations made at the New York University's 56th Annual Conference on Labor, on May 8–9, 2003, as well as some additional contributions, this volume brings to bear considerable expertise and analysis of the status, prospects, and particularly the controversy surrounding class actions.

One criticism of class actions concerns the potential damage that might be done to a corporate defendant. However, in 'The Price of Discrimination: The Nature of Class Action Employment Discrimination Litigation and Its Effects,' Professor Michael Selmi offers evidence that class actions neither affect losing companies' share prices nor, for that matter, typically result in meaningful corporate change.

Any discussion of litigation must also take into account on of its principal alternatives, arbitration. As a starting point for that discussion, in 'Measuring the Value of Class and Collective Action Employment Settlements: A Preliminary Assessment' Professor Samuel Estreicher and Jones Day's Kristina Yost evaluate the oft-stated view that class actions make possible relief for small-size claims that would go unredressed individual arbitration or lawsuits. The authors report that settlements of employment class actions suggest a monetary value to average and median claims that, as prima facie matter, could support individual actions either in arbitration or court.

In a detailed analysis, 'Class and Representative Actions,' noted lawyers Richard T. Seymour and John F. Aslin detail the reasons behind the observed decline in Federal Rule of Civil Procedure (Rule 23) class actions, in part because of the expense and complexity of such cases.

EMPLOYMENT CLASS AND COLLECTIVE ACTIONS

The decline in class actions may mean difficulties in resolving discrimination cases, in the view of Professor Suzette M. Malveaux. In 'Fighting to Keep Employment Discrimination Class Actions Alive: How *Allison v. Citgo's* Predomination Requirement Threatens to Undermine Title VII Enforcement,' she suggests that the conflicting holdings of federal courts of appeals regarding class actions might best be resolved with an ad hoc balancing test, favored by a few, rather than the bright line holding used in several controversial decisions.

As detailed by Daniel F. Piar in 'The Uncertain Future of Title VII Class Actions after the Civil Rights Act of 1991,' revisions to federal statutes designed to provide additional remedies to individuals ironically served to increase the obstacles to class litigation.

The poster child for the contemporary challenges and complexities of class actions is the Ninth Circuit panel decision in *Dukes v. Wal-Mart Stores*. In 'A Classless Act: The Ninth Circuit's Erroneous Class Certification in *Dukes v. Wal-Mart, Inc.*,' Aaron B. Lauchheimer analyzes this California class action and argues that certifying a wide-ranging, nationwide class is usually not appropriate.

Rachel Tallon Pickens offers a different perspective on *Dukes* in 'Too Many Riches?: *Dukes v. Wal-Mart* and the Efficacy of Monolithic Class Actions.' She argues that manageability concerns in a wide-ranging, though monolithic, class should not necessarily inhibit certification of the class.

One lesson of the *Dukes* is that compliance and internal enforcement present important challenges for large employers, concludes Professor Melissa Hart in 'The Possibility of Avoiding Discrimination: Considering Compliance and Liability.' She adds, however, that these very points must be considered central elements for limiting discrimination of the workplace.

Often left out of the discussion of class actions is the preclusive effect of a judgment on absent class members. Professor Tobias Barrington Wolff addresses this omission in 'Preclusion in Class Action Litigation.' Unfortunately, courts have given short shrift to this issue.

Increasing collective actions are being brought under the Fair Labor Standards Act, Age Discrimination in Employment Act, and Equal Pay Act. As detailed by Mark S. Dichter in 'Opt-In Class Actions: Collective Litigation Under the FLSA, ADEA and EPA,' these are opt-in actions rather than the class Rule 23 opt-out action where members of the class are bound unless they affirmatively exclude themselves from the action.

Steven Arenson and Craig J. Ackermann advocate an alternative to the expense and complexity of class actions in 'Not without Class: Test Cases In Lieu of Class Certification as a Paradigm for Litigating Multi-Plaintiff Harassment Cases.' They assess the use of a different approach, namely, using test cases as patterns, combined with multi-party joinder.

Also looking at the possibility of test cases, in '"Pattern or Practice" Discrimination Litigation,' Michael Delikat explains that pattern or practice test cases that apply to discriminatory harassment have so far not been accepted by appellate courts, although they have been heard in federal trial courts.

The difficulties of disabled people have been multiplied, write Professors Michael Ashley Stein and Michael E. Waterstone in 'Disability, Disparate Impact, and Class Actions.' They point out that the increasing difficulty in predicating collective employment actions on a unifying group-based identity when dealing with disadvantaged persons with disabilities, in part because disability law has heretofore not been litigated on the basis of group identity.

Proposals have been floated relating to the shifting of the burden of proof in actions under the Fair Labor Standards Act and state wage payment laws. In 'Collective and Class Action Issues under the Fair Labor Standards Act and State-Based Wages Statutes,' Adam T. Klein concludes that these proposals are unfair to workers.

In a related discussion, 'Working with the Equal Employment Opportunity Commission,' Wayne N. Outten suggests that, in principle, joining forces with the US Equal Employment Opportunity Commission in a litigation confers advantages, but it also involves challenges and pitfalls.

When the topic of arbitration is broached, the case of *Green Tree v. Bazzle* is not far behind. In '*Green Tree v. Bazzle* in the Supreme Court: "How to Succeed in Blocking Class Actions in Arbitration Without Really Saying So,"' Daniel B. Edelman addresses whether agreements that provide for arbitration of disputes can be read to authorize class-wide arbitration if the agreement is silent on that particular point.

Henry D. Lederman looks at the *Green Tree* case in the context of California case law. In 'Arbitration Agreements, Unconscionability, and Bans on Class Actions: Dueling Magic Wands? The California Experience,' he writes that the California Supreme Court's answer to the conundrum posed by *Green Tree v. Bazzle* is, yes. That is, when an agreement that sends disputes to arbitration is silent on class actions, arbitrators have authority to proceed on a classwide basis.

Another issue surrounding arbitration is its fairness to employees, especially when the employee is employed under an agreement that both requires arbitration and requires the employee to bear some of the cost. In 'When Is Cost an Unlawful Barrier to Alternative Dispute Resolution? The Ever Green Tree of Mandatory Employment Arbitration,' Professors Michael H. LeRoy and Peter Feuille explain that courts have begun to scrutinize this type of employment arrangement.

The fairness to employees issue also arises in connection with the matter of individuation, writes Professor W. Mark. C. Weidenmaier. In 'Arbitration and the Individuation Critique,' he suggests that aggregating claims in arbitration may blunt the critique that individuals are not likely to fare well in arbitration because of the advantage that accrues to so-called 'repeat players.'

At root, the best defense against any litigation is to make sure that there is no cause in the first place. G. Roger King, Jeffrey D. Winchester, Lori A. Clary, and Kimberly J. Potter explain the value of an internal human services audit in 'Building An Internal Defense Against Class Action Lawsuits: HR Practices Audits.' Such an audit can be an important step in forestalling class litigation-in part, by identifying and ending inappropriate practices.

Mark Twain's negative comment about statistics notwithstanding, it is possible to 'prove' diametrically opposed positions with similar-sounding statistics, as detailed in '"Statistical Dueling" with Unconventional Weapons: What Courts Should Know about Experts in Employment Discrimination Class Actions.' Expert witnesses William T. Bielby and Pamela Coukos offer this primer, which explains the need to analyze the power of a statistical claim.

One issue underlying the tangled matters of class actions is the tension between state and federal interests. In 'Symposium: Emerging Issues in Class Action Law: Backdoor Federalization,' Professors Samuel Issacharoff and Catherine M. Sharkey suggest that the Supreme Court has supported federal efforts to preempt areas that have been matters of concern for the individual states, particularly in matters relating to commerce.

Looking ahead, Allan Erbsen seeks resolution. Writing in 'From "Predominance" to "Resolvability": A New Approach to Regulating Class Actions,' he points out that the core of class actions contains a contradiction, to wit, the tension between commonality and individuation. Rather than a predominance balancing test, he suggests that a better approach might be a resolvability test that reconciles the practical and theoretical constraints of class litigation.

D.S.
Ithaca, New York
April 3, 2008

CHAPTER 1

The Price of Discrimination: The Nature of Class Action Employment Discrimination Litigation and Its Effects

Michael Selmi*

1.1 INTRODUCTION

The last decade has seen an explosion of employment discrimination class action lawsuits that have been resolved through record breaking settlements. The best known of these cases is the 176 million dollar (USD) settlement involving Texaco, one that came on the heels of the much publicized discovery of tape-recorded meetings that seemingly indicated the use of explicit racial epithets by management-level employees.[1] There have also been substantial settlements involving Coca-Cola (USD 192 million), Home Depot (USD 104 million), Shoney's (USD 105 million), Publix Markets (USD 81 million), and State Farm Insurance Co. (USD 157 million).[2] A recently

---

*Michael Selmi is Professor of Law, George Washington University Law School, and Distinguished Visiting Professor of Law, Suffolk University Law School. He holds a J.D. from Harvard University.
[1] The *Texaco* case is discussed *infra* section 1.3.1.
[2] The *Home Depot* case is discussed *infra* section 1.3.2. For discussions of the other settlements see Philip Hager, 'State Farm to Pay Women USD 157 Million for Job Bias,' LA Times, April 29, 1992, at A1; Allen R. Myerson, 'Supermarket Chain to Pay USD 81 Million to Settle a Bias Suit,' NY Times, January 25, 1997, at A1; Henry Unger, 'Coke to Settle Racial Suit with USD 192.5 Million Deal,' Atlanta J-Const,

David Sherwyn and Samuel Estreicher (eds), *Employment Class and Collective Actions*, pp. 1–106.
© 2009, Kluwer Law International BV, Printed in Great Britain.

filed sex discrimination suit against Wal-Mart appears poised to set a new record.[3]

Despite the proliferation of these high profile cases, we know surprisingly little about their effects on either the firms that have been sued or the plaintiff classes. For example, we do not know whether the lawsuits produce substantial benefits to the plaintiff class, prompt any changes in corporate culture, or exact costs sufficient to serve as an adequate deterrent against discrimination. Because all of the large cases have been resolved through settlements rather than trial, we also do not know whether the cases involve provable claims of discrimination. In this chapter, I will seek to expand our knowledge by analyzing the effect these large class action lawsuits have on firms and plaintiffs. The first part of the chapter involves an empirical analysis designed to assess whether the lawsuits or their settlements affect shareholder value, as measured by their effect on stock prices.[4] In the second part of the chapter, I will present three case studies of lawsuits, involving *Texaco, Home Depot*, and *Denny's*, to explore whether the lawsuits produce substantial changes within the corporations or provide meaningful benefits to the plaintiff class.[5]

This study challenges many of the prevailing views on employment discrimination class action litigation. The statistical study demonstrates that the lawsuits do not substantially influence stock prices, either at their filing or their settlement, and when there is an effect, it tends to be short-lived. Yet, although the lawsuits do not result in significant financial losses to shareholder value, managers still often take them seriously – more seriously than is typically warranted by the financial impact of the suits. Stated somewhat differently, while investors do not appear to be significantly interested in the lawsuits, managers frequently are. Taking the lawsuits seriously, however, does not mean that the managers implement meaningful reform; on the

---

November 17, 2000, at A1; Lynne Duke, 'Shoney's Bias Settlement Sends $105 Million Signal,' Wash Post, February 3, 1993, at A1. As discussed in more detail below, the reported settlement amounts often exaggerate the actual cost of the settlement by stating the maximum possible cost over an extended period of time. See *infra* text accompanying notes 264–273.

[3] See Reed Abelson, '6 Women Sue Wal-Mart, Charging Job and Promotion Bias,' NY Times, June 20, 2001, at C1.

[4] See *infra* section 1.2.

[5] See *infra* section 1.3.

CHAPTER 1. THE PRICE OF DISCRIMINATION

contrary, I will suggest that the settlements frequently produce little to no substantive change within the corporations. Moreover, many of the changes that are implemented tend to be cosmetic in nature and are primarily designed to address public relations problems. As demonstrated in the case studies, many companies, such as Texaco and Home Depot, fail to enact meaningful changes in their employment practices, and monetary recoveries generally constitute the primary direct benefit the lawsuits provide to the plaintiff class.

When divided by the size of the class, these benefits tend to be relatively modest, averaging about USD 10,000 per class member – well below what a plaintiff could expect to recover in a successful individual suit.[6] Furthermore, given the size of the defendant corporations, the damages also fail to pose a significant deterrent threat to firms. To give but one example, the record-setting settlement involving *Coca-Cola* amounted to less than 0.15% of the firm's capitalization.[7] Although the damage amounts are often insufficient to compensate plaintiffs or deter defendants, other parties involved in the litigation fare significantly better. Attorneys routinely receive fee awards that are four to six times their actual fees, and a host of groups loosely tied to the diversity industry are likewise collecting a disproportionate share of the settlement funds through diversity training, purchases from minority suppliers, and contributions to various minority groups either as part of the settlement or to repair public relations damage.[8]

---

[6] See discussion *infra* subsection 1.4.1. In a previous study, I documented that discrimination settlements obtained by the Equal Employment Opportunity Commission in 1997 averaged USD 23,000, while the mean trial recovery in litigation initiated by private plaintiffs was approximately USD 100,000. Michael Selmi, 'Public vs. Private Enforcement of Civil Rights: The Case of Housing and Employment,' 45 UCLA L Rev 1401, 1435 (1998).

[7] The relation between the settlement and a firm's market value is set forth in Table 1.3, *infra*. See also Constance L. Hays, 'Coke's Black Employees Step Up Pressure to Resolve a Racial Discrimination Lawsuit,' NY Times, March 23, 2000, at C1 (noting that a penny a share amounted to USD 37 million in pretax earnings). At the time of the settlement, Coca-Cola's stock price hovered at about USD 60, with the settlement theoretically shaving approximately six cents off the price. Davan Maharaj, 'Coca-Cola to Settle Racial Bias Lawsuit Workplace: Soft Drink Giant Agrees to Pay $192.5 Million over Allegations it Treated Blacks Unfairly,' LA Times, November 17, 2000, at A1.

[8] In both the *Texaco* and *Denny's* cases, minority-and women-owned businesses obtained substantial increases in business with the companies. See *infra* text accompanying notes 103, 204, 214.

The limited effect the suits have on stock prices also provides an empirical challenge to the ability of the labor market to eliminate discrimination. Gary Becker hypothesized long ago that firms that engaged in employment discrimination would ultimately be driven out of the market because of their inefficient discriminatory tastes.[9] But if lawsuits alleging discrimination, settlements of those suits, or the remedial changes that follow the settlement have no significant effect on firm value, then it is difficult to see how the market would provide an adequate deterrent to discrimination. Neither the aggregate data nor the case studies suggest that there is reason to expect the market to punish firms because of their discriminatory employment practices.

These findings reflect a substantial shift in the nature of employment discrimination litigation, and indeed in the nature of discrimination itself. Not so long ago, class-action employment-discrimination suits were defined as a quintessential form of public law litigation where monetary relief was generally viewed as one component of necessary remedial relief, and a far less important component than the institutional reform the suit ultimately produced.[10] Yet today the lawsuits have largely become just another variation of a tort claim where monetary relief is the principal, and often the only, goal of the litigation. Along with this shift in emphasis has come a dramatic change in our perspective on the persistence of discrimination. There is no longer any concerted effort to eliminate discrimination; instead, efforts

---

[9] See Gary Becker, *The Economics of Discrimination*, (2nd edn, 1971) 44, (performing an economic analysis showing that firms with the lowest 'discrimination coefficient' will be able to undersell all others).

[10] In his seminal article on public law litigation, Professor Abram Chayes identified employment discrimination as one of the 'avatars' of public law litigation. See Abram Chayes, 'The Role of the Judge in Public Law Litigation,' 89 Harv L Rev 1281, 1284 (1976). For similar perspectives, see Robert Belton, 'A Comparative Review of Public and Private Enforcement of Title VII of the Civil Rights Act of 1964,' 31 Vand L Rev 905 (1978) (describing Title VII as implicating public law rights); Larry Kramer, 'Consent Decrees and the Rights of Third Parties,' 87 Mich L Rev 321, 321 (1988) (identifying consent decrees in employment discrimination cases as a hallmark of public law); Maimon Schwarzschild, 'Public Law by Private Bargain: Title VII Consent Decrees and the Fairness of Negotiated Institutional Reform,' 1984 Duke LJ 887, 887 ('Large-scale Title VII remedies are typical of "public law" litigation....').

CHAPTER 1. THE PRICE OF DISCRIMINATION

are directed at providing monetary compensation for past discrimination without particular concern for preventing future discrimination, or even remedying past discrimination, through injunctive relief. For firms, discrimination, claims are now like accidents – a cost of doing business, which necessarily implies that a certain level of discrimination will persist.

One reason for the change in the nature of the litigation is that employment discrimination class actions have evolved into a purely private realm with little to no government oversight – indeed, as I will suggest, with hardly any oversight at all. With some exceptions, most courts never become involved in fashioning an appropriate remedy or overseeing the implementation of the consent decree, so enforcement is largely left to private plaintiffs' attorneys or their recent offshoots, diversity task forces, neither of which has a sufficient interest in the ongoing proceedings to ensure that change actually occurs.[11]

This study contains two distinct but related parts. The first part involves an empirical study of the effect class action employment discrimination lawsuits have on firms. This part of the study relies on the event study technique, a statistical methodology that seeks to measure the effect of a particular event, in this case the filing and settlement of class action litigation, on firm value. The event studies model has been widely used to assess the impact of litigation in previous studies.[12] The second part of this study will involve three case studies to see how firms react to class action litigation. The three case studies involve three distinct responses to class action litigation by *Texaco*, *Home Depot*, and *Denny's*. I will suggest that each provides a model response under particular circumstances, models that I label public relations (*Texaco*), recalcitrance (*Home Depot*), and reform (*Denny's*). In the final part of the article, I will offer some suggestions for reform, including increased monetary damages for the plaintiffs and monitoring of the settlement, to restore the original public purpose to the litigation. However, much of this article is descriptive in nature, with the primary intent of analyzing the nature of class action employment discrimination litigation today.

---

[11] Diversity task forces have been adopted in the cases involving *Texaco*, *Coca-Cola*, and *Mitsubishi*. The task forces are discussed in more detail in subsection 1.4.3.
[12] See sources cited *infra* n. 13.

1.2 THE EMPIRICAL STUDY

If the filing or settling of class action discrimination lawsuits adversely affects defendant firms, that effect should be reflected in lower stock prices. To measure that effect, this chapter uses the event study, a methodology that has been widely employed in economics and finance to measure the impact of specific events on firm value.[13] An event study is a statistical technique designed to isolate the impact of an event on a firm's stock price, and, as described in more detail below, it does so by measuring the stock's return after the event is announced against the return that would have been expected had the event not occurred.[14] In this way, it is possible to determine what effect, if any, the particular event had on the stock price. The methodology of the study will be explained further following a discussion of the underlying hypothesis and the data on which the study is based.

1.2.1 The Hypothesis

This study measures the effect the filing and settlement of a class action lawsuit have on a firm's stock price, with the expectation that either event will negatively affect the stock price. The filing of a class

---

[13] See e.g., Sanjai Bhagat et al., 'The Costs of Inefficient Bargaining and Financial Distress: Evidence from Corporate Lawsuits,' 35 J Fin Econ 221 (1994) [hereinafter Bhagat et al., 'Costs'] (analyzing the effect of interfirm lawsuits on the value of corporate litigants); Sanjai Bhagat et al., 'The Shareholder Wealth Implications of Corporate Lawsuits,' 27 Fin Mgmt, Winter 1998, at 5 [hereinafter Bhagat et al., 'Shareholder Wealth'] (analyzing the effect of filings and settlements on corporations); John M. Bizjak & Jeffrey L. Coles, 'The Effect of Private Antitrust Litigation on the Stock-Market Valuation of the Firm,' 85 Am Econ Rev 436 (1995); Joni Hersch, 'Equal Employment Opportunity and Firm Profitability,' 26 J Hum Res 139 (1991) (measuring the effect of discrimination lawsuits); Michael I. Muoghalu et al., 'Hazardous Waste Lawsuits, Stockholder Returns, and Deterrence,' 57 S Econ J 357 (1990); David W. Prince & Paul H. Rubin, 'The Effects of Product Liability Litigation on the Value of Firms,' 4 Am L & Econ Rev 44 (2002); W. Kip Viscusi & Joni Hersch, 'The Market Response to Product Safety Litigation,' 2 J Reg Econ 215 (1990) (assessing the impact of product safety litigation on firm value).

[14] For an overview of event study methodology, see John Y. Campbell, *The Econometrics of Financial Markets*, (1997) 149–180 and A. Craig MacKinlay, 'Event Studies in Economics and Finance,' 35 J Econ Lit 13 (1997).

CHAPTER 1. THE PRICE OF DISCRIMINATION

action discrimination suit against a corporation presents the possibility that the firm will experience significant costs from the suit, either from a settlement or judgment. In addition to the financial cost, firms may also suffer reputational costs from being identified as a firm that discriminates. This should be particularly true if the lawsuit generates national news, as is true for all of the cases analyzed here. The prediction that the filing of suit will adversely affect stock prices is consistent with many prior studies examining the effect of various kinds of lawsuits – product liability, securities, and discrimination – on stock prices, most of which have found that the lawsuits result in a loss of shareholder value.[15]

Settlements should also diminish stock prices, particularly if the value of the settlement is higher than what the market was expecting. Here again the financial costs are not the only costs the lawsuits can exact from firms. Employment discrimination settlements often require changes in institutional practices, and they may also require firms to engage in some form of what might be labeled affirmative action, by requiring that members of the affected class receive employment preferences.[16] Even if the settlement does not require affirmative action, the perception may be just as important as the reality. Investors may believe that the firm will be required to engage in affirmative action and may also view affirmative action as inconsistent with efficient employment practices. All of these factors should lead to a decrease in the stock price based on the settlement of the lawsuit,[17] and this study is designed to test these hypotheses.

---

[15] See e.g., Bhagat et al., 'Shareholder Wealth,' *supra* n. 13, at 6 ('We find that no matter who brings a lawsuit against a firm...defendants experience economically meaningful and statistically significant wealth losses upon the filing of the suit.'); Bizjak & Coles, *supra* n. 13, at 437 (finding that filings of private antitrust suits result in a wealth loss for defendants of 0.6% of the firm's equity value); Hersch, *supra* n. 13, at 150 (finding a significant negative effect for class action filings).

[16] See *United States v. Paradise*, 480 US 149, 185 (1987) (requiring one-for-one promotions for members of discriminated class to remedy past discrimination); *Local 28 of Sheet Metal Workers' Int'l Ass'n v. EEOC*, 478 US 421, 447 (1986) (permitting remedial race-conscious relief).

[17] There are two ways in which the stock price might increase due to a settlement. The price may increase to the extent the settlement is lower than the market was expecting. Some studies have confirmed such an effect that mitigates the initial drop in the stock price at the time of filing. See e.g., Bhagat et al., 'Costs,' *supra* n. 13, at 245 (finding that the loss attributed to the filing of a suit was often regained upon settlement). This effect is generally dependent on an initial wealth loss attributable

1.2.2 The Data

This study involves class action employment discrimination lawsuits filed or settled between November 1991 and August 2001 in which the defendants were publicly traded corporations on the New York Stock Exchange. The study's beginning date was selected to coincide with the passage of the Civil Rights Act of 1991, which for the first time made damages available to plaintiffs who successfully sued under Title VII of the 1964 Civil Rights Act.[18] Prior to the passage of the Act, plaintiffs were limited to equitable relief, typically back pay, which rarely offered the prospect of substantial damages.[19] The availability of damages significantly increased the cost of discrimination and likewise produced a sharp increase in class action litigation.[20]

The study focuses on class action lawsuits rather than individual lawsuits because, with few exceptions, only class action litigation raises the threat of costs that would be substantial enough to interest an investor or to deter firms from discriminatory practices. Even after the passage of the 1991 Act, most individual cases are resolved for under USD 25,000,[21] and given the sheer volume of individual cases, it is not reasonable to expect investors to react to each case that receives some publicity. Class action lawsuits, on the other hand, have the potential to cost the firm millions of dollars as well as to generate adverse publicity, and the initial uncertainty regarding their potential monetary impact is the kind of information that should be of interest to investors. Additionally, class action lawsuits remain relatively rare. Approximately

---

to the filing, and would be captured in the current study. Additionally, as noted below, it is conceivable that the stock price would increase if the settlement were seen as a sign that inefficient employment practices would be eliminated.

[18] 42 USC 1981a (2000).

[19] See *Albemarle Paper Co. v. Moody*, 422 US 405 (1975) (discussing the remedial objectives of Title VII).

[20] See David Segal, 'Lawyers Stake a Claim on Bias Lawsuits; With More Cases in Litigation, Firms Cash In on Billable-Hour Bonanza,' Wash Post, January 27, 1997, at A1 (discussing the impact that the Civil Rights Act of 1991 had on class action litigation).

[21] This figure is based on settlements obtained by the EEOC. See Selmi, *supra* n. 6, at 1432–1433. For cases that are resolved at trial, the awards tend to be substantially higher, particularly for private plaintiffs for whom the median award between 1992 and 1995 was USD 91,000. *Id.* at 1434. It is important to note, however, that only about 8% of the cases are resolved through trial. *Id.* at 1433.

CHAPTER 1. THE PRICE OF DISCRIMINATION

seventy-five employment discrimination lawsuits that include class action allegations are filed in any given year, compared to approximately 20,000 individual cases.[22] The scarcity of class action lawsuits means that such suits should send a potent signal to interested parties, particularly when the potential size of the award is taken into account.

Since the statistical part of this study focuses on the reaction of investors, the data include class action lawsuits that were reported in *The New York Times*, *The Wall Street Journal*, the *Washington Post*, and the *Los Angeles Times*. These four newspapers were selected because of their national scope, which makes it reasonable to assume that information published in these papers would reach investors in one way or another, either directly through the newspapers themselves or through wire or news services affiliated with the newspapers.[23] Because the sample includes only those cases that were reported in the national press, it likely overrepresents large and noteworthy cases, while overlooking

---

[22] Based on figures compiled by the Administrative Office of the U.S. Courts, seventy employment class action suits were filed in 1997, eighty-five in 1998, and seventy-four in 1999. Administrative Office of the U.S. Courts, Judicial Business of the Courts tbl.X-5 (1998); U.S. Office of the Courts, Judicial Business of the Courts tbl.X-5 (1999).

[23] A limited survey supported this assumption. I checked to determine whether information published in one of the above-referenced newspapers was carried in other major newspapers and, invariably, five or six other major city newspapers ran a similar story on the same day the story was reported in one of the four papers relied on for this study, with several papers typically carrying the story a day or so later. A number of prior studies seeking to measure the effect of events on stock prices have focused exclusively on stories reported in The Wall Street Journal. See e.g., Bhagat et al., 'Shareholder Wealth,' *supra* n. 13, at 15; Hersch, *supra* n. 13, at 141. While The Wall Street Journal is likely the best single source of information for investors, restricting the study to one paper appears unnecessary, particularly since the number of individuals holding stock has increased substantially in the last decade. See Cheryl Russell & Marcia Mogelonsky, 'Riding High on the Market,' Am Demographics, April 2000, at 45, 48 (noting that in 1998, nearly 49% of households owned stock, up from 32% a decade earlier). Nevertheless, with only a few exceptions, most of the lawsuits analyzed in this study were reported in *The Wall Street Journal*, and a separate analysis of the cases that only appeared in that paper found no significant difference from the results generally reported in this study. When the story appeared in more than one newspaper, the stories generally ran on the same day. On the few occasions when the stories ran on different days, I relied on the earliest date as the event date.

smaller and less publicized cases. By the same measure, the cases included in this study should have the greatest potential to influence shareholder value precisely because of the publicity they received. As a result, restricting the data to large nationally reported cases is a measure that should bias the study in favor of finding an effect on firm value.[24] I also chose to focus only on firms that were traded on the New York Stock Exchange so as to control for broad market changes in the stock index. This proved to be a modest limitation since there were only three class action lawsuits reported by the national press for firms traded on other exchanges.[25]

Limiting the study to publicly traded companies proved a more significant restriction than excluding companies traded on exchanges other than the NYSE. Although such a limitation is obviously necessary for a study measuring the effect on stock prices, it had the effect of eliminating several of the largest class action suits, including a case against *State Farm* that settled for approximately USD 157 million, an USD 81 million suit against *Publix*, and two high profile sexual harassment cases against *Mitsubishi Motors* that ultimately settled for a total of USD 45 million.[26] Neither State Farm nor Publix is publicly traded, and

---

[24] An exception to this principle might arise due to the size of the firms that are included in the analysis, all of which are large firms. While these firms are likely to garner the most publicity, they are also in the best position to absorb the financial costs of the suit. In contrast, smaller firms may have more to lose through a class action lawsuit to the extent the information relating to the company was available to investors. This is less likely with smaller companies because, in addition to getting less news coverage, they are also typically covered by fewer stock analysts.

[25] The three cases involved *O'Charley's* and *Rent-A-Center*, both of which trade on Nasdaq, and *Crown Central Petroleum*, which trades on the American Stock Exchange. See 'Settlement Reached in Suit Over Alleged Racial Bias,' Wall St J, July 23, 1996, at B4 (discussing a USD 7.5 million settlement with *O'Charley's*); 'Crown Central is Sued for Alleged Gender, Race Discrimination,' Wall St J, July 1, 1997, at C23 (describing the filing of the class-action suit); 'Rent-A-Center, Inc.,' Wall St J, July 10, 2000, at A15 (noting a USD 2 million settlement for sex discrimination suit involving *Rent-A-Center*). *Rent-A-Center* subsequently entered a settlement in a different case for USD 47 million. Kirsten Downey Grimsley, 'Rent-A-Center to Pay USD 47 Million to Settle Sex-Bias Suit,' Wash Post, March 9, 2002, at A9.

[26] Glenn Ruffenach, 'Publix Supermarkets Will Pay USD 81.5 Million to Settle Bias Suit,' Wall St J, January 27, 1997, at B4; Kathy Bergen & Carol Kleiman, 'Mitsubishi Will Pay USD 34 Million: The Biggest Settlement in a Sexual Harassment Suit Is Seen as a Wake-Up Call,' Chi Trib, June 12, 1998, at A1; Hager, *supra* n. 2. There were two

CHAPTER 1. THE PRICE OF DISCRIMINATION

Mitsubishi is traded only on Japan's Nikkei stock exchange. Additionally, suits against governments, which make up a significant portion of the class actions that have been filed or settled in the last decade, were likewise excluded from the study.[27]

The stock prices were drawn from publicly available sources, including Yahoo! Finance, and siliconinvestor.com. Where data were missing from those sources, newspapers and publications that list historical stock prices were used to supplement the data. The Standard and Poor's 500 Index was used to measure the expected returns over time.

This study isolates two relevant events: the filing of a lawsuit and the notice of a settlement. In some cases, only one event was reported in the press, typically the filing of the lawsuit, but there were also several cases where the settlement was reported while the original case filing was not. Other significant litigation events are occasionally reported in the newspapers, but they are generally reported infrequently, and they are not as likely to influence investment decisions. For example, the required court approval of a settlement agreement was occasionally noted in national newspapers, but it was rare that the approval differed from the original notice of settlement; therefore, these notices do not seem likely to impact investor decisions.[28] Newspapers also frequently report when the Equal Employment Opportunity Commission joins or seeks to join an existing lawsuit, or when a class was certified, but these occurrences were too rare to measure, and, again, not clearly of interest to investors.[29]

---

cases involving *Mitsubishi*. One filed by the EEOC settled for USD 34 million, and a private suit settled for USD 9.5 million. 'Mitsubishi Harassment Settlement Approved,' NY Times, June 26, 1998, at D20.

[27] The largest discrimination settlement to date arose, in fact, from a suit filed against the United States in a twenty-three-year-old case involving the US Information Agency and the Voice of America. Bill Miller & David A. Vise, 'U.S. Settles Job Bias Case; A Record $508 Million is Due Women in USIA Dispute,' Wash Post, March 23, 2000, at A1.

[28] The only exception involved the sex discrimination suit against *Smith Barney*, which the district judge initially refused to approve. Peter Truell, 'Judge Rejects Proposed Pact in Sex Harassment Case,' NY Times, June 25, 1998, at D20. The Court ultimately approved a revised agreement. Patrick McGeehan, 'Judge Approves Class-Action Settlement for Sex Harassment at Smith Barney,' Wall St J, July 27, 1998, at B6.

[29] It is conceivable that investors would assume that the resources of the EEOC would significantly affect the outcome of the litigation, though this assumption

The cases that are included in the database are described in the accompanying Appendices One and Two. The study includes thirty-three class action lawsuits filed against publicly traded corporations and twenty-six settlements against publicly traded corporations.[30] Only six of the cases appear in both files, as many of the cases have yet to be resolved, while other cases settled during the study's time-frame were originally filed before the selected starting date. Race discrimination cases accounted for nearly 65% of the class action filings, with nearly three times as many race claims (twenty-two) as sex discrimination claims (eight). There were only two age discrimination claims, as well as one claim based on national origin, though several cases included multiple allegations. Two-thirds (twenty-two) of the cases have been filed since 1996, the year of the much publicized settlement involving *Texaco*.

The settlements are more evenly divided among race, sex, and age discrimination claims, with ten, nine, and four respectively. The aggregate value of the settlements totals more than USD 1 billion, with a mean recovery of USD 44.3 million and a median of USD 28 million. The mean recovery for race discrimination claims was USD 58.9 million, with a median of USD 28 million. The sex discrimination claims yielded about half as much, with a mean recovery of USD 24.9 million and a median recovery of USD 10 million. Consistent with past studies, the age discrimination claims produced the largest settlements, with a mean recovery of USD 71.12 million and a median of USD 46.75 million. In this instance, however, the mean figure for age discrimination cases was significantly skewed by a USD 183 million settlement against *Lockheed-Martin*. It is also worth noting that all of the cases were the product of a negotiated settlement; none of the cases were resolved

---

often proves incorrect. Particularly in the last decade, the EEOC has often jumped into litigation well after the case has commenced, or even after it has settled (as it did against *Texaco*) and seems to do so primarily as a public relations vehicle. See *infra* text accompanying notes 303–305. Nevertheless, it is certainly possible that investors would treat EEOC intervention as meaningful, but this study did not measure that effect.

[30] This number of cases falls within the range used in previous event studies. See e.g., Bhagat et al., 'Shareholder Wealth,' *supra* n. 13, at 16 (using a sample size of twenty-nine for defendant settlements); Bizjak & Coles, *supra* n. 13, at 442 (using a sample size of twenty-six cases); Mark S. Johnson et al., 'Stock Price Reaction to Regulation in the Meat Packing Industry,' 45 J Agric Econ 31, 35 (1993) (using a sample size of twenty-three).

CHAPTER 1. THE PRICE OF DISCRIMINATION

through a trial. Indeed, in only one case, involving *Lucky Stores* in 1992, was there a trial to determine the defendant's liability.[31] There was also no case where the defendant prevailed at trial. When these cases are resolved, it is invariably by settlement rather than trial.

1.2.3 The Statistical Analysis

As previously noted, the statistical portion of this study relies on a technique known as an event study. Event studies, in turn, rely on the efficient markets hypothesis, which states in its strong form that new information is quickly incorporated into stock prices.[32] This assumption has been borne out in many prior event studies that have found that new information is typically incorporated into a stock price within one to three days of the event having been reported.[33]

An event study seeks to measure the effect of a particular event, in this instance the filing or settling of class action employment discrimination litigation, on a firm's stock price. For the purposes of the statistical analysis, an event is defined as the publication of the story in one

---

[31] See *Stender v. Lucky Stores*, 803 F. Supp. 259 (ND Cal. 1992) (holding that the plaintiff-employees met their burden of proving sex discrimination).

[32] The seminal work defining the efficient markets hypothesis is Eugene F. Fama, 'Efficient Capital Markets: A Review of Theory and Empirical Work,' 25 J Fin 383 (1970). Although the efficient markets hypothesis is not without its critics, the model underlies most event studies. See e.g., Bizjak & Coles, *supra* n. 13, at 438 (relying on efficient markets hypothesis to measure the effect of antitrust litigation); Kathleen Engelmann & Bradford Cornell, 'Measuring the Cost of Corporate Litigation: Five Case Studies,' 17 J Legal Stud 377, 378 n. 3 (1988) ('We are implicitly assuming that markets are efficient.'); Viscusi & Hersch, *supra* n. 13, at 216 ('The underlying assumption is that stock markets operate in an efficient manner.').

[33] See Eugene F. Fama, 'Efficient Capital Markets II,' 46 J Fin 1575, 1601 (1991) ('The typical result in event studies on daily data is that, on average, stock prices seem to adjust within a day to event announcements.'); Muoghalu et al., *supra* n. 13, at 362 (reporting that stock prices adjusted within a day of announcement); Wallace N. Davidson III et al., 'The Effectiveness of OSHA Penalties: A Stock-Market-Based Test,' 33 Indus Rel 283, 290 (1994) (finding that 'the stock market reaction is confined to a very narrow period (e.g., the three-day interval)'). Occasionally there can be a delay before the information is incorporated. See Viscusi & Hersch, *supra* n. 13, at 222 (finding a delay of five days before an effect was felt by Agent Orange litigation).

of the four newspapers described earlier, and the date of publication is defined as the event date. For each event, the day the story was published is defined as day 0, and the previous trading day is represented as -1, and together these two days make up the event period.[34] A two-day event period helps capture any changes that might have occurred the day before the particular event. This is especially important in cases where information has leaked into the market prior to the official announcement, and event studies commonly use a two-day period.[35] This study relies on the dummy variable technique and uses ordinary least squares (OLS) regression analysis.[36]

The event period provides the means to identify whether the filing or settlement impacts a firm's stock price during the two-day event period with the expectation that the impact will be negative. While a simplistic assessment can be made by comparing the stock price the day the announcement was made with the price several days earlier, this assessment may ascribe a correlation to the event when the change in the stock price is actually the result of an overall market change, or a continuation of a firm's stock price trajectory. Therefore, to isolate the effect of the event, it is necessary to calculate what are defined as abnormal returns, the returns that would not otherwise be expected based on past or future patterns.[37] There are various ways to calculate the expected return, one of which is based on the progression of a firm's stock price, while the more common technique relies on market trends.[38] This study relies on a market model by measuring a stock's past performance against the general market return. In other words, the

---

[34] To the extent the story was first published over the weekend, the next Monday was treated as the event date, with the prior Friday defined as the day before.

[35] See MacKinlay, *supra* n. 14, at 14–15 (suggesting a three-day event period); Sanjai Bhagat & Roberta Romano, 'Event Studies and the Law: Part I: Technique and Corporate Litigation,' 4 Am L & Econ Rev 141, 143–145 (2002) (discussing and defining the event period); Bhagat et al., 'Shareholder Wealth,' *supra* n. 13, at 15 (using a two-day event period); Davidson et al., *supra* n. 33, at 290 (using a three-day event period); Johnson et al., *supra* n. 30, at 34 (using a three-day event window).

[36] See Campbell, *supra* n. 14, at 157–159; Prince & Rubin, *supra* n. 13, at 51–52 (discussing the event study methodology and the use of dummy variables to calculate abnormal returns).

[37] See Fama, *supra* n. 33, at 1601–1602 (discussing the role of abnormal returns).

[38] See MacKinlay, *supra* n. 14, at 14–15 (discussing two common choices for modeling the normal return).

CHAPTER 1. THE PRICE OF DISCRIMINATION

model captures the expected returns as measured against the changes in the broad market, and I rely on the Standard and Poor's 500 Index as a general market indicator.

Two aspects of the market model bear mentioning. First, the model assumes a linear relation between the stock price and the market measure, so that if the S&P 500 goes up 100 points it is possible to predict the corresponding expected return of the particular stock. Second, the market model provides an imperfect measure since it will rarely offer a strong prediction of a particular stock price, a limitation discussed further below.[39] The expected returns are calculated by using a standard market parameter of the 120 days prior to the event and forty-five days after the announcement day period to provide a statistical estimate of the normal return that would have been expected had the event not occurred. The actual return is then compared to the expected return to determine the abnormal return.

1.2.3.1 The Results

This statistical analysis requires a four-step process, described in detail in Appendix Three. As indicated in Table 1.1, the analysis found that there was no significant effect on stock prices from either the filing of a lawsuit or the announcement of a settlement, and these findings held true regardless of the nature of the suit or the magnitude of the settlement.

TABLE 1.1: Class Action Filings, November 1991-August 2001

	Class Action Filings	Dummy Variable Coefficient	Standard Error of Coefficient	t Statistic	P_value	Cumulative Prediction Error (CPE)
1	AA	0.0218	0.0175	1.2435	0.2154	0.0435
2	ABS	0.0383	0.0138	2.7761	0.0061	0.0766
3	ABS_92	_0.0041	0.0760	_0.0541	0.9569	_0.0082
4	C_FEB97	0.0161	0.0435	0.3702	0.7117	0.0322

---

[39] See *infra* text accompanying notes 45–47.

EMPLOYMENT CLASS AND COLLECTIVE ACTIONS

	Class Action Filings	Dummy Variable Coefficient	Standard Error of Coefficient	t Statistic	P_value	Cumulative Prediction Error (CPE)
5	**CBS_VIA**	**_0.0316**	**0.0177**	**_1.7825**	**0.0765**	**_0.0632**
6	CC_INITIAL	_0.0156	0.0162	_0.9668	0.3351	_0.0313
7	DAL	_0.0094	0.0164	_0.5752	0.5660	_0.0188
8	F_JUN93	_0.0022	0.0113	_0.1954	0.8453	_0.0044
9	FTU	_0.0064	0.0073	_0.8811	0.3795	_0.0129
10	GE_FEB97	0.0028	0.0065	0.4298	0.6679	0.0056
11	GPE	0.0075	0.0183	0.4130	0.6802	0.0151
12	HD	_0.0062	0.0430	_0.1439	0.8858	_0.0124
13	IBC_APR00	0.0239	0.0211	1.1343	0.2583	0.0478
14	KO_APR99	_0.0114	0.0119	_0.9524	0.3423	_0.0227
15	KO_JUN00	0.0226	0.0191	1.1849	0.2377	0.0452
16	LMT_RACE	0.0024	0.0217	0.1111	0.9117	0.0048
17	JWN_APR92	_0.0007	0.0184	_0.0383	0.9695	_0.0014
18	MCDONNELL	_0.0075	0.0130	_0.5771	0.5646	_0.0150
19	**MET**	**_0.0321**	**0.0186**	**_1.7298**	**0.0855**	**_0.0643**
20	MLM_MAY94	_0.0210	0.0144	_1.4636	0.1452	_0.0420
21	MRK_JAN99	_0.0028	0.0105	_0.2656	0.7909	_0.0056
22	MS_JAN97	0.0423	0.0318	1.3312	0.1850	0.0847
23	**MSFT_JAN01**	**0.0356**	**0.0209**	**1.7034**	**0.0904**	**0.0713**
24	MSFT_OCT00	_0.0145	0.0204	_0.7080	0.4800	_0.0289
25	PEP_SEP94	0.0014	0.0104	0.1312	0.8958	0.0027
26	POM	_0.0007	0.0067	_0.1026	0.9184	_0.0014
27	TX_MAR94	0.0004	0.0063	0.0632	0.9497	0.0008
28	TX_MAR00	_0.0165	0.0153	_1.0754	0.2838	_0.0329

CHAPTER 1. THE PRICE OF DISCRIMINATION

	Class Action Filings	Dummy Variable Coefficient	Standard Error of Coefficient	t Statistic	P_value	Cumulative Prediction Error (CPE)
29	TX_FEB97	0.0060	0.0098	0.6168	0.5382	0.0121
30	UA	0.0018	0.0177	0.1012	0.9195	0.0036
31	WEN_APR94	_0.0039	0.0087	_0.4449	0.6570	_0.0077
32	WMT	0.0076	0.0136	0.5567	0.5785	0.0152
33	XRX	0.0035	0.0484	0.0724	0.9423	0.0070
	Cases in bold are significant at 10%.					
	Cumulative Average Prediction Error (CAPE) = SUM(CPE)/N	0.0029	CAPE test statistic = SUM(t_Stat)/sqrt(N)		0.1125	

There was, however, some variation among the individual lawsuits, and seven of the individual equations produced statistically significant results at the 0.10 level. Four of the filings – those against *Albertson's*, *CBS*, *MetLife*, and *Microsoft* – had statistically significant effects on the stock prices, although these four cases display no obvious pattern. For example, two of the cases involved allegations of sex discrimination, while two involved race discrimination. To the extent a pattern exists, all of the cases were filed during the two-year period 2000–2001, and three were filed in 2001. The fact that the recent cases had a significant effect on stock prices may be attributable to an increased awareness regarding the potential financial impact of the suits as a result of the recent string of high profile cases such as *Texaco* and *Coca-Cola*. Nonetheless, there were ten other cases filed during the same time period that were not significant.

Table 1.2 indicates a similar lack of aggregate significance in the settlement cases, and notably the size of the settlement was not related to whether the case had a significant effect. For example, the USD 120 million settlement agreement entered into by *Interstate Brands* (the makers of Wonder Bread) had no greater effect on the company's stock price than the USD 8 million settlement agreed to by *AlliedSignal*.

17

EMPLOYMENT CLASS AND COLLECTIVE ACTIONS

Three of the individual settlements produced statistically significant results: the *Texaco* settlement involving race discrimination, a USD 33 million agreement involving *Winn-Dixie* that included allegations of both race and sex discrimination, and a race discrimination resolution entered into by *Morgan Stanley* that did not include any monetary award. Of these, only the *Texaco* settlement had a negative effect on the firm's stock price, while the other two agreements positively affected the price.

TABLE 1.2: Class Action Settlements
November 1991 to August 2001

	Class Action Settlements	Dummy Variable Coefficient	Standard Error of Coefficient	t Statistic	P_value	Cumulative Prediction Error (CPE)
1	AB	_0.0178	0.0345	_0.5155	0.6069	_0.0356
2	ABS_92	_0.0028	0.0112	_0.2476	0.8048	_0.0056
3	ASC	0.0150	0.0096	1.5522	0.1225	0.0299
4	AXP_AUG92	_0.0012	0.0179	_0.0691	0.9450	_0.0025
5	ALD_NOV99	_0.0018	0.0096	_0.1893	0.8501	_0.0036
6	BA_DOL	0.0109	0.0141	0.7745	0.4397	0.0218
7	BA_JAN99	0.0167	0.0186	0.8996	0.3696	0.0335
8	CBS_VIA	_0.0047	0.0208	_0.2243	0.8228	_0.0093
9	CHV_NOV96	0.0023	0.0076	0.3085	0.7581	0.0047
10	EIX_OCT96	_0.0036	0.0087	_0.4185	0.6761	_0.0073
11	FTU	0.0063	0.0078	0.8114	0.4183	0.0127
12	HD	_0.0046	0.0085	_0.5365	0.5923	_0.0091
13	IBC	_0.0193	0.0222	_0.8699	0.3856	_0.0387
14	KO	0.0100	0.0165	0.6057	0.5456	0.0200
15	LMT_AGE	_0.0011	0.0082	_0.1378	0.8906	_0.0023
16	MER_FEB00	_0.0141	0.0189	_0.7434	0.4583	_0.0281
17	MER_MAY98	_0.0035	0.0152	_0.2295	0.8188	_0.0070

	Class Action Settlements	Dummy Variable Coefficient	Standard Error of Coefficient	t Statistic	P_value	Cumulative Prediction Error (CPE)
18	**MWD**	**0.0346**	**0.0195**	**1.7732**	**0.0780**	**0.0691**
19	MD_J JUL 98	_0.0016	0.0143	_0.1118	0.9111	_0.0032
20	NSC	_0.0105	0.0181	_0.5813	0.5618	_0.0210
21	PZL_NOV98	_0.0057	0.0161	_0.3515	0.7257	_0.0113
22	SHOY	_0.0236	0.0186	_1.2689	0.2063	_0.0472
23	SWY	0.0004	0.0147	0.0250	0.9801	0.0007
24	**TX_NOV96**	**_0.0219**	**0.0083**	**_2.6448**	**0.0090**	**_0.0439**
25	**WIN_JUL99**	**0.0214**	**0.0111**	**1.9310**	**0.0552**	**0.0428**
26	WXS_FEB95	0.0071	0.0108	0.6511	0.5159	0.0141
	Cases in bold are significant at 10%.					
	Cumulative Average Prediction Error (CAPE) = SUM(CPE)/N	_0.0010		CAPE test statistic = SUM(t_Stat)/sqrt(N)	0.0377674	

1.2.3.2 Explaining the Statistical Analysis

The above findings cast doubt on several of the reigning myths regarding employment discrimination litigation. For many years, it has been argued that the costs of employment discrimination lawsuits are devastating to corporations and should therefore be limited so as to reduce the harm the suits produce.[40] Yet based on the data analyzed here, there is no indication that firms suffer a significant loss of shareholder value

---

[40] See generally Richard Epstein, *Forbidden Grounds: The Case Against Employment Discrimination Law* (1992); Phillip Howard, *The Death of Common Sense* (1994) 134; Walter K. Olson, *The Excuse Factory: How Employment Law Is Paralyzing the American Workplace* (1997).

as a result of the filing of a lawsuit; indeed, the filing of a lawsuit appears to be of little direct interest to investors. This is not because investors are unconcerned about the costs of the lawsuits, but as discussed in more detail below, because the potential costs appear too insignificant for the purposes of determining investment decisions. Moreover, given that, even with the settlements, the loss to firm value does not generally exceed the costs of the lawsuit, there appears to be little reputational damage that results from being accused of discrimination. As detailed in the next section, firms often react quickly to reduce possible reputational damage that might arise from the lawsuits, and often do so effectively, and their swift actions may limit collateral damage from the suits.[41]

The absence of significant effects stemming from the filing of a lawsuit may not seem unusual, because a filing sends no particular message to investors other than that a firm will incur legal costs. The filing of a lawsuit does not indicate that a firm is actually discriminating, or that it will be found liable. Many lawsuits terminate shortly after they are filed, typically without any relief at all. This is not, however, true of the majority of cases tracked in this article.[42] While a number of cases are still pending, and some have likely been resolved without any attendant publicity, the vast majority of cases that were resolved resulted in significant relief for the plaintiff class. Based on this sample, the success rate of class action employment litigation appears to exceed the rate for employment discrimination cases more generally.[43] This is

---

[41] See *infra* subsection 1.3.1 (describing Texaco's swift reaction to negative litigation-related news).

[42] Of the cases in this study, in only the *Nordstrom* case was the dismissal reported in the news. See Sylvia Wieland Nogaki, 'Nordstrom Bias Suit Dropped,' Chi Trib, November 15, 1992, at C14 (reporting that the race discrimination suit was dropped by all but one of the thirteen plaintiffs due to a lack of financing).

[43] Employment discrimination cases have long had success rates lower than other classes of civil claims. See Theodore Eisenberg, 'Litigation Models and Trial Outcomes in Civil Rights and Prisoner Cases,' 77 Geo LJ 1567, 1578 (1989) (documenting a success rate of 22% for employment discrimination cases). In a recent comprehensive analysis of trial and appellate outcomes, Professors Clermont and Eisenberg concluded, 'Job discrimination plaintiffs are one of the least successful classes of plaintiffs at the trial-court level, in that they fare worse at trial than almost any other category of civil case.' Kevin M. Clermont & Theodore Eisenberg, 'Plaintiphobia in the Appellate Courts: Civil Rights Really Do Differ from Negotiable Instruments,' 2002 Ill L Rev (forthcoming 2003).

likely attributable to the costs and difficulties of filing and litigating class action cases, perhaps evidenced by the fact that only a handful of law firms regularly file discrimination class actions, and one law firm in particular is responsible for a disproportionate number of suits.[44] It also appears that investors do not anticipate that the filing of a lawsuit will result in litigation fees sufficiently large to adversely impact the firm. This may be true either because the fees are not expected to be particularly high given the size of the firm or because the fees are treated as an operating cost that has already been factored into the stock price. Somewhat contrary to common perceptions, the assumption that litigation costs will be relatively modest appears to be supported by the realities of the litigation. For example, in the hotly contested litigation involving *Home Depot*, a case that settled on the eve of trial, the defendant's fees were estimated to have totaled USD 5 million.[45] These fees are not insignificant, but in the context of a firm the size of Home Depot, they are not especially consequential either.[46]

The fact that the settlements had no significant effect on the stock price may seem more puzzling but can also be explained in a number of ways. First, it is important to highlight a limitation on a study of this nature where only limited controls are imposed to measure the movement of a stock price. Although I have used standard event studies methodology, the statistical model does not always offer a substantial explanation of an expected return to a stock price, in large part because it is often difficult to predict stock price movements. What this study measures is whether a stock price moves differently from what was expected, but given that stock price movements often belie our expectations, it can be difficult to accurately predict expected returns.

Another reason a firm's stock price may not be affected by the settlement is that the stock market may have been anticipating a larger monetary award than was ultimately obtained.[47] In the case of

---

[44] The law firm is now called Saperstein Goldstein Demchak & Bellar, and is discussed in more detail in subsection III(B). Of the suits tracked in this study, the Saperstein firm was involved in the *Home Depot, Denny's, Shoney's, State Farm, Publix, Lucky's, Albertson's, Safeway,* and *Southern California Edison* cases.
[45] See Vera Titunik, 'Facing Hammer, Home Depot Decides to Deal,' Am Law, November 1997, at 38 (noting that Home Depot spent USD 5 million in legal fees prior to trial).
[46] See *infra* text accompanying n. 49.
[47] See Engelmann & Cornell, *supra* n. 32, at 393 (noting that when settlements are lower than expected, firm value may increase); Prince & Rubin, *supra* n. 13, at 48

Coca-Cola, the largest and the most recent class action settlement to date, it is possible that the market was expecting a judgment in excess of the actual reported award of USD 192.5 million – particularly since the *Texaco* case had only recently received so much attention and Coca-Cola was enmeshed in a difficult public relations battle involving the negative implications of the lawsuit.[48]

It also seems clear that the damages, even at this level, are simply too small to affect corporations the size of Coca-Cola, Texaco, Home Depot, or most of the other firms involved in this study. For example, the USD 104 million settlement agreed to by *Home Depot* amounted to two weeks' pretax profit.[49] Table 1.3 provides a representative sampling of the relation of the settlement to the firm's capitalization. Except for the case involving *Shoney's*, the remaining settlements all fell below 3.5% of a firm's capitalization, with both the *Home Depot* and *Coca-Cola* falling below 1%. Previous studies have found that the size of the firm positively affects results so that the lawsuits have less of an impact on large firms,[50] and all of the firms included in the sample were large firms.

Table 1.3: Size of Judgment as Percentage of Firm Capitalization

Company Name	Settle. Amt. (in USD millions)	Firm Capital. (in USD millions)	Percent
American Stores	107.00	3,077.73	3.48
First Union	58.50	25,536.99	0.23
Home Depot	104.00	11,478.85	0.91

(noting that positive returns from settlements may indicate investors were expecting higher monetary relief).

[48] See Maharaj, *supra* n. 7 (describing the *Coca-Cola* settlement and noting that the amount was well within investor expectations).

[49] Chris Roush, *Inside Home Depot: How One Company Revolutionized an Industry through the Relentless Pursuit of Growth* (1999) 78.

[50] See Bhagat et al., 'Shareholder Wealth,' *supra* n. 13, at 25 (finding that the defendant wealth effect is positively related to the size of the firm).

CHAPTER 1. THE PRICE OF DISCRIMINATION

Company Name	Settle. Amt. (in USD millions)	Firm Capital. (in USD millions)	Percent
Interstate Bakeries	28.30	1,066.50	2.65
Coca-Cola	192.50	140,643.07	0.14
Lockheed Martin	183.00	8,610.78	2.13
Shoney's	134.00	903.37	14.83

It is also possible, for both the filings and the settlements, that information had leaked into the market prior to the official event, thus allowing investors to adjust their expectations prior to the actual announcements. There is even the possibility that substantial insider trading may have affected stock prices before the official announcements.[51] While it remains possible that information leaked out into the market before the news was reported, there is no empirical evidence to support the theory, and it seems more likely that the events did not have a significant effect on prices rather than that substantial insider trading occurred.

The fact that neither the filings nor the settlements have a significant effect on stock prices suggests that there is no market penalty associated with being accused of discrimination or from having reached a negotiated settlement in a discrimination suit. It would certainly be possible to imagine that investors would disinvest from discriminatory firms, but there is little evidence to suggest that investors shun firms that have been accused of discrimination or that have settled discrimination cases.[52] The fact that discrimination suits do not extract significant value from firms, while perhaps contrary to common perceptions, may be understandable once we realize that social investing

---

[51] Insider trading has been shown to move stock prices, often significantly. See Lisa K. Meulbroek, 'An Empirical Analysis of Illegal Insider Trading,' 47 J Fin 1661, 1663 (1992) (demonstrating the effect of insider trading on stock prices). How insider trading is recognized by the market is less clear, though there does seem to be evidence that it is recognized, perhaps by its volume. See *id.* at 1693–1695.

[52] The one exception, discussed in the next section, is the case against *Texaco* that involved widely publicized tapes that appeared to include racial epithets. When the story first broke, there was widespread selling of the stock, but the disinvestment proved only temporary, and most of the lost value was restored within a month of the initial allegations. See *infra* text accompanying notes 92–94.

remains a very small part of the investment world, and even within the realm of social investors, employment practices generally do not factor into the investment decision.[53]

In addition to the monetary costs of the suits, firms are undoubtedly concerned with the potential reputational costs of the lawsuits, but there appear to be few actual consequences outside of the unusual case that receives extremely high publicity, typically resulting from overt forms of racial discrimination.[54] Indeed, based on past studies of lawsuits in other areas, it appears that employment discrimination lawsuits have less stigma attached to them than other kinds of lawsuits such as product liability claims. One study involving product recalls found a significant effect on firm value that exceeded the direct costs of the recall,[55] and other studies have likewise found that the value lost as a result of interfirm corporate lawsuits often exceeds the costs of the lawsuit, largely because of the reforms companies may need to make as a result of the litigation.[56] However, because discrimination claims rarely lead to substantial corporate reform, most investors will not be concerned with the fact that a firm has been accused of discrimination other than as it relates to the potential direct costs of that discrimination.

Based on the statistical analysis, it appears that neither the filing nor the settlement of a lawsuit significantly affects a firm's stock price. Later in this article, I will suggest some implications of this study for the

---

[53] See Lawrence E. Mitchell, *Corporate Irresponsibility: America's Newest Export* (2001) 167–168 (discussing socially responsible investing). TIAA-CREF, the largest pension fund in the country with many participants who ought to be sympathetic to social investing, reports that its social investment account totals USD 4.4 billion while its stock accounts are valued at USD 87.5 billion. TIAA-CREF, TIAA-CREF Mutual Funds: Social Choice Equity Fund Profile, at <www.tiaa-cref.org> (last visited September 2, 2008). Many social investment funds do not screen for labor practices.

[54] This has occurred in a handful of cases over the last few years, including *Texaco* and *Denny's*, discussed in the next section, as well as *Shoney's*, *Mitsubishi*, and to a lesser extent *Coca-Cola*.

[55] Gregg Jarrell & Sam Peltzman, 'The Impact of Product Recalls on the Wealth of Sellers,' 93 J Pol Econ 512, 533 (1985).

[56] See Bhagat et al., 'Costs,' *supra* n. 13, at 229 ('Our results indicate that plaintiffs can and do damage defendants through litigation, but that plaintiffs gain far less than defendants lose.'); see also David M. Cutler & Lawrence H. Summers, 'The Costs of Conflict Resolution and Financial Distress: Evidence from the Texaco-Pennzoil Litigation,' 19 Rand J Econ 157, 164 (1988) (finding that the lawsuit jointly cost shareholders USD 1 billion).

theory that discrimination litigation serves as an adequate deterrent against discrimination and for the prospect that the market will eradicate discriminatory firms (as has long been argued by law and economics scholars).[57] But before doing so, I want to discuss three case studies to determine what effect employment discrimination class actions have within firms.

1.3 DO THE LAWSUITS PRODUCE MEANINGFUL CHANGE? THREE CASE STUDIES

The previous section sought to determine how, or whether, class action litigation affects stock prices of defendant firms. Stock prices, however, provide only one measure of the potential impact of a lawsuit, and in this section I present three case studies to explore how the lawsuits affect internal company practices, including the changes made by the firms as a result of the settlement agreements. This analysis inevitably provides only a limited insight into the company's response to the lawsuit, because it does not take into account whether the corporate culture has changed other than as measured in numerical changes in personnel, purchasing agreements, and other quantifiable factors. Measuring changes in corporate culture is a difficult task that requires extensive observation both before and after the lawsuits, something that is generally infeasible by anyone other than the company itself – though a company's own biases often preclude an honest assessment of just how much things have actually changed.[58] Nevertheless, the case studies provide significant insight into what changes the lawsuits prompted. They also provide three distinct models for how companies respond to the suits – what I label the public relations model, the recalcitrance model, and the reform model.

---

[57] See *infra* section 1.4.
[58] This part of the study is based on available public information, primarily from court decisions and journalist accounts, including several book-length treatments. For a variety of reasons, I decided not to rely on interviews, although I have spoken with a number of attorneys who have been involved in the cases, and those conversations have likely influenced some of my thinking.

1.3.1 *Texaco*: The Public Relations Model

1.3.1.1 *The Lawsuit and the Tapes*

Although the case against Texaco is perhaps now the most famous employment discrimination case to arise in the last decade, the controversy began in a much quieter fashion. The suit was originally filed in 1994 by two African-American employees who sought class action status for their salary and promotion claims, and when the suit was filed it received virtually no national attention.[59] At the time of the suit, Texaco was one of the United States oil companies with more than 19,000 employees, of whom approximately 22% were minorities, a percentage that placed Texaco roughly in the middle of its oil company peers.[60] Texaco also claimed that 19.4% of its executive-level employees were minorities,[61] a figure that was disputed by the plaintiffs, and after investigating the company's practices, both the Equal Employment Opportunity Commission[62] and the Department of Labor found Texaco's promotional policies deficient.[63]

The case, initiated by a law firm that had not handled a civil rights case in twenty years, was largely statistical in nature, involving both claims of disparate treatment and disparate impact.[64] From the available evidence, it appears that the claims with the greatest chance for success were based on the disparate impact theory, though it is difficult to say

---

[59] Alison Frankel, 'Tale of the Tapes,' Am Law, March 1997, at 64, 68–69 ('This case crawled along virtually unnoticed for two-and-a-half years.').

[60] David Ivanovich et al., 'Oil Industry Struggling with Diversity,' Houston Chron, November 17, 1996, at A1.

[61] Kurt Eichenwald, 'The Two Faces of Texaco,' NY Times, November 10, 1996, at C1.

[62] Frankel, *supra* n. 59, at 71.

[63] The Department of Labor had conducted two investigations and found Texaco's promotion policies deficient in both. See *id.* (discussing Department of Labor reviews that found 'wide disparities between the promotion rates for whites and nonwhites at Texaco').

[64] In a decision awarding attorneys' fees, the district court summarized the case as follows: 'The amended complaint charged that... Texaco had, by certain employment policies and practices, engaged in conduct that had a disparate impact upon and abridged the rights of salaried African-American employees of Texaco in promotions, compensation, and the terms and conditions of their employment,

CHAPTER 1. THE PRICE OF DISCRIMINATION

more than that; during the two years the case was active, most of the litigation involved discovery disputes, and no class had been certified prior to the settlement.[65] It is significant that the strongest claims involved disparate impact allegations, since such claims are tried before a judge rather than a jury and are limited to equitable relief rather than damages.[66] Based on an account by one of the plaintiffs, during the mediation and prior to the revelation of the taped conversations, the plaintiffs' statistical expert valued the case at between USD 10–30 million.[67] Other reports have suggested that the plaintiffs estimated their salary claim to be worth USD 71 million in back pay.[68] The suit became bogged down early on by a lengthy and decidedly unproductive government-supported mediation, during which the case took a dramatic turn that had little to do with its underlying merits.[69]

On November 4, 1996, *The New York Times* published a story based on a transcript of a secretly tape-recorded meeting attended by management officials that included what appeared to be racial epithets, as well as evidence indicating an intent on the part of Texaco officials to destroy documents that had been requested by the plaintiffs in the

---

including training and job assignments.' *Roberts v. Texaco*, 979 F. Supp. 185, 189 (SDNY 1997). The statistical portion of the case was based on a disparate impact claim, which likewise formed the basis for the class allegations. See Frankel, *supra* n. 59, at 69 (noting that 'the plaintiffs lawyers tried to show the court that the reason for the disparate impact was racial discrimination').

[65] See *Roberts*, 979 F. Supp. at 189 (noting that a class certification hearing was scheduled for December 6, 1996).

[66] See 42 USC 2000e-2(k) (2000).

[67] Bari-Ellen Roberts, 'Roberts vs. Texaco: A True Story of Race and Corporate America,' (1998) 232. The author quotes one of the plaintiffs' attorneys, in preparing for the mediation, as saying, 'We think Texaco ought to pay ten million dollars in back wages to the black employees it has been discriminating against for the past five years and another ten million dollars to compensate. Throw in attorneys' fees and other odds and ends and it comes to thirty million dollars... how's that sound?'

[68] Frankel, *supra* n. 59, at 69 ('The plaintiffs' statistician concluded in his expert witness report that Texaco's African Americans were paid USD 71 million less than comparable nonminority employees....').

[69] Based on Roberts' book, until the tapes were disclosed, there did not appear to be any particular hope that the case would be resolved short of either summary judgment or trial, as the parties remained engaged in seriously contested litigation. Roberts, *supra* n. 67, at 188–245.

27

case.[70] The tapes were made by Texaco executive Richard Lundwell, ostensibly to aid him in preparing minutes of the meeting, and were turned over to the plaintiffs by Lundwell after he was involuntarily retired by the company.[71] The plaintiffs' attorneys in turn leaked the transcripts to *The New York Times*, which ran a story about the tapes on its front page, and the reaction to the tapes was both immediate and dramatic.

On the day the news was reported, Texaco's stock price dropped 2.6% on the New York Stock Exchange.[72] While the stock price stabilized quickly thereafter, the direct economic impact of the newly disclosed tape recordings was a drop in the value of the stock of approximately USD 1 billion.[73] Several large public investors also reacted negatively to the revelation of the tapes, and a number of other agencies threatened to terminate their investments.[74] Shortly

---

[70] See Kurt Eichenwald, 'Texaco Executives, On Tape Discussed Impeding a Bias Suit,' NY Times, November 4, 1996, at A1. The article stated that on the tapes 'executives are heard referring to black employees as "black jelly beans" and "niggers."' Id. The 'black jelly beans' apparently was borrowed from a metaphor used in diversity training, and an enhanced version of the tape indicated that the racial epithet had not been used but instead had been a reference to St. Nicholas' beard. See *infra* n. 79.

[71] Eichenwald, *supra* n. 70. Mr. Lundwell initially sought to trade the tapes to the plaintiffs' attorney in exchange for their representation of him in an age discrimination suit against his former employer. The plaintiffs' attorney declined to represent Lundwell but did refer him to an attorney, and once Lundwell had retained an attorney he turned the tapes over to the plaintiffs' attorneys in the *Roberts* case. For the most comprehensive report of the tapes incident, see Frankel, *supra* n. 59, at 64.

[72] Kurt Eichenwald, 'U.S. Inquiring Into Texaco's Actions in Suit,' NY Times, November 5, 1996, at Dl.

[73] Alexander Cockburn, 'Oil's Sweet Music; Racial Discrimination Lawsuit Against Texaco,' The Nation, December 9, 1996, at 9.

[74] The Philadelphia comptroller's city-pension board unanimously voted to sell all of its Texaco stock, valued at more than USD 5.6 million. Sally Goll Beatty, 'Texaco's Effort to Repair Image Comes Under Fire After First Ad,' Wall St J, November 27, 1996, at B2. Lauren R. Rublin, The Trader, Barron's, November 25, 1996, at MW3. A Texas legislator called on his state to sell nearly USD 250 million of Texaco stock held by the state's retirement funds. Demetrius Patterson, 'Pressure on Texaco Continues,' Chi Sun-Times, November 10, 1996, at 2. New York State Comptroller H. Carl McCall took the 'wait and see' approach. He was reluctant to act too quickly to sell the state's Common Retirement Fund's shares, valued at about USD 114 million. See Rublin, *supra*; Joann S. Lublin, 'Texaco's Board Takes Limited Role in Handling Race-Discrimination Case,' Wall St J, November 18, 1996, at A3.

CHAPTER 1. THE PRICE OF DISCRIMINATION

after *The New York Times* story broke, Jesse Jackson announced that his organization, the Rainbow PUSH Action Network, would buy Texaco stock to gain a voice in the company, and would likewise initiate a study of the affirmative action policies of other companies that had directors in common with Texaco, such as Gillette and Campbell's Soup.[75] Many outraged Texaco customers contacted the company's chairman directly, vowing to destroy their Texaco credit cards[76] and expressing their intent to stop doing business with the company.[77] This action was echoed by local and national efforts to boycott Texaco, while a number of prominent civil rights leaders urged consumers not only to boycott Texaco, but to picket as well.[78]

A week after the initial story broke, *The New York Times* reported that an enhanced version of the tape recording indicated that no racial epithet had been used in the conversation, although the allegations of document tampering remained.[79] In a masterful bit of public relations, the plaintiffs' attorneys declared that the new version of the tapes did not change matters, and one day later major civil rights groups called for a national boycott, demanding that Texaco settle the lawsuit quickly and establish an effective affirmative action plan to address its racist

---

[75] Steven A. Holmes, 'Size of Texaco Discrimination Settlement Could Encourage More Lawsuits,' NY Times, November 17, 1996, at A20. It appears that, to date, the study has not been completed and none of those companies has been sued for racial discrimination.

[76] Allanna Sullivan & Peter Fritsch, 'Texaco Punishes Officials Over Racist Epithets,' Wall St J, November 7, 1996, at A2.

[77] Kurt Eichenwald, 'The First Casualties in Scandal at Texaco,' NY Times, November 7, 1996, at Dl.

[78] Kurt Eichenwald, 'For Texaco, an Unsought Role on a Big Stage,' NY Times, November 14, 1996, at D1. Also, a group of San Diego clergy and business leaders called for Texaco customers to cut their Texaco credit cards. They further called for a national boycott of *Texaco* products. Eichenwald, *supra* n. 77.

[79] See Kurt Eichenwald, 'Investigation Finds No Evidence of Slur on Texaco Tapes,' NY Times, November 11, 1996, at A1. It is worth noting that the original version of the tapes were played widely on television and radio, and most listeners believed the word used was the racial epithet, as was also the case when Texaco's chairman originally heard the tape. *Id*. The Texaco officials were later acquitted on criminal charges of obstruction of justice relating to the document destruction allegations. Adam Bryant, '2 in Texaco Case Found Not Guilty,' NY Times, May 13, 1998, at A1.

culture.[80] The threat of a national boycott prompted another sell-off of Texaco's stock, which declined USD 2 (2.1%), closing at USD 95.375 the day the boycott was announced.[81] The timing of the controversy surrounding the tapes added an additional sense of urgency to the protests, as California's anti-affirmative action Proposition 209 had been ratified by the voters only two weeks earlier and *Texaco* was quickly seen as an important test case for preserving corporate affirmative action.[82]

In what has now become a textbook reaction to negative litigation-related news, Texaco's chief executive officer, Peter Bijur, reacted quickly to defuse the public outrage that followed the disclosure of the tapes. Bijur, who had only been at the helm for several months when the news first broke,[83] immediately condemned the acts of the managers that had been reported on the tape, fired two of them, and stripped two other retirees of their pension benefits.[84] He also appointed a prominent New York attorney to investigate the allegations sparked by the tapes,[85] a retired and well-respected judge, Leon Higginbotham, to investigate the corporate culture, and declared that the company would take additional actions to ensure that Texaco became a model employer.[86] On November 11, 1996, *The Wall Street Journal* reported Texaco had entered into formal settlement talks and was 'hoping to bring a quick end to a widening scandal.'[87] On that day, Texaco's stock gained USD 1.375,[88] indicating shareholders viewed the potential settlement as softening the total financial impact the case might have on Texaco's future. As noted earlier, those gains were all but eliminated by the announcement of the boycott, though the stock rebounded the following day based on news reports that the settlement was progressing. Even though the tapes proved far less incriminating

---

[80] Kurt Eichenwald, 'Calls Issued for Boycott of Texaco,' NY Times, November 13, 1996, at D1.
[81] *Id.*
[82] Eichenwald, *supra* n. 77.
[83] 'Rooting Out Racism,' Bus Wk, January 10, 2000, at 66.
[84] See Eichenwald, *supra* n. 77 (reporting Bijur's announcement that the company had taken action against the manager and retirees).
[85] Allanna Sullivan & Peter Fritsch, 'Texaco is Trying to Reach a Settlement in 1994 Racial-Discrimination Lawsuit,' Wall St J, November 11, 1996, at A3.
[86] Eichenwald, *supra* n. 77, at D1.
[87] Sullivan & Fritsch, *supra* n. 85.
[88] 'Texaco Seeks to Settle; Stock Up,' NY Times, November 12, 1996, at D22.

CHAPTER 1. THE PRICE OF DISCRIMINATION

than originally anticipated, the pressure on the company remained intense, and its potential liability for the lawsuit was then estimated to exceed USD 500 million.[89] Reports indicated that Texaco had lagged behind its peers in hiring and promoting African Americans,[90] and it was clear that Texaco was fast becoming a poster child for racism in corporate America.[91]

Several days later, on November 15, 1996, *Texaco* settled the lawsuit for an amount that was estimated to total USD 140 million, a record-setting agreement that caused an additional significant drop of nearly 3% in the stock price.[92] Yet, continuing its schizophrenic ride, the stock quickly recovered half of the lost value the next day, and by November 25, the stock was trading at a price that was nearly 4% higher than its pre-tape level. An important industry journal later observed 'Five months after Texaco Inc. was plunged into its worse-ever public relations disaster...it appears to have emerged relatively unscathed. Between early November – when news of damaging evidence in a race discrimination suit broke – and the end of March, Texaco's stock skyrocketed 10% as oil prices slid 11%.'[93] By the middle of 1997, less than a year after the tapes were revealed, Texaco's stock price reached an all-time high.[94]

The settlement agreement included a USD 115 million settlement fund to compensate the class members' monetary claims, attorneys' fees, and costs, and to cover the costs of administering the agreement. Texaco also agreed to increase the salaries of all class members by 11.34%, in addition to whatever salary increase the individual was entitled to under Texaco's normal review procedures,[95] a process that was estimated to cost the company an additional USD 22 million.[96]

---

[89] Sullivan & Fritsch, *supra* n. 85.
[90] *Id.* In 1995, only 3.75% of Texaco's officials and managers were black, compared to at least 6% at Amoco Corp., Chevron Corp., Exxon Corp., and Mobil Corp.
[91] See Eichenwald, *supra* n. 80 (discussing calls for a boycott of Texaco).
[92] See 'Texaco Stock Skids after Settlement Terms Disclosed,' NY Times, November 19, 1996, at D4 (reporting that Texaco shares fell by USD 2.75, or 2.7%).
[93] Courtney Chubb, 'Texaco Outlook Shines Despite Race Problems,' Oil Daily, April 7, 1997, at 1.
[94] Sharon Walsh, 'Investors Focus on Diversity at Texaco Annual Meeting; Company Faces,' 94 Discrimination Filings, Wash Post, May 14, 1997, at D9 (reporting that it was announced in Texaco's annual meeting that its stock price had 'reached an all-time high today').
[95] *Roberts v. Texaco, Inc.*, 979 F. Supp. 185, 191–192 (SDNY 1997).
[96] *Id.* at 191 n. 6.

In addition to the direct monetary terms, the company agreed to establish a diversity task force to evaluate, revise, and develop the company's employment policies and practices so as to ensure fair hiring and promotion of minority workers.[97] The task force would comprise seven members, three appointed by the plaintiffs, three by Texaco, with the chairperson jointly selected by the two parties. The task force was intended to act as an ongoing oversight committee with a five-year term and was estimated to add an additional USD 35 million to the settlement.[98] As discussed in more detail below, the task force was seen as both an integral and innovative part of the settlement agreement, and is now becoming a standard feature in many large class action resolutions.[99] When the various aspects of the settlement were added together, the settlement was valued at USD 170 million. While the settlement amount was unquestionably large, the amounts were to be paid out over a five-year period – and the company's 1996 revenue alone exceeded USD 30 billion.[100] It is estimated that members of the plaintiff class averaged USD 63,000 as part of the settlement, and the lead plaintiffs received substantially higher awards for their participation in the

---

[97] See Peter Fritsch et al., 'Record Settlement Includes Task Force Possessing Broad Oversight Power,' Wall St J, November 18, 1996, at A3 (discussing the settlement reached and the powers of the diversity task force); see also Kurt Eichenwald, 'Texaco to Make Record Payout in Bias Lawsuit,' NY Times, November 16, 1996, at A1 (mentioning that 'the task force will have the authority to evaluate employment policies and practices and to develop new procedures on hiring and promoting minority workers').

[98] Eichenwald, *supra* n. 97.

[99] Both Mitsubishi and Coca-Cola have similar groups. See Sherri Day, 'Anti-Bias Task Force Gives Coca-Cola Good Marks, But Says Challenges Remain,' NY Times, September 26, 2002, at C3 (mentioning that 'the seven-person diversity panel is only the second independent body appointed by a court to monitor race and human resources relations within a company'); Kirstin Downey Grimsley, 'Mitsubishi Settles for USD 34 Million; Amount is Record in Harassment Suits,' Wash Post, June 12, 1998, at A1 (discussing 'the creation of a three-person panel of outside monitors to ensure policies banning sexual harassment' as part of the *Mitsubishi* settlement); see also *infra* text accompanying notes 129–132.

[100] 'Texaco to Pay USD 176.1 Million in Bias Suit,' Wall St J, November 18, 1996, at A3.

CHAPTER 1. THE PRICE OF DISCRIMINATION

case.[101] A little-known fact about the settlement is that a substantial portion was covered by insurance.[102]

As a demonstration of its commitment to repairing its image, Texaco also agreed to implement changes that went beyond the formal terms of the settlement agreement. Texaco committed itself to increasing its minority employees by the year 2000 to 29% of the firm's total (from its 1996 level of 23%), and to increase its employment of African Americans from 9% to 13%.[103] The firm also pledged to increase the promotion of women and minorities throughout the firm, and to increase its spending with minority- and women-owned businesses to USD 200 million a year from its previous annual level of USD 135 million.[104] To ensure the goals were met, the company agreed to tie a portion of its managers' bonuses to meeting diversity goals, and also agreed to enroll all of its employees in diversity training.[105] Texaco also established scholarship programs for minorities and women interested in engineering, increased its recruiting of women and minorities, and became the principal sponsor of UniverSoul Big Top Circus, the nation's only circus owned by African Americans.[106]

Attorneys' fees form a critical, and often controversial, part of any settlement agreement, and the *Texaco* case was no exception. The

---

[101] See 'Texaco Discrimination Settlement Endorsed,' NY Times, March 26, 1997, at D6 (noting that the awards exceeded USD 63,000 on average for 1,348 salaried African-American employees); Leon E. Wynter & Allanna Sullivan, 'Business & Race: Recipients of Checks From Texaco Suit Chart Their Futures,' Wall St J, November 5, 1997, at B1 (stating that Bari-Ellen Roberts, one of the lead plaintiffs, received a USD 150,000 settlement check while Paulette Grant received 'close to a USD 100,000 payout').

[102] See Stephanie D. Esters, 'Texaco Case to Bolster EPLI Market, Nat'l Underwriter: Prop. & Casualty/Risk & Benefits Mgmt. Edition,' December 2, 1996, at 1, 45 ('Jim Sword, a Texaco representative, said the company would not discuss the details of its insurance coverage for the settlement, but said "we feel we are adequately covered."').

[103] Kurt Eichenwald, 'Texaco Plans Wide Program for Minorities,' NY Times, December 19, 1996, at D1.

[104] 'Texaco Diversity Plan Is Endorsed by Heads of Activist Groups,' Wall St J, December 19, 1996, at B11.

[105] Eichenwald, *supra* n. 103.

[106] See Adam Bryant, 'How Much Has Texaco Changed?,' NY Times, November 2, 1997, at C1 (discussing the implementation of Texaco's diversity programs, as well as future goals set by Texaco to further increase minority hiring).

plaintiffs' attorneys sought a fee award of 25% of the USD 115 million settlement fund, or a total of more than USD 28 million.[107] Based on their detailed filings, the plaintiffs' actual fees[108] and expenses[109] totaled just over USD 4 million, with an expectation that they would spend an additional USD 700,000 administering the settlement.[110] The plaintiffs' attorneys therefore initially sought a fee award that was just over six times their actual fees and costs. The district court ultimately awarded USD 19.1 million in fees, or 5.5 times the actual fees, as well as another USD 1 million to be used for future services relating to the decree.[111]

Although the results of the lawsuit were undeniably impressive, the fee award by any measure was extraordinary, particularly given that most courts, at the direction of the Supreme Court, have severely limited the availability of fee enhancements in civil rights cases.[112] One of the interesting aspects of the fee award, not uncommon in class action settlements, is that there was no party to contest the application for fees. The fee award came directly out of the settlement fund, and therefore was of little interest to the defendants. Conversely, the plaintiff class was in an awkward position to challenge the fees of the attorneys who had brought them such a significant settlement. Even so, at 16.5% of the damage award, the fee award was substantially below (in fact, approximately half) the one-third contingency that remains common among plaintiffs' attorneys.[113]

1.3.1.2 Texaco's Progress

Although the company's settlement and additional commitments received widespread news coverage, its implementation of the planned

---

[107] *Roberts v. Texaco, Inc.*, 979 F. Supp. 185, 193 (SDNY 1997).

[108] *Id.* at 194 n.13 (stating that plaintiffs' counsel's time charges were just under USD 3.5 million).

[109] *Id.* at 193 n.12 (stating that plaintiffs' counsel's disbursements were USD 778,137.34).

[110] *Id.* at 195.

[111] *Id.* at 197.

[112] See *City of Burlington v. Dague*, 505 US 557 (1992) (holding that a fee enhancement to reflect the contingent nature of the representation exceeding the lodestar amount was impermissible).

[113] See Herbert M. Kritzer, 'The Wages of Risk: The Returns of Contingency Fee Legal Practice,' 47 DePaul L Rev 267, 285 (1998) (stating that the standard contingency fee figure is one-third).

CHAPTER 1. THE PRICE OF DISCRIMINATION

changes has gone virtually unexamined. In this section, I will explore the fruits of the settlement, including changes Texaco has made in response to the lawsuit. I will suggest that much of the company's implementation involves a carefully structured public relations campaign that obscures how limited the company's changes have actually been – changes implemented with little to no oversight. Moreover, although the plaintiff class clearly has benefited from the suit, others who were not parties to the suit – women, minority contractors, and the diversity industry – have benefited at least as much, and in some instances far more than the plaintiff class.

Table 1.4, which is based on the reports issued by the Texaco Diversity Task Force ('Task Force'), indicates the percentages of female and minority employees, new hires, and promotions.

TABLE 1.4: Texaco Progress Since Settlement

Category	1997	1998	1999	2000
Minority Workers	20.3	21.1	22.4	23.2
Female Workers	26.7	26.0	26.6	27.2
Minority & Female Execs	15.0	18.9	20.0	19.8
Minority Execs.	8.5	10.4	10.5	10.1
New Minority Hires	na	37.7	44.4	33.4
New Female Hires	na	40.4	49.4	40.6
Minority Promotions	24.9	21.4	28.8	24.9
Female Promotions	43.6	38.7	57.6	39.4

Between 1997 and 2000, the percentage of minority employees, which includes minority group members other than African Americans, increased from 20.3% to 22.4% of the total, although minorities represented 44.0% of Texaco's new hires in 1999. African Americans constituted 10.0% of the employees in 1999,[114] an increase from 9.1%

---

[114] Texaco Task Force on Equality and Fairness, Third Annual Report of the Equality and Fairness Task Force for the Year Ending June 30, 2000 (2000), available

35

in 1996,[115] but still below the modest goal that had been established by the company.[116] Although minorities received nearly 25% of the promotions in 1997 and 21.4% in 1998, the number of minority executives increased from 8.5% to 10.4%, and in 1998 the company failed to meet the executive-level goal it had established, though it exceeded the goal the following year. Women generally fared much better, accounting for nearly 50% of the new hires[117] and 57.6% of the promotions in 1999, although the total number of female executives increased more modestly from 8.5% to 10.4% in 1998.[118] In the year 2000, Texaco's efforts at diversifying its workforce stalled, as the percentage of new hires and promotions declined across the board as did the percentage of employees and executives.[119] With one year remaining on the settlement

---

at <www.texaco.com/archive/diversity/taskforce> (last visited September 2, 2008) [hereinafter Third Annual Report].

[115] Texaco Task Force on Equality and Fairness, First Annual report of the Equality and Fairness Task Force for the Year Ending June 30, 1998 (1998), available at <www.texaco.com/archive/diversity/taskforce/tf<uscore>report.html> (last visited January 2, 2003) [hereinafter First Annual Report].

[116] See Third Annual Report, *supra* n. 114 (stating that the 10% mark fell 'just 0.2% points below the goal of 10.2%').

[117] Of the 316 new hires in 1999, 156 (49.4%) were women. *Id*. Although women and minorities constituted a substantial portion of the new hires, both groups had higher separation rates than their white counterparts, and women left the firm at a significantly higher rate than their workplace representation. The First Task Force Report explained: 'At the end of 1997 the percentage of voluntary separations of women was notably higher than their percentage representation in the Texaco workforce, namely 49.3% versus 34.4%.' First Annual Report, *supra* n. 115, XI. The separation rate for African-American employees was 13.0% compared to their 9.9% representation in the workforce. *Id*.

[118] Texaco Task Force on Equality and Fairness, Second Annual Report of the Equality and Fairness Task Force for the Year Ending June 30, 1999, XI (1999), available at <www.texaco.com/archive/diversity/taskforce/tf<uscore>es99.html> (last visited November 14, 2002) [hereinafter Second Annual Report].

[119] The percentage of new female hires decreased from 49.4% in 1999 to 40.6% in 2000, while new minority hires decreased from 44.0% to 33.4%. Promotions decreased from 57.6% in 1999 to 39.4% in 2000 for women and went from 29.9% in 1999 to 24.9% in 2000 for minorities. In 1999, 10.5% of executives were women and 10.5% were minorities. In 2000, 10.6% of executives were women and 10.1% were minorities. Compare Third Annual Report *supra* n. 114, with Texaco Task Force on Equality and Fairness, Fourth Annual Report of the Equality and Fairness Task Force for the Year Ending June 30, 2001, XI (2001), available at <www.texaco.com/

CHAPTER 1. THE PRICE OF DISCRIMINATION

agreement, Texaco had failed to meet any of its numerical goals and remained substantially behind most of the original goals it had set for itself.[120]

An important aspect of the underlying case involved salary discrepancies for African-American employees, and part of the settlement agreement required Texaco to analyze its salary record to identify employees who were deserving of adjustments based on established objective criteria. In 1997, Texaco made fifty-two salary adjustments among nearly 7,500 salaries reviewed, but nearly half of the adjustments went to white men and only three of the adjustments went to African-American employees.[121] The Task Force saw this as a sign that 'salary-related issues are relatively limited at Texaco, and the adverse impact of salary-related issues is not disproportionately concentrated among minorities.'[122] The report failed to note, however, that the salary claim was a core component of the plaintiffs' class action allegations.[123]

As noted earlier, outside of the confines of the settlement agreement, Texaco developed a Minority and Women's Business Development Program ('MWBE') to increase its purchases from and affiliations with women and minorities. In its annual reports, the Task Force has reported Texaco's expenditures in an inconsistent fashion, which makes it difficult to conduct an accurate analysis. Nevertheless,

---

archive/diversity/taskforce/tf<uscore>2001<uscore>employ2.html> (last visited November 14, 2002) [hereinafter Fourth Annual Report].

[120] During the fifth and final year of the consent decree, Texaco merged with Chevron to become Chevron-Texaco. The Task Force subsequently filed a Fifth Annual Report, but because of the merger, it is difficult to assess any progress that was made during the final year of the decree. See Texaco Task Force on Equality and Fairness, Fifth Annual Report of the Equality and Fairness Task Force for the Year Ending June 30, 2002, (2002), available at <www.chevrontexaco.com>.

[121] *Id.* Subsequent salary adjustments have been of similar size, though the Task Force ceased reporting the racial or gender breakdown of those who received the adjustments. See Fourth Annual Report, *supra* n. 119.

[122] First Annual Report, Executive Summary: Employment Selection and Performance Management, *supra* n. 115.

[123] From the report, it is not possible to determine whether this analysis took into account the across-the-board increase agreed to as part of the settlement agreement. See *supra* text accompanying n. 95. It is possible that the across-the-board increase cured whatever salary discrepancy existed. However, if this were the case, the Diversity Task Force should have mentioned the increase was responsible for having eliminated any salary disparities, or at least its role in reducing the disparities.

37

Texaco's MWBE initiative appears to have been successful in channeling millions of dollars to women- and minority-owned businesses and is certainly the most successful aspect of Texaco's reforms. In 1998, Texaco spent a total of USD 230.2 million with MWBEs,[124] and in 1999, 8.8% of Texaco's discretionary expenditures went to MWBEs, for a total of USD 188 million.[125] This level of expenditures placed Texaco in the top quartile of Fortune 500 firms that participated in a purchasing study, and was nearly double the average expenditure of survey participants.[126] Women-owned firms, however, received nearly twice as many contract funds as African-American-owned companies.[127]

In addition to these tangible goals, the company also enacted many qualitative changes. Pursuant to the settlement agreement, the company instituted mandatory diversity training for all of its employees, with periodic refresher training. The company also instituted formal mentoring programs, appointed an ombudsman, engaged in more aggressive recruiting, and established seemingly dozens of task forces to address a wide range of workplace issues. The company also implemented basic management techniques such as formal job posting, which had previously been done on a fairly haphazard basis, along with more formal job descriptions and performance evaluations. Texaco, partly to meet its diversity plan obligations and partly to improve public relations, also hired UniWorld Group, a black-owned advertising agency, to create ads that would boost the company's image among minorities.[128]

As previously mentioned, a cornerstone of the settlement involved the creation of the Diversity Task Force to oversee the implementation of the decree. The Task Force was widely heralded at the time, and has

---

[124] Second Annual Report, Executive Summary: Employment Selection and Performance Management, *supra* n. 118.

[125] Third Annual Report, Executive Summary: Employment Selection and Performance Management, *supra* n. 114.

[126] *Id.* The survey was the 1999 Center for Advanced Purchasing Studies (CAPS) survey.

[127] *Id.* In 1999, African-American-owned firms received USD 37.1 million, while women-owned firms obtained contracts valued at USD 89.8 million. *Id.*

[128] Sally Goll Beatty, 'Texaco Hires Black Agency to Create Ads,' Wall St J, November 21, 1996, at A3.

CHAPTER 1. THE PRICE OF DISCRIMINATION

been copied in a number of other settlement agreements.[129] At the same time, it is often difficult to determine where the Task Force's loyalties or responsibilities lie, or what the Task Force has actually accomplished. For example, the annual reports issued pursuant to the Texaco decree could easily have been written by Texaco's public relations department. In assessing the company's hiring practices, the monitors continually praise Texaco even though the company repeatedly falls short of its modest goals. The following excerpt from the Second Annual Report exemplifies the nature of the reports:

> The overall percentage of minorities in the workforce increased from 20.3% to 21.1% during 1998. This 0.8% point change is short of the 1.4% growth originally planned, but indicates that the Company made progress in 1998 despite the downturn in business and the overall workforce reduction.... The percentage of women declined from 26.7% to 26.0% in 1998.... The decline in the percentage of women stemmed from the impact of reductions among service departments...that traditionally employ higher percentages of women than other components of Texaco.[130]

The last sentence appears particularly glaring to an experienced employment attorney because one would certainly want to know why the reductions had occurred more heavily in female-dominated job categories. Although there may be a valid explanation, the decline in female representation certainly merited a closer analysis. This statement is by no means an isolated incident, as each diversity report is replete with similar statements and excuses for Texaco's failure to meet its goals.[131] Moreover, after four years, the Task Force has yet to make a

---

[129] One of the plaintiffs' attorneys stated that 'he believed the creation of a task force to oversee the company's employee relations programs was the most important aspect of the settlement.' Sharon Walsh, 'Texaco Settles Bias Suit: USD 176 Million Payment Is Largest Ever: Diversity Promised,' Wash Post, November 16, 1996, at A1. A number of employer-oriented publications have urged the creation of such committees to provide internal company oversight. See e.g., Timothy S. Bland & Robert D. Hall, 'Do the Math: Class Action Lawsuits,' HR Mag, June 1, 2001, at 121, 125 ('It may be a good idea to consider voluntarily setting up a modified version of [the internal oversight committees at Texaco and Coca-Cola] within your company.').

[130] See Second Annual Report, *supra* n. 118.

[131] For example, the Task Force explained the company's failure to meet its modest goal of 10.4% African-American employees in 2000 as follows:

> It has apparently become difficult to retain employees who have been with the Company only a few months or a few years due to uncertainty about the

single substantial suggestion for how Texaco might change its practices, but rather has opted to embrace any changes implemented by Texaco of its own accord.[132]

Beyond the monetary relief awarded to the plaintiffs, which was substantial, it is difficult to conclude that Texaco has made much progress in reforming its culture – particularly when the focus is on its African-American employees rather than female employees or minority suppliers. Equally clear is that once the monetary settlement was reached, the case was of little interest to the American public, media,[133] investors, or the attorneys who brought the case. Instead, the attorneys turned the case over to a salaried task force that by all appearances works for Texaco rather than for the plaintiffs. As I will discuss in more detail later, this model – where the money that changes hands is more important than structural reforms – has transformed civil rights class action litigation into something more akin to torts or consumer class actions, and in the process has largely deprived the cases of their public nature.[134]

1.3.2 *Home Depot*: The Recalcitrance Model

If *Texaco* represents the 'public relations' model of class action discrimination litigation, the cases against *Home Depot* provide a distinctly different approach, which I label the 'recalcitrance model.' In this model, the company refuses to acknowledge any problems or potential liability even while agreeing to make substantial changes and paying large sums of money in settlement.[135] A key component

---

merger with Chevron and a 'full employment' job market among college-educated professionals. In this regard, Texaco's successful, activist approach to diversifying its workforce makes it particularly vulnerable to minority losses.

Fourth Annual Report, *supra* n. 119.

[132] In its Third Annual Report, the Task Force did suggest that Texaco extend the diversity training to supervisors, which it did during the following year. Third Annual Report, *supra* n. 114, I.

[133] Since the case settled, only two articles have appeared in major publications. See Bryant, *supra* n. 106 (assessing Texaco's early efforts); Sherwood Ross, 'Texaco Pumping Up its Diversity,' Newsday, December 28, 1998, at C2 (discussing Texaco's diversity efforts).

[134] See *infra* subsection 1.4.3.2.

[135] Other cases have been premised on a similar model. For example, *Lucky Stores*, on which the *Home Depot* lawsuit was largely based, settled a sex discrimination case for

of this model is that the settlement largely ends the matter, as the company and the plaintiffs ignore the underlying allegations and any prospects for institutional change once the money has exchanged hands. An important difference from the *Texaco* public relations model is that, while Texaco has devoted considerable effort and expense to create the appearance of transformation, in the recalcitrance model there is little pretense of a follow-up. The *Home Depot* case also differs from the *Texaco* litigation in that it never received anywhere near the national attention that was heaped upon Texaco, since it was devoid of any sensational allegations and instead involved classic allegations of stereotypical sex discrimination. This allowed Home Depot to lie below the radar throughout the litigation, and as a result the case had no effect on the company's stock price even on a temporary basis.

1.3.2.1 The Case

Home Depot is now the largest retailing chain of home improvement stores in the world, and during the 1990s was one of the fastest growing retailers in the United States.[136] In March 1994, a sex discrimination class action lawsuit was filed against the company's Western Division, which included 17,000 female employees in 150 stores located in ten western states. The case, which also sought class action status on behalf of as many as 200,000 failed applicants, was filed in federal court in San Francisco and drew one of the few federal judges with plaintiffs' class action experience.[137]

The stakes of the case were raised by the attorneys representing the plaintiff class. Indeed, perhaps the most significant fact of the case was

---

USD 107 million in 1994 but today refuses to discuss its progress on female hiring or promotions. See Stuart Silverstein, 'In Supermarkets' Executive Department, A Lack of Variety,' LA Times, May 2, 1999, at C1.

[136] See 'Hewlett-Packard Co.: Home Depot Is to Receive 40,000 New PCs in Its Stores,' Wall St J, October 9, 2002, at A12 (Home Depot's 1,456 stores make it the world's largest home improvement chain); Don Longo, 'A Tribute to a History-Making Retailer,' Nat'l Home Center News, December 27, 1999, at 5; Patricia Sellers, 'Exit the Builder, Enter the Repairman,' *Fortune*, March 19, 2001, at 86 (noting Home Depot's two decades of nonstop expansion).

[137] See Max Boot, 'For Plaintiffs' Lawyers, There's No Place Like Home Depot,' Wall St J, February 12, 1997, at A17 (noting that Judge Illston had been 'a class-action lawyer who worked on cases with one of the [plaintiffs' counsel]').

that it was brought by the law firm of Saperstein, Goldstein, Demchak, and Baller, the unquestioned champion of class action employment discrimination litigation. The Saperstein law firm has litigated more employment discrimination class action cases than any other firm in the country.[138] The firm is known not only for the volume of its litigation but also for the success of its settlements, including record-breaking agreements with *State Farm Insurance Company* and the race-discrimination case against *Denny's* discussed in the next section. The firm has produced settlements of USD 100 million or more in a number of other cases, including a series of sex discrimination cases against grocery store chains, on which the *Home Depot* case was patterned.[139] The firm's experience provides a sharp contrast to the attorneys who handled the *Texaco* case, who had limited experience in employment discrimination class actions.[140] Saperstein's litigation style also proved quite different. While not beyond relying on the media, the firm seems content to allow its cases to stay out of the media, as evidenced by the fact that the *Home Depot* case never received front page status.

The case against *Home Depot* was a classic case of sex discrimination, with an equally time-tested defense. The primary allegation was that women were routinely assigned to cashier positions, and were not allowed to work on the sales floor.[141] Unlike the sales floor positions,

---

[138] See Roush, *supra* n. 49, at 69 (noting that the Saperstein firm 'handles more employee discrimination class-action suits and recovers more money for workers in those cases than any other firm in the United States').

[139] The law firm brought, and successfully resolved, cases against *Albertson's*, *Lucky Stores*, *Publix*, and *Safeway*, most of which were premised on the notion that women were generally consigned to insignificant jobs in the delicatessen or bakery. The law firm has been profiled in a number of articles. See e.g., Benjamin A. Holden, 'Doing Well: A Law Firm Shows Civil Rights Can Be a Lucrative Business,' Wall St J, June 10, 1993, at A1; Russell Mitchell, 'The SWAT Team of Bias Litigation,' Bus Wk, January 23, 1995, at 88; see also Susan Sturm, 'Lawyering for a New Democracy: Lawyers and the Practice of Workplace Equity,' 2002 Wis L Rev 277, 299–307 (discussing the work of Barry Goldstein of the Saperstein firm).

[140] See *supra* text accompanying n. 63.

[141] In the preliminary statement of the complaint, the plaintiffs stated: 'In general, Home Depot reserves the most desirable work assignments and positions, and the training necessary to achieve them and to advance within the company, for males, including its male employees.' See Class Action Complaint for Injunctive and Declaratory Relief and Damages, at P 2, 2, *Frank v. Home Depot, Inc.*, No. C-95-2182 SI (ND Cal. August 29, 1997) (combined with *Butler v. Home Depot*, 1997 WL 605754 (ND Cal. August 29, 1997)).

CHAPTER 1. THE PRICE OF DISCRIMINATION

the cashier positions rarely led to promotional opportunities, despite Home Depot's avowed philosophy of promoting from within. According to one of the plaintiffs' experts, 70% of the employees in operations jobs, such as cashiers, were women, while 70% of the sales force were men, and 94% of the store managers in the Western Division were men.[142] Plaintiffs alleged discrimination in pay and training, as well as sexual harassment, but their core theory was that Home Depot did not believe women were sufficiently knowledgeable or conveyed the proper image to work on the sales floor.[143] This was a theory borrowed directly from Saperstein's successful litigation against grocery stores, where the companies routinely assigned women to the bakery department rather than other departments, such as produce or meat, from which promotions were made.[144]

Just as the plaintiffs stated a classic case of sex discrimination, the defendants responded with a classic defense. The company sought to explain the workforce disparities by arguing that women were not interested in working on the sales floor but routinely applied for cashier positions, and had prior experience at the positions.[145] Home Depot also claimed that it preferred to hire employees with construction-trade experience, which few women had.[146] These defenses, which are common in sex discrimination cases, were borrowed from a well-known class action case from the 1980s against Sears, in which the company successfully argued that the lack of women in commission jobs was due to their lack of interest.[147]

---

[142] Chris Roush, 'Focus on Discrimination Case, Both Sides Confident,' Atlanta J-Const, March 4, 1997, at F8.

[143] See Nicole Harris, 'A Woman's Place Is at the Cash Register?,' Bus Wk, June 30, 1997, at 89 ('The suits allege that women are funneled into cashier slots, which does not give them the experience needed to move up, and results in unequal pay.').

[144] See *id.* (mentioning that the suit will be argued by Saperstein, winners of a recent similar suit against *Publix Super Markets*); see also Boot, *supra* n. 137 (explaining that the Saperstein firm has turned its sights on the *Home Depot* class action after winning a large settlement against *Publix Super Markets*).

[145] *Id.*; see also Roush, *supra* n. 142.

[146] Allen R. Myerson, 'Home Depot Pays USD 87.5 Million for Not Promoting Women,' NY Times, September 20, 1997, at A7.

[147] *EEOC v. Sears, Roebuck & Co.*, 839 F.2d 302 (7th Cir. 1988). A more recent variant of this argument involved the litigation over the famed restaurant *Joe's Stone Crab's* refusal to hire women for its dining room staff, which the restaurant unsuccessfully claimed was due to a lack of female applicants. *EEOC v. Joe's Stone Crab, Inc.*, 220 F.3d

43

Another potentially larger case was filed against Home Depot in Louisiana by a different set of attorneys. The Louisiana suit involved 22,000 female employees in 310 Home Depot stores east of the Mississippi.[148] The suit attracted the attention of the Equal Employment Opportunity Commission, which sought to intervene.[149] Despite the size of the case and the presence of the EEOC, the Louisiana case always paled in significance to the California case, and was ultimately settled for a fraction of the cost.[150]

The evidence in both cases consisted largely of statistical analyses, but because of the nature of sex discrimination the cases could be pursued on a theory of intentional discrimination. The plaintiffs' central contention was that women were intentionally confined to dead-end jobs because they were women, the kind of claim that had formed the basis of suits going back to the early years of Title VII. In this type of case, the statistics, such as the fact that 70% of women worked as cashiers, are used as evidence of the company's intent to discriminate by assigning women to particularly undesirable jobs.[151] The attorneys also put together strong anecdotal evidence, particularly from one of the named plaintiffs, who had been assigned to a cash register despite her prior experience in a lumberyard. Nevertheless, the core of the case depended on seven expert witnesses and

---

1263 (11th Cir. 2000). For a discussion of the lack of interest defense, see Vicki Schultz, 'Telling Stories about Women and Work: Judicial Interpretations of Sex Segregation in the Workplace in Title VII Cases Raising the Lack of Interest Argument,' 103 Harv L Rev 1749 (1990).

[148] See Ronette King, 'Bias Lawsuit Has LA Roots,' Times-Picayune, April 27, 1997, at F1.

[149] See *id.* (detailing the EEOC's planned intervention).

[150] In discussing the California case, the company's general counsel noted, 'We spared no expense. It was the biggest case we ever had. Nothing here [in Atlanta, Home Depot's headquarters] was as important as what was happening in California.' Roush, *supra* n. 49, at 71. See also Jacqueline Bueno, 'Home Depot's Agreement to Settle Suit Could Cut 3rd-Quarter Earnings by 21%,' Wall St J, September 22, 1997, at B18 (indicating that out of the USD 104 million total settlement amount, USD 17 million was used to settle three other lawsuits, including the New Orleans suit).

[151] Roush, *supra* n. 142; see also *Joe's Stone Crab, Inc.*, 220 F.3d at 1273–1283 (discussing the role of statistical analysis in identifying disparate impact).

CHAPTER 1. THE PRICE OF DISCRIMINATION

extensive statistical analysis.[152] While the plaintiffs also included claims of disparate impact discrimination, the suits centered on the intentional discrimination claims – thus raising the prospect of damages that could total USD 300,000 per plaintiff.[153] Together the suits presented Home Depot with a potential liability of more than USD 100 billion.

Given this potential liability, one might expect Home Depot's stock price to have suffered, but throughout the litigation Home Depot's stock price continued its decade-long ascent. When the California case was filed, Home Depot's stock price declined, but the loss was recovered the following day.[154] In its annual reports, Home Depot mentioned the suit only after it settled the case, and did so only in relation to the cost of the settlement.[155] One reporter noted, 'With tens of millions likely at stake, Wall Street hasn't paid much attention to the case.'[156]

Just three days before trial, and after a two-day mandatory mediation with an experienced defense attorney, the California case settled.[157] The terms of the settlement included USD 65 million to the

---

[152] Both sides pulled out all the stops when it came to hiring experts. The plaintiffs' experts included Drs Susan Fiske and William Bielby, two of the best-known experts on the nature of sex discrimination, as well as a statistician, a labor economist, an organizational psychologist, an expert in survey research, and an expert on organizational diversity. The defendants lined up an equally formidable roster of experts: Nobel economist Gary Becker was assisted by two of the most famous labor economists, Edward Lazear and Sherwin Rosen, along with an additional labor economist, the most renowned defendants' counterpart to Dr. Fiske, Dr. Barbara Gutek, and three others. See Proposed Consent Decree, at 8–9, *Butler v. Home Depot, Inc.*, No. 94-4335 SI (ND Cal. January 14, 1998).

[153] Under the damage provisions of Title VII, plaintiffs are entitled to recover up to USD 300,000 in compensatory and punitive damages against employers with more than 500 employees. 42 USC 1981a (2002).

[154] The suit was announced on September 20, 1994, and the stock price fell USD 1.25 that day. On the following day, the price rose USD 1.625. See Tom Walker, 'Market Shares of Home Depot Rebound,' Atlanta J-Const, December 22, 1994, at E7.

[155] See 'Home Depot, Inc.,' 1997 Annual Report (1998), available at <www.homedepot.com/HDUS/EN<uscore>US/compinfo/financial/annual/1997/discussion.html>.

[156] Roush, *supra* n. 142.

[157] Although it is difficult to form an opinion based on two isolated cases, it is worth noting that the mediations in *Home Depot* and *Texaco* were as different as the cases themselves. One of the plaintiff's portrayals of the New-Age federal mediator who

plaintiff class, with an additional USD 22.5 million for attorneys' fees, or 25.7% of the settlement amount. The 6,569 members of the class who filed claims averaged recoveries of USD 9,683.[158] Although during the litigation the applicant class was estimated to include as many as 200,000 individuals, only 336 applicant class-members were determined to have submitted valid claims for compensation.[159] The company also agreed to spend an additional USD 17 million to settle three other pending lawsuits, including the case that had been filed in Louisiana. To cover the costs of the suit, the company took a one-time pretax charge of USD 104 million, which reduced its earnings by eight cents per share.[160] The settlement had no apparent effect on the stock price; on the first day of trading after the settlement was announced, Home Depot's shares gained 12.5 cents to reach USD 53.75 per share.[161]

At the time of the settlement, the company had devoted approximately USD 5 million to its defense.[162] Assuming the plaintiffs' attorneys had incurred comparable expenses, they received a substantial premium for their work, similar to the premium received by plaintiffs' counsel in the *Texaco* litigation.[163] One important difference, however, was that the fees in the *Home Depot* litigation were specified as part of the settlement, and were valued separately from the class settlement funds.

---

worked on the *Texaco* case for months to no avail is both hilarious and a bit frightening, given how much was at stake and his obvious ineffectiveness. See *Roberts, supra* n. 67, at 233–237. In contrast, the mediator in the *Home Depot* case was respected by both sides and was able to fashion a settlement by getting the company to focus on its long-term business interests. See *Roush, supra* n. 49, at 76–77 (discussing the mediator's understanding of *Home Depot*'s goals in arriving at an amicable settlement).

[158] See Joint Report to the Court Regarding the Status of the Implementation of the Consent Decree and the Distribution of the Settlement Fund, at 2, *Butler v. Home Depot, Inc.*, No. 94-4335 SI (ND Cal. January 14, 1998) [hereinafter Joint Report].
[159] *Id.*
[160] See Bueno, *supra* n. 150.
[161] *Id.*
[162] See Titunik, *supra* n. 45, at 38 ('The company had already invested some USD 5 million in a full-throttle defense.').
[163] See *supra* notes 107–111 and accompanying text.

CHAPTER 1. THE PRICE OF DISCRIMINATION

1.3.2.2 The Aftermath

Another distinct contrast with the *Texaco* litigation is that the essence of the *Home Depot* settlement was money. The agreement did not provide for any specified jobs for class members, nor did it require any specific goals. Rather, it took the unusual step of allowing Home Depot to establish the goals it would seek to meet based on criteria set forth in the decree.[164] Similarly, no diversity task force was created. Instead, an African-American female on the Board of Directors was given the responsibility of overseeing the company's implementation of the settlement agreement.[165] Home Depot has also been reluctant to provide any information regarding the changes it has made, and the initial progress report required under the terms of the consent was filed under seal.[166] In contrast, Texaco's diversity task force reports are readily available on their website.[167]

Based on the limited progress reports and on information Home Depot has made available in a 'Social Responsibility Report,' it appears that women have made small gains within the company's employment structure since the suit was settled. Companywide, the percentage of women employed at Home Depot did not increase at all between 1996–1999, but has remained at 35% every year.[168] The percentage of women working as sales associates in the Western Division, however, increased

---

[164] See Consent Decree, P XIII, *Butler v. Home Depot, Inc.*, No. 94-4335 SI (ND Cal. January 14, 1998). Essentially, the benchmark was a typical applicant-flow benchmark where the company agreed to hire female sales associates consistent with their representation in the qualified pool of applicants. *Id.* at 41. This does not, of course, account for the depressed pool of applicants that likely resulted from Home Depot's past practices.

[165] See Cheryl Ann Lambert, 'Corporate Boards Take On Bigger Role,' Nat'l Home Center News, April 13, 1998, at 38 ('Home Depot tapped its only African-American member, Dr. Johnetta Cole, to supervise implementation of the company's new hiring and promotions policies following the settlement of a class-action discrimination lawsuit.'). Dr. Cole, who was Home Depot's first African-American board member, was appointed in 1995, one year after the class action suits were filed. *Id.*

[166] Joint Report, *supra* n. 158.

[167] The reports can be found at <www.chevrontexaco.com/archive/diversity>.

[168] The total number of women employed has increased, but the percentage has remained constant. Home Depot Social Responsibility Report (1999), available at <http://trilliuminvest.com/resolutions/issue-report-on-equal-employment-opportunity-home-depot-2/> (last visited September 2, 2008).

37.5% between 1996 and March 2000, from 16% to 22%.[169] A similar increase was registered companywide, where the percentage of female sales associates rose from 14% to 20%.[170] The Joint Report filed with the Court also indicates that women accounted for 37% of the sales associates who were hired from an internal pool, while only 19% of those who were hired from an external pool were women.[171] The report, however, provides no comparative statistics to past practices, nor does it provide any indication of how these percentages translate to actual jobs or how they relate to the percentage of female applicants. Indeed, the one-and-a-half page report states only that 'these percentages are several times higher than the percentage of women in these positions before the Consent Decree was approved.'[172] Even so, it appears that Home Depot failed to meet half of its own benchmarks.[173]

According to the parties, the lawsuit has produced two primary innovations: Home Depot now posts its jobs companywide, and it also has created an in-store system that allows existing employees and applicants to bid for new jobs or promotions.[174] This system replaces what had been a decentralized process that allowed store managers to steer applicants to particular jobs (though even under the new system, managers continue to make the final selections based on a list of

---

[169] See 'Second Joint Report to the Court Regarding the Status of the Implementation of the Consent Decree,' at 2, *Butler v. Home Depot, Inc.*, No. 94-4335 SI (ND Cal. January 14, 1998).

[170] *Id.*

[171] *Id.*

[172] *Id.* at 3.

[173] Pursuant to the consent decree, the company established its own benchmarks for positions that had been contested. See Joint Report to the Court Regarding the Status of the Implementation of the Consent Decree and the Distribution of Settlement Funds, at app. E, *Butler v. Home Depot, Inc.*, No. 94-4335 SI (ND Cal. January 14, 1998) (on file with author). In its report to the court, the company failed to meet its following benchmarks: internal sales associates, 50% benchmark, 37% hired; external sales associates, 23% benchmark, 19% hired; and external assistant managers, 20% benchmark, 14% hired. See *id.*; 'Second Joint Report to the Court Regarding the Status of the Implementation of the Consent Decree,' at 2, *Butler v. Home Depot, Inc.*, No. 94-4335 SI (ND Cal. January 14, 1998).

[174] The system is described in detail in Susan Sturm, 'Second Generation Employment Discrimination: A Structural Approach,' 101 Colum L Rev 458, 512–513 (2001) and Cora Daniels, 'To Hire a Lumber Expert, Click Here,' *Fortune*, April 3, 2000, at 267.

CHAPTER 1. THE PRICE OF DISCRIMINATION

qualified applicants).[175] The company also instituted a process that requires managers to interview at least three candidates for every position – a system that has been in place for government hiring for at least forty years.[176] While the system may be an improvement over the company's past practices, it can hardly be defined as innovative. As was the case with *Texaco*, one significant result of the lawsuit has been to force superior (although commonplace) management techniques on a company that was steeped in inefficient old habits. The company, however, has maintained that it was planning to overhaul its practices even without the lawsuit, and contends that it simply did what it was planning to do, though within a slightly shorter time period.[177]

---

[175] Sturm, *supra* n. 174, at 513.

[176] The 'rule of three,' which requires employers to interview three candidates for every position, has been standard procedure for government employment for many years. See e.g., *Sarabia v. Toledo Police Patrolman's Assoc.*, 601 F.2d 914, 915 (6th Cir. 1979) ('The Toledo Division of Police has traditionally followed the 'rule of three' which requires that the civil service commission certify the names of the three candidates standing highest on the eligibility list for each position to be filled.'); *Wilson v. Kelley*, 294 F. Supp. 1005, 1010 (ND Ga. 1968) (stating that the rule of three is 'common to the federal and most state systems').

[177] One report noted that a few months before the settlement, 'Home Depot had begun designing a computerized job application system and objective tests for applicants at its stores....' See Titunik, *supra* n. 45, at 38. It is certainly possible that the lawsuit prodded the company to go forward with changes it was contemplating, but it seems clear that the changes did not originate with the plaintiff class or its attorneys. See *id.* (quoting plaintiffs' attorney James Finberg as stating, 'When we heard they were working on [the system], we were very encouraged'); see also Sturm, *supra* n. 174, at 512 (quoting mediation counsel as noting that the settlement became possible 'once we realized there were programs they were working on that would blend nicely with what the plaintiffs wanted us to do'). It should be noted that Professor Susan Sturm has praised the work of plaintiffs' counsel in the *Home Depot* litigation for its role as a 'problem solver,' and she clearly views the hiring system as a substantial contribution of the lawsuit. See Sturm, *supra* n. 174, at 509–519, 557–559; Sturm, *supra* n. 139, at 302–304. Several differences in analytical methods likely explain the divergent assessments of the *Home Depot* litigation. First, Professor Sturm relied primarily on interviews with counsel and other active players in the litigation, which likely afforded her a different perspective on the process of change for Home Depot. Additionally, Professor Sturm's analysis was made largely independent of the quantitative data and was also performed before the parties moved to terminate the decree prior to its expiration. Finally, and as discussed further below, Professor Sturm emphasizes the attorney's role as problem solver

In a remarkable end to the litigation, the parties jointly moved to terminate the consent decree eighteen months before it was due to expire. The five-page document supporting the motion offers only summary statistical information on the most recent six-month period, and provides no indication of how women have fared overall in either sales positions or promotions.[178] Perhaps most revealing, the report acknowledges that Home Depot had failed to meet its own benchmarks, which the parties sought to explain by noting the 'dynamic nature of the qualified pool.'[179] Despite these obvious limitations, the court approved the motion shortly after it was filed.[180]

Although there are similarities with the *Texaco* case, the differences are far more pronounced. Home Depot has provided extremely limited information on its progress, and maintains that it never had any need for improvement. Unlike Texaco, the company has not sought any recognition as a 'best place for women to work,' though *Fortune* magazine continues to list the company as one of the most admired retailers in the country.[181] This is in part due to the limited attention the lawsuit brought, which meant that Home Depot had less of a need to repair its public image than Texaco did. It may also have something to do with the difference in the underlying basis for the suit. While there is a clear

---

in a changing environment, whereas I have taken a more traditional approach of looking at the direct benefits produced to the class.

[178] See Joint Notice of Motion and Motion to Terminate Consent Decree, *Butler v. Home Depot, Inc.*, No. 94-4335 SI (ND Cal. January 14, 1998). The report notes:

> For the most recent reporting period, from September 17, 2001 through March 17, 2002, 32% of the Home Depot associates registered in the AQP [Adjusted Qualified Pool] for sales positions were women, while 39.3% of the associates placed in sales positions were women. For the same period, 17.5% of the internal applicants for department supervisor in the AQP were female, while 23.8% of the persons selected to be department supervisors were female. While 19.9% of the AQP for assistant store manager were women, 26.7% of the people selected were female.

Id. at 4. The 'Adjusted Qualified Pool' reflects unspecified adjustments to the actual applicant pool. *Id.*

[179] *Id.* at 5.

[180] See 'Home Depot Hiring Supervision Lifted,' LA Times, June 25, 2002, at C4 (noting that the decree was lifted more than a year early).

[181] See Matthew Boyle, 'America's Most Admired Companies,' *Fortune*, March 4, 2002, at 70, 78 (ranking Home Depot first in its industry and sixth overall).

CHAPTER 1. THE PRICE OF DISCRIMINATION

societal consensus against race discrimination – and no company wants to be labeled as racist – there is far less of a consensus regarding sex discrimination, particularly when that discrimination is based on common stereotypes.[182] The case of women suing to gain access to the lumberyard feels different from a case based on intentional race discrimination, particularly when that discrimination includes racial epithets.

1.3.2.3 Denny's: The Reform Model

The final case study does not involve an employment discrimination case but rather concerns a number of lawsuits brought pursuant to the federal public accommodations statute, known as Title II.[183] Although the allegations involved discrimination in service, the reforms pursued by Denny's reflect the aspirations of the employment discrimination suits already discussed. Additionally, as analyzed in detail below, *Denny's* provides the best example of what I call the 'reform model,' as the company implemented wide-ranging and meaningful changes in response to a series of high-profile lawsuits involving its discriminatory service policies. At the same time, as in the *Texaco* case, many of the most meaningful changes occurred outside the context of the USD 54 million in settlements that ended the class action litigation, and instead arose out of an agreement made with a national civil rights group intended to reshape its business practices. The cases against *Denny's* thus provide some insight into the way actual reform can be accomplished.

1.3.2.3.1 The Cases The allegations against Denny's originally arose in 1991 when a number of African-American college students in Northern California, returning from a local NAACP conference, alleged that they were required to pay a cover charge and prepay for their meals late at night, while white customers were able to eat without

---

[182] See Michael Selmi, 'Why Are Employment Discrimination Cases So Hard to Win?,' 61 La L Rev 555, 568 (2001) ('Despite the fact that two-income families now comprise the majority of American families, as a society we remain ambivalent over the role of working women.').
[183] 42 USC 2000(a) (2000).

51

either a cover charge or prepayment.[184] This allegation received little national attention, although it did provoke a Justice Department investigation that ultimately unearthed more than 4,300 complaints nationwide.[185] Well-known civil rights firms, including the Saperstein firm, undertook representation of the class action in California and sought class members through various publication notices.[186] The Justice Department, which has no authority under the public accommodations statute to seek monetary relief, entered into a consent decree with *Denny's* in April, 1993, that called for a variety of reforms and nondiscriminatory pledges.[187]

On the same day the Justice Department decree was entered, six African-American Secret Service officers – dressed in their uniforms and on their way to guard President Clinton at the Naval Academy – were forced to wait to order at a Denny's in Annapolis, Maryland, while the white officers traveling with them were served rapidly, including second helpings. The African-American officers were not served before they had to leave for their detail.[188] This case attracted national headlines and thrust Denny's firmly into the spotlight as a prime example of how racism remained alive and well in corporate America. The allegations continued mounting, including claims of discrimination made by a federal judge and his wife, as well as by a children's choir named after Martin Luther King, Jr., that was refused sit-down service at a Virginia restaurant.[189] The Maryland case was transformed into a nationwide

---

[184] *United States v. TW Services, Inc.*, No. C-93-20208JW, 1993 US Dist. LEXIS 7882, at 3 (ND Cal. April 1, 1993).

[185] 'Justice Department to Test Chain: Denny's Vows to Avoid Bias,' The Plain Dealer, May 5, 1994, at 6C.

[186] See Benjamin A. Holden, 'Denny's Chain Settles Suits by Minorities,' Wall St J, May 24, 1994, at A3; Benjamin A. Holden, 'Doing Well: A Law Firm Shows Civil Rights Can Be a Lucrative Business,' Wall St J, June 10, 1993, at A1 (discussing Saperstein's role in the lawsuit).

[187] See TW Svcs., Inc., 1993 US Dist. LEXIS 7882. The decree required training, compliance testing, the creation of a civil rights monitor, and the inclusion of minorities in company advertisements.

[188] See Jim Adamson et al., *The Denny's Story: How a Company in Crisis Resurrected its Good Name* (2000) 6–9 (describing the incident).

[189] See Carlos Sanchez & Marion E. Odum, 'Two Denny's Said to Refuse Service to Black Choir,' Wash Post, June 5, 1993, at B1; Jerry Urban, 'Denny's Again Accused of Bias: Judge, Wife Describe Incidents at Restaurant in California,' Houston Chron, at A31.

CHAPTER 1. THE PRICE OF DISCRIMINATION

class action for claims that arose outside of California and was led by the Washington Lawyers' Committee for Civil Rights and assisted by a prominent Washington law firm.[190] By June 1994, fifteen major public accommodations race-bias suits had been filed against Denny's, including the two class-action suits described above.[191]

These allegations came at a precarious financial juncture for Denny's, whose parent company was straddled with huge debt accumulated from a leveraged buyout in the late 1980s.[192] At the time of the lawsuit, Denny's was the largest family-dining chain in the country, serving more than one million customers a year at 1,400 restaurants, including one-third that were franchise-owned.[193] In addition to its flagship Denny's chain, the parent company owned a number of other restaurant chains, including Hardee's, El Pollo Loco, Coco's, and Carrow's, most of which were struggling financially.[194] In 1993, customer traffic at Denny's fell 4.1%, largely as a result of the racial discrimination allegations lodged against the company.[195] That same year Denny's parent, Flagstar, reported a staggering loss of USD 1.72 billion, or USD 40.93 a share, on revenue of USD 3.97 billion.[196] Given Flagstar's severe financial troubles, it is difficult to assess the effect the lawsuits may have had on the company's stock price, although it does not appear that the stock price was affected by either the filings or the settlement of the lawsuits.[197]

Two other important facts contributed to Denny's desire to resolve the suits and reform its image. Perhaps the most critical fact was that

---

[190] See Michael Briggs, 'Pattern of Bias Alleged in Suit Against Denny's,' Chi Sun-Times, July 14, 1993, at A30.

[191] *Id.*

[192] Faye Rice, 'Denny's Changes Its Spots,' *Fortune*, May 13, 1996, at 133, 134.

[193] See Stephen Labaton, 'Denny's Gets a Bill for the Side Orders of Bigotry,' NY Times, May 29, 1994, at D4.

[194] Robert Frank, 'Flagstar Loss Is $1.65 Billion on Big Charge,' Wall St J, January 25, 1994, at A3.

[195] See Rice, *supra* n. 192, at 142 (stating that Denny's operating income fell 30% in 1993, the year of the worst racial incidents).

[196] George White, 'Flagstar to Sell or Close as Many as 180 Denny's and El Pollo Locos Restaurants,' LA Times, January 25, 1994, at D1.

[197] One newspaper analyst concluded, 'The negative publicity hasn't hurt Denny's revenues or Flagstar's stock price, which has strengthened in recent months and is currently trading in the $11–$12 range on the Nasdaq market.' Jim Clarke, 'Denny's Takes Steps to Overcome Racism,' St. Petersburg Times, October 18, 1993, at 8.

Denny's chairman Jerry Richardson, a football star in the 1950s, was seeking to establish a new NFL franchise in Charlotte, North Carolina, and the bias allegations were seen as a threat to his efforts.[198] Additionally, the lawsuits arose during the Rodney King trial, a time when the country was acutely aware of the persistence of a racial divide many had wished away years earlier. As a result, the company moved quickly to stem the damage from the mountain of allegations and did so on a number of fronts.

Rather than settling the cases, the company's first move was to begin negotiating an agreement with the NAACP that would conspicuously and tangibly promote minority interests. The NAACP was not a party to any of the lawsuits but for a decade had encouraged corporations to enter into voluntary 'Fair Share' agreements as a way of demonstrating a company's commitment to diversity.[199] Negotiations over the NAACP Fair Share agreement began shortly after the original complaints were filed and nearly eighteen months before the lawsuits were finally settled.[200] There was, in fact, some sense among the parties to the lawsuits that *Denny's* sought to use the Fair Share agreement, along with the nonmonetary Justice Department consent decree, to fend off further settlement negotiations.[201]

The terms of the NAACP Fair Share agreement ('NAACP Pact'), signed on July 1, 1993, exceeded the terms of all of the previous agreements the NAACP had negotiated.[202] The NAACP Pact was said to be worth more than USD 1 billion to minority businesses and interests, and established specific goals and time frames for the company to

---

[198] See Benjamin A. Holden, 'Parent of Denny's Restaurants, NAACP Agree on Plan to Boost Minorities' Role,' Wall St J, July 1, 1993, at A3 (noting that the discrimination suits had 'greatly damaged Mr Richardson's chances' to obtain a football franchise).
[199] See Adamson et al., *supra* n. 188, at 56 (describing the Fair Share agreements between Denny's and the NAACP).
[200] See Paul W. Valentine, 'Denny's Signs Agreement with NAACP; Estimated USD 1 Billion Pact to Increase Minority Jobs,' Wash Post, July 2, 1993, at Al (detailing the Fair Share agreement).
[201] See Holden, *supra* n. 198 (explaining that plaintiffs' attorney John Relman 'was skeptical about the new agreement').
[202] See Andrea Adelson, 'Denny's Parent Vows Larger Role for Blacks,' NY Times, July 2, 1993, at D2. NAACP director Benjamin F. Chavis, Jr. observed, 'In my 30 years in the civil rights movement, I've never seen the commitments made by this C.E.O. [Flagstar's Jim Richardson] today.'

CHAPTER 1. THE PRICE OF DISCRIMINATION

meet.[203] As part of the agreement, Flagstar promised to maintain employment of African Americans at or above the then-current level of 20%, to double the number of minority-owned restaurants by 1997, to hire 325 more African-American restaurant and corporate managers earning annual salaries in excess of USD 42,000, and to increase purchases from minority-owned firms from 2% to 12% of its discretionary budget by the year 2000.[204] At the time of the agreement, only fifty-four of Denny's 1,485 restaurants (3.7%) were minority-owned, and only one of those was owned by an African American.[205] As will be detailed shortly, Denny's has met or exceeded all of the goals established in the Fair Share agreement.

While the company was negotiating the Fair Share pact, the litigation was proceeding, and the evidence against Denny's was mounting, including evidence that discrimination against African Americans had been known, tolerated, and perhaps encouraged by the corporate office.[206] Nevertheless, the truth of the allegations began to fade in

---

[203] Valentine, *supra* n. 200.

[204] See Sam Fulwood III, 'Denny's Signs Pact Assuring Minority Hires,' LA Times, July 2, 1993, at Dl (discussing the agreement between Denny's parent company and the NAACP). Under the agreement, the 325 new management positions will come with average annual salaries of USD 42,000, and Flagstar 'will spend 10% of its marketing budget with minority-owned media, 12% of its purchasing budget with minority firms and 15% of its professional services – such as banking, accounting and legal services – with minority firms.' *Id.* See also Rice, *supra* n. 192, at 134 (Flagstar had only two minority-owned firms among its network of some 20 suppliers in 1992); 'Denny's Signs Pact with NAACP: Minorities Given Jobs and Business Opportunities,' Seattle Post-Intelligencer, July 2, 1993, at C5 (reporting on the agreement that covered 120,000 employees at Denny's and Flagstar's other restaurants).

[205] 'A New Recipe for Denny's,' LA Times, July 3, 1993, at B7.

[206] See Labaton, *supra* n. 193. Lawyers for the black customers in the class action suit said that the evidence they uncovered before settlement talks ended the brief discovery period included:

(1) corporate headquarters ignoring frequent customer complaints;
(2) sworn testimony describing instances in which managers taught restaurant operators how to discourage black customers and employees were given 'strategies' to avoid 'blackouts';
(3) some former managers were told about a company policy requiring that certain customers pay cover charges or prepay their meals in advance;
(4) managers of Denny's in Delaware and Pennsylvania kept logs that described periods when the restaurant had too many black customers;

55

importance as Denny's quickly became the nation's icon of racial bigotry, an image that was likely to further erode its financial condition given that members of minority groups made up approximately 10% of its customer base, accounting for more than USD 150 million in annual revenue.[207]

Shortly after the Fair Share agreement was signed, the company moved to settle the lawsuits, focusing on the class action cases that had drawn the most attention. On May 23, 1994, after a federal judge had consolidated several of the cases, the two class actions and one other complaint were settled for a total of USD 54.4 million – the highest settlement ever obtained in a public accommodations case.[208] The settlement included USD 34.8 million for the California case, including USD 6.8 million (19.5%) in attorneys' fees, while the nationwide class action filed by the six Secret Service agents received a monetary award of USD 19.6 million, including USD 1.9 million (9.6%) in attorneys' fees.[209] When the settlements were distributed approximately a year later, more than 290,000 individuals received checks for either USD 177.71 or USD 132.28, depending on the particular case.[210]

The consent decrees, along with the separate decree entered into with the Justice Department, concentrated on the public accommodations aspect of the cases. They required a variety of non-discrimination language and training, as well as a requirement that 25% of Denny's promotional materials include individuals who were identifiably

---

(5) employees were told to seat blacks where they could not easily be seen by other customers and away from exits because they had a tendency to walk out without paying; and

(6) testimony from a former assistant manager in San Jose, California, who said she got the clear impression that the district manager was being pressured by his supervisor to control and limit black clientele. *Id.*

[207] See Labaton, *supra* n. 193 ('Some executives said they feared the publicity had begun to discourage blacks, who represent 10 percent of the chain's customers. . . . ').
[208] See Jeff Leeds, 'Denny's Restaurants Settle Bias Suits for USD 54 Million,' LA Times, May 25, 1994, at A1 (quoting Assistant Attorney General Deval L. Patrick, who described the USD 54.4 million settlement as 'the largest, most-sweeping nationwide settlement of a public accommodations case in history').
[209] *Id.*
[210] See 'Denny's Paying Off Bias Suits,' Dallas Morning News, December 12, 1995, at 17D. The USD 177.71 checks were distributed to members of the California class, whereas the USD 132.28 checks went to members of the nationwide class. *Id.*

CHAPTER 1. THE PRICE OF DISCRIMINATION

non-white.[211] The decrees also required the creation of an Office of the Civil Rights Monitor (OCRM) to serve as the legal entity responsible for ensuring that Denny's complied with the consent decree.[212] OCRM was empowered to send testers into Denny's restaurants to monitor for discriminatory behavior, to receive and act on all complaints concerning behavior at Denny's from anywhere in the country, and to require Denny's to cooperate in any of OCRM's discretionary investigations.[213]

1.3.2.3.2 Denny's Reform Efforts The company moved quickly to comply with the terms of the agreements and to repair its broken image. In 1994, Flagstar made 124 new minority hires in management and executive positions – 103 of whom were African Americans.[214] The company also appointed its first African-American member to its board of directors and its first African-American executive – the Vice President for Human Resources.[215] Denny's increased the number of African Americans in its management ranks by 56% from the previous year,[216] and, by the end of 1994, 13% of its employees were African American.[217] Flagstar also entered into new contracts with nineteen minority suppliers, including fourteen African-American-owned firms, representing USD 21.3 million worth of business a year (3.5% of the corporation's purchases). The company also negotiated a number of Denny's franchise agreements that would result in seven new black owners operating thirty-two restaurants, although by the end of the

---

[211] Twenty-five percent of persons in these ads and promotional materials specifically had to be African American. The decrees also required Denny's to compute the number of seconds that non-white faces appeared on the screen. Adamson et al., *supra* n. 188, at 52–53.

[212] Calvin Sims, 'Restaurant Chain Settles Charges of Racial Bias,' NY Times, March 26, 1993, at A14.

[213] Adamson et al., *supra* n. 188, at 52–53. The consent decree originally entered into with the Justice Department contained most of the same terms, adding little that was new other than the monetary relief. However, the scope of the private suits greatly expanded the jurisdiction of the Civil Rights Monitor.

[214] Ann LoLordo, 'Denny's Improving Slowly on Minority Relations,' Balt Sun, September 20, 1994, at A1.

[215] *Id.*

[216] *Id.*

[217] See 'Denny's Parent Arranges for Black-Owned Outlets,' Chi Trib, November 9, 1994, at 1N.

year the company had actually closed its only African-American-owned franchise.[218] The company also exceeded its goal of USD 100,000 in charitable contributions to civil rights groups,[219] and established a pilot program at South Seattle Community College to provide training for minority students in a culinary-arts program.[220]

In 1995, Denny's increased its percentage of African-American managers and executives from 7% to 12%,[221] and its minority contracts increased five-fold from 1993 levels to USD 50 million.[222] The same year, Denny's initiated a diversity training program for all of its 50,000 employees, and sought to improve its image through a USD 5 million series of television and print advertisements intended to convey a message welcoming back their African-American clientele. Along the same lines, the company became a primary sponsor for Soul Train (contributing USD 500,000 for its 25th anniversary television special)[223] and the Harlem Globetrotter basketball team.[224] Flagstar also announced a major leadership change, as Jerry Richardson resigned as chairman of the corporation to devote all of his time to the ownership of his new football franchise, the Charlotte Panthers.[225]

Richardson was replaced by Jim Adamson, who has been widely acclaimed for moving the company forward on diversity issues. His policy was simple, and he repeated it wherever he went: 'If you

---

[218] LoLordo, *supra* n. 214.

[219] *Id.*

[220] Aly Colon, 'Denny's Acts on Pledge Against Bias – SSCC Is Site of Pilot Program,' Seattle Times, August 17, 1994, at D1.

[221] LoLordo, *supra* n. 214. Reports on the agreement after twelve months emphasized the 'slow but steady progress' being made by Denny's. For instance, while the Fair Share agreement arranged for the NAACP and minority organizations to help the company recruit new hires and suppliers for the corporation, and even though some African-American-owned businesses were referred by the NAACP, 'other blacks who won contracts...did so through their own efforts and persistence.' *Id.*

[222] See 'Denny's Begins New Era; Settlement Payout Closes Discrimination Chapter,' Bus Wire, December 11, 1995, at C8.

[223] Del Jones, 'Serving a New Image: Denny's Strives to Eliminate Racist Elements,' USA Today, November 2, 1995, at 1A.

[224] Roger Thurow, 'Bouncing Back: A Sports Icon Regains Its Footing By Using the Moves of the Past,' Wall St J, January 21, 1998, at A1 (noting that 'Denny's...began promoting the Globetrotters three years ago').

[225] See 'Flagstar Chief Quits Restaurant Chain to Focus Full Time on New NFL Team,' Atlanta J-Const, May 3, 1995, at 1F.

discriminate, I'm going to fire you.'[226] To make good on his promise, the company began to include provisions in its franchisee contracts that provided for termination if the franchisee 'put the [Denny's] brand at risk.'[227] By November 2, 1995, Denny's had dropped a California franchisee for customer discrimination, and had fired a number of its managers, including the manager of the restaurant that had denied service to the Secret Service agents.[228] In addition to penalties, Adamson also offered incentives: He tied 20% of managers' bonuses to the reduction in the number of discrimination complaints the company received.[229]

In 1996, Denny's secured additional franchise agreements, bringing the total African-American-owned franchises to twenty-seven, out of 512 franchises nationwide (5.3%).[230] At the close of 1996, minority purchasing contracts exceeded USD 80 million – an eight-fold increase since 1993.[231] As a result of Denny's progress, the NAACP named Jim Adamson its 1996 'CEO of the Year.'[232] The award, however, was perhaps bittersweet, as it arrived while the company was in the midst of its most dire financial straits, including a Chapter 11 filing for bankruptcy protection and reorganization under the name Advantica.[233]

Despite its financial difficulties, Denny's remained steadfast in its commitment to meeting the terms of the Fair Share agreement. In 1998, when *Fortune* magazine published its first list of the 'Best 50 Companies for Asians, Blacks, and Hispanics,' Advantica placed second – a remarkable turnaround from just five years earlier.[234] At the time of the report, nearly 33.3% of Advantica officers and managers were minorities,[235] and 37% of the 748 Denny's franchises nationwide

---

[226] Jones, *supra* n. 223.
[227] *Id.*
[228] *Id.*
[229] *Id.*
[230] See Rice, *supra* n. 192, at 133.
[231] 'Denny's Contributes USD 625,000 to United Negro College Fund,' PR Newswire, January 16, 1997.
[232] See also 'Denny's Diversity Initiatives,' at <www.allbusiness.com/company-activities-management/company-structures/7188772-1.html> (last visited September 2, 2008) [hereinafter Diversity Initiatives].
[233] See Anne Faircloth, 'Guess Who's Coming to Denny's,' *Fortune*, August 3, 1998, at 108–110 (discussing many of the hardships facing the reorganized company).
[234] *Id.*
[235] David Segal, 'Denny's Serves Up a Sensitive Image; Restaurant Chain Launches PR Drive to Show Minorities It Has Changed Its Ways,' Wash Post, April 7, 1999, at E1.

were minority-owned, of which 109 franchises, or 14.5%, were African-American owned.[236] Yet the diversity initiatives were not enough to salvage the company's financial condition, and in the middle of a booming stock market Advantica's stock price dropped 69%.[237] The company dropped to sixth on the *Fortune* list in 1999, but by 2000 it had climbed to the top of the list, where it remained in 2001.[238] It is worth noting that despite its efforts, Texaco has never made the *Fortune* list.

Denny's continued transformation can be seen in the latest statistics. Four of its eleven board members are minorities, as are 31.1% of its officials and managers and 48% of its employees.[239] Approximately 19% of the company's contracts for services went to minority-owned businesses,[240] and 42% of all Denny's franchise restaurants are now owned by minority franchisees.[241] Collectively, 109 minority franchisees own 450 Denny's restaurants; sixty-three of these are owned by African Americans.[242] All of these figures exceed the goals originally established by the Fair Share agreement, and have garnered the company a bevy of awards beyond the recognition from *Fortune*.[243]

The story, however, does not yet have a happy ending, as Denny's continues to struggle financially and has not been able to shake its tattered image. Despite record sales of more than USD 2 billion, last year the company was delisted by the over-the-counter exchange where it had previously traded, and toward the end of 2002 traded for about

---

[236] Pamela Yip, 'Olajuwon Group Buys Denny's in 12 States,' Houston Chron, March 28, 1998, at I.

[237] John H. Christy, 'The Forbes 500s: Wall Street,' *Forbes*, April 21, 1997, at 286 (listing the company under the 'Flagstar' name).

[238] See Christine Y. Chen & Jonathan Hickman, 'America's 50 Best Companies for Minorities,' *Fortune*, July 10, 2000, at 190; Fabiana Esposito et al., 'America's 50 Best Companies for Minorities,' *Fortune*, July 9, 2001, at 122.

[239] Esposito et al., *supra* n. 238, at 122.

[240] See Toni Heinzl, 'Denny's Embraces Diversity: Discrimination Lawsuits Triggered a Transformation at the Restaurant Chain,' Omaha World-Herald, November 16, 1999, at 9.

[241] Diversity Initiatives, *supra* n. 232.

[242] *Id.*

[243] For example, the National Association for Female Executives ranked Denny's thirteenth in its 2002 survey of the Top 25 Companies for Executive Women, at <www.mfha.net/products/2008_Community_Report.pdf> (last visited December 2, 2008).

CHAPTER 1. THE PRICE OF DISCRIMINATION

USD 1 on the over-the-counter bulletin board.[244] Nor has the company's transformation stemmed the tide of lawsuits, as Denny's remains plagued by suits alleging discriminatory service, including a high-profile lawsuit filed by Syracuse University students that, although ultimately dismissed, generated a new round of adverse publicity.[245] It would certainly be too much to suggest that the company's diversity efforts caused, or even contributed, to its financial slide, but it appears that, at least in this instance, although diversity may have been good for business it has not been good enough.

1.4 THE BENEFITS AND EFFECTS OF CLASS ACTION LITIGATION

The case studies, together with the statistical study, offer important insights into how class action employment discrimination has changed, particularly over the last decade, as the litigation has begun to resemble common tort rather than traditional civil rights actions. As discussed in more detail below, this is perhaps most evident in the relief that is now commonly afforded the plaintiff class. Monetary damages, often at minimal levels when calculated on an individual basis, constitute the primary – and frequently the only – relief intended to compensate for past discrimination. The lawsuits rarely require corporations to modify their existing practices, and whatever changes occur tend to be driven by a company's own interests or by public relations concerns rather than the requirements of a consent decree. This is likely one reason why neither the lawsuits nor the settlements tend to affect shareholder value in any meaningful way.

Even though the nature of the litigation has substantially changed, this study suggests that the nature of discrimination identified in the

---

[244] Advantica now trades under the ticker symbol 'DINE,' and current prices can be accessed on <yahoo.finance.com>. Advantica has sold off many of its poorer performing chains and has substantially increased the number of stores that are franchise-owned. See Advantica Restaurant Group, Inc., 2000 SEC Form 10-K3 (March 27, 2001).

[245] See *Lizardo v. Denny's, Inc.*, 270 F.3d 94, 99 (2nd Cir. 2001) (upholding the dismissal of a Syracuse civil rights suit); *Laroche v. Denny's, Inc.*, 62 F. Supp. 2d 1375, 1383–1384 (SD Fla. 1999) (finding that Denny's engaged in discrimination when it told a group of African-American correctional officers that it was out of food).

subset of class action cases studied here surprisingly has stayed much the same. At least with respect to systemic discrimination challenged by class action litigation, the kind that is most likely to catch the public eye remains overt racial discrimination – along the lines of *Texaco* and *Denny's* – the kind that we would like to believe is part of our past rather than our present. The gender discrimination cases evince a similar pattern by continuing to focus on the assignment of women to undesirable jobs based on stereotypical perceptions of their interests – the very kind of discrimination that has been at the heart of sex discrimination litigation for the past thirty years.[246]

These insights raise an important question regarding the social utility of class action litigation involving employment discrimination. This kind of litigation has always had the twin purposes of remedying past discrimination while deterring future discrimination. In this section, I will explore both of these purposes by first analyzing the effect the lawsuits have had both on corporations and on the plaintiff classes and then by examining the roles played by the other actors in the process – namely the attorneys, the new diversity task forces, and the government. I will suggest that the turn to large damage awards as the primary remedial tool has diminished both the public nature and the efficacy of the litigation. In the final section, I will discuss some possible reforms that might return a public interest dimension to the class action litigation, with an eye toward serving the underlying purposes of the law. These reforms include increasing damages to strengthen the deterrent effect of antidiscrimination litigation and providing a monitoring function to ensure that the settlement not only serves the interests of the class but is also implemented faithfully.

---

[246] The case against *Sears*, on which many of these cases were based, initially began in 1973. See Alice Kessler-Harris, *In Pursuit of Equity: Women, Men and the Quest for Economic Citizenship in the Twentieth Century* (2001) 292. For some early discussions of the role sex stereotyping and sex segregation had on women's opportunities, see generally Francine D. Blau, *Equal Pay in the Office* (1977) 100 ('Predominantly female occupations may be characterized by fewer possibilities for promotion and more numerous ports of entry than comparable male jobs. . . . '); Cynthia Fuchs Epstein, *Woman's Place: Options and Limits in Professional Careers* (1970) 152–166 (discussing sex typing in occupations); Ruth Bader Ginsburg, 'Sex Equality and the Constitution,' 52 Tulane L Rev 451 (1978) (describing role of sex stereotypes in the development of Supreme Court jurisprudence).

CHAPTER 1. THE PRICE OF DISCRIMINATION

1.4.1 The Plaintiffs: Do They Come out Ahead?

The benefits that accrue to the plaintiff class comprise an important measure of the effect of class action litigation. The basic remedial principle underlying Title VII has always been to place the injured party in the position she would have been in absent the discrimination.[247] Prior to the passage of the Civil Rights Act of 1991, when damages were not available for claims filed under Title VII, successful class action plaintiffs were typically afforded some monetary relief to compensate for lost wages, as well as injunctive relief designed to alter the employer's discriminatory practices.[248] Many of the cases before the 1991 Act involved discriminatory employment tests, so often the settlements required the employer to design new tests that had less of a discriminatory impact.[249] The remedial relief also typically provided a preference to victims of discrimination in future hiring or promotions, so as to place them in the position they would have been in had they not been discriminated against.[250] Goals and timetables were commonplace in these settlement agreements.[251] In these cases, relief was generally reserved to individuals

---

[247] *Ford Motor Co. v. EEOC*, 458 US 219, 230 (1982) (stating that Title VII 'aims' to make the victims of unlawful discrimination whole 'by restoring them..."to a position where they would have been were it not for the unlawful discrimination"' (quoting *Albemarle Paper Co. v. Moody*, 422 US 405, 421 (1975))).

[248] For a discussion of the remedies that were traditionally available, see Clyde Summers, 'Effective Remedies for Employment Rights: Preliminary Guidelines and Proposals,' 141 U Pa L Rev 457 (1992).

[249] See e.g., *Firefighters Inst. for Racial Equal. v. City of St. Louis*, 616 F.2d 350 (8th Cir. 1980) (requiring the development of a new test if the city was unable to validate the existing exam); *Freeman v. City of Philadelphia*, 751 F. Supp. 509, 512 (ED Pa. 1990) ('The Consent Order obligates the City to solicit and evaluate proposals for a new police officer recruit exam which minimizes adverse impact on nonwhites....'); *Kirkland v. New York State Dep't of Corr. Servs.*, 520 F.3d 420, 426 (2nd Cir. 1975) (noting that the district court had ordered development of 'lawful nondiscriminatory tests').

[250] See e.g., *Firefighters Inst. for Racial Equal. v. St. Louis*, 588 F.2d 235 (8th Cir. 1978) (ordering promotions in a fire department); *United States v. City of Chicago*, 549 F.2d 415 (7th Cir. 1977) (ordering hiring and promotion of class members in a police department).

[251] See e.g., *Donaghy v. City of Omaha*, 933 F.2d 1448, 1451–1452 (8th Cir. 1991) (discussing hiring goals of the 1980 consent decree); *Officers for Justice v. Civil Serv. Comm'n*, 688 F.2d 615, 635–636 (9th Cir. 1982) (validating promotions goals and timetables); *United States v. City of Alexandria*, 614 F.2d 1358, 1368 (5th Cir. 1980)

who could establish a valid claim of discrimination based on a defined procedure. Determining who was eligible for relief has always been a burdensome task, but at least with respect to obtaining monetary relief, the burden on the party seeking relief has often been minimal. Establishing that he or she had applied during a particular time period and was not disqualified from the position for some nondiscriminatory reason was often enough to establish one's eligibility for monetary relief.[252] The standards, however, for obtaining a job or promotion were often more stringent, typically requiring proof of one's qualifications.[253]

1.4.1.1 Structural Reforms after the Civil Rights Act of 1991

The cases that were filed after the Civil Rights Act of 1991 have a distinctly different focus from cases that preceded the Act. Monetary relief now forms the core of the remedial package, and beyond monetary relief there is little attempt to remedy past discrimination by other methods. This is true of the cases studied earlier: Neither Texaco nor Home Depot offered any specific jobs or promotions to members of the plaintiff class, and neither case required any particular changes in the employers' practices.[254] Instead, the companies themselves (Texaco under the auspices of its Diversity Task Force) were charged with studying their practices to determine what changes, if any, were necessary. In both cases, the companies ultimately hired more

---

(requiring job performance goals); *Kirkland v. N.Y. State Dep't of Corr. Servs.*, 711 F.2d 1117, 1123–1124 (2nd Cir. 1983) (providing race conscious promotional relief).

[252] These procedures generally tracked those outlined by the Supreme Court for determining individual remedies. See *Int'l Bhd. of Teamsters v. United States*, 431 U.S. 324, 360 (1977).

[253] See e.g., *Officers for Justice v. Civil Serv. Comm'n*, 979 F.2d 721, 727–728 (9th Cir. 1992), cert. denied, 507 US 1004 (1993) (allowing banding of scores for promotional relief); *Ass'n Against Discrimination v. City of Bridgeport*, 710 F.2d 69, 74–75 (2nd Cir. 1983) (discussing the relation between back pay and job relief); *United States v. City of Chicago*, 549 F.2d 415, 436–437 (7th Cir. 1977) (upholding promotional quotas for a police department).

[254] The *Home Depot* decree required the development of the new hiring process described earlier. See *supra* text accompanying notes 173–174. But given that Home Depot was developing the program at the time of the settlement, it is more accurate to state that the decree required the company to implement the plan it was developing.

CHAPTER 1. THE PRICE OF DISCRIMINATION

women and minorities. However, there was no effort to offer jobs to those who might have been discriminated against in the past, nor was there any specific effort to make up for the past years of discriminatory hiring or promotions. At most, the companies appeared to stop discriminating without remedying their past discrimination (other than through monetary relief).[255] Other lawsuits demonstrate similar characteristics. The case against *Coca-Cola* was modeled on the *Texaco* litigation, and the consent decree required no specific changes in the corporation's practices.[256] Progress has been difficult to measure in the extensive litigation against grocery store chains, the vast majority of which were initiated by the Saperstein law firm that was primarily responsible for the *Home Depot* case, because many of the companies have refused to provide any information about their employment practices or workforce statistics, even after the cases settled.[257]

The two cases in which reform did occur – *Shoney's* and *State Farm* – were both filed before the enactment of the Civil Rights Act of 1991, and the *Shoney's* case was initially prosecuted by a non-profit public interest group, the NAACP Legal Defense and Education Fund.[258] The *State Farm* case, which for many years was the largest employment discrimination settlement, resulted in large monetary awards of approximately USD 190,000 to class members and also required that at least 50% of new agents had to be women.[259]

---

[255] As noted earlier, Home Depot agreed to hire women as sales associates in proportion to their representation in the qualified pool of applicants. See *supra* n. 164. This remedy, however, only protects against future discrimination by requiring nondiscriminatory hiring, but does not compensate for the years when Home Depot had been discriminating. In order to remedy that discrimination, Home Depot should be required to hire at levels that exceed current applicant levels.
[256] See *Abdallah v. Coca-Cola*, 133 F. Supp. 2d 1364, 1368–1374 (ND Ga. 2001) (summarizing programmatic relief). The only programmatic relief that appeared to be mandatory was diversity training. *Id.* at 1370.
[257] See Stuart Silverstein, 'In Supermarkets' Executive Department, A Lack of Variety,' LA Times, May 2, 1999, at C1 (noting that only one of the four major supermarket chains that had been sued agreed to provide information on diversity in executive ranks).
[258] See Al Kamen, 'Shoney's Faces Suit on Hiring,' Wash Post, April 5, 1989, at F1 (noting that the suit was filed by the NAACP Legal Defense and Educational Funds).
[259] See Hager, *supra* n. 2 ('Under the settlement, the 814 women are to receive an average of USD 193,000' and 'at least 50% of the new agents hired in California over a 10-year period...were to be women.').

65

This shift in remedial focus from structural change to monetary relief highlights one of the central ways in which employment discrimination class action litigation has become just another tort. In the analogous tort area of products liability, money damages are the primary remedy for past injury and defendants are not required by the terms of the settlement to change their practices, nor does the plaintiff have an ongoing monitoring role once the lawsuit has ended.[260] Whatever changes the company implements are self-initiated to limit its exposure to additional lawsuits. The litigation costs associated with additional accidents or injuries thus provide the incentive to alter corporate practices, but accidents are treated as an inevitable part of the business to be controlled but not eliminated. In the same way, discrimination has now become part of the cost of doing business. It appears that as a society we no longer desire to eradicate discrimination, but instead have placed a price on it – which effectively assumes discrimination will persist.[261] Although this evolution has largely gone unnoticed, it represents a sea change in the way we think about discrimination – and is in many ways consistent with Derrick Bell's emphasis on the permanence of discrimination.[262]

1.4.1.2 Monetary Relief

Assessing the effect of the shift in remedial focus requires analyzing the monetary relief that is provided to plaintiffs as part of the settlements. Even though as a society we may not want to condone the persistence of discrimination, in our imperfect world we may accept a tradeoff between structural reforms and monetary relief if that tradeoff provides the best prospects for antidiscrimination enforcement, particularly if the monetary relief is substantial. Many plaintiffs would undoubtedly

---

[260] See Linda S. Mullenix, 'Resolving Aggregate Mass Tort Litigation: The New Private Law Dispute Resolution Paradigm,' 33 Val U L Rev 413, 428 (1999) (noting that injunctive relief and consent decrees are almost never used in mass tort settlements); Richard A. Nagareda, 'Turning from Tort to Administration,' 94 Mich L Rev 899, 919–930 (1996) (discussing the structure of mass tort settlements).
[261] In the distinction drawn by Robert Cooter, the new era of litigation emphasizes prices rather than sanctions, where prices increase with the amount of external harm caused by the act, and sanctions are instead tied to the actor's state of mind. Robert Cooter, 'Prices and Sanctions,' 84 Colum L Rev 1523, 1537–1538 (1984).
[262] Derrick Bell, *Faces at the Bottom of the Well: The Permanence of Racism* (1992).

CHAPTER 1. THE PRICE OF DISCRIMINATION

prefer money damages to the prospect of a job or a promotion, especially when they have already located alternative employment.

All of the cases discussed in this study, including those in the statistical study, settled for substantial financial amounts – awards that generally far exceed what had been obtained prior to the enactment of the new damage provisions of the Civil Rights Act of 1991. But the amounts that are reported by the parties are often misleading in that they represent the defendants' maximum possible exposure, typically spread across a multi-year timeframe, and often exceed what the defendant will actually pay out. When the settlement amounts are reported, they generally include the money that will be distributed to the plaintiff class as well as attorneys' fees, third-party expenditures on diversity efforts and minority suppliers, and other potential costs that may never be realized – such as the potential costs of raising salaries should a study determine that past practices in setting salaries were discriminatory.

As set forth in Table 1.5, the recent *Coca-Cola* settlement illustrates how a settlement amount can be inflated to overrepresent its value to the plaintiff class.[263]

Table 1.5: Coca-Cola Settlement

Item	Amt. (in USD millions)
Compensatory Damages	58.7
Back Pay Fund	23.7
Promotional Achieve. Fund	10.0
Salary Equity Adjustments	43.5
Diversity Initiatives	36.0
Attorney's Fees	20.6
Total	192.5

Source: *Ingraham v. Coca-Cola*

---

[263] In a recent, and rare, reversal of a district court's approval of a consent decree, the Ninth Circuit expressed concern regarding the way in which the value of the settlement was calculated. See *Staton v. Boeing Co.*, 313 F.3d 447, 482 (9th Cir. 2002) (noting that much of the value of 'injunctive relief... cannot be accurately traced to the decree').

The *Coca-Cola* settlement was routinely reported to be worth USD 192.5 million, but the projected totals are actually USD 193 million.[264] Of that amount, USD 58.7 million was set aside for compensatory damages, which were defined as compensating emotional distress, hostile environment discrimination, and other non-wage discrimination.[265] There is also a USD 23.7 million back pay fund to compensate for lost wages due to discriminatory policies, some of which would be paid in stock options.[266] The remaining monetary amounts were less well-defined. The USD 10 million Promotional Achievement Award Fund would be awarded to class members who remained with the company and received promotions over the next ten years.[267] A pay equity fund in the amount of USD 43.5 million – nearly twice the size of the back pay fund – would be paid out over ten years to remedy pay disparities that were identified by statistical experts.[268] The amount of the pay equity fund was an estimate, and the amounts actually distributed could be far lower, as occurred in the *Texaco* case, where the company's actual expenditures toward pay equity were only a fraction of the initial estimates.[269] The total defined in the settlement approved by the court amounts to USD 156 million, and the remaining USD 36 million is dedicated to various diversity initiatives, many of which the company likely would have implemented even without the settlement. This was especially true in the case of Coca-Cola, which even prior to the lawsuit had contributed millions of dollars to African-American groups and had a strong reputation within the civil rights community.[270] Attorneys' fees accounted for an additional USD 20.7 million, or 20% of the total

---

[264] See e.g., 'Coca-Cola Agrees to Pay USD 192.5 Million, Make HR Policy Changes to Settle Lawsuit,' Daily Lab Rep, November 17, 2000, at AA1; Betsy McKay, 'Coca-Cola Agrees to Settle Bias Suit for USD 192.5 Million,' Wall St J, November 17, 2000, at A3; Unger, *supra* n. 2.

[265] See *Ingram v. Coca-Cola Co.*, 200 FRD 685, 694 n. 11 (ND Ga. 2001); 'Coca-Cola Agrees to Pay $192.5 Million,' *supra* n. 264.

[266] 'Coca-Cola Agrees to Pay USD 192.5 Million,' *supra* n. 264.

[267] Ingram, 200 FRD at 695.

[268] *Id.* at 688.

[269] *Id.*; see also *supra* text accompanying notes 121–122.

[270] In one news report, Congressman John Lewis, himself a veteran of the civil rights movement, was quoted as saying, 'The reason Atlanta is Atlanta today, and Birmingham is Birmingham and Little Rock is Little Rock, is to a large degree because of the leadership of Coca-Cola.' Nikhil Deogun, 'A Race Bias Suit Tests Coke,' Wall St J, May 18, 1999, at B1.

CHAPTER 1. THE PRICE OF DISCRIMINATION

current cash settlement fund dedicated to compensation for the plaintiff class and the attorneys.[271] While this amount is again considerably lower than the standard one-third contingency fee, the *Coca-Cola* case was settled within a year of the initial filing and no substantial motions were ever filed.[272] By the attorneys' own estimates, the fee award was between three and four times their actual fees.[273] As a percentage of the total settlement, only about 43% of the amount would go directly to the plaintiffs, with another USD 53.5 million, or 28%, contingent on future events.

Even when broken down by its components, the *Coca-Cola* settlement provided substantial payoffs to the plaintiffs – estimated to be USD 38,000 per class member.[274] While the average payments are often based on estimates of the potential class size, they provide one of the best measures of the benefits that ultimately redound to class members. Table 1.6 provides a representative sampling of settlements based on the various amounts that were distributed to the individual class members and the attorneys.[275]

---

[271] Ingram, 200 FRD at 694.

[272] There were, however, a number of significant discovery disputes. See *Abdallah v. Coca-Cola Co.*, 186 FRD 672 (ND Ga. 1999) (resolving disputes regarding interviews of prospective class members); *Abdallah v. Coca-Cola Co.*, No. 1:98CV3679-RWS (ND Ga. 1999) (granting a motion for a protective order).

[273] Ingram, 200 FRD at 696 ('Counsel estimate that the time expended results in a lodestar amount for this case of between $5.2 and $6 million.').

[274] Henry Unger, 'Coca-Cola Soon to Mail Class-Action Checks,' Atlanta J-Const, July 12, 2001, at E1.

[275] The sources for Table 1.6 are: Lisa Backman, 'Publix Pays Women $81 Million,' Tampa Trib, January 25, 1997, at 1 (*Publix*); 'Excerpts: Deal Includes "Make-Whole" Back Pay Fund', Atlanta J-Const, November 17, 2000 (averages figures for *Boeing* and *Shoney's*); *Haynes v. Shoney's, Inc.*, 89-30093-RV, 1993 WL 19915, 46 (ND Fla. 1993) (*Shoney's* attorneys' fees); Benjamin A. Holden, 'American Stores to Settle Sex-Bias Suit By Paying As Much as $107.3 Million,' Wall St J, December 17, 1993, at A2 (*Lucky Stores*); Joint Report, *supra* n. 158, at 2 (*Home Depot* averages); Ingram, 200 FRD at 694 n.11 (*Coca-Cola* fees); Paul Nyhan, 'Bias Pact Rejected, Federal Appeals Court Throws Out USD 15 Million Settlement from 1999,' Seattle Post-Intelligencer, November 27, 2002, at C1 (*Boeing*); 'Shoney's Bias Suit Settled,' NY Times, January 28, 1993, at D19 (*Shoney's*); Chris Roush, 'Home Depot OKs Bias Settlement,' Atlanta J-Const, September 20, 1997, at A1 (*Home Depot* fees); Stuart Silverstein, 'Edison Will Pay USD 18.25 Million to Settle Racial Bias Class Action,' LA Times, October 2, 1996, at D1 (Edison International); 'Texaco Discrimination Settlement Endorsed,' *supra* n. 101 (*Texaco*); Unger, *supra* n. 274 (*Coca-Cola* payments). As noted previously,

69

EMPLOYMENT CLASS AND COLLECTIVE ACTIONS

Table 1.6: Class Action Settlement Distributions

Case	Amount for class (in USD millions)	Ave. Amt. (in USD)	Atty's Fees (in USD millions)
Texaco	117.10	63,000	20.1 (14.6%)
Shoney's	105.00	4,850	29.0 (21.6%)
Coca-Cola	83.00	38,000	20.7 (29.0%)
Home Depot	65.00	9,683	22.5 (25.7%)
Publix	63.00	840	18.0 (22.2%)
Lucky Stores	60.50	5,000	13.8 (18.6%)
Edison Int'l	11.25	4,700	7.0 (38.4%)
Boeing	7.30	14,280	4.0 (35.4%)

Source: Public sources, newspapers, court opinions.

The 'Amount for Class' category includes only those payments designated for the class, excluding attorneys' fees, payments on diversity initiatives, and possible payments to class members that are contingent on future events. The average payments are based on reported estimates for non-class representatives and vary widely from a high of USD 63,000 in the *Texaco* case to a low of USD 70 in the sex discrimination case involving Publix Markets.[276] Only two of the cases provided an average payment in excess of USD 20,000; the median award was USD 9,683, obtained in the *Home Depot* case. In many of the cases, the class representatives received far higher payments than the average – as much as USD 300,000 in the *Coca-Cola* litigation.[277]

---

the *Boeing* settlement was overturned by the Ninth Circuit Court of Appeals and sent back to the district court for additional justification. The case is included here as an indication of what the plaintiffs were offered rather than what they will ultimately receive.

[276] See Myerson, *supra* n. 2 ('The women employees will divide $63.5 million, generally receiving from $70 to $840 depending on their experience at Publix....').

[277] See e.g., Betsy McKay, 'Coca-Cola Agrees to Settle Bias Suit for $192.5 Million,' Wall St J, November 17, 2000, at A3 ('The four plaintiffs who filed the lawsuit... will each receive an award of no more than $300,000 each....').

Given that these lawsuits primarily produce monetary relief for class members, a substantial question exists as to whether these payouts render the cases socially valuable or whether they should be seen as modest wealth transfers between the defendants and the plaintiffs and their attorneys. Professor Bill Rubenstein has recently suggested that class action litigation has become less adversarial and more transactional in nature, in which the transaction involves the sale of the plaintiffs' rights to sue.[278] Employment discrimination class actions provide additional support for his thesis, with the important caveat that in addition to buying the plaintiffs' right to sue, the defendants are also required to cease their discriminatory practices, at least to the extent those practices can be identified.

Table 1.6 also provides information on the attorneys' fees obtained in the cases, including the percentage of the total amounts paid to the class and the attorneys. Without question, the attorneys for the plaintiff classes receive a substantial portion of the wealth transfer. Yet even though the fees tend to be extremely high in absolute terms, as a percentage of the recovery most of the awards fall well within the accepted range of 20–30% for class action litigation,[279] and all but two fall well below the standard one-third contingency fee. It is interesting that the two smallest damage awards produced the two highest fee awards as a percentage of the recovery, perhaps suggesting that attorneys seek a minimum fee independent of the underlying monetary awards.

1.4.1.3 Diversity Initiatives

In the new era of employment discrimination litigation, neither monetary relief nor structural reform exhausts the terms of the agreements.

---

[278] See William B. Rubenstein, 'A Transactional Model of Adjudication,' 89 Geo LJ 371, 419 (2001) ('The core premise of the transactional model is that complex multiparty litigation resembles a transaction more than it resembles a conventional adversarial lawsuit. What is bought and sold are rights-to-sue.').

[279] Deborah R. Hensler et al., *Class Action Dilemmas: Pursuing Public Goals for Private Gain* (2000) 78 ('The most widely cited standard [for fees in class actions] is 25–30 percent.'); Russ M. Herman & Stephen J. Herman, 'Percentage-of-Benefit Fee Awards in Common Fund Cases,' 74 Tul L Rev 2033, 2044 n. 51 (2000) (noting that the most common fee is between 20% and 30% of the class action settlement fund); Janet Cooper Alexander, 'Do the Merits Matter? A Study of Settlements in Securities Class Actions,' 43 Stan L Rev 497, 573 (1991) (estimating that attorneys' fees in securities class actions average 26.8% of the settlement fund).

Rather, as part of the settlements, employers now commonly engage in a variety of diversity initiatives, ranging from increasing their commitments to minority suppliers to diversity training for their employees. As mentioned above, companies have also agreed to contribute funds to colleges or other public interest groups, and have sponsored minority groups such as the Harlem Globetrotters and a black-owned circus.[280] Virtually every settlement now requires some form of diversity initiative, and these efforts can add significantly to the cost of the settlement. This was certainly true for the *Texaco* and *Denny's* litigations, where the companies directed millions of dollars to women and minority suppliers, and likewise comprised a substantial portion of the total settlement amount in the cases involving *Coca-Cola* and *Shoney's*. In a recent proposed settlement involving *Boeing*, the amount the company agreed to devote to unspecified affirmative action efforts was nearly half as large as the amount dedicated to class relief.[281]

These diversity initiatives raise a number of troubling concerns, not the least of which is their value to the plaintiff class. Diversity training is now commonplace in corporate America, and it is quite likely that the costs attributed to the settlement for diversity training are simply costs the employer would have incurred even if it had not been sued. It is estimated that more than 70% of large corporations have initiated diversity training in the last decade, and most of those that have not yet instituted some form of training are expected to do so in the near future.[282] Even though diversity training is now a standard business practice, its benefits remain largely speculative as there has been sparse empirical evidence to document its value.[283] The diversity

---

[280] See *supra* text accompanying notes 223–224.

[281] The settlement involving *Boeing* provided for USD 6.65 million to class members and USD 3.65 million for diversity efforts. 'Settlement Is Approved in Boeing Bias Lawsuit,' NY Times, October 10, 1999, at C20. The Ninth Circuit recently reversed the district court's approval of the consent decree and remanded the case for additional justification or a renegotiated settlement. See *Staton v. Boeing Co.*, 313 F.3d 447, 482 (9th Cir. 2002).

[282] See Elizabeth Lasch-Quinn, *Race Experts: How Racial Etiquette, Sensitivity Training, and New Age Therapy Hijacked the Civil Rights Revolution* (2001) 163 (estimating that 70% of Fortune 500 companies had adopted diversity training by 1995).

[283] Professor Susan Bisom-Rapp recently reviewed the existing literature and concluded that there was little support for the purported beneficial effects of diversity training. Susan Bisom-Rapp, 'An Ounce of Prevention Is a Poor Substitute for a Pound of Cure: Confronting the Developing Jurisprudence of Education and

CHAPTER 1. THE PRICE OF DISCRIMINATION

industry itself, an unregulated and amorphous collection of groups, has come under sharp criticism for the lack of validation for its programs.[284] At a minimum, it seems safe to conclude that diversity training is a poor substitute for structural reform.

No doubt the popularity of diversity initiatives in settlement agreements is attributable to the benefits they provide to employers rather than employees. This is particularly true of the third-party transfer payments. While the employees may gain some value from the increased use of minority suppliers or advertisers, or the promotion of a circus or a basketball team, the employers use these efforts as important public relations tools designed to repair or enhance their image. These programmatic expenditures come at little cost to the company as they generally represent a shift of suppliers or sponsored programs rather than any new financial obligations. This is not to suggest that these expenditures are undesirable, only that they should not be counted as an unqualified benefit to the plaintiff class, especially if the money that is distributed to third parties could have been available to the plaintiffs.

1.4.2 Corporations and Class Action Litigation

Even if the benefits to the plaintiff class are modest, class action litigation may still be socially beneficial to the extent it alters corporate

---

Prevention in Employment Discrimination Law,' 22 Berkeley J Emp & Lab L 1 (2001). Professor Bisom-Rapp concludes:

> The empirical and anecdotal evidence discussed in the last section renders the legal profession's reflexive and undiscerning endorsement of anti-discrimination training highly suspect. While the desire to find a 'quick fix' for the problem of employment discrimination is understandable, that educational efforts positively affect entrenched bias is a hypothesis that has yet to be proven.

Id. at 44; see also Mark Bendick Jr. et al., 'Workforce Diversity Training: From Anti-Discrimination Compliance to Organizational Development,' 24 Hum Resource Plan 10, 12 (2001) (identifying only two studies designed to measure the efficacy of diversity training).

[284] For two extensive critiques of the industry, see Lasch-Quinn, *supra* n. 282, and Frederick R. Lynch, *The Diversity Machine: The Drive to Change the 'White Male Workplace'* (1997). Although these critiques are hardly models of objectivity, their descriptions of the evolution of the diversity industry are valuable and expose its lack of a theoretical foundation.

practices to prevent and eradicate discrimination. This may occur in several distinct ways – through reforms the suits prompt, through the market reaction by investors, or by deterring employers from discriminatory practices. As already touched on, and discussed in more detail below, the fact that the lawsuits do not significantly affect shareholder value suggests they have a limited deterrent effect. Other factors, such as the presence of insurance and the apparent random quality of the lawsuits, likewise suggest that the litigation will offer limited prospects for deterrence. This section will explore what this study tells us about the effect the lawsuits have had on corporations, and about the continuing presence of discrimination.

1.4.2.1 *The Nature of Discrimination and its Reform*

Before analyzing the deterrent effects of the lawsuits, it is worth exploring what these lawsuits reveal about the nature of contemporary discrimination. Understanding the nature of that discrimination will enable us to better define the effect that litigation has had over the last several decades. One of the surprising conclusions of this study is just how little has changed. While institutional discrimination has unquestionably receded in the last two decades, the cases discussed in this study all involve allegations of discrimination that implicate policies resembling those of an earlier era, including policies involving overt racial animus and sex-stereotyping. Indeed, all of the cases receiving widespread attention in the last decade have involved allegations of overt intentional discrimination.

Texaco, *Denny's*, and *Shoney's* all involved classic cases of overt racial discrimination, complete with racial epithets, code words, and the Ku Klux Klan. Not coincidentally, the cases against *Denny's* and *Texaco* (and to a lesser extent against *Shoney's*) are the only cases that captured any sustained national attention during the last decade, and they did so based on what appeared to be evidence of discrimination from a bygone era – racial epithets secretly recorded on tape, and the refusal to serve black Secret Service agents wearing their dress uniforms.[285] The case against *Shoney's* involved explicit directives from

---

[285] See *supra* text accompanying notes 70–72 (discussing the tape recordings in the *Texaco* case) and n. 184 (discussing a Maryland Denny's refusal to serve African-American Secret Service agents).

CHAPTER 1. THE PRICE OF DISCRIMINATION

the company to keep African-American workers out of the dining room, as well as allegations that the chief executive officer at one time supported the Ku Klux Klan and offered to match his employees' contributions to that organization.[286] Both Shoney's and Denny's, as well as many of the other companies discussed in this study, are headquartered in the South, giving the cases an additional tie to the segregation-era cases.[287]

As noted previously, Denny's and Shoney's are two companies that have gone to great lengths to actually change their cultures, and Texaco has gone to considerable lengths to change its image. One lesson to be drawn from these cases is that allegations of race discrimination, particularly those steeped in intentional discriminatory practices, still resonate far more than any other claim of discrimination. Indeed, our social norms have turned so strongly against overt acts of racial discrimination that the effects of those norms persist even after the allegations turn out to be false, as in the *Texaco* case.[288] The case against *Coca-Cola* provides another example of a company reacting quickly to the public perception that it was riddled with racially discriminatory practices.[289] Yet these efforts are not always successful. Despite its substantial reform efforts, for example, Denny's has been unable to shake its tainted image. In one recent case, the Sixth Circuit Court of Appeals took judicial notice of Denny's past history, noting, 'Defendant's past history of discriminatory conduct, both to its minority patrons and employees alike, is well known in the jurisprudence and public forums.'[290]

---

[286] It was reported that Shoney's former Chairman, Raymond L. Danner, had 'once offered to match any employee's contributions to the Ku Klux Klan.' Ronald Smothers, '$105 Million Poorer Now, Chain Mends Race Policies,' NY Times, January 31, 1993, at A16.

[287] Denny's is headquartered in South Carolina, while Shoney's is headquartered in Tennessee. In addition, Home Depot and Coca-Cola are both headquartered in Atlanta, Winn-Dixie and Publix in Florida, Wal-Mart in Arkansas, and Texaco has substantial operations in Texas.

[288] See *supra* text accompanying notes 79–80 (explaining that the tape records did not actually contain racial epithets).

[289] See Maharaj, *supra* n. 7.

[290] *Logan v. Denny's Inc.*, 259 F.3d 558, 577 (6th Cir. 2001). The court's reference to Denny's history elicited a stern rebuke from a dissenting judge: 'Even more disturbing...is the majority opinion's reference to articles from the news media and

The sex-discrimination cases provide a sharp contrast to the continued salience of race discrimination. Home Depot, as with all of the grocery chains charged with similar sex-discrimination practices, never garnered much public attention or faced a boycott, and as a result was able to institute as reform, practices already under consideration. Evidence from the series of grocery-store lawsuits also indicates that the industry has remained resistant to change. Women continue to be seriously underrepresented at the management level, and two recent studies identified the grocery industry as the leading industry in terms of discrimination against women.[291]

The fact that so many of the cases filed during the last decade have involved traditional claims of intentional discrimination is contrary to the prevailing view of the nature of contemporary discrimination. There has long been an assumption that overt forms of discrimination have been displaced by more subtle forms, aptly described as 'second-order' discrimination.[292] This may be true of individual cases of discrimination, and may also be true of most forms of systemic discrimination, but the cases discussed in this study demonstrate that there remains a substantial level of overt intentional discrimination. The major class action cases that have arisen over the last decade are not

---

the purported litigation history of Denny's restaurants to increase the burden upon defendants....' *Id.* at 582 (Batchelder, J., dissenting).

[291] See Silverstein, *supra* n. 135 (discussing studies conducted in Georgia and Washington). It also appears that, in general, the grocery stores have not been hurt despite the bevy of lawsuits aimed at the industry. For one analysis, see Michael Sasso, 'Discrimination Lawsuits Haven't Deterred Shoppers,' The Ledger, January 21, 2001, at E1 ('In the three months following the settlement... Publix's sales were actually up about 9 percent from the same three months in 1996. Meanwhile, profits were up 22 percent over the same quarter in 1996.').

[292] See Sturm, *supra* n. 174, at 468–474 (describing second-generation discrimination). In the mid-1980s, Charles Lawrence wrote an influential article describing how racial discrimination was more commonly the product of unconscious forces rather than overt, animus-based discrimination. Charles Lawrence III, 'The Id, the Ego, and Equal Protection: Reckoning with Unconscious Racism,' 39 Stan L Rev 317, 322–24 (1987). In my own work, I have likewise described how discrimination has become more subtle in nature. Michael Selmi, 'Proving Intentional Discrimination: The Reality of Supreme Court Rhetoric,' 86 Geo LJ 279, 290 (1997) ('Following the passage of the historic Civil Rights Acts in the mid-1960s, discrimination began to take on new and more subtle forms, and overt or blatant racial classifications gradually became the exception rather than the rule in legal challenges....').

CHAPTER 1. THE PRICE OF DISCRIMINATION

about discriminatory promotion tests or practices or even glass ceilings, but more often involve subjective employment practices that create distinct patterns of segregated jobs largely based on traditional stereotypes regarding the abilities and interests of women and minorities.[293] For the most part, there is nothing subtle or novel about the discrimination alleged in any of these cases. Rather they tend to raise familiar claims and arguments. As noted earlier, the *Texaco, Denny's,* and *Shoney's* cases all involved explicit claims of racial discrimination. Another case, involving *Mitsubishi*, grabbed national headlines based on explicit and pervasive sexual harassment.[294] The case against *Publix Markets* involved all of the classic forms of sex stereotyping, ranging from women's lack of interest in working long hours to men's need for higher salaries to care for their families.[295]

At the same time, because none of the cases was tried, it is difficult to know whether the cases targeted actual patterns of discrimination (or at least what the law would define as unlawful discrimination). All of the cases identified statistical imbalances in the workforce, but a

---

[293] The cases involving supermarkets have all raised nearly identical claims. See e.g., Christine Blank, 'Ingles Hit by Class-Action Sex Bias Suit,' Supermarket News, March 9, 1998, at 4 ('The suit...alleges that women are relegated to cashier, clerk, deli and bakery positions....'); Myerson, *supra* n. 2 ('The discrimination suit was filed...by 12 women who said they were concentrated at the cash registers, while men sold and stocked the merchandise – positions with more potential for advancement.'); Krysten Crawford, 'Barnhart v. Safeway,' The Recorder, April 6, 1994, at 2 ('[The plaintiffs] alleged that Safeway consistently overlooked women when making management promotions, assigned them to lower-paying jobs in the deli or bakery....'); Jane Gross, 'Big Grocery Chain Reaches Landmark Sex-Bias Accord,' NY Times, December 17, 1993, at A1 ('The women said they were channeled into dead-end jobs, either working the cash registers or in relatively new departments like bakeries and delicatessens....').

[294] See Kristen Downey Grimsely et al., 'Fear on the Line at Mitsubishi: Women Recount Allegations of Sexual Harassment at Auto Plant,' Wash Post, April 29, 1996, at A1.

[295] For an extensive analysis of the *Publix* case, see Anne Hull, 'A Woman's Place,' St Petersburg Times, February 2, 1997, at 1A. The statistical basis for the promotional claims at issue in *Publix* was gathered by walking into the store to observe the pictures of the managers and assistant managers that were hanging in the stores, more than 90% of whom were white men. *Id.* The case included allegations of widespread harassment, overt statements of paying men more because of their family responsibilities, and many cases of women who were denied opportunities readily available to men. *Id.*

77

statistical imbalance by itself is rarely sufficient to establish a defendant's liability.[296] The three case studies provide mixed evidence of discrimination. In the *Texaco* case, the primary allegations involving salary and promotion discrimination were not substantiated by the salary studies conducted under the terms of the settlement agreement or by the company's subsequent promotion patterns.[297] The *Home Depot* case appears to provide a stronger case of discrimination in its assignment policy, but this is also the kind of claim that courts have not been especially receptive to over the years, largely because of their own stereotypical biases regarding jobs that are appropriate for women.[298] Yet, based on the plaintiffs' statistical evidence, it does seem that Home Depot engaged in a pattern of discriminatory conduct. It also seems that such conduct remains a surprisingly prominent part of the corporate landscape, particularly with respect to what are treated as traditional male and female jobs. The case against *Denny's* was almost certainly the strongest of the cases studied here, but, because it focused on public accommodations rather than employment, it is difficult to draw any conclusions regarding employment discrimination other than to say that Denny's was unquestionably capable of substantially improving its record with respect to the hiring and promotion of minorities once it made a concerted effort. The *Shoney's* case, which in many ways parallels the case against Denny's, also provides extensive evidence of systemic discrimination by a corporation with a culture permeated by discriminatory beliefs.[299]

---

[296] Most of the cases were premised on a theory of intentional discrimination that resulted from a pattern or practice of discrimination. In these cases, statistics alone can be used to establish a prima facie case of discrimination, and statistics generally provide the substance of the claim. *Hazelwood Sch. Dist. v. United States*, 433 US 299, 307–308 (1977) ('Where gross statistical disparities can be shown, they alone may in a proper case constitute prima facie proof of a pattern or practice of discrimination.'). The defendant is then afforded an opportunity to either rebut the statistics or to offer an alternative explanation for the observed disparities. *Id.* at 310.

[297] See *supra* text accompanying notes 121–124 (discussing salary adjustments and promotions made by Texaco).

[298] See Selmi, *supra* n. 182, at 568–569 ('Courts are also often influenced by what they might consider the proper roles for women....').

[299] See Duke, *supra* n. 2 (noting that the company President 'was so adamant about holding down the number of black employees that managers hid blacks "from view"... when he paid them visits').

CHAPTER 1. THE PRICE OF DISCRIMINATION

It may be that these cases reveal more about class action litigation than they do about the nature of discrimination. One reason claims of overt discrimination continue to predominate among the large class actions is that these claims have a substantially higher probability of success than other forms of discrimination – a critical factor in attracting the profit-motivated attorneys who currently bring the large class action cases. In contrast, cases that involve subtle discrimination are far more difficult to prove, and often do not lend themselves to class action treatment because they involve complicated issues of proof that are often individualized. Claims premised solely on a disparate impact theory may also fail to attract profit-motivated attorneys because only equitable relief, typically in the form of back pay, is available in these cases.[300] Traditionally, requiring defendants to pay attorneys' fees to successful plaintiffs was intended to create an incentive for attorneys to pursue civil rights cases, including those involving employment discrimination that may not otherwise be financially lucrative.[301] However, as we saw earlier, attorneys in class action cases are today routinely obtaining fee awards of three to five times their actual fees,[302] suggesting that the statutory fee provisions are unlikely to provide a comparable incentive.

What this means is that the difficult cases – those involving subtle discrimination or disparate impact claims – are candidates either for government prosecution or non-profit public interest organizations, neither of which has been actively pursuing large class action claims over the last decade. During this time, the government's litigation behavior has been almost comically inept. For example, the EEOC sought to intervene in the *Texaco* litigation only after the tapes were revealed, and in fact only after the case was settled.[303] The agency never sought to intervene in the California *Home Depot* litigation, but instead

---

[300] 42 USC 1981a(a)(1) (2000) (permitting damages for 'unlawful intentional discrimination' while specifically excluding 'an employment practice that is unlawful because of its disparate impact').

[301] See Michael Selmi, 'The Value of the EEOC: Reexamining the Agency's Role in Employment Discrimination Law,' 57 Ohio St LJ 1, 27–32 (1996) (discussing incentives for private attorneys).

[302] See *supra* text accompanying notes 111, 162 (discussing attorneys' fees in the *Texaco* and *Home Depot* cases).

[303] See Kurt Eichenwald, 'Agency Seeks a Role in Texaco Case,' NY Times, November 21, 1996, at D4 ('A Federal agency asked yesterday to be allowed to intervene in a discrimination suit settled last week by Texaco....').

sought intervention in the relatively dormant Louisiana litigation. Its intervention became moot when the case settled shortly after the California agreement was entered into by the parties.[304] Moreover, while the Justice Department negotiated the first agreement with Denny's, the government ultimately played no significant role in transforming the company's practices other than to insist on the creation of the Office of the Civil Rights Monitor. Even in cases where the government was an active party, such as the case against *Publix Markets*, it was always a secondary player that had a limited role in the litigation.[305] As discussed below, the government's failure to play an effective role has contributed to the lack of public accountability in the current class action litigation.

1.4.2.2 The Deterrence Hypothesis: Do the Lawsuits Deter Discrimination?

This study also raises an important question regarding whether our current system creates adequate incentives to deter discrimination within the workplace. Although deterrence is one of the central purposes of antidiscrimination law, it is invariably difficult to determine whether any form of litigation serves this purpose. One important limitation is that no system can attain perfect deterrence, if by perfect deterrence we mean that all discriminators, but only discriminators, are deterred by the law. Rather, for any legal system designed to deter socially undesirable conduct, there will inevitably be either over or underdeterrence, and as a matter of social policy it will be necessary to choose between these imperfect alternatives.[306]

---

[304] See Kirstin D. Grimsley, 'Home Depot Settles Gender Bias Lawsuits,' Wash Post, September 20, 1997, at D1 (noting that the EEOC sought to intervene in a suit filed against Home Depot in New Orleans).

[305] There is an important exception. Although the case was begun by private attorneys, the sexual harassment litigation against Mitsubishi was driven primarily by the EEOC. See *EEOC v. Mitsubishi*, 990 F. Supp. 1059 (CD Ill. 1998); Marion Crain & Ken Matheny, 'Labor's Divided Ranks: Privilege and the United Front Ideology,' 84 Cornell L Rev 1542, 1546–1550 (1999) (discussing the EEOC's role in the lawsuit).

[306] See generally Louis Kaplow & Steven Shavell, 'Fairness Versus Welfare,' 114 Harv L Rev 961, 1261–1262 (2001) ('Perfect deterrence generally will not be achieved because, among other factors, some actors may regard the probability of capture as

CHAPTER 1. THE PRICE OF DISCRIMINATION

In the context of antidiscrimination law, the choice may seem easy insofar as there is no strong claim for a system that underdeters. Discrimination serves no positive social purpose, and our national commitment has long been to eliminate rather than merely to reduce or contain discrimination. In this respect, we plainly ought to prefer overdeterrence to underdeterrence, and we may even conclude that maximum deterrence would be optimal deterrence.[307] Yet while a desire to eliminate discrimination at any cost may be our theoretical ideal, we certainly expect employers to make cost calculations in establishing their levels of care. We would not expect, for example, a firm to overhaul its hiring practices if the cost of doing so would exceed the firm's potential liability, nor would we expect employers to implement antidiscrimination precautions at any cost, and as a result the costs of compliance are inevitably taken into account in a firm's profit-maximizing decisions.[308]

A system that overdeters is not without its problems. To the extent that antidiscrimination litigation punishes employers that are not engaging in discrimination, firms may become overly cautious in their employment practices. In some cases, employers may be hesitant to hire African Americans or women so as to avoid class action suits

---

very low, may not find the prospect of punishment very distasteful, or may act in the heat of the moment to pursue a higher perceived gain.'). For a general discussion on levels of deterrence, see Keith N. Hylton, 'Punitive Damages and the Economic Theory of Penalties,' 87 Geo LJ 421 (1998).

[307] See Michael Selmi, 'Discrimination as Accident: Old Whine, New Bottle: A Response to Professor Wax,' 74 Ind LJ 1233, 1248 (1999) (arguing that as a society we should prefer overdeterrence to underdeterrence).

[308] In a related context, Professor Kip Viscusi has explained, 'A risk-free society is neither feasible nor desirable because of the inordinate costs of eliminating risk.... The optimal level of risk is not zero but is rather an efficient level of risk that reflects the appropriate balancing between the benefits and costs of risk reduction.' See W. Kip Viscusi, *Overview, in Regulation Through Litigation* (W. Kip Viscusi ed., 2002) 1–4. While we may be reluctant to discuss discrimination in this manner, the reality is that we should not expect employers to seek to eliminate discrimination at any cost, and indeed, the limitation on damages in Title VII limits a firm's economic incentive to take certain costly precautions. See *infra* text accompanying notes 316–318. For a discussion of the incentive effects liability regimes might have on discriminatory behavior, see generally J. Hoult Verkerke, 'Notice Liability in Employment Discrimination Law,' 81 Va L Rev 273 (1995).

based on their employment practices.[309] Alternatively, employers may engage in quota hiring as a way of avoiding suits, as has long been alleged by opponents of affirmative action,[310] and they may also engage in inefficient employment practices by placing a value on the avoidance of lawsuits ahead of other company interests. Mid-level managers are particularly prone to this sort of behavior, as they are more likely to suffer repercussions for highly visible lawsuits than for the less-visible reduction in productivity that may result from emphasizing the avoidance of litigation.

This overview demonstrates some of the difficulties in identifying an optimal deterrence system, but there remains the question of whether the current system provides for socially desirable levels of deterrence. In its most basic formulation, deterrence is a function of the probability of detection and the likely penalty, which includes the prospect of the firm being held liable.[311] As a practical matter, this

---

[309] See Richard A. Posner, 'The Efficiency and the Efficacy of Title VII,' 136 U Pa L Rev 513, 519 (1987) (noting that Title VII makes hiring black workers more costly). This should only occur to the extent an employer fears suits regarding its treatment of employees more than it fears suits over its hiring practices. Litigation, however, seems to warrant precisely this perspective. For many years, suits involving hiring practices have paled in importance to those involving treatment of employees. See John J. Donohue III & Peter Siegelman, 'The Changing Nature of Employment Discrimination Litigation,' 43 Stan L Rev 983, 1015–1021 (1991). Indeed, the vast majority of the cases included in the statistical analyses involved allegations of discriminatory treatment of employees rather than job applicants, and the *Home Depot* case likewise suggests that even successful claims of applicants are likely to have substantially lower settlement value than those involving treatment of employees.

[310] See e.g., Paul Craig Roberts & Lawrence M. Stratton, *The New Color Line: How Quotas and Privilege Destroy Democracy* (1995) 133–135. For an excellent refutation of this argument, see Ian Ayres & Peter Siegelman, 'The Q-Word as Red Herring: Why Disparate Impact Liability Does Not Induce Hiring Quotas,' 74 Texas L Rev 1487 (1996).

[311] See e.g., James D. Cox, 'Private Litigation and the Deterrence of Corporate Misconduct,' Law & Contemp Probs, Autumn 1997, at 2 ('Central variables to this [deterrence] equation are the size of the fine and the joint probabilities of detection, prosecution, and conviction for the violation.'). The literature on deterrence is extensive. For a recent sampling, see Richard Craswell, 'Deterrence and Damages: The Multiplier Principle and Its Alternatives,' 97 Mich L Rev 2185 (1999) (reexamining the need for a damage multiplier when detection is less than perfect); A. Mitchell Polinsky & Steven Shavell, 'Punitive Damages: An Economic Analysis,' 111 Harv L

CHAPTER 1. THE PRICE OF DISCRIMINATION

theoretical construct is of limited utility because an essential element of the equation is invariably missing. Although the probability of detection is routinely discussed as if it were measurable, the actuality of the likelihood of detection is never known because we do not know how many firms escape detection. This problem is compounded by the present study, which fails to shed light on whether the lawsuits that are filed target actual discrimination. Not only is there no way to quantify the number of firms that escape detection, but we also do not know how many of the targeted firms were actually engaging in discriminatory conduct. This, too, may limit the law's deterrent effects. When lawsuits do not target actual discrimination, employers may determine that their efforts to prevent discrimination will go unrewarded and would therefore be wasteful. If a suit is as likely regardless of whether the company actually discriminates, then there is little a company can do to stave off a lawsuit. As the authors of a study on class action litigation recently concluded: 'Whenever the justice system rewards litigation without regard to its legal or factual merit, the deterrent potential of litigation is squandered.'[312]

Even with these limitations, there is reason to believe that our current system is less than socially optimal. As noted earlier, class action cases still constitute an insignificant portion of the cases that are filed in any given year, amounting to only about seventy-five cases filed in federal court annually, a level that is down substantially from those of a decade earlier.[313] Based on the paucity of class action filings, the probability of detection appears to be extremely low.[314]

Rev 869 (1998) (discussing the role of punitive damages in deterring conduct); Cass R. Sunstein et al., 'Do People Want Optimal Deterrence?,' 29 J Legal Stud 237 (2000) (reporting the results of a study showing that potential jurors are unlikely to link punitive damages awards to the probability of detection).

[312] Hensler et al., *supra* n. 279, at 119.

[313] See Administrative Office of the US Courts, *supra* n. 22.

[314] It may be that the limited number of suits reflects the limited presence of discrimination in contemporary labor markets. However, given that the lawsuits target statistical workforce imbalances, there is reason to expect a far larger universe of possible lawsuits. Existing data continue to demonstrate substantial levels of segregation by race and gender, which are precisely the kind of data that ought to produce more class action lawsuits. On the persistence of workforce segregation, see Francine D. Blau, 'Trends in the Well-Being of American Women 1970–1995,' 36 J Econ Literature 112, 132 (1998) (discussing segregation levels for women), and

When combined with the fact that the lawsuits may be opportunistically targeted rather than designed to eradicate discrimination, it seems unlikely that firms face a serious deterrent threat based on the likelihood of detection. The uncertainty that pervades the process – both as to the likelihood of a suit and its merits – undoubtedly provides an additional limitation on the deterrent value of the litigation.[315]

Not only does the detection threat appear weak, but the probable penalty is also too low to serve as an effective deterrent, a fact confirmed by the statistical study. Any deterrent effect the suits might have should be evidenced by a declining or depressed stock price for those companies that have been sued; otherwise the suits will likely be treated as little more than a cost of doing business. One reason the damages are too low is that current law caps the damages for an employment discrimination case filed under Title VII at a maximum of USD 300,000 per plaintiff for large companies, with lower caps for smaller employers.[316] Employment discrimination cases are, in fact, one of the few classes of federal cases for which damages are capped, and the caps have not been revised since they were first instituted more than a decade ago. Intentional claims of race discrimination can avoid the damage caps if they are filed under section 1981, though surprisingly few cases are brought pursuant to that statute.[317] In the class action area, this is partly due to the fact that most systemic discrimination claims include allegations based on a disparate impact theory, a theory that cannot be pursued under section 1981.[318]

By their nature, damages caps are arbitrary and have no necessary relation to the damage a company's discrimination is likely to cause either to the immediate victims or to society at large, and as a result, the damage caps almost certainly pose an additional restriction on the law's deterrent effect.[319] As noted earlier, at least for the companies

---

Glenn C. Loury, *The Anatomy of Racial Inequality* (2002) 73–91 (discussing job-level segregation of African-American men).

[315] See generally John E. Calfee & Richard Craswell, 'Some Effects of Uncertainty on Compliance with Legal Standards,' 70 Va L Rev 965 (1984) (analyzing the impact of uncertainty on deterrence).

[316] See 42 USC 1981a(b)(3) (2000).

[317] See Selmi, *supra* n. 301, at 45 (noting private attorneys' underutilization of 1981).

[318] *Gen. Bldg. Contractors Ass'n v. Pennsylvania*, 458 US 375, 383 (1982).

[319] See Don Dewees et al., *Exploring the Domain of Accident Law: Taking the Facts Seriously* (1996) 194 (arguing that damage caps result in underdeterrence of accidental torts).

studied in this article, the aggregate settlement amounts are often too small to provide meaningful deterrence. The USD 100 million settlement with Home Depot amounted to two weeks of pretax profit,[320] and the USD 54 million settlement with Denny's – a corporation that was on the brink of financial collapse – amounted to roughly 3% of its annual revenue, or about two weeks of revenue.[321]

The existence of insurance further complicates the firm's potential liability. Following the passage of the Civil Rights Act of 1991, insurance carriers began to offer Employment Practices Liability Insurance ('EPLI') to cover the costs of discrimination claims.[322] While the policy coverages vary, many include punitive damages as well as all other forms of monetary relief, and many large employers now carry the insurance.[323] The effect insurance may have on the law's deterrence function is a subject of considerable speculation, and one that is not unique to employment discrimination cases.[324] Even though the presence of insurance may suppress incentives to prevent discrimination, insurance carriers can play a preventive role through their

---

[320] See *supra* n. 49 and accompanying text.

[321] In 1993, Denny's revenues were USD 1.53 billion. See Labaton, *supra* n. 193.

[322] See e.g., Joan Gabel et al., 'Evolving Conflict Between Standards for Employment Discrimination Liability and the Delegation of That Liability: Does Employment Practices Liability Insurance Offer Appropriate Risk Transference?,' 4 U Pa J Lab & Emp L 1, 28–30 (2001) (discussing the evolution of policies); Francis J. Mootz III, 'Insurance Coverage of Employment Discrimination Claims,' 52 U Miami L Rev 1, 57–59 (1997) (describing the substance of these policies).

[323] It is estimated that approximately 30% of large corporations carry employment practices liability insurance. See Reed Abelson, 'Surge in Bias Cases Punish Insurers, and Premiums Rise,' NY Times, January 9, 2002, at C1 (noting that 'roughly 30 percent of the companies surveyed in 1999 . . . had some sort of employment practices liability coverage'). It is not always easy to determine whether insurance was part of a settlement. Of the cases discussed in this study, *Texaco* and *Lucky's* have acknowledged insurance contributed to the settlement. See *supra* text accompanying n. 102; 1993 Annual Report of American Stores, at 50 (reporting that USD 31.6 million of USD 74.3 million paid out for judgment came from insurance carriers).

[324] See e.g., Tom Baker, 'Reconsidering Insurance for Punitive Damages,' 1998 Wis L Rev 101, 108–110 (examining the effect of insurance coverage for punitive damages on deterrence); Cox, *supra* n. 311, at 21–37 (discussing the effect of director's and officer's insurance on corporate conduct); Gary T. Schwartz, 'The Ethics and the Economics of Tort Liability Insurance,' 75 Cornell L Rev 313, 336–359 (1990) (evaluating the effect of insurance in tort cases).

underwriting practices and the various incentives they provide to the insured.[325] Overall, however, it seems that the combination of limited damages, a low probability of detection, and the availability of insurance substantially reduces the litigation's deterrent effects.

There are, of course, non-monetary sanctions that could also serve as deterrents. In the discrimination area, it has long been assumed that the reprobation that accompanies a finding of liability would provide a strong deterrent, and in a related fashion, society's moral condemnation attending accusations of discrimination should provide additional incentives for managers to ensure that their practices conform to the requirements of the law.[326] This study, however, cautions against relying on these non-monetary sanctions – moral condemnation seems to follow only explicit racial discrimination, with less application to sex stereotyping or subtle forms of race or sex discrimination. As demonstrated by the statistical study in Section 1.2, unless the lawsuit involves overt claims of race discrimination, a company that is sued for discrimination, or that settles litigation, does not appear to suffer any distinct reputational damage.[327] In this respect, despite the various legal developments regarding what constitutes discrimination over the last several decades, as a society we remain steeped in a notion of discrimination that is animus-based, a definition that excludes much of what the law defines as discrimination.[328] Although many managers will sincerely declare a desire to do the right thing, their definition of

---

[325] See Cox, *supra* n. 311, at 28 ('There is reason to believe that insurers, acting out of their own financial interest, have also complemented reasonable social interests by limiting their coverage to claims that are risks of the type that are both inherent to business organizations and pose no serious potential for moral hazard on the part of the insured.').

[326] See e.g., Cynthia A. Williams, 'Corporate Compliance with the Law in an Era of Efficiency,' 76 NC L Rev 1265, 1369 (1998) ('The serious reputational harm that can be done to a firm by... well-publicized civil liability (as in the recent discrimination settlement at Texaco) imposes real costs on a firm that are virtually impossible to quantify....'). For a discussion of the ways a law firm's reputation on issues involving race can affect its behavior, see David B. Wilkins & G. Mitu Gulati, 'Why Are There So Few Black Lawyers in Corporate Law Firms? An Institutional Analysis,' 84 Cal L Rev 493, 554–565, 601–602 (1996).

[327] See *supra* text accompanying notes 54–56.

[328] See Selmi, *supra* n. 292, at 334–335 (explaining that, while the US Supreme Court has developed doctrines that recognize discrimination can be subtle, as a practical matter the Court only finds discrimination when it is overt).

what constitutes the right thing is quite often narrowly drawn. This leaves monetary sanctions as the primary deterring force, limited as they may be.

1.4.2.3 Will the Market Drive out Discrimination?

In addition to the deterrent value of the litigation, competitive market forces might also work to eradicate systemic labor market discrimination. In one of the most influential insights from the law and economics school, Gary Becker posited that competitive labor markets should drive out discriminatory firms because discrimination is an inefficient labor practice that would create competitive disadvantages for the discriminating firms.[329] Labor market discrimination involves relying on characteristics that are unrelated to a firm's productivity concerns, and thus, over time, discriminatory firms should be priced out of the market by nondiscriminating firms that have lower production costs.[330] Because labor costs themselves are often difficult for investors to isolate,[331] a class action lawsuit alleging employment discrimination should provide a strong market signal that the firm is engaging in inefficient employment practices, the very kind of information that investors or competitors could and should exploit.[332] Moreover,

---

[329] Becker, *supra* n. 9, at 43–45.

[330] See *id.* at 44 (performing an economic analysis showing that firms with the lowest 'discrimination coefficient' will be able to undersell all others). Stewart Schwab makes the important observation that even competitive markets may not drive out discrimination. As he explains, 'Markets cater to tastes...[and] it seems wrong to say, in general, that competitive markets will drive out a taste. Rather, markets drive out tastes that people are not willing to pay for, and markets sustain tastes where value exceeds cost.' Stewart J. Schwab, 'Employment Discrimination,' in 3 Encyclopedia of Law & Economics 31 (2000).

[331] See Paul Osterman, *Securing Prosperity* (1999) 36 (noting that the stock market traditionally undervalues soft investments in people).

[332] Although Becker's thesis has been the subject of considerable criticism and controversy, it remains the dominant theory regarding the economics of discrimination in economics, law, and sociology. See e.g., Robert Max Jackson, *Destined for Equality: The Inevitable Rise of Women's Status* (1998) 86–90 (embracing Becker's premises as part of a sociological study); George R. Boyer & Robert S. Smith, 'The Development of the Neoclassical Tradition in Labor Economics,' 54 Indus & Lab Rel Rev 199, 199 (2001) (describing Becker as a pioneer of the influential neoclassical school of labor

given how infrequent class action suits remain, the filing of a lawsuit should provide a particularly powerful market signal.

Yet, as demonstrated by the statistical study, the lawsuits rarely have any significant effect on stock prices, a fact that casts doubt on Becker's strong hypothesis that the market will eliminate discriminatory firms. Becker's thesis, however, did not focus on the filing of lawsuits, but rather on the costs of discrimination. It may be that stock prices reflect those costs even without the presence of a lawsuit. However, if this were the case, one would expect stock prices to increase after a settlement, because a settlement would send a signal that the discriminatory practices had been eliminated.[333] The data do not support this hypothesis, with the exception of the two cases in which the settlement boosted stock prices.[334] Thus, the statistical study suggests that there is no reason to believe that discriminatory firms will be driven from the market, or even that discriminatory practices will be eliminated.

I have so far been concentrating on the way in which the statistical study is inconsistent with Becker's thesis, but there is another interpretation of Becker's thesis that may find support in the data and case studies. Becker originally premised his thesis on a definition of discrimination that involves explicit intentional discrimination based on animus – whites not wanting to hire African Americans because of their distaste or dislike for them.[335] Today, however, much of the existing labor market discrimination occurs in less overt forms. Animus discrimination appears to account for only a small level of current labor market discrimination, notwithstanding the contrary evidence found within the class actions discussed in this study.

---

economics); Keith N. Hylton & Vincent D. Rougeau, 'The Community Reinvestment Act: Questionable Premises and Perverse Incentives,' 18 Ann Rev Banking L 163, 172–174 (1999) (using Becker's theory to evaluate the Community Reinvestment Act); Jack F. Williams & Jack A. Chambless, 'Title VII and the Reserve Clause: A Statistical Analysis of Salary Discrimination in Major League Baseball,' 52 U Miami L Rev 461, 509–510 (1998) (utilizing Becker's hypothesis in the context of salary discrimination in Major League Baseball).

[333] See Hersch, *supra* n. 13, at 140 (arguing that where a corporation's stock price reflects the effects of a pending lawsuit, news of a settlement should improve the stock price).

[334] See *supra* notes 88–111 and accompanying text.

[335] Becker, *supra* n. 9, at 40.

CHAPTER 1. THE PRICE OF DISCRIMINATION

Based on this evidence, as well as the reaction to the Texaco tapes and the overtly discriminatory policies of Denny's, one might conclude that Becker's thesis has largely proved correct, at least with respect to animus-based discrimination – much of which has been driven from the market.[336] When systemic animus-based discrimination does appear today, the market's reaction is both strong and swift, as demonstrated by the sharp stock price decline Texaco suffered after the tapes were first revealed.[337] This does not necessarily suggest that competitive market pressures were responsible for driving out animus-based discrimination, as Becker predicted. Rather, it seems more likely that our social norms regarding discrimination have substantially evolved, and this change in norms best explains the relative paucity of systemic animus-based discrimination as well as the societal reaction when it does appear.[338] This may also explain why we do not see a similar reaction to sex discrimination suits: Our social norms regarding sex discrimination have not been transformed to the same extent as those regarding race, and we remain strikingly ambivalent about women's presence in the workplace.[339]

In contrast to Becker's emphasis on the inefficiency of discrimination, others have argued that some forms of discrimination may be efficient and would likely persist until a lawsuit was filed to end the practice. For example, discrimination that is intended to satisfy customer expectations or demand can be efficient so long as the gain in customer satisfaction exceeds the loss due to inefficient labor practices.[340] Under

---

[336] I am grateful to Dick Pierce for his discussion on this point.

[337] See *supra* notes 71–74 and accompanying text. As described in the Denny's case study, it is more difficult to isolate the effect that the lawsuits had on the stock price of Denny's corporate parent, although business clearly suffered as a result of the adverse publicity the lawsuits generated. See *supra* n. 197 and accompanying text.

[338] It is important to distinguish between systemic and individual animus-based discrimination. While systemic animus-based discrimination may no longer substantially affect the workplace, individual acts of animus-based discrimination certainly do persist, and can cumulate to significant levels.

[339] For a recent thorough analysis of the ambiguity regarding women's role in the marketplace, see Joan Williams, *Unbending Gender: Why Family and Work Conflict and What to Do About It* (2000).

[340] Schwab, *supra* n. 330, at 578 ('Perhaps a more important explanation for long-run discrimination is that profit-maximizing employers in competitive markets will cater to the discriminatory tastes of employees or customers.'). For a recent study exploring the relationship between customer discrimination and firm profits, see

some circumstances, employees may also prefer, and work better in, a racially homogeneous workplace either because their and their co-workers' interests will more likely be aligned, or because some employees may gain status by having a workplace that is structured along race or gender lines. Richard McAdams, for example, has suggested that white workers gain status at the expense of black workers when black workers are assigned to the least desirable jobs,[341] and Richard Epstein has argued that homogeneous workforces are often more productive than a diverse workforce.[342]

The case studies provide some support for the notion that firms' discriminatory practices may have been consistent with either customer or employee preferences. It is conceivable, for example, that Home Depot structured its assignment system based on the preferences of its customers, assuming that customers of either gender might prefer to receive advice on the sales floor from men.[343] The policies instituted

---

Harry J. Holzer & Keith R. Ihlanfeldt, 'Customer Discrimination and Employment Outcomes for Minority Workers,' 113 Q J Econ 835 (1998). The authors of the study found a strong correlation between the race of customers and the race of employees, particularly with respect to African Americans. *Id.* at 862.

[341] Richard H. McAdams, 'Cooperation and Conflict: The Economics of Group Status Production and Race Discrimination,' 108 Harv L Rev 1003, 1045–1046 (1995).

[342] Richard Epstein asserts that homogenous workplaces can produce a more harmonious collective life based on such small details as 'the music played in the workplace, the food that is brought in for lunch, the holidays on which the business is closed down, the banter around the coffeepot, the places chosen for firm outings....' Epstein, *supra* n. 40, at 68. Epstein, however, presents no empirical evidence to substantiate the likelihood that a homogenous workplace will produce greater benefits than a diverse workplace, or that even where conflicts arise over these issues that they cannot be worked out amicably and at low cost. This is an issue on which the empirical data appear to be limited and conflicting. In a review of the existing literature, two authors concluded that 'diversity [in the workplace] thus appears to be a double-edged sword, increasing the opportunity for creativity as well as the likelihood that group members will be dissatisfied and fail to identify with the group.' Francis J. Milliken & Luis L. Martins, 'Searching for Common Threads: Understanding the Multiple Effects of Diversity in Organizational Groups,' 21 Acad of Mgmt Rev 402, 403 (1996).

[343] According to the company, its customers are evenly split between men and women. See Jacqueline Bueno, 'Home Depot Is Going to Court to Fight Sex-Discrimination Suit,' Wall St J, September 19, 1997, at B5 ('Home Depot...estimates its customer base is evenly split between men and women.').

CHAPTER 1. THE PRICE OF DISCRIMINATION

by Denny's and Shoney's could also plausibly be explained by customer preferences assuming that white customers may have preferred not to eat with or be waited on by African Americans. That said, it is important to emphasize that the corporations in these case studies never justified their policies based on customer or employee preference,[344] and there is no evidence to indicate that the policies in the cases discussed were designed to satisfy those preferences. At most, the policies appeared to be based on the presumed preferences of customers, which were almost certainly consistent with the preferences of the owners who instituted the discriminatory policies.[345]

1.4.3 Reforming the Process

The picture I paint of class-action discrimination suits may seem unduly negative, but I want to emphasize that this is an instance where the evidence is clearly mixed. Class-action litigation has brought jobs and monetary relief to thousands of individuals, and has likely ended or significantly altered many discriminatory practices. These are all socially desirable outcomes and alone may justify the costs of the current system. Those costs, however, are not insubstantial, as measured by the limited benefits that actually accrue to class members, the emphasis on diversity programs and other reform efforts that primarily serve public relations purposes rather than structural reform, the limited deterrent effects of the lawsuits, the lack of any accountability and oversight in the aftermath of litigation, and the extraordinary fees obtained by attorneys. Given all of the existing constraints, the

---

[344] A likely reason the companies did not rely on customer preference is that courts have consistently rejected customer preference as a legitimate justification for discriminatory policies. See e.g., *EEOC v. Joe's Stone Crab, Inc.*, 220 F.3d 1263, 1283 (11th Cir. 2000) (treating a restaurant's policy of hiring only male waiters to create a European ambience as an intentional discrimination claim); *Wilson v. Southwest Airlines*, 517 F. Supp. 292, 304 (ND Tex. 1981) (rejecting an airline's policy of only hiring women as flight attendants based on notions of customer preference).

[345] Shoney's Chief Executive Officer, Raymond Danner, frequently offered customer preferences as a rationale for its policies, but it was clear that the policies were designed primarily to satisfy his own preferences. See Steve Watkins, *The Black O: Racism and Redemption in an American Corporate Empire* (1997) 108, 171–172 (describing Shoney's racially discriminatory policies as 'Danner's Laws').

EMPLOYMENT CLASS AND COLLECTIVE ACTIONS

current system may still be, on balance, the best system we can reasonably expect. However, I believe some reforms could better align the system with its fundamental purposes while simultaneously increasing its accountability. I will concentrate on two important reforms: increasing the damages that are available in employment discrimination lawsuits and restoring the public accountability of litigation.

1.4.3.1 Higher Damages Should Be Available

The current litigation regime fails to adequately deter discrimination in part because the damages are too low to make a significant difference to large firms. One possible reform would be to change the remedies that are available for employment discrimination. This might be accomplished in three different ways. First, the damage caps might be raised, perhaps from the current maximum of USD 300,000–500,000, or some similar figure. Second, the damage caps could be eliminated. Third, the statute could be altered so that it more closely resembles the antitrust enforcement scheme so that treble damages are available.

At a minimum, the existing damage caps should be raised, if for no other reason than to take account of inflation, which has substantially eroded the statute's deterrent effect over the last decade. By itself, however, this reform would accomplish little more than to return the statute to the force it held earlier in the decade when it did not seem to serve as an adequate deterrent against discrimination. The statute's deterrent effects would be enhanced far more successfully if the damage caps were removed altogether. In this way, defendants would be required to bear the full costs of their discrimination, which has always been seen as a critical feature of any system designed to deter misconduct.[346] In addition to removing the caps, there is a substantial argument that a serious commitment to deterring discrimination might require the availability of treble damages, such as are available for successful antitrust prosecutions.[347] Alternatively, rather than adopting a treble damages provision, it might be possible to borrow the remedial scheme applicable in age discrimination cases, which

---

[346] See Polinsky & Shavell, *supra* n. 311, at 874–875.
[347] 15 USC 15a (2000).

CHAPTER 1. THE PRICE OF DISCRIMINATION

provides for a doubling of the back pay award for established willful violations.[348]

A treble or double damages provision serves two purposes that are as applicable to employment discrimination suits as they are to antitrust prosecutions. First, such a provision creates a stronger deterrent than would otherwise exist, and second, it helps attract attorneys who will ultimately receive a portion of any successful prosecution. Antitrust cases are notoriously complex and difficult to prosecute, and studies have found that the treble damages available in antitrust cases has, in fact, increased private prosecutions.[349] Applying treble damages to employment discrimination cases would surely have a similar effect, though as discussed below, that is not necessarily reason alone to justify increasing the damage levels.

In addition to possibly enhancing the deterrence value, providing for treble damages would also send an important expressive message. There has recently been a renewed interest among scholars in the expressive element of law, defined as the messages and the values conveyed by our legal structure.[350] Providing treble damages for employment discrimination would send a message of moral outrage

---

[348] The Age Discrimination Act borrows the remedial scheme from the Fair Labor Standards Act (FLSA), which allows for liquidated damages in the amount equal to the back pay loss in the case of willful violations. 29 USC 626(b) (2001) (applying 29 USC 216 (2000) of the FLSA).

[349] For several discussions regarding the effect of antitrust enforcement, see William Breit & Kenneth G. Elzinga, 'Private Antitrust Enforcement: The New Learning,' 28 JL & Econ 405, 430–436 (1985) (suggesting that private parties over-enforce antitrust laws); Steven C. Salop & Lawrence J. White, 'Economic Analysis of Private Antitrust Litigation,' 74 Geo LJ 1001, 1002 (1986) (noting that private enforcement cases outnumbered government cases six to one).

[350] See e.g., Matthew D. Adler, 'Expressive Theories of Law: A Skeptical Overview,' 148 U Pa L Rev 1363, 1364 (2000) (arguing that expressive theories of law claim that linguistic meaning is an irreducible moral factor); Robert Cooter, 'Expressive Law and Economics,' 27 J Legal Stud 585, 597–606 (1998) (developing an economic theory of expressive law); David A. Dana, 'Rethinking the Puzzle of Escalating Penalties for Repeat Offenders,' 110 Yale LJ 733, 777–780 (2001) (discussing the expressive element of law in the context of environmental penalties); Richard H. McAdams, 'A Focal Point Theory of Expressive Law,' 86 Va L Rev 1649, 1652 (2000) (expounding a theory of how legal signals guide societal expectations); Cass R. Sunstein, 'On the Expressive Function of Law,' 144 U Pa L Rev 2021, 2022 (1996) (discussing the expressive function of the law and its relationship to societal norms).

toward the persistence of discrimination that as a society we often proclaim but fail to support with tangible policy initiatives. The existing damage caps send a far more limited message to potential discriminators by placing a price on discrimination – a price that seems far too low either to deter most employers or to adequately compensate the public for the social harm that results from persistent and pervasive discrimination. The current limits do not convey an adequate societal condemnation of discrimination. Rather, they suggest that discrimination should be treated as a controllable cost of doing business, which is indeed what discrimination has largely become.

Increasing the damages available for employment discrimination so as to increase the deterrent value of antidiscrimination litigation is likely to be met with two immediate objections, though they arise from opposite perspectives. First, those who desire more deterrence may be skeptical about the possible effect that removing the caps or providing for treble damages would have, given the limited influence even large damage awards currently have on firms. In both the *Texaco* and *Home Depot* cases, the settlement amounts were well below the theoretical outer limits of their potential liability, as measured by the number of class members and the possible damage awards,[351] and it is far from clear that raising those outer limits will substantially deter a greater amount of discrimination. Nevertheless, the prospect of greater damages should provide a stronger incentive for firms to implement sound precautionary measures designed to prevent discrimination, though admittedly it is difficult to say precisely how much stronger. Nevertheless, this is a sufficiently important social goal that merits altering the existing damages regime.

Second, a more forceful objection will arise from those who are skeptical about the need for greater deterrence. It seems that there is no existing societal consensus that discrimination remains a prominent feature of the labor market. Indeed, one of the most striking findings of this study was the absence of any such concern regarding ongoing discrimination in the media reports. For this article, I read hundreds of newspaper and magazine articles. However, outside of sensational allegations of overt race and sex discrimination, no story suggested that the increase in litigation or the resulting massive settlements were a

---

[351] See *supra* text accompanying n. 89 (estimating Texaco's liability to exceed USD 500 million); *supra* text accompanying n. 153 (estimating Home Depot's liability to be as high as USD 100 billion).

CHAPTER 1. THE PRICE OF DISCRIMINATION

sign that the companies were, in fact, engaging in systemic discrimination. The articles invariably discussed the cases in statistical terms and likewise described the settlements as business decisions that were not necessarily tied to a need for serious reform. No story mentioned the fact that discriminatory business practices were inefficient and therefore harmful to the underlying business, with the limited exception of the articles about the *Denny's* and *Shoney's* cases (and to a lesser extent *Texaco*), which discussed the discrimination suits as potentially discouraging to minority customers.[352] While the lawsuits were not necessarily defined as frivolous, they were also not seen as rooting out discriminatory practices. Instead, the lawsuits were typically treated as transfers of wealth, with the attorneys' fees always playing a prominent role in the media portrayals.[353]

These issues touch on a fundamental paradox raised by this study: Although the existing damages regime appears inadequate to deter discrimination, increasing the damages may increase litigation without actually deterring additional discrimination. Ultimately, resolving this conundrum through legislative reform will require considerably more information – and a stronger societal consensus – regarding the persistence of discrimination than currently exists. Nevertheless, there seems to be little reason to limit the damages available in discrimination suits. Lifting the damage caps will at least require companies to concentrate on the actual cost of discrimination rather than the artificial limits currently imposed by statute.

1.4.3.2 *Restoring Public Accountability to Class Action Litigation*

One of the most troubling conclusions of this study is the lack of oversight and enforcement of the class action settlements involving

---

[352] See e.g., Calvin Sims, 'Giving Denny's a Menu for Change,' NY Times, January 1, 1994, at A43 (noting that the decline in traffic at Denny's restaurants was partly due to the lawsuits).

[353] See e.g., Stephanie Armour, 'Bias Suits Put Spotlight on Workplace Diversity: Critics Cite Lucrative Fees; Advocates Say Cases Bring Progress,' USA Today, January 10, 2001, at 1B (discussing the scope of attorneys' fees versus the difficulty of finding lawyers to take discrimination cases); Segal, *supra* n. 20 (discussing the new incentives for plaintiffs' lawyers to bring discrimination suits created by large settlement prospects).

employment discrimination. The cases discussed in this article were all brought and developed by private parties, as is true for the vast majority of class action employment discrimination lawsuits filed during the last decade.[354] As noted earlier, the government occasionally seeks to join a lawsuit, as it did in the *Texaco* and *Shoney's* litigations, but with the exception of the *Mitsubishi* case the government has not played a significant role in either the litigation or the subsequent monitoring of any of the cases. However, without a government presence there appears to be no substantive monitoring at all.

Diversity task forces have become one of the primary means of implementing and enforcing settlement agreements, but these task forces provide little meaningful oversight. The task forces rarely object to the company's proposals or their reported progress. Rather, as indicated in the *Texaco* discussion, the task forces quickly become an arm of the company, amounting to little more than a public relations cheerleader that conveys a false picture of independence and review.[355] The lack of independence is likely due to the task force's dependence on the company for access to information and its fees, and, although the task force may provide its report to the court, the plaintiffs' attorneys, and any government agency that was involved in the case, there appears to be no independent oversight of any kind by any of the interested parties. Indeed, the task forces are designed to remove any obligation on the parties to monitor the consent decree.

Like the diversity industry that the task forces resemble, the monitoring business is fast becoming a lucrative enterprise for a small group of individuals, many of whom cycle through the various corporate monitoring groups.[356] The current task forces are comprised substantially of former government officials from the Clinton and Bush administrations who now make their living touting the accomplishments of

---

[354] For example, of the eighty-five class action employment discrimination cases filed in 1998, the government brought only one. Administrative Office of the U.S. Courts, Judicial Business of the Courts tbl.X-5 (1998).

[355] See *supra* text accompanying notes 128–132 (discussing the Diversity Task Force created to oversee the implementation of the settlement decree).

[356] It is estimated that the members of the Texaco Task Force received annual compensation of USD 75,000, while the Chair received USD 125,000. Henry Unger, 'Judge Instructs Coke Task Force,' Atlanta J-Const, August 22, 2001, at 3D.

former defendants.[357] These high-profile individuals provide unquestionably positive public relations for the companies, but it is less clear that they provide meaningful oversight. Based on my research, there has not been a single substantial issue or objection raised by either a diversity task force or any of the plaintiffs' attorneys in any of the cases discussed earlier.[358]

The situation is considerably worse in those cases that do not implement diversity task forces. In their litigation, the Saperstein law firm has not required the creation of diversity task forces, and in fact requires little reporting from its defendants at all. During the four years it was under a consent decree, Home Depot appears to have filed only one progress report, which provided no data and which the plaintiffs' attorneys summarily approved with the conclusory statement that the numbers were better than before.[359] Similarly, progress reports were provided only to plaintiffs' counsel, and to the court in the *Shoney's* case, and public information was made available only at the urging of activist shareholder groups.[360] Despite the lack of public reporting, many of the earlier cases involving Shoney's and State Farm did result

---

[357] For example, Deval Patrick, the former head of the Civil Rights Division for the Department of Justice, resigned his position as general counsel for Texaco, a stint he entered after having served as the head of Texaco's Diversity Task Force, to move to Coca-Cola, where he oversees the implementation of its new diversity initiatives. Patrick was replaced on the Texaco Diversity Task Force by Thomas Williamson, the former Labor Department Solicitor in the Clinton Administration and now a partner at a prominent Washington law firm. Clinton's former Labor Secretary, Alexis Herman, was named to oversee Coca-Cola's Diversity Task Force, a group that includes two other former Clinton Department officials. See *id.* (noting that the former head of the EEOC and Assistant Attorney General for Civil Rights were on the Task Force). Lynn Martin, labor secretary in the first Bush Administration, played a prominent role in Mitsubishi's reform efforts.

[358] The exception is Mitsubishi, where the task force made a number of suggestions to the company and seemed much less an arm of the company than has been the case for the Texaco task force. See Final Report to the Parties and the Court, *EEOC v. Mitsubishi Motor Mfg.*, 102 F.3d 869 (7th Cir. 1996) (on file with the author).

[359] See *supra* notes 167–173 and accompanying text.

[360] See *Haynes v. Shoney's, Inc.*, No. 89-30093-RV, 1993 US Dist. LEXIS 749, at 120 (ND Fla. January 25, 1993) (requiring progress reports to be filed with plaintiffs' counsel); 'Providing Minority Status Reports; Shoney's OKs Operations Plan,' Chattanooga Free Press, February 13, 1997, at E3 (reporting that activist shareholder groups pressed for release of information on the company's progress).

in meaningful reform, while the later cases brought by the firm, including all of the grocery store cases, seem to have resulted in far less tangible (if any) benefits from revised employment practices.[361] This may have to do with the changes in the law that made damages available, changes in personnel in the law firm, or other factors, but the change seems unmistakable. Indeed, there is some danger that employment discrimination class actions are becoming more like the much-maligned consumer class actions. Coupons have already been used as part of a settlement involving *Winn-Dixie*,[362] stock options covered some of the damages in the *Coca-Cola* settlement,[363] and in the last few years attorneys who had previously specialized in personal injury litigation and securities fraud have gravitated towards employment discrimination cases.[364]

The current situation marks a dramatic change from the past, when class action employment discrimination litigation was thought to represent one of the hallmarks of public law litigation, brought by lawyers

---

[361] See Silverstein, *supra* n. 135 (analyzing the lack of women and minorities at management levels in the supermarket industry).

[362] See Mark Albright, 'Judge to Review Winn-Dixie Suit Deal,' St Petersburg Times, July 27, 1999, at 1E ('A substantial slice of Winn-Dixie's settlement, $6.2 million, will be paid not in cash but in coupons offering 10 percent discounts on goods at Winn-Dixie stores.').

[363] *Abdallah v. Coca-Cola Co.*, 133 F. Supp. 1364, 1376–1378 (ND Ga. 2001).

[364] As noted earlier, some of the attorneys who brought the Texaco case made their names in consumer class actions. Also, attorneys who previously specialized in personal injury and securities fraud have recently become involved in discrimination class actions. See Betsy McKay, 'Aggressive Lawyer Joins Race Lawsuit Against Coca-Cola,' Wall St J, April 17, 2000, at B34 (noting that plaintiffs' attorney Will Gary, who 'doesn't generally handle employment discrimination cases,' had joined the lawsuit); Jess Bravin, 'Lawyers Noted for Investor Class Actions Ally with Employment and Bias Specialists,' Wall St J, October 13, 2000, at B6 ('Milberg, Weiss, Bershad, Hynes and Lerach, a law firm best known for its securities class action practice, is pushing into the growth area of employment law ... in bringing discrimination suits.'). Not everyone sees the turn to personal injury lawyers as a negative development. See Anne Bloom, *Taking on Goliath: Why Personal Injury Litigation May Represent the Future of Transnational Cause Lawyering*, in Cause Lawyering and the State in a Global Era (A. Sarat & S. Sheingold, eds, 2001) 110, 115 (suggesting that personal injury attorneys may have much to offer because of their resources and risk-taking orientation).

CHAPTER 1. THE PRICE OF DISCRIMINATION

who were primarily interested in pursuing justice rather than profit.[365] The recent cases reject this model in favor of a purely private dispute resolution system that is principally about money. In other words, employment discrimination claims are now just another form of tort where the principal objective is to recover money rather than to reform the corporation through ongoing monitoring. This is perhaps most evident in the case against *Home Depot*, where the company steadfastly refused to provide meaningful information to the public and the plaintiffs' attorneys agreed to vacate the consent decree early – even though Home Depot had not met the goals it had established for itself.[366] Similarly, recall that in the *Texaco* case none of the primary beneficiaries (women and suppliers) of Texaco's reform initiatives were parties to the lawsuit. African Americans, including African-American suppliers, have gained little from the *Texaco* litigation other than the initial (though substantial) monetary recoveries.[367]

An important reason the cases do not produce more change is that they lack any public accountability, which contradicts the original and continuing purposes of class action litigation. With one temporary exception, judges have routinely signed off on the settlement agreements proposed by the parties without engaging in any serious inquiry, and often no independent judicial decision is produced at the time the settlements are approved.[368] Moreover, courts are increasingly appointing mediators to negotiate settlements, which diminishes the likelihood that a court will conduct meaningful review because the mediator will often be seen as acting on behalf of the court. Perhaps an ideal enforcement system would combine high damage awards to plaintiffs with a financial incentive to attorneys that is sufficient to

---

[365] See e.g., Joel F. Handler, *Social Movements and the Legal System: A Theory of Law Reform and Social Change* (1978) 140–149 (describing law reform efforts through employment discrimination litigation); see *supra* n. 6.

[366] See *supra* text accompanying notes 177–180.

[367] See *supra* text accompanying notes 125–127.

[368] See *supra* n. 28. As previously noted, the Ninth Circuit recently rejected a district court's approval of a consent decree, in large part because of the failure of the district to review the settlement with care. See *supra* n. 263. This is not a problem that is unique to employment discrimination. See Judith Resnick, 'The Prerequisites of Entry and Exit,' 30 UC Davis L Rev 835, 849 (1997) (noting that a class action study indicated that in all of the 28 cases studied, settlements were approved generally without change).

attract competent counsel without luring those whose interests are primarily financial in nature. This may be an impossible equilibrium to obtain, but there are clearly some reforms that could restore public accountability to the process and thereby ensure that antidiscrimination litigation serves the goal of preventing and remedying discrimination.

First, rather than establishing diversity task forces that report directly to the company, a court should appoint an independent monitor to oversee implementation of the consent decree. This is the model that had previously been used for discrimination suits and that was successfully employed in the *Mitsubishi* litigation. That case relied on a court-appointed three-person task force charged with reviewing the company's employment practices.[369] In this scheme, the monitor is seen as an arm of the court rather than an arm of the company, and is far more likely to engage in independent assessment than a group that has been appointed (and is directly compensated) by the company itself. The court might also establish an independent monitor or perhaps a magistrate to provide a serious review of the terms of the settlement, a power currently provided under the Federal Rules of Civil Procedure.[370] It is not clear how much will be gained by asking someone else to do the court's job,[371] although for a variety of reasons, a court is in a distinctly inferior position to actively oversee the implementation of the agreement.[372] An independent monitor or trustee may provide

---

[369] See *supra* n. 305.

[370] Fed. R. Civ. P. 53(a).

[371] Judith Resnik has suggested that the presence of a court-appointed monitor might be required during class action settlement negotiations, in large part to assure that attorneys' fees are not discussed until after settlement on the claim is reached. See Judith Resnik, 'Money Matters: Judicial Market Interventions Creating Subsidies and Awarding Fees and Costs in Individual and Aggregate Litigation,' 148 U Pa L Rev 2119, 2181 (2000). Charles Silver and Lynn Baker contend that attorneys representing a class should be treated as trustees or guardians, but acknowledge that fiduciaries do not always perform their tasks consistent with their duties. Charles Silver & Lynn Baker, 'I Cut, You Choose: The Role of Plaintiffs' Counsel in Allocating Settlement Proceeds,' 84 Va L Rev 1465, 1509 (1998).

[372] Given their docket pressures and their lack of access to the information the attorneys have compiled, courts are unlikely to fail to approve a settlement absent clear evidence of abuse, and are even less likely to become involved in the implementation of the agreement. See Christopher R. Leslie, 'A Market-Based Approach to Coupon Settlements in Antitrust and Consumer Class Action Litigation,' 49 UCLA L Rev 991, 1053 (2002) ('For a variety of systemic and case-specific reasons,

CHAPTER 1. THE PRICE OF DISCRIMINATION

some reasonable certainty that the goals of the decree actually will be sought and possibly attained. Such a monitor should be paid a fee on an hourly basis determined by the court, so as to provide an adequate incentive for the monitor to oversee the process and for the defendants to provide meaningful and expeditious reform. Similar suggestions have been made to curb the abuses seen in other forms of class actions, particularly mass torts,[373] which again highlight the evolution of employment discrimination class action from civil rights claims with public overtones to private tort-like litigation.

Additionally, a court should not permit settlements that provide for attorneys' fees out of a common settlement fund, nor should the court allow the parties to negotiate a fee at the time they negotiate the settlement for the class members.[374] Fee negotiations should be conducted only after the class settlement is obtained, and the monetary amounts for the claim fund and attorneys' fees should always be kept separate and distinct.[375] Allowing the attorneys to petition a court for a

---

courts are loathe to reject proposed settlements in class action litigation.'); Silver & Baker, *supra* n. 371, at 1515 (noting that courts typically require clear abuse before they reject a settlement). Courts appear even more reluctant to disrupt settlements in discrimination cases because, unlike other class action attorneys, the plaintiffs' attorneys in discrimination claims have the air of protecting the public interest, and thus there has been little occasion to challenge their judgment.

[373] On calls for increased monitoring of class action settlements, see Nagareda, *supra* n. 260, at 948–952 (calling for hard-look review of settlements); Deborah R. Hensler & Thomas D. Rowe, Jr., 'Beyond "It Just Ain't Worth It": Alternative Strategies for Damage Class Action Reform,' Law & Contemp Probs, Spring/Summer 2001, at 137, 148–152 (arguing for a more rigorous review of settlements); John C. Coffee, Jr., 'Rescuing the Private Attorney General: Why the Model of the Lawyer as Bounty Hunter Is Not Working,' 42 Md L Rev 215, 248 (1983) (calling for institutionalizing a monitoring role at the settlement stage).

[374] The role of attorneys' fees in class action litigation is widely recognized as both critically important to ensuring adequate representation and deeply troubling. For a recent discussion of proposals to regulate attorneys' fees, see Samuel Issacharoff, 'Governance and Legitimacy in the Law of Class Actions,' 1999 Sup Ct Rev 337, 386–389.

[375] At one time, this was the rule of the Third Circuit. See *Prandini v. Nat'l Tea Co.*, 557 F.2d 1015, 1017 (3rd Cir. 1977). The *Prandini* decision was implicitly overturned by the Supreme Court decision in *Evans v. Jeff D.*, 475 US 717, 765 (1986). See *Ashley v. Atl. Richfield Co.*, 794 F.2d 128, 137–138 (3rd Cir. 1986). For a discussion of the rule and the pertinent cases, see Resnik, *supra* n. 371, at 2179–2181. The Supreme Court, it

part of the settlement fund, as was done in the *Texaco* case, places the attorneys in an adversarial position to their clients without any interested party available to defend the client's interests. Even better, but far less practical, the question of attorneys' fees would not be negotiated until after the settlement was approved. A defendant, however, is unlikely to agree to such an approach because it does not provide the finality a defendant typically seeks through the settling of a class action claim.[376]

An alternative method of compensating the attorneys would be for courts to return to the lodestar approach that governs most individual claims of employment discrimination. Under a lodestar approach, an attorney is compensated for the actual time she devotes to a case based on a reasonable hourly rate.[377] Applying the lodestar approach would almost certainly depress the supply of profit-motivated attorneys available to litigate employment discrimination claims, and in doing so it would likely leave too few attorneys available to bring the class action cases – particularly considering the low current filing levels despite the tremendous increase in damages and publicity that the class action cases have received in the last few years. The lodestar approach also brings its own set of undesirable incentives, including divorcing the attorney from the value of the settlement and increasing the emphasis on overlitigating cases. These limitations have caused courts to abandon the lodestar approach in other class action areas,[378] and there is no reason to believe the approach would prove substantially more successful for employment discrimination claims. Instead, courts

---

should be noted, has approved of the practice of negotiating the fees and class relief simultaneously. See *Evans*, 475 US at 734–735.

[376] My own experience negotiating class action settlements is that defendants typically care far less about who gets the money than they do about how much money they have to pay out.

[377] For a recent discussion and comparison of the lodestar method with the percentage of recovery method, see Jill E. Fisch, 'Lawyers on the Auction Block: Evaluating the Selection of Class Counsel by Auction,' 102 Colum L Rev 650, 657–659 (2001).

[378] See Samuel Issacharoff, 'Class Action Conflicts,' 30 UC Davis L Rev 805, 827 (1997) ('Basically, all courts except the Florida Supreme Court...have abandoned the failed lodestar experiment.'). The statute aimed at curbing some of the abuses of securities litigation requires that attorneys be paid from a common settlement fund. See 15 USC 78u-4(a)(6) (2000).

CHAPTER 1. THE PRICE OF DISCRIMINATION

should carefully scrutinize fee claims, and rely on the lodestar method as a check on the reasonableness of the fee request.[379]

It is important to emphasize that none of the attorneys involved in the cases previously discussed appeared to engage in collusive activity or put their own interests ahead of their clients. Rather, what is troubling is the lack of public accountability and the seeming lack of real progress on the terms of the decrees, despite what the parties often represent to the court and the public. It is worth noting here that the courts have never played a substantial role in employment discrimination settlements. With few exceptions, fairness hearings have been used to create a record rather than to determine the actual fairness of an agreement. Consequently they are rarely eventful and rarely even attended by dissident class members.[380] Yet when employment discrimination cases were treated as involving public rather than purely private interests – particularly when the cases were brought by non-profit civil rights organizations or the government – the filing of the settlement agreement often marked the beginning of the proceedings rather than the end, as these attorneys carefully reviewed the defendants' progress to ensure that the terms of the agreement were being fulfilled.[381] Contempt proceedings and less formal objections were common, and the fruit of the litigation was often found in a change to an employer's employment practices, or to secure jobs or promotions for class members, rather than simply to change the size of the

---

[379] This is increasingly the practice in securities litigation, where the statute restricts attorneys to a percentage of the recovery. See Fisch, *supra* n. 377, at 661 ('Courts are increasingly evaluating the reasonableness of their fee calculations by using the percentage of recovery method and then cross-checking their results with the lodestar method.').

[380] Some of the recent cases have drawn objectors, but the court has invariably overruled the objections. See e.g., *Ingram v. Coca-Cola*, 200 FRD 685, 692–693 (ND Ga. 2001) (holding that the proposed settlement was fair, reasonable, and adequate).

[381] See John Payton, 'Redressing the Exclusion and Discrimination Against Black Workers in the Skilled Construction Trades: The Approach of the Washington Lawyers' Committee for Civil Rights Under Law,' 27 How LJ 1397, 1437–1441 (1984) (discussing the importance of monitoring of workplace reforms). For a discussion of the role monitoring and monitors play in implementing structural reform through consent decrees, see Lloyd C. Anderson, Implementation of Consent Decrees in Structural Reform Litigation, 1986 U Ill L Rev 725, 732–735.

settlement fund. Today the success of the private class action litigation is measured solely by the size of the monetary pie with little attention devoted to securing actual reform. Perhaps this is a worthy tradeoff, and it is certainly what is to be expected from profit-motivated attorneys who have an interest in securing a return on their investment. Unless there is money to be earned from the monitoring of the settlement agreement, there is no reason to expect attorneys to engage in substantial active monitoring – particularly when they are paid in advance, as in the *Home Depot* litigation.[382]

One additional reform that might help restore public accountability to the process would be to craft a role for the government in monitoring class action settlements. For example, the EEOC might be appointed by a court, or allowed to intervene in the case, for the purposes of overseeing the implementation of consent decrees, and challenging a corporation's actions or its failure to meet the terms of the decree. Alternatively, a non-profit agency such as the NAACP Legal Defense Fund could be appointed to serve this role as an active monitor without any financial interests tied to the litigation. This initiative could be funded by proceeds from the settlement, and would be one way of providing an independent and disinterested voice to ensure that the terms of the settlement agreement were fulfilled.[383] In this respect, the government or a non-profit agency would simply replace the private diversity task force as the overseer of the settlements. Even if the EEOC were not given a role in the formation of the settlement, its role in the enforcement of the decree may encourage the parties to work toward an acceptable and stronger agreement.[384]

---

[382] See *supra* text accompanying notes 157–158 (describing the payment to the plaintiffs' lawyers pursuant to the settlement agreement).

[383] In a different context, Alon Klement has recently made the intriguing suggestion that monitors should be afforded a financial stake in the outcome of the case. See Alon Klement, 'Who Should Guard the Guardians? A New Approach for Monitoring Class Action Lawyers,' 21 Rev Litig 25 (2002). The difficulty with this suggestion, particularly in the employment discrimination setting where monetary relief should only be one aspect of the remedy provided, is that it would likely replicate the existing problems by adding what would, in effect, be another attorney to divide the settlement fund.

[384] As Professor Sturm has argued, there are other ways to protect public accountability without direct intervention by the government or other parties. For example, a firm's reputation or ties to the community may prove to be an important source of

1.5 CONCLUSION

This study sought to measure the effect of class action employment discrimination lawsuits on corporations and plaintiffs by conducting a statistical study and developing three case studies. The statistical study demonstrates that shareholder value is not typically affected by either the filing or the settlement of the lawsuits, and this finding holds true regardless of the nature of the lawsuit or the size of the settlement. This finding also suggests that no significant penalty results from either engaging in or being accused of discrimination, and that if we want to provide a stronger form of deterrence, it will be necessary to make higher damage awards available for employment discrimination suits. The case studies highlight additional limitations of seeking to implement reform through litigation. In many cases, it appears that employment discrimination litigation has become a private affair that is largely about money and public relations, and rarely concerned with implementing broad institutional reform. It also seems that only those cases that include sensational allegations, generally involving racial epithets or blatant discrimination, can capture national attention. Under these circumstances, it is possible that a company such as Denny's will seek to transform itself. However, these instances are infrequent, as is the prospect of corporate reform arising from private class action litigation. All of this suggests that neither the harm nor the benefit of the private class action litigation is substantial. Instead, the cases are primarily about transfers of wealth, transfers that are often channeled to entities other than the parties to the suit. In any event, these transfers are too inconsequential to affect corporate balance sheets.

The reforms suggested here – increasing damages while also imposing a monitoring function over the settlements – are limited in nature and would offer modest improvements without the prospect of transforming the litigation regime. This study's primary value is descriptive in nature and suggests that we may want to reconsider our underlying assumptions about class action discrimination litigation. Most important, we should not rely on the litigation to eliminate or deter discrimination, but instead should see it in a more limited light as a process of wealth transfers with a substantial public relations

---

accountability. See Sturm, *supra* n. 139, at 305–307. At the same time, without an external check, there may be little threat to a firm's reputation, particularly if the firm is able to produce substantial monetary relief.

dimension that can occasionally lead to significant change, but only to the extent a firm finds that it is in its interests to reform its employment practices. In this respect, the litigation has become just another form of tort, which reflects our declining national commitment to eradicate discrimination – discrimination that, based on this study, remains a significant presence in the labor market.

CHAPTER 2

Measuring the Value of Class and Collective Action Employment Settlements: A Preliminary Assessment

Samuel Estreicher* and Kristina Yost**

2.1 INTRODUCTION

There has been a recent debate in the literature on the relative merits of arbitration, individual litigation, and class action litigation in providing adequate remedies for disputes arising out of the employment relationship. For the last decade and a half, the debate centered on whether arbitration provided a fair forum for plaintiffs, despite the relative informality of the process, the employer's ability to tailor procedures, and the claimed propensity of arbitrators to curry the favor of repeat-player employers. The empirical literature has not borne out these criticisms. Almost without exception, the studies find that employment arbitration is quicker, less costly, and results in a win-loss rate that is no different than in litigation, with median awards somewhat lower (perhaps due to the fact that low-value claims are able to proceed to hearing in the more informal process of arbitration).[1]

---

* Samuel Estreicher is Dwight D. Opperman Professor of Law, New York University School of Law.
** Kristina Yost is a J.D. candidate, University of Virginia School of Law.
[1] See David Sherwyn, Samuel Estreicher & Michael Heise, Assessing the Case for Employment Arbitration: A New Path for Empirical Research, 57 Stan. L. Rev. 1557 (2005); Theodore Eisenberg & Elizabeth Hill, Arbitration and Litigation of Employment Claims: An Empirical Comparison, Disp. Resol. J., November 2003-January

David Sherwyn and Samuel Estreicher (eds), *Employment Class and Collective Actions*, pp. 107–137.
© 2009, by Samuel Estreicher and Kristina Yost.

With the introduction by employers of express provisions in employment arbitration agreements barring class action claims,[2] the debate has shifted to the relative merits of individual arbitration versus class action litigation of employment claims. Proponents of class action litigation make two empirical arguments for the superiority of their preferred mode of dispute resolution over individual arbitration. First, it is maintained, class actions are likely to do a better job of providing compensation for claimants (and thus deterring employer wrongdoing) because by aggregating claims in a single proceeding, the employer will not be able to benefit from the costs of delay or costs of relitigating underlying liability in individual proceedings. Second, it is further argued, class actions provide the only practicable vehicle for obtaining redress of certain low-value claims that, if required to be asserted on an individual basis, would never be championed, thus allowing the employer to escape with impunity. Thus, plaintiff advocates argue, with some support in the courts,[3] there

---

2004 at 44; Lewis L. Maltby, Private Justice: Employment Arbitration and Civil Rights, 30 COLUM. HUM. RTS. L. REV. 29 (1998); Alexander J.S. Colvin, Empirical Research on Employment Arbitration: Clarity Amongst the Sound and Fury?, EMP. RTS. & EMP. POL'Y J. (forthcoming, 2007); but cf. Lisa B. Bingham, Is There A Bias in Arbitration of Nonunion Employment Disputes? An Analysis of Actual Cases and Outcomes, 6 INT'L J. CONFLICT MGMT. 369 (1995) (comparing employee damage awards in arbitration to the amounts actually demanded).

[2] This occurred in response to the Supreme Court's ruling in *Green Tree Fin. Corp. v. Bazzle*, 539 U.S. 444 (2003), that in the absence of an express limitation in the arbitration agreement, the arbitrator in the first instance has the authority to decide whether the agreement authorizes a class-wide proceeding.

[3] See *Muhammed v. County Bank of Rehoboth Beach*, 189 N.J. 1, 16–17, 21, 912 A.2d 88, 97, 100 (2006) (' "By permitting claimants to band together, class actions equalize adversaries and provide a procedure to remedy a wrong that might otherwise go unredressed".... Other courts have referred to such small damage cases as "negative value" suits recognizing that they "would be uneconomical to litigate individually".... The finance charge for the loan in this matter was USD 60. The class of people whom plaintiff seeks to represent may have similar claims about that size. In fact, plaintiff had to roll-over her loan two times, bringing her compensatory claims to USD 180 that, with the possibility of treble damages available under CFA, may add up to a maximum of less than USD 600. One may be hard-pressed to find an attorney willing to work on a consumer-fraud complaint involving complex arrangements between financial institutions of other jurisdictions when the recovery is so small.') Cf. *Gentry v. Superior Court*, 42 Cal. 4th 443, 458, 165 P.3d 556 (2007)

CHAPTER 2. A PRELIMINARY ASSESSMENT

should be a nearly blanket rule banning agreements precluding class action treatment for certain types of employment claims.

Unfortunately, very little empirical work has been done to test either of these propositions. We begin in this paper the process of bringing some facts to light on potential recoveries in employment class actions. This is intended as preliminary assessment, to stimulate further research.

Few class actions go to trial. Most settle well before trial. Some settlements may be private because they occur prior to class certification, but the overwhelming number of class actions cannot be settled without judicial approval. The actual terms of settlement, once approved by the court, should be part of the public file in the case. Moreover, in many cases, the terms have been publicized in the labor and employment press.

For this study, we have assembled a data set of major employment settlements reached since 1993. Employment claims are those arising under Title VII of the Civil Rights Act of 1964 (Title VII), the Age Discrimination in Employment Act of 1967 (ADEA), the Americans with Disabilities Act of 1990 (ADA), and other federal and state anti-discrimination laws, the Fair Labor Standards Act (FLSA) and similar state wage-hour laws, and the Employee Retirement Income Security Act (ERISA).

Our essential finding is that, contrary to assumptions of some academic commentators and courts, average individual potential recoveries and (with the exception of certain ERISA and state wage-hour claims) median potential individual recoveries are not trivial, negative-value amounts. One therefore cannot assume as a prima facie matter that such claims would not be pursued by individual employees, whether in arbitration or litigation. Much, of course, depends on institutional design – the costs of access to the forum and whether attorney representation is required. Class actions arguably reduce access costs and provide a mechanism for funding legal counsel but do so in a manner which through aggregation of claims may reduce the value of individual claims and entail a considerable loss of party autonomy. We hope to provoke additional empirical research on

---

(discussing lower court decision 'reject[ing] the argument that even an award as large as $37,000 would be "ample incentive" for an individual lawsuit for overtime pay, and would obviate the need for a class action, pointing to the expense and practical difficulties of such individual suits.').

EMPLOYMENT CLASS AND COLLECTIVE ACTIONS

whether class actions do a better job at providing compensation, both as to amount (net of costs) and time from claim to recovery, than individual arbitration, and whether any such difference outweighs the loss of party autonomy inherent in class adjudication.

2.2 PROCEDURE FOR SETTLEMENT

In class action practice, settlement procedure is more complicated than it is in a single-party case. Under Rule 23 of the Federal Rules of Civil Procedure, after a class has been certified, the court must approve any settlement before it becomes final.[4] Before the court can do so, it must conduct a hearing and find that the settlement is 'fair, reasonable, and adequate.'[5] Rule 23 also requires that notice be given to all class members who would be bound by the settlement.[6] This allows class members to object to the settlement.[7] The court also must approve, under separate motion, any award of attorney fees.[8] Most of the settlements in our data set were resolved in this manner, and have therefore been approved by courts.

There is, however, a small difference to be noted between employment settlements generally and FLSA settlements. Under Rule 23, and therefore most class actions, typically all members of the class are included in the final settlement unless they opt-out at the certification stage under 23(b)(3).[9] Under the FLSA, in order for a class member to be included in a settlement, he or she must specifically opt-in to the class.[10] However, FLSA litigants often bring a hybrid Rule 23 class action (respecting the state wage-hour claims) coupled with an opt-in collective action (respecting the FLSA claim); the effect is that the settlement may ultimately be applied to class members who have not specifically opted in. In pure FLSA collective actions, because of the opt-in structure, generally each class member has to consent to the

---

[4] Fed. R. Civ. P. 23(e)(1)(A).
[5] Fed. R. Civ. P. 23(e)(1)(C).
[6] Fed. R. Civ. P. 23(e)(1)(B).
[7] Fed. R. Civ. P. 23(e)(4)(A).
[8] Fed. R. Civ. P. 23(h).
[9] Fed. R. Civ. P. 23(c)(2)(B).
[10] 29 U.S.C. § 216(b).

CHAPTER 2. A PRELIMINARY ASSESSMENT

settlement before it can be valid.[11] Furthermore, FLSA settlements typically have to be approved either by the Department of Labor or by the court after determining the settlement is fair.[12]

Some employment discrimination cases are separately prosecuted by the Equal Opportunity Employment Commission (EEOC) and the procedure for settling those cases is also somewhat different. First, the EEOC is exempt from the class representation requirements of Rule 23 and able to represent a class without meeting those requirements.[13] Though these technical requirements of Rule 23 do not apply, in some cases courts still conduct an evaluation of EEOC settlements and notice is to be provided in the same fashion as a typical Rule 23 action. Similarly, EEOC settlements usually provide that each party must pay its own attorney fees, rather than the fees being deducted from the total settlement, unless a plaintiff has separate private counsel.

2.3 METHODOLOGY

Our data set is composed of class action settlements of employment claims that were approved by courts from 1993 through July, 2007, and reported in various labor and employment and class action reports. While we do not purport to include every settlement reached during this period,[14] we were able to locate a large number of important settlements.[15]

---

[11] Donald H. Nichols, Sign Up and Settle: FLSA Collective Actions, NATIONAL EMPLOYMENT LAWYERS ASSOCIATION, 2004 FIFTEENTH ANNUAL CONVENTION, June 25, 2004, at 4.

[12] See *Lynn's Food Stores, Inc. v. U.S.*, 679 F.2d 1350, 1352–1353 (11th Cir. 1982)

[13] See *General Tel. Co. of the Northwest v. EEOC*, 446 U.S. 318 (1980).

[14] A major reason why some settlements have not been included is that terms have been kept under seal or subjected to confidentiality provisions by the parties. (We are going to need some data on this down the road.)

[15] The data were drawn from Mealey's Class Action Reports and BNA's Daily Labor Report, Class Action Report and Employment Discrimination Report. Some data was also used from Attorney Fee Awards in Common Fund Class Actions, 24 NO. 2 CLASS ACTION REP. 4, (2003). Finally, we performed the same search of class action settlements performed in Theodore Eisenberg & Geoffrey Miller, The Role of Opt-Outs and Objectors in Class Action Litigation: Theoretical and Empirical Issues, 57 VAND. L. REV. 1529 (2004). To check on the accuracy of reporting in these commercial services, we randomly chose twelve settlements and examined the settlement documents as found in the court files.

EMPLOYMENT CLASS AND COLLECTIVE ACTIONS

The information we used from these reports was primarily the gross aggregate settlement amount, attorney's fees, costs, class size (number of employees or former employees in the class), the type of claim, job title of plaintiffs asserting claim, and any information on the disposition of residual, i.e., unclaimed, amounts and incentive payments for lead plaintiffs. When not all of the information about a settlement was available in the commercial reports, we tried to obtain the missing information from court records and other news articles. If the information could not be found, we have indicated that fact in our results.

The data were then separated by type of claim and average (and median) individual potential recoveries were calculated. We use the term 'potential recovery' because our sources do not always reveal the amounts particular individuals received or will receive. To calculate the net aggregate settlement amount, attorney fees and costs, where known, were subtracted from the gross settlement. (Costs were not obtainable for every settlement.) Average individual potential recoveries were then calculated by dividing the net settlement amount by the total number of class members. Lead plaintiff payments and other distribution schemes were not taken into account in making this calculation but will be discussed later in this paper. At this point, averages were also calculated for gross settlement amounts, net settlement amounts, attorney fees, and class size, as well as a few other categories.

Because some of the settlements were unusually high or low, we also calculated medians and standard deviations for gross settlements, individual potential recoveries and attorney fees. Finding median amounts was very helpful in taking account of these types of cases because the median weighs each settlement once rather than giving undue effect to a very high or very low award.

There are two tables in this paper that contain most of the important data.

Table 2.1 is the more inclusive presentation of the data we have accumulated. If we had data on a gross settlement amount, but not on attorney fees or class size, the gross settlement was still included in the average and median gross settlement figures in Table 2.1, even though we were unable to calculate an average or median individual potential recovery without the class size information.

In Table 2.2, we present results for settlements for which we had all necessary information. This means that if we had a gross settlement

CHAPTER 2. A PRELIMINARY ASSESSMENT

amount but not class size or attorney fees, the gross settlement was not included in the average or median gross settlement amounts. Also, for this table, we excluded any settlements that did not list the amount of attorney's fees or class size, so the average and median individual potential recoveries only include settlements for which attorney fees could be subtracted from the gross settlement. Also, for discrimination awards, EEOC settlements were excluded from this data set because the EEOC can pursue litigation even where employment contracts require arbitration; hence, the policy debate is limited to private litigation versus private arbitration.[16] Furthermore, the EEOC does not take attorney fees, so including these settlements would artificially inflate individual potential recoveries.[17]

There are potential errors or biases in the data sources we used. One source of error may be simply reporting errors by BNA and the other commercial services. To increase our confidence level, we used Westlaw, Lexis, or PACER to verify the reported settlement amounts for a random sample of the settlements in this data set; we found no significant incidence of error. A second source of bias is what might be called publication bias – settlements are likely to published by the commercial services where lawyers, principally plaintiff lawyers, alert the services of their having received judicial approval. Presumably, they report only the more favorable awards to the BNA publications. This could skew our data set to be more favorable to plaintiffs than in average or median employment class action cases (counting all class action filings).

Other unknown factors include:

- the state of settlement;
- the timing from filing of claim to ultimate recovery;

---

[16] *EEOC v. Waffle House, Inc.*, 534 U.S. 279, 293–94 (2002) ('No one asserts that the EEOC is a party to the contract, or that it agreed to arbitrate its claims. It goes without saying that a contract cannot bind a nonparty. Accordingly, the proarbitration policy goals of the FAA do not require the agency to relinquish its statutory authority if it has not agreed to do so.') (citations omitted). It should be noted that only those settlements to which the EEOC was a named party in the lawsuit were excluded.

[17] Our results broken down by type of claim are discussed in Part IV, B. Observations about attorney fees are presented in Part IV, C. The data are also separated by state to see if there any significant differences in the settlements or potential individual recoveries across states. These results can be seen in Part IV, D and Table 2.9.

- the value of any injunctive relief; and
- what happens to any residual of the total settlement amount.

While we do know the state in which settlements were approved, this may not be the same state where the plaintiff initially filed the lawsuit. There are also three other variables for which we have only partial information: the amount of any lead plaintiff awards; the disposition of unclaimed sums; and the income of plaintiffs in FLSA suits.

In some cases, the parties may have stipulated the disposition of any unclaimed residual, but we are not able to include that information in our tables because of uncertainty over whether there in fact will be unclaimed sums and how large the residual amount will be. Out of the settlements where we have information about the disposition of any residuals, five agreements awarded the residual to a non-profit or government organization such as a women's rights organization, a scholarship fund, or a food bank, two redistributed the residual back to the class, two allowed the residual to go back to the defendant, and one mandated that any residual be applied towards paying for arbitration costs.

2.4 FINDINGS

2.4.1 General Findings

The general findings have been split into two tables, Table 2.1 including all settlements, and Table 2.2 including only those for which we have all the relevant information, such as attorney fees and class size. These tables include claims under Title VII, the FLSA, ERISA, state wage-hour laws, and other miscellaneous state and federal statutes. As can be seen in Table 2.1, the average gross settlement for all employment claims is approximately USD 43 million, while the median is only USD 8 million. Table 2.2 concerns only those settlements where we can calculate individual potential recoveries. Here, the average gross settlement increases to USD 58 million; the median is USD 9.5 million. Averages are especially misleading here because a few large settlements are raising the average and raising it more so in the smaller data.

CHAPTER 2. A PRELIMINARY ASSESSMENT

As also shown in Table 2.2, the average individual potential recovery for all claims is around USD 25,000 while the median is significantly lower, at USD 5,000.[18] The gap between median and average individual potential awards indicates that several extremely large settlements are raising the average, while most of the claims are more centered around the median. The differential is also partially explained by the wide spread of awards, shown by the standard deviation of USD 130,000.

TABLE 2.1: Statistics for All Settlements in Data Set

Category of Claim	Sub-Category	Number of Settlements in Data Set[19]	Average Gross Settlement for Category	Median Gross Settlement for Category	Average Net Recovery
Discrimination	All	50	USD 42,955,654	USD 7,875.000	USD 37,421,212
	Race	14	USD 19,738,956	USD 5,700,000	USD 15,787,484
	Sex	13	USD 22,409,831	USD 11,750,000	USD 17,375,806
	Age	3	USD 20,950,000	USD 5,500,000	USD 13,235,000
	EEOC	12	USD 7,916,817	USD 635,000	USD 7,797,100
	Other	8	USD 120,087,500	USD 42,250,000	USD 111,912,500
FLSA[20]	All	31	USD 23,500,186	USD 11,400,000	USD 20,184,922
	Off the Clock	10	USD 18,455,968	USD 5,900,000	USD 14,587,613

---

[18] This is a relatively low amount when compared with mean demands in employment arbitration and single-plaintiff litigation. A study by Lewis Maltby recently found the mean demands in arbitration and litigation to be USD 165,128 and USD 756,738, respectively. Maltby, *supra* n. 1, at 48. His mean recoveries were slightly lower amounts, USD 49,030 for arbitration and USD 530,611 for individual litigation, but still higher than the individual potential recoveries we have found here. *Id.*

[19] It should be noted that the total number of settlements within all sub-types do not total the number of settlements within each type of claim. This is because settlements for which we did not know the sub-type of claim or where more than one sub-type of claim were asserted were not included within any sub-type, but were included in the data set for the broad type of claim in general.

[20] If the class brought an FLSA claim and one or more state-FLSA equivalent claims, then the settlement was included under the FLSA category.

115

EMPLOYMENT CLASS AND COLLECTIVE ACTIONS

Category of Claim	Sub-Category	Number of Settlements in Data Set[19]	Average Gross Settlement for Category	Median Gross Settlement for Category	Average Net Recovery
	Classification	16	USD 29,402,813	USD 18,750,000	USD 27,261,288
	Other	2	USD 1,500,270	USD 1,500,270	USD 1,435,557
State Wage-Hour[21]	All	21	USD 24,385,573	USD 11,000,000	USD 19,474,093
	Off the Clock	10	USD 8,577,641	USD 8,250,000	USD 7,073,277
	Classification	7	USD 56,021,429	USD 14,900,000	USD 42,784,106
	Other	4	USD 8,592,657	USD 5,975,000	USD 6,583,407
ERISA	All	59	USD 75,454,308	USD 16,850,000	USD 56,184,468
	Stock Drop	30	USD 45,084,083	USD 16,100,000	USD 23,599,579
	Cash Balance	5	USD 393,748,600	USD 7,200,000	USD 302,555,362
	Other	24	USD 48,239,720	USD 26,000,000	USD 40,137,074
Other Claims[22]	All	27	USD 12,162,104	USD 3,500,000	USD 10,228,566
ALL CLAIMS		188	USD 41,669,255	USD 8,500,000	USD 32,705,783

---

[21] In some cases, these state-FLSA equivalent claims have been brought in conjunction with claims under other state laws.

[22] The settlements within the 'other claims' category include claims under the Seaman's Wage Act, state apparel statutes, and contract/pension plan suits, as well as others.

TABLE 2.2: Statistics for Settlements Where Class Size and Attorney Fees Are Known

Category of Claim	Sub-Category	Number of Settlements in Data Set	Average Gross Settlement for Category	Median Gross Settlement for Category	Average Net Recovery for Category	Average Number of Class Members for Category	Average Individual Potential Recovery for Category	Median Individual Potential Recovery for Category	Standard Deviation of Individual Potential Recovery
Discrimination	All	24	USD 51,895,391	USD 8,550,000	USD 45,734,856	13,634	USD 18,127	USD 10,304	USD 23,956
	Race	10	USD 15,344,538	USD 5,700,000	USD 12,086,705	1,285	USD 27,479	USD 14,903	USD 33,956
	Sex**	6	USD 31,565,666	USD 30,500,000	USD 24,400,666	6,342	USD 10,995	USD 11,245	USD 7,513
	Age	3	USD 20,950,000	USD 5,500,000	USD 13,235,000	761	USD 10,154	USD 7,576	USD 10,023
	Other	5	USD 167,960,000	USD 53,500,000	USD 158,132,100	54,806	USD 12,766	USD 5,038	USD 14,363
FLSA	All	15	USD 21,244,643	USD 9,500,000	USD 16,056,702	10,958	USD 6,066	USD 5,476	USD 5,478
	Off the Clock	6	USD 32,420,000	USD 10,000,000	USD 23,218,750	15,765	USD 5,213	USD 5,000	USD 4,633

EMPLOYMENT CLASS AND COLLECTIVE ACTIONS

Category of Claim	Sub-Category	Number of Settlements in Data Set	Average Gross Settlement for Category	Median Gross Settlement for Category	Average Net Recovery for Category	Average Number of Class Members for Category	Average Individual Potential Recovery for Category	Median Individual Potential Recovery for Category	Standard Deviation of Individual Potential Recovery
	Classification	8	USD 16,590,625	USD 10,900,000	USD 12,367,254	8,597	USD 7,139	USD 6,584	USD 6,406
	Other	1							
State Wage-Hour	All	12	USD 28,511,784	USD 12,723,207	USD 19,196,728	14,728	USD 11,262	USD 4,859	USD 15,843
	Off the Clock	6	USD 9,956,902	USD 10,973,207	USD 7,568,248	28,009	USD 3,015	USD 1,211	USD 4,200
	Classification	5	USD 54,280,000	USD 14,900,000	USD 35,390,248	1,538	USD 21,812	USD 18,625	USD 20,601
	Other	1							
ERISA	All	22	USD 131,647,109	USD 33,375,000	USD 108,066,844	36,992	USD 63,379	USD 2,787	USD 259,877
	Stock Drop	9	USD 32,251,389	USD 30,750,000	USD 27,577,398	47,514	USD 1,917	USD 937	USD 2,071

CHAPTER 2. A PRELIMINARY ASSESSMENT

		Cash Balance						
	3	USD 574,181,000	USD 6,400,000	USD 446,091,603	91,133	USD 2,171	USD 1,252	USD 2,528
	Other	10	USD 88,343,089	USD 58,454,000	USD 79,099,919	8,423	USD 137,056	USD 12,024	USD 382,780
Other Claims	All	12	USD 18,460,173	USD 1,950,00	USD 15,875,809	23,561	USD 9,414	USD 984	USD 16,962
ALL CLAIMS		85	USD 58,343,770	USD 9,500,000	USD 47,694,472	21,552	USD 24,751	USD 5,034	USD 130,589

In looking at the settlements and average individual potential recoveries by type of claim, clearly the highest individual potential recoveries tend to go to discrimination and ERISA plaintiffs. The average individual potential recoveries are highest for ERISA claims, at USD 63,379, followed by discrimination claims, at USD 18,127. In examining the median recoveries, however, discrimination plaintiffs tend to receive more. The median discrimination individual potential recovery is the highest of any type of claim, at USD 10,304, while the ERISA median individual potential recoveries are the lowest of any claim, at USD 2,787. FLSA and state wage-hour potential recoveries tend to be lower, and are similar in amounts both for median individual potential recoveries. This can be seen in Figure 2.1 below.

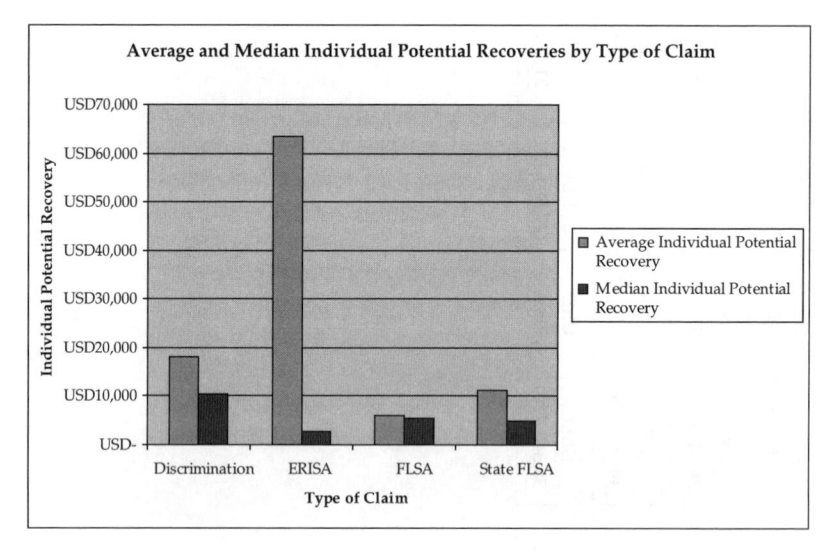

Figure 2.1

One important variable to note is the presence of lead plaintiff incentive payments in some of these settlements. Because we did not have such data for most of the settlements, we have thus far not factored this element into our computations. In some cases, adding in these amounts will reduce the individual potential recoveries, especially in the settlements involving smaller classes. Table 2.3 summarizes the effect of accounting for incentive payments to lead plaintiffs in calculating

CHAPTER 2. A PRELIMINARY ASSESSMENT

individual potential recoveries. (It can readily be seen that subtracting these figures has a substantial effect on the individual potential recoveries involving smaller classes, but only has a minor effect on the recoveries involving larger classes.)

TABLE 2.3: The Effect of Incentive Payments to Lead Plaintiffs on Individual Potential Recoveries (in 14 Settlements)

Total Incentive Payments	Individual Potential Recovery Adjusting for Incentive Payments	Individual Potential Recovery (without Adjustment)	Difference	Number of Class Members
USD 285,000	USD 55,000	USD 75,000	**USD 20,000**	6
USD 680,000	USD 4,947	USD 5,400	**USD 453**	1,500
USD 360,000	USD 48,000	USD 75,000	**USD 27,000**	8
USD 360,000	USD 1,910	USD 1,925	**USD 15**	20,000
USD 300,000	USD 8,559	USD 9,910	**USD 1,351**	222
USD 975,000	USD 88,500	USD 108,000	**USD 19,500**	50
USD 15,000	USD 1,878	USD 2,061	**USD 183**	5000
USD 90,000	USD 2,631	USD 2,761	**USD 130**	23,632
USD 170,000	USD 24,993	USD 25,000	**USD 7**	25000
USD 40,000	USD 43	USD 44	**USD 1**	136,000
USD 1,705,000	USD 20,209	USD 21,214	**USD 1,005**	1697
USD 500,000	USD 27,818	USD 62,000	**USD 34,182**	13
USD 20,000	USD 20,158	USD 20,158	**USD 0**	505
USD 56,000	USD 28,055	USD 27,423	**USD 632**	800

2.4.2 Findings by Type of Claim

2.4.2.1 Discrimination Claims

According to our data, discrimination claims are potentially the most valuable claims for plaintiffs in employment litigation. The average discrimination settlement is USD 43 million when all settlements are included; the average individual recovery is USD 18,127. However, these individual plaintiff recoveries also have a relatively high standard deviation of approximately USD 23,956. This means that the individual recoveries in discrimination class action settlements are fairly varied. The data on discrimination suits in Table 2.4 reveals a wide spread, with the highest individual potential recovery being USD 108,000 and the lowest only USD 40. The USD 108,000 figure is likely also raising the average individual potential recovery, which partially explains the considerably lower median of USD 10,304.

TABLE 2.4: Spread of Discrimination Settlements

Size of Average Plaintiff Potential Recovery	Number of Settlements Within Size Range in Data
Under USD 1,000	2
USD 1,000–10,000	9
USD 10,000–100,000	12
USD 100,000–108,000	1

Another important factor is the size of the class. Discrimination classes tend to be smaller than ERISA or FLSA classes, with some exceptions. The average class size for a discrimination suit is similar to an FLSA class, with 13,634 members. The average class size for an FLSA claim is 11,000 potential claimants, and an enormous 37,000 for ERISA cases. These statistics do not fully reflect the true size of the differential, however, because there are several very large classes in our data set with over 10,000 class members. Furthermore, the average class size for each sub-type of discrimination class action is significantly lower. For a race claim, the

CHAPTER 2. A PRELIMINARY ASSESSMENT

average class size is 1,285, for a sex claim it is 6,342 and for an age claim it is only 761.

Class size is an important determinant of the size of potential individual recoveries. Gross discrimination settlements tend to be quite large, and with smaller classes, the individual plaintiff awards are similarly large.

There are also some other differences to note among sub-categories of discrimination claims.[23] The settlements are typically fairly different for each of these types of discrimination claims, with gender bias claims resulting in higher individual potential recovery, followed by age claims, and then race claims, as can be seen in Table 2.1. These amounts are all lower than the overall average gross settlement for discrimination claims of USD 43 million. This is likely because the average settlement for all discrimination suits reflects settlements which may larger than the average for particular subtypes because they include claims asserting more than one type of discrimination. The average gross settlements are all centered around USD 20 million or so for each sub-category.

Although there are these minor differences in settlement amounts, the disparities become more noticeable when looking at average and median individual potential recoveries. The average individual potential recovery for a race claim is around USD 27,000, but is only around USD 10,000 or sex and age claims. The median individual recoveries are also quite different, at USD 14,000 for race bias, USD 11,000 for sex, and USD 7,000 for age. Interestingly, race claims consistently produce higher individual potential recoveries than the sex or age claims.

There is also typically more variation in the size of potential individual recoveries for race claims than for sex and age claims. The standard deviation for race claims is over USD 30,000, while only around USD 10,000 for age claims, USD 7,000 for sex claims, and USD 14,000 for other claims. This may also partially explain the high average individual potential recovery for race claims when compared to other types of discrimination claims.

---

[23] Unfortunately, our sample of disability and national origin discrimination settlements is too small to note any trends about them, so the main discussion will revolve around race, sex, and age claims.

TABLE 2.5: Standard Deviations of Discrimination Claims by Sub-category

Sub-category	Standard Deviation
Sex	USD 7,513
Age	USD 10,023
Race	USD 33,956
Other or Combination	USD 14,363

2.4.2.2 FLSA and State Wage-Hour Claims

The average gross settlements, median settlements and class sizes vary slightly for state wage-hour and FLSA claims. The average and median gross settlements are slightly higher for state than federal claims. The average class size also tends to be higher for state claims. The average individual potential recovery varies quite a bit more between state and federal settlements: USD 11,262 for a state claim, but a much lower USD 6,066 for a federal claim. The median individual potential recovery, however, is similar for a federal claim, at USD 5,476 but is lower for a state claim, at USD 4,859.

There is a large differential between gross settlement amounts for off the clock and mis-classification suits, especially for settlements asserting only state law claims. For settlements asserting FLSA claims, gross settlements in off the clock cases average around USD 32 million, whereas gross settlements in a classification suit are on average worth USD 16.6 million. The median gross settlement amounts do not necessarily reflect this pattern, with federal off the clock claims yielding approximately the same settlements as the classification claims.

For settlements asserting only state law claims, gross settlements in off the clock cases average about USD 9.95 million, in contrast to USD 54.2 million for a classification claim. One explanation for this is that almost all of the state classification suits in our data set were settled in California, where settlements may typically be larger. By contrast, our federal claims data set contains settlements from a wide range of states. The median gross settlements show the same trend for state claims, but the differential between off the clock and classification claims is a bit smaller.

For both state and federal claims, classification suits tend to yield higher individual potential recoveries than off the clock suits. The

CHAPTER 2. A PRELIMINARY ASSESSMENT

differential is quite large for state claims: average individual potential recovery for an off the clock suit is USD 3,015, whereas it is USD 21,812 for a classification suit. The federal claims settlements do not diverge quite so much, but the classification claims still typically pay out about USD 2,000 more per plaintiff than the off the clock claims.

This large differential in potential individual payouts is likely a function of income level, which tends to be considerably higher for claimants in classification suits than for claimants in off the clock suits. We used proxies for deriving average incomes of plaintiffs in the classification and off the clock suits based on occupation, approximate location, and approximate date of the settlement. We obtained salary information from the Department of Labor's Occupational Employment Statistics (OES) Survey. For most cases, mean income figures for individuals having the identical job title involved were found. For a few cases, the exact job title salary was not listed, so the mean incomes of two very closely titled occupations were averaged together.

Almost all of the cases used involving classification claims in our data set were settled in California, which is largely due to the very large number of FLSA and state wage-hour actions brought in that state. For federal cases, we used the OES mean income levels for the largest metropolitan area in the particular federal district the case was brought in. This meant we used Los Angeles income levels for cases settled in the Central District of California, Oakland statistics for cases settled in the Northern District, and San Diego statistics for cases settled in the Southern District. For the state cases, we used the statewide average, since the specific area of settlement was unknown. Only one of the classification cases was settled in a different state, Minnesota, and that income information was found using statewide OES data and averaging together the mean income levels of two occupations closely titled to the occupation in question in the case.

For the off the clock data set, there were again several settlements from California, for which the same data from the OES Survey was used. There was one case in Washington and one case in New Jersey for which we used statewide data from the OES. For the Tennessee federal case, we used Nashville data, being the largest metropolitan area in that district, from the OES survey.

Tables 6 and 7 give the average and median incomes for classification and off the clock claims. Figures 2 and 3 summarize the correlation between income level and the average per plaintiff awards for both classification and off the clock claims.

TABLE 2.6: Average and Median Income Levels for Classification Claims
Classification Claims – Federal and State

Number of Settlements	10
Average Income	USD 59,889
Median Income	USD 57,864

TABLE 2.7: Average and Median Income Levels for Off the Clock Claims – Federal and State

Number of Settlements	7
Average Income	USD 35,983
Median Income	USD 38,741

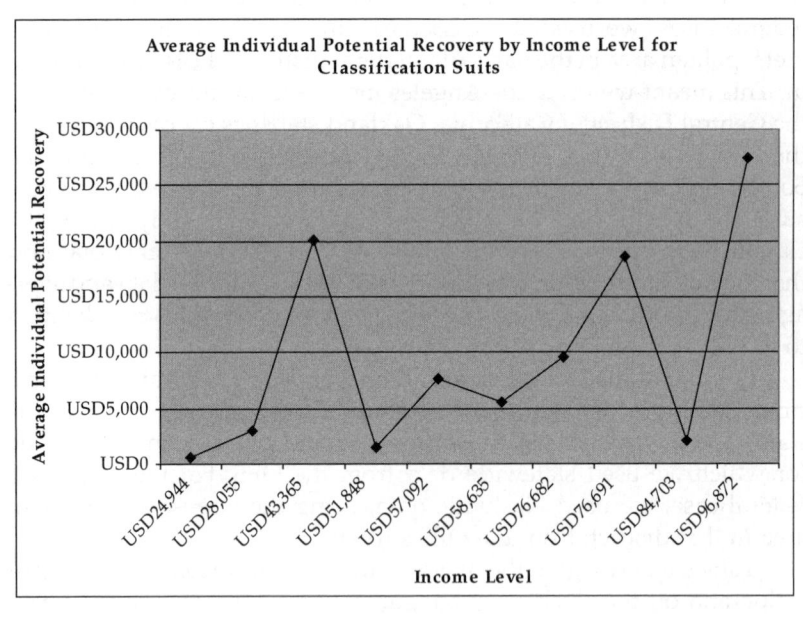

Figure 2.2

CHAPTER 2. A PRELIMINARY ASSESSMENT

Average Individual Potential Recovery by Income Level for Off the Clock Suits

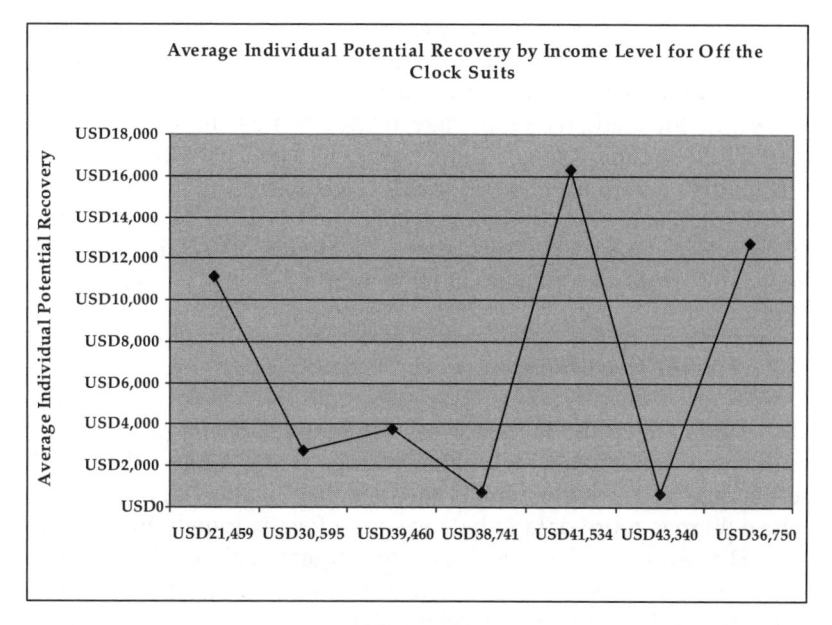

[Chart showing Average Individual Potential Recovery plotted against income levels: USD21,459; USD30,595; USD39,460; USD38,741; USD41,534; USD43,340; USD36,750]

Figure 2.3

The graph in Figure 2.2 suggests a positive correlation between salary and the amount of the individual potential recovery for classification claims. With some exceptions, claimants with higher income levels tend to be associated with higher individual potential recoveries. But for two outlier recovery amounts, there would be a linear relationship between the two variables. In fact, these outlier data points are probably due to the specific facts involved in those lawsuits and the methodology of approximating income levels by job title.[24] In comparing the classification

---

[24] In one particular outlier lawsuit, the employees were called 'business consultants' and 'business analysts' but the facts specifically alleged that the titles were created solely to uphold the illusion that the employees were managerial when in fact they mostly performed administrative tasks such as filling out forms. Since we used job title to approximate what plaintiffs' income levels were, this means that the salary level we have listed, USD 84,703, is probably grossly inflated. If we actually had data on what these plaintiffs were earning, it likely would have correlated better with the individual potential recovery in that lawsuit. In the other outlier, off the clock claims were alleged along with classification claims, which may have made the overall recovery lower.

line with the off the clock line in Figure 2.3, there is clearly a stronger correlation between income and average individual potential recovery in the classification than in the off the clock cases.[25]

Despite the median and average awards being generally lower for the off the clock claims, they are still over USD 5,000, with the exception of the median award for state off the clock claims of USD 1,211. Importantly, while the lowest off the clock claim is only USD 44, every other settlement is for at least USD 600, so this low figure may be bringing the average for off the clock claims down slightly.

2.4.2.3 ERISA Claims

ERISA claims have the largest gross settlements of any of the major employment settlements, with the average being USD 131,647,109. The average gross settlement is also smaller in the larger data set because there is more data to balance out a few extremely high settlements. However, the class size is also the largest, with 36,992 members on average. It is important to note that the overall average ERISA settlement is significantly larger than the stock drop sub-type in our data, largely because there are quite a few ERISA settlements in our data set which did not specifically fall into either sub-category of ERISA suits. Moreover, one of these uncategorized settlements was an extreme outlier, with an individual potential recovery of USD 1,225,074.[26]

---

[25] There are also fewer data points on income level for off the clock suits, largely because occupation is a much more important factor in the classification suits, so it is reported more often. This may simply make finding a trend in the off the clock data more difficult. However, with the data we have here, there does not appear to be any type of correlation, positive or negative, between income level and average plaintiff award for this type of claims. Furthermore, while there are potentially explanative reasons for the outliers in the classification graph, there are not any significant reasons for the off the clock outliers. The only potential explanation for one of the outliers is that the settlement covered employees in four states, but it was settled in New Jersey and we used income level data from that state. It could therefore be possible that the income level for that particular settlement is slightly inflated because the income is higher in New Jersey than the other states involved.

[26] As well, the cash balance settlements tend to be larger than the stock drop settlements, but the sample size of our data also contains fewer cash balance settlements, making the figures less reliable. Further, one of the five cash balance settlements was for USD 1.7 billion, so this clearly skewed the data, making the average gross cash

CHAPTER 2. A PRELIMINARY ASSESSMENT

Interestingly, the average and median potential recoveries for all types of ERISA claims are the lowest of any type of employment settlement. The median individual potential recoveries are USD 937 for a stock drop case and USD 1,252 for a cash balance case. There were no significant differences in median individual recoveries across subcategories. The data indicate that there are three average plaintiff awards that are under USD 100 (two stock drop cases and one unknown), which are likely bringing these numbers down.

The standard deviation between ERISA awards was also the largest, at USD 259,877. This shows that, similar to discrimination claims, there is a wide disparity among settlements. Table 2.8 can be used to compare the award disparity in ERISA cases to that in discrimination cases.

TABLE 2.8: Spread of ERISA Settlements

Size of Average individual Potential Recovery	Number of Settlements Within Size Range
Under USD 1,000	9
USD 1,000–10,000	8
USD 10,000–100,000	4
USD 100,000–USD 1,225,074	1

2.4.2.4 Other Claims

It is difficult to note any major trends among the diverse set of claims that constitutes this category, ranging from the Seaman's Wage Act to state apparel statutes, to pension plan claims. The average gross settlement is around USD 18 million and the average plaintiff award is approximately USD 9,000. The median individual potential recovery is also quite low, at USD 984. All three of these figures are lower than the average and median statistics for all employment settlements. There are no specific inferences to be drawn from this difference, however, because the claims in this category are so widely varied.

---

balance settlement around USD 574 million. Most cash balance cases also contain very large classes, so the individual potential recoveries are more on par with those of stock drop plaintiffs, both being around USD 2,000 per plaintiff.

2.4.3 Observations about Attorney Fees

On a pure numerical level, ERISA claims produce the highest attorney fees, with state wage-hour claims coming in second, followed by FLSA and discrimination claims. The median attorney fees show a somewhat different trend, with state wage-hour claims receiving the highest fees, followed by ERISA claims, and then discrimination and FLSA claims. However, in looking at what claims produce the highest fee as a percent of net recovery, discrimination cases are clearly highest, being approximately 30% of the ultimate recovery. Attorney fees in state wage-hour cases are generally about 29% of the total recovery, FLSA cases about 27%, and ERISA cases only about 23%. It is expected that ERISA cases would produce such high fees numerically but represent a low percentage of overall recovery, since the average gross settlement for ERISA claims is so high. This indicates that the fees for ERISA claims may be higher but only because the gross settlements are higher as well.[27]

However, the reasons behind the attorney fees and percentages of net recovery in other types of cases are less clear. Discrimination cases may be thought to be riskier than FLSA cases, which may partially account for the higher contingency fee percentage. The higher fees in state wage-hour cases when compared to the federal cases may simply be due to the cases being settled in different locations. Most of the state FLSA settlements came from California, while the federal settlements came from all over the nation.

For discrimination claims, the fees were fairly consistent among the claims, with age claims yielding slightly higher fees. However, since the number of age bias settlements in our data is small, it is likely one larger fee award that raised the average. In ERISA cases, the fees are larger for cash balance settlements, but that is largely a result of the larger gross cash balance settlements and the small sample size. There is no significant difference in fees between classification and off the clock FLSA claims. In the state cases, the value of the fees appears to be greater for classification claims, but the percentage of gross settlement is higher for off the clock claims.

---

[27] E.g., Theodore Eisenberg & Geoffrey Miller, Attorney Fees in Class Action Settlements: An Empirical Study, J. EMPIRICAL LEGAL STUD., March 2004, at 27.

CHAPTER 2. A PRELIMINARY ASSESSMENT

TABLE 2.9: Attorney Fee Statistics for Settlements Where Known

Category of Claim	Sub-category	Number of Settlements within Data Set	Average Gross Settlement	Median Gross Settlement	Average Attorneys Fees	Median Attorney Fees	Average Net Recovery	Fee as % of Gross Settlement
Discrimination	All	33	USD 46,500,107	USD 8,400,000	USD 5,972,735	USD 2,165,000	USD 40,462,853	0.302
	Race	13	USD 21,211,183	USD 5,900,000	USD 4,300,575	USD 1,450,000	USD 16,955,752	0.317
	Sex	10	USD 24,150,814	USD 13,375,000	USD 5,162,427	USD 3,000,000	USD 18,613,387	0.362
	Age	3	USD 20,950,000	USD 5,500,000	USD 7,711,000	USD 2,000,000	USD 13,235,000	0.335
	Other	7	USD 136,342,857	USD 53,500,000	USD 9,490,786	USD 10,850,000	USD 127,001,500	0.184
FLSA	All	18	USD 19,408,901	USD 9,500,000	USD 4,452,439	USD 2,165,208	USD 15,419,327	0.266*
	Off the Clock	7	USD 25,233,526	USD 10,000,000	USD 4,949,420	USD 1,837,500	USD 21,141,248	0.258

EMPLOYMENT CLASS AND COLLECTIVE ACTIONS

Category of Claim	Sub-category	Number of Settlements within Data Set	Average Gross Settlement	Median Gross Settlement	Average Attorneys Fees	Median Attorney Fees	Average Net Recovery	Fee as % of Gross Settlement
	Classification	9	USD 18,858,333	USD 12,800,000	USD 4,969,491	USD 3,200,000	USD 14,076,448	0.269*
	Other	2	USD 1,500,270	USD 1,500,270	USD 386,270	USD 386,270	USD 1,435,557	0.278
State FLSA	All	15	USD 26,028,744	USD 12,723,207	USD 8,673,102	USD 3,550,000	USD 17,678,552	0.288
	Off the Clock	8	USD 8,568,059	USD 9,000,000	USD 2,742,275	USD 3,000,000	USD 6,508,498	0.307
	Classification	5	USD 54,280,000	USD 14,900,000	USD 18,877,500	USD 3,725,000	USD 35,390,248	0.275
	Other	2	USD 16,513,000	USD 16,513,000	USD 3,920,000	USD 3,920,000	USD 12,494,500	0.246
ERISA	All	50	USD 73,098,170	USD 15,143,944	USD 14,073,879	USD 2,978,405	USD 58,851,983	0.233
	Stock Drop	20	USD 24,008,625	USD 12,500,000	USD 4,589,008	USD 3,015,000	USD 19,292,424	0.259

CHAPTER 2. A PRELIMINARY ASSESSMENT

	Cash Balance	5	USD 393,748,600	USD 7,200,000	USD 90,997,639	USD 2,028,000	USD 302,555,362	0.251
	Other	25	USD 48,239,720	USD 26,000,000	USD 6,277,023	USD 3,078,810	USD 41,758,954	0.209
Other Claims	All	23	USD 14,116,948	USD 5,087,607	USD 2,550,130	USD 1,350,000	USD 11,467,639	0.292
ALL CLAIMS		139	USD 45,129,453	USD 9,987,500	USD 8,413,148	USD 2,500,000	USD 36,715,048	0.269

* Excludes fee as percentage of gross settlement in one settlement because the attorney fees were awarded separately and most of the settlement was based on injunctive relief rather than monetary damages so the gross settlement amount was significantly lower than the actual value of the settlement.

2.4.4 Findings by State of Settlement

Based on the differences in laws, courts, and attorneys in various states it may be helpful to analyze the settlements by the state in which they were approved. Generally, there are some clear differences across states, but much of this difference can be attributed to the differences in sample size among the states. The vast majority of these claims are all federal claims, with settlements ultimately approved in district courts in those states. Yet, there are a few settlements involving state claims that were settled in state courts. A large number of these settlements were approved in California, whereas a few were approved in New York, New Jersey, and Pennsylvania. Table 2.10 summarizes the results. In this table, average and median recoveries were calculated using as much data as was available since the sample of settlements for each state was not particularly large. This means that the average individual potential recoveries were calculated for awards where attorney's fees were not known, which likely inflated the results.

TABLE 2.10: Average and Median Individual Potential Recoveries by State

State*	Number of Settlements	Average Potential Recovery Award	Median Potential Recovery Individual Award
Alabama	2	USD 109,315	USD 109,315
California	35	USD 12,469	USD 8,000
Colorado	2	USD 41,326	USD 41,326
District of Columbia	4	USD 8,378	USD 8,378
Florida	2	USD 291	USD 291
Georgia	2	USD 22,606	USD 22,606
Idaho	2	USD 4,448	USD 4,448
Illinois	7	USD 5,016	USD 4,444
Kansas	5	USD 9,559	USD 5,839
Louisiana	2	USD 8,965	USD 8,965

CHAPTER 2. A PRELIMINARY ASSESSMENT

State	Number of Settlements	Average Potential Recovery Award	Median Potential Recovery Individual Award
Maryland	2	USD 16,347	USD 16,347
Minnesota	3	USD 4,709	USD 5,400
New Jersey	5	USD 247,503	USD 2,118
New York	12	USD 72,068	USD 5,610
Ohio	4	USD 15,525	USD 1,329
Oklahoma	2	USD 35,429	USD 35,429
Pennsylvania	10	USD 13,526	USD 6,634
Tennessee	3	USD 6,940	USD 6,545
Texas	4	USD 34,208	USD 45,281
Washington	8	USD 11,339	USD 2,812

* Only states in which there was per plaintiff data on at least two settlements were included in this table.

For many of the states with higher average and median individual potential recoveries we had fewer settlements in our data set. The states with at least five settlements are italicized in the table. Among those states, the average individual potential recoveries by state are quite varied, as can be seen above. Of these, New York and New Jersey are the highest, at USD 72,068 and USD 247,503 respectively. Yet, the median individual potential recoveries are significantly lower, at USD 5,610 for New York and USD 2,118 for New Jersey. This is likely because there was one settlement in each of those states that was unusually high, raising the ultimate average awards.

The other states with more data points have averages and medians within a smaller range. Washington, California, and Pennsylvania all have averages within USD 3,000 of each other. The medians for Pennsylvania and California are also similar, at around USD 6,000 and USD 8,000 respectively. The median for Washington is lower, at approximately USD 3,000. Of these states with the larger sample sizes, the lowest average award is in Illinois, where the average is a mere USD 5,016 and the median is USD 4,444.

2.4.5 A Brief Comparison of Our Results to Recent Studies of Individual Recoveries in Arbitration

A recent study of American Arbitration Association (AAA) awards in 1999 and 2000 by Theodore Eisenberg and Elizabeth Hill suggests that arbitration awards achieved by employees may be higher than the potential individual recoveries in employment class actions (to the extent reflected in our data set). Eisenberg and Hill separated their results by Civil Rights and Non-Civil Rights Employment Disputes, and split up claims made by higher-paid employees from those made by lower-paid employees.[28] Since our data has not been separated in these ways, comparisons are of necessity rough.

Eisenberg and Hill found the average AAA award for a non-Civil Rights claim was USD 211,720 in the case of higher-paid employees, and USD 30,732 for a lower-paid employee.[29] Further, they found the median award for a higher-paid employee to be USD 94,484, and for a lower-paid employee, USD 13,450.[30] For Civil Rights claims, the mean was USD 32,500 for a higher pay employee and USD 259,795 for a lower pay employee.[31] The median awards for these actions were USD 32,500 for a higher-paid employee and USD 56,096 for a lower-paid employee.[32] Another recent paper by Alexander J.S. Colvin that examined empirical research on arbitration yielded similar results.[33]

These results are uniformly higher than the results we have found for mean and median individual potential recoveries in class action lawsuits. The highest average potential individual recovery in our data set is around USD 63,000 for an ERISA claim, but the rest of our mean and median results are all below USD 20,000.

2.5 CONCLUSION

While our data set does not include every settlement of employment law class or collective action over the past fourteen years, it

---

[28] Eisenberg & Hill, *supra* n. 1, at 51.
[29] *Id.*
[30] *Id.*
[31] *Id.*
[32] *Id.*
[33] Colvin, *supra* note 1.

CHAPTER 2. A PRELIMINARY ASSESSMENT

includes a large sample of them. Although the numbers vary by type of claim, state of settlement, and income level of plaintiffs in some cases, the individual potential recoveries are typically rather substantial in these settlements, suggesting that – from the standpoint of size of individual claim alone – it cannot be said that these are claims that would not be individually pursued in arbitration. Much work needs to be done to determine if these potential recoveries would be obtainable in individual litigation or arbitration, or whether there is something special about the class action vehicle that makes possible such potential recoveries. We would also need to account for a selection bias in class action cases – that plaintiff lawyers may under-report less favorable settlements and are highly selective in picking cases for class action treatment. If so, the characteristics of individual and class claims may differ in systematic ways. In the interim, our data shows that potential individual recoveries for many types of employment disputes are valuable enough to place in question the arguments that these are 'negative value' cases that will be brought forward, if at all, only through the class action vehicle.

CHAPTER 3

Class and Representative Actions

By Richard T. Seymour* and John F. Aslin**

3.1 INTRODUCTION

The number of Rule 23 class actions[1] alleging employment discrimination has declined sharply, as shown in the accompanying table.[2] These data are based on the civil cover sheets and do not include cases in which the original non-class complaints are later amended to include class allegations. Class filings over the last five years have been relatively flat. They are a tiny fraction of all filings of employment discrimination lawsuits. There may be several reasons for the slowness of the last decade's rebound even in the face of sharp increases in the assertion of individual claims. First, every knowledgeable observer would agree that there has been an enormous reduction in open forms of discrimination alerting every victim to the cause of her or his injury. Where there is a discriminatory pattern, its existence is not readily apparent to applicants and employees, and attorneys

---

*Richard T. Seymour is principal of Richard T. Seymour Law Office. He holds a J.D. from Harvard Law School.
**John F. Aslin is a partner in Perkins Coie. He holds a J.D. from Georgetown University.
[1] This article focuses on the appellate treatment of class actions in fair employment cases and does not discuss significant developments in the law of class actions in other contexts. It should be used as a starting point for research.
[2] Table 3.1 is drawn from: Administrative Office of the United States Courts, Annual Report of the Director. Table 32 in the **1977** report; Table **X-5** in each report from **1978** to **1985**; Table **X-5** in unpublished printouts compiled and maintained by the Administrative Office from **1986** to date.

David Sherwyn and Samuel Estreicher (eds), *Employment Class and Collective Actions*, pp. 139–201.
© 2008, by the American Bar Association. Reprinted with permission.

may be reluctant to bring class claims in the mere hope that formal discovery will reveal such a pattern. Second, class litigation has become much more expensive over the past twenty years, as defendants have increasingly employed statistical, economic, and psychological experts and plaintiffs have, as a practical matter, been required to do likewise. Third, because of the increased stakes and complexity of class litigation, it can take many years to resolve class claims, whereas individual claims are often resolved within a year or two from their filing. Fourth, the standards for certifying a class have become more tightly focused over the past two decades. Two of the leading cases are *General Telephone Co. of the Southwest v. Falcon*,[3] and *East Texas Motor Freight Systems, Inc. v. Rodriguez*.[4]

3.2 NECESSITY OF FOLLOWING CLASS PROCEDURES BEFORE GRANTING CLASS RELIEF

Lowery v. Circuit City Stores, Inc.,[5] affirmed the decertification of a Rule 23(b) (2) class seeking common-law damages as well as traditional Title VII relief, and held that individual plaintiffs may not maintain a private, non-class cause of action for pattern or practice discrimination, and may not avail themselves of the presumption of discrimination flowing from the proof of such a pattern or practice. The court held that individual claims are typically resolved by the inferential model, and that evidence of a pattern or practice may be relevant to prove that the challenged action took place in circumstances giving rise to an inference of discrimination, or pretext, but that such evidence cannot establish all of the four elements of a prima facie case.[6] Citing a treatise, the court also stated its views of the differences between individual and class pattern or practice cases with respect to remedies:

> Class action pattern or practice suits primarily seek to redress widespread discrimination and the harm suffered by the group of individuals subjected to that discrimination. Accordingly, the relief typically sought in

---

[3] 457 U.S. 147, 28 FEP Cases 1745 (1982).
[4] 431 U.S. 395, 14 FEP Cases 1505 (1977).
[5] 158 F.3d 742, 759–762, 77 FEP Cases 1319 (4th Cir. 1998), vacated and remanded on other grounds, 527 U.S. 103 1 (1999).
[6] *Id.* at 761.

class action pattern or practice suits is injunctive and may include such aspects as, for example, affirmative action plans and the altering of a seniority system.... The need for such remedies can be determined without referring to matters such as the qualifications of a particular employee. On the other hand, in a private, non-class disparate treatment case, the plaintiff seeks to remedy individual harm. Accordingly, the relief typically sought involves reinstatement, hiring, back pay, damages, etc. Such remedies typically require the examination of the circumstances surrounding a single employment action involving the plaintiff.[7]

The court did not refer to any of its class pattern-and-practice cases involving individualized relief.[8]

3.3 RULE 23 CLASS ACTIONS

3.3.1 Suitability of the Issues for Class Treatment

Munoz v. Orr[9] affirmed the grant of summary judgment to the Title VII class action defendant. The court stated, 'Disparate treatment claims can be brought as class actions as well. Plaintiffs in a class action disparate treatment case must show a "pattern or practice" of discrimination by the employer, i.e., that "racial discrimination was the company's standard operating procedure – the regular rather than the unusual practice."... Proving a pattern or practice is necessary to establishing a prima facie case in a disparate treatment class action: "Proving isolated or sporadic discriminatory acts by the employer is insufficient to establish a prima facie case.'[10] The court stated that disparate-impact claims may be brought either by individuals or a class.[11] The court held

---

[7] *Id.*
[8] See *EEOC v. Northwest Airlines, Inc.*, 188 F.3d 695, 701–702, 80 FEP Cases 123 1 (6th Cir. 1999); *EEOC v. Dinuba Medical Clinic*, 222 F.3d 580, 587–588, 83 FEP Cases 1655 (9th Cir. 2000), affirmed the judgment for the EEOC. The court held that the EEOC may seek common-law damages for persons who did not file charges of discrimination, but who are situated similarly to the charging party, without becoming a class representative under Rule 23.
[9] 200 F.3d 291,299, 8 1 FEP Cases 13 18 (5th Cir.), cert. denied, _____U.S._____, 121 S. Ct. 45, 148 L. Ed. 2d 15 (2000).
[10] Citations omitted.
[11] *Id.* at 299–300.

that the plaintiffs showed only isolated statistical disparities, not systemic discrimination.[12]

3.3.2 Suitability of the Class Representative

Holmes v. Pension Plan of Bethlehem Steel Corp., an ERISA benefits case, affirmed the denial of class certification.[13] The court held that, in addition to the Rule 23 requirements, 'class actions are also subject to more generally applicable rules such as those governing standing and mootness.'[14] The court stated:

> So long as a class representative has a live claim at the time he moves for class certification, neither a pending motion nor a certified class action need be dismissed if his individual claim subsequently becomes moot. ... If, on the other hand, the putative class representative's claim becomes moot before he moves for class certification, then any subsequent motion must be denied and the entire action dismissed.[15]

Robinson v. Sheriff of Cook County[16] affirmed the dismissal of the Title VII plaintiffs' claims and the denial of class certification. The original plaintiff, Charles Robinson, had brought a disparate-impact class action challenging the hiring process for correctional officers.

Challenging Robinson's suitability as a class representative, the Sheriff presented evidence that Robinson's application had been turned down because of his very poor employment record, which among other things contained an unexplained twenty-seven-month gap between jobs. The judge rejected Robinson as class representative but permitted Belinda Taylor to join the suit as a plaintiff and take Robinson's place as class representative.

Her claim was later dismissed, and she was barred from serving as a class representative, because she had not filed an EEOC charge.[17] The court held that the suitability of the class representative is bound up with questions of typicality and adequacy of representation where the

---

[12] *Id.* at 302–303.
[13] 213 F.3d 124, 135–136 (3rd Cir. 2000).
[14] *Id.* at 135.
[15] *Id.* at 135–136.
[16] 167 F.3d 1155, 1156, 79 FEP Cases 203 (7th Cir.), cert. denied, 528 U.S. 824 (1999).
[17] This aspect is commonly called the 'Single-Filing' Rule.

CHAPTER 3. CLASS AND REPRESENTATIVE ACTIONS

weakness of the named plaintiffs claim is apparent prior to certification of the class.[18] The court explained:

> Under Rule 23, the class representative's claim must be typical of the claims of the class, and he must also be an adequate representative of the class. (Fed. R. Civ. P. 23(a)(3), (4).) The first of these requirements is really an aspect of the second; if his claim is atypical, he is not likely to be an adequate representative; his incentive to press issues important to the other members of the class will be impaired. ... And if when class certification is sought it is already apparent – as it was here because of Robinson's employment history as shown on the application that he submitted to the Sheriff's office – that the class representative's claim is extremely weak, this is an independent reason to doubt the adequacy of his representation. ... One whose own claim is a loser from the start knows that he has nothing to gain from the victory of the class, and so he has little incentive to assist or cooperate in the litigation; the case is then a pure class action lawyer's suit. ... Finally, if the class representative's claim is both weak and typical – if the case as a whole is as weak as the representative's individual claim – then the case should be dismissed, with or without class certification. ... The plaintiffs' lawyer, who we assume is the real mover and shaker in this suit, would not be happy to have this case certified as a class action and then dismissed; that would have res judicata effect on any unnamed class members who did not opt out.[19]

The court distinguished between a plaintiff's possible loss and a clear prospect of loss. 'But if his claim is a *clear* loser at the time he asks to be made class representative, then approving him as class representative can only hurt the class.'[20] The court also drew an adverse inference from the fact that the proposed class had 387 members and the plaintiffs' attorney was not able to intervene any other proposed class representative with a claim that was not time-barred.[21]

3.3.3 Discretion to Consider Factors Not Specified in Rule 23

Lowery v. Circuit City Stores, Inc.,[22] affirmed the decertification of a Rule 23(b)(2) class seeking common-law damages as well as traditional

---

[18] *Id.* at 1157.
[19] *Id.* (citations omitted).
[20] *Id.* at 1158 (emphasis in original).
[21] *Id.*
[22] 158 F.3d 742 (4th Cir.).

Title VII relief. The court rejected plaintiffs' argument that, once the Rule 23(a) criteria are met, district courts have no discretion to deny certification:

> The Plaintiffs first argue that the district court erroneously decertified the class action because, if the four requirements of Federal Rule of Civil Procedure 23(a) are satisfied, the district court is not at liberty to consider other factors in deciding whether to certify a class. In effect, Plaintiffs argue that, once the requirements of Rule 23(a) are met, the district court loses its discretion to certify or decertify the class. This argument, however, does not comport with either the language of Rule 23 or this court's precedent. First, Rule 23 states that an action 'may' be maintained as a class action if the listed requirements are met. (See Fed. R. Civ. P. 23(a) and (b).) The Rule does not say that, once the requirements are met, the district court 'must' certify and maintain the suit as a class action.[23]

The court's second reason was that it had previously held that the lower courts have broad discretion in deciding whether to certify a class. 'This broad discretion necessarily implies that the district court may appropriately consider factors other than those listed in Rule 23 in determining whether to certify a class action.'[24] The court returned to this question:[25]

> We note that, in affirming the district court's decertification of the class due to concerns about case manageability, we do not mean to imply that the factors for certifying a Rule 23(b)(3) class should be imported into Rule 23(b)(2) classes. Nevertheless, because efficiency is one of the primary purposes of class action procedure ... we hold that in appropriate circumstances a district court may exercise its discretion to deny certification if the resulting class action would be unmanageable or cumbersome.

Davoll v. Webb[26] affirmed the denial of class certification for a proposed class of former, present, and future members of the Denver Police Department who have or will have disabilities, who will be denied reasonable accommodation, and who meet certain other requirements. The court upheld the trial court's determination that the class was not sufficiently definite, because it would have required individual

---

[23] *Id.* at 757.
[24] *Id.* at 758.
[25] See *Id.* at 758 n. 5.
[26] 194 F.3d 1116, 1146–1147, 9 AD Cases 1533, 24 EB Cases 1088 (10th Cir. 1999).

CHAPTER 3. CLASS AND REPRESENTATIVE ACTIONS

hearings to determine whether a given person was in the class. The court elaborated on its holding:

> We understand plaintiffs' concern that by denying their class certification motion and upholding the United States pattern and practice action, this decision may be interpreted as holding that only the government can bring a class-wide ADA employment suit. Such an interpretation would be unfounded. Given the deferential standard by which we review class certification, it is possible the district court could have certified the class in its discretion, or could have modified the proposed definition so that it was sufficiently definite. Of course, we do not decide those questions, as our holding here is limited to the issue directly before us.
>
> At the same time, we do note that a pattern and practice action brought by the United States pursuant to section 707 of Title VII, 42 U.S.C. 2000e-6, is not subject to the requirements of Fed. R. Civ. P. 23.[27]

3.3.4 Numerosity under Rule 23(a)(1)

Stokes v. Westinghouse Savannah River Co.[28] affirmed the denial of Rule 23 class certification on the plaintiffs ERISA claims. 'Not only can members of so small a class just as well present their own claims, there is ample evidence from which to conclude that their circumstances differed in material respects.'

3.3.5 Commonality under Rule 23(a)(2)

Caridad v. Metro-North Commuter Railroad[29] reversed the denial of class certification for a Title VII racial discrimination class 'challenging the delegation to supervisors, pursuant to company-wide policies, of the authority to make subjective decisions regarding employee discipline and promotion.'[30] The court stated that decisions on class certification are subject to review for abuse of discretion, but that 'we are "noticeably less deferential to the district court when that court has

---

[27] *Id.* at 1147-1147 n. 20 (citation omitted).
[28] 206 F.3d 420, 431, 82 FEP Cases 391,24 EB Cases 2737 (4th Cir. 2000).
[29] 191 F.3d 283, 80 FEP Cases 627 (2nd Cir. 1999), cert. denied sub nom. *Metro-North Commuter Railroad v. Norris*, 529 U.S. 1 107 (2000).
[30] *Id.* at 286.

denied class status than when it has certified a class."'[31] The court cautioned that 'a motion for class certification is not an occasion for examination of the merits of the case.'[32] The court held that 'the fact that the Class Plaintiffs challenge the subjective components of company-wide employment practices does not bar a finding of commonality under either the disparate treatment or disparate impact model.'[33] The court continued, holding that there should not be a preliminary inquiry into the merits at the class-certification stage:

> Of course, class certification would not be warranted absent some showing that the challenged practice is causally related to a pattern of disparate treatment or has a disparate impact on African-American employees at Metro-North. Where the decision-making process is difficult to review because of the role of subjective assessment, significant statistical disparities are relevant to determining whether the challenged employment practice has a class-wide impact. ... Regardless of their ultimate persuasiveness on the issue of liability, the statistical report and anecdotal evidence submitted by the Class Plaintiffs are sufficient to demonstrate common questions of fact regarding the discriminatory implementation and effects of Metro-North's company-wide policies regarding promotion and discipline. The District Court relied on the report of Metro-North's statistical expert, Dr. Evans, to conclude that the Class Plaintiffs' statistics were inadequate because they failed to take into account the fact that various Metro-North positions have materially different rates of discipline and promotion. Though Metro-North's critique of the Class Plaintiffs' evidence may prove fatal at the merits stage, the Class Plaintiffs need not demonstrate at this stage that they will prevail on the merits. Accordingly, this sort of 'statistical dueling' is not relevant to the certification determination. ... We conclude that the Class Plaintiffs' statistical evidence supports a finding of commonality on the issue of discipline with respect to those African-American employees who were disciplined while working in one of the 48 positions in which African-Americans are more likely to be disciplined than Whites. In addition, the statistical evidence supports a finding of commonality on the promotion claim. The Class Plaintiffs submitted evidence that tends to establish that being Black has a statistically significant effect on an employee's likelihood of being promoted; indeed, being Black reduces an employee's likelihood of promotion by approximately 33 percent. In conducting her analyses, the

---

[31] *Id.* at 291 (citation omitted).
[32] *Id.* (citation omitted).
[33] *Id.* at 292.

CHAPTER 3. CLASS AND REPRESENTATIVE ACTIONS

> Class Plaintiffs' expert controlled for various factors that one would expect to be relevant to the likelihood of disciplinary action and promotion.... More detailed statistics might be required to sustain the Plaintiffs' burden of persuasion ... but this report, in conjunction with the anecdotal evidence, satisfies the Class Plaintiffs' burden of demonstrating commonality for purposes of class certification.[34]

The court held that the district court had improperly resolved disputed questions of fact in crediting the defendant's expert evidence over that of the plaintiffs.[35]

McAuley v. International Business Machines Corp., Inc.,[36] affirmed the restriction of an ERISA early retirement class to former employees of the Lexington plant of the defendant, because plaintiffs relied on 'particularized allegations of oral misrepresentations' that were made only at that plant. 'Although plaintiffs also rely upon the allegedly misleading written representations from the Summary Plan Descriptions, the necessity that allegations of representations be uniform among class members supports the district court's restriction of the class to former employees of the Lexington plant.'[37]

Rutstein v. Avis Rent-A-Car Systems, Inc.,[38] reversed the certification under Rule 23(b)(3) of a class of Jewish individuals and businesses who were discriminated against in attempts to set up or maintain business accounts. The court held that there were too many case-specific factors bearing on the question of discrimination against individual customers for class treatment to be suitable.[39] The court explained:

> Whether Avis maintains a policy or practice of discrimination may be relevant in a given case, but it certainly cannot establish that the company intentionally discriminated against every member of the putative class. The individual issues that must be addressed include not only whether Avis actually denied a particular plaintiff a corporate account, gave the plaintiff a less advantageous account, or cancelled the plaintiffs account,

---

[34] *Id.* at 292–293 (citations omitted).

[35] *Id.* at 293. Judge Walker dissented. *Id.* at 296–297.

[36] 165 F.3d 1038, 104647,22 EB Cases 2425 (6th Cir. 1999), cert. dismissed, 527 U.S. 1066 (1999).

[37] *Id.* See the discussion of *Lang v. Kohl's Food Stores. Inc.*, 217 F.3d 9 19, 924–925, 83 FEP Cases 311 (7th Cir. 2000), below in the section on 'Representative Actions.'

[38] 211 F.3d 1228 (11th Cir. 2000).

[39] *Id.* at 1235.

but also whether the particular plaintiff was of the age required by Avis to qualify for a corporate account; whether the plaintiff met the financial criteria for a corporate account; whether the nature of the plaintiffs expected use of Avis vehicles would make the transaction cost-justified for Avis; whether the plaintiff would be renting cars from Avis in a criminally high-risk or low-risk geographical area; whether the Avis employee who allegedly denied the plaintiff a corporate account judged the caller applicant to be lying about his or her qualifications based on information not related to the caller's ethnicity; and so on, and so on. All of these issues are clearly case-specific, and they will all have to be addressed in one way or another in order for each plaintiff to demonstrate a prima facie case of intentional discrimination.[40]

With respect to pattern-and-practice cases, the court distinguished between employment and consumer cases, holding that the presumption of discrimination arising from proof of a pattern of discrimination is more suitable in employment discrimination cases, where it replaces the prima facie case under *McDonnell Douglas*, than in a car rental case:

> To understand this point is to see why the Teamsters rationale cannot apply in the instant case. In contrast to a *McDonnell Douglas* case, a plaintiff in this non-employment discrimination case will have to demonstrate that (1) he or she is a member of racial minority; (2) the defendant had an intent to discriminate on the basis of race; and (3) the discrimination concerned one or more of the activities enumerated in the statute. The second requirement is more demanding than any of the requirements imposed on plaintiffs in a *McDonnell Douglas* case, requiring, as it does, that the plaintiff bring forth evidence of actual intent on the part of the defendant. A finding that Avis has a policy or practice of discrimination could not possibly function as a meaningful substitute for the establishment of an actual intent to discriminate against an individual plaintiff on the basis of his or her ethnicity. This is because the legitimate reasons why Avis might have judged an individual plaintiff to be 'unqualified' for a corporate account are far more various and individualized than in the employment context. The requirement that an individual demonstrate that he or she is 'qualified' for a job under *McDonnell Douglas* is not particularly rigorous; the same does not hold true in the instant case where Avis may have refused to contract with a plaintiff for any number of reasons having nothing to do with the plaintiff's ethnicity. Thus, even if plaintiffs could establish a generalized policy or practice of discrimination, they still

---

[40] *Id.*

would not have established that the policy was implemented (and, thus, that Avis actually intended to discriminate) in their individual cases.[41]

The court also stated that the *Teamsters* approach is more appropriate for equitable relief than for damages.[42]

3.3.6 Typicality under Rule 23(a)(3)

The most recent Supreme Court decision involving a class of employees is *United States v. National Treasury Employees Union*.[43] The class included all Executive Branch employees below grade GS-16 who, but for the ban on receiving honoria for speeches and articles, would receive honoraria within the definition of the statute. The opinions in the case make clear that some members of the class were limited as to activities that had no connection with their jobs, while others were limited as to activities closely connected to their official responsibilities. The Court did not discuss the effect of such differences on typicality. It reversed the relief as overbroad because it enjoined the ban as to all Executive Branch employees, not just those in the class.[44]

Amchem Products. Inc. v. Windsor,[45] an asbestos products liability case, held that the 'claims or defenses' aspect of the typicality requirement, like the 'common questions' under Rule 23(b)(3), are the questions that would be significant if the case were to be litigated, not questions that pertain to interest in a settlement. *Caridad v. Metro-North Commuter Railroad*,[46] reversed the denial of class certification. It stated that the commonality and typicality requirements tend to merge, and quoted *General Telephone Co. of the Southwest v. Falcon*:[47] 'Both serve as guideposts for determining whether ... the named plaintiffs claim and the class claims are so interrelated that the interests of the class members will be fairly and adequately protected in their absence.' The

---

[41] *Id.* at 1239 (footnote omitted).
[42] *Id.* See the discussion below as to class actions seeking common-law damages.
[43] 5 13 U.S. 454, 10 IER Cases 452 (1995), which invalidated the ban in 5 U.S.C. App. 6 501(b) on federal employees' receipt of honoraria for making speeches and writing articles.
[44] *Id.* at 477–480.
[45] 521 U.S. 591, 623 n. 18 (1997).
[46] 191 F.3d 283, 291 (2nd Cir.).
[47] 457 U.S. 147, 157 n. 13 (1982).

court held that the typicality element 'does not require that the factual background of each named plaintiff's claim be identical to that of all class members; rather, it requires that the disputed issue of law or fact "occupy essentially the same degree of centrality to the named plaintiffs claim as to that of other members of the proposed class." '[48] Applying these standards to the case and finding the typicality requirement satisfied, the court stated:

> Nineteen of the named Plaintiffs allege that they have been subjected to discipline pursuant to Metro-North's company-wide 'PDS' as a result of racial discrimination. The fact that two of these Plaintiffs admitted that they had committed the infractions giving rise to the challenged disciplinary actions does not defeat a finding of typicality; indeed, one of the claims levied by the putative class is that African-American workers are disciplined for violations for which White workers are not. For these Plaintiffs, the question of whether Metro-North's system-wide PDS has resulted in a pattern and practice of discrimination or affects African-Americans more severely than other employees is central to their claims. Likewise, for the seven named Plaintiffs who alleged that they were not promoted as the result of racial discrimination, the question of whether Metro-North's policy of delegating discretion to department supervisors to make subjective decisions regarding employee promotions is administered in a racially discriminatory manner or has a disparate impact on African-American workers is crucial to their claims, as well as to those of the proposed class.[49]

The court held that the district court had improperly resolved disputed questions of fact in crediting the defendant's expert evidence over that of the plaintiffs.[50]

3.3.7 Adequacy of Representation under Rule 23(a)(4)

Amchem Products, Inc. v. Windsor[51] involved a proposed settlement on behalf of a proposed class of persons (some asymptomatic) occupationally exposed to asbestos in the past, and their family members, who

---

[48] *Id.* at 293 (citation omitted).
[49] *Id.* at 293.
[50] *Id.* Judge Walker dissented. *Id.* at 296–297. See the discussion of *Robinson v. Sheriff of Cook County*, 167 F.3d 1 155, 1 157 (7th Cir.), in § 7-3 (e), above.
[51] 521 U.S. 591, 604–605 (1997).

CHAPTER 3. CLASS AND REPRESENTATIVE ACTIONS

may be expected to have severe health problems of one type or another in the future, and who have not made claims of their own or been included in any of the previous asbestos litigation. The Court stated that the proposed class could not meet the requirement of adequacy of representation:

> As the Third Circuit pointed out, named parties with diverse medical conditions sought to act on behalf of a single giant class rather than on behalf of discrete subclasses. In significant respects, the interests of those within the single class are not aligned. Most saliently, for the currently injured, the critical goal is generous immediate payments. That goal tugs against the interest of exposure-only plaintiffs in ensuring an ample, inflation-protected fund for the future.[52] The disparity between the currently injured and exposure-only categories of plaintiffs, and the diversity within each category are not made insignificant by the District Court's finding that petitioners' assets suffice to pay claims under the settlement. ... Although this is not a 'limited fund' case certified under Rule 23(b)(l)(B), the terms of the settlement reflect essential allocation decisions designed to confine compensation and to limit defendants' liability. For example, as earlier described ... the settlement includes no adjustment for inflation; only a few claimants per year can opt out at the back end; and loss-of-consortium claims are extinguished with no compensation. The settling parties, in sum, achieved a global compromise with no structural assurance of fair and adequate representation for the diverse groups and individuals affected. Although the named parties alleged a range of complaints, each served generally as representative for the whole, not for a separate constituency.[53]

The Court emphasized that representatives of subclasses have a responsibility not to the entire class, but solely to the members of their subgroup.[54] The terms of the settlement and the structure of the negotiations did not provide any assurance that the named plaintiffs 'operated under a proper understanding of their representational responsibilities.'[55]

---

[52] Cf. *General Telephone Co. of Northwest v. EEOC*, 4 46 U. S. 318, 331,22 FEP Cases 1196 (1980)('In employment discrimination litigation, conflicts might arise, for example, between employees and applicants who were denied employment and who will, if granted relief, compete with employees for fringe benefits or seniority. Under Rule 23, the same plaintiff could not represent these classes.').
[53] *Id.* at 626–627 (parallel citation to FEP Cases added).
[54] *Id.* at 627.
[55] *Id.* at 627–628.

Munoz v. Orr,[56] affirmed the grant of summary judgment to the Title VII class action defendant, and rejected the plaintiffs' argument that the failure of the class claims should result in decertification of the class because the plaintiffs would thereby have been shown to be inadequate class representatives.

> First, individual claims based on particularized evidence of discrimination may still be possible for some class members. Second, we cannot say that the named plaintiffs have failed to adequately represent the interests of the class over fourteen years of federal litigation. Decertification is not appropriate merely because the statistical evidence proved inadequate to raise a genuine issue of material fact. The named plaintiffs have zealously sought to vindicate what they see as wrongs to the class and have not failed in their duty of representation.[57]

Frank v. United Airlines, Inc.,[58] reversed the determination of the lower court that the plaintiffs were precluded from making facial, age, and gender discrimination claims as to the defendant's height-and-weight policy because of the 1979 decision on behalf of the defendant, and subsequent settlement, in a class action brought by the Airline Pilots Association against the defendant. The court held that there was a conflict among the class members in the earlier settlement, because all of the relief went to class members affected by the 1977 weight policy, who received reinstatement and back pay. These class members had no interest in appealing the adverse judgment. There was no relief for the persons who would be affected by a future weight policy, who did have an interest in appealing the adverse judgment. 'Consequently, when the class representatives chose not to appeal the adverse ruling on the facial validity of the weight policy, they abandoned any representation of the interests of those present and potential future class members in order to protect present class members seeking back pay and reinstatement.'[59] As a result, that settlement did not preclude the present class.[60]

---

[56] 200 F.3d 291, 307 n. 7 (5th Cir.).

[57] See the discussion of *Robinson v. Sheriff of Cook County*, 167 F.3d 1155, 1156 (7th Cir.), in §7-3 (e) above.

[58] 216 F.3d 845, 852–853, 83 FEP Cases 1 (9th Cir. 2000).

[59] *Id.* (footnote and citations omitted).

[60] *Id.* at 853. Judge O'Scannlain concurred in part and dissented in part. *Id.* at 857–864.

3.3.8 Acting and Refusing to Act on Common Grounds under Rule 23(b)(2)

Amchem Products, Inc. v. Windsor,[61] reiterated in dictum the old observation: 'Civil rights cases against parties charged with unlawful, class-based discrimination are prime examples' of cases suitable for treatment under Rule 23(b)(2).

Jefferson v. Ingersoll International Inc.[62] vacated the certification under Rule 23(b)(2) of a Title VII class seeking common-law damages. The court noted that the lack of notice and of opt-outs in (b)(2) classes gives class counsel 'a much freer hand' than in (b)(3) class actions,[63] but exposes the defendant to a much greater danger of collateral attack 'by class members who contend that they should have been notified and allowed to proceed independently.'[64] The court stated, 'Defendants who want the outcome of a damages action (no matter which side wins) to be *conclusive* favor Rule 23(b)(3), because it alone insulates the disposition from collateral attack by dissatisfied class members.'[65]

Frank v. United Airlines, Inc.,[66] reversed the determination of the lower court that the plaintiffs were precluded from making facial age and gender discrimination claims as to the defendant's height-and-weight policy because of the 1979 decision on behalf of the defendant, and subsequent settlement, in a class action brought by the Air Line Pilots Association against the defendant. The court observed that no class members in the earlier case had been allowed to opt out, and stated that the lack of an opportunity to opt out in itself barred claim preclusion. 'Under *Eisen*, class members in a Rule 23(b)(3) class may be bound to the result of that action only if the notice and opt-out requirements applicable to Rule 23(b)(3) actions are satisfied. Because ALPA did not satisfy the requirements applicable to a Rule 23(b)(3) class action, ALPA cannot preclude the Rule 23(b)(3) class action in this case.'

---

[61] 521 U.S. 591, 614 (1997).
[62] 195 F.3d 894, 896–897, 81 FEP Cases 170 (7th Cir. 1999).
[63] *Id.* at 896.
[64] *Id.*
[65] *Id.* at 896–897 (emphasis in original). Other related aspects of this case are discussed throughout this chapter.
[66] 216 F.3d 845, 852 (9th Cir.).

3.3.9 Predominance of Class Questions and Superiority of Class Treatment under Rule 23(b)(3)

Amchem Products, Inc. v. Windsor[67] stated that although:

> the text of Rule 23(b)(3) does not exclude from certification cases in which individual damages run high, the Advisory Committee had dominantly in mind vindication of 'the rights of groups of people who individually would be without effective strength to bring their opponents into court at all.'[68]

The Court held that the 'common questions' contemplated by Rule 23(b)(3) do not include the interests class members assertedly have in the settlement, in receiving their shares of the proceeds without further risk, or whether the settlement is fair.

> The benefits asbestos-exposed persons might gain from the establishment of a grand-scale compensation scheme are a matter fit for legislative consideration ... but it is not pertinent to the predominance inquiry. That inquiry trains on the legal or factual questions that qualify each class member's case as a genuine controversy, questions that pre-exist any settlement.[69]

The Court stated that the predominance inquiry 'tests whether proposed classes are sufficiently cohesive to warrant adjudication by representation.'[70] If a common interest in a fair compromise were enough to satisfy the requirement, the requirement 'would be stripped of any meaning in the settlement context.'[71] The Court then held that facts sufficient to satisfy the commonality requirement, such as a shared exposure to asbestos, were not enough to satisfy the more demanding predominance test:

> Even if Rule 23(a)'s commonality requirement may be satisfied by that shared experience, the predominance criterion is far more demanding. ... Given the greater number of questions peculiar to the several categories of class members, and to individuals within each category, and the significance of those uncommon questions, any overarching dispute about the

---

[67] 521 U.S. 591, 617 (1997).
[68] Citation omitted.
[69] *Id.* at 622–623 (footnote omitted).
[70] *Id.* at 623.
[71] *Id.*

health consequences of asbestos exposure cannot satisfy the Rule 23(b)(3) predominance standard.

The Third Circuit highlighted the disparate questions undermining class cohesion in this case:

> Class members were exposed to different asbestos- containing products, for different amounts of time, in different ways, and over different periods. Some class members suffer no physical injury or have only asymptomatic pleural changes, while others suffer from lung cancer, disabling asbestosis, or from mesothelioma. ... Each has a different history of cigarette smoking, a factor that complicates the causation inquiry.
>
> The [exposure-only] plaintiffs especially share little in common, either with each other or with the presently injured class members. It is unclear whether they will contract asbestos-related disease and, if so, what disease each will suffer. They will also incur different medical expenses because their monitoring and treatment will depend on singular circumstances and individual medical histories.[72]
>
> Differences in state law, the Court of Appeals observed, compound these disparities.[73]

The Court observed that '[n]o settlement class called to our attention is as sprawling as this one.'[74] The Court made clear, however, that Rule 23(b)(3) class actions remained available for a wide variety of cases seeking damages. 'Predominance is a test readily met in certain cases alleging consumer or securities fraud or violations of the antitrust laws. ... Even mass tort cases arising from a common cause or disaster may, depending upon the circumstances, satisfy the predominance requirement.'[75] The greatest caution is required 'when individual stakes are high and disparities among class members great.'[76] The Court affirmed the Third Circuit's rejection of the settlement class. Justice Breyer, joined by Justice Stevens, concurred in part and dissented in part.[77] *Frank v. United Airlines, Inc.*,[78] discussed in the preceding section, suggested that no Rule 23(b)(3) class would be bound by

---

[72] *Id.* at 626.
[73] *Id.* at 623–624.
[74] *Id.* at 624.
[75] *Id.* at 625.
[76] *Id.*
[77] *Id.* at 629–641.
[78] 216 F.3d 845, 852 (9th Cir.).

the result of an adverse class determination entered in a Rule 23(b)(2) class in which class members did not have the opportunity to opt-out.

3.3.10 'Hybrid' Class Actions under Rules 23(b)(2) and 23(b)(3)

Jefferson v. Ingersoll International Inc.[79] vacated the certification under Rule 23(b)(2) of a Title VII class seeking common-law damages as well as an injunction. The court discussed the possibility of a 'hybrid' class certification:

> Divided certification also is worth consideration. It is possible to certify the injunctive aspects of the suit under Rule 23(b)(2) and the damages aspects under Rule 23(b)(3), achieving both consistent treatment of class-wide equitable relief and an opportunity for each affected person to exercise control over the damages aspects. *Beacon Theatres, Inc. v. Westover*,[80] and *Dairy Queen, Inc. v. Wood*,[81] would require the district judge to try the damages claims first, to preserve the right to jury trial, a step that would complicate the management of separate classes – and mean, as a practical matter, that the damages claims and the Rule 2 3(b)(3) class would dominate the litigation – but the damages-first principle holds even when there is a single class under a single subdivision of Rule 23. That the seventh amendment gives damages the dominant role just strengthens the conclusion that Rule 23(b)(3) must be employed. Instead of divided certification-perhaps equivalently to it – the judge could treat a Rule 23(b)(2) class *as if* it were under Rule 23(b)(3), giving notice and an opportunity to opt out on the authority of Rule 23(d)(2).[82]

3.3.11 Adequacy of Notice under Rule 23(e)

Amchem Products, Inc. v. Windsor,[83] stated that the Court recognized 'the gravity of the question whether class action notice sufficient under the Constitution and Rule 23 could ever be given to legions so

---

[79] 195 F.3d 894, 898 (7th Cir.).
[80] 359 U.S. 500 (1959).
[81] 369 U.S. 469 (1962).
[82] Emphasis in original; citation and parallel citations omitted. Other related aspects of this case are discussed throughout this chapter.
[83] 521 U.S. 591, 628 (1997).

CHAPTER 3. CLASS AND REPRESENTATIVE ACTIONS

unselfconscious and amorphous' as the proposed settlement class, where many members may not even know of their exposure or realize the extent of the harm they may incur. 'Even if they fully appreciate the significance of class notice, those without current afflictions may not have the information or foresight needed to decide, intelligently, whether to stay in or opt-out.'[84] That problem is compounded because the proposed class includes family members exposed to the asbestos through the person who had occupational exposure. 'Family members of asbestos-exposed individuals may themselves fall prey to disease or may ultimately have ripe claims for loss of consortium. Yet large numbers of people in this category-future spouses and children of asbestos victims – could not be alerted to their class membership. Current spouses and children of the occupationally exposed may know nothing of that exposure.'[85] The Court stated that it did not need to rule definitively on the issue because of the other problems requiring affirmance of the Third Circuit's rejection of the proposed settlement class.[86]

3.4 SETTLEMENT CLASSES

Amchem Products, Inc. v. Windsor,[87] an asbestos products liability case, involved the propriety of a settlement class where the action was never intended to be litigated, and the Complaint, Answer, proposed settlement agreement, and joint motion for conditional class certification were all filed on the same day. The Court stated that settlement is relevant to the class determination, but only to a limited extent:

> Confronted with a request for settlement-only class certification, a district court need not inquire whether the case, if tried, would present intractable management problems (see Fed. Rule Civ. Proc. 23(b)(3)(D)), for the proposal is that there be no trial. But other specifications of the rule – those designed to protect absentees by blocking unwarranted or overbroad class definitions – demand undiluted, even heightened, attention in the settlement context. Such attention is of vital importance, for a court asked to certify a settlement class will lack the opportunity, present when a case is litigated, to adjust the class, informed by the proceedings as they unfold.[88]

---

[84] *Id.*
[85] *Id.*
[86] *Id.*
[87] 521 U.S. 591, 601–602 (1997).
[88] *Id.* at 620.

The rule 'as now composed' must be followed,[89] not the standard of whether the settlement is 'fair.'[90]

3.5 CHANGES IN CLASS CERTIFICATION AND DEFINITION

Culver v. City of Milwaukee[91] held that in some circumstances, the dismissal of a putative class action or decertification of a class action might impose on plaintiffs' counsel the obligation to provide notice to all members of the now uncertified class. The obligation does not apply where it is clear that there is no prejudice, such as where the class size is small and all members were likely to learn of the dismissal or decertification through other means. The court also held that, where it is necessary to subdivide the class into mutually exclusive subclasses and the plaintiff or plaintiffs counsel fail to do so and to invite members of the other subclass to join as representatives, their failure makes representation of the class inadequate.[92]

Walker v. Mortham[93] affirmed in part, vacated in part, and remanded, the dismissal of plaintiffs' racial discrimination claims. Because some of the plaintiffs may still prevail on their claims, destroying the reason for the lower court's decertification of the class, the court held that on remand the lower court is free to consider recertification of the class if at least one plaintiff is entitled to judgment.

3.6 INDIVIDUALIZED RELIEF FOR CLASS MEMBERS

The courts have generally required a prima facie showing that particular class members are within the class for purposes of relief, and have required the defendant to meet a 'preponderance of the

---

[89] *Id.*

[90] *Id.* Justice Breyer, joined by Justice Stevens, concurred in part and dissented in part. *Id.* at 629–641.

[91] 277 F.3d 908, 914–915 (7th Cir. 2002).

[92] *Id.* at 912–913.

[93] 158 F.3d 1177, 1196–1197, 78 FEP Cases 573 (11th Cir. 1998), cert. denied, 528 U.S. 809 (1999).

CHAPTER 3. CLASS AND REPRESENTATIVE ACTIONS

evidence' standard to overcome that showing. In government enforcement cases, which are not in themselves class actions, the same standards have been applied to determine entitlement to individual relief.

Berger v. Iron Workers Reinforced Rodmen[94] affirmed in part, and reversed in part, the lower court's award of back pay to a class of African-American rodmen discriminatorily denied membership in the union. The court stated:

> Class action lawsuits brought under Title VII are typically bifurcated into two phases, a liability phase and a damages phase, as was done in this case. The first phase establishes whether the employer is liable to the class because of a pattern or practice of discrimination.... The second phase addresses questions of class membership and the degree of damage suffered by individual class members.[95]

EEOC v. Joe's Stone Crab, Inc.,[96] reversed the finding of disparate-impact discrimination and vacated and remanded the dismissal of the EEOC's intentional-discrimination claim. The court stated that 'in determining pattern or practice liability, the government is not required to prove that any particular employee was a victim of the pattern or practice; it need only establish a prima facie case that such a policy existed.'[97] It stated that proof of such a pattern and practice creates a rebuttable presumption of discrimination and entitlement to relief. 'The employer may overcome this presumption only with clear and convincing evidence that job decisions made when the discriminatory policy was in force were not made in pursuit of that policy.'[98]

Reynolds v. Roberts[99] vacated the judgment for the Title VII plaintiff class of back pay in the sum of USD 17,450,077 plus interest in the sum of USD 17,282,410, because there had been no individualized determination that all class members had been affected by racial discrimination in hiring and promotions, and the Alabama Department of Transportation's entry into a consent decree was not the functional equivalent of

---

[94] Local 201,170 F.3d 1111, 1124, 79 FEP Cases 1018 (D.C. Cir. 1999)(per curiam).
[95] Citation omitted.
[96] 220 F.3d 1263, 1273–1274, 84 FEP Cases 195 (llth Cir. 2000).
[97] *Id.* at 1287 (footnote omitted).
[98] *Id.* at 1287 n. 22. Judge Hull concurred in part and dissented in part. *Id.* at 1287–1297.
[99] 202 F.3d 1303, 1312–1319 (11th Cir. 2000).

such an admission. Consent Decree I provided both affirmative and prohibitory injunctive relief for class members with respect to hiring, promotions, classifications, and pay.[100] The Preamble stated that Consent Decree I was entered in final and complete resolution of all class issues asserted in the case, with the exception of back pay and non-monetary relief for individual class members as provided in Article 20.[101] Article 20, paragraph 1, stated:

> Further negotiations and proceedings are required to resolve the claims for monetary and non-monetary remedies for individual members of the class[es] (including the named plaintiffs and interveners), provided however, that this Decree does not in and of itself entitle any such class member to such remedies. Such claims shall be resolved first by settlement negotiations and then, to the extent not resolved by settlement negotiations, by the Court.[102]

The court rejected the lower court's finding that the phrase 'final and complete resolution' in the Preamble meant that Consent Decree I should not be regarded as silent on the issue of liability, and stated that this phrase simply meant that the plaintiffs did not need to offer any further proof of discrimination to justify the class-wide injunctive relief.[103]

> A defendant who consents to the entry of an injunction (or other form of judgment) does not *necessarily* agree that it has committed the wrongful acts alleged in the plaintiff's complaint. Common practice is that defendants who consent to the entry of injunctive orders do so without admitting liability. ... If every consent decree constituted an admission of liability, defendants would have little incentive to settle the case.[104]

The court then rejected the lower court's finding that the phrase amounted to an admission of discrimination against individual class members, entitling them to recovery if they merely showed a disparity between their pay and that of similarly situated white employees. It held that this interpretation was 'flatly inconsistent' with the Consent Decree's provisions stating that, absent agreement, each class member must demonstrate entitlement to individual relief, and observed that

---

[100] *Id.* at 1307.
[101] *Id.* at 1308.
[102] *Id.*
[103] *Id.* at 1314.
[104] *Id.* at 1315 (citation omitted; emphasis in original).

this interpretation was also inconsistent with the explanations of plaintiffs' counsel at the fairness hearing.[105]

The court held that the entitlement of class members to individualized relief was not governed by *Pettway v. American Cast Iron Pipe Co.*[106] It stated that the question in Pettway was the extent to which findings of classwide discrimination could be taken into account in determining individual class members' claims for relief. 'Here, because the parties settled the plaintiffs' claims for prospective relief (concerning the hiring and promotion criteria the Department should use), there is no adjudication that the Department discriminated against the plaintiff classes on the basis of race in deciding whether to hire or promote.'[107] The court's discussion made clear that there was also no stipulation or admissions that class members were presumptively entitled to relief. The court held with an important caveat that, to obtain individualized relief under these circumstances, each class member must establish her or his own prima facie case of discrimination, and that this should be done by following the *McDonnell Douglas* model for the prima facie case.[108] The court continued:

> If it appears that, as a matter of policy or practice, the Department's hiring or promotion decisions were based on race, a class member may rely on such fact in countering the Department's lawful excuse for not hiring or promoting the member.[109]

---

[105] *Id.* at 1315–1316.
[106] 494 F.2d 21 1, 7 FEP Cases 11 15 (5th Cir. 1974).
[107] 202 F.3d 1303, 13 19 n. 26.
[108] *Id.* at 1319.
[109] Whether the Department followed a discriminatory policy in deciding whether to hire or promote a person is an issue that may be susceptible to resolution in a consolidated proceeding involving representative members of each of the three plaintiff classes, so that the findings of fact yielded by such proceeding would operate as collateral estoppel in the litigation of the individual class members' claims under the framework provided by McDonnell Douglas.... See *Gulf Tampa Drydock Co. v. Germanischer Lloyd*, 634 F.2d 874, 877 n. 4 (5th Cir. 1981)(stating that collateral estoppel 'would preclude a party from relitigating an issue decided against him in a prior action, even if the party asserting the estoppel was a stranger to the prior action ... unless it appears that the party against whom the estoppel is asserted [did not have] a full and fair opportunity to litigate the issue in the prior proceeding and that application of the doctrine [would] result in an injustice.').

3.7 CLASS ACTIONS SEEKING COMMON-LAW DAMAGES

Ortiz v. Fibreboard Corp.[110] reversed the approval of a Rule 23(b)(l)(B) limited-fund class damages settlement for asbestos exposure. The court distinguished between mandatory and opt-out classes for purposes of damages claims:

> The inherent tension between representative suits and the day-in-court ideal is only magnified if applied to damage claims gathered in a mandatory class. Unlike Rule 23(b)(3) class members, objectors to the collection of a mandatory (b)(l)(B) action have no inherent right to abstain. The legal rights of absent class members (which in a class like this one would include claimants who by definition may be unidentifiable when the class is certified) are resolved regardless either of their consent, or, in a class with objectors, their express wish to the contrary. And in settlement-only class actions the procedural protections built into the Rule to protect

---

We emphasize that a finding, in such consolidated proceeding, that the Department implemented a racially discriminatory policy, would not *necessarily* create an inference that a given class member was denied employment or a promotion because of race. That is, a finding that the employer has been discriminating against job applicants and employees does not, standing alone, entitle a person to relief; other facts must be present –including that the person seeking relief was qualified for the position in question – if that person is to carry the day. In *Pettway v. American Cast Iron Pipe Co.*, 494 F.2d 211 (5th Cir. 1974)(Pettway III), which we discussed above the district court found, after a full trial on the merits, that the defendant essentially froze all of its black employees in less desirable positions by using testing requirements unrelated to business necessity. See *Id.* at 217–243. The former Fifth Circuit held that those facts supported a 'reasonable inference' that an individual member was the victim of discrimination. *Id.* at 260.

In the instant case, it is undisputed that the Department hired thousands of blacks; these black employees, in fact, make up the merit and non-merit classes of employees. It is also clear that the Department promoted some members of the merit-employee class and gave some members of the non-merit employee class merit status. In light of this, there can be no inference that the Department's policies and practices injured every member of the plaintiff classes by discriminating against him or her on account of race. It is for this reason that, in litigating an individual class member's case, the establishment of the facts that give rise to a McDonnell Douglas presumption of discrimination is important.

[110] 527 U.S. 815, 846–847 (1999).

CHAPTER 3. CLASS AND REPRESENTATIVE ACTIONS

the rights of absent class members during litigation are never invoked in an adversarial setting.[111]

Amchem Products, Inc. v. Windsor,[112] stated that Rule 23 might allow class treatment for at least some mass tort cases.

Robinson v. Metro-North Commuter R. R. Co.[113] reversed the denial of class certification. The plaintiffs were black present and former employees who sought to represent a class of about 1,300 employees seeking traditional Title VII relief as well as compensatory damages. 'Specifically, they challenge Metro-North's company-wide policy of delegating to department supervisors discretionary authority to make employment decisions related to discipline and promotion. Relying on statistical and anecdotal evidence, the Class Plaintiffs argue that this delegated authority has been "exercised in a racially discriminatory manner and has a disparate impact on African American employees."'[114] The court rejected the 'incidental damages' – only approach to Rule 23(b)(2) contained in the dicta of the Fifth Circuit in *Allison v. Citgo Petroleum Corp.*,[115] and stated:

> Thus, the question we must decide is whether this bright-line bar to (b)(2) class treatment of all claims for compensatory damages and other non-incidental damages (e.g., punitive damages) is appropriate. For the reasons we discuss below, we believe that it is not and therefore decline to adopt the incidental damages approach set out by the Fifth Circuit in Allison and followed by the district court below. Rather, we hold that when presented with a motion for (b)(2) class certification of a claim seeking both injunctive relief and non-incidental monetary damages, a district court must 'consider[ ] the evidence presented at a class certification hearing and the arguments of counsel,' and then assess whether (b)(2) certification is appropriate in light of 'the relative importance of the remedies sought, given all of the facts and circumstances of the case.' . . . The district court may allow (b)(2) certification if it finds in its 'informed, sound judicial discretion' that (1) 'the positive weight or value [to the plaintiffs] of

---

[111] (Citation omitted; footnote omitted.) Chief Justice Rehnquist, joined by Justices Scalia and Kennedy, concurred. Justice Breyer, joined by Justice Stevens, dissented.
[112] *Ibid.*
[113] 267 F.3d 147, 86 FEP Cases 1580 (2nd Cir. 2001), cert. denied, 529 U.S. 1107 (2002).
[114] *Id.* at 155.
[115] 151 F.3d 402 (5th Cir. 1998), but see the opinion on denial of rehearing defining the real issues decided, 151 F.3d at 420.

the injunctive or declaratory relief sought is predominant even though compensatory or punitive damages are also claimed,'[116] and (2) class treatment would be efficient and manageable, thereby achieving an appreciable measure of judicial economy.

Although the assessment of whether injunctive or declaratory relief predominates will require an ad hoc balancing that will vary from case to case, before allowing (b)(2) certification a district court should, at a minimum, satisfy itself of the following: (1) even in the absence of a possible monetary recovery, reasonable plaintiffs would bring the suit to obtain the injunctive or declaratory relief sought; and (2) the injunctive or declaratory relief sought would be both reasonably necessary and appropriate were the plaintiffs to succeed on the merits. Insignificant or sham requests for injunctive relief should not provide cover for (b)(2) certification of claims that are brought essentially for monetary recovery.[117]

The court held that 'where non-incidental monetary relief such as compensatory damages are involved, due process may require the enhanced procedural protections of notice and opt out for absent class members.'[118] The court held that the lower court erred in failing to bifurcate the case and certify a 23(b)(2) class for purposes of liability.[119] The court explained the utility of a partial (b)(2) certification of liability issues only:

Here, litigating the pattern-or-practice liability phase for the class as a whole would both reduce the range of issues in dispute and promote judicial economy. For example, if the class should succeed and, even assuming that the remedial stage is ultimately resolved on a non-class basis, the issues and evidence relevant to these individual adjudications would be substantially narrowed:

By proving that the defendant engaged in a pattern or practice of discrimination, not only is the plaintiff class's eligibility for appropriate prospective relief established, a prima facie case with regard to the remedial phase of the suit, in which relief for individuals is considered, is also made out. Thus, the court presumes that the employer unlawfully discriminated against individual class members. In pattern or practice cases, however, the presumption shifts to the employer not only the burden of production, but also the

---

[116] Allison, 15 1 F.3d at 430 (Dennis, J., dissenting).
[117] 267 F.3d 147, 164 (citations omitted).
[118] *Id.* at 165.
[119] *Id.* at 167.

CHAPTER 3. CLASS AND REPRESENTATIVE ACTIONS

> burden of persuading the trier of fact that it is more likely than not that the employer did not unlawfully discriminate against the individual.[120]

> If, on the other hand, Metro-North succeeds at the liability stage, the question of whether it engaged in a pattern or practice of intentional discrimination that injured its African American employees would be completely and finally determined, thereby eliminating entirely the need for a remedial stage inquiry on behalf of each class member.[121]

The court rejected the district court's assumption that the focus of the liability trial would be an individual-by-individual, supervisor-by-supervisor morass:

> However, as we have discussed, the liability phase is largely preoccupied with class-wide statistical evidence directed at establishing an overall pattern or practice of intentional discrimination.[122] To the extent that evidence regarding specific instances of alleged discrimination is relevant during the liability stage, it simply provides 'texture' to the statistics. Such anecdotal evidence is not introduced to establish that the particular instances of discrimination actually occurred nor that the particular employees were in fact victims of discrimination.[123] Indeed, to ensure that the liability phase remains manageable, the district court may limit the anecdotal evidence as it deems appropriate.[124]

The court rejected the argument that partial certification would necessitate the use of separate juries in violation of the Re-Examination Clause of the Seventh Amendment:

> As one commentator has observed, avoiding this calls for sound case management, not [outright] avoidance of the procedure.... First, the court needs to carefully define the roles of the two juries so that the first jury does not decide issues within the prerogative of the second jury. Second, the court must carefully craft the verdict form for the first jury so that the second jury knows what has been decided already. If the first jury makes

---

[120] *Craik v. Minn. State Univ. Bd.*, 731 F.2d 465, 470 (8th Cir.1984)(internal citation omitted).
[121] 267 F.3d at 168.
[122] See Allison, 151 F.3d at 434 (Dennis, J., dissenting).
[123] See Price Waterhouse v. Hopkins, 490 U.S. 228, 244–245 n. 10, 109 S. Ct. 1775, 104 L. Ed. 2d 268 (1989), superseded by statute on other grounds.
[124] See Fed. R. Evid. 403. 267 F.3d 147, 168.

sufficiently detailed findings, those findings are then akin to instructions for the second jury to follow.[125]

The court held that the lower court abused its discretion by failing to certify the disparate-impact claim for class treatment under Rule 23(b)(2). It rejected the defendant's argument that Rule 23(b)(2) class certification would defeat the Seventh Amendment's Trial by Jury Clause. The court held that the right to jury trial would be preserved by trying first to a jury all issues in common between the disparate-treatment and disparate-impact claims:

> Where a legal and equitable claim in a suit share a common factual issue, trial of the equitable claim first to a judge would foreclose the later presentation of the common issue to a jury, and thereby violate the trial-by-jury guarantee. ... Thus, when as here, a pattern-or-practice claim seeking compensatory damages is pled with a disparate impact claim, the pattern-or-practice claim must be tried first to a jury if there are common factual issues necessary to the resolution of each claim.[126]

Finally, the court dealt with Metro-North's argument that the plaintiffs were inadequate class representatives because they had already settled their individual claims, while reserving their right to seek class-wide relief. The court observed that the plaintiffs would benefit from class-wide injunctive relief, and the defendant was not asserting inadequacy of representation as to such relief. The court continued:

> Metro-North's contention that the Class Plaintiffs may thereafter fail to 'vigorously' pursue the individual relief stages is both speculative and premature, and, we believe, is an insufficient basis for rejecting class certification at this juncture. Rather, the preferable course is for the district court to revisit the question of the Class Plaintiffs' 'fitness' to represent the class if and when the individual-relief stages of the claims occur. Then, if the district court deems it appropriate, it can direct that class members who are entitled to seek individual relief be named as additional class representatives.[127]

Lowery v. Circuit City Stores, Inc.,[128] affirmed the decertification of a Rule 23(b)(2) class seeking common-law damages as well as traditional Title

---

[125] Steven S. Gensler, Bifurcation Unbound, 75 Wash. L. Rev. 705, 736–737 (2000) (footnotes omitted). *Id.* at 169 n. 13.
[126] *Id.* at 170 (citation omitted).
[127] *Id.* at 171 (citations omitted).
[128] 158 F.3d 742, 758–759 (4th Cir.).

CHAPTER 3. CLASS AND REPRESENTATIVE ACTIONS

VII relief. The court expressed strong concerns with the workability and fairness of trying the claims of groups of class members before separate juries:

> Here, the district court had legitimate concerns that trying the suit as a class action would be unwieldy and unfair to Circuit City. First, the district court rightly questioned whether the Plaintiffs' proposed trial procedure would be an efficient or accelerated method of disposing of the claims. While holding two-week trials with separate juries on the class members' claims would have doubtlessly been more efficient and accelerated than bringing dozens of individual suits, that fact does not require the district court to certify a class action that would nevertheless be inefficient and cumbersome. Second, the district court had legitimate concerns about fairness. The Plaintiffs' proposed trial method would allow the Stage 1 jury to determine punitive damages before the Stage 2 jury hears evidence of actual harm to the class members or Circuit City's proffered justifications for its adverse employment decisions. It would have been entirely possible that the evidence adduced in Stage 1 would have resulted in stiff punitive damages, while the evidence of actual harm presented in Stage 2 would have shown that Circuit City's actions were not sufficient to merit compensatory damages, or even egregious enough to have merited punitive damages. We cannot conclude that such concerns led the district court to abuse its discretion in decertifying the class.

The court then rejected the plaintiffs' policy arguments against decertification:

> The Plaintiffs also argue, as do several of the amici curiae, that decertification was inappropriate because (1) the statute of limitations began running against the class members; (2) each former class member will now have to retain counsel and file a separate suit; (3) class action procedure is an important tool for the effective enforcement of civil rights laws; and (4) courts routinely certify Title VII classes under Rule 23(b)(2). Similarly, amici NAACP and the EEOC argue that Rule 23(b)(2) was intended to facilitate the bringing of class actions in civil rights cases, and that class actions are a favored means for both ending systemic discrimination and obtaining full relief for all the victims of such discrimination. Although these statements may be absolutely true, they are beside the point. If we were to hold these factors to be the predominant considerations for certifying a civil rights class, then nearly every suit alleging a pattern or practice of discrimination would be certified for class action because these factors would exist in nearly every case. However, the Supreme Court has rejected the proposition that merely alleging a pattern or

practice of discrimination automatically entitles plaintiffs to class certification.[129]

The court held that 'individuals do not have a private, non-class cause of action for pattern or practice discrimination under section 1981 or Title VII,' and reversed the lower court's finding of a pattern and practice of racial discrimination.[130] While plaintiffs may prove a pattern of discrimination in helping them prove an individual claim of discrimination under the inferential model of *McDonnell Douglas Corp. v. Green*,[131] the court held that only in a class action are persons entitled to use proof of such a pattern to shift the burden of persuasion under *International Brotherhood of Teamsters v. United States*.[132] Finally, the court reversed the parts of the injunction entered below that granted classwide relief:

> First, although the district court appropriately decertified the class action, the provisions of the injunction grant class-wide remedies. The injunction requires Circuit City to promote all persons at HQ without regard to their race, and requires Circuit City to set up a Department of Diversity Management and revise its program of promoting employees. To ensure that the provisions of the injunction are carried out, it includes labyrinthine provisions for reporting and enforcement. Many aspects of the new programs are subject to Plaintiffs' approval, for which Plaintiffs' counsel may apply quarterly for fees and expenses incurred in the monitoring and enforcement of the order. Oversight by the Plaintiffs and the district court would occur for at least five years, and possibly longer if it were deemed necessary to carry out the purposes of the injunction. Such sweeping remedies far surpass those needed – and are far more burdensome than needed – to provide the prevailing Plaintiffs with complete relief.[133]

Celestine v. Petroleos de Venezuella SA[134] affirmed the grant of summary judgment to the defendant on the plaintiffs' claims of denial of promotion and training. Although there were 206 individual plaintiffs, the court held that, in light of the earlier denial of class certification, the lower court did not abuse its discretion in barring the plaintiffs from proceeding with their claims on a pattern-and-practice basis and

---

[129] *Id.* at 759 (citations omitted).
[130] *Id.*
[131] 41 1 U.S. 792, 5 FEP Cases 965 (1973).
[132] 43 1 U.S. 324, 14 FEP Cases 15 14 (1977). 158 F.3d 742, 760–762.
[133] *Id.* at 766–767.
[134] 266 F.3d 343, 355–356, 86 FEP Cases 1462 (5th Cir. 2001).

CHAPTER 3. CLASS AND REPRESENTATIVE ACTIONS

requiring them to proceed on an individual basis under the *McDonnell Douglas* model.

Smith v. Texaco, Inc.,[135] a decision that followed and elaborated upon *Allison v. Citgo Petroleum Co.*,[136] has been withdrawn because of the settlement of all claims in the underlying action, while the matter was still pending on further review by the Circuit.[137]

Lemon v. International Union of Operating Engineers, Local No. 139[138] vacated the Rule 23(b)(2) certification of a Title VII class of minority and of female union members because plaintiffs' request for money damages was not incidental. Plaintiffs alleged that the union operated its hiring hall in a racially and sexually discriminatory manner. The court stated that a class seeking injunctive or declaratory relief is presumed to be cohesive and have homogenous interests 'such that the case will not depend on adjudication of facts particular to any subset of the class nor require a remedy that differentiates materially among class members.'[139]

The court stated that an additional claim for money damages, 'even if the plaintiffs seek uniform, class-wide equitable relief as well, jeopardizes that presumption of cohesion and homogeneity because individual claims for compensatory or punitive damages typically require judicial inquiry into the particularized merits of each individual plaintiffs claim.'[140] The court described 'incidental' damages as those that do not depend on intangible or subjective differences in class members' circumstances, and do not require additional hearings.[141] The court did not discuss the individual determinations sometimes needed to determine which class members shall receive remedial hirings, promotions, constructive seniority, or other individualized injunctive relief in response to proof of a pattern of discrimination, or the individual hearings sometimes required to determine back pay. It held that awards of damages require hearings of each individual's claim. It explained:

> Even if the plaintiffs prove that Local 139 administered the referral hall in a discriminatory manner and won injunctive and declaratory relief on that

---

[135] 263 F.3d 394, 86 FEP Cases 1619 (5th Cir. 2001).
[136] 151 F.3d 402 (5th Cir.), reh 'g denied, 151 F.3d 434 (5th Cir. 1998).
[137] *Smith v. Texaco, Inc.*, 281 F.3d 477, 88 FEP Cases 51 (5th Cir. 2002).
[138] 216 F.3d 577, 83 FEP Cases 63 (7th Cir. 2000).
[139] *Id.* at 580.
[140] *Id.*
[141] *Id.* at 581.

169

ground, each individual plaintiff pursuing damages claims still would need to establish that Local 139's discrimination caused her personal injury and would need to show the magnitude of injury to determine compensatory damages. Similarly, to win punitive damages, an individual plaintiff must establish that the defendant possessed a reckless indifference to the plaintiff's federal rights – a fact-specific inquiry into that plaintiff's circumstances.[142]

The court described the options available to the district court on remand. First, the court can consider certifying the class under Rule 23(b)(3) for all purposes, with mandatory personal notice and an opportunity to opt out. 'In this category of lawsuit, the class members may seek either predominantly legal or equitable remedies, but each member must share common questions of law or fact with the rest of the class, therefore making class-wide adjudication of the common questions efficient compared to repetitive individual litigation of the same questions.'[143] Second, the court can consider 'divided certification,' with a Rule 23(b)(2) class for equitable relief and a Rule 23(b)(3) class for damages, with notice and an opportunity to opt out. The court explained that the damages claim had to be adjudicated first before a jury 'to preserve the Seventh Amendment right to a jury trial, even if adjudication of these claims decides the equitable claims as well.'[144] Third, the court might certify the class for all purposes under Rule 23(b)(2) but 'exercise its plenary authority under Rules 23(d)(2) and 23(d)(5) to provide all class members with personal notice and opportunity to opt out, as though the class was certified under Rule 23(b)(3).'[145]

Jefferson v. Ingersoll International Inc.[146] vacated the certification under Rule 23(b)(2) of a Title VII class seeking common-law damages. The court stated that it agreed with the 'principal holding' of *Allison v. Citgo Petroleum Corp.*[147] that Rule 23(b)(2) class certification can be used

---

[142] *Id.* (citation omitted).
[143] *Id.*
[144] *Id.* at 582 (citations omitted).
[145] *Id.* (citations omitted).
[146] 195 F.3d 894, 897–899 (7th Cir.).
[147] 151 F.3d 402, 41 1–16, 81 FEP Cases 501 (5th Cir.), reh'g denied, 151 F.3d 434 (5th Cir. 1998).

CHAPTER 3. CLASS AND REPRESENTATIVE ACTIONS

in connection with claims for compensatory or punitive damages 'only when monetary relief is incidental to the equitable remedy-so tangential that the principle of *Beacon Theatres* and *Dairy Queen* does not apply, and that the due process clause does not require notice.'[148]

The court held that the interpretation of *Allison*'s statement on denial of rehearing en banc was unimportant because the subsequent decision in *Ortiz* is controlling, and it described *Ortiz* as saying, 'in no uncertain terms that class members' right to notice and an opportunity to opt out should be preserved whenever possible.'[149] The court explained that this entitlement of class members is not absolute, but that there are limits to the exceptions:

> This entitlement may be overcome only when individual suits would confound the interest of other plaintiffs – when, for example, there is a limited fund that must be distributed ratably, the domain of Rule 23(b)(1), or when an injunction affects everyone alike, the domain of Rule 23(b)(2). *Ortiz* disapproved a creative use of Rule 23(b)(1) that employed the 'limited fund' rationale to eliminate notice and opt-out rights; the Court's analysis applies equally when a request for an injunction is being used to override the rights of class members to notice and an opportunity to control their own litigation.[150]

The court described the class actions appropriate for certification under Rule 23(b)(2) as those 'all or none' cases in which there is a request for an injunction or for declaratory relief that will affect all alike,[151] and stated that in these cases the class representatives and their counsel are required to act as fiduciaries for the absent class members.[152] When common-law damages are sought, the court stated that the considerations differ:

> Money damages under 1981a(b) are neither injunctive nor declaratory, and they do not affect a class as a whole. It is possible for one applicant for employment to recover substantial damages while another recovers nothing (for example, because the second person would have been rejected under nondiscriminatory conditions, or found a better job elsewhere). Class members sensibly may decide that direct rather than vicarious

---

[148] *Id.* at 898.
[149] *Id.* at 898–899.
[150] *Id.* at 897.
[151] *Id.* at 897–898.
[152] *Id.* at 897.

representation is preferable, and they may reject the aid of self-appointed fiduciaries. Rule 23(c)(2) gives them that right.[153]

The court stated that it 'is an open question' in the Supreme Court and in the Circuit 'whether Rule 23(b)(2) *ever* may be used to certify a no-notice, no-opt-out class when compensatory or punitive damages are in issue',[154] and that the task of the court is to select the most appropriate subdivision of Rule 23, not merely to choose the earliest subdivision that is potentially applicable, and that this means that Rule 23(b)(3) should be used 'when substantial damages have been sought.'[155] The court directed the district court on remand to determine whether the common-law damages sought are more than incidental to the equitable relief. 'If the answer is yes, then the district court should either certify the class under Rule 23(b)(3) for all purposes or bifurcate the proceedings – certifying a Rule 23(b)(2) class for equitable relief and a Rule 23(b)(3) class for damages (assuming that certification under Rule 23(b)(3) otherwise is sound, a question we do not broach).'[156] The court continued:

> If, however, the district judge believes that the damages sought here are merely incidental to the equitable relief, then the judge must face and resolve the question that we have elided: whether certification of a class under Rule 23(b)(2) ever is proper when the class seeks money *damages* (as opposed to equitable monetary *relief* such as back pay). The district judge may consider following still a third course on remand: modifying or vacating the class certification now that the Equal Employment Opportunity Commission has appeared as plaintiffs' champion.[157]

The court held that the EEOC's application for leave to intervene did not moot the dispute about the use of Rule 23(b)(2), even though the EEOC is not required to follow the requirements of Rule 23 in obtaining relief for groups of victims. The court stated that the EEOC might not seek, or might not obtain, the same relief as the class; it might dismiss its action; it might settle its action on terms that leave the class members dissatisfied; and many of the class members are pursuing section 1981 claims.

---

[153] *Id.*
[154] *Id.* (emphasis in original; citations omitted).
[155] *Id.* at 898.
[156] *Id.* at 899.
[157] *Id.* (emphasis in original).

CHAPTER 3. CLASS AND REPRESENTATIVE ACTIONS

Disappointed job applicants may find that their own suit remains useful. Whether to maintain parallel litigation is their choice: the Court concluded in General Telephone that 'where the EEOC has prevailed in its action, the court may reasonably require any individual who claims under its 'judgment to relinquish his right to bring a separate private action.' ... The Court did not hold that an action by the EEOC supersedes pending private litigation or disables victims of discrimination from preferring relief under section 1981a(b) to whatever relief the Commission secures. The agency's claim is both logically and legally distinct from the private suit.[158]

3.8 OPT-OUTS FROM RULE 23 CLASS ACTIONS

Frank v. United Airlines, Inc.,[159] discussed in the preceding section, suggested that no Rule 23(b)(3) class would be bound by the result of an adverse class determination entered in a Rule 23(b)(2) class in which class members did not have the opportunity to opt out.

3.9 REPRESENTATIVE ACTIONS

Class actions under the Equal Pay Act and under the Age Discrimination in Employment Act as to all defendants except Federal agencies are not governed by Rule 23, Fed. R. Civ. P., but by 6 16(b) of the Fair Labor Standards Act,[160] which provides that persons may bring suit on behalf of themselves 'and other employees similarly situated.' The statute expressly requires that members of the putative class are not included in the suit unless they file with the court their written consent to becoming a party.

Stokes v. Westinghouse Savannah River Co.,[161] affirmed the denial of representative status on the plaintiffs ADEA claims. 'Not only can members of so small a class just as well present their own claims, there is ample evidence from which to conclude that their circumstances differed in material respects.'

---

[158] *Id.* Other related aspects of this case are discussed throughout this chapter.
[159] 216 F.3d 845, 852 (9th Cir.).
[160] 29 U.S.C. 5 216(b).
[161] 206 F.3d 420, 431 (4th Cir.).

Lang v. Kohl's Food Stores, Inc.,[162] affirmed the judgment on a jury verdict for the Equal Pay Act collective-action defendant. The plaintiffs were female bakery and deli clerks, who were classified as department clerks in the collectively bargained pay scale and claimed that they should be paid the same as produce clerks, most of whom were male, who were classified as regular clerks in the CBA pay scale. The decision presented an 'outlier' situation that was decided pursuant to the court's construction of the Equal Pay act, but some of the court's reasoning rested on the nature of the case as a representative action. In holding that the trial court did not abuse its discretion in requiring the parties to focus their proof on the duties of the jobs at issue in median stores, and thus preventing both sides from comparing the duties of one job at smaller stores to the duties of the other job at larger stores, the court stated:

> To get anywhere, plaintiffs had to make a categorical comparison between 'department clerk' positions and 'regular clerk' positions. Class treatment is appropriate only if there are common issues of fact – that is, only if it is possible to compare all 'department clerk' positions in bakery and deli departments with all 'regular clerk' positions in produce departments. The district court's outlier ruling ensured that the premise of class certification (granted at plaintiffs' behest) would not be subverted. It was not an abuse of discretion.[163]

Thiessen v. General Electric Capital Corp[164] reversed the decertification of the ADEA collective action. Preliminarily, the court held that the lower court properly adopted the ad hoc, case-by-case approach to determining whether the plaintiffs and opt-in plaintiffs were similarly situated, instead of attempting to import the standards of Rule 23 into 29 U.S.C. § 216(b).[165] The court held that the lower court's failure to focus on the fact that plaintiffs were challenging an alleged pattern and practice of discrimination 'adversely impacted its "similarly situated" analysis and resulted in an abuse of discretion.'[166]

---

[162] 217 F.3d 919, 924–925 (7th Cir.).
[163] *Id.* at 925.
[164] 267 F.3d 1095 (10th Cir. 2001), cert. denied, _____U.S._____, 122 S. Ct. 2614, 153 L. Ed. 2d 799 (2002).
[165] *Id.* at 1105.
[166] *Id.*

CHAPTER 3. CLASS AND REPRESENTATIVE ACTIONS

Pattern-or-practice cases differ significantly from the far more common cases involving one or more claims of individualized discrimination. In a case involving individual claims of discrimination, the focus is on the reason(s) for the particular employment decisions at issue. ... In contrast, the initial focus in a pattern-or-practice case is not on individual employment decisions, 'but on a pattern of discriminatory decision-making.'[167] Thus, the order and allocation of proof, as well as the overall nature of the trial proceedings, in a pattern-or-practice case differ dramatically from a case involving only individual claims of discrimination.[168]

The court emphasized the benefit, to individual class members in Stage I proceedings, of the presumption of discrimination that arises from the finding of a pattern of discrimination in Stage I.

Given the pattern-or-practice nature of plaintiffs' claim, this factor necessarily encompasses factual issues relevant to both the first and second stages of trial, e.g., whether the blocker policy continued after Lanik's alleged repudiation and, if it did, whether a link existed between that policy and the individual employment decisions affecting the named plaintiffs. The problem is that the district court effectively made findings regarding these issues in the guise of determining whether plaintiffs were 'similarly situated.' ... By doing so, the district court essentially deprived plaintiffs of their right to have the issues decided by a jury, or to at least have the court determine, under summary judgment standards, whether there was sufficient evidence to send the issue to the jury. Further, the district court failed to take into account the fact that, if plaintiffs were able to establish a pattern or practice of discrimination, they would be entitled to a presumption that the individual employment actions taken against them were the result of such discrimination. Indeed, the district court effectively deprived plaintiffs of this procedural advantage as well.[169]

The court held that the lower court's determinations were flawed by failing to take into account the pattern-and-practice nature of the case.

Although it is true that defendants asserted 'highly individualized' defenses to each of the instances of individual discrimination asserted by plaintiffs, those defenses would not become the focal point until the second stage of trial and could be dealt with in a series of individual trials, if necessary. With respect to the first stage of trial and the initial issues of whether they had in place a pattern or practice of discrimination and

---

[167] *Id.*
[168] *Id.* at 1106 (citations omitted).
[169] *Id.* at 1106–1107.

whether it continued after the fall of 1994, defendants had only a few common defenses.[170]

The court explained:

> Thus, the presence of the 'highly individualized' defenses clearly did not, as the district court concluded, outweigh 'any potential benefits in proceeding as a collective action.' As previously noted, there was a significant procedural advantage for plaintiffs to proceed in a collective action: if they prevailed in the first stage of trial, they would be entitled to a presumption of discrimination in subsequent proceedings to decide the merits of their individual claims. By bowing to the individualized defenses relevant only to the second stage of trial, the district court deprived plaintiffs of this opportunity.
>
> The district court's consideration of the third factor (trial management concerns) was also adversely affected by its failure to recognize the pattern-or-practice nature of plaintiffs' claim. Most notably, the district court failed to acknowledge that plaintiffs' proposed trial plan, though perhaps deficient in some respects, was consistent with the framework outlined in *Teamsters* for pattern-or-practice claims. The court also failed to make any effort to modify the plaintiffs' proposed trial plan. Finally, the district court was wrong in concluding that trying the case in two phases, as suggested by plaintiffs, 'render[ed] individualized consideration of the claims impossible.'[171]

The court concluded that, because of the pattern-and-practice nature of plaintiffs' case, the 'plaintiffs were, in fact, "similarly situated" for purposes of § 216(b).'[172]

3.10 RULE 23(F) APPEALS OF DECISIONS GRANTING OR DENYING CLASS CERTIFICATION

On December 1, 1998, new Rule 23(f) went into effect. It provides that:

> A court of appeals may in its discretion permit an appeal from an order of a district court granting or denying class action certification under this rule if application is made to it within ten days after entry of the order. An

---

[170] *Id.* at 1107.
[171] *Id.*
[172] *Id.* at 1107–1108.

CHAPTER 3. CLASS AND REPRESENTATIVE ACTIONS

appeal does not stay proceedings in the district court unless the district judge or the court of appeals so orders.

One of the issues to be resolved in litigation is whether this provision allows the courts of appeals to exercise jurisdiction over rulings other than the Rule 23 decision itself, to the extent that the correctness of those rulings affects the propriety of the Rule 23 decision. The issue takes on added importance where the district court has denied a permissive appeal of those rulings under 28 U.S.C. § 1292(b).

Jefferson v. Ingersoll International Inc.[173] granted leave to appeal the certification of a Title VII class under Rule 23(b)(2) where the class was seeking common-law damages. The court held that this situation fits within its third category of permissible interlocutory appeals under Rule 23(f), 'situations in which the legal question is important, unresolved, and has managed to escape resolution by appeals from final judgments.' It explained: 'Both sides cite a welter of district court decisions (many in this circuit) addressing the subject, but none has reached this court since the Civil Rights Act of 1991, and only one has reached another court of appeals.' It then decided the case on the basis of the petition and the response, vacated the class certification and remanded the case to the district court for further action. 'We have seen enough to how that the district court must confront rather than dodge the fundamental legal question.'[174] Other related aspects of this case are discussed throughout this chapter.

Blair v. Equifax Check Services, Inc.[175] affirmed the certification of a class action under the Fair Debt Collection Practices Act. The court described three circumstances under which a court of appeals should exercise its discretion to allow a Rule 23(f) appeal from the grant or denial of class certification. The first involves the 'death knell' situation – 'though we must be wary lest the mind hear a bell that is not tolling' – in which the denial of certification may doom the action. The court stated that some small putative class actions continue as individual actions after the denial of class certification, and appeal the denial at the end of the case. 'But when denial of class status seems likely to be fatal, and when the plaintiff has a solid argument in opposition to the district court's decision, then a favorable exercise of appellate discretion is

---

[173] 195 F.3d 894, 896–897 (7th Cir.).
[174] *Id.*
[175] 181 F.3d 832, 834–835 (7th Cir. 1999).

indicated.'[176] The second situation arises when the plaintiff has a very weak case but the grant of class status puts 'considerable pressure on the defendant to settle.'[177] The court observed that '[m]any corporate executives are unwilling to bet their company that they are in the right in big-stakes litigation, and a grant of class status can propel the stakes of a case into the stratosphere.'[178] The court observed that some plaintiffs and judges are willing to use class actions as a device to wring settlements from defendants with justified but unpopular legal positions, and that some courts have remade substantive doctrine in order to make the class actions more manageable.[179] The court continued:

> So, in a mirror image of the death-knell situation, when the stakes are large and the risk of a settlement or other disposition that does not reflect the merits of the claim is substantial, an appeal under Rule 23(f) is in order. Again the appellant must demonstrate that the district court's ruling on class certification is questionable – and must do this taking into account the discretion the district judge possesses in implementing Rule 23, and the correspondingly deferential standard of appellate review. However dramatic the effect of the grant or denial of class status in undercutting the plaintiffs claim or inducing the defendant to capitulate, if the ruling is impervious to revision there's no point to an interlocutory appeal.[180]

The court stated that the third and final situation is when an appeal may help the development of the law. In this category, it is not so important that the district judge may have made a mistake. 'Some questions have not received appellate treatment because they are trivial; these are poor candidates for the use of Rule 23(f). But the more fundamental the question and the greater the likelihood that it will escape effective disposition at the end of the case, the more appropriate is an appeal under Rule 23(f).'[181] The court stated that stays would be infrequent, so the allowance of interlocutory appeals under Rule 23(f) should not delay the underlying cases too much.[182] The court held that the ten-day period for filing a Rule 23(f) application runs from the denial of a timely

---

[176] *Id.* at 834.
[177] *Id.*
[178] *Id.*
[179] *Id.*
[180] *Id.* at 835.
[181] *Id.*
[182] *Id.*

motion for reconsideration as well as from the entry of the underlying order.[183]

3.11 APPEALABILITY OF CLASS DETERMINATION

Carter v. West Publishing Co.[184] reversed the grant of Title VII class certification, holding that the lower court's determination of standing was a necessary part of the class certification analysis and was therefore subject to review under Rule 23(f) as well. Because no class plaintiff filed a timely EEOC charge, and because neither the continuing violation nor the equitable tolling theory applied, no class plaintiff had standing to pursue the class claims.[185]

3.12 JUDICIAL APPROVAL OF CLASS SETTLEMENTS

Devlin v. Scardelletti[186] held that a nonplaintiff class member who objected to a proposed class settlement could appeal from the grant of final approval without first having to intervene. The court stated that it had never restricted the right to appeal to named parties, where the appellant was bound by the order in question. The right of an objector to appeal from final approval of a class settlement, however, is limited to appealing the lower court's rejection of the appellant's objections.

In Re: Vitamins Antitrust Class Actions[187] affirmed the denial of intervention to nonsettling class members who opted out of the class while their appeal was pending. The settlement agreement contained a 'most favored nations' clause that required the settling defendants to match, as to the settling class, any more favorable relief they provided in a subsequent settlement to a plaintiff who was not part of the class settlement. The nonsettling class members were denied intervention but allowed to participate as amici curiae. The court held that opt-outs do not have standing to challenge a Rule 23(b)(3) settlement

---

[183] *Id.* at 837.
[184] 225 F.3d 1258, 1262–1263, 83 FEP Cases 1523 (11th Cir. 2000).
[185] *Id.* at 1263–1266.
[186] ____ U.S. ____, 122 S. Ct. 2005 (2002).
[187] 215 F.3d 26 (D.C. Cir. 2000).

because they have preserved their full legal rights by opting out.[188] 'As opt-out plaintiffs they have no interest in the specifics of the settlement except for their desire to be free of a troublesome MFN clause.'[189] The court observed that their interest was not congruent with the interests that Rule 23 requires the court to address. Even the district court's power to ensure that a settlement is fair, adequate and reasonable does not convey a general power to evaluate the effect of the settlement on the public interest. 'But the district court's duty is to the class members themselves; it lacks the power to conduct a free-ranging analysis as to the broader implications of the proposed settlement agreement.'[190] The court rejected the appellants' argument that the MFN clause did not serve the interests of class members, and that something of greater value to class members must have been traded away because there was no evidence that the defendants resisted the clause. 'In fact the defendants may well not have much resisted, affirmatively liking a Ulysses-tied-to-the-mast arrangement that enables them to convincingly stiff opt-outs who demand more. ... In any event, appellants do not deny that their sole actual concern is that the MFN clause limits their ability to reach a settlement more lucrative than that offered to the class. Consequently, their arguments fall outside of the zone of interests protected by Rule 23(e).'[191] The court held that the right to opt out did not carry with it the 'right to be free of ancillary effects flowing from a class settlement.'[192] The court stated that the Due Process Clause allows nonparties to challenge settlement agreements if the agreement causes them 'plain legal prejudice' or 'strips the party of a legal claim or cause of action,' but the MFN clause did not have such an effect because the appellants preserved their right to litigate their claims independently.[193] The court stated that there is uncertainty over whether standing is necessary for permissive intervention, but that there was no right to take an appeal from such a denial in itself, and relied on the uncertainty of the standing question in deciding not to exercise pendent appellate jurisdiction over the question whether the lower

---

[188] *Id.* at 28–29.
[189] *Id.* at 29.
[190] *Id.* at 30.
[191] *Id.*
[192] *Id.*
[193] *Id.* at 31 (citations omitted).

court abused its discretion in denying permissive intervention but according appellants status as amici.[194]

Frank v. United Airlines, Inc.,[195] discussed above, held that the absence of a fairness hearing for the post-judgment settlement of an earlier case meant that it was never examined by a judge for fairness to the class; and could not bind the class in the later case. 'We are simply not allowed to give preclusive effect to a post-judgment settlement that was never subjected to the scrutiny contemplated by Rule 23(e) and never entered as a judgment.'

3.13 CONCLUSIVENESS OF CLASS SETTLEMENTS, DECREES, AND DECISIONS ON THE MERITS

Munoz v. Orr[196] affirmed the grant of summary judgment to the Title VII class action defendant, and held that no individual claims would have survived summary judgment. The court stated that 'the only possible individual claims would be those appearing in the complaint, i.e., those of Jesus and Manuel Mufioz, Jr.'[197] These individual claims were properly before the court of appeals because the defendant's last motion for summary judgment had successfully requested dismissal of the Complaint as a whole, not just of the class claims, and this put plaintiffs on notice that their individual claims were also at stake. The court held that individual disparate-impact claims could not have survived summary judgment because such claims would have been duplicative of the class claims and because they would have been predicated on the same statistical evidence found inadequate for class purposes.[198] The court held that the individual disparate-treatment claims pleaded or set forth in the plaintiffs' affidavits failed, because all of the promotion denials arose from the Merit Promotion Plan, including its automated component. 'Plaintiffs would have to show, therefore, either that there is a genuine issue as to whether the promotion plan indicates intentional discrimination or that the promotions denied them were somehow capable of being isolated from the

---

[194] *Id.* at 31–32.
[195] 216 F.3d 845, 852 (9th Cir.).
[196] 200 F.3d 291, 305–307 (5th Cir.).
[197] *Id.* at 306.
[198] *Id.*

promotion system and that purposeful discrimination was behind those employment actions.'[199] The court held, however, that there was no allegation or evidence of purposeful discrimination. Citing *Cooper v. Federal Reserve Bank of Richmond*,[200] the court continued: 'We note that the failure of proof on the class claim does not bar all individual class members from bringing their own suits, provided that they do not base their claims solely on issues already adjudicated in this action and that they can show individualized proof of discrimination.'[201]

3.14 CHANGES IN THE CLASS ACTION RULES

On September 24, 2002, the United States Judicial Conference recommended that the Supreme Court approve revisions to Rule 23 that are discussed below. These rules took effect on December 1, 2003, with the changes noted at the end of this discussion of the rules as proposed.[202]

Rule 23. Class Actions

3.14 (a) Determining by Order Whether to Certify a Class Action; Appointing Class Counsel; Notice and Membership in Class; Judgment; Multiple Classes and Subclasses.

3.14 (a)(1)(a) When a person sues or is sued as a representative of a class, the court must – at an early practicable time – determine by order whether to certify the action as a class action.

3.14 (a)(1)(b) An order certifying a class action must define the class and the class claims, issues, or defenses, and must appoint class counsel under Rule 23(g).

3.14 (a)(1)(c) An order under Rule 23(c)(l) may be altered or amended before final judgment.

3.14 (a)(2)(a) For any class certified under Rule 23(b)(l) or (2), the court may direct appropriate notice to the class.

---

[199] *Id.* at 307.
[200] 467 U.S. 867, 880, 35 FEP Cases 1 (1984).
[201] *Id.* (citation omitted).
[202] Important further explanatory materials can be found in the explanatory Recommendation of the Advisory Committee, at 123–132 of its Report, and in the Summary of Comments and Testimony beginning at 133.

CHAPTER 3. CLASS AND REPRESENTATIVE ACTIONS

3.14 (a)(2)(b) For any class certified under Rule 23(b)(3), the court must direct to class members – the best notice practicable under the circumstances, including individual notice to all members who can be identified through reasonable effort. The notice must concisely and clearly state in plain, easily understood language:

- the nature of the action;
- the definition of the class certified;
- the class claims, issues, or defenses;
- that a class member may enter an appearance through counsel if the member so desires;
- that the court will exclude from the class any member who requests exclusion, stating when and how members may elect to be excluded; and
- the binding effect of a class judgment on class members under Rule 23(c)(3).

3.14 (a)(3) The judgment in an action maintained as a class action under subdivision (b)(l) or (b)(2), whether or not favorable to the class, shall include and describe those whom the court finds to be members of the class. The judgment in an action maintained as a class action under subdivision (b)(3), whether or not favorable to the class, shall include and specify or describe those to whom the notice provided in subdivision (c)(2) was directed, and who have not requested exclusion, and whom the court finds to be members of the class.

3.14 (a)(4) When appropriate (a) an action may be brought or maintained as a class action with respect to particular issues, or (b) a class may be divided into subclasses and each subclass treated as a class, and the provisions of this rule shall then be construed and applied accordingly.

3.14 (b) Notes from the Revision Committee

Subdivision (c). Subdivision (c) is amended in several respects. The requirement that the court determine whether to certify a class 'as soon as practicable after commencement of an action' is replaced by requiring determination 'at an early practicable time.' The notice provisions are substantially revised.

Paragraph (1). Subdivision (c)(l)(A) is changed to require that the determination whether to certify a class be made 'at an early practicable time.' The 'as soon as practicable' exaction neither reflects prevailing practice nor captures the many valid reasons that may justify deferring the initial certification decision.[203]

Time may be needed to gather information necessary to make the certification decision. Although an evaluation of the probable outcome on the merits is not properly part of the certification decision, discovery in aid of the certification decision often includes information required to identify the nature of the issues that actually will be presented at trial. In this sense, it is appropriate to conduct controlled discovery into the 'merits,' limited to those aspects relevant to making the certification decision on an informed basis. Active judicial supervision may be required to achieve the most effective balance that expedites an informed certification determination without forcing an artificial and ultimately wasteful division between 'certification discovery' and 'merits discovery.' A critical need is to determine how the case will be tried. An increasing number of courts require a party requesting class certification to present a 'trial plan' that describes the issues likely to be presented at trial and tests whether they are susceptible of class-wide proof.[204]

Other considerations may affect the timing of the certification decision. The party opposing the class may prefer to win dismissal or summary judgment as to the individual plaintiffs without certification and without binding the class that might have been certified. Time may be needed to explore designation of class counsel under Rule 23(g), recognizing that in many cases the need to progress toward the certification determination may require designation of interim counsel under Rule 23(g)(2)(A).

Although many circumstances may justify deferring the certification decision, active management may be necessary to ensure that the certification decision is not unjustifiably delayed.

Subdivision (c)(1)(C) reflects two amendments. The provision that a class certification 'may be conditional' is deleted. A court that is not satisfied that the requirements of Rule 23 have been met should refuse certification until they have been met. The provision that permits alteration or amendment of an order granting or denying class certification is amended to set the cut-off point at final judgment rather than 'the decision on the merits.' This change avoids the possible ambiguity in

---

[203] See Willging, Hooper, and Niemic, Empirical Study of Class Actions in Four Federal District Courts: Final Report to the Advisory Committee on Civil Rules 26–36 (Federal Judicial Center 1996).

[204] See Manual For Complex Litigation Third, § 21.213, 44; § 30.11, 214; § 30.12, 215.

CHAPTER 3. CLASS AND REPRESENTATIVE ACTIONS

referring to 'the decision on the merits.' Following a determination of liability, for example, proceedings to define the remedy may demonstrate the need to amend the class definition or subdivide the class. In this setting, the final judgment concept is pragmatic. It is not the same as the concept used for appeal purposes, but it should be flexible, particularly in protracted litigation.

The authority to amend an order under Rule 23(c)(l) before final judgment does not restore the practice of 'one-way intervention' that was rejected by the 1966 revision of Rule 23. A determination of liability after certification, however, may show a need to amend the class definition. Decertification may be warranted after further proceedings.

If the definition of a class certified under Rule 23(b)(3) is altered to include member who have not been afforded notice and an opportunity to request exclusion, notice-including an opportunity to request exclusion-must be directed to the new class members under Rule 23(c)(2)(B).

Paragraph (2). The first change made in Rule 23(c)(2) is to call attention to the court's authority – already established in part by Rule 23(d)(2) to direct notice of certification to a Rule 23(b)(1) or (b)(2) class. The present rule expressly requires notice only in actions certified under Rule 23(b)(3). Members of classes certified under Rules 23(b)(1) or (b)(2) have interests that may deserve protection by notice.

The authority to direct notice to class members in a (b)(1) or (b)(2) class action should be exercised with care. For several reasons, there may be less need for notice than in a (b)(3) class action. There is no right to request exclusion from a (b)(1) or (b)(2) class. The characteristics of the class may reduce the need for formal notice. The cost of providing notice, moreover, could easily cripple actions that do not seek damages. The court may decide not to direct notice after balancing the risk that notice costs may deter the pursuit of class relief against the benefits of notice.

When the court does direct certification notice in a (b)(1) or (b)(2) class action, the discretion and flexibility established by subdivision (c)(2)(A) extend to the method of giving notice. Notice facilitates the opportunity to participate. Notice calculated to reach a significant number of class members often will protect the interests of all. Informal methods may prove effective. A simple posting in a place visited by many class members, directing attention to a source of more detailed information, may suffice. The court should consider the costs of notice in relation to the probable reach of inexpensive methods.

If a Rule 23(b)(3) class is certified in conjunction with a (b)(2) class, the (c)(2)(B) notice requirements must be satisfied as to the (b)(3) class.

The direction that class-certification notice be couched in plain, easily understood language is a reminder of the need to work unremittingly at the difficult task of communicating with class members. It is difficult to provide information about most class actions that is both accurate and easily understood by class members who are not themselves lawyers. Factual uncertainty, legal complexity, and the complication of class-action procedure raise the banners high. The Federal Judicial Center has created illustrative clear-notice forms that provide a helpful starting point for actions similar to those described in the forms.

3.14 (c) Rule 23(e) Class Actions: Settlement, Voluntary Dismissal, or Compromise.

3.14 (c)(1)(a) The court must approve any settlement, voluntary dismissal, or compromise of the claims, issues, or defenses of a certified class.

(b) The court must direct notice in a reasonable manner to all class members who would be bound by a proposed settlement, voluntary dismissal, or compromise.

3.14 (c)(1)(c) The court may approve a settlement, voluntary dismissal, or compromise that would bind class members only after a hearing and on finding that the settlement, voluntary dismissal, or compromise is fair, reasonable, and adequate.

3.14 (c)(2) The parties seeking approval of a settlement, voluntary dismissal, or compromise under Rule 23(e)(1) must file a statement identifying any agreement made in connection with the proposed settlement, voluntary dismissal, or compromise.

3.14 (c)(3) In an action previously certified as a class action under Rule 23(b)(3), the court may refuse to approve a settlement unless it affords a new opportunity to request exclusion to individual class members who had an earlier opportunity to request exclusion but did not do so.

3.14 (c)(4)(a) Any class member may object to a proposed settlement, voluntary dismissal, or compromise that requires court approval under Rule 23(e)(1)(A).

3.14 (c)(4)(b) An objection made under Rule 23(e)(4)(A) may be withdrawn only with the court's approval.

3.14 (d) Committee Notes on Settlement Subdivision (e). Subdivision (e) is amended to strengthen the process of reviewing proposed class-action settlements. Settlement may be a desirable means of resolving a class action. However, court review and approval are essential to assure adequate representation of class members who have not participated in shaping the settlement.

CHAPTER 3. CLASS AND REPRESENTATIVE ACTIONS

Paragraph (1). Subdivision (e)(1)(A) expressly recognizes the power of a class representative to settle class claims, issues, or defenses.

Rule 23(e)(l)(A) resolves the ambiguity in former Rule 23(e)'s reference to dismissal or compromise of 'a class action.' That language could be – and at times was – read to require court approval of settlements with putative class representatives that resolved only individual claims.[205] The new rule requires approval only if the claims, issues, or defenses of a certified class are resolved by a settlement, voluntary dismissal, or compromise.

Subdivision (e)(1)(B) carries forward the notice requirement of present Rule 23(e) when the settlement binds the class through claim or issue preclusion; notice is not required when the settlement binds only the individual class representatives. Notice of a settlement binding on the class is required either when the settlement follows class certification or when the decisions on certification and settlement proceed simultaneously.

Reasonable settlement notice may require individual notice in the manner required by Rule 23(c)(2)(B) for certification notice to a Rule 23(b)(3) class. Individual notice is appropriate, for example, if class members are required to take action – such as filing claims – to participate in the judgment, or if the court orders a settlement opt-out opportunity under Rule 23(e)(3).

Subdivision (e)(1)(C) confirms and mandates the already common practice of holding hearings as part of the process of approving settlement, voluntary dismissal, or compromise that would bind members of a class. Subdivision (e)(1)(C) states the standard for approving a proposed settlement that would bind class members. The settlement must be fair, reasonable, and adequate.[206]

Further guidance can be found in the Manual for Complex Litigation. The court must make findings that support the conclusion that the settlement is fair, reasonable, and adequate. The findings must be set out in sufficient detail to explain to class members and the appellate court the factors that bear on applying the standard.

Settlement review also may provide an occasion to review the cogency of the initial class definition. The terms of the settlement

---

[205] See Manual for Complex Litigation Third, § 30.41.

[206] A helpful review of many factors that may deserve consideration is provided by In re: Prudential Ins. Co. America Sales Practice Litigation Agent Actions, 148 F.3d 283, 316–324 (3rd Cir. 1998).

themselves, or objections, may reveal divergent interests of class members and demonstrate the need to redefine the class or to designate subclasses. Redefinition of a class certified under Rule 23(b)(3) may require notice to new class members under Rule 23(c)(2)(B).[207]

Paragraph (2). Subdivision (e)(2) requires parties seeking approval of a settlement, voluntary dismissal, or compromise under Rule 23(e)(1) to file a statement identifying any agreement made in connection with the settlement. This provision does not change the basic requirement that the parties disclose all terms of the settlement or compromise that the court must approve under Rule 23(e)(1). It aims instead at related undertakings that, although seemingly separate, may have influenced the terms of the settlement by trading away possible advantages for the class in return for advantages for others. Doubts should be resolved in favor of identification.

Further inquiry into the agreements identified by the parties should not become the occasion for discovery by the parties or objectors. The court may direct the parties to provide to the court or other parties a summary or copy of the full terms of any agreement identified by the parties. The court also may direct the parties to provide a summary or copy of any agreement not identified by the parties that the court considers relevant to its review of a proposed settlement. In exercising discretion under this rule, the court may act in steps, calling first for a summary of any agreement that may have affected the settlement and then for a complete version if the summary does not provide an adequate basis for review. A direction to disclose a summary or copy of an agreement may raise concerns of confidentiality. Some agreements may include information that merits protection against general disclosure, and the court must provide an opportunity to claim work-product or other protections.

Paragraph (3). Subdivision (e)(3) authorizes the court to refuse to approve a settlement unless the settlement affords class members a new opportunity to request exclusion from a class certified under Rule 23(b)(3) after settlement terms are known. An agreement by the parties themselves to permit class members to elect exclusion at this point by the settlement agreement may be one factor supporting approval of the settlement. Often there is an opportunity to opt out at this point because the class is certified and settlement is reached in circumstances that lead to simultaneous notice of certification and notice of settlement. In these cases, the basic opportunity to elect exclusion applies without further

---

[207] See Rule 23(c)(1)(C).

CHAPTER 3. CLASS AND REPRESENTATIVE ACTIONS

complication. In some cases, particularly if settlement appears imminent at the time of certification, it may be possible to achieve equivalent protection by deferring notice and the opportunity to elect exclusion until actual settlement terms are known. This approach avoids the cost and potential confusion of providing two notices and makes the single notice more meaningful. However, notice should not be delayed unduly after certification in the hope of settlement.

Rule 23(e)(3) authorizes the court to refuse to approve a settlement unless the settlement affords a new opportunity to elect exclusion in a case that settles after a certification decision if the earlier opportunity to elect exclusion provided with the certification notice has expired by the time of the settlement notice. A decision to remain in the class is likely to be more carefully considered and is better informed when settlement terms are known.

The opportunity to request exclusion from a proposed settlement is limited to members of a (b)(3) class. Exclusion may be requested only by individual class members; no class member may purport to opt out other class members by way of another class action.

The decision whether to approve a settlement that does not allow a new opportunity to elect exclusion is confided to the court's discretion. The court may make this decision before directing notice to the class under Rule 23(e)(l)(B) or after the Rule 23(e)(l)(C) hearing. Many factors may influence the court's decision. Among these are changes in the information available to class members since expiration of the first opportunity to request exclusion, and the nature of the individual class members' claims.

The terms set for permitting a new opportunity to elect exclusion from the proposed settlement of a Rule 23(b)(3) class action may address concerns of potential misuse. The court might direct, for example, that class members who elect exclusion are bound by rulings on the merits made before the settlement was proposed for approval. Still, other terms or conditions may be appropriate.

Paragraph (4). Subdivision (e)(4) confirms the right of class members to object to a proposed settlement, voluntary dismissal, or compromise. The right is defined in relation to a disposition that, because it would bind the class, requires court approval under subdivision (e)(1)(C).

Subdivision (e)(4)(B) requires court approval for withdrawal of objections made under subdivision (e)(4)(A). Review follows automatically if the objections are withdrawn on terms that lead to modification of the settlement with the class. Review also is required if the objector formally withdraws the objections. If the objector simply abandons pursuit of the objection, the court may inquire into the circumstances.

Approval under paragraph (4)(B) may be given or denied with little need for further inquiry if the objection and the disposition go only to a protest that the individual treatment afforded the objector under the proposed settlement is unfair because of factors that distinguish the objector from other class members. Different considerations may apply if the objector has protested that the proposed settlement is not fair, reasonable, or adequate on grounds that apply generally to a class or subclass. Such objections, which purport to represent class-wide interests, may augment the opportunity for obstruction or delay. If such objections are surrendered on terms that do not affect the class settlement or the objector's participation in the class settlement, the court often can approve withdrawal of the objections without elaborate inquiry.

Once an objector appeals, control of the proceeding lies in the court of appeals. The court of appeals may undertake review and approval of a settlement with the objector, perhaps as part of appeal settlement procedures, or may remand to the district court to take advantage of the district court's familiarity with the action and settlement.

3.14 (e) Rule 23 Class Actions: Class Counsel.

3.14 (e)(1) Appointing Class Counsel.

3.14 (d)(1)(a) Unless a statute provides otherwise, a court that certifies a class must appoint class counsel.

3.14 (e)(1)(b) An attorney appointed to serve as class counsel must fairly and adequately represent the interests of the class.

3.14 (e)(1)(C) In appointing class counsel, the court
(i) must consider:

- the work counsel has done in identifying or investigating potential claims in the action;
- counsel's experience in handling class actions, other complex litigation, and claims of the type asserted in the action;
- counsel's knowledge of the applicable law; and
- the resources counsel will commit to representing the class;

(ii) may consider any other matter pertinent to counsel's ability to fairly and adequately represent the interests of the class;

(iii) may direct potential class counsel to provide information on any subject pertinent to the appointment and to propose terms for attorney fees and nontaxable costs; and

CHAPTER 3. CLASS AND REPRESENTATIVE ACTIONS

(iv) may make further orders in connection with the appointment.

3.14 (e)(2) Appointment Procedure.

3.14 (e)(2)(a) The court may designate interim counsel to act on behalf of the putative class before determining whether to certify the action as a class action.

3.14 (e)(2)(b) When there is one applicant for appointment as class counsel, the court may appoint that applicant only if the applicant is adequate under Rule 23(g)(1)(B) and (C).

If more than one adequate applicant seeks appointment as class counsel, the court must appoint the applicant best able to represent the interests of the class.

3.14 (e)(2)(c) The order appointing class counsel may include provisions about the award of attorney fees or nontaxable costs under Rule 23(h).

3.14 (f) Committee Notes on Appointment of Counsel.

Subdivision (g). Subdivision (g) is new. It responds to the reality that the selection and activity of class counsel are often critically important to the successful handling of a class action. Until now, courts have scrutinized proposed class counsel as well as the class representative – under Rule 23(a)(4). This experience has recognized the importance of judicial evaluation of the proposed lawyer for the class, and this new subdivision builds on that experience rather than introducing an entirely new element into the class certification process. Rule 23(a)(4) will continue to call for scrutiny of the proposed class representative, while this subdivision will guide the court in assessing proposed class counsel as part of the certification decision. This subdivision recognizes the importance of class counsel, states the obligation to represent the interests of the class, and provides a framework for selection of class counsel. The procedure and standards for appointment vary depending on whether there are multiple applicants to be class counsel. The new subdivision also provides a method by which the court may make directions from the outset about the potential fee award to class counsel in the event the action is successful.

Paragraph (I) sets out the basic requirement that class counsel be appointed if a class is certified and articulates the obligation of class counsel to represent the interests of the class, as opposed to the potentially conflicting interests of individual class members. It also sets out the factors the court should consider in assessing proposed class counsel.

Paragraph (1)(A) requires that the court appoint class counsel to represent the class. Class counsel must be appointed for all classes, including each subclass that the court certifies to represent divergent interests.

Paragraph (1)(A) does not apply if 'a statute provides otherwise.' This recognizes that provisions of the Private Securities Litigation Reform Act of 1995,[208] contain directives that bear on selection of a lead plaintiff and the retention of counsel. This subdivision does not purport to supersede or to affect the interpretation of those provisions, or any similar provisions of other legislation.

Paragraph 1(B) recognizes that the primary responsibility of class counsel, resulting from appointment as class counsel, is to represent the best interests of the class. The rule thus establishes the obligation of class counsel, an obligation that may be different from the customary obligations of counsel to individual clients. Appointment as class counsel means that the primary obligation of counsel is to the class rather than to any individual members of it. The class representatives do not have an unfettered right to 'fire' class counsel. In the same vein, the class representatives cannot command class counsel to accept or reject a settlement proposal. To the contrary, class counsel must determine whether seeking the court's approval of a settlement would be in the best interests of the class as a whole.

Paragraph (1)(C) articulates the basic responsibility of the court to appoint class counsel who will provide the adequate representation called for by paragraph (l)(B). It identifies criteria that must be considered and invites the court to consider any other pertinent matters. Although couched in terms of the court's duty, the listing also informs counsel-seeking appointment about the topics that should be addressed in an application for appointment or in the motion for class certification. The court may direct potential class counsel to provide additional information about the topics mentioned in paragraph (1)(C) or about any other relevant topic. For example, the court may direct applicants to inform the court concerning any agreements about a prospective award of attorney fees or nontaxable costs, as such agreements may sometimes be significant in the selection of class counsel. The court might also direct that potential class counsel indicate how parallel litigation might be coordinated or consolidated with the action before the court.

The court may also direct counsel to propose terms for a potential award of attorney fees and nontaxable costs. Attorney fee awards are an

---

[208] Pub. L. No. 104-67, 109 Stat. 737 (1995)(codified in various sections of 15 U.S.C.).

CHAPTER 3. CLASS AND REPRESENTATIVE ACTIONS

important feature of class action practice, and attention to this subject from the outset may often be a productive technique. Paragraph (2)(C) therefore authorizes the court to provide directions about attorney fees and costs when appointing class counsel. Because there will be numerous class actions in which this information is not likely to be useful, the court need not consider it in all class actions.

Some information relevant to class counsel appointment may involve matters that include adversary preparation in a way that should be shielded from disclosure to other parties. An appropriate protective order may be necessary to preserve confidentiality.

In evaluating prospective class counsel, the court should weigh all pertinent factors. No single factor should necessarily be determinative in a given case. For example, the resources counsel will commit to the case must be appropriate to its needs, but the court should be careful not to limit consideration to lawyers with the greatest resources.

If, after review of all applicants, the court concludes that none would be satisfactory class counsel, it may deny class certification, reject all applications, recommend that an application be modified, invite new applications, or make any other appropriate order regarding selection and appointment of class counsel.

Paragraph (2). This paragraph sets out the procedure that should be followed in appointing class counsel. Although it affords substantial flexibility, it provides the framework for appointment of class counsel in all class actions. For counsel who filed the action, the materials submitted in support of the motion for class certification may suffice to justify appointment so long as the information described in paragraph (g)(1)(C) is included. If there were other applicants, they ordinarily would file a formal application detailing their suitability for the position.

In a plaintiff class action, the court usually would appoint as class counsel only an attorney or attorneys who have sought appointment. Different considerations may apply in defendant class actions.

The rule states that the court should appoint 'class counsel.' In many instances, the applicant will be an individual attorney. In other cases, however, an entire firm, or perhaps numerous attorneys who are not otherwise affiliated but are collaborating on the action will apply. No rule of thumb exists to determine when such arrangements are appropriate; the court should be alert to the need for adequate staffing of the case, but also to the risk of overstaffing or an ungainly counsel structure.

Paragraph (2)(A) authorizes the court to designate interim counsel during the pre-certification period if necessary to protect the interests of the putative class. Rule 23(c)(1)(B) directs that the order certifying the class includes appointment of class counsel. Before class certification, however, it will usually be important for an attorney to take action to prepare for the certification decision. The amendment to Rule 23(c)(1) recognizes that some discovery is often necessary for that determination. It also may be important to make or respond to motions before certification. Settlement may be discussed before certification. Ordinarily, the lawyer who filed the action handles such work. In some cases, however, there maybe rivalry or uncertainty that makes formal designation of interim counsel appropriate. Rule 23(g)(2)(A) authorizes the court to designate interim counsel to act on behalf of the putative class before the certification decision is made. Failure to make the formal designation does not prevent the attorney who filed the action from proceeding in it. Whether or not formally designated interim counsel, an attorney who acts on behalf of the class before certification must act in the best interests of the class as a whole. For example, an attorney who negotiates a precertification settlement must seek a settlement that is fair, reasonable, and adequate for the class.

Rule 23(c)(1) provides that the court should decide whether to certify the class 'at an early practicable time,' and directs that class counsel should be appointed in the order certifying the class. In some cases, it may be appropriate for the court to allow a reasonable period after commencement of the action for filing applications to serve as class counsel. The primary ground for deferring appointment would be that there is reason to anticipate competing applications to serve as class counsel. Examples might include instances in which more than one class action has been filed, or in which other attorneys have filed individual actions on behalf of putative class members. The purpose of facilitating competing applications in such a case is to afford the best possible representation for the class. Another possible reason for deferring appointment would be that the initial applicant was found inadequate, but it seems appropriate to permit additional applications rather than deny class certification.

Paragraph (2)(B) states the basic standard the court should use in deciding whether to certify the class and appoint class counsel in the single applicant situation-that the applicant be able to provide the representation called for by paragraph (1)(B) in light of the factors identified in paragraph (1)(C).

If there are multiple adequate applicants, paragraph (2)(B) directs the court to select the class counsel best able to represent the interests of the class. This decision should also be made using the factors outlined in paragraph (1)(C), but in the multiple applicant situation the court is to go beyond scrutinizing the adequacy of counsel and make a comparison of the strengths of the various applicants. As with the decision whether to appoint the sole applicant for the position, no single factor should be dispositive in selecting class counsel in cases in which there are multiple applicants. The fact that a given attorney filed the instant action, for example, might not weigh heavily in the decision if that lawyer had not done significant work identifying or investigating claims. Depending on the nature of the case, one important consideration might be the applicant's existing attorney-client relationship with the proposed class representative.

Paragraph (2)(C) builds on the appointment process by authorizing the court to include provisions regarding attorney fees in the order appointing class counsel. Courts may find it desirable to adopt guidelines for fees or nontaxable costs, or to direct class counsel to report to the court at regular intervals on the efforts undertaken in the action, to facilitate the court's later determination of a reasonable attorney fee.

3.14 (g) Rule 23 Class Actions: Attorney Fees Award.

In an action certified as a class action, the court may award reasonable attorney fees and nontaxable costs authorized by law or by agreement of the parties as follows:

3.14 (g)(1) Motion for Award of Attorney Fees.

A claim for an award of attorney fees and nontaxable costs must be made by motion under Rule 54(d)(2), subject to the provisions of this subdivision, at a time set by the court. Notice of the motion must be served on all parties and, for motions by class counsel, directed to class members in a reasonable manner.

3.14 (g)(2) Objections to Motion.

A class member, or a party from whom payment is sought, may object to the motion.

3.14 (g)(3) Hearing and Findings.

The court may hold a hearing and must find the facts and state its conclusions of law on the motion under Rule 52(a).

3.14 (g)(4) Reference to Special Master or Magistrate Judge.

The court may refer issues related to the amount of the award to a special master or to a magistrate judge as provided in Rule 54(d)(2)(D).

3.14 (h) Committee Notes on Attorney Fee Awards Subdivision (h) Subdivision (h) is new. Fee awards are a powerful influence on the way attorneys initiate, develop, and conclude class actions. Class action attorney fee awards have heretofore been handled, along with all other attorney fee awards, under Rule 54(d)(2), but that rule is not addressed to the particular concerns of class actions. This subdivision is designed to work in tandem with new subdivision (g) on appointment of class counsel, which may afford an opportunity for the court to provide an early framework for an eventual fee award, or for monitoring the work of class counsel during the pendency of the action.

Subdivision (h) applies to 'an action certified as a class action.' This includes cases in which there is a simultaneous proposal for class certification and settlement even though technically the class may not be certified unless the court approves the settlement pursuant to review under Rule 23(e). When a settlement is proposed for Rule 23(e) approval, either after certification or with a request for certification, notice to class members about class counsel's fee motion would ordinarily accompany the notice to the class about the settlement proposal itself.

This subdivision does not undertake to create new grounds for an award of attorney fees or nontaxable costs. Instead, it applies when such awards are authorized by law or by agreement of the parties. Against that background, it provides a format for all awards of attorney fees and nontaxable costs in connection with a class action, not only the award to class counsel. In some situations, there may be a basis for making an award to other counsel whose work produced a beneficial result for the class, such as attorneys who acted for the class before certification but were not appointed class counsel, or attorneys who represented objectors to a proposed settlement under Rule 23(e) or to the fee motion of class counsel. Other situations in which fee awards are authorized by law or by agreement of the parties may exist.

This subdivision authorizes an award of 'reasonable' attorney fees and nontaxable costs. This is the customary term for measurement of fee awards in cases in which counsel may obtain an award of fees under the 'common fund' theory that applies in many class actions, and is used in many fee-shifting statutes. Depending on the circumstances, courts have approached the determination of what is reasonable in different ways. In particular, there is some variation among courts about whether in 'common fund' cases the court should use the lodestar or a percentage method of determining what fee is reasonable.

CHAPTER 3. CLASS AND REPRESENTATIVE ACTIONS

The rule does not attempt to resolve the question whether the lodestar or percentage approach should be viewed as preferable.

Active judicial involvement in measuring fee awards is singularly important to the proper operation of the class-action process. Continued reliance on case law development of fee-award measures does not diminish the court's responsibility. In a class action, the district court must ensure that the amount and mode of payment of attorney fees are fair and proper whether the fees come from a common fund or are otherwise paid. Even in the absence of objections, the court bears this responsibility.

Courts discharging this responsibility have looked to a variety of factors. One fundamental focus is the result actually achieved for class members, a basic consideration in any case in which fees are sought on the basis of a benefit achieved for class members. The Private Securities Litigation Reform Act of 1995 explicitly makes this factor a cap for a fee award in actions to which it applies.[209] For a percentage approach to fee measurement, a result achieved is the basic starting point.

In many instances, the court may need to proceed with care in assessing the value conferred on class members. Settlement regimes that provide for future payments, for example, may not result in significant actual payments to class members. In this connection, the court may need to scrutinize the manner and operation of any applicable claims procedure. In some cases, it may be appropriate to defer some portion of the fee award until actual payouts to class members are known. Settlements involving non-monetary provisions for class members also deserve careful scrutiny to ensure that these provisions have actual value to the class. On occasion, the court's Rule 23(e) review will provide a solid basis for this sort of evaluation, but in any event, it is also important to assess the fee award for the class.

At the same time, it is important to recognize that in some class actions the monetary relief obtained is not the sole determinant of an appropriate attorney fees award.[210]

---

[209] See 15 U.S.C. § 5 772-1(a)(6); 78u-4(a)(6)(fee award should not exceed a 'reasonable percentage of the amount of any damages and prejudgment interest actually paid to the class').

[210] Cf. *Blanchard v. Bergeron*, 489 U.S. 87, 95 (1989)(cautioning in an individual case against an 'undesirable emphasis' on 'the importance of the recovery of damages in civil rights litigation' that might 'shortchange efforts to seek effective injunctive or declaratory relief').

Any directions or orders made by the court in connection with appointing class counsel under Rule 23(g) should weigh heavily in making a fee award under this subdivision. Courts have also given weight to agreements among the parties regarding the fee motion, and to agreements between class counsel and others about the fees claimed by the motion. Rule 54(d)(2)(B) provides: 'If directed by the court, the motion shall also disclose the terms of any agreement with respect to fees to be paid for the services for which claim is made.' The agreement by a settling party not to oppose a fee application up to a certain amount, for example, is worthy of consideration, but the court remains responsible to determine a reasonable fee. 'Side agreements' regarding fees provide at least perspective pertinent to an appropriate fee award.

In addition, courts may take account of the fees charged by class counsel or other attorneys for representing individual claimants or objectors in the case. In determining a fee for class counsel, the court's objective is to ensure an overall fee that is fair for counsel and equitable within the class. In some circumstances, individual fee agreements between class counsel and class members might have provisions inconsistent with those goals, and the court might determine that adjustments in the class fee award were necessary as a result.

Finally, it is important to scrutinize separately the application for an award covering nontaxable costs. If costs were addressed in the order appointing class counsel, those directives should be a presumptive starting point in determining what an appropriate award is.

Paragraph (1). Any claim for an award of attorney fees must be sought by motion under Rule 54(d)(2), which invokes the provisions for timing of appeal in Rule 58 and Appellate Rule 4. Owing to the distinctive features of class action fee motions, however, the provisions of this subdivision control disposition of fee motions in class actions, while Rule 54(d)(2) applies to matters not addressed in this subdivision.

The court should direct when the fee motion must be filed. For motions by class counsel in cases subject to court review of a proposed settlement under Rule 23(e), it would be important to require the filing of at least the initial motion in time for inclusion of information about the motion in the notice to the class about the proposed settlement that is required by Rule 23(e). In cases litigated to judgment, the court might also order class counsel's motion to be filed promptly so that notice to the class under this subdivision (h) can be given.

Besides service of the motion on all parties, notice of class counsel's motion for attorney fees must be 'directed to the class in a reasonable

CHAPTER 3. CLASS AND REPRESENTATIVE ACTIONS

manner.' Because members of the class have an interest in the arrangements for payment of class counsel whether that payment comes from the class fund or is made directly by another party, notice is required in all instances. In cases in which settlement approval is contemplated under Rule 23(e), notice of class counsel's fee motion should be combined with notice of the proposed settlement, and the provision regarding notice to the class is parallel to the requirements for notice under Rule 23(e). In adjudicated class actions, the court may calibrate the notice to avoid undue expense.

Paragraph (2). A class member and any party from whom payment is sought may object to the fee motion. Other parties – for example, nonsettling defendants – may not object because they lack a sufficient interest in the amount the court awards. The rule does not specify a time limit for making an objection. In setting the date objections are due, the court should provide sufficient time after the full fee motion is on file to enable potential objectors to examine the motion.

The court may allow an objector discovery relevant to the objections. In determining whether to allow discovery, the court should weigh the need for the information against the cost and delay that would attend discovery. See Rule 26(b)(2). One factor in determining whether to authorize discovery is the completeness of the material submitted in support of the fee motion, which depends in part on the fee measurement standard applicable to the case. If the motion provides thorough information, the burden should be on the objector to justify discovery to obtain further information.

Paragraph (3). Whether or not there are formal objections, the court must determine whether a fee award is justified and, if so, set a reasonable fee. The rule does not require a formal hearing in all cases. The form and extent of a hearing depend on the circumstances of the case. The rule does require findings and conclusions under Rule 52(a).

Paragraph (4). By incorporating Rule 54(d)(2), this provision gives the court broad authority to obtain assistance in determining the appropriate amount to award. In deciding whether to direct submission of such questions to a special master or magistrate judge, the court should give appropriate consideration to the cost and delay that such a process might entail.

3.14 (i) Changes Made after Publication and Comment.

3.14 (i)(1) Rule 23(c)(1)(B) is changed to incorporate the counsel-appointment provisions of Rule 23(g). The statement of the method and time for requesting exclusion from a (b)(3) class has been moved to the notice of certification provision in Rule 23(c)(2)(B).

3.14 (i)(2) Rule 23(c)(2)(A) is changed by deleting the requirement that class members be notified of certification of a (b)(1) or (b)(2) class. The new version provides only that the court may direct appropriate notice to the class.

3.14 (i)(3) Rule 23(c)(2)(B) is revised to require that the notice of class certification define the certified class in terms identical to the terms used in (c)(1)(B), and to incorporate the statement transferred from (c)(1)(B) on 'when and how members may elect to be excluded.'

Rule 23(e)(1) is revised to delete the requirement that the parties must win court approval for a precertification dismissal or settlement.

3.14 (i)(4) Rule 23(e)(2) is revised to change the provision that the court may direct the parties to file a copy or summary of any agreement or understanding made in connection with a proposed settlement. The new provision directs the parties to a proposed settlement to identify any agreement made in connection with the settlement.

3.14 (i)(5) Rule 23(e)(3) is proposed in a restyled form of the second version proposed for publication.

3.14 (i)(6) Rule 23(e)(4)(B) is restyled.

3.14 (i)(7) Rule 23(g)(1)(C) is a transposition of criteria for appointing class counsel that was published as Rule 23(g)(2)(B). The criteria are rearranged and expanded to include consideration of experience in handling claims of the type asserted in the action and of counsel's knowledge of the applicable law.

3.14 (i)(8) Rule 23(g)(2)(A) is a new provision for designation of interim counsel to act on behalf of a putative class before a certification determination is made.

3.14 (i)(9) Rule 23(g)(2)(B) is revised to point up the differences between appointment of class counsel when there is only one applicant and when there are competing applicants. When there is only one applicant the court must determine that the applicant is able to fairly and adequately represent class interests. When there is more than one applicant the court must appoint the applicant best able to represent class interests.

3.14 (i)(10) Rule 23(h) is changed to require that notice of an attorney-fee motion by class counsel be 'directed to class members,' rather than 'given to all class members.'

Table 3.1: Number of Employment Discrimination Class Actions Filed Nationwide in the Following Reporting Periods

Twelve Months Preceding June 30	Number of Job Discrimination Class Actions Commenced in These 12 Months
1976	1,174
1977	1,138
1978	739
1979	515
1980	326
1981	302
1982	224
1983	156
1984	135
1985	82
1986	68
1987	48
1988	46
1989	50
1990	42
1991	32
1992 (12 mos. to 9/30/92)	30
1993 (12 mos. to 12/31/93)	44
1994 (12 mos. to 9/30/94)	56
1995 (12 mos. to 9/30/95)	71
1996 (12 mos. to 12/31/96)	77
1997 (12 mos. to 12/31/97)	79
1998 (12 mos. to 12/31/98)	86
1999 (12 mos. to 12/31/99)	72
2000 (12 mos. to 12/31/00)	89

CHAPTER 4

Fighting to Keep Employment Discrimination Class Actions Alive: How *Allison v. Citgo*'s Predomination Requirement Threatens to Undermine Title VII Enforcement

Suzette M. Malveaux[*,**]

4.1 INTRODUCTION

The class action device is critical to the enforcement of Title VII of the Civil Rights Act of 1964. For decades, Title VII class actions have resulted in extensive reforms in employers' policies and millions of dollars in monetary relief for thousands of employees nationwide.[1]

---

[*] Suzette M. Malveaux is Associate Professor, The Catholic University of America, Columbus School of Law. She holds a J.D. from New York University School of Law.
[**] This paper was previously published by the Berkeley Journal of Employment and Labor Law, Suzette Malveaux, Fighting to Keep Employment Discrimination Class Action Alive: How Allison v. Citgo's Predomination Requirement Threatens to Undermine Title VII Enforcement, Berkeley Journal of Employment and Labor Law, Vol. 26 No. 2 (2005).
[1] See Press Release, Texaco, 'Texaco Announces Settlement in Class Action Lawsuit' (November 15, 1996) (African-American class received USD 176 million in settlement with Texaco), available at <www.texaco.com/sitelets/diversity>; *Ingram v. Coca-Cola Co.*, 200 FRD 685, 687–688 (ND Ga. 2001) (describing 'far reaching' programmatic relief of settlement in Title VII class action against Coca-Cola); Julie Dunn & Andy Vuong,

David Sherwyn and Samuel Estreicher (eds), *Employment Class and Collective Actions*, pp. 203–239.
© Regents of the University of California. Reprinted from Berkeley Journal of Employment and Labour Law Vol. 26 No. 2, 405-429, by permission of the Regents of the University of California.

203

However, this traditional tool of enforcement has come under attack. The Civil Rights Act of 1991, which provides compensatory and punitive damages, and attendant jury trials in cases alleging intentional discrimination, was designed to enhance enforcement and expand remedies.[2] Its enactment, however, has created a schism among the courts over the propriety of class certification where employees seek monetary damages as well as injunctive relief for Title VII claims.

The courts of appeals hotly contest what the proper standard is for determining whether monetary damages or injunctive relief predominates, a necessary inquiry for determining whether plaintiffs are entitled to class certification under Rule 23(b)(2) of the *Federal Rules of Civil Procedure*. The Fifth Circuit concluded in *Allison v. Citgo Petroleum Corp.*,[3] that monetary relief predominates unless it is 'incidental,' and that compensatory and punitive damages are by 'nature' not 'incidental.'[4] This narrow interpretation of Rule 23 has been adopted by the Third, Seventh,[5] and Eleventh Circuits.[6] On the opposite end of the spectrum is the Second Circuit's

---

'Retail Titans Battle Bias More Workers Sue Warehouse Stores Rapid Growth is Blamed Wal-Mart, Home Depot and Costco Have Dealt with Claims that They Discriminated against Workers Based on Race and Sex,' *Denver Post*, September 19, 2004, at K1 (describing Home Depot USD 5.5 million settlement in employment discrimination class action and others); Mark Diana, 'Beginning of the End of Money Damage Class Actions? The Future of Big Money Employment Discrimination Class Actions, on the Rise since the 1991 Civil Rights Act Was Passed, Is Unsettled,' NJLJ, March 25, 2002 at S2 (discussing 'extraordinary settlements' against Coca-Cola (USD 192.5 million), Home Depot (USD 87 million), Publix (USD 82 million), and Texaco (USD 176 million)); Nadya Aswad & Joyce Cutler, 'Home Depot Agrees to Pay USD 65 Million to Settle Sex Discrimination Class Action,' Daily Lab Rep (BNA) No. 183, at A-11 (September 22, 1997)); Lesley Frieder Wolf, 'Evading Friendly Fire: Achieving Class Certification after the Civil Rights Act of 1991,' 100 Colum L Rev 1847, 1847 n. 3 (2000) (citing multi-million dollar settlements against employers such as Home Depot, Boeing, Amtrak and others).

[2] See The Civil Rights Act of 1991 2–3, Pub. L. No. 102-166 (1991).

[3] 151 F.3d 402, 415–418 (5th Cir. 1998).

[4] *Id.* at 417.

[5] An alternative approach is suggested by the Seventh Circuit. While the Seventh Circuit has adopted *Allison*'s 'incidental' predomination test for (b)(2) classes, this circuit has put forward various ways a district court may be able to certify such cases under (b)(3). See *Jefferson v. Ingersoll Int'l, Inc.*, 195 F.3d 894, 898–899 (7th Cir. 1999); *Lemon v. Int'l Union of Operating Eng'rs*, Local 139, 216 F.3d 577, 581–582 (7th Cir. 2000).

[6] See *Barabin v. Aramark Corp.*, No. 02-8057, 2003 WL 355417, at 1 (3rd Cir. Jan. 24, 2003); *Jefferson v. Ingersoll Int'l, Inc.*, 195 F.3d 894, 898 (7th Cir. 1999); accord, e.g., In re

CHAPTER 4. FIGHTING TO KEEP EMPLOYMENT DISCRIMINATION

standard set forth in *Robinson v. Metro-North Commuter Railroad Co.*, which permits the courts to use a liberal 'ad hoc'-approach when determining predomination.[7] This approach is also embraced by the Ninth Circuit.[8]

This division between the circuits is reason for great concern. Employees are currently subject to inconsistent and inadequate standards of justice. The more restrictive formulation set forth in *Allison* threatens to undermine the enforcement of civil rights in three ways. First, the Fifth Circuit's adoption of an 'incidental' standard of damages and its conclusion that compensatory and punitive damages are not per se 'incidental' make it much harder for plaintiffs seeking such damages to get a case certified as a class action under provision (b)(2), or even (b)(3) in some circuits, of the federal class action rule. Deprivation of this enforcement mechanism will result in unchecked systemic employment discrimination because of the critical role the class action plays in Title VII enforcement. Second, the propensity of the Fifth Circuit (and other circuits) to deny certification to plaintiffs seeking class-wide monetary relief under (b)(2) forces plaintiffs to forgo relief to which they are entitled as a cost of class certification. Consequently, deterrence objectives are undermined and defendants receive a windfall. Finally, the heightened standard for certification under (b)(2) compels employees to seek certification under (b)(3), a provision which imposes greater costs, burdens, and scrutiny. These additional hurdles may be just enough to prevent some plaintiffs from vindicating their civil rights.

Given the importance of the class action mechanism to civil rights enforcement, it is imperative that the predomination approach – taken by the majority of circuits that have ruled on this issue – be abandoned in favor of the more equitable ad hoc balancing approach established by the Second Circuit in *Robinson*. Under the latter approach, plaintiffs will be able to effectively vindicate their statutory rights under Title VII, courts will retain their discretionary power under Rule 23, and Congressional intent articulated in the Civil Rights Act of 1991 will be honored. The latest amendments to Rule 23 and the recently enacted

---

Allstate Ins. Co., 400 F.3d 505, 507 (7th Cir. 2005); *Murray v. Auslander*, 244 F.3d 807, 812 (11th Cir. 2001). Cf. *Coleman v. Gen. Motors Acceptance Corp.*, 296 F.3d 443, 446–447 (6th Cir. 2002) (in race discrimination case brought under Equal Credit Opportunity Act, court reserved judgment as to whether compensatory damages are ever recoverable in a 23(b)(2) class action, but concluded that if they were, such damages dominated over the injunctive relief sought because of the 'highly individualized determinations that would be required to determine those damages').

[7] *Robinson*, 267 F.3d 147, 162–164 (2nd Cir. 2001).

[8] *Molski v. Gleich*, 318 F.3d 937, 949–950 (9th Cir. 2003).

Class Action Fairness Act of 2005 only bolster the protections against judicial abuse of power in class certification determinations, thereby preserving due process. Thus, the minority's ad hoc balancing approach to predomination is preferable to the majority's bright-line one.

4.2 THE DEVELOPMENT OF THE CIRCUIT CONFLICT OVER THE INTERPRETATION OF RULE 23'S PREDOMINATION REQUIREMENT AFTER THE ENACTMENT OF THE CIVIL RIGHTS ACT OF 1991

4.2.1 The Central Role of Rule 23(b)(2) Certification in Civil Rights Enforcement

The class action mechanism has been the cornerstone of civil rights enforcement, particularly in Title VII actions, for the past forty years. Rule 23 governs cases brought in federal court on behalf of a class of people. In order to represent a class, plaintiffs must meet all four criteria of Rule 23(a): numerosity, commonality, typicality, and adequacy of representation,[9] and one of three criteria set forth in Rule 23(b). Rule 23(b)(1) is designed primarily to protect the interests of defendants who may be forced to follow inconsistent or incompatible judgments and absent class members whose rights may be compromised in the absence of a class action.[10] The most common provision utilized for Title VII class

---

[9] These prerequisites are set forth in Rule 23(a):

> One or more members of a class may sue or be sued as representative parties on behalf of all only if:
>
> (1) the class is so numerous that joinder of all members is impracticable;
> (2) there are questions of law or fact common to the class;
> (3) the claims or defenses of the representative parties are typical of the claims or defenses of the class; and
> (4) the representative parties will fairly and adequately protect the interests of the class. Fed. R. Civ. P. 23(a).

[10] Rule 23(b)(1) certification is appropriate where the prosecution of separate actions would create a risk of either:

> (A) inconsistent or varying adjudications with respect to individual members of the class which would establish incompatible standards of conduct for the party opposing the class, or

CHAPTER 4. FIGHTING TO KEEP EMPLOYMENT DISCRIMINATION

actions has been provision (b)(2), which applies where 'the party opposing the class has acted or refused to act on grounds generally applicable to the class, thereby making appropriate final injunctive relief or corresponding declaratory relief with respect to the class as a whole[.]'[11] Conduct that is 'generally applicable' means that the party opposing the class 'has acted in a consistent manner towards members of the class so that his actions may be viewed as part of a pattern of activity, or to establish a regulatory scheme, to all members.'[12] Rule 23(b)(3) certification is meant to provide a representative action where the class is less cohesive than those certified under (b)(1) or (b)(2), but efficiency and manageability make certification desirable.[13] Specifically, certification is appropriate under Rule 23(b)(3) where 'the court finds that questions of law or fact common to the members of the class predominate over any questions affecting only individual members, and that a class action is superior to other available methods for the fair and efficient adjudication of the controversy.'[14] Because a (b)(3) class is by nature less cohesive and often involves monetary damages, class members are entitled to notice and the right to opt out of the class.[15]

(B) adjudications with respect to individual members of the class which would as a practical matter be dispositive of the interests of the other members not parties to the adjudications or substantially impair or impede their ability to protect their interests[.] Fed. R. Civ. P. 23(b)(1).

[11] Fed. R. Civ. P. 23(b)(2).
[12] Charles A. Wright et al., 'Federal Practice & Procedure,' 1775 at 43–46 (3rd edn, 2005).
[13] See Fed. R. Civ. P. 23(b)(3) advisory committee notes to 1966 amendment (Rule 23(b)(3) is intended to provide aggregate litigation where 'class-action treatment is not as clearly called for as in those described above, but it may nevertheless be convenient and desirable depending upon the particular facts. Subdivision (b)(3) encompasses those cases in which a class action would achieve economies of time, effort, and expense, and promote uniformity of decision as to persons similarly situated, without sacrificing procedural fairness or bringing about other undesirable results' (citing Chafee, 'Some Problems of Equity,' 201 (1950))).
[14] Fed. R. Civ. P. 23(b)(3).
[15] See Fed. R. Civ. P. 23(c)(2)(B)('For any class certified under Rule 23(b)(3), the court must direct to class members the best notice practicable under the circumstances, including individual notice to all members who can be identified through reasonable effort. The notice must . . . state . . . that a class member may enter an appearance through counsel if the member so desires, that the court will exclude from the class any member who requests exclusion . . . and the binding effect of a class judgment on class members under Rule 23(c)(3).').

Because civil rights cases have historically sought to curtail discrimination on a broad scale, they are uniquely suited for (b)(2) certification.[16] Plaintiffs in these cases have customarily sought injunctive and declaratory relief for systemic conduct based on race and other protected statuses. This benefits the class as a whole. Such cohesiveness makes notice and the right to opt out unnecessary,[17] especially where plaintiffs only seek class-wide injunctive or declaratory relief.[18] It is well recognized that provision (b)(2) in particular 'was promulgated ... essentially as a tool for facilitating civil rights actions.'[19] The Supreme Court has more recently recognized the centrality of Rule 23(b)(2) to civil rights class actions as well.[20]

---

[16] See, e.g., *Kyriazi v. W. Elec. Co.*, 647 F.2d 388, 393 (3rd Cir. 1981) (explaining that a Title VII class action seeking injunctive and declaratory relief for systemic discrimination is 'obviously the paradigm of a Rule 23(b)(2) class action'); *East Tex. Motor Freight Sys., Inc. v. Rodriguez*, 431 US 395, 405 (1977) (stating that race discrimination cases 'are often by their very nature class suits, involving class-wide wrongs').

[17] See *Wetzel v. Liberty Mut. Ins. Co.*, 508 F.2d 239, 250–251 (3rd Cir. 1975).

[18] See *Jones v. CCH-LIS Legal Info. Servs.*, No 97-CIV-4372, 1998 WL 671446, at 2 (S.D.N.Y. Sept. 28, 1998); see e.g., *Jefferson v. Windy City Maint., Inc.*, No. 96-C-7686, 1998 WL 474115, at 10 (ND Ill. Aug. 4, 1998); *Vaszlavik v. Storage Tech. Corp.*, 183 FRD 264, 272 (D. Colo. 1998) (ERISA case).

[19] 5 James Wm. Moore et al., 'Moore's Federal Practice,' 23.43[1][b], at 23–192 (3rd edn 2005); see advisory committee's note to Proposed Rule of Civil Procedure 23, 39 FRD 69, 102 (1966) (explaining that Rule 23(b)(2) certification was intended to apply to civil rights cases where 'final relief of an injunctive nature or of a corresponding declaratory nature, settling the legality of the behavior with respect to the class as a whole, is appropriate'); *Eubanks v. Billington*, 110 F.3d 87, 92 (DC Cir. 1997) ('Title VII and other civil rights class actions are frequently certified pursuant to Rule 23(b)(2).'); *Holmes v. Cont'l Can Co.*, 706 F.2d 1144, 1152 (11th Cir. 1983) (noting that civil rights class actions are usually certified pursuant to Rule 23(b)(2)); *Kincade v. Gen. Tire & Rubber Co.*, 635 F.2d 501, 506 n. 6 (5th Cir. 1981) (same); *Barefield v. Chevron*, No. C-86-2427-TEH, 1988 WL 188433 (ND Cal. December 6, 1988) (explaining it is 'often acknowledged, (b)(2) was deliberately drafted to facilitate the vindication of civil rights through the class action device'); see also Harvey S. Bartlett III, 'Determining Whether a Title VII Plaintiff Class's 'Aim is True': The Legacy of Allison v. Citgo Petroleum Corp. for Employment Discrimination Class Certification Under Rule 23(b)(2)', 74 Tul L Rev 2163, 2170–2171 (2000) (concluding that some courts treat employment discrimination cases as 'categorically certifiable' under Rule 23(b)(2), as opposed to analyzing them on a case-by-case basis).

[20] See *Amchem Prods., Inc. v. Windsor*, 521 US 591, 614 (1997) ('Civil rights cases against parties charged with unlawful, class-based discrimination are prime examples' of (b)(2) classes).

CHAPTER 4. FIGHTING TO KEEP EMPLOYMENT DISCRIMINATION

4.2.2 The Impact of the Civil Rights Act of 1991

Despite the pivotal role (b)(2) certification has played in the enforcement of civil rights in general, and Title VII rights in particular, the propriety of such certification is being questioned in the wake of the Civil Rights Act of 1991. Prior to 1991, employees had limited recourse for Title VII actions; they could pursue only equitable relief, such as injunctions, declarations, reinstatement, back pay, and front pay. The Civil Rights Act of 1991 enhanced employees' remedies, enabling them to seek compensatory and punitive damages and a jury trial in Title VII cases alleging intentional discrimination.[21]

The Act, however, did not immediately awaken the giant; rather, employees continued to successfully bring class actions seeking certain monetary and injunctive relief under Rule 23(b)(2).[22] The courts agreed that in order for a case to be certified under (b)(2), monetary relief could not 'predominate' over the equitable relief sought – a standard articulated by the Advisory Committee Notes that accompany Rule 23. However, the inclusion of compensatory and punitive damages and jury trials to Title VII ultimately led to a major division among the courts.[23] The Fifth Circuit's ruling in *Allison* marked the moment at which the giant awoke and the propriety of (b)(2) certification for employees seeking monetary damages and injunctive relief came into sharp focus.

4.2.3 *Allison v. Citgo*

The Fifth Circuit, in *Allison*, was the first appellate court to hold that plaintiffs who pursued compensatory and punitive damages in

---

[21] 42 USC 1981a, 1981(c) (2001).
[22] See e.g., *Orlowski v. Dominick's Finer Foods, Inc.*, No. 95 C1666, 1997 US Dist. LEXIS 1984 (ND Ill. Feb. 21, 1997), aff'd, 172 F.R.D. 370 (ND Ill. 1997) (certifying a (b)(2) case where monetary relief was sought because it did not predominate and court counseled that disputes over which type of relief predominates should be avoided); *Jones v. CCH-LIS Legal Info. Servs.*, No 97-CIV-4372, 1998 WL 671446, at 2 (SDNY September 28, 1998) (focusing on appropriateness of certifying (b)(2) class in civil rights case and not focusing on whether monetary damages predominated over injunctive relief).
[23] See Richard A. Nagareda, 'The Preexistence Principle and the Structure of the Class Action,' 103 Colum L Rev 149, 236 n. 368 (2003) (explaining 'Judicial efforts to give practical meaning to this passage have led to a dizzying array of approaches.').

addition to injunctive relief were precluded from seeking class-wide relief under Rule 23(b)(2). The Fifth Circuit held that:

> Monetary relief predominates in (b)(2) class actions unless it is incidental to requested injunctive or declaratory relief. By incidental, we mean damages that flow directly from liability to the class as a whole on the claims forming the basis of the injunctive or declaratory relief.[24]

More specifically, the court defined 'incidental' damages as:

(1) 'concomitant with, not merely consequential to, class-wide injunctive or declaratory relief';
(2) 'capable of computation by means of objective standards and not dependent in any significant way on the intangible, subjective differences of each class member's circumstances'; and
(3) 'not requiring additional hearings to resolve the disparate merits of each individual's case;' and not introducing 'new and substantial legal or factual issues', or entailing 'complex individualized determinations.'[25]

The Fifth Circuit's definition of incidental damages has also been adopted by the Third, Seventh, and Eleventh Circuits.[26]

Using this approach, the Fifth Circuit in *Allison* affirmed the district court's conclusion that neither the compensatory nor punitive damages were sufficiently incidental to the injunctive and declaratory relief to warrant (b)(2) certification.[27] The Fifth Circuit concluded that the amount of compensatory damages could not be determined by objective standards, but rather required specific, individualized proof of actual injury for each class member.[28] The Fifth Circuit concluded that because the punitive damages were dependent upon the determination of the compensatory damages, the former also required individualized proof and were based on subjective differences.[29]

---

[24] *Allison v. Citgo Petroleum Corp.*, 151 F.3d 402, 415 (5th Cir. 1998).
[25] *Id.*
[26] See *Barabin v. Aramark Corp.*, No. 02-8057, 2003 WL 355417, at 2 (3rd Cir. Jan. 24, 2003); In re Allstate Ins. Co., 400 F.3d 505, 507 (7th Cir. 2005); *Murray v. Auslander*, 244 F.3d 807, 812 (11th Cir. 2001).
[27] *Allison*, 151 F.3d at 416.
[28] *Id.* at 416–417.
[29] *Id.* at 416–418.

CHAPTER 4. FIGHTING TO KEEP EMPLOYMENT DISCRIMINATION

Allison has been interpreted by some as the death knell for Title VII (b)(2) class actions seeking compensatory and punitive damages in addition to equitable relief.[30] Absent Supreme Court intervention on the issue, this interpretation is not unreasonable in certain circuits. *Allison's* definition of incidental damages is interpreted in such a way that compensatory and punitive damages automatically fail to qualify, thereby making it practically impossible to seek such remedies in a (b)(2) class.[31] The adoption of such a 'rigid bright-line' test strips district courts of their discretion to certify a class action when appropriate and to conduct a 'rigorous analysis' as required.[32] Courts are left with little room to navigate (b)(2) certification in Title VII cases.[33]

---

[30] See e.g., *id.* at 431 (Dennis, J., dissenting) ('The majority's rule, contrary to the intent of the drafters and Congress, threatens a drastic curtailment of the use of (b)(2) class actions in the enforcement of Title VII and other civil rights acts.'); see also Bartlett III, *supra* n. 19, at 2165, 2184 ('That Allison represents the demise of the effectiveness of the Civil Rights Act of 1991 remains inescapable...'); Wolf, *supra* n. 1, at 1848 (the combination of the Civil Rights Act of 1991 and current case law, e.g., *Allison*, 'threatens to drastically curtail – if not eliminate altogether – employment discrimination class actions); see generally Nikaa Baugh Jordan, "Allison v. Citgo Petroleum: The Death Knell for the Title VII Class Action?," 51 Ala L Rev 847 (2000).

[31] See *Allison*, 151 F.3d at 426 (Dennis, J., dissenting).

[32] See *id.* (Dennis, J., dissenting); see also *Gen. Tel. Co. of Southwest v. Falcon*, 457 US 147, 161 (1982) (district courts must conduct a 'rigorous analysis' in determining the appropriateness of class certification); *U.S. Parole Comm'n v. Geraghty*, 445 US 388, 408 (1980) (explaining that district courts are not obligated to construct subclasses).

[33] The plot has thickened even further. In the case of In the Matter of Monumental Life Insurance Co., Industrial Life Ins. Litigation, the Fifth Circuit addressed the scope of *Allison* in a non-employment case. Plaintiffs brought suit against three insurance companies for discriminating against African-Americans in setting premiums for low-value life insurance policies. The district court found that plaintiffs' damages predominated over the injunctive relief sought and therefore denied certification under Rule 23(b)(2). In re Indus. Life Ins. Litig., 208 FRD 571, 572–574 (E.D. La. 2002), rev'd sub nom. In re Monumental Life Ins. Co., 365 F.3d 408 (5th Cir. 2004). However, the Fifth Circuit reversed, concluding that because the damages could be calculated mechanically based on 'factors developed and maintained in the course of defendants' business,' such damages did not predominate. In re Monumental Life Ins. Co., 365 F.3d 408, 418–420, n. 20 (5th Cir. 2004), cert. denied, *American Nat'l Ins. Co. v. Bratcher*, 125 S.Ct. 277 (2004). In Monumental Life Insurance, the Fifth Circuit concluded that a refund-type case, involving 'factors such as premium rate, issue age, and benefits paid' presented an ideal situation for calculating damages using

Moreover, the Fifth Circuit's cramped interpretation of what constitutes predomination is unwarranted. Based on the text of Rule 23, the accompanying Advisory Committee Notes to Rule 23(b)(2), and the underlying policies of both Rule 23(b)(2) and the Civil Rights Act of 1991, the Fifth Circuit was not compelled to read predomination so narrowly.[34] Rule 23 is silent on the issue of whether monetary relief is permitted in a (b)(2) class; nothing in the Rule's text suggests that certification under such circumstances is impermissible.[35] The Advisory Committee Notes interpreting provision (b)(2) shed some light on the issue, noting that (b)(2) 'does not extend to cases in which the appropriate final relief relates exclusively or predominately to money damages.'[36] This, of course, means that the Advisory Committee anticipated that some amount of monetary damages would be permissible in a (b)(2) class, so long as they did not predominate.[37] Given the Committee's endorsement of civil rights cases as prototypical

---

objective standards. 365 F.3d at 420 n. 20. While the majority conceded, 'one is left wondering in what circumstances (if any) the dissent would permit monetary damages in a rule 23(b)(2) class,' 365 F.3d at 420 n. 20, thereby belying the fact that the Fifth Circuit itself has yet to define the precise scope of Allison, the case confirms its narrow approach in employment cases. The Monumental Life Insurance majority made clear that its facts were distinguishable from those in Allison: 'This is not . . . like Allison, a title VII case in which class members' claims for compensatory and punitive damages necessarily implicated[] subjective differences of each plaintiff's circumstances.'" 365 F.3d at 419. The impact of Monumental Life Insurance on district court rulings in employment cases will be important to follow.

[34] See *Allison v. Citgo Petroleum Corp.*, 151 F.3d 402, 431–432 (5th Cir. 1998) (Dennis, J., dissenting), reh'g en banc denied with clarification, No. 96-30489, 1998 US App. LEXIS 24651 (5th Cir. October 2, 1998).

[35] See Fed. R. Civ. P. 23; see also *Parker v. Local Union No. 1466*, 642 F.2d 104, 107 (5th Cir. 1981) (explaining that while Rule 23(b)(2) explicitly refers to injunctive and declaratory relief, the text does not exclude the possibility of monetary relief).

[36] Fed. R. Civ. P. 23(b)(2) advisory committee's note.

[37] Plaintiffs have also been successful in obtaining back pay awards in (b)(2) classes prior to the enactment of the Civil Rights Act of 1991 because of the equitable nature of such relief. See *Allison*, 151 F.3d at 415 ('Back pay, of course, had long been recognized as an equitable remedy under Title VII.') (describing cases); see e.g., *Williams v. Owens-Ill., Inc.*, 665 F.2d 918, 928–929 (9th Cir. 1982) (describing back pay as equitable and incidental and distinguishing between compensatory damages), amended by, No. 79-4110, 1982 WL 308873 (9th Cir. June 11, 1982).

CHAPTER 4. FIGHTING TO KEEP EMPLOYMENT DISCRIMINATION

(b)(2) class actions,[38] it follows that the Committee must have foreseen the possibility of civil rights (b)(2) class actions involving monetary damages. The underlying policy rationale for Rule 23(b)(2) is to provide an effective tool for the vindication of civil rights,[39] which countenances certification where employees seek compensatory and punitive damages, as well as equitable relief. Finally, the purpose of the Civil Rights Act of 1991 favors a liberal interpretation of (b)(2) certification because it was enacted to bolster, not limit, employees' ability to seek relief for intentional employment discrimination.[40] This is true in the class context as well. For all the above stated reasons, the Fifth Circuit and others need not, and should not, read Rule 23(b)(2) so restrictively.[41]

4.2.4 Robinson v. Metro-North

In contrast, the Second Circuit, in *Robinson v. Metro-North Commuter R.R. Co.*, explicitly rejected *Allison*'s test and set forth an alternative analytical framework for certification under Rule 23(b)(2) when monetary damages are sought.[42] *Robinson* adopted an 'ad hoc' approach, whereby the district court must assess whether (b)(2) certification is appropriate in light of the 'relative importance of the remedies sought,

---

[38] See Fed. R. Civ. P. 23 advisory committee's note to subdivision (b)(2). (citing civil rights cases as illustrative).
[39] 5 James Wm. Moore et al., *supra* n. 19, 23.43[1][b], at 23–192 (3rd edn, 2005).
[40] See *Pollard v. E.I. du Pont de Nemours & Co.*, 532 US 843 (2001).
[41] Melissa Hart offers some compelling reasons for why the courts have sought to restrict (b)(2) certification of civil rights cases. She concludes that the courts are swayed by three things:

(1) the perception that class actions are unfair;
(2) the perception that employment class actions are unnecessary; and
(3) the concern that employment class actions are meritless.

See Melissa Hart, 'Will Employment Discrimination Class Actions Survive?,' 37 Akron L Rev 813 (2004).
[42] *Robinson v. Metro-North Commuter R.R.*, 267 F.3d 147, 164 (2nd Cir. 2001) ('The question we must decide is whether this bright-line bar to (b)(2) class treatment of all claims for compensatory damages and other non-incidental damages (e.g., punitive damages) is appropriate.... We believe that it is not and therefore decline to adopt the incidental damages approach set out by the Fifth Circuit in Allison and flowed by the district court below.').

given all of the facts and circumstances of the case.'[43] The court may certify a (b)(2) class, where in its 'informed sound judicial discretion,' it finds that:

> The positive weight or value [to the plaintiffs] of the injunctive or declaratory relief sought is predominant even though compensatory or punitive damages are... claimed... and (2) class treatment would be efficient and manageable, thereby achieving an appreciable measure of judicial economy.[44]

The Second Circuit elaborated that even using an ad hoc approach, a court must ensure two criteria are met to satisfy (b)(2) certification where plaintiffs seek monetary damages and injunctive relief:

> Even in the absence of a possible monetary recovery, reasonable plaintiffs would bring the suit to obtain the injunctive or declaratory relief sought; and 2) the injunctive or declaratory relief sought would be both reasonably necessary and appropriate were the plaintiffs to succeed on the merits.[45]

The *Robinson* approach is designed to promote judicial efficiency and to provide a case-by-case assessment of certification.[46] While the *Robinson* court conceded that (b)(2) certification of classes involving non-incidental monetary damages could present due process risks for absent class members, it encouraged courts to consider providing notice and opt-out rights to alleviate this concern.[47] The Ninth Circuit is the only other circuit to adopt *Robinson*'s analytical framework.[48]

4.2.5 Hybrid Approaches to Class Certification

Some courts, while adopting the *Allison* predomination test, have encouraged alternative means, such as bifurcation and hybrid certification,[49] for aiding employees seeking monetary damages and

---

[43] *Id.* at 164 (quoting *Hoffman v. Honda of Am. Mfg., Inc.*, 191 FRD 530, 536 (SD Ohio 1999)).
[44] *Id.*
[45] *Id.*
[46] *Id.* at 165.
[47] *Id.* at 165–167.
[48] See *Molski v. Gleich*, 318 F.3d 937, 949–950 (9th Cir. 2003).
[49] It is not unusual to bifurcate a civil rights case by having a jury consider the pattern and practice liability at Stage I and individual damages at Stage II. These

CHAPTER 4. FIGHTING TO KEEP EMPLOYMENT DISCRIMINATION

injunctive relief in obtaining class certification. For example, the Seventh Circuit, in *Jefferson v. Ingersoll International Inc.*, suggests ways that due process concerns might be overcome where plaintiffs seek significant monetary damages.[50] Because some class members might have a significant financial stake in the litigation, they may prefer not to be bound by a class judgment and instead to forge litigation on their own. Under such circumstances, certification under (b)(2) with no notice or right to opt out threatens to deprive absent class members of due process. Rather than deny certification altogether, *Jefferson* suggests that the district court consider: certifying the entire case under Rule 23(b)(3); certifying the entire case under Rule 23(b)(2) and provide notice and opt-out rights; or certifying class-wide liability and equitable issues under Rule 23(b)(2) while certifying damages issues under Rule 23(b)(3).[51] These alternatives are well within a court's discretion, address manageability concerns, and give employees the benefit of the class action device as a civil rights enforcement tool. They have been employed by many courts.[52]

---

are referred to as Teamsters hearings. See *Int'l Bhd. of Teamsters v. United States*, 431 US 324, 360–361 (1977); Manual for Complex Litigation (Fourth) 32.42 (2004).

[50] *Jefferson v. Ingersoll Int'l Inc.*, 195 F.3d 894, 898–899 (7th Cir. 1999). In Ingersoll, the district court granted (b)(2) certification where plaintiffs sought money damages. The Seventh Circuit vacated the certification order and remanded so that the district court could consider if the damages sought were 'incidental.' The Seventh Circuit, however, offered alternatives for how such a case could still be certified as a class action, even if the monetary damages predominated. See *id.*, 897–898.

[51] *Id.* at 897–899; see also *Lemon v. Int'l Union of Operating Eng'rs Local 139*, 216 F.3d 577, 581–582 (7th Cir. 2000); *Eubanks v. Billington*, 110 F.3d 87, 92–96 (DC Cir. 1997).

[52] See e.g., *Warnell v. Ford Motor Co.*, 189 F.R.D. 383, 387–389 (ND Ill. 1999) (certifying a Title VII case under (b)(2) and (b)(3)); *Smith v. Univ. of Wash.*, 233 F.3d 1188, 1196 (9th Cir. 2000) (holding that hybrid certification is available in Ninth Circuit), cert. denied, 532 US 1051 (2001); *Officers for Justice v. Civil Serv. Comm'n*, 688 F.2d 615, 632–633 (9th Cir. 1982), cert. denied, 459 US 1217 (1983); *Beck v. Boeing Co.*, 203 FRD 459, 465–468 (WD Wash. 2001) (certifying the liability phase under (b)(2) and the damages phase under (b)(3)), aff'd in part and vacated in part, 60 F. App'x 38 (9th Cir. 2003) (holding court abused its discretion by certifying damages phase under (b)(3) prematurely, while recognizing possibility of hybrid certification); *Barefield v. Chevron*, No. C-86-2427-TEH, 1988 WL 188433 (ND Cal. December 6, 1988); *Eubanks v. Billington*, 110 F.3d 87 (DC Cir. 1997); *Taylor v. Dist. of Columbia Water & Sewer Auth.*, 205 FRD 43, 48–50 (DDC 2002); *Wilson v. United Int'l Investigative Servs. 401(k) Savings Plan*, No. Civ.A. 01-CV-6126, 2002 WL 734339, at 6–7 (ED Pa. April 23,

4.2.6 The Supreme Court's Due Process Concerns

The circuit split continues because the Supreme Court has yet to determine the due process prerequisites for putative class members seeking significant monetary damages as well as injunctive relief under a (b)(2) class.[53] In *Phillips Petroleum Co. v. Shutts*, the Supreme Court did, however, address the issue of whether a court could bind absent class members who asserted claims 'wholly or predominantly for money damages' absent contacts with the forum state.[54] There, the Court concluded that before an absent class member's cause of action was extinguishable, due process mandated that the class member 'receive notice plus an opportunity to be heard and participate in the litigation' and 'at a minimum' be given 'an opportunity to remove himself from the class.'[55] And, of course, an absent class member's interests had to be adequately represented.[56] Because the Court explicitly limited its ruling to the scenario where plaintiffs sought wholly or predominantly monetary damages, there remained the question of what due process was required when plaintiffs sought some monetary damages as well as equitable relief in a mandatory class action – i.e., the '*Shutts* problem.'[57]

Unfortunately, this problem has not yet been solved. In *Ticor Title Insurance Co. v. Brown*,[58] the Supreme Court granted certiorari in hope of resolving, inter alia, whether notice and opt-out rights were required by due process in mandatory class actions.[59] Although the Court ultimately dismissed the writ as improvidently granted, it did note that there is 'at least a substantial possibility' that 'in actions seeking monetary damages, classes can be certified only under Rule 23(b)(3),

---

2002) (certifying injunctive relief under (b)(2) and damages under (b)(3) to avoid due process concerns in ERISA class action).

[53] See also Nagareda, *supra* n. 23 (discussing the problem of punitive damages within a limited fund case under Rule 23(b)(1) and arguing that this violates *Ortiz* and works against the interest of class members).

[54] *Phillips Petroleum Co. v. Shutts*, 472 US 797 (1985).

[55] *Id.* at 812.

[56] *Id.* (citing *Hansberry v. Lee*, 311 US 32, 42–43 (1940)).

[57] See Linda S. Mullenix, 'Getting to Shutts,' 46 U Kan L Rev 727, 730 (1998).

[58] *Ticor Title Ins. Co. v. Brown*, 510 US 810 (1993).

[59] Mandatory class actions are those brought pursuant to (b)(1) or (b)(2) where putative class members do not have a right to opt-out.

which permits opt-out, and not under Rules 23(b)(1) and (b)(2), which do not.'[60] In *Adams v. Robertson*, the Court admitted its 'continuing interest' in the *Shutts* problem but again concluded that the petition for writ of certiorari was improvidently granted.[61] In *Ortiz v. Fibreboard Corp.*, when presented with the issue of whether opt-out rights were necessary in mandatory class actions, the Supreme Court declined to address the issue and instead decided the case on other grounds.[62] The Supreme Court noted, however, that the 'inherent tension between representative suits and the day-in-court ideal is only magnified if applied to damage claims gathered in a mandatory class' because the 'legal rights of absent class members...are resolved regardless of either their consent, or...their express wish to the contrary.'[63] The Supreme Court's dicta suggest that courts' efforts to bolster due process procedural protections for class members seeking monetary damages in mandatory class actions are prudent. Nothing indicates, however, that the Supreme Court would never find it appropriate to permit (b)(2) certification where plaintiffs seek some degree of monetary damages and injunctive relief.

In sum, the enactment of the Civil Rights Act of 1991 has resulted in a serious schism among the courts over the correct interpretation of when monetary damages predominate, thereby foreclosing Rule 23(b)(2) certification in employment discrimination cases. In the absence of firm guidance from the Supreme Court on this issue, the courts will continue to provide inconsistent and incomplete justice for employees seeking to fully protect their Title VII statutory rights through the pursuit of compensatory and punitive damages and jury trials.

4.3 THE RESTRICTIVE INTERPRETATION OF THE PREDOMINATION REQUIREMENT THREATENS TO UNDERMINE CIVIL RIGHTS ENFORCEMENT

The narrow interpretation of the predomination requirement threatens to undermine enforcement of Title VII in various ways.

---

[60] *Ticor Title Ins. Co. v. Brown*, 511 US 117, 121 (1994).
[61] *Adams v. Robertson*, 520 US 83, 92 n. 6 (1997).
[62] *Ortiz v. Fibreboard Corp.*, 527 US 815 (1999).
[63] *Id.* at 846–847.

Specifically, enforcement will be jeopardized by fewer class certifications, fewer monetary damages being awarded, and greater costs and burdens to plaintiffs challenging systemic intentional discrimination.

4.3.1 Fewer Employment Discrimination Class Actions Will Be Certified

As never before, plaintiffs challenging systemic employment discrimination by filing class actions are facing additional, and sometimes insurmountable, hurdles. The terrain has become littered with cases rejected as class actions because plaintiffs sought monetary damages as well as injunctive relief on a class-wide basis. Although employees may pursue individual Title VII claims or have their interests represented by the Equal Employment Opportunity Commission,[64] these alternatives to a class action offer no solace because of the superiority of the class action device in vindicating civil rights.[65]

The class action device is an essential and irreplaceable component of the Title VII enforcement scheme for several reasons. First, while an employee may bring her own individual action, an employer can more easily mask and justify discrimination when challenged on an individual level. By bringing a pattern or practice claim against an employer, an employee can more easily identify and expose discriminatory conduct.[66] Second, as private attorneys general, plaintiffs in a class action can craft remedies and injunctive relief that are far greater

---

[64] See Daniel F. Piar, 'The Uncertain Future of Title VII Class Actions after the Civil Rights Act of 1991,' 2001 BYU L Rev 305, 345 (2001) (claiming individual suit is, for the individual, 'an equivalent opportunity for justice' to the class action).

[65] The Equal Employment Opportunity Commission, which is tasked with Title VII enforcement in pattern or practice cases, offers no solace either. This government agency may easily be restricted by limited resources and political will. See Hart, *supra* n. 41, at 844; but see, Piar, *supra* n. 64, at 345–346.

[66] See, e.g., *Graniteville Co. (Sibley Division) v. EEOC*, 438 F.2d 32, 38 (4th Cir. 1971). The Fourth Circuit observed: 'Sophisticated general policies and practices of discrimination are not susceptible to such precise delineation by a layman who is in no position to carry out a full-fledged investigation himself' although 'long observation of plant practice may bring the realization that he and his black coemployees are not getting anywhere.' *Id.*

in scope than those in an individual case.[67] Third, the class action mechanism enables individuals with small resources and claims to pool them together and share risk and burdens so that they can pursue such claims. In the absence of such a scheme, it is unlikely that a 'negative value suit' – an action in which the attorney's fees exceed the available damages – would be pursued by an individual, and, even more unlikely, by an attorney. Finally, a finding of class-wide liability shifts the burden of proof in favor of plaintiffs.[68] By proving a pattern or practice of discrimination, each class member enjoys a rebuttable presumption that he was victimized by the discrimination as an individual.[69] The defendant has the burden of proving otherwise.[70] Given the power of this procedural device, victims of employment discrimination have been able to obtain significant relief for over four decades. The fewer class actions certified the less effective civil rights enforcement will be.

4.3.2 Fewer Monetary Damages Will Be Awarded to Those Who Deserve Them

The restrictive predomination requirement jeopardizes employees' ability to obtain full relief. While the Fifth Circuit and others contend that the inclusion of compensatory and punitive damages normally

---

[67] See *Zepeda v. INS*, 753 F.2d 719, 727–729 (9th Cir. 1983) (in absence of class certification, injunction was limited to individual plaintiffs); *Nat'l Center for Immigrant Rights v. INS*, 743 F.2d 1365, 1371–1372 (9th Cir. 1984) (same), vacated on other grounds, 481 US 1009 (1987); *Bresgal v. Brock*, 843 F.2d 1163, 1170–1171 (9th Cir. 1987) (noting that in absence of certification, class-wide relief was only available to named plaintiffs); *Lowery v. Circuit City Stores, Inc.*, 158 F.3d 742, 766–767 (4th Cir. 1998), vacated and remanded on other grounds, 527 US 1031 (1999) (systemic injunction going beyond providing individual plaintiffs relief reversed); but see Piar, *supra* n. 64, at 345–346 (arguing that 'sweeping changes are therefore possible (though usually only prospectively) in nonclass cases').

[68] *Int'l Bd. of Teamsters v. United States*, 431 US 324, 360 (1977).

[69] *Cooper v. Fed. Reserve Bank of Richmond*, 467 US 867, 875–876 (1984) (citing *Franks v. Bowman Transp. Co.*, 424 US 747, 772 (1976)).

[70] *Teamsters*, 431 US at 361–362; *Franks v. Bowman Transp.*, 424 US 747, 772–773 (1976); *Cooper v. Fed. Reserve Bank of Richmond*, 467 US at 875–876; *Robinson v. Metro-North Commuter R.R. Co.*, 267 F.3d 147, 168 (2nd Cir. 2001), cert. denied, 535 US 951 (2002). This burden-shifting scheme is not available through other multi-aggregate party

forecloses (b)(2) and (b)(3) class certification in Title VII cases, this interpretation is unwarranted. Such an interpretation puts plaintiffs in a dilemma that Congress could not have intended. Employees are confronted with the untenable choice of foregoing the monetary damages to which they are entitled under the Civil Rights Act of 1991 to ensure classwide injunctive relief, or abandoning class treatment altogether; thereby abandoning their mandate to challenge widespread systemic discrimination as private attorneys-general. It was not Congress' intention to compel victims of intentional discrimination to choose between their right to monetary damages and complete injunctive relief.

In enacting the Civil Rights Act of 1991, Congress sought to bolster the rights of victims of intentional discrimination and expand the remedies available to them, in both the individual and class action context.[71] This was accomplished by providing for compensatory and punitive damages and a jury demand.[72] One of the legislature's major goals of amending the Civil Rights Act of 1964 was to overturn *Wards Cove Packing Co., Inc. v. Atonio*,[73] and *Martin v. Wilks*,[74] decisions in which the Supreme Court limited remedies for discrimination.[75] The legislative history makes clear that Congress valued the class action and anticipated its continued viability after the 1991 amendments. Notwithstanding the minority view that permitting damages in class actions alleging intentional discrimination on the basis of statistical proof would unfairly burden employers and coerce them into covertly

---

tools such as consolidation under Rule 42. But see Piar, *supra* n. 64, at 346 (equating efficiencies of class action with Rule 42's provision for consolidation and severance).

[71] Civil Rights Act of 1991, Pub. L. No. 102-166, 2(1), 105 Stat. 1071 (codified as amended at 42 USCA 1981 (1994)) (finding 'additional remedies under Federal law are needed to deter unlawful...intentional discrimination in the workplace'); *id.* 3(1), (4) (stating that Congress passed the Act 'to provide appropriate remedies for intentional discrimination...in the workplace...and expand[] the scope of relevant civil rights statutes in order to provide adequate protection to victims of discrimination'); see also HR Rep. No. 102-40 (I), at 4, as reprinted in 1991 USCCAN 549, 602, 603, 607 (recognizing a damages remedy is necessary for deterrence).

[72] See *Pollard v. E.I. du Pont de Nemours & Co.*, 532 US 843, 852 (2001) (explaining the intention of the Act is to expand remedies, not contract them).

[73] 490 US 642 (1989).

[74] 490 US 755 (1989).

[75] HR Rep. No. 102-40 (I), at 4 (1991), as reprinted in 1991 USCCAN at 595.

CHAPTER 4. FIGHTING TO KEEP EMPLOYMENT DISCRIMINATION

applying quotas to avoid litigation,[76] Congress did not take steps to curtail the availability of class-wide damages.[77]

Despite the legislature's intent to the contrary, the Fifth Circuit and others have put plaintiffs in a no-win situation, in which some feel compelled as a cost of certification to forgo damages altogether, to choose between compensatory or punitive damages, or to limit the amount of potential damages by using formulas.

For example, plaintiffs may seek punitive damages because they arguably do not require the individualized determinations that compensatory damages do. To the extent that the Fifth Circuit in *Allison* permits a punitive damage award on a class-wide basis where each plaintiff is affected by a discriminatory policy in the same way,[78] class counsel may chose to strategically forgo compensatory damages. In *Dukes v. Wal-Mart Stores, Inc.*,[79] for example, plaintiffs alleged that Wal-Mart engaged in company-wide discrimination in pay and promotions against a class of approximately 1.5 million women, in violation of

---

[76] See HR Rep. No. 102-40 (II), at 68 (1991), as reprinted in 1991 USCCAN 549, 694, 754 (finding that 'not only would HR 1 allow the recovery of punitive and compensatory damages in individual disparate treatment cases, it would allow recovery of such damages and jury trials for class action disparate treatment suits'); see also HR Rep. No. 102-40 (I), at 127 (1991), as reprinted in 1991 USCCAN at 656 ('Further, the concerns with "quotas"... are heightened by inclusion of punitive and compensatory damages. Class action intentional discrimination claims are also based on statistical imbalances; employers will again feel inordinate pressure to engage in race-and sex-based preferential treatment.').

[77] See e.g., HR Rep. No. 102-40(I), at 143, as reprinted in 1991 USCCAN at 672 ('Class actions claiming intentional discrimination will be based – as they are under current law – on racial and sexual statistical imbalances in the workforce.'); HR Rep. No. 102-40 (II), at 68, as reprinted in 1991 USCCAN at 754 ('Not only would H.R. 1 allow the recovery of punitive and compensatory damages in individual disparate treatment cases, it would allow recovery of such damages and jury trials for class action disparate treatment suits.'); 137 Cong. Rec. E2086-01 (1991) (statement of Rep. Doolittle (quoting letter from Zachary Fasman, Attorney of Paul, Hastings, Janofsky & Walker, to Bill Goodling, Congressman)) ('The proponents of this legislation consistently have argued that the expanded remedies in question will apply only to cases of intentional discrimination. In fact, the bill would allow compensatory and punitive damages in class actions premised upon the disparate treatment theory of discrimination.').

[78] *Allison v. Citgo Petroleum Corp.*, 151 F.3d 402, 417 (5th Cir. 1998).

[79] 222 FRD 137 (ND Cal. 2004).

EMPLOYMENT CLASS AND COLLECTIVE ACTIONS

Title VII. In the largest private-employer civil rights case in American history, the district court certified a class action where plaintiffs chose to forgo compensatory damages and instead sought class-wide injunctive and declaratory relief, lost pay, and punitive damages.[80] Wal-Mart has challenged the propriety of class certification, and the Ninth Circuit has granted its Rule 23(f) petition for review.

In *Beck v. Boeing Co.*, female employees challenged the Boeing Company with gender-based employment discrimination in promotions and compensation under Title VII and various other federal civil rights laws.[81] Plaintiffs chose not to seek back pay, individualized equitable relief, or punitive damages for their promotions claims, but instead pursued injunctive relief for a pattern or practice of discriminatory promotion-making.[82] Plaintiffs, however, did seek back pay, injunctive relief, and punitive damages for a pattern or practice of discriminatory compensation, which would flow from a finding of class-wide liability.[83] Defendants argued that plaintiffs were inadequate representatives because they failed to seek all potential relief in a mandatory class action – thereby jeopardizing absent class members' ability to pursue such relief in the future because of *Shutts*.[84] The district court rejected defendants' argument on the grounds that the court could certify a notice and opt-out class under (b)(3) for the punitive damages portion of the litigation.[85] Moreover, the court recognized that in bringing only certain types of relief in a (b)(2) class, plaintiffs were identifying the injunctive relief as primary.[86] Plaintiffs used statistics and testimony from Boeing's most senior executives to demonstrate that Boeing's decision making affected the class as a whole. This convinced the court that individualized, fact-specific inquiries were unnecessary and that punitive damages could be awarded on a class-wide basis.[87] Thus, the district court certified the class for the liability phase

---

[80] *Id.* at 141, 170.
[81] *Beck v. Boeing Co.*, 203 FRD 459, 460–461 (WD Wash. 2001), aff'd in part & vacated in part, 60 F. App'x 38 (9th Cir. 2003) (unpublished).
[82] *Id.* at 461, 465.
[83] *Id.*
[84] *Id.* at 465.
[85] *Id.*
[86] *Id.*
[87] *Id.* at 466–467.

CHAPTER 4. FIGHTING TO KEEP EMPLOYMENT DISCRIMINATION

under (b)(2) and the punitive damages phase under (b)(3).[88] Plaintiffs' success, however, was short-lived. The Ninth Circuit vacated the court's certification in part, concluding that it abused its discretion by certifying the class for punitive damages claims in Phase II of the litigation. The Ninth Circuit held that it was premature for the court to have certified the Phase II punitive damages class.[89]

Unitary punitive damage awards are appropriate because 'the purpose of punitive damages is not to compensate the victim, but to punish and deter the defendant, [therefore] any claim for such damages hinges, not on facts unique to each class member, but on the defendant's conduct toward the class as a whole.'[90] Moreover, punitive damages are more likely to be considered incidental when treated as an outgrowth of defendant's systemic misconduct:

> The addition of a class-wide claim for punitive damages, to claims for injunctive and declaratory relief, and lost pay, does not render the monetary aspect of the case predominant. Rather, such relief may be treated as ancillary to the claims for injunctive and declaratory relief which remain at the heart of this action.[91]

However, while punitive damages may lend themselves to class certification, plaintiffs should not be limited to such damages in order to get a class certified.

---

[88] Ironically, the district court did not certify the request for back pay for the claims of pay discrimination, concluding that individualized inquiries would be necessary. *Id.* at 468.

[89] *Beck v. Boeing Co.*, 60 F. App'x 38, at 39–40 (9th Cir. 2003) (unpublished).

[90] *Barefield v. Chevron, U.S.A., Inc.*, No. C-86-2427-TEH, 1988 WL 188433, at 3 (ND Cal. December 6, 1988) (citing *Jenkins v. Raymark Indus., Inc.*, 782 F.2d 468, 474 (5th Cir. 1986), reh'g denied, 785 F.2d 1034 (5th Cir. 1986) (applied in asbestos case)). Note, however, that in *Smith v. Texaco*, the Fifth Circuit suggested that in Title VII cases, in accordance with Allison and Jenkins, punitive damages, like compensatory damages, rely on individual inquiries when considering predominance. Despite the fact that the *Smith v. Texaco* opinion was withdrawn and the case dismissed, the Fifth Circuit may retain this view. *Smith v. Texaco, Inc.*, 263 F.3d 394, 408–413, n. 23 (5th Cir. 2001), withdrawn, 281 F.3d 477 (5th Cir. 2002). Interestingly, the court in Allison even conceded that class-wide awards of punitive damages may be appropriate under some circumstances. See *Allison v. Citgo Petroleum Corp.*, 151 F.3d 402, 417 (5th Cir. 1998).

[91] *Barefield*, 1988 WL 188433, at 3 (ND Cal. December 6, 1988) (citing *Fontana v. Elrod*, 826 F.2d 729, 730 (7th Cir. 1987) (certifying a (b)(2) class seeking punitive damages));

EMPLOYMENT CLASS AND COLLECTIVE ACTIONS

Other plaintiffs have pursued compensatory damages but sought to reduce their complexity to increase the likelihood of certification, despite the fact that such an approach may yield lower damages for the class. While some courts require substantial evidence to justify the award of compensatory damages,[92] others may grant such damages for 'garden variety' emotional harm and distress claims, without requiring medical or other expert testimony.[93] However, such 'garden variety' compensatory claims will likely yield lesser, if not nominal, damages for class members.[94] In an effort to assuage the court of manageability concerns, plaintiffs compromise the amount of damages to which they may be entitled. Again, plaintiffs choose between full relief and class certification.[95]

Stolz v. United Bhd. of Carpenters Local 971, 620 F. Supp. 396, 406–407 (D Nev. 1985) (certifying a (b)(2) class seeking punitive damages); *Edmondson v. Simon*, 86 FRD 375, 383 (ND Ill. 1980) (certifying a (b)(2) class seeking compensatory and punitive damages); accord *Butler v. Home Depot, Inc.*, No. C-94-4335 SI, 1996 WL 421436 (ND Cal. January 25, 1996). Some courts have also awarded punitive damages on a class-wide basis in cases outside of the employment and civil rights contexts. See e.g., *Hilao v. Estate of Marcos*, 103 F.3d 767, 786 (9th Cir. 1996) (human rights violations); In re Exxon Valdez, 229 F.3d 790 (9th Cir. 2000) (environmental claims), reh'g granted, 270 F.3d 1215 (9th Cir. 2001); *Day v. NLO*, 851 F. Supp. 869, 884–885, 887 (SD Ohio 1994) (permitting plaintiff class to seek punitive damages for injuries allegedly resulting from radiation exposure).

[92] See e.g., *Allison*, 151 F.3d at 417; *Patterson v. P.H.P. Healthcare Corp.*, 90 F.3d 927, 938–940 (5th Cir. 1996) (citing cases); *Price v. City of Charlotte*, 93 F.3d 1241, 1250–1256 (4th Cir. 1996) (citing cases).

[93] For example, in *Burrell v. Crown Central Petroleum*, plaintiffs who chose not to put forth medical or psychiatric evidence to prove emotional harm and distress damages were excused from having to produce such information in discovery. See *Burrell v. Crown Cent. Petroleum*, 177 FRD 376 (ED Tex. 1997). The court concluded that where the 'crux of the case is the work-related income loss resulting from discrimination[,]' then 'mental anguish is incidental to the work-related economic damages like lost wages.' Id. at 380.

[94] See e.g., *Burrell*, 177 FRD at 384.

[95] Such a quandary could be ameliorated in the Ninth Circuit, where the courts permit plaintiffs to seek compensatory damages for emotional harm and distress without introducing economic loss or medical evidence. Instead, the plaintiff's own testimony and inferences from the circumstances may form the basis for proof of an individual's emotional harm and distress. See *Phiffer v. Proud Parrot Motor Hotel, Inc.*, 648 F.2d 548, 552–553 (9th Cir. 1980); *Johnson v. Hale*, 940 F.2d 1192, 1193 (9th Cir. 1991); *Passantino v. Johnson & Johnson Consumer Prods., Inc.*, 212 F.3d 493, 513 (9th Cir.

CHAPTER 4. FIGHTING TO KEEP EMPLOYMENT DISCRIMINATION

Whether plaintiffs forgo compensatory or punitive damages or both, or limit their potential relief, defendants are protected by the uncertainty created by the courts' narrow predomination test. Where plaintiffs are risk averse, defendants found guilty of intentional discrimination are inoculated from the risk of having to pay significant damages. Because plaintiffs appropriately fear that they will not be able to get a (b)(2) case certified if they seek monetary damages as well as injunctive relief, defendants enjoy a windfall.

Moreover, the restrictive predomination interpretation not only gives defendants a monetary boon, it also undermines deterrence objectives. If compensatory and punitive damages are per se not 'incidental,' plaintiffs are less likely to obtain certification when they seek the most significant damage awards.[96] Ironically, in the most egregious discrimination cases – where systemic intentional misconduct results in extensive emotional harm and warrants punitive damages – defendants enjoy the most protection from class-wide exposure. Alternatively, where plaintiffs seek back pay – an equitable remedy that merely makes the plaintiffs whole – defendants are more likely to incur class-wide liability because such mandatory relief is considered 'incidental.' Thus, defendants have a greater risk of a monetary penalty when there is less money at stake. Deterrence objectives of Title VII and the Civil Rights Act of 1991 are not served where defendant's only real exposure to class-wide relief involve those cases concerning the least amount of money.

2000). Class members who suffer in similar ways could reasonably be rewarded similar compensatory damages. For example, in a multi-party case, *Lambert v. Ackerley*, 180 F.3d 997, 1011 (9th Cir. 1999), each plaintiff received an identical award of USD 75,000 where 'the jury likely concluded that the emotional harm to each plaintiff was roughly equal given the similar treatment each plaintiff suffered at the hands of the defendants.' A similar approach could be taken for class members.

[96] To the extent that class members have incurred different amounts of compensatory and punitive damages because of their individual circumstances, it follows that certification of a mandatory class action might be less desirable – especially in cases involving extensive monetary damages – because of a breakdown in class cohesion. Those class members who have a greater financial stake in the litigation would seek to have their due process rights protected through notice and the right to opt-out, features required under (b)(3). However, these protections and others could be provided in a (b)(2) class, subject to the court's discretion.

Finally, plaintiffs who sacrifice damages for the sake of (b)(2) certification risk being attacked as inadequate class representatives. Where a plaintiff fails to pursue all of the claims available to the class, such as compensatory and punitive damages claims, absent class members may be precluded from later raising such claims individually because of res judicata.[97] For example, in *Zachery v. Texaco Exploration and Production, Inc.*,[98] the named plaintiffs decided to drop their claims for compensatory and punitive damages to maximize the chance of getting their Title VII case for class-wide disparate treatment certified under Rule 23(b)(2). The court denied certification because it was 'greatly concerned' that the named plaintiffs' unilateral decision to drop the damages claims would preclude class members in the future from being able to seek the monetary damages to which they were entitled.[99]

Moreover, because the law is not yet settled on the question of whether a class member is entitled to opt out from a (b)(2) class seeking monetary damages, the court in *Zachery* was hesitant to permit plaintiffs to 'gamble away...class members' potential rights to compensatory' and punitive damages.[100] Given that the named plaintiffs chose not to pursue the monetary damages that some class members wanted and might not have had the opportunity to seek individually, the court concluded that the named plaintiffs were inadequate representatives due to a conflict of interest.[101]

---

[97] See *Cooper v. Federal Reserve Bank of Richmond*, 467 US 867, 874 (1984) (holding that a class action decision generally binds the parties in subsequent decisions).

[98] 185 FRD 230, 242–244 (WD Tex. 1999).

[99] *Id.* at 243 ('It is a very real possibility, if not a probability, that another court of competent jurisdiction could determine that the proposed class members would be barred from bringing individual actions for damages arising from intentional acts of discrimination if the class obtained a finding of intentional discrimination in this Court.').

[100] *Id.* at 244 (discussing *Ticor Title Ins. Co. v. Brown*, 511 US 117, 118–121 (1994) (per curiam) (6-3 decision)).

[101] *Id.* at 244, 245; see Bartlett III, *supra* n. 19, at 2165 (discussing the competing goals of 23(b)(2) class certification and 23(b)(3) class certification in terms of the interests of the parties); Piar, *supra* n. 64, at 323–324 (discussing same); but see *Farmers Group, Inc. v. Geter*, Nos 09-03-404 CV, 09-03-396 CV, 2004 WL 2365394, at 6 (Tex. App.-Beaumont, October 21, 2004) (not finding possible conflict of interest as grounds for inadequacy). See also *Miller v. Baltimore Gas & Elec. Co.*, 202 F.R.D. 195, 203 (D Md. 2001) (court

CHAPTER 4. FIGHTING TO KEEP EMPLOYMENT DISCRIMINATION

Plaintiffs and their attorneys should not be forced into the dilemma of having to forgo monetary damages to obtain class certification. Due process requires that in order for an absent class member to be bound by a class judgment, his interests must have been adequately represented in the class proceedings. Plaintiffs who seek to curtail intentional employment discrimination on a large scale, however, are being forced to choose between pursuing all available claims or being deemed inadequate because they decided to forgo certain claims or relief to improve their chance of class certification. Equating adequacy with strategy, however, may lead to untoward results. Certainly, in any class action there are bound to be differences among the named plaintiffs and the other class members about various strategic decisions, including what claims to bring and relief to seek. The court must protect the interests of the class as a whole; if there is a minority of class members who diverge from the whole, the court may take measures to protect its separate interests. For example, such differences might be better resolved by certifying subclasses or specific issues under Rule 23(c)(4), rather than denying certification altogether.

In sum, *Allison*'s restrictive predomination interpretation threatens to decrease the amount of monetary damages to which victims of employment discrimination are entitled. In an effort to save the class action mechanism, which is critical to civil rights enforcement, plaintiffs are compelled to choose between two conflicting alternatives. Plaintiffs are forced to choose between certification and full relief. On the one hand, plaintiffs must forgo certain relief (primarily compensatory and punitive damages) to improve their chances of certification. On the other hand, plaintiffs must seek complete relief so as not to be deemed inadequate or to preclude class members from certain remedies based on *Shutts*.[102]

---

denied plaintiff's motion for leave to amend class complaint to drop claims for compensatory and punitive damages, concluding that the motion 'raises serious questions regarding the ability of the named plaintiffs to represent the putative class adequately'); *Cooper v. Southern Co.*, 390 F.3d 695, 721 (11th Cir. 2004) (named plaintiffs' willingness to forego damages to achieve class certification called into question their adequacy to represent the class).

[102] See *Baltimore Gas & Electric Co.*, 202 FRD at 203 (describing 'Hobson's Choice').

4.3.3 Plaintiffs Will Have to Meet the More Rigorous and Costly Certification Standards of Rule 23(b)(3)

Since the Fifth Circuit and other courts increasingly have been denying victims of employment discrimination (b)(2) certification where they seek compensatory and punitive damages as well as injunctive relief, plaintiffs have been compelled to seek (b)(3) certification, which imposes a more formidable standard that has not historically been used in Title VII cases. This movement has subjected plaintiffs to greater costs and burdens.

First, the cost of pursuing a (b)(3) class is greater than a (b)(2) class, which may chill Title VII enforcement for some plaintiffs and their counsel. Pursuit of a (b)(3) case may cost more than a (b)(2) one because the named plaintiffs are required to send personal notice to each individual class member who can be identified through reasonable effort, pursuant to Rule 23(c)(2)(B). Because class counsel must attempt to identify, locate, and contact every potential class member, notice can be prohibitively expensive, which in turn may discourage class counsel from bringing meritorious civil rights cases. Appropriate notice may be ordered at the discretion of the court for a (b)(2) class, pursuant to Rule 23(c)(2)(A) and Rule 23(d), and may take many forms, including much less expensive methodologies such as publication notice or postings on websites.[103] However, notice under (b)(3) – a cost plaintiffs usually bear[104] – must be the 'best notice practicable under the circumstances,

---

[103] The Advisory Committee Note to the 2003 Amendments explains that the court's 'authority to direct notice to class members in a (b)(1) or (b)(2) class action should be exercised with care.' The Advisory Committee cautions the court to consider the costs of notice and encourages informal and inexpensive means when possible:

> The court may decide not to direct notice after balancing the risk that notice costs may deter the pursuit of class relief against the benefits of notice.... When the court does direct certification notice in a (b)(1) or (b)(2) class action, the discretion and flexibility established by subdivision (c)(2)(A) extend to the method of giving notice.... Informal methods may prove effective. A simple posting in a place visited by many class members, directing attention to a source of more detailed information, may suffice. The court should consider the costs of notice in relation to the probable reach of inexpensive methods.

Fed. R. Civ. P. 23 advisory committee's note to 2003 amendments subdiv. (c), para. (2).
[104] See 'Manual for Complex Litigation' (Fourth) 32.42 (2004); see also *Eisen v. Carlisle & Jacquelin*, 417 US 156, 177 (1974).

CHAPTER 4. FIGHTING TO KEEP EMPLOYMENT DISCRIMINATION

including individual notice to all members who can be identified through reasonable effort.'[105] For example, notice to the class can easily cost hundreds of thousands of dollars, depending on the size and nature of the case.[106] Thus, the cost of (b)(3) notice may chill plaintiffs from bringing class-wide civil rights cases, resulting in the under-enforcement of Title VII.

Second, the provision of opt-out rights under provision (b)(3) may undermine the plaintiffs' ability to settle. If a significant number of class members opt out, thereby denying the defendant the 'peace' he bought, a settlement fair, reasonable, and adequate to the class may be jeopardized.

Third, those plaintiffs who are able and willing to bear the higher cost of notice and the risk that opt-outs may undermine a potential settlement, also face a more difficult certification standard under Rule 23(b)(3) in certain circuits. Because Rule 23(b)(3) is designed to provide aggregate litigation where there is the least amount of cohesiveness among class members, it requires that:

(1) common questions predominate over individual ones; and
(2) the class action is superior to other mechanisms.[107]

Although the question of whether a pattern or practice of discrimination exists often suffices as a common question under Rule 23(a)(2), individual determinations of compensatory and punitive damages often dwarf this common question under Rule 23(b)(3). Plaintiffs' ability to overcome the (b)(3) hurdle often depends on the extent to which courts believe that compensatory and punitive damages must be determined on an individualized basis and through labor-intensive hearings.[108] Those courts which conclude that individualized hearings on damages are necessary will likely also conclude that

---

[105] Fed. R. Civ. P. 23(c)(2)(B).

[106] See e.g., *Ahearn v. Fibreboard Co.*, 162 F.R.D. 505, 528 (ED Tex. 1995) (cost of notice to absent class members was approximately USD 22 million).

[107] See Linda S. Mullenix, 'No Exit: Mandatory Class Actions in the New Millennium and the Blurring of Categorical Imperatives,' 2003 U Chi Legal F 177, 215, 215 (because Rule 23(b)(2) classes 'do not need to meet the more stringent 23(b)(3) requirements of predominance and superiority, certification under the mandatory classes is viewed as easier, and more desirable').

[108] Courts are also impacted by whether they believe individual class members must still prove liability after a class-wide liability determination.

a class action is not superior to other mechanisms because of manageability problems.[109]

The courts may be developing another schism over their willingness to certify cases under (b)(3) where plaintiffs seek compensatory and punitive damages as well as injunctive relief for Title VII violations. For example, the Fifth Circuit and Eleventh Circuits – which are apt to conclude that damages must be determined on an individualized basis – are also more likely to deny (b)(3) certification on the grounds that individualized inquiries predominate over common ones.[110] The Third and Seventh Circuits, however, have demonstrated a greater willingness to certify (b)(3) classes under similar circumstances.[111] For example, in *Chiang v. Veneman*, plaintiffs challenged the United States Department of Agriculture for lending discrimination, in violation of the Equal Credit Opportunity Act. The Third Circuit held that (b)(3)'s predominance and superiority requirements were met despite the fact that plaintiffs sought approximately USD 2.8 billion in damages, which plaintiffs conceded involved individualized proof.[112] In *Lemon v. International Union of Operating Engineers, Local 139*, the Seventh Circuit vacated a district court's class certification order under (b)(2), concluding that individualized inquiries were necessary to determine compensatory and punitive damages in this Title VII case. The Seventh Circuit, however, then directed the district court to consider various alternative class certification options under (b)(3). Thus, plaintiffs are again being subjected to different standards of justice, depending upon the circuit in which their case is brought.

The additional challenges of (b)(3) certification in certain circuits threaten to discourage plaintiffs from pursuing meritorious civil rights

---

[109] Moreover, courts may be concerned that bifurcation violates the Seventh Amendment's Re-examination Clause, now that both stages of Title VII cases are tried to a jury. See e.g., *Allison v. Citgo Petroleum Corp.*, 151 F.3d 402, 422–425 (5th Cir. 1998). The Reexamination Clause states that 'no fact tried by jury, shall be otherwise reexamined in any Court of the United States, than according to the rules of the common law.' US Const. amend. VII; see also *Gasoline Prods. Co. v. Champlin Ref. Co.*, 283 US 494, 500 (1931) (regarding same).
[110] See e.g., *Allison*, 151 F.3d 402; *Cooper v. Southern Co.*, 390 F.3d 695, 721–723 (11th Cir. 2004).
[111] See e.g., *Lemon v. Int'l Union of Operating Eng'rs*, Local No. 139, 216 F.3d 577, 581–582 (7th Cir. 2000); *Chiang v. Veneman*, 385 F.3d 256, 273 (3rd Cir. 2004).
[112] *Chiang*, 385 F.3d at 273.

cases, resulting in the under-enforcement of Title VII. Under the restrictive predomination test, some plaintiffs will be prohibited from bringing a case under either (b)(2) or (b)(3). For those class members who cannot bring their cases individually, they will be precluded from vindicating their statutory rights at all. Thus, the ad hoc predomination test is necessary to preserve the Title VII enforcement scheme.

4.4 THE *ROBINSON* AD HOC BALANCING TEST IS A SUPERIOR PREDOMINATION TEST FOR THE ENFORCEMENT OF TITLE VII

The Second Circuit's ad hoc balancing approach enforces Title VII and its underlying purposes better than the *Allison* restrictive predomination approach. First, the *Robinson* approach more aptly recognizes the underlying rationale of the (b)(2) class and its basis in class cohesiveness. As a number of scholars have noted, the presence of monetary damages – even nonincidental ones – does not necessarily trample the cohesiveness of a class bound by a common injury where injunctive or declaratory relief is appropriate to the class as a whole.[113] Recognizing both the words and spirit of Title VII, the *Robinson* ad hoc balancing test properly compares the value of the monetary damages to the injunctive and declaratory relief sought. Utilizing an overly-narrow definition of incidental, the *Allison* test improperly gives inordinate weight to the individualized nature of monetary damages and insufficient weight to the value of class-wide injunctive and declaratory relief.

The *Robinson* ad hoc approach sufficiently addresses potential due process concerns by promoting the use of traditional safeguards such as bifurcation of class-wide liability and individual damages

---

[113] See Hart, *supra* n. 41, at 827 ('The fact that individual members may also have individual damage claims against the employer does not necessarily diminish the significance of the shared burden. Nor does the existence of individual damages claims create intragroup conflict...'); W. Lyle Stamps, 'Getting Title VII Back on Track: Leaving Allison Behind for the Robinson Line,' 17 BYU J Pub L 411, 432–433, 447–448 (2003) (calling the *Allison* approach overly inclusive because neither the text nor plain meaning of advisory committee note requires that monetary damages be secondary, insignificant or dependent upon injunctive or declaratory relief to be appropriate under (b)(2)).

determinations,[114] importation of notice and the right to opt out of mandatory classes, and the use of significant judicial discretion and oversight.[115] Moreover, use of Rule 23(c)(4) to permit certification solely of class-wide liability issues under (b)(2) properly recognizes a district court's power to certify certain issues as a tool for managing complex litigation, rather than as an end run around Rule 23.[116]

The *Robinson* ad hoc approach protects victims of employment discrimination by preserving one of the most powerful enforcement mechanisms available – the class action device. Damage limits of up to USD 300,000 under Title VII have led some to believe that employment discrimination cases are no longer negative value suits – not worth the cost of litigation.[117] Empirical research indicates, however, that the availability of attorneys' fees, monetary damages, and litigation on an individual basis does not overcome the negative value suit dilemma faced by those denied class certification.[118] Furthermore, without strength in numbers in employment discrimination actions, individual employees are understandably deterred from bringing suit by fear of retaliation and personal exposure.[119] Even if plaintiffs may have a greater incentive to pursue their individual claims because of Title VII's

---

[114] Various courts have promoted the use of bifurcation and hybrid claims to preserve class certification where plaintiffs seek monetary damages as well as injunctive and declaratory relief under Title VII, as discussed *supra* in Part II E. Various scholars have promoted the same. See e.g., Robert M. Brava-Partian, 'Due Process, Rule 23 and Hybrid Classes: A Practical Solution,' 53 Hastings LJ 1359, 1363–1378 (2002); Meghan E. Changelo, 'Reconciling Class Action Certification with the Civil Rights Act of 1991,' 36 Colum JL & Soc Probs 133, 152–162 (2003).

[115] See Hart, *supra* n. 41, at 814; Stamps, *supra* n. 113, at 434.

[116] See *Robinson v. Metro-North Commuter R.R.*, 267 F.3d 147, 167–169 (2nd Cir. 2001); *Allison*, 151 F.3d at 421–422 (accusing plaintiffs of attempting to 'manufacture predominance through the nimble use of subdivision (c)(4)' through severance of individual specific issues). See also Piar, *supra* n. 64, at 324–335 (describing attempt to reconcile the Civil Rights Act of 1991 remedies with Rule 23(b)(2) as distorting both).

[117] Piar, *supra* n. 64, at 314, 331.

[118] See Stamps, *supra* n. 113, at 444–447 (concluding that *Allison* approach would 'effectively eviscerate Title VII enforcement' and that 'many individual plaintiffs may be effectively barred from bringing their claims due to the small recoveries available compared to litigation expenses').

[119] *Id.* at 446.

CHAPTER 4. FIGHTING TO KEEP EMPLOYMENT DISCRIMINATION

USD 300,000 damage cap, plaintiffs are not able to spread the costs of litigation as class members would be able to in the class action context.[120] Thus, the class action device permits employees to challenge widespread discriminatory practices that would otherwise go unaddressed. Moreover, the increase in individual suits that may follow from fewer class certifications would create further backlog in the courts, undermining judicial economy and efficiency.[121]

The *Robinson* ad hoc approach has been criticized because certification has the potential to pressure innocent defendants overwhelmed by the confluence of bad publicity, exorbitant litigation costs, and tremendous risk into unfavorable settlements.[122] While class certification often changes the bargaining power of the parties to the detriment of defendants, there is no reason to believe that defendants, who often control the evidence, would not be able to defeat truly meritless claims through the use of dispositive motions.

Although the *Robinson* scheme 'sacrifices simplicity for flexibility,'[123] such flexibility is crucial to the enforcement of Title VII. The *Robinson* ad hoc approach affords proper deference to the trial court in its certification determination. It is well established that courts enjoy broad discretion in this determination, given the highly factual nature of this inquiry.[124]

The *Robinson* scheme has been criticized for not sufficiently taking into account potential efficiency and manageability concerns that could arise from certification of compensatory and punitive damages in a (b)(3) class following certification of class-wide liability in a (b)(2) class.[125]

---

[120] Bartlett III, *supra* n. 19, at 2183.

[121] See Stamps, *supra* n. 113, at 447.

[122] Piar, *supra* n. 64, at 343–345; Martin H. Redish, 'Class Actions and the Democratic Difficulty: Rethinking the Intersection of Private Litigation and Public Goals,' 2003 U Chi Legal F 71, 77 (2003) (characterizing private class action attorneys as 'bounty hunters'); George Priest, 'The Economics of Class Actions,' 9 Kan J Law & Pub Pol'y 481, 482 (2000); Nagareda, *supra* n. 23, at 163; Charles Silver, '"We're Scared to Death": Class Certification and Blackmail,' 78 NYU L Rev 1357, 1357 (2003).

[123] See Hart, *supra* n. 41, at 829; see also Changelo, *supra* n. 104, at 151.

[124] See Stamps, *supra* n. 113, at 436; 5 James Wm. Moore et al., *supra* n. 19, P 23.80[1] (3rd edn 2005); 2 Herbert B. Newberg & Alba Conte, 'Newberg on Class Actions,' 4.14, at 97 (4th edn 2002).

[125] Changelo, *supra* n. 104, at 159–160 ('The test provided by the Robinson court is overly complex and therefore unlikely to be efficiently or consistently applied by lower courts.').

EMPLOYMENT CLASS AND COLLECTIVE ACTIONS

Robinson arguably fails to provide, even with the protection of notice and opt-out rights, how the determination of class-wide damages for numerous individuals would efficiently take place in the context of a (b)(3) class that was bifurcated from a (b)(2) class determining a pattern or practice of discrimination.[126] As a solution, Meghan Changelo wisely proposes that the courts adopt the Ninth Circuit's approach in *Brown v. Ticor Title Insurance Co.*,[127] which permits individuals to litigate their damages in individual trials at the remedial stage, rather than on a class-wide basis.[128] Many courts disallow this approach on the grounds that damages claims should have been asserted in the context of the (b)(2) liability class and are therefore waived.[129] Courts could permit such bifurcation by giving res judicata effect to a (b)(2) class-wide liability finding and allowing class members to bring damages claims in individual subsequent actions.[130] This solution would be palatable, however, only if courts permitted plaintiffs to seek injunctive and declaratory relief on a class-wide basis, without being deemed inadequate for failure to seek monetary damages.

Overall, the Second Circuit's ad hoc approach is superior to the Fifth Circuit's bright-line one because the former ensures that plaintiffs can effectively vindicate their Title VII statutory rights, courts can exercise their proper discretion under Rule 23, and Congress' will, as articulated in the Civil Rights Act of 1991, is respected.

4.5 THE IMPACT OF RECENT LEGISLATION ON PREVENTING POTENTIAL JUDICIAL ABUSE OF CLASS CERTIFICATION

To the extent that the most recent amendments to Rule 23 and the recently enacted Class Action Fairness Act of 2005 curtail potential judicial abuse of discretion, district courts will not be able to abuse their power easily under the *Robinson* ad hoc certification scheme.

---

[126] *Id.* at 159.

[127] *Brown v. Ticor Title Insurance Co.*, 982 F.2d 386 (9th Cir. 1992), cert. dismissed as improvidently granted, 511 US 117 (1994).

[128] *Id.* at 392 (9th Cir. 1992).

[129] See e.g., *Zachery v. Texaco Exploration and Prod., Inc.*, 185 FRD 230, 243 (WD Tex. 1999).

[130] Changelo, *supra* n. 104, at 159–161.

CHAPTER 4. FIGHTING TO KEEP EMPLOYMENT DISCRIMINATION

Such safeguards, designed to reign in judicial and attorney misconduct, should temper any great concern that the Second Circuit's ad hoc balancing test will go unchecked.

4.5.1 Amended Rule 23

Amended Rule 23, which went into effect on December 1, 2003, contains multiple safeguards to ensure that class members' rights are protected. Moreover, the amendments often confirm or add to the court's discretion – demonstrating a certain degree of confidence in the judicial system's ability to responsibly make class certification decisions. For example, the court is no longer required to make certification decisions 'as soon as practicable,' but instead 'at an early practicable time.'[131] While this change may seem minor, it stems from the important recognition that courts often need sufficient time to permit class discovery and to entertain dispositive motions before deciding certification.[132] The amended rule encourages district courts to make prompt and well-informed decisions. Additional time for the class certification decision would give courts the opportunity to weigh all the factors necessary in an 'ad hoc' certification approach.

For the first time, the Rule explicitly states that a district court 'may direct appropriate notice to the class' for mandatory class actions.[133] While Rule 23(c)(2)(A) merely codifies existing practice, the amendment makes clear that courts have the power, when certifying a (b)(2) class, to require notice when appropriate.[134] A court no longer need solely rely on its discretionary power under Rule 23(d) to provide notice for (b)(2) classes to address due process concerns. The amended Rule also indicates that the courts can be entrusted with more discretion and flexibility when handling class actions and protecting class members' due process rights.

The amendments to Rule 23 force the district court to define the class it is certifying and to more rigorously prove that the certification criteria are met. Rule 23(c)(1)(B) requires the court to 'define the class

---

[131] Fed. R. Civ. P. 23(c)(1)(A).
[132] Fed. R. Civ. P. 23 advisory committee's note.
[133] Fed. R. Civ. P. 23(c)(2)(A).
[134] Fed. R. Civ. P. 23 advisory committee's note.

and the class claims, issues or defenses,' in its order.[135] Rule 23(c)(1)(C) no longer allows the court to conditionally certify a class. While the court may alter or amend its certification order prior to final judgment, the court may no longer evade the certification criteria by conditioning certification upon circumstances that may never occur. The eradication of conditional certification should assuage concerns of certification as a form of legalized blackmail.[136] The fact that courts must now more rigorously prove that the certification criteria are met ensures that courts applying the *Robinson* ad hoc approach will have to carefully consider and justify their decisions. This safeguard reduces the concern that courts applying the ad hoc approach will improperly certify class actions.

Amendments to the Rule also provide additional protection for classes certified under provision 23(b)(3). For example, Rule 23(c)(2)(B) requires that (b)(3) notice 'concisely and clearly state in plain, easily understood language' certain information, including the right of exclusion and the binding effect of class judgments. Additionally, Rule 23(e)(3) permits courts to provide (b)(3) class members with a second chance to opt out under certain settlements.

Finally, and perhaps most significant, the new provisions (g) and (h) protect the most fundamental due process concern of class certification – adequacy of representation – by imposing more rigorous standards for selection of class counsel. Rule 23(g) requires that class counsel 'fairly and adequately represent the interests of the class.' While Rule 23(g) expands upon Rule 23(a)'s adequacy requirement and codifies established practice articulated in case law, the new provision also requires the court to follow a formal appointment procedure and to consider certain enumerated factors.[137] Rule 23(h)

---

[135] See also Fed. R. Civ. P.23(c)(3).

[136] See L. Elizabeth Chamblee, 'Unsettling Efficiency: When Non-Class Aggregation of Torts Creates Second-Class Settlements,' 65 La L Rev 157, 222–225 (2004) (discussing the inequitable bargaining advantage plaintiffs certified as a class have over defendants and noting that 'although the danger of blackmail exists with respect to class certification, the 2003 amendments to Rule 23 lessen this danger').

[137] Rule 23(g) requires that courts consider:

(1) 'the work counsel has done in identifying or investigating potential claims in the action';
(2) 'counsel's experience in handling class actions, other complex litigation, and claims of the type asserted in the action';

CHAPTER 4. FIGHTING TO KEEP EMPLOYMENT DISCRIMINATION

further monitors the selection of class counsel through its enhanced examination of attorneys' fees. Thus, through the most recent additions to Rule 23, adequacy of representation – the linchpin to class litigation – is further protected.

The amendments to Rule 23 reign in the possibility for the class action device to be misused. While many of the provisions simply codify existing practice, the amendments clarify the proper boundaries for class certification and management. These protections ensure that a court's use of the ad hoc approach will be properly checked. While the amendments serve to reinforce the court's boundaries, many of them expand and bolster the court's discretion in the class certification process. This is not surprising given the long-held deference courts have enjoyed when making class certification determinations.

4.5.2 The Class Action Fairness Act of 2005

The Class Action Fairness Act of 2005, perhaps the most sweeping legislation impacting how class actions will be litigated, was enacted on February 18, 2005.[138] The Act, purportedly designed to curtail 'abuses of the class action device' that have transpired over the last decade,[139] should help to curb potential state judicial abuse of discretion in certification decisions. Perhaps the most significant and controversial component of the Act is its liberalization of the jurisdictional requirements for class actions brought in federal courts on the grounds of diversity. The Act permits certain class actions with national implications to be heard more easily in federal court by requiring only minimal diversity among the parties for original jurisdiction to exist and by creating a more lenient device for removal of class actions from state to federal court.[140] The impetus behind this provision is a perception that state courts are less likely than federal courts to conduct a rigorous

---

(3) 'counsel's knowledge of the applicable law'; and
(4) 'the resources counsel will commit to representing the class.' Fed. R. Civ. P. 23(g).

[138] Class Action Fairness Act of 2005, Pub. L. No. 109-2, 119 Stat. 4.
[139] S. 5, 109th Cong. 2 (2005).
[140] See 28 USC 1332(d) (2005).

analysis when determining the propriety of class certification.[141] Thus, by making it easier for such cases to be heard in federal court, where certification issues might presumably by more rigorously analyzed, the number of certifications improvidently granted should diminish.

Assuming that this liberalization of the jurisdictional standards results in fewer improper class certifications of civil rights cases (and not just fewer civil rights class actions),[142] the Act should curtail some mischief by those state courts who would abuse their discretion. By shifting some class cases from state to federal court, the Act would seem to suggest that Congress has some measure of confidence that the federal courts will exercise their discretion responsibly. The Act – while not a ringing endorsement of class actions – seems at least a vote of confidence in the federal judiciary's overall ability to fairly assess the propriety of class certification. And where the federal courts have been less diligent, such as in the settlement of consumer class actions, the Act has developed considerable new safeguards.[143] Thus, to the extent that the Act has facilitated a shift of class actions from state to federal court, the Act demonstrates Congress' confidence in the federal judiciary's discretion.

4.6 CONCLUSION

One of the most important tools for effective civil rights enforcement is in jeopardy. Should the majority's rigid interpretation of the predomination requirement prevail, employees fighting systemic intentional discrimination will be denied one of their most powerful weapons in their arsenal for justice – the class action.

Specifically, the restrictive interpretation threatens to undermine civil rights enforcement by diminishing the number of class actions,

---

[141] See e.g., SR Rep. No. 109–114, at 14 (2005), as reprinted in 2005 USCCAN 314–315 (commenting that state courts are more lax in certification and noting high caseloads and a lack of judicial resources in state courts).

[142] This, of course, is a real concern given the overwhelming docket under which the federal courts labor today and the propensity for some federal courts to be hostile to such claims. See Hart, *supra* n. 41, at 835–846 (ascribing fewer employment discrimination class actions to the perception that such cases are unfair, unnecessary and unmeritorious).

[143] See 28 USC 1711–1715 (2005).

CHAPTER 4. FIGHTING TO KEEP EMPLOYMENT DISCRIMINATION

depriving employees of full relief, and imposing greater costs and burdens on those employment discrimination class actions that do survive. Deterrence and fairness will be undermined. The ad hoc approach, on the other hand, respects the courts' discretion and properly reconciles the goals of the Civil Rights Act of 1991 and Rule 23. The ad hoc approach's flexibility allows plaintiffs to seek full relief, while enjoying due process protections available through hybrid certification and discretionary notice and opt-out rights. The recent amendments to Rule 23 and the Class Action Fairness Act of 2005 only curb potential judicial abuse, and confirm the propriety of allowing federal courts wide latitude in making class certification determinations. The class action is vital to curtailing employment discrimination. Consequently, should the Supreme Court have occasion to consider the propriety of the predomination test in the future, it should embrace the ad hoc balancing test adopted by the minority of circuits to preserve this essential tool.

CHAPTER 5

The Uncertain Future of Title VII Class Actions after the Civil Rights Act of 1991

Daniel F. Piar*,**

5.1 INTRODUCTION

In recent years, employment discrimination class actions have become well-publicized, high-stakes events.[1] Enormous monetary exposures, sensational allegations, and aggressive litigation tactics have brought these cases to prominence in legal circles, the business community, and the public eye. There are signs, however, that this trend could be slowed or even halted by a ten-year-old civil rights law whose implications in this area are just beginning to be felt in the federal courts.

Employment discrimination class actions are typically brought under Title VII of the Civil Rights Act of 1964. As initially passed, the 1964 Act provided only equitable relief to victims of employment discrimination. The Civil Rights Act of 1991 expanded these remedies by providing compensatory and punitive damages to victims of

---

* Daniel F. Piar is Professor of Law at John Marshall Law School, Atlanta. He holds a J.D. from Yale Law School.
** This paper was previously published by the BYU Law Review. Daniel F. Piar, The Uncertain Future of Title VII Class Actions After the Civil Rights Act of 1991, 2001 BYU L. Rev. 305 (2001).
[1] See David McNaughton, The Lawyer Taking on Coke: Cyrus Mehri Looks for a 'Public Dimension,' in This Case, Race Relations in the United States, Atlanta J & Const, May 2, 1999, at P-1.

David Sherwyn and Samuel Estreicher (eds), *Employment Class and Collective Actions*, pp. 241–286.
© BYU Law Review. Reprinted with permission.

241

intentional discrimination in the workplace. The 1991 Act also bestowed the right to a jury trial on both parties in such cases.

Ironically, however, the same law that was designed to provide additional remedies to individuals may have made it more difficult for them to bring class claims. The availability of substantial monetary damages to Title VII plaintiffs may destroy the homogeneity of remedy required to maintain a class action under *Federal Rule of Civil Procedure 23(b)(2)*, a concern that was not present when injunctive relief was the predominant remedy under the statute. The individualized issues of proof and liability raised by the availability of damages may destroy the commonality necessary to maintain a class action under Rule 23(b)(3) and may render other means of adjudication superior to a class action within the meaning of the Rule. And the availability of a jury trial under Title VII may raise Seventh Amendment bars to the bifurcation schemes that were traditionally used to manage class claims of discrimination. As one court has summarized, 'Certification of many Title VII cases as class actions may no longer be appropriate, given the expanded damages now made available under Title VII by the Civil Rights Act of 1991.'[2]

This chapter will examine the ways in which the Civil Rights Act of 1991 has altered the landscape of Title VII class actions and will analyze the ways in which courts have attempted – with varying degrees of plausibility – to surmount the obstacles to class litigation raised by the 1991 Act. It will also suggest ways in which these obstacles might be avoided in the future, if, indeed, they should be avoided at all.

5.2 TITLE VII AND THE CIVIL RIGHTS ACT OF 1991

Title VII of the Civil Rights Act of 1964 prohibits employment discrimination based on race, religion, sex, color, and national origin.[3] In the decades since 1964, Title VII cases have become a staple of the federal court system and a prominent means of addressing both real

---

[2] *Taylor v. Flagstar Bank*, 181 FRD 509, 519 n. 4 (MD Ala. 1998) (citation omitted); see also *Zachery v. Texaco Exploration and Prod., Inc.*, 185 FRD 230, 237 (WD Tex. 1999) (noting that the class action 'may no longer be a valid vehicle' for employment discrimination claims seeking money damages).

[3] See 42 USC 2000e-2 (1994).

CHAPTER 5. UNCERTAIN FUTURE OF TITLE VII CLASS ACTIONS

and perceived discrimination on the job.[4] As initially passed, Title VII provided only declaratory, injunctive, and other equitable relief (principally back and front pay) to victims of discrimination.[5] This remedial scheme was consistent with those in other federal workplace discrimination statutes before and since, which have frequently omitted compensatory or punitive damages provisions.[6]

The Civil Rights Act of 1991 strengthened Title VII's remedial scheme by authorizing compensatory and punitive damages in cases of intentional employment discrimination.[7] While understanding the damages provisions of the 1991 Act is essential to understanding its impact on Title VII class actions, there is no indication in the legislative history that Congress considered the effect these provisions might have on class litigation as opposed to individual claims.

The 1991 Act's enhanced damages provisions were designed to compensate victims of discrimination for humiliation, trauma, physical distress, medical expenses, and other economic and non-economic harms caused by workplace discrimination. They were also intended

---

[4] In 1999, employment discrimination cases in general accounted for 8.6% of all federal civil filings. See Administrative Office of the US Courts, Judicial Business of the United States Courts, Table C-2A (1999).

[5] 42 USC 2000e-5(g) (1994). Back pay is compensation for past income lost as a result of discrimination. Front pay is compensation for lost future income (i.e., money that the plaintiff would have made in the future absent unlawful discrimination). Front pay is considered a monetary substitute for the remedies of reinstatement or promotion and is typically awarded where hostility between the parties makes reinstatement infeasible or where no job openings are available at the time of judgment to enforce a remedial promotion. See *Cassino v. Reichold Chems., Inc.*, 817 F.2d 1338, 1346 (9th Cir. 1987); *Briseno v. Central Technical Community College Area*, 739 F.2d 344, 348 (8th Cir. 1984). Both back pay and front pay are generally regarded as equitable remedies rather than money damages. See *United States v. Georgia Power Co.*, 474 F.2d 906, 921 (5th Cir. 1973) (back pay); *Kramer v. Logan County Sch. Dist.*, 157 F.3d 620, 626 (8th Cir. 1998) (front pay).

[6] See e.g., National Labor Relations Act 10(c), 29 USC 160(c) (1994) (providing affirmative relief, including back pay, for victims of unfair labor practices); Fair Labor Standards Act 16(b), 29 USC 216(b) (1994) (providing back pay, affirmative relief, and liquidated damages for claimants); Age Discrimination in Employment Act 7(b), 29 USC 626(b) (1994) (adopting remedies provisions of Fair Labor Standards Act); Uniformed Services Employment and Reemployment Rights Act 2(a), 38 USC 4323(d) (1994) (providing injunctive relief and liquidated damages for victims of anti-military discrimination).

[7] See 42 USC 1981a (1994). Intentional discrimination cases are also known as 'disparate treatment' cases. In cases of unintentional discrimination, or 'disparate impact' cases, remedies remained equitable under the 1991 Act. See 42 USC 1981a(a)(1) (1994).

to punish and deter employers who acted 'with malice or with reckless indifference to the federally protected rights of an aggrieved [employee].'[8] In passing these provisions, Congress intended to 'confirm that the principle of anti-discrimination is as important as the principle that prohibits assaults, batteries, and other intentional injuries to people'[9] and to 'ensure compensation commensurate with the harms suffered by victims of intentional discrimination.'[10]

The 1991 revisions also were motivated by a remedial anomaly in race discrimination cases. The Civil Rights Act of 1866,[11] which forbids racially motivated interference with the right to enter contracts, had long been held to confer a right of action for job discrimination on the theory that such discrimination constituted interference with the right to enter contracts of employment.[12] Because unlimited compensatory and punitive damages were available under 1981,[13] plaintiffs claiming employment discrimination based on race could recover full damages, while those claiming other forms of discrimination could not. Congress therefore made damages available for all Title VII plaintiffs in part to address this perceived inconsistency.[14]

Finally, the 1991 amendments were seen as an enforcement mechanism: the House Report declares that the additional remedies are necessary to 'encourage citizens to act as private attorneys general' in enforcing Title VII.[15] To protect the Seventh Amendment rights of

---

[8] 42 USC 1981a(b)(1) (1994).

[9] HR Rep. No. 102-40(I), at 15 (1991).

[10] Id. at 18. Among the anecdotes included in the House report was that of a sexual harassment victim who endured sleeplessness, severe neck pain, and nausea at work but was awarded only one dollar in nominal damages under the pre-1991 remedial scheme. Id. at 66–67. Another harassment victim was fired for being pregnant, lost her insurance, and was shunned by her hospital, which threatened the seizure of her property to pay her medical bills. She prevailed in her discrimination case and was compensated for lost income and medical expenses but received nothing for her 'years of stress and humiliation.' HR Rep. No. 102-40(II), at 25–26 (1991).

[11] Act of April 9, 1866, Ch. 31, 1, 14 Stat. 27 (codified at 42 USC 1981 (1994)).

[12] See e.g., *Johnson v. Railway Express Agency, Inc.*, 421 US 454, 460 (1975).

[13] See id. at 459–460.

[14] See HR Rep. No. 102-40(I), at 65 (1991).

[15] Id. at 64–65. That effort has been successful. Employment discrimination filings, which as of 1990 had stabilized at approximately 8,000-9,000 cases per year in the federal courts, increased to 12,962 filings in 1993, 19,059 in 1995, and 22,490 in 1999. Compare Administrative Office of the US Courts, Judicial Business of the United

CHAPTER 5. UNCERTAIN FUTURE OF TITLE VII CLASS ACTIONS

parties involved in such claims, the Act made trial by jury available in cases seeking compensatory and punitive damages.[16] The sum of compensatory and punitive damages under the 1991 Act is capped on a sliding scale ranging from USD 50,000-300,000, depending on the size of the employer.[17]

The language of the House Report on the 1991 Act places great emphasis on the nature and extent of the harms suffered by some victims of discrimination.[18] It is clear that the House majority felt strongly that intentional discrimination should be redressed with both compensation and retribution where appropriate, and there is every indication that Congress viewed itself as the white knight of those whom the law protected. In subsequent litigation, however, both litigants and courts would wrestle with the potentially serious (and apparently unforeseen) restrictions imposed by these individual remedies on the maintenance of Title VII class actions.

5.3 THE RULE 23 REQUIREMENTS FOR CLASS ACTIONS

The original Title VII remedies fit neatly within the procedural scheme established for the certification and maintenance of class actions under *Rule 23 of the Federal Rules of Civil Procedure*.[19] A class must pass two major tests to be certified under Rule 23. First, it must possess the four attributes required by Rule 23(a): numerosity, typicality, commonality, and adequacy of representation. Specifically:

(1) the class must be 'so numerous that joinder of all members is impracticable' (numerosity);
(2) there must be 'questions of law or fact common to the class' (commonality);

States Courts, Table C-2A (1997) with Administrative Office of the US Courts, Judicial Business of the United States Courts, Table C-2A (1999). While these are not all Title VII claims, Title VII remains the broadest and most widely used employment discrimination statute.

[16] See HR Rep. No. 102-40(II), at 29 (1991).
[17] See 42 USC 1981a(b)(3) (1994).
[18] See HR Rep. No. 102-40(I), at 66–69 (1991); HR Rep. No. 102-40(II), at 25–28 (1991).
[19] See *Jefferson v. Ingersoll Int'l, Inc.*, 195 F.3d 894, 896 (7th Cir. 1999).

(3) the claims or defenses of the class representatives must be 'typical of the claims or defenses of the class' (typicality); and
(4) the representative parties must be able to 'fairly and adequately protect the interests of the class' (adequacy of representation).[20]

Once these requirements are met, the class then must fit within one of the three categories established under Rule 23(b).[21]

Rule 23(b)(1) generally applies when individual adjudication would risk establishing inconsistent standards of behavior for the party opposing the class or when adjudication of the class representatives' claims

---

[20] Fed. R. Civ. P. 23(a).

[21] Fed. R. Civ. P. 23(b) provides as follows:

(b) Class Actions Maintainable. An action may be maintained as a class action if the prerequisites of subdivision (a) are satisfied, and in addition:
(1) the prosecution of separate actions by or against individual members of the class would create a risk of:
(A) inconsistent or varying adjudications with respect to individual members of the class which would establish incompatible standards of conduct for the party opposing the class, or
(B) adjudications with respect to individual members of the class which would as a practical matter be dispositive of the interests of the other members not parties to the adjudications or substantially impair or impede their ability to protect their interests; or
(2) the party opposing the class has acted or refused to act on grounds generally applicable to the class, thereby making appropriate final injunctive relief or corresponding declaratory relief with respect to the class as a whole; or
(3) the court finds that the questions of law or fact common to the members of the class predominate over any questions affecting only individual members, and that a class action is superior to other available methods for the fair and efficient adjudication of the controversy.

The matters pertinent to the findings include:

(A) the interest of members of the class in individually controlling the prosecution or defense of separate actions;
(B) the extent and nature of any litigation concerning the controversy already commenced by or against members of the class;
(C) the desirability or undesirability of concentrating the litigation of the claims in the particular forum;
(D) the difficulties likely to be encountered in the management of a class action.

CHAPTER 5. UNCERTAIN FUTURE OF TITLE VII CLASS ACTIONS

would either dispose of the interests of other potential plaintiffs or impede their ability to recover. The textbook 23(b)(1) class involves a set of claims against a limited fund whose resources might be exhausted by initial plaintiffs to the detriment of subsequent claimants.[22] Rule 23(b)(1) typically does not apply in employment discrimination class actions. There is little risk of establishing inconsistent standards of behavior for a defendant employer, as the standards to be enforced are clear: do not discriminate. Similarly, class discrimination claims are not claims upon a limited fund as the Rule 23 Advisory Committee understood the concept but are efforts to remedy and deter certain types of harm by recovering equitable, compensatory, or punitive relief for persons who have been wronged.

Rule 23(b)(2) applies when a defendant has 'acted or refused to act on grounds generally applicable to the class, thereby making appropriate final injunctive relief or corresponding declaratory relief with respect to the class as a whole.'[23] Under the original Title VII remedies, which were entirely equitable, Rule 23(b)(2) was the principal basis for certifying employment discrimination class actions.[24] Indeed, the 1966 Advisory Committee comments to Rule 23(b)(2) singled out civil rights classes as paradigmatic: 'Illustrative [of 23(b)(2) classes] are various actions in the civil-rights field where a party is charged with discriminating unlawfully against a class....'[25] Rule 23(b)(2) comes with an important caveat, according to the Advisory Committee: 'The subdivision does not extend to cases in which the appropriate final relief relates exclusively or predominantly to money damages.'[26] While the Advisory Committee did not attempt to define the term 'predominantly' (which appears nowhere in Rule 23(b)(2) itself), this 'predominance' requirement has been central to efforts to assess the impact of the 1991 Act on class litigation, as discussed below.

The final Rule 23(b) category is Rule 23(b)(3), which permits certification where a court finds that 'questions of law or fact common to the members of the class predominate over any questions affecting only individual members, and ... a class action is superior to other available

---

[22] See Fed. R. Civ. P. 23 advisory committee's notes, 39 FRD 69, 101 (1966).
[23] Fed. R. Civ. P. 23(b)(2).
[24] See e.g., *Amchem Prods., Inc. v. Windsor*, 521 US 591, 614 (1997); *Jefferson v. Ingersoll Int'l, Inc.*, 195 F.3d 894, 896 (7th Cir. 1999).
[25] Fed. R. Civ. P. 23 advisory committee's notes, 39 FRD 69, 102 (1966).
[26] *Id.*

methods for the fair and efficient adjudication of the controversy.'[27] The 'commonality' required by this section is a stricter test than that of commonality under Rule 23(a) and requires that the class members be 'more bound together by a mutual interest in the settlement of common questions than... divided by the individual members' interest in the matters peculiar to them.'[28] Rule 23(b)(3) also requires a finding that a class action is superior to other methods of adjudication, such as the prosecution of consolidated or individual claims. Rule 23(b)(3) permits courts to consider a variety of factors in deciding whether to certify a class, including the interests of class members in controlling their claims individually, the existence of individual litigation concerning the same claims, the desirability of concentrating class claims in the particular forum, the manageability of the class, and the desirability of certifying the class to avoid 'negative value suits,' in which the cost of individual litigation would outweigh the potential individual recovery.[29]

Rule 23(b)(3) classes are subject to an important 'opt-out provision' imposed by Rule 23(c)(2). Under this provision, each potential member of a 23(b)(3) class is entitled to notice of the action, notice that all non-excluded class members will be bound by the class judgment, and notice of the member's right to be excluded from the class upon request, leaving excluded members to a private right of action.[30] This provision exists as a hedge against the individual interests of potential 23(b)(3) class members, especially with respect to their right to pursue and recover individual monetary damages. As the Advisory Committee noted, in many Rule 23(b)(3) cases, the interests of individuals in pursuing their own claims 'may be so strong here as to warrant denial of a class action altogether.'[31] Even where those interests are not strong enough to bar a class action, Rule 23(b)(3) recognizes that individual interests may still exist and must be respected as a matter of due process by allowing potential class members to choose to pursue their own claims instead of joining in with the class.[32]

---

[27] Fed. R. Civ. P. 23(b)(3); see also *Gorence v. Eagle Food Ctrs., Inc.*, No. 93 C 4862, 1994 WL 445149, at 7 (ND Ill., August 16, 1994).
[28] *Id.* at 11.
[29] See Fed. R. Civ. P. 23(b)(3)(A)-(D); see also *Castano v. American Tobacco Co.*, 84 F.3d 734, 748 (5th Cir. 1996).
[30] See Fed. R. Civ. P. 23(c)(2).
[31] Fed. R. Civ. P. 23 advisory committee's notes, 39 FRD 69, 104–105 (1966).
[32] See *id.* at 104–105; see also *Ortiz v. Fibreboard Corp.*, 527 US 815, 846–847 (1999).

CHAPTER 5. UNCERTAIN FUTURE OF TITLE VII CLASS ACTIONS

These Rule 23 requirements provide the procedural framework for class actions, and the interplay between those requirements, the remedies now afforded under Title VII, and the constitutional rights of the parties leads to the current uncertainties concerning the maintainability of Title VII class actions.

5.4 TITLE VII CLASS ACTIONS BEFORE THE CIVIL RIGHTS ACT OF 1991

Before the passage of the 1991 Act, the courts had developed fairly well-defined procedures for certifying and managing Title VII class actions. These procedures were famously outlined and approved by the Supreme Court in *International Brotherhood of Teamsters v. United States*.[33] Title VII class actions before 1991 typically involved allegations that the employer had engaged in a pattern and practice of intentional discrimination, were typically certified under Rule 23(b)(2), and were typically handled in two phases. In the first, or liability phase, the plaintiffs had the burden of proving prima facie the existence of a pattern or practice of discrimination – in other words, that discrimination was the employer's 'standard operating procedure.'[34] This could be achieved through various combinations of statistical and anecdotal evidence.[35] The employer then could attempt to rebut the plaintiffs' showing by demonstrating that the plaintiffs' proof was 'inaccurate or insignificant.'[36] If the plaintiffs' proof withstood challenge, then the pattern and practice was considered proven and the court could grant classwide prospective relief, including injunctions and other remedial orders.[37] To address individual claims, such as those for back pay or reinstatement, this initial phase was followed by a remedial phase in which the court (or, in some cases, a special master) would

---

[33] 431 US 324 (1977).
[34] *Id.* at 336.
[35] See *id.* at 337. (statistical evidence); *EEOC v. McDonnell Douglas Corp.*, 960 F. Supp. 203, 205 (ED Mo. 1996) (holding that liability phase can encompass ' "direct statistical evidence, anecdotal evidence ... and any other evidence that bears on the issue of whether a pattern of discrimination existed" (quoting *Sperling v. Hoffman-LaRoche, Inc.*, 924 F. Supp. 1346, 1352 (DNJ 1996))).
[36] *International Bd. of Teamsters v. United States*, 431 US 324, 360–362 (1977).
[37] See *id.* at 361.

determine the appropriate remedies for the individual class members. In this second phase, each class member only had to show:

(1) that he experienced an adverse employment action, and
(2) the extent of any resulting loss.

Because of the pattern and practice established in the first phase, each class member in the second phase enjoyed a rebuttable presumption that the adverse action and resulting loss were the products of discrimination. The employer then could attempt to rebut the presumption as to each class member and thereby avoid liability to that class member by proving that the disputed employment action had been taken for a nondiscriminatory reason.[38]

For the most part, this paradigm worked smoothly under the equitable remedy scheme of the original 1964 Act. Class certification was largely unproblematic under Rule 23(b)(2) because declaratory and injunctive relief could be held to predominate absent the availability of money damages. (While individual class members could recover money in the form of back or front pay, this was considered an equitable remedy that would not detract from the predominance of declaratory and injunctive relief.[39]) Moreover, the availability of only equitable remedies meant that there was no right to a jury trial, and thus courts were free to use devices such as special masters to handle individual claims as efficiently as possible in the second phase.[40] All of this would change dramatically with the advent of the damages and jury trial remedies afforded by the Civil Rights Act of 1991.

5.5 TITLE VII CLASS ACTIONS AFTER THE CIVIL RIGHTS ACT OF 1991

The damages remedies provided by the 1991 Act have introduced serious complications in the certification and management of Title VII class actions under Rule 23. While plaintiffs had typically sought and obtained certification under Rule 23(b)(2) in such cases, the availability

---

[38] See *id.*; *Allison v. Citgo Petroleum Corp.*, 151 F.3d 402, 409 (5th Cir. 1998).
[39] See *supra* n. 6; *Jefferson v. Ingersoll Int'l, Inc.*, 195 F.3d 894, 896 (7th Cir. 1999).
[40] See 42 USC 2000e-5(f)(5) (1994 & Supp. III 1997) (authorizing use of special masters); *Kraszewski v. State Farm Gen. Ins. Co.*, 912 F.2d 1182, 1183 (9th Cir. 1990).

CHAPTER 5. UNCERTAIN FUTURE OF TITLE VII CLASS ACTIONS

of substantial and individualized money damages has raised difficult questions about the predominance of declaratory and injunctive relief required by Rule 23(b)(2). It has also raised procedural and constitutional questions about the need for or the availability of an opt-out procedure for 23(b)(2) cases in which individual claimants might want to reserve their monetary claims.

As to 23(b)(3) classes, the highly individualized nature of claims for compensatory and punitive damages has raised questions under the commonality requirement of that rule, while courts have struggled to determine whether a class of persons can be said to have sufficient matters in common when each of them seeks a personalized remedy. Similarly, the presence of scores, hundreds, or even thousands of unique claims for damages has greatly complicated the manageability of Title VII classes, especially where the relevant damages issues must be resolved by juries upon the demand of either party. The presence of such claims increases the risk that a class action will degenerate in practice into a series of minitrials, thereby becoming unmanageable and defeating the efficiencies that class actions were designed to realize. In addition, the high limits on damages under the 1991 Act – up to USD 300,000 per plaintiff, depending on the size of the employer – may have eliminated the threat of negative value suits, which has been one of the primary bases for 23(b)(3) certification.

The 1991 changes have also raised questions about the availability of the *Teamsters*-style bifurcation that had been used in declaratory or injunctive-based class actions in the past. Attempts to apply such a process in light of the 1991 Act's jury trial right may violate the Seventh Amendment rights of the litigants. Because of the nature of proof in employment discrimination cases, multiple juries might be required to decide identical or substantially related issues of fact in evaluating the various phases of such trials.

Finally, the high damages limits under the 1991 Act have paved the way for 'blackmail' class actions, in which a defendant's monetary exposure can be used by plaintiffs and their lawyers to force a settlement regardless of the merits of the case.

Trial courts have begun to address these issues with some regularity in Title VII cases, but these matters have only recently begun to make their way to the appellate courts. The varying approaches taken by the courts – as well as their varying degrees of persuasiveness – indicate that these questions will continue to vex both litigants and judges for some time to come.

5.5.1 The 23(b)(2) Class: The Problems of Predominance and Opt-Out Rights

5.5.1.1 Rule 23(b)(2) and Money Damages

Rule 23(b)(2) was designed for classes in which declaratory or injunctive relief is the predominant remedial issue. As the Federal Rules Advisory Committee explained in its comments to Rule 23(b)(2), this section 'does not extend to cases in which the appropriate final relief relates exclusively or predominantly to money damages.'[41] Thus, a key question in the post-1991 litigation of Title VII class actions has been whether the availability of money damages means that such damages 'predominate' over injunctive relief to render Rule 23(b)(2) unsuitable as a means of certifying a class.

One difficulty in answering this question has been determining the definition of 'predominantly.' The language of Rule 23(b)(2) does not absolutely rule out money damages for a 23(b)(2) class, and the Advisory Committee comments would apparently allow 23(b)(2) certification in some circumstances where money damages are sought, so long as they are not the 'exclusive' or 'predominant' form of relief. On the other hand, the Supreme Court has stated in dicta that there is 'at least a substantial possibility' that classes seeking money damages can never be certified under Rule 23(b)(2) due to the lack of an opt-out provision by which individual claimants can elect to pursue their remedies apart from the class.[42] Absent a more definitive holding, courts continue to be tasked with the job of determining when money damages 'predominate' over other types of relief in considering 23(b)(2) certification.

5.5.1.2 The Allison v. Citgo Approach

To date, the most thorough appellate analysis of this issue in the Title VII context is the Fifth Circuit's opinion in *Allison v. Citgo Petroleum Corp.*[43]

---

[41] Fed. R. Civ. P. 23 advisory committee's notes, 39 FRD 69, 102 (1966).
[42] *Ticor Title Ins. Co. v. Brown*, 511 US 117, 121 (1994). The lack of clear authority on this point was noted by the court in *Zachery v. Texaco Exploration and Production, Inc.*, 185 FRD 230, 244 (WD Tex. 1999) ('There is no clear cut decision as to whether Rule 23(b)(2) contains an opt-out procedure.').
[43] 151 F.3d 402 (5th Cir. 1998).

CHAPTER 5. UNCERTAIN FUTURE OF TITLE VII CLASS ACTIONS

Allison was an attempted Title VII race discrimination class action challenging hiring, promotion, training, and compensation practices at Citgo's Lake Charles, Louisiana, facility. The plaintiffs alleged both disparate impact and disparate treatment and sought declaratory, injunctive, and equitable relief as well as compensatory and punitive damages for a potential class of over 1,000 members.[44] The district court denied class certification, and the ensuing appeal raised numerous issues about the applicability of Rule 23 in light of the Civil Rights Act of 1991.

Both the district court and the Fifth Circuit relied on the predominance requirement of Rule 23(b)(2) in denying the plaintiffs' request for 23(b)(2) certification.[45] Because of Rule 23(b)(2)'s emphasis on classwide declaratory and injunctive relief, the appeals court found that the rule was designed to 'concentrate the litigation on common questions of law and fact' in order to evaluate and impose 'uniform group remedies.'[46] In the court's view, this urge toward uniformity was demonstrated by the lack of an opt-out provision such as the one found under Rule 23(b)(3): 23(b)(2) class actions will bind class members without their consent precisely because all of them are affected in substantially the same way by the conduct complained of and will require substantially the same remedies to cure the problem.[47]

Based on this principle of uniformity, the panel concluded that monetary relief will be found to 'predominate' in 23(b)(2) actions 'unless it is incidental to requested injunctive or declaratory relief.'[48] By 'incidental,' the court explained, it meant 'damages that flow directly from liability to the class as a whole on the claims forming the basis of

---

[44] See *id.* at 407.

[45] See *id.* at 412–416; *Celestine v. Citgo Petroleum Corp.*, 165 FRD 463, 468–469 (WD La. 1995).

[46] *Allison*, 151 F.3d at 414.

[47] See *id.* at 413. Some courts have nonetheless imposed an opt-out requirement on 23(b)(2) classes. See e.g., *Robinson v. Sears, Roebuck & Co.*, No. 4:98CV00739, 2000 WL 1036245 (ED Ark. 2000); *Smith v. Texaco, Inc.*, 88 F. Supp. 2d 663, 680 (ED Tex. 2000) (extending opt-out rights to 23(b)(2) portion of hybrid Title VII class action); *Martens v. Smith Barney, Inc.*, 181 FRD 243, 260 (SDNY 1998) (holding that courts have discretion to extend opt-out rights to 23(b)(1) and (b)(2) classes). It is not clear that this is proper, however, and the Supreme Court has recognized the 'substantial possibility' that Rule 23(b)(2) cannot be used to certify a class where money damages are sought. *Ticor Title Ins. Co. v. Brown*, 511 US 117, 121 (1994).

[48] *Allison*, 151 F.3d at 415.

the injunctive or declaratory relief.'[49] One index of the 'incidental' character of damages is the ease with which they can be calculated. 'Ideally, incidental damages should be only those to which class members automatically would be entitled once liability to the class (or subclass) as a whole is established.'[50] The determination of such 'incidental' damages 'should not require additional hearings to resolve the disparate merits of each individual's case; it should neither introduce new and substantial legal or factual issues, nor entail complex individualized determinations.'[51]

Having determined the standard to be applied under Rule 23(b)(2), the *Allison* court then held that compensatory damages were neither uniform nor ministerial enough to avoid 'predominating' under Rule 23(b)(2). Because compensatory and punitive damages are not presumed from the violation of a person's rights, even a plaintiff who could prove that he was discriminated against would be required to present 'specific individualized' proof to establish his entitlement to damages. Damages for injuries stemming from discrimination – which may include compensation for emotional trauma, accompanying physical injury, and any other tangible or intangible consequences of discriminatory treatment – 'cannot be calculated by objective standards' and would introduce 'new and substantial legal and factual issues' beyond those required to make a liability determination.[52] Accordingly, such damages would not flow automatically from a finding of liability to the class, and such a class could not be certified under Rule 23(b)(2).

5.5.1.3 The Allison Dissent and the Issue of Back Pay

The *Allison* majority's view of Rule 23(b)(2) is not a novel one.[53] The dissent nonetheless attacked the holding, claiming that the majority

---

[49] *Id.*

[50] *Id.*

[51] *Id.* The court noted that as a matter of precedent this was not inconsistent with cases allowing back pay under Rule 23(b)(2) because back pay is 'an integral part of the statutory equitable remedy.' *Id.* (quoting *Johnson v. Georgia Highway Express, Inc.*, 417 F.2d 1122, 1125 (5th Cir. 1969)).

[52] *Id.* at 417–418.

[53] Other courts in non-Title VII cases have read Rule 23(b)(2) much as the Allison court did and have denied 23(b)(2) certification where individualized damages

CHAPTER 5. UNCERTAIN FUTURE OF TITLE VII CLASS ACTIONS

had created a rule that would absolutely preclude class certification in 23(b)(2) cases seeking damages.[54] That misstates the holding of the majority, which noted that the Advisory Committee had apparently meant to leave open the possibility of damages recoveries in some circumstances under Rule 23(b)(2), subject to the 'predominance' analysis.[55] More plausible was the dissent's argument that the disallowance of damages could not be squared with the routine certification under Rule 23(b)(2) of classes seeking to recover back pay: 'Although back pay has often been characterized as an equitable remedy for practical purposes, functionally there is little to distinguish back pay awards from compensatory damages. Both require complex individualized determinations.'[56] This argument has superficial appeal but is not altogether persuasive. It is arguable that back pay proceedings are qualitatively different from damages determinations. Back pay determinations typically do not require highly complex factual or legal adjudications. Instead, they involve only a determination of how much pay an employee lost and whether any offsets should be applied, for such things as interim earnings or failure to mitigate damages. While not entirely formulaic, such determinations are made according to methods of calculation that are well developed and can be applied with some degree of classwide efficiency, especially because they need not be determined by juries.[57] At the least, one can plausibly argue that the calculation of such remedies is inherently more uniform than the

---

determinations would be required if liability were found. See *Washington v. CSC Credit Servs. Inc.*, 199 F.3d 263 (5th Cir. 2000) (following Allison and holding that it would be error to certify 23(b)(2) class under Fair Credit Reporting Act where monetary damages would not flow from declaratory relief but would require separate adjudication); *Boughton v. Cotter Corp.*, 65 F.3d 823, 827 (10th Cir. 1995) (holding that certification of 23(b)(2) class not required in environmental contamination case where relief sought was primarily individualized money damages); *Marascalco v. International Computerized Orthokeratology Soc'y, Inc.*, 181 FRD 331 (ND Miss. 1998) (denying 23(b)(2) certification in action for breach of warranty and fraud; plaintiffs each sought damages in excess of USD 5 million, and availability of individual relief would depend on varying individual circumstances going to elements of fraud).

[54] See *Allison*, 151 F.3d at 426–427 (Dennis, J., dissenting).
[55] See *id.* at 411.
[56] *Id.* at 427 n. 1 (Dennis, J., dissenting).
[57] See Barbara Lindemann & Paul Grossman, *Employment Discrimination Law*, 1848–1856 (3rd edn 1996). These calculations are perhaps most complex in cases involving claims of discriminatory failure to hire or failure to promote, in which there may be

assessment of compensatory or punitive damages, which might involve medical, psychiatric, and other types of tangible and intangible proof that could differ widely among class members.

Moreover, even assuming that back pay and damages are conceptually similar for purposes of Rule 23(b)(2), that does not mean that both should be available to a 23(b)(2) class. The monetary relief available to a 23(b)(2) Title VII class, in the majority's view, is equitable (e.g., back pay). That relief is therefore determined by the court, without the additional procedural complications of a jury trial. Considering that the availability of equitable monetary remedies in class actions is entrenched as a matter of precedent, it would seem consistent with the homogeneity of fact and remedy contemplated by Rule 23(b)(2) to eschew the extra layer of fact finding and complication that would be imposed on such proceedings by jury damages determinations. In other words, the availability of some monetary recovery under Rule 23(b)(2) does not mean that there should be more, especially when that 'more' is at odds with the homogeneity that Rule 23(b)(2) was supposed to represent.

5.5.1.4 Other Appellate Views: Jefferson v. Ingersoll International, Inc. and Lemon v. International Union of Operating Engineers

To date, only one other appellate court has considered the Rule 23(b)(2) issue in a post-1991 Title VII class action. In *Jefferson v. Ingersoll International, Inc.*,[58] the Seventh Circuit heard an interlocutory appeal from a Title VII class certification under Rule 23(b)(2). The appeals court reversed and remanded the case to the trial court with instructions to consider, among other things, whether the money damages sought by the class were 'more than incidental' to the requested equitable relief, and, if not, whether 23(b)(2) certification is ever permissible when money damages are sought. In so doing, the court agreed with *Allison* that 23(b)(2) certification would be appropriate only where 'monetary relief is incidental to the equitable remedy – so tangential ... that the

---

more class members than available positions, and some method must therefore be used for allocating limited back pay to the class. Nonetheless, these procedures are also fairly well-established. See *id.*
[58] 195 F.3d 894, 897 (7th Cir. 1999).

CHAPTER 5. UNCERTAIN FUTURE OF TITLE VII CLASS ACTIONS

due process clause does not require notice [and the opportunity to opt out].'[59] The Seventh Circuit therefore recognized that there are circumstances under Title VII in which the pursuit of money damages will prevent 23(b)(2) certification. The Seventh Circuit's opinion did not, however, purport to direct how this issue should be resolved on remand.

The Seventh Circuit later applied *Jefferson* to decertify another class in *Lemon v. International Union of Operating Engineers*,[60] while continuing to avoid deciding the Rule 23 issues. In *Lemon*, members of a local union filed a Title VII class action, alleging that the union discriminated against women and minorities in its hiring referral system. The district court certified the class under Rule 23(b)(2) without imposing an opt-out provision, but the appellate court reversed. Relying on *Jefferson*, the court held that the seeking of individual damages 'jeopardizes [the] presumption of cohesion and homogeneity' by requiring 'judicial inquiry into the particularized merits of each individual plaintiff's claim.'[61] Further, it would violate due process to deprive individual class members of the chance to opt out of such a class where money damages were at issue, precisely because of this potential divergence of interests.[62] Accordingly, the court held that the trial judge had abused his discretion by certifying a 23(b)(2) class without giving the class members a chance to opt out.

On remand, as it had in *Jefferson*, the court directed the trial judge to consider three options:

(1) certifying the class under Rule 23(b)(3);
(2) certifying the equitable issues under Rule 23(b)(2) and the legal issues under Rule 23(b)(3); or
(3) certifying a Rule 23(b)(2) class but imposing an opt-out provision.[63]

---

[59] *Id.* at 898–899. The court also suggested (without deciding) that the injunctive aspects of the case could be severed from the other claims and certified separately under Rule 23(b)(2). The issue of bifurcation of class claims is discussed *infra* 5.5(c).
[60] 216 F.3d 577 (7th Cir. 2000).
[61] *Id.* at 580.
[62] See *id.*
[63] See *id.* at 581–582.

EMPLOYMENT CLASS AND COLLECTIVE ACTIONS

As in *Jefferson*, the appeals court did not consider whether any of the three options themselves might be improper (for example, whether a class seeking money damages can be certified under Rule 23(b)(2) at all), nor did it tell the lower court how the issue should be resolved.[64]

5.5.1.5 Other Post-1991 Cases Restricting 23(b)(2) Certification

District courts that have considered 23(b)(2) certification under Title VII both before and after *Allison* have generally agreed that the predominance analysis is necessary, and a number of those courts have rejected attempts to certify employment discrimination classes under Rule 23(b)(2) where compensatory and punitive damages were sought.[65]

---

[64] The Eastern District of Arkansas relied upon Jefferson and Lemon and adopted their proposed third option, certifying a Title VII class under Rule 23(b)(2) and imposing an opt-out provision. See *Robinson v. Sears, Roebuck & Co.*, No. 4:98CV00739, 2000 WL 1036245 (ED Ark. July 3, 2000). The court went on to adopt a Teamsters-style approach to the adjudication of the case without addressing the consequent Seventh Amendment problems (discussed *infra*) or the contradictions inherent in the adjudication of individualized damages claims under Rule 23(b)(2) for those class members who did not opt out.

[65] See *Adams v. Henderson*, 197 FRD 162, 171 (D Md. 2000) (denying 23(b)(2) certification to Title VII class; money damages 'predominate' under 23(b)(2) when presence of monetary claims suggests that notice and right to opt out are necessary); *Zapata v. IBP, Inc.*, 167 FRD 147, 162 (D Kan. 1996) (finding that monetary relief therefore predominated although plaintiffs alleged that only monetary relief would make class members whole for racially hostile work environment and denying 23(b)(2) certification); *Griffin v. Home Depot, Inc.*, 168 FRD 187, 190–191 (ED La. 1996) (holding without analysis that predominant relief sought by sex discrimination class is 'economic and not injunctive' and denying 23(b)(2) certification); *Gorence v. Eagle Food Ctrs., Inc.*, No. 93 C 4862, 1994 WL 445149, at 7 (ND Ill. August 16, 1994) (denying 23(b)(2) certification where complaint and class certification memorandum sought declaratory and injunctive relief but prayer for relief mentioned only compensatory, punitive and liquidated damages, and promotions and finding that plaintiffs' 'primary motivation' deemed money damages); *Faulk v. Home Oil, Inc.*, 184 FRD 645 (MD Ala. 1999) (following Allison in denying 23(b)(2) certification in race discrimination case).

CHAPTER 5. UNCERTAIN FUTURE OF TITLE VII CLASS ACTIONS

5.5.1.6 Post-1991 Cases Granting 23(b)(2) Certification

Other courts have granted 23(b)(2) certifications under Title VII. In *Warnell v. Ford Motor Co.*,[66] the plaintiffs sought certification of a class of women alleging sexual harassment. The court certified the class under Rule 23(b)(2), noting that the plaintiffs sought a permanent injunction and a declaration of liability against Ford, and holding without further analysis that the accompanying claims for money damages were 'incidental' to these equitable claims.[67] The Northern District of California certified a 23(b)(2) class in *Butler v. Home Depot, Inc.*[68] despite the plaintiffs' substantial claims for money damages. Relying primarily on an analogy to pre-1991 cases involving back pay awards, the court held that class certification under 23(b)(2) is not precluded where monetary relief is sought. The court then somewhat startlingly held that the mere allegation of a policy and practice of denying equal opportunities to women 'is sufficient to satisfy the Rule 23(b)(2) requirement.'[69] The court therefore severed and certified claims regarding liability, injunctive relief, and classwide punitive damages, deferring a ruling on class treatment of individual damages.[70] A similar approach was followed in *Shores v. Publix Super*

---

[66] 189 FRD 383 (ND Ill. 1999).

[67] See *id.* at 389 (quoting *Senn v. United Dominion Indus., Inc.*, 951 F.2d 806, 813 (7th Cir. 1992). The Warnell court rejected Allison in part based on the Fifth Circuit's published denial of petition for rehearing in that case. See *infra* 5.5(c)(2).

[68] 70 Fair Empl. Prac. Cas. (BNA) 51 (ND Cal. 1996).

[69] *Id.* at 55.

[70] The problems raised by bifurcated trials under the Civil Rights Act of 1991 are discussed *infra* Part V.C. It should nonetheless be pointed out here that the Butler court's inclusion of 'classwide' punitive damages in the phase-one determination may have been incorrect. Arguably, liability for punitive damages depends on individual circumstances. It cannot be imposed as a result of a classwide determination of pattern-and-practice liability, which does not purport to determine whether any single class member has been a victim of discrimination, much less whether each class member has been treated with 'malice or with reckless indifference to the federally protected rights of an aggrieved individual' as required to justify a punitive award. *Allison v. Citgo Petroleum Corp.*, 151 F.3d 402, 417–418 (5th Cir. 1998); see also 42 USC 1981a(b)(1) (1994). The language of the 1991 Act seems to confirm this: the Act provides for punitive awards to 'a complaining party,' not to a class as a whole. 42 USC 1981a(b)(1) (1994 & Supp. III 1997). If a class and a

Markets, Inc.[71] There the court certified a class under Rule 23(b)(2) based on its finding that the class had already satisfied the 'commonality' requirement of Rule 23(a). The court then bifurcated the trial into a first phase covering liability and a second phase covering damages. The court acknowledged that it had 'not determined what means it will employ to efficiently resolve Stage II damages claims. Nor has it determined how punitive damages will be handled.'[72]

At least one of these cases is consistent with the holding of *Allison* despite coming out the opposite way on the facts. In *Arnold v. United Artists Theatre Circuit, Inc.*,[73] the court certified a 23(b)(2) class alleging disability discrimination in movie theater access under the Americans with Disabilities Act of 1990 and California state law. The California statute allowed compensatory damages for each violation, and the court considered whether such damages predominated over the requested injunctive relief. Significantly, each plaintiff sought only the USD 250 statutory minimum damage award for each violation. Comparing such an award with cases in which back pay was permitted in 23(b)(2) class actions, and noting that 23(b)(2) was 'specifically designed' for civil rights classes, the court concluded that the action was maintainable as a 23(b)(2) class because the damages assessment would not require 'a complicated, individual-specific calculus.'[74]

As discussed below, the named plaintiffs' forswearing of full money damages on behalf of a class raises important questions about the appropriateness of class certification that were not addressed in *Arnold*. Nonetheless, the *Arnold* decision is largely consistent with *Allison* and related cases. Because the amount of damages at issue was small, it is plausible to consider such damages as incidental to the more sweeping injunctive relief sought, which was the physical alteration of over seventy movie theaters to accommodate disabled patrons.[75] Further, because the amount of damages was fixed as to

---

'party' were the same thing, then the damages caps imposed by 42 USC 1981a(b)(3) would limit class recovery to USD 300,000 because that limit caps recovery for a 'party.' That clearly was not what Congress intended.

[71] 69 Empl. Prac. Dec. (CCH), P 44,477 (MD Fla. 1996).
[72] *Id.* P 87,689.
[73] 158 FRD 439 (ND Cal. 1994).
[74] *Id.* at 452.
[75] See *id.* at 444–445.

CHAPTER 5. UNCERTAIN FUTURE OF TITLE VII CLASS ACTIONS

each plaintiff, the determination of damages would be a mechanical matter once liability was established and would not require additional fact finding or the analysis of complex issues of law.

5.5.1.7 Forgoing Money Damages: Zachery v. Texaco

The complications introduced by money damages in 23(b)(2) cases could be avoided if class members simply did not seek money damages at all in disparate treatment cases.[76] Such an attempt was rejected, however, in *Zachery v. Texaco Exploration and Production, Inc.*[77] The plaintiffs in *Zachery* sought certification of a class of alleged victims of intentional and unintentional race discrimination in pay, promotions, and hiring. As part of their litigation strategy, the named plaintiffs dropped their claims for compensatory and punitive damages and sought 23(b)(2) certification.[78] The court nonetheless denied class certification because of concerns that the unnamed plaintiffs might thereby be stripped involuntarily of their right to recover damages. Central to this holding was the apparent unavailability of an opt-out procedure under 23(b)(2). The *Zachery* court noted that the Supreme Court had raised this issue in *Ticor Title Insurance Co. v. Brown*[79] but then had chosen not to decide it, meaning that there was 'no clear cut decision' on the availability of an opt-out procedure in 23(b)(2) cases.[80] This meant that should relief be granted to a 23(b)(2) class that excluded money damages it would be possible that no class member would be able to recover such damages because the entire class would necessarily be bound by the judgment. A plaintiffs' victory in the class action might therefore stand as a bar to any subsequent actions by the class members to recover the money damages that their representatives had forsworn.[81] Thus, the court concluded that the decision to drop monetary damages could not be 'imposed upon the absent class members

---

[76] In a pure disparate impact case, only equitable relief is available, and damages are therefore not an issue.
[77] 185 FRD 230 (WD Tex. 1999).
[78] See *id.* at 242.
[79] 511 US 117, 120–121 (1994).
[80] See *Zachery*, 185 FRD at 244 (citing *Ticor Title Ins. Co.*, 511 US at 120–121).
[81] See *id.* at 243–244.

without raising a very serious conflict of interest' and refused to certify the class.[82]

The *Zachery* decision encapsulates many of the problems inherent in trying to reconcile the damages provisions of the 1991 Act with 23(b)(2) class certification. The individualized nature of such relief is at odds with the homogeneity of harm and remedy presupposed by 23(b)(2) certification. At the same time, attempts to forgo such relief may be barred by the lack of an opt-out provision – a provision that is not part of 23(b)(2) precisely because of the common interests and remedies of the archetypal 23(b)(2) class.

5.5.1.8 The End of the 23(b)(2) Title VII Class?

For all of these reasons, it would appear that the more persuasive authority has denied 23(b)(2) certification in Title VII class actions. Because the 23(b)(2) class is a homogeneous class as to which homogeneous relief can be granted, the presence of individualized claims seems incompatible with that type of action. Those cases that have nonetheless certified 23(b)(2) classes have done so in express or implicit reliance on pre-1991 cases and their treatment of equitable back pay relief – a type of relief that is generally less complex and less individualized than compensatory or punitive damages and which is therefore less at odds with the fundamental purposes of Rule 23(b)(2).

In addition to the incompatibility of individualized damages with the 23(b)(2) model, the apparent or arguable lack of an opt-out procedure for 23(b)(2) classes should preclude attempts to bind class members to the adjudication of their monetary claims in a 23(b)(2) case. Unlike Rule 23(b)(3), which entitles potential class members to notice of the class action and the opportunity to 'opt out' of the class to pursue their claims individually, Rule 23(b)(2) class actions bind all class

---

[82] *Id.* at 244. Another court has characterized this problem as a 'catch-22': if the plaintiffs do not seek full relief, they could be accused of being inadequate class representatives. If they do seek full relief, then under *Zachery* they may fail to meet the 23(b)(2) requirements for certification. *Smith v. Texaco, Inc.*, 88 F. Supp. 2d 663, 679 (ED Tex. 2000). The Smith court sidestepped this dilemma by certifying only the equitable claims under Rule 23(b)(2) with an opt-out provision and certifying the damages claims under Rule 23(b)(3). See *infra* Part V.C (discussing this type of split certification).

members with or without their consent. This is consistent with the homogeneity of harm and remedy contemplated by Rule 23(b)(2): if all class members are harmed in a similar way and if that harm can be remedied through the same declaratory or injunctive relief, then it makes sense to apply that relief once to all class members rather than allowing individualized adjudication and risking inconsistent or inefficiently repetitive outcomes. Where damages claims are at issue, however, courts have been wary of the right to opt out as a matter of due process and have frequently looked to Rule 23(b)(3) rather than 23(b)(2) to address such claims.[83] If the 1991 remedies are a square peg, Rule 23(b)(2) is a round hole, and, as the two presently exist, they cannot be fitted without distorting them both.

5.5.2 23(b)(3) Classes – Commonality, Manageability, and Negative Value

The certification of Title VII class actions under Rule 23(b)(3) has also become problematic in the wake of the 1991 Act's damages provisions. In particular, the 1991 remedies have raised questions concerning commonality, manageability, and negative value in adjudicating 23(b)(3) certification.

5.5.2.1 Commonality

A primary issue under Rule 23(b)(3) has been that of commonality: whether, when each plaintiff or class member seeks compensatory and punitive damages, 'questions of law or fact common to the members of the class predominate over any questions affecting only individual members.'[84] Under the 1991 Act, entitlement to compensatory and

---

[83] See e.g., *Ortiz v. Fibreboard Corp.*, 527 US 815 (1999); *Jefferson v. Ingersoll Int'l, Inc.*, 195 F.3d 894, 897 (7th Cir. 1999). See *infra* 5.5(b).

[84] Fed. R. Civ. P. 23(b)(3). This requirement of 'commonality' under Rule 23(b)(3) should not be confused with the 'commonality' requirement of Rule 23(a), which asks whether there are 'questions of law or fact common to the class.' The 23(a) 'commonality' standard has generally been viewed as less rigorous than the one in Rule 23(b)(3). See *Gorence v. Eagle Food Ctrs., Inc.*, No. 93 C 4862, 1994 WL 445149 at 11 (ND Ill. August 16, 1994).

perhaps punitive damages will turn on each plaintiff's private experience of discrimination as well as on personal factors (such as psychiatric history, medical history, family situation, or other social particularities) that may influence the type or degree of emotional or other harm resulting from that discrimination. Accordingly, when such damages are sought, there is a strong possibility that questions affecting individual members will predominate, thereby precluding 23(b)(3) certification.

Nonetheless, it seems clear that a claim for damages will not inevitably preclude 23(b)(3) certification. The Advisory Committee appears to have taken a balanced view of this issue, with an eye toward promoting judicial efficiency. As the Committee explained, a primary purpose of the rule is the achievement of economies of scale for courts and litigants:

> The court is required to find, as a condition of holding that a class action may be maintained under this subdivision [23(b)(3)], that the questions common to the class predominate over the questions affecting individual members. It is only where this predominance exists that economies can be achieved by means of the class-action device.[85]

Thus, the presence of individual damages claims would not necessarily bar 23(b)(3) certification, so long as the resulting class was an efficient collective means of disposing of those claims. The Committee continued:

> In this view, a fraud perpetrated on numerous persons by the use of similar misrepresentations may be an appealing situation for a class action, and it may remain so despite the need, if liability is found, for separate determination of the damages suffered by individuals within the class. On the other hand, although having some common core, a fraud case may be unsuited for treatment as a class action if there was material variation in the representations made or in the kinds or degrees of reliance by the persons to whom they were addressed.[86]

The availability of Rule 23(b)(3) certification will therefore turn less on the mere availability of money damages than on the possibility of achieving efficiency by the adjudication of common damages claims through use of the class device.

---

[85] Fed. R. Civ. P. 23, advisory committee's notes, 39 FRD 69, 103 (1966).
[86] Id.

CHAPTER 5. UNCERTAIN FUTURE OF TITLE VII CLASS ACTIONS

Courts confronting the 23(b)(3) commonality issue following the 1991 Act have reached mixed results. Here, too, *Allison* provides the only direct appellate authority to date under Title VII. The *Allison* court rejected 23(b)(3) certification of the class before it, holding that the individual-specific damages issues raised by the plaintiffs meant that a class action would likely degenerate into 'multiple lawsuits separately tried':

> The plaintiffs' claims for compensatory and punitive damages must therefore focus almost entirely on facts and issues specific to individuals rather than the class as a whole: what kind of discrimination was each plaintiff subjected to; how did it affect each plaintiff emotionally and physically, at work and at home; what medical treatment did each plaintiff receive and at what expense; and so on and so on. Under such circumstances, an action conducted nominally as a class action would 'degenerate in practice into multiple lawsuits separately tried.'[87]

The Eleventh Circuit has also rejected 23(b)(3) certification in a discrimination case, *Rutstein v. Avis Rent-A-Car Systems, Inc.*[88] While *Rutstein* is not an employment discrimination case, it would seem to leave little room for 23(b)(3) certification in any discrimination case in which individualized damages are sought.

The plaintiffs in *Rutstein* sued under 42 USC 1981, alleging that Avis followed a 'Yeshiva policy' designed to deny services to individuals and businesses with Jewish-sounding accents or Jewish-sounding names. The district court certified the case as a 23(b)(3) class action, but the Eleventh Circuit reversed based both on the elements of proof and the damages sought. As to proof, the court noted that each plaintiff, in order to prevail, would have to prove that he or she was intentionally discriminated against by the defendant. Thus,

---

[87] *Allison v. Citgo Petroleum Corp.*, 151 F.3d 402, 419 (5th Cir. 1998) (quoting *Castano v. American Tobacco Co.*, 84 F.3d 734, 745 n.19 (5th Cir. 1996) (citing Fed. R. Civ. P. 23 advisory committee's notes)). The Seventh Circuit, in *Jefferson v. Ingersoll Int'l, Inc.*, appeared to hint that 23(b)(3) certification could be appropriate in Title VII class actions precisely because of the availability of money damages, which made 23(b)(3) a more suitable choice than 23(b)(2) due to the opt-out provision. 195 F.3d 894, 898 (7th Cir. 1999). The Seventh Circuit directed the district court on remand to consider 23(b)(3) certification as one possibility but stated in the same breath that it 'did not broach' the question whether 23(b)(3) certification was 'sound' in the case before it. *Id.* at 899.
[88] 211 F.3d 1228 (11th Cir. 2000).

'each plaintiff will have to bring forth evidence demonstrating that the defendant had an intent to treat him or her less favorably because of the plaintiff's Jewish ethnicity.'[89] Likewise, the fact that each plaintiff sought compensatory and punitive damages made the case inappropriate for class treatment:

> To establish that they are entitled to some compensation, plaintiffs will have to prove that they actually suffered some injury, whether it be emotional or otherwise. The idea that individual injury could be settled on a classwide basis is preposterous. Plaintiffs' claims for damages must 'focus almost entirely on facts and issues specific to individuals rather than the class as a whole: what kind of discrimination was each plaintiff subjected to[, and] how did it affect each plaintiff emotionally and physically, at work and at home.'[90]

This requirement meant that 'most, if not all, of the plaintiffs' claims will stand or fall, not on the answer to the question whether [Avis] has a practice or policy of [ethnic] discrimination, but on the resolution of ... highly case-specific factual issues.'[91] This also made *Teamsters*-style adjudication inappropriate because 'the establishment of a policy or practice of discrimination cannot trigger the defendant's liability for damages to all the plaintiffs in the putative class,'[92] which would still require individual determinations.

While the *Rutstein* court was careful to point out that 'this is not a case alleging employment discrimination,' its holding would seem to leave little room for the certification of any class – including a Title VII class – in which the plaintiffs or potential class members seek individualized damages.[93]

Some district courts have likewise rejected 23(b)(3) certification in Title VII cases on grounds of lack of commonality. In *Adams v. Henderson*, the court held that the presence of individual damages claims would require 'individualized liability inquiries,' thereby making it unsuitable

---

[89] *Id.* at 1235.
[90] *Id.* at 1239–1240 (quoting Allison, 151 F.3d at 419).
[91] *Id.* at 1234 (quoting *Jackson v. Motel 6 Multipurpose, Inc.*, 130 F.3d 999, 1006 (11th Cir. 1997) (decertifying class alleging discrimination in lodging where liability to class members would turn on individualized circumstances of denial of motel rooms to each class member)).
[92] *Id.* at 1239.
[93] See *id.* at 1241.

CHAPTER 5. UNCERTAIN FUTURE OF TITLE VII CLASS ACTIONS

for 23(b)(3) certification.[94] The court in *Zapata v. IBP, Inc.* denied such certification, noting that 'claims for compensatory damages...greatly complicate the management of a class' and that the assessment of psychological damages 'would necessarily require an individual, subjective analysis.'[95] The court in *Gorence v. Eagle Food Centers, Inc.* noted that the assessment of discrimination and 'individualized damages' would require it to 'hold a series of mini-trials' and denied 23(b)(3) certification.[96] And in *Faulk v. Home Oil Co.*, the court adopted the reasoning of the *Allison* court to deny 23(b)(3) certification to a potential class of race discriminatees.[97]

By contrast, in *Griffin v. Home Depot, Inc.*, the court denied a motion to dismiss the class allegations in a sex discrimination complaint, holding that on the pleadings 'one can postulate that there is sufficient commonality of facts to satisfy Rule 23(b)(3).'[98] This amounts to a holding that 23(b)(3) certification is not automatically precluded in Title VII class actions – a holding not at odds with the Advisory Committee's view of damages in 23(b)(3) cases but perhaps inconsistent with *Allison*'s recognition that damages determinations arising out of employment discrimination tend, by definition, to be more individualized than typical.

5.5.2.2 Manageability

Hand-in-hand with the issue of commonality under Rule 23(b)(3) has gone the issue of manageability. One factor for consideration under Rule 23(b)(3) is 'the difficulties likely to be encountered in the management of a class action.'[99] In the Title VII context, this has for the most part meant the logistical difficulties attendant to trying the individualized damages claims of hundreds or even thousands of class members. The *Allison* court sketched the problem concisely: 'This action must be

---

[94] 197 FRD 162, 172 (D Md. 2000).
[95] 167 FRD 147, 163 (D Kan. 1996).
[96] No. 93 C 4862, 1994 WL 445149 at 11 (ND Ill. August 16, 1994).
[97] 184 FRD 645, 661–662 (MD Ala. 1999).
[98] 168 FRD 187, 191 (ED La. 1996).
[99] Fed. R. Civ. P. 23(b)(3)(D).

tried to a jury and involves more than a thousand potential plaintiffs spread across two separate facilities, represented by six different unions, working in seven different departments, and alleging discrimination over a period of nearly twenty years.'[100] While each party is entitled to trial by jury in such cases, it is unthinkable that a single jury could try this or even a much smaller class action in which individual issues must be resolved as to each plaintiff. Accordingly, courts in a variety of settings have rejected the class device where the need for individual jury fact finding would render class adjudication unmanageable.[101] At least one court, on the other hand, has expressed a preference for class adjudication over individual adjudication in the Title VII context. In *Smith v. Texaco, Inc.*,[102] the court certified a 23(b)(3) class of approximately 200 employees alleging race discrimination in employment. In doing so, the court noted that, should the claims be tried individually, 'this one district court will be totally and fully occupied for the larger part of at least 200 weeks in the trial of these claims alone.'[103] The court therefore concluded that 'individual actions would take up far more judicial resources than a single class[,] ... [and] a class action is a superior means for managing this case because of the efficiencies involved in addressing the claims of about 200 class persons.'[104]

The distinction drawn by the *Smith* court between class and individual adjudication may be more rhetorical than actual: it is neither obvious nor inevitable that the litigation of hundreds or thousands of individual damages claims in a class action will be less time consuming than whatever individual lawsuits might be brought if class certification were denied. In either scenario, individualized, jury-based fact finding must be undertaken as to each plaintiff or class member who

---

[100] *Allison v. Citgo Petroleum Corp.*, 151 F.3d 402, 419 (5th Cir. 1998).

[101] See e.g., *Zimmerman v. Bell*, 800 F.2d 386, 390 (4th Cir. 1986) (holding that it is proper to deny certification in securities fraud case due to 'excessive managerial burden' imposed by individualized issues of knowledge and reliance); *Alabama v. Blue Bird Body Co.*, 573 F.2d 309, 328 (5th Cir. 1978) (upholding denial of certification in antitrust case where, inter alia, certification might bring in 'thousands of possible claimants,' leading to a 'multitude of mini-trials').

[102] 88 F. Supp. 2d 663 (ED Tex. 2000).

[103] *Id.* at 682.

[104] *Id.* at 683.

seeks to recover compensatory or punitive damages. Left to their own devices, however, some members of a large group of individual plaintiffs might lose interest in pressing their claims, realize that they did not have claims and so not bring them, or be unable to find counsel to represent them should their case not be sufficiently strong. Accordingly, the denial of a certification to a class of 200 members does not mean that two hundred individual lawsuits would be brought. This makes the rationale of the Smith court less persuasive than it might first appear.

5.5.2.3 Negative Value

Finally, the damages afforded by the 1991 Act have diminished the force of another strong rationale for granting 23(b)(3) certification: the specter of the negative value lawsuit. One benefit of the class action device is that it permits plaintiffs to aggregate small claims. Although such claims individually may be worth less than the cost of litigation, when combined as a class they may be worth the efforts of an attorney, which grants the plaintiffs access to the courts that they might not otherwise have. In certifying 23(b)(3) classes in various settings, courts have sometimes relied on the fact that a denial of certification could effectively bar the bringing of such small-value individual claims. The danger of negative value suits has even been described as 'the most compelling rationale'[105] for granting 23(b)(3) certification in an appropriate case. The 1991 Act, however, has effectively removed this issue from the Title VII arena. Given the significant statutory damages available under the 1991 Act (ranging from USD 50,000-300,000 per plaintiff, depending on the size of the employer), as well as the availability of attorney's fees to the prevailing party,[106] the possibility of negative value suits is now virtually nonexistent in Title VII cases.[107]

---

[105] *Castano v. American Tobacco Co.*, 84 F.3d 734, 748 (5th Cir. 1996).

[106] See 42 USC 2000e-5(k) (1994).

[107] See *Allison v. Citgo Petroleum Corp.*, 151 F.3d 402, 420 (5th Cir. 1998) ('The relatively substantial value of these claims (for the statutory maximum of USD 300,000 per plaintiff) and the availability of attorney's fees eliminate financial barriers that might make individual lawsuits unlikely or infeasible.').

5.5.3 Procedural and Constitutional Problems of Bifurcation and Partial Certification

Courts have attempted to circumvent Rule 23 concerns by applying various schemes of bifurcation or partial certification to Title VII classes after the 1991 Act. The most frequent scheme of this type is the certification of liability determinations and equitable relief under Rule 23(b)(2), with the court reserving judgment on how to handle damages claims or ordering their certification separately under Rule 23(b)(3).[108] Another option, and one raised by the plaintiffs in *Allison*, is to certify a class only as to the disparate impact claims, leaving the disparate treatment claims for individual trials or later class treatment.[109] Such schemes, however, pose serious problems under Rule 23 and the Seventh Amendment. In many cases, these difficulties have been ignored or minimized by the courts, and one suspects that in some cases courts are either unable or unwilling to confront the profound changes wrought in the class action landscape by the 1991 Act.

5.5.3.1 Procedural Issues

Much of the current judicial approach to Title VII class actions has evolved from the class action management scheme approved in *International Brotherhood of Teamsters v. United States*[110] and discussed above. The difficulties with such bifurcated proceedings under the 1991 Act are both procedural and constitutional: procedural because of concerns about Rule 23(b)(3)'s commonality requirement and the misuse of Rule 23(c)(4) to evade that requirement and constitutional because of concerns about the Seventh Amendment rights of the parties in cases that could employ scores or even hundreds of juries under some circumstances.

The *Teamsters* paradigm was both sensible and effective when only equitable remedies were available. It allowed for focused resolution of the dominant equitable issues, and, while individual relief could be

---

[108] See e.g., *Smith v. Texaco Inc.*, 88 F. Supp. 2d 667, 682 (ED Tex. 2000); *Shores v. Publix*, 69 Empl. Prac. Dec. (CCH), P 44,477 (MD Fla. 1996); *Butler v. Home Depot, Inc.*, 70 Fair Empl. Prac. Cas. (BNA) 51 (ND Cal. 1996).
[109] See *Allison*, 151 F.3d at 422.
[110] 431 US 324 (1977).

CHAPTER 5. UNCERTAIN FUTURE OF TITLE VII CLASS ACTIONS

time consuming to administer, at least it was not complicated by individualized damages issues. The paradigm also worked when neither party had the right to a jury trial, as special masters could be used to streamline the proceedings in the damages phase. This paradigm appears to have become ingrained in the psyches of many litigants and judges, but its application is questionable in the wake of the 1991 Act.

The Fifth Circuit faced these issues squarely in *Allison* and rejected (though not categorically) the use of bifurcated or partial class proceedings in Title VII class actions. The *Allison* plaintiffs first suggested certifying all damages issues under Rule 23(b)(3) and the rest of the case under Rule 23(b)(2). This suggestion was rejected based on the Fifth Circuit's 23(b)(3) 'commonality' analysis. The court noted that the case before it involved over one thousand potential class members at two facilities, represented by six unions, in seven departments, over a twenty-year period. Each of these thousand claimants sought compensatory and punitive damages, which would require individualized determination. The court therefore concluded that Rule 23(b)(3) certification would be inappropriate in light of this lack of commonality. The court also noted that the availability to each plaintiff of attorney's fees and up to USD 300,000 in damages eliminated the possibility of a 'negative value suit,' one of the most frequent rationales for certifying a 23(b)(3) class.[111] Thus, because 23(b)(3) certification was inappropriate, the attempt to 'split' certification between Rules 23(b)(2) and 23(b)(3) was also improper.[112]

The *Allison* plaintiffs suggested a second bifurcation scheme: certifying both their disparate impact and pattern-and-practice claims

---

[111] See *Allison*, 151 F.3d at 419–420 (quoting *Castano v. American Tobacco Co.*, 84 F.3d 734, 748 (5th Cir. 1996)). The court also noted that multiple juries would be needed to try the thousand or so damages claims, thereby raising Seventh Amendment issues. See *infra* 5(c)(3).

[112] The Seventh Circuit in *Jefferson v. Ingersoll Int'l, Inc.*, 195 F.3d 894, 898 (7th Cir. 1999), suggested, without deciding, that classes of this type could be handled by certifying the injunctive aspects under Rule 23(b)(2) and the damages aspects under Rule 23(b)(3). This suggestion was made as part of the court's discussion of how courts might preserve what it viewed as essential opt-out rights where money damages are sought. See *id.* The court also noted, however, that it expressed no view on whether Rule 23(b)(3) certification would be proper in Title VII class actions, which it would have to be for such a scheme to work. See *id.* at 899.

under Rule 23(b)(2) or 23(b)(3), trying those issues to a jury, and allowing the court to rule on the certification of the remaining claims – such as those for damages – after the jury's findings on these initial issues.[113] The court rejected this proposal as well, stating that there was no reason to believe that adjudication of the first phase – the pattern-and-practice and disparate impact issues – would make possible the class certification of damages issues in the second phase in light of its previous determination that the damages issues were uncertifiable because of their individualized nature. Noting that under *Teamsters* there are no common issues between a first-stage pattern and practice finding of liability (that merely creates a rebuttable presumption of discrimination against affected individuals) and the second remedial phase (that requires individuals to prove that the presumption should apply to them and that they suffered damages),[114] the court declined to certify the initial phase of the litigation 'when there is no foreseeable likelihood that the claims for compensatory and punitive damages could be certified in the class action sought by the plaintiffs.'[115]

The court pointed out that what the plaintiffs were suggesting was an end run around the commonality requirements of Rule 23(b)(3): by temporarily setting aside individual-specific damages issues (presumably by invoking Rule 23(c)(4)),[116] the plaintiffs could pretend for purposes of the first phase that common issues, rather than individual-specific issues, would predominate for purposes of 23(b)(3) certification. The *Allison* court refused to indulge this make-believe commonality based on Fifth Circuit precedent, which forbids attempts to 'manufacture predominance through the nimble use of subdivision (c)(4).'[117] Otherwise, a court in any case could sever issues until only common issues remained, and 'the result would be automatic certification in every case where there is a common issue, a result that could not have been intended.'[118]

---

[113] See *Allison*, 151 F.3d at 420–421.
[114] See *Cooper v. Federal Reserve Bank*, 467 US 867, 877–880 (1984).
[115] *Allison*, 151 F.3d at 421.
[116] See Fed. R. Civ. P. 23(c)(4), which provides that 'when appropriate...an action may be brought or maintained as a class action with respect to particular issues.'
[117] *Allison*, 151 F.3d at 422 (quoting *Castano v. American Tobacco Co.*, 84 F.3d 734, 745 n. 21 (5th Cir. 1996)).
[118] *Id.*

CHAPTER 5. UNCERTAIN FUTURE OF TITLE VII CLASS ACTIONS

Other courts have not been so scrupulous. In *Butler v. Home Depot*, for instance, the court certified a class under Rule 23(b)(2) as to 'liability and relief applicable to the class as a whole including declaratory and injunctive relief, and whether defendant is liable for punitive damages.'[119] The court admitted, however, that it had not determined how to handle the phase-two damages determinations: 'The precise procedures to be used during the second phase, if any, will be determined later in this litigation.'[120] Similarly, in *Shores v. Publix* the court approved a 'hybrid' class, relying on pre-1991 Eleventh Circuit precedent.[121] In the first phase, liability would be resolved under Rule 23(b)(2), while in the second phase, damages would be determined under a Rule 23(b)(3) opt-out procedure. Like the *Butler* court, the *Shores* court admitted that it 'has not determined what means it will employ to efficiently resolve Stage II claims. Nor has it determined how claims for punitive damages will be handled.'[122]

It is remarkable that at least these two courts have certified bifurcated Title VII classes while frankly acknowledging that they have no idea how to handle the damages issues. This may reflect a habit of *Teamsters*-style adjudication in Title VII class cases that has prevented some courts from grasping the implications of the 1991 Act. On a darker view, it may reflect a desire to set the class process in motion and force a settlement before thorny and time-consuming issues such as individual damages have to be addressed. In both *Butler* and *Shores*, the result of certification was an expensive settlement, and hence the strategy (if there was one) was successful.

---

[119] *Butler v. Home Depot, Inc.*, No. C-94-4335 SI, 1996 WL 421436 at 1 (ND Cal. January 25, 1996). As noted *supra*, the Butler court's apparent belief that there is such a thing as 'classwide' punitive damages may be incorrect.

[120] *Id.* The parties never reached this issue: in September, 1997, the case was settled for USD 65 million. See 'Home Depot Agrees to Pay $65 Million to Settle Sex Discrimination Class Action, Daily Labor Report' (BNA), September 22, 1997, at A-11.

[121] 69 Empl. Prac. Dec. (CCH) P 44,477, 87,688 (citing *Cox v. American Cast Iron Pipe Co.*, 784 F.2d 1546 (11th Cir. 1986)).

[122] *Shores v. Publix Super Markets, Inc.*, 69 Empl. Prac. Dec. (CCH), P 44,477, 87,689 (MD Fla. 1996). As in Butler, the court never got that far. The case was settled in January, 1997, for a total of USD 81.5 million. See 'Publix Markets Agrees to Pay $81.5 Million to Settle Sex Bias Suit,' Daily Labor Report (BNA), January 27, 1997, at AA-1.

5.5.3.2 The Integrity of Rule 23

There are other sound reasons to prefer individual suits to class actions that would, in any event, degenerate into individual suits. Individual suits preserve the integrity of Rule 23 by not stretching it to cover classes that lack the required commonality and manageability. They also avoid the danger that sweeping issues of liability may turn on the whims of a single jury. In a bifurcated class action, one jury will decide the existence of a pattern and practice of discrimination. If that jury decides against the employer, it then establishes a presumption of discrimination that applies to every member of the class who can prove an adverse job action in the individual adjudication phase. While the presumption is rebuttable, that presumption will have significantly heightened the burden on the employer and will increase the chance that it will be found liable to each of the individual plaintiffs. Depending on the size of the employer and the size of the class, a significant step will then have been taken toward the employer being found liable for millions upon millions of dollars in individual liability (in *Allison*, up to USD 300 million).[123] Spreading this risk among multiple juries in individual cases will ensure that such momentous issues of liability are determined by a process involving the collective judgment of many juries, not the potential caprice of one.

Courts in other contexts have recognized the value of nonclass, case-by-case adjudication of matters that threaten defendants with massive liability. In *Matter of Rhone-Poulenc-Rorer, Inc.*,[124] the Seventh Circuit held that a case involving potentially bankrupting liability for manufacturers of antihemophiliac factor concentrate was unsuitable

---

[123] Further, this risk is one-sided: should the phase-one jury rule against the plaintiffs, that decision has no res judicata effect as to the class members' individual claims of discrimination because all that the decision means is that the employer does not discriminate against employees as a matter of standard practice. See *Cooper v. Federal Reserve Bank*, 467 US 867, 877–880 (1984). Each class member remains free to file his own lawsuit (if timely), and the employer may gain little peace of mind by prevailing in this phase of the class action. In essence, the plaintiffs have two chances instead of one to press their claims, and they and their lawyers have little incentive not to 'shoot the moon' in seeking class certification.

[124] 51 F.3d 1293 (7th Cir. 1995).

CHAPTER 5. UNCERTAIN FUTURE OF TITLE VII CLASS ACTIONS

for class treatment, in part because trying the case as a class action would place the fate of the industry in the hands of six people:

> If these [individual] trials are permitted to go forward ... the pattern that results will reflect a consensus, or at least a pooling of judgment, of many different tribunals. For this consensus or maturing of judgment the district judge proposes to substitute a single trial before a single jury.... One jury ... will hold the fate of an industry in the palm of its hand.... [This] need not be tolerated when the alternative exists of submitting an issue to multiple juries constituting in the aggregate a much larger and more diverse sample of decision-makers. That would not be a feasible option if the stakes to each class member were too slight to repay the cost of suit, even though the aggregate stakes were very large and would repay the costs of a consolidated proceeding. But this is not the case....[125]

A case like *Allison* is not so different from a case like *Rhone-Poulenc*. The total exposure in money damages alone in *Allison* was USD 300 million (USD 300,000 per class member times 1,000 potential members). It is a frightening prospect to place a small handful of jurors in charge of such potentially crippling liability, especially where there are sound reasons why such a thing would be a misuse of Rule 23. For this reason, the possibility of individual lawsuits rather then implausible *Teamsters*-style classes is to be preferred (or at least not bemoaned): plaintiffs who have colorable claims (and some who do not) will still get their day in court because their suits are potentially valuable, the judicial system will not necessarily be substantially more burdened, and defendants can have their potential liability determined by something more than a single set of jurors.

5.5.3.3 Constitutional Issues

The issues raised by bifurcating class actions after 1991 are not only procedural but also constitutional. In a further effort to have their class certified, the *Allison* plaintiffs proposed certifying only their disparate impact claim, as to which money damages are not available, as a means of sidestepping the problems posed by their seeking individualized damages under their disparate treatment claim. While such a proposal presents far fewer Rule 23 problems than other attempts at certification,

---

[125] *Id.* at 1299–1300, quoted with approval in *Castano v. American Tobacco Co.*, 84 F.3d 734, 748 (5th Cir. 1996).

275

the availability of a jury trial under the 1991 Act also implicates the Seventh Amendment. This difficulty, the *Allison* court found, was insurmountable.

As the *Allison* court explained, the Seventh Amendment preserves the right to trial by jury in 'suits at common law' where legal rights are to be determined.[126] Where the right to a jury exists, the Seventh Amendment prohibits the reexamination of one jury's findings by another fact finder.[127] Although a disparate impact claim does not implicate legal rights (the remedy being confined to equitable relief), the jury trial right conferred by the 1991 Act extends to 'all factual issues necessary to determine liability' and damages under the companion disparate treatment claim.[128] Thus, where disparate impact and disparate treatment claims are joined (as they were in *Allison*), 'the Seventh Amendment requires that all factual issues common to these claims be submitted to a jury for decision on the legal claims before final court determination of the equitable claims.'[129]

The *Allison* court held that the certification of only the disparate impact claims would be barred by the Seventh Amendment because of the risk that subsequent fact finders in the disparate treatment litigation would be required to revisit the first jury's determinations both in determining liability toward individual plaintiffs and in determining their damages. This problem is a function of the particular nature of proof in Title VII cases. In a disparate impact case, the plaintiffs must first produce evidence that a challenged policy or practice of the employer adversely affects a protected group. The employer may rebut this evidence by showing 'that the challenged practice is job related for the position in question and consistent with business necessity.'[130] In a class disparate treatment case, the plaintiffs must first show prima facie that discrimination is the employer's standard practice, a showing that can be made by a combination of statistical and anecdotal evidence.[131] The employer then can attempt to rebut this evidence, in the course of which it would almost inevitably attempt to show that the

---

[126] US Const. amend. VII.
[127] See *Allison v. Citgo Petroleum Corp.*, 151 F.3d 402, 423 (5th Cir. 1998).
[128] *Id.*
[129] *Id.*
[130] 42 USC 2000e-2(k)(1)(A)(i) (1994).
[131] See *Int'l Bd. of Teamsters v. United States*, 431 US 324, 338–341 (1977); *EEOC v. McDonnell Douglas Corp.*, 960 F. Supp. 203, 205 (ED Mo. 1996).

CHAPTER 5. UNCERTAIN FUTURE OF TITLE VII CLASS ACTIONS

actions that are the subject of the plaintiffs' illustrative anecdotes were taken for legitimate, nondiscriminatory reasons.

These methods of proof provide considerable potential for overlap between the fact finding in a disparate impact case and the fact finding in a disparate treatment case, especially where the same employer practices and policies are challenged under both theories of liability. As the *Allison* court explained:

> It is the rare case indeed in which a challenged practice is job-related and a business necessity, yet not a legitimate nondiscriminatory reason for an adverse employment action taken pursuant to that practice. Thus, a finding that a challenged practice is job related and a business necessity in response to a disparate impact claim strongly, if not wholly, implicates a finding that the same practice is a legitimate nondiscriminatory reason for the employer's actions in a pattern or practice claim.[132]

Under the Title VII scheme of proof, then, 'significant overlap of factual issues is almost inevitable whenever disparate impact and pattern or practice claims are joined in the same [class] action.'[133] Because consideration of these overlapping issues by different juries would violate the Seventh Amendment, the *Allison* court declined to certify the class only as to disparate impact.[134]

Other courts have certified bifurcated classes in spite of these Seventh Amendment problems. Some courts have done so with little analysis, brushing aside the Seventh Amendment issues by declaring that the first-and second-phase determinations are legally distinct.

---

[132] *Allison*, 151 F.3d at 424.

[133] *Id.* (citing *Segar v. Smith*, 738 F.2d 1249, 1268–1270 (DC Cir. 1984)).

[134] For another discussion of these Seventh Amendment issues, see Keith R. Fentonmiller, 'Damages, Jury Trials and the Class Action under the Civil Rights Act of 1991,' 12 Lab. L. 421, 437–447 (1997). Had the Allison plaintiffs not joined disparate impact and disparate treatment claims in the same case, this issue would not have been present. It appears to be an open question what would happen if a class sued on a disparate impact theory and then tried to bring a separate disparate treatment case under the same facts. Most likely, the same Seventh Amendment issues would arise because there would still be factual overlap between these claims, whether or not they were joined. It is doubtful that a class disparate impact claim could be tried to judgment before the statute of limitations expired on disparate treatment claims under the same facts (unless the plaintiffs could rely on a theory of continuing violation); thus, the possibility of consecutive disparate impact and disparate treatment suits involving the same facts would seem remote.

EMPLOYMENT CLASS AND COLLECTIVE ACTIONS

For instance, in *Butler v. Home Depot*, the court certified a class under Rule 23(b)(2) as to 'liability and relief applicable to the class as a whole, including declaratory and injunctive relief, and whether defendant is liable for punitive damages.'[135] If liability were established, the second phase would decide 'individual compensatory damages.'[136] The only aspect of divided certification addressed by the court was the Seventh Amendment issue, which it disposed of by observing (based largely on pre-1991 cases) that courts have 'routinely' adopted such a bifurcated approach. According to the *Butler* court, the mere fact that the second phase would involve 'individual claims' meant that it would not involve the same issues as the first phase would.[137] The court did not, however, analyze the methods of proof under Title VII to the degree that *Allison* did and thus may not have considered the matter as thoroughly. In *EEOC v. McDonnell Douglas Corp.*,[138] a class action under the Age Discrimination in Employment Act, the court rejected Seventh Amendment concerns much as the *Butler* court did. Noting that the phase-one finding of liability did no more than establish a presumption of discrimination, the court held that phase-two issues of individual liability were therefore 'separate and distinct' issues of fact.[139] As in *Butler*, the court did not address the details of the ADEA's proof scheme, which mirrors that of Title VII,[140] in making this holding.

Decisions like these appear questionable (or at least hasty) in light of the 1991 Act and the concerns raised by *Allison*. The *McDonnell Douglas* court undermined its own holding when it noted the various means of proof that an employer could use to rebut the plaintiffs' phase-one case:

> Although the Defendant will not be able to present evidence regarding each individual termination at the liability trial, it can 'introduce direct statistical evidence, anecdotal evidence, illustrative evidence of individual dismissals and any other evidence that bears on the issue of whether a pattern of discrimination existed.'[141]

---

[135] *Butler v. Home Depot, Inc.*, No. C-94-4335 SI 1996 WL 421436, at 1 (ND Cal. January 25, 1996).
[136] *Id.* at 6.
[137] *Id.*
[138] 960 F. Supp. 203 (ED Mo. 1996).
[139] See *id.* at 205.
[140] *Brennan v. Metropolitan Opera Ass'n., Inc.*, 192 F.3d 310, 316 (2nd Cir. 1999).
[141] *EEOC v. McDonnell Douglas Corp.*, 960 F. Supp. 203, 205 (ED Mo. 1996) (quoting *Sperling v. Hoffmann-LaRoche, Inc.*, 924 F. Supp. 1346, 1353 (DNJ 1996)).

CHAPTER 5. UNCERTAIN FUTURE OF TITLE VII CLASS ACTIONS

This raises the question, however: if an employer introduces anecdotal evidence or 'illustrative evidence of individual dismissals,' then presumably, in determining the existence of a pattern of discrimination, a jury may find that there was discrimination behind those events. In the second phase, when the liability to the particular employees who were involved in these events is adjudicated, the liability jury would be free to decide that there was no discrimination present, thereby discounting evidence that the first jury found dispositive. Thus, while the questions of pattern and practice and individual liability are indeed separate issues in the sense that the answer to the first question (did the employer discriminate as a matter of practice?) does not resolve the second (was this particular class member discriminated against?), the scheme of proof in employment discrimination cases raises the risk that different juries may make different findings based on the same facts– a situation that is prohibited under the Seventh Amendment.

It may be that the Seventh Amendment problems in *Allison* were simply ones of scale. The court appears to have assumed that multiple juries would be needed to resolve the individual claims – a safe assumption in a class covering 1,000 potential members. It is conceivable, however, that a Title VII class could be small enough to have all of its claims heard by a single jury. Rule 23 requires no minimum number of class members for certification, and Rule 23 classes have been certified with as few as thirteen members.[142] While a small class may not solve the problems of predominance and commonality, it would at least avoid Seventh Amendment problems by making it possible to use a single fact finder throughout.

5.5.3.4 *The Allison Denial of Rehearing*

As a coda to the bifurcation issues raised by *Allison*, it is worth examining the court's somewhat cryptic denial of rehearing. The logic of *Allison* would seem to preclude most types of divided or partial certifications, but the *Allison* court apparently did not intend to prohibit

---

[142] See e.g., *Dale Elec., Inc. v. R.C.L. Elec., Inc.*, 53 FRD 531, 534–535 (DNH 1971) (certifying class of thirteen members in patent infringement case); *Cypress v. Newport News Gen. & Nonsectarian Hosp. Ass'n*, 375 F.2d 648, 653 (4th Cir. 1967) (certifying class of eighteen minority physicians in race discrimination case).

such schemes absolutely. In denying rehearing, the court acknowledged that some forms of partial certification might survive:

> The trial court utilized consolidation under rule 42 rather than class certification under Rule 23 to manage this case.... We are not called upon to decide whether the district court would have abused its discretion if it had elected to bifurcate liability issues that are common to the class and to certify for class determination those discreet liability issues.[143]

This has the ring of a declaration that will become famously puzzled over in the years ahead. Some courts have taken it to undermine the main opinion's holdings entirely, reducing them to dicta.[144] Others have read it more narrowly as an acknowledgment that the principles discussed in the main opinion are not absolute.[145] The latter view appears more likely: had the Fifth Circuit wanted to nullify large portions of its opinion, it could simply have withdrawn them. Moreover, its holdings concerning the nature of Rule 23 were not dicta because the decision appealed from was a denial of Rule 23 certification. The Fifth Circuit itself relied on *Allison* as precedent in a later case, following *Allison*'s holdings as to Rule 23(b)(2) predominance in reversing certification of a class under the Fair Credit Reporting Act.[146]

Yet, if nullification is not what the statement means, determining what it does mean is still challenging. One possibility is that liability issues could be certified as 'stand-alone' class claims only to the extent that they do not implicate the manageability and Seventh Amendment concerns addressed in the main opinion. But such 'liability issues' virtually by definition (according to the *Allison* court) could not be issues that shared any facts in common with the determination of

---

[143] *Allison v. Citgo Petroleum Corp.*, 151 F.3d 402, 434 (5th Cir. 1998). The trial court explained: 'In some instances it may be appropriate to consolidate cases with similar facts and issues under Fed. R. Civ. P. 42. However, it will be necessary for the unnamed potential class members to file their own lawsuits rather than intervene in the present action.' *Celestine v. Citgo Petroleum Corp.*, 165 FRD 463, 471 (WD La. 1995). Examples of such consolidation might be trying simultaneously all promotion claims involving the same decisionmaker or all claims of discriminatory discipline involving the same supervisor and the same employee conduct.

[144] See e.g., *Warnell v. Ford Motor Co.*, 189 FRD 383, 389 (ND Ill. 1999).

[145] See e.g., *Jefferson v. Ingersoll Int'l, Inc.*, 195 F.3d 894, 898 (7th Cir. 1999); *Faulk v. Home Oil Co.*, 184 FRD 645, 660–661 (MD Ala. 1999); *Riley v. Compucom Sys., Inc.*, No. CIV. A398CV1876L, 2000 WL 343189, at 3 n. 6 (ND Tex. March 31, 2000).

[146] See *Washington v. CSC Credit Servs.*, 199 F.3d 263, 269–270 (5th Cir. 2000).

CHAPTER 5. UNCERTAIN FUTURE OF TITLE VII CLASS ACTIONS

compensatory or punitive damages because of the constraints of Rule 23 and the Seventh Amendment. Thus, such issues would have to be either damages issues that were not individualized, such as liquidated damages claims, or equitable issues that did not implicate fact issues that could arise in evaluating the disparate treatment claims of the individual plaintiffs. Such claims, if they exist, would therefore be very narrow indeed. One possible example would be claims for relief from specific policies and procedures that were challenged only on a disparate impact theory. For these sorts of claims, damages would not be available, the facts necessary to prove such a claim would not be at issue in any individual's disparate treatment case (because there would be no such cases), and certification as to that discreet issue could proceed. Thus, the *Allison* plaintiffs may have hampered themselves by the breadth of their challenge: if class status is the goal, then *Allison* suggests that a narrower focus may be a surer road to success and a pure disparate impact case the safest route of all.

5.5.4 The Problem of the Blackmail Class

A final problem introduced by the 1991 Act is the problem of the blackmail class – the risk that the monetary exposure presented by the availability of compensatory and punitive damages to each class member will force defendants to settle regardless of any wrongdoing. The plaintiffs in *Allison* tried overtly to exploit this issue, arguing on appeal that partial certification would 'facilitate' settlement. The *Allison* court rejected that argument: 'We should not condone a certification-at-all-costs approach to this case for the simple purpose of forcing a settlement. Settlements should reflect the relative merits of the parties' claims, not a surrender to the vagaries of an utterly unpredictable and burdensome litigation procedure.'[147] These are laudable goals, but they are routinely trampled on in class litigation. Class actions are frequently settled for reasons having nothing to do with their merits: faced with potentially overwhelming liability, bad publicity, and enormous legal fees (even if it prevails), an employer may capitulate and settle the case even though it may lack merit and even though it

---

[147] *Allison*, 151 F.3d at 422 n. 17.

ultimately may not be maintainable as a class action.[148] Nor are plaintiffs' lawyers shy about this goal. In the author's own experience, class plaintiffs' lawyers have been heard privately to say that their goal is to bankrupt the defendant or, more colorfully, to 'blow them off the New York Stock Exchange.' This approach has been recognized in class cases as the principle of 'judicial blackmail.'[149] While liability in Title VII cases does not always rise to the potentially crippling liability present in mass tort litigation, the USD 300 million at stake in *Allison* is momentous, and, for any given employer, the prospect of a multimillion dollar legal bill or a nine-figure damages exposure is surely an incentive to settle regardless of the merits of the claims.[150] Indeed, settlements of class actions for millions, tens of millions, or hundreds of millions of

---

[148] As noted *supra*, this problem is illustrated starkly by cases such as *Shores v. Publix Super Markets, Inc.*, 69 Empl. Prac. Dec. (CCH), P 44,477 (MD Fla. 1996), and *Butler v. Home Depot, Inc.*, 70 Fair Empl. Prac. Cas. (BNA) 51 (ND Cal. 1996), in which courts certified portions of class actions while acknowledging that they did not know how to manage the remainder of the case. The class process with all of its risk and expense was set in motion; yet, it was by no means clear that the use of the class device was proper under the circumstances.

[149] As the Rutstein court stated: 'There is nothing to be gained by certifying this case as a class action . . . except the blackmail value of a class certification that can aid the plaintiffs in coercing the defendant into a settlement.' *Rutstein v. Avis Rent-A-Car Sys., Inc.*, 211 F.3d 1228, 1240 n. 21 (11th Cir. 2000). See also *In Re Matter of Rhone-Poulenc-Rorer, Inc.*, 51 F.3d 1293, 1298 (7th Cir. 1995); *Castano v. American Tobacco Co.*, 84 F.3d 734, 746 (5th Cir. 1996).

[150] While it is probably impossible to quantify how many settled class actions have merit and how many do not, statistics concerning individual discrimination suits may be informative. Of the discrimination charges submitted to the mandatory pre-lawsuit administrative procedure before the United States Equal Employment Opportunity Commission, the agency in fiscal 1999 found probable cause to believe that discrimination had occurred in only 5.7% of charges. That was the highest rate in the last eight years, and 'cause' findings have historically been as low as 1.6%. See United States Equal Employment Opportunity Commission, Title VII of the Civil Rights Act of 1964: Changes FY 1992-FY 1999 (visited October 27, 2000) <www.eeoc.gov/stats/vii.html>. Of the employment discrimination lawsuits disposed of in federal court from October 1, 1998, through September 30, 1999, (both class actions and non-class actions) approximately 80% were dismissed by the courts before trial, while only 5.8% were eventually tried. It is difficult to escape an inference that a huge number of meritless cases are being brought, and there is no apparent reason why class actions should be any exception to the general rule.

CHAPTER 5.   UNCERTAIN FUTURE OF TITLE VII CLASS ACTIONS

dollars are becoming increasingly common[151] and are increasingly accompanied by employers' public statements that it was less expensive to settle the case than to litigate it with the attendant risks.[152] Careful attention to the requirements of Rule 23 and the Seventh Amendment is therefore desirable to police the class action scene and to protect against abuses of class proceedings by plaintiffs and their lawyers.

5.6 FOR BETTER OR FOR WORSE?

Nearly ten years after the passage of the Civil Rights Act of 1991, its implications are just beginning to be felt in the area of Title VII class actions. While many lower courts have shown themselves willing to ignore or able to work around these implications, there is every indication that as more of these cases reach the appellate level more and more courts may adopt the kinds of restrictions recognized in *Allison*. Thus, there is a real possibility that a law that was passed to expand the relief available to individual victims of discrimination may have the effect of restricting their ability to bring claims on behalf of those similarly situated.

It is a different question whether this irony is a problem that demands a solution. There are sound reasons to tolerate a rule that limits the maintenance of Title VII class actions. The problem of the 'blackmail class' is not an academic one: the costs of such suits to employers are enormous and are unrelated to whether or not they have done anything wrong. Contrary to the Fifth Circuit's optimistic footnote in *Allison*, settlement of such cases often has nothing to do with the merits of the claims and everything to do with the financial and public relations risks presented by the overwhelming scale of such

---

[151] In the author's city of Atlanta, for example, the past two years have brought the filing of race discrimination class actions against the Coca-Cola Company (twice), Lockheed Martin Corporation (one suit each on behalf of hourly and salaried employees), Waffle House (a prominent restaurant chain), and Georgia Power Company (the principal local utility).

[152] See 'Judge Approves $12.1 Million Settlement in Part-Time Workers' Lawsuit Against UPS,' *Daily Labor Report* (BNA), April 14, 1999, at A-6; 'EEOC Says San Francisco Grocery Chain Agreed to Settle Bias Claims for $1.3 Million,' *Daily Labor Report* (BNA), January 23, 1988, at A-11.

actions. The limits placed on class actions by the 1991 Act may in turn limit the ease with which corporations can be browbeaten by an aggressive set of plaintiffs and their equally aggressive attorneys.

This is not necessarily bad news for the cause of individual rights. While the 1991 Act may limit class actions, it arguably makes it easier for individual plaintiffs to get access to the courts. The availability of damages and attorney's fees provides incentives for plaintiffs' lawyers to take such cases on a contingent-fee basis, which means that plaintiffs can bring suit without spending their own money to do so.[153] In other words, employment discrimination suits are no longer negative value suits. While this diminishes their suitability for class treatment, it increases their odds of being brought individually, which for the individual is an equivalent opportunity for justice.

Further, class actions are not necessary for certain types of wide-ranging relief. Insofar as plaintiffs seek to end discriminatory practices in the workplace, such results are possible in individual suits. For example, a plaintiff who challenges a particular employment practice on his own behalf may succeed in having it declared invalid, to the benefit of both himself and all other current and future employees. Sweeping changes are therefore possible (though usually only prospectively) in non-class cases. Moreover, the EEOC may file suit itself or intervene in a private suit to seek relief on behalf of others similarly situated to the plaintiff.[154] When the EEOC seeks such relief, even for a large class of persons, it is not required to satisfy the provisions of Rule 23 with its attendant constraints.[155] Finally, in multiplaintiff cases, various efficiencies can be achieved through the use of *Federal Rule of Civil Procedure 42*, which permits the severance and consolidation of

---

[153] They have done so in increasing numbers. See *supra* n. 15.

[154] The EEOC has stated publicly that it intends to become more active in the pursuit of class-style claims. See EEOC: 'Expanded Mediation, More Class Actions in Agency's Future, Officials Tell ABA Meeting,' *Daily Labor Report* (BNA), March 26, 1999, at C-1. It has also taken an active role in the maintenance and settlement of several highly publicized class actions in past few years. See 'Mitsubishi Settles EEOC Suit for $34 Million, Agency Says Class, Amount Largest Ever,' *Daily Labor Report* (BNA), June 12, 1998, at AA-1; 'Publix Markets Agrees to Pay $81.5 Million to Settle Sex Bias Suit,' *Daily Labor Report* (BNA), January 27, 1997, at AA-1; 'EEOC, Texaco Settle Bias Charges with Plan for Monitoring Promotions,' *Daily Labor Report* (BNA), January 6, 1997, at AA-1.

[155] See *General Tel. Co. v. EEOC*, 446 US 318 (1980).

CHAPTER 5. UNCERTAIN FUTURE OF TITLE VII CLASS ACTIONS

individual claims. While such plaintiffs could not represent others, they still could bring aggregated claims that could be dealt with on a mass scale and could result in equitable relief that would benefit similarly situated employees. All of this means that the constraints imposed on Title VII class actions by the law and the civil rules are entirely compatible with a balancing of the interests of employees and employers as participants in the federal antidiscrimination scheme. It also means that Title VII class actions might not be missed as much as one might think should the 1991 Act render them unsustainable in many cases, as seems likely.[156]

Because the trend, at least at the appellate level, is toward restricting Title VII class actions, it becomes a political question whether those restrictions should be eased or lifted. If Congress wanted to encourage or facilitate Title VII class actions, most, if not all, of the barriers to class certification could be obviated if the damages portions of the 1991 Act were modified or repealed. Many federal employment discrimination statutes lack a punitive or compensatory damages provision, or both. If only liquidated damages were available under Title VII (based, for instance, on a multiple of back pay or simply on a sliding scale like the damages caps already in place), then the individualized damages that make class certifications problematic would be significantly streamlined. This would not alleviate the Seventh Amendment problem in large cases involving multiple juries. Nonetheless, it would be a step toward minimizing Seventh Amendment issues, leaving more room for waivers and other devices that might facilitate a constitutional resolution of the issues.

5.7 CONCLUSION

The Civil Rights Act of 1991 has raised complex questions in the field of Title VII class actions, and it will likely take years, if not decades, before these issues are fully resolved. Until they are, or until Congress

---

[156] For a contrary view, see Harvey S. Bartlett III, 'Determining Whether a Title VII Plaintiff Class's "Aim Is True": The Legacy of Allison v. Citgo Petroleum Corp. for Employment Discrimination Class Certification Under Rule 23(b)(2),' 74 Tul L Rev 2163 (2000).

takes action to counter the apparent trend, these types of cases appear to be on their way to becoming significantly curtailed, at least where individual money damages are sought. Whether these developments will slow the filing and settlement of such cases only time will tell, but litigants who wish to bring or oppose such cases can no longer afford to ignore the implications of the 1991 remedies for class litigation.

CHAPTER 6

A Classless Act: The Ninth Circuit's Erroneous Class Certification in *Dukes v. Wal-Mart, Inc.*

Aaron B. Lauchheimer[*,**]

6.1 INTRODUCTION

In June 2004, the United States District Court for the Northern District of California certified the largest private civil rights lawsuit in United States history – *Dukes v. Wal-Mart, Inc.*[1] The proposed class is composed of at least 1.5 million women,[2] all of whom work or have worked at one of approximately 3,400 Wal-Mart stores across the United States.[3] The plaintiffs claim that Wal-Mart sexually discriminated against them because they

---

[*] A graduate of Brandeis University, Aaron B. Lauchheimer was a 2006 J.D. candidate, Brooklyn Law School, at the time of this writing.
[**] This article was previously published in the Brooklyn Law Review. "A Classless Act: The Ninth Circuits Erroneous Class Certification in Dukes v. Wal-mart, Inc." by Aaron B. Lauchheimer, Brooklyn Law Review, Vol. 71, No. 1, 2005.
[1] *Dukes v. Wal-Mart Stores, Inc.*, 222 F.R.D. 137, 142 (N.D. Cal. 2004); David Kravets, Class Action Against Wal-Mart Approved, The Legal Intelligencer, June 23, 2004, at 4.
[2] See *Dukes*, 222 F.R.D. at 142. The 1.5 million women are represented by six plaintiffs: Betty Dukes, Patricia Surgeson, Christine Kwapnoski, Deborah Gunter, Edith Arana, and Cleo Page. See Pl.'s Mot. for Class Certification, at 3 n. 1, *Dukes v. Wal-Mart, Inc.* (N.D. Ca. 2003) (No. C-01-2252 MJJ).
[3] *Dukes*, 222 F.R.D. at 142, n.1. Wal-Mart operates four types of stores: Discount Stores, Supercenters, Sam's Clubs and Neighborhood Markets. *Id.* at 141, n. 1.

David Sherwyn and Samuel Estreicher (eds), *Employment Class and Collective Actions*, pp. 287–327.
© Brooklyn Law Review. Reprinted with permission.

EMPLOYMENT CLASS AND COLLECTIVE ACTIONS

were paid less than men 'in comparable positions,' 'received fewer promotions to in-store management than did men' and those who received promotions 'waited longer than their male counterparts to advance.'[4] The plaintiffs are seeking class-wide injunctive and declaratory relief, lost pay and punitive damages pursuant to 42 USC, S 2000(e) et seq. ('Title VII').[5]

The district court certified the class in *Dukes* using the criteria set forth in the Federal Rules of Civil Procedure.[6] Rule 23(a), governing class certification, contains four requirements[7] that must be met in order for a class to be certified. These requirements are:

(1) the class is so numerous that joinder of all members is impracticable;
(2) there are questions of law or fact common to the class;
(3) the claims or defenses of the representative parties are typical of the claims or defenses of the class; and
(4) the representative parties will fairly and adequately protect the interests of the class.[8]

These factors are also known as: numerosity, commonality, typicality, and adequacy.[9] Rule 23(b) provides that the class must fulfill one of three additional requirements:

(1) That separate actions by individual members of the class would produce inconsistent judgments.
(2) That the party opposing the class 'has acted or refused to act on grounds generally applicable to the class' making injunctive and/or declaratory relief appropriate.
(3) That any issues pertaining to individual members of the class are outweighed by issues that pertain to the class as a whole, and that a class action lawsuit is the best method to adjudicate the issue or issues.[10]

Class action lawsuits are an exception to the rule that litigation is normally conducted only on behalf of individuals and not individuals

---

[4] *Id.*
[5] *Id.*
[6] *Id.* at 143. FED. R. CIV. P. 23(a), 23(b)(2).
[7] Dukes, 222 F.R.D. at 143 (citing *Zinser v. Accufix Research Inst., Inc.*, 253 F.3d 1180, 1186 (9th Cir. 2001), amended 275 F.3d 1266 (9th Cir. 2001)).
[8] Fed. R. Civ. P. 23(A).
[9] Dukes, 222 F.R.D. at 143.
[10] Fed. R. Civ. P. 23(b).

CHAPTER 6. A CLASSLESS ACT

representing a group and, as such, a class must be carefully evaluated before it is certified.[11] In *General Telephone Co. of the Southwest v. Falcon*,[12] the Supreme Court concluded that in a Title VII class action lawsuit, a court must conduct a 'rigorous analysis'[13] to ensure 'that the prerequisites of Rule 23(a) have been satisfied.'[14] The *Dukes* court, however, deemphasized the importance of the Supreme Court's 'rigorous analysis' standard and held that a court maintains 'broad discretion in determining whether a class should be certified.'[15] By stressing the court's ability to use 'broad discretion,'[16] the *Dukes* court found that the class met all of the requirements of Rule 23(a). In doing so, the court pointed to evidence of a strong and centralized corporate culture[17] at Wal-Mart, which enabled it to control all of the stores and their operations.[18] Such control laid the groundwork for the entire class to suffer an injury, which resulted from a specific discriminatory

---

[11] *Gen. Tel. Co. of the Southwest v. Falcon*, 457 US 147, 155 (1982) (quoting *Califano v. Yamasaki*, 442 US 682, 700–01 (1979)).

[12] *Id.*

[13] *Id.* at 161. See also *Zinser v. Accufix Research Inst., Inc.*, 253 F.3d 1180, 1186 (9th Cir. 2001), amended by 275 F.3d 1266 (9th Cir. 2001).

[14] *Falcon*, 457 US at 161. See also *In re Domestic Air Transp. Antitrust Litig.*, 137 F.R.D. 677, 684 (N.D. Ga. 1991) (stating that the court would 'scrutinize the evidence plaintiffs propose to use in proving their claims without unnecessarily reaching the merits of underlying claims.').

[15] *Dukes*, 222 F.R.D. at 143 (citing *Armstrong v. Davis*, 275 F.3d 849, 871 n. 28 (9th Cir. 2001)).

[16] *Id.*

[17] As evidence of Wal-Mart's strong corporate culture, the Dukes court noted that:

> every new employee nation-wide goes through the same orientation process and ... is trained about the Wal-Mart culture. Thereafter, employees at Wal-Mart stores attend a daily meeting ... where managers discuss company culture and employees do the Wal-Mart cheer. Employees also receive weekly training on culture topics at mandatory store meetings.

Id. at 151 (citations omitted). While the court pointed to these characteristics as evidence of a strong corporate culture, there is no connection between a corporation maintaining a strong corporate culture, on the one hand, and, making local store managers responsible for hiring and promotion decisions, on the other hand.

[18] *Id.* at 145–153. This evidence was used to satisfy the commonality requirement of Fed. R. Civ. P. 23(a). *Id.* at 145.

practice.[19] Because the class possibly contains 1.5 million women, neither side challenged the class' ability to meet Rule 23(a)'s numerosity requirement. Such a large class, though, can backfire against a class, as will be discussed in section 6.5. The court also held that the class met the requirement of Rule 23(b)(2), finding that the primary purpose of the litigation is to seek injunctive and declaratory relief, even though class members are seeking punitive damages.[20] According to Rule 23(b)(2), injunctive relief must outweigh any punitive damages sought in order to maintain class action status.[21] In this case, the court held that the injunctive relief related to ending sexual discrimination at Wal-Mart 'predominates'[22] over any possible punitive award, even one that could be in the billions of dollars.[23]

---

[19] *Id.* at 167–168. This evidence was used to satisfy the typicality requirement of Fed. R. Civ. P. 23(a). *Id.* at 166–168.

[20] Dukes, at 170–171. Fed. R. Civ. P. 23(b)(2) only provides for injunctive and declaratory relief and not punitive damages. See Fed. R. Civ. P. 23(b)(2). A 1991 Amendment to Title VII allowed for punitive damages if the plaintiff could prove that the employer discriminated 'with malice or with reckless indifference' 42 USC ß 1981a(b)(1) (1991).

[21] The monetary damages must be 'secondary to the primary claim for injunctive or declaratory relief.' *Molski v. Gleich*, 318 F.3d 937, 947 (9th Cir. 2003) (citing *Probe v. State Teachers' Ret. Sys.*, 780 F.2d 776, 780 (1986)).

[22] The monetary damages must be 'secondary to the primary claim for injunctive or declaratory relief.' *Molski v. Gleich*, 318 F.3d 937, 947 (9th Cir. 2003) (citing *Probe v. State Teachers' Ret. Sys.*, 780 F.2d 776, 780 (1986)).

[23] Given the potential size of the class, it would seem quite obvious that any punitive damages award would be in the billions of dollars and would clearly outweigh any declaratory or injunctive relief that would be granted to the class. One can assume that this case would result in an award in the billions of dollars given the fact that in 1999 a 10,000-employee sexual discrimination lawsuit settled for USD 25 million; if this award was divided equally among claimants, each claimant received USD 2,500. See William C. Martucci et al., Class Action Litigation in the Employment Arena – the Corporate Employers' Perspective, 58 J. MO. B. 332, 336 (2002). Assuming an equivalent settlement per person here, the total award in this case would be USD 3.75 billion. At the high end of the scale, a 1992 sexual discrimination case against State Farm involving 814 women settled for USD 157 million. *Id.* at 336, Appendix. Therefore, each claimant received USD 192,874.69. *Id.* Extrapolating this value to the Wal-Mart case would result in a total settlement value of USD 289,312,039,312. Wal-Mart's market capitalization is only around USD 210.62 billion. See <http://finance.yahoo.com/q?s=WMT> (last visited December 2, 2008). Therefore, any

CHAPTER 6. A CLASSLESS ACT

This chapter argues that the Northern District of California incorrectly certified the class in *Dukes v. Wal-Mart Stores*.[24] Section 6.3 proceeds with an in-depth description of *Dukes*. Section 6.4 then continues with a discussion of Rule 23 and its requirements. Section 6.5 discusses why the court was incorrect in finding that the class in *Dukes* met the requirements of commonality and typicality. Because this chapter only challenges the court's finding in *Dukes* regarding commonality and typicality, any issues regarding numerosity or adequacy of representation are not discussed. Section 6.5 also discusses the court's use of expert witness testimony in certifying the class, and the importance of using a *Daubert* analysis in order to analyze potential expert witness testimony to certify a class. Section 6.6 discusses the Title VII issues that are present in this case, and explains why the court should have denied class certification based on these issues. Section 6.7 argues that the court incorrectly ignored the issue of blackmail settlements and that the class should not have been certified because of the concern regarding blackmail settlements.[25] Section 6.8 proposes a method for certifying class action lawsuits similar to the *Dukes* case. More specifically, the proposal will suggest that certification not be granted for 'wall to wall' or 'across the board' class action lawsuits. Keeping in line with many other cases involving corporate parents, the proposal will limit the instances in which a class action lawsuit can be brought to cases where, unlike in *Dukes*, specific corporate policies existed that promoted a definite practice and where the corporate parent actively engaged in the day to day hiring, firing and promoting of employees. The method will finally propose that allegations of sexual discrimination are best left to be heard on a more individual level, or at the very least, that class action lawsuits should be brought on a smaller scale, rather than as one class action lawsuit encompassing 1.5 million women.

---

award approaching the high end of the scale would bankrupt Wal-Mart and possibly force Wal-Mart to layoff thousands of employees. This result cannot be considered secondary to any injunctive or declaratory relief sought by the class.

[24] Pursuant to Fed. R. Civ. P. 23(f), the Ninth Circuit agreed to hear Wal-Mart's appeal of the lower court's class certification. A decision in that case is pending. Principal Br. For Wal-Mart Stores, Inc., *Dukes v. Wal-Mart Stores, Inc.* at 1–2 (9th Cir. 2004) (Nos 04-16688 & 04-16720).

[25] Briefly, blackmail settlements occur when a group of plaintiffs tries to gather as many potential class members as possible in order to scare the defendant into settling, rather than risk facing a jury award.

6.2 DUKES V. WAL-MART: AN IN-DEPTH OVERVIEW

In *Dukes*, the named plaintiffs include six women, each of whom worked for Wal-Mart either as an hourly or salaried worker in stores across the country.[26] Despite claiming to represent women across the country, all of the representative plaintiffs worked in stores in California, three of whom worked at stores outside of California before moving to California.[27] Additionally, only one of the lead plaintiffs, Christine Kwapnoski, briefly occupied a salaried position.[28] All of the women worked at a Wal-Mart store since at least 1997.[29]

All of the named plaintiffs describe a set of policies that, they allege, point to a general policy by Wal-Mart to sexually discriminate against women.[30] More specifically, the plaintiffs claim that as females, Wal-Mart's policies hindered their ability to receive promotions.[31] Plaintiffs also claim that female Wal-Mart employees received less pay than men for performing the same tasks.[32] As a general basis for their claims, plaintiffs argue that Wal-Mart employed an excessively subjective decision-making process regarding their employment and possible promotions, which created an environment for sexual discrimination.[33] Wal-Mart's policy mandated that an hourly worker could only become a manager by participating in the Management Training Program.[34] The plaintiffs allege that, until recently, managers chose which employees would participate in the Program through a

---

[26] See Def.'s Opp'n to Mot. for Class Certification, at 17–18, n. 9, *Dukes v. Wal-Mart, Inc.* (N.D. Cal. 2003) (No. C-01-2252 MJJ).
[27] Plaintiff Page worked in a Supercenter in Oklahoma before moving to California. Plaintiff Gunter worked in a Discount Store in Texas before moving to California and Plaintiff Kwapnoski worked in a Sam's Club in Missouri before transferring to a Sam's Club in California. See *id.*
[28] *Id.* at 17–18 n. 9. It should be noted that she only held an entry-level managerial position as a Receiving Area Manager. *Id.*
[29] See Pl.'s Mot. for Class Certification, at 1, *Dukes v. Wal-Mart, Inc.* (N.D. Cal. 2003) (No. C-01-2252 MJJ).
[30] See *id.* at 1–4.
[31] *Id.*
[32] *Id.*
[33] See *Dukes*, 222 F.R.D. at 149–50.
[34] See *id.* at 148. In order to participate in the Management Training Program, an hourly employee must rise to the level of a Support Manager. See *id.*

CHAPTER 6. A CLASSLESS ACT

'tap on the shoulder' system.[35] Under this system, managers chose candidates to participate in the Management Training Program by deciding for themselves who might make a good manager, rather than by relying on set guidelines.[36] The named plaintiffs allege that this type of system suffered from 'excessive subjectivity'[37] in that male managers would pick male hourly employees to participate in the Management Training Program, more frequently than female employees.[38]

Wal-Mart claims that, as the corporate parent, it cannot be held responsible for decisions made by store managers because the managers made decisions based on a certain amount of subjectivity.[39] Moreover, despite the plaintiffs' contentions regarding the nexus between excessive subjectivity and sexual discrimination, Wal-Mart cited a Ninth Circuit case, *Coleman v. Quaker Oats Co.*, to show that excessive subjectivity is not necessarily evidence of sexual discrimination.[40] In *Coleman*, plaintiffs claimed that Quaker Oats committed age discrimination when, in the process of carrying out a large-scale layoff, it laid off two-thirds of workers over age forty.[41] In determining whom to lay off, Quaker Oats considered an employee's rankings in six areas and his/her overall ranking.[42] The Ninth Circuit held in *Coleman* that Quaker Oats did not use an excessively subjective evaluation system in order to mask its true intention of firing the older employees.[43]

---

[35] See Pl.'s Mot. for Class Certification, at 2, *Dukes v. Wal-Mart, Inc.* (N.D. Cal. 2003) (No. C-01-2252 MJJ). The plaintiff's allege that this policy existed until recently citing that in January 2003, Wal-Mart moved from a 'tap on the shoulder' program to posting job vacancies in the Management Program. See *Dukes*, 222 F.R.D. at 149.

[36] See Pl.'s Mot. for Class Certification, at 2, *Dukes v. Wal-Mart, Inc.* (N.D. Cal. 2003) (No. C-01-2252 MJJ).

[37] *Dukes*, 222 F.R.D. at 149.

[38] See Pl.'s Mot. For Class Certifcation at 2, *Dukes v. Wal-Mart Stores, Inc.* (N.D. Cal. 2003) (No. C-01-2252 MJJ).

[39] See Def.'s Opp'n to Mot. for Class Certification, at 4, 6–7, 14–15, 23–24, *Dukes v. Wal-Mart, Inc.* (N.D. Cal. 2003) (No. C-01-2252 MJJ).

[40] See *id.* at 32 n. 19 (citing *Coleman v. Quaker Oats Co.*, 232 F.3d 1271, 1285 (9th Cir. 2000) ('While a subjective evaluation system can be used as a cover for illegal discrimination, subjective evaluations are not unlawful per se and "their relevance to proof of discriminatory intent is weak" ')) (quoting *Sengupta v. Morrison-Knudson Co.*, 804 F.2d 1072, 1075 (9th Cir. 1986)).

[41] *Coleman*, 232 F.3d 1271, 1278–1279.

[42] *Id.* at 1278.

[43] *Id.* at 1285.

Similarly, Wal-Mart argues that even though it used a subjective system to evaluate employees, such a system does not necessarily mean that it maintained sexually discriminatory practices.

At Wal-Mart, managers are given a certain amount of leeway with regard to some aspects of pay and promotion.[44] Wal-Mart asserts that when making decisions regarding pay, although it sets a range for each class of employee, store managers are able to depart from that scale.[45] Wal-Mart argues, therefore, that because store managers control their individual stores as they see fit, Wal-Mart, as the corporate parent, cannot be held responsible for the individual pay decisions made by each store manager.[46]

Similarly, Wal-Mart also claims that it cannot be held responsible for promotion decisions, because store managers make those decisions on a store-by-store basis.[47] The plaintiffs even admit that store managers make promotion decisions on their own by choosing which hourly employees will participate in the Management Training Program.[48] Wal-Mart claims that the purpose of this policy is to allow store managers to identify those people who they believe will make the best managers.[49] Wal-Mart argues that managers are best equipped to determine who would make a good manager, not a corporate officer who has virtually no knowledge of each of the stores' employees.[50]

---

[44] See generally *Dukes*, 222 F.R.D. 137 (N.D. Cal. 2004).

[45] See Def.'s Opp'n to Class Certification, at 14–15, *Dukes v. Wal-Mart, Inc.* (N.D. Cal. 2003) (No. C-01-2252 MJJ). After store managers decide to depart from the pay scale, the district manager can then question the store manager's decision, after the fact, if the hourly rate departs from the standard minimum by more than 6%. See Pl.'s Mot. For Class Certification at 17 (N.D. Cal. 2003) (No. C-01-2252 MJJ).

[46] See Def.'s Opp'n to Mot. for Class Certification, at 4, 6–7, 14–15, 23–24, *Dukes v. Wal-Mart, Inc.* (N.D. Cal. 2003) (No. C-01-2252 MJJ).

[47] *Dukes*, 222 F.R.D. at 150.

[48] *Id.* at 148.

[49] See *Id.* at 148. Wal-Mart only sets minimum standards for promoting employees to the Management Training Program. Those standards include the employee: 'have an "above average" evaluation, have at least one year in their current position, be current on training, not be in a "high shrink" department or store, be on the company's "Rising Star" list, and be willing to relocate.' *Id.*

[50] The court later faults Wal-Mart for not overseeing promotion decisions made by store managers given its ability to oversee such things as the type of music played in each store. *Id.* at 151–53.

CHAPTER 6. A CLASSLESS ACT

In looking at the *Dukes* case, the court faced a number of issues that speak to the heart of Rule 23 and class certification. Issues of subjectivity in hiring, promotion and pay practices at Wal-Mart raise concerns as to whether a class can meet all the requirements of Rule 23. If in fact Wal-Mart maintained excessively subjective practices in hiring, promotion, and pay, then proving commonality and typicality would appear to be quite difficult. Given the 'increased skepticism – particularly among members of the federal judiciary – toward the class action as an effective dispute-resolution mechanism in the employment context,'[51] courts must carefully consider all of Rule 23's requirements before certifying a class.

6.3 RULE 23

6.3.1 An Overview

Rule 23 of the Federal Rules of Civil Procedure provides the framework for class action litigation.[52] A class action lawsuit is a unique form of litigation because it seeks relief on behalf of a large group of people not limited to the named plaintiffs.[53] The reasons for allowing class action litigation are fourfold:

(1) It promotes judicial economy.
(2) It provides a single remedy for a group when it is uneconomical to seek multiple remedies in individual lawsuits.
(3) It provides greater plaintiff access to courts through spreading of litigation costs.
(4) It protects defendants from inconsistent jury verdicts.[54]

As discussed earlier, Rule 23(a) contains four requirements that a class must meet in order to be certified: numerosity, commonality, typicality and adequacy.[55] If a class meets all four of these requirements, it then must meet one of the three further requirements of Rule 23(b).[56]

---

[51] Melissa Hart, Will Employment Discrimination Class Actions Survive? 37 Akron L. Rev. 813 (2004).
[52] Fed. R. Civ. P. 23.
[53] *Gen. Tel. Co. of the Southwest v. Falcon*, 457 US 147, 155 (1982).
[54] 5 James Wm. Moore et al., Moore's Federal Practice P 23.02 (3rd edn 2005).
[55] See Fed. R. Civ. P. 23(a).
[56] See Fed. R. Civ. P. 23(b).

Typically, civil rights lawsuits fall under the rubric of Rule 23(b)(2) where the 'party opposing the class has acted or refused to act on grounds generally applicable to the class,'[57] as described by the Advisory Committee notes to Rule 23,[58] because all the class members are claiming that the defendant has wronged them in a common way.[59]

In determining if a class meets the requirements of Rule 23 for certification, courts are split as to how they should evaluate the class' allegations. In *General Telephone. Co. of the Southwest v. Falcon*,[60] the Supreme Court held that courts should perform a 'rigorous analysis' to ensure that a class meets each of the requirements of Rule 23(a).[61] In an earlier decision, though, the Court held in *Eisen v. Carlisle & Jacquelin*[62] that a judge cannot go so far as to 'conduct a preliminary inquiry into the merits of a suit in order to determine whether it may be maintained as a class action.'[63] It has been noted, though, that judges apply this holding inconsistently.[64] Since *Falcon*, courts have had a difficult time finding a middle ground between *Eisen* and *Falcon*.[65] One court went so far as to require a

---

[57] See Fed. R. Civ. P. 23(b)(2).

[58] See Fed. R. Civ. P. 23 advisory committee's note:

> This subdivision is intended to reach situations where a party has taken action or refused to take action with respect to a class, and final relief of an injunctive nature or of a corresponding declaratory nature, settling the legality of the behavior with respect to the class as a whole, is appropriate.... Illustrative are various actions in the civil-rights field where party is charged with discriminating unlawfully against a class, usually one whose members are incapable of specific enumeration.

[59] See Fed. R. Civ. P. 23(b)(2).
[60] 457 US 147 (1982).
[61] *Id.* at 161.
[62] *Eisen v. Carlisle & Jacquelin*, 417 US 156 (1974).
[63] *Id.* at 177.
[64] Robert G. Bone & David S. Evans, Class Certification and the Substantive Merits, 51 Duke L.J. 1251, 1254 (2002). In fact, Bone and Evans argue that rather than apply the requirements of Rule 23, judges decide certification based on 'the value of the class action' and that 'judges seem more willing to overlook evidentiary weaknesses and certify a class the more strongly they believe in the importance of the class action for enforcement of the substantive law.' *Id.* at 1272.
[65] 'We have noted that the "boundary between a class determination and the merits may not always be easily discernible." ' *Retired Chicago Police Ass'n v. City of Chi.*, 7 F.3d 584, 599 (7th Cir. 1993) (quoting *Eggleston v. Chicago Journeyman Plumbers' Local Union No. 130*, 657 F.2d 890, 895 (7th Cir. 1981)).

party seeking to certify a class to show 'under a strict burden of proof, that all requirements of *[Fed. R. Civ. P.] 23(a)* are clearly met.'[66]

6.3.2 Commonality

The commonality requirement of Rule 23(a)(2) is meant to ensure that all potential class members have their case adequately heard when joinder of all plaintiffs would be 'impracticable.'[67] In determining whether a particular class meets this requirement, the Supreme Court directed lower courts to focus on whether there are common facts and legal issues among class members.[68] A class can satisfy this requirement by sharing only one common legal issue or fact.[69]

Courts have acknowledged that class action cases concerning sexual discrimination in the employment context generally meet the commonality requirement when decisions regarding employment are centralized to a particular place or within a particular group.[70] In *Dean v. Boeing Co.*, the plaintiff sued Boeing on behalf of female employees at a limited number of plants in the United States.[71] The District Court of Kansas held that the commonality requirement was met in part because there was a common question of law or fact to all plaintiffs in that all of the women worked at Boeing's Kansas operations.[72] Likewise, in *Penk v. Oregon State Board of Higher Education*,[73]

---

[66] *Reed v. Bowen*, 849 F.2d 1307, 1309 (10th Cir. 1988) (quoting *Rex v. Owens ex rel. Okla.*, 585 F.2d 432, 435 (10th Cir. 1978)).

[67] Fed. R. Civ. P. 23(a)(1).

[68] 5 James Wm. Moore et al., Moore's Federal Practice P 23.23 (3rd edn 2005).

[69] *Id.*

[70] See *Talley v. ARINC, Inc.*, 222 F.R.D. 260, 267 (D. Md. 2004) (stating that finding commonality is more prevalent in an employment discrimination lawsuit when, 'the alleged pattern or practice was sufficiently centralized and defined so as to eliminate the need for individualized inquiries on liability.'). The court cited cases where commonality existed when there was a centralized decision-making process in a single location or evidence of a corporate wide policy of discrimination. See e.g., *Newsome v. Up-To-Date Laundry, Inc.*, 219 F.R.D. 356, 361–362 (D. Md. 2004); *Hewlett v. Premier Salons Int'l, Inc.*, 185 F.R.D. 211, 216–217 (D. Md. 1997).

[71] *Dean v. Boeing Co.*, No. 02-1019-WEB, 2003 US Dist. LEXIS 8787, at *4 (D. Kan., April 24, 2003).

[72] *Id.* at *47.

[73] *Penk v. Or. State Bd. of Higher Educ.*, 93 F.R.D. 45 (D. Or. 1981).

the proposed class consisted of 'all women faculty members who have taught or are teaching at Oregon's eight institutions of higher education.'[74] Given the centralized nature of a public school system, the District Court of Oregon found that 'the Board, and not each individual institution, assures compliance with Oregon's law against educational discrimination.'[75]

On the other hand, when the decision-making process is decentralized or stratified, courts tend to find that commonality does not exist because the employees are dealt with on a more local level, rather than by a corporate parent. In *Droughn v. FMC Corp.*,[76] the defendants constituted three different areas of employment, each engaged in distinct tasks, with 48,000 employees across thirty-two states and thirteen countries.[77] FMC employees alleged that FMC engaged in sexual and racial discrimination.[78] The Eastern District Court of Pennsylvania held that the proposed class could not be certified, because:

> FMC, consistent with its structurally diverse and geographically widespread organization, has adopted a decentralized approach to personnel practices. Not only is there no evidence of employment practices emanating from national corporate headquarters, but there is also nothing to suggest that the Chemical Group maintains a firm grip on employment policy within different segments of the division.[79]

Similarly, in *Talley v. ARINC, Inc.*,[80] the District Court of Maryland rejected plaintiffs' class, because no 'cohesive pattern' of discrimination existed to find that the class satisfied the commonality requirement.[81] By highlighting the stratified nature of these company's employment practices, these courts show that maintaining a practice of making employment decisions at the local level is a legitimate defense for a corporate parent.

---

[74] *Id.* at 48.
[75] *Id.* at 50.
[76] *Droughn v. FMC Corp.*, 74 F.R.D. 639 (E.D. Pa. 1977).
[77] *Id.* at 641.
[78] *Id.*
[79] *Id.* at 642.
[80] 222 F.R.D. 260 (D. Md. 2004).
[81] *Id.* at 267. Talley is discussed *infra* in greater detail.

6.3.3 Typicality

When evaluating whether or not a class has met the typicality requirement of Rule 23(a)(3),[82] courts often note that 'the commonality and typicality requirements of Rule 23(a) tend to merge,'[83] because:

> both serve as guideposts for determining whether under the particular circumstances maintenance of a class action is economical and whether the named plaintiff's claim and the class claims are so interrelated that the interests of the class members will be fairly and adequately protected in their absence.[84]

However, this is not to say that courts do not evaluate typicality independently or that the typicality requirement does not have its own set of criteria.[85] When evaluating typicality, courts look to see whether 'other members of the class...have the same or similar grievances as the plaintiff.'[86] Put otherwise, 'the typicality requirement assesses the sufficiency of the named plaintiff.'[87] By focusing on the plaintiff's claims,

---

[82] Rule 23(a)(3) requires that:

> the court finds that the questions of law or fact common to the members of the class predominate over any questions affecting only individual members, and that a class action is superior to other available methods for the fair and efficient adjudication of the controversy.

Fed. R. Civ. P. 23(a)(3).

[83] *Gen. Tel. Co. of the Southwest v. Falcon*, 457 US 147, 158 n. 13 (1982). See also *Rowe v. Phila. Coca-Cola Bottling Co.*, No. 01-6965, 2003 US District LEXIS 19561, at *17 (E.D. Penn. September 30, 2003); *Campos v. INS*, 188 F.R.D. 656, 659 (S.D. Fla. 1999); *Adames v. Mitsubishi Bank, Ltd.*, 133 F.R.D. 82, 90 (E.D.N.Y. 1989); *Thonen v. McNeil-Akron, Inc.*, 661 F. Supp. 1271, 1273–1274 (N.D. Ohio 1986). All of these cases cite Falcon for the proposition that the commonality and typicality requirements of Rule 23 'tend to merge.'

[84] Falcon, 457 US at 157 n. 13.

[85] But it is true that some courts view the typicality requirement as being redundant. See e.g., *Bullock v. Bd. of Ed. of Montgomery County*, 210 F.R.D. 556, 560 (D. Md. 2002) (stating that the typicality requirement 'has been observed to be a redundant criterion.').

[86] *Paxton v. Union Nat'l Bank*, 688 F.2d 552, 562 (8th Cir. 1982). See *Carpe v. Aquila, Inc.*, No. 02-0388-CV-W-FJG, 2004 US Dist. LEXIS 21590, at *6 (W.D. Mo. September 13, 2004); *Evans v. Am. Credit Sys.*, 222 F.R.D. 388, 394 (D. Neb. 2004); *Bullock v. Bd. of Ed. of Montgomery County*, 210 F.R.D. 556, 560 (D. Md. 2002).

[87] In re Chrysler Corp. Paint Litig., No. 1239, 2000 US District LEXIS 2332, at *16 (E.D. Pa. March 2, 2000).

courts can discern between claims that have a common basis from those that require an individual evaluation, and therefore, are inappropriate for class action status.

Historically, courts have held that 'across-the-board' employment class action lawsuits fulfilled the typicality requirement of Rule 23.[88] 'Across-the-board' class action lawsuits consist of claims by a group of people that a system-wide policy of discrimination exists, and that the entire system must be challenged and not an individual part of it.[89] This means that a representative plaintiff could bring a class action lawsuit implicating an employer's discriminatory practice, even if the representative plaintiff was only affected by one instance of such practice.[90] However, in *Falcon*, the Supreme Court rendered 'across-the-board' employment discrimination lawsuits obsolete 'by insisting on actual, not presumed, compliance with the typicality... provisions of Rule 23.'[91] In distinguishing between an individual's claim of discrimination and class-wide discrimination, the Court stated:

> Conceptually, there is a wide gap between (a) an individual's claim that he has been denied a promotion on discriminatory grounds, and his otherwise unsupported allegation that the company has a policy of discrimination, and (b) the existence of a class of persons who have suffered the same injury as that individual, such that the individual's claim will be typical of the class claims. For plaintiff to bridge the gap, he must prove much more than the validity of his own claim.[92]

Ultimately, for a class to meet the typicality requirement, the court must determine that the potential class members' interests are 'fairly encompassed' with the named plaintiffs' interests.[93]

Turning to post-*Falcon* class actions in the employment context, courts have found that an employment class has fulfilled the typicality

---

[88] *Miller v. Hygrade Food Prods. Corp.*, 89 F. Supp. 2d 643, 648 (E.D. Pa. 2000) (discussing the history of across the board employment lawsuits).
[89] See *Johnson v. Ga. Highway Express, Inc.*, 417 F.2d 1122, 1124 (5th Cir. 1969) (reversing the lower court's decision to narrow the scope of the case because even though different facts and circumstances applied to different employees, the named plaintiff challenged system-wide discrimination on behalf of all African-American workers).
[90] Miller, 89 F. Supp. at 648.
[91] *Goodman v. Lukens Steel Co.*, 777 F.2d 113, 122 (3rd Cir. 1985), aff'd 482 US 656 (1987) (citing Falcon, 457 US 147 (1982)).
[92] Falcon, 457 US at 157–158.
[93] *Id.* at 160.

requirement of Rule 23 when the discrimination emanated from a 'centrally administered policy.'[94] This is demonstrated in *Mathers v. Northshore Mining Co.*,[95] where the District Court of Minnesota held that a group of women who 'worked in eight particular departments'[96] met the typicality requirement.[97] By specifying that the class members worked in a limited number of departments within the company's mining operation, the court emphasized that it certified the class because of a policy administered by the corporation.[98] It should be noted that many courts have stated that 'typicality is not demanding,'[99] and, as such, courts sometimes give little or no explanation regarding this requirement of class certification. Additionally, the opposing party sometimes does not attempt to challenge the class' assertion that it meets the typicality requirement.[100]

Despite the low threshold that courts demand for the typicality requirement, given the issues raised by the Court in *Falcon*, courts have denied class certification based on a class' inability to meet the typicality requirement.[101] As mentioned earlier, in cases where a class did not satisfy the typicality requirement, the representative plaintiff or plaintiffs often had a unique claim[102] or attempted to implicate an individual incident of discrimination as indicative of a companywide policy of discrimination.[103] In both *ARINC* and *Abrams v. Kelsey-Seybold Medical Group*, the representative plaintiffs attempted to take their

---

[94] *Resnick v. Am. Dental Ass'n*, 90 F.R.D. 530, 539 (N.D. Ill. 1981).

[95] *Mathers v. Northshore Mining Co.*, 217 F.R.D. 474 (D. Minn. 2003).

[96] *Id.* at 486.

[97] *Id.*

[98] *Id.*

[99] *Stirman v. Exxon Corp.*, 280 F.3d 554, 562 (5th Cir. 2002) (citing *James v. City of Dallas*, 254 F.3d 551, 571 (5th Cir. 2001)). See also *Forbush v. J.C. Penney Co.*, 994 F.2d 1101, 1106 (5th Cir. 1993)).

[100] 7A Charles Alan Wright & Arthur R. Miller, Federal Practice and Procedure § 1764 (2nd edn 1986).

[101] See generally ARINC, 222 F.R.D. at 268; *Abrams v. Kelsey-Seybold Med. Group Inc.*, 178 F.R.D. 116, 129 (S.D. Tex. 1997).

[102] See *Boyce v. Honeywell*, 191 F.R.D. 669, 676 (M.D. Fla. 2000) (stating that 'the claims asserted by the eight named plaintiffs...cover a vast array of individual circumstances' and therefore 'this case does not appear to implicate a common, general policy...which has a discriminatory impact on the class.').

[103] See ARINC, 222 F.R.D. at 268 ('This case does not present the factual scenario of a discriminatory practice being applied so as to broadly discriminate against persons

individual claims and apply them to all members of a similarly situated group of people.[104] In *Abrams*, Kelsey-Seybold operated twenty outpatient clinics in the Houston area. The plaintiffs alleged racial discrimination in employment decisions regarding promotions and layoffs.[105] Although the plaintiffs reduced the class size three times, the Southern District Court of Texas still found that, based on the Supreme Court's holding in *Falcon*, the claims were individual in nature and not applicable to the whole class.[106]

Likewise, ARINC was a government contractor with over 3,000 employees in twenty-four states.[107] All of the plaintiffs in the lawsuit worked either at ARINC's headquarters in Annapolis, Maryland or in its Washington, DC office.[108] The plaintiffs attempted to represent all African-American employees, alleging racial and sexual discrimination in promotions and layoffs.[109] The District Court of Maryland held, however, that the plaintiffs improperly attempted to combine several individual claims of sexual and racial discrimination, when in reality, each plaintiff's claim required individualized proof.[110]

6.4 THE COURT'S DECISION IN *DUKES V. WAL-MART*

6.4.1 The Finding of Commonality

As discussed above, commonality focuses on whether there are common facts and legal issues among class members.[111] In *Dukes*, the court held that commonality existed between the class representatives and the potential class members because they all suffered from

---

in the identical manner'); Abrams, 178 F.R.D. at 129 (S.D. Tex. 1997) ('In cases alleging classwide disparate treatment in particular employment actions, plaintiffs must show a company-wide policy or practice, beyond individualized claims of discrimination.').

[104] See generally ARINC, 222 F.R.D 260; Abrams, 178 F.R.D. 116.
[105] Kelsey-Seybold Med. Group, Inc., 178 F.R.D. at 119.
[106] *Id.* at 129.
[107] ARINC, 222 F.R.D. at 263.
[108] *Id.* at 265.
[109] *Id.* at 263.
[110] *Id.* at 268.
[111] 5 James Wm. Moore et al., Moore's Federal Practice para. 23.23 (3rd edn 1999).

CHAPTER 6. A CLASSLESS ACT

the same subjective corporate policies regarding compensation and promotion.[112] The class representatives presented three types of evidence to prove this allegation. First, they pointed to Wal-Mart's 'excessively subjective'[113] policies regarding compensation and promotions. Second, they offered 'expert statistical evidence,'[114] which demonstrated a connection between gender disparities and discrimination. Finally, they presented the court with 'anecdotal evidence'[115] regarding management's tolerance for or promulgation of discrimination.[116] The court stated that considered together, 'this evidence more than satisfies plaintiffs' burden'[117] in meeting Federal Rule of Civil Procedure 23's commonality requirement.

Notwithstanding the court's holding, the plaintiffs failed to meet the commonality criteria. Just because class representatives worked for the same corporation as potential class members, it does not follow that they all suffered from a common policy of discrimination. As discussed earlier, plaintiffs alleged that Wal-Mart policies prevented them from receiving promotions and that Wal-Mart awarded greater compensation for men who performed the same tasks as women. There is a significant difference, though, between an individual allegedly suffering from corporate-wide discrimination in promotion and pay practices and a group of people all suffering from the same injury such that there are common questions of law and fact pertaining to all of the plaintiffs.[118]

This idea is especially apparent in a corporation like Wal-Mart, 'the largest employer in the world,'[119] because it would be very difficult for an employee in Maine, for example, to suffer from the same discrimination as an employee in Oregon. Wal-Mart utilizes a tiered managerial system,[120] which makes it virtually impossible for corporate

---

[112] *Dukes v. Wal-Mart Stores, Inc.*, 222 F.R.D. 137, 145 (N.D. Cal. 2004).
[113] *Id.*
[114] *Id.*
[115] *Dukes*, 222 F.R.D. at 145.
[116] *Id.*
[117] *Id.*
[118] Hart, *supra* n. 51, at 819 (quoting *Gen. Tel. Co. of the Southwest v. Falcon*, 457 US 147, at 157 (1982)).
[119] *Dukes*, 222 F.R.D. at 141.
[120] *Id.* at 146. At the bottom of the managerial system are assistant managers and specialty department managers. *Id.* These managers report to the store manager,

headquarters to control decisions made at the local level.[121] Individual Wal-Mart store managers are solely responsible for setting compensation levels for hourly positions and 'are granted substantial discretion in making salary decisions.'[122] In fact, in *McCree v. Sam's Club*,[123] which involved Sam's Club, one of the four types of Wal-Mart stores,[124] the Middle District Court of Alabama recognized Sam's Club's policy whereby store managers determined the eligibility criteria for Sam's Clubs' management training program.[125] In deciding whether the plaintiffs could show that this policy was discriminatory, the court stated,

> Plaintiffs do not attempt to show that this policy is in itself... discriminatory, but merely argue that it must allow for discriminatory practices by local stores because of the raw statistics furnished. Such speculation does not satisfy the court that this case is an appropriate one for class action.[126]

On the contrary, the *Dukes* court certified the class relying on statistics regarding the percentage of women who held hourly positions versus the percentage of women who held salaried positions, as well as statistical evidence of discrimination and statistical evidence regarding compensation.[127] It is surprising, therefore, that the *Dukes* court did not follow the court's decision in *McCree* and deny certification based on a lack of evidence of a national policy of discrimination at Wal-Mart.

Another way that courts have described the commonality requirement is that all of the plaintiffs must suffer from a common policy that results in a common injury.[128] In cases where courts certified a class in

---

who in turn reports to the district manager. *Id.* at 145. Wal-Mart operates four different types of stores and all stores are divided into seven divisions. *Id.* at 145. Each division is divided into regions, for a total of forty-one regions nationwide, with each region containing roughly 80–85 stores. *Id.* This results in a total of almost 3,500 stores. *Id.*

[121] See Def.'s Opp'n to Mot. for Class Certification at 4, *Dukes v. Wal-Mart, Inc.* (N.D. Cal. 2003) (No. C-01-2252 MJJ).
[122] Dukes, 222 F.R.D. at 146.
[123] *McCree v. Sam's Club*, 159 F.R.D. 572 (M.D. Ala. 1995).
[124] Dukes, 222 F.R.D. at 141 n. 1.
[125] See McCree, 159 F.R.D. at 577.
[126] *Id.*
[127] Dukes, 222 F.R.D. at 146, 154–156.
[128] See *Talley v. ARINC, Inc.*, 222 F.R.D. 260, 268 (N.D. Md. 2004) (stating that for a class to be certified it must 'present the factual scenario of a discriminatory

CHAPTER 6. A CLASSLESS ACT

an 'across-the-board' case, plaintiffs all suffered from the same policy and suffered a common injury.[129] An example of this is found in *Newsome v. Up-to-Date Laundry*. Plaintiffs, were denied the opportunity to work overtime and received less pay.[130] Although no explicit policy forbidding African-Americans from working overtime existed, defendants openly used racial slurs, and plaintiffs presented statistical evidence that they were subject to less favorable conditions and terms than other workers.[131] In effect, the plaintiffs suffered from an unspoken policy that amounted to racial discrimination. Unlike the plaintiffs in Newsome, who suffered from a common policy, the *Dukes* plaintiffs cannot point to a Wal-Mart policy, latent or overt, that encourages sexual discrimination. Plaintiffs in *Dukes* rely on the argument that Wal-Mart's policies contained 'excessive subjectivity,' which, in effect, led to sexual discrimination.[132] However, the Ninth Circuit held in *Coleman*, that 'subjective evaluations are not unlawful per se and their relevance to proof of discriminatory intent is weak.'[133]

Other courts have also held that when promotion decisions were made on a local level, the parent company was not liable and the class was not certified.[134] In those cases, the courts held that although corporate headquarters determined hiring and promotion guidelines, because local managers implemented those policies, 'the circumstances of each proposed class representative's case will depend on how a specific manager treated that proposed class representative at his or her store.'[135] Plaintiffs' attempt to hold Wal-Mart responsible for

---

practice being applied so as to broadly discriminate against persons in the identical manner.').

[129] See e.g., *Newsome v. Up-to-Date Laundry, Inc.*, 219 F.R.D. 356, 361–362 (N.D. Md. 2004); *Buchanan v. Consolidated Stores Co.*, 217 F.R.D. 178, 187 (D. Md. 2003); *Hewlett v. Premier Salons Int'l*, 185 F.R.D. 211, 216–217 (D.C. Md. 2003).

[130] Newsome, 219 F.R.D. at 360.

[131] See Id.

[132] Dukes, 222 F.R.D. at 151.

[133] *Coleman v. Quaker Oats Co.*, 232 F.3d 1271, 1285 (9th Cir. 2000) (quoting *Sengupta v. Morrison-Knudson Co.*, 804 F.2d 1072, 1075 (9th Cir. 1986)).

[134] See e.g., *Rhodes v. Cracker Barrel Old Country Store, Inc.*, 213 F.R.D. 619, 682 (N.D. Ga. 2002); *Reid v. Lockheed Martin Aeronautics Co.*, 205 F.R.D. 655, 670 (N.D. Ga. 2001); *Donaldson v. Microsoft Corp.*, 205 F.R.D. 558, 567 (W.D. Wash. 2001).

[135] Rhodes, 213 F.R.D. at 676 (stating that 'several other courts have found that the commonality requirement is not satisfied where geographic diversity or an absence of centralized decision-making exists, or where different decision-makers made the

decisions made on a local level is misguided because district managers had the ability to oversee pay and promotion decisions made by store managers,[136] and therefore, they should be held responsible for any sexual discrimination, not corporate headquarters.

The court in *Dukes* further emphasized that the 'subjective manner' in which store managers made hiring and promotion decisions militated for class certification.[137] The court pointed to the 'considerable discretion'[138] given to store managers to make those decisions and the fact that this discretion was 'deliberate and routine,'[139] which made Wal-Mart 'susceptible to being infected by discriminatory animus.'[140] In describing Wal-Mart's employment practices as discriminatory,[141] the court neglected to discuss *Reid v. Lockheed Martin Aeronautics*.[142] In *Reid*, plaintiffs sued Lockheed Martin on behalf of African-American employees working in facilities across the country, claiming that the company engaged in racial discrimination by allowing facility managers to use subjective criteria when making employment decisions.[143] The Northern District of Georgia denied certification, because the *Reid* plaintiffs, like the plaintiffs in *Dukes*, had essentially claimed that Lockheed Martin had a 'centralized policy of decentralization'[144] under which facility

---

challenged decisions'). See also Donaldson, 205 F.R.D. at 567; Reid, 205 F.R.D. at 669; *Zachery v. Texaco Exploration & Prod., Inc.*, 185 F.R.D. 230, 238 (W.D. Tex. 1999), stating:

> the fact that employment decisions are handled by one's immediate supervisor based on subjective criteria would be useful evidence in an individual disparate treatment claim, but works against class certification of a disparate impact claim when the proposed class is subject to the same local autonomy in geographically dispersed facilities.

[136] See Def's Opp. to Class Certification, at 14–15, *Dukes v. Wal-Mart, Inc.* (N.D. Cal. 2003) (No. C-01-2252 MJJ).
[137] *Dukes*, 222 F.R.D. at 145.
[138] *Id.* at 153.
[139] *Id.* at 149.
[140] *Id.*
[141] See *Watson v. Fort Worth Bank & Trust*, 487 US 977, 990–991 (1988); *Sengupta v. Morrison-Knudsen Co.*, 804 F.2d 1072, 1075 (9th Cir. 1986); *Casillas v. United States Navy*, 735 F.2d 338, 345 (9th Cir. 1984) (cases where courts rejected plaintiffs' attempts to attack employment practices as discriminatory).
[142] *Reid v. Lockheed Martin Aeronautics Co.*, 205 F.R.D. 655 (N.D. Ga. 2001).
[143] *Id.* at 657–659.
[144] *Id.* at 670.

CHAPTER 6. A CLASSLESS ACT

managers had the autonomy to use subjective criteria when making employment decisions.[145] The court held that this is an insufficient basis to maintain a multi-facility class action lawsuit because 'Title VII prohibits discriminatory employment practices, not an abstract policy of discrimination.'[146] *Reid* and *Dukes* are factually and legally analogous: both involve an abstract claim of discrimination whereby the plaintiffs attempted to hold a corporate parent liable, when in reality, no substantive corporate policy existed that could implicate the corporate parent.

Furthermore, *Dukes* cited *Watson v. Fort Worth Bank & Trust*[147] as proof that subjective decision-making is a basis for class certification when the factual scenario in *Watson* should have led the *Dukes* court to the exact opposite conclusion.[148] In *Watson*, a woman sued an individual bank for racial discrimination on the grounds that the bank used subjective criteria in its employment decisions that led to discrimination.[149] A key fact in *Watson*, which the *Dukes* court failed to mention, was that *Watson* did not involve a class action lawsuit. Apart from this, the *Reid* court emphasized the fact that claims of subjective decision-making give rise to individual claims, and not class action lawsuits.[150] The *Dukes* court, therefore, incorrectly cited *Watson* and the proposition that it stands for – that claims of subjective decision making are appropriate in cases involving a single facility or location and not multi-facility – to support 'across-the-board' class action lawsuits.

Although the *Dukes* court held that a subjective decision-making process could serve as a basis for a discrimination claim, there are cases where courts rejected the use of this argument even when the case

---

[145] *Id.*
[146] *Id.* at 670 (citing *Gen. Tel. Co. of Southwest v. Falcon*, 457 US 147, 159 n. 15 (5th Cir. 1982) (emphasis in original)).
[147] *Watson v. Fort Worth Bank & Trust*, 487 US 977 (1988).
[148] See *Dukes* at 149.
[149] See *id.* at 977.
[150] See Reid, 205 F.R.D. at 670 (stating that using subjective criteria 'does not mean that subjective employment practices necessarily give rise to a broad, multi-facility class; rather, it leads to the opposite conclusion.'). The Reid court cited a number of cases where other courts emphasized this point. See e.g., *Stastny v. S. Bell Tel. & Tel. Co.*, 628 F.2d 267, 279 (4th Cir. 1980), stating that

> evidence of subjectivity in employment decisions may well serve to bolster proof on the merits of individual claims of disparate treatment... it cuts

307

involved an individual plaintiff. In *Sengupta v. Morrison-Knudsen Co.*, the Ninth Circuit rejected the claim that subjective decision-making alone can be used to prove discrimination.[151] In *Sengupta*, the plaintiff claimed that Morrison-Knudsen utilized subjective criteria in its employee evaluations, which led to racial discrimination and plaintiff's discharge.[152] In dismissing the plaintiff's claim, the court in *Sengupta* held that subjectivity is not grounds for proving discrimination, because 'its relevance to proof of a discriminatory intent is weak.'[153] Furthermore, in *Casillas v. United States Navy*, the plaintiff claimed that the Navy used subjective decision-making practices as a cover for national origin discrimination and that the Navy used these practices to prevent his promotion.[154] The Ninth Circuit flatly rejected plaintiff's claim, stating that 'we have explicitly rejected the idea that an employer's use of subjective employment criteria has a talismanic significance.'[155]

As the final basis for deciding that the plaintiffs fulfilled the commonality requirement of Rule 23, the *Dukes* court noted Wal-Mart's 'strong...distinctive, centrally controlled, corporate culture.'[156] The court claimed that this strong corporate culture led to 'uniformity of operational and personnel practices,'[157] and that these practices

---

against any inference for class action commonality purposes that local facility practices were imposed or enforced state-wide with respect to a statewide class;

Zachery v. Exploration & Prod., Inc., 185 F.R.D. 230, 238 (W.D. Tex. 1999), stating that

the fact that employment decisions are handled by one's immediate supervisor based on subjective criteria would be useful evidence in an individual disparate treatment claim, but works against class certification of a disparate impact claim when the proposed class is subject to the same local autonomy in geographically dispersed facilities (emphasis in original).

[151] *Sengupta v. Morrison-Knudsen Co.*, 804 F.2d 1072, 1075 (9th Cir. 1986). (stating 'the use of subjective employment criteria is not unlawful per se' and 'their relevance to proof of a discriminatory intent is weak.').
[152] *Id.* at 1073–1075.
[153] *Id.* at 1075.
[154] *Casillas v. United States Navy*, 735 F.2d 338, 340–342 (9th Cir. 1984).
[155] *Id.* at 345.
[156] Dukes, 222 F.R.D. at 151 (N.D. Cal. 2004).
[157] *Id.*

CHAPTER 6. A CLASSLESS ACT

'include gender stereotyping.'[158] There is an inherent tension, though, with claiming, on the one hand, that the decision-making process at Wal-Mart is subjective, and on the other hand, that a strong corporate culture existed at Wal-Mart that led to a 'uniformity of operational and personnel practices.'[159] The court even acknowledged this contradiction,[160] but attempted to reconcile it by holding that the subjective decision-making on the local level allows gender bias to become a common part of the Wal-Mart system. This holding was in direct contrast with the *Reid* court's more reasonable summary of similar plaintiffs' arguments, in which it was observed that, 'the best characterization of Plaintiffs' theory is that Defendants had a centralized policy of decentralization, which is insufficient on these facts to satisfy commonality... with respect to Plaintiffs' proposed multi-facility cases.'[161] In certifying the class, the *Dukes* court effectively acknowledged that subjective decision-making practices are not grounds for a class action lawsuit, and used animus against Wal-Mart's 'strong corporate culture' as a way of glossing over the legal gaps in the court's reasoning.[162]

6.4.2 The Typicality Finding

Turning to Rule 23's typicality requirement, the *Dukes* court found that, although the plaintiffs worked in Wal-Mart stores across the country, they fulfilled this requirement because they were subject to 'excessively subjective decision-making in a corporate culture of

---

[158] *Id.* at 150.

[159] *Id.*

[160] 'The Court recognizes that there is a tension inherent in characterizing a system as having both excessive subjectivity at the local level and centralized control.' *Id.* at 152.

[161] Reid, 205 F.R.D. at 670.

[162] There are numerous websites whose sole purpose is to portray Wal-Mart as an evil corporate giant. See e.g., Walmart Sucks, <www.walmartsucks.org> (last visited December 30, 2004); Walmart Blows, <www.walmart-blows.com> (last visited October 15, 2005); Walmart Watch, <www.walmartwatch.com> (last visited December 30, 2004). Cities have also gone on the offense against Wal-Mart by passing zoning laws that prevent 'big box' stores such as Wal-Mart from opening. See e.g., Wake-Up Wal-Mart, Zoning changes prohibit big-box stores, at <http://wakeupwalmart.com/news/20050527-tcre.html> (last visited October 31, 2005).

uniformity and gender stereotyping.'[163] In other words, even though one plaintiff worked in a store in New York and another in a store in California, both suffered from a 'common practice,'[164] and thereby fulfilled Rule 23's requirement that 'claims or defenses of the representative parties are typical of the claims or defenses of the class.'[165]

A problem with the *Dukes* court's decision regarding typicality is that, on the one hand, it held that the named representatives and all possible plaintiffs suffered from typical claims, but on the other hand, acknowledged that the claims are 'individual-specific.'[166] This leads to a serious problem: if the plaintiffs' claims were 'individual-specific,' then the court will have to examine each plaintiff's claim, which defeats the purpose of a class action lawsuit.[167] Courts have routinely denied class certification where the court deemed necessary a review of each plaintiff's individual claims.[168] Moreover, the court in *Abrams v. Kelsey-Seybold Medical Group, Inc.*, went as far as to say that 'a class may

---

[163] *Dukes*, 222 F.R.D. at 167.

[164] *Id.* at 167–168.

[165] Fed. R. Civ. P. 23(a)(3).

[166] *Dukes*, 222 F.R.D. at 167. In acknowledging defendant's objection based on the individual-specific nature of the plaintiffs' claim, the court responded that 'some degree of individualized specificity must be expected in all cases.' *Id.*

[167] See *Rhodes v. Cracker Barrel Old Country Store, Inc.*, 213 F.R.D. 619, 682 (N.D. Ga. 2003) (in discussing one reason for not certifying the class, the court stated that 'the proposed class representatives' and members' disparate treatment claims will require individualized factual determinations. Plaintiffs consequently cannot satisfy the typicality requirement with respect to their disparate treatment claims.').

[168] See *Id.* (concluding its analysis of the typicality requirement by stating that 'Plaintiffs consequently cannot satisfy the typicality requirement with respect to their disparate treatment claims.'). See also *Talley v. ARINC, Inc.*, 222 F.R.D. 260, 268 (D. Md. 2004)

> Plaintiffs have aggregated several individual complaints that require individualized proof and give rise to individualized defenses.... This case does not present the factual scenario of a discriminatory practice being applied so as to broadly discriminate against persons in the identical manner.

Abrams v. Kelsey-Seybold Med. Group, Inc., 178 F.R.D. 116, 129 (S.D. Tex. 1997) ('The courts have made it clear that in cases alleging classwide disparate treatment in particular employment actions, plaintiffs must show a company-wide policy or practice, beyond individualized claims of discrimination.').

not be based on discrimination occurring in different departments, involving different decision makers.'[169]

While the representative plaintiffs could conceivably bring a claim against their individual store managers, or even possibly against all Wal-Mart stores in California, 'the consensus among other courts... is that a plaintiff may represent a multi-facility class only when centralized and uniform employment practices affect all facilities in the *same way*.'[170] In situations where:

> employment practices were set by a plant manager located at each division facility... the court held that the plaintiffs could only represent those... employees employed at the first facility, and it excluded... those... employees that worked at the other three facilities.[171]

As mentioned earlier, the situation in *Reid* is extremely similar to the situation in *Dukes* whereby plaintiffs attempted to represent class members at several locations in several different states.[172] In *Reid*, the court denied the plaintiffs' motion for class certification, because each plant determined employment practices and, in a multi-facility case, a plaintiff can only represent workers from his own facility, unless centralized policies existed.[173] It would only seem logical, therefore, that in a case like *Dukes*, which involves over 3,400 stores and in which each store manager had 'substantial discretion'[174] regarding employment decisions, that the court should have denied class certification as well. This assertion is further bolstered by the court's decision in *ARINC*, where the court held that 'a class may not be based on discrimination occurring in different departments, involving different decision makers.'[175] Surely, if a class cannot be certified when discrimination occurs in different departments, then a class cannot be certified when discrimination allegedly occurred in over 3,400 stores across the country. Accordingly, the *Dukes* court erroneously and without reason ignored the rulings of its sister courts.

---

[169] Abrams, 178 F.R.D. at 129.
[170] *Reid v. Lockheed Martin Aeronautics Co.*, 205 F.R.D. 655, 667–668 (N.D. Ga. 2001) (emphasis added).
[171] Citing *Webb v. Westinghouse Elec. Co.*, 78 F.R.D. 645, 651 (E.D. Pa. 1978).
[172] *Id.* at 659.
[173] See *id.* at 669.
[174] Dukes, 222 F.R.D. at 153 (N.D. Cal. 2004).
[175] Abrams, 178 F.R.D. at 129 (S.D. Tex. 1997).

EMPLOYMENT CLASS AND COLLECTIVE ACTIONS

For a class to satisfy the typicality requirement, the named plaintiffs must represent the interests of all other potential plaintiffs.[176] Whereas the *Dukes* court cited cases that have allowed different types of plaintiffs to represent an entire class,[177] the *Dukes* case is in fact different from those cases. The plaintiffs' class in *Dukes* is composed of hourly and salaried employees, even though the hourly employees' case is based on discrimination allegedly perpetrated by the salaried mangers.[178] In other cases where the plaintiffs sought to be certified as a class composed of members with competing interests, the courts have held that the competing class members could not be in the same class.[179]

Another issue raised during the court's discussion of typicality in *Dukes* is whether the class representatives could represent the entire class even though only one of the representatives held a managerial position in a Sam's Club store.[180] The plaintiffs arranged their class so that Christine Kwapnoski, the only plaintiff to have held a managerial position, represented other managers, even though she only held an entry-level managerial position at a Sam's Club.[181] The *Dukes* court asserted that it is irrelevant whether or not there is a representative for each level of management,[182] and specifically that Kwapnoski, as an entry-level manager, was not a member of upper management.[183] Other courts have said that

---

[176] *Gen. Tel. Co. of the Southwest v. Falcon*, 457 US 147, 157 n. 13 (1982).

[177] See *Hartman v. Duffey*, 19 F.3d 1459, 1471 (D.C. Cir. 1994); *Meyer v. MacMillan Publ'g Co.*, 95 F.R.D. 411, 414 (S.D.N.Y. 1982); *Taylor v. Union Carbide Corp.*, 93 F.R.D. 1, 6 (S.D. W. Va. 1980).

[178] See Def.'s Opp'n to Mot. for Class Certification at 34, *Dukes v. Wal-Mart Stores, Inc.*, 222 F.R.D. 137 (2004) (No. 01-2252).

[179] See *id.* (citing *Donaldson v. Microsoft Corp.*, 205 F.R.D. 558, 568 (W.D. Wash. 2001) (denying class certification and holding that 'a conflict of interest may arise where a class contains both supervisory and non-supervisory employees.')); *Appleton v. Deloitte & Touche L.L.P.*, 168 F.R.D. 221, 233 (M.D. Tenn. 1996) (preventing plaintiffs from representing class members, the court stated, 'members of the proposed class who are supervisors have likely been responsible for evaluating the performances of other members of the class – evaluations these nonsupervisory personnel may challenge as discriminatory.').

[180] *Dukes*, 222 F.R.D. at 166.

[181] See Def.'s Opp'n to Mot. for Class Certification at 17–18 n. 9, *Dukes v. Wal-Mart Stores, Inc.*, 222 F.R.D. 137 (2004) (No. 01-2252).

[182] See *Dukes*, 222 F.R.D. at 167 (N.D. Cal. 2004) (citing *Taylor v. Union Carbide Corp.*, 93 F.R.D. 1, 6 (S.D. W. Va. 1980).

[183] *Id.* at 166–167.

if there are conflicts between different managerial positions, then one manager cannot represent a different managerial position.[184] Once again, rather than apply a 'rigorous analysis'[185] to the typicality requirement of Rule 23, the court chose to emphasize the 'permissive'[186] nature of the typicality requirement. The court failed to recognize that while class actions should be certified when appropriate, the Court in *Falcon* demanded 'rigorous analysis'[187] of all applications for class action status because class action lawsuits are 'an exception to the usual rule that litigation is conducted by and on behalf of the individual named parties only.'[188]

In sum, the *Dukes* court found a basis for holding that the plaintiffs met the commonality and typicality requirements of Rule 23 based on the 'broad discretion to determine whether a class should be certified'[189] and the 'permissive'[190] nature of the typicality requirement.

6.5 THE COURT'S USE OF EXPERT WITNESSES AND THE LACK OF A *DAUBERT* ANALYSIS

Courts rely on expert witnesses to determine whether the assertions made by plaintiffs seeking class action status are accurate.[191] Federal Rules of Evidence 702 and 703 govern the admissibility of expert

---

[184] See Def.'s Opp'n to Mot. for Class Certification at 34 (citing *Clayborne v. Omaha Pub. Power Dist.*, 211 F.R.D. 573, 587–588, 597–598 (D. Neb. 2002)); *Morgan v. United Parcel Serv. of Am.*, 169 F.R.D. 349, 357–358 (E.D. Mo. 1996) (holding that center managers could not adequately represent higher-level managerial employees due to potential conflicts of interest).

[185] Falcon, 457 US at 159 n. 15 (1982); *Zinser v. Accufix Research Inst.*, 253 F.3d 1180, 1186 (9th Cir. 2001).

[186] Dukes, 222 F.R.D. at 167 (citing *Staton v. Boeing Co.*, 327 F.3d 938, 957 (9th Cir. 2003)).

[187] Falcon, 457 US at 159 n. 15; Zinser, 253 F.3d at 1186.

[188] Falcon, 457 US at 155 (quoting *Califano v. Yamasaki*, 442 US 682, 700–701 (1979)).

[189] Dukes, 222 F.R.D. at 143 (citing *Armstrong v. Davis*, 275 F.3d 849, 871 n. 28 (9th Cir. 2001).

[190] See *id.* at 167 (citing Staton, 327 F.3d at 957).

[191] See *Daubert v. Merrell Dow Pharm.*, 509 US 579, 589 (1993) (citing FED. R. EVID. 702) ('If scientific, technical, or other specialized knowledge will assist the trier of fact to understand the evidence or to determine a fact in issue "an expert" may testify thereto.') (emphasis in original); L. Elizabeth Chamblee, Between 'Merit Inquiry'

witness testimony.[192] In *Daubert v. Merrell Dow Pharmaceuticals*, plaintiffs claimed that their children were born with birth defects as a result of a drug manufactured by Merrill Dow Pharmaceuticals.[193] Merrell Dow challenged expert witness testimony presented by the plaintiff regarding the link between the drug and birth defects on the grounds that the testimony did not meet the criteria set forth in the precedental case of *Frye v. United States*.[194] In *Frye*, the Court held that expert witness testimony is only admissible if the witness uses techniques that 'have gained general acceptance' by the scientific community.[195] In *Daubert*, however, the Court held that Federal Rule of Evidence 702 allows judges 'some gatekeeping responsibility' in admission of expert testimony.[196] This 'gatekeeping' role is meant to ensure that expert testimony is relevant to the issue and that the expert witness meets certain qualifications.[197] In addition to being relevant to the issue and the expert witness being qualified, the evidence must also assist the factfinder.[198]

---

and 'Rigorous Analysis': Using Daubert to Navigate the Gray Areas of Federal Class Action Certification, 31 FLA. ST. U. L. REV. 1041, 1050 (2004).

[192] See Fed. R. Evid. 702, 703. The Advisory Committee Notes list five factors to determine the reliability of expert witness testimony.

(1) Whether the expert's technique or theory can be or has been tested – that is, whether the expert's theory can be challenged in some objective sense, or whether it is instead simply a subjective, conclusory approach that cannot reasonably be assessed for reliability.
(2) Whether the technique or theory has been subject to peer review and publication.
(3) The known or potential rate of error of the technique or theory when applied.
(4) The existence and maintenance of standards and controls.
(5) Whether the technique or theory has been generally accepted in the scientific community.

[193] Daubert, 509 US at 582.
[194] *Frye v. United States*, 293 F. 1013 (D.C. Cir. 1923).
[195] *Id.* at 1014.
[196] Daubert, 509 US at 589 n. 7 (quoting Rehnquist's opinion, concurring in part, dissenting in part, *id.* at 600).
[197] *Id.* at 589. The Supreme Court clarified this requirement to apply to all expert witnesses and not testimony just based on science. See *Kumho Tire Co. v. Carmichael*, 526 US 137, 147–148 (1999).
[198] See Fed. R. Evid. 702.

CHAPTER 6. A CLASSLESS ACT

In *Dukes*,[199] the court held a *Daubert* hearing regarding the admissibility of the testimony of the plaintiffs' expert witness relating to the presence of stereotypes and discrimination at Wal-Mart[200] and concluded that only part of one witness' testimony should be stricken.[201] At the separate hearing, the court, in stating the legal standard for reviewing expert witness testimony at the class certification stage, held 'that a lower *Daubert* standard should be employed at this [class certification] stage of the proceedings.'[202] The plaintiffs relied on three expert witnesses in order to prove that gender stereotyping and disparities exist at Wal-Mart.[203] The testimony of one of the expert witnesses, Dr. Bielby, a sociologist, is especially troubling for a number of reasons. Dr. Bielby assessed various Wal-Mart policies based on 'subjective beliefs,'[204] rather than 'the methods and procedures of science.'[205] In looking at various Wal-Mart policies, Dr. Bielby concluded that 'managers make decisions with considerable discretion and little oversight'[206] and 'that subjective decisions such as these, as well as discretionary wage decisions are likely to be biased "unless they are assessed . . . with clear criteria and careful attention to the integrity of the decision-making process." '[207] Dr. Bielby based his opinion on what the court termed 'social science research.'[208]

In turning to the issue of social science research, other social scientists have reached the exact opposite conclusion than that of Dr. Bielby, though Wal-Mart surprisingly did not use this evidence in its case.[209] One group of researchers found that the 'distinction between an "objective" and "subjective" evaluative measurement is neither

---

[199] See *Dukes v. Wal-Mart Stores, Inc.*, 222 F.R.D. 189 (N.D. Cal. 2004).
[200] *Id.* at 191–193.
[201] *Id.* at 195 (excluding part of the evidence submitted by Dr. Richard Drogin because he made an error in his mathematical computations).
[202] *Id.* at 191 (quoting *Thomas & Thomas Rodmakers, Inc. v. Newport Adhesives & Composites, Inc.*, 209 F.R.D. 159, 162 (C.D. Cal. 2002)).
[203] See Dukes, 222 F.R.D. at 153–156. More specifically, the court used the expert witness' testimony to conclude that the plaintiffs met the commonality requirement of Rule 23(a)(1). *Id.* at 166.
[204] Daubert, 509 US at 590.
[205] *Id.*
[206] *Dukes*, 222 F.R.D. at 153 (citing Bielby Decl. 37–41).
[207] *Id.* (quoting Bielby Decl. at 39).
[208] *Id.*
[209] See David Copus, Beware the Power of Junk Science, 177 N.J.L.J. 764 (2004).

meaningful nor useful in human performance.'[210] Another group of researchers found that 'the distinction between subjective and objective is problematic and somewhat arbitrary.'[211] The most persuasive statement against Dr. Bielby, though, is that of the *Dukes* court itself. In addressing the defendant's objections to Dr. Bielby's testimony, the court stated:

> Defendant also challenges Dr. Bielby's opinions as unfounded and imprecise. It is true that Dr. Bielby's opinions have a built-in degree of conjecture. He does not present a quantifiable analysis; rather, he combines the understanding of the scientific community with evidence of Defendant's policies and practices, and concludes that Wal-Mart is 'vulnerable' to gender bias. Defendant rightly points out that Dr. Bielby cannot definitively state how regularly stereotypes play a meaningful role in employment decisions at Wal-Mart.[212]

This statement indicates that Dr. Bielby's testimony should fail under the *Daubert* analysis because it was based on 'subjective belief or unsupported speculation.'[213] Amazingly, however, at the special hearing, the *Dukes* court decided that Dr. Bielby's testimony 'was sufficiently probative to assist the Court in evaluating the class certification requirements at issue in this case.'[214]

In reaching its conclusion, the court cited previous cases where the court admitted expert witness testimony, even though the testimony could not definitively state a conclusion.[215] A majority of the cases relied on by the court dealt with a single employee or a group of employees suing an employer and not a class action lawsuit.[216] Taking into account the fact that class action lawsuits are the exception to

---

[210] Fredrick Muckler & Sally A. Seven, Selecting Performance Measures: 'Objective' versus 'Subjective' Measurement, 34 HUMAN FACTORS 441 (1992).

[211] J. Kevin Ford et al., Study of Race Effects in Objective Indices and Subjective Evaluations of Performance: A Meta-Analysis of Performance Criteria, 99 Psychol. Bull. 330, 331 (1986).

[212] *Dukes*, 222 F.R.D. at 154 (emphasis added) (citations omitted).

[213] Daubert, 509 US at 590 (1993).

[214] *Dukes*, 222 F.R.D. at 192.

[215] *Id.* (citing *Price Waterhouse v. Hopkins*, 490 US 228, 235–236 (1989); *Costa v. Desert Palace Inc.*, 299 F.3d 838, 861 (9th Cir. 2002), aff'd, 539 US 90 (2003).

[216] *Dukes*, 222 F.R.D. at 192. (citing *Price Waterhouse v. Hopkins* and *Butler v. Home Depot, Inc.* to show that courts have admitted expert witness testimony based on social science) (citations omitted).

CHAPTER 6. A CLASSLESS ACT

the rule,[217] the court should have rejected Dr. Bielby's testimony on account of its 'built-in degree of conjecture,'[218] and the fact that it resembles 'junk science'[219] and not 'scientifically valid principles.'[220]

6.6 THE COURT'S DECISION REGARDING TITLE VII ISSUES

Congress amended Title VII with the Civil Rights Act of 1991.[221] As part of the amendment, Congress granted victims of alleged intentional discrimination the right to seek compensatory and punitive damages.[222] Whatever the intentions of Congress, the 1991 Amendment created significant difficulties for plaintiffs involved in a class action employment discrimination lawsuit seeking compensatory or punitive damages.[223] As stated in Rule 23(b)(2) of the Federal Rules of Civil Procedure, plaintiffs who seek class certification pursuant to Rule 23(b)(2), can do so only if they are seeking 'final injunctive relief or corresponding declaratory relief with respect to the class as a whole.'[224]

These competing provisions result in a difficult situation for classes seeking to be certified while also requesting monetary damages. As a result, the Advisory Committee for the Federal Rules of Civil Procedure, in looking at the Civil Rights Act of 1991 in conjunction with Rule 23(b)(2), stated that class certification

---

[217] *Gen. Tel. Co. of the Southwest. v. Falcon*, 457 US at 155 (quoting *Califano v. Yamasaki*, 442 US 682, 700–701 (1979)).

[218] *Dukes*, 222 F.R.D. at 154 (citing Bielby Decl. P63). 'Conjecture' is defined by Merriam-Webster's On-Line dictionary as an 'inference from defective or presumptive evidence' or 'a conclusion deduced by surmise or guesswork.' Merriam-Webster's On-Line, available at <www.m-w.com/cgi-bin/dictionary?book=Dictionary&va=conjecture> (last visited October 15, 2005).

[219] *Lust v. Merrell Dow Pharm., Inc.*, 89 F.3d 594, 597 (9th Cir. 1996).

[220] *Daubert v. Merrell Dow Pharm., Inc.*, 43 F.3d 1311, 1316 (9th Cir. 1995) (hereinafter Daubert II). See also Chamblee, *supra* n. 198, at 1048 (stating that courts normally use a low threshold when deciding on class certification, but that 'they should use a higher standard to filter unreliable evidence.').

[221] See The Civil Rights Act of 1991, 42 USC § 1981a(a)(1) (1991).

[222] See 42 USC § 1981a(b)(1) (1991).

[223] See Hart, *supra* n. 52, at 813.

[224] Fed. R. Civ. P. 23(b)(2).

pursuant to Rule 23(b)(2) 'does not extend to cases in which the appropriate final relief relates exclusively or predominantly to monetary damages.'[225] Despite this explicit warning, the *Dukes* court overlooked possible Title VII issues and permitted the plaintiffs to proceed with their claims.[226] In fact, the court concluded that it had 'little difficulty'[227] holding that the equitable relief predominated over the monetary relief sought.[228]

This result is surprising given the outcome in *Allison v. Citgo Petroleum Corp.*, which some have described as 'the best-known articulation'[229] regarding employment class actions following the passage of the Civil Rights Act of 1991. In *Allison*, plaintiffs sued Citgo Petroleum Corporation, claiming that the supervisors at one plant engaged in racial discrimination in their employment decisions.[230] The Fifth Circuit denied class certification because the monetary damages sought by the plaintiffs 'were not incidental'[231] to the injunctive

---

[225] Fed. R. Civ. P. 23 advisory committee's notes.

[226] *Dukes v. Wal-Mart Stores, Inc.*, 222 F.R.D. 137, 170–71 (N.D. Cal. 2004).

[227] *Id.* at 171.

[228] *Id.* The court's conclusion is even more surprising, because the court relied on *Young v. Pierce*, 544 F. Supp. 1010, 1028 (E.D. Tex. 1982). It would appear that the court incorrectly relied on this decision given that there is a more recent case that dealt with the Civil Rights Amendment of 1991. Young was decided before Congress passed The Civil Rights Act of 1991. Although the Dukes plaintiffs seek injunctive and declaratory relief, they also seek monetary damages, a remedy unavailable in Young. The Dukes court, therefore, should have relied on cases after 1991 in order to determine if the injunctive and declaratory relief outweighed the monetary relief sought by the plaintiffs. See *infra* n. 141 for post-1991 cases involving the Civil Rights Act of 1991. Once again, it would appear that the Dukes court went to great lengths to certify this class, despite clear case precedent that would appear to point to the opposite result.

[229] Hart, *supra*, at 821–822.

[230] See *Allison v. Citgo Petroleum Corp.*, 151 F.3d 402, 407 (5th Cir. 1998).

[231] *Id.* at 425. In laying the foundation for denying class certification, the court stated (*Id.* at 415):

> The recovery of incidental damages should typically be concomitant with, not merely consequential to, class-wide injunctive or declaratory relief. Moreover, such damages should at least be capable of computation by means of objective standards and not dependent in any significant way on the intangible, subjective differences of each class member's circumstances.

CHAPTER 6. A CLASSLESS ACT

or declaratory relief being sought.[232] As a basis for its holding, the court wrote that:

> The underlying premise of the [23](b)(2) class – that its members suffer from a common injury properly addressed by class-wide relief – 'begins to break down when the class seeks to recover back pay or other forms of monetary relief to be allocated based on individual injuries.' Thus, as claims for individually based money damages begin to predominate, the presumption of cohesiveness decreases while the need for enhanced procedural safeguards to protect individual rights of class members increases.[233]

Therefore, it is difficult to understand the court's findings on this issue in *Dukes*. Even though the plaintiffs were seeking punitive damages in the form of lost pay, the court had 'little difficulty' in determining that the claim for punitive damages was incidental to the injunctive or declaratory relief sought. This was so despite the fact that based on prior cases a jury award has the potential to bankrupt Wal-Mart.

The *Dukes* court's stated rationale for dismissing any Title VII damages problem is a further demonstration of its disregard for precedent and its intense desire to certify the *Dukes* class.[234] In making its decision, the court in *Dukes* relied solely on the depositions of the class representatives in determining that the punitive damages being sought were secondary to the equitable or injunctive relief being sought.[235] It would seem almost inconceivable that a court would rely so heavily on the affidavits of the very people seeking class certification in deciding whether or not to certify what would be largest

---

[232] The factual situation in Allison is quite similar to the one in *Dukes*. The Allison court described the situation as follows:

> Plaintiffs seek to certify a class of a thousand potential plaintiffs spread across two separate facilities... working in seven different departments, challenging various policies and practices.... Some plaintiffs may have been subjected to more virile discrimination than others: with greater public humiliation, for longer periods of time, or based on more unjustifiable practices, for example. *Id.* at 417.

[233] *Id.* at 413 (citations omitted).

[234] The *Dukes* court stated that it based its findings on 'ample legal precedent.' Dukes, 222 F.R.D. at 142 (N.D. Cal. 2004). The contention of this Note is that the court either misapplied legal precedent or construed it in such a way, so as to guarantee that the class would be certified.

[235] See *Id.* at 171.

private civil rights lawsuit in United States legal history. The court in *Allison* spent almost ten pages discussing various Title VII issues when deciding whether or not to certify a class of 'more than 1,000 potential members,'[236] a class that the court described as a 'potentially huge and wide-ranging class.'[237] The court in *Dukes* devoted only three pages[238] to its discussion of any potential Title VII issues, despite the fact that *Dukes* involved a 'proposed class that covers at least 1.5 million women'[239] which the court called 'historic in nature.'[240] The court did not discuss whether damages would have to be determined on an individual basis or could be calculated based on 'objective standards.'[241] This disparity is only a further indication that the *Dukes* court casually dismissed significant legal issues in favor of certifying the class.

6.7 BLACKMAIL SETTLEMENTS

The concern over blackmail settlements is an additional policy reason for supporting the denial of class certification in a case involving such a large number of plaintiffs and a possibly enormous award. The idea behind a blackmail settlement is that a class will seek to be certified in order to 'coerce the defendant into settlement.'[242] In a speech in 1972, Judge Henry Friendly coined the term 'blackmail settlement.'[243] The concern regarding blackmail settlements is one that many courts and authors have recognized[244] and courts began raising concerns

---

[236] *Id.* at 407.
[237] *Id.*
[238] See *Dukes*, 222 F.R.D. at 170–172.
[239] *Id.* at 142.
[240] *Id.*
[241] See *Allison*, 151 F.3d at 425. Even when other courts have certified class actions in Title VII cases, the courts considered the approach taken in *Allison*. See e.g., *Robinson v. Metro-North Commuter R.R. Co.*, 267 F.3d 147, 163–167 (2nd Cir. 2001); *Warnell v. Ford Motor Co.*, 189 F.R.D. 383, 388–389 (N.D. Ill. 1999); *Faulk v. Home Oil Co.*, 186 F.R.D. 660, 662–65 (M.D. Ala. 1999).
[242] *Rutstein v. Avis Rent-A-Car Sys., Inc.*, 211 F.3d 1228, 1241 n. 21 (11th Cir. 2000).
[243] Charles Silver, 'We're Scared to Death': Class Certification and Blackmail, 78 N.Y.U. L. Rev. 1357 (2003) (quoting Henry J. Friendly, Federal Jurisdiction: A General View 120 (1973)).
[244] See e.g., *Coopers & Lybrand v. Livesay*, 437 US 463, 467 (1978); *Newton v. Merrill Lynch, Pierce, Fenner & Smith, Inc.*, 259 F.3d 154, 167–169 (3rd Cir. 2001); *Castano v.*

CHAPTER 6. A CLASSLESS ACT

surrounding blackmail settlements shortly after Judge Friendly coined the phrase.[245] In 1998, Congress passed Rule 23(f) of the Federal Rules of Civil Procedure, which allows defendants to seek an interlocutory appeal of a district court's class certification.[246] The Advisory Committee Notes state that one reason for allowing an interlocutory appeal is that 'an order granting certification ... may force a defendant to settle rather than incur the costs of defending a class action and run the risk of potentially ruinous liability.'[247] Courts have used Rule 23(f) and the guidance provided by the Advisory Committee notes to decertify classes when it appeared that class certification would pressure a defendant into settling.[248]

As mentioned earlier, the potential award in this case could be in the billions of dollars given the fact that in 1999 a sexual discrimination lawsuit brought by 10,000 employees settled for USD 25 million, which

---

Am. Tobacco Co., 84 F.3d 734, 746 (5th Cir. 1996). See also Thomas E. Willging et al., Empirical Study of Class Actions in Four Federal District Courts: Final Report To The Advisory Committee On Civil Rules 60 (Federal Judicial Center 1996) (in looking at class actions across four federal district courts, the authors found that 'a substantial majority of certified class actions were terminated by class-wide settlements.').

[245] One of the earliest examples of a court discussing pressure to settle was in *Kline v. Coldwell, Banker & Co.*, where the court stated:

> I doubt that plaintiffs' counsel expect the immense and unmanageable case that they seek to create to be tried. What they seek to create will become (whether they intend this result or not) an overwhelmingly costly and potent engine for the compulsion of settlements, whether just or unjust.

Kline v. Coldwell, Banker & Co., 508 F.2d 226, 238 (9th Cir. 1974). The Seventh Circuit has notably been at the forefront of not certifying or decertifying class action lawsuits because of the issue of blackmail settlements. See generally In re Bridgestone/Firestone, Inc., 288 F.3d 1012, 1015–1016 (7th Cir. 2002); *West v. Prudential Sec., Inc.*, 282 F.3d 935, 937 (7th Cir. 2002); In re Rhone-Poulenc Rorer, Inc., 51 F.3d 1293, 1298–1299 (7th Cir. 1995).

[246] See Fed. R. Civ. P. 23(f).

[247] Fed. R. Civ. P. 23(f) advisory committee's note.

[248] The raison d'être for Rule 23(f) ... provides a mechanism through which appellate courts, in the interests of fairness, can restore equilibrium when a doubtful class certification ruling would virtually compel a party to abandon a potentially meritorious claim or defense before trial.

Waste Mgmt. Holdings, Inc. v. Mowbray, 208 F.3d 288, 293 (1st Cir. 2000).

means that if divided equally, each claimant received USD 2,500.[249] Assuming a jury awarded each claimant in *Dukes* USD 2,500, the total award in this case would be USD 3.75 billion. Therefore, although neither the defense nor the court in *Dukes* raised the issue of blackmail settlements, it is an important issue, which should be discussed given the magnitude of the case and possible size of the settlement.

Although Rule 23(a)(1) requires that 'the class be so numerous that joinder of all members is impracticable,'[250] an excessively large class can prove to be a double-edged sword when it comes to blackmail settlements. In *Coopers & Lybrand v. Livesay*, plaintiffs sued an accounting firm, because they purchased securities based on a faulty prospectus certified by the firm.[251] In denying class certification, the Supreme Court said that 'certification of a large class may so increase the defendant's potential damages liability and litigation costs that he may find it economically prudent to settle and to abandon a meritorious defense.'[252] Picking up on the Court's ruling in *Livesay*, the Third Circuit, in *Newton v. Merrill Lynch*,[253] held that where 'there are hundreds of thousands of class members,'[254] 'the size of the class and number of claims may place acute and unwarranted pressure on defendants to settle.'[255] A number of other courts have also discussed the problems of an excessively large class and blackmail settlements.[256] In recognizing that the pressure to settle is problematic in class action lawsuits, it is surprising, to say the least,

---

[249] A recent article reported that Wal-Mart is seeking to settle this case, but no settlement amounts have been made public. See Justin Scheck, 'Wal-Mart Said to Be in Talks to Settle Huge Class Action', at <www.law.com/jsp/article.jsp?id=1110202461600> (last visited October 15, 2005).
[250] Fed. R. Civ. P. 23(a).
[251] *Coopers & Lybrand v. Livesay*, 437 US 463, 465 (1978).
[252] *Id.* at 476.
[253] *Newton v. Merrill Lynch, Pierce, Fenner & Smith, Inc.*, 259 F.3d 154 (3rd Cir. 2001).
[254] *Id.* at 182.
[255] *Id.* at 168 n. 8.
[256] See e.g., *Parker v. Time Warner Entm't. Co.*, 331 F.3d 13, 22 (2nd Cir. 2003) ('It may be that the aggregation in a class action of large numbers of statutory damages claims...could create a potentially enormous aggregate recovery for plaintiffs, and thus an in terrorem effect on defendants, which may induce unfair settlements.') (emphasis in original); In re Bridgestone/Firestone Inc., 288 F.3d at 1012, 1015–1016 ('Aggregating millions of claims...makes the case so unwieldy, and the stakes so large, that settlement becomes almost inevitable.').

CHAPTER 6. A CLASSLESS ACT

that neither the defense nor the court in *Dukes* addressed the issue in motions filed or the opinion rendered. However, in June 2004, the Ninth Circuit, agreed to hear an interlocutory appeal of this case[257] pursuant to Rule 23(f), so it is possible, if not quite likely, that the Ninth Circuit will address this issue given the purpose of Rule 23(f) as described in the Advisory Committee Notes.[258]

6.8 A PROPOSED GUIDE FOR CERTIFYING EMPLOYMENT CLASS ACTIONS

The guide that I propose for class certifications is based on the holdings of other circuits. By way of a brief outline, I propose five issues that courts should address when deciding whether or not to certify a class. The first issue deals with why courts should utilize a standard closer to 'rigorous analysis'[259] than to 'broad discretion'[260] when deciding whether or not to certify a class. The second issue involves whether or not a court should hold a parent company liable for the actions of individual managers if the individual manager is responsible for decision-making. I identify examples of cases where individuals brought successful and unsuccessful lawsuits against Wal-Mart for sexual discrimination and explain why such an avenue is more appropriate than a class action lawsuit. Next, I recommend that courts consider the realities of certifying a huge class in relation to the commonality requirement. I then propose that courts carefully consider the requirements for typicality in the context of large class action lawsuits so as to ensure that the requirements are truly met. Finally, I discuss the importance of considering the possible impact that class certification can have on settlement negotiations and the issue of blackmail settlements.

A number of courts have proposed various levels of scrutiny when making a decision regarding class certification. The levels

---

[257] Bob Egelko, Review OKd in Wal-Mart Case: Court to Rule on Class-Action Status of Sex-Bias Lawsuit, S. F. CHRON., August 14, 2004, at A-14.
[258] Fed. R. Civ. P. 23(f) advisory committee's note.
[259] *Gen. Tel. Co. of the Southwest v. Falcon*, 457 US 147, 162 (1982); *Zinser v. Accufix Research Inst., Inc.*, 253 F.3d 1180, 1186 (9th Cir. 2001), amended 275 F.3d 1266 (9th Cir. 2001).
[260] *Dukes v. Wal-Mart Stores, Inc.*, 222 F.R.D. 137, 143 (N.D. Cal. 2004) (citing *Armstrong v. Davis*, 275 F.3d 849, 871 n. 28 (9th Cir. 2001)).

range from 'broad discretion,'[261] which the *Dukes* court used, to 'rigorous analysis,'[262] as the Supreme Court prescribed. When deciding between these two extremes, the Court gave lower courts guidance by stating that class action lawsuits are 'an exception to the usual rule that litigation is conducted by and on behalf of the individual named parties only.'[263] This note proposes that, because class action lawsuits are the exception to the rule, courts should utilize a higher degree of scrutiny than 'broad discretion.'[264] The *Dukes* court tries to leave itself some breathing room by stating that it could reconsider 'certification throughout the legal proceedings before the court.'[265] In a study sponsored by the Federal Judicial Center, though, the Center strongly suggested that once a court certifies a class, it is unlikely that a court will go back and decertify it based on 'traditional rulings on motions or trials.'[266] Therefore, rather than relying on an escape hatch, courts should acknowledge the purpose of a class action lawsuit and rigorously analyze a motion for class certification.

In numerous cases, courts have declined to certify the class either when a class attempted to hold a corporate parent liable for the actions of an individual store, or when the corporate parent had little or no control over the individual store or unit.[267] In each of these cases, the corporation had a policy of decentralized decision-making and the courts found that as a result of this policy, it was inappropriate to hold the corporate parent liable for decisions made in an individual store. A more appropriate method of adjudication in these types of cases is for individual plaintiffs to bring individual lawsuits against a particular store.

Several cases exist where Wal-Mart employees successfully sued individual stores for sexual harassment. In *Dudley v. Wal-Mart Stores,*

---

[261] *Id.*

[262] Falcon, 457 US at 162; Zinser, 253 F.3d at 1186.

[263] *Id.* at 155 (quoting *Califano v. Yamasaki*, 442 US 682, 700–701 (1979)).

[264] *Dukes*, 222 F.R.D. at 143 (citing *Armstrong v. Davis*, 275 F.3d 849, 872 n. 28 (9th Cir. 2001)).

[265] *Id.*

[266] See Willging et al., *supra*, at 80.

[267] See *Rhodes v. Cracker Barrel Old Country Store, Inc.*, 213 F.R.D. 619 (N.D. Ga. 2003); *Reid v. Lockheed Martin Aeronautics Co.*, 205 F.R.D. 655 (N.D. Ga. 2001); *Donaldson v. Microsoft Corp.*, 205 F.R.D. 558 (W.D. Wash. 2001); *Zachery v. Texaco Exploration & Prod., Inc.*, 185 F.R.D. 230 (W.D. Tex. 1999).

CHAPTER 6. A CLASSLESS ACT

Inc., the court consolidated thirteen plaintiffs' cases, all of whom alleged racial discrimination against a single Wal-Mart store.[268] At trial, a jury found in favor of two of the eleven plaintiffs, awarding them a total of USD 375,000.[269] Of course, a number of employees' claims failed, but that is to be expected, just as in any other lawsuit. In *Moulds v. Wal-Mart Stores, Inc.*, plaintiffs alleged racial and sexual discrimination against a Wal-Mart store.[270] The Eleventh Circuit found for Wal-Mart on the grounds that it had a legitimate reason for choosing another employee for promotion over plaintiff.[271] It is apparent, therefore, that plaintiffs do have the ability to challenge Wal-Mart's practices and win, but on a scale that is far more manageable than 1.5 million women.

The numerosity requirement appears to act as a double-edged sword. A class wants to be sufficiently large so as to satisfy the numerosity requirement; however, if a class is too large, there are potential issues of manageability and commonality that could preclude certification. Many other courts have identified class diversity as, at least, a partial reason for denying certification.[272] As the class size gets larger, there is less of a chance that every class member suffered from the same discrimination. The court in *Donaldson* stated that 'where a putative class involves extensive diversity in terms of geography, job requirements, or managerial responsibilities'[273] commonality does not exist.[274] By tying the issue of commonality to numerosity, the *Donaldson* court demonstrated that, while a large class fulfilled the numerosity requirement of Rule 23,[275] it was ultimately class diversity that caused the court to find that the class lacked commonality.

In the employment context, it is very difficult to fulfill the typicality requirement, as it is nearly impossible to prove that a large class of plaintiffs all suffered from a common policy of discrimination. This is especially true when a corporation uses a decentralized subjective decision-making process. If a plaintiff claims that he/she was subjected

---

[268] *Dudley v. Wal-Mart Stores, Inc.*, 166 F.3d 1317, 1319 (11th Cir. 1999).
[269] *Id.*
[270] *Moulds v. Wal-Mart Stores, Inc.*, 935 F.2d 252 (11th Cir. 1991).
[271] *Id.* at 256–267.
[272] See Reid, 205 F.R.D. at 666; Donaldson, 205 F.R.D. at 567; Zachery, 185 F.R.D. at 239–240.
[273] Donaldson, 205 F.R.D. at 567.
[274] *Id.*
[275] *Id.* at 565.

to discrimination on a local level, due to subjective decision-making procedures, then that is evidence of an 'individual disparate treatment claim,'[276] but insufficient for class action status.[277] The Supreme Court raised the legal standard by requiring 'significant proof'[278] if the subjective decision-making process is used as a basis for class certification.[279] If courts are to certify a class based on a claim that a corporation used subjective decision-making procedures, then plaintiffs should either have to offer evidence revealed during discovery or present expert witness testimony that is scrutinized using a *Daubert* analysis. In this way, a court would fulfill the directive of the Supreme Court to obtain 'significant proof'[280] of the plaintiffs' claims.

Courts finally must acknowledge that if they certify a large class, most plaintiffs will settle the case, rather than leave their fate to the flip of a coin. A number of courts have refused to certify or have even decertified a class when they believed that certification would force the defendant to settle.[281] Courts, therefore, must ensure that the plaintiffs have viable claims, and if they do, that the parties have exhausted all settlement possibilities before deciding on class certification.[282]

6.9 CONCLUSION

The Ninth Circuit's decision in *Dukes* is an excellent example of a class action certification gone wrong. In certifying the class, the court ignored the Supreme Court's decree that class action lawsuits are the exception to the rule.[283] The court mischaracterizes Wal-Mart's

---

[276] Zachery, 185 F.R.D. at 238.
[277] *Id.*
[278] Falcon, 457 US at 159 n. 15 (1982).
[279] *Id.* See also Chamblee, *supra.*
[280] Falcon, 457 US at 159 n. 15.
[281] "'Hydraulic pressure...to settle' is now a recognized objection to class certification." Charles Silver, "We're Scared to Death": Class Certification and Blackmail, 78 N.Y.U. L. REV. 1357, 1358 (2003) (quoting *Newton v. Merrill Lynch, Pierce, Fenner & Smith, Inc.,* 259 F.3d 154, 164 (3rd Cir. 2001)).
[282] See Fed. R. Civ. P. 1 (The purpose of the Rules is 'to secure the just, speedy, and inexpensive determination of every action.') Encouraging parties to settle avoids a long, drawn-out litigation process.
[283] Falcon, 457 US at 155 (citing *Califano v. Yamasaki,* 442 US 682, 700–701 (1979)).

CHAPTER 6. A CLASSLESS ACT

intentions as trying to 'insulate'[284] itself merely because of the lawsuit's size, when, in reality, Wal-Mart's main concern is the manageability of the case.[285] Protecting and ensuring women's rights is a noble and worthy cause, but it does not outweigh legal precedent. Rather than certifying the class, which will most likely force Wal-Mart to settle, unless the class is decertified on appeal, the court would have better served these women by denying class certification and suggesting that they pursue their cases on a smaller, more manageable scale. By bringing their actions individually, these plaintiffs would have their claims heard and the litigation would be conducted in its normal fashion, namely 'by and behalf of the individual named parties only.'[286]

---

[284] *Dukes v. Wal-Mart Stores, Inc.*, 222 F.R.D. 137, 142 (N.D. Cal. 2004).
[285] See Def.'s Opp'n to Mot. For Class Certification, at 5, *Dukes v. Wal-Mart, Inc.* (N.D. Ca. 2003) (No. C-01-2252 MJJ).
Even if plaintiffs could survive Rule 23(a), they cannot survive Rule 23(b). Plaintiffs essentially argue that it is irrelevant whether this litigation is manageable or not because they are invoking Rule 23(b)(2). Plaintiffs are wrong. The Ninth Circuit, in a discrimination case involving a class of 15,000 (just 1% of the alleged class herein), disapproved a settlement and remanded, directing the district court to consider manageability if the case proceeded at all: 'We have some concerns, largely relating to litigation management, as to whether the case could be maintained as a class action if the litigation continues.' *Id.* (quoting *Staton v. Boeing Co.*, 327 F.3d 938, 953 (9th Cir. 2003)).
[286] Falcon, 457 US at 155 (citing Califano, 442 US at 701).

CHAPTER 7

Too Many Riches? *Dukes v. Wal-Mart* and the Efficacy of Monolithic Class Actions

Rachel M. Pickens*

7.1 INTRODUCTION

In May 1994, Betty Dukes secured employment as a cashier at the Wal-Mart store in Pittsburg, California.[1] For the next three years, Dukes advanced in the store and received salary increases and positive reviews.[2] However, in September 1997, Dukes' positive Wal-Mart experience came to an abrupt end when she 'began to experience harsh and discriminatory treatment' from the customer service manager and the store manager.[3] Dukes eventually complained about this discriminatory treatment to the district manager, but was rebuffed.[4] After complaining, Dukes suffered retaliation from store management, culminating in her demotion.[5] When Dukes was again eligible for

---

* Rachel M. Pickens is an Associate Attorney at McDermott Newman PLLC. She holds a J.D. from Chapman University School of Law.
** This paper was previously published by the University of Detroit Mercy Law Review, 'Too Many Riches? Dukes v.Wal-Mart and Efficacy of Monolithic Class Actions', by Rachel Tallon Pickens, 83 U.Det.Mercy L.Rev.71.
[1] *Plaintiffs' First Amended Complaint P 29, Dukes v. Wal-Mart Stores, Inc., 222 F.R.D. 137 (N.D. Cal. 2004) (No. C-01-2252 MJJ), 2001 WL 34134868.*
[2] *Ibid.*
[3] *Id.*, 30.
[4] *Id.*, 31.
[5] *Id.*, 33.

David Sherwyn and Samuel Estreicher (eds), *Employment Class and Collective Actions*, pp. 329–352.
© University of Detroit Mercy Law Review [and Joe Christiansen, Inc.].
Reprinted with permission.

promotion, '[she] was discouraged from seeking other positions because of the way she and other women had been treated by Wal-Mart.'[6] Dukes exhausted her administrative remedies by filing charges with the California Department of Fair Employment and Housing (DFEH) and the United States Equal Employment Opportunity Commission.[7] Subsequently, Dukes chose to take legal action against Wal-Mart. Dukes' decision was the first step in the largest employment discrimination lawsuit in United States history.[8]

On June 19, 2001, Dukes and five former and current female employees filed suit against Wal-Mart Stores, Inc., alleging workplace bias.[9] Three years later, the United States District Court for the Northern District of California certified a class composed of 'all women employed [at] any Wal-Mart domestic retail store at any time since December 26, 1998, who have been or may be subjected to Wal-Mart's challenged pay and management track promotions policies and practices.'[10]

Following entry of the district court's certification order, Wal-Mart sought review of the same by the United States Court of Appeals for the Ninth Circuit.[11] The Ninth Circuit granted certiorari[12] and heard oral argument on August 8, 2005.[13] At the time this article was initially prepared, the Ninth Circuit had not issued a decision. This article suggests that the district court's order certifying the class against Wal-Mart should stand. Specifically, this article will address the numerical extent of class actions to determine whether *Dukes v. Wal-Mart* exceeds the same.

---

[6] *Id.*, 37.

[7] *Id.*, 39–40.

[8] *Dukes v. Wal-Mart Stores, Inc.*, 222 F.R.D. 137, 141–42 (N.D. Cal. 2004).

[9] *Plaintiffs' First Amended Complaint, supra* n. 1, 1. Wal-Mart operates approximately 3,400 stores nationally and employs more than one million people. *Dukes*, 222 F.R.D. at 141.

[10] *Dukes*, 222 F.R.D. at 188.

[11] Press Release, The Impact Fund, Plaintiffs Oppose Wal-Mart's Request for Immediate Appeal of Class Certification Ruling in Nation-wide Sex Discrimination Case (July 19, 2004), available at <www.impactfund.org/pages/press1/prs/071904.htm>.

[12] Bob Egelko, Review OKd in Wal-Mart Case, S. F. Chronicle, August 14, 2004, at A14, available at <www.sfgate.com/cgi-bin/article.cgi?file=/chronicle/archive/2004/08/14/MNG0H87RF71.DTL>.

[13] David Kravets, Wal-Mart, Facing Billions in Damages, Wants Bias Case Tossed, North County Times, August 5, 2005, available at <www.nctimes.com/articles/2005/08/06/business/news/15_13_578_5_05.txt>. See also United States Court of Appeals for the Ninth Circuit, <www.ca9.uscourts.gov/> (last visited November 23, 2005) (audio recording of the oral arguments).

The author maintains that the sheer size of a putative class is not prohibitive of a class action. Rather, where a large class seeks to be certified, manageability is the sine qua non for certification. Since the manageability of a class action often requires inquiry into the facts of the proposed action, the district courts are best suited to determine the efficacy of monolithic class actions. Absent clear error in the manageability determination, monolithic class actions certified by the district courts should stand. Accordingly, the Ninth Circuit should not reverse the *Dukes v. Wal-Mart* certification decision.

First, the general principles of federal class actions will be discussed. Specifically, section 7.2 will set forth the prerequisites and requirements of a class action under *Federal Rule of Civil Procedure 23*. Likewise, this article will address the manageability concept used in class action certification decisions. Section 7.3 will set forth the procedural history of *Dukes v. Wal-Mart*. Section 7.4 suggests a formulation for determination of when a class action is too large based upon manageability standards. Finally, section 7.5 sets forth an argument for maintaining *Dukes v. Wal-Mart* and other monolithic class actions.

7.1.1 Addendum

On February 6, 2007, the United States Court of Appeals for the Ninth Circuit upheld the District Court's certification decision in *Dukes v. Wal-Mart*. The Ninth Circuit noted that the case 'involves the largest certified class in history'. *Dukes v. Wal-Mart*, 509 F.3d 1168, 1190 (C.A. 9, 2007). However, the Court found that the class size did not render the class unmanageable. *Id.* The Court therefore declined to create a per se rule regarding the numerical limit of putative classes. Therefore, the Ninth Circuit's decision allows manageability to be the touchstone of class action certification decisions.

7.2 CLASS ACTIONS GENERALLY

Class actions allow courts to resolve common claims of general interest in a single action.[14] Class actions are controversial procedural

---

[14] David Hill Koysza, Preventing Defendants from Mooting Class Actions by Picking off Named Plaintiffs, 53 *Duke L.J.* 781 (2003) (citing *Fed. R. Civ. P. 23* advisory committee's note (1937)).

devices that are the topic of tremendous debate.[15] The class action mechanism has come under attack as a viable procedural device for forcing compliance with the law. There is 'a significant and increasing hostility to the class action mechanism' prevalent today.[16] Indeed, legal scholarship is replete with writings which castigate the class action. Noted jurists and scholars, including Henry Friendly, Richard Posner, and Frank Easterbrook, claim that class actions create 'blackmail settlements.'[17] With regard to employment discrimination cases, scholars contend that the Civil Rights Act of 1991's[18] 'high damage limits ... have paved the way for "blackmail" class actions.'[19]

Nevertheless, the class action mechanism promotes several public policies. First, class actions encourage judicial economy and maximize efficiency by preventing duplicative lawsuits and preventing inconsistent adjudications.[20] Likewise, class actions have social utility insofar as

---

[15] See e.g., Martin H. Redish, Class Actions and the Democratic Difficulty: Rethinking the Intersection between Private Litigation and Public Goals, *2003 U. Chi. Legal F. 71 (2003)* (noting that the class action 'in recent years ... has become the focal point of much political and legal debate').

[16] Stephen D. Susman, Class Actions: Consumer Sword Turned Corporate Shield, *2003 U. Chi. Legal F. 1*, 2 (2003).

[17] See Charles Silver, 'We're Scared to Death': Class Certification and Blackmail, *78 N.Y.U L. Rev. 1357*, 1357–1359 (2003); see also Henry J. Friendly, Federal Jurisdiction: A General View 120 (1973) (wherein Friendly argues that class actions create 'blackmail settlements'). Friendly believes that the aggregation of small claims, not large enough to bring on an individual basis, create tremendous exposure for a corporate defendant who is forced to settle the claim without reference to the merits. Silver, *supra*, at 1362–1363. Friendly likewise maintains that such settlements do not benefit the claimants because the individual recoveries are usually very small. *Id.* at 1362. Posner, Chief Judge of the Seventh Circuit, has decertified a class to protect an industry from bankruptcy. See *In re Rhone-Poulenc Rorer, Inc., 51 F.3d 1293*, 1299–1300 (7th Cir. 1995).

[18] Civil Rights Act of 1991, Pub. L. No. 102–166, 1745, 105 Stat. 1071, *42 U.S.C. 1981* (2003).

[19] Daniel F. Piar, The Uncertain Future of Title VII Class Actions After the Civil Rights Act of 1991, *2001 BYU L. Rev. 305*, 314 (2001).

[20] See e.g., *Buford v. Am. Fin. Co., 333 F. Supp. 1243 (N.D. Ga. 1971)*; *Schrader v. Selective Serv. Sys. Local Bd., 329 F. Supp. 966 (W.D. Wis. 1971)*; *Hernandez v. Motor Vessel Skyward, 61 F.R.D. 558 (S.D. Fla. 1973)*; *In re Four Seasons Sec. Laws Litig., 63 F.R.D. 422 (W.D. Okla. 1974)*; *Mungin v. Fla. E. Coast Ry. Co., 318 F. Supp. 720 (M.D. Fla. 1970)*; *Kekich v. Travelers Indem. Co., 64 F.R.D. 660 (W.D. Pa. 1974)*; *Haley v. Medtronic, Inc., 169 F.R.D. 643 (C.D. Cal. 1996)*; *Green v. Wolf Corp., 406 F.2d 291 (2nd Cir. 1968)*; *N. Acceptance Trust 1065 v. AMFAC, Inc., 51 F.R.D. 487 (D. Haw. 1971)*.

CHAPTER 7. TOO MANY RICHES

they allow an aggregation of private individuals to enforce laws.[21] Moreover, class actions allow numerous individuals who have been slightly harmed to bring a single action to protect their rights.[22] In such situations, bringing a civil case to vindicate wrongs or enforce rights is often cost prohibitive, as it would cost more money to prosecute the case than would be recovered.[23] Proponents of the class action mechanism argue that class actions further public interests, as the defendant bears the costs of the harm and the recovery deters future transgressions.[24] Indeed, class actions 'provide a mechanism for the economic and expeditious disposal of those claims subsequently brought to court, as claims need not be litigated on an individual basis.'[25]

Class actions have particular utility in the civil rights arena, as they offer a vehicle for rectifying civil rights abuses. Courts have found that class actions are 'preferable' to individual actions brought under Title VII of the Civil Rights Act of 1964.[26] In the Civil Rights Act of 1991,[27] Title VII was expanded to include compensatory and punitive damages to victims.[28] Nevertheless, the 1991 amendments to Title VII did not diminish the efficacy of class actions in civil rights cases. In fact, the Federal Rules Advisory Committee explicitly noted that broad civil rights cases are appropriate under Rule 23.[29]

---

[21] Redish, *supra* n. 15, at 87–88 (noting that 'private class actions for money damages can yield significant social benefits').

[22] *Id.* (citing Ryan Patrick Phair, Resolving the 'Choice-of-Law Problem' in Rule 23(b)(3) Nationwide Class Actions, *67 U. Chi. L. Rev. 835, 837 (2000)* ('By spreading the costs of litigation across a class, a greater number of litigants are able to pool their resources in an effort to vindicate their rights.')).

[23] John Bronsteen & Owen Fiss, The Class Action Rule, *78 Notre Dame L. Rev. 1419 (2003)*.

[24] Id. at 1419–1422. Bronsteen & Fiss agree that class actions serve important public policies, but argue that Rule 23 is insufficient to protect against risks of abuse. As such, they argue that Rule 23 should continue to be amended. *Id. at 1419–1421.*

[25] Chris Brummer, Sharpening the Sword: Class Certification, Appellate Review, and the Role of the Fiduciary Judge in Class Action Lawsuits, *104 Colum. L. Rev. 1042, 1046 (2004)*.

[26] Civil Rights Act of 1964, Pub. L. No. 88–352, Title VII, 78 Stat. 241 (1964), *42 U.S.C. 2000e (2003)*. See e.g., *Hill v. Am. Airlines, Inc., 479 F.2d 1057, 1059–1060 (5th Cir. 1973)*.

[27] Civil Rights Act of 1991, Pub. L. No. 102–166, 1745, 105 Stat. 1071, *42 U.S.C. 1981 (2003)*.

[28] Piar, *supra* n. 19.

[29] Fed. R. Civ. P. 23(b) advisory committee's notes ('Illustrative [of a (b)(2) class] are various actions in the civil rights field where a party is charged with discriminating unlawfully against a class').

7.2.1 Rule 23

Rule 23 of the Federal Rules of Civil Procedure sets forth the requirements for a federal class action.[30] Rule 23(a) establishes the prerequisites for a class action, which are commonly referred to as numerosity, commonality, typicality, and adequacy.[31] In *General Telephone Co. of the Southwest v. Falcone*, the Supreme Court mandated strict compliance with Rule 23(a).[32] Nevertheless, courts often interpret Rule 23 liberally.[33] For instance, to satisfy the numerosity prerequisite, the class would have to be 'so numerous that joinder of all of the members is impracticable.'[34] There is no set number of class members required to satisfy the numerosity requirement; rather, 'whether joinder is impracticable depends on the facts and circumstances of each case.'[35] Courts have recognized that numerosity is not a 'strict numerical test.'[36] The plain language of Rule 23(a) suggests that numerosity requires a certain minimum number; the rule itself places no numerical limit on the size of a class.

The remaining prerequisites for a class action – commonality, typicality, and adequacy – are aimed at 'insuring that the named plaintiff [or plaintiffs] can be trusted to represent the interests of his fellow class members.'[37] The commonality prerequisite requires that there be

---

[30] *Fed. R. Civ. P. 23.*

[31] *Fed. R. Civ. P. 23(a).*

[32] *457 U.S. 147 (1982).*

[33] *Black v. Rhone-Poulenc, Inc., 173 F.R.D. 156, 159 (S.D. W. Va. 1996)* ('The recent trend in class certification decisions is to interpret Rule 23 flexibly and give it a liberal construction.') (citing *Kidwell v. Transp. Communs. Int'l Union, 946 F.2d 283, 305 (4th Cir. 1991),* cert. denied, *503 U.S. 1005 (1992)).*

[34] *Id.* (quoting *Brady v. Thurston Motor Lines, 726 F.2d 136, 145 (4th Cir. 1984)).* The numerosity requirement operates to 'limit class actions to circumstances in which they are necessary to uphold a value that is important enough to justify the dangers to absent class members inherent in any class action.' Bronsteen & Fiss, *supra* n. 23, at 1423.

[35] *Dukes v. Wal-Mart Stores, Inc., 222 F.R.D. 137, 144 (N.D. Cal. 2004)* (quoting *Arnold v. United Artists Theatre Circuit, Inc., 158 F.R.D. 439, 448 (N.D. Cal. 1994));* see also *Pederson v. La. State Univ., 201 F.3d 388, 397 n. 11 (5th Cir. 2000)* (noting that trial courts conducting numerosity analyses 'must not focus on sheer numbers alone').

[36] *Bittinger v. Tecumseh Prod. Co., 123 F.3d 877, 884 n.1 (6th Cir. 1997).*

[37] Bronsteen & Fiss, *supra* n. 23, at 1424.

'questions of law or fact common to the class.'[38] As applied, the commonality prerequisite is not rigorous. In fact, courts have consistently held that the commonality prerequisite 'is not demanding.'[39]

The typicality prerequisite requires that the claims of the named plaintiff be typical of the claims of the class as a whole.[40] Like the commonality prerequisite, the typicality requirement is not stringently applied.[41] Indeed, the claims of the class representatives need not be identical to the class as a whole; rather, a 'strong similarity of legal theories' suffices.[42]

The adequacy prerequisite requires that the class representatives 'fairly and adequately protect the interests of the class.'[43] Unlike the other prerequisites, the adequacy requirement is somewhat stringent. Courts will find that the adequacy requirement is not satisfied where a conflict of interest or a potential conflict exists, or if the class representative is not trustworthy.[44]

Once the prerequisites to a class action have been satisfied, the court must find that the case meets the criteria of Rule 23(b) to certify a class action.[45] Rule 23(b) requires that the matter fall within one of

---

[38] Fed. R. Civ. P. 23(a)(2).

[39] *Mullen v. Treasure Chest Casino, L.L.C.*, 186 F.3d 620, 625 (5th Cir. 1999), cert. denied, 528 U.S. 1159 (2000); see also *Keele v. Wexler*, 149 F.3d 589, 594 (7th Cir. 1998) (noting that 'factual variations among class members' grievances do not defeat a class action'); *Hanlon v. Chrysler Corp.*, 150 F.3d 1011 (9th Cir. 1998) (stating that the requirement of commonality is 'minimal'); *Lightbourn v. County of El Paso*, 118 F.3d 421, 426 (5th Cir. 1997), cert. denied, 522 U.S. 1052 (1998) ('The commonality test is met when there is at least one issue, the resolution of which will affect all or a significant number of the putative class members.') (citing *Forbush v. J.C. Penney Co.*, 994 F.2d 1101, 1106 (5th Cir. 1993)).

[40] Fed. R. Civ. P. 23(a)(2).

[41] See e.g., *Lightbourn*, 118 F.3d at 426 (noting that the test for typicality 'is not demanding').

[42] *Appleyard v. Wallace*, 754 F.2d 955, 958 (11th Cir. 1985); see also *Paxton v. Union Nat'l Bank*, 688 F.2d 552, 561 (8th Cir. 1982) ('The rule does not require that every question of law or fact be common to every member of the class.').

[43] Fed. R. Civ. P. 23(a)(4).

[44] See e.g., *Retired Chicago Police Ass'n v. City of Chicago*, 7 F.3d 584, 598 (7th Cir. 1993), cert. denied, 519 U.S. 932 (1996); *Savino v. Computer Credit, Inc.*, 164 F.3d 81, 87 (2nd Cir. 1998) ('To judge the adequacy of representation, courts may consider the honesty and trustworthiness of the named plaintiff.'); see also Deborah L. Rhode, Class Conflicts in Class Actions, 34 Stan. L. Rev. 1183, 1186–1191 (1982).

[45] Fed. R. Civ. P. 23(b).

three situations to maintain a class action.[46] The first category of maintainable class actions covers situations where separate actions would create a risk of inconsistent adjudications.[47] The second category of maintainable class actions occurs where an individual action would be 'dispositive of the interests' of individuals not party to the litigation.[48] The third category allows class actions where injunctive relief is appropriate because the defendant has acted on 'grounds generally applicable to the class.'[49] This final category is referred to as Rule

---

[46] *Id.* ss. b provides:

> (b) Class Actions Maintainable. An action may be maintained as a class action if the prerequisites of subdivision (a) are satisfied, and in addition:
> (1) the prosecution of separate actions by or against individual members of the class would create a risk of
>   (A) inconsistent or varying adjudications with respect to individual members of the class which would establish incompatible standards of conduct for the party opposing the class, or
>   (B) adjudications with respect to individual members of the class which would as a practical matter be dispositive of the interests of the other members not parties to the adjudications or substantially impair or impede their ability to protect their interests; or
> (2) the party opposing the class has acted or refused to act on grounds generally applicable to the class, thereby making appropriate final injunctive relief or corresponding declaratory relief with respect to the class as a whole; or
> (3) the court finds that the questions of law or fact common to the members of the class predominate over any questions affecting only individual members, and that a class action is superior to other available methods for the fair and efficient adjudication of the controversy. The matters pertinent to the findings include:
>   (A) the interest of members of the class in individually controlling the prosecution or defense of separate actions;
>   (B) the extent and nature of any litigation concerning the controversy already commenced by or against members of the class;
>   (C) the desirability or undesirability of concentrating the litigation of the claims in the particular forum;
>   (D) the difficulties likely to be encountered in the management of a class action.

[47] Fed. R. Civ. P. 23(b)(1)(A).
[48] Fed. R. Civ. P. 23(b)(1)(B).
[49] Fed. R. Civ. P. 23(b)(2).

23(b)(3)'s 'catch-all' provision.[50] Pursuant to the same, a class action may be maintained where common questions of law or fact predominate over individual claims and the class action mechanism is superior to alternative methods for dispute resolution.[51]

7.2.2 Class Action Manageability

When a class is certified under Rule 23(b)(3), concerns about manageability arise.[52] Subsection (D) of Rule 23(b)(3) mandates that the district court consider 'the difficulties likely to be encountered in the management of a class action.'[53] Subsection (D) essentially requires the district court to determine whether the proposed class action is manageable in light of 'the whole range of practical problems that may render the class action format inappropriate for a particular suit.'[54]

Courts are divided as to whether manageability is properly considered under Rule 23(b)(2).[55] The Fourth Circuit[56] and several district courts have held that manageability concerns are appropriate considerations under Rule 23(b)(2) certification decisions.[57] These courts found that manageability concerns are appropriate in part because they ensure that certified class actions are efficient.[58] Likewise,

---

[50] Melissa Hart, Will Employment Discrimination Class Actions Survive?, 37 *Akron L. Rev.* 813, 816 (2004) (citing 8 Alba Conte & Herbert B. Newberg, Newberg on Class Actions 24:81, at 315 (4th edn 2003)).

[51] *Fed. R. Civ. P. 23(b)(3).*

[52] *Fed. R. Civ. P. 23(b)(3)(D).*

[53] *Fed. R. Civ. P. 23(b)(3)(D).*

[54] *Eisen v. Carlisle & Jacquelin,* 417 U.S. 156, 164 (1974).

[55] *Shook v. El Paso County,* 386 F.3d 963, 972–973 (10th Cir. 2004) ('The circuits do not speak with one voice on whether courts may look to manageability considerations in evaluating Rule 23(b)(2) class certification.').

[56] *Lowery v. Circuit City Stores, Inc.,* 158 F.3d 742, 757–759 (4th Cir. 1998), vacated, 527 U.S. 1031 (1999).

[57] *Id.* at 758 (citing 7B Charles Alan Wright, Arthur R. Miller, & Mary Kay Kane, Federal Practice and Procedure 1785, at 119, 122 (2nd edn, 1986 and Supp.1998) ('some courts have ruled it is appropriate to take account of considerations not expressly addressed in Rule 23, including manageability in Rule 23(b)(2) cases')).

[58] *Id. at 759* (noting that because 'efficiency is one of the primary purposes of class action procedure...in appropriate circumstances a district court may exercise its discretion to deny certification if the resulting class action would be unmanageable or cumbersome.').

adherents to this view believe that the district courts are best situated to assess any potential manageability problems.[59] Several other courts have followed the *Lowery* decision.[60] On the contrary, the Fifth and Ninth Circuits have held that manageability is not a proper consideration for Rule 23(b)(2) class action certification decisions.[61] Courts adhering to this view rely upon the plain text of Rule 23. Rule 23 'makes manageability an issue important only in determining the propriety of certifying an action as a (b)(3), not a (b)(2), class action.'[62]

When assessing the manageability of class actions, the district court may consider a variety of issues. Manageability analyses often require inquiries into the facts of the proposed class action. In fact, courts often assess the nature of the proposed class, the computation of damages, and the mechanics of administering the suit in determining manageability.[63] Under the auspices of Title VII,[64] manageability means 'the logistical difficulties attendant to trying the individualized damages claims of hundreds or even thousands of class members.'[65] Where a court finds that a proposed class action is unmanageable, claims that the class action is superior to other adjudications are untenable.[66] Accordingly, manageability is the sine qua non for class action maintainability.

---

[59] *Ibid.*

[60] See *Shook*, 386 F.3d at 973 (citing *Walsh v. Ford Motor Co.*, 807 F.2d 1000, 1019 n. 111 (D.C. Cir. 1986); *Simer v. Rios*, 661 F.2d 655, 669 n. 24 (7th Cir. 1981); *Seidel v. Gen. Motors Acceptance Corp.*, 93 F.R.D. 122, 126 (W.D. Wash. 1981); *Duncan v. Tennessee*, 84 F.R.D. 21, 34 (M.D. Tenn. 1979)).

[61] *Ibid.*, see also *Forbrush v. J.C. Penney Co.*, 994 F.2d 1101, 1105 (5th Cir. 1993); *Elliott v. Weinberger*, 564 F.2d 1219 (9th Cir. 1977), aff'd in pertinent part sub nom. *Califano v. Yamasaki*, 442 U.S. 682, 701 (1979).

[62] *Elliott*, 564 F.2d at 1229.

[63] George T. Anagnost, Notice and Manageability Requirements Interpreted in Class Actions, 48 Tul. L. Rev. 726 (1974).

[64] Civil Rights Act of 1964, Pub. L. No. 88–352, Title VII, 78 Stat. 241 (1964), 42 U.S.C. 2000e (2003).

[65] Piar, *supra* n. 19, at 330.

[66] See *Perez v. Metabolife Int'l, Inc.*, 218 F.R.D. 262, 273 (S.D. Fla. 2003) ('Severe manageability problems are a prime consideration that can defeat a claim of superiority.').

CHAPTER 7. TOO MANY RICHES

One potential manageability problem is posed by nationwide class actions where choice of law problems may exist.[67] Another manageability concern is the number of class members. Interestingly, a large class does not necessarily militate against manageability. In *Smith v. Texaco*, the court certified a 200-member class in a racial discrimination case.[68] The *Smith* court noted that failing to certify the proposed class would mean 'this one district court will be totally and fully occupied for the larger part of at least 200 weeks in the trial of these claims alone.'[69] Accordingly, the court found that the class action mechanism would provide the best and most efficient means for managing the case.[70]

7.2.3 Certification Decisions

Traditionally, employment discrimination class actions are 'certified under 23(b)(2) because they typically involve a request by a group of plaintiffs that the defendant employer be enjoined from further discriminatory conduct.'[71] However, employment discrimination class actions have also been certified pursuant to the Rule 23(b)(3) 'catch-all' provision.[72]

The seminal class action certification, following the Civil Rights Acts of 1991, is the Fifth Circuit's decision in *Allison v. Citgo Petroleum Corp*.[73] The *Allison* plaintiffs brought suit against Citgo, alleging discriminatory hiring, promoting, training, and compensation practices.[74] In addition to declaratory, injunctive, and equitable relief, the *Allison* plaintiffs sought compensatory and punitive damages.[75] The *Allison*

---

[67] In *re Warfarin Sodium Antitrust Litig.*, 391 F.3d 516, 529 (3rd Cir. 2004) ('the district court must determine whether variations in state laws present the types of insuperable obstacles which render class action litigation unmanageable.'). See also *Amchem Products v. Windsor*, 521 U.S. 591 (1997).

[68] 88 F. Supp. 2d 663 (E.D. Tex. 2000). But see *Eisen v. Carlisle & Jacqueline*, 479 F.2d 1005, 1019 (2nd Cir. 1973) (noting in dicta that a vast and diversified class was unmanageable).

[69] *Smith*, 88 F. Supp. 2d at 682.

[70] *Id*. at 683.

[71] Hart, *supra* n. 50, at 816 (citing Conte & Newberg, *supra* n. 50, 24:81, at 315).

[72] *Ibid*.

[73] 151 F.3d 402 (5th Cir. 1998).

[74] *Id*. at 407.

[75] *Ibid*.

court denied certification of the class under Rule 23(b)(2), on the basis that the individual damages sought by the plaintiffs predominated over the equitable relief sought by the class as a whole.[76] Likewise, the court declined to certify the *Allison* class pursuant to Rule 23(b)(3) on the basis that the individual damages sought predominated over the common questions of law and fact.[77] Courts and scholars rely on *Allison* as the benchmark for class action certification.[78]

Determination of whether class certification is appropriate is largely discretionary.[79] The trial court has tremendous discretion to certify a class action where the mandates of Rule 23 are satisfied.[80] Indeed, trial courts are 'uniquely situated to make class certification decisions'[81] in light of the district courts' 'inherent power to manage and control pending litigation.'[82]

Although trial court judges are well situated to assess the efficacy of certification under Rule 23, courts of appeal may second guess district court judges' certification decisions. Rule 23(f) allows interlocutory appeals of certification decisions.[83] Section (f) was added to Rule 23 in the 1998 amendments to prevent settlement pressure.[84] The courts of appeal apply an abuse of discretion standard in assessing the district court's certification order.[85]

---

[76] *Id.* at 416.

[77] *Id.* at 420.

[78] See generally Hart, *supra* n. 50, at 825.

[79] See *Dukes v. Wal-Mart Stores, Inc.*, 222 F.R.D. 137, 143–144 (N.D. Cal. 2004) (noting that 'Rule 23 confers "broad discretion to determine whether a class should be certified"') (citations omitted); see also *Black v. Rhone-Poulenc, Inc.*, 173 F.R.D. 156, 159–160 (S.D. W. Va. 1996).

[80] *Dukes*, 222 F.R.D. at 143–144.

[81] *Id.* at 143 (citing *Hartman v. Duffy*, 19 F.3d 1459, 1471 (D.C. Cir. 1994) (citations omitted)).

[82] *Id.* at 143–144 (citing *In re Monumental Life Ins. Co.*, 365 F.3d 408, 414 (5th Cir. 2004)) (citations omitted).

[83] Fed. R. Civ. P. 23(f).

[84] Fed. R. Civ. P. 23(f) (advisory committee's notes); see also *Klay v. Humana, Inc.*, 382 F.3d 1241, 1275 (11th Cir. 2004) (noting that settlement 'pressures were the main reason behind the enactment of Rule 23(f)'); Brian Anderson & Patrick McLain, A Progress Report on Rule 23(f): Five Years of Immediate Class Certification Appeals, Legal Backgrounder, March 19, 2004, at 1.

[85] *Chiang v. Veneman*, 385 F.3d 256, 264 (3d Cir. 2004).

7.3 THE CASE AT BAR: *DUKES V. WAL-MART*

Wal-Mart is the largest corporation in the United States and the world's largest retailer.[86] Wal-Mart 'is three times the size of the No. 2 retailer, France's Carrefour. Every week, 138 million shoppers visit Wal-Mart's 4,750 stores; last year, 82% of American households made at least one purchase at Wal-Mart.'[87] Indeed, Wal-Mart dwarfs its domestic competitors: Wal-Mart's 2003 sales were four times greater than Home Depot and five times more than Target.[88] At 1.4 million employees, Wal-Mart is the country's largest private employer.[89] Unfortunately, the industry leader has also been dubbed the 'discrimination leader.'[90] Wal-Mart is alleged to subject its female employees to 'a sexually demeaning atmosphere, where female employees are told that "women do not make good managers," that "a trained monkey" could do their jobs, and that women with kids could not be managers.'[91]

Dukes v. Wal-Mart Stores, Inc. was filed in the Northern District of California on June 19, 2001.[92] Six current and former employees of Wal-Mart, on behalf of themselves and others similarly situated, brought the suit, alleging *inter alia* that the monolithic employer violated Title VII of the Civil Rights Act of 1964.[93] The stated purpose of the

---

[86] See e.g., Ritu Bhatnagar, *Dukes v. Wal-Mart* as a Catalyst for Social Change, 19 Berkeley Women's L.J. 246, 250 (2004) (citations omitted).

[87] Anthony Bianco & Wendy Zellner, Is Wal-Mart Too Powerful?, BusinessWeek, October 6, 2003, at 101, 102; see also Ellen Israel Rosen, The Wal-Mart Effect: The World Trade Organization and the Race to the Bottom, 8 Chap. L. Rev. 261, 262 (2005).

[88] See Rosen, *supra* n. 87, at 262 n. 4 (citing The Home Depot, Inc., 2003 Annual Report 1 (2004) ('showing 2003 fiscal sales were $ 64.8 billion'); Target Corp., 2003 Annual Report i (2004) ('showing total revenues for 2003 were $ 48.163 billion')).

[89] *Id.* at 262 n. 5 (citing Bianco & Zellner, *supra* n. 87, at 102).

[90] Press Release, Equal Rights Advocates, Wal-Mart Stores, Inc., the Nation's Largest Private Employer, Sued for Company-Wide Sex Discrimination (June 19, 2001), available at <www.walmartclass.com/staticdata/press_releases/r1.html> ('The industry leader should not be the discrimination leader. If Wal-Mart's top competitors are able to promote qualified women to more than half of their management jobs, why can't Wal-Mart?').

[91] *Ibid.*

[92] *Plaintiffs' First Amended Complaint, supra* note 1.

[93] *Id.*, 4–11. 'Title VII of the Civil Rights Act of 1964 prohibits discrimination in employment on the basis of race, sex, religion and national origin.' Hart, *supra* n. 50, at 815 (citing Civil Rights Act of 1964, 701–716, 78 Stat. 241, 253–266 (1964)

suit is to 'end...Wal-Mart's discriminatory practices, make whole relief for the class, and [to secure] punitive damages.'[94] In addition, plaintiffs' attorneys also hope to expose Wal-Mart's questionable labor practices and encourage labor reforms.[95]

The suit alleged that Wal-Mart engages in systematic and rampant gender discrimination in the workplace.[96] Specifically, plaintiffs alleged that 'Wal-Mart discriminates against its female employees by advancing males more quickly than female employees, by denying female employees equal job assignments, promotions, training and compensation, and by retaliating against those who oppose its unlawful practices.'[97] Plaintiffs' allegations relied heavily upon statistical data tending to corroborate their contentions. For instance, the First Amended Complaint alleged that the workforce is predominately female, but management positions are predominately staffed by male employees.[98] Moreover, plaintiffs alleged uneven distribution of employees throughout store departments in accordance with traditional gender roles – men are 'disproportionately assigned' to the 'furniture,...hardware, sporting

---

(current version at *42 U.S.C. 2000e-5* (2000)). Plaintiffs' First Amended Complaint also contained a claim under the California Fair Employment & Housing Act, *Cal. Gov't. Code 12940* (West 2004), alleging that Wal-Mart racially discriminated against *Plaintiff Dukes. Plaintiffs' First Amended Complaint, supra* note 1, P 4. For the purposes of this discussion, Plaintiff Dukes' individual claim for racial discrimination is not relevant.

[94] *Plaintiffs' First Amended Complaint, supra* n. 1, 3.

[95] Bhatnagar, *supra* n. 86, at 247 n. 17 (citing Telephone Interview by Ritu Bhatnagar with Jocelyn Larkin, Attorney, The Impact Fund (January 21, 2004); Telephone Interview by Ritu Bhatnagar with Debra Smith, Attorney, Equal Rights Advocates (January 20, 2004)). The reforms sought by plaintiffs' attorneys include 'paying more workers for overtime, revamping the entire hiring and promotions system, and improving the pay structure so that salaries are higher and assigned on a more objective basis.' *Id.* at 247. Debra Smith, one of plaintiffs' attorneys, noted, 'We are hoping that by hitting the largest retailer in the world...several of the 1.6 million [female employees] will be raised out of poverty and paid a living wage.' *Id.*

[96] Bhatnagar, *supra* n. 86, at 247.

[97] *Plaintiffs' First Amended Complaint, supra* n. 1, P 2.

[98] *Id.*, 1 (stating that women comprise 'over 72% of the hourly sales employees, yet only one-third of management positions.'). The First Amended Complaint also alleged that male employees comprise only 28% of hourly sales positions, 'yet hold[] two-thirds of all store management positions and over 90% of the top Store Manager positions.' *Id.*

goods, guns, produce, and stocking' departments, while women are assigned to the 'front-end cashier, customer service, health and beauty aids, cosmetics, house ware, stationary [sic], toys, layaway, [and] fabrics and clothes' departments.[99]

Plaintiffs further alleged that male employees are consistently offered more opportunities for training and promotion than female employees.[100] These opportunities were believed to provide avenues for male employees to advance through the company.[101] Moreover, plaintiffs alleged that female employees are consistently paid less for the same work and the corporation's 'segregated assignment practices exacerbate such unequal pay, because men are more likely to be assigned to departments that pay better than departments to which women are assigned.'[102] A statistical analysis conducted by one of plaintiffs' experts revealed that full-time female hourly employees 'made about $1,150 less per year than men in similar jobs.'[103] Strikingly, 'female store managers made an average of...$16,400 less than' their male counterparts.[104]

Plaintiffs alleged that the disparities in gender distribution throughout Wal-Mart are 'the result of purposeful discrimination' against female employees.[105] Indeed, plaintiffs' First Amended Complaint alleged company-wide misogyny:

> This pattern of unequal assignments, pay, training, and advancement opportunities is not the result of random or non-discriminatory factors. Rather, it is the result of an on-going and continuous pattern and practice of intentional sex discrimination in assignments, pay, training and promotions, and reliance on policies and practices that have an adverse impact on female employees that cannot be justified by necessity, and for which alternative policies and practices with less discriminatory impact could be utilized that equally serve any asserted justification.[106]

---

[99] *Id.*, 23.
[100] *Id.*, 24.
[101] *Ibid.*
[102] *Id.*, 25.
[103] Bhatnagar, *supra* n. 86, at 249 (citing Steven Greenhouse, Wal-Mart Faces Lawsuit over Sex Discrimination, N.Y. Times, February 16, 2003, at A22).
[104] *Ibid.*
[105] *Plaintiffs' First Amended Complaint, supra* note 1, P 1.
[106] *Id.*, 28.

EMPLOYMENT CLASS AND COLLECTIVE ACTIONS

The plaintiffs' prayer for relief included requests for injunctive relief, compensatory, declaratory, and punitive damages.[107] The prayer also requested attorneys' fees and pre-and post-judgment interest.[108] Most notably, the plaintiffs requested 'certification of the case as a class action on behalf of the proposed plaintiff class and designation of plaintiffs as representatives of the class.'[109] Plaintiffs alleged that a class action was the proper vehicle for the suit, because joinder of all members of the proposed class would be impracticable.[110] At the time of filing, plaintiffs believed that the proposed class would include approximately 700,000 present and former Wal-Mart employees.[111]

On June 21, 2004, three years after plaintiffs filed their First Amended Complaint and after extensive discovery, Judge Martin J. Jenkins of the United States District Court for the Northern District of California granted in part and denied in part plaintiffs' Motion for Class Certification.[112] A class consisting of 'all women employed at any Wal-Mart domestic retail store at any time since December 26, 1998, who have been or may be subjected to Wal-Mart's challenged pay and management track promotions policies and practices' was certified, with limitations.[113] The estimated class contains nearly 1.6 million women, rendering it the largest employment discrimination case in American history.[114]

The district court certified the proposed class under Rule 23(b)(2).[115] The court found that certification of employment discrimination claims under Rule 23(b)(2) was appropriate because it effectuated

---

[107] *Id.* (citing the Prayer for Relief PP 1–5).
[108] *Id.* (citing the Prayer for Relief PP 10–11).
[109] *Id.* (citing the Prayer for Relief P 1).
[110] *Id.*, 14.
[111] *Id.* Plaintiffs have obtained 110 voluntary declarations from Wal-Mart's female employees. See Bhatnagar, *supra* n. 86, at 247 n. 11 (construing Alexei Oreskovic, Wal-Mart Hopes Judge Doesn't Buy Huge Class, Recorder, September 23, 2003, at 1).
[112] *Dukes v. Wal-Mart Stores, Inc.*, 222 F.R.D. 137 (N.D. Cal. 2004).
[113] *Id.* at 188 (explaining the certifying class 'for purposes of liability, injunctive and declaratory relief, punitive damages, and lost pay except that class members for whom there is no available objective data documenting their interest in challenged promotions shall be limited to injunctive and declaratory relief with respect to plaintiffs' promotion claim.').
[114] Steven Greenhouse & Constance L. Hays, Wal-Mart Sex-Bias Suit Given Class Action Status, N.Y. Times, June 23, 2004, at A1, available at <www.globalexchange.org/campaigns/sweatshops/2149.html>; see also Bhatnagar, *supra* n. 86, at 247.
[115] *Dukes*, 222 F.R.D. at 188.

Congress' intent in drafting the subsection.[116] The court noted that 'Congress added subsection (b)(2) in 1966 "primarily to facilitate the bringing of class actions in the civil rights area." '[117] Further, 'the drafters of Rule 23 specifically contemplated that suits against discriminatory hiring and promotion policies would be appropriately maintained under Rule 23(b)(2).'[118]

The district court decision focused on commonality and manageability.[119] Although the court noted that manageability is not a requirement under Rule 23(b)(2), it 'is implicit in any type of class certification.'[120] Moreover, the court stated bluntly that 'no court would certify a class unless it believed that the case could proceed in a manageable fashion.'[121] The court found it incumbent upon itself to 'very carefully assess the manageability issues presented by this unique case.'[122]

In the certification order, District Judge Jenkins dismissed Wal-Mart's contention that the size of the class precluded certification, noting that Title VII of the Civil Rights Act of 1964 'contains no special exception for large employers.'[123] In the eyes of the district court, the purpose of Title VII and Rule 23(b) would be defeated if large employers were 'insulated' from civil rights class actions.[124] Judge Jenkins did concede that a large putative class 'raises concerns regarding manageability' that a court is compelled to consider.[125] The court noted that the sheer size of the proposed class raised serious issues regarding the manageability of a class action.[126] Nevertheless, the court found that neither the liability stage nor the remedial stage would be unmanageable because of

---

[116] *Id.* at 170.

[117] *Id.* (citing *In re Monumental Life Ins. Co.*, 365 F.3d 408, 417 n. 16 (5th Cir. 2004)).

[118] *Id.* (citing *Domingo v. New England Fish Co.*, 727 F.2d 1429, 1443 n. 11 (9th Cir. 1984); see also *Coley v. Clinton*, 635 F.2d 1364, 1378 (8th Cir. 1980); *Wetzel v. Liberty Mutual Ins. Co.*, 508 F.2d 239, 250 (3rd Cir. 1975)).

[119] *Id.* at 170.

[120] *Id.* at 173.

[121] *Ibid.*

[122] *Ibid.*

[123] *Id.* at 142.

[124] *Id.* (noting that '[Federal Rule] 23(b)(2) was added in 1966 primarily to facilitate the bringing of civil rights class actions.').

[125] *Ibid.*

[126] *Id.* at 173 (noting that the proposed class is 'huge both in sheer numbers of class members and in its nationwide geographic scope....').

the sheer size of the proposed class.[127] The court found that while 'the proposed class size is extremely large, the types of claims asserted are relatively limited in the context of other judicially sanctioned class actions.'[128]

The district court's certification of the *Dukes* class launched a debate into the efficacy of large-scale Title VII class actions. Opponents of such class actions impute nefarious purposes to the class members and plaintiffs' attorneys:

> There is little doubt that the only reason the plaintiffs' lawyers sought class certification was to coerce the defendant into settling the case without regard to the merits of the plaintiffs' claims. Class actions of this magnitude are virtually never appropriate because they could never be brought to trial; yet they serve the purposes of the plaintiffs' bar by imposing tremendous settlement pressure on defendants.[129]

Following the district court's certification of the *Dukes* class, Wal-Mart sought interlocutory review of the decision pursuant to Rule 23(f).[130] The United States Court of Appeals for the Ninth Circuit granted certiorari, and heard oral argument on August 8, 2005.[131] Wal-Mart and amici curiae, filing supporting briefs, argued inter alia that the sheer size of the class proposed will have dire effects on American business.[132] Notably, the Washington Legal Foundation filed an amicus curiae brief arguing that 'the plaintiffs have failed to demonstrate that the case could manageably be tried as a class action.'[133]

---

[127] See *id.* at 173. The bifurcated liability and remedial approach was established in *International Brotherhood of Teamsters v. United States*, 431 U.S. 324, 360–362 (1977). The Teamsters approach has been consistently applied in cases seeking to eliminate 'systemic employment discrimination.' Hart, *supra* n. 50, at 817 (citing Conte & Newberg, *supra* n. 50, 24:124, at 485) ('The majority of courts have held the bifurcation of class liability and relief phases of Title VII suits to be an appropriate means of litigating employment discrimination claims.').

[128] *Dukes*, 222 F.R.D. at 142 n. 4.

[129] Press Release, Wash. Legal Found., Court Urged to Decertify Massive Class Action Suit (December 9, 2004), available at <www.wlf.org/upload/120904RS.pdf>.

[130] See Press Release, The Impact Fund, *supra* n. 11.

[131] Egelko, *supra* n. 12. See also *supra* n. 13 and accompanying text.

[132] See Press Release, Wash. Legal Found., *supra* n. 129.

[133] *Ibid.*

CHAPTER 7. TOO MANY RICHES

7.4 THE SHEER SIZE OF THE PROPOSED CLASS IS NOT DETERMINATIVE OF THE EFFICACY OF THE ACTION

Dukes v. Wal-Mart raises the issue of the numerical extent of the class action. Wal-Mart opposed the certification of the *Dukes'* class in part because of the sheer size of the proposed class.[134] The author contends that the formulation set forth by the district court is the proper gauge of the numerical limits of the class action. Accordingly, a monolithic class action that otherwise satisfies the requirements of Rule 23 should be certified upon proper motion. The only situation when a putative class becomes too big to be certified is when the sheer size of the class renders the class unmanageable. Manageability should be the touchstone of any court's certification decision, regardless of whether the proposed action arises under subsection (b)(2) or (b)(3).

Where a proposed class is numerically large, the sheer size of the class does not preclude certification.[135] Indeed, a vast class is 'not negatively determinative of the issue of the superiority of a class action.'[136] On the contrary, at least one judge has found that a large class militates in favor of granting certification. 'Sheer size legitimizes and vindicates the bringing of a representative action since otherwise there may be no means for resolving such disputes fairly and efficiently.'[137] Moreover, a failure to certify a large proposed class may adversely affect the judiciary by overwhelming the district courts with numerous individual suits.[138]

Whether a proposed class is too large to be maintained should be determined by the manageability of the action. In certifying a class

---

[134] *Dukes v. Wal-Mart Stores, Inc.*, 222 F.R.D. 137, 142 (N.D. Cal. 2004).

[135] *Johnson v. Uncle Ben's, Inc.*, 71 F.R.D. 19, 21 (S.D. Tex. 1975), aff'd in part, rev'd in part, 628 F.2d 419 (5th Cir. 1980); *Viking Travel, Inc. v. Air France*, No. 76 VC 2195, 1982 U.S. Dist. LEXIS 18350 (E.D.N.Y. July 23, 1982).

[136] *Reader v. Magma-Superior Copper Co.*, 515 P.2d 860, 863 (Ariz. 1973.) (Struckmeyer, J., dissenting) (quoting *Eisen v. Carlisle & Jacquelin*, 391 F.2d 555, 563 (2nd Cir. 1968)). The Magma-Superior case involved Arizona's Rule 23, which conformed with the 1966 amendments to *Federal Rule of Civil Procedure Rule 23*. Id.

[137] *Ibid.*

[138] See e.g., *Lailhengue v. Mobil Oil Co.*, 657 So. 2d 542, 546 (La. Ct. App. 1995) ('If not brought as a class action, the sheer number of actual or potential claims would be enough to unduly burden this Judicial District and this Court, whether the claims are brought as separate suits or by joinder.').

347

action, 'the critical determinant is that of its manageability – judicially, administratively and practically.'[139] In *Coleman v. Cannon Oil Co.*, the court certified a class action in the face of the defendants' arguments 'that the sheer number of people who could be class members renders the suit unmanageable as a class action.'[140] In rendering its decision, the court noted 'that the law on the question is mixed but that the practice of many courts of subordinating any speculations about manageability and proof of damages to the policy that animates Rule 23 is to be preferred to premature speculations about draconian case management.'[141]

Courts have certified monolithic class actions in the past. For example, 'the consumer class-actions against Microsoft may have had at least a million members. Moreover, the Holocaust-era slave labor suits encompassed a class of at least 500,000 members.'[142]

Courts have certified large class actions in the past, even for mere settlement purposes. Wal-Mart, Home Depot, Texaco, Microsoft, and Coca-Cola have all been party to large employment discrimination suits.[143] Accordingly, courts should certify even vast class actions absent some finding that the sheer size would render the action unmanageable.

7.5 *DUKES V. WAL-MART* SHOULD BE MAINTAINED UNDER RULE 23

A federal class action is the proper vehicle for *Dukes v. Wal-Mart*. The Federal Rules Advisory Committee explicitly noted that broad civil

---

[139] *Katz v. Carte Blanche Corp.*, 53 F.R.D. 539, 541 (W.D. Pa. 1971).

[140] 141 F.R.D. 516, 519 (M.D. Ala. 1991).

[141] *Id.* at 520.

[142] Anthony J. Sebok, Wal-Mart Wants to Declassify Lawsuit. Dukes v. Wal-Mart Would be Largest U.S. Discrimination Case, CNN.Com, August 11, 2004, <www.cnn.com/2004/LAW/08/11/sebok.walmart.suit/>.

[143] See John M. Husband, An Overview of Federal Employment Class Actions and Collective Actions, 33 Colo. Law. 97 (December 2004) (citing Robert Luke, Heavy Legal Hitters: Bias Litigation Taking Big Risks for Big Rewards, Atlanta J.-Const., Aug. 4, 2002; Butler v. Home Depot Inc., No. C-94-433551 (N.D. Cal. Sept. 19, 1997); *Roberts v. Texaco Inc.*, 979 F. Supp. 185, 185 (S.D.N.Y 1997); *Vizcaino v. Microsoft Corp.*, 142 F. Supp. 2d 1299 (W.D. Wash. 2001); *Abdallah v. Coca-Cola Co.*, 133 F. Supp. 2d 1364 (N.D. Ga. 2001)).

CHAPTER 7. TOO MANY RICHES

rights cases are appropriate under Rule 23.[144] In addition, some have argued that class actions are necessary to enforce anti-discrimination laws.[145] When employment discrimination classes are not certified, plaintiffs generally do not bring their claims individually.[146] While the bases for individual avoidance of discrimination claims have not been established, possible explanations for this phenomenon include the cost of litigation, fear of individual involvement in such suits, and retribution from the employer.[147] Thus, it appears that allowing an aggregation of claims is necessary to ensure compliance with Title VII.

In addition, the class action mechanism is particularly useful in employment discrimination claims, where the standard of proof is heightened. In employment discrimination cases, plaintiffs must 'demonstrate that the employer operates a pattern of discrimination in the workplace.'[148] Individual claimants may not be able to meet their burden because of evidentiary problems.[149] Aggregation of claims allows Title VII plaintiffs to establish a company-wide pattern of discrimination.[150]

Dukes v. Wal-Mart is therefore appropriate under Rule 23. The case seeks to aggregate individual claims of discrimination to demonstrate company-wide discrimination on the part of Wal-Mart. Allowing *Dukes* to proceed will ensure that company-wide data on Wal-Mart's employment practices will be presented to the trier of fact. Moreover, maintaining *Dukes* will force Wal-Mart to comply with the mandates of Title VII.

Although the size of the class is monumental, that is simply insufficient to decertify the *Dukes* class. In rendering the certification decision, Judge Jenkins conducted a rigorous analysis of the proposed class and concluded that the case would not become unmanageable

---

[144] See *Fed. R. Civ. P. 23(b)* advisory committee's notes ('Illustrative [of a (b)(2) class] are various actions in the civil-rights field where a party is charged with discriminating unlawfully against a class.').

[145] Hart, *supra* n. 50, at 841–842.

[146] *Id.* at 842 (citing W. Lyle Stamps, Getting Title VII Back on Track: Leaving Allison Behind for the Robinson Line, *17 BYU J. Pub. L. 411, 445 (2003)*).

[147] *Id.* at 842 n. 137 (citing Stamps, *supra* n. 146).

[148] *Id.* at 843.

[149] *Ibid.*

[150] *Ibid.*

merely because of the large class size.[151] Decertification of the *Dukes* class would be tantamount to creating an exception to Rule 23 for large employers. Wal-Mart should not be rewarded for its size. Indeed, the vast size of the class 'is not the result of any error by the district court but the predictable result of a class-wide pattern and practice of discrimination perpetrated by [Wal-Mart].'[152] As stated eloquently by plaintiffs in their Opening Brief to the United States Court of Appeals for the Ninth Circuit, 'while Wal-Mart is eager to reap the financial benefits conferred by its mammoth size, it must also accept accountability on the same scale when it violates the rights of its workers.'[153] Wal-Mart's protestations that the *Dukes* class action is too large to be maintained seem disingenuous – any follies perpetrated by the largest private employer in the country are likely to have significant ramifications.

Moreover, judicial economy dictates that the *Dukes* class be maintained. Decertification of the class could yield over one million individual actions brought against Wal-Mart for violations of Title VII. Such a volume of suits would invariably clog the federal dockets unnecessarily, as a litany of judges and juries would be called upon to decide the same question: whether Wal-Mart violated Title VII through its employment practices. Individual actions would also result in inconsistent adjudications for members of the *Dukes* class.

To be sure, the *Dukes'* litigation is the subject of tremendous debate, and has given rise to claims of judicial blackmail. In a brief filed with the United States Court of Appeals for the Ninth Circuit, the Equal Employment Advisory Council (EEAC) argues that the sheer size of the Wal-Mart class creates the potential for blackmail contemplated by Judge Posner in *Rhone-Poulenc*.[154] The EEAC contends that the potential liability of a class so large forces defendants like Wal-Mart into settlement 'whether or not they have done anything wrong.'[155]

---

[151] *Dukes v. Wal-Mart Stores, Inc.*, 222 F.R.D. 137, 173–174 (N.D. Cal. 2004).

[152] *Opening Brief for Appellees and Cross-Appellants, Dukes v. Wal-Mart Stores, Inc.*, 222 F.R.D. 137 (9th Cir. 2004) (Nos 04-16688 & 04-16720).

[153] Ibid.

[154] *Brief for Amici Curiae EEAC at 25, Dukes v. Wal-Mart Stores, Inc.*, 222 F.R.D. 137 (9th Cir. 2004) (Nos 04-16688 & 04-16720).

[155] Ibid.

However, other scholars have noted that criticisms of the class action in other contexts 'are largely inapt as applied to employment discrimination claims.'[156] In addition, some scholars have argued, 'the risks of... blackmail settlements have been overstated.'[157] Indeed, one scholar has stated that claims of legal extortion are 'unsupported on any basis currently articulated in judicial opinions or legal scholarship.'[158] Moreover, an empirical study of class actions conducted by the Federal Judicial Center found no support for the contention that 'the certification decision... coerces settlements with any frequency.'[159] A review of the study demonstrates that 'certification increases the likelihood of settlement, but it does not ensure it.'[160]

In addition, a close examination of the blackmail claim reveals that it is predicated, at least in part, upon a belief that pressure to settle in and of itself justifies the legal extortion claim. While 'all American civil justice systems generate settlement pressure by forcing parties to risk losing at trial,' in the class action context critics impute some nefarious motive behind the pressure to settle large claims.[161] Therefore, one scholar has found that 'the fear of losing at trial (whether coupled with risk aversion or not) does not justify a blackmail claim.'[162] If a large corporate defendant is concerned about the pressure to settle, perhaps that corporation should not have engaged in improper or illegal behavior. Stated differently, 'companies that break billion-dollar promises should face billion dollar losses at trial, as should companies that commit billion-dollar torts.'[163] Such is the case in *Dukes v.*

---

[156] Hart, *supra* n. 50, at 836. But cf. Piar, *supra* n. 19, at 344 (arguing that blackmail settlements occur in the employment litigation context, as evidenced by several large settlements).

[157] Bruce Hay & David Rosenberg, 'Sweetheart' and 'Blackmail' Settlements in Class Actions: Reality and Remedy, *75 Notre Dame L. Rev. 1377, 1379 (2000).*

[158] Warren F. Schwartz, Long-Shot Class Actions: Toward a Normative Theory of Uncertainty, 8 Legal Theory 297, 298 (2002).

[159] Thomas E. Willging, et al., Empirical Study of Class Actions in Four Federal District Courts: Final Report to the Advisory Committee on Civil Rules 61 (1996); see also Silver, *supra* n. 17, at 1359 (arguing that trial judges utilize class actions to induce settlements from defendants in unfavorable legal positions).

[160] Silver, *supra* n. 17, at 1399. The study found that approximately 13% to 37% of certified class actions are disposed of by trial or other non-settlement dispositions. *Id.*
[161] *Id.* at 1366.
[162] *Id.* at 1367.
[163] *Ibid.*

Wal-Mart. Wal-Mart should not be able to thwart plaintiffs' quest for justice with unsubstantiated speculation about blackmail settlements. If Wal-Mart did not engage in employment practices violative of Title VII, it can establish the same and be vindicated at trial. Likewise, Wal-Mart should not be rewarded for its size. The fact that the size of the *Dukes* class is monolithic is a function of Wal-Mart's retail dominance. Accordingly, the *Dukes* class should be maintained.

7.6 CONCLUSION

Monolithic class actions such as *Dukes v. Wal-Mart* should be maintained, absent a finding that the proposed class action would be unmanageable by the district court. The district courts are exceptionally well situated to assess the manageability of class actions in their certification decisions. Accordingly, the district court's findings should not be disturbed on appeal, absent clear error.

With regard to *Dukes v. Wal-Mart*, Judge Jenkins' certification decision should not be disrupted by the United States Court of Appeals for the Ninth Circuit. Judge Jenkins rigorously assessed the efficacy of maintaining the *Dukes* class action in certifying the class, concluding that the sheer size of the proposed class did not render the suit unmanageable. Moreover, *Dukes v. Wal-Mart* should be maintained because it is the type of case envisioned by the drafters of Rule 23 and Title VII. Allowing this case to proceed will allow the trier of fact to ascertain whether in fact Wal-Mart engaged in company-wide gender discrimination and to force compliance with federal law.

CHAPTER 8

The Possibility of Avoiding Discrimination: Considering Compliance and Liability

Melissa Hart*,**

8.1 INTRODUCTION

It is not really surprising that Wal-Mart is the defendant in the largest employment discrimination lawsuit in United States' history. Wal-Mart is, after all, the largest private employer in the world, with a workforce that is nearly 1% of the United States' working population.[1] At the same time, Wal-Mart has become notorious for its unfriendly workplace policies. So, when *Dukes v. Wal-Mart Stores, Inc.* was certified in June 2004, authorizing the named plaintiffs to represent more than 1.5 million current and former Wal-Mart employees in their claims of gender discrimination in pay and promotion,[2] it might have seemed almost inevitable.

---

* Melissa Hart is associate professor, University of Colorado Law School. She holds a J.D. from Harvard Law School.
** Previously published in Connecticut Law Review, Vol. 39 #4 p. 1621 (2007).
[1] See Ellen Israel Rosen, The Wal-Mart Effect: The World Trade Organization and the Race to the Bottom, 8 Chap. L. Rev. 261, 262 n. 5 (2005); David Neumark et al., The Effects of Wal-Mart on Local Labor Markets 1 (Nat'l Bureau of Econ. Research, Working Paper No. 11782, 2005), available at <www.nber.org/papers/w11782>.
[2] *Dukes v. Wal-Mart Stores, Inc.*, 222 F.R.D. 137 (N.D. Cal. 2004). The Ninth Circuit affirmed the certification decision on February 6, 2007. *Dukes v. Wal-Mart, Inc.*, 474 F.3d 1214 (9th Cir. 2007). Wal-Mart has announced it will seek rehearing en banc.

David Sherwyn and Samuel Estreicher (eds), *Employment Class and Collective Actions*, pp. 353–382.
© Connecticut Law Review. Reprinted with permission.

But litigation is never – or perhaps should never be – inevitable. In the context of federal antidiscrimination law, in particular, the law's primary goal is arguably 'not to provide redress but to avoid harm.'[3] If this is truly the goal of Title VII and other similar laws, it must be possible for an employer who wishes to do so to comply with the law's obligations and thereby to avoid liability, and even perhaps to avoid some kinds of litigation entirely.

The past decade has seen a growing number of large class action suits challenging the aggregate effects of multiple individual employment decisions.[4] These cases are an extremely important tool for challenging the subtle but pervasive discrimination that continues to limit women's job opportunities. The patterns of exclusion and inequality presented in *Dukes* mirror patterns that still hamper women's opportunities in many workplaces. They are not inevitable or excusable patterns. By seeking to hold employers accountable for the persistent gender divide in work opportunities, litigation like *Dukes* holds transformative potential. In pushing employers to take steps to counteract the harmful impact of unexamined stereotypes, these suits destabilize settled assumptions about the limits of legal change and the inevitability of workplace inequality.

One of the very things that makes these cases so significant – the challenge to broad cultural norms – has the potential to undermine their success. The challenge to widespread cultural stereotypes raises concerns about where to locate legal boundaries. In particular, cases like *Dukes* push us to the question of what an employer can do to avoid liability in litigation of this sort. Employers have raised the specter that there is no legitimate way to avoid liability under Title VII if these suits are permissible, and some courts are clearly bothered by this possibility as well.

This chapter will consider the problem of compliance: What can an employer do to avoid liability for excessively subjective decision-making that leads to gender-biased outcomes in pay and promotions? It

---

See Wal-Mart to Appeal Discrimination Suit Status, CNNMoney.Com, February 6, 2007, <money.cnn.com/2007/02/06/news/companies/walmart/ index.htm>.

[3] *Faragher v. City of Boca Raton*, 524 U.S. 775, 806 (1998); see also *Kolstad v. Am. Dental Ass'n*, 527 U.S. 526, 545 (1999).

[4] Like many of the topics discussed at the Wal-Mart Matters symposium, this is an area where one could say that you do not need Wal-Mart to study the Wal-Mart effect. See e.g., V. Sridhar & Vijay Prashad, Wal-Mart with Indian Characteristics, 39 Conn. L. Rev. 1785 (2007); Chris Tilly, Wal-Mart and its Workers: NOT the Same All Over the World, 39 Conn. L Rev. 1805 (2007).

CHAPTER 8. CONSIDERING COMPLIANCE AND LIABILITY

will first explore the significance of *Dukes* and the kind of challenge it mounts as an important step in antidiscrimination litigation. It will then consider the standard defense arguments – that only quotas or strict objective tests will protect them – and will reject those solutions as potentially illegal and certainly unnecessary. Next, it will explore the kinds of requests that litigants like the *Dukes* plaintiffs make – not only for monetary remedies, but also for structural reforms. It will place those remedial options in the context of the Supreme Court's jurisprudence on employer compliance with Title VII. Finally, this article will consider the dilemma presented by the possibility that compliance is not achieving the goals of equal employment opportunity. There has been a significant scholarly critique of the Court's emphasis on employer training programs and other internal antidiscrimination policies, and recent empirical work raises questions about the effectiveness of many employer-driven diversity efforts. These are serious concerns that cannot be ignored, but in spite of these concerns, compliance efforts and the internal enforcement mechanisms they generate must be considered as a central element of efforts to limit discrimination in the workplace.

8.2 LITIGATION TRENDS: *DUKES* AND OTHER CHALLENGES TO ENTRENCHED STEREOTYPES

Dukes v. Wal-Mart Stores, Inc. is part of a litigation trend that includes similar suits against well-recognized national retailers like Home Depot[5] and Costco,[6] as well as dozens of other chain stores, grocery stores and other relatively large, geographically dispersed employers.[7] Each of these suits raises a challenge to the defendant employer's policy of allowing local decision-makers to make important employment decisions in a largely unguided subjective manner. The suits also challenge the

---

[5] See *Butler v. Home Depot, Inc.*, No. 94-4335, 1996 WL 421436 (N.D. Cal. January 25, 1996).

[6] See *Ellis v. Costco Wholesale Corp.*, 372 F. Supp. 2d 530 (N.D. Cal. 2005).

[7] See e.g., Melissa Hart, Learning from Wal-Mart, 10 Emp. Rts. & Emp. Pol'y J. 355, 372 (2007) (discussing recent cases involving employment discrimination); Michael Selmi, Sex Discrimination in the Nineties, Seventies Style: Case Studies in the Preservation of Male Workplace Norms, 9 Emp. Rts. & Emp. Pol'y J. 1, 2 & n. 4, 5 (2005) (same); Michael Zimmer, Systemic Empathy, 34 Colum. Hum. Rts. L. Rev. 575, 599–600 (2003) (same).

individual results of that unguided decision-making. What these suits are fundamentally doing is contesting the continued operation of entrenched gender stereotypes in workplace decision-making.

This part will begin by briefly describing the claims in *Dukes v. Wal-Mart Stores, Inc.*, and the facts the plaintiffs focused on to support their legal claims. Because the allegations in *Dukes* are typical of the claims brought in other recent class action suits, they help to illuminate the particular kind of persistent discrimination such litigation targets. This part will then explore the role these suits push employers to play in challenging entrenched cultural norms.

8.2.1 Statistical Disparities, Centralized Policies, and Stories of Bias at Wal-Mart

In 2001, the *Dukes* plaintiffs filed suit on behalf of current and former female employees of Wal-Mart, alleging that for years women at Wal-Mart stores had been paid less than their male counterparts every year and in every Wal-Mart region and that they had been denied opportunities for promotion during that same time and on the same broad geographic scale.[8] The plaintiffs charged that:

> Wal-Mart discriminates against its female employees by advancing male employees more quickly than female employees, by denying female employees equal job assignments, promotions, training and compensation, and by retaliating against those who oppose its unlawful practices.[9]

They alleged that the retail giant had violated Title VII of the Civil Rights Act of 1964 both through intentional discrimination and through maintenance of policies that, while facially neutral, operate in a manner that disproportionately harms female employees and that cannot be justified as necessary to Wal-Mart's business.[10] They supported these claims with a narrative and a theory of discrimination that have become increasingly common in efforts to combat workplace inequality.

---

[8] See Motion for Class Certification at 1, *Dukes. v. Wal-Mart Stores, Inc.*, 222 F.R.D. 137 (N.D. Cal. 2004) (No. C-01- 2252) [hereinafter Motion for Certification].

[9] Plaintiffs' Third Amended Complaint <pmark> 2, *Dukes v. Wal-Mart Stores, Inc.*, 222 F.R.D. 137 (N.D. Cal. 2004) (No. C-01-2252) [hereinafter Third Amended Complaint].

[10] *Id.* at 102, 104.

CHAPTER 8. CONSIDERING COMPLIANCE AND LIABILITY

The narrative and theory of *Dukes v. Wal-Mart Stores, Inc.*, like those in other similar litigation, have three central elements: an attack on the aggregate results of multiple individual decisions; identification of a number of company policies that either foster discriminatory attitudes or at least allow them to thrive unchecked; and detailing of anecdotal instances of explicit gender bias and stereotyping. The plaintiffs' goal is to demonstrate how the individual decisions that form the basis of the statistical showing are attributable to the policies and cultural attitudes of the employer. By making this showing, plaintiffs enable the courts to evaluate the aggregate consequences of individual decisions and expose patterns of discriminatory outcomes that might be difficult or impossible to challenge through individual suits.[11]

The first step in the *Dukes* plaintiffs' argument was to demonstrate a statistically significant disparity in pay and promotion between men and women at Wal-Mart. Plaintiffs' statistical expert looked at men and women hired at the same time into the same position over a five-year period and found that, on average, women in hourly positions made USD 1,100 less annually than men. In salaried management positions the annual pay gap was USD 14,500.[12] Relevant non-discriminatory factors could not explain these pay differences.[13] The statistical disparities in promotion of women at Wal-Mart were similarly stark. Wal-Mart has a large female employee population at the lowest sales ranks; in 2001, women comprised 67% of hourly workers and 78% of hourly department managers.[14] The percentage of women is considerably different, however, in the salaried management ranks. Only 35.7 % of assistant managers, 14.3% of store managers and 9.8% of district managers were female.[15]

As to both pay and promotion, the plaintiffs pointed to substantial evidence that these disparities are attributable to the unguided discretion vested in store managers. Wal-Mart's policies for setting pay combine a fixed base rate for each job with manager discretion for fairly substantial adjustments. The company 'provides no guidance on what circumstances would justify such an adjustment. Without proper

---

[11] See Hart, *supra* n. 7, at 365.
[12] Motion for Certification, *supra* n. 8, at 25.
[13] *Id.* at 27–28.
[14] *Id.* at 7.
[15] *Id.*; see also *Dukes v. Wal-Mart Stores, Inc.*, 222 F.R.D. 137, 146 (N.D. Cal. 2004).

criteria, inappropriate gender-based factors therefore can, and do, affect pay decisions.'[16] Wal-Mart offered similarly little information or guidance to managers about standards for promotion. Opportunities for promotion to most management positions were not posted; permission to apply for them often had to be obtained from supervisors; and access was limited by invitation-only training programs.[17] Evidence suggests that supervisors relied on difficult-to-define criteria – like teamwork skills and ability to get along with others – that are especially susceptible to gender bias and stereotypes.[18]

Other evidence presented by the *Dukes* plaintiffs showed that, as to both pay and promotion, Wal-Mart's corporate management consistently disregarded the developing gender disparities.[19] For example, variations from a range of 'normal' pay for any particular job show up on exception reports, allowing corporate headquarters to see where significant differences in pay have developed. While corporate management 'is aware of how its Store Managers are using their discretion' in setting pay 'it has done nothing to rein them in or ensure this discretion is exercised fairly.'[20] The company has been unwilling to engage in monitoring of gender disparities in compensation.[21] As to the gender differences in promotion rates, consultants hired by Wal-Mart over the years have pointed to the lack of gender equality in the management levels of the company and a task force created by the company in 1996 suggested mechanisms for increasing representation of women in management.[22] Wal-Mart ignored these recommendations and disbanded the group in 1998.[23] An internal group of Wal-Mart women told the company as long ago as 1992 that they were concerned that gender stereotypes throughout the company were limiting opportunities for

---

[16] Motion for Certification, *supra* n. 8, at 9.
[17] Dukes, 222 F.R.D. at 148–149.
[18] *Ibid.*; see also Motion for Certification, *supra* n. 8, at 25–26.
[19] Motion for Certification, *supra* n. 8, at 2.
[20] *Id.* at 19.
[21] See Expert Report of Dr.William T. Bielby, *Dukes v. Wal-Mart Stores, Inc.*, 222 F.R.D. 137 (N.D. Cal. 2004) [hereinafter Bielby Report].
[22] See Motion for Certification, *supra* n. 8, at 15; Wal-Mart Didn't Act on Internal Sex-Bias Alert, Documents Show, Bloomberg.com, July 15, 2005, <www.bloomberg.com/apps/news?pid= 71000001&refer=us&sid=aGS8a.3TSjRQ>.
[23] See Wal-Mart Didn't Act, *supra* n. 22.

CHAPTER 8. CONSIDERING COMPLIANCE AND LIABILITY

women's advancement.[24] Wal-Mart did not act on these recommendations and expressions of concern.

The largely unguided and unchecked allocation of pay and promotion opportunities described by the plaintiffs' evidence is at odds with Wal-Mart's highly centralized and controlled corporate environment. Both Wal-Mart's personnel management structure and, especially, the company's corporate culture are tightly managed out of corporate headquarters in Bentonville, Arkansas. The retail giant's United States' operations are divided into forty-one national regions supervised by vice presidents who meet at least weekly with central corporate leadership in Bentonville.[25] Each region is also covered by a regional personnel manager, based at corporate headquarters, who monitors personnel policies and assists in the recruitment and selection of individual store managers.[26] The regions are divided into districts, each run by a manager who works directly with his regional personnel manager on personnel decisions.[27] This system connects human resources decisions directly back to corporate headquarters along several lines.

This centralized personnel structure is one of the tools Wal-Mart uses to ensure the dissemination of and continued emphasis on its corporate culture. From the first orientation to mandatory weekly store meetings, employees are trained in Wal-Mart's culture.[28] Store managers use standardized 'corporate "culture" lessons and accompanying training materials' to run these meetings.[29] The company newsletter, *Wal-Mart World*, includes a section on corporate culture,[30] and Wal-Mart's website has a section devoted to culture.[31] Every store

---

[24] Motion for Certification, *supra* n. 8, at 15–16.

[25] *Id.* at 5; see also Cheryl L. Wade, Transforming Discriminatory Corporate Cultures: This is Not Just Women's Work, 65 Md. L. Rev. 346, 366–367 (2006) (describing Wal-Mart's management structure and noting in particular the expectation that '[e]ach level of management was in "close and constant touch." ').

[26] See Motion for Certification, *supra* n. 8, at 2.

[27] See *id.* at 5.

[28] See *Dukes v. Wal-Mart Stores, Inc.*, 222 F.R.D. 137, 151 (N.D. Cal 2004); see also Barbara Ehrenreich, Nickel and Dimed: On (Not) Getting By in America 143–144 (2001) (describing the orientation process).

[29] Motion for Certification, *supra* n. 8, at 11.

[30] Bielby Report, *supra* n. 21, at 7.

[31] See Wal-Mart Stores, Wal-Mart Culture, <www.walmartstores.com/GlobalWM StoresWeb/ navigate.do?catg=251> (last visited March 30, 2007).

manager is expected to monitor a real-time computer link connected to the home office to keep immediately up-to-date with corporate policy.[32] Moreover, store-level managers at both Wal-Mart and Sam's Club are frequently transferred from one facility to another, and even from one state to another.[33] This movement within the company helps to ensure that a consistent message carries across retail outlets. 'By constantly moving people around, the Wal-Mart blood circulates to the extremities.'[34] Similarly, Wal-Mart's strong preference for promoting from within ensures that most managers will have been 'thoroughly steeped' in the company culture.[35] Wal-Mart reinforces this lesson by rewarding commitment to the corporate culture in evaluation and allocation of opportunities.[36]

As a final step in their argument, the *Dukes* plaintiffs offered anecdotal evidence that business at Wal-Mart was often conducted in contexts that either explicitly or implicitly excluded women and that women faced considerable bias at stores throughout the nation. The incident that is credited with being the impetus for the *Dukes* class action suit was the moment when a female store manager saw her male counterpart's pay stub and realized he was making thousands of dollars more than she was for doing the same job. When this single working mother questioned her manager about the disparity, he explained that the male employee had a family to support and therefore was appropriately paid more.[37] Another member of the class said

---

[32] Motion for Certification, *supra* n. 8, at 8, 9.

[33] *Id.* at 12.

[34] See Cora Daniels, *Women v. Wal-Mart*; How Can the Retailer Reconcile its Storied Culture with the Anger of These Female Workers?, Fortune, July 21, 2003 at 78, available at LEXIS, News Library, FORTUN File.

[35] See Motion for Certification, *supra* n. 8, at 11–12; see also Don Soderquist, The Wal-Mart Way: The Inside Story of the Success of the World's Largest Company 39–40 (2005).

[36] See Motion for Certification, *supra* n. 8, at 11; see also Robert Slater, The Wal-Mart Decade 109 (2003) (quoting current Wal-Mart CEO as saying '[y]ou have to be less tolerant of people who don't get the culture').

[37] See Liza Featherstone, Selling Women Short: The Landmark Battle for Workers' Rights at Wal-Mart 16 (2004); see also Third Amended Complaint, *supra* n. 9, <pmark> 65, (describing another employee who was told that a male co-worker was paid more 'because he had a family to support').

CHAPTER 8. CONSIDERING COMPLIANCE AND LIABILITY

that she was advised that if she wanted to get a better job at Wal-Mart she should ' "doll up" ' and ' "blow the cobwebs off" her makeup.'[38] Another testified that her boss repeatedly justified his favoritism for men by explaining that 'God made Adam first.'[39] One woman was discouraged from applying for a position as manager of the sporting-goods department with the explanation that customers would feel more comfortable with a man in the position.[40] Other women reported that women were generally steered to 'traditionally female' departments, which often came with fewer advancement opportunities.[41] One class member testified that during an interview she was informed that 'it was a man's world and that men control managerial positions at Wal-Mart.'[42] Class members explained that work meetings in stores and divisions around the country were held at Hooters restaurants and, in some cases, at strip clubs.[43] At meetings of Sam's Club executives, women employees were regularly referred to as 'girls' and as 'little Janie Qs.'[44]

The pieces of the *Dukes* plaintiffs' narrative fit together to describe an environment with a strong and central corporate culture that emanates directly out of headquarters and that requires managerial compliance with all sorts of directives, but without any kind of attention to or concern about gender bias in promotion and compensation. The anecdotes of discriminatory attitudes and biased treatment at Wal-Mart stores around the country portray a culture that permitted or even encouraged local managers to act on stereotypes and bias in exercising discretion on pay and promotion decisions. The statistical inequities in both compensation and management opportunities demonstrate that Wal-Mart's corporate decision to remain at best indifferent to concerns of gender equality in the workplace had real consequences for its female employees.

---

[38] Third Amended Complaint, *supra* n. 9, at 64.
[39] Daniels, *supra* n. 34, at 78.
[40] Third Amended Complaint, *supra* n. 9, at 57.
[41] *Id.* at 93.
[42] *Id.* at 52.
[43] Daniels, *supra* n. 34; see also Geri L. Dreiling, The Women of Wal-Mart (2004), <www.alternet.org/rights/19901>/ (describing one female employee's experience with repeated visits to strip clubs on business trips).
[44] Motion for Certification, *supra* n. 8, at 6.

8.2.2 Potential for Challenging Culturally Entrenched Stereotypes

There are obviously elements of the *Dukes* plaintiffs' narrative that are entirely unique to Wal-Mart. The basic framework of the challenge, however, is much the same as that in *Ellis v. Costco*, where plaintiffs allege that an entirely subjective system with no written standards for doling out promotion opportunities[45] or *Butler v. Home Depot*, where a system that granted a largely male supervisory staff the discretion to make decisions about pay and promotion allegedly kept women in lower paying, lower status positions at the company,[46] or *Shores v. Publix Super Markets*, where women were allegedly relegated to low-paying positions and denied access to management at the grocery store chain by a system of pay and promotions that relied on the unguided discretion of supervisory personnel.[47] In all of these cases, and in many others,[48] the pay and promotion policies being challenged 'have as a common feature that they have entrusted to managers very broad discretion to make promotion and compensation decisions with little or no oversight.'[49] This is a core theme in recent Title VII class litigation, and it is this aspect of the claims that gives them great potential as a tool to push on the glass ceiling that continues to limit women's opportunities at work.

These claims of excessive subjectivity in decision-making are attacks both on the employer practices that allowed subjectivity to intrude into workplace decisions and on the substantive content of the subjective judgments being made. The former is a challenge to particular workplace policies of the defendant employer. So, for

---

[45] *Ellis v. Costco Wholesale Corp.*, 372 F.2d 530, 533 (N.D. Cal. 2005).

[46] *Butler v. Home Depot, Inc.*, No. C-94-4335 SI, 1996 WL 421436, at *1 (N.D. Cal. January 25, 1996).

[47] *Shores v. Publix Super Markets, Inc.*, No. 95- 1162-CIV-T-25(E), 1996 U.S. Dist. LEXIS 3381, at *15 (M.D. Fla. March 12, 1996).

[48] See e.g., *Palmer v. Combined Ins. Co.*, 217 F.R.D. 430, 435 (N.D. Ill. 2003) (seeking certification of class challenging employer's central policy of delegating unfettered discretion and ignoring consequences); *Beckmann v. CBS*, 192 F.R.D. 608, 614 (D. Minn. 2000) (describing challenge to a centrally formulated and disseminated personnel policy that leaves discretion to individual managers to make personnel decisions); see also Melissa Hart, Subjective Decisionmaking and Unconscious Discrimination, 56 Ala. L. Rev. 741, 787 notes 247, 248 (2005) (collecting cases).

[49] Motion for Certification, *supra* n. 8, at 16.

CHAPTER 8. CONSIDERING COMPLIANCE AND LIABILITY

example, the *Dukes* plaintiffs point to Wal-Mart's failure to post training and promotion opportunities; its lack of clear written criteria for advancement, evaluation, and pay differentials; and its residual reliance on a willingness to relocate as a requirement for management positions as specific policies and practices that make the retail giant an appropriate litigation target. As one of the plaintiffs' experts has explained, the difficulty with these employment practices is that they have 'structured the decision-making context in ways that allowed cognitive bias to place women at a systematic disadvantage.'[50] Among the plaintiffs' litigation goals is to force Wal-Mart to adopt policies that will limit the opportunity for bias and stereotype to intrude into workplace decisions. They are challenging what Susan Sturm has described as 'second generation discrimination' that is 'structurally embedded in the norms and cultural practices of an institution'[51] and are seeking institutional reforms that will disrupt persistent patterns of inequality.

These challenges attack not only what Michael Selmi has described as 'corporate indifference to gender inequality,'[52] but also the stereotypical attitudes of the individual supervisors who have been making decisions at the company for years. In this regard, class action claims challenging the aggregate effects of unguided subjective decision-making are attacks on gender stereotyping and bias more generally.[53] They contest not only the institutional culture of a particular workplace, but also the widespread stereotypes and biases that exist outside the

---

[50] William T. Bielby, Can I Get a Witness? Challenges of Using Expert Testimony on Cognitive Bias in Employment Discrimination Litigation, 7 Emp. Rts. & Emp. Pol'y J. 377, 385 (2003).

[51] Susan Sturm, Lawyers and the Practice of Workplace Equity, 2002 Wis. L. Rev. 277, 280–281; see also Susan Sturm, Second Generation Employment Discrimination: A Structural Approach, 101 Colum. L. Rev. 458, 468 (2001) [hereinafter Sturm, Second Generation Discrimination] (defining second generation employment discrimination).

[52] Michael Selmi, Sex Discrimination in the Nineties, Seventies Style: Case Studies in the Preservation of Male Workplace Norms, 9 Emp. Rts. & Emp. Pol'y J. 1, 46 (2005); see also Tristin K. Green, Discrimination in Workplace Dynamics: Toward a Structural Account of Disparate Treatment Theory, 38 Harv. C.R.-C.L. L. Rev. 91, 145 (2003) (noting that recent litigation focuses on 'the employer's role in enabling the forms of discriminatory bias that hinder opportunities of women and minorities in the modern workplace').

[53] I explore this aspect of the claims in more detail in Hart, *supra* n. 7, at 372–374.

workplace and that are imported into worksites through individual decision-makers.

These claims require for their success that workplace decisions be evaluated in the aggregate. Looking at broad swaths of pay and promotion decisions reveals patterns of inequality that may be masked if decisions are considered in isolation.[54] The decision whether or not to certify a class to pursue these claims is therefore fundamental. Many district courts have certified class action suits that challenge the consequences of unguided subjective decision-making, recognizing, as both the district court and the Ninth Circuit did in *Dukes*, that an employer can have corporate policies that tolerate and even encourage the operation of stereotypes in decision-making and that the widespread discrimination that results is properly attributable to the employer.[55] Others have viewed these claims as simply an impermissible effort to aggregate dozens or hundreds of individual claims with the class action device.[56]

Underlying the decisions from courts that have been unwilling to certify these class action suits is an anxiety about holding employers liable on a class-wide scale for the type of discrimination at issue in these claims. As one court has put it:

> a decision by a company to give managers the discretion to make employment decisions, and the subsequent exercise of that discretion by some managers in a discriminatory manner, is not tantamount to a decision by a company to pursue a systemic, companywide policy of intentional discrimination.[57]

---

[54] See e.g., *Dukes v. Wal-Mart Stores, Inc.*, 222 F.R.D. 137, 150–151 (N.D. Cal. 2004); see also Sturm, *supra* n. 51, at 469 ('[B]ehavior that appears gender neutral when considered in isolation may actually produce gender bias when connected to broader exclusionary patterns.').

[55] See e.g., *Dukes v. Wal-Mart, Inc.*, 474 F.3d 1214, 1231 (9th Cir. 2007); Dukes, 222 F.R.D. at 150–151; see also Hart, *supra* n. 48, at 787 n. 247.

[56] See Hart, *supra* n. 48, at 787.

[57] *Sperling v. Hoffman-LaRoche, Inc.*, 924 F. Supp. 1346, 1363 (D.N.J. 1996); see also *Wright v. Circuit City Stores, Inc.*, 201 F.R.D. 526, 541 (N.D. Ala. 2001) ('[T]he purported class is comprised of a large group of diverse and differently situated employees whose highly individualized claims of discrimination do not lend themselves to class-wide proof.'); *Robertson v. Sikorsky Aircraft Corp.*, No. 397CV1216(GLG), 2000 WL 33381019, at *5 (D. Conn. July 5, 2001):

> [W]hat we have here are evaluations and decisions made by hundreds of supervisors and managers on a variety of things besides promotions, such

CHAPTER 8. CONSIDERING COMPLIANCE AND LIABILITY

The concern reflected in these comments is with the move from holding a single manager responsible for his stereotyped decisions (or even finding the employer liable for this individual bias under established standards of proof in individual discrimination cases) to holding the employer responsible for the aggregate of many managers' decisions. A core element of this concern is that it may be difficult to distinguish an employer that should be held liable under this theory from one that should not. Are employers obligated to eliminate stereotypes from all decision-making in the workplace in order to avoid this kind of aggregate liability, or simply to make legitimate efforts to do so? How can we tell when an employer is doing enough?

8.3 AVOIDING LITIGATION LIABILITY: WHAT SHOULD EMPLOYERS DO?

Class actions challenging the results of excessive subjectivity in employment decision-making raise fundamental questions about the responsibility employers should have for eliminating or minimizing the impact of persistent gender stereotypes when they operate at work. The considerable potential of these suits to challenge widespread cultural norms has a flip side that presents a significant question: because this kind of litigation targets a broad social phenomenon, is it reasonably possible to distinguish employers who are part of the problem from those who are not? This question presents a formidable challenge and contributes to judicial resistance to recognizing these claims at all. Given the real possibility of continued – or even increasing – judicial resistance to this type of litigation, there is a serious need for some articulation of what employer practices would be sufficient to demonstrate legal compliance sufficient to forestall a suit like *Dukes*.

My concern here is not so much with remedies in litigation, but with whether there are steps an employer can take to avoid liability, or even to avoid litigation altogether and whether those same steps will necessarily diminish workplace inequality. The topics are certainly not unrelated, and the question of what litigation remedies are appropriate

---

as job assignments, salary determinations, merit increases, etc. From a practical standpoint, it is impossible to put these all under one roof.

in these cases is also difficult and hotly contested.[58] Some have noted that in many instances employment discrimination lawsuits appear to be simply opportunities to transfer money from one party to the other in compensation for past wrongs, rather than serious catalysts for workplace change.[59] Others who are perhaps more optimistic have pointed to the inclusion of 'systemic prospective relief aimed at reducing future discrimination' in consent decrees approving settlement in several cases.[60] It is clear that, even taking this more optimistic view, once the discussion is focused on remedies in litigation, money becomes a central element of the conversation.

Perhaps for that reason, among others, recent scholarship has emphasized the role that employers, consultants and non-litigation arbiters have come to play in crafting solutions to continuing discrimination.[61] Increasingly, it seems possible that the best hope of organizational – and consequently societal – change in this arena may come from outside litigation. At the same time, litigation and the significant threat it poses to employers will likely always play a fundamental part in forcing change that might otherwise be considered too costly or too complicated. Moreover, independent of this coercive potential, there is the possibility that the remedies plaintiffs seek in litigation, the expert

---

[58] Much of the litigation in *Dukes*, particularly in the appellate arguments in the Ninth Circuit, has been focused on the appropriateness of a remedial scheme that allocates money damages to class members based on a formula, rather than based on individualized proof of damages. Wal-Mart has asserted that this formulaic allocation of damages is unconstitutional, and that courts' use of such a model calls the legality of Federal Rule of Civil Procedure 23 into question. The Ninth Circuit rejected these arguments in affirming the certification decision. See *Dukes*, 474 F.3d at 1237–1242. While the arguments surrounding damages allocation are fascinating, they are beyond the scope of this paper.

[59] See e.g., Michael Selmi, The Price of Discrimination: The Nature of Class Action Employment Discrimination Litigation and Its Effects, 81 Tex. L. Rev. 1249, 1300–1301 (2003).

[60] Tristin K. Green, Targeting Workplace Context: Title VII as a Tool for Institutional Reform, 72 Fordham L. Rev. 659, 688 n. 129 (2003); Sturm, Second Generation Discrimination, *supra* n. 51, at 529–530; Sturm, The Practice of Workplace Equity, *supra* n. 51, at 280–281.

[61] See e.g., Rachel Arnow-Richman, Public Law and Private Process: Toward an Incentivized Organizational Justice Model of Equal Employment Quality for Caregivers, 2007 Utah L. Rev. 25; Sturm, Second Generation Discrimination, *supra* n. 51, at 566.

CHAPTER 8. CONSIDERING COMPLIANCE AND LIABILITY

reports that inform those remedial requests, and consent decrees from settled cases can provide guidance to employers and consultants seeking pre-emptive workplace reform. Thus litigation and non-litigation solutions should not be considered as entirely independent and neither is likely to be entirely sufficient.

This section will examine a range of compliance alternatives, including the steps defendants incorrectly assert that they would have to take to avoid class action lawsuits as well as solutions that plaintiffs and courts have proposed in litigation. It will then consider how tight the relationship is and should be between eliminating inequality and avoiding liability. That is, if an employer adopts the kinds of policies that plaintiffs, experts and courts are suggesting as tools for the elimination of stereotype and bias in decision-making and yet statistical disparities persist, should the employer be liable under Title VII in a *Dukes*-type suit or not?

8.3.1 Quotas and Objective Testing: The Defendants' Parade of Horribles

Defendants warn of a 'parade of horribles' if courts begin to permit class action challenges to the aggregate impact of excessive unguided subjective decision-making.[62] They assert that, if claims like those made in *Dukes* are allowed, employers will be pushed into one of two unpalatable choices: the adoption of quota systems to avoid the statistical imbalances that support the claims or the rigid elimination of all subjective elements of employee selection and evaluation.[63] Neither of these options is viable and so, employers suggest, the claims themselves must not be legitimate.

Defendants are about half correct. Neither quotas nor strictly objective testing is a workable solution in the current legal and political context. Not only is there widespread opposition to quotas as a matter of social policy, but Title VII quite explicitly states that nothing in the statute should be interpreted to require employers to give preferential

---

[62] See Jocelyn Larkin & Christine E. Webber, Challenging Subjective Criteria in Employment Class Actions 7 (2005), available at <www.impactfund.org/pdfs/Subjective%20Criteria.pdf>.
[63] *Ibid.*

367

treatment to members of a protected class because of an existing workforce imbalance in representation of that class among its employees.[64] Experience teaches that when employers do adopt quotas to avoid statistical imbalances in workforce representation of different groups, they may face legal challenges to the quotas themselves.[65] Further, the Supreme Court has made it clear that even employer-initiated affirmative action plans are valid only if they do not involve strict numerical quotas.[66] Thus, any interpretation of Title VII, or any claim made under the statute, that required an employer to adopt a strict statistical balance of men and women in particular positions would be unlikely to survive scrutiny.

The elimination of subjective aspects of selection and evaluation of employees would face similar attack. Every Federal Court of Appeals has recognized that 'subjective evaluations "are more susceptible of abuse and more likely to mask pretext." '[67] Courts have also been careful, however, to acknowledge that '[h]onorable employers frequently use subjective criteria... [i]ndeed, in many situations they are indispensable to the process of selection in which employers must engage.'[68] The Supreme Court has explicitly endorsed the use of subjective evaluations, emphasizing that '[s]ome qualities-for example, common sense, good judgment, originality, ambition, loyalty, and

---

[64] 42 U.S.C. 2000e-2(j) (2000); see also *Wards Cove Packing Co. v. Atonio*, 490 U.S. 642, 652 (1989) ('The only practicable option for many employers would be to adopt racial quotas, insuring that no portion of their work forces deviated in racial composition from the other portions thereof; this is a result that Congress expressly rejected in drafting Title VII.'); *Watson v. Fort Worth Bank & Trust*, 487 U.S. 977, 992–994 & n. 2, (1988) (the Court of Appeals' theory would 'leav[e] any class of employers with "little choice" ' but to engage in a subjective quota system of employment selection. This, of course, is ' "far from the intent of Title VII" ').

[65] See e.g., *Martin v. Wilks*, 490 U.S. 755, 755 (1989) (discussing annual racial hiring goals challenged under Title VII).

[66] See e.g., *Grutter v. Bollinger*, 539 U.S. 306, 309 (2003) (stating that 'universities cannot establish quotas for members of certain racial or ethnic groups'); *Gratz v. Bollinger*, 539 U.S. 244, 272 (2003); *Johnson v. Santa Clara Trans. Agency*, 480 U.S. 616, 616–617 (1987).

[67] *Weldon v. Kraft, Inc.*, 896 F.2d 793, 798 (3rd Cir. 1990) (quoting *Fowle v. C&C Cola*, 868 F.2d 59, 64–65 (3rd Cir. 1989)); see also Hart, *supra* n. 48, at 767 n. 132 (listing a host of federal court decisions warning of the discriminatory potential of subjective evaluation methods).

[68] *Sengupta v. Morrison-Knudson Co.*, 804 F.2d 1072, 1075 (9th Cir. 1986).

CHAPTER 8. CONSIDERING COMPLIANCE AND LIABILITY

tact-cannot be measured accurately through standardized testing techniques.'[69] Thus, an argument that subjective elements of employment decision-making should be eliminated entirely is unlikely to carry much weight in any court. Moreover, for much the reasons the courts have recognized, a shift to purely objective testing would not make sense as a matter of employment policy. In most job categories, there are aspects of qualification for the position that are not amenable to objective measure and eliminating their consideration would diminish the ability of employers to select qualified employees.

Further, an employer who trades all subjective evaluation for an entirely objective system of testing puts itself at risk of litigation for that decision. Title VII law entitles employees to challenge employer practices that have a disparate impact on a particular group. To succeed in a disparate impact claim, an employee must identify a particular practice and then show that the challenged practice has a statistically significant negative impact on members of a protected class.[70] While not all objective evaluation systems have this kind of disparate impact, the risk is not inconsiderable.[71] To avoid the risks associated with a disparate impact challenge to an objective test, employers have to spend considerable resources validating the tests and ensuring that they are consistent with the employer's business necessity. Making this kind of showing would be particularly complicated in a circumstance where the employer in fact believes that a different measure-one with some subjective element-would produce outcomes more consistent with business needs.

8.3.2 Best Practices?: Workplace Policies that May Reduce the Negative Effects of Stereotype and Bias and Limit the Risk of Liability

Defendant employers are correct that neither quotas nor elimination of subjectivity is a viable solution to the problems targeted by class

---

[69] Watson, 487 U.S. at 991.

[70] See 42 U.S.C. § 2000(e)(2)(k) (2000); New York City Trans. *Auth. v. Beazer*, 440 U.S. 568, 568–569 (1979); *Griggs v. Duke Power Co.*, 401 U.S. 424, 431 (1971).

[71] See e.g., Michael Selmi, Was the Disparate Impact Theory a Mistake?, 53 UCLA L. Rev. 701, 705–706, 755 (2006) (noting evidence that most written tests have some disparate impact).

action suits challenging the aggregate impact of excessive subjectivity in decision-making. They are not necessarily correct, however, that these are the only employer practices that could decrease the negative effects of stereotyping and bias at work. In fact '[l]ists of 'best practices' in diversity management have proliferated recently.'[72] Moreover, remedies proposed by plaintiffs in litigation and often incorporated into consent decrees suggest steps employers might take to avoid lawsuits like *Dukes*.[73] The kinds of changes often voluntarily made by employers facing these suits – the kinds of changes Wal-Mart has made in the past few years-provide similar guidance. As well, some of the Supreme Court's recent Title VII jurisprudence offers instruction to employers about implementation of antidiscrimination training and prevention programs as an important aspect of compliance.

These diverse sources offer some consensus about areas in which workplace regulation may help to both prevent discrimination and limit the likelihood of liability in litigation. These areas include neutral and well-advertised posting of management positions and training opportunities; written standards of both expectation and evaluation; monitoring and appraisal of workplace statistics; and antidiscrimination policies and training. Of course, no checklist of policies will or should automatically insulate an employer from liability for discrimination. Courts must consider how policies in fact operate in the particular context of a given workplace. But the practices described here may offer a starting point for considering what kinds of basic steps employers should be taking to reduce the likelihood of stereotyping in workplace decisions. It seems quite likely that an employer that implements this range of practices will be less susceptible to class litigation challenging organizational discrimination. This section will

---

[72] Alexandra Kalev et al., Best Practices or Best Guesses? Assessing the Efficacy of Corporate Affirmative Action and Diversity Policies, 71 Amer. Soc. Rev. 589, 589 (2006). See generally United States Equal Opportunity Commission, Best Practices of Private Sector Employers (1998), available at <www.eeoc.gov/abouteeoc/task reports/practice.html>. In this context, a 'best practice' is generally understood to mean a practice that 'promotes equal employment opportunity and addresses one or more barriers that adversely affect equal employment opportunity.' *ibid.*

[73] See Green, *supra* n. 60, at 705 (noting that 'consent decrees like those recently agreed upon can provide valuable foundational information for other organizations seeking to avoid Title VII liability').

elaborate on these employer practices and their relevance in a few notable recent cases, including *Dukes*.

8.3.2.1 Advertising and Posting Positions

One of the most commonly criticized employer practices that tends to permit subjective judgments to limit women's opportunities is the failure to make job opportunities widely available through posting and some form of objective initial screening of applicants.[74] A central allegation of the *Dukes* litigation, for example, was that the retail giant allowed individual supervisors to select candidates for management training and other promotion gateway opportunities through a 'tap on the shoulder.'[75] This kind of selection system for training and promotions is extremely likely to replicate the existing composition of managerial ranks.[76] Instead, employers seeking to eliminate subtle discrimination in the workplace should maintain some form of neutral, public job posting that 'communicates clear and accurate information to employees about the training and experience required to become eligible for a job, about job conditions, and about how the job fits into a career path in the organization.'[77]

Since the *Dukes* suit was first initiated, Wal-Mart seems to have taken substantial steps toward such a publicly available posting system.[78] Similarly, the settlement decree in the Home Depot litigation included implementation of a less subjective promotion application process in which employees and applicants would enter their job preferences into a computerized database, which would automatically place qualified applicants into an interview pool.[79] In the wake of the

---

[74] See e.g., *Dukes v. Wal-Mart Stores, Inc.*, 222 F.R.D. 137 (N.D. Cal. 2004); *Shores v. Publix Super Markets, Inc.*, No. 95-1162-CIV-T-25(E), 1996 U.S. Dist. LEXIS 3381, at *31–32 (M.D. Fla. Mar. 12, 1996); Abigail Goldman, Costco Manager Files Sex-Bias Suit, L.A. Times, August 18, 2004, at C1, available at LEXIS, News Library, LAT File.
[75] See *Dukes*, 222 F.R.D. at 148; Motion for Certification, *supra* n. 8, at 8.
[76] See e.g., Bielby Report, *supra* n. 21, at 11; Scott A. Moss, Women Choosing Diverse Workplaces: A Rational Preference with Disturbing Implications for Both Occupational Segregation and Economic Analysis of Law, 27 Harv. Women's L. J. 1, 32–33 (2004).
[77] Bielby Report, *supra* n. 21, at 15.
[78] See Wal-Mart Didn't Act, *supra* n. 22.
[79] See Green, *supra* n. 60, at 684.

Wal-Mart class certification decision, at least one major employment defense firm explicitly recommended to its clients that it 'adopt or modify a posting system so that promotional opportunities (or more of them) are publicized internally.'[80] While publicizing promotion opportunities will not eliminate subjectivity in assessment of candidates for these opportunities, it will at least give women the opportunity to apply for senior positions that, in a tap on the shoulder world, they often never learn of at all.

8.3.2.2 Establishing Written Standards

An emerging consensus about best practices for equal employment opportunity also focuses on the need to develop written standards for evaluation and to require supervisors conducting evaluations to provide explanations in writing. Without written guidelines, neither those doing evaluations nor those being evaluated know what measures are being applied. This information vacuum allows different standards of evaluation to be applied to different candidates and diminishes accountability.

The absence of written criteria may also be a significant factor in class litigation. For example, the allegations in *Ellis v. Costco* focus in substantial part on the fact that the warehouse store does not provide written criteria or procedures for filling its highest-paying store management positions and that, as a consequence, '[c]andidates who aspire to these positions often have little or no idea how these positions are filled or what they need to do to obtain them.'[81] When senior management does describe the promotion criteria, these criteria are highly subjective.[82] Wal-Mart's approach has been much the same, with individual managers applying their own assessments of the criteria most relevant for promotion. Factors like 'teamwork, ethics, integrity, ability to get along with others, and willingness to volunteer,' which

---

[80] James J. Oh, *Dukes v. Wal-Mart*: A Foreboding Class Certification Decision For Employers, ASAP, (Littler Mendelson, Chicago, Ill.), July 2004, <www.littler.com/collateral/print/A59F4C0F A2B09CDB3C0F709269E2D5BE.html>.

[81] Plaintiffs' Motion for Class Certification and Appointment of Counsel at 1, *Ellis v. Costco Wholesale Corp.*, 2007 U.S. Dist. LEXIS 2103 (N.D. Cal. January 11, 2007) (No. C-04- 3441).

[82] *Id.* at 9–10.

CHAPTER 8. CONSIDERING COMPLIANCE AND LIABILITY

some managers at Wal-Mart described as the standards they used for doling out advancement opportunities, are concededly relevant to all kinds of jobs, but evaluation of those qualities is likely to be biased 'unless they are assessed in a systematic and valid manner, with clear criteria and careful attention to the integrity of the decision-making process.'[83] Requiring managers to provide written explanations for decisions may counter the operation of unthinking bias because it will require them to articulate the reasons for the decision. Similarly, 'requiring a supervisor to anchor an evaluation of a particular skill or characteristic of an employee with examples of specific observed behaviors rather than vague impressions can diminish the influence of subconscious stereotyping.'[84]

Written standards can also counteract misunderstandings about corporate policies or preferences that have discriminatory impact. Without written standards, outdated policies that have been abandoned in part because of their impact on women or minority candidates can have continuing detrimental effects as they live on in practice if not in formal policy. In Wal-Mart's case, for example, there was evident internal confusion about whether higher-level management positions required a willingness to relocate anywhere in the country. It is clear that the company's original policies required a willingness to relocate, and in fact that new managers were consistently relocated around the country.[85] That official policy seems to have been dropped in recent years, but testimony from the *Dukes* litigation makes clear that some evaluating supervisors still consider it to be one of the requirements for promotion.[86] Since it had been recognized even within Wal-Mart itself that this policy disadvantaged female applicants for management positions, clear written directives about its discontinuation would have been one step to opening more promotion opportunities to women.

---

[83] Bielby Report, *supra* n. 21, at 14. Supporting this general perspective, legal scholarship on cognitive bias and its effects at work draws on and contextualizes a well-developed body of psychological research documenting the intrusion of biases into workplace decisions. See e.g., Linda Hamilton Krieger, The Content of Our Categories: A Cognitive Bias Approach to Discrimination and Equal Employment Opportunity, 47 Stan. L. Rev. 1161, 1186–1211 (1995).
[84] Larkin & Webber, *supra* n. 62, at 8.
[85] Bielby Report, *supra* n. 21, at 18.
[86] *Id.* at 17–18.

8.3.3 Establishing Antidiscrimination Policies and Education

Of all the possible employer responses to the problem of discrimination, the one that has received the most sustained attention is the development of antidiscrimination training and internal prevention programs. This is the one area in which the Supreme Court has affirmatively suggested that employers may avoid liability (or at least decrease their liability risks) through policy implementation. No doubt at least in part as a consequence of the Court's encouragement, employers have been fairly aggressive in implementing antidiscrimination education and prevention policies.[87] But these are also, as I discuss further below,[88] the kinds of employer policies that have received the most sustained skeptical review from scholars evaluating their effectiveness as a mechanism for challenging workplace inequalities.

What guidance there is from the Supreme Court on the measures an employer can take to comply with the federal law's antidiscrimination mandates focuses primarily on when an employer will be held vicariously liable for sexual harassment undertaken by a supervisor. In that context, the Supreme Court has recognized that Title VII was intended not only to provide a cause of action to injured employees, but also to 'encourage the creation of anti-harassment policies and effective grievance mechanisms.'[89] In a pair of 1998 decisions, the Court held that an employer would be vicariously liable for supervisory sexual harassment, but that the employer could avoid liability if it could demonstrate that:

(1) it had taken effective steps to prevent harassment and to correct for harassment if and when it was made aware of it; and
(2) that the complaining employee had unreasonably failed to take advantage of available preventative or corrective measures.[90]

In a similar vein, the Court held in 2000 that an employer would not be liable for punitive damages if it engaged in good faith efforts to comply

---

[87] See Cynthia Estlund, Rebuilding the Law of the Workplace in an Era of Self-Regulation, 105 Colum. L. Rev. 319, 335–336 (2005).
[88] See *infra* section 7.3.3.
[89] *Burlington Indus. v. Ellerth*, 524 U.S. 742, 764 (1998).
[90] *Faragher v. City of Boca Raton*, 524 U.S. 775 (1998); Burlington Indus., 524 U.S. at 764; see also *Pa. State Police v. Suders*, 542 U.S. 129, 145–146 (2004).

CHAPTER 8. CONSIDERING COMPLIANCE AND LIABILITY

with Title VII and that an employer's creation of antidiscrimination policies and education of its employees about the importance of these policies would constitute such good faith.[91]

Even before these Supreme Court opinions offered incentives to employers to establish antidiscrimination training and prevention policies, diversity training was a relatively popular human resources practice among larger companies.[92] The theory behind this training is that if you sensitize people to the problem of stereotyping and suggest behavioral changes that will cut down on the incidence of bias, you may be able to reduce the negative effects of these phenomena.[93] Over the past three decades, companies have also grown increasingly likely to have established procedures for addressing complaints of discrimination internally. Creation or enhancement of this type of internal program is a common component of consent decrees settling class action discrimination claims.

8.3.3.1 Monitoring and Ensuring Accountability

A consistent message in evaluating the efficacy of employer efforts to reduce workplace discrimination is that any program must include strong central support and clear channels of accountability.[94] In order to be most effective, internally driven antidiscrimination practices must involve 'a process of self-assessment that would lead to genuine accountability and organizational self-monitoring.'[95] Regular

---

[91] *Kolstad v. Am. Dental Ass'n*, 527 U.S. 526, 545–546 (1999).
[92] See e.g., Kalev et al., *supra* n. 72, at 593.
[93] See *ibid*.
[94] See e.g., U.S. Equal Employment Opportunity Comm'n, Best Practices of Private Sector Employees 7 (1997), available at <www.eeoc.gov/abouteeoc/task reports/practice.html> [hereinafter Good for Business] ('Management must have a positive and unequivocal commitment to equal employment opportunity. Without commitment from top-level management to front-line supervisors, nothing can reasonably be expected to be done.'); U.S. Glass Ceiling Comm'n, Good for Business: Making Full Use of the Nation's Human Capital 39 (1995).
[95] Susan Sturm, Race, Gender and the Law in the Twenty-First Century Workplace: Some Preliminary Observations, 1 U. Pa. J. Lab. & Emp. L. 639, 676 (1998). More than a decade ago, the federal Glass Ceiling Commission made the point that any successful effort to shatter the glass ceiling would include CEO support, an emphasis on accountability, explicit confrontation of preconceptions and stereotypes,

375

monitoring and oversight of how promotion criteria are developed and applied is essential to diminishing the discriminatory effects of stereotyping in workplace decisions.[96] One of the most troubling among the employment practices challenged in *Dukes* was Wal-Mart's unwillingness to acknowledge and assess available information about pay and promotion disparities or to address the perceptions of its female employees that gender discrimination limited their opportunities in the company.[97] Available research shows that the negative impact of bias and stereotyping on employment decision-making:

> can be minimized when decision-makers know that they will be held accountable for the criteria used to make decisions, for the accuracy of the information upon which the decisions are based, and for the consequences their actions have for equal employment opportunity.[98]

Thus, organizations that incorporate evaluation of patterns of segregation or differential status by gender into their personnel systems are more likely to catch troubling patterns of inequality relatively early. Similarly, monitoring employees' perceptions of the workplace culture may counter 'subtle forms of bias and related problems not immediately apparent from analyses of more objective workforce data.'[99] For these reasons, human resources experts recommend that companies designate specific individuals or committees with explicit responsibility for monitoring diversity progress and concerns.[100] Further, settlement decrees in employment discrimination cases regularly

---

mechanisms for tracking progress and a comprehensive scope. Good for Business, *supra* n. 94, at 39.

[96] See e.g., Kalev et al., *supra* n. 72, at 592 (noting that '[s]cholars and consultants alike advise ongoing coordination and monitoring of diversity progress by dedicated staff members or task forces').

[97] Similar allegations were made in *Ellis v. Costco Wholesale Corp*. See Plaintiffs' Motion for Class Certification and Appointment of Counsel, *supra* n. 81, at 15–16.

[98] Bielby Report, *supra* n. 21, at 19; see also Green, *supra* n. 52, at 147; Christine Jolls & Cass R. Sunstein, The Law of Implicit Bias, 94 Cal. L. Rev. 969, 986–987 (2006) (discussing mechanisms for 'debiasing,' including prohibitions on implicit bias). Courts have long recognized this as an option for safeguarding against bias. See e.g., *Pouncy v. Prudential Ins. Co. of Am.*, 499 F. Supp. 427 (S.D. Tex. 1980).

[99] Bielby Report, *supra* n. 21, at 24; see also Larkin & Webber, *supra* n. 62, at 7–8; Good For Business, *supra* n. 94, at 40.

[100] See e.g., Good for Business, *supra* n. 94, at 39–40; Kalev et al., *supra* n. 72, at 592–593.

require the creation of systems to monitor employment decision-making patterns and often include outside review processes.[101]

8.3.4 What if Compliance Does Not Work?

An employer that adopted a human resources policy incorporating this range of 'best practices' would be extremely unlikely to face serious risk of liability under a theory like that presented in *Dukes*. If these kinds of practices are in fact working to diminish the discriminatory consequences of stereotyping and bias, then it seems entirely appropriate that employers would not be liable for class claims seeking structural reform.[102] Moreover, even absent clear evidence that these practices are working to eliminate discrimination, courts are unlikely to find employers responsible for class-wide discrimination when they have adopted policies that track what many have identified as 'best practices.' But what if the issue is not an absence of evidence that certain policies do work and instead the existence of evidence that they do not? In this section, I will consider what the link can and should be between the effectiveness of compliance efforts for equal opportunity goals and their effectiveness for liability prevention.

Dukes, like other similar suits, challenged the aggregate effects of unguided, excessively subjective decision-making. The theory behind the suits is that the employer practice of permitting unguided subjectivity allowed the stereotypes and biases of individual managers to intrude into workplace decisions. An employer that established written standards for evaluation that required written explanations for evaluation and that monitored the outcomes of pay and promotion decision-making would not be guilty of permitting 'unguided' decision

---

[101] Green, *supra* n. 60, at 685–686 (describing consent decree provisions in several cases). As Michael Selmi has noted, there may be good reason to look to outside monitoring rather than creating diversity review processes that report only internally. Selmi, The Price of Discrimination, *supra* n. 59, at 1327–1328.

[102] Liability for intentional discrimination in individual cases is a separate question. One could certainly imagine a workplace that operated on terms that forestalled a class action claim challenging the aggregate effects of unguided subjectivity in decision-making but in which individuals might still face occasional instances of discrimination. My focus here is exclusively on class action litigation seeking structural reform.

making. An employer that ensured posting of positions, with publicly available minimum standards and careful attention to a decision-maker's obligation to explain his decisions would be less likely to suffer the problems that attend excessive subjectivity in selection of candidates for hiring or promotion. So, there is a chance that an employer who adopted these types of policies would have created a workplace in which stereotypes and bias were visibly the exception to general practice. This assumption is one of the principal justifications for the liability theory in suits like *Dukes*, which allege that the absence of these employer practices is responsible for the operation of continued stereotyping and bias in allocation of opportunities.

Moreover, it is this assumption, at least in part, that undergirds the Supreme Court's vicarious liability decisions. In holding that training and prevention programs should limit an employer's liability for the discriminatory acts of its employees, the Court emphasized that Title VII's primary goal was 'to avoid harm.'[103] If an employer is making reasonable efforts to limit the harm that Title VII seeks to prevent, the Court reasoned it should be 'give[n] credit' for those efforts.[104] But what if this assumption proves wrong? What if 'best practices' either have no impact on diversity in the workplace or even have negative consequences for women's employment opportunities?

A wave of recent scholarship on diversity training programs has raised the concern that these programs are enabling employers to avoid liability despite the fact that they do little to actually diminish stereotypes and bias in the workplace.[105] These critics of what sometimes appears to be unexamined judicial deference to the existence of

---

[103] *Faragher v. City of Boca Raton*, 524 U.S. 775, 806 (1998).
[104] *Ibid.*
[105] See Samuel R. Bagenstos, The Structural Turn and the Limits of Antidiscrimination Law, 94 Cal. L. Rev. 1, 28 (2006); Susan Bisom-Rapp, An Ounce of Prevention is a Poor Substitute for a Pound of Cure: Confronting the Developing Jurisprudence of Education and Prevention in Employment Discrimination Law, 22 Berkeley J. Emp. & Lab. L. 1, 3 (2001); Susan D. Carle, Acknowledging Informal Power Dynamics in the Workplace: A Proposal for Further Development of the Vicarious Liability Doctrine in Hostile Work Environment Sexual Harassment Cases, 13 Duke J. Gender L. & Pol'y 85, 86–87 (2006); Joanna L. Grossman, The Culture of Compliance: The Final Triumph of Form over Substance in Sexual Harassment Law, 26 Harv. Women's L. J. 3, 3 (2003); Anne Lawton, Operating in an Empirical Vacuum: The Ellerth and Faragher Affirmative Defense, 13 Colum. J. Gender & L. 197, 197–198 (2004).

CHAPTER 8. CONSIDERING COMPLIANCE AND LIABILITY

employer antidiscrimination policies raise a number of powerful cautionary points about the risks of reliance on these internal mechanisms for enforcement of the equality ideals embodied in federal antidiscrimination laws.

Some note that the Supreme Court's justification for its liability standards – that the existence of antidiscrimination programs will reduce the incidence of discrimination – rests on an empirically testable assumption that has not truly been tested and that may very well prove to be incorrect.[106] If an employer is to avoid liability because of the existence of these policies, it should perhaps only be if the policies in fact work to reduce discriminatory conduct.[107] Without some attention to this issue, there is a risk that internal programs will be merely 'symbolic responses – responses designed to create a visible commitment to law, which may, but do not necessarily, reduce employment discrimination.'[108] In fact, a recent empirical study offers evidence that diversity training does not lead to an increase in diversity.[109]

To the extent that this evidence undercuts the proffered justification for doctrines that limit liability because of these programs, it might be cause for rethinking those doctrines.

Others make the related point that the judiciary's acceptance of employer-created training and prevention programs carries the risk

---

[106] See Theresa M. Beiner, Sex, Science and Social Knowledge: The Implications of Social Science Research on Imputing Liability to Employers for Sexual Harassment, 7 Wm. & Mary J. Women & L. 273, 275 (2000); Susan Bisom-Rapp, Fixing Watches with Sledgehammers: The Questionable Embrace of Employee Sexual Harassment Training by the Legal Profession, 24 U. Ark. Little Rock L. Rev. 147, 148 (2001); Linda Hamilton Krieger & Susan Fiske, Behavioral Realism in Employment Discrimination Law, 94 Cal. L. Rev. 997, 1017–1019 (2006).

[107] Krieger & Fiske, *supra* n. 106, at 1061 ('When a court, like the Supreme Court in Faragher and Ellerth, justifies its adoption of an affirmative defense to otherwise meritorious harassment cases on the grounds that anti-harassment training programs and grievance procedures will prevent harassment from occurring, social science evidence on this question is of undeniable import in evaluating the defense's merit as a normative legal rule.').

[108] Lauren B. Edelman, Legal Ambiguity and Symbolic Structures: Organizational Mediation of Civil Rights Law, 97 Am. J. Soc. 1531, 1542 (1992); see also Bisom-Rapp, *supra* n. 106, at 23–24 (discussing the risk that diversity training becomes 'mere window dressing').

[109] Kalev et al., *supra* n. 72, at 590, 604.

that self-regulation will descend into deregulation.[110] Sociologist Lauren Edelman and her colleagues have conducted significant empirical evaluations of the ways in which implementation of antidiscrimination laws through internal human resources managers tends to shift the focus of the laws to a more managerial approach and how these internal shifts are then exported into judicial understandings of compliance.[111] Other concerns include the risk that, by letting employers off the hook for admittedly egregious incidents of discrimination by individual employees, courts are limiting the law's ability to address that underlying discrimination and may even be masking its occurrence.[112] Finally, there is some disturbing evidence that the existence of antidiscrimination and anti-harassment policies can have unintended negative effects in the workplace by reinforcing stereotypes or exacerbating underlying tensions.[113]

There has been less empirical research done of other 'best practices' for equal employment opportunity. The recent study that demonstrated little positive impact from diversity training did show significant positive results when employers adopted structures of accountability, such as diversity committees or staff positions and affirmative action plans.[114] When courts are evaluating the reasonableness of employer efforts to counter discrimination in the workplace, this kind of empirical information should inform their analysis. As the relative effectiveness of different programs becomes better known, an employer's decision to adopt a less effective alternative in lieu of one with demonstrably better outcomes starts to seem less reasonable.

---

[110] Estlund, *supra* n. 87, at 337.

[111] See e.g., Lauren B. Edelman et al., Internal Dispute Resolution: The Transformation of Civil Rights in the Workplace, 27 Law & Soc'y Rev. 497, 499 (1993).

[112] See Susan Bisom-Rapp, Bulletproofing the Workplace: Symbol and Substance in Employment Discrimination Law Practice, 26 Fl. St. U. L. Rev. 959, 962 (1999).

[113] Bisom-Rapp, *supra* n. 106, at 29–41; see also Kalev et al., *supra* n. 72, at 604.

[114] Kalev et al., *supra* n. 72, at 590; see also Susan Bisom-Rapp, Margaret S. Stockdale & Faye J. Crosby, A Critical Look at Organizational Responses to and Remedies for Sex Discrimination, in Sex Discrimination in Employment: Multidisciplinary Perspectives 280–283 (Faye J. Crosby et al. eds, forthcoming 2007) (describing success rates of employer compliance efforts); Susan Sturm, The Architecture of Inclusion: Advancing Workplace Equity in Higher Education, 29 Harv. J. L. & Gender 247 (2006) (describing a program at the University of Michigan that produced measurable results in improving women's experiences and opportunities in the sciences through internal mechanisms of accountability and inclusion).

CHAPTER 8. CONSIDERING COMPLIANCE AND LIABILITY

Given the information currently available, for example, caution about the unthinking embrace of internal employer training and prevention efforts is essential. Certainly, the mere existence of an antidiscrimination policy or educational program – or of any other practice – should not automatically insulate an employer from liability. Wal-Mart, for example, was not completely without any diversity programs or initiatives, but the programs it did have in place were (especially compared with its to-the-minute operations more generally) haphazard and underemphasized.[115] Courts must be able – and willing – to conduct some independent evaluation of the effectiveness of an employer's policy in assessing what kind of impact it should have on liability.[116] Moreover, training and prevention programs should be tied to other organizational practices designed to minimize the negative impact of stereotyping and bias in employment decisions.

Ultimately, though, if an employer has adopted the kinds of policies that experts – even plaintiffs' experts – recommend as best practices for meeting the demands of equal employment opportunity, there will be a point at which liability under a class-wide structural theory of discrimination will not be appropriate. This may be true even if the kinds of programs an employer has adopted have not led to the kinds of diversity gains that proponents of equal opportunity would hope for. If suits like *Dukes* are to continue to survive, courts will want to know how to distinguish an employer whose policies and practices are in line with the requirements of the law from those whose policies are not. A precise elaboration of where that distinction lies may not be possible, but consciousness about the existence of the distinction should frame both litigation arguments and compliance recommendations.

8.4 CONCLUSION

The Wal-Mart gender discrimination litigation may never get to trial. It is statistically most likely, in fact, that it will not do so.

---

[115] Bielby Report, *supra* n. 21, at 22–25.

[116] See e.g., *Williams v. Spartan Communications*, 2000 WL 331605, at *3 (4th Cir. March 30, 2000) (No. 99-1566) (looking at the context in which an antidiscrimination policy was disseminated and concluding that it did not meet the employer's affirmative defense because the employee reasonably believed the employer was not committed to the goals expressed in the policy).

If the certification decision survives further review, the case will probably settle. Employment discrimination class actions almost never actually get tried.[117] But *Dukes v. Wal-Mart Stores, Inc.* will have had a significant impact even if it never does go beyond class certification. The case has received considerable media attention, and Wal-Mart's reform efforts, implemented largely in response to the litigation, have also generated press attention. Research suggest that employers, with increasingly sophisticated personnel advisors, are likely to look at the efforts of other companies in determining what employment policies make sense for avoiding discrimination litigation and liability. So perhaps the *Dukes* litigation will ultimately have contributed to a better understanding of the contours of compliance in this central and complex area of equal employment opportunity.

In any event, those supportive of claims like *Dukes* must have responses to the concerns raised by employers and skeptical courts about the limits of antidiscrimination law. I believe that part of that effort must include some recognition that it is possible for an employer to structure its workplace in such a way as to avoid liability in this type of litigation. This is not to say that an employer would be immune from any form of antidiscrimination litigation, but rather that it could take steps to substantially eliminate the risk of this particular kind of litigation, which pushes the employer to adopt structures that counter the effects of cultural stereotypes and bias in the workplace. Without some notion of what an employer whose workplace culture and policies complied with the requirements of Title VII would look like, there is a significant risk that courts will react against the apparently unbounded nature of these claims.

---

[117] See Melissa Hart, Will Employment Discrimination Class Actions Survive?, 37 Akron L. Rev. 813, 814 (2004).

CHAPTER 9

Preclusion in Class Action Litigation

Tobias Barrington Wolff*,**

9.1 INTRODUCTION

For years, courts and commentators have engaged in a fierce debate over the circumstances under which a class action judgment should have binding effect upon absent class members.[1] Despite this

---

* Tobias Barrington Wolff is professor of law, University of California at Davis. He holds a J.D. from Yale University.
** Previously published by Columbia Law Review. Tobias Barrington Wolff, Preclusions in Class Action Litigation, 105 Colum. Law Rev. 717, (2005).
[1] Much of that debate has focused on the availability of collateral attacks where adequate representation was arguably lacking in an initial proceeding. See e.g., *Stephenson v. Dow Chem. Co.*, 273 F.3d 249, 257–261 (2nd Cir. 2001) (permitting 'future claimant' to escape effects of class settlement due to inadequate representation in initial proceeding), affirmed by an equally divided Court, in part, and vacated on other grounds, in part, 539 US 111 (2003); *Epstein v. MCA*, Inc. (Epstein II), 126 F.3d 1235, 1241 (9th Cir. 1997) (holding that representation that is actually inadequate will prevent class action from binding absentees), vacated, *Epstein v. MCA*, Inc. (Epstein III), 179 F.3d 641, 648 (9th Cir. 1999) (holding that collateral attack is never available provided that procedures were in place to ensure adequacy of representation in initial proceeding); *State v. Homeside Lending*, 826 A.2d 997, 1007–1018 (Vt. 2003) (permitting Vermont residents to bring suit, despite Alabama judgment purporting to resolve all claims in nationwide class action, for reasons of inadequate representation and lack of personal jurisdiction); Marcel Kahan and Linda Silberman, The Inadequate Search for 'Adequacy' in Class Actions: A Critique of Epstein v. MCA, Inc., 73 N.Y.U. L. Rev. 765, 774 (1998) [hereinafter Kahan and Silberman, Inadequate

David Sherwyn and Samuel Estreicher (eds), *Employment Class and Collective Actions*, pp. 383–497.
© Columbia Law Review. Reprinted with permission.

intensity of focus, the related question of exactly what preclusive effect such a binding judgment should have on the claims of those absentees has remained largely unexamined.[2] The omission is a serious one. The preclusive effects of a proposed class proceeding, considered ex ante, can sometimes have a dramatic impact upon the certification calculus. Nonetheless, insofar as courts have taken note of preclusion questions at all in considering requests for class certification, they have most

---

Search] (criticizing Epstein II and arguing that opportunities to opt out at certification and settlement provide adequate protection to class members); Henry Paul Monaghan, Antisuit Injunctions and Preclusion Against Absent Nonresident Class Members, 98 Colum. L. Rev. 1148, 1162–1178 (1998) (arguing that collateral review of adequacy is necessary where forum's only basis for exercising personal jurisdiction is provision of notice and opportunity to opt out, which assumes minimal participation by absentee). The requirements of notice, personal jurisdiction, and opt-out rights have also been the focus of much attention. See *Phillips Petroleum Co. v. Shutts*, 472 US 797, 809–812 (1985) (establishing notice and opt-out requirements for out-of-state absentees in damages class action where forum would otherwise lack personal jurisdiction); *Twigg v. Sears, Roebuck and Co.*, 153 F.3d 1222, 1226–1229 (11th Cir. 1998) (holding that class member is not bound to class action judgment because notice was insufficient to alert him that his interests would be compromised); Samuel Issacharoff, Preclusion, Due Process, and the Right to Opt Out of Class Actions, 77 Notre Dame L. Rev. 1057 (2002) [hereinafter Issacharoff, Preclusion] (discussing certification standards and due process limitations on binding litigants to different types of class proceedings).

[2] The best discussion of the issue is to be found in Wright, Miller, and Cooper, which does a good job both in identifying some of the areas of class litigation where preclusion doctrine requires careful attention and in offering commonsense solutions. See 18A Charles Alan Wright, Arthur R. Miller, and Edward H. Cooper, Federal Practice and Procedure § 4455, at 448–494 (2nd edn 2002 and Supp. 2004). Even so, the volume's treatment of the issue is succinct and undertheorized (of necessity, given the nature of the treatise format). There has been no comprehensive treatment of the issue in any law review article and only occasional mention of it in the context of other discussions. The best partial treatment of which I am aware can be found in Richard Nagareda's discussion of the class action as a mechanism for regulating the 'market' among defendants in obtaining claim preclusive repose. See Richard A. Nagareda, The Preexistence Principle and the Structure of the Class Action, 103 Colum. L. Rev. 149, 159–181 (2003). Nagareda does not purport to offer a comprehensive treatment of claim and issue preclusion in aggregate litigation, but is attentive to the importance of the problem, which is rare. Some courts have attempted to grapple with the nuances of preclusion in class litigation, as I discuss at length below, but no satisfying judicial approach has emerged.

CHAPTER 9. PRECLUSION IN CLASS ACTION LITIGATION

frequently avoided any serious engagement with the issue by placing broad reliance upon the ubiquitous maxim, aptly stated by Justice Ginsburg in the *Matsushita* case, that '[a] court conducting an action cannot predetermine the res judicata effect of the judgment; that effect can be tested only in a subsequent action.'[3] The Court further entrenched this maxim in the *Semtek* case, where it placed a construction upon Federal Rule of Civil Procedure 41(b) that limited the operative effect of a dismissal 'upon the merits' under that provision to the federal court in which the dismissal is actually issued. '[I]t would be peculiar,' the Court reasoned in explaining that result, 'to find a rule governing the effect that must be accorded federal judgments by other courts ensconced in rules governing the internal procedures of the rendering court itself.'[4] Relying uncritically upon these tenets, courts regularly take it as a matter of course that the preclusive effect of a judgment is not a subject with which a rendering court should concern itself but, rather, is a feature of a judgment that can only be determined with certainty – and should only receive serious attention – in a subsequent proceeding. The broad and imprecise fashion in which courts and commentators have deployed this preclusion maxim in class proceedings has led to serious error that calls for a reexamination of the ubiquitous preclusion maxim that has pretermitted that inquiry.

To be sure, there are some preclusion questions that a rendering court cannot answer with finality. Will a subsequent attempt by a litigant to obtain a remedy in another proceeding constitute an alternative legal theory on the same claim, rather than an analytically and transactionally

---

[3] *Matsushita Elec. Indus. Co. v. Epstein*, 516 US 367, 396 (1996) (Ginsburg, J., concurring in part and dissenting in part) (citing 7B Wright, Miller, and Cooper, *supra* n. 2, § 1789, at 245).

[4] *Semtek Int'l Inc. v. Lockheed Martin Corp.*, 531 US 497, 503 (2001); see also *id.* at 505–506 (construing provision). Rule 41(b) reads:

> Involuntary Dismissal: Effect Thereof. For failure of the plaintiff to prosecute or to comply with these rules or any order of court, a defendant may move for dismissal of an action or of any claim against the defendant. Unless the court in its order for dismissal otherwise specifies, a dismissal under this subdivision and any dismissal not provided for in this rule, other than a dismissal for lack of jurisdiction, for improper venue, or for failure to join a party under Rule 19, operates as an adjudication upon the merits.

Fed. R. Civ. P. 41(b).

distinct prayer for relief?[5] Will a contested issue be essential to the final judgment, and will it remain the 'same' issue over time, such that it could serve as the basis for a later estoppel?[6] When questions about the extent of a judgment's future preclusive effect depend upon events that lie outside the rendering forum's knowledge or control, their likely outcome can be a matter of legitimate and serious ex ante dispute. In such cases, litigants must compare the likely benefit of a lawsuit as presently conceived with the risk that a judgment will produce adverse consequences in the future. The inability to answer such questions with certainty until a subsequent proceeding, and the risk that a litigant will choose unwisely, are basic structural features of preclusion doctrine.[7]

In the context of individual litigation, such risk is manageable. Just as an individual litigant in a civil proceeding does not enjoy any right of adequate representation that could enable him to escape the effects of a judgment, and hence assumes the risk that his lawyers will make bad litigation choices on his behalf, so a litigant assumes the risk that the

---

[5] See e.g., *Herendeen v. Champion Int'l Corp.*, 525 F.2d 130, 134–135 (2nd Cir. 1975) (adopting more formalistic definition and permitting lawsuit for pension benefits to proceed, even though plaintiff had previously filed unsuccessful lawsuit for same benefits, because second suit based cause of action on different contract and hence constituted distinct 'claim'); Restatement (Second) of Judgments § 24 (1982) (offering pragmatic definition of series of transactions).

[6] The Restatement provides:

> When an issue of fact or law is actually litigated and determined by a valid and final judgment, and the determination is essential to the judgment, the determination is conclusive in a subsequent action between the parties, whether on the same or a different claim.

Restatement (Second) of Judgments § 27.

[7] Professor Burbank makes reference to this dynamic in calling for an approach to preclusion in the federal courts that will minimize the risk associated with such uncertainty:

> Preclusion rules affect litigation strategy. It is therefore important that litigants know what the rules are. Before filing a complaint asserting federal rights in a federal court, or in response to the successful removal of such a case to federal court, the plaintiff should be able to predict with considerable assurance the rules of claim preclusion that will govern a judgment.

Stephen B. Burbank, Interjurisdictional Preclusion, Full Faith and Credit and Federal Common Law: A General Approach, 71 Cornell L. Rev. 733, 767 (1986) [hereinafter Burbank, Interjurisdictional Preclusion].

CHAPTER 9. PRECLUSION IN CLASS ACTION LITIGATION

judgment that results from a lawsuit may compromise other important interests that he possesses.[8] We trust individual litigants to make the necessary choices in navigating these risks. When litigants make bad choices, or when they fail to consider the preclusive consequences of a lawsuit at all, we consider it an appropriate expression of litigant autonomy to bind them to the result.

In a class action, however, these observations cease to be merely prosaic. There is a deep tension between the doctrine of preclusion as it is frequently applied in individual litigation and the conditions that serve to limit the use of the class action device. When absent class members are bound to a judgment, they are bound by virtue of the commonality of interest that makes it possible to find individual plaintiffs who will serve as proper representatives for them all.[9] A court's evaluation of factors like adequacy of representation, typicality, and superiority requires it to compare the respective interests and incentives of all the members of the class.[10] When a court conducts such an evaluation, it must do so not only with respect to the likely course of the litigation currently before it, but also with respect to the likely future impact of a judgment upon the interests of class members. In other words, a court must assess, early in the proceedings, what the likely preclusive effect of a judgment will be upon members of the class it has been asked to certify.

Introducing preclusion doctrine into the certification inquiry can present two complications. The first is a time-frame problem. The type of early prognostication inherent in class action procedures is at odds with the retrospective posture that courts often treat as a necessary feature of preclusion analysis, calling for a degree of certainty about

---

[8] I mean here a right that might qualify the effect of the judgment upon the individual litigant. Of course, a litigant may possess a right to recover against incompetent counsel under the law of malpractice.

[9] See *Hansberry v. Lee*, 311 US 32, 42–45 (1940) (finding that Due Process Clause prohibits binding class members to judgment without adequate protections for representation of their interests); cf. *Phillips Petroleum Co. v. Shutts*, 472 US 797, 812 (1985) (reiterating requirement that interests of class members be adequately represented).

[10] See Fed. R. Civ. P. 23(a) (requiring showing of typicality of lead plaintiff's claims in comparison to those of class, and ability of lead plaintiff and class counsel to represent the class adequately); *id.* 23(b)(3) (requiring showing that class action is superior to other forms of relief).

the likely effect of a judgment in subsequent proceedings that the preclusion maxim quoted above appears to foreclose.[11] The second is a doctrinal problem. Even leaving considerations of timing to one side, if the doctrines of claim and issue preclusion that are associated with individual litigation were to apply unaltered to class proceedings, the preclusion inquiry would sometimes reveal significant obstacles to class certification, often in the form of conflicts among the interests of class members in their incentive to settle an action rather than litigate to judgment.

No court can legitimately rule on a request for certification in a class action – at least, a class action that may proceed to a litigated outcome[12] – without achieving a clear understanding of the likely preclusive effect that a judgment in the case would have upon the members of the class and the options that the court has at its disposal for altering or constraining those effects. Nonetheless, many courts regularly proceed without achieving any such understanding. Some flatly refuse to certify a class when preclusion obstacles become apparent, complaining that the time-frame problem prevents any resolution of the issues in the initial forum and concluding that there is an unmanageable 'risk' that absentees will suffer adverse preclusion consequences in future proceedings. Others – most others – simply fail to address the matter at all, creating the possibility that the interests of absentees will be improperly compromised in future cases. The first approach is inadequate and may prevent socially desirable class actions from being certified. The second constitutes a form of judicial malfeasance. The fact that most certifying courts have not been

---

[11] In one of its few statements on the issue, the Court alludes to this problem in the closing passages of the Cooper decision, stating, 'Rule 23 is carefully drafted to provide a mechanism for the expeditious decision of common questions. Its purposes might well be defeated by an attempt to decide a host of individual claims before any common question relating to liability has been resolved adversely to the defendant.' *Cooper v. Fed. Reserve Bank of Richmond*, 467 U.S. 867, 881 (1984). I discuss the Cooper decision at length *infra* section 2(a).

[12] Settlement-only class actions may greatly diminish preclusion-based problems. Indeed, the resolution of preclusion may provide an important example of a 'relevant' feature of a settlement-only class action in the certification process. See *Amchem Prods., Inc. v. Windsor*, 521 U.S. 591, 619 (1997) ('Settlement is relevant to a class certification.'). I discuss these issues above section 3(a)(3).

CHAPTER 9. PRECLUSION IN CLASS ACTION LITIGATION

mindful of preclusion issues in the past cannot authorize further inattention.[13]

Several steps are required to address this problem. The first is to understand it with precision. To that end, section 9.2 of this chapter discusses the different types of preclusion problems that can arise at the outset of a class proceeding. Foremost among these are potential conflicts of interest. When members of an otherwise cohesive class possess different configurations of factually related claims beyond those presented for class certification, the threat of claim and issue preclusion can give them starkly different incentives to prosecute or settle the action. Still other preclusion problems can affect the entire class uniformly. Strategic litigation choices – like a decision to eschew a federal cause of action in order to stay in state court, or a failure to request a particular form of injunctive relief when seeking institutional reform – raise questions about the limits of the representational role in a class proceeding. Section 9.2 takes up these issues in detail.

The next step is to develop more precise tools for discussing preclusion in general and, in particular, for challenging the pervasive and uncritical reliance upon the view that preclusion questions can only be addressed in any meaningful way in a subsequent proceeding. As section 9.3 explains, preclusion questions embrace three distinct inquiries:

(1) a determination as to the exercise of positive legal authority undertaken by the rendering forum;
(2) an inquiry into the actual course of the proceedings in the rendering forum; and
(3) an inquiry into the relationship between the matters resolved in the first lawsuit and the claims or issues raised in a subsequent proceeding.

Contrary to the familiar maxim, only the third of these inquiries lies entirely outside the knowledge or control of the rendering forum. As to the first two, the initial court can exert considerable influence on the future preclusive effects of its own judgment, and often does. This is especially the case when a court seeks to impose constraints upon the preclusive effect that its judgment will have in subsequent proceedings,

---

[13] Cf. Larry Kramer, Choice of Law in Complex Litigation, 71 N.Y.U. L. Rev. 547, 547 (1996) (challenging received view that 'ordinary choice-of-law practices should yield in suits consolidating large numbers of claims').

rather than seeking to predetermine the judgment's affirmative consequences. Section 9.3 offers a more precise positive law account of preclusion doctrine and then explores the tools of limitation that are available to a rendering forum in controlling the future preclusive effect of its own judgments.

With these tools in place, the final step is to determine the proper roles of both the rendering and the recognizing courts in navigating these preclusion issues. In the case of the initial forum, the fact that the court has the power to overcome barriers to certification through the 'negative' or constraining use of preclusion doctrine does not mean that exercising that power always represents the preferred course. When a diligent court identifies potential preclusion problems at the outset of a class proceeding, it should determine the steps that it can take to avoid those problems, but it should also assess the impact of those steps upon other adjudicatory values like fairness to the defendant and the integrity of its own judgments. It is necessary, in other words, to determine whether joinder policies or preclusion policies should predominate when analyzing the propriety of class certification in such a case. As section 9.4 explains, although many class actions could be certified despite what might first appear to be intractable preclusion problems, not all should be.

In the case of a recognizing forum, the primary task will most frequently be to determine the proper response to an initial tribunal's complete inattention to preclusion problems. The number of courts that have even attempted to address preclusion issues at the initial stages of a class proceeding remains small, and the poor track record of some courts in observing other certification requirements suggests that the failure of the rendering forum to address the preclusive consequences of certification will continue to be a serious problem in class litigation. Section 9.5 concludes by arguing that a recognizing court has an appropriate role to play in enforcing constraints upon the preclusive effects of prior class action judgments through a less disruptive application of the adequacy of representation principles that have heretofore been associated with full-scale collateral attacks.

9.2 DEFINING THE PROBLEM

It is necessary, before commencing an in-depth examination of the role of preclusion in class action litigation, to address the Supreme

CHAPTER 9. PRECLUSION IN CLASS ACTION LITIGATION

Court's decision in *Cooper v. Federal Reserve Bank of Richmond*.[14] *Cooper* is the only occasion on which the Court has purported to speak in any detail about the operation of preclusion doctrine in class litigation, and the Court articulated a deceptively simple set of postulates in that case to arrive at the outcome that it produced. The meaning and import of the resulting decision are often misunderstood. Unsurprisingly, *Cooper* has proven inadequate as a framework for the analysis of subsequent preclusion disputes. I preface my examination of the conflicts of interest and representational problems that claim and issue preclusion can generate in a class proceeding with a discussion of the limited usefulness of *Cooper* in moving that analysis forward.

9.2.1 The *Cooper* Case

The dispute in *Cooper* centered around claims of race and gender discrimination at a branch of the Federal Reserve Bank of Richmond located in Charlotte, North Carolina. The case was initially filed by the Equal Employment Opportunity Commission (EEOC), which charged the bank with a 'pattern or practice' violation of Title VII of the Civil Rights Act of 1964 for refusing to promote black and female workers. Four employees later intervened, each asserting the same pattern or practice claim under Title VII along with a claim of individual discrimination under 42 USC § 1981, which authorized the award of more extensive damages than Title VII did at the time.[15] The district court certified the intervenors as representatives of a class consisting of all employees within a specified time period who had been 'discriminated against in promotion, wages, job assignments and terms and conditions of employment because of their race.'[16] The district court issued a ruling in favor of the class on the pattern or practice claim and in favor of two of the four class representatives on their individual claims

---

[14] 467 U.S. 867.
[15] Before the passage of the Civil Rights Act of 1991, Title VII only provided equitable relief and section 1981 was the primary vehicle for obtaining compensatory damages for racial discrimination in private employment contracts. See George Rutherglen, The Improbable History of Section 1981: CLIO Still Bemused and Confused, 2003 Sup. Ct. Rev. 303, 338–339 and notes 125–137 (describing remedial history of Title VII and section 1981).
[16] Cooper, 467 U.S. at 869–870 and n. 3.

of discrimination, but the court of appeals reversed on the merits and ruled in favor of the bank in all respects.[17]

A second group of employees also sought to intervene in the trial at a later point in the proceedings, but the district court denied their request. These employees then filed separate, individual claims of discrimination against the bank. The court of appeals found that the judgment in the class proceeding, as modified by its own reversal on the merits, precluded the unsuccessful intervenors from maintaining their individual claims of discrimination. It was on this portion of the Fourth Circuit's ruling that the Supreme Court granted certiorari.[18]

The Court's ruling on the preclusion question, and the attendant propositions for which *Cooper* is most frequently cited, comes in two parts. First, as a general matter, the Court issued a broad statement in which it purported to hold that the doctrines of claim and issue preclusion operate with full force in class action proceedings:

> There is of course no dispute that under elementary principles of prior adjudication a judgment in a properly entertained class action is binding on class members in any subsequent litigation. Basic principles of res judicata (merger and bar or claim preclusion) and collateral estoppel (issue preclusion) apply. A judgment in favor of the plaintiff class extinguishes their claim, which merges into the judgment granting relief. A judgment in favor of the defendant extinguishes the claim, barring a subsequent action on that claim. A judgment in favor of either side is conclusive in a subsequent action between them on any issue actually litigated and determined, if its determination was essential to that judgment.[19]

Note the sequence of the reasoning here. The passage begins with an observation about the binding effect of class actions – a 'properly entertained class action is binding on class members' – that is little more than a tautology. While the capacity of representative litigation to bind absentees is a relatively recent development in our adjudicatory tradition,[20] that capacity is now well established, and the assertion that class actions are binding when 'properly entertained' tells us little.

---

[17] *EEOC v. Fed. Reserve Bank of Richmond*, 698 F.2d 633, 638, 669–670, 671–673 (4th Cir. 1983), reversed sub nom. Cooper, 467 U.S. 867.
[18] Cooper, 467 U.S. at 873 n. 6.
[19] *Id.* at 874 (citations omitted).
[20] The authoritative account of the historical evolution of class suits in this respect is Geoffrey C. Hazard, Jr. et al., An Historical Analysis of the Binding Effect of Class Suits, 146 U. Pa. L. Rev. 1849 (1998).

CHAPTER 9. PRECLUSION IN CLASS ACTION LITIGATION

This reminder of a class action's binding effect is followed by a series of broad statements about the consequent applicability of 'basic principles' of preclusion doctrine. The implicit suggestion is that the application of 'basic' preclusion principles, in full force, must follow naturally from a determination that a judgment is binding upon class members. This logical fallacy exemplifies one of the pervasive sources of imprecision that this article seeks to correct, and it is no coincidence that the error makes a prominent appearance in the Court's major statement on the issue to date.

The second proposition in *Cooper* concerns the relationship between a 'pattern or practice' claim and a specific allegation of discrimination by an individual. Reversing the appellate court's dismissal of the discrimination claims brought by the second group of intervenors, the Court held that an adverse finding on a pattern or practice claim is not logically inconsistent with a finding of isolated instances of disparate treatment within a business. While the two types of claim might be expected to share significant areas of factual overlap, the Court explained, it is possible for the one to exist in the absence of the other.[21] As an observation about evidentiary findings and logical relationships between claims, this holding is obviously correct. How that observation translates into the actual holding on preclusion doctrine that *Cooper* embodies, however, is a different question. Mapping that translation requires careful attention to the posture of the claims on appeal, an issue as to which the Court's opinion is inattentive.

First, there is some tension between the Court's assertion that 'basic principles of res judicata (merger and bar or claim preclusion) . . . apply' in a class action and the actual holding of the case. Under 'basic

---

[21] The Court put the point in these terms: Proving isolated or sporadic discriminatory acts by the employer is insufficient to establish a prima facie case of a pattern or practice of discrimination; rather it must be established by a preponderance of the evidence that 'racial discrimination was the company's standard operating procedure – the regular rather than the unusual practice.'

> Given the burden of establishing a prima facie case of a pattern or practice of discrimination, it was entirely consistent for the District Court simultaneously to conclude that Cooper and Russell had valid individual claims even though it had expressly found no proof of any classwide discrimination [in the relevant segments of the business].

Cooper, 467 U.S. at 875–876, 878 (citations omitted).

principles of res judicata,' a litigant is ordinarily required to assert all the claims for relief that relate to a given transaction or series of transactions in a single proceeding. If the litigant fails to satisfy this requirement, the maintenance of her claims need not be 'logically inconsistent' with the prior action for a merger or bar to apply. A party attempting to split two requests for relief on the same claim into separate proceedings, or attempting to assert two related claims in successive lawsuits, will ordinarily face a preclusion defense regardless of whether the relief she requests in the second suit would be logically consistent with the result in the first. Nonetheless, the *Cooper* Court permitted the individual class members to assert their discrimination claims in a subsequent proceeding, even though those claims arose out of the same series of transactions as did the class claim – their termination or nonadvancement within the workplace. The Court's opinion does not give a careful account of the preclusion reasoning that led it to this conclusion. Rather, the opinion simply announces the limited effect of the class judgment as if claim preclusion self-evidently required the result. The class judgment:

> (1) bars the class members from bringing another class action against the Bank alleging a pattern or practice of discrimination for the relevant time period [i.e. reasserting the class claim] and (2) precludes the class members in any other litigation with the Bank from relitigating the [issue] whether the Bank engaged in a pattern and practice of discrimination against black employees during the relevant time period. The judgment is not, however, dispositive of the individual claims the ... petitioners have alleged in their separate action.[22]

While this result may represent the correct rule in a Title VII class action, it does not flow inevitably from an application of basic claim preclusion principles.

Second, the Court did not deal at all with any impact that the anticipated preclusive effects of the judgment might have had upon the propriety of the initial class certification in this case. There is a good reason for this omission. Not only was the issue of certification not raised on appeal, but it was not even contested below. The class in *Cooper* was certified on a 'consent order' – an unusual procedure when a class action is certified for trial rather than settlement. The Supreme Court did not discuss this fact at all in its opinion, and the Fourth

---

[22] *Id.* at 880.

CHAPTER 9. PRECLUSION IN CLASS ACTION LITIGATION

Circuit mentioned it only in passing.[23] Thus, there was never any opportunity in *Cooper* to consider the ex ante impact that preclusion effects might have upon the propriety of certifying the class, and the Supreme Court's opinion clearly cannot be read to speak to the issue.

---

[23] See *EEOC v. Fed. Reserve Bank of Richmond*, 698 F.2d 633, 637 (4th Cir. 1983) ('The petition [of the four lead plaintiffs] to intervene was allowed and the intervenors were, by a consent order, certified as the class representatives'), reversed sub nom. *Cooper*, 467 U.S. 867.

One must return to the original record in the case to uncover the sequence of events that led to this certification by consent. The complaint was filed against the bank by the EEOC and alleged discrimination on the basis of both race and sex for a twelve-year period beginning in July 1965, shortly after Title VII took effect. See Joint Appendix Petition for Writ of Certiorari Filed August 4, 1983 Certiorari Granted October 31, 1983 at 24a–26a, Cooper (No. 83-185) [hereinafter Cooper Record] (copy of consent order). When the four individual plaintiffs intervened to seek class certification, they agreed to narrow the complaint in two important respects: They dropped the classwide allegations of sex discrimination and limited the time frame for the race discrimination claim to a period beginning in January 1974, just three years before the action was filed. *Id.* at 26a–27a. (One of the named plaintiffs, Sylvia Cooper, retained the right to pursue her individual sex discrimination claim in the action. See *id.* at 27a.) The court's order suggests that the bank agreed not to contest the certification of the class in exchange for this reduction in its potential exposure. See *id.* at 26a ('The plaintiff-intervenors and the defendant have agreed upon a designation of the class to include all black persons who worked for the defendant at any time since January 3, 1974. The plaintiff-intervenors no longer seek to raise in this action any issues of sex discrimination.'). As a consequence, the district court issued its certification ruling on consent and offered no analysis in support of its order, merely reciting the requirements of Rule 23 and announcing in a conclusory manner that those requirements were satisfied. See *id.* at 27a–29a.

The district court can perhaps be forgiven for this lax procedure. The independent obligation of trial courts to ascertain the propriety of class certification even in the face of agreement by the parties, set forth definitively in Amchem, was not clearly established in 1978 when the court issued its order. Even so, perfunctory analysis by district courts remains pervasive, even in contested certification proceedings, as a recent article by Professor Robert Klonoff demonstrates. See Robert H. Klonoff, The Judiciary's Flawed Application of Rule 23's 'Adequacy of Representation' Requirement, 2004 Mich. St. L. Rev. 671, 673–674 (conducting empirical study and concluding that 'the vast majority of courts conduct virtually no gatekeeping function and approve class representatives and class counsel with little or no analysis').

EMPLOYMENT CLASS AND COLLECTIVE ACTIONS

Third, even leaving aside the unusual circumstances surrounding the certification ruling, the preclusion question decided by the Court in *Cooper* was a limited one in other respects. The case presented only a federal question claim for employment discrimination. The federal courts were thus free to shape substantive preclusion policy in administering this action in ways that might not have been available in a suit encompassing state law claims. Moreover, the particular type of federal claim at issue in the case – an allegation of a pattern or practice of discriminatory behavior by an employer – posed a claim preclusion question that was exceptional.[24]

A pattern or practice claim is a gestalt cause of action. As the Court put it in *General Telephone Co. of Southwest v. Falcon*, such a claim alleges 'the existence of a class of persons who have suffered the same injury' of discriminatory treatment, revealing a 'policy of ... discrimination [that] is reflected [throughout the defendant's] employment practices.'[25] Thus, the assertion of a pattern or practice claim encompasses allegations of a series of individual instances of discrimination, any one of which might itself serve as a basis for relief in an individual lawsuit. As a consequence, it is not merely the case that pattern or practice claims are well suited to classwide treatment, as is the case with many civil rights suits;[26] they call out for such treatment. An individual who has suffered discrimination could ordinarily obtain complete relief in an individual action, making a separate pattern or practice claim redundant. An individual who has not suffered discrimination would have no standing to raise a pattern or practice claim by invoking the injuries

---

[24] The *Cooper* plaintiffs raised only disparate treatment claims. The Supreme Court formally recognized disparate impact claims in 1971, six years before the original complaint in Cooper was filed. See *Griggs v. Duke Power Co.*, 401 US 424, 430–434 (1971) (concluding that legislative intent behind Title VII was to deal with consequences of allegedly discriminatory employment practices and not merely motivation).

[25] 457 US 147, 157–158 (1982); see also *Cooper*, 467 US at 877–878 (pattern or practice claim alleges ' "a companywide practice" ' or 'a consistent practice within a given department' (quoting *Falcon*, 457 U.S. at 159)).

[26] The oft-cited Advisory Committee's note on the 1966 amendment to Rule 23(b)(2) makes this point with respect to civil rights actions generally, offering as its principle illustration 'various actions in the civil-rights field where a party is charged with discriminating unlawfully against a class, usually one whose members are incapable of specific enumeration.' Fed. R. Civ. P. 23(b)(2) advisory committee's note on 1966 amendment.

CHAPTER 9. PRECLUSION IN CLASS ACTION LITIGATION

of others, any more than she would be an appropriate representative for such a claim in a class proceeding.[27] The question of what preclusive effect to attach to a pattern or practice claim is thus most appropriately addressed in the class action context, and the *Cooper* Court used the dispute before it to set forth the appropriate policy on the litigation of such claims. The opinion's almost exclusive reliance upon Title VII precedents, with only the most perfunctory mention of preclusion doctrine, is an accurate reflection of the issues to which the Court addressed itself.[28]

Finally, there was a much simpler ground available for a ruling on the issue of preclusion, had that been the Court's true concern: The district court itself had authorized the intervening class members to proceed with their individual claims with no preclusion bar. Recall that it was the second group of claimants – the 'Baxter intervenors' – whose dismissal on claim preclusion grounds gave rise to the appeal in *Cooper*. The district court had denied the request of those class members to intervene in the remedy phase of the original action and press their individual claims because they were not employed at the pay grades as to which the district court had found a pattern of discrimination during the liability phase.[29] The court denied their motion 'without prejudice to any underlying rights the intervenors may have,' however, and went on to state its belief that nothing in the class proceeding would prevent the would-be intervenors from pursuing their individual claims:

> The pendency of this action has apparently tolled the rights of the would be intervenors to file separate individual actions preceded by claims filed with the EEOC as to Title VII rights, and it has also apparently tolled their rights to file suit under 42 USC § 1981.
>
> I see no reason why, if any of the would be intervenors are actively interested in pursuing their claims, they cannot file a Section 1981 suit next

---

[27] Falcon, 457 U.S. at 157–159 (describing requirements of adequacy and typicality in pattern or practice class claim). For an individual who has suffered disparate treatment, a pattern or practice claim might nonetheless be attractive as a way of expanding the scope of the evidence that will be available at a trial. Even so, it would constitute a redundant remedy.

[28] The entirety of the Court's discussion of preclusion precedent and theory is contained in a single paragraph, part of which is quoted above, that simply offers a string cite of the 'usual suspects' on the subject. See *Cooper*, 467 U.S. at 874.

[29] Cooper Record, *supra* n. 23, at 287a–288a (copy of order denying motion for leave to intervene).

week, nor why they could not file a claim with EEOC next week. More pertinently, since the EEOC is a party to this case and seems to have an active interest in seeing that the claims of the four intervenors are pursued, I see no reason why all formalities of processing the claim and the subsequent proceedings of conciliation and mediation could not be accomplished in very short order, like two weeks or less, so that this whole question could become moot in a few weeks.[30]

On the strength of these statements, the class members did not appeal the denial of their motion to intervene in what was at that point a successful pattern or practice suit, and instead filed a separate action to pursue their individual claims. In something of a judicial bait and switch, the Fourth Circuit reversed the district court's finding for the class on the pattern or practice claim and then found that claim preclusion barred the Baxter intervenors from maintaining their individual claims in a separate suit, despite the obvious intention of the district court to avoid that result, dismissing the portions of the district court's order quoted above as 'plain dictum.'[31] In a final confirmation of the true nature of its focus in the case, the Supreme Court failed to analyze these aspects of the proceedings, referring only briefly to the district court's 'pointed refus[al] to decide the individual claims of the Baxter petitioners' in holding that the decision whether to join such claims under Rule 23 was 'a matter of judicial administration that should be decided in the first instance by the District Court.'[32]

Cooper, in short, is a Title VII opinion, not an opinion about the preclusive effects of class action judgments. The Court confronted a limited question – whether plaintiffs automatically lose their ability to raise individual claims of employment discrimination when a pattern or practice claim fails – and it offered an answer informed primarily by Title VII policy, making no attempt to explain its result with reference to general preclusion principles. While the opinion may have some elements of preclusion doctrine embedded in its holding, it provides little guidance for the array of preclusion problems that can arise – and that courts have begun to confront – in the increasingly diverse range of class action litigation.

---

[30] *Id.* at 288a–289a.
[31] *EEOC v. Fed. Reserve Bank of Richmond*, 698 F.2d 633, 673–675 (4th Cir. 1983), reversed sub nom. *Cooper*, 467 US 867.
[32] *Cooper*, 467 U.S. at 881.

9.2.2 Conflicts of Interest

The potential for conflicts of interest within a putative class is the most acute problem that preclusion doctrine poses to class litigation. Such a conflict most commonly arises when different groups within a class possess different configurations of claims relating to the same transaction. Suppose, for example, that a class was certified on behalf of all purchasers of an automobile containing a design defect that reduced the car's resale value. Suppose further that some subset of the class had suffered an additional harm as a result of the defect – say, an automobile accident – giving rise to a factually related claim for relief that was unsuitable for class treatment. If the common claim for economic damages was certified and litigated on behalf of the entire class, the resulting judgment may have adverse preclusive effects on the related accident claims. Only those members of the class who possessed the accident claim will be subject to such adverse preclusive effects. As a result, a conflict of interest arises between the two groups of claimants as to the risks and benefits of litigation.

Claim preclusion and issue preclusion implicate this conflict in related but distinct fashions. In the case of claim preclusion, the potential for conflict arises from the prohibition on the 'splitting' of claims. That doctrine ordinarily prevents a plaintiff from asserting two related claims in successive proceedings, even if the first claim is successful. If an individual is a member of a class that has litigated the economic damages claim in our example, and then that same individual seeks to assert her accident claim in a subsequent, individual proceeding, merger (if the plaintiff class prevailed) or bar (if it failed) may prevent recovery. Under this scenario, some members of the class in the initial proceeding are asked to sacrifice their related claims in order to permit the class claim to move forward.

In the case of issue preclusion, the potential for conflict arises from the overlap of factual or legal issues among the multiple claims. If there is a sufficient overlap of issues between one claim that is common to an entire class and other claims possessed only by some class members, an adverse determination of key issues in the common claim could preclude absentees from establishing the required elements in their related claims. This is so, of course, even where claim preclusion would not impose an absolute barrier to recovery. Thus, in our example, suppose that the plaintiff class loses on its claim for economic damages because the finder of fact concludes that the automobiles in question were not defective. If the members of the class with accident claims seek to maintain individual lawsuits for their personal injuries, they may be estopped from relitigating the issue of defect and hence unable to recover. Under this scenario, some members of the class are asked to assume a greater risk when they participate in the class proceeding, since an adverse finding on key issues in the resolution of the common claim may fatally undermine their ability to recover on their individual claims.

Some of these preclusion problems may seem to beg simple responses. Where claim preclusion is concerned, perhaps an individual claim that is unsuitable for classwide treatment is best described as one that 'could not have been brought' in the class proceeding and hence should not be subject to claim preclusion. Similarly, established limitations on issue preclusion like those making reference to the ability and incentives of litigants to contest or appeal an issue might sometimes mitigate the potential for conflict within the class.[33] Such responses may ultimately correspond to defensible doctrinal solutions in some instances. That is not always the case, however, and the apparent simplicity of these responses is deceptive.

Class certification and preclusion both entail inquiries that are difficult to discuss in the abstract.[34] In embarking upon a discussion of the intersection of these two doctrines, it will be useful to have a vocabulary of claims, claimants, and facts to draw upon for reference.[35] I begin with an overview of two of the areas of class litigation in which courts have

---

[33] See 18A Wright, Miller, and Cooper, *supra* n. 2, § 4455, at 465 ('[I]t may be appropriate to reduce the complexity of class litigation by imposing special limits on the basic transactional approach to defining a claim or cause of action.'); see also Restatement (Second) of Judgments §§ 28–29 (1982) (setting forth broadly worded qualifications to use of issue preclusion in an F2 proceeding); 18A Wright, Miller, and Cooper, *supra* n. 2, § 4455, at 490 (offering example of class action relating to economic damages and concluding that prosaic limitations on issue preclusion would militate against any estoppel in individual action by class member for personal injury).

[34] Professor Cooper's plaintive footnote in his report from the front lines of the Advisory Committee, where he despairs of providing a concise explanation of Amchem, is emblematic where class actions are concerned. See Edward H. Cooper, The (Cloudy) Future of Class Actions, 40 Ariz. L. Rev. 923, 925 n. 2 (1998).

[35] See David L. Shapiro, Civil Procedure: Preclusion in Civil Actions 22–24 (2001) [hereinafter Shapiro, Preclusion] (offering a simple factual scenario as a frequent point of reference in subsequent discussions of preclusion doctrine).

CHAPTER 9. PRECLUSION IN CLASS ACTION LITIGATION

begun to confront the potential conflicts of interest created by preclusion doctrine most directly: Title VII suits in the wake of the Civil Rights Act of 1991, and tort class actions in the wake of *Amchem Products, Inc. v. Windsor*.[36]

9.2.2.1 Title VII and the Civil Rights Act of 1991

Perhaps the highest profile area of class litigation where preclusion problems have begun to appear involves Title VII. The problems arise out of the 1991 amendment to the Civil Rights Act of 1964 and an attempt to expand the relief available to aggrieved plaintiffs that has produced unforeseen complications.

Under the original version of the Civil Rights Act, the principal remedies available to a plaintiff in a Title VII case were injunctive or declaratory relief and equitable restitution in the form of back pay. With the Civil Rights Act of 1991, Congress significantly expanded the range of remedies under Title VII, authorizing plaintiffs who suffer from intentional discrimination to request compensatory damages for emotional or other harms, punitive damages, and a jury trial for the resolution of these claims.[37] Though crafted as a pro-plaintiff reform, the 1991 Act has had the unforeseen consequence of throwing into doubt the amenability of Title VII claims to class certification. This doubt has unfolded in two stages. The first concerns the proper treatment of these expanded Title VII actions under Rule 23(b) and is the issue that has received the lion's share of attention. The second, which implicates preclusion doctrine, has resulted from associated attempts by class counsel to circumvent these Rule 23(b) problems.

When the relief available in a Title VII action was primarily injunctive in nature, with restitutional damages occupying only a subsidiary role, Rule 23(b)(2) served as the principal vehicle for the prosecution of employment discrimination claims. Proceeding under (b)(2) enabled plaintiffs to certify a class without satisfying the additional requirements of predominance and superiority and freed them from providing the costly notice and opt-out rights that Rule 23(b)(3) would demand. When Congress expanded the relief for intentional discrimination to

---

[36] 521 U.S. 591 (1997).
[37] 42 USC § 1981a (2000).

include compensatory and punitive damages, a question arose as to whether (b)(2) treatment remained appropriate for these suits.[38] As a purely doctrinal matter, the scope of Rule 23(b)(2) may not extend to suits in which compensatory damages constitute a substantial portion of the relief requested by the class.[39] As a constitutional matter, notice to class members and an opportunity to opt out may be required for multistate class actions that involve the adjudication of substantial monetary claims, even when those claims are admixed with an overarching request for injunctive relief.[40]

The most dramatic response to this change in the Title VII landscape has come from the Fifth Circuit in its much-noted decision in *Allison v. Citgo Petroleum Corp.*, which upheld a district court's denial of certification in a run-of-the-mill employment discrimination suit because of the complications introduced by the 1991 Act.[41] The plaintiffs in the case had raised both disparate impact and disparate treatment claims against a Citgo plant, seeking both injunctive and monetary damages, and the district court refused to certify on the grounds that the addition of the damages claims made certification under Rule 23 impossible. The Fifth Circuit held that the district court did not abuse its discretion in finding Rule 23(b)(2) unavailable for the certification of the hybrid injunctive and monetary claims in the case, and it strongly suggested that (b)(2) might never be available

---

[38] As Judge Easterbrook recently wrote, 'the statutory authorization in 1991 of damages recoveries for employees in Title VII cases has complicated what used to be an almost automatic class certification in pattern-or-practice cases.' *Allen v. Int'l Truck & Engine Corp.*, 358 F.3d 469, 470 (7th Cir. 2004).

[39] See Fed. R. Civ. P. 23(b)(2) advisory committee's n. on 1966 amendment ('The subdivision does not extend to cases in which the appropriate final relief relates exclusively or predominantly to money damages.'); *Ticor Title Ins. Co. v. Brown*, 511 U.S. 117, 121 (1994) (per curiam) (suggesting possibility that class action seeking substantial money damages can only be certified under (b)(3) and dismissing writ of certiorari for review of constitutional question as improvidently granted).

[40] See *Phillips Petroleum Co. v. Shutts*, 472 US 797, 811–812 (1985) (establishing notice and opportunity to opt out as minimal requirements for establishing personal jurisdiction in class suit for damages); *Jefferson v. Ingersoll Int'l Inc.*, 195 F.3d 894, 897–899 (7th Cir. 1999) (assuming that due process requires these procedures when substantial monetary claims are at stake). The constitutional issue is a bit more complicated, as explained above section 3(b)(3)(b).

[41] 151 F.3d 402, 410–426 (5th Cir. 1998).

CHAPTER 9. PRECLUSION IN CLASS ACTION LITIGATION

for Title VII claims that include requests for substantial monetary damages.[42] It also affirmed the lower court's finding that this hybrid action – and, the court implied, almost any such action – could not satisfy the requirements of superiority and predominance under Rule 23(b)(3).[43] These two holdings – both part of the 'first stage' of the doctrinal response to the 1991 Act as that term is used above – have placed significant limitations on the ability of any plaintiff in the Fifth Circuit to maintain a Title VII action for classwide relief that includes a request for damages. The Seventh Circuit has followed the Fifth in its Rule 23(b) holding[44] (though the Second Circuit has declined to[45]), and the cases have been the subject of much controversy.[46]

After issuing these core holdings, the *Allison* court went on to reject several alternative strategies offered by the plaintiffs by which they hoped to utilize a bifurcated action to finesse the certification problem. In each of these strategies, plaintiffs proposed to litigate only the portions of the case that could be certified under Rule 23(b)(2) in the initial phase of the suit and to leave the resolution of the damages claims for

---

[42] *Id.* at 417–418 and n. 13.

[43] *Id.* at 418–420.

[44] See Ingersoll, 195 F.3d at 897–899.

[45] *Robinson v. Metro-N. Commuter R.R. Co.*, 267 F.3d 147, 162–167 (2nd Cir. 2001) (rejecting uncompromising rule of Allison and Ingersoll in favor of 'ad-hoc approach').

[46] See e.g., Linda S. Mullenix, No Exit: Mandatory Class Actions in the New Millennium and the Blurring of Categorical Imperatives, 2003 U. Chi. Legal F. 177, 207–214 (criticizing ungenerous approach of Allison and Ingersoll); Brad Seligman and Jocelyn D. Larkin, Lessons in Class Certification, Trial, October 2001, at 36, 36–37 (describing impact of Allison and its progeny on Title VII litigation).

Subsequent decisions by the Fifth Circuit have blunted some of the more far-reaching consequences of Allison's Rule 23(b) holding. The court has held that a court's certification inquiry must proceed on a 'claim-by-claim' rather than an 'holistic' basis in order to preserve the ability of Title VII plaintiffs to pursue class actions whenever possible. See *Bolin v. Sears, Roebuck & Co.*, 231 F.3d 970, 976 (5th Cir. 2000). It has adopted more forgiving standards for determining when Title VII damages calculations may be made consistently with the requirements of Rule 23(b)(2), see In re Monumental Life Ins. Co., 365 F.3d 408, 416–420 (5th Cir. 2004), and, in an unpublished opinion, one panel has authorized certification of an 'inconsistent adjudications' Title VII suit under Rule 23(b)(1)(A) to avoid Allison problems, see *Smith v. Crystian*, 91 F. Appx. 952, 954–955 (5th Cir. 2004).

later in the proceeding.[47] The appellate court rejected these attempts on the strength of an aggressive reading of the Seventh Amendment. The Amendment requires factual questions that overlap claims for damages and equitable relief in a single action to be submitted to a jury for resolution.[48] The court found that the region of overlap between disparate impact and pattern or practice claims was so great that it would require the empanelling of a jury in any initial, equitable resolution of the disparate impact claims.[49] That being so, the court went on to find, later juries empanelled to decide damages claims in the succeeding phase of litigation would inevitably run afoul of the Reexamination Clause by making independent findings on those overlapping issues.[50] The Fifth Circuit thus concluded that the difficulty of avoiding Seventh Amendment problems prevented the use of bifurcation to litigate both the equitable and the monetary Title VII claims in a single class action proceeding.

Finally, as if tying up a loose end, the Fifth Circuit added the following sentence at the close of its Seventh Amendment analysis: 'Nor may [the damages claims] be advanced in a *subsequent* class action without being barred by res judicata and collateral estoppel, because all of the common factual issues will already have been decided, or could have been decided, in the prior litigation.'[51] It is this part of the Fifth

---

[47] There was some confusion as to whether the plaintiffs proposed litigating both the disparate impact claim and the liability portions of the disparate treatment claim in such a bifurcated action, or instead sought to litigate only the disparate impact claim. The Fifth Circuit concluded that the district court had discretion to reject either scenario. See Allison, 151 F.3d at 420–426.

[48] See *Dairy Queen, Inc. v. Wood*, 369 U.S. 469, 472–473 (1962) (holding that right to jury trial on legal issues applies regardless of whether legal claims are 'incidental' to equitable claims); *Beacon Theaters, Inc. v. Westover*, 359 U.S. 500, 510–511 (1959) (holding that 'only under the most imperative circumstances ... can the right to a jury trial of legal issues be lost through prior determination of equitable claims').

[49] Allison, 151 F.3d at 422–425.

[50] This finding was a debatable one, as the dissent pointed out. See *id.* at 433–434 (Dennis, J., dissenting) (arguing that issues to be determined during proposed stages of litigation 'are separate and distinct and the second jury will not reexamine issues decided by the first jury'). Indeed, the opinion is rather vague in its Seventh Amendment analysis and does not make this last step in its reasoning explicit, see *id.* at 423–425, leaving it to the dissent to spell out the steps of the majority's logic by way of refuting them, see *id.* at 433 (Dennis, J., dissenting).

[51] *Id.* at 425 (citing *Montana v. United States*, 440 U.S. 147, 153 (1979); *Nilsen v. City of Moss Point*, 701 F.2d 556, 559–564 (5th Cir. 1983) (en banc)).

CHAPTER 9. PRECLUSION IN CLASS ACTION LITIGATION

Circuit's opinion, addressing the second 'stage' of the doctrinal response to the 1991 Act, that is relevant for present purposes.

For reasons that should be obvious, the court's perfunctory statement about the preclusive consequences of conducting two separate proceedings was wrong in several ways at once. Issue preclusion never applies to issues that 'could have been decided' in a prior litigation; it requires actual litigation of issues that were necessary to a prior judgment.[52] Claim preclusion does not necessarily operate to preclude litigation of factually related claims in subsequent class proceedings, as *Cooper* itself made clear in construing an earlier version of the same statute that was at issue in *Allison*. Perhaps the court was proceeding on some misguided instinct that it should not be possible to accomplish through successive lawsuits what the Seventh Amendment would prevent a court from doing in a single, bifurcated proceeding.[53] (This instinct was misguided, of course, because the Supreme Court had already rejected that proposition some twenty years earlier.[54])

---

[52] See Restatement (Second) of Judgments § 27 (1982) ('When an issue of fact or law is actually litigated and determined by a valid and final judgment, and the determination is essential to the judgment, the determination is conclusive in a subsequent action between the parties, whether on the same or a different claim.'); *id.* § 27 cmt. e ('A judgment is not conclusive in a subsequent action as to issues which might have been but were not litigated and determined in the prior action.').

[53] Professor Woolley examines a similar proposition in his article discussing Judge Posner's opinion in In re Rhone-Poulenc Rorer Inc., 51 F.3d 1293 (7th Cir. 1995), and the role of the Reexamination Clause in the certification of 'issue classes.' See Patrick Woolley, Mass Tort Litigation and the Seventh Amendment Reexamination Clause, 83 Iowa L. Rev. 499 (1998) [hereinafter Woolley, Reexamination Clause]. Woolley concludes that the Seventh Amendment should be interpreted in a dynamic and nonrigid fashion that would permit the use of issue classes, bifurcation, and other mechanisms involving overlapping issues, provided that doing so will not create undue confusion for juries. See *id.* at 517–542.

[54] *Parklane Hosiery Co. v. Shore*, 439 U.S. 322, 333–337 (1979), in which the Court authorized the limited use of offensive nonmutual issue preclusion in federal question cases, presented a Seventh Amendment situation similar to this 'shadow' question in Allison. Parklane involved two proceedings, the first an enforcement action brought by the government and tried before the bench in equity, the second a damages action brought by a class of stockholders and tried before a jury. The plaintiffs sought to benefit from a finding in the earlier enforcement action that Parklane had issued a false and misleading proxy statement. Parklane argued that applying an estoppel in a damages action would violate its right to trial by

Whatever its thought process, the majority should have realized that it was traveling a confused path when it produced this convoluted misstatement on preclusion. But it did not, and *Allison* has produced confusion over the preclusive effect that the certification of a (b)(2) class action for equitable relief will have upon plaintiffs' subsequent attempts to recover on individual damages claims in a Title VII case.[55]

Indeed, though *Allison*'s own statement on the preclusion issue is somewhat nonsensical, the 1991 Act does give rise to issue preclusion consequences that require close attention. A court's resolution of a disparate impact claim in a stand-alone proceeding will often involve issues of fact that overlap the elements of an intentional discrimination claim. An unfavorable result in the equitable proceeding therefore threatens to preclude class members from litigating their damages claims in individual suits, since an adverse finding on an overlapping issue might prevent a class member from establishing an element of his claim.[56] A victory in the equitable proceeding, however, would not offer the concomitant benefit of a guaranteed victory in the damages claims, since a plaintiff in a disparate treatment claim will always have

---

jury under the Seventh Amendment. The Court disagreed, finding that 'if an issue common to both legal and equitable claims was first determined by a judge, relitigation of the issue before a jury [in a separate action] might be foreclosed by res judicata or collateral estoppel,' even if a different result would obtain if the two claims were joined in the same action. *Id.* at 334.

Thus, to the extent that Allison's statement about preclusion relied upon a belief that any limitation imposed by the Seventh Amendment in the structuring of a single, bifurcated action must be replicated by preclusion doctrine in successive actions, that belief was mistaken.

[55] See George Rutherglen, Fed. Judicial Ctr., Major Issues in the Federal Law of Employment Discrimination 98–99 (4th edn 2004), available at <www.fjc.gov/public/pdf.nsf/lookup/EmplDis4.pdf/$file/EmplDis4.pdf> (on file with the Columbia Law Review) ('The overall effect of the [Allison] decision certainly is not to increase the availability of class actions in Title VII cases, and the ironic consequence is that the expanded remedies created by the Civil Rights Act of 1991 might restrict the procedures formerly available to victims of discrimination.').

[56] The Supreme Court makes a related point in Cooper in discussing the factual relatedness of classwide and individual discrimination claims. See *Cooper v. Fed. Reserve Bank of Richmond*, 467 U.S. 867, 880 (1984) ('[T]he prior adjudication [of the classwide pattern or practice claim] may well prove beneficial to the Bank in the [individual discrimination] action.').

CHAPTER 9. PRECLUSION IN CLASS ACTION LITIGATION

to establish additional facts relating to her individual circumstances: causation, the absence of a nonpretextual explanation for the adverse employment action, and so forth.[57] Given these risks, are the interests of the class well served by authorizing class counsel to litigate the equitable claim?

If only some members of the class have viable damages claims for individual discrimination, as will usually be the case, the problem becomes more acute. The plaintiffs whose high-value damages claims are placed in jeopardy by the potential issue-preclusive effects of the equitable action will likely be risk averse, willing to settle the (b)(2) action for modest structural reforms in order to avoid endangering their damages claims. The plaintiffs who have no hope of substantial monetary recovery, in contrast, will be more interested in going for broke in seeking a litigated outcome, since they have no adverse preclusion consequences to fear. If issue preclusion operates in its normal mode in such cases, an ex ante conflict can arise between the incentives of class members with viable damages claims and those without in any (b)(2) action, even if those damages claims are neither litigated in the action nor directly threatened through an application of claim preclusion.

In one post-*Allison* decision, *Zachery v. Texaco Exploration & Production, Inc.*, a district court that apprehended some of these potential conflicts proclaimed itself powerless to guard against the 'very real possibility, if not . . . probability, that another court of competent jurisdiction could determine that the proposed class members would be barred from bringing individual actions for damages' if it were to certify a class for injunctive relief.[58] Invoking the ubiquitous maxim that a court 'cannot conclusively determine the res judicata effect of [its own] decision,' the district court concluded that its only option was to 'assess the risk of such a determination and weigh it in the consideration of the certification of a class.'[59] The court then denied certification altogether, explaining that it was unable to assure itself

---

[57] Professors Silver and Baker offer a useful discussion of these potentially divergent incentives in employment litigation. See Charles Silver and Lynn Baker, I Cut, You Choose: The Role of Plaintiffs' Counsel in Allocating Settlement Proceeds, 84 Va. L. Rev. 1465, 1491–1494 (1998).
[58] 185 F.R.D. 230, 243 (W.D. Tex. 1999).
[59] *Id.*

that a Title VII action could be structured in a way that would serve the interests of the class.[60]

Thus, following the Civil Rights Act of 1991, litigation of Title VII cases presents a series of preclusion-related problems. There is a claim preclusion question: Does the decision to assert only claims for injunctive relief on behalf of a class of employees require the plaintiffs to sacrifice (or 'risk' sacrificing) their individual damages claims outright? It presents an issue preclusion question: Would an adverse result in an injunctive suit have issue preclusive effects that could sound the death knell for individual damages claims, and how does that risk affect the suitability of the action for class treatment? It presents a question about conflicts of interest: If only some members of the class have damages claims to lose, whether through claim or issue preclusion, is it possible to accommodate the interests of both groups of employees in a single injunctive action? It also presents a question about the desirability of class treatment in the first instance: If the use of a class action to litigate claims for equitable relief will inevitably entail a serious risk of sacrificing the damages claims of class members, does that risk call into question the propriety of proceeding under Rule 23? Contrary to the Fifth Circuit's precipitous conclusion in *Allison*, it is entirely possible to answer these questions in a fashion that enables plaintiffs to pursue the forms of relief contemplated in the 1991 Act, as sections 9.3 and 9.4 explain.

9.2.2.2 Tort Class Actions

The range of preclusion problems that arises out of the bifurcated litigation typical of Title VII cases has also begun to find more general expression in class actions involving tort claims. This has been particularly true following the Supreme Court's decision in *Amchem*, which imposed strict constraints on the certification of personal injury claims and has encouraged a concomitant change in the character of tort class actions.[61] *Amchem* did not produce an appreciable reduction in the rate

---

[60] See *id.* at 244–245 ('The class members the Plaintiffs seek to represent must be given the opportunity to pursue intentional discrimination claims and seek monetary damages, and certifying this class may very well deny them just that chance.').

[61] The most immediate impact of Amchem has been felt in the federal courts, as the holding of the case related only to Rule 23. Since many states have chosen to track the

CHAPTER 9. PRECLUSION IN CLASS ACTION LITIGATION

at which class action lawsuits are brought to federal court (other than a short lived blip that surrounded the decision itself).[62] Even so, the constellation of claims asserted in these suits appears to be shifting as plaintiffs' attorneys attempt to craft class proceedings that will satisfy

---

Federal Rules closely and view federal decisions construing those rules as authoritative, the Court's ruling has also had a doctrinal impact upon state class litigation. See e.g., *Hoffman v. Cohen*, 538 A.2d 1096–1098 (Del. 1988) (noting that rules of procedure in Delaware were patterned after Federal Rules and so cases construing Federal Rules are persuasive authority); *Riley v. New Rapids Carpet Ctr.*, 294 A.2d 7, 11 (N.J. 1972) (describing New Jersey's class action provision as 'a replica of Rule 23 of the Federal Rules of Civil Procedure as amended in 1966').

[62] In 2002, the Advisory Committee on Civil Rules commissioned the Federal Judicial Center to perform a comprehensive study aimed at determining the effects of *Amchem* and *Ortiz v. Fibreboard Corp.*, 527 U.S. 815 (1999), on federal class actions. See Bob Niemic and Tom Willging, Fed. Judicial Ctr., Effects of *Amchem/Ortiz* on the Filing of Federal Class Actions: Report to the Advisory Committee on Civil Rules (September 9, 2002), available at <www.fjc.gov/public/pdf.nsf/lookup/AmChem.pdf/$file/AmChem.pdf> (on file with the Columbia Law Review) [hereinafter FJC Filing Rate Report]. The study examined the rates at which class actions were brought to federal court (through original filing or removal) from January 1994 to June 2001 and used a time series regression model in an attempt to identify significant causal relationships between the changes in filing rates and the Supreme Court's two major opinions on certification. See *id.* at 4–5 (describing contents of database used in study); *id.* at 34–35 (describing methodology employed in data analysis).

The rate at which class action lawsuits were brought to federal court increased steadily over the course of the study period. The only significant deviation from this trend was a decrease in the filing rate of nonsecurities class actions immediately following the Court's decision in Amchem, followed by a renewal of the upward trend in the wake of Ortiz. See *id.* at 6–10 (describing overview of findings). While it is difficult to draw robust conclusions about the causal effect of a single Supreme Court decision on a decision as complex as whether and where to file a class action lawsuit, the study tentatively concluded that the correlation between Amchem and the brief decrease in filing rates was not purely coincidental. See *id.* at 1–2 (summarizing findings). The increase in filing rates following Ortiz is counterintuitive, since the decision imposed further limitations upon the use of alternative class action strategies to circumvent the holding of Amchem. To the extent that the two are causally linked, the upward trend might best be explained by the fact that Ortiz clarified the doctrinal landscape following Amchem and ended a period during which plaintiff attorneys may have refrained from filing new class actions while they reassessed the best strategies to employ.

EMPLOYMENT CLASS AND COLLECTIVE ACTIONS

the new restrictions.[63] If this trend continues, preclusion issues promise to figure prominently in the assessment of these more tailored tort classes.

---

[63] It is difficult to offer any comprehensive assessment of the breadth and scope of class action lawsuits, particularly since reliable data often are not available from state court systems. See FJC Filing Rate Report, *supra* n. 62, at 3 (excluding rates of state filings from class action study due to lack of available data). Nonetheless, there is good reason to think that the profile of class action lawsuits is undergoing a change. Some key state jurisdictions have begun to impose and enforce Amchem-like restrictions on the use of omnibus class actions, See e.g., *S.W. Refining Co. v. Bernal*, 22 S.W.3d 425, 433–436 (Tex. 2000) (requiring strict enforcement of predominance and superiority requirements in damages class action), and federal courts have been turning away nationwide class actions that attempt to sweep a broad array of claims into a single proceeding, See e.g., In re Bridgestone/Firestone, Inc. Tires Prods. Liab. Litig. (Bridgestone/Firestone I), 288 F.3d 1012, 1018–1021 (7th Cir. 2002) (rejecting nationwide class action in product defect case due to serious predominance and manageability problems created by divergent choice of law rules); In re Methyl Tertiary Butyl Ether ('MTBE') Prods. Liab. Litig., 209 F.R.D. 323, 343–345 (S.D.N.Y. 2002) (refusing to certify multistate class action where need for individually tailored environmental remediation for every class member made certification under Rule 23(b)(2) inappropriate). The most noteworthy exception in the federal courts to this recent trend – the massive nationwide class action settlement being administered in the Eastern District of Pennsylvania to address the heart valve damage inflicted by the diet drugs commonly known as Fen-Phen – has been a spectacular failure that will not likely invite emulation. See In re Diet Drugs (Phentermine, Fenfluramine, Dexfenfluramine) Prods. Liab. Litig., MDL No. 1023, Civil Action No. 99-20593, 2000 WL 1222042, at *1 (E.D. Pa. August 28, 2000) (granting certification for nationwide settlement-only class action encompassing approximately 6 million consumers with potential heart valve injuries); Class Counsel's Memorandum of Law in Support of Joint Motion by Wyeth, Class Counsel, and the Seventh Amendment Liaison Committee for the Entry of an Order Preliminarily Approving the Seventh Amendment to the Nationwide Class Action Settlement Agreement and for the Entry of Related Orders: (1) Directing the Resumption of the Parallel Processing Program; (2) Approving a Procedure for Resolving Outstanding Post-Audit Determination; and (3) Approving the Eighth Amendment to the Settlement Agreement at 38–39, In re Diet Drugs (MDL No. 1023, Civil Action No. 99-20593) (describing settlement as hovering on brink of complete collapse).

More broadly, class counsels' decisions about where to file a lawsuit and how to structure the action will always be influenced by their assumptions about the reception that they are likely to receive from the certifying judge – a common sense proposition to which the Federal Judicial Center recently lent credence with an

CHAPTER 9. PRECLUSION IN CLASS ACTION LITIGATION

One of the most notable trends among tort class actions has been a shift toward proceeding under Rule 23(b)(1) or (2), rather than (b)(3), even when class members possess substantial damages claims. In a move paralleling some of the core issues that played out in *Allison*, class counsel in a broad range of cases have either sought to characterize damages claims as appurtenant or subordinate to equitable claims when the damages claims might be suitable for class treatment, or else to carve damages claims out of a suit entirely and litigate only equitable claims when class treatment of the damages claims is clearly not possible.[64] Courts confronting such efforts in the posture of a recognizing forum – that is, in an F2 proceeding where a defendant seeks to rely upon an F1 judgment for a preclusion defense – are fairly consistent in their reactions, generally rejecting expansive claim preclusion defenses but entertaining issue preclusion arguments more seriously.[65] When

---

attorney survey seeking to quantify the criteria that class counsel use in choosing between a federal and a state forum. See Thomas E. Willging and Shannon R. Wheatman, Fed. Judicial Ctr., Attorney Reports on the Impact of Amchem and Ortiz on Choice of a Federal or State Forum in Class Action Litigation 5-10 (April 2004), available at <www.fjc.gov/public/pdf.nsf/lookup/AmOrt02.pdf/$file/AmOrt02.pdf> (on file with the Columbia Law Review) [hereinafter FJC Forum Choice Report] (summarizing results of attorney survey, which found strong tendency to seek out most hospitable forum). Although the study found that Amchem and Ortiz were not foremost in the minds of most attorneys selecting between federal and state fora, the decisions have had some effect. See *id.* at 6. As more omnibus class actions are rejected on the authority of those two decisions, one can expect that class counsel will attempt to pare down their lawsuits in order to satisfy the newly imposed standards.

[64] See e.g., Samuel Issacharoff, Class Action Conflicts, 30 U.C. Davis L. Rev. 805, 820–824 (1997) [hereinafter Issacharoff, Conflicts] (describing pre-Ortiz attempts to use the limited-fund class action to get around notice, opt-out, and predominance requirements).

[65] See e.g., *Hiser v. Franklin*, 94 F.3d 1287, 1290–1294 (9th Cir. 1996) (applying Alaska law to deny claim preclusion defense of prison officials in civil rights suit initiated by a prisoner alleged to be precluded by consent decree in an earlier suit); In re Jackson Lockdown/MCO Cases, 568 F. Supp. 869, 891–893 (E.D. Mich. 1983) (disallowing claim preclusion defense but entertaining issue preclusion defense in individual suit by prisoner following class action); *Jahn ex rel. Jahn v. ORCR, Inc.*, 92 P.3d 984, 985 (Colo. 2004) (en banc) (adopting 'absolute' rule that suits for injunctive relief filed under state rule 23(b)(2) never have claim preclusive effect on damages claims).

courts confront these issues in an initial proceeding, however – that is, as an F1 forum – they frequently repeat the complaint of powerlessness heard above in the *Zachery* decision and profess themselves unable to protect the rights of class members against possible preclusion in the future.

A recent decision from the Southern District of New York, *In re Methyl Tertiary Butyl Ether ('MTBE') Products Liability Litigation*,[66] is typical of the latter trend. In 2000 and 2001, property owners around the country brought suit over the contamination of their well water by MTBE, a gasoline additive. Collectively, these plaintiffs named an enormous group of oil companies as defendants, comprising every producer of MTBE that they could identify. The suits were consolidated by the Judicial Panel on Multidistrict Litigation and transferred to Judge Shira Scheindlin's court,[67] where the plaintiffs asked to be certified as class representatives for a suit encompassing all property owners in Florida, California, New York, and Illinois whose well water was contaminated

---

Some courts have precluded individual claimants for failure to intervene in a class action and assert their individual claims, but most such opinions are sufficiently old as to have limited continuing relevance. See e.g., *Int'l Prisoners' Union v. Rizzo*, 356 F. Supp. 806, 809–810 (E.D. Pa. 1973) (barring prisoner who received notice of class proceeding but failed to intervene and raise individual claims from pursuing claims in subsequent suit).

To the extent that such opinions rely upon a general duty of class members to appear and intervene when they have notice of a suit, they are undermined by *Martin v. Wilks*, 490 U.S. 755, 762–765 (1989), which disclaimed any general duty to intervene on the part of affected individuals with notice of a pending action. The particular intervention issue decided by the Court in Martin was one of the topics that Congress addressed in the Civil Rights Act of 1991, reversing portions of the Court's holding. See 42 USC §§ 2000e2(n)(1)(B) (2000). Even that statutory imposition of a duty to intervene was controversial at the time it was enacted. Respected commentators expressed the view that the provision might violate the due process rights of interested nonparties, and Congress was sufficiently concerned to insert a (redundant) proviso foreclosing any application of the statute that would violate the Constitution. See 42 USC § 2000e-2(n)(2)(D) (stating that nothing in the subsection shall be construed to 'authorize or permit the denial to any person of the due process of law required by the Constitution'); Owen M. Fiss, The Allure of Individualism, 78 Iowa L. Rev. 965, 971–972 (1993) (discussing majority opinion in Martin as articulating a 'right of participation' that appears to have constitutional stature).

[66] 209 F.R.D. 323 (S.D.N.Y. 2002).

[67] *Id.* at 328–330 (recounting procedural history of case).

CHAPTER 9. PRECLUSION IN CLASS ACTION LITIGATION

by detectable levels of MTBE.[68] The plaintiffs proceeded under state tort theories along with a claim for failure to notify under the federal Toxic Substances Control Act, seeking injunctive relief to remediate each of their individual cases of contamination. Various unnamed class members, from whom class counsel obtained declarations in support of certification, made clear that they also had claims for individual damages that they wanted to preserve,[69] even though the lead plaintiffs apparently acknowledged that such claims could not be litigated on a classwide basis.[70]

There were more than a few obstacles to this multistate, multi-incident, multidefendant omnibus class action, and the court denied certification on many different grounds.[71] It addressed the question of preclusion under the rubric of adequacy of representation. As with the Title VII examples discussed above, this request for purely injunctive relief raised both claim and issue preclusion concerns for the related damages claims. In the case of claim preclusion, it raised the possibility, albeit one usually rejected in F2 courts, that the maintenance of an injunctive class action would bar individual class members from pursuing damages claims, even if those claims could not have been asserted in the class proceeding. In the case of issue preclusion, the suit raised the more serious concern that adverse findings on the request for injunctive

---

[68] *Id.* at 334–335 (stating class definition).

[69] The declarations were filed in support of the argument that the MTBE problem was widespread. As the court explained, 'Plaintiffs also provide declarations from other residents from New York, Florida, California and Illinois to illustrate the extent of the MTBE problem as well as the proliferation of MTBE-related lawsuits. Many of the declarants seek to recover for personal injuries allegedly caused by MTBE.' *Id.* at 334. As the court later explained, those damages claims were potentially lucrative: '[S]everal declarants – who are class members by definition – have already ... [employed tort lawyers, on a contingency basis,] and have achieved results.' *Id.* at 350.

[70] The plaintiffs only sought injunctive relief before Judge Scheindlin, see *id.* at 328–329, though they did attempt to fit their injunctive claims under Rule 23(b)(3) as an alternative method of proceeding, see *id.* at 349–351.

[71] See e.g., *id.* at 337–338 (denying certification because class members did not meet typicality requirement); *id.* at 342–345 (describing impropriety of class treatment due to necessarily individualized nature of injunctive relief); *id.* at 348–349 (denying certification due to impossibility of binding absent plaintiffs to adverse result, since time when MTBE contamination occurs usually cannot be determined).

relief might preclude the property owners from establishing the elements of their damages claims in subsequent individual proceedings.

One might have expected the court to conclude that it could resolve the concern over claim preclusion rather easily, given the willingness of most F2 courts to entertain individual claims that could not have been litigated on a classwide basis in an earlier proceeding.[72] This conclusion might not hold true in all cases, as the next subparts discuss, but it would often provide a sufficient ex ante answer to claim preclusion problems, leaving only the need to scrutinize the issue preclusive implications of the proceeding. And issue preclusion did raise some legitimate concerns in the *MTBE* litigation. The levels of contamination alleged by members of the class varied widely, suggesting that only some members of the class (and perhaps only a small number) had substantial, positive-value claims for monetary damages.[73] The potential for adverse issue preclusive effects was patent here, as would be true in almost any tort case where class counsel proposes to pursue only a limited form of classwide relief, since the elements necessary to establish liability would be the same regardless of the form of the remedy requested. The primary focus of the *MTBE* court's attention should have been issue preclusion.

But the court did not discuss issue preclusion at all. Instead, it based its preclusion ruling entirely on concerns over claim preclusion. While it acknowledged the significant number of cases in which F2 courts have rejected claim preclusion defenses based upon earlier injunctive class actions, the court dismissed those cases as 'alleging

---

[72] Wright, Miller, and Cooper are in accord:

> The basic effort to limit class adjudication as close as possible to matters common to members of the class frequently requires that nonparticipating members of the class remain free to pursue individual actions that would be merged or barred by claim preclusion had a prior individual action been brought or the relief demanded in the class action... [A]n individual who has suffered particular injury as a result of practices enjoined in a class action should remain free to seek a damages remedy even though claim preclusion would defeat a second action had the first action been an individual suit for the same injunctive relief.

18A Wright, Miller, and Cooper, *supra* n. 2, § 4455, at 461–462.

[73] In re MTBE, 209 F.R.D. at 338–339 (embracing finding that only 'few absent class members' have sufficient levels of contamination to support substantial damages claims).

CHAPTER 9. PRECLUSION IN CLASS ACTION LITIGATION

civil rights violations' (primarily on behalf of prisoners), rather than tort claims.[74] Even if 'most [F2] courts' would probably embrace the treatment of claim preclusion embodied in the civil rights precedents, the district court concluded, it 'could not *ensure*' that the *MTBE* plaintiffs would be able to pursue their damages claims in subsequent actions.[75] In support of this proposition, the court pointed to several cases in which other F1 courts had found class representatives to be inadequate because of their willingness to forgo damages claims in the hope of satisfying the requirements of certification – a slightly different issue, as section 9.4 explains. Invoking the ubiquitous preclusion maxim for good measure, the court concluded that the risk of adverse claim preclusion consequences in future cases was unmanageable, rendering the named plaintiffs inadequate to represent the class.[76]

Judge Scheindlin was not venturing into unoccupied terrain in issuing this ruling. A growing number of other courts, while failing to analyze the potentially significant conflicts of interest that issue preclusion might produce in class proceedings, have placed dispositive weight on the specter of claim preclusion. Although there are very few reported decisions in which an F2 court has actually recognized a claim preclusion defense preventing a plaintiff from recovering on a claim not litigated in an earlier class proceeding,[77] many F1 courts still refuse to allow class actions to proceed on the basis of a vague apprehension of 'risk' that such a parade of horribles might nonetheless result for the hapless plaintiffs currently before them.[78]

---

[74] *Id.* at 339. The court did not explain how this difference in the underlying claim might bear upon the preclusion analysis, though the instinct that it might be relevant was not entirely unwarranted as section 4 *infra* explains.
[75] *Id.* at 339–340 (emphasis added).
[76] *Id.* at 340 ('[O]nly subsequent courts will determine the res judicata effect of any judgment' (citing 7B Wright, Miller, and Cooper, *supra* n. 2, § 1789, at 245 and n. 16)).
[77] I am aware of only one such decision – *Int'l Prisoners' Union v. Rizzo*, 356 F. Supp. 806, 809 (E.D. Pa. 1973) – and that case placed significant reliance upon a finding that the plaintiff had notice of the earlier suit, had an opportunity to intervene in that action and assert his individual claim, and made a considered choice not to do so.
[78] See e.g., *Clark v. Experian Info. Solutions, Inc.*, No. Civ.A.8:00-1217-24, 2001 WL 1946329, at *3–*4 (D.S.C. March 19, 2001) (stating that offering only some claims for class certification when other, more lucrative claims could not be certified 'defeats adequate representation since it places absent class members at the risk of having other claims forever barred by res judicata'); *Thompson v. Am. Tobacco Co.*, 189 F.R.D. 544, 550–551 (D. Minn. 1999) (refusing to certify because the 'possible

This is not an acceptable way to administer an adjudicatory system. We would ordinarily be unsatisfied if a court refused to provide relief on the basis of its own professed 'uncertainty' as to the proper resolution of a legal question.[79] The few situations in which we formally recognize uncertainty as an appropriate basis for refusing to proceed – usually under the rubric of abstention – are exceptional in nature, frequently impelled by concerns over comity between sovereigns, and generally accompanied by the promise of comparable relief in an alternative forum.[80] The denials of certification discussed above have

---

prejudice to class members' resulting from claim preclusion in the future 'is simply too great'); *Feinstein v. Firestone Tire and Rubber Co.*, 535 F. Supp. 595, 606 (S.D.N.Y. 1982) (refusing to certify class action for economic losses where plaintiffs also had personal injury claims because of 'significant risks' that class members would 'later [be told] that they had impermissibly split a single cause of action'); *Millett v. Atl. Richfield Co.*, No. Civ.A. CV-98-555, 2000 WL 359979, at *9 (Me. Super. Ct. March 2, 2000) (explaining that asserting claims for injunctive relief while leaving personal injury claims unraised places class members at risk of subsequent claim preclusion defense); *Small v. Lorillard Tobacco Co.*, 679 N.Y.S.2d 593, 601–602 (App. Div. 1998) (stating that paring down class claims to avoid certification problems creates impermissible 'risk' of adverse preclusive effects).

A substantial number of courts do continue to resist the siren song of this diffuse, risk-based argument when considering class actions outside the 'civil rights' context. See e.g., *Coleman v. Gen. Motors Acceptance Corp.*, 220 F.R.D. 64, 79–84 (M.D. Tenn. 2004) (considering many of these authorities and distinguishing or rejecting them); *Jahn ex rel. Jahn v. ORCR, Inc.*, 92 P.3d 984, 987–991 (Colo. 2004) (en banc) (adopting restrictive interpretation of state Rule 23(b)(2) for all types of action).

[79] There is, of course, an ongoing discussion of the virtue of judicial passivity when it comes to the constitutional review of legislative enactments in contentious areas of social disputation. See Michael C. Dorf, Legal Indeterminacy and Institutional Design, 78 N.Y.U. L. Rev. 875, 892–895 (2003) (summarizing and critiquing debate over 'passive virtue' of restraint in judicial review, most frequently associated with James Thayer and Alexander Bickel). The principles of political theory that motivate that debate obviously are not implicated here.

[80] The Court has considered and rejected the suggestion that uncertainty as to the proper resolution of state law claims might offer a sufficient basis for a federal court to decline to exercise its diversity jurisdiction. See *Meredith v. Winter Haven*, 320 U.S. 228, 234–237 (1943) ('[W]e can discern in [Congress' diversity jurisdiction policy] no recognition of a policy which would exclude cases from the jurisdiction merely because they involve state law or because the law is uncertain or difficult to determine.'). Where other public policy concerns militate in favor of abstention, and an adequate remedy exists in another forum, the Court has left the door open for

CHAPTER 9. PRECLUSION IN CLASS ACTION LITIGATION

none of these mitigating qualities,[81] and they rely upon a declaration of uncertainty that is no less disquieting for its attenuated quality. These courts have said, in effect, 'I know that you have proposed a class action that may be properly maintainable, but I won't allow you to proceed because I must protect the absentees from the possibility that a subsequent court might misapply my judgment.' This is abdication masquerading as diligence.

But it would be inappropriate to single these courts out exclusively for criticism. These are, after all, the rare judges who have taken time at the certification stage to recognize and consider the preclusive effect of their judgments upon class members. That fact alone distinguishes them from the great majority of trial courts, which pass over the issue completely. These judges have been operating from a presumption – a flawed presumption, as section 9.3 explains, but one with a formidable pedigree in the form of the ubiquitous preclusion maxim – that it is impossible for a rendering forum to resolve preclusion problems in any meaningful fashion, leaving the rights of class members always contingent upon the whims of a future, recognizing forum. Given the appalling state of class litigation in some courts,[82] one can sympathize

---

declining jurisdiction, *id.*, though it has viewed such arguments with skepticism. A good discussion of this line of cases may be found in Lewis Yelin, Note, Burford Abstention in Actions for Damages, 99 Colum. L. Rev. 1871, 1883–93 (1999); see also 28 USC § 1367(c)(1) (2000) (recognizing 'novel[ty]' of state law claim as appropriate basis for declining to exercise court's discretionary supplemental jurisdiction).

[81] Indeed, if Judge Easterbrook's opinion in Bridgestone/Firestone II finds general acceptance, these courts' professions of uncertainty might also bind others that do not share their reticence. See In re Bridgestone/Firestone Tires Prods. Liab. Litig. (Bridgestone/Firestone II), 333 F.3d 763, 769 (7th Cir. 2003) (issuing injunction to prevent any trial court from certifying nationwide class that Seventh Circuit had previously held uncertifiable).

[82] The Class Action Fairness Act of 2005, which gained passage immediately before this Article went to press, includes findings in which Congress expressed particularly harsh criticism toward the negligent and manipulative use of the class action in some courts. See Class Action Fairness Act of 2005, Pub. L. No. 109-2, § (2)(a)(1)–(4), 119 Stat. 4, 4–5.

Indeed, even if the courts in the cases discussed above realize that their vague gestures of 'uncertainty' and 'risk' are less than satisfying as explanations for a denial of certification, one can imagine them casting their gaze over the rocky landscape of class litigation created by some of their sister courts and borrowing from Alfred Hitchcock's Mother Sebastian in assuring themselves that they will be safe from

EMPLOYMENT CLASS AND COLLECTIVE ACTIONS

with the desire of these judges not to yoke the class members under their supervision to an uncertain fate.[83] Even so, the solutions that these courts have produced are entirely inadequate, at once conjuring obstacles to certification from claim preclusion that might be unnecessary, and failing to address issue preclusion problems that might create actual conflicts within an otherwise cohesive class.

9.2.3 Representation and Strategic Litigation Choices

Not all claim preclusion problems arise out of attempts to pare a class action down to a certifiable core, nor do they all lend themselves to the response that contested claims in a subsequent proceeding 'could not have been brought' in the original forum. Class counsel may have strategic objectives that require them to choose between more than one viable approach in structuring a class action, and the choice between those different approaches may have claim preclusive implications for the class. Scenarios of this description do not necessarily create intra-class conflicts like those explored above. Rather, they present questions about the limits of class counsel's authority to bind absentees to costly decisions in a class proceeding.

9.2.3.1 Stay-in-State-Court Suits

Class counsel sometimes perceive a strategic benefit in pressing only certain legal arguments in their request for relief, deliberately choosing to forgo potentially meritorious claims. An important example of such 'argument splitting' is the decision to plead only state grounds for relief and forgo federal claims in order to keep an action in state court.

---

censure: 'The enormity of your stupidity protects us.' Notorious (RKO Radio Pictures 1946).

[83] Professor Burbank captures a similar sentiment in rejecting the argument that the preclusive effect of federal diversity judgments should be determined by the legal standards of the recognizing forum, rather than those of the rendering forum:

From the perspective of litigants... a system of preclusion rules for diversity judgments keyed to the locus of subsequent litigation would be hopeless, either because it would be unpredictable or because it would be, functionally, a sham.

Burbank, Interjurisdictional Preclusion, *supra* n. 7, at 797.

CHAPTER 9. PRECLUSION IN CLASS ACTION LITIGATION

Avoiding a federal forum through such selective pleading may redound to the benefit of the plaintiffs for a variety of reasons.

Some class counsel employ this technique simply because they assume that state courts will offer greater judicial flexibility, or lesser judicial diligence, in the supervision of class litigation – to be blunt, they assume that they can get away with more in state court than in federal court.[84] There are certainly many accounts of notorious state court systems that provide particularly hospitable homes for plaintiffs' attorneys,[85] and the Class Action Fairness Act (CAFA) that was recently signed into law includes findings that would support some broader generalizations about the relative merits of these forums.[86] One variation on this forum manipulation that has received a great deal of attention occurs when one attorney files a nationwide class action on a federal claim and others then file parallel proceedings in state court, on state law claims, commencing a rush to settlement in hopes of securing generous fees with the promise of a global release.[87]

But not all efforts to stay in state court have a nefarious ring to them. In a dispute of national scope, for example, class counsel may perceive a strategic benefit in bringing many statewide class actions,

---

[84] See Linda S. Mullenix, Abandoning the Federal Class Action Ship: Is There Smoother Sailing for Class Actions in Gulf Waters?, 74 Tul. L. Rev. 1709, 1712–1719 (2000) [hereinafter Mullenix, Abandoning the Ship] (describing plaintiffs' increased reliance upon state fora on the assumption that state courts will be more receptive to their claims).

[85] See e.g., Susan P. Koniak and George M. Cohen, Under Cloak of Settlement, 82 Va. L. Rev. 1051, 1057–1068 (1996) (criticizing Alabama state courts for inadequate supervision of class members' interests in home mortgage lending cases); Mullenix, Abandoning the Ship, *supra* n. 84, at 1756–1758, 1767 (concluding that Florida remains a strongly pro-plaintiff jurisdiction but that Texas and Louisiana have begun cracking down on lax certification standards).

[86] See § (2)(a)(1)-(4), 119 Stat. at 4–5.

[87] This is a simplified description of the course of events in the Matsushita litigation. See *Epstein v. MCA*, Inc. (Epstein II), 126 F.3d 1235, 1251–1255 (9th Cir. 1997) (recounting history of proceedings). Similar races to judgment in parallel proceedings – sometimes exhibiting the appearance of collusion between class counsel and defendants – have been common. See e.g., In re Lease Oil Antitrust Litig. (No. II), 200 F.3d 317, 321 (5th Cir. 2000) (holding that global release in settlement of nationwide class action in Alabama state court does not require dismissal of exclusively federal claims in parallel proceeding due to jurisdictional competency requirement in Alabama law).

instead of a single nationwide proceeding. While conventional wisdom holds that plaintiffs' attorneys have an incentive to sweep as many plaintiffs as possible into a single proceeding in order to raise the stakes (and hence their fees), this tenet does not always hold true. If the stakes in a dispute are sufficiently high, even a statewide class action can be a 'bet the company' lawsuit for the defendant, with potential exposure that exceeds its insurance coverage and could jeopardize its viability. It may give class counsel a stronger hand to bring multiple statewide suits in such a case, rather than initiating a single, nationwide proceeding that could be resolved, and potentially dismissed, all at once.[88] If nonmutual offensive issue preclusion is available, of course, bringing multiple statewide actions may strengthen plaintiffs' hand even further. The distinctive tools that a federal cause of action offers in a federal forum – nationwide service of process, consolidation of multidistrict litigation – may work against the plaintiffs' interests here, making relinquishment of the federal claim an attractive option. Along similar lines, some states have standards for certification and notification that are more permissive than their federal counterparts, making state court the only forum in which a class action can occur.[89]

---

[88] Professor Issacharoff describes a related phenomenon in discussing the disincentives that sometimes exist to the filing of legitimate and socially desirable class settlements. See Issacharoff, Conflicts, *supra* n. 64, at 817–820. Some courts have effectively required, as a prerequisite to approval of a settlement-only class proceeding, that the parties stipulate that the class could also have been certified for litigation. See *id.* at 817–818. In a class action aimed at the effects within a single state of a claim with national implications, Issacharoff points out [t]he problem...that this stipulation may carry estoppel effects elsewhere...The defendant may rightfully fear that conceding the certifiability of a litigation class in one state may preclude a defense to class certification in another state.

Id. at 818. Issacharoff appears to be confusing the doctrines of issue preclusion and judicial estoppel here, however, as traditional issue preclusion would not be available in a case where certification is conceded, rather than adversarially contested. See Linda J. Silberman, Allan R. Stein, and Tobias B. Wolff, Civil Procedure: Theory and Practice 31–33 (Supp. 2004–2005) (describing difference between doctrines of judicial estoppel and issue preclusion); see also *New Hampshire v. Maine*, 532 US 742, 749 (2001) (embracing doctrine of judicial estoppel for federal courts).

[89] Compare e.g., *Eisen v. Carlisle and Jacquelin*, 417 U.S. 156, 175–176 (1974) (holding that class action filed under Rule 23(b)(3) must provide individualized notice to identifiable class members, even when doing so renders lawsuit impracticable), with, e.g., *Cartt v. Superior Court*, 124 Cal. Rptr. 376, 381–388 (Ct. App. 1975)

CHAPTER 9. PRECLUSION IN CLASS ACTION LITIGATION

In civil rights cases and other forms of impact litigation, plaintiffs may also forgo federal claims and a federal forum in order to minimize the harm associated with a bad outcome. This strategy has been the hallmark of much of the constitutional litigation on behalf of gay men and lesbians in the past twenty years, particularly as it concerns relationship rights and sexual privacy. Since 1993, when the Hawaii Supreme Court held that the state's exclusion of gay couples from civil marriage required strict judicial scrutiny,[90] a significant number of cases, including some class actions, have been filed seeking to secure equal access to marriage, or to the legal and economic benefits that attach to the institution, for gay and lesbian couples.[91] In a reversal of the strategy that led to the issuance and implementation of *Brown v. Board of Education*,[92] most of these cases have been filed in state courts and have sought relief only on the basis of state constitutions, deliberately eschewing the argument that the U.S. Constitution invalidates discrimination against gay couples.[93] Civil rights attorneys who litigate

---

(distinguishing Eisen and applying more permissive standard under California law for notification of class members in negative-value consumer class action).

[90] *Baehr v. Lewin*, 852 P.2d 44, 67 (Haw. 1993). On remand, the Hawaii trial court found that the state could not meet its burden and ordered that gay and lesbian couples receive equal access to marriage. Before that decision could go into effect, however, the people of Hawaii amended their constitution and removed the substantive basis for the original decision. See *Baehr v. Miike*, 994 P.2d 566 (Haw. 1999) (unpublished table decision), available at <www.hawaii.gov/jud/20371.htm> (on file with the Columbia Law Review) (detailing history of case on remand and dismissing following enactment of state constitutional amendment).

[91] See e.g., *Clinton v. California* (Marriage Cases), No. CGC-04-429548 (Cal. Super. Ct. filed March 12, 2004) (on file with the Columbia Law Review) (seeking equal access to civil marriage for same-sex couples).

[92] 347 US 483 (1954), enforced, 349 US 294 (1955).

[93] See e.g., *Brause v. Bureau of Vital Statistics*, No. 3AN-95-6562 CI, 1998 WL 88743, at *1 (Alaska Super. Ct. February 27, 1998) (holding that Alaska constitution requires that gay couple enjoy equal access to civil marriage), superseded by Alaska Const. Art. I, §25 ('To be valid or recognized in this State, a marriage may exist only between one man and one woman.'); *Goodridge v. Dep't of Pub. Health*, 798 N.E.2d 941, 948 (Mass. 2003) (holding that Massachusetts constitution requires that same-sex couples enjoy equal access to civil marriage); *Tanner v. Or. Health Scis. Univ.*, 971 P.2d 435, 448 (Or. Ct. App. 1998) (finding that same-sex couples are entitled to equal employment benefits from state employers under Oregon constitution); *Baker v. State*, 744 A.2d 864, 867 (Vt. 1999) (holding that Vermont constitution requires

in this field have long been apprehensive about the reception that federal constitutional arguments relating to marriage might receive if they were to reach the Supreme Court of the United States, fearing that they might provoke another *Bowers v. Hardwick*.[94] Given the significance that would attach to a ruling by a federal appellate court that the Constitution gives same-sex couples an equal right to marry, there is good reason to think that the Supreme Court would grant review of any such decision. Accordingly, the plaintiffs in these suits have avoided the U.S. Constitution.

The decision to disclaim any federal grounds for relief can, of course, have a real impact on a plaintiff's prospects for recovery. In the case of parallel statutory causes of action, federal law may have fewer defenses or offer more extensive damages than state law. In civil rights litigation, state charters may impose special barriers to the recognition of certain constitutional claims, particularly where the rights of gay couples are concerned.[95] Unlike the scenarios examined in section 9.2.2, these stay-in-state-court suits all involve the abandonment of claims that *could* be raised in an initial class action proceeding. The strategic decisions in these cases aim to maximize

---

state to afford same-sex couples the same rights and benefits that are available to opposite-sex married couples).

[94] 478 U.S. 186 (1986), overruled by *Lawrence v. Texas*, 539 U.S. 558, 578–579 (2003). In Bowers, the Court rejected a gay man's argument that private consensual sexual activity between two gay men fell within the penumbra of constitutional privacy protected by the Due Process Clause, despite the apparent holdings of the Court in *Griswold v. Connecticut*, 381 U.S. 479 (1965), *Eisenstadt v. Baird*, 407 U.S. 438 (1972), and *Roe v. Wade*, 410 U.S. 113 (1973), that similar sexual activity between heterosexual partners was protected. The language employed by the Bowers Court in explaining its holding was notoriously derisive, as the Supreme Court forthrightly admitted when it repudiated the decision seventeen years later.

[95] In a recent Alaska case, for example, a group of same-sex couples in committed relationships brought suit under the Alaska constitution requesting the same employment benefits from state employers that were available to married couples. The Alaska constitution expressly forbids same-sex couples from marrying, see Alaska Const. Art. I, § 25, imposing a potential obstacle to any state law claim to equal treatment. Even so, the plaintiffs have declined to raise federal constitutional claims, arguing instead that the equality provisions of the state constitution give them a right to equal employment benefits despite their inability to marry. See *Alaska Civil Liberties Union v. Alaska* (AkCLU), No. S10459 (Alaska filed May 22, 2002). The author served as co-counsel for the plaintiffs in the AkCLU case from its initiation.

CHAPTER 9. PRECLUSION IN CLASS ACTION LITIGATION

the plaintiffs' expected outcome or serve some larger social purpose, not to eliminate claims that would prevent class certification.

9.2.3.2 Unpled Equitable Claims

The failure to raise significant claims in a class proceeding is not always part of an elaborate litigation strategy. Class counsel may decide not to raise a claim if she believes it to have limited significance or little chance of success, simply as a matter of resource allocation, or she may omit claims through inattention or negligence. Once again, when such claims could have been brought in an initial proceeding, a serious question arises as to the response that class members should encounter if they attempt to assert them in subsequent lawsuits.

A prison litigation case from the Ninth Circuit, *Hiser v. Franklin*,[96] offers a useful illustration. In 1981, a group of plaintiffs initiated a state court class action on behalf of all present and future inmates in the Alaska prison system, alleging civil rights violations. The suit ended in a 1990 consent decree that addressed a broad range of issues, including the impact of confinement conditions upon prisoners' access to the courts. Some months later, Timothy Hiser, who was not incarcerated when the initial class settlement was approved, brought suit against Alaska prison officials, claiming that they were denying him reasonable access to the courts by preventing him from photocopying documents. Hiser requested damages and individual equitable relief for the denials and also sought to maintain a claim on behalf of all inmates to have the photocopying policy reformed throughout the prison. The district court cited the consent decree and dismissed all of Hiser's claims on claim preclusion grounds, but the Ninth Circuit reversed in full and allowed him to proceed, finding that Alaska preclusion law would not bar the action.[97]

The Ninth Circuit's decision to allow Hiser to proceed with his individual claims for relief is not difficult to justify under a straightforward application of claim preclusion rules, since the factual predicate for his claim – the prison's denial of photocopying services to him – did not exist at the time of the earlier judgment. Indeed, the certification of a class that includes future inmates would now warrant

---

[96] 94 F.3d 1287 (9th Cir. 1996).
[97] *Id.* at 1289–1290.

particular scrutiny under *Amchem* insofar as the suit purported to settle or compromise claims for damages.[98] The classwide challenge to the prison's photocopying policy, however, presented a different kind of question. The policy, and hence the factual predicate for the claim, predated Hiser's incarceration and could have been made a part of the original litigation.[99] Whether the omission of photocopying from the broader court access claim was a strategic choice or an oversight in the first suit, class counsel did not raise the issue when they could have, and they brokered a consent decree without making a classwide challenge to photocopying polices a part of the negotiating mix. The argument for applying the 'could have been raised' doctrine of claim preclusion to an unpled equitable claim of this type is strong, as the Ninth Circuit recognized. In permitting Hiser to proceed with his class claim nonetheless, the Ninth Circuit did not question the applicability of this form of merger in representative litigation, and instead relied upon a finding that merger was not implicated in the case before it because the claim did not arise out of the same series of transactions as the broader access-to-court claims litigated in the original proceeding.[100]

Both stay-in-state-court suits and unpled equitable claims raise questions about the limits of lead counsel's representational role in class litigation. In individual litigation, strategic decisions about the claims that counsel will raise in structuring a complicated case are an accepted and inevitable part of the representational relationship – as are oversights and mistakes, within reasonable parameters. The autonomy that affords a litigant such wide discretion in choosing how to structure the lawsuit in an adversarial system also offers the primary justification for binding the litigant to the result. In a class proceeding, where absentees have little or no opportunity to approve the decisions of their lawyers, the court's independent duty to ensure the adequacy

---

[98] Amchem rejected a settlement-only class action that sought to resolve the damages claims of future victims of asbestosis, ruling that the trial court had not employed safeguards adequate to protect the interests of that diffuse group and expressing skepticism about the certification of any class action in which some class members did not yet exist as such. *Amchem Prods., Inc. v. Windsor*, 521 U.S. 591, 619–629 (1997).

[99] See Hiser, 94 F.3d at 1292.

[100] See *id.* at 1292–1293. This finding may have been something of a stretch, and one member of the panel dissented from this portion of the ruling. See *id.* at 1294 (Rymer, J., concurring in part and dissenting in part).

CHAPTER 9. PRECLUSION IN CLASS ACTION LITIGATION

of class counsel's representation serves as the principal substitute for litigant autonomy. From *Hansberry v. Lee* onward, the bulk of the attention in adequacy analysis has focused on conflicts of interest, whether among class members or between absentees and class counsel.[101] On occasion, courts and commentators have also explored the standards that should govern an adequacy challenge based on lack of competence or diligence.[102] The preclusion problems explored in this part demonstrate the need for a third mode of adequacy analysis that speaks to the extent of class counsel's authority to make purely strategic decisions on behalf of absentees.

Before addressing that issue, however, it is necessary to articulate a more coherent approach to the structure of preclusion analysis than has been evident in class action litigation thus far. Any resolution of the preclusion problems discussed in this article will only be enduring if it rests on a firm foundation.

9.3 THE STRUCTURE OF PRECLUSION ANALYSIS

My principal aim in this part is to unseat the hegemony of the maxim that '[a] court conducting an action cannot predetermine the res judicata effect of the judgment.'[103] The important but limited core of descriptive truth that this maxim embodies has metastasized

---

[101] *Hansberry v. Lee*, 311 U.S. 32 (1940), established the absence of conflicting interests between a representative plaintiff and absentees as a constitutional requirement in class litigation. For subsequent judicial treatments of the issue, See for example, *Stephenson v. Dow Chem. Co.*, 273 F.3d 249, 258–259 (2nd Cir. 2001) (permitting collateral attack to Agent Orange settlement by claimants whose injuries did not manifest during settlement period and who were thus denied relief, on grounds that their interests were adverse to those of the rest of the class in the original action), affirmed by an equally divided court, in part, 539 U.S. 111 (2003); *Gonzales v. Cassidy*, 474 F.2d 67, 72 (5th Cir. 1973) (permitting collateral attack on adequacy grounds where representation afforded class member in first action was hostile and adverse).

[102] See e.g., *Epstein v. MCA, Inc.* (Epstein II), 126 F.3d 1235, 1251–1255 (9th Cir. 1997) (detailing inadequate course of representation offered by class counsel in state action while parallel federal proceeding was pending), vacated, *Epstein v. MCA, Inc.* (Epstein III), 179 F.3d 641 (9th Cir. 1999).

[103] *Matsushita Elec. Indus. Co. v. Epstein*, 516 U.S. 367, 396 (1996) (Ginsburg, J., concurring in part and dissenting in part) (citing 7B Wright, Miller, and Cooper, *supra* n. 2, § 1789, at 245).

throughout the law of preclusion, crowding out the vital contributions of the rendering forum in superintending the preclusive implications of the lawsuits that it shepherds to judgment. In a class action, where a court's authority to determine the scope of the litigation is especially conspicuous and its responsibility to supervise the course of the litigation at its maximum, this denuded conception of the rendering forum's role in determining the future impact of its judgment is especially pernicious. The most basic reform that is needed in this arena is for rendering fora to recognize and claim their proper role as expositors of positive law in assessing and controlling the preclusive effects of their own judgments.[104]

9.3.1 A Positive Law Account of Preclusion Doctrine

Much of the confusion that surrounds the analysis of a judgment's prescriptive scope – particularly the confusion surrounding the time-frame problem that the ubiquitous preclusion maxim purports to describe – stems from a failure to think carefully about adjudication as an exercise of positive legal authority. Indeed, rendering courts sometimes seem to treat the future preclusive effects of their own judgments as a species of 'brooding omnipresence':[105] a system of legal rules that is mysteriously unconnected to the exercise of sovereign authority – the court's own judgment – to which those rules will later be applied. One of the important conceptual lessons of *Erie*[106] is that courts serve as

---

[104] The cognitive problem here is as widespread as the one that Walter Wheeler Cook took aim at when he leveled his challenge to the a priori approach to choice of law analysis, which predominated through the first half of the twentieth century. See Walter Wheeler Cook, The Logical and Legal Bases of the Conflict of Laws 6–8 (1942) (describing traditional method of conflicts analysis, which attempted to derive solutions from 'the general or essential nature of law and legal rights'). Indeed, the problem is more serious in some respects. According to Cook, common law courts were aware that 'the absurd and socially bad result' produced by the a priori method in some cases '[was] not due to inherent lack of power on the part of our states, but merely to the operation of certain rules of positive law.' *Id.* at 13. Cases like those discussed in the previous sections lead me to conclude that this realization has not taken root in the analysis of preclusion doctrine by most rendering courts.

[105] *S. Pac. Co. v. Jensen*, 244 U.S. 205, 222 (1916) (Holmes, J., dissenting).

[106] *Erie R.R. Co. v. Tompkins*, 304 U.S. 64 (1938).

CHAPTER 9. PRECLUSION IN CLASS ACTION LITIGATION

wellsprings of positive legal authority, just as legislatures do. That lesson is most frequently identified with the broad rules of decision that courts issue as expositors of common law principles. But it has equal application to the more specialized rules of decision that the preclusive effect of a court's judgment attaches to the parties to a dispute.

9.3.1.1 *Preclusion as a Rule of Decision*

When a court issues a judgment, that sovereign act has two different types of impact upon the parties: its mandate and its preclusive effect. The 'mandate' consists of a judgment's immediate and executory impacts upon the persons and property of the parties. A judicial mandate transforms the parties' rights and responsibilities – it imposes an executory obligation to pay money, obliges the parties to take or refrain from taking certain actions, or transforms their civil status. When a court spreads the mandate of its judgment, that action attaches a new set of obligations and entitlements to the parties.[107]

The 'preclusive effect' of a judgment does not exert any such immediate or executory impact. Rather, a judgment's preclusive effect prescribes a rule of decision for the resolution of future disputes: It proclaims one or more elements of a cause of action to be satisfied, provides an affirmative defense to the assertion of transactionally related claims, or establishes a rule of evidence for the resolution of factual disputes.[108] The specialized rule of decision bound up in the preclusive effect of a judgment is much more limited in its prescriptive scope than the rules of decision generally issued by legislatures. A judgment's rule of decision can only be invoked against the parties bound by the proceeding, or their privies, and it relates only to a

---

[107] As the Restatement points out, when enforcement of a judgment is sought across territorial jurisdictions, this 'coercive' effect of the mandate can only be realized through the cooperation of a subsequent forum. See Restatement (Second) of Judgments Ch. 2 introductory n. at 23 (1982) ('[O]utside the territorial limits of a court's jurisdiction, the coercive effectiveness of its judgment depends upon the judgment's being given recognition by the authorities of another government, under a principle of comity or by virtue of legal provisions such as the Full Faith and Credit Clause of the Constitution.').

[108] Burbank makes a similar observation, in passing, in his article on interjurisdictional preclusion. See Burbank, Interjurisdictional Preclusion, *supra* n. 7, at 771 ('Claim preclusion includes defenses to rights asserted under the substantive law.').

specific, temporally bounded set of issues or transactions. The Supreme Court's decision in Baker v. General Motors Corp. contains its most nuanced discussion of the positive law foundations of preclusion law in this respect.[109] In addition, determining the contents of a judgment's prescriptive scope may depend upon the actual course of the proceedings giving rise to the judgment, a type of inquiry that has no analog in determining the scope of a legislative enactment.[110] Despite this

---

[109] 522 U.S. 222 (1998). Baker involved an attempt by General Motors to take an injunction obtained against a former employee that prohibited the employee from testifying about certain product defect issues and to apply that prohibition against subsequent claimants who had no involvement in the earlier proceeding. Id. at 226–231. The Court rejected this attempt, holding that only litigants who were parties to the earlier proceeding could be bound, as a matter of preclusion law, to the evidentiary issues determined therein. Id. at 237–239. As to all other litigants, the Court found, subsequent courts were entitled to determine for themselves what role the earlier injunction should play in constraining the evidence available at trial, free from the unyielding mandate of Full Faith and Credit. Id. at 234–236, 238–241. In explaining the principles that required this result, the Baker Court offered an analysis of the limits of the prescriptive scope of the rule of decision bound up in the disputed injunction. The passage nicely captures the relationship between the parties to the action and the prescriptive scope of the judgment and, by implication, the distinction between the judgment's rule of decision and its mandate:

> Michigan's judgment...cannot reach beyond the Elwell-GM controversy to control proceedings against GM brought in other States, by other parties, asserting claims the merits of which Michigan has not considered. Michigan has no power over those parties, and no basis for commanding them to become intervenors in the Elwell-GM dispute. Most essentially, Michigan lacks authority to control courts elsewhere by precluding them, in actions brought by strangers to the Michigan litigation, from determining for themselves what witnesses are competent to testify and what evidence is relevant and admissible in their search for the truth.

Id. at 238 (citation omitted); see also id. at 239 n. 12 ('If the Bakers had been parties to the Michigan proceedings and had actually litigated the privileged character of Elwell's testimony, the Bakers would of course be precluded from relitigating that issue in Missouri.').

[110] The Supreme Court resolved early on, in Fletcher v. Peck, that it would not permit challenges to the scope or validity of a law based upon a detailed inquiry into the process giving rise to that law. 10 U.S. (6 Cranch) 87, 130–131 (1810). But this decision was a matter of constitutional policy, not metaphysical inevitability. There is no logical or analytical impediment to an analogous inquiry into 'legislative due

CHAPTER 9. PRECLUSION IN CLASS ACTION LITIGATION

narrowness of scope, however, a judgment's preclusive effect still operates as a rule of decision – an element, defense, or rule of evidence – in adjudicating a claim for relief made in a subsequent lawsuit.[111] Indeed, the very reason for specifying a legal category to describe a judgment's 'preclusive effect,' as distinct from the judgment's 'mandate,' is to distinguish between those features of a judgment that operate as rules of decision in subsequent adjudications and those that have immediate or executory impacts upon the rights and obligations of the parties.

Choice of law analysis offers a useful guide to developing a more precise positive account of preclusion law, since both doctrines address the application of sovereign authority across jurisdictions in prescribing rules of decision. In choice of law analysis, the source of sovereign authority is legislative and regulatory, and the jurisdictional line is territorial. A conflicts regime provides an approach for identifying situations where more than one sovereign wishes to apply its regulatory authority to a state of affairs in the world – that is, it identifies when a 'true conflict' exists – and then offers rules for determining which

---

process' that would ask, for example, whether a law can be applied to a segment of the population that was denied an opportunity to be heard on the matter (through disenfranchisement), or, in the case of a ballot initiative, whether the public received adequate notice of the meaning and effect of a ballot initiative before being asked to vote. See e.g., *Jones v. Bates*, 127 F.3d 839, 855–863 (9th Cir. 1997) (exploring these issues in challenge to California ballot initiative on term limits for elected officials), reversed en banc, 131 F.3d 843 (9th Cir. 1997).

[111] The Court has used the language of evidence and jurisdiction in drawing this distinction between a judgment's mandatory and prescriptive features.

> [The Full Faith and Credit Clause and its implementing act] establish a rule of evidence, rather than of jurisdiction. While they make the record of a judgment, rendered after due notice in one State, conclusive evidence in the courts of another State, or of the United States, of the matter adjudged, they do not affect the jurisdiction, either of the court in which the judgment is rendered, or of the court in which it is offered in evidence. Judgments recovered in one State of the Union, when proved in the courts of another government, whether state or national, within the United States, differ from judgments recovered in a foreign country in no other respect than in not being reexaminable on their merits, nor impeachable for fraud in obtaining them, if rendered by a court having jurisdiction of the cause and of the parties.

Wisconsin v. Pelican Ins. Co., 127 U.S. 265, 291–292 (1888); see also *Baker*, 522 U.S. at 242 (Scalia, J., concurring in judgment) (reiterating this language in discussing enforcement of out-of-state injunctions).

sovereign's authority should predominate – that is, it directs how to resolve the conflict. The first task is interpretive, requiring a determination as to what extraterritorial scope the legislature intended its laws to have. The second task is normative, requiring a set of principles for assessing competing regulatory claims. Larry Kramer offers the most precise account of these structural features of the choice of law process. He describes the first, interpretive task of conflicts analysis in the following terms:

> A lawsuit with multistate contacts is still just a lawsuit: the plaintiff still alleges that because something happened he or she is entitled to relief; the court still must determine whether the facts alleged are true and whether, if they are true, some rule of law confers a right to recover. Making this determination is still a problem of interpretation. The only difference is that some of the facts are connected to different states, and the court must determine if that affects whether the law or laws at issue confer a right. While this determination may sometimes be difficult, it does not alter the nature of the problem confronting the court, which remains to decide what rights are conferred by positive law.[112]

In the absence of express statements about a law's intended extraterritorial effect – the usual case – a state's choice of law regime 'establishes the state's rules of interpretation for questions of territorial scope.'[113]

Preclusion doctrine shares important structural parallels with choice of law analysis. Preclusion, too, addresses the application of

---

[112] Larry Kramer, Rethinking Choice of Law, 90 Colum. L. Rev. 277, 290 (1990) [hereinafter Kramer, Rethinking]; see also Larry Kramer, Return of the Renvoi, 66 N.Y.U. L. Rev. 979, 1005 (1991) [hereinafter Kramer, Renvoi] (reproducing this passage as a predicate to describing proper treatment of another state's choice of law rules in conflicts analysis).

[113] Kramer, Renvoi, *supra* n. 112, at 982. There are plenty of smart people in the field who take issue with Kramer's account of the structure of choice of law analysis. Lea Brilmayer is well known for her broad attack on the capacity of positive accounts of choice of law to say anything useful or 'objective' about the purposes underlying a law and the interests that the law serves. See e.g., Lea Brilmayer, Conflict of Laws §§ 2.5.1–2.5.5 (2nd edn 1995). Kim Roosevelt, though embracing a positivist approach, questions Kramer's assertion that a choice of law regime provides default rules for the territorial scope of legislation. See Kermit Roosevelt III, The Myth of Choice of Law: Rethinking Conflicts, 97 Mich. L. Rev. 2448, 2480–2481 (1999). I do not view either type of criticism as detracting from the purposes to which I put Kramer's analysis in the discussion that follows.

CHAPTER 9. PRECLUSION IN CLASS ACTION LITIGATION

sovereign authority across jurisdictional lines. The source of sovereign authority here is judicial rather than legislative, and the relevant jurisdictional line marks the boundary between different adjudicatory proceedings within a given court system.[114] These differences in the form of the authority being exercised call for a different interpretive focus in assessing a judgment's prescriptive scope. But the judgment of a court still serves as a sovereign source of prescriptive authority: It sets forth a specialized rule of decision for future disputes involving the parties bound by a particular proceeding. That specialized rule of decision can produce a 'conflict of laws' with a general rule prescribed by legislation, just as with two legislative enactments in a classic choice of law problem. When a prior judgment is one of the competitors in such a conflict of prescriptive authority, however, the method for resolving that conflict is much simpler than would be true of an ordinary choice of law problem. With few exceptions, a court will apply the rule of decision bound up in a jurisdictionally sufficient judgment, to the exclusion of any conflicting legislative rule. The same holds true when a judgment is given effect across territorial lines, as will frequently be the case in successive lawsuits in which class actions are involved. While federal law is generally silent on the resolution of conflicts between state legislative enactments, and the Constitution allows for a diversity of choice of law regimes, the Full Faith and Credit Clause and its enforcement statute establish a uniform policy for the interjurisdictional treatment of state court judgments[115] under which a valid judgment's rule of decision:

(1) must be given the same effect that it would receive in a court of the rendering state; and

---

[114] I use the terms 'legislative' and 'legislation' here to denote the exposition of general laws of liability allocation and conduct regulation. Of course, courts often serve as the sole source of such laws when they interpret the common law. My characterization of the structure of choice of law analysis is meant to describe such general rules, whether judicial or legislative in origin – a common convention in choice of law discussions. See e.g., Kramer, Renvoi, *supra* n. 112, at 1005–1006 (employing hypothetical concerning 'legislative' scope that combines common law and statutory elements).

[115] For ease of reference, I will use state court judgments and the full faith and credit requirement in discussing preclusion doctrine between jurisdictions. In the case of federal judgments, the recognition requirement arises from federal common law. See *Semtek Int'l Inc. v. Lockheed Martin Corp.*, 531 U.S. 497, 508 (2001).

(2) always trumps a legislative rule when domestic preclusion law would require that result.[116]

The burden of the analysis in preclusion doctrine thus resides in the first, interpretive task described above: determining whether the rule of decision established by the earlier exercise of sovereign authority – the judgment – has application in a subsequent dispute.

Where ordinary choice of law analysis is concerned, the authority of a legislature to specify the interjurisdictional reach that it intends for its laws is a matter of common understanding.[117] The problem is that legislatures exercise that authority only rarely,[118] requiring courts to develop methods of interpretation for divining, or imputing, the interjurisdictional application that the legislature intended for its law.[119] Where preclusion doctrine is concerned, the situation is essentially reversed. A rendering court has the opportunity that is usually denied to a legislature to focus its attention on a narrow, defined set of circumstances in assessing and controlling the prescriptive scope that any rule of decision resulting from its exercise of sovereign authority will have in the resolution of future disputes. Even so, courts rarely exercise this power. Although the positive role of courts as expositors of common

---

[116] See Baker, 522 U.S. at 232–233 (describing obligation of states to enforce intended claim and issue preclusive effect of valid judgments from other states); *id.* at 233–234 (rejecting any 'public policy' exception for enforcement of judgments, in contrast to recognition of statutory enactments in choice of law analysis).

[117] See Kramer, Renvoi, *supra* n. 112, at 1006–1008 (describing role of legislature in prescribing multistate elements of its laws and observing that need to interpret these features of a law in conducting choice of law analysis is 'uncontroversial').

[118] As Kramer has put it:

> Sometimes a law will specify what elements of a claim must be connected to or located in the state for the law to apply. With such laws, the court need not look beyond the face of the statute to determine prima facie applicability. Unfortunately, the great majority of laws are silent with respect to extraterritorial reach, and determining their prima facie applicability is more difficult.

Kramer, Rethinking, *supra* n. 112, at 293.

[119] See Kramer, Renvoi, *supra* n. 112, at 1008 ('[D]etermining whether a law applies in a multistate case requires interpreting it in a way that is not qualitatively different from other legal problems [and] the proper method of interpretation looks to purposes.'); Kramer, Rethinking, *supra* n. 112, at 294 ('Since the legislature's failure to specify the statute's extraterritorial reach is an oversight, the court must infer what limits – if any – there ought to be on the extraterritorial reach of the law.').

CHAPTER 9. PRECLUSION IN CLASS ACTION LITIGATION

law principles has long since become a transparent part of our conceptual vocabulary, the power of courts to play a positive legal role in determining the prescriptive scope of their judgments' preclusive effect remains poorly understood.[120]

This failure of understanding is all the more striking in the class action context, where the opportunity for a court to determine whether and to what extent its judgment will establish a rule of decision for absent class members is so conspicuously on display. The certification hearing represents a singular concentration of attention by the court and the parties on the future preclusive effect of the court's judgment. Even so, the ubiquitous preclusion maxim continues to dissuade rendering courts from recognizing the opportunity that the certification process offers for shaping that preclusive effect.[121]

---

[120] Professor Burbank has made a similar observation in his discussion of the federal rulemaking process, where he has criticized the 'literature specific to the proposed Federal Rules of Evidence' for 'obscuring the distinction between power and prudence in court rulemaking.' Stephen B. Burbank, The Rules Enabling Act of 1934, 130 U. Pa. L. Rev. 1015, 1022 (1982) [hereinafter Burbank, Rules Enabling Act].

[121] Wright, Miller, and Cooper, despite their otherwise sophisticated and thoughtful treatment of preclusion in class litigation, themselves contribute to this problem in the closing passages of their discussion on the issue, writing:

> These limitations on preclusion by a class judgment are wrapped up with the general proposition that 'the court conducting the action cannot predetermine the res judicata effect of the judgment.' Even though a court hearing a class action may at times undertake to reject an assertion that the judgment will not be binding on nonparticipating class members, final enforcement of preclusion ordinarily occurs only with the decision of the court hearing a later action. The class-action court can easily defeat preclusion, however, either by adopting a narrow class definition to ensure adequate representation or by decertifying the class at the close of trial or on appeal on the ground that the class was not adequately represented.

18A Wright, Miller, and Cooper, *supra* n. 2, § 4455, at 493–944 (citations omitted). While technically correct, the assertion that 'final enforcement of preclusion' ordinarily must wait for a recognizing forum simply perpetuates the fallacy of the ubiquitous preclusion maxim by overstating its significance. It implicitly suggests that the only tools available to a rendering court in addressing preclusion are a narrow class definition, which rendering courts have already proclaimed to be insufficient in giving them confidence that their judgments will not be misinterpreted, or decertification of the class at the close of the proceedings, an extreme and disruptive step that rendering courts cannot be relied upon to undertake.

9.3.1.2 The Components of Preclusion Analysis

When a recognizing forum is called upon to determine the impact that a prior judgment will have upon the resolution of a current dispute, there are three distinct types of inquiry that it must perform. The first is to assess the exercise of positive legal authority that the initial forum undertook in rendering the judgment, an inquiry that will itself consist of several components. The court must determine what claims and transactions were placed in issue in the pleadings of the prior action. It must take stock of the preclusion doctrines that would have applied in the rendering forum – the availability of nonmutual issue preclusion, the approach to defining a transaction or series of transactions, the treatment of a statute of limitations dismissal, and so forth. It must determine whether the rendering forum placed any constraints upon the preclusive effect that its judgment should have in subsequent proceedings. Second, the court must inquire into the actual course of proceedings in the rendering forum to determine, for example, whether a contested issue was actually litigated and determined, or whether the parties were afforded a full and fair opportunity to litigate a contested claim.[122] Third, the court must examine the relationship between the matters that were resolved in the initial proceeding and the claims or issues presently before it in order to decide how the rules of decision embodied in the first judgment should apply to the current dispute – whether the current claims are part of the same series of transactions that were adjudicated by the rendering forum, for example, or whether an issue resolved by the rendering forum is identical to an issue raised in the present lawsuit in all pertinent respects.

The core of truth contained in the ubiquitous preclusion maxim derives primarily from the third of these inquiries. As a descriptive matter, it is obviously not possible for a rendering forum to conduct an analysis of claims and issues that have not yet been raised, in a lawsuit that has not yet been filed. To employ more formal language, it is not possible for the rendering forum to predetermine how the

---

[122] This requirement is captured in the Restatement's allowance for the use of extrinsic evidence in determining the prescriptive scope of a prior judgment. See Restatement (Second) of Judgments §27 cmt. f (1982) ('If it cannot be determined from the pleadings and other materials of record in the prior action what issues, if any, were litigated and determined by the verdict and judgment, extrinsic evidence is admissible to aid in such a determination.').

CHAPTER 9. PRECLUSION IN CLASS ACTION LITIGATION

specialized rule of decision embodied in its judgment will come to be interpreted and applied in future disputes. The relevant body of information for this final step in the preclusion inquiry lies outside the rendering court's knowledge and experience. Indeed, insofar as the phrase 'predetermine the res judicata effect of a judgment' implies some control over the mandate of a future court as well as the application of the judgment's rule of decision, such an action would lie outside the power and jurisdiction of a rendering court as well as its knowledge and experience.[123]

This observation is at once consequential and trivially true. It identifies an important feature of the manner in which sovereigns exercise power, but one that is neither novel nor limited to preclusion analysis. On an analytical level, the assertion that a court cannot 'predetermine' the effect of its judgment in this limited sense of the term is no different from the observation that a legislature cannot predetermine how a rule of decision in one of its laws will come to be applied in future disputes. These observations do not reveal any profound limitations on the power of a rendering forum. They constitute a prosaic statement about the manner in which the prescriptive force of a rule of decision becomes actualized in particular cases, a statement that applies with equal force to legislative enactments.[124]

---

[123] This is the import of the distinction that the Court draws between the substantive content of a judgment and the method for its enforcement in *Baker v. General Motors Corp.*:

> Full faith and credit ... does not mean that States must adopt the practices of other States regarding the time, manner, and mechanisms for enforcing judgments. Enforcement measures do not travel with the sister state judgment as preclusive effects do; such measures remain subject to the evenhanded control of forum law.
>
> Orders commanding action or inaction have been denied enforcement in a sister State when they purported to accomplish an official act within the exclusive province of that other State or interfered with litigation over which the ordering State had no authority. Thus, a sister State's decree concerning land ownership in another State has been held ineffective to transfer title, although such a decree may indeed preclusively adjudicate the rights and obligations running between the parties to the foreign litigation.

522 U.S. 222, 235 (1998) (citations omitted).

[124] I take Professor Kramer to be making a similar observation in his approach to choice of law when he argues that, '[f]rom an analytical standpoint ... both

Clarifying the limited import of the preclusion maxim in this respect allows for a clearer analysis of a rendering court's capacity to exert influence over those elements of the preclusion inquiry that do lie within its ambit – in particular, the extent of the positive legal authority that attaches to the court's judgment. Consider the legislative parallel once again. A legislature's inability to identify the actual disputes to which its laws will apply does not call into question its ability to prescribe the scope of those laws in a meaningful fashion. Similarly, a court's inability to predetermine the future cases in which the preclusive effects of its judgment will play a determinative role does not call into question the ability of the court to exert other types of influence in prescribing the judgment's scope. There are some important respects in which these situations are not strictly parallel. A court operates under prescriptive limitations that a legislature does not. But the broad assertion that is implicit in the ubiquitous preclusion maxim – that a court's inability to predetermine the precise role that its judgment will play in resolving future disputes is indicative of a deeper inability of the court to play any meaningful or authoritative role in determining the preclusive effect of that judgment – is logically and descriptively incorrect.

The preclusion rules of a jurisdiction can best be understood as a source of authorization for a court to attach prescriptive force to its judgment, along with a set of default rules that determine the extent of that prescriptive force in the absence of any express statement by the rendering forum.[125] A court cannot give its judgment prescriptive force in excess of that authorized by the applicable preclusion rules – it cannot proclaim that the judgment in a particular case will be available as a future rule of evidence through offensive nonmutual issue preclusion, for example, if the applicable law does not authorize offensive issue

---

"choosing" and "applying" [law] entail the same process of interpretation.' Kramer, Rethinking, *supra* n. 112, at 289. In both types of situation, Kramer observes, a court must determine 'whether a party has a claim (or defense)' in light of the inherent limits on the ability of a legislature to specify the precise situations that its laws are designed to govern. *Id.*

[125] I deliberately invite a parallel here with Kramer's description of choice of law rules as providing default 'rules of interpretation for questions of extraterritorial scope' in determining the prescriptive reach of a legislative enactment. See Kramer, Renvoi, *supra* n. 112, at 1011; see also Kramer, Rethinking, *supra* n. 112, at 289–311 (developing an approach based on statutory interpretation for determining whether a law is 'prima facie applicable' to a multistate dispute).

CHAPTER 9. PRECLUSION IN CLASS ACTION LITIGATION

preclusion in the absence of mutuality. This is one respect in which a rendering court has considerably less freedom than a legislature, which can assign a different prescriptive scope to every law it passes, if it wishes. Within the parameters established by the applicable preclusion doctrine, however, the rendering court has many tools at its disposal through which to shape the course of the proceedings and control the positive effects of its judgment.

The most important such tools, for present purposes, are those through which the rendering forum can impose constraints – that is, the mechanisms by which it can employ less than the full extent of the authorization that the applicable preclusion doctrine provides in attaching prescriptive force to its judgment. Perhaps the most familiar tool that a rendering court can use to constrain the positive legal effect of its own judgment in this manner is the dismissal without prejudice, governed by Rule 41 in the federal system. Rule 41 expressly grants federal courts the authority to designate any dismissal as 'an adjudication [not] upon the merits' or 'without prejudice.'[126] As the Supreme Court's *Semtek* decision has confirmed, such a designation deprives a dismissal of any preclusive force as a rule of decision in subsequent proceedings.

The *Semtek* case called upon the Court to decide what source of authority governs the preclusive effect of a judgment issued by a federal court sitting in diversity, and what role Rule 41 plays in prescribing that effect. The Court held that federal common law governs the preclusive effect of all federal judgments, but that it is ordinarily appropriate to incorporate state preclusion standards as a rule of decision when determining the prescriptive effect of a diversity judgment, rather than imposing an independent federal standard.[127] In

---

[126] Fed. R. Civ. P. 41(b) ('Unless the court in its order for dismissal otherwise specifies, a dismissal under this subdivision... operates as an adjudication upon the merits.' (emphasis added)); *id.* 41(a)(2) ('Unless otherwise specified in the order, a dismissal under this paragraph is without prejudice.' (emphasis added)).

[127] *Semtek Int'l Inc. v. Lockheed Martin Corp.*, 531 U.S. 497, 506–509 (2001). While the Court cited the work of Ronan Degnan in setting forth this result, *id.* at 508, it actually embraced Professor Burbank's prescriptions. Degnan had argued for a uniform federal standard in assessing the preclusive effect of federal diversity judgments, while Burbank urged that federal common law adopt state preclusion rules in most such cases. Compare Ronan Degnan, Federalized Res Judicata, 85 Yale L.J. 741, 755–773 (1976) (calling for uniform federal rule), with Burbank, Interjurisdictional

437

keeping with that holding, the Court imposed a restrictive definition on Rule 41. Rather than serving as an independent source of authority for developing a federal rule of decision on the preclusive impact of judgments, the Court found a dismissal 'upon the merits' under Rule 41(b) speaks only to the ability of the parties to refile their claim in the same federal district court in which the dismissal was issued.[128] A federal diversity court, in other words, receives no authority from Rule 41 to make an independent determination about the affirmative prescriptive force that a dismissal on statute of limitations grounds, or any other basis, should have in future proceedings. Rather, it must depend upon the authority that a state court in the same forum would exercise in identifying the preclusion rules that apply to its judgments.[129]

Even in setting forth these restrictive conclusions about the sources of a federal diversity court's preclusion authority, however, the Supreme Court confirmed the continuing ability of a district court to decline to exercise that authority to its fullest extent. While Rule 41(b) does not authorize a court to develop an independent standard for determining the affirmative 'effect that must be accorded federal judgments by other courts,'[130] the Court explained, a dismissal 'upon the merits' under that provision 'is undoubtedly a necessary condition, [even though] not a sufficient one, for claim preclusive effect in other courts.'[131] A dismissal without prejudice or 'not upon the merits,' in other words, is not merely a 'factor' that a recognizing forum would look to in deciding whether to accord preclusive effect to a judgment. Such a dismissal has a determinative impact upon the prescriptive scope of a judgment, depriving the judgment of a necessary condition for serving as a rule of decision in other courts.[132] Professor Burbank

---

Preclusion, *supra* n. 7, at 736–739 (urging incorporation of state standards in federal common law of preclusion).

[128] Semtek, 531 U.S. at 504–506.

[129] *Id.* at 506–509 (calling for federal reference to state preclusion law in determining effect of federal diversity judgment, at least in absence of exceptional circumstances implicating strong federal interest).

[130] *Id.* at 503; see also *id.* at 505–506 (construing Rule 41(b)).

[131] *Id.* at 506.

[132] This approach to preclusion analysis is consistent with the posture that the Court has adopted in other important interjurisdictional cases. In Marrese, for example, the Court reaffirmed the primacy of the rendering court's policies in determining the preclusive effect of a judgment, even when the F1 proceeding involves a state law

CHAPTER 9. PRECLUSION IN CLASS ACTION LITIGATION

has characterized this tool of limitation as a necessary corollary to any regime in which federal judgments must be respected.[133]

This particular mechanism for predetermining the preclusive effect of one's own judgment is a common one. Courts regularly issue dismissals without prejudice with the expectation that their judgments will neither impose any immediate mandate upon the parties nor serve as a rule of decision in future cases.[134] Indeed, in the case of claim preclusion, the Restatement has formally recognized such designations as an appropriate basis for permitting a plaintiff to 'split' her claims between multiple proceedings.[135] Nonetheless, even the efficacy of a dismissal without prejudice is sometimes challenged, as happened

---

claim in a state court and the F2 proceeding involves an exclusively federal claim in a federal court. See *Marrese v. Am. Acad. of Orthopaedic Surgeons*, 470 U.S. 373, 380–382 (1985). Given the powerful federal interest embodied in the grant of exclusive jurisdiction, the Court might have concluded that the preclusive effect of the prior judgment should be determined by federal law in the federal proceeding, with the outcome contemplated by state law merely constituting one factor for consideration. See *id.* at 387–391 (Burger, C.J., concurring in judgment) (calling for federal preclusion rule with only minimal consideration of state law in such a case). Instead, the Court found that the Full Faith and Credit Clause and its implementing statute 'generally allow States to determine the preclusive scope of their own courts' judgments' in the first instance. *Id.* at 385.

[133] Burbank writes:

> Save for any constitutional constraints, neither validity nor finality need play a part in domestic preclusion law. But if, as it appears, there is a federal common law obligation not to disregard federal judgments [across jurisdictions], it requires as a corollary that the federal courts have the power to define the conditions precedent to status as a 'judgment' having the potential for preclusive effect. Moreover, the need here is not simply for federal law-in-reverse, acting only as a check against hostile or inconsistent state law. The nature of the problem demands a uniform, and uniformly federal, solution.

Burbank, Interjurisdictional Preclusion, *supra* n. 7, at 764.

[134] See e.g., *Equitable Fire and Marine Ins. Co. v. Bradford Builders, Inc.*, 174 So. 2d 44, 45 (Fla. Dist. Ct. App. 1965) ('To support a defense of res judicata, it must be clear that the court in the previous action intended that the disposition there was to be without right to further proceedings by the plaintiff.').

[135] Restatement (Second) of Judgments § 26(1)(b) (1982) ('[T]he general rule [against claim splitting] does not apply [when] ... [t]he court in the first action has expressly reserved the plaintiff's right to maintain the second action.'); see also *id.* § 26(1)(b) cmt. b (discussing application of this proposition to dismissals 'without prejudice').

in the *Cooper* case. When the district court refused to allow the Baxter class members to intervene and press their individual claims for damages in the original action in *Cooper*, it issued an order that carved those claims out of any subsequent preclusive effect that might flow from the action.[136] In other words, the district court imposed a constraint upon the prescriptive scope of its judgment as a rule of decision in the future resolution of those claims. While it is unclear how such a constraint would have applied to the issue preclusive effects of the judgment – a question that I address in the next subpart – the court's intention to prevent the judgment from having claim preclusive effect in the form of a subsequent defense of merger or bar was clear. Even so, the Fourth Circuit disregarded this feature of the district court's order, dismissing it as 'plain dictum'[137] and reaffirming the misguided instinct that rendering courts cannot exercise such control over their own judgments.[138]

That misguided instinct is particularly out of place in a class action proceeding. Rule 23 grants district courts the authority to multiply the binding effect of their proceedings enormously, sweeping in huge numbers of absent plaintiffs who will be subject to the court's mandate and bound to the rules of decision embodied in the court's judgment. As a consequence, Rule 23 is hedged about with elaborate protections aimed at ensuring that the court will exercise that authority only to an extent consistent with the interests of the absentees. The Rule makes certification discretionary, not mandatory, as a confirmation of the court's role in exercising its own judgment as to whether and to what extent a case should move forward on a classwide basis. Rule 23(d) even makes express provision for the court to 'make appropriate orders...requiring...that notice be given [to the class]...of the proposed extent of the judgment'[139] in setting the conditions for

---

[136] Cooper Record, *supra* n. 23, at 288a–289a (copy of order denying motion for leave to intervene).

[137] *EEOC v. Fed. Reserve Bank of Richmond*, 698 F.2d 633, 675 (4th Cir. 1983), reversed sub nom. *Cooper v. Fed. Reserve Bank of Richmond*, 467 U.S. 867 (1984).

[138] It is worth noting that the Fourth Circuit did not engage in a substantive review of the district court's designation of its order as 'without prejudice.' Rather, it dismissed that designation as ineffectual. A ruling that the district court should not have allowed the Baxter intervenors to maintain separate individual actions would have been quite different from the Fourth Circuit's statement that the district court was powerless to do so once having certified the class.

[139] Fed. R. Civ. P. 23(d)(2).

CHAPTER 9. PRECLUSION IN CLASS ACTION LITIGATION

certification, reiterating the role of the court in prescribing the contours of the action. To urge a court to exercise restraint when invoking its authority to bind absentees to a judgment, but then to deny the court the ability to control the preclusive effect of its judgment as one such tool of restraint, is both anomalous and illogical.[140] The role of the rendering court as an expositor of positive law in the certification process is broad enough to cover both functions.

In his canonical article addressing the source and content of the obligation to grant interjurisdictional recognition to judgments, Professor Burbank offers a broad observation that nicely captures the dilemma that litigants increasingly face when attempting to navigate the threat of preclusion during the certification process.

> [B]roadly preclusive trans-substantive rules are tolerable only to the extent that they are sufficiently nonformal, or contain sufficient qualifications or exceptions, to permit the avoidance of preclusion in circumstances where it would be unjust. But the characteristics that may make modern preclusion law tolerable in the administration of substantive law are the very characteristics that bedevil litigants, who desire clear and certain rules in planning litigation strategy.
>
> These considerations suggest that a court administering a modern domestic body of preclusion law must be alert to the loss of substantive rights caused by the failure of that body of law to provide fair notice of its implications for a particular context or by the failure of the jurisdiction's law as a whole to afford a fair opportunity to pursue claims of substantive right. Moreover, both concerns are more pressing when the preclusion law is not only trans-substantive, but trans-systemic.[141]

---

[140] One might express Rule 23's concern over constraining the scope of class proceedings as a question of the court's institutional legitimacy, as well as a concern over the rights of affected parties. Professor Nagareda makes this point in his discussion of the class action as a regulatory device.

> The claim preclusive effect of class settlements is what carries the potential to push them perilously close to civil justice reform legislation. It is because class counsel do not have nearly the kind of institutional legitimacy as legislators do to alter the rights of the populace that class settlements cannot do all that Congress might by way of legislation – whether to impose a compressed bureaucratic damage schedule or any other type of civil justice reform that one might consider desirable on instrumental grounds.

Nagareda, *supra* n. 2, at 174.
[141] Burbank, Interjurisdictional Preclusion, *supra* n. 7, at 815–816.

In the special circumstance of representative litigation, where the principle of litigant autonomy is not available to reinforce the moral authority of harsh or imperfect outcomes, these sentiments are more pressing still.[142] The most effective means of providing class members with the clarity and certainty that Burbank has urged is the prospective imposition of constraints upon the preclusive effects of class judgments.

9.3.1.3 Settlement and Preclusion

The assertion that a trial court has the authority to place constraints upon the preclusive effect of its own judgment that are calibrated to the needs of a particular class proceeding may sound unfamiliar. In fact, however, that authority has a close cousin that occupies a well-established position in the doctrinal landscape of representative litigation: the class settlement.

In most circumstances, a settlement between two individual litigants is a simple contract. While such agreements are always made against a backdrop of sovereign authority, the active participation of the state generally is required in a settlement agreement between individuals only when a party seeks assistance in enforcing its terms.[143]

---

[142] Owen Fiss has discussed this feature of representative litigation as embodying the difference between a 'right of participation' and a 'right of representation.' Fiss, *supra* n. 65, at 970–971. As Fiss correctly observes, representation and participation offer overlapping but distinct theoretical justifications for binding individuals to adjudicatory outcomes – justifications with very different practical implications in hard cases. One's assessment of the importance of participation as a means of reinforcing the dignity and worth of the individual in a given adjudicatory context, as opposed to its importance as a proxy for ensuring adequate representation of interests, may dictate one's view as to whether the costs of imperfect or harsh outcomes should fall upon unlucky individuals or should be spread more broadly as a systemic cost by permitting collateral challenge or relitigation. See *id.* at 978–979 (discussing varying importance of individual participation in different contexts); see also Douglas Laycock, Due Process of Law in Trilateral Disputes, 78 Iowa L. Rev. 1011, 1020 (1993) (identifying individual notice and opportunity to participate as 'the essence of due process').

[143] The standard illustration of the relationship between contractual arrangements and state authority centers around the Court's treatment of racially restrictive covenants. See *Shelley v. Kraemer*, 334 U.S. 1, 14–23 (1948). The classic discussion of Shelley is Louis Henkin, *Shelley v. Kraemer*: Notes for a Revised Opinion, 110 U. Pa. L. Rev.

CHAPTER 9. PRECLUSION IN CLASS ACTION LITIGATION

The same is not true of a class settlement. A settlement in a class action binds all the members of the class, just as a judgment would, even though absent class members never manifest the sort of individual consent or agreement that contract law would ordinarily require. This result is possible only because a class settlement constitutes an exercise of judicial authority, just as a judgment does. It is through the issuance of a certification order that a court acquires the power to bind absentees to a settlement agreement – a fact reinforced by Rule 23(e)'s requirement that a court provide further process to class members and then review and approve any settlement before such an agreement can take effect.[144] These features of the class settlement lie at the heart of the Court's pronouncement in *Amchem* that the requirements of Rule 23, and the due process principles to which they give voice, 'demand undiluted, even heightened, attention in the settlement context.'[145] Individuals can compromise their interests in all kinds of foolish ways when they act on their own behalf, but class representatives act with the authority of the state when they compromise the interests of absentees and they must act within the limitations of that authority.[146]

---

473 (1962), wherein Professor Henkin explores the broad implications of finding 'state action' in the state's enforcement of obligations between private citizens.

[144] See Fed. R. Civ. P. 23(e)(1)(A) ('The court must approve any settlement, voluntary dismissal, or compromise of the claims, issues, or defenses of a certified class.'); *id.* 23(e)(1)(B)-(4)(B) (detailing process that court must provide before approving class settlement).

[145] *Amchem Prods., Inc. v. Windsor*, 521 U.S. 591, 620 (1997).

[146] In this connection, the Supreme Court's suggestion in Matsushita that some jurisdictions might treat class action settlements as 'a question of pure contract law,' if taken literally, is incoherent. *Matsushita Elec. Indus. Co. v. Epstein*, 516 U.S. 367, 379 n. 6 (1996). 'Pure contract law' speaks only to the circumstances under which an individual binds her own person to a voluntary obligation. When individuals can bind others through their actions, another juridical category is at work. Agency law, family law, the law of business organizations, and the law of representative litigation all describe circumstances under which one individual might bind another to a contractual obligation. Each of those juridical categories possesses its own set of internal doctrinal requirements, and each must abide by external constitutional constraints. A jurisdiction might well choose not to adopt any special canons of construction for a class settlement, relying only on general contract principles to interpret the settlement's terms. This appears to be how some courts have construed Matsushita's footnote. See e.g., In re Lease Oil Antitrust Litig. (No. II), 200 F.3d 317, 320 (5th Cir. 2000) (citing Matsushita footnote and interpreting 'pure contract law' approach to mean that 'a settlement will be enforced according to

Settlement agreements almost always contain some form of release, and this is equally true of class settlements. A release is, in effect, the contractual version of claim preclusion: an agreement not to assert specified claims against one's adversary in any future proceeding.[147] Like claim preclusion, a settlement release is invoked as an affirmative defense if a covered claim is asserted in a subsequent lawsuit.[148] Unlike claim preclusion, however, a settlement release typically specifies, often in great detail, the claims to which it will apply. Naturally, parties sometimes argue, and litigate, over whether the terms of a release in an earlier settlement apply to a newly raised claim. Even when disagreements emerge as to the proper interpretation of a release in a particular dispute, however, no one doubts the ability of two contracting parties to make meaningful prospective choices about what claims they will include in such an agreement.

When a release is contained in a settlement that has been approved by a court on behalf of a class, it is the sovereign authority of the court that binds the absentees to the surrender of future claims. Thus, courts regularly use their authority to place carefully calibrated constraints upon the extent to which a class action will compromise the claims of class members in future proceedings.[149] They simply do so through the device of an order approving a settlement agreement, rather than an order limiting the preclusive effect of a judgment terminating a fully litigated action.

Indeed, the capacity to specify in precise detail the scope of the release that a settlement will include is one of those features of a settlement that is clearly 'relevant' to the certification calculus, as that term

---

its terms' without reference to broader class concerns). But when a lead plaintiff and her counsel exercise the authority to bind absentees to a settlement agreement, something more than 'pure contract law' is at work.

[147] See Restatement (Second) of Judgments §27 reporter's note to cmt. e (1982) ('A stipulation or consent judgment may have preclusive effect in a subsequent action if the parties have so agreed. In such a case the effect results not from the rule of this Section but from an agreement manifesting an intention to be bound.' (citations omitted)).

[148] See e.g., Fed. R. Civ. P. 8(c) ('In pleading to a preceding pleading, a party shall set forth affirmatively... release [and] res judicata').

[149] See e.g., *Trotsky v. L.A. Fed. Sav. and Loan Ass'n*, 121 Cal. Rptr. 637, 646 (Ct. App. 1975) (holding that court should exercise caution in approving settlement that includes general release of claims not raised in complaint or litigated in action, even though it has power to do so).

CHAPTER 9. PRECLUSION IN CLASS ACTION LITIGATION

was used in *Amchem*.[150] A settlement-only class action can greatly reduce the potential conflicts of interest that preclusion doctrine might otherwise introduce, precisely because it allows class counsel to remove much of the uncertainty associated with preclusion and to predetermine how the claims of class members will be affected in future lawsuits. The constraints on the preclusive effects of the judgment in a litigated action that I advocate here aim to resolve potential Rule 23 problems in the same manner.

To be clear, there are important differences between a court-approved settlement agreement and the judgment that results from a litigated action, on both a formal and a practical level. In particular, preclusion doctrine sometimes gives voice to institutional values that are not implicated by settlement, even in the case of a class proceeding. The contours of a judgment's preclusive effect – and the permissible forms of the constraints that a rendering forum can impose upon it – may differ markedly from the typical scope of a negotiated release. I discuss these issues in section 9.4. My point here is a more basic one. The aggressive reading that so many courts have given to the ubiquitous preclusion maxim appears to be founded upon a belief that rendering courts operate under some inherent disability when it comes to placing meaningful or effective constraints upon the preclusive effect that their own judgments will have in future cases. In the last subpart, I demonstrated that there is no logical or theoretical basis for such a belief. Commonly accepted practice in the approval of class action settlements further demonstrates that, in fact, courts regularly disprove the existence of any such categorical disability on the imposition of preclusion constraints by using their sovereign authority to achieve the same result in a closely analogous manner.[151]

---

[150] See *Amchem*, 521 U.S. at 619–620 (explaining that decision to proceed as a settlement-only class action is relevant to those elements of certification calculus that are inherently dependent upon the fact of litigation, like the manageability of the action).

[151] Cook offered a trenchant observation in setting forth the 'scientific' method that he employed in his challenge to traditional choice of law analysis that is equally apt here:

> We shall therefore undertake to formulate general statements as to what the 'law' of a given country 'can' or 'cannot' do in the way of attaching legal consequences to situations and transactions by observing what has actually been done. In making our observations we shall, however, find it necessary to

9.3.2 Tools of Limitation in Class Action Proceedings

It is not difficult to offer a basic description of the tools by which trial courts might constrain the preclusive effects of their own judgments in appropriate cases. Indeed, rendering courts already employ such tools in isolated instances.[152] It is only the threat of the ubiquitous preclusion maxim that dissuades courts from incorporating these constraints into the regular administration of class action proceedings, even when doing so is obviously the most sensible course. One decision from a Wisconsin appellate court, *Milwaukee Women's Medical Service, Inc. v. Scheidler*,[153] nicely captures the tenor of the response that many trial courts must expect when they attempt to incorporate such limitations into the orders that they craft. I begin here with a brief account of that case as a reminder of the judicial mindset that has prevented the simple steps that I describe from being widely implemented.

The *Milwaukee Women's Medical Service* decision involved a pair of lawsuits: one a federal class action, the other an individual litigation brought in state court. The federal proceeding was a nationwide class action initiated in the Northern District of Illinois in 1986 on behalf of all women seeking reproductive health services.[154] The plaintiffs in the federal action included a trio of Wisconsin-based women's health care providers collectively referred to as 'Summit,' while the defendants included Joseph Scheidler, an anti-abortion activist whom the

---

focus our attention primarily upon what courts have done, rather than upon the description they have given of the reasons for their action. Whatever generalizations we reach will therefore purport to be first of all an attempt to describe in as simple a way as possible the concrete judicial phenomena observed, and their 'validity' will be measured by their effectiveness in accomplishing that purpose. In other words, they will be regarded as 'true' only in so far as they enable us to handle effectively the concrete materials with which we must deal.

Cook, *supra* n. 104, at 8.

[152] Wright, Miller, and Cooper appear to assume the propriety of utilizing such constraints in discussing the use of narrow definitions of class certification, though they neither identify that analytic step expressly nor offer a defense for the propriety of its use – an unfortunate omission. See *supra* n. 72.

[153] 598 N.W.2d 588 (Wis. Ct. App. 1999).

[154] The federal action eventually gave rise to the Supreme Court's decision in *National Organization for Women, Inc. v. Scheidler*, 510 U.S. 249 (1994).

CHAPTER 9. PRECLUSION IN CLASS ACTION LITIGATION

plaintiffs accused of engaging in racketeering activities in the early 1980s in order to intimidate and threaten women away from clinic entrances.[155] In 1997, when the federal action was in its eleventh year, Summit brought a separate, individual lawsuit against Scheidler and fifty-two other defendants in Wisconsin state court on the basis of more recent protests that the defendants had targeted at the plaintiffs' local facilities. In that action, Summit requested an order to keep the defendants from blocking their Wisconsin clinic entrances or harassing their patients. After failing to secure a preliminary injunction, Summit settled the state action with the defendants and joined in a stipulation of dismissal.[156]

The stipulation, and the court's attendant order, included a carelessly worded release broadly providing that '*all claims* against [the defendants] *relating to conduct which occurred prior to the signing of this stipulation* are hereby dismissed [as to Summit], with prejudice.'[157] Although Summit sought to settle only the claims in the Wisconsin action, the broad release appeared to encompass the pending RICO claims. Seeking to capitalize upon Summit's mistake, Scheidler took the stipulation to the federal proceeding and sought to have Summit dismissed as a named plaintiff on collateral estoppel grounds.[158] In response, Summit then returned to the state trial court and asked for a modification of the stipulation and order, arguing that the broad language in the release was an error and did not reflect the more limited intentions of the parties. The trial court agreed, amending the order and stipulation so that it released only claims 'asserted in the [state court] Complaint.' To reinforce the limited scope of its amended order, the court added: '[I]t is not the intent of this court that this order have any effect upon *National Organization for Women, Inc., et al. v. Joseph M. Scheidler, et al.*, Case No. 86 C 7888 in the United States District Court for the Northern District of Illinois, Eastern District.'[159]

---

[155] *Id.* at 252–253.

[156] Milwaukee Women's Med. Serv., 598 N.W.2d at 590–591.

[157] *Id.* at 590 (emphasis added).

[158] *Id.* at 590–591. Actually, the proper basis for Scheidler's motion was presumably release, not collateral estoppel, since the two lawsuits dealt with different protesting activities separated by more than a decade and the state proceeding did not finally resolve any factual issues.

[159] *Id.* at 591–592.

447

EMPLOYMENT CLASS AND COLLECTIVE ACTIONS

The Wisconsin appeals court rejected the amendment to the stipulation and vacated the amended order. The appellate court spent much of its decision discussing the standard for granting relief from a final judgment under Wisconsin's equivalent of Federal Rule 60(b), which is not pertinent here. As an alternative ground, however, the appellate court also categorically repudiated the trial court's effort to place constraints upon the effects of its order of dismissal. The appellate court discarded the trial court's limiting clause as dicta, explaining that a rendering court does not have 'power' to impose such constraints – a proposition that it explained solely through an invocation of the ubiquitous preclusion maxim.[160] A concurring judge, seeking to place an additional gloss upon this holding, further explained that the trial court 'could not affect how the United States District Court for the Northern District of Illinois ... will interpret or apply the parties' stipulation or the trial court's order based on that stipulation.'[161]

The series of steps by which the Wisconsin appellate court reached its result form a roadmap of the errors of reasoning in preclusion doctrine discussed in this article. The trial court's dismissal was only an order implementing a stipulated settlement, not a judgment following an adjudication, so there should have been little problem in placing limitations upon the terms of its negotiated release – assuming, as the trial court did, that it was proper as a matter of contract law to revisit the stipulation's language.[162] As for the pure claim preclusive effect of the order, a 1997 judgment in the state court action should not have affected the claims raised in the federal suit at all. The two sets of claims arose from facts separated in time by a span of years, presumably bringing them comfortably outside any impact that the state court judgment might have on transactionally related claims. Thus, the

---

[160] The entire passage reads:

> Finally, we note that the circuit court's attempt to narrow the legal effect, if any, of its second order by adding language explaining the circuit court's own intent that the order not 'have any effect upon [the federal action]' amounted to dicta. A court rendering a first judgment does not have the power to determine that judgment's effect; the successor court will make its own decision.

Id. at 593 (citation omitted).
[161] Id. at 594 (Fine, J., concurring in part and dissenting in part).
[162] See id. at 592–593 (analyzing trial court's amendment of stipulation under principles of contract law).

CHAPTER 9. PRECLUSION IN CLASS ACTION LITIGATION

'constraint' that the trial court imposed upon the claim preclusive effect of its order did not detract from any effect that would actually have resulted had the state lawsuit been litigated to judgment. Finally, the appellate court's explanation for rejecting the trial court's order in the face of these facts concisely exemplifies the failure of understanding that has perpetuated the reign of the ubiquitous preclusion maxim. The majority and concurrence opined that the trial court had no 'power' to 'affect how [another court] will interpret or apply' the stipulation and order.[163] That is quite true – and entirely irrelevant to the power of the trial court to enter the order that it did. As the last section explained, neither legislatures nor courts can control the manner in which the rules of decision that they enact will come to be applied in future cases. They can, however, place constraints upon the prescriptive scope of those rules of decision. The state trial court was not attempting to issue an order mandating the federal district court to 'interpret or apply' its judgment in a particular fashion. It was seeking to clarify the positive legal effect of the consent judgment so that the federal court would know exactly what rule of decision it was being called upon to interpret and apply. In rejecting that attempt, the appellate court chastised the trial court for an error that it did not make.

When trial judges must fear such categorical repudiation as the thanks for exercising sensible restraint, it is small wonder that even diligent courts have not yet begun to implement the simple and straightforward steps that might allow them to resolve preclusion problems during class certification.

9.3.2.1 *Constraining a Judgment's Preclusive Effect*

When a court apprehends a preclusion problem at the outset of a proposed class action, there are two questions that it must ask: What constraints on the prescriptive scope of a judgment in this action would ameliorate the problem; and would those constraints be permissible, and appropriate, under the preclusion and joinder policies that apply to the dispute? The second question is the subject of section 9.4, and I leave it to one side for now. In this subpart, my focus is the forms of the constraints that a court can impose upon a certification order and judgment in addressing ex ante preclusion problems.

---

[163] *Id.* at 593–594.

9.3.2.1.1 Constraints Relating to a Parallel Proceeding The narrowest type of preclusion constraint that a court can impose is one that identifies a particular proceeding for which the court does not wish its judgment to have claim or issue preclusive effect. The attempt by the trial court in *Milwaukee Women's Medical Service* to amend its earlier judgment so as not to interfere with the pending RICO case offers an example of such a constraint, and also of the type of situation where it is most likely to be pertinent – where two parallel actions involving related claims are being litigated simultaneously.

Parallel class action proceedings are not unusual, particularly where federal law creates a cause of action with close analogs among the laws of the various states, as in the regulation of anticompetitive activities or certain types of corporate malfeasance in publicly traded companies.[164] When a nationwide class action is initiated in federal court on federal claims, follow-on class actions in state court are often not far behind. Class counsel in these state actions typically assert only state law claims in order to avoid having the cases removed to federal court and consolidated with the original action through the Multidistrict Litigation Panel. These stay-in-state-court suits may raise claims that could not have been certified in the federal action because of choice of law complications, or they may be entirely duplicative, with class counsel hoping to race ahead of the federal action to judgment or settlement. Either way, a judgment in such an action carries a risk of compromising the claims of plaintiffs in the federal suit through claim or issue preclusion, even where there is exclusive jurisdiction over the federal claims.[165]

A diligent state court might conclude that some follow-on class actions of this description are suitable for certification and would

---

[164] E.g., Richard A. Posner, Antitrust in the New Economy, 68 Antitrust L.J. 925, 940–943 (2001) (discussing parallel federal and state antitrust regimes and capacity of state officials to enforce federal antitrust laws, and arguing for broad federal preemption and elimination of state parens patriae actions).

[165] As Wright, Miller, and Cooper explain:

> Difficult choices must be made ... if the plaintiff knowingly chose a court of more limited jurisdiction when a court of broader jurisdiction was available, or chose a narrower remedy over a broader remedy. It has been urged that the plaintiff should be required to seek out the most comprehensive proceeding available, so that the dimensions of the claim are measured by that possibility.

18 Wright, Miller, and Cooper, *supra* n. 2, § 4412, at 277–278.

CHAPTER 9. PRECLUSION IN CLASS ACTION LITIGATION

serve the interests of the class – as, for example, in the case of a statewide suit seeking to raise valuable state law claims that could not be asserted in a nationwide federal action. At the same time, the state court might conclude that it would be inappropriate for a judgment in a state proceeding to compromise federal claims that are being thoroughly litigated in a federal forum.[166] Where there is exclusive jurisdiction over the federal claims, a straight application of preclusion doctrine might provide protection from merger or bar through the 'jurisdictional competency' exception that some states employ,[167] but the exception is not firmly established in every state[168] and does not generally apply to issue preclusion in any event.[169] As a consequence, a state court must always think about the preclusive consequences of certifying such a parallel proceeding.

Cases of this description appear to be particularly good candidates for the imposition of a constraint on the prescriptive scope of the state court's judgment. Following the lead of the Wisconsin trial court in *Milwaukee Women's Medical Service*, the court could provide in its certification order that nothing in any judgment or dismissal of the action it has certified would have any preclusive impact upon the parallel action currently pending in federal court. Such an order would have the

---

[166] In his first Epstein opinion, Judge William Norris adopted this limitation as a federal common law constraint on the capacity of state court class settlements to compromise exclusively federal claims. See *Epstein v. MCA, Inc.* (Epstein I), 50 F.3d 644, 662–666 (9th Cir. 1995) (arguing that state courts do not have 'the power to extinguish exclusively federal claims by approving a class action settlement that could have been extinguished by adjudicating the class action'), reversed sub nom. *Matsushita Elec. Indus. Co. v. Epstein*, 516 US 367 (1996).

[167] See Restatement (Second) of Judgments § 26(1)(c) (1982) (describing general rule that preclusion should not attach where 'plaintiff was unable to rely on a certain theory of the case or to seek a certain remedy or form of relief in the first action because of the limitations on the subject matter jurisdiction of the courts').

[168] See e.g., In re Heckert, 272 F.3d 253, 258–260 (4th Cir. 2001) (holding that West Virginia law demands that prior state court judgment exert claim preclusive effect upon subsequent federal bankruptcy proceeding, despite exclusive federal jurisdiction in bankruptcy proceedings); In re Genesys Data Techs., Inc., 245 F.3d 312, 314–315 (4th Cir. 2001) (same for prior state court judgment from Hawaii).

[169] See e.g., *Freeman v. San Diego Ass'n of Realtors*, 322 F.3d 1133, 1142 n. 8 (9th Cir. 2003) (observing that California does not apply claim preclusion where exclusively federal claims could not have been raised in initial action, but conducting issue preclusion analysis even so because that doctrine continues to apply).

added benefit of helping to focus the attention of the court on the propriety of any global release (i.e., one including federal claims) that the parties might attempt to incorporate into a proposed settlement – a mechanism by which class counsel in parallel state proceedings sometimes seek to entice the defendants to settle quickly, to the benefit of class counsel's fee award but not always to the benefit of the class.[170]

9.3.2.1.2 Constraints Relating to a Specific Cause of Action Where no parallel action exists, or where an order specifying a particular lawsuit would not resolve the preclusion problem, a court might consider carving a particular cause of action out of the preclusive impact of the proceeding it is certifying. Such an order might limit itself to preserving the right of class members to raise certain types of claims in any future proceedings without fear of merger or bar, or it might also place limits on the issue preclusive effect of the court's judgment. The choice would depend upon the nature of the preclusion problem that the court sought to address.

An order of the first type might be appropriate for some stay-in-state court civil rights litigation. A state court might decide that it is desirable for a civil rights suit raising important and novel questions under the state's constitution to be heard in state court. In such a case, the court could view the decision of class counsel not to plead federal grounds for relief in order to eliminate the possibility of removal as wholly legitimate. At the same time, the court might conclude that members of the class should not have to forgo any possibility of federal relief in order to obtain a state forum for their state claims. The court could thus provide in its certification order that any judgment in the case would have no impact through merger or bar upon the ability of class members to pursue federal relief in a future case, even though the federal claims could have been asserted on a classwide basis in the state forum. It would not be necessary, and probably would not be

---

[170] Judge Friendly's observation on this score remains one of the most cogent. See *Nat'l Super Spuds, Inc. v. N.Y. Mercantile Exch.*, 660 F.2d 9, 18 (2nd Cir. 1981) (Friendly, J.) ('If a judgment after trial cannot extinguish claims not asserted in the class action complaint, a judgment approving a settlement in such an action ordinarily should not be able to do so either.'). It was a global release in a parallel state court proceeding that produced the dispute which ultimately gave rise to the Court's decision in Matsushita. See 516 U.S. at 369–372 (recounting case history); *Epstein v. MCA, Inc.* (Epstein II), 126 F.3d 1235, 1251–1255 (9th Cir. 1997) (same).

CHAPTER 9. PRECLUSION IN CLASS ACTION LITIGATION

appropriate, to extend the effect of that exception to issue preclusion, since the state court is presumably as competent as any federal court to resolve contested issues of fact. The preclusion dilemma in this case arises from the court's desire to preserve a state forum for important state claims without categorically depriving the class of a federal cause of action. An exception that is limited to merger and bar would accomplish that goal.

In contrast, such an order would not eliminate the problems associated with conflict of interest cases where class members who possess high-value damages claims have much more to lose from the issue preclusive effects of an adverse judgment than do class members who are only able to benefit from injunctive relief. Consider the Title VII case that the district court refused to certify in *Zachery v. Texaco Exploration & Production, Inc.*[171] The Supreme Court's decision in *Cooper* already made it clear that merger and bar would not operate in a disparate impact case to compromise the class members' individual claims of discriminatory treatment when those claims could not have been certified in the original action, a fact that the *Zachery* court understood.[172] But issue preclusion would still threaten to compromise the high-value claims of those individuals, giving them a much stronger incentive to settle for a lesser form of injunctive relief rather than litigating through to judgment, thus placing them in conflict with the rest of the class. Where the rendering court concludes that it is desirable for the disparate impact suit to proceed on a classwide basis, it would have to specify that its certification order and judgment are without prejudice from either claim or issue preclusion to the ability of individual class members to pursue individual damages claims alleging discriminatory treatment. Once again, the nature of the preclusion problem – here, a conflict of interest arising from the threat of issue preclusion – dictates the scope of the order needed to ameliorate that problem.

9.3.2.1.3 Constraints Relating to the Entire Action Exempting a particular cause of action from the prescriptive scope of a future judgment in a certified class sometimes will not suffice, or will not be practicable, in the effort to eliminate an ex ante preclusion problem. Where this is so, a court may have to consider the imposition of a broader limitation that will restrict the preclusive effect of its judgment in

---

[171] 185 F.R.D. 230 (W.D. Tex. 1999).

[172] *Id.* at 243 (discussing *Cooper* and claim preclusion).

any future action – the type of constraint that is the most likely to raise concerns under the broader policies embodied in the forum's preclusion doctrines, as the next part discusses.

Actions seeking to pursue defective product claims on behalf of a class of consumers – which are becoming increasingly common, despite the many barriers to certification that they present – might present preclusion problems redressable only through such broad measures. When a defective product is released into the market, it will generally give rise to two types of claims: the economic damages associated with the reduced value of the product, which will often be readily calculable on a classwide basis; and the consequential damages that occur when the defect actually causes the product to fail, which may include claims for personal injuries and property damage that will be unsuited for class treatment. In the *Bridgestone/Firestone* litigation, for example, the economic harm that consumers suffered when the tires they had purchased were revealed to be defective was not an inherently difficult claim to resolve on a class-wide basis.[173] The personal injuries and property damages of consumers who actually experienced a tire failure, however, would have entailed highly individualized determinations of causation, comparative fault, and damages, which would be unsuited for class treatment. Nonetheless, a plaintiff seeking to pursue only economic damages would have to establish certain elements, like the defective nature of the tires or the inadequate level of care exhibited by the defendant in their manufacture, that are shared in common with the more valuable claims. As a result, a class certified to resolve only the economic damages claims would raise a serious conflict between the absentees who want maximum value for their unusable tires and the absentees who possess valuable claims for consequential damages and would not want to risk an adverse judgment on such a relatively insignificant item.[174]

---

[173] See In re Bridgestone/Firestone Tires Prods. Liab. Litig. (Bridgestone/Firestone I), 288 F.3d 1012, 1014–1016 (7th Cir. 2002) (discussing claims for economic harm). The Seventh Circuit concluded that a nationwide class on these claims was nonetheless impossible because of the multiple state law regimes that would apply to the dispute and the diversity of tire models encompassed in the omnibus action. *Id.* at 1018–1020.

[174] Instead of acknowledging and confronting the conflicts of interest that preclusion doctrine created within the class, the Seventh Circuit finessed the issue by accepting the assertion of class counsel that all individuals possessing high-value damages claims were 'sure to opt out and litigate independently,' *id.* at 1016, and hence could

CHAPTER 9. PRECLUSION IN CLASS ACTION LITIGATION

This is not to say that high-stakes claimants would derive no material benefit from an economic damages class action in a defective products case. The aggregate recovery in such a suit would be large enough to focus substantial energy and resources upon the issues common to both types of claim, and high-stakes claimants would

---

safely be assumed away in considering class certification. This is a remarkable proposition. While it is probably true that most individuals who suffer serious injury or harm would consider pursuing litigation on their own, it is quite another matter to assume breezily that all those individuals will in fact exercise their right to opt out and hence require no further consideration by the certifying court. Many people do not pay attention to the notices that they receive, and some people who do receive a notice may make unwise or uninformed decisions, either from a failure to understand the consequences of not opting out or from a simple lack of good judgment. See Debra Lyn Bassett, Implied 'Consent' to Personal Jurisdiction in Transnational Class Litigation, 2004 Mich. St. L. Rev. 619, 626–628 (describing challenges that recipients of notice frequently experience in understanding its meaning). As I discuss at greater length in section 3(b)(3)(b), notice and opt out are poor proxies for the type of robust litigant autonomy that justifies binding individuals to bad litigation choices.

One rather suspects that Judge Easterbrook would have been less cavalier about the status of the high-stakes class members had their presence in the suit been dispositive of the certification analysis. In fact, the Seventh Circuit's opinion makes much more sense if one reads into it an implicit recognition that no class could be certified in an action of this type unless it was understood to include a constraint on the issue preclusive effect that any judgment would have upon the high-value claims of injured absentees.

The Seventh Circuit, per Judge Easterbrook, recently passed up another opportunity to address the conflicts of interest that issue preclusion can generate. In *Allen v. International Truck and Engine Corp.*, 358 F.3d 469 (7th Cir. 2004) (Easterbrook, J.), the court reversed a district court's denial of certification in a Title VII case. The district court had found that it was impossible to certify a suit seeking only injunctive relief on behalf of a 350-person class because the divergent facts surrounding the individual damages claims in the case would make the lawsuit unmanageable. *Id.* at 470–471. The Seventh Circuit reversed on the manageability finding and sent the case back. *Id.* at 471–472. It did not, however, address the divergent settlement interests that employees with high-value damages claims and those without such claims would apparently possess. Since the court ruled, following its decision in *Jefferson v. Ingersoll International Inc.*, 195 F.3d 894 (7th Cir. 1999), that the class members must have an opportunity to opt out in a bifurcated action of this sort, its failure to address the divergent settlement interests of class members may proceed from the same instinct that apparently informed Judge Easterbrook's opinion in Bridgestone/Firestone II: the assumption that class members with high-value claims will opt out when doing so is necessary to protect their interests.

benefit from those efforts. Nonetheless, a serious conflict of interest would remain when the decision arose whether to litigate or settle, and it would be necessary to restrict the issue preclusive effects of the judgment in order to remove that conflict. The range of individual claims that might be compromised by the class suit, however – personal injury, wrongful death, loss of consortium, property damages to the vehicle, and so forth – would not lend itself to the type of specific delineation that resolved the conflict between disparate impact and disparate treatment claims in the Title VII context. Here, the court would need to impose a broader constraint, providing that any judgment in the certified action would be without prejudice, either from issue preclusion or from merger or bar, to the ability of class members to pursue any claims not raised in the complaint itself. In essence, such an order would restrict the action from having any preclusive effect upon the class beyond the final resolution of the claims actually raised therein.

These three forms of limitation – constraints relating to a parallel proceeding, to a specific type of claim, and to the entire action certified for class treatment – are tools with which a court might be able to eliminate the ex ante problems that preclusion doctrine can pose to the certification of a class. There may be legitimate objections to the use of these tools in some cases, as they might be inconsistent with the broader preclusion policies that govern the action. Those potential objections are the subject of section 9.4. If a court determines that these 'negative' or constraining applications of preclusion doctrine are not available to it, and that no alternatives exist for addressing an ex ante preclusion problem, then it may be justified in concluding that a class action is not appropriate. But the posture of vague powerlessness toward preclusion problems that some courts have adopted in refusing to certify a class action can no longer be tolerated.

9.3.2.2 *The Seventh Amendment and Reexamination*

It is worth taking a moment to discuss the Seventh Amendment's Reexamination Clause, since the same error that led the Fifth Circuit to make its confused statement about reexamination and preclusion in *Allison* might also lead a certifying court to have misplaced concerns about the use of preclusion constraints like those discussed above.[175] The Clause

---

[175] See *supra* notes 51–60 and accompanying text.

CHAPTER 9. PRECLUSION IN CLASS ACTION LITIGATION

provides that 'no fact tried by a jury, shall be otherwise reexamined in any Court of the United States, than according to the rules of the common law.'[176] The amendment has not been incorporated against the states and so applies only to federal courts,[177] though a few states have similar provisions in their own constitutions.[178] In some of the cases explored above in which a preclusion constraint might be appropriate – for example, a class action for economic damages in which some absentees possess related claims for personal injuries – the initial proceeding will be tried before a jury. Suppose that the class loses before the jury in such a case on an explicit finding that it had failed to prove a key factual issue, and a class member then sought to pursue his individual claim for personal injuries in a subsequent suit, taking advantage of the preclusion constraint imposed by the court in the initial action. The question might arise whether the second suit, by raising a factual issue that the jury in F1 decided adversely, would run afoul of the Seventh Amendment's prohibition on reexamination.

The Court has often said that the Seventh Amendment 'preserve[d] the right to jury trial as it existed in 1791.'[179] While this formulation has at times been read to impose a 'static' limitation demanding strict adherence to the jury practices of the late eighteenth century, that mode of interpretation has given way to a 'dynamic' approach that preserves the basic prerogatives of the jury but allows for procedural innovation.[180] In *Gasperini*, the Court applied that dynamic mode of interpretation to the Reexamination Clause, rejecting the view that 'the meaning of the Seventh Amendment [was] fixed at 1791' and formally acknowledging that procedures 'not in conformity with practice

---

[176] U.S. Const. Amend. VII.
[177] See *Gasperini v. Ctr. for the Humanities, Inc.*, 518 U.S. 415, 432 (1996) (holding that Seventh Amendment 'governs proceedings in federal court, but not in state court'). The Reexamination Clause does apply to federal court review of state court jury findings, however. See *Bose Corp. v. Consumers Union of United States, Inc.*, 466 US 485, 508 n. 27 (1984).
[178] See e.g., S.C. Const. Art. V, § 5 ('[The Supreme Court of South Carolina] shall have appellate jurisdiction only in cases of equity, and in such appeals they shall review the findings of fact as well as the law, except in cases where the facts are settled by jury and the verdict not set aside.'); W. Va. Const. Art. III, § 13 ('No fact tried by a jury shall be otherwise reexamined in any case than according to rule of court or law.').
[179] *Curtis v. Loether*, 415 US 189, 193 (1974).
[180] See Woolley, Reexamination Clause, *supra* n. 53, at 502–506 (describing development of the Court's Seventh Amendment doctrine).

457

at common law when the Amendment was adopted' remain consistent with the Clause when they are 'necessary and proper to the fair administration of justice.'[181] Thus, in framing a Seventh Amendment inquiry, it is useful to ask whether a procedural innovation is inconsistent with a core function of the civil jury as it functioned at common law, and also what role the proposed innovation will play in promoting other adjudicatory values. Much of this article is devoted to addressing the second of these inquiries. As to the first, it would be exceedingly difficult to argue that the type of preclusion constraint that I have suggested here derogates from the common law prerogatives of the jury, or from the purposes animating the Reexamination Clause.

When American courts received the common law from England, pleading practice in civil proceedings still required conformity with the traditional forms of action. In English law courts, a bundle of claims that we would now describe as 'transactionally related' had long required the issuance of separate writs in order to obtain different

---

[181] 518 U.S. at 435, 436 n. 20. In an early commentary on the Seventh Amendment and the reform of civil procedure in American courts, Professor Austin Scott embraced this 'dynamic' interpretive approach to the amendment when discussing the many variations among the jury practices of early American courts. He wrote:

> First. Whatever was an incident or characteristic of trial by jury in a particular jurisdiction at the time of the adoption of the constitutional guaranty in that jurisdiction is not thereby abolished. In determining what is meant by trial by jury under the Seventh Amendment, inasmuch as the practice was different in the different colonies, the federal courts look to the common law of England rather than to the law of any particular colony; and incidents of trial by jury, known in England at the time of the adoption of the Seventh Amendment, are not done away with by its adoption.
>
> Second. Although the incidents of trial by jury which existed at the time of the adoption of the constitutional guaranty are not thereby abolished, yet those incidents are not necessarily made unalterable. Only those incidents which are regarded as fundamental, as inherent in and of the essence of the system of trial by jury, are placed beyond the reach of the legislature. The question of the constitutionality of any particular modification of the law as to trial by jury resolves itself into a question of what requirements are fundamental and what are unessential, a question which is necessarily, in the last analysis, one of degree.

Austin Wakeman Scott, Trial by Jury and the Reform of Civil Procedure, 31 Harv. L. Rev. 669, 671 (1918) (citation omitted).

CHAPTER 9. PRECLUSION IN CLASS ACTION LITIGATION

types of judicial remedy.[182] This requirement migrated to the American colonial courts and persisted through the eighteenth century. As Professor Millar has explained, with rare exception, the common law limited the 'joinder of causes of action [in early American courts] ... to the case where all fell within the same form of action.'[183] In a judicial system shackled by such constraints, claims for economic harm and personal injury, or contract and tort, frequently could not be joined in a single proceeding. When an individual suffered a harm that sounded in more than one form of action, she would thus need to bring multiple suits with multiple juries to obtain complete relief.[184] It was only with the enactment of the amended Field Code of 1852 that a court system in the United States expressly permitted the joinder of all claims that 'arise out of the same transaction, or transactions connected with the same subject of action,' before a single jury.[185] Even then, this innovation was slow to spread from New York to

---

[182] A rich account of the writ system may be found in Sir John Baker, 6 The Oxford History of the Laws of England, 1483–1558, at 323–349 (2003) [hereinafter Baker, Oxford History]. While Baker writes exclusively of the Tudor period in this volume, the relevant structural features of the writ system remained essentially unchanged through the end of the eighteenth century. See J.H. Baker, An Introduction to English Legal History 37–51 (4th edn 2002) (describing evolution of English common law courts). As Baker explains, the diverse array of original writs 'had come to be regarded not only as "the foundation of every suit" but as the foundations of the law itself, on which the whole law depended.' Baker, Oxford History, *supra*, at 323 (citation omitted). 'The writs exerted their dominion not only over procedure but over the common-law mind. If there was no writ, there was no remedy.' Id.

[183] Robert Wyness Millar, Civil Procedure of the Trial Court in Historical Perspective 111 (1952) [hereinafter Millar, Historical Perspective].

[184] See *id.* at 112. Millar states,

> [U]nless there existed the common origin indicated, it would not permit, for example, the joinder of a claim in contract with one in tort, or one for injury to character with one for injury to the person, or one for the recovery of real property with one for the recovery of personal property.

Id.

[185] *Id.* at 111 (quoting Act of April 16, 1852, Ch. 392, 1852 N.Y. Laws 655). The Field Code, which was first enacted into law in New York in 1848, was named for David Dudley Field, 'one of [the code's] chief architects and certainly its most ardent supporter.' Robert G. Bone, Mapping the Boundaries of a Dispute: Conceptions of Ideal Lawsuit Structure from the Field Code to the Federal Rules, 89 Colum. L. Rev. 1, 10 n. 13 (1989).

other states during the eighty-six years that elapsed before the adoption of the Federal Rules.[186]

These rigid rules of common law pleading and joinder were combined with concomitantly narrow rules of preclusion. A judgment in one action would preclude parties from relitigating the same legal theory, applying what we would call a 'direct estoppel'[187] that marked the proceedings as final. But judgments did not attach the sort of transproceeding finality to factual determinations that we associate with modern issue preclusion. 'Estoppel by record' – the closest analog to modern issue preclusion in actions at law – was grounded in a desire to protect the integrity of the initial proceeding as manifest in the written record. The preclusive effect that attached to that determination was such as was necessary to prevent an unsuccessful party from undermining the integrity of that record. Estoppel by record thus prohibited a second attempt to obtain the same form of relief that was once denied, which would constitute an affront to the verdict recorded in the first proceeding. It also prohibited a party's disavowal of the sworn testimony and admissions that he offered in a prior proceeding, which would attack the integrity of the original testimonial record. The first concern was not implicated when parties brought successive suits for different forms of relief under properly distinct forms of action. The second is a species of concern that we now police through perjury laws, judicial estoppel, and the use of inconsistent testimony for impeachment. Our current concerns over inefficient relitigation and the value of repose, and our tendency to place special reliance upon the view of the facts propounded by the first tribunal to hear a dispute between parties, were not the motivating purposes behind the estoppel employed by common law courts.[188] While the 'verdict' of a jury could serve

---

[186] See Millar, Historical Perspective, *supra* n. 183, at 113–114 (describing gradual liberalization of joinder standards in other states before adoption of Fed. R. Civ. P. 18).

[187] Woolley, Reexamination Clause, *supra* n. 53, at 523 ('The rules [of direct estoppel] are designed to prevent a party from relitigating facts decided between the same parties on the same cause of action.').

[188] As one commentator writes:

Originally, parties were permitted to relitigate issues. Indeed, common law writ systems invited such multiple litigation. The litigation followed a certain hierarchy, however. A litigant might sue first for possession of property, later for a sort of ownership. The parties could not deny the matters in the record of a suit; they

CHAPTER 9. PRECLUSION IN CLASS ACTION LITIGATION

as the basis for an estoppel in appropriate cases,[189] that estoppel by record bore little relationship to modern preclusion doctrine.[190]

> were estopped from doing so. Until recently, that concern could be found reflected in the frequent use of 'estoppel by record' to refer to issue preclusion. The record consisted of matters that had been sworn to by witnesses in testimony or by the jury in delivering its verdict. At first, one might conclude that the record, therefore, included only matters of fact. To modern legal minds, juries consider questions of fact alone, leaving any decision on the relevant law to the judge. Such distinctions result from a [more] developed legal system than that which devised estoppel...
>
>> Even in America, the distinction between questions of law and fact only developed after the colonial period. Estoppel by record, therefore, was not a doctrine regarding facts but concerned court decision-making both of fact and law.
>>
>> Estoppel by record had little to do with relitigation and ignored any distinction between law and fact. Instead, the doctrine sought to protect the integrity of the court. Other courts, presented with different causes of action, might come to different conclusions, both of the law and the facts. However, in each court (it is too early to talk of jurisdiction), there existed a record, and that record bound the parties to the court's findings. Those notions of independent court determinations and of court integrity play large roles in unraveling the present state of the issue preclusion doctrine.
>
> Colin Hugh Buckley, Issue Preclusion and Issues of Law: A Doctrinal Framework Based on Rules of Recognition, Jurisdiction and Legal History, 24 Hous. L. Rev. 875, 877–879 (1987) (citations omitted); see also Joseph H. Koffler and Alison Reppy, Handbook of Common Law Pleading 406 (1969) ('The Ground upon which the Estoppel rests... is a determination of the Merits of the Action, which, by Reason of the Admitted Facts shown upon the Record, the Unsuccessful Party is precluded from again bringing into question.').
>
> [189] See e.g., Robert Wyness Millar, The Historical Relation of Estoppel by Record to Res Judicata, 35 Ill. L. Rev. 41, 47–49 (1940) (describing historical forms of pleading preclusion by reason of former judgment).
>
> [190] Most importantly, estoppel by record did not depend upon the existence of a final judgment on the merits. See id. at 55 ('[I]t is clear that the only part played by the judgment in the realm of estoppel was in perfecting, confirming and authenticating the record of the antecedent episode of the proceeding which constituted the estoppel. The judgment, itself, operating under the principle of res judicata, was quite another thing.'). A judgment was necessary to mark the termination of the prior suit (and delimit the content of the record available for estoppel), but the content of that judgment was immaterial. Id.
>
> Professor Millar points out that a more modern, transproceeding style of estoppel was sometimes available in equity courts, where the resolution of an issue

As Professor Millar has put it, 'the ghost of [common law estoppel] may still occasionally walk... but it would be difficult to maintain that it preserves today its corporeal identity.'[191]

When the Seventh Amendment established a constitutional prohibition on reexamination, it did not supersede or alter the need to bring multiple, separate actions to vindicate multiple rights. Concern over successive actions was not the motivating force behind the amendment. Rather, as Professor Woolley explains, the amendment sought to guard against the possibility that federal judges might usurp the role of the jury within a given proceeding,[192] particularly in the case of the Supreme Court and its capacity to exercise appellate jurisdiction 'both as to Law and Fact' under Article III.[193] Indeed, Alexander Hamilton's oft-quoted reassurance on this score, from *The Federalist No. 81*, offers the possibility of a second trial by jury as the innocuous alternative to the concentration of unaccountable federal authority that direct judicial

---

'plainly decided as a step toward the award or denial of the relief sought by a plaintiff might foreclose the re-litigation of the same question in a later suit, though this was other than a repetition of the earlier.' *Id.* at 56. But, he explains, this form of preclusion operated only 'outside the peculiar sphere of common-law estoppel.' *Id.* The chancery derived authority for this form of preclusion 'not from the common-law principle, which it did not know, but... from the Roman principle of res judicata.' *Id.*

[191] *Id.* at 59.
[192] See Woolley, Reexamination Clause, *supra* n. 53, at 508–510.
[193] U.S. Const. Art. III, §2, cl. 2 ('[T]he supreme Court shall have appellate Jurisdiction, both as to Law and Fact, with such Exceptions, and under such Regulations as the Congress shall make.'). Justice Scalia emphasizes the primacy of this concern in his Gasperini dissent: The desire for an explicit constitutional guarantee against reexamination of jury findings was explained by Justice Story, sitting as Circuit Justice in 1812, as having been specifically prompted by Article III's conferral of 'appellate Jurisdiction, both as to Law and Fact' upon the Supreme Court. '[O]ne of the most powerful objections urged against [the Constitution],' he recounted, was that this authority 'would enable that court, with or without a new jury, to re-examine the whole facts, which had been settled by a previous jury.' *United States v. Wonson*, 28 F. Cas. 745, 750 (No. 16,750) (CC Mass.). The Reexamination Clause put to rest 'apprehensions' of 'new trials by the appellate courts,' Wonson, 28 F. Cas., at 750, by adopting, in broad fashion, 'the rules of the common law' to govern federal-court interference with jury determinations. *Gasperini v. Ctr. for Humanities, Inc.*, 518 U.S. 415, 450–451 (1996) (Scalia, J., dissenting).

CHAPTER 9. PRECLUSION IN CLASS ACTION LITIGATION

review of jury findings threatened.[194] It is thus unclear whether the Seventh Amendment should ever place limitations on the maintenance of successive suits, at least in the absence of a blatant attempt to usurp the function or integrity of the jury.[195]

What is more, the Amendment clearly does not operate to foreclose successive jury trials where mutuality of parties is absent.[196] How should one view a class proceeding against this requirement of mutuality? Nothing remotely resembling the modern class action – with its shadowy absentees who are bound by the judgment but never fully embodied as parties in the lawsuit – existed in a world of common law forms of action, power-based personal jurisdiction, and the capias ad respondendum. To argue that the sparse words of the Reexamination Clause should be read categorically to foreclose successive class action proceedings with some areas of factual overlap – as Judge Posner did in his much noted *Rhone-Poulenc* opinion, which imposed significant Seventh Amendment obstacles to the use of issue-only classes in complex cases[197] – is simply not sustainable.[198]

---

[194] Hamilton wrote:

> If... the re-examination of a fact once determined by a jury should in any case be admitted under the proposed Constitution, it may be so regulated as to be done by a second jury, either by remanding the cause to the court below for a second trial of the fact, or by directing an issue immediately out of the Supreme Court.

The Federalist No. 81, at 489 (Alexander Hamilton) (Clinton Rossiter ed., 1961).

[195] *Parklane Hosiery Co. v. Shore*, 439 U.S. 322 (1979), could be read as support for that proposition. See *supra* n. 54 (discussing Parklane's holding that a prior action can exert dispositive preclusive effect upon a jury trial without violating the Trial by Jury Clause).

[196] Mutuality of parties was, of course, a consistent and ubiquitous prerequisite for preclusion at common law. Justice Traynor recounts this historical requirement in his famous Bernhard opinion, even as he condemns it as 'facile' and formally disavows it. See *Bernhard v. Bank of Am. Nat'l Trust and Sav. Assoc.*, 122 P.2d 892, 894–895 (Cal. 1942).

[197] In re Rhone-Poulenc Rorer Inc., 51 F.3d 1293, 1303–1304 (7th Cir. 1995). Judge Posner has shown a willingness to entertain issue-only class actions where, to use the Seventh Circuit's distinctive turn of phrase, the issue may be 'carv[ed] at the joint' in such a way as to prevent factual overlap with successive actions. See e.g., *Mejdrech v. Met-Coil Sys. Corp.*, 319 F.3d 910, 911–912 (7th Cir. 2003) (Posner, J.) (affirming district court's certification of issue-only class in pollution case where class treatment of common issue will not need to be revisited in individual damages determinations).

[198] Professor Scott makes a similar point in discussing the Trial by Jury Clause: 'The question, it is submitted, should be approached in a spirit of open-mindedness, of

As I discuss in section 9.4, a jurisdiction's preclusion policies may sometimes embody systemic commitments that will counsel against imposing certain types of constraint upon the preclusive effects of a class judgment. But, as Professor Woolley has aptly stated, 'there is no basis for concluding that the burden inherent in requiring parties to present evidence more than once raises an issue of constitutional dimension.'[199] This is all the more true where the specific manifestation of that burden – permitting parties to bring multiple actions in order to secure multiple forms of relief – was one of the defining features of the common law system in force when the Seventh Amendment was ratified.[200]

9.3.2.3 Alternative Mechanisms for Addressing Preclusion Problems

Imposing constraints upon the preclusive effect of a judgment is not the only mechanism that a court can employ in seeking to address ex ante preclusion problems. When the problem is a conflict of interest arising

---

readiness to accept any changes which do not impair the fundamentals of trial by jury. It is a question of substance, not of form.' Scott, *supra* n. 181, at 671.

[199] Woolley, Reexamination Clause, *supra* n. 53, at 533.

[200] I therefore disagree with the American Law Institute's seemingly uncompromising view on reexamination in its forthcoming statement on the principles of aggregate litigation. In discussing the role of the Reexamination Clause, the current draft of the ALI report takes the position that:

> aggregation should not occur if a jury determination made in the aggregate proceeding would, as a practical matter, have to be reconsidered in subsequent individual proceedings. This concern implicates the foundational point... that the determination of a common overlapping issue on an aggregate basis should have preclusive effect, a stance implying that putative aggregation that would lack preclusive effect should not be pursued.

Am. Law Inst., Principles of the Law of Aggregate Litigation §2.08 cmt. a, at 55 (Preliminary Draft No. 1, August 13, 2004); see also *id.* at 56 ('[A]ggregation should not occur where the relationship of issues under applicable substantive law is such as to create a need for reconsideration in subsequent proceedings of the determination of a given issue made in the aggregate proceeding.'). In my view, this is a vast overstatement of the role that the reexamination inquiry should play in the certification decision, both as a matter of constitutional mandate and as a matter of remedial policy. I discuss the latter issue in section 9.4 *infra*.

CHAPTER 9. PRECLUSION IN CLASS ACTION LITIGATION

from the different risk structures that the threat of adverse preclusion consequences appears to present to different groups within a class, the creation of subclasses might sometimes form part of an appropriate response. More broadly, some courts have invoked notice and opt-out rights in analyzing the preclusive reach of a class action judgment, though these devices are less likely to bear upon the appropriate ex ante response to a preclusion problem.

9.3.2.3.1 Subclasses Subclassing has been one of the first responses that diligent certifying courts have considered to apparent conflicts of interest since the Supreme Court gave the practice prominent and approving treatment in *Amchem* and *Ortiz v. Fibreboard Corp.*[201] When claim and issue preclusive effects create widely varying risk structures for the members of a class, those variations translate to different incentives to settle the action or to prosecute it vigorously, and so may render it impossible for the class to receive adequate representation in a single, unitary action. Creating a subclass with separate representation for each distinct interest group might help to cure this adequacy problem.

But there are practical impediments to the use of subclasses to alleviate preclusion-related conflicts. Foremost among these is a potentially serious ascertainability problem. Rule 23 contains an implied requirement that the members of a class or subclass be specifically identifiable through the use of some objective criteria and that the process of identification be administratively feasible. Ascertaining the identities of class members with potentially meritorious individual claims might be prohibitively difficult. Objective criteria might be available in some circumstances, as in the *MTBE* case, where levels of MTBE contamination might have served as a reliable proxy for the

---

[201] 527 U.S. 815 (1999). In both cases, the Court reversed proposed class action settlements, offering the trial court's failure to create separately represented subclasses for each distinct interest group as one explanation for why the right of class members to adequate representation was not satisfied. See *Amchem Prods., Inc. v. Windsor*, 521 U.S. 591, 627 (1997) ('The settling parties, in sum, achieved a global compromise with no structural assurance of fair and adequate representation for the diverse groups and individuals affected. Although the named parties alleged a range of complaints, each served generally as representative for the whole, not for a separate constituency.'); see also *Ortiz*, 527 U.S. at 846–848 (applying holding of Amchem to (b)(1)(B) limited-fund class action and criticizing failure to certify subclasses with separate representation for each distinct interest group in conflicted class).

identification of class members with positive-value damages claims.[202] In other cases, however, such identification would not be possible. Consider a Title VII disparate impact suit in which some of the class members have viable claims for intentional discrimination. In many instances, the only facts by which one could identify the class members with high-value claims would coincide with the proof required to establish the elements of those same claims – for example, through a prima facie showing of discriminatory intent when some adverse employment action has been taken against them. Where it is necessary to make complicated evidentiary findings or to employ state of mind or other subjective criteria in order to identify the members of a vital subclass, it may be inappropriate, or impossible, to proceed.[203]

Subclasses might also turn out to be of limited use in addressing one of the most frequent manifestations of a preclusion-related conflict of interest: divergent incentives on the part of class members in the choice between settling and litigating through to judgment. Conflicts of this sort often arise in cases like those discussed in section 9.2 where plaintiffs' counsel seek to pursue equitable relief under Rule 23(b)(2) and carve out individual damages claims that are not suitable for class treatment. The primary purpose of subclassing in such a case is to ensure that members of each interest group receive separate representation in the decision whether to settle the case or risk the issue preclusive effects of an adverse judgment.

The problem is that settlement with only part of the class might be of little use to the defendant in a (b)(2) action, where a demand for equitable relief from the remaining subset of the plaintiffs might still require the defendant to take actions that would benefit the entire group. Such non-atomizable relief is, after all, the defining feature of

---

[202] See In re Methyl Tertiary Butyl Ether ('MTBE') Prods. Liab. Litig., 209 F.R.D. 323, 349–350 (S.D.N.Y. 2002) (discussing relationship between damages claims and exposure levels).

[203] See e.g., *id.* at 337 n. 20, explaining that class definition requiring plaintiffs to 'prevail on the merits in order to qualify as a class member... "would preclude certification of just about any class of persons"' (quoting *Forbush v. J.C. Penney Co.*, 994 F.2d 1101, 1104–1106, 5th Cir. 1993); *Zapka v. Coca-Cola Co.*, No. 99 CV 8238, 2000 WL 1644539, at *3 (N.D. Ill. October 27, 2000) (refusing to certify class where membership is defined in terms of state of mind regarding advertising).

CHAPTER 9. PRECLUSION IN CLASS ACTION LITIGATION

a class action under Rule 23(b)(2).[204] Having separate representation will be of considerably less benefit to risk-averse class members if the defendant has no incentive to negotiate a separate settlement with them.[205] Separate counsel may serve an informational function, helping to ensure that the court will take the potential threat to damages claims into account when assessing whether a proposed settlement is fair and reasonable.[206] But that is a limited benefit.

Finally, subclassing is a cumbersome business. If done properly, it involves the introduction of a greater number of wholly independent lawyers into a class action, with all the attendant increase in paper and posture that multiple class counsel can bring. As Professor Issacharoff has observed:

> In an extreme form, this [pro-subclass] reading of *Amchem* would create a spiral of subclasses and sets of counsel that would not only swamp the incentive to invest in bringing a class action, but would impose tremendous transactional costs on an already vulnerable procedure that turned heavily on its ability to realize economies of scale.[207]

The conflicts of interest that can arise from preclusion problems in class litigation are both real and serious, but it will often be the case that only a small portion of a class will be at risk of losing valuable individual

---

[204] See Fed. R. Civ. P. 23(b)(2) (authorizing certification of class where 'the party opposing the class has acted or refused to act on grounds generally applicable to the class, thereby making appropriate final injunctive relief or corresponding declaratory relief with respect to the class as a whole').

[205] Patrick Woolley makes a similar point in discussing his proposal that absentees be granted robust intervention rights in class action proceedings. See Patrick J. Woolley, Rethinking the Adequacy of Adequate Representation, 75 Tex. L. Rev. 571, 617 (1997) ('Because individual structural reform claims can be inextricably intertwined with each other, defendants have no incentive to agree to a partial settlement.').

Silver and Baker explore other types of free-rider problems in their discussion of plaintiff incentives in complex class actions. See Silver and Baker, *supra* n. 57, at 1528–1530.

[206] See Fed. R. Civ. P. 23(e)(1)(C) ('The court may approve a settlement, voluntary dismissal, or compromise that would bind class members only after a hearing and on finding that the settlement, voluntary dismissal, or compromise is fair, reasonable, and adequate.').

[207] Samuel Issacharoff, Governance and Legitimacy in the Law of Class Actions, 1999 Sup. Ct. Rev. 337, 380 [hereinafter Issacharoff, Governance and Legitimacy].

claims. Where this is so, the expense and inefficiency that subclassing threatens to introduce make that procedure less attractive.

There may be some cases in which subclassing will provide an adequate or superior method of dealing with intraclass conflicts arising from preclusive effects. In most instances, however, it will make more sense simply to impose constraints upon the preclusive effects themselves.

9.3.2.3.2 Notice and Opt-Out Notice and opt-out rights are even less fitting candidates for ameliorating the adverse consequences that can flow from preclusion doctrine in class litigation. When offered as a means of addressing potential sources of unfairness to class members in an ongoing proceeding, notice and opt out operate on the presumption that absentees will read the contents of a notification and possess the capacity to make a meaningful decision about how best to protect their own interests.[208] The level of sophistication that an absentee would have to exhibit in order to make an informed decision about the risk that preclusion doctrine poses to her individual claims, however, would make notice and opt-out poorly suited to the protection of those interests, even, or perhaps especially, if the notice were to include a detailed description of the nature of the doctrinal risk.[209] To the extent that notice and opt-out rights have played a role in the

---

[208] Rule 23 now contains prolix requirements for the contents of class notice in a (b)(3) action:

> For any class certified under Rule 23(b)(3) ... [t]he notice must concisely and clearly state in plain, easily understood language:
>
> – the nature of the action,
> – the definition of the class certified,
> – the class claims, issues, or defenses,
> – that a class member may enter an appearance through counsel if the member so desires,
> – that the court will exclude from the class any member who requests exclusion, stating when and how members may elect to be excluded, and
> – the binding effect of a class judgment on class members under Rule 23(c)(3). Fed. R. Civ. P. 23(c)(2)(B).

[209] See 18A Wright, Miller, and Cooper, *supra* n. 2, § 4455, at 486 ('The opportunity to opt out of a state class action is only as good as the clarity of the notice and the sophistication and incentives of class members. In realistic terms, the opt-out opportunity provides no real protection to many members of many classes.').

CHAPTER 9. PRECLUSION IN CLASS ACTION LITIGATION

reported decisions addressing these issues, that role has instead related to the ex post consideration of a class judgment's preclusive impact.

Individual notice and opt-out rights serve two distinct functions in a class proceeding. The first function is jurisdictional. In a class action that spans multiple states or otherwise involves absent plaintiffs who have no minimum contacts with the rendering forum, notice and the opportunity to opt out provide the minimal manifestation of consent that is necessary for the rendering forum to bind the absentees to its judgment. The Supreme Court's decision in *Phillips Petroleum Co. v. Shutts*, which is so frequently cited for the proposition that notice and opt-out rights are a constitutional requirement in a damages class action, dealt almost exclusively with the function of those procedures in conferring personal jurisdiction where it would otherwise be lacking.[210]

The second function that opt-out rights serve is to reintroduce an element of litigant autonomy into an ongoing class action. In theory, notifying the absentees about developments in a class proceeding (like a proposed settlement), and giving them the opportunity to opt out, provides a check on the adequacy of class counsel's representational efforts and reinforces the moral authority of binding absentees to the result.[211] The reiteration of the court's discretion to provide opt-out rights during settlement that is contained in the recent revisions to Rule 23 aims at such process-reinforcing goals.[212]

In practical terms, these two functions often have little to do with each other. The constitutional requirements of personal jurisdiction aim primarily at protecting litigants against inconvenience and expense. Even in that capacity, personal jurisdiction rules exhibit a highly formal structure and a fetishistic treatment of state boundaries that often make them better as gatekeepers for the substantive law that will apply to a dispute than as protection against inconvenience. These constraints on choice of forum, which were the primary concern in *Shutts*, have little

---

[210] 472 U.S. 797, 811–812 (1985).

[211] Professor Fiss makes a similar point in his discussion of representation and individualism. See Fiss, *supra* n. 65, at 977 ('Notice is provided to members of the class, but only as a way of checking on the adequacy of representation, not to protect the individual's right to participation.').

[212] See Fed. R. Civ. P. 23(e)(1)(B), (e)(3) (requiring that court provide notice to class members before approving settlement and reaffirming power of court to order second opt-out opportunity in (b)(3) cases).

relation to the fairness or integrity of an ongoing proceeding. The manifestation of consent that *Shutts* requires is a blunt instrument that seeks only a 'yes' or 'no' answer best suited to the threshold question of forum choice. The established place that notice and opt out occupy in the certification process as a means of establishing jurisdiction thus says little about the usefulness of those devices in reinforcing process values once the action is underway.[213]

Those few courts that have concluded that notice and opt-out rights are of central importance in analyzing preclusion in class action litigation have tended to conflate the jurisdiction-conferring and process-reinforcing functions of those devices. A few such courts, for example, have held that a class action for equitable relief, certified without individual notice and opt-out rights, can never extinguish the individual damages claims of class members through merger or bar because notice and the opportunity to opt out are threshold constitutional requirements for the extinguishment of damages claims in representative litigation.[214] When the equitable proceeding in question presents no personal jurisdiction problems, however,[215] opt-out rights have little constitutional relevance to the claim preclusive effect of the judgment, and there is little reason to think that providing notice and opt-out rights to the members of an equitable class action would give them a meaningful opportunity to decide whether to place their individual damages claims at risk.[216]

---

[213] See Issacharoff, Governance and Legitimacy, *supra* n. 207, at 369 ('The ability to opt out rises to constitutional dimensions only with [Shutts], in which the ability to opt out is considered a mild signifier of consent to jurisdiction – although not to adequacy of representation – in a forum that otherwise had no contact with the injuries claimed by some portion of the absent class members.').

[214] See e.g., *Jahn ex rel. Jahn v. ORCR, Inc.*, 92 P.3d 984, 987–992 (Colo. 2004) (en banc) (holding that action certified under Rule 23(b)(2) can never have claim preclusive effect on individual damages claims). The Seventh Circuit suggests as much in *Jefferson v. Ingersoll Int'l Inc.*, 195 F.3d 894, 897–899 (7th Cir. 1999).

[215] See *Jahn*, 92 P.3d at 985 (describing scope of class, which includes only residents from a single nursing home in Colorado).

[216] Commentators differ greatly as to the need for and utility of opt-out rights, even in the case of damages claims where class members have no contact with the proposed forum. Compare David Rosenberg, Adding a Second Opt-Out to Rule 23(b)(3) Class Actions: Cost Without Benefit, 2003 U. Chi. Legal F. 19, 19–24 (criticizing utility of opt-out rights in settlement of damages class actions), David Rosenberg, Mandatory-Litigation Class Action: The Only Option for Mass Tort Cases,

CHAPTER 9. PRECLUSION IN CLASS ACTION LITIGATION

Notice and opt-out rights function best when they present class members with relatively straightforward choices: Do you wish to have your claims litigated in this class proceeding; or do you think this settlement offers you fair value for the injuries you have suffered? They are not well suited to operate as a proxy for robust expressions of litigant autonomy on complicated doctrinal matters like those associated with preclusive effects.[217]

9.3.2.4 The Incentives of Counsel and the Need for Judicial Supervision

There is a practical impediment to identifying and confronting preclusion problems during certification: It will sometimes be the case that neither plaintiffs' counsel nor the defendant will have a clear incentive to raise the issue. Where this is so, the court will have to be diligent in recognizing potential preclusion problems on its own initiative.

The natural party to bring preclusion problems to the attention of the court in a litigated action might seem to be the defendant, since a preclusion analysis might expose conflicts of interest within the class that could defeat certification. The problem is that it will often be necessary, in making a convincing argument on this score, to accentuate

---

115 Harv. L. Rev. 831, 896–897 (2002) (issuing broad call for binding class actions without opportunity to opt out), and David L. Shapiro, Class Actions: The Class as Party and Client, 73 Notre Dame L. Rev. 913, 950–960 (1998) [hereinafter Shapiro, Class Actions] (arguing against mandatory opt-out rights where class may properly be treated as independent entity rather than aggregate of individual claims), with John C. Coffee, Jr., Class Action Accountability: Reconciling Exit, Voice, and Loyalty in Representative Litigation, 100 Colum. L. Rev. 370–380 (2000) (endorsing opt-out rights as appropriate opportunity for exit where ability of class members to count upon loyalty of their representatives or voice their interests effectively are compromised), and Issacharoff, Preclusion, *supra* n. 1, at 1073–1080 (urging that opt-out rights be provided in high-stakes cases where individual litigants are more likely to make meaningful individual choices).

[217] See 18A Wright, Miller, and Cooper, *supra* n. 2, § 4455, at 486 (concluding that '[i]t requires extraordinary faith to rely on the opportunity to opt out to justify preclusion without actually adequate representation in any setting' and noting that '[t]o rely on the opportunity to opt out from litigation in a state court that could not command personal jurisdiction over absent class members for any other purpose is even more extraordinary').

the importance and viability of the class members' unpled claims. That may be a very unattractive prospect for a defendant. While there may be nothing illogical about attacking the merits of the classwide claims while at the same time pointing out the theoretical existence of meritorious individual claims, one can easily imagine many defense lawyers deciding that the potential benefit of raising the argument is outweighed by the potential harm to their credibility. This is particularly true in light of the fact that the result of conducting a preclusion analysis at the outset of a class proceeding might be an order expressly constraining the effects of the judgment, rather than a denial of certification. Unless the merits of plaintiffs' claims are undeniable and the viability of any constraining order in serious doubt, there may be little reason for defendants to place preclusion issues before the court.

Class counsel is also an imperfect agent here. In theory, of course, class counsel would have a duty to bring any preclusion problems to the court's attention in order to avoid potential harm to the absentees' future interests and resolve a potential impediment to class certification by requesting a constraining order that would expressly avoid those bad results. In practice, many plaintiff lawyers may be dissuaded from doing so by the risk that a court will respond by denying certification rather than imposing a curative constraint. Indeed, even responsible class counsel might sometimes conclude, whether rightly or not, that any threat to the interests of individual claimants within a class would be outweighed by the benefits of the class action and could possibly be addressed by a subsequent forum in any event.[218] While some class counsel would undoubtedly be willing to risk their own fees to protect the interests of the class, Rule 23 must also guard against less responsible actors.

---

[218] Some state courts have demonstrated a greater willingness than is usually evident in the federal system to allow class counsel to certify broad actions, particularly for low-value claims, and allow any problems to be sorted out in subsequent challenges to the judgment. See e.g., *Cartt v. Superior Court*, 124 Cal. Rptr. 376, 382–385 (Ct. App. 1975) (permitting negative-value class action to proceed despite problems in providing notice on theory that aggrieved class members can challenge adequacy of notice in subsequent proceedings). But see *S.W. Ref. Co. v. Bernal*, 22 S.W.3d 425, 435 (Tex. 2000) (rejecting 'approach of certify now and worry later' and requiring Texas state courts to adhere strictly to class action requirements). I discuss the role of the rendering forum in policing the preclusive effects of class judgments in section 9.5 below.

CHAPTER 9. PRECLUSION IN CLASS ACTION LITIGATION

The responsibility thus falls to the certifying court to inquire into the preclusive effects of a class proceeding, even if neither party raises the issue as an initial matter. Such an independent duty of judicial supervision has become a more broadly acknowledged feature of class litigation since the Supreme Court proclaimed it to be indispensable in the review of settlement-only proceedings.[219] The responsibility is a more modest one here, for the parties should have every incentive to litigate the threat of adverse preclusion effects vigorously once the issue is before the court.

9.4 HARMONIZING JOINDER AND PRECLUSION POLICIES

It remains to be determined when the tools set forth above should be put to use – in other words, how joinder and preclusion policies should be harmonized – in a complex class action. When attempting to bring together two concepts, one of which is quite familiar and one largely unexplored, there is a natural tendency to place the more familiar concept in the dominant position and then attempt to bring the less familiar concept into conformity with it. That tendency could offer a powerful temptation in the present context. We have a rich vocabulary for discussing the familiar requirements for certifying a class action, while the role of preclusive effects in that calculus has received only scant and superficial attention. Having recognized the threat that preclusion doctrine can pose to certification, it would be easy to take the theoretical and doctrinal tools laid out in section 9.3 and frame a preclusion analysis solely in terms of the most expedient way to overcome preclusion problems so as to enable a class action to proceed. Indeed, this tendency is already discernible among those authorities that have attempted to navigate the issue. Wright, Miller, and Cooper, for example, offer the following exhortation where the claim preclusive effect of an injunctive class action is concerned:

> The basic effort to limit class adjudication as close as possible to matters common to members of the class frequently requires that nonparticipating members of the class remain free to pursue individual actions that would

---

[219] See *Amchem Prods., Inc. v. Windsor*, 521 U.S. 591, 621–622 (1997) (describing danger that settlement proponents will not fairly represent downsides of proffered bargain to court, and concomitant need for court to be independently vigilant).

be merged or barred by claim preclusion had a prior individual action been brought from the relief demanded in the class action... [A]n individual who has suffered particular injury as a result of practices enjoined in a class action should remain free to seek a damages remedy even though claim preclusion would defeat a second action had the first action been an individual suit for the same injunctive relief.[220]

As section 9.2 discusses, this proposed solution to the treatment of injunctive class actions represents the dominant approach among the few courts that have considered the issue, and it may well be the best course in most cases. But Wright, Miller, and Cooper frame the analysis in an oversimplified manner, assuming without analysis that preclusion doctrine should give way to certification when the two come into conflict.

The clarification of preclusion doctrine's ex ante impact upon the certification process, and the demystification of the rendering forum's role in managing that impact, need not and should not equate to the subordination of a forum's preclusion policies to all competing concerns. The question 'How should preclusion doctrine be managed in order to permit a class action to be filed?' could as easily be met with the rejoinder 'Which class actions should be prohibited in order to give proper expression to the principles underlying the forum's preclusion doctrines?' When a court considers the imposition of constraints upon its judgment in order to eliminate a preclusion problem that might prevent class certification, it must also assess the impact of those constraints upon the jurisdiction's preclusion policies and determine whether joinder or preclusion should take precedence when the two come into conflict.

9.4.1 Preclusion Policies

The task of assessing how a proposed constraint on the preclusive effect of a class proceeding should be measured against a jurisdiction's

---

[220] 18A Wright, Miller, and Cooper, *supra* n. 2, § 4455, at 461–462. The omitted text consists mostly of a discussion of the Cooper case. See also *Bolin v. Sears, Roebuck and Co.*, 231 F.3d 970, 976 (5th Cir. 2000) ('To determine whether damages predominate, a court should certify a class on a claim-by-claim basis, treating each claim individually and certifying the class with respect to only those claims for which certification is appropriate.').

CHAPTER 9. PRECLUSION IN CLASS ACTION LITIGATION

policy commitments in that field requires one to look beyond the simple rules of the doctrine to examine the systemic preclusion values that the jurisdiction has embraced. In a trivial sense, every decision by a court to place limitations upon the preclusive effect of a class judgment will run contrary to the ordinary practice of the jurisdiction. That observation is not helpful in seeking to determine the acceptable metes and bounds of such constraints. Rather, the goal must be to identify those doctrines that reveal a considered and definite choice between competing values. When a jurisdiction has placed particular emphasis on one or more systemic values in crafting the preclusion rules for its judicial system, a certifying court should be hesitant to impose a constraint that operates in derogation of those values.

One such systemic value relates to the imperative to choose the most efficient forum when initiating a lawsuit. Some jurisdictions adopt preclusion doctrines that threaten plaintiffs with harsh penalties if they fail to select a forum in which all of their claims can be litigated in a single proceeding. In states that have refused to adopt the 'jurisdictional competency' exception, for example, a plaintiff who initiates a suit in a court of limited subject matter jurisdiction may find himself precluded from filing a related claim later on, even if that claim could not have been brought in the original action due to the limitations of the forum.[221] Some courts have penalized plaintiffs for 'splitting' claims when they utilize a small claims court or other specialized tribunal of limited jurisdiction and then attempt to file a related claim in a court of general jurisdiction.[222] In the context of exclusive federal jurisdiction, *Marrese* offers the possibility that a plaintiff who brings a state claim in

---

[221] See *supra* n. 168 and accompanying text.
[222] See e.g., *Humphrey v. Tharaldson Enters*, 95 F.3d 624, 626–627 (7th Cir. 1996) (precluding plaintiff from raising federal discrimination claims where plaintiff chose to litigate related claims in a state administrative tribunal, even though tribunal could not have heard federal claims, because more convenient forum was available). Indeed, the Restatement offers this result as the expected outcome when a plaintiff has access to a court of general jurisdiction but chooses to file in a limited forum:

> The same considerations apply when the first action is brought in a court which has jurisdiction to redress an invasion of a certain interest of the plaintiff, but not another, and the action goes to judgment on the merits.... The plaintiff, having voluntarily brought his action in a court which can grant him only limited relief, cannot insist upon maintaining another action on the claim.

Restatement (Second) of Judgments § 24 cmt. g (1982).

state court may forfeit his right to assert exclusively federal claims in a subsequent federal proceeding, though the opinion also does hint that there may sometimes be a sufficient interest in preserving a federal forum for such claims to override state policy when this situation arises.[223] One court has even adopted a similar rule in supplemental jurisdiction cases, holding that when a federal court declines to hear related state law claims in a federal question suit, the plaintiff must nonsuit the federal claims and refile the entire suit in state court or else lose the chance to assert the state law claims.[224] New Jersey's much-noted experiment with the 'entire controversy' doctrine, which subjected plaintiffs to nonmutual claim preclusion for failing to join all available defendants on transactionally related claims, might also

---

[223] See *Marrese v. Am. Acad. of Orthopaedic Surgeons*, 470 US 373, 386 (1985) ('Resolution of this question will depend upon the particular federal statute as well as the nature of the claim or issue involved in the subsequent federal action.'); *supra* n. 168 (citing cases where court of appeals found state judgments to have claim preclusive effect on subsequent bankruptcy proceeding despite exclusive jurisdiction of federal courts).

[224] A California appellate court adopted this harsh policy in *Mattson v. City of Costa Mesa*:

> The initial choice by the plaintiff to file suit in federal court will not necessarily result in splitting his cause of action, because the federal court may well exercise pendent jurisdiction over the non-federal claim. However, when the federal court has been requested to and has declined to exercise pendent jurisdiction over the non-federal claim, the plaintiff is presented with a new choice. He may proceed to trial on the federal claim or, usually, he may elect to dismiss the federal claim without prejudice and litigate both claims in the state court. Once it is known that the federal court will not exercise pendent jurisdiction over the state claim, plaintiff's proceeding to trial in the federal court on the federal claim alone will necessarily result in splitting the plaintiff's cause of action, and that fact should be apparent to the plaintiff.

164 Cal. Rptr. 913, 921–922 (Ct. App. 1980) (citations omitted). This unusual holding probably does not survive the Court's opinion in *Semtek International Inc. v. Lockheed Martin Corp.*, 531 U.S. 491 (2001). The federal court's dismissal under § 1367 in this case was a dismissal for lack of subject matter jurisdiction – albeit one involving the special case of a discretionary jurisdictional grant. The federal courts treat such a dismissal as 'without prejudice' for the refiling of those claims, see Fed. R. Civ. P. 41(b), and Semtek confirms that such a designation has dispositive effect in a subsequent proceeding, see *supra* notes 126–133 and accompanying text.

CHAPTER 9. PRECLUSION IN CLASS ACTION LITIGATION

be characterized as embodying a strong policy in favor of having all related claims heard in a single proceeding.[225]

Jurisdictions that embrace such policies assign a higher value to the repose for defendants, consistency of result, and responsible behavior by plaintiffs that come from requiring a single, comprehensive adjudication than they ascribe to the expertise and comity associated with preserving a specialized forum for the adjudication of certain types of claims. A certifying court that imposed a preclusion constraint intended solely to preserve the benefits of a specialized forum – as, for example, with the stay-in-state-court civil rights suit described in section 9.3.2 – would be acting in derogation of that policy decision. If the jurisdiction has made a clear choice in its preclusion policies to elevate repose, consistency, and responsible litigation choices over the benefits of specialized fora, the certifying court might have to conclude that those policies militate strongly against the use of preclusion constraints to enable a class of civil rights plaintiffs to bring state claims in a state forum while also preserving the right of individuals to seek federal relief.

Another body of preclusion policies relates to what might be called equality of downside risk. The doctrine of offensive non-mutual issue preclusion most clearly implicates these concerns. When a defendant suffers from broad liability exposure to a large number of potential claimants, the threat of an offensive use of issue preclusion with no requirement of mutuality makes every lawsuit a high-stakes proposition. While any individual plaintiff may stand to gain only a modest recovery from a victory in such a case, the defendant might stand to lose a fortune from any defeat. This imbalance in the downside risk of litigation can strengthen the plaintiff's hand significantly in settlement negotiations.[226] Some jurisdictions reject the use of offensive non-mutual issue preclusion because they conclude that the unfairness to the defendant resulting from this imbalance in downside risk

---

[225] See generally Allan R. Stein, Commentary: Power, Duty and the Entire Controversy Doctrine, 28 Rutgers L.J. 27 (1996) (describing entire controversy doctrine and benefits and disadvantages of such aggressive joinder policies).

[226] See Michael D. Green, The Inability of Offensive Collateral Estoppel to Fulfill Its Promise: An Examination of Estoppel in Asbestos Litigation, 70 Iowa L. Rev. 141, 207–216 (1984) (enumerating costs to fairness values associated with use of nonmutual offensive issue preclusion in mass tort litigation and calling into serious question concomitant benefits).

outweighs the benefits – of efficiency, consistency of result, or integrity of judgments – that the doctrine promises.[227]

Such a policy determination might be relevant to a certifying court faced with a conflict of interest of the type that a defective products case may pose. As section 9.3.2 explains, when a class wishes to pursue a claim for economic damages or equitable relief in a defective products case without compromising the ability of injured class members to pursue more valuable individual claims, the certifying court will likely need to impose a constraint upon its judgment that would remove all prejudice to the class from issue preclusion or merger and bar outside of the claims actually litigated in the action. Such an order – which, in practical terms, would prohibit the defendants from invoking the class action version of 'nonmutual' defensive issue preclusion in subsequent suits by absentees – would serve to eliminate the conflict in settlement incentives that the class would otherwise experience. But it would also have the effect of shifting disproportionate risk to the defendant, who would face the threat of widespread offensive issue preclusion by individual plaintiffs if the class secured a favorable judgment but would enjoy no preclusion benefits if the class lost.[228]

In a jurisdiction that has chosen to forgo offensive nonmutual issue preclusion in order to avoid imposing the unfairness of unequal downside risk upon defendants, these consequences would militate against the issuance of such broad constraints upon the preclusive effects of a class action judgment. If a class cannot be certified on claims for economic damages or equitable relief in a defective products case (or similar tort suit) without the use of these constraints, the court might have to conclude that the applicable preclusion policies foreclose the resolution of those claims on a classwide basis. Indeed, even in jurisdictions

---

[227] See Shapiro, Preclusion, *supra* n. 35, at 110–116 (discussing offensive nonmutual issue preclusion in light of these systemic preclusion values).

[228] Such an arrangement is somewhat reminiscent of the 'premodern class actions' in which 'absent class members could, in effect, join into the lawsuit' only after a representative plaintiff achieved a victory while suffering no detriment in the event of a loss. Issacharoff, Governance and Legitimacy, *supra* n. 207, at 364–365. There is a key difference, of course, in that class members in the above scenario would be bound by the resolution of the certified claim. But in a case where the certified claim is of low value and the individual claims are large, the impact upon the defendant is not dissimilar. The Bridgestone/Firestone cases probably fit this description. See *supra* notes 173–174 and accompanying text.

CHAPTER 9. PRECLUSION IN CLASS ACTION LITIGATION

that do not place determinative weight on inequality of downside risk when setting their mutuality requirements, these concerns about fairness to the defendant would surely be recognized as legitimate.[229] Thus, the extra burden to the defendant that would flow from imposing broad, unilateral constraints on issue preclusion in a defective products case will likely be a consideration in almost any certification analysis. In a suit for economic damages under Rule 23(b)(3), for example, the need for the defendant to bear disproportionate risk from issue preclusion in order for the suit to proceed should factor into the superiority determination.

A court could mitigate these consequences by extending its broad constraint on issue preclusion to benefit the defendant as well as the class. But a bilateral constraint of this kind would raise its own set of concerns. For starters, it would eliminate all efficiency benefits from the class action beyond the resolution of the certified claim itself. It would also significantly amplify the likelihood of inconsistent factual determinations – on the same issues and between the 'same' parties – across multiple suits. In the case of a unilateral constraint, inconsistent determinations would, by definition, be possible only if the defendant prevailed in the class suit, since the absentees could invoke the judgment as an offensive estoppel if they prevailed in the first action. In the case of a bilateral constraint on issue preclusion, in contrast, every individual suit would present an opportunity for a finding inconsistent with the class judgment, regardless of the outcome in the first proceeding. For a jurisdiction that places particular weight upon preserving the integrity of its judgments and avoiding inconsistent resolutions – policies that might find expression in a liberal doctrine of offensive nonmutual issue preclusion – this type of bilateral constraint on the preclusive effects of the class judgment would be disfavored.[230]

In short, in a defective products or other tort suit where some class members possess substantial damages claims that are not suitable for classwide treatment, any attempt to use constraints on the preclusive effect of the judgment to eliminate the conflicts of interest within the

---

[229] See *Parklane Hosiery Co. v. Shore*, 439 U.S. 322, 330–333 (1979) (discussing fairness concerns that offensive use of nonmutual issue preclusion introduces).

[230] In his monograph on preclusion doctrine, Professor Shapiro, for one, has taken the position that 'the virtues of [nonmutual issue preclusion] exceed the defects so long as the limitations are marked with sufficient clarity and uniformly applied by all tribunals within the jurisdiction.' Shapiro, Preclusion, *supra* n. 35, at 115.

class is likely to operate in tension with the jurisdiction's broader preclusion policies, regardless of what configuration of policies the jurisdiction embraces. When the use of such constraints is the only way to make any part of a complicated tort case suitable for class treatment, class counsel should be required to offer a convincing argument as to why certification is nonetheless desirable.

As with any form of governmental interest analysis, these inquiries into the values underlying a jurisdiction's preclusion doctrine could be subject to manipulation[231] – though perhaps less so than in other fields, given the relatively concise vocabulary of concepts that tends to be utilized in preclusion analysis.[232] Still, one might argue that placing a powerful new tool in the hands of a rendering forum and then offering policy analysis as the principal restriction on that tool is an invitation for aggressive courts to certify ever more inappropriate class actions. It seems more likely, however, that any court that is strongly inclined to certify at all costs will simply continue the dominant practice of ignoring preclusion concerns altogether. The proper audience for this discussion, at least for the present, is made up of those rendering courts – and also those recognizing courts, as I discuss in section 9.5 – that diligently seek to balance the ability of plaintiffs to obtain effective relief against the other important policies that a jurisdiction has adopted. For those courts, the form of policy analysis described in this section provides a practicable method for determining which constraints will operate in tension with a jurisdiction's broader preclusion commitments.

---

[231] The debate about such manipulation in the choice of law field is fully joined. See Lea Brilmayer, Governmental Interest Analysis: A House Without Foundations, 46 Ohio St. L.J. 459, 466–476 (1985) (issuing broad critique of interest analysis in choice of law as devoid of constraints and excessively malleable); Kramer, Rethinking, *supra* n. 112, at 299–301 (arguing that criticisms of governmental interest analysis apply with at least some force to all instances where courts must interpret and apply laws in cases presenting 'unforeseen or uncontemplated circumstances'); Robert A. Sedler, Interest Analysis as the Preferred Approach to Choice of Law: A Response to Professor Brilmayer's 'Foundational Attack', 46 Ohio St. L.J. 483, 483 (1985) (defending interest analysis as best option for securing fairness to litigants and reasonable outcomes); Patrick J. Borchers, Professor Brilmayer and the Holy Grail, 1991 Wis. L. Rev. 465, 476–489 (reviewing Lea Brilmayer, Conflict of Laws: Foundations and Future Directions (1991)) (criticizing the alternatives that Brilmayer has offered to interest analysis as equally subject to manipulation).
[232] See Shapiro, Preclusion, *supra* n. 35, at 13–18 (discussing range of interests generally associated with preclusion doctrine).

CHAPTER 9. PRECLUSION IN CLASS ACTION LITIGATION

9.4.2 Sources of Law and the Rules Enabling Act

If a class action cannot be certified without the use of a preclusion constraint that the jurisdiction appears to disfavor, the certifying court must determine whether the plaintiffs' interest in proceeding as a class is nonetheless strong enough to justify the use of the constraint. The specific responsibility of the court in such a case is to determine the policy that the forum has embraced for making aggregate relief, as opposed to individual relief, available to the class of claimants before it. The Rules Enabling Act, with its proviso forbidding any application of a rule of procedure that would 'abridge, enlarge or modify any substantive right,'[233] makes the task of assessing that policy interest more complicated.[234] Although Rule 23 occupies a central position as the tool by which broad joinder is effectuated in representative litigation, it is not an appropriate authority to look to for the type of robust interest in aggregate relief that is necessary here.

Seventy years after the enactment of the Rules Enabling Act, there is still no general agreement concerning the proper interpretation of the statute's 'substantive rights' proviso. The two dominant approaches come to us from John Hart Ely and Stephen Burbank. Ely set forth the view that the limitations contained in the Act are primarily an

---

[233] 28 USC § 2072(b) (2000). Many states have a parallel provision to the Act that includes a reservation clause for substantive rights. See e.g., Tex. Gov't Code Ann. § 22.004(a) (Vernon 2004) (stating that Texas Supreme Court cannot 'abridge, enlarge, or modify the substantive rights of a litigant' using its rulemaking power); Tex. R. Civ. P. 815 (stating that Texas Rules of Civil Procedure cannot abridge, enlarge, or modify any substantive right). As Professor Burbank has explained, there may be significant theoretical and practical differences between the application of this proviso in the federal system and in a state court. See Burbank, Rules Enabling Act, *supra* n. 120, at 1091–1092. Nonetheless, I will treat the Rules Enabling Act and its state counterparts as interchangeable, a simplifying gesture that is adequate for the broad discussion of joinder policy that follows.

[234] Professor Burbank has demonstrated that those who drafted the Rules Enabling Act likely viewed subsection (a) of the statute, which granted authority to prescribe only 'general rules of practice and procedure,' as the primary source of limitation contained in the Act, with the proviso of subsection (b) serving merely to confirm that limited authority. See Burbank, Rules Enabling Act, *supra* n. 120, at 1077–1090; see also 28 USC § 2072(a)-(b). Nevertheless, since the second subsection has become the primary focus of judicial attention in discussing limitations on the Federal Rules, I will follow the more common convention.

expression of federalism values. He therefore advocated an interpretive approach that would treat substantive state policies as 'trumps,' available on a roving basis to override otherwise applicable Federal Rules.[235] Burbank, in contrast, has argued that the Act is primarily an embodiment of separation of powers principles – specifically, a judgment that decisionmaking authority for matters of substantive policy should ordinarily be reserved to Congress rather than the federal courts. Burbank would interpret the proviso to impose more unitary limitations upon the Rules, branding as ultra vires any interpretation that would have predictable and identifiable effects of the type normally reserved for substantive lawmaking, but otherwise not bowing to contrary state policies, 'substantive' or otherwise.[236]

Although the Act's proviso appeared to lapse into partial desuetude for some time following the narrow construction that the Court placed upon it in *Sibbach v. Wilson & Co.*,[237] it has recently received

---

[235] See John Hart Ely, The Irrepressible Myth of Erie, 87 Harv. L. Rev. 693, 718–738 (1974) (suggesting that substantive state law should prevail over federal procedural rules).

[236] See Burbank, Rules Enabling Act, *supra* n. 120, at 1025 ('[T]he famous first two sentences of the Act... were intended to allocate power between the Supreme Court as rulemaker and Congress and thus to circumscribe the delegation of legislative power'); *id.* at 1122–1125 (criticizing manner in which Ely frames 'substantive rights' question which improperly places federalism values at center of analysis and produces interpretations of Federal Rules that can vary across jurisdictions).

[237] U.S. 1 (1941). Sibbach involved an application of Federal Rule of Civil Procedure 35, the provision that authorizes physical and mental examinations of persons. The plaintiff in the case, who was asserting personal injury claims, was ordered to undergo a physical examination during discovery, and she argued that this application of Rule 35 violated her right to privacy. *Id.* at 7–8. The Court rejected the argument and adopted an interpretation of the Enabling Act proviso under which a party could assert an abridgment of her substantive rights only when a Rule imposed a mandatory requirement upon her that impacted her primary, extralitigation activities. Since the plaintiff in Sibbach could have chosen not to comply with the discovery order, the Court held, she had no basis for arguing that the application of Rule 35 had infringed her substantive rights. See *id.* at 13–14 (explaining that test for such rules is whether they truly regulate procedure). The fact that this refusal would have resulted in a discovery sanction, such that the plaintiff's 'choice' lay between complying with the order or losing the right to pursue her claim, did not change the Court's assessment of the Rule's nonmandatory character. See *Schlagenhauf v. Holder*, 379 U.S. 104, 114 (1964) (applying Sibbach's holding to defendant); Burbank, Rules Enabling Act, *supra* n. 120, at 1176–1184 (arguing that Sibbach

CHAPTER 9. PRECLUSION IN CLASS ACTION LITIGATION

renewed attention in a pair of cases that happen to address the two halves of the present doctrinal inquiry: *Ortiz* and *Semtek*. In *Ortiz* – the class action case in which the Court invalidated a limited fund variation on the asbestos settlement previously rejected in *Amchem* – the settling parties had attempted to misuse Rule 23(b)(1)(B) as a device for reducing the total amount of monetary relief that would be available to class members by manufacturing a 'limited fund' of available assets by stipulation.[238] The majority invoked the Act's substantive rights language in rejecting this attempt and cautioned against any interpretation of Rule 23 that would dramatically limit the relief available to class members under the applicable liability regime.[239] In *Semtek*, the Court invoked the Act in explaining its refusal to read an independent set of preclusion doctrines into Rule 41(b), suggesting that an interpretation of the Rule that would eliminate a remedy otherwise allowed by the applicable preclusion law might constitute an 'abridgement' of rights under the proviso.[240]

These recent statements imply that the remedial expectations that a party enjoys under a given preclusion regime constitute one of those 'substantive rights' that the Federal Rules cannot alter. In extreme cases, where a Federal Rule threatens to extinguish or dramatically limit a form of relief that a claimant would otherwise enjoy, that result is intuitively satisfying and probably in accord both with Ely, who would identify such remedial expectations as substantive policies sufficient to trump an otherwise applicable rule, and with Burbank, who has already expressed the view that preclusion doctrines exceed the regulatory authority of the federal rulemakers when they 'dramatically affect the ability of litigants to enforce their substantive rights.'[241]

---

was rightly decided, though wrongly explained, in light of purposes originally animating Rules Enabling Act).

[238] *Ortiz v. Fibreboard Corp.*, 527 U.S. 815, 850–853 (1999).

[239] *Id.* at 845.

[240] *Semtek Int'l Inc. v. Lockheed Martin Corp.*, 531 U.S. 497, 503–504 (2001) ('In the present case ... if California law left petitioner free to sue on this claim in Maryland even after the California statute of limitations had expired, the federal court's extinguishment of that right (through Rule 41(b)'s mandated claim preclusive effect of its judgment) would seem to violate this limitation.').

[241] Burbank, Rules Enabling Act, *supra* n. 120, at 1128.

> (Clearly preclusive doctrines like a statute of limitations, laches, or res judicata dramatically affect the ability of litigants to enforce their substantive rights

Now, it would be a mistake to overestimate the relevance of the substantive rights language in interpreting Rule 23, even following these suggestive dicta. At this late date, it is untenable to urge a reading of the Rules Enabling Act that would prohibit Rule 23 from having any impact whatsoever on the ability of class members to employ the full range of remedial options that would be available to them in individual litigation, and neither *Ortiz* nor *Semtek* compels that result.[242] Indeed, the Court's suggestion in *Semtek* that a jurisdiction's preclusion rules constitute one of the substantive rights protected by the Act's proviso clearly cannot be read too literally. Taken to its logical conclusion, this proposition would seem to foreclose a federal court from designating a dismissal as without prejudice whenever a state court would not do likewise, since allowing the plaintiff another bite at the apple would presumably 'enlarge or modify' his remedial rights. The *Semtek* Court itself rejected this result, however, when it reaffirmed the ability of a federal court to utilize the without prejudice designation in Rule 41 to dispositive effect.[243]

---

and... determine in a practical sense whether those rights exist at all, at least when viewed from the point in time at which they are asserted. (citation omitted)).

[242] The Court said as much in one of its earliest interpretations of the Act:

Undoubtedly most alterations of the rules of practice and procedure may and often do affect the rights of litigants. Congress' prohibition of any alteration of substantive rights of litigants was obviously not addressed to such incidental effects as necessarily attend the adoption of the prescribed new rules of procedure upon the rights of litigants who, agreeably to rules of practice and procedure, have been brought before a court authorized to determine their rights.

Miss. Publ'g Corp. v. Murphree, 326 U.S. 438, 445 (1946). Professor Woolley argues that certain Federal Rules can entail the articulation of supporting preclusion doctrines that will survive the Rules Enabling Act. See Patrick Woolley, The Sources of Federal Preclusion Law After Semtek, 72 U. Cin. L. Rev. 527, 590–591 (2003) (arguing that 'preclusion rules [aimed at] enforcing procedural obligations [lie] within the scope of the REA'). But see Semtek, 531 U.S. at 506 n. 2 (flagging the possibility that a district court's ' "dismissal upon the merits" [in a diversity action] under circumstances where a state court would decree only a "dismissal without prejudice," ' might conceivably 'abridge[ ] a "substantive right" and thus exceed[ ] the authorization of the Rules Enabling Act'); Stephen B. Burbank, Semtek, Forum Shopping, and Federal Common Law, 77 Notre Dame L. Rev. 1027, 1042 n. 66 (2002) (discussing this passage).

[243] Semtek, 531 US at 505–506.

CHAPTER 9. PRECLUSION IN CLASS ACTION LITIGATION

Nonetheless, these passages do have some bearing upon the present question. They suggest that, when a proposed constraint on the preclusive effect of a class action judgment derogates from a jurisdiction's broader preclusion policies, a court cannot rely upon its joinder rules alone to serve as an independent counterweight in analyzing the propriety of the proposed constraint. Rather, the court will have to rely upon more clearly 'substantive' sources of law – in particular, the liability regime that applies to the dispute – in determining the extent to which the benefits of aggregate relief can serve to offset any burden that the constraint places upon preclusion values.[244] This observation is particularly important in the case of a federal diversity court. When a diversity court considers a proposed constraint upon the preclusive effect of a class action judgment that would burden preclusion commitments under state law, the court cannot look to Rule 23 as an independent source of authority to counterbalance that burden.[245] It must rely instead upon the state liability regime.[246]

---

[244] Burbank makes a similar point in his discussion of the federal common law origins of preclusion doctrine for federal judgments. See Burbank, Interjurisdictional Preclusion, *supra* n. 7, at 766 ('So long as preclusion law affects substantive rights, there is a federal interest in the definition of the federal rights adjudicated in a federal judgment.'); see also *id.* at 790 (discussing the importance of 'disciplining the process by which federal policies finding expression in the permissible legal sources are considered, as against competing policies, in determining whether federal common law applies').

[245] The Class Action Fairness Act of 2005, Pub. L. No. 109–2, 119 Stat. 4, might complicate the analysis. As an independent federal statute, the CAFA is not bound by the proviso of the Rules Enabling Act, and any independent joinder policies that the CAFA entails are available to influence or control assessments about the propriety of employing particular constraints on preclusion to facilitate class certification. It is unclear, however, what independent policy it would be appropriate to read into the statute in this respect. On the one hand, the CAFA aims to curb the abuses of overly ambitious state court actions, which might suggest that the statute would be cautious about replicating such actions in federal court. See § (2)(a)(1)–(4), 119 Stat. at 4–5 (criticizing certification practices in state and local courts). On the other hand, that very concern over state court abuses might counsel in favor of reading broad joinder policies into the statute so that the maximum number of claims coming within its jurisdictional provisions could be adjudicated in a federal forum.

[246] Professor Burbank makes a similar point in his discussion of the sources of authority for preclusion rules in federal diversity court:

> If the Constitution or acts of Congress, fairly read, provide for or require federal common law, state law does not apply [in a federal diversity court].

There are many situations in which a jurisdiction's liability rules will have something to say about the desirability of liberal joinder rules in a class action proceeding. The circumstance that has received the most attention in this respect is the negative-value claim, where aggregate litigation may represent the only economically viable opportunity for obtaining relief. The Supreme Court has thus far resisted the argument that negative-value suits should enjoy more permissive treatment under mandatory Rule 23 requirements like notice and adequacy of representation.[247] When a court must decide whether to impose a

---

> The same is true whether a uniform federal rule is called for or a particular state rule is found to be hostile to or inconsistent with federal interests. In other cases where the Constitution does not so ordain, state law applies, not 'of its own force' and not by judicial grace or borrowing, but because Congress has borrowed it.

Burbank, Interjurisdictional Preclusion, *supra* n. 7, at 762.

Burbank has also suggested the possibility that Federal Rules might embrace a broader set of federal common law interests where such interests are pertinent to their proper spheres of regulatory concern:

> Federal Rules of Civil Procedure can thus serve as sources of federal common law, not only by leaving interstices to be filled but also by expressing policies that are pertinent in areas not covered by the Rules. Even when legal regulation in a certain area is forbidden to the Rules, the policies underlying valid Rules may help to shape valid federal common law.

Id. at 774; see also *id.* at 773 ('In authorizing the Court to promulgate Federal Rules, Congress must have contemplated that the federal courts would interpret them, fill their interstices, and, when necessary, ensure that their provisions were not frustrated by other legal rules.'). But that power is a limited one that must be tied to legitimate sources of regulatory authority. See *id.* at 789–790 ('Federal courts are not free to conjure up "interests"; rather, they must tie them to policies already articulated in, or at least articulable from, valid legal prescriptions.').

Rule 23 does not embody a policy in favor of the broadest joinder possible. Rather, it is hedged about with many qualifications aimed at constraining its potentially far reaching effects. In Burbank's terms, there is no federal interest in a 'uniform... decisional law' of broad joinder that would 'displace particular state law rules in areas untouched by the Federal Rules.' *Id.* at 773.

[247] See *Eisen v. Carlisle and Jacquelin*, 417 U.S. 156, 176 (1974) ('There is nothing in Rule 23 to suggest that the notice requirements can be tailored to fit the pocketbooks of particular plaintiffs... Rule 23 speaks to notice as well as to adequacy of representation and requires that both be provided.').

CHAPTER 9. PRECLUSION IN CLASS ACTION LITIGATION

discretionary constraint on the preclusive effect of a class action judgment, however, the question is different. The purpose of such a constraint is to bring a class action into compliance with the mandatory requirements of the Rule, not to circumvent them. The relevant question is whether liberal joinder is consistent with the constellation of remedial policies that apply to the dispute.[248] In a small-stakes suit, where recovery would be effectively impossible without aggregation, that exigency alone militates in favor of employing a preclusion constraint in order to eliminate a conflict of interest that might otherwise make certification impossible.[249]

Particular liability schemes may speak even more directly to the propriety of liberal joinder. Consider the Civil Rights Act of 1991. The express purpose of Congress in passing the Act was to expand the remedies available to individuals who suffer from employment discrimination. The Act was enacted against an acknowledged backdrop of class litigation as the primary vehicle for obtaining relief for employees.[250] As section 9.2(b)(1) discusses, the statute had the

---

State courts have not always followed the Court's lead in this regard. In his innovative opinion in *Cartt v. Superior Court*, for example, Justice Kaus rejected the Court's reasoning in Eisen and found instead that a court is justified in applying looser notification standards to a negative-value consumer class action suit where doing so is necessary to make any recovery available to class members and the likelihood of subsequent challenges to the adequacy of the notice is remote. 124 Cal. Rptr. 376, 381–385 (Ct. App. 1975).

[248] In this vein, Wright, Miller, and Cooper suggest that:

> [w]hen the only realistic opportunity to litigate is an aggregated opportunity, whether called a class action or something else, it is not difficult to adopt a new conception of the underlying claim. The claim is not so much an individual claim as a share in a class claim.

18A Wright, Miller, and Cooper, *supra* n. 2, §4455, at 486; see also Shapiro, Class Actions, *supra* n. 216, at 923–25 (discussing 'entity' theory of class litigation and attractiveness of that theory in negative-value class action).

[249] Some commentators have argued that the same exigencies that warrant flexibility in the certification of negative-value class actions also warrant stricter adherence to finality, and fewer opportunities for collateral attack, following the close of the proceeding. See 18A Wright, Miller, and Cooper, *supra* n. 2, §4455, at 486–487 ('This view [of limited collateral attack opportunities] is particularly beguiling with respect to individual claims that would not in fact be litigated individually.').

[250] Cf. Burbank, Interjurisdictional Preclusion, *supra* n. 7, at 815 ('It seems unlikely that legislatures often think about preclusion law when they are enacting schemes of

unintended consequence of complicating the certification calculus in those cases where class members might have viable claims for individual damages. When a certifying court in a Title VII case wishes to employ a preclusion constraint in order to permit a class action to go forward without compromising the claims of individual class members, the 1991 Act must be read to embody a substantive joinder policy in favor of permitting that step. Such a policy is a natural concomitant to the statute's remedial purposes.

A state law regime that assigns damages among multiple defendants on an actuarial basis – like market-share liability – is another example of a liability rule that would embody a clear preference for liberal joinder in the face of potential preclusion problems. The more comprehensively an actuarial liability rule is applied in adjudicating claims, the more accurate the apportionment of damages will be among the defendants.[251] The broad application of such a liability rule to the claims that it properly embraces will promote fairness and avoid over-deterrence.[252] Where preclusive effects would prevent the certification of an otherwise desirable class action in the absence of an ex ante constraint, an actuarial liability rule should thus be read to include a policy in favor of broad joinder and hence in favor of using the constraint.

Thus, the *MTBE* court was correct when it voiced its instinct that the nature and source of the liability rule might be relevant to the

---

substantive rights. But they do legislate against a background of judge-made preclusion law.').

[251] I take Professor David Rosenberg to be making a similar point in his discussion of aggregate litigation and risk based claims. See David Rosenberg, Individual Justice and Collectivizing Risk-Based Claims in Mass-Exposure Cases, 71 N.Y.U. L. Rev. 210, 236–244 (1996).

[252] There may be other reasons for caution in applying such a liability rule broadly in aggregate litigation. In the case of 'immature' claims, for example, it might be difficult to achieve a high level of confidence in the scientific evidence for causation, or the proper measure of damages, without the benefit of a large number of fully litigated individual actions. In such a case, the precipitous certification of a class, or the broad use of nonmutual preclusion, might be contraindicated. See e.g., *Kaufman v. Eli Lilly and Co.*, 482 N.E.2d 63, 66–70 (N.Y. 1985) (discussing availability of issue preclusion following test cases in DES litigation, where scientific evidence for causation was disputed); see also Issacharoff, Governance and Legitimacy, *supra* n. 207, at 342–343 (describing asbestos claims as the quintessential 'mature' tort because strengths and weaknesses of the science, valuation of claims, and litigation options are now so well-established).

CHAPTER 9. PRECLUSION IN CLASS ACTION LITIGATION

resolution of a preclusion problem in class litigation.[253] The court was also correct in concluding that precedents from the civil rights arena might not speak directly to the preclusion problems posed by a massive, multi-incident tort suit. In a civil rights dispute like the prison riot cases that the *MTBE* court distinguished away, any injunctive suit would be frustrated and its relief undermined by the possibility of multiple inconsistent adjudications. A policy in favor of broad joinder is substantively related to the underlying rights being vindicated in a civil rights action seeking institutional reform. This is the classic example of a 'true' class action, where providing a benefit to one class member necessarily redounds to the benefit of the others.[254] When an ex ante constraint is required in such a case to preserve the damages claims of individual class members from adverse preclusive consequences and to eliminate conflicts of interest within the class, the underlying liability rule militates in favor of employing the constraint. In a multi-incident tort suit like *MTBE*, in contrast, the relief sought by the plaintiff class was not interdependent and contingent; rather, it was highly atomized.[255] The liability regime thus included no special imperative that would have favored the use of ex ante constraints to overcome preclusion problems and ensure class certification. Such constraints might still have been allowable, but they enjoyed no special preference.

Since the *MTBE* court was operating under the baleful influence of the ubiquitous preclusion maxim, it failed to set forth these distinctions with any precision. The court's core instinct, however, was sound.

---

[253] See In re Methyl Tertiary Butyl Ether ('MTBE') Prods. Liab. Litig., 209 F.R.D. 323, 339–340 (S.D.N.Y. 2002); see also *supra* notes 74–75 and accompanying text.

[254] See Hazard et al., *supra* n. 20, at 1921–1923 (describing treatment of 'true' and 'spurious' class actions prior to enactment of Rule 23); Issacharoff, Governance and Legitimacy, *supra* n. 207, at 359–363 (characterizing such actions as 'compelled participation cases whose coerced quality is justified by the inability for any legal resolution to proceed absent complete resolution'). The standard work on the history of representative or aggregative litigation is Yeazell's. See Stephen C. Yeazell, From Medieval Group Litigation to the Modern Class Action (1987) (tracing history of representative or aggregative litigation); see also Robert G. Bone, Personal and Impersonal Litigative Forms: Reconceiving the History of Adjudicative Representation, 70 B.U. L. Rev. 213, 236–238 (1990) (reviewing Yeazell and characterizing suits involving contingent relief, as in many civil rights actions, as involving 'general right').

[255] In re MTBE, 209 F.R.D. at 342–345 (discussing individualized nature of injunctive relief).

When a certifying court would have to impose a constraint on the preclusive effect of its judgment in order for certification to be proper, and the requisite constraint would operate in clear derogation of a jurisdiction's broader preclusion commitments, the court must look to substantive joinder policies like those embodied in certain liability rules in order to determine whether it should employ the constraint or, instead, decline to certify the class.

9.5 THE ROLE OF THE RECOGNIZING FORUM

Any discussion of the proper theoretical and doctrinal treatment of class litigation would be of limited utility if it did not make allowance for the inevitable fact that its suggestions would frequently be disregarded. Classes that should not be certified routinely are. The push for ever more ambitious class-wide resolutions of personal injury and other highly individualized claims has easily kept pace with the rate at which the legal community has internalized the norms of limitation that should apply to such actions. Indeed, the primary reason for the intense focus on the binding effect of class action judgments that I referred to in the introduction to this chapter has been the failure of rendering courts to pay careful enough attention to the adequacy of representation afforded to absentees, particularly as it relates to conflicts of interest within the class.[256] There is a more robust dialogue between academy, bench, and bar in the field of complex litigation than in many others, owing to such institutions as the Rules Advisory Committee and the Federal Judicial Conference, and also in part to the growing practice of soliciting expert testimony from legal academics during the certification hearing.[257] Even so, any proposal for reform in the standards that rendering courts should apply to the certification process must anticipate gradual and incomplete acceptance, at best.

---

[256] See Klonoff, *supra* n. 23, at 677–689 (conducting broad empirical study of adequacy analysis by certifying courts and concluding that slipshod analysis is more the norm than the exception).

[257] See e.g., *West v. Prudential Sec., Inc.*, 282 F.3d 935, 938 (7th Cir. 2002) (instructing district courts to resolve competing opinions of experts on question of certification). The apparent willingness of some law professors to attest to the propriety of certifying the most wildly overreaching class actions has itself become a focus of critical inquiry within the academy, and properly so.

CHAPTER 9. PRECLUSION IN CLASS ACTION LITIGATION

As a consequence, recognizing forums will continue to play an important role in defining and enforcing the proper scope of a class judgment's preclusive effects. While a subsequent tribunal cannot undo the effect of an improper denial of certification of the type that has occurred in recent Title VII litigation,[258] it will sometimes be able to mitigate an initial court's failure to consider the impact of preclusion on the interests of absentees following entry of judgment when a class action does move forward. The appropriate means for undertaking such mitigating efforts is through scrutiny of the adequacy of the representation that class members were afforded in the first action.

It remains a matter of serious dispute whether an F2 court may recognize a full-scale collateral attack and set aside a class judgment on adequacy grounds. The Supreme Court recently failed to answer the question in *Dow Chemical Co. v. Stephenson*,[259] the circuits remain split,[260] and commentators divide sharply between those who would err in favor of ensuring that class members have a reliably fair opportunity to recover[261] and those who fear that permitting collateral attacks would harm all plaintiffs by fatally undermining the finality of judgments, thereby dissuading defendants from settling.[262] The form of adequacy analysis that I contemplate here, however, is much less disruptive than a full-scale collateral attack would be. It is, in essence, a more nuanced form of the preclusion analysis that is already an accepted part of a recognizing court's role in reviewing prior judgments.

In addition to the familiar limitations on claim and issue preclusion that F2 courts already apply,[263] a court that is asked to give effect to a class action judgment may need to ask what prospective constraints the rendering court should have imposed upon the judgment in order for the representation of all class members to have been minimally

---

[258] See *supra* section 9.2.2.1.

[259] 539 U.S. 111, 112 (2003) (per curiam) (dividing four to four on appeal from Second Circuit opinion that permitted collateral attack by Agent Orange victims on grounds of inadequate representation in initial class proceeding).

[260] See *supra* n. 1 and accompanying text.

[261] See e.g., Monaghan, *supra* n. 1, at 1200–1202; Patrick J. Woolley, The Availability of Collateral Attack for Inadequate Representation in Class Suits, 79 Tex. L. Rev. 383, 389–397 (2000) [hereinafter Woolley, Availability] (arguing in favor of permitting collateral attack upon showing of inadequate representation).

[262] See e.g., Kahan and Silberman, Inadequate Search, *supra* n. 1, at 779.

[263] See e.g., Restatement (Second) of Judgments §§ 28–29 (1982).

adequate in the initial proceeding. Where the failure of the F1 court to apply such a constraint has resulted in the inadequate representation of class members' interests, the F2 court should limit the preclusive effect of the judgment as if the initial tribunal had acted properly. The F2 court would not reopen claims actually adjudicated in the first action, as in a full-scale collateral attack. Rather, the court would constrain the judgment's effect upon the claims not litigated in that action to the extent necessary to cure the prejudice that the absentees would otherwise suffer from the inadequate representation of their interests.[264]

Many recognizing courts have already embraced this role in cases involving damages claims brought by individuals who were members of an earlier injunctive class action. While certifying courts can still be skittish about the issue, subsequent courts have been fairly consistent in holding that a judgment from an equitable class proceeding should not preclude individual damages claims that were not litigated in the first action. Some courts have simply invoked the 'could not have been brought' language in explaining why claim preclusion does not apply to such cases,[265] but others have explained their holding under the rubric of adequacy of representation.[266] What I am suggesting here is a more generalized application of the rule implicit in that practice.[267]

---

[264] Wright, Miller, and Cooper speak in favorable, if general, terms of this form of adequacy analysis:

> The conduct of a class action may often create conflicts between the best interests of non-participating class members and the substantive or procedural arguments that seem best calculated to maintain the momentum of the class action itself. Such conflicts may often be difficult to identify, and may not always warrant denial of preclusion. They should not be ignored, however, and at least should be considered in attempting to apply the more objective requirement that the class have been adequately represented in fact.

18A Wright, Miller, and Cooper, *supra* n. 2, §4455, at 474.

[265] See e.g., In re Jackson Lockdown/MCO Cases, 568 F. Supp. 869, 891–893 (E.D. Mich. 1983) (permitting inmates to assert individual claims that could not have been brought in prior class proceeding).

[266] See e.g., *Ferguson v. Alaska Dep't of Corr.*, 816 P.2d 134, 138–139 (Alaska 1991) (invoking adequacy as one basis for refusing to preclude inmate from litigating individual claim arguably precluded by prior injunctive class proceeding).

[267] The Restatement captures some elements of this more generalized application when it allows for issue preclusion to be withheld from a judgment when 'the party sought to be precluded, as a result of...special circumstances, did not have an

CHAPTER 9. PRECLUSION IN CLASS ACTION LITIGATION

The most difficult problem that a rendering court is likely to face in this posture involves the issue preclusive effect of a prior judgment. Consider a class action for equitable relief in which some members of the class also possess substantial damages claims. As should now be second nature, such an action will often create an ex ante conflict of interest between the absentees with no damages claims, who would have less to lose from an adverse judgment and hence would adopt a tougher negotiating position on settlement, and those possessing high-value claims, who would be risk averse and eager to settle the equitable proceeding cheaply. Suppose that the initial tribunal certifies the class without acknowledging the interests of the absentees who possess high-value claims or otherwise taking any steps to protect them. The case is then fully litigated and results in a judgment for defendant. The rendering court in this case has failed to ensure adequate representation for the class members with high-value claims. Instead, their interest in avoiding an adverse judgment that would compromise their damages claims has been subordinated to the interest of other class members in maximizing the benefits from the equitable suit.[268] To resolve this conflict, the rendering court should have imposed an ex ante constraint that would have prevented its judgment from having issue preclusive effect on individual damages claims. To cure the first court's error, the F2 court must now impose an ex post constraint to the same effect.

A stay-in-state-court case – where class counsel forgoes a federal claim in order to defeat removal – might call for a different kind of adequacy analysis. If a class member in such a case seeks to raise the abandoned federal claim in an F2 forum, there is no conflict of interest to point to in the initial proceeding, since by hypothesis the class was affected uniformly by class counsel's decision to pursue only state law

---

adequate opportunity or incentive to obtain a full and fair adjudication in the initial action.' Restatement (Second) of Judgments § 28(5)(c). One could thus interpret the analysis that follows as an explanation of when the Restatement's qualification is properly implicated in class litigation.

[268] This conflict of interest recalls the one between asbestos claimants seeking immediate payments and those wanting to ensure the availability of funds for future relief, which the Court found fatal in Amchem. See *Amchem Prods., Inc. v. Windsor*, 521 U.S. 591, 626 (1997) ('[F]or the currently injured, the critical goal is generous immediate payments. That goal tugs against the interest of exposure-only plaintiffs in ensuring an ample, inflation-protected fund for the future.').

relief. And when the federal claim is one that could have been raised in the state court – or, in the case of exclusively federal claims, when the entire action could have been filed in federal court – traditional claim preclusion doctrine may offer no obvious basis for avoiding merger or bar. Here, the adequacy analysis undertaken by the recognizing forum must focus upon the limits of counsel's representational role in a class proceeding. The court must ask whether it constituted a legitimate strategic decision for class counsel in F1 to trade the federal claim for a state forum on behalf of the class.[269] The line of Sixth Amendment decisions that federal courts have developed in assessing adequacy of representation in the criminal context – and, in particular, in assessing decisions by counsel to abandon certain claims or defenses – would likely be an important source to draw upon in such an inquiry.[270]

If the answer is no – if counsel acted incompetently in eschewing the federal claim or else was acting from selfish or nefarious motives – then the F2 court should permit the federal claim to proceed.[271] Class

---

[269] Professor Issacharoff appears to recognize the need for adequacy review of strategic decisions in class litigation. See Issacharoff, Governance and Legitimacy, *supra* n. 207, at 385–386 (discussing methods by which class counsel can 'overtly' and 'covertly' make allocation decisions on behalf of a class, including the decision 'to forgo some claims' or 'not to prosecute individual-based damages' claims that might prevent certification, and recognizing need for both leeway and limitations).

[270] Those cases articulate a strict standard for challenging 'strategic' decisions. See *Strickland v. Washington*, 466 U.S. 668, 687–688 (1984), requiring a showing that counsel's advice 'was not "within the range of competence demanded of attorneys in criminal cases"' (quoting *McMann v. Richardson*, 397 U.S. 759, 771 (1970); *id.* at 690–691 ('[S]trategic choices made after thorough investigation of law and facts relevant to plausible options are virtually unchallengeable; and strategic choices made after less than complete investigation are reasonable precisely to the extent that reasonable professional judgments support the limitations on investigation.'). In applying this standard, the Court has tended to rely heavily upon an assessment of the diligence that counsel exhibited in arriving at a strategic decision and to shy away from second guessing the wisdom of decisions that are well informed. See e.g., *Wiggins v. Smith*, 539 U.S. 510, 523–529 (2003) (finding defense attorney's investigation of mitigating evidence in capital case to be inadequate and, hence, his decision not to put on mitigation case was inadequate and entitled to little deference).

[271] Wright, Miller, and Cooper appear to endorse this form of collateral adequacy attack for certain unpled claims. See 18A Wright, Miller, and Cooper, *supra* n. 2, § 4455, at 474, discussing *Haas v. Harris*, 436 F. Supp. 279 (D.R.I. 1977), reversed sub nom. *Haas v. Howard*, 579 F.2d 654 (1st Cir. 1978) (offering favorable account of

CHAPTER 9. PRECLUSION IN CLASS ACTION LITIGATION

counsel's actions would constitute inadequate representation in such a case, and the recognizing forum should cure the error that the rendering forum committed when it allowed the suit to proceed without imposing a preclusion constraint. But if responsible counsel could have chosen to relinquish federal claims in favor of a state forum in F1 – for example, if the relief that the federal claim offered was largely duplicative and the benefits of preserving a state forum were substantial – then the F2 court might have to conclude that merger and bar apply. This result may seem counterintuitive, as it appears that class members are being penalized for having competent counsel in the first proceeding. Indeed, if class counsel in such a case never even requested that the certifying court impose a constraint upon its judgment that would preserve the federal claims, the absentees might be able to challenge that decision itself as inadequate, counsel's legitimate strategic motives notwithstanding.[272] But if the F1 court considered and rejected such a constraint – perhaps concluding that it would be inconsistent with the jurisdiction's broader preclusion commitments – and class counsel made a legitimate strategic decision in continuing to litigate in state court nonetheless, there would seem to be no basis for invoking adequacy of representation to prohibit a subsequent merger or bar.[273]

---

district court opinion that limited res judicata effect of earlier judgment where class counsel's failure to raise argument rendered representation inadequate). Some courts disagree. See e.g., *Nathan v. Rowan*, 651 F.2d 1223, 1227–1228 and n. 8 (6th Cir. 1981) (barring federal claims that went unpled in state class action, apparently through inadvertence, under ' "might have been offered" aspect of res judicata').

[272] But see Nathan, 651 F.2d at 1227–1228 (refusing to recognize failure of plaintiff in state class action to seek leave to amend complaint and add federal claims as constituting inadequate representation).

[273] In some cases, this mode of analysis might implicate the continuing debate over whether a rendering court can conclusively determine the adequacy of the representation that class members have received in a proceeding before it – a question that collapses into one variant of the collateral attack problem. See Marcel Kahan and Linda Silberman, Matsushita and Beyond: The Role of State Courts in Class Actions Involving Exclusive Federal Claims, 1996 Sup. Ct. Rev. 219, 262–266 (concluding that 'adequacy of representation should be raised directly, and not be permitted to be raised collaterally,' provided that class members had a 'fair opportunity to raise the issue'); Woolley, Availability, *supra* n. 261, at 389–397 (arguing against ability of rendering forum to issue conclusive determination of adequacy, at least where class members lack minimum contacts or other jurisdictional nexus with forum).

In each of these cases, the question for the F2 court is no longer whether a class action should have been certified at all in light of its impact upon preclusion values in the initial forum. Rather, the question is what preclusion constraints the rendering forum would have had to apply in order to afford constitutionally adequate representation to the absentees, given the class that was actually certified. This modest form of adequacy based collateral challenge, which leaves intact the claims actually litigated in the original action, poses none of the threats to finality and predictability that are associated with full-scale collateral attacks. It merely constitutes a variation on the type of retrospective interpretation of judgments that the ubiquitous preclusion maxim – even in its properly limited form – already warns parties to expect.

9.6 CONCLUSION

Many of the doctrinal proposals set forth in this article are new. The insights that lie at their core, however, should sound familiar. The power of a court to constrain the preclusive effects of its own judgment in a class proceeding rests on the same theoretical foundation as the court's power to enter a prosaic dismissal without prejudice, or to approve a class settlement containing a narrowly tailored release of claims. As courts confront requests to certify increasingly ambitious class actions, and as class counsel increasingly tailor the causes of action that they assert in an effort to comply with the other requirements of certification, the threat of adverse preclusive effects will require courts to employ that power with care and precision. It is a testament to the tenacity of the ubiquitous preclusion maxim that most courts consistently fail to consider the threat of preclusion at all, while those few that do make the attempt frequently throw up their hands in helplessness.

Improving upon this inadequate state of affairs will require a more thoughtful and realistic description of the array of interests possessed by the members of a class outside the four corners of the complaint. We have seen the need for this type of reform many times. An example from a related juridical context makes the point succinctly. Linda Silberman has famously noted that a judge who places more weight upon a litigant's forum contacts when analyzing personal jurisdiction than when analyzing choice of law operates under the mistaken assumption that an accused cares more about 'where he will be hanged than

CHAPTER 9. PRECLUSION IN CLASS ACTION LITIGATION

whether.'[274] The quip brilliantly captures the manner in which a misguided, formalistic doctrinal myopia can lead judges to misdescribe reality and unwittingly harm the interests of litigants. A similar danger is becoming manifest in the treatment of preclusion in class litigation. When a court fails to consider the consequences of certification for the unpled claims of absentees, its attempt to uncover hidden treasure for the class may wind up digging the hole for a premature burial. Choice of law has now begun to assume its proper place as a regular inquiry at the threshold of the certification process. Preclusion should not be far behind.

---

[274] Linda J. Silberman, Shaffer v. Heitner: The End of an Era, 53 N.Y.U. L. Rev. 33, 88 (1978).

CHAPTER 10

Opt-In Class Actions: Collective Litigation under the FLSA, ADEA, and EPA

Mark S. Dichter*

10.1 COLLECTIVE LITIGATION UNDER THE FLSA, ADEA, AND EPA

An action to recover relief under the Fair Labor Standards Act (FLSA), Age Discrimination in Employment Act (ADEA) and Equal Pay Act (EPA) can be brought in any federal or state court of competent jurisdiction, by any one or more employees.[1] An action can also be brought by an individual, or by a group, on behalf of other employees who are 'similarly situated.'[2] Unlike a class action under Fed. R. Civ. P. 23, however, or a comparable state law class action equivalent, group actions brought under the FLSA, ADEA, or EPA, known as 'collective actions,' are governed by 29 U.S.C. §216 and the case law that has developed under that Section. The rules governing 'collective actions' under 921 6(b) of the FLSA apply equally to cases brought under the ADEA and EPA (the EPA is a subsection of the FLSA, while the ADEA specifically incorporates the remedy provisions of the FLSA). While there are some similarities between class and collective actions, there

---

* Mark S. Dichter is chair of the global labor and employment practice of Morgan, Lewis & Bockius.
[1] 29 U.S.C. §216(b).
[2] Ibid.

David Sherwyn and Samuel Estreicher (eds), *Employment Class and Collective Actions*, pp. 499–547.
© 2009, Kluwer Law International BV, Printed in Great Britain.

are also significant differences. Those differences, and other issues specific to collective litigation under the FLSA, ADEA, and EPA, are discussed below.

10.1.1 Similarities and Differences between Class Actions and Collective Actions

10.1.1.1 Class Actions under Rule 23

Class actions are governed by Rule 23 of the Federal Rules of Civil Procedure (Fed. R. Civ. P.). Fed. R. Civ. P. 23(a) provides that:

> One or more members of a class may sue or be sued as representative parties on behalf of all only if:
>
> (1) the class is so numerous that joinder of all members is impracticable;
> (2) there are questions of law or fact common to the class;
> (3) the claims or defenses of the representative parties are typical of the claims or defenses of the class; and
> (4) the representative parties will fairly and adequately protect the interests of the class.

All of these prerequisites, commonly known as numerosity, commonality, typicality, and adequacy of representation, must be satisfied. Fed. R. Civ. P. 23(b) further requires that there be a showing that:

> (1) the prosecution of separate actions would prejudice non-parties or create incompatible adjudications; or
> (2) the defendant has taken action in some way generally applicable to the class as a whole; or
> (3) common questions of law or fact predominate.

10.1.1.2 Collective Actions under 29 U.S.C. § 216(b)

Collective actions under the FLSA, including the EPA, are not governed by Rule 23, but are instead governed by 29 U.S.C. § 216(b), which provides that such claims:

> May be maintained against any employer (including a public agency) in any Federal or State court of competent jurisdiction by any one or more employees for and in behalf of himself or themselves and other employees similarly situated. No employee shall be a party plaintiff to any such action

CHAPTER 10. OPT-IN CLASS ACTIONS

unless he gives his consent in writing to become such a party and such consent is filed in the court in which such action is brought.[3]

Claims brought under the ADEA are also governed by 29 U.S.C. § 216(b) and, thus, must be brought as collective actions. See 29 U.S.C. § 626(b):

> ([T]he provisions of this chapter [Age Discrimination in Employment] shall be enforced with the powers, remedies, and procedures provided in sections 211(b), 216 (except for subsection (a) thereof), and 217 of this title, and subsection (c) of this section.)

Therefore, ADEA cases interpreting § 216(b) are generally applicable to FLSA cases, and vice versa.

10.1.1.3 The Applicability of Rule 23 to Collective Actions

As noted above, § 216(b) authorizes plaintiffs to proceed collectively on behalf of others who are 'similarly situated.' A majority of the courts have held that the conjunctive requirements of Rule 23 need *not* be met in establishing that a class of similarly-situated individuals exists for the purposes of a § 216(b) action.[4] Instead, as discussed below, an arguably much easier standard applies.[5]

---

[3] 29 U. S. C. § 216(b).

[4] See e.g., *Gamer v. G.D. Searle Pharms. & Co.*, 802 F. Supp. 41 8,421 (M.D: Ala. 1991), (characterizing the requirements under Rule 23 –9 and § 216(b) as 'irreconcilable'); see also *La Chapelle v. Owens-Ill. Inc.*, 513 F.2d 286, 288 (5th Cir. 1975). ('There is a fundamental, irreconcilable difference between the class action described by Rule 23 and that provided for by FLSA § [216](b)'); *Foster v. Food Emporium*, No. 99 Civ. 3860, 2000 WL 1737858, at *1 (S.D.N.Y. April 26, 2000). ('The strict requirements of Rule 23 . . . do not apply to FLSA collective actions.'); *Schmidt v. Fuller Brush Co.*, 527 F.2d 532, 536 (8th Cir. 1975), (adopting the rationale of *La Chapelle*); *Lusardi v. Xerox Corp.*, 118 F.R.D. 351, 358 (D.N.J. 1987), (citation omitted). ('The requirements for pursuing a section 216(b) class action are independent of and unrelated to the requirements of a class action filed pursuant to Rule 23, Fed. R. Civ. P.'); *White v. Osmose, Inc.*, 204 F. Supp. 2d 1309, 1315 (M.D. Ala. 2002)('[The strict requirements of F.R.C.P. 23 are inapplicable to an opt-in collective action under the FLSA').

[5] See G, *Heagney v. European Am. Bank*, 122 F.R.D. 125, 127 n. 2, (E.D.N.Y. 1988), (noting that the 'similarly situated' requirement of collective actions under 216(b) is less stringent than the Fed. R. Civ. P. 23(b)(3) requirement that common questions predominate); *Thiebes v. Wal-Mart Stores. Inc.*, No. Civ. 98-802, 1999 WL 1081357, at *3 (D. Or. December 1, 1999),(same); *Sheffield v. Orius Corn*, 211 F.R.D. 411, 412 (D. Or. 2002),(stating that the standard for certifying a collective action under section 216(b) is more liberal than under Rule 23).

501

EMPLOYMENT CLASS AND COLLECTIVE ACTIONS

Contrary to this majority view, however, some district courts have held that ADEA plaintiffs proceeding under § 216(b) must satisfy all of the requirements of Fed. R. Civ. P. 23 to the extent that they do not conflict with § 216(b).[6] In *Shushan v. Univ. of Colo. at Boulder*, the court held that, due to the lack of guidance from Congress concerning the appropriate standard for determining who is similarly situated under § 216(b), district courts should apply the class action standards established by Rule 23. *Shushan* and its progeny remain a distinctly minority view, however, with which other federal courts have expressly disagreed.[7]

10.1.1.4 The Legal Differences between Rule 23 Class Actions and § 216(b) Collective Actions

10.1.1.4.1 The Need to Opt-In The principal difference between an action under § 216(b) and a Rule 23 class action is that an individual who wants to be a part of the § 216(b) 'class' must 'opt in' to participate and be bound by a judgment. In contrast, Rule 23 class members are generally bound by the judgment in an action unless they affirmatively opt out.[8] An individual 'opts in' simply by filing with the court a written document consenting to become a party in the action.[9]

---

[6] See *Shushan v. Univ. of Colo. at Boulder*, 132 F.R.D. 263, 265 (D.Colo. 1990); see also *Wilkerson v. Martin Marietta Corn.*, 875 F. Supp. 1456, 1461 (D. Colo. 1995), (holding that potential ADEA class must meet both requirements of § 216(b) and non-conflicting requirements of Fed. R. Civ. P. 23); *H&R Block, Ltd. v. Housden*, 186 F.R.D. 399, 400–01 (E.D. Tex. 1999)(noting the Fed. R. Civ. P. 23 analysis applied in *Shushan*).

[7] See e.g., *Jackson v. N.Y. Tel. Co.*, 163 F.R.D. 429, 432 (S.D.N.Y. 1995), (finding that 'the application of the Rule 23 requirements to the question of whether potential plaintiffs are similarly situated is at odds with the well-reasoned conclusions of other courts').

[8] *Gamer*, 802 F. Supp. at 421; see also *Heagney*, 122 F.R.D. at 130 (noting that § 216(b), in contrast to Rule 23 class actions, 'does not fix the rights of absent parties'); *Vazquez v. Tri-State Mgmt. Co.*, No. 01C5926, 2002 WL 58718, at *2 (N.D. Ill. January 14, 2002),('[C]lass actions under the FLSA can only be maintained when and if potential claimants opt in. In contrast, class actions under Rule 23 bind all members of the class unless they opt out.').

[9] 29 U.S.C. § 216(b).

CHAPTER 10. OPT-IN CLASS ACTIONS

Consent to opt-in to a collective action must be in writing and be filed in the court where the suit is filed.[10]

10.1.1.4.2 Notice to Class or Collective Action Members of Dismissal of Claims   Fed. R. Civ. P. 23(e) generally requires the court to give notice to all putative class members if an action is dismissed. This may also be true in the context of a settlement. Moreover, notice may be required regardless of whether a class is ever certified, on the theory that putative class members may have relied upon the filing of the action in not bringing their own claims.[11] In that regard, Fed. R. Civ. P. 23(e) expressly provides:

> A class action shall not be dismissed or compromised without the approval of the court, and notice of the proposed dismissal or compromise shall be given to all members of the class in such manner as the court directs.

However, courts have refused to adopt an absolute rule requiring notice to every potential class member in every case in which class allegations are voluntarily amended or dismissed.[12] Where a court determines that putative class members have not developed a reliance interest in the lawsuit and where prejudice to absent class members

---

[10] *Sperlinn v. Hoffman-La Roche, Inc.*, 862 F.2d 439,444 (3rd Cir. 1988); *Hipp v. Liberty Nat'l Life Ins. Co.*, 252 F.3d 1208, 1217 n. 7 (11th Cir. 2001); In re Food Lion, Inc 15 1 F.3d 1029 (unpub. op.), available at 1998 WL 322682, at **12–13 (4th Cir. June 4, 1998). 'A consent meeting these requirements is valid regardless of its form.' *Id.*, see also UFCW Local 1529, No. GC 86-298-D-0, 1987 WL 48301, at * 1 (N.D. Miss. July 10, 1987), (finding valid consents that provided:

> I hereby consent to be included as a plaintiff in a lawsuit against my employer alleging violations of the Fair Labor Standards Act... I consent to become a plaintiff in the suit on behalf of myself and all other employees similarly situated.

[11] See *Roper v. Consurve, Inc.*, 578 F.2d 1106, 11 10 (5th Cir. 1978), ('prior to certification a class action cannot be dismissed... unless there is notice to the putative class... as required by Rule 23(e)'); *Anderberg v. Masonite Corp.*,176 F.R.D. 682, 687–690 (N.D.G a. 1997),(notice to putative class members may be appropriate, even in instances of dismissal prior to certification, when there is evidence of collusion between the parties or reliance on the part of absent class members).

[12] In re Cardizem CD Antitrust Litig., No. 99-MD-1278, 2000 WL 33180833, at *6 (E.D. Mich. September 21, 2000). ('Courts have adopted a functional approach to Rule 23(e)'s application.').

would not result, a court may determine that notice to all potential class members is unnecessary.[13]

While individual courts have 'inherent powers' to impose their own protections, including notice requirements, no such notice of dismissal, even to members of the collective action who have already opted in, is required under § 216(b).[14]

10.1.1.4.3 *Tolling the Statute of Limitations*   Under Fed. R. Civ. P. 23, the statute of limitations may be tolled pending a determination as to whether the plaintiffs can maintain a proper class.[15] Moreover, in many actions brought in the Fed. R. Civ. P. 23 context (e.g., Title VII actions), the statute of limitations is tolled as to all participants upon the filing of the complaint by even a single named plaintiff.[16]

Filing suit under the FLSA, on the other hand, does not toll the statute of limitations.[17] Indeed, there is a basis for arguing that even the

---

[13] *Ibid.*

[14] *Bayles v. Am. Med. Response, Inc.*, 962 F. Supp. 1346, 1348 (D. Colo. 1997)(addressing arguments made by plaintiffs' counsel after a decertification of the case, and noting that § 216(b) does not require any notice of dismissal, even for the opt-in plaintiffs in the action). See also *Moonev v. Aramco Services Co.*, 54 F.3d 1207, 1214 (5th Cir. 1995), (stating that if a conditional certification is not continued and the 'class' is decertified, the opt-in plaintiffs are dismissed without prejudice).

[15] *American Pipe Constr. Co. v. Utah*, 414 U.S. 538, 561 (1974), (statute of limitations for the claims of all putative class members is tolled until class certification is denied); *Crown, Cork & Seal, Inc. v. Parker*, 462 U.S. 345 (1983).

[16] *Salazar v. Brown*, No. G87-961, 1996 WL 302673, at * 10 (W.D. Mich. April 9, 1996); In re Cardizem CD Antitrust Litig., No. 99-MD-1278, 2000 WL 33180833, at *5 (E.D. Mich. September 21, 2000), (stating that when a class action complaint is filed, the statute of limitations is tolled for absent class members, and begins to run again if the court refuses to certify the class.).

[17] *Salazar*, 1996 WL 302673, at * 10. Only filing a consent to participate, or 'opt in,' with the court, will toll the statute of limitations. See *Redman v. U.S. West Bus. Resources, Inc.*, 153 F.3d 691, 695 (8th Cir. 1998). ('In the case of a collective action under the FLSA, the action is commenced when a party files his or her written consent to become part of the action'); *Grayson v. Kmart Corp.*, 79 F.3d 1086, 1105 (11th Cir. 1996)('ADEA opt-in plaintiffs are deemed to commence their civil action only when they file their written consent to opt into the class action'); *Atkins v. General Motors Corn.*, 701 F.2d 1124, 1130 n. 5 (5th Cir. 1983)(same); *Lee v. Vance Exec. Protection. Inc.*, 243 F.3d 538, 2001 WL 108760, at *5 (4th Cir. February 8, 2001), (unpub. op.), (recognizing that consents filed after the complaint do not relate back to the filing date of the complaint for purposes of the statute of limitations).

CHAPTER 10. OPT-IN CLASS ACTIONS

named plaintiffs in an FLSA action must file their own consents, and that simply filing the complaint is not enough.[18]

10.1.1.5 The Legal Similarities between Rule 23 Class Actions and § 216(b) Collective Actions

'Although [§ 216(b)] nowhere mentions "class," "class actions," or "certifications," courts have repeatedly employed Rule 23 terminology when determining issues relating to § 216(b).'[19] Courts often refer to the § 216(b) plaintiffs as a 'class,' and concerns of effective and efficient case management, and conservation of judicial resources, apply to both class and collective actions.

Class and collective actions also have some procedural similarities. For example:

> [L]ike a member of a plaintiff class under rule 23 . . . the section 216 plaintiff does not formally appear before the court or file a pleading; he simply files his written consent. He is therefore not named in the caption and he would not ordinarily be served with papers filed after he files the written consent.[20]

10.1.2 The Three-Step Process through Which Nationwide Collective Actions Are Born

Under Fed. R. Civ. P. 23, 'as soon as practicable after the commencement of an action,' the court is to determine whether class treatment is appropriate.[21] Additionally, in class actions brought under Rule 23(b)(3), in which common questions of law or fact predominate, the Federal Rules of Civil Procedure specifically direct the court to send notice to putative class members informing them that:

(a) the court will exclude the member from the class if the member so requests by a specific date;

---

[18] See e.g., *Whalen v. W.R. Grace Co.*, 56 F.3d 504, 506 (3rd Cir. 1995), ('Unlike a class action under Fed. R. Civ. P. 23, under § 16(b), no person can become a party plaintiff . . . unless he or she has affirmatively "opted into" the class by filing a written consent with the court.').

[19] *Wyatt v. Pride Offshore, Inc.*, Civ. A. No. 96-1998, 1996 WL 509654, at *1 (E.D. La. September 6, 1996)(citation omitted).

[20] Fed. R. Civ. P. 5(a). *Shushan*, 132 F.R.D. at 264 (citation omitted).

[21] Fed. R. Civ. P. 23(c)(1).

(b) the judgment, whether favorable or not, will include all members who do not request exclusion; and

(c) any member who does not request exclusion may, if the member desires, enter an appearance through counsel.[22]

In other words, in class actions brought under Rule 23(b)(3), a person is bound by the results of the action, and any judgment entered therein, unless he or she specifically 'opts out.'

Section 216 does not contain any similar guidelines or directives as to how or when an action under the FLSA, ADEA, or EPA can or should become more than a single plaintiff case. Instead, a body of case law has arisen, and continues to evolve, which together sets forth some general principles, including a three-step process, through which large 'collective actions' are created and develop.

First, there must be some showing that there is sufficient evidence that a group of 'similarly situated' individuals exists who can be lumped together in one action. If the plaintiff satisfies this minimal burden, a conditional class is created. Second, the plaintiffs can send notice to current and former employees who fall within the scope of the 'conditional class' of similarly situated individuals.[23] Discovery can be sought to assist in this process, including discovery relating to the names and addresses of the current and former employees. Third, after the notice(s) go out, individuals opt in, and all discovery is complete, the court has another opportunity to decide whether the 'class' really is similarly situated for purposes of dispositive motions, trial or settlement. If the court does not find such similarity exists, the 'class' can be 'decertified' or redefined.

This three-step process, and other issues that arise in the creation, expansion and maintenance of collective actions, are discussed in greater detail below.

---

[22] Fed. R. Civ. P. 23(c)(2).

[23] As discussed in Section 10.2.1 plaintiffs are not required to obtain court approval before sending notice. Practically, however, plaintiffs often cannot send the notices without the assistance of the court in obtaining the names and addresses of the similarly situated individuals. However, court involvement in the notice stage of a § 216(b) proceeding is typical.

CHAPTER 10. OPT-IN CLASS ACTIONS

10.1.2.1 The Supreme Court's Treatment of Notice in § 216(b) Actions

Because § 216(b) affirmatively permits employees to proceed on behalf of those who are alleged to be similarly situated, the Supreme Court has reasoned that trial courts have 'the requisite procedural authority to manage the process of joining' additional parties.[24] Court-supervised notice, the Court explained, assures that the notification procedure will be accomplished in an orderly, sensible, efficient, and accurate manner.[25] 'Court authorization of notice serves the legitimate goal of avoiding a multiplicity of duplicative suits and setting cutoff dates to expedite disposition of the action.'[26]

Court supervision is not required, however, and, barring local rules or a court order to the contrary, court approval is not needed before notice can be sent. Practically, however, plaintiffs are often in a position where they cannot send notice without assistance from the court, because they do not have access to the names and addresses of the allegedly similarly situated individuals to whom they wish notice to be sent. Accordingly, plaintiffs typically have had to make a basic showing that similarly situated individuals do exist, and then ask the court for assistance in obtaining the names and addresses of those or other allegedly similarly situated individuals. Once those names and addresses are obtained, notice seeking to expand the action can be sent.

10.1.2.2 The 'Similarly Situated' Requirement of § 216(b)

10.1.2.2.1 Initially Determining 'Similarly Situated' Is a Minimal Burden Neither the FLSA nor its implementing regulations define the § 216(b) requirement that plaintiffs be 'similarly situated.' The courts, however, have created a body of jurisprudence holding that plaintiffs can meet this threshold burden by making a 'modest factual showing' or a showing 'sufficient to demonstrate that they

---

[24] *Hofmann-La Roche Inc. v. Sperling*, 493 U.S. 165, 169 (1989)(ADEA case).
[25] *Id.* at 170–171.
[26] *Id.* at 172.

and potential plaintiffs together were victims of a common policy or plan that violated the law.'[27]

In *Foster*, the plaintiffs, who claimed they had been denied compensation for overtime work, met this burden by showing that they all were hourly employees in stores owned by the defendant and identified certain practices that they alleged were common to all eighty-two stores owned by the defendant in the New York metropolitan area.[28]

10.1.2.2.2 The 'Two-Tiered' System of Similarly Situated As noted by the Eleventh Circuit in *Hipp v. Liberty Nat'l Life Insur. Co.*, several courts have adopted a two-tiered system for evaluating whether a 'class' of individuals is 'similarly situated.'[29] Under this system, the court

---

[27] Foster, 2000 WL 1737858, at * 1 (requiring only a 'modest factual showing'); *Hoffman v. Sbarro. Inc.*, 982 F. Supp. 249, 262 (S.D.N.Y. 1997); see also Wyatt, 1996 WL 50965, at *2; m, 252 F.3d at 1217, (holding that plaintiffs have the burden of showing that their positions are similar to the positions held by putative class members); Grayson, 79 F.3d at 1096 (same); *Whitworth v. Chiles Offshore Corp.*, No. Civ. A. 92-1504, 1992 WL 235907, at *1 (E.D. La. September 2, 1992), (citation omitted),(holding that a collective action cannot be maintained if 'the action arises from circumstances purely personal to the plaintiff'); Lusardi, 11 8 F.R.D. at 359 ('[f]or prospective plaintiffs to be similarly situated, there must be a factual nexus which binds them together as victims of an alleged policy or practice'); Jackson, 163 F.R.D. at 431 (plaintiffs 'need merely provide some factual basis from which the court can determine if similarly situated potential plaintiffs exist'); *Bontempo v. Westwood One Broad. Serv., Inc.*, No. 01 C 8969, 2002 WL 192591 1, at *1 (N.D. Ill. May 3, 2002), (noting that 'plaintiff need only make a modest factual showing sufficient to demonstrate that plaintiff and potential plaintiffs together were victims of a common policy or plan that allegedly violated the FLSA'); *Harrington v. Educ. Mgmt. Corp.*, No. 02 Civ. 0787(HB), 2002 WL 1009463, at *2 (S.D.N.Y. May 17, 2002), (holding that the plaintiff met his 'modest preliminary burden' by submitting a single affidavit explaining why putative plaintiffs are similarly situated).

[28] Foster, 2000 WL 1737858, at *2. See also *Realite v. Ark. Rest. Corp.*, 7 F. Supp. 2d 303, 304–305 (S.D.N.Y. 1998), (certifying a class of hourly paid non-managerial employees of fifteen restaurants because, although they held different positions, they were victims of a common scheme that violated the law); *Severtson v. Phillips Beverage Co.*, 137 F.R.D. 264,267 (D. Minn. 1991). ('Requiring a showing that there is some factual basis for the class allegations... hardly places an unreasonable burden on the plaintiffs'); Vazquez, 2002 WL 58718, at *3, (certifying a class of employees who worked more than forty hours in one week, did not receive time-and-a-half pay, and received pay stubs that their employer altered to reflect payment of overtime compensation.).

[29] 252 F.3d at 1217–1219.

addresses the similarly situated question at two distinct stages in the litigation.[30] First, to justify sending initial notice, the plaintiff must make only a minimal initial showing that there are likely to be similarly situated potential plaintiffs.[31] After the class has been notified and discovery completed, the plaintiff must then establish that some class of plaintiffs is indeed similarly situated so that the court can certify the class.[32] Under this two-tiered approach, while the majority of the district courts that have applied it have granted conditional certification for the purpose of sending notice, a number have ultimately denied certification at stage two.[33] Indeed, that is exactly what happened in the *Thiessen* case.[34] On appeal, however, without invalidating the two-tier approach adopted by the district court, the Tenth Circuit reversed the decertification decision because the lower court did not conduct the proper analysis.[35]

10.1.2.2.3 A Minimal Burden, but a Burden Nonetheless Although the pre-notice burden on the plaintiffs to establish a similarly situated class is relatively light, courts still require some initial showing. For example, in *Wertheim v. Arizona*,[36] the court noted that it did not interpret the

---

[30] See *Thiessen v. Gen. Elec. Capital Corp.*, 996 F. Supp. 1071, 1080 (D. Kan. 1998); see also *Garza v. Chic. Transit Auth.*, No. OO-C-0438, 2001 WL 503036, at *2 (N.D. Ill. May 8, 2001).

[31] See ex., *Jackson*, 163 F.R.D. at 431. ('The inquiry at the inception of the lawsuit is less stringent than the ultimate determination that the class is properly constituted.'); *Harrington v. Educ. Mgmt. Corp.*, No. 02 Civ. 0787(HB), 2002 WL 1343753, at *1 (S.D:N.Y. June 19, 2002), (noting that 'opt-in notice at this early stage of litigation – at the outset of discovery – is to be construed broadly in furtherance of the remedial purposes of the FLSA').

[32] *Hall v. Burk*, No. Civ. 301CV2487H, 2002 WL 413901, at *2 (N.D. Tex. March 11, 2002); see also *Barnett v. Countrywide Credit Indus. Inc.*, No. CIV.A.3:Ol-CV-1182-M, 2002 WL 1023 161, at * 1 (N.D.T ex. May 21, 2002), (noting that if the court finds that the class no longer contains similarly situated persons after notice and discovery has occurred, it may decertify the class).

[33] See Thiessen, 996 F. Supp. at 1080 n. 12 (listing several cases).

[34] *Thiessen v. Gen. Elec. Capital Corp.*, 996 F. Supp. 107 1, 1083 (D. Kan. 1998)(granting conditional class certification) *Thiessen v. Gen. Elec. Capital Cow.*, 13 F. Supp. 2d 113 1, 1141 (D. Kan. 1998)(decertifying opt-in class and dismissing opt-in plaintiffs' claims).

[35] See *Thiessen v. Gen. Elec. Capital Corp.*, 267 F.3d 1095, 1106–1111 (10th Cir. 2001).

[36] No. Civ. 92-0453, 1992 WL 566321, at *5 (D. Ariz. August 4, 1992).

Supreme Court's ruling in *Sperling* as requiring the court to authorize notice 'to the broadest possible class of persons, based solely on the plaintiffs unsupported allegations, and decline to make even a preliminary determination of whether the potentially huge number of opt-in plaintiffs that may result actually are or may be similarly situated to the plaintiff.' The Court in *Wertheim* did not consider such an approach to be consistent with orderly management of the litigation, the recognized purpose for allowing early court-approved notice to potential plaintiffs.[37] Similarly, in *Severtson v. Phillips*, plaintiffs alleged that their former employer had a pattern and practice of terminating older, more highly-compensated workers in violation of the ADEA.[38] Plaintiffs eventually sought court-authorized notice to potential class members. Because the plaintiffs were seeking assistance from the court to expand the litigation, '[a]s a matter of sound case management,' the court noted that it had a duty to 'make a preliminary inquiry as to whether a manageable class exists.'[39] Likewise, in *White*, the court refused to certify a nationwide class of current and former employees who were allegedly 'similarly situated' with respect to their job duties and pay because there was no evidence that the employer's policies necessarily led to FLSA violations nationwide.[40] The court explained that certifying such a broad class would not 'partake of the economy of scale envisioned by the FLSA collective action procedure.'[41] Thus, the court limited notice to potential plaintiffs in Alabama.[42] The court also noted that 'courts ... have a responsibility to avoid the stirring up of litigation through unwarranted solicitation.'[43]

---

[37] *Ibid.*
[38] 137 F.R.D. at 266.
[39] *Ibid.*
[40] 204 F. Supp. 2d at 1318.
[41] *Ibid.*
[42] *Ibid.*
[43] *Id.* (quoting Severtson, 137 F.R.D. at 266). See also *Marsh v. Butler County Sch. Sys.*, No. CIV.A.02-A-788-N, 2003 WL 136192, at *6 (M.D. Ala. January 14, 2003), (noting that a plaintiff must show a commonality between his claims and those of the potential plaintiffs that is 'beyond the mere facts of job duties and pay provisions, because without such a requirement, it is doubtful that § 216(b) would further the interests of judicial economy.'); Sheffield, 21 1 F.R.D. at 413, ('Putative class members must share more than a common allegation that they were denied overtime or paid below the minimum wage. The class members must put forth a common legal theory upon which each member is entitled to relief'.).

CHAPTER 10. OPT-IN CLASS ACTIONS

10.1.2.2.4 District Courts Have Broad Discretion District courts are given wide latitude by appellate courts with respect to how they structure case management details, including the scope of actions and the propriety of notice of claims to potential class members.[44]

10.1.2.3 *Discovery Permitted to Assist in the Notice Process*

10.1.2.3.1 Allowing Plaintiffs to Discover Names, Addresses, and Other Information about Defendant's Current and Former Employees to Support Allegations that Potential Plaintiffs Are Similarly Situated and that Notice Is Warranted In general, the courts have held that 'some discovery is necessary prior to a determination of class certification' in an FLSA collective action.[45] Indeed, once a plaintiff has made a sufficient showing indicating the existence of other, similarly situated putative plaintiffs, the discovery of names and addresses and the sending of notice can, and often do, proceed simultaneously.[46] For example, in

---

[44] See e.g., In re Food Lion. Inc., 1998 WL 322682, at *11.

> (Given that this consolidated action had almost one thousand claims in the beginning of proceedings, this 'court will afford the district court significant latitude in its handling of pretrial matters and in its case management directives.)

White, 204 F. Supp. 2d at 13 12, ('District courts have discretionary power to authorize the sending of notice to potential class members in a collective action brought pursuant to § 216(b)'); Hipp, 252 F.3d at 1219, ('The decision to create an opt-in class under § 216(b), like the decision to certify a class under Rule 23, remains soundly within the discretion of the district court').

[45] *Tracy v. Dean Witter Revnolds, Inc.*, 185 F.R.D. 303, 304 (D. Colo. 1998); see also *Bradford v. Bed, Bath & Beyond, Inc.*, 184 F. Supp. 2d 1342, 1346 (N.D. Ga., January 5, 2002), (determining that employees were 'similarly situated' only after discovery occurred).

[46] See *Mooney v. Aramco Services Co.*, 54 F.3d 1207, 1213–1216 (5th Cir. 1995); *Lusardi v. Xerox Corp.*, 118 F.R.D. 351, 352 (D.N.J. 1987), mandamus manted in part, appeal dismissed, *Lusardi v. Lechner*, 855 F.2d 1062 (3rd Cir. 1988), vacated in part and remanded, *Lusardi v. Xerox Corp.*, 122 F.R.D. 463 (D.N.J. 1988), aff d in part. appeal dismissed, *Lusardi v. Xerox Corp.*, 975 F.2d 964 (3rd Cir. 1992); Bontempo, 2002 WL 192591 1, at *2, (allowing plaintiff to proceed with opt-in notice and ordering defendants to produce names and addresses of potential class members); Barnett, 2002 WL 1023 161, at *2, (simultaneously approving notice to potential class members and ordering defendant to produce names and addresses of potential class members).

Realite,[47] current and former hourly restaurant employees brought suit for minimum wage and overtime violations of the FLSA. The employees worked in fourteen restaurants in Manhattan and one in New Jersey. After the Court approved the sending of notice to prospective opt-ins, the defendant opposed the content of the notice on the grounds that the notice was inappropriate because the named plaintiffs were not similarly situated. Through the allegations in the complaint and affidavits, the Court found that the hourly paid employees at the fifteen restaurants had established that they were 'similarly situated.'[48] The Court held that early notice to potential plaintiffs, even before the defendant has had an opportunity to complete discovery, both effectuated the FLSA's remedial purpose and promoted case efficiency.[49] Accordingly, where a showing of similarly situated individuals is made, and even in some cases if it is not, it may be difficult to avoid some discovery or the sending of notice. The next battle then becomes limiting the extent and scope of the notice or discovery.

The case of *Walters v. Raymond James & Assocs., Inc.*,[50] is instructive on this issue. In that case, the court found that plaintiffs' first attempt to establish that there was a group of similarly situated employees failed. Nevertheless, the Court ordered defendant to produce documents to assist plaintiff in making such a showing, including:

(1) all documents relating to complaints by employees of failure to pay overtime;
(2) names of all such complaining employees;
(3) documents relating to exit interviews of non-exempt employees; and
(4) documents relating to investigations of any complaints of non-payment of overtime.

---

[47] 7 F. Supp. 2d at 306, 37.
[48] *Id.* at 308.
[49] See also *Schwed v. Gen. Elec. Co.*, 159 F.R.D. 373, 375 (N.D.N.Y. 1995)(noting that the remedial nature of the ADEA makes pre-discovery notice appropriate); *Jackson*, 163 F.R.D. at 43 1 (listing cases that support the use of notice at an early stage in FLSA actions); *Bailey v. Ameriquest Mortgage Co.*, No. CIV. 01-545 (JRTFLN), 2002 WL 100388, at *2 (D. Minn. January 23, 2002)(permitting discovery of names, addresses and telephone numbers of current and former account executives nationwide prior to determining whether plaintiffs met the 'similarly situated' requirement).
[50] No. 97-141 5-Civ-T-24C, slip. op. at 4 (M.D. Fla. January 13, 1998).

CHAPTER 10. OPT-IN CLASS ACTIONS

The plaintiffs also sought, but were denied, access to the following categories of documents for offices beyond the office where the opt-in plaintiffs worked:

(1) names and addresses of current/former employees;
(2) non-exempt employee time sheets;
(3) profit and loss statements;
(4) compensation records of non-exempt employees;
(5) non-exempt employee payroll updates;
(6) overtime compensation documentation for non-exempt employees;
(7) discipline resulting from non-compliance with overtime policy; and
(8) sign-in and sign-out sheets.

The court noted that:

> [a]s these requests seek information that is not relevant to plaintiff's preliminary burden of showing that there are other employees who are similarly situated, the requests are overly broad for this stage of the proceedings and are denied at this time.

10.1.2.3.2 Types of Information Found to Be Discoverable The required disclosure regarding potential 'class' members could include:

(1) Names;
(2) Addresses;
(3) Phone numbers; and
(4) Other information, such as hours worked, wages paid, and job descriptions.

10.1.2.3.3 Discovery of Names and Addresses The Supreme Court has held that a district court that permitted the plaintiffs discovery regarding the names and addresses of other potential plaintiffs was 'correct' in doing so.[51] Specifically, in *Hoffman-LaRoche*, the Supreme Court allowed an ADEA plaintiff, who had been discharged by his employer as a result of a reduction in force, to discover, at the beginning of the case, the names and addresses of other employees similarly discharged.[52] Following up

---

[51] Hoffrnann-La Roche, 493 U.S. at 170. ('The District Court was correct to permit discovery of the names and addresses of the discharged employees.').
[52] *Ibid.*

on the Supreme Court's confirmation of District Court discretion in this area, many courts have permitted the discovery of names and addresses.[53]

(1) In *Tucker*,[54] the Middle District of Florida permitted discovery as to the names and addresses of employees that were, inter alia, not exempt under the FLSA and who were not paid overtime pay to which they were entitled. The court noted that such discovery should be permitted so that the plaintiff could attempt to make a showing that other plaintiffs, particularly those out of the geographic area of the named plaintiff, were similarly situated.[55] The court did, however, limit such discovery to those individuals who were similarly situated to plaintiffs 'with respect to their job requirements and with regard to their pay provisions.'[56] For that reason, the court allowed discovery only with respect to three separate job categories – not the defendant's entire workforce as the plaintiffs had requested.

(2) Similarly, the Middle District of Tennessee required the defendant to provide the plaintiff with the names and addresses of:

> All present and former employees... who were paid on an hourly basis or under a fluctuating pay plan... within the three (3) years prior to the date the Complaint was filed in this case.[57]

The Court ruled that the twenty-four affidavits submitted by the plaintiffs constituted 'a sufficient showing that [defendant] failed to properly compensate [plaintiffs] as required by the FLSA.'[58]

(3) In *Adams*,[59] the United States Claims Court denied discovery of the names of potential additional plaintiffs in an FLSA action brought

---

[53] See e.g., *Tucker v. Labor Leasing. Inc.*, 155 F.R.D. 687, 689 (M.D. Fla. 1994)(at the start of discovery, and pre-notice and certification, allowing discovery of names and addresses of limited group of current employees); Contra *Adams v. United States*, 21 Cl. Ct. 795, 797 (Cl. Ct. 1990),(during discovery refusing to allow discovery of names and addresses of allegedly similarly-situated individuals).
[54] 155 F.R.D. at 689.
[55] *Ibid.*
[56] *Ibid.*
[57] *Belcher v. Shoney's, Inc.*, 927 F. Supp. 249, 252 (M.D. Tenn. 1996).
[58] *Id.* at 252–253.
[59] 21 Cl. Ct. at 797.

under §216(b) for overtime pay allegedly due to special agents. The Adams court noted that, unlike *Hoffman-LaRoche v. Sperling*, there was no relatively narrow, well defined issue or a specifically-defined group of potential plaintiffs, as '[r]ecovery is sought under four distinct theories.'[60] The case involved several different types of special agents who brought claims alleging that they were misclassified as exempt employees for purposes of the FLSA. The court denied the requested discovery, in part, because the issue of whether each plaintiff was in fact exempt would likely turn on unique circumstances, making 'each theory of recovery ... employee-specific.'[61]

(4) In *Bailey v. Ameriquest Mortgage Co.*,[62] a group of account executives brought an FLSA action to recover unpaid overtime compensation. The District of Minnesota affirmed a magistrate's order compelling discovery of the names; addresses, telephone numbers, branch locations and dates of employment for all account executives.[63] In doing so, the court relied upon *Hoffman-LaRoche v. Sperling*,[64] and rejected the defendant's argument that before compelling disclosure, the court had to determine that the account executives were similarly situated.[65]

10.1.2.4 Approaches to Arguing in Favor of Notice

10.1.2.4.1 Notice Permitted Based Solely on Class-Wide Allegations of Illegality   At least one court has permitted notice to potential plaintiffs based solely on an allegation of class-wide practices in violation of the ADEA.[66] In *Allen*, in response to the defendant's objection that notice was inappropriate, the court noted that differences in treatment between the potential plaintiffs – some were demoted, some were forced into early retirement, and some were transferred – was mainly

---

[60] *Ibid.*
[61] *Ibid.*
[62] 2002 WL 1835642, at *2 (D. Minn. August 5, 2002).
[63] *Ibid.*
[64] 493 U.S. at 170.
[65] *Ibid.*
[66] *Allen v. Marshall Field & Co.*, 93 F.R.D. 438, 442–443 (N.D. Ill. 1982).

relevant to the amount of damages, not to the question of which plaintiffs were similarly situated.[67]

10.1.2.4.2 Notice Permitted Based upon Allegations and Supporting Proof Yet another approach requires both an allegation of class-wide discrimination and modest factual support for the allegation in the form of affidavits.[68] In *Grayson*, the plaintiffs met this burden by producing affidavits from statistical experts, which supported their allegations of class-wide discrimination.[69] On the other side of the issue, in *Ray v. Motel 6 Operating, Ltd.*,[70] the court refused to grant notice to potential class members, and held that discovery as to whether notice would be appropriate was unnecessary, based on an 'extensive' showing that the employees were not similarly situated. In *Ray*, the court cited extensive evidence that the potential class members worked at different locations, in different states, the locations varied widely in size and operations, and that the allegedly illegal overtime plan was not camed out through central management.[71]

In these cases, which reached opposite conclusions, the courts were focused on the factual showing that was, or was not, made as to whether individuals were similarly situated. This appears to be the approach taken by the majority of the courts that have considered the propriety of 'class-based' discovery and notice in FLSA actions.

10.1.2.5 Arguments that Can Be Used to Oppose the Sending of Notice

Because both the initial justification for sending notice and the subsequent ultimate certification of the 'class' depend on the plaintiffs

---

[67] *Ibid.* See also Belcher, 927 F. Supp. at 251, (noting the disagreement between the position taken by the Allen court and the courts requiring some factual showing to warrant notice to potential plaintiffs).

[68] See Grayson, 79 F.3d at 1097 (citation omitted), (requiring 'detailed allegations supported by affidavits which successfully engage defendants' affidavits to the contrary').

[69] *Id.* at 1097.

[70] 1996 WL 93823 1, at *4 (D. Minn. March 18, 1996).

[71] *Ibid.*

CHAPTER 10. OPT-IN CLASS ACTIONS

ability to show that a group of similarly situated individuals exists, the following arguments can be made:

(1) to avoid 'class-based' discovery or the sending of notice; and
(2) to discontinue conditional certification or to decertify a class.

10.1.2.5.1 Challenges to Allegations Made without Supporting Evidence that a Potential Class Exists

(1) The District of Maryland denied plaintiffs' motion to send notice in *D'Anna v. M/A-COM, Inc.*,[72] where plaintiffs' allegations of ADEA violations were 'broad and vague' and lacked 'factual support' for the existence of a potential class. Plaintiff alleged that representatives of M/A terminated individuals over the age of forty and that these terminations, as well as the termination of plaintiff, were motivated by discriminatory animus.[73]

(2) In *Klegerman v. F.G. Apparel, Inc.*,[74] plaintiff sued his employer alleging that his termination resulted from age bias in violation of the ADEA. Plaintiff alleged that 'in addition to firing plaintiff, defendant fired other persons between the ages of forty and seventy because of their age, and replaced these terminated persons with younger employees under the age of forty.'[75] The court held that these allegations failed to establish that there were any similarly situated plaintiffs such that notice would be appropriate.[76]

(3) In *Hayes v. Singer Co. Inc.*,[77] two opt-in plaintiffs in a §216(b) action sued Singer Company for unpaid overtime wages. While both plaintiffs previously worked at a Tallahassee store, plaintiffs requested that notice be distributed to all Singer employees in Florida.[78] The Eleventh Circuit affirmed the district judge's refusal to grant state-wide notice based only on 'counsel's unsupported assertions that FLSA

---

[72] 903 F. Supp. 889, 894 @. Md. 1995).
[73] *Ibid.*
[74] No. 85 C 7887, 1986 WL 253 1, at * 1 (N.D. Ill. February 11, 1986).
[75] *Id.* at *6.
[76] *Ibid.*
[77] 696 F.2d 884, 885 (11th Cir. 1983).
[78] *Id.* at 884.

violations were widespread and that additional plaintiffs would come from other stores.'[79]

(4) In *Severtson*,[80] a case in which five plaintiffs alleged they had been terminated because of their age in violation of the ADEA, the court initially held that notice and discovery of names and addresses was not appropriate because plaintiffs offered only conclusory allegations of age discrimination and their personal observations of the firing. older employees and replacing them with younger ones. Upon rehearing, the court approved notice finding sufficient plaintiffs' evidence, in the form of affidavits and other documents, that:

> (a) five plaintiffs' terminations were part of a company-wide action;
> (b) corporate headquarters made all employment decisions; and
> (c) plaintiffs had observed other age-based terminations and gave names and other details.[81]

(5) In *Hall*,[82] the plaintiff asserted that her employer violated the FLSA because she and other employees did not receive salaries or overtime payments in accordance with the employer's fluctuating work week plan. The court denied the plaintiff's motion to send notice because the plaintiff 'failed to present sufficient evidence that similarly situated plaintiffs exist[ed].'[83] The court reasoned that instead of submitting affidavits or names of potential plaintiffs, the plaintiff merely put forth a 'conclusory allegation' that the employer improperly deducted from the employees' salaries.[84]

10.1.2.5.2 Challenges Based upon the Argument that a Representative Plaintiff is Not Similarly Situated to Putative Class Members, or because Individualized Facts Would Apply to Each Plaintiff A defendant can also attempt to defeat notice or discovery, or move to decertify a 'class,' by showing that a named plaintiff or plaintiffs are not similarly situated to

---

[79] *Id.* at 887.
[80] 137 F.R.D. at 266.
[81] *Severtson v. Phillips Beverage Co.*, 141 F.R.D. 276, 279–280 (D. Minn. 1992).
[82] 2002 WL 41 3901, at * 1.
[83] *Id.* at *3.
[84] *Ibid.*

other putative plaintiffs. A defendant can also prevail by showing that no, or very few, individuals are similarly situated because of different fact scenarios or theories of recovery.

(1) In *Bayles v. American Medical Response, Inc.*,[85] employees of an ambulance service alleged failure to pay overtime and the improper deduction of meal and sleep time hours from their pay. The District of Colorado decertified the conditionally certified class, to whom notice had already been sent, finding that only those class members who were dispatchers were 'similarly situated,' and that, for the rest of the class, the case was 'fraught with questions requiring distinct proof as to individual plaintiffs,' [including call volume and the policies each employee had agreed to].[86]

(2) In *Lusardi*,[87] the court found that putative §216(b) ADEA class members were not similarly situated because of dramatic differences of age, job posting, compensation, alleged adverse employment action, and geographic location between them, as well as variation in the defenses that could apply to each.

(3) In *Sheffield*,[88] the court found that putative class members were not similarly situated because each of their claims would require 'extensive consideration of individualized issues of liability and damages.' The class members worked at different subsidiaries, held different job titles and enjoyed different payment structures.[89] Moreover, the plaintiffs failed to establish that they were commonly affected by a uniform plan or scheme to deny overtime compensation and minimum wages.[90]

10.1.2.5.3 Challenges Based on Geographic Factors, Such as No Evidence of Nationwide, Statewide, or Class-Wide Wrongdoing Defendants can also challenge the propriety of notice or discovery or seek to decertify a 'class,' by showing that no evidence of a geographically broad-based

---

[85] 950 F. Supp. 1053, 1067 (D. Colo. 1996).
[86] *Ibid.*
[87] 118 F.R.D. at 351–375.
[88] 211 F.R.D. at 413.
[89] *Ibid.*
[90] *Ibid.*

practice or policy exists, or by affirmatively producing evidence that significant differences exist among facilities, locations, or even departments.

(1) To succeed in establishing a statewide or nationwide action, plaintiffs must allege some facts in support of their contention that a policy was company-wide. As Judge Shlatter of the District of Colorado noted:

> Even if it is true that some individuals failed to receive appropriate compensation for hours which were worked overtime, that fact alone does not lead me to conclude that there must be some unlawful national policy out there somewhere.[91]

In response to such an argument, defendants can argue that allegedly unlawful decisions were made locally, by individual offices and managers and were not company-wide, thus limiting the breadth of the notice class.

(2) In *Ray*,[92] the court refused to grant notice to potential class members, citing evidence that the class members worked at different locations in different states, the locations themselves varied in size and types of operations, and that the actual amounts of overtime allegedly worked varied from plaintiff to plaintiff, which 'demonstrate[d] a lack of commonality for damages.'[93]

(3) In *Tucker*,[94] the plaintiffs worked at the Jacksonville terminal of a company that allegedly owed them unpaid overtime. They alleged that the defendant failed to pay overtime at all of its locations and requested permission to send nationwide notice.[95] The court denied the plaintiffs' request for notice holding that the plaintiffs had to show that employees located elsewhere were similarly situated before a notice could be issued outside the Jacksonville, Florida, terminal.[96] The court did

---

[91] Tracy, 185 F.R.D. at 311.
[92] 1996 WL 938231, at *4.
[93] *Ibid.*
[94] 155 F.R.D. at 689.
[95] *Ibid.*
[96] *Ibid.*

CHAPTER 10. OPT-IN CLASS ACTIONS

allow discovery to enable the plaintiff to make such a showing if possible.[97]

(4) Contesting the existence of any company-wide policy is important because such a policy may serve to overcome factual differences between the plaintiffs, who may be similarly situated as to the policy, and increase the likelihood that a court will authorize broad-based notice. As the Court noted in *Crain v. Helmerich & Payne International Drilling Co.*:[98]

> That the plaintiffs and the potential claimants may have worked in different areas of the country, on different types of rigs, and performed different jobs is not dispositive.... [W]hat matters is that the fundamental allegation – that according to company policy the time spent in job related meetings and training was uncompensated – is 'common to all the [FLSA] plaintiffs and dominates each of their claims.

(5) Just as the existence of nationwide policy provides strong support for broad-based notice or discovery, the existence of state-, department-, or division-specific policies or procedures, which differ among themselves in content and for application, provides strong support that narrowly circumscribed discovery or notice is appropriate.[99] In *Wertheim*, the plaintiff worked for the Department of Public Safety ('DPS') for the State of Arizona. Plaintiffs moved to send notice of a collective action to all state workers who were not paid for overtime worked.[100] The court denied the request, finding that DPS used its own system of classifying employees as exempt or non-exempt and, consequently, plaintiff failed to establish class wide wrongdoing for all state employees.[101]

(6) Courts have also held that that evidence that a company expressly prohibited a certain complained of practice and enforced

---

[97] *Ibid.*; see also Haynes, 696 F.2d at 888 (upholding denial of request for statewide notice where plaintiffs, employees at the same area store, presented no evidence to support allegations of statewide FLSA violations).

[98] No. Civ. A. 92-0043, 1992 WL 91946, at *3 (E.D. La. April 16, 1992) (citation omitted).

[99] Wertheim, 1992 WL 566321, at * 1.

[100] *Ibid.*

[101] *Id.* at *2.

the prohibition, or required a certain practice and enforced it, creates a strong inference that an action or inaction contrary to the policy was an isolated phenomenon. For example, an official company policy that outlines and requires lawful procedures for overtime payment may allow an employer to argue that any unlawful practices were effectuated on a local, and not company-wide, level. In *Ulvin v. Northwestern National Life Insurance Co.*,[102] the court held that members of an ADEA collective action were not similarly situated where the company's RIF plan specifically provided that age could not be used as a factor.[103]

(7) In *White*,[104] the plaintiff, an hourly-paid foreman, alleged that he and other foremen and crewmen did not receive proper compensation. He argued that the appropriate class of plaintiffs should include current and former foremen and crewmen nationwide.[105] The court refused to certify a nationwide class, concluding that the evidence did not necessarily indicate that widespread illegal policies or practices existed.[106] Moreover, such a broad certification would not 'partake of the economy of scale envisioned by the FLSA collective action procedure.'[107] Thus, the court conditionally certified only foremen in Alabama.[108]

10.1.2.5.4 Challenges Based upon Factual Differences in Pay Status, Job Requirements, Duties, Departments, Etc. Even if broad, statewide or nationwide notice or discovery is sought, and perhaps even likely to be ordered, a defendant can seek to limit the scope of the notice or discovery to discrete categories of jobs, or to individuals with the same pay status, (i.e., commission, salaried, hourly), having the same job requirements, (i.e., working at remote locations), or performing the same duties, (i.e., driving a truck).

---

[102] 141 F.R.D. 130, 131 @. Minn. 1991).

[103] *Ibid.* (noting further that 'the plan's implementation was to be achieved on a decentralized level by local management'). See also Ray, 1996 WL 93823 1, at * 4 (refusing to grant notice to potential class members, citing evidence that allegedly illegal overtime policy was instituted on local rather than company-wide level).

[104] 204 F. Supp. 2d at 1311.

[105] *Id.* at 1314.

[106] *Id.* at 1318.

[107] *Ibid.*

[108] *Ibid.*

10.1.2.5.4.1 Limits Based upon Different Job Requirements or Duties

(a) In *Mooney v. Arabian American Oil Co.*,[109] the court, on defendant's motion, and after a conditional issuance of notice and a four-year discovery period, dismissed the claims of the opt-in plaintiffs, who were alleging age discrimination, under the ADEA, finding that they were not similarly situated. The Court found:

> Plaintiffs were employed by at least ninety-three different Aramco departments scattered over eleven separate locations in Saudi Arabia. Virtually every plaintiff worked in a different division of the company and held a distinct job title requiring different job skills. Moreover, Plaintiffs differ significantly in employment characteristics such as job tenure (varying from one to thirty-four years), employment history, salary grade, qualifications, and education. In addition, the court found that the Plaintiffs were discharged from their employment in several different years upon the recommendation of different decision-making supervisors for a variety of stated reasons.[110]

(b) In the securities industry, a defendant might argue that sales assistants, wire operators, and cashiers are not similarly situated due to the differences in their job tasks. Employees might be distinguished, as well, on the basis of whether they were registered with an exchange or possessed securities licenses.

(c) In *Donihoo v. Dallas Airmotive, Inc.*,[111] the court held that sending notice of an FLSA collective action brought by the plaintiff, a customer service representative allegedly misclassified as exempt, to every salaried employee was inappropriate. The Court further held that determining exempt status under the FLSA for each individual class member from among several potential categories requires an examination of an employee's job duties that 'is not appropriate in a class lawsuit under Section 216(b).'[112]

---

[109] No. Civ.A. H-87-498, 1993 WL 739661, at *1. (S.D. Tex. August 25, 1993).
[110] *Id.* at * 9.
[111] No. Civ. A.3:97-CV-0109-P, 1998 WL 91256, at *1 (N.D. Tex. February 23, 1998).
[112] *Ibid.*

10.1.2.5.4.2 Limits Based upon Different Pay Provisions Employers may be able to distinguish employees on the basis of whether they are exempt or non-exempt, or paid on commission, salary, or an hourly basis. In addition, whether and how employees get bonuses, comp time, sleep time, and meal breaks may also affect their eligibility for overtime compensation under the FLSA.

> (a) In *Wertheim*,[113] the plaintiff alleged that his employer deliberately misclassified him as an exempt employee to avoid paying him overtime. Plaintiff wanted to send notice to all employees to whom overtime compensation was due; but the court noted that such a definition of the class would include both non-exempt employees who were not correctly paid, as well as 'exempt' employees who were misclassified.[114] The court restricted notice to those employees who, like the named plaintiff, were classified as exempt.[115]
>
> (b) In *Bayles*,[116] ambulance service employees brought a collective action under the FLSA against their employers for overtime due them for uncompensated meal and sleep time accrued during twenty-four hour shifts. The court noted that 'this case is fraught with questions requiring distinct proof as to individual plaintiffs. Issues requiring individualized proof, such as call volume, sleep habits, conditions at particular stations, and treatment under [the employer's] mealtime policy, dominate plaintiffs' claims.'[117] Consequently, the court found that the group was not 'similarly situated' as required by §216(b).

10.1.2.5.5 Other Bases for Challenges

> (1) Coverage under a Collective Bargaining Agreement: In *Adams*,[118] the United States Claims Court noted that certain individuals were covered by collective bargaining agreements which might address whether someone was exempt or

---

[113] 1992 WL 56632 1, at * 1.
[114] *Id.* at *3.
[115] *Ibid.*
[116] 950 F. Supp. at 1053.
[117] *Id.* at 1067.
[118] 21 Cl. Ct. at 797.

CHAPTER 10. OPT-IN CLASS ACTIONS

non-exempt and, thus, potential plaintiffs may not be similarly situated.

(2) Conflict of Interest: In *White*,[119] the court concluded that the conditionally certified class should not include both crewmen and foremen because the foremen were responsible for keeping track of and accurately reporting their crew members' payroll information.[120] Thus, the foremen could be held individually liable for potential claims of crewmen, which created an 'inherent conflict of interest' between the two groups.[121]

10.1.2.5.6 Temporal Limits (Statute of Limitations) upon the Scope of Discovery or Notice The FLSA has a three-year statute of limitations for willful violations.[122] Accordingly, a number of courts have limited notice to a three-year period.[123] The notice period applies retroactively from the date the original complaint was filed.[124]

A longer statute of limitations period may be permissible where a complaint also contains a claim for overtime or wages under a state law with a longer statue of limitations. In *Realite*,[125] the Court allowed notice to be sent to all employees within a six-year period because the claim for overtime, inter alia, was brought under both the FLSA and the New York state labor laws, which have a six-year statute of limitations.[126]

---

[119] 204 F. Supp. 2d at 1314.

[120] *Ibid.*

[121] *Ibid.*

[122] 29 U.S.C. § 255(a).

[123] *Dole v. Elliot Travel & Tours. Inc.*, 942 F.2d 962, 966–67 (6th Cir. 1991), citing Mc Laughlin v. Richland Shoe Co., 486 U.S.'1 28 (1988)); see also Vazquez, 2002 WL 58718, at *4 (limiting notice to a three-year period).

[124] See Belcher, 927 F. Supp. at 252 (noting that since the applicable statute of limitations under the FLSA is three years for a willful violation, notice should be restricted to people employed within the three years prior to when the complaint was filed); White, 204 F. Supp. 2d at 13 18 (applying three-year notice period retroactively from date of original lawsuit).

[125] 7 F. Supp. 2d at 308.

[126] See also Harrington, 2002 WL 1343753, at *2 (permitting notice to go back six years for employees in New York, pursuant to a New York state labor law, and limiting notice to three years for employees outside of New York).

10.1.2.6 Other Miscellaneous Points about Notice

10.1.2.6.1 Nondisclosure Agreements and the Attorney-Client Privilege
Several years ago a former general manager and co-manager of a Sbarro's restaurant sought to bring a 'collective action' lawsuit under the FLSA on behalf of all current and former managers for unpaid overtime compensation. They claimed that the company improperly classified them as 'executives' in an effort to deny them overtime. In response to the lawsuit, Sbarro attorneys sought a court order prohibiting the plaintiffs' attorneys from obtaining information from other current and former Sbarro employees.[127] The company argued that the lawyers were trying to obtain information from the employees in violation of the attorney-client privilege and a nondisclosure agreement that covered all Sbarro employees.[128] With respect to the nondisclosure agreements, the court found that the litigation did not involve 'competition-related information... such as... secret recipes,' and thus that the nondisclosure agreements would not be breached if the managers in question were notified about the lawsuit.[129] With respect to the attorney-client the court recognized that '[t]here is often a tension between the need to obtain information efficiently during litigation and the danger that informal discovery will breach the attorney-client privilege'[130] The court noted that this conflict has led many courts to restrict communications between plaintiffs' attorneys and employees of a corporate defendant.[131] The court concluded, however, that this was not the appropriate outcome in this case because the corporate employees in question were potential plaintiffs in the litigation.[132] The court explained that imposing significant restrictions on the ability of the plaintiffs' attorneys to communicate with corporate employees would hamper those employees ability to 'litigate their own rights.'[133] The court also cited the fact that Sbarro's attorneys had not identified a single example of an attorney-client communication with any potential

---

[127] *Hoffman v. Sbarro, Inc.*, No. 97 Civ. 4484, 1997 WL 736703, at *1-*2 (S.D.N.Y. November 26,1997).
[128] *Id.* at * 1.
[129] *Id.* at *1–*2.
[130] *Id.* at *2 (citation omitted).
[131] *Ibid.*
[132] *Ibid.*
[133] *Ibid.*

member of the class.[134] This ruling cleared the way for the managers to bring a large collective action that resulted in a settlement of approximately USD 3.5 million.[135]

10.1.2.6.2 Potentially Applicable Local Rules of Civil Procedure As discussed below, local jurisdictions may have their own rules of civil procedure that address the issue(s) of class discovery, notice and for contact with potential plaintiffs.[136] Accordingly, a careful search of the local civil procedures rules should be done in every FLSA action.

10.1.3 Communication with Class Plaintiffs

10.1.3.1 Generally

Section 216(b) does not expressly address the issue of communication with putative class members. Instead, the provision's silence has led the courts to take up the issue specifically with respect to the sending of notice. In *Hoffinan-LaRoche v. Sperling*,[137] the Supreme Court upheld the district court's order authorizing notice to potential ADEA class members on the ground that the order constituted a proper exercise of the district court's authority. However, the Court specifically declined to address 'any conflicts between court-authorized notice and communications with potential plaintiffs' because that issue was 'not implicated' in the case before the Court.[138] Indeed, the question as to whether parties or their counsel may communicate with putative class members in the collective action context remains unanswered in many jurisdictions.[139] However, even when courts permit pre-certification communication

---

[134] *Ibid.*

[135] Manny Topol, Court Takes Labor Violations Seriously, Newsday, March 1, 1999, available at 1999 WL 8159745.

[136] See e.g., M.D. Fla. L.R. Civ. P. 404(e).

[137] 493 U.S. 165 (1989).

[138] *Id.*, at 487 n. 2.

[139] See Bontempo, 2002 WL 192591 1, at *2, (ordering defendants to refrain from 'any and all communication' regarding FLSA claims with current or putative class members during notice stage); but see *O'Brien v. Morse*, No. 02 C 50026, 2002 WL 1290392, at *2 (N.D. Ill. June 11, 2002), (denying plaintiffs request that during the notice stage defendant refrain from communicating with potential class members);

with putative plaintiffs in a collective action, they can restrict such communication if the communication misleads potential plaintiffs or contradicts or undermines the court's notice.[140]

While *Sperling* counsels that court authorized notice is not mandatory, the ethical question of the solicitation of claims may prompt counsel to seek such prior approval. In the Middle District of Florida, the local rules of civil procedure specifically prohibit plaintiffs' attorneys from communicating with potential members of a class without court approval.[141] Such rules may be used by defense attorneys to prevent or delay communications between FLSA plaintiffs' attorneys and potential collective action members. Whether an argument based on this type of rule will succeed will depend on whether the court in question construes the rule to apply to collective actions in addition to traditional class actions. One Florida district court, which addressed this issue in the context of an FLSA collective action, without deciding the question, stated that the local rule may not be applicable to collective actions.[142] The court reasoned that since the rule is entitled 'Class Action,' refers only to Rule 23, and does not refer to any other statute, rule or any other type of representative suit it is possible that the rule does not apply.[143]

Unlike § 216(b), Rule 23 provides some direction as to communication with class members, specifically regarding the sending of notice.[144] Moreover, the Supreme Court has made clear that prior to certification

---

Parks v. Eastwood Ins. Servs. Inc., 235 F. Supp. 2d 1082, 1083 (C.D. Ca. 2002), (permitting pre-certification communication with prospective plaintiffs in a collective action, noting that 'for purposes of defense communication with § 216(b) prospective plaintiffs, the situation is analogous to a pre-certification Rule 23 class action, when the prospective plaintiffs are still unrepresented parties').

[140] See *Id.* at *1085.

[141] See M.D. Fla. L.R. Civ. P. 4.04(e),

> (In every case sought to be maintained by any party as a class action, all parties thereto and their counsel are hereby forbidden, directly or indirectly, orally or in writing, to communicate concerning such action with any potential or actual class member, not a formal party to the case without approval by order of the Court.).

[142] *Tucker v. Labor Leasing. Inc.*, 872 F. Supp. 941, 949 (M.D. Fla. 1994).

[143] *Ibid.*

[144] See Fed. R. Civ. P. 23.

CHAPTER 10. OPT-IN CLASS ACTIONS

communication with putative class members is permissible.[145] In *Gulf Oil*, the Supreme Court held that in a Rule 23 class action, an order suppressing almost all communication by counsel for the parties with potential class members violated Rule 23 of the Federal Rules of Civil Procedure unless it was shown that there was a need for the restriction in speech and that the order was carefully drawn to limit speech as little as possible. In *Gulf Oil*, notice of a conciliation agreement reached between Gulf Oil and the EEOC in an earlier race discrimination class action was sent to approximately 600 eligible employees. Shortly after the conciliation agreement was signed, respondents filed a class action alleging race discrimination on behalf of a similar group of present and former employees of Gulf Oil. Soon after being served with the complaint, counsel for Gulf Oil filed a motion seeking an order limiting communications by parties and their counsel with class members. Defense counsel had become aware that counsel for respondents had met with putative class members and recommended that they not sign the releases pursuant to the conciliation agreement, and that they return the checks. The district court entered an order prohibiting all communications between the parties or their counsel and any actual or potential class member who was not a formal party without the court's prior approval. The Supreme Court held that the district court order was improper and in excess of the authority provided to the court by the Rule 23.

Post certification class members are deemed to be represented by class counsel unless they opt out. Therefore, courts often impose orders restricting the ability of an employer or its counsel to communicate with class members about the litigation, the claims raised in the litigation, or, even more broadly, matters relating to the claims of the litigation.[146] Additionally, ethical rules governing the conduct of attorneys may prevent contact with plaintiffs who are represented by counsel.[147]

---

[145] See *Gulf Oil Co. v. Bernard*, 452 U.S. 89, 101–105 (1981).

[146] See *Fulco v. Continental Cablevision. Inc.*, 789 F. Supp. 45, 48 (D. Mass. 1992)(imposing order restricting communication with class plaintiffs post certification); *Bontempo*; 2002 WL 192591 1, at *2 (ordering defendants to refrain from 'any and all communication' regarding FLSA claims with current or putative class members).

[147] *Haffer v. Temple Univ.*, 115 F.R.D. 506, 510 (E.D. Pa. 1987)(holding that defendant's communication with plaintiff class members violated anti-contact rules given the existence of an attorney-client relationship); *Tedesco v. Mishkin*, 629 F. Supp. 1474, 1482–1484 (S.D.N.Y. 1986)(same).

EMPLOYMENT CLASS AND COLLECTIVE ACTIONS

Nevertheless, it is within the province of the district court to authorize the communication and thereby take it outside the strictures of rules prohibiting contact.[148] While none of these restrictions would arguably apply before individuals have opted-in to an FLSA action, it would be prudent to assume that they would apply once a consent form has been filed.

10.1.3.2 Special Considerations Regarding Communication with Managerial Employees

In a case where a single plaintiff who is a manager or assistant manager claims an entitlement to overtime, a key aspect of the employer's investigation of that claim would be to speak with the employees supervised by that manager and with any other management employee who would have knowledge of the plaintiffs work activities. Under those circumstances, there would be no dispute that such communications are proper and necessary. In the context of a class or collective wage and hour action, however, courts are very concerned about defense counsel using an opportunity to speak with class members or potential class members to either discourage participation in the action or to obtain damaging admissions.

As stated above, under Rule 23 employer defendants can communicate with putative class members before the class is certified.[149] But, they do so at their peril. When conducting an investigation and interrogating putative class members, an employer and its counsel must always be sensitive to the reality that class counsel will subsequently have access to the class members. In order to reduce the chances of alienating such witnesses or creating hostility, some preventive steps should be taken. In conducting an interview, disclosure should be made to class members as to the identity of the interviewer where the employer uses outside counsel, including who counsel is representing and what information the interviewer is trying to gather. The interviewee needs to know that he or she need not cooperate if that is his or

---

[148] *United States v. Lopez*, 4 F.3d 1455, 1461–1462 (9th Cir. 1993), (holding that court order can except a lawyer from the anti-contact rule).

[149] See Gulf Oil, 452 U.S. at 89; *Abdallah v. Coca-Cola Co.*, 186 F.R.D. 672, 674 n. 1 (N.D. Ga. 1999), (indicating that absent a showing of abuse (or a local court order), the defendant may continue to communicate with putative class members prior to class certification).

her desire, and that anything that the individual says will not impact in any way upon his or her employment. It is good practice to obtain a written acknowledgment of such disclosures from the interviewee with an attestation to his or her acquiescence to the interview.

In the collective action context, an individual does not become a plaintiff unless and until he or she takes affirmative action to opt in to the litigation. Accordingly, much like the situation in a Rule 23 class action before the class has been certified, an employer is generally free to communicate with potential plaintiffs free of restrictions unless and until the individual affirmatively opts in to the litigation, or the court has legitimate concerns of potential abuse.[150] If the court has legitimate concerns for potential abuse, it may issue a protective order prohibiting or limiting communications with potential plaintiffs.[151] The United States District Court for the Central District of California recently came to largely the same conclusion in *Parks v. Eastwood*.[152] The Court in that case, like the court in *O'Brien*, concluded that since pre-certification communications with putative class members in a Rule 23 class action is permitted unless restrictions are necessary to correct serious misconduct, the same should hold true in the § 216(b) context.[153] The Parks court thus concluded that pre opt-in communications with potential plaintiffs in a § 216(b) collective action are permissible unless the communications undermine or contradict the court's § 216(b) notice to potential plaintiffs.[154]

The court stated that if an undermining or contradictory communication is sent, the court, in its discretion, could impose sanctions, require payment for curative notices, regulate or restrict future ex parte communications, or order other appropriate relief.[155]

As a result, the cautionary measures described above with regard to pre-certification communications in a Rule 23 class action apply equally to pre opt-in communications with potential plaintiffs in a § 216(b) collective action. Indeed, as in the Rule 23 context, class counsel

---

[150] *O'Brien v. Morse*, 2002 WL 1290392 at *2 (citing Gulf Oil).
[151] *Ibid.*
[152] 235 F. Supp. 2d 1082 (C.C. Cal. December 3, 2002).
[153] *Id.* at 1084 (citing Gulf Oil).
[154] *Id.* at 1085.
[155] *Ibid.*

in a § 216(b) collective action will likely have access to the interviewee at some point later in the litigation. It is important to note, however, that at least one court has forbidden a defendant from communicating with putative class members even before notice of the right to opt-in was issued.[156] Accordingly, in the collective action context, it is critical to determine whether there exists any authority in the jurisdiction in which the action was filed prohibiting even pre opt-in communications with potential plaintiffs. In the absence of such authority, the majority rule and the better reasoned analysis is that a defendant can communicate with potential plaintiffs before they affirmatively opt in to the litigation in largely the same manner as a defendant would communicate with putative class members in a Rule 23 class action before the class has been certified.

Once a class has been certified under Rule 23, the broad orders restricting communication often imposed by courts can create serious problems in defending the litigation. For example, courts might limit:

- an employer's ability to speak to a class member about the claims of another class member (i.e., preventing the defendant from speaking to a manager about the activities of his or her assistant manager, or vice versa) as would naturally occur in a single plaintiff case;
- disciplinary communications arising with respect to core issues of the litigation, for example, a failure to delegate or properly supervise, a failure to effectively schedule employees or otherwise to overspend the budget, all of which relate directly to the exempt status of the individual; or
- the ability of the employer to express its expectations of how class members should perform their jobs (i.e., 'managers should be delegating certain tasks, or should not be engaging in a certain task' where those tasks help define the manager's exempt status).

One can see how this affects not only an employer's ability to mount its defense, but the employer's ability to manage its employees and run its business on a day-to-day basis.

---

[156] See *Bontempo*, 2002 WL 192591 1 at *2.

An employer is afforded little flexibility in dealing with these problems when the individual with whom the communications are sought is represented by counsel by virtue of being a member of a certified Rule 23 class or filing a consent to become a plaintiff in a collective action. In a collective action under Section 216(b), an individual who has filed a consent to join in the action becomes a plaintiff in the case. He or she is thus a represented party in the same manner as he or she would be if he or she filed an individual action against the employer. In such circumstances, the employer has little ability to communicate with the collective action plaintiff in the absence of plaintiffs' counsel. A defendant seeking to communicate ex parte with such an individual would, in the absence of agreement by plaintiffs' counsel, be forced to either petition the court for an order either excluding the individual from the collective action or authorizing the communications at issue. Even if permission were granted to speak with the individual, however, the employer must be cognizant of the fact that it is speaking with a plaintiff – i.e., an adverse party – and therefore may be deemed to have waived the attorney-client privilege with respect to the communications.

10.1.4 FLSA Statute of Limitations

10.1.4.1 Two-Year Statute of Limitations for Non-willful Violations; Three-Year Statute of Limitations for Willful Violations

The Portal-to-Portal Act provides the following statute of limitations for the FLSA:

> [I]f the cause of action accrues on or after May 14, 1947 – may be commenced within two years after the cause of action accrued, and every such action shall be forever barred unless commenced within two years after the cause of action accrued, except that a cause of action arising out of a willful violation may be commenced within three years after the cause of action accrued.[157]

---

[157] 29 U.S.C. 255(a).

EMPLOYMENT CLASS AND COLLECTIVE ACTIONS

10.1.4.2 When the Statute of Limitations Runs

10.1.4.2.1 Generally In the context of a collective action, the statute of limitations runs as to each individual plaintiff until that plaintiff files a consent form with the court.[158]

10.1.4.2.2 No Relation Back Plaintiffs filing untimely consents cannot have their claims relate back to the original complaint.[159]

10.1.4.2.3 Continuing Violations In the context of the FLSA, an employer's failure to adequately compensate an employee accrues at each payday, i.e., with each paycheck, that follows the allegedly uncompensated work period.[160] In other words, the employer's conduct constitutes a continuing violation from the time between when the overtime is actually worked and the time the employee is paid.[161]

---

[158] *Grayson v. Kmart Corp.*, 79 F.3d 1086, 1105 (11th Cir. 1996)('[O]pt-in plaintiffs commence an ADEA civil action, not when the complaint is filed, but when the plaintiff files a written consent to opt into the class action.'); *O'Connell v. Champion Int'l Corp.*, 812 F.2d 393, 394 (same). "'Until a plaintiff, even a named plaintiff, has filed a written consent, [ ]he has not joined in the class action, at least for statute of limitations purposes.'" In re Food Lion, Inc., 1998 WL 322682, at *13, (4th Cir. June 4, 1998),(quoting *Songu-Mbriwa v. Davis Mem'l Goodwill Indus. Inc.*, 144 F.R.D. 1,2 (1992), (ruling on an Equal Pay Act claim brought under 8 2 16(b)), dismissed by, No. 95-7060, 1996 WL 467692 (D.C. Cir. August 15, 1996)); see also Bailey, 2002 WL 1835642, at *l, (statute of limitations for putative plaintiffs continues to run until they file consent forms with the court); *Tate v. Showboat Marina Casino*, No. 02 C 3432,2002 WL 31443 124, at *6 (N.D. Ill. October 31, 2002)('[A] plaintiffs case is deemed to have commenced only when his or her own signed consent has been filed.').

[159] See In re Food Lion, Inc., 1998 WL 322682, at *12, (holding that the wording of the FLSA precludes potential plaintiffs from arguing that their untimely consents 'relate back' to the filing of the original complaint).

[160] *Allison v. Frito-Lay. Inc.*, No. 91-41 93-C, 1992 WL 123799, at *3 (D. Kan. March 27, 1992); see also *Kowalski v. Kowalski Heat Treating. Co.*, 920 F. Supp. 799, 806 (N.D. Ohio 1996), (holding that failure to pay overtime constitutes a continuing violation). 'Such actions are considered continuing violations which accrue with each paycheck.' Allison, 1992 WL 123799, at *3 (citation omitted).

[161] *Ibid.* (barring any plaintiffs' claims that were not for paydays falling within either a two- or three-year period of the filing of consent for that plaintiff); Kowalski, 920 F. Supp. at 806 (holding that the statute of limitations did not toll until two years after the date of the last paycheck); *Hasken v. Louisville*, 234 F. Supp. 2d 688, 691 (W.D. Ky.

CHAPTER 10. OPT-IN CLASS ACTIONS

10.1.4.3 Tolling the Statute of Limitations

10.1.4.3.1 Tolling, Generally   The doctrine of equitable tolling applies to every federal statute of limitation including, arguably, the limitation under the FLSA.[162]

10.1.4.3.1.1   Conduct that May Toll the Statute

(a) Employer Misrepresentations – The statute of limitations will be tolled for misrepresentations made to plaintiffs by defendants, 'even if... not made negligently or fraudulently.'[163] For example, an employer may not tell an employee to refrain from filing an action because his or her wage claim would be paid in order to have the employee miss a statute of limitations deadline.

(b) Failure to Inform Employees of Their FLSA Rights – The statute may also be tolled if the employer fails to display a poster advising employees of their wage rights as required by 29 C.F.R. § 516.4.[164]

(c) Employer's Failure to Comply with Court Order – In *Meyers v. Cooper Cellar Corp.*,[165] the court equitably tolled the FLSA statute of limitations, where the defendant did not respond to the court's order to provide plaintiff with a list of similarly situated plaintiffs.

(d) Court's Failure to Rule on a Motion for an Extended Period – Lack of action on behalf of courts can also constitute grounds for tolling. In *Madrigal v. Green Giant Co.*[166] the statute was

---

2002), (noting that in an action for overtime compensation under the FLSA, a new statute of limitations begins to run each time the employer fails to pay overtime).

[162] See *Kamens v. Summit Stainless, Inc.*, 586 F. Supp. 324, 328 (E.D. Pa. 1984), (citing *Holmberg v. Armbrecht*, 327 U.S. 392, 397 (1946)).

[163] *Ibid.* (citation omitted).

[164] *EEOC v. Ky. State Police Dep't.*, 80 F.3d 1086, 1095 (6th Cir. 1996)(holding district court did not abuse discretion in tolling statute of limitations for class of mandatorily retired police officers alleging violations of ADEA and related claims, where officers had not been made aware through posting or distribution of their rights under ADEA); *Archer v. Sullivan County TennesSee* Nos. 95–5214, 95–5215, 1997 WL 720406, at *9 (6th Cir. November 14, 1997)(finding that a failure to post a notice could help support a case for equitable tolling).

[165] No. 3:95-CV- 541, 19'96 WL 766505, at *3 (E.D. Tenn. September 27, 1996).

[166] No. C-78-157, 198 1 WL 233 1, at *6 (E.D. Wash. July 27, 1981).

tolled because the court failed to rule on a motion to send notice for over two years.

10.1.4.3.1.2 Employer Conduct that Has Been Held Not to Give Rise to Tolling The Fourth Circuit has held that an employer's attempts to mitigate the negative effects of a termination on an employee do not toll the statute of limitations.[167] In *Price*, the plaintiff failed to file his lawsuit alleging violations of the ADEA until after the statute of limitations had expired. The plaintiff argued that the defendant should be equitably estopped from asserting the statutory limit, stating that after his termination, communications between the plaintiff and the company indicated that the company was continuing to investigate potential re-employment.[168] The Fourth Circuit affirmed the district court's granting of summary judgment for the defendant, noting that:

> [a]n employee's hope for rehire, transfer, promotion, or a continuing employment relationship – which is all that [the plaintiff] asserts here – cannot toll the statute absent some employer conduct likely to mislead an employee into sleeping on his rights.[169]

10.1.4.3.2 Plaintiffs' Burden It is the plaintiffs' burden to demonstrate, by a preponderance of the evidence, facts that justify equitable tolling of the statute of limitations.[170] In *Allison*, a class of truck drivers filed suit against the defendant based upon its policy requiring drivers to remain 'on-call' during times when they were off-duty. The plaintiffs then petitioned the court to toll the statute of limitations, based upon their reliance on the defendant's representations that defendant wanted to settle the case. The court noted that a plaintiff might succeed in tolling the statute of limitations if he could establish that the defendant provided assurances of settlement and, in reliance on those assurances, the plaintiff did not file his claim until after the statute of limitations had run. Nevertheless, the court denied the plaintiffs' request, finding that they failed to demonstrate that they had in fact

---

[167] *Price v. Litton Bus. Sys., Inc.*, 694 F.2d 963, 965–966 (4th Cir. 1982).
[168] *Id.* at 964–965.
[169] *Id.* at 965–966 (citation omitted).
[170] *Allison*, 1992 WL 123799, at *4.

CHAPTER 10. OPT-IN CLASS ACTIONS

held off filing their suit in reliance on any representations or actions of the defendant regarding settlement possibilities.[171]

10.1.4.4 Attorneys' Fees

10.1.4.4.1 The General Rule § 216(b) requires that '[t]he court in such an action shall, in addition to any judgment awarded to the plaintiff or plaintiffs, allow a reasonable attorney's fee to be paid by the defendant, and the costs of the action.'[172]

10.1.4.4.2 Method(s) of Calculating Fees Generally; What Is a 'Reasonable' Fee?

10.1.4.4.2.1 The 'Lodestar' Approach

(a) 'The most useful starting point for determining the amount of a reasonable fee is the number of hours reasonably expended on the litigation multiplied by a reasonable hourly rate.' This approach, coupled with the possibility of a 'multiplier,' is the lodestar approach to determining a reasonable attorneys' fee.[173]

(b) The plaintiff bears the initial burden of establishing the market rate used to compute the lodestar amount.[174] The burden then shifts to the defendant, who has an opportunity to prove that fees should be calculated at a lower rate.[175]

10.1.4.4.2.2 The 'Common Fund' Approach The lodestar approach is not the only approach that has been used to calculate attorneys' fees in § 216(b) collective actions. Specifically, the common fund approach – where the amount of the 'reasonable fee' is based upon a fair percentage of the fund obtained for the class – has been used, but only in the context

---

[171] *Id.* at *4.
[172] 29 U.S.C. 5 216(b); see *Christiansburg Garment Co. v. EEOC* 434 U.S. 412, 415 n. 5 (1978), (characterizing the FLSA as a fee-shifting statute).
[173] *Hensley v. Eckerhart,* 461 U.S. 424, 433 (1983).
[174] *LeTourneau v. Pan Am. Fin. Servs., Inc.,* 15 1 F.3d 1033, available at 1998 WL 538 130, at *2 (7th Cir. August 21, 1998).
[175] *Ibid.*

EMPLOYMENT CLASS AND COLLECTIVE ACTIONS

of the *settlement* of a §216(b) action, as opposed to the award of attorneys' fees following a *judgment* against a defendant.

The common or equitable fund doctrine is used to compute attorneys' fees under '[t]he theory... that an attorney whose actions have conferred a benefit upon a given group or class of litigants may file a claim for reasonable compensation for his efforts.'[176] Although it could be argued that a common fund approach should be employed to determine attorneys' fees following a judgment in a §216(b) collective action, such an argument is contrary to the express language of 29 U.S.C. §216(b), which is clearly a fee-shifting statute.[177] The lodestar method is typically used in statutory fee shifting cases to ensure that counsel undertaking socially beneficial litigation are adequately compensated for their effort, regardless of the monetary recovery achieved for the class.[178] Accordingly, the lodestar method, rather than the common fund approach, is typically used to calculate attorneys' fees following a judgment in plaintiffs' favor in a 216(b) action.[179]

As stated in section 4(c), below, however, the common fund approach may be appropriate to determine attorneys' fees in the context of certain settlements of 216(b) actions.

10.1.4.4.3 What Is Reasonable?

Regardless of whether a lodestar or common fund approach is applied, the amount of the attorneys' fee must be 'reasonable.' When employing the lodestar method to determine the award of attorneys' fees in a 216(b) ADEA action, the

---

[176] *County of Suffolk v. Long, Island Lighting, Co.*, 907 F.2d 1295, 1326 (2nd Cir. 1990), (quoting *City of Detroit v. Grinnell Corn.*, 560 F.2d 1093, 1098 (2nd Cir. 1977)).

[177] See 29 U.S.C. §216(b), (permitting an attorney's fee 'in addition to any judgment awarded to the plaintiff').

[178] In re General Motors Corp. Pick-Up Fuel Tank Prods. Liability Litin., 55 F.3d 768,8 19 (3rd Cir.), cert. denied, 516 U.S 824 (1995).

[179] See *Lyle v. Food Lion. Inc.*, 954 F.2d 984, 988 (4th Cir. 1992).

> (The Supreme Court has held that '[t]he contingent-fee model, premised on the award to an attorney of an amount representing a percentage of the damages, is...inappropriate for the determination of fees under §1988,' and we are satisfied that this implies that the contingent-fee approach is inappropriate under the FLSA as well.

(endorsing lodestar method in FLSA cases); *Ruenkarnol v. Stifel*, No. 77-2162, 1980 WL 2191, at * 2 (D.N.J. June 13, 1980)(same).

CHAPTER 10. OPT-IN CLASS ACTIONS

11th Circuit examined the meaning of 'reasonable' in *Jones v. Cen. Soya Co.*[180] The Court found the following factors could or should be reviewed in assessing the reasonableness of fees under the lodestar method:

(1) Required time and labor;
(2) Difficulty and novelty of questions presented;
(3) Skill required for proper rendering of services;
(4) Preclusion of other employment for attorney because of this representation;
(5) Customary fee;
(6) Fixed versus contingent fee;
(7) Limitations on time due to client requests or circumstances;
(8) Amount involved and results obtained;
(9) Ability, reputation, and experience of attorney;
(10) 'Undesirability' of case;
(11) Nature and length of attorney's professional relationship with client; and
(12) Awards in similar cases.

The Supreme Court has endorsed the use of these factors in setting and, if necessary, adjusting an award for attorney's fees in lodestar cases.[181]

When a common fund approach is used to determine attorneys' fees, however, different factors are used to assess the reasonableness of fees. In common fund cases, a court should consider the following factors:

(1) the size of the fund created and the number of persons benefited;
(2) the presence or absence of substantial objections by members of the class to the settlement terms and/or fee request;
(3) the skill and efficiency of the attorneys involved;
(4) the complexity and duration of the litigation;
(5) the risk of nonpayment;

---

[180] 748 F.2d 586,588 (11th Cir. 1984)(adopting factors used by the Fifth Circuit in *Johnson v. Ga. Highway Express, Inc.*, 488 F.2d 714'7 17–19 (5th Cir. 1974)).

[181] *Henslev v. Eckerhart*, 461 U.S. 424, 434 n. 9 (noting that, in addition to 'results obtained' by counsel:

> [t]he district court also may consider other factors identified in Johnson [], though it should note that many of these factors usually are subsumed within the initial calculation of hours reasonably expended at a reasonable hourly rate).

(6) the amount of time devoted to the case by plaintiffs' counsel; and
(7) the awards in similar cases.[182]

An award of 25–30% of the fund is typically reasonable.[183]

10.1.4.4.4 Is a Settlement in an FLSA Collective Action a Common Fund? Although the common fund approach is inappropriate in determining attorneys' fees following a *judgment* in plaintiffs' favor in a §216(b) action, it is, however, appropriate in determining attorneys' fees in certain *settlements* of §216(b) collective actions.[184] Specifically, where the settlement of a collective action calls for the payment of plaintiffs' damages and attorneys' fees from the same source, (i.e., a 'common fund'), the common fund approach is appropriate.[185] 'Where there is a common fund in a class settlement, application of a percentage method to calculate an attorney's fee award is now favored.'

In the *Erie County* case, for example, the settlement provided that defendant would pay a lump sum of USD 350,000 in consideration for a full and general release, including a release from liability or attorneys' fees in the case at issue.[186] Counsel for plaintiffs, however, argued that the lodestar method should be employed to calculate their fees.[187] The court rejected plaintiffs' claims and used the common fund approach to calculate fees because the settlement called for the payment of damages and fees from the same source.[188] As the court noted:

> Unlike the usual common fund case, this case was brought under the ADEA, a federal discrimination stake which contains a fee shifting provision. That this case is appropriately analyzed under common fund

---

[182] *Gunter v. Ridgewood Energy Corp.*, 223 F.3d 190, 194 (3rd Cir. 2000).

[183] *Paul, Johnson, Alston & Hunt v. Graulty*, 886 F.2d 268 (9th Cir. 1989); *Erie County Retirees Assn. v. county of Erie*, 192 F. Supp. 2d 369 (W.D. Pa. 2002); *Kidrick v. ABC Television & Appliance Rental, Inc.*, No. 3:97CV19 1999 WL 1027050 (N.D. W.Va. May 12, 1999).

[184] See *Erie County Retirees Assn. v. County of Erie*, 192 F. Supp. 2d 369 (W.D. Pa. 2002); *Kidrick v. ABC Television & Appliance Rental. Inc.*, No. 3:97CV19 1999 WL 1027050 (N.D. W. Va. May 12, 1999).

[185] *Id.*, Kidrick, 1999 WL 1027050 a *1 (citing *Boeing Co. v. Van Gemert*, 444 U.S. 472, 478 (1980); *Camden I Condominium Assn., Inc. v. Dunkle*, 946 F.2d 768, 774 (11th Cir. 1991)).

[186] 192 F. Supp. 2d at 372, 378 n. 4.

[187] *Id.* at 377.

[188] *Id.* at 377–378.

principles, therefore, is not due to the underlying nature of the action but rather to the common fund nature of the Settlement the parties have reached.[189]

The court ultimately awarded a fee of 38% of the total fund, or USD 133,000.[190]

In the *Kidrick* case, plaintiffs' counsel sought a fee award under the common fund approach following the settlement of an FLSA collective action and concurrent state law class action.[191] Upon determining that the settlement called for the payment of damages and fees from the same fund, the court ordered a fee award representing 30.6% of the total fund.[192]

10.2 OVERVIEW OF FLSA CASES: AN INCREASING FAVORITE OF THE PLAINTIFFS' BAR

10.2.1 Enterprise Rent-A-Car

Judge Susan C. Bucklew, in the United States District Court for the Middle District of Florida, ordered notice of a collective action to be mailed to as many as 12,000 people who worked as 'management assistants' at leasing counters nationwide (except in California) for Enterprise and its subsidiaries.[193] Such assistants allegedly worked between fifty and sixty hours per week, but Enterprise had classified them as non-exempt and refused to pay overtime until August 1997.[194]

10.2.2 Chapter Albertson's

A federal action filed in April 1997 sought unspecified damages on behalf of a class of grocery store managers in twenty states for failure

---

[189] *Id.* at 382.

[190] *Id.* at 383.

[191] Kidrick, 1999 WL 1027050 a * 1.

[192] *Ibid.*

[193] *Hanison, et al. v. Enterprise Rent-A-Car*, No. 98-CV-233 (M.D. Fla. (Tampa) July 1, 1998).

[194] Enterprise Rent-A-Car Sued by Employees in Florida Georgia and Alabama for Failing to Pay Overtime Wages, U.S. Newswire, February 3, 1998, available at 1998 WL

to pay overtime. The suit covered over 150,000 current and former workers.[195] In October 1998, the Ninth Circuit ruled that the union-represented employees could proceed with their federal claims without first invoking grievance arbitration procedures.[196] Albertson's reportedly settled the suits in December 1999. It estimated total liability at USD 37 million, according to a one-time charge against third-quarter earnings. The settlement calls for payments of at least USD 2,500 for plaintiffs who participated in depositions and at least USD 1,000 for those who were named as plaintiffs but did not participate in depositions.[197]

10.2.3 Longs Drug Stores

Pharmacists for Longs Drug Stores filed an FLSA collective action in the U.S. District Court for the Northern District of California on behalf of current and former pharmacists at its stores in California, Hawaii, Nevada, and Colorado.[198] The complaint alleged that Longs knew or should have known that the pharmacists were working 'off-the-clock,' including working through lunch break, but not receiving overtime pay. Longs allegedly misled the pharmacists by telling them that they were exempt employees.[199] Longs ultimately settled this suit

---

5682740; Plaintiffs Win National Class Motion in Enterprise Rent-A-Car Overtime Lawsuit, U.S. Newswire, July 7, 1998, available at 1998 WL 13603424; Diane Stafford, Lawsuit Challenges Overtime Policies – Enterprise Rent-A-Car Could be Forced to Pay Back Wages to Thousands,' Kan. City Star, July 9, 1998, at B1. Judge Bucklew dismissed this case in September, 2002 after the parties settled for an undisclosed amount. Harrison, No. 98-CV-233 (M.D. Fla. (Tampa) September 22, 2000).

[195] Mike Maharry, Puvallup Worker Testifies Against Senate Labor Bill/Albertson's Employee Cites Alleged Abuses She Suffered as Reason Why Congress Should Not Amend Overtime Rules, Morning News Trib., February 14, 1997, at B8; E. Scott Reckard, Lawsuits Allege Albertson's Forced Unpaid Overtime, L.A. Times, April 22, 1997, at D10; Retail Food Stores: Court Allows Grocery Managers to Join Wage-Hour Class Suit Against Albertson's, 62 Daily Lab. Rep. (BNA) A-9 (April 1, 1998).

[196] *Albertsons, Inc. v. UFCW*, No. 97-35500 (9th Cir. October 8, 1998).

[197] Albertson's Settles Suits, available at 1999 WL 984902 1, The Journal Record, December 2, 1999.

[198] See *Janice v. Longs Drug Stores Corp.*, No. 99-CV-1100 (N.D. Cal. March 10, 1999).

[199] See Pharmacists Sue Longs for Off the Clock Violations, Select Fed. Filings Newswires, March 11, 1998, at 15:07:00.

CHAPTER 10. OPT-IN CLASS ACTIONS

for over USD 5 million in March 2002.[200] Longs must pay each member of the class who filed a claim 3.25 hours of overtime at the rate of USD 20.66 per hour for each full week of active employment between March 10, 1995, and April 30, 1999, less paid vacation and sick leave.[201] In addition to the over USD 5 million that Longs paid to settle the instant case, the company reportedly also paid USD 3.1 million to avoid a lawsuit contemplated by the Department of Labor.[202]

10.2.4 Wal-Mart

Wal-Mart, the world's largest retailer, has been the subject of several FLSA lawsuits in recent years. In 2000, the company settled a collective action alleging failure to pay overtime wages to 69,000 class members. The settlement reportedly cost Wal-Mart USD 50 million.[203] Most recently, in a similar lawsuit in Oregon, a federal jury determined that Wal-Mart failed to pay overtime to over 350 employees between 1994 and 1999. A separate trial will occur to determine the damages owed to these employees.[204]

10.2.5 Prudential

In January 1998, a former sales assistant brought an FLSA collective action against Prudential on behalf of current and former sales assistants in federal court in Florida. The complaint alleged that sales assistants were only allowed to report forty hours on their time

---

[200] *Janice v. Longs Drug Stores*, No. 99-CV-1100 (N.D. Cal. March 29, 2002).
[201] *Ibid*.
[202] Overtime Checks in the Mail to Longs Drugs Pharmacists, Drug Topics, April 6, 1998, at 12, available at 1998 WL 9218430; U.S. Labor Dept., Longs Drug Stores Reach Agreement Over Unpaid Overtime, U.S. Newswire, March 24, 1998, available at 1998 WL 5684096.
[203] See *Yates v. Wal-Mart Stores. Inc.*, 58 F. Supp. 2d 1217 (D. Colo. 1999); Bruce Ruben, Wal-Mart Faces New Group of Class Actions, Corp. Legal Times 56 (col. 3), (August 2002).
[204] William McCall, Wal-Mart Liable in Suit Over Staff Pay, Contra Costa Times Fri., December 20, 2002, 1, available at 2002 WL 10395 1380.

sheets, regardless of how many hours they actually worked.[205] Prudential settled the lawsuit for up to USD 4.5 million, which allows all hourly employees in 270 Prudential retail offices nationwide to make claims for unpaid overtime for a three-year period. Prudential sent initial checks and notices of the action and settlement to over 5,200 employees for amounts ranging from USD 40 to USD 360. The settlement also includes USD 950,000 in attorneys' fees for plaintiffs counsel.[206]

10.2.6 Sbarro

Current and former restaurant managers alleged that Sbarro violated their rights under the FLSA when it made certain deductions from their salaries, although it had characterized them as exempt employees, pursuant to Sbarro's cash shortfall reimbursement policy. Sbarro claimed that the employees were subject to the executive exception to the FLSA. U.S. District Judge Sonia Sotomayor held that the executive exception did not apply. Judge Sotomayor also concluded that the case could proceed as a collective action, and authorized the mailing of notice to potential class members.[207] The class action reportedly settled in January 1999. Although the parties have not disclosed the amount of the settlement pursuant to a confidentiality agreement, the company took USD 3.5 million in pre-tax write-offs related to the settlement in 1998.[208]

10.2.7 Paine Webber

In January 1998, a former sales assistant brought an FLSA collective action on behalf of current and former sales assistants against

---

[205] *Meyers v. Prudential Securities*, No. 8:96 CV2549 (M.D. Fla.). Firms Face Wane and Hour Violation Charges, Registered Representative, January 30, 1998, available at 1998 WL 1 187 1003.
[206] Robert Keefe, Prudential Mails Millions to Settle Overtime Lawsuit, St. Petersburg Times, July 26, 1997, at 8E.
[207] See Hoffman, 982 F. Supp. at 249–264; Bill Alden, Class Action Over Overtime Payments is Cleared, N.Y.L.J. 1 (col. 3) October 29, 1997.
[208] Manny Topol, Court Takes Labor Violations Seriously, Newsday, March 1, 1999, available at 1999 WL 8159745.

CHAPTER 10. OPT-IN CLASS ACTIONS

Paine Webber in federal court in Florida, alleging the company failed to pay employees overtime.[209] PaineWebber settled for between USD USD 1.5-3.5 million.[210] The company sent class members initial checks in amounts ranging from USD 22.50-324. The settlement included USD 700,000 in attorneys' fees.[211]

10.2.8 Dean Witter

Dean Witter was sued by a class of non-exempt employees at the company's Denver Tech Center claiming they were not paid for overtime hours worked. In discovery, the plaintiffs' attorney allegedly uncovered over 5,600 hours of reported but unpaid overtime over a three-year period.[212] Dean Witter settled this case in May 2001, shortly before trial was set to begin, for an undisclosed amount.[213]

10.2.9 Saipan Class Action

In 1999, twenty-three workers brought a USD 1 billion FLSA collective action, on behalf of 25,000 similarly situated garment workers on the island of Saipan in the U.S. Commonwealth of the Northern Marianna Islands, against twenty-one major retailers and manufacturing contractors, including Wal-Mart, J.C. Penny, Sears, and The Limited. The complaint alleged that the defendants maintained a pattern, practice, or policy of failing to pay overtime, deducting excessive sums for unsanitary food and housing, and failing to keep adequate records.[214] In September 2001, nineteen major retailers, including Nordstrom and J. Crew, settled claims against them for USD 8.75 million and agreed to

---

[209] Firms Face Wage and Hour Violation Charges, Registered Representative, January 30, 1998, available at 1998 WL 1171003.
[210] Rex Henderson, Brokers Face Overtime Complaints, The Tampa Tribune, July 18, 1998, available at 1998 WL 13769183.
[211] Firms Face Wane and Hour Violation Charges, Registered Representative, January 30, 1998, available at 1998 WL 1171003.
[212] Firms Settle Alleged Overtime Violations, Registered Representative, September 30, 1998, available at 1998 WL 11871131.
[213] *Tracy v. Dean Witter Reynolds Inc.*, No. 1:97cv257 (D. Col. May 29, 2001).
[214] See *Does I Thru XXIII v. Advanced Textile Corp.*, 214 F.3d 1058, 1063 (9th Cir. 2000).

545

establish various standards in their garment factories, including provisions for clean food, drinking water, and overtime pay.[215] Most recently, in September 2002, additional retailers, including Target, Abercrombie & Fitch, J.C. Penney, Lane Bryant, Limited Brands, and Talbots also joined the settlement. Levi Strauss refused to settle at that time, and reportedly continues to battle the lawsuit.[216]

10.2.10 Hooters Restaurants

On June 21, 2001, a class of waitresses filed a collective action against the Hooters restaurant and bar chain in the Southern District of Florida alleging that company requirements that employees purchase unsubsidized uniforms and other accessories violate the FLSA in light of the USD 2.13/hour wage paid to servers.[217] The court dismissed the case when Hooter's settled the lawsuit out of court in November 2001, for an undisclosed amount.[218]

10.2.11 Perdue Farms, Inc.

In May 2002, Perdue reportedly settled an FLSA collective action lawsuit with the Department of Labor for USD 10 million. The settlement affected 25,000 employees who brought suit, arguing that they did not receive pay for the eight minutes they spent each day 'donning and doffing' their protective gear necessary for their jobs in the poultry-processing plants. The Labor Department found that these estimated

---

[215] See Margot Patterson, American Dream Lures Saipan Workers, Nat'l Cath. Rep., September 7, 2001, at 7, available at 2001 WL 8698130; Clothes Retailers Agree to Settle a Lawsuit Over Work Conditions, Wall St. J., March 29, 2000, available at 2000 WL-WSJ 3023419.

[216] Robert Collier & Jenny Strasburg, Clothiers Fold On Sweatshop Lawsuit, The San Francisco Chronicle, September 27, 2002, available at 2002 WL 4031564; Melissa Levy, Target Settles Lawsuit Over Pacific Factories, Star Tribune, September 27, 2002, available at 2002 WL 538132.

[217] See *Arcaro v. Hooters*, No. 01-CV-26 16 (S.D. Fla. June 21, 2001).

[218] See *Arcaro*, No. 01-CV-2616 (S.D. Fla. November 19, 2001); James E. Guyette, Lawsuit Says Pep Boys Cheated Hourly Workers, Motor Age, November 1, 2002, available at 2002 WL 133310190.

CHAPTER 10. OPT-IN CLASS ACTIONS

eight minutes calculated into approximately USD 500 in wages per worker per year. Under the agreement, Perdue must change its current and future compensation policies at its fifteen poultry processing plants in the United States. In addition, the company must provide back pay for the years 2000–2002 to current and former employees.[219]

10.2.12 Aetna Services, Inc.

In September 2002, the District Court for the District of Connecticut certified a class of Aetna's systems engineers who claimed that the company wrongly classified them exempt from overtime pay, in violation of the FLSA and the Connecticut Minimum Wage Act. The class was conditionally certified as a 'collective action' under the FLSA, with 281 potential plaintiffs. Only twenty-two individuals, however, opted in to the litigation in the forty-five-day time period allotted by the court. Aetna then moved to limit plaintiffs' state law claims to only the twenty-two individuals who had elected to opt in to the FLSA collective action, while plaintiffs moved to certify a 'class' of 281 members entitled to damages under state law. The court denied Aetna's motion to limit plaintiffs' state law claims to only the twenty-two individuals who had filed consent forms under § 216(b), and granted plaintiffs' motion to certify a class of 281 individuals. Accordingly, the class includes 281 system engineers who did not receive overtime compensation from Aetna from January 1996 through January 1999.[220]

---

[219] Melissa Sepos, Purdue Settles Lawsuit with Labor Department, Delaware Law Weekly, May 15, 2002.

[220] Aetna Systems Engineers Certified in Class Action, The Connecticut Law Tribune, col. 1218, October 21, 2002. This case is still pending in Connecticut. *Scott v. Aetna, Inc.*, No. 99-CV-46 (D. Conn. December 19, 2002).

CHAPTER 11

Not without Class: Test Cases in Lieu of Class Certification as a Paradigm for Litigating Multi-plaintiff Harassment Cases

By Steven Arenson* and Craig J. Ackermann**

11.1 INTRODUCTION

Although pattern or practice claims[1] for workplace harassment are authorized by Title VII of the Civil Rights Act of 1964,[2] plaintiffs' attorneys increasingly face procedural obstacles to bringing such claims.

---

* Steven Arenson is a partner in Arenson, Dittmar & Karban. He holds a J.D. from Columbia University School of Law.
** Craig J. Ackerman is a founding partner of Ackerman and Tilajef. He holds a J.D. from University of Texas School of Law.
[1] See *International Brotherhood of Teamsters v. United States*, 431 U.S. 324 (1977). Under the Teamsters framework, common liability issues in a Title VII pattern or practice claim (i.e., whether discrimination was the company's standard operating procedure) are tried at stage I, followed by individualized mini-trials on the defendant's individualized defenses and each plaintiff's individualized damages at stage II. *Id.* at 360–362.
[2] See *EEOC v. Dial Soap Corp.*, 156 F. Supp. 2d 926, 945–946 (N.D. Ill. 2001) (discussing framework for litigating Title VII sexual harassment pattern or practice claim); *EEOC v. Mitsubishi Motor Company of America, Inc.*, 990 F. Supp. 1059, 1069–1070 (C.D. Ill. 1998) ('Title VII authorizes a pattern or practice action for sexual harassment.'); *Warnell v. Ford Motor Company*, 189 F.R.D. 383, 387 (N.D. Ill. 1999); *EEOC v. Foster Wheeler Constructors, Inc.*, 1999 W.L. 528200 (N.D. Ill. 1999).

David Sherwyn and Samuel Estreicher (eds), *Employment Class and Collective Actions*, pp. 549–580.
© 2009, Kluwer Law International BV, Printed in Great Britain.

EMPLOYMENT CLASS AND COLLECTIVE ACTIONS

The Fourth and Fifth Circuit Courts of Appeals have now held that individuals do not have a right to bring non-class action pattern or practice claims.[3] No federal appellate courts have held otherwise. Thus, in these two circuits and possibly in others,[4] plaintiffs' attorneys must now certify a class under Federal Rule of Civil Procedure 23 prior to bringing pattern or practice claims for workplace harassment.

Class certification may also be foreclosed. In *Allison v. Citgo Petroleum,* the Fifth Circuit Court of Appeals suggested that Title VII class actions seeking damages cannot be certified because the individualized determinations necessarily required by claims for compensatory and punitive damages always predominate over class issues, rendering the litigation unmanageable and inappropriate as a Rule 23 class action.[5] While the Second Circuit Court of Appeals and several federal district courts have rejected or ignored *Citgo*[6] numerous federal district courts,

---

[3] See *Lowery v. Circuit City Stores, Inc.*, 158 F.3d 742, 759–761, vacated on other grounds, 527 U.S. 1031 (1999), reinstated in part, vacated in part, 206 F.3d 431, 448 (4th Cir. 2000) ('individuals do not have a private, non-class cause of action for pattern or practice discrimination under § 1981 or Title VII'); *Celestine v. Citgo Petroleum Corp.*, 266 F.3d 343, 355–356, n. 4 (5th Cir. 2001) (holding pattern and practice claims can only be asserted by the Equal Employment Opportunity Commission or through a class action).

[4] See *Gilty v. Village of Oak Park*, 919 F.2d 1247, 1252 (7th Cir. 1990) (pattern or practice evidence is only collateral to evidence of specific discrimination against individual plaintiffs); *Victory v. Hewlett-Packard Co.*, 34 S.Fupp.2d 809 (E.D.N.Y. 1999) (arguing that pattern or practice suits cannot be established outside of a class action suit); In Re West Dist. Xerox Litigation, 850 F.Supp. 1079, 1083 (W.D.N.Y. 1994) ('trials of that discrete [pattern or practice] issue generally occur in the context of class actions or suits brought by the government,' which follows the *Teamsters* paradigm).

[5] See *Allison v. Citgo Petroleum Corp.*, 15 1 F.3d 402, 410 (5th Cir. 1998), rehearing denied and prior opinion withdrawn, 151 F. 3d 434 (5th Cir. 1998); see also *Jefferson v. Ingersoll Int'l Inc.*, 195 F.3d 894, 898 (7th Cir. 1999) (relying on *Allison* without embracing the suggestion that class actions seeking monetary relief cannot be certified); *Lemon v. International Operating Engineers, Local 119*, 216 F.3d 577 (7th Cir. 2000).

[6] See *Robinson et al. v. Metro North Railway*, 267 F.3d 147 (2nd Cir. 2001); see also *Warnell v. Ford Motor Company, supra; Hoffman v. Honda of America, Inc.*, 191 F.R.D. 530 (S.D.Oh. 1999) (same). The court in *Warnell* held that the *Allison* panel's opinion on rehearing rendered all of the panel majority's discussion regarding Rule 23 in its earlier decision dicta. See *Warnell*, 189 F.R.D. at 389. This argument has been expressly rejected by the Seventh Circuit Court of Appeals and by a federal district court within the Fifth Circuit. See *Jefferson*, 195 F.3d at 898; see also *Riley v. CompuCom Systems, Inc.*, 82 Fair Emp. Pract. Cas. (BNA) 996 (N.D.Tex. 2000) at 996, n. 6.

CHAPTER 11. NOT WITHOUT CLASS

relying on *Citgo*, have denied certification of Title VII class actions where plaintiffs sought to recover compensatory and punitive damages.[7] Although it is premature to conclude that *Citgo* will herald the end of Title VII class actions,[8] the decision clearly constitutes a significant impediment to the certification of Title VII class actions in those circuits that adopt its logic.[9]

In light of the barriers to class certification posed by *Citgo* and its progeny and the barriers to non-class action pattern or practice suits posed by Lowery and its progeny, what procedural vehicle may be used to litigate effectively and efficiently the claims of a large group of individuals against a common employer?

In this paper, we argue that multi-party joinder coupled with use of 'test cases' offers a fair, sensible and efficient means of litigating large-scale harassment cases. More specifically, the proposed alternative contemplates a consolidated action, with numerous plaintiffs alleging various claims, that is managed through the court's well-established

---

[7] See e.g., *Riley*, 82 Fair Emp. Pract. Cas. (BNA) 996 (N.D.Tex. 2000) (denying class certification under *Citgo* where plaintiffs sought compensatory and punitive damages); *Latson v. GC Services*, 77 Empl.Pract.Dec. (CCH), 46, 201 (S.D.Tex. 2000) (same); *Faulk v. Home Oil Co., Inc.*, 184 F.R.D. 645 (M.D.Ala. 1999) (same); *McClain v. Lufiin Industries, Inc.*, 187 F.R.D. 267 (E.D.Tex. 1999) (relying on *Citgo* but allowing certification because compensatory and punitive damages were not sought); *Zachary v. Texaco Exploration and Production*, 185 F.R.D. 230, 1999 W.L. 167098 (W.D.Tex. 1999) (denying certification on 'adequacy' grounds because named plaintiffs did not seek compensatory and punitive damages for the class).

[8] Cf. Lesley Frieder Wolf, Evading Friendly Fire: Achieving Class Certification after the Civil Rights Act of 1997, 100 Columbia Law Review 1847, 1852 (2000):

> (In the wake of this decision [*Citgo*], there is reason to believe that class certification has become an impossibility where employment discrimination plaintiffs seek damages, injunctive relief, and to exercise their right to demand a jury trial.);

Nikaa Baugh Jordan, *Allison v. Citgo Petroleum*: The Death Knell for the Title VII Class Action?, 51 Ala.L.Rev. 847 (2000) (predicting that *Citgo* will result in a diminishing number of class certifications nation-wide).

[9] See Deborah Sudbury, Douglas Towns, Elizabeth Baumgarten, Keeping the Monster in the Closet: Avoiding Employment Class Actions, Employee Relations Law Journal, Vol. 26, No. 2 (Autumn 2000), 14 ('The impact of the *Allison* case is significant – class claims under Title VII seeking predominantly compensatory and punitive damages for numerous putative class members are unlikely to be certified.'); see also Daniel F. Pines, The Uncertain Future of Title VII Class Actions after the Civil Rights Act of 1991, 2001 B.Y.U. Law Review 305 (2001).

joinder[10] and severance powers[11] to allow for a discrete number of individual test case trials to be conducted seriatim with full damages, including punitive damages, available to each plaintiff. Collateral estoppel is applied, where appropriate, to narrow triable issues in subsequent trials. Discovery and trial are focused at the outset on a select number of 'test cases' that share common liability issues enabling the court and the parties to benefit from the substantial economies offered by the use of collateral estoppel. Litigation of the non-test cases is stayed during the period of discovery and trial of the test cases, yielding a substantial savings of time, money and effort for the court and the parties.

Although we discuss the test-case paradigm in detail below, we do not intend this paper to be an exhaustive examination of the issues involved in litigating large-scale harassment cases through the use of test cases. We hope, instead, to highlight some of the key issues involved in using the test case method in multi-plaintiff harassment cases.

We present the argument in six parts. In 11.2, we define, and distinguish between, 'test cases' and 'bellwether trials' as used in this paper. In 11.3, we show that there is ample authority in the rules of civil procedure, case law and legal treatises – although generally not in the employment context – supporting the use of test cases in complex multi-plaintiff litigation. In 11.4, we demonstrate how a test case approach to discovery and trial can be implemented in a large-scale harassment case. Specifically, we discuss:

(1) the importance of mastering the facts of your case prior to formulating and proposing a test case model;
(2) the formulation of the test case through the identification of a discrete unit within the larger group of plaintiffs, the identification of a unifying theme, and the identification of the test case plaintiffs;

---

[10] See Fed. R. Civ. P. 19 (joinder of persons needed for just adjudication); Fed. R. Civ. P. 20(a) (authorizing permissive joinder of parties where plaintiffs assert any right to relief arising out of the same transaction or occurrence, or series of transactions or occurrences, and where any questions of law or fact common to all these persons will arise in the action); see also Fed. R. Civ. P. 42(a) (authorizing consolidation of actions involving common questions of law or fact); Fed. R. Civ. P. 24(b) (authorizing permissive intervention when an applicant's claim has a question of law or fact in common with named plaintiffs' claims).

[11] See Fed. R. Civ. P. 42(b) (authorizing separate trials of any claim or issue for the sake of efficiency).

(3) test case discovery; and
(4) test case pre-trial submissions.

In 11.5, we examine the use of collateral estoppel as a means of narrowing the triable issues in the trials subsequent to the first test plaintiffs trial.

In 11.6, we discuss the availability of successive punitive-damages awards under the test case model. Finally, in 11.7, we analyze how the test case approach can enhance the prospects for settlement by, among other things, enabling the parties to reach that critical settlement-inducing point in a case at an accelerated pace without the huge expenditure of resources typically made in a large multi-plaintiff case. While the test case model raises a variety of issues and challenges, we do not believe they are insurmountable. We conclude, therefore, that multi-party joinder, combined with a test case model, offers a compelling alternative to the class action procedure when litigating a large-scale harassment case.

11.2 DEFINING THE TERMS 'TEST CASES' AND 'BELLWETHER TRIALS'

Like Rule 23 class actions, test cases and bellwether trials are procedural vehicles used by courts for the adjudication of complex, multi-plaintiff litigation. The terms, 'test case,' and 'bellwether trial' are, however, flexible and used by judges and scholars in a wide variety of ways. We therefore begin the analysis by defining the terms, 'test case' and 'bellwether trial.'

11.2.1 Test Case

A test case begins when a court, sua sponte or upon motion of one or all parties, severs one plaintiff's claim or a small group of plaintiffs' claims from the remaining plaintiffs' claims for purposes of expedited discovery and trial in a multi-plaintiff collective action.[12] After the

---

[12] See generally, D. Alan Rudlin, Packaging Toxic Tort Cases for Trial – Use of Test Cases, Bifurcation and Class Actions, 406 Practicing Law Institute 185 (1991):

(the test case technique entails the selection of a relatively few sample plaintiffs from the entire group of plaintiffs. The test plaintiffs' claims are then fully litigated prior to those of the remaining plaintiffs.)

selection of the 'test plaintiffs,' the remaining plaintiffs' cases are stayed pending resolution of the test cases. Fact and expert discovery is then focused on trial preparation of the test plaintiffs' claims.[13] While a test case have binding effects on subsequent plaintiffs' cases through the application of offensive collateral estoppel, the results of the test case, are automatically generalized to the later proceedings. Instead, the parties must litigate whether certain issues should be precluded from relitigation in subsequent trials based on collateral estoppel principles.[14] Thus, as used in this paper, the term, 'test case,' means 'a test case for practical purposes,[15] where neither the test plaintiffs nor the results of their trials are considered "representative" of the non-test plaintiffs or their claims'.

11.2.2 Bellwether Trial

In this paper, the term, 'bellwether trial' means a type of test case involving an initial plaintiff or group of plaintiffs whose claims are deemed, based on competent scientific or statistical evidence, to be 'representative' of a larger pool of plaintiffs.[16] In contrast to test cases, the results obtained in bellwether trials are automatically generalized to all the remaining plaintiffs. Thus, while discovery and trial of bellwether plaintiffs' claims may resemble discovery and trial of a test case for practical purposes, the selection process of the bellwether plaintiffs is far more complicated, implicating due process concerns. Because a bellwether verdict will have binding effects on the remaining plaintiffs, the court must ensure that the bellwether plaintiffs' claims

---

[13] See Kenneth Chiate, Smart Ways To Settle Complex Cases (2003) <http://library.lp.findlaw.com/articles/file/00078/001255/title/subject~to . . . /litigationappeals_1_27>, 4–5 (describing ways test cases expedite trial and simplify complex mass tort litigation and further advising that once a test cases is selected counsel should seek a stay in the remaining cases).

[14] See e.g., *Bogus v. American Speech & Hearing Ass'n*, 582 F.2d 277, 290 (3rd Cir. 1978); *Yeager's Fuel, Inc. v. Pennsylvania Power & Light Co.*, 162 F.R.D. 482, 488–489 (E.D.Pa. 1995).

[15] See *Kronisch v. Howard Sav. Inst.*, 143 N.J.Super. 423, 427, n. 1 (N.J.Super.A.D. 1976).

[16] See *Perez v. Wyeth Laboratories, Inc.*, 161 N.J. 1, 734 A.2d 1245, fh. 2 (N.J. 1999):

> (The term bellwether is derived from the ancient practice of belling a wether (a male sheep) selected to lead his flock. The ultimate success of the wether

CHAPTER 11. NOT WITHOUT CLASS

are 'representative' of the larger group of plaintiffs from whom they were selected to satisfy due process concerns.[17]

11.3 LEGAL AUTHORITY SUPPORTING TEST CASES

Although the test case model has not often been implemented in the area of employment litigation, it is a recognized approach to managing large, multi-plaintiff cases.

The architects of Federal Rule of Civil Procedure 23 have for years recognized that counsel in complex actions, involving numerous parties and claims, may prefer to proceed with test cases rather than litigation through the class action device. The Advisory Committee's Note to Rule 23 specifically provides: 'One or more actions agreed to by the parties as test or model actions may be preferred to a class action.'[18]

While the Advisory Committee's Note clearly supports 'test or model actions' in multi-plaintiff cases where the parties have agreed on the framework,[19] it neither advocates nor rejects a test case paradigm where only one party, or only the court, supports the idea.

---

selected to wear the bell was determined by whether the flock had confidence that the wether would not lead them astray.)

In Re Chevron, 109 F.3d 1016 (5th Cir. 1997) – (discussing need for scientific or statistical evidence justifying selection of 'representative' bellwether plaintiffs).
[17] *Ibid*.
[18] See Fed. R. Civ. P. 23, Advisory Committee Note (emphasis added).
[19] See e.g., *Ambrahamson v. U.S.*, 228 F.3d 1360, 1365 (CA Fed. 2000) (The trial court designated four test-plaintiffs, each of whom had received lump-sum payments through an IBM exit incentive buy-out, and who claimed that taxes were wrongfully deducted, and, upon agreement of the parties, stayed the remaining 2,627 cases. Each of the test cases was representative of one of IBM's programs.); see also The Matter of Bevill, Bresler & Shulman, Inc., 67 B.R. 557 (D.N.J. 1986) (the parties agreed to select several 'test cases' to be adjudicated by the court on motions for summary judgment). Some courts have required the parties' agreement to the test case framework as a prerequisite to the application of offensive collateral estoppel in later cases. See e.g., *Sommers v. Abraham Lincoln Federal Sav. and Loan Ass'n*, 66 F.R.D. 581, 20 Fed.R.Sew.2d 386 (E.D. Pa. 1975) ('The alternative of a test case with 'one-way' res judicata, such as was approved in *Katz v. Carte Blanche*, 496 F.2d 747 (3rd Cir. 1974), cert. den. 419 U.S. 885, 95 S.Ct. 152, 42 L.Ed.2d 125 (1974), is unavailable since defendants have not indicated that they would accede to such a procedure, a precondition of the *Katz* test case alternative.')

EMPLOYMENT CLASS AND COLLECTIVE ACTIONS

Even without the parties' consent, federal courts are authorized to order test cases in multi-party actions. Rule 42 of the Federal Rules of Civil Procedure empowers courts to consolidate,[20] or sever[21] individual claims for the sake of efficiency and convenience and gives courts broad authority to 'make such orders concerning the proceedings therein as may tend to avoid unnecessary cost or delay.'[22] In mass tort cases, courts frequently invoke their discretion under Rule 42 to order joint trials on common claims.[23]

Federal district courts have also used their broad discretion under Rule 42 to manage large-scale discrimination cases. Indeed, in its decision on rehearing in *Citgo*, a race discrimination case involving over potential one thousand claimants, the Fifth Circuit noted:

---

[20] Fed.R.Civ.P. 42(a) provides:

> ...when actions involving a common question of law or fact are pending before the court, it may order a joint hearing or trial of any or all the matters in issue in the actions; it may order all the actions consolidated; and it may make such orders concerning proceedings therein as may tend to avoid unnecessary costs or delay.

[21] Fed.R.Civ.P. 42(b) provides:

> ...the court, in furtherance of convenience or to avoid prejudice, or when separate trials will be conducive to expedition and economy, may order a separate trial of any claim, cross-claim, counterclaim, or third-party claim, or of any separate issue or of any number of claims, cross-claims, counterclaims, third-part claims, or issues, always preserving inviolate the right of trial by jury as declared by the Seventh Amendment to the Constitution or as given by a statute of the United States.

[22] See Fed. R. Civ. P. 42(a); *Pittman v. Memorial Herman Healthcare*, 324 F.Supp. 446 (S.D.Tex. 2000) ('under the Federal Rules, district courts are vested with broad discretionary authority to consolidate cases in the interests of efficiency and judicial economy'); In Re Air Crash Disaster at Stapleton Airport, 720 F.Supp. 1505, 1513 (D.Colo. 1989) (noting that Rule 42(a) gives courts broad case management authority to avoid cost or delay); see also Fed. R. Civ. P. 20 (joinder); Fed. R. Civ. P. 24 (intervention).

[23] See e.g., *Easton v. City of Boulder*, 776 F.2d 1441, 1446 (10th Cir. 1985) (courts enjoy broad discretion to sever liability from damages); see also *Hines v. Joy Mfg. Co.*, 850 F.2d 1146, 1152–1153 (6th Cir. 1988) (severance of products liability claims not abuse of discretion); *Arnold v. Eastern Air Lines, Inc.*, 681 F.2d 186, 192 (4th Cir. 1982) (severance of liability in air crash cases not an abuse of discretion), cert. denied sub nom., 460 U.S. 1102, 103 S.Ct. 1801, 76 L.Ed.2d 366 (1983).

CHAPTER 11. NOT WITHOUT CLASS

The trial court utilized consolidation under rule 42 rather than class certification under rule 23 to manage this case. We review that decision for abuse of discretion and we find no abuse in this case.[24]

Moreover, several authorities in the area of complex litigation also recognize the legitimacy of the test case framework and advocate the use of test cases without requiring agreement by the parties. For example, the Manual for Complex Litigation states:

> Because complex cases involve numerous parties and issues, a fair and efficient trial structure is needed. Suggestions should be sought from counsel for approaches to structuring that will improve the trial process. They may include... the trial of one or more test cases. With appropriate provision being made concerning, the estoppel effect of the judgment.[25]

Similarly, Professor Moore notes in his treatise that, 'a test case can be an appealing alternative to a class suit.'[26]

In the mass tort context, courts have long advocated the use of test or bellwether cases as an effective method for handling complex, multi-plaintiff cases.[27] Courts also have successfully used bellwether trials in complex anti-trust matters.[28]

---

[24] See *Citgo*, 151 F.3d at 434 (emphasis added).

[25] See Manual For Complex Litigation § 21.63 (3rd edn 1995) (emphasis added); see also *id.*, § 33.27–33.28.

[26] See 3B Moore, Federal Practice, § 23.45(3) at 813.

[27] See e.g., In Re *Chevron*, 109 F.3d 1016 (5th Cir. 1997) (trial court's plan was to conduct a bellwether trial of thirty claimants, fifteen chosen by each side, in case involving 3,000 claimants); *Katz v. Carte Blanche Corp.*, 496 F.2d 747, 758–762 (3rd Cir. 1974) (en banc), cert. denied; 419 U.S. 885, 95 S.Ct. 152 (1974) (test case an available alternative effecting balance of factors considered in deciding whether to certify a class action); *Perez v. Wyeth Laboratories, Inc.*, 161 N.J. 1, 734 A.2d 1245 (N.J. 1999), reversing *Perez v. Wyeth Laboratories, Inc.*, 313 N.J.Super. 646, 713 A.2d 588, N.J. Super.L. (1997) (In approving the use of five bellwether cases in a consolidated action involving fifty recipients of Norplant birth control, the Court stated:

> The notion that the trial of some members of a large group of claimants may provide a basis for enhancing prospects of settlement or for resolving common issues or claims is a sound one that has achieved general acceptance by both the bench and bar. References to bellwether trials have long been included in the Manual for Complex Litigation. See Manual for Complex Litigation § 33.27–33.28 21.63 (3rd edn 1995)).

[28] See e.g., In re Ampicillin Antitrust Litigation, 88 F.R.D. 174, 176–178 (D.D.C. 1980) (bellwether trials endorsed as an 'aid to judicial economy and manageability' and, in

EMPLOYMENT CLASS AND COLLECTIVE ACTIONS

Despite the above-cited approval for the test-case model, my research reveals only two reported decisions in the employment discrimination context where the test case approach has been used.[29] In *Isaacs v. Caterpillar, Inc.*,[30] the plaintiffs brought suit alleging that Caterpillar engaged in a pattern or practice of coercing older management employees into retirement in violation of the Age Discrimination in Employment Act (ADEA). While thirty-two plaintiffs initially brought suit, the case grew to seventy plaintiffs as more plaintiffs elected to opt in under the ADEA's collective opt-in mechanism. After discovery was completed, the plaintiffs in *Isaacs* moved the court to hold a 'test case' trial. The motion contemplated trial of 'a selected group of plaintiffs' cases' as a means to promote the expeditious resolution of the entire litigation.[31] The Court granted the motion for a test case, designated the organizational areas from which the plaintiffs would be chosen, decided to conduct a trial of eleven of the seventy plaintiffs, and then ordered the parties to make alternating selections of the test plaintiffs.[32]

---

the event the parties could not agree on the selection of bellwether plaintiffs, the court would decide how they would be selected).

[29] The test case model has been used, however, to litigate the rights of government employees in the Federal Court of Claims. See *Clincher v. United States*, 499 F.2d 1250, 1253 (Cl.Crt. 1974), cert. denied, 420 U.S. 991, 95 S.Ct. 1427, 43 L.Ed.2d 672 (1976) ('The test case, brought by one or more plaintiffs, has been the traditional method of litigating the rights of Government employees in the [Court of Claims]'); *Armitage v. United States*, 18 Cl.Ct. 310 (1989) (in using a test case model to litigate claims of federal employees for back pay, the court observed: 'The advantages of such an approach are considerable. This action could proceed promptly with a minimum of discovery, and with none of the requirements of class notification and identification. In short, a result could be reached on the merits in significantly less time'). More recently, however, the Federal Court of Claims has favored class certification over the use of test cases. See *Taylor v. United States*, 41 Fed. Cl. 440 (1998)(noting the risks of the test case approach); *Berkeley v. United States*, 45 Fed. Cl.224 (1999) (noting the limitations of the test case approach).

[30] 765 F.Supp. 1359 (C.D.Ill. 1991).

[31] *Id.* at 1362.

[32] *Id.* at 1362, 1374–1376. In Isaacs, the precise issue before the Court was whether the plaintiffs' failure to re-tender consideration, which they had received upon signing releases, constituted ratification of the releases they had signed. In certifying this question to the court of appeals, the Court noted that there would be an initial 'test trial' of eleven of the seventy plaintiffs. *Ibid.*

Isaacs contains virtually no discussion of the nuances of the test case model. While the court noted the test case would involve 298 witnesses, 1,463 exhibits and take over fifty trial days, the judge did not discuss the effect, if any, of rulings in the test case on the claims of the remaining fifty-nine class members.[33] Similarly, in *Vaszlavik v. Storage Technology Corp.*,[34] the Court certified an ADEA collective action brought by twelve plaintiffs on behalf of a large group of former employees of Storage Technology who were terminated in various reductions in force and were over the age of forty. The Court elected to conduct an initial trial of the plaintiffs' pattern or practice claims, as well as of 'all claims of the representative plaintiffs, including the remedial phase of their pattern or practice claims.'[35] The Court reasoned that this approach would 'not only provide complete relief to the representative plaintiffs,' it would 'also provide 'test cases' that may aid in the settlement of the class-plaintiffs' claims should plaintiffs prevail in the liability phase.'[36] *Vaszlavik* is the only reported decision of which we are aware in which a court ordered a test case to try a pattern or practice claim. Yet, as in *Isaacs*, the opinion fails to discuss the test case framework in any detail and the implications, if any, of a verdict for plaintiffs on the remaining plaintiffs' claims.

Vaszlavik and *Isaacs* demonstrate that courts have broad discretion to fashion creative case-management approaches, including utilization of the test case framework, particularly in the context of ADEA opt-in collective actions.

11.4 PUTTING THE TEST CASE APPROACH TO WORK

Imagine a fifty-two year-old Chinese man appears in your office. He wants to speak with a lawyer though he barely speaks English. He tells you that he makes clothes in a factory in San Francisco, where most of the other workers are also Chinese. He hands you a piece of paper onto which a picture has been photocopied. The picture is of an Asian man on his knees with a white man standing over him holding a gun to his head. Underneath the picture, there is writing in Chinese. He tells

---

[33] *Ibid.*
[34] 175 F.R.D. 672 (D.Col. 1997).
[35] *Id.*, 175 F.R.D. at 681.
[36] *Ibid.*

you it says 'might makes right.' On the lower right hand corner of the paper there is more Chinese writing. He tells you it says 'The Management.' He tells you that yesterday this paper was posted at the same time as other company announcements were posted on the bulletin board in the main working area where he and about 120 other people work. He says that for years the company, which you recognize as a household name, has been abusing the workers in this factory. He gives various examples of verbal harassment on the basis of race and national origin and tells you there are many other workers who want to meet with you.

After several meetings with large groups of workers, you are retained on an individual basis by 180 workers to pursue claims of employment discrimination. Your initial investigation reveals evidence of a hostile work environment on the basis of race, national origin, sex and age, as well as numerous claims for discrimination in pay and promotions on the basis of race, national origin, age and sex. There is also evidence of retaliation in the form of termination against workers who complain.

Your investigation further reveals that the factory is located in a two-story building where approximately 120 people work on the first floor cutting and sewing clothing and the on-site management's offices are on the second floor. In the basement, approximately sixty employees work, almost all of whom are women. They fold and pack the clothing into boxes prior to shipment. Though in a basement, these workers all saw the picture on the main-floor bulletin board and they also complain of a hostile-work environment based on race, national origin and, particularly, sex. The basement workers are supervised, you learn, by a supervisor and an assistant supervisor who essentially run the folding and packing department.

How do you begin to formulate an effective litigation strategy that enables you to represent 180 plaintiffs without engaging in an enormously expensive and protracted battle against a large defendant with unlimited resources?

Step 1: Know Your Case

Indispensable to the successful formulation and implementation of a test case approach to litigating a large-multi-plaintiff case is a detailed knowledge of the facts of each of the individual cases. It is only through and with such knowledge that an effective and defensible plan may be presented to the Court. Critical to achieving mastery of the facts of each case is a thorough client interview. Whether this is done prior to filing the complaint, prior to the commencement of discovery, or in response to discovery requests served by the defendant, each of the plaintiffs must be interviewed individually. In short, you must conduct a comprehensive and exacting inventory of the cases before you can determine how best to present them.

Ideally, each client interview yields a written narrative, drafted by the interviewing attorney, reviewed and signed by the client, and produced to the defendant. Detailed answers to the defendant's first set of interrogatories are a vehicle for presenting such information. Individual affidavits are another. Once produced to the defendant, all parties are then in possession of a common statement of facts for each individual case. As discussed more fully below, this is critical when proposing the test case model to the Court.

Step 2: Formulating the Test Case

A. Identify a Discrete Unit

In the course of interviewing your clients, a discrete unit within the larger group of plaintiffs may be identified. This unit can take the form of a separate department, division, or work area within the company. For example, in the hypothetical set of facts outlined above, the folding and packing department located in the basement of the factory, staffed almost exclusively by women and supervised by two identifiable supervisors, is a discrete unit well suited to a test case. By virtue of its self-contained nature, discovery can be focused and the overall manageability of the case enhanced.

B. Identify a Unifying Theme

While a discrete department is helpful, even more critical to the formulation of a successful test case is the identification of a common claim that renders the test-case plaintiffs similarly situated factually and legally.

For example, imagine that as you interviewed all of the plaintiffs, you learned of a variety of allegations, including verbal harassment on the basis of race (Asian) and national origin (China), sexual harassment against men and women in the form of physical touching and verbal harassment, discrimination in pay and promotions on the basis of age, race, and national origin, and retaliation in the form of denial of pay and promotions and termination against workers who complain. Each case, in a sense, is distinct, yielding claims for individualized damages. Nevertheless, unifying themes may emerge. For example, your interviews reveal that:

(1) everyone (180 plaintiffs) saw the offensive picture on the bulletin board;
(2) most of the plaintiffs (approximately 160) have been exposed to anti-Chinese verbal harassment;
(3) about thirty plaintiffs have suffered some form of age-based verbal harassment or discrimination in pay or promotions;
(4) about thirty-five plaintiffs complain of retaliatory terminations, and an additional fifty-five plaintiffs complain of retaliatory denials of pay or promotions; and
(5) approximately seventy-five plaintiffs, men and women, complain of physical or verbal sexual harassment.

Imagine that among these various themes, one theme stands out: The female packing and folding department workers uniformly speak of a work environment pervaded by sexually offensive conduct and comments perpetuated by the supervisor and assistant supervisor in charge of the department. Some women are touched, others are propositioned, and others are insulted. Complaints, you are told, are met with swift retaliation in the form of termination or denial of work. None of the women in this department, you learn, have ever been advised of any company anti-harassment or anti-retaliation policies, nor have they been advised of the existence of a human resources department where they may register complaints.

Thus, the individual client interviews reveal at least two unifying themes emerging out of the discrete folding and packing department:

(1) the creation and toleration by the company of a sexually hostile work environment against women; and
(2) the company's failure to provide effective anti-harassment policies and procedures which, among other things, protect employees from retaliation.

Both of these themes work well with the test case model because of their susceptibility to the application of collateral estoppel. Whether the company created an *objectively* hostile work environment on the basis of sex may be fully and fairly litigated in the first trial. Because evidence of the harassment suffered and witnessed by four women in the department is relevant to the issue of the objective hostility in the trial of the first test plaintiff, all, or most, of the women in this department may testify in the first trial about their experiences. If a jury finds in the first trial that an *objectively* hostile work environment was created by the company, then the other female plaintiffs in the department may successfully argue that the company is collaterally estopped from contesting this issue in subsequent cases.

Similarly, were a jury to find in the first trial that the company failed to provide female workers in the folding and packing department with effective anti-harassment and anti-retaliation policies and procedures, after a full and fair presentation of the evidence, including appropriate expert testimony, other plaintiffs are well situated to argue that the company should be collaterally estopped from contesting this issue in subsequent trials.

C. Identifying the Test Plaintiffs

Identifying and selecting the test plaintiffs who will be the subject of the initial test case discovery and trials is critical. In the course of interviewing the plaintiffs, you have asked each plaintiff not only about the harassment and discrimination he or she has suffered but also about that which they have witnessed. Among the women in the folding and packing department, several women are acknowledged by most to have suffered particularly severe harassment. In addition, during your one-on-one interviews, after a level of trust and confidence has been established, several women who initially were reluctant to speak tell of particularly offensive acts of physical touching and solicitation by supervisors.

Once a group of test-plaintiff candidates has emerged, each candidate must be carefully evaluated and scrutinized. Any area in which a defendant may press to impeach the credibility of a test plaintiff must be investigated and considered.

Out of the forty women in the test case department, approximately ten women should be identified as potential test plaintiffs. An important decision is whether each of the ten women should have similar factual allegations of a sexually hostile work environment (i.e., all were touched or all were mocked), or whether the ten should have varying claims of a sexually hostile work environment (i.e., some with direct sexual advances and some with adverse treatment as a result of their being viewed as sexually unattractive by the supervisors). While greater similarity may enhance the likelihood that collateral estoppel will be applied to subsequent trials, greater diversity in the allegations provides plaintiffs' counsel with more options as the factual record develops as discovery proceeds.

Despite the unlikelihood that a defendant will consent to plaintiffs' selection of the initial test plaintiffs, it is helpful for plaintiffs' counsel to identify the potential test plaintiffs prior to presenting the test case plan to the Court and the defendant. First, the selection of the individual test plaintiffs helps frame the issues to be presented in the test cases and the issues to which collateral estoppel may apply. Second, critical to persuading the Court to adopt a test case model is presenting the Court with a concrete proposal that is factually specific and feasible. Identifying the potential test plaintiffs enables the Court to evaluate the test case plan in practical terms. It is at this point that submission to the Court of the signed statements of the proposed test plaintiffs, each of which is replete with factual detail supporting the hostile work environment claims, is crucial. These statements provide a common ground for discussion and argument about the fairness, efficiency, and advisability of the proposed test case model.

The defendant is likely to argue that the plaintiffs should not unilaterally select the test plaintiffs, contending that the plaintiffs will choose their best cases to be tried first to the disadvantage of the defendant. Indeed, given the significance of this selection and the subsequent impact of collateral estoppel, this issue can prove to be especially contentious.

In the class action context, there are four basic approaches to selecting representative plaintiffs for the plaintiffs' class:

(1) plaintiffs' counsel selects the plaintiffs;
(2) each side selects an equal number of plaintiffs;
(3) both sides nominate plaintiffs and the judge selects the plaintiffs; or
(4) representatives are randomly selected from established categories of plaintiffs.[37]

---

[37] See *Sterling v. Velsicol Chem. Corp.*, 855 F.2d 1188, 1196 (6th Cir. 1988) (identifying the four basic approaches used by the court in the selection of representative plaintiffs in a class action).

A central concern for a defendant where the plaintiffs are permitted to select the initial test plaintiffs is the 'representativeness' of the selected plaintiffs.[38] Allowing plaintiffs' counsel to choose the test plaintiffs unilaterally where the results are not automatically generalized to the remaining plaintiffs raises no constitutional concerns. Because factual issues may be 'narrowed' in later trials under the doctrine of collateral estoppel – not as a result of a 'representativeness' determination – after all parties have had the opportunity to address the advisability of applying collateral estoppel, due process concerns are not implicated.

Moreover, the issues to which collateral estoppel may apply – for example, the creation of an objectively hostile work environment and the defendant's failure to have effective anti-harassment policies and procedures – involve evidence that is 'pattern or practice' or 'class' type evidence about the treatment of a group of workers, and not merely one individual plaintiff. The evidence supporting any single plaintiff's claim of a sexually hostile work environment in the department out of which the test case arises will undoubtedly include testimony from the best plaintiffs about their experiences of harassment. Thus, inevitably the jury determinations in the first test trial will be based, at least in part, on testimony from the 'best' individual plaintiffs, regardless of whether the Court permits the plaintiffs to select these individuals as the initial test plaintiffs. This supports allowing the plaintiffs to select the initial test plaintiffs.

Even where plaintiffs select their best case as the first test case, the jury finds in that case that an objectively hostile work environment has been created and the Court precludes the defendant from relitigating the issue of objective hostility in the subsequent trial, the subsequent plaintiffs must still prove, among other things, subjective hostility.

In addition, the defendant retains all of its affirmative defenses, including that the plaintiff welcomed the allegedly harassing conduct, that the defendant exercised reasonable care to prevent and correct promptly any sexually harassing behavior, and that the plaintiff unnecessarily failed to take advantage of any preventive or corrective opportunities or to otherwise avoid harm.[39] Thus, what the plaintiffs' gain by

---

[38] See *Perez*, 161 N.J. at 7, n. 2, *Chevron* 109 F.3d at 1019–1020.

[39] See *Faragher v. City of Boca Raton*, 18 S.Ct. 2275 (1998), *Burlington Industries, Inc. v. Ellerth*, 118 S.Ct. 2257 (1998). Were the jury in the first trial to find that the defendant failed to provide effective policies and procedures to prevent and correct the

selecting the initial test plaintiffs, even where the defendant is collaterally estopped from relitigating certain issues, is mitigated by each plaintiffs continuing burden of proof on a variety of individualized issues – subjective hostility, damages – and the defendant's retention of its affirmative defenses.

That the plaintiffs have the burden of proof for each of their claims further supports the position that the plaintiffs should select the initial trial plaintiffs. Typically, a plaintiff is given free reign to select and order the witnesses to be presented at trial and, subject to the rules of evidence, the other proof to be offered. Allowing the plaintiffs to select the initial test plaintiffs is in accord with the general practice of allowing plaintiffs to shape their case. Instead of asserting all their claims in a single collective action, the plaintiffs each could have filed suit separately and at different times within the governing statute of limitation, thereby 'selecting' which of the plaintiffs' cases would be heard first. Arguably, allowing the plaintiffs in a single collective action to select the test plaintiffs has no greater effect.

The defendant may argue that any selection of test plaintiffs must await the completion of discovery on all plaintiffs, when the defendant has had a full opportunity to assess each case individually.

Such an approach, however, would undermine a central advantage of the test case model – streamlined, accelerated discovery. Indeed, such an approach, if implemented, would convert the test case model into a test trial model, and impose on the parties all of the delay and expense that typically attends years of protracted discovery.

If, prior to proposing a test case approach, the plaintiffs have provided the defendant with detailed and comprehensive statements of the factual contentions of each plaintiff – whether through answers to defendant's interrogatories or plaintiffs' sworn affidavits – plaintiffs may credibly argue that the defendant already has obtained a measure of discovery sufficient to apprise it of the substance of each plaintiffs allegations and therefore to prepare an effective discovery and defense strategy for the test cases.

Ultimately, even if the defendant were permitted to conduct discovery on each of the plaintiffs in the entire case and to make all of their dispositive motions, the question of which aspects of the case should

---

sexually harassing behavior at issue, the defendant may be collaterally estopped from relitigating this issue, which could preclude the defendant from asserting a Faragher-Ellerth defense in subsequent trials.

be tried first – let alone which of the individual plaintiffs should be selected – would still be vigorously contested by the parties. The Court would still be confronted with choosing one side's trial plan. Making this choice prior to full-blown discovery being conducted, without making any decision about the preclusive effect of the results of an initial trial, fosters judicial economy and manageability, enhances the prospects of settlement and increases the overall options available to the Court and the parties in handling a complex, multi-party litigation.

Step 3: Test Case Discovery – Ordered Not Limited Discovery

A key feature of the test case model is test case discovery that is targeted at preparing the ten test plaintiffs for trial. Depositions are focused on the ten test plaintiffs, the witnesses each test plaintiff intends to call at trial, the test case department supervisors and other relevant representatives of the defendant. Discovery that is unrelated to the test cases is stayed. By focusing discovery, the test case approach can yield substantial savings of money, time and effort for all parties.

A defendant faced with such targeted discovery may object on due process grounds. Several federal courts have held that discovery in civil cases is a constitutionally mandated component of due process and fundamental fairness.[40]

Test case discovery, however, does not seek to limit discovery; it seeks ordered discovery. Under the test case model, the defendant will eventually conduct full discovery on all plaintiffs and all claims. The question is not whether the defendant will conduct discovery on every plaintiff, rather, the question is when this discovery will take place. A temporary stay on discovery unrelated to the test plaintiffs does not raise any due process concerns because ordered discovery is not limited discovery. The defendant will depose every plaintiff in due course.

The concept of ordered discovery is not unique to the test case model. In the class action context, the *Manual for Complex Litigation*

---

[40] See *Columbus-America Discovery Group v. Atlantic Mutual Insurance Co.*, 924 F.2d 450 (4th Cir. 1992) Due process mandates that a judicial proceeding give all parties an opportunity to be heard on the *critical and decisive allegations* which go to the *core* of the parties' claim or defense and to present evidence on contested facts')(emphasis in original), cert. denied, 507 U.S. 1000 (1993); In Re Bankers Trust Co., 752 F.2d 874, 886–887 (3rd Cir. 1984).

EMPLOYMENT CLASS AND COLLECTIVE ACTIONS

recommends that courts place appropriate limits on class-wide discovery:

> The party seeking discovery from the class should... be required to demonstrate the need for such discovery.... Moreover, ... the court should place appropriate limits on the form and extent of the discovery from the class to assure that it serves the legitimate purpose and is not used as a device to harass either the class representatives or the class member.[41]

A defendant may also challenge discovery focused on the test plaintiffs on the ground that it impairs the defendant's ability to prepare an effective defense. One way to respond to this concern is to require the plaintiffs to provide the defendant with written notice, prior to the commencement of depositions, of:

(1) the identity of each test plaintiff;
(2) each separate claim asserted by each test plaintiff;
(3) the identity of each defendant against whom each claim is asserted;
(4) the names of all witnesses each test plaintiff intends to call at trial; and
(5) those issues as to which there is the potential for collateral estoppel to be applied.

Another measure that a court can take to ensure that a defendant has a full opportunity to prepare its defense is to allow the defendant to depose any and all witnesses it deems necessary to such a defense, including witnesses the test plaintiffs have not identified as trial witnesses who may rebut or undermine the test plaintiffs' claims. Test case discovery is thus expanded but remains focused on the claims of the test plaintiffs.

Beyond the obvious advantages of streamlined test case discovery for plaintiffs – avoiding years of costly depositions and discovery battles in connection with *all* members of a large multi-plaintiff action prior to the trial of *any* of the plaintiffs – test case discovery can yield a significant reduction in the expenses incurred in connection with expert witnesses.

---

[41] Manual for Complex Litigation, § 30.233. See *also Lusardi v. Xerox Corp.*, 118 F.R.D. 351 (D.N.J. 1987) (in an age discrimination case brought under ADEA the court focused discovery on the thirteen named plaintiffs and fifty-one randomly selected members out of a 1,300-member class).

Typically, plaintiffs' counsel in an employment discrimination case will introduce expert testimony on damages from a psychologist or an economist. An expert psychologist or economist may charge anywhere from USD 10,000–20,000 or more. In large-scale cases, plaintiffs' counsel will often not be able to afford the cost of over 100 expert reports. Using a test case model, however, plaintiffs' counsel need only – at least initially – designate experts and serve expert reports on behalf of the test plaintiffs. This, like several other aspects of the test case model, in effect neutralizes some of the financial advantages of defendants (i.e., the ability to fund litigation for many years) and reduces the possibility that plaintiffs' counsel will be unable financially to sustain the litigation of a large-scale case. For this reason alone, plaintiffs' lawyers should carefully examine the potential benefits of a test case.

Step 4: Test Case Pre-Trial Submissions

Under the test case model, summary judgment motions, motions in limine, and pre-trial memoranda are limited to the test plaintiffs. In addition, at some point prior to the close of discovery, a small number of the test plaintiffs can be selected as the plaintiffs whose cases will be tried first. If, for example, three test plaintiffs are selected as the initial trial plaintiffs, then pre-trial submissions can be limited to the three trial plaintiffs. If the trial plaintiffs are selected sufficiently in advance of expert discovery, experts' reports can initially be limited to the trial plaintiffs, yielding even greater savings to the parties.

11.5 COLLATERAL ESTOPPEL AND THE TEST CASE MODEL

Central to the test case model is the availability of collateral estoppel as a means to narrow the triable issues in subsequent trials. 'Collateral estoppel allows one who was not a party to an action involving a common defendant or plaintiff to use a finding from that action to preclude relitigation of the issue in the pending case.'[42] The doctrine of issue preclusion is not limited to situations where the parties are the same in a subsequent suit. 'Nonmutual issue preclusion is now

---

[42] *Batson v. Lederle Laboratories*, 290 N.J.Super. 49, 52 (1996).

permitted in federal courts, in most state courts, and in the overwhelming majority of state decisions that recently reconsidered the question.'[43] The modern rule permitting non-mutual collateral estoppel as against a party that has had a 'full and fair opportunity to litigate the issue in the first action' is contained in Chapter 29 of the Restatement (Second) of Judgments (Issue Preclusion in Subsequent Litigation with Others). Under Chapter 29, non-mutual collateral estoppel may be used either defensively or offensively. When used by a defendant to bar a plaintiff from relitigating an issue the plaintiff has previously litigated and lost against a different defendant, it is referred to as defensive collateral estoppel.[44] When used by a plaintiff to bar a defendant from asserting a defense or otherwise relitigating an issue which the defendant previously litigated and lost against a different plaintiff, it is referred to as *offensive* collateral estoppel.[45] Under the principles of non-mutual, offensive collateral estoppel,[46] a defendant who loses the first in a series of suits involving the 'same issue' may be bound by adverse findings on that issue in later suits. In *Parklane Hosiery Co. v. Shore*, the Court observed that collateral estoppel 'has the dual purpose of protecting litigants from the burden of relitigating an identical issue with the same party or his privy and of promoting judicial economy by preventing needless litigation.'[47] The Supreme Court recognized that non-mutual offensive collateral estoppel poses risks of unfairness to defendants in some cases such as where the defendant had little practical incentive to aggressively defend the first action or where the result of the first action is inconsistent with the results of other related cases. The Court held that the preferable approach would be to allow the courts broad discretion to determine whether the doctrine should apply in the particular case.[48] A growing body of case law holds non-mutual offensive collateral estoppel applicable in connection with

---

[43] C. Wright, A. Miller & E. Cooper, Federal Practice and Procedure, § 4463 (1981 & 2001 Supp.). See *id.* §§ 4463–4465.
[44] *Parklane Hosiery Co. v. Shore*, 439 U.S. 322, 329 (1979).
[45] *Ibid.*
[46] One court has characterized the term 'non-mutual offensive collateral estoppel' as 'concededly cumbersome.' Chicago Truck Drivers, Helpers and Warehouse Union (Independent) *Pension Fund v. Century Motor Freight, Inc.*, 125 F.3d 526, 53 1 (7th Cir. 1997).
[47] *Id.*, 439 U.S. at 326.
[48] *Ibid.*

CHAPTER 11. NOT WITHOUT CLASS

individual and class claims of employment discrimination. In *Meredith v. Beech Aircraft Corp.*,[49] the Tenth Circuit upheld application of non-mutual offensive collateral estoppel to preclude an employer from relitigating the issue of the employer's allegedly non-discriminatory reasons for denying the plaintiff a promotion where the same issue had been litigated and determined in a prior suit involving a co-worker of the plaintiff. The Tenth Circuit observed that the employer had been a party to the prior action and had a full and fair opportunity to defend; the issue was identical in the two cases; and the prior case had been finally adjudicated on the merits.[50] Notably, the Tenth Circuit held that the District Court erred in applying collateral estoppel against the plaintiff on the question whether she would have been selected absent discrimination in that she was neither a party to the prior action nor in privity with the prior plaintiff.[51]

A federal district court considered the appropriateness of non-mutual offensive collateral estoppel in *Petit v. City of Chicago*,[52] consolidated class actions by white police officers complaining of racially preferential promotions. The plaintiffs sought to preclude the city from relitigating pro-plaintiff findings made in another suit by white officers. The court rejected the city's objections to non-mutual offensive collateral estoppel, including that only one of multiple plaintiffs prevailed in the earlier suit; that the plaintiffs in the current suits adopted a 'wait and see approach' about requesting collateral estoppel; and that it would be unfair to allow the plaintiffs 'to take advantage of plaintiff-favorable findings' in the other cases 'while not being bound by the defendant-favorable findings.'[53] To the last objection, the court responded that such a disparity, 'is part of the nature of applying collateral estoppel in non-mutual situations; the estoppel can only be applied against the party that participated in the prior litigation.'[54]

---

[49] 18 F.3d 890 (10th Cir. 1994).
[50] *Id.* at 894.
[51] *Id.* at 895. See also *Harrison v. Eddy Potash. Inc.*, 248 F.3d 1014 (10th Cir. 2001) (court affirmed district court's determination that doctrine of collateral estoppel prohibited defendant employer from relitigating factual issue of whether plaintiff–employee consented to the sexual advances of her supervisor because such issue had been litigated and determined in a prior trial on claims of battery and assault).
[52] 2001 WL 914457 (N.D. Illinois 2001).
[53] *Id.* at *7–*8.
[54] *Id.* at *8.

The court found that applying collateral estoppel would not be unfair in the circumstances presented:

> The city has known for a number of years that rulings in one of the CPD discrimination cases might have a preclusive effect on one or more of the other cases.... [S]ince discovery was coordinated, the same evidence that was available to the City at the *Reynolds* trial is the evidence that will be available at the *Erwin* and *Petit* trials. The city had every incentive and opportunity to present its best case at the *Reynolds* trials. Plaintiffs, though, have not yet had the opportunity to present their best case – their presentation and strategy may differ significantly from the *Reynolds* trials.... The split nature of the verdict in *Reynolds* is not a basis for finding the application of collateral estoppel to be unfair in the present circumstances.[55]

The court accordingly determined that applying non-mutual offensive collateral estoppel would not be unfair and would be warranted to the extent that the issues resolved in the prior trial were truly identical.[56]

---

[55] *Id.* at *8.

[56] To the same effect, see *United States v. Tropic Seas, Inc.*, 887 F. Supp. 1347, 1358–1359 (D. Haw. 1995) (private-party intervenors were entitled to preclusive effect of prior state court determination of identical issue of housing discrimination); *Ward v. Harte*, 794 F. Supp. 109 (S.D.N.Y. 1992)(plaintiff entitled to preclusive effect of prior state administrative determination of identical issue of housing discrimination); *Jennings v. Roscrow*, 1987 WL 11341 (N.D. Ill. 1987)(plaintiff entitled to preclusive effect of prior determination of housing discrimination entered in contempt proceeding pursuant to consent decree in housing discrimination suit by federal government); *Georgia State Conf. of Branches of NAACP v. State of Georgia*, 570 F. Supp. 314, 327–329 (S.D. Ga. 1983)(offensive collateral estoppel applicable on issues of state's authority and obligation to end segregation in suit complaining of racial and handicap discrimination in pupil – assignment); *Monroe v. United Air Lines, Inc.*, 565 F. Supp. 271, 273 (N.D. Ill. 1983)(age discrimination plaintiff entitled to preclusive effect of pro-plaintiff findings on common issues by jury in prior trial. Consistent with *Parklane Hosiery*, courts have declined to apply offensive collateral estoppel in circumstances where the prior results were inconsistent, *Kortenhaus v. Eli Lilly & Company, supra,* 549 A.2d at 440 (prior verdicts regarding defendant's alleged negligence in approving DES were inconsistent), *Gentner v. Cheyney University of Pa:*, 1997 WL 529058 at *3 (E.D. Pa. 1997)(jury gave inconsistent answers to special interrogatories in prior trial), where it was uncertain whether the issue previously determined was identical to that currently posed, *Davis v. West Community Hospital*, 786 F.2d 677, 682 (5th Cir. 1986)(uncertainty whether issues were identical); and where the issues were in fact not identical, *Petit v. City of Chicago, supra,* 2001 WL 9 14457 at *9–*11.

CHAPTER 11. NOT WITHOUT CLASS

The application of collateral estoppel to the findings made at the trial of the first test plaintiffs could dramatically narrow the issues relating to, among other things, the plaintiffs' hostile environment sexual harassment claims. In order to establish a sex-based hostile work environment claim under Title VII, a plaintiff must generally satisfy the following elements: the conduct that plaintiffs were subjected to would not have taken place but for the employee's sex; the conduct was severe and pervasive; a reasonable person would believe that the conduct was severe and pervasive enough to alter the conditions of employment; and the working environment was sexually hostile or abusive.[57] In hostile work environment cases, the trier of fact must find both that:

(1) an objectively reasonable person would find the environment hostile; and
(2) that the victim subjectively perceived the environment as hostile.[58]

The 'objective hostility' component of a pattern or practice sexual harassment claim could be litigated in a test case and any finding of 'objective hostility' would be potentially applicable in later trials through the doctrine of offensive collateral estoppel.[59] Thus, through

---

[57] See generally, *Faragher v. City of Boca Raton*, 18 S.Ct. 2275 (1998); *Burlington Industries, Inc. v. Ellerth*, 118 S.Ct. 2257 (1998); *Oncale v. Sundowner Offshore Services, Inc.*, 188 S.Ct. 998 (1998); *Harris v. Forklift Sys. Inc.*, 114 S.Ct.367 (1993); *Meritor Savings Bank v. Vinson*, 106 S.Ct. 2399 (1986).

[58] See *Harris v. Forklift Sys. Inc.*, 510 U.S. 17, 21–22, 114 S.Ct. 367, 126 L.Ed.2d 295 (1993).

[59] A test case trial on the issue of 'objective hostility' in a sense resembles stage I of a sexual harassment pattern or practice suit where the issue for the jury is whether the company created and fostered a sexually hostile working environment as its standard operating procedure. See e.g., *EEOC v. Mitsubishi Motor Manufacturing of America, Inc.*, 990 F.Supp. 1059, 1070 (C.D.111. 1998) ('Title VII authorizes a pattern or practice action for sexual harassment.'); *Warnell v. Ford Motor Company*, 189 F.R.D. 383 (N.D.111. 1999) (certifying Rule 23 class action of 850 women with claims of pattern and practice sexual harassment); *EEOC v. Foster Wheeler Constructors, Inc.*, 1999 W.L. 528200 (N.D.111 1999) (adopting bifurcated two stage procedure for Title VII pattern and practice claim); *Bremiller v. Cleveland Psychiatric Institute*, 195 F.R.D. 1, (N.D.Oh. 2000) (court refused to decertify Rule 23 sexual harassment class action); *Jenson v. Eveleth Taconite Co.*, 139 F.R.D. 657 (D.Minn.); *Jenson v. Eveleth Taconite Co.*, 130 F.3d 1287 (8th Cir. 1997), cert. denied, 118 S.Ct 2370 (1988).

the use of non-mutual offensive collateral estoppel, the trial of the first test plaintiff could resolve critical issues for all of the forty women in the folding and packing department and, in several instances, all of the plaintiffs in the entire case. These issues include:

(1) whether the company created and tolerated an *objectively* hostile work environment on the basis of sex in the folding and packing department;
(2) whether the company created and tolerated an *objectively* hostile work environment on the basis of race or national origin in the folding and packing department;
(3) whether in the case of supervisory harassment the company took reasonable care to prevent sexual, racial, or national origin harassment in the folding and packing department;
(4) whether in the case of supervisory harassment the company took reasonable care to correct sexual, racial, or national origin harassment in the folding and packing department;
(5) whether in the case of co-worker harassment, if any, the company knew or should have known of the harassment and failed to take prompt remedial action;
(6) whether supervisors and managers, who had the authority to establish policy, participated in, or showed willful indifference to the harassment, discrimination, or retaliation in the folding and packing department;
(7) whether the company had implemented effective policies against discrimination and harassment prior to the commencement of this lawsuit; and
(8) whether the company knew or should have known of sexual harassment and discrimination in folding and packing department based on a prior history of discrimination and harassment or notice of discrimination and harassment at the company.

Significantly, any determination by the Court as to the applicability of collateral estoppel to any particular issue will be made only after each side has had an opportunity fully to brief the issue. It is at that time, prior to the Court's ruling on whether the defendant should be precluded from relitigating in the second trial an issue determined at the first trial, that the defendant may assert any potential arguments about the fairness or unfairness of applying the doctrine of collateral estoppel to a particular issue. The defendants would be free to argue, among other things, that:

(1) they did not have a full and fair opportunity to litigate the issue at hand in the first test case;
(2) the issue sought to be precluded from litigation in the second proceeding is not identical to the issue determined in the first test case;
(3) procedural opportunities exist in the second proceeding that were unavailable in the first test case that are likely to cause a different result; and
(4) other circumstances justify affording them an opportunity to relitigate the issue determined in the first trial.[60]

To ensure that the defendant has a 'full and fair opportunity to litigate,' all plaintiffs for whom plaintiffs' counsel may seek to apply collateral estoppel may have to be called as witnesses in the first test case trial, whether the conduct they experienced was witnessed by the first test plaintiff. Depending on the size of the relevant department, this could make the first test case trial fairly lengthy.

Courts may be reluctant to apply offensive collateral estoppel with respect to 'objective hostility' where the subsequent plaintiffs' claims are not sufficiently similar to those asserted by the first test plaintiff. Is 'objective hostility' always the 'same issue' for each plaintiff in a particular work unit? Employers may argue it is not. A plaintiff in a hostile work environment case cannot establish her claim based solely on harassment inflicted on co-workers but not witnessed by her.[61] For each plaintiff, then, the question of whether the work environment was hostile may depend primarily on the alleged harassment inflicted on or witnessed by that particular plaintiff. If a court adopts this approach, it may be reluctant to preclude relitigation of the 'objective hostility' issue in later trials.

---

[60] See generally *Parklane*, 439 U.S. 322 (1979); In Re Dawson, 136 N.J. 1, 20–21, 641 A.2d 1026 (1994) (listing factors to be considered in assessing applicability of collateral estoppel); Restatement (Second) of Judgments, Section 29 (1982) (same). See also *Meredith v. Beech Aircraft Corp.*, 18 F.3d 890 (10th Cir. 1994) (applying offensive collateral estoppel in the employment context after weighing similar factors).
[61] See *Leibowitz v. New York Trans. Authority*, 252 F.3d 179 (2nd Cir. 2001).

Depending on the weight of the evidence supporting a finding of objective hostility and other issues to which collateral estoppel might be applied, a court may also be reluctant to apply collateral estoppel where an appeal from the first trial has been taken prior to a decision from the appellate court regarding the validity of the findings at the first trial.

Thus, barring an expedited appeal, the parties may be forced to delay the commencement of the second test case trial until a decision is issued by the appellate court on the appeal taken from the first test case trial. While a pending appeal does not automatically preclude the application of collateral estoppel, pre-appeal issue preclusion arguably could lack the certainty and reliability on which collateral estoppel is predicated. This delay could undermine some of the efficiency offered by the test case trials.[62]

Application of collateral estoppel under the test case model is further undermined by the possibility of inconsistent verdicts in the initial test case trials.[63] The Restatement explains:

> Inconsistent prior determination. Giving a prior determination of an issue conclusive effect in subsequent litigation is justified not merely as avoiding further costs of litigation but also by underlying confidence that the result reached is substantially correct. Where a determination relied on as preclusive is itself inconsistent with some other adjudication of the same issue, that confidence is generally unwarranted. The inference, rather, is that the outcomes may have been based on equally reasonable resolutions of doubt as to the probative strength of the evidence or the appropriate application of a legal rule to the evidence. That such a doubtful determination has been given effect in the action in which it was reached does not require that it be given effect against the party in litigation against another adversary.[64]

---

[62] Of course, during the period of appellate review, other test case preparation could be handled, such as the expert discovery and pre-trial submissions of the next group of test trial plaintiffs.

[63] See e.g., In re Bedectin Products Liability Litigation, 749 F.2d 300,305 (6th Cir. 1984) (offensive collateral estoppel inappropriate in mass-tort litigation with conflicting prior judgments); *Setter v. AH Robins Co.*, 748 F.2d 1328, 1330 (8th Cir. 1984) (upholding trial court's refusal to apply offensive collateral estoppel because defendant had prevailed in twelve of twenty-one prior cases); *Prudential Securities v. Arain*, 930 F.Supp. 151 (S.D.N.Y. 1996) (stating that 'non-mutual collateral estoppel may not be applied offensively' where, inter alia:

(1) the judgment relied upon is inconsistent with other decisions; or
(2) it would be unfair for other reasons).

[64] Restatement of Judgments 2d, 29, comment f.

Accordingly, if the defendant prevailed on the existence of an objectively hostile work environment in the first test case, the plaintiffs would likely be barred from applying offensive collateral estoppel even if a subsequent test plaintiff prevailed on the same issue. If the defendant loses the first case on objective hostility, it arguably loses this issue once and for all. Thus, the possible application of collateral estoppel raises the stakes for all parties in the first test case trial.

11.6 PUNITIVE DAMAGES AND THE TEST CASE MODEL

The prospect of successive punitive-damages awards in each of the individual trials of both test and non-test plaintiffs is a powerful factor in the test case model that should be considered by all parties and the court.

In a collective action brought by numerous plaintiffs under Title VII, each plaintiff has the individual right to assert claims for, among other things, compensatory and punitive damages. In 1991, Congress amended Title VII of the Civil Rights Act of 1964 to permit victims of intentional discrimination to recover, among other things, punitive damages.[65] Most state and municipal anti-discrimination statutes similarly provide for punitive damages.[66]

Under the test case model, each plaintiff whose claims are brought to trial presents separate and distinct claims for damages, including punitive damages.[67] Thus, the defendant is faced with the prospect of successive punitive damage awards as each test plaintiff goes to trial. No constitutional or legal barrier exists to successive punitive damage awards arising from the same course of conduct. The contention that repetitive awards are prohibited has been rejected in the context of toxic tort cases where there are hundreds of punitive damage

---

[65] See 42 U.S.C. § 1981a.

[66] See e.g., New Jersey Law Against Discrimination, N.J.S.A. 105-1; California Civil Code § 52; Texas – Labor Code, § 21.051. See also Title 8 of the Administrative Code of the City of New York.

[67] See e.g., *Baker v. National State Bank*, 16 1 N.J. 220 (1999) (each punitive damage claim under the New Jersey Law Against Discrimination is separate and distinct); *Allen v. R& H Oil & Gas Co.*, 63 F.3d 1326 (5th Cir. 1995).

claimants.[68] As observed by Professor Phillips, multiple punitive damage verdicts present 'no inherent due process problem... because each of the claimants has been separately injured and, therefore, each may justly claim retribution from the defendant.'[69] While courts have long acknowledged the potential for punitive damages overkill,[70] they have at the same time upheld the permissibility of successive awards.[71]

The daunting prospect of successive punitive damages awards to test case plaintiffs is likely to trigger objections from the defendant. Despite statutory caps on punitive damages and the court's remittitur power, the problem of punitive damages overkill is a real concern.

Moreover, the availability of successive punitive awards could result in the initial trial plaintiffs receiving greater punitive awards than subsequent plaintiffs due to the subsequent juries having been informed of the amounts previously awarded and of punitive damages claims still pending. This, in turn, arguably could present plaintiffs' counsel with a conflict of interest in choosing which plaintiffs should proceed to trial first, where the likelihood of a higher punitive damages award is greater.

---

[68] See e.g., *Dunn v. Hovic*, 1 F.3d 1371, 1385–1386 (3rd Cir. 1993), modified on other grounds, 13 F.3d 58 (3rd Cir. 1993); *Roginsky v. Richardson-Merrell*, 378 F.2d 832, 839–841 (2nd Cir. 1967). See also, Andrea G. Nadel, Note, Propriety of Awarding Punitive Damages to Separate Plaintiffs Bringing Successive Actions Arising Out of Common Incident or Circumstances Against Common Defendant or Defendants ('One Bite' or 'First Comer' Doctrine), 11 A.L.R. 4th 1261, 1262 (1982 & Supp. 1992) (noting that courts

> have generally held that no principle exists which prohibits a plaintiff from recovering punitive damages against a defendant or defendants simply because punitive damages have previously been awarded... for the same conduct, or because other actions are pending... which could result in an award of punitive damages);

Jerry J. Phillips, Multiple Punitive Damages Awards, 39 Vill. L. Rev. 433 n. 7 (1994)(gathering cases).

[69] 39 Vill. L. Rev. at 437–438.

[70] See e.g., *Roginsky v. Richardson-Merrell*, 378 F.2d at 832 ('we have the greatest difficulty in perceiving how claims for punitive damages in such a multiplicity of actions throughout the nation can be so administered as to avoid overkill').

[71] See e.g., *Ripa v. Owens-Corning Fiberglass Corp.*, 282 N.J. Super. 373, 396 (App. Div. 1995) (after discussing some of the problems attending multiple punitive damage awards, the Court stated: 'No – appellate court has found that repetitive punitive damages awards against asbestos defendants for the same course of conduct violate due process.').

Where multiple separate plaintiffs claim punitive damages there are numerous valid concerns and difficulties. A balanced approach can be fashioned, however, by requiring that each plaintiff's punitive award must bear a rational relationship to his or her individual harm. This requirement links the punitive award of any individual plaintiff – first, middle or last in the succession of claimants – to the specific harm suffered by that plaintiff. Each plaintiff is awarded what he or she deserves – punitive damages that are a function of actual harm suffered as reflected by the compensatory damages awarded.[72]

Thus, the prospect of punitive-damages overkill is addressed:

(1) by the requirement that punitive damages awards be proportional to individual harm;
(2) by the availability of remittitur;
(3) statutory caps; and
(4) the defendant's opportunity to present evidence that prior awards affect its ability to pay.

Given the availability of these limiting mechanisms, under the test case model, trials of punitive damage claims can be conducted on a case-by-case basis in tandem with each test plaintiff's compensatory damage claim by the same jury passing upon that plaintiffs claim.

11.7 ENHANCED SETTLEMENT PROSPECTS UNDER THE TEST CASE MODEL

The test-case approach achieves quickly and cost-effectively two objectives that often compel settlement:

(1) it enables counsel and the parties to gain sufficient knowledge about the strengths and weaknesses of the case; and
(2) it forces the parties to face an accelerated trial date.[73]

---

[72] See generally, State Farm Mutual Automotive Insurance Co. c. Campbell, 123 S.Ct. 1513 (2003) (discussing need for punitive damages awards to be proportional to individual harm by a factor of less than 10:1).
[73] See Kenneth Chiate, Smart Ways To Settle Complex Cases (2003), 2.

In so doing, the test case model can bring the parties to the critical settlement-inducing point in a large-scale harassment case relatively early and before resources are wasted.[74]

'A test case serves as a barometer for testing the theories in the overall case.'[75] This too, facilitates settlement. The test-case approach also provides counsel and the parties with an opportunity to 'test' each other. A compressed discovery schedule leading to an early trial date often results in the intensification of the usual rigors of litigation. Quickly, counsel and the parties can assess their adversaries. Such an assessment often informs the decision to settle.

The test-case model may also enhance settlement prospects as a result of benchmark verdicts. If a group of test cases are tried to verdict, the results of such trials can be beneficial for litigants who desire to settle their claims by providing information on the value of other plaintiffs' cases as reflected by the jury verdicts.[76] An early resolution of the test plaintiffs' claims is likely to give the parties a basis to evaluate the merits and value of the remaining claims, particularly of other similar cases, thereby facilitating settlement.[77]

11.8 CONCLUSION

Thus, the test-case model offers a viable alternative to the class action procedure for litigating large-scale harassment cases. Courts, particularly when faced with a complex litigation, look to counsel for creative approaches to effective case management. Multi-party joinder leading to an early trial of select cases with the potential of narrowing the triable issues in subsequent proceedings through the application of collateral estoppel presents such an approach.

---

[74] *Id.* at 1.

[75] *Id.* at 4; See also, Alan Rudlin, Packaging Toxic Tort Cases for Trial – Use of Test Cases, Bifurcation and Class Actions, 406 Practicing Law Institute 185, 199–200 (1991).

[76] See e.g., *Henses v. Ostow Corp.*, 30 Ohio App. 3d 108, 506 N.E. 939 (Ohio App. 9 Dist. 1986) ('A successful lawsuit on behalf of some individuals can be used by others similarly situated as a means of procuring a settlement From the defendant'); See generally, Manual of Complex Litigation, 5 33.27–33.28 (3rd edn 1995) (recognizing that a key benefit to be derived from the trial of some members of a large group of claimants is providing a basis for enhancing prospects for settlement).

[77] See 3B Moore, Federal Practice (1978), § 23.45[3] at 23-356–23-357.

CHAPTER 12

'Pattern or Practice' Discrimination Litigation

Michael Delikat[*]

12.1 INTRODUCTION

Pattern or practice theory originally developed as the basis to award remedial injunctive relief in cases of broad-scale discrimination. In such cases, upon a finding of a pattern or practice of discrimination, the court could enjoin it. At a time when all relief, including individual back-pay relief, under Title VII was considered to be equitable in nature, the theory also became an efficient means of handling the prima facie and pretext issues for the individual claims being aggregated in such cases.

Pattern or practice theory is a staple of class action litigation, because evidence of an alleged pattern or practice will often supply the commonality required under Rule 23 of the Federal Rules of Civil Procedure; however, the EEOC is empowered to litigate pattern or practice claims on a representative basis without meeting the requirements of Rule 23, even though pattern or practice cases partake of most of the characteristics of class litigation.

Pattern or practice theory is applicable both to intentional (disparate treatment) and unintentional (disparate impact) claims. A further purpose of the pattern or practice proof is to engender a presumption of discrimination that carries over to each individual affected by the pattern or practice. In most cases, upon the establishment of a pattern

---

[*] Michael Delikat is partner and chair of the Employment Law Department of Orrick, Herrington & Sutcliffe. He holds a J.D. from Harvard Law School.

David Sherwyn and Samuel Estreicher (eds), *Employment Class and Collective Actions*, pp. 581–591.
© 2009, Kluwer Law International BV, Printed in Great Britain.

or practice of discrimination, the burden of any individual claimant is eased to showing that the claimant is in the class affected by the pattern or practice and has incurred provable damages. In cases where only lost earnings and benefits are in issue, the quantification of damages may be determined by formula.

Pattern or practice theory arose originally in cases where objectively measurable facts of employment selection or exclusion were in issue. In those cases, generally, readily ascertainable actions (hiring, promotions, transfers and so on) are usually the basic data subjected to pattern or practice analysis. There may be disputes about the composition of the basic data, but these are usually resolvable without great difficulty. There will often, however, be extensive and expensive statistical dueling over the significance of the data that are assembled.

The amendments to Title VII of the Civil Rights Act of 1991, allowing compensatory and punitive damages and jury trials in cases of intentional discrimination, have complicated pattern or practice litigation of disparate treatment claims. This has occurred because of the greater complexity of individualized issues those added remedies introduce. The courts have been divided over the suitability of such claims for pattern or practice litigation.

Recently, pattern or practice theory has been extended by some of the federal trial courts to claims of discriminatory harassment. To our knowledge, no appellate court has yet accepted this application of the theory.

This extension raises serious questions about, inter alia,

- procedure (how one evaluates the significance of fundamental data that are not established events but only allegations that need to be proved),
- utility (whether any presumption carrying over to the resolution of individual claims is valid, and, if not, whether pattern or practice theory accomplishes anything in these cases),
- the statute of limitations (whether application of the theory in this context is an inappropriate device to restart time-barred claims),
- and the Seventh Amendment to the Constitution of the United States (whether it is possible to structure bifurcation so as to avoid having different juries try the same factual issues in considering the validity of individual allegations advanced as part of the pattern or practice proof and then repeating the same inquiry in determining the individual claims for the purposes of awarding relief).

CHAPTER 12. 'PATTERN OR PRACTICE' DISCRIMINATION LITIGATION

Because, like class litigation in general, the procedure for litigating pattern or practice claims is protracted, cumbersome, and expensive, few such cases are ever tried. In particular, we are unaware of any pattern or practice claim of discriminatory harassment that has ever been tried. Instead, the prospect of litigating these cases to conclusion is so daunting that they almost always settle at some point. Indeed, at the time of writing, the EEOC announced the settlement of its pattern or practice sexual harassment case against Dial Corp., discussed in 12.4, on the eve of trial. In what was 'expected to be one of the hardest fought sexual harassment trials in the commission's history,' Dial agreed to pay identified claimants approximately USD 100,000 out of a total settlement of USD 10 million. This was less than the USD 34 million settlement obtained by the EEOC in the *Mitsubishi* case discussed at 12.4, but individual payments to affected workers at Dial were reported to be higher. Dial also entered into a consent decree that, among other things, provided for an independent outside monitor to oversee its sexual harassment prevention process and claims procedure.[1]

12.2 ORIGINS OF PATTERN OR PRACTICE THEORY

The seminal case establishing the framework for pattern or practice litigation is *Int'l Brotherhood of Teamsters v. United States*.[2] In *Teamsters*, the Attorney General instituted litigation under section 707(a) of the Civil Rights Act of 1964; 42 USC 52000e-6(a)[3] against a nationwide over-the-road trucking company and the Teamsters Union. The government alleged that the company had engaged in a pattern or practice of discriminating against Blacks and Hispanics who were hired as servicemen or local city drivers, which were lower paid than line, over-the-road drivers. It further alleged that the seniority system in the collective bargaining agreement locked in the effects of discrimination

---

[1] (Daily Labor Report, April 30, 2003).
[2] 431 US 324 (1977).
[3] 42 USC 52000e-6(a) provides in pertinent part:

> Whenever the Attorney General has reasonable cause to believe that any person or group of persons is engaged in a pattern or practice of resistance to the fill enjoyment of any of the rights secured by this subchapter...the Attorney General may bring a civil action....requesting such relief....as he deems necessary to insure the full enjoyment of the rights herein described.

in hiring because a city driver who transferred to a line driver job had to forfeit all accumulated seniority.

At the time of trial, the effects of these policies produced the following statistical dispersion of the company's 6,472 employees: 314 (5%) were Black and 257 (4%) were Hispanic. However, only eight of the 1,828 line drivers (0.4%) were Black and only five (0.3%) were Hispanic. Moreover, all of the Black line drivers had been hired after the litigation had commenced. The District Court found after a trial that the government had sustained its burden of proving a pattern or practice of employment discrimination after the Court of Appeals affirmed the company and union appealed to the Supreme Court contending that the evidence introduced at trial was insufficient to show that the company engaged in a pattern or practice of discrimination and that the seniority system contained in the collective bargaining agreement as non-discriminatory.

The Supreme Court began its analysis by stating that the 'question of whether the company engaged in a pattern or practice of discriminatory hiring practices involves controlling legal principles that are relatively clear.' The ultimate question, according to the Supreme Court was whether there was a pattern or practice of treating minorities less favorably than whites because of racial differences. To prove a pattern or practice:

> the Government had to prove more than the mere occurrence of isolated or sporadic discriminatory acts. It had to establish by a preponderance of the evidence that racial discrimination was the company's standard operating procedure – the regular rather than unusual practice.[4]

Analyzing the legislative history of Title VII, the Court pointed out that the words 'pattern or practice' in section 707(a) should be interpreted by reference to their usual meaning. Quoting remarks made on the Senate floor by Senator Humphrey:

> A pattern or practice would be present only where the denial of rights consists of something more than an isolated, sporadic incident, but is repeated, routine, or of a generalized nature.

Using this framework, the Court found that the government carried its burden of proof by the aforementioned statistical showing (which had been impacted by the seniority provision in the collective bargaining agreement) bolstered by the testimony of individuals who recounted

---

[4] 431 US at 337.

CHAPTER 12. 'PATTERN OR PRACTICE' DISCRIMINATION LITIGATION

over forty specific instances of discrimination. Having met that burden of proof, an inference was created that any particular employment decision made with respect to an individual discriminatee was made in pursuit of that unlawful policy. Although the company attempted to attack the government's statistical analysis, the Court found that the simple fact was that minorities were overwhelmingly excluded from line-driver jobs. As the Court stated:

> In any event, fine tuning of the statistics could not have obscured the glaring absence of minority line drivers. As the Court of Appeals remarked, the company's inability to rebut the inference of discrimination came not from a misuse of statistics but from 'the inexorable zero.'[5]

So, once a pattern or practice of discrimination is found, every class member was presumptively entitled to relief subject to a showing by the company that its actions towards that class member were not based on its policy of discrimination.

12.3 PATTERN OR PRACTICE LITIGATION BY THE EEOC AND PRIVATE PLAINTIFFS

Teamsters was a pattern or practice case brought by the Attorney General pursuant to section 707(a). A pattern or practice claim may also be brought by the EEOC or by a class of private plaintiffs and the *Teamsters* burden of proof standard has been applied, more recently with some variation. To state a claim however, a pattern or practice plaintiff must prove more than the mere occurrence of isolated or sporadic discriminatory acts. It has to establish that discrimination is the company's standard operating procedure – the regular rather than the unusual practice.

As the Eleventh Circuit recently pointed out in *EEOC v. Joe's Stone Crab, Inc.*[6] pattern or practice discrimination is one of two theories of intentional discrimination under Title VII (the other being individual disparate treatment claims). To prove discriminatory intent necessary for a pattern or practice claim a plaintiff need not prove that a defendant harbored some special 'animus' or 'malice' towards the protected

---

[5] 431 US at 342.
[6] 220 F.3d 1263 (11th Cir. 2000).

group. However, a plaintiff must show that the adverse action by defendant was made deliberately because of the protected characteristic (e.g., race, sex). As the Eleventh Circuit noted in *Joe's Stone Crab*:

> [I]f Joe's deliberately and systematically excluded women from food server positions based on a sexual stereotype.... it then could be found liable under Title VII for intentional discrimination regardless of whether it also was motivated by ill will or malice toward women.[7]

The Court went on to state that it is enough to show in a pattern or practice case that employment decisions were generally made deliberately because of sex, regardless of whether a formal or express policy of discrimination existed from the employer. But intent is the gravamen of the cause of action.

Several older cases also demonstrate the importance of a strong statistical showing to establish a prima facie case of pattern or practice discrimination. In *Sagers v. Yellow Freight System, Inc.*,[8] the statistics showed an almost complete exclusion of minorities; before July 1968, Yellow Freight had only one black road driver throughout its nationwide system that employed more than 8,400 employees. Similarly, in *Jones v. Lee Way Motor Freight*,[9] the Court relied on statistics to establish a prima facie proof of pattern or practice of discrimination. These statistics indicated that at no time between July 1, 1964, and March 1, 1968, did the company employ a single 'Black' line driver in spite of the fact that there were between 353–542 men employed.

The common factor in these private plaintiff cases finding a prima facie case of pattern or practice of discrimination was statistical evidence that demonstrated the exclusion of virtually all minorities or women. Discrimination was the employers' standard operating procedure, the regular rather that the unusual practice of the employer.[10]

---

[7] 220 F.3d at 1284.
[8] 529 F.2d 721 (5th Cir. 1976).
[9] 431 F.2d 245 (10th Cir. 1970), cert denied, 401 US 954 (1971).
[10] Teamsters, 431 US at 336.

CHAPTER 12. 'PATTERN OR PRACTICE' DISCRIMINATION LITIGATION

12.4 CAN A PATTERN OR PRACTICE THEORY BE ASSERTED IN DISCRIMINATORY HARASSMENT CLAIMS?

Teamsters and its progeny were discriminatory hiring cases built on strong statistical proof establishing that discrimination was the standard operating procedure. Several district court cases, although none have been reviewed by a Circuit Court of Appeals, suggest that this theory of liability can also be asserted in the context of discriminatory harassment.

Jenson v. Eveleth Taconite Co.,[11] a private class action under Rule 23, was the first case to recognize pattern or practice litigation of sexual harassment. The plaintiff class alleged that the employer engaged in a pattern or practice of sex discrimination in hiring, job assignment, promotion, compensation, discipline, and training. In addition, plaintiffs alleged a pattern or practice sex discrimination in the form of hostile environment sexual harassment. The court held that harassment was so pervasive that the employer was chargeable with knowledge of it, and that the employer's failure to take adequate preventive steps meant that it tolerated and facilitated the harassment, such that it had made sexual harassment the 'standard operating procedure' at the plant.[12]

More recently, the EEOC has pursued pattern or practice litigation in the context of sexual harassment. *EEOC v. Mitsubishi Motor Mfg. of America, Inc.*,[13] presented the legal question of whether the EEOC could assert a pattern or practice claim on behalf of sexual harassment claimants for compensatory and punitive damages under the Civil Rights Act of 1991.

The EEOC alleged that Mitsubishi created and maintained a sexually hostile and abusive work environment because it tolerated, from the time the plant opened, acts of sexual harassment, and that Mitsubishi's 'standard operating procedure' was to ignore complaints of sexual harassment. Mitsubishi argued that the individual issues necessary to resolve an individual claim of sexual harassment precludes the establishment of pattern or practice liability.

---

[11] 824 F. Supp. 847 (D. Minn. 1993).
[12] Jenson, 824 F. Supp. at 886–888.
[13] 990 F. Supp. 1059 (C.D.Ill. 1998).

The District Court made quick work of Mitsubishi's argument holding that while it is true that in an individual case of sexual harassment a plaintiff must prove that the conduct they are challenging was subjectively unwelcome, in a pattern or practice case, 'the rules of engagement' are different. The Court set forth a modified framework for proving a harassment pattern or practice case: In Phase I, the EEOC will be permitted to establish a pattern or practice by proving an objectively reasonable person would find:

(1) A pattern or practice of sexual harassment defined as a situation where individuals in the workplace, as a whole, must accept a gender hostile environment.
(2) A company policy of tolerating a workforce permeated with severe and pervasive sexual harassment.

As the Court stated: 'the landscape of the total work environment, rather than the subjective experiences of each individual claimant, is the focus for establishing a pattern or practice of unwelcome sexual harassment which is severe and pervasive.'

Once Phase I liability is established, the *Mitsubishi* Court found (slightly altering the *Teamsters* formulation) that a burden of production shifts to the employer to come forward with evidence demonstrating that individual members of the potential class did not subjectively perceive the environment as hostile. Once the employer comes forward with its individual defenses, those members of the class who are challenged carry the ultimate burden of proving and persuading the tier of fact that they were subjectively affected. For those individuals not challenged, the presumption turns into a liability finding and the Court can then move to the individual damages phase.

The case arose out of a single automobile assembly plant in which the company had employed in excess of 1,200 women since the beginning of operations. The EEOC identified a list of 289 alleged victims of sexual harassment. The purported claimants, therefore, represented approximately 24.1% – almost one-quarter – of all of the women ever employed in the plant. The EEOC alleged that Mitsubishi engaged in a 'pattern or practice' of discrimination because it:

> created and maintained a sexually hostile and abusive work environment at [a plant] because it tolerated, from the facility's inception, individual acts of sexual harassment by its employees by refusing to take notice

CHAPTER 12. 'PATTERN OR PRACTICE' DISCRIMINATION LITIGATION

of, investigate, or discipline the workers who sexually harassed other employees.[14]

The *Mitsubishi* court did not determine whether the prevalence of claims presented by the EEOC raised a triable inference of a pattern or practice of intentional discrimination; indeed, it was not asked to do so. Rather, relying heavily upon *Jenson*,[15] the court held that the necessity to prove subjective harassment on an individualized basis in sexual harassment claims was not a barrier to pattern or practice litigation of such claims, and that a finding of a pattern or practice of severe and pervasive sexual harassment would be justified if:

> based on the sum of the individual testimony by the class, the trier of fact determines that an objectively reasonable person would have to spend the workday running a 'gauntlet of sexual abuse in return for the privilege of being allowed to work and make a living.'[16]

The imputation of such a pattern or practice of sexual harassment to the company would be justified, the court said, '[w]hen harassing behavior occurs frequently enough and is both common and continuous,' or when there is 'evidence that many of a company's first-line supervisors had actual knowledge of the harassing behaviors,' or when the employer 'has a policy or practice of tolerating a work environment that it knows or should have known is permeated with sexual harassment, but does not take steps to address the problem on a company-wide basis.'[17]

Most recently, in *EEOC v. Dial Corp.*,[18] the EEOC brought suit alleging a pattern or practice of tolerating sexual harassment in another single manufacturing plant. The EEOC, after it filed the action, sent a letter to approximately 400 current and former female employees who had worked at the plant, 'notifying them of the lawsuit and seeking "to identify any female employees who were affected by sex harassment and who may be entitled to recover in this lawsuit." '[19] Approximately 100 respondents to this solicitation were identified as 'claimants' in the

---

[14] Mitsubishi Motor Mfg. of America, Inc., 990 F. Supp. at 1069.
[15] *Supra.*
[16] Mitsubishi Motor Mfg. of America, Inc., 990 F. Supp. at 1073–1074.
[17] Mitsubishi Motor Mfg. of America, Inc., 990 F. Supp. at 1074–1075.
[18] 156 F. Supp. 2d 926 (N.D. Ill. 2001).
[19] Dial Corp., 156 F. Supp. 2d at 938.

action by the EEOC, and that prior to the summary judgment motion, defendant deposed all or most of these claimants.

As in *Mitsubishi*, Dial argued that the pattern or practice theory of liability was never viable in sexual harassment cases because such claims were inherently individualized and because it had no identifiable policy in favor of harassment that adversely affected a class of readily identifiable victims. Hence, the EEOC was not challenging a policy and practice of general application but was simply attempting to aggregate a large number of highly individualized claims that were not susceptible to class-type treatment. Dial further contended that individualized issues predominated over any common questions where the claimants alleged different conduct, by different alleged perpetrators, over the course of more than twelve years on different shifts.

Denying Dial's motion for summary judgment, relying upon *Mitsubishi* and *Jenson*,[20] the court swept the objections aside, holding that pattern or practice liability depended not upon the particularized experience of the individual claimant but upon 'the landscape of the total work environment.'[21] Thus, according to the court, it was not the aggregating of the individual claims of sexual harassment, but the existence of Dial's policy of tolerating sexual harassment that is the basis for establishing pattern or practice liability.

The court then went on to find triable issues of fact as to:

(1) whether the EEOC's allegations were of events severe enough to rise to the level of actionable sexual harassment;
(2) whether a reasonable person would deem the working environment in the plant to be abusive so as to alter the terms and conditions of employment;
(3) whether the employer maintained a policy of tolerating co-worker harassment;
(4) whether the employer was negligent in remedying co-worker harassment; and
(5) whether the employer's prevention efforts were sufficient to permit the *Ellerth/Faragher* defense to supervisory harassment.

As such, and despite the inherently individualized nature of sexual harassment claims, the *Jenson*, *Mitsubishi*, and *Dial* courts found that

---

[20] *Supra*.
[21] *Id.*, 946 (quoting Mitsubishi, 990 F. Supp. at 1074).

CHAPTER 12. 'PATTERN OR PRACTICE' DISCRIMINATION LITIGATION

pattern or practice theory of liability was viable in sexual harassment claims. Whether other courts and ultimately the appellate courts will agree with this conclusion remains to be seen, and there remain significant problems in attempting to pursue sexual harassment claims under a pattern or practice framework. What is clear is that in light of its successes in *Mitsubishi* and *Mitsubishi*, the EEOC will continue to attempt to expand the reach of this theory to multi-facility employers and different fact patterns.

CHAPTER 13

Disability, Disparate Impact, and Class Actions*

Michael Ashley Stein** and Michael E. Waterstone***

13.1 INTRODUCTION

Future workplace policies should plan for 'all jobs to include some physical activity' unrelated to job qualifications in order to 'dissuade unhealthy people from coming to work at Wal-Mart.'[1]

The period following enactment of Title VII of the Civil Rights Act of 1964[2] was a high-water mark in group-based employment discrimination theories. In a typical narrative of a Title VII case, an individual from a racial or ethnic minority group led a class action against a common employer. The class comprised members of its own minority group, other minority groups, or sometimes all minority groups. Collectively they alleged that employment policies had excluded them from workplace opportunities. Not only were individuals permitted

---

*Previously published by Duke Law Journal, 56 Duke L.J. 861 (2006).
**Michael Ashley Stein is Cabell Research Professor, William & Mary School of Law, and visiting professor, Harvard Law School. He holds a Ph.D. from Cambridge University and a J.D. from Harvard Law School.
***Michael E. Waterstone is associate professor, Loyola Law School, Los Angeles. He holds a J.D. from Harvard Law School.
[1] Steven Greenhouse & Michael Barbaro, Wal-Mart Memo Suggests Ways to Cut Employee Benefit Costs, N.Y. Times, October 26, 2005, at C1 (publishing a memorandum from Wal-Mart's Executive Vice President for Benefits to its Board of Directors).
[2] 42 U.S.C. § 2000e-2000e-17 (2000).

David Sherwyn and Samuel Estreicher (eds), *Employment Class and Collective Actions*, pp. 593–661.
© Duke Law Journal. Reprinted with permission.

to proceed as a class and thereby challenge a variety of employment policies; they were encouraged to do so.

Group dynamics were crucial to these cases. Courts recognized that, historically, employment practices had harmed entire communities of minority workers.[3] To ameliorate this situation, plaintiff classes were defined by their members' exclusion. In other words, the effects of subordination defined the group and bound its members together. This was true even when a class requested relief that, due to its variety and scope, was subsequently addressed individually rather than communally. Throughout this period, group-based employment discrimination theories played a crucial role in restructuring the workplace.

Undergirding the definition of group identity for these classes was the notion of panethnicity. Panethnicity is a heuristic used by mainstream society, including employers and judges, through which groups that are not inherently related are treated as having a common, overarching identity. Viewing Chinese Americans, Japanese Americans, and Korean Americans who possess distinct historical, linguistic, and cultural norms, as Asian Americans is an example of panethnicity. Although the concept is a social construct, post-Title VII cases recognized panethnic identities when applying disparate impact theory and the class action device. Both of those legal frameworks, however, have subsequently been eroded by stringent judicial interpretation; Title VII disparate impact cases are now chiefly directed toward a single remedial policy, and class certification analysis applies the federal pleading requirements of commonality and adequacy in a manner that constricts group identity. As a result, it has become increasingly difficult to predicate collective employment action on a unifying group-based identity. This is true even when actions aim to enjoin discriminatory practices that the group commonly experiences.

The deconstruction of group-based theory has immensely disadvantaged persons with disabilities. Unlike race-and sex-based employment discrimination theories, disability law has not been litigated on the basis of group identity. Under the Americans with Disabilities Act (ADA),[4] individual claims to accommodate specific impairments in particular

---

[3] As noted by the Supreme Court, the purpose of Title VII was to 'achieve equality of employment opportunities and remove barriers that have operated in the past to favor an identifiable group of white employees over other employees.' *Griggs v. Duke Power Co.*, 401 U.S. 424, 429–430 (1971).

[4] 42 U.S.C §§ 12101–12213 (2000).

CHAPTER 13. DISABILITY, DISPARATE IMPACT, AND CLASS ACTIONS

jobs have all but eclipsed a coherent theory of disability-related disparate impact law. Moreover, the class action device, which historically played a central role in group-based discrimination theory (while often going hand in hand with robust disparate impact litigation), has been virtually nonexistent under the statute's employment provisions. We therefore advocate for pandisability theory as an appropriate response to the common and unifying interest of the disability classification in eradicating common subordination, however individually those harms must be resolved. Because prejudice and stereotypes arise from misperceptions about the characteristics of a class of individuals, it is appropriate and effective to pursue classwide solutions. Put most elementarily, we argue that group-based discrimination requires group-based action.

We frame our arguments within the context of a growing debate on the efficacy of disparate impact law in light of prevailing workplace realities. Commentators agree that for racial minorities and for women, success in the working world is contingent on eradicating, in turn, facially discriminatory and facially neutral policies. After confronting the more obvious forms of discrimination through disparate treatment theory, the thrust of employment discrimination litigation has been directed at altering workplace hierarchies whose bases are harder to discern. Scholars also agree that barriers in the modern workplace are more deeply embedded in unstated cultural norms and manifest in more nuanced modes of discrimination. They sharply divide, however, on whether disparate impact theory can alter these latter, subtler norms. A nihilist school claims that nothing can be done regarding entrenched workplace culture,[5] whereas a more optimistic perspective

---

[5] See e.g., Samuel R. Bagenstos, The Structural Turn and the Limits of Antidiscrimination Law, 94 Cal. L. Rev. 1 (2006) (averring that disparate treatment and impact models of discrimination are ill-suited to redistribute power and remedy unintentional discrimination); Christine Littleton, Reconstructing Sexual Equality, 75 Cal. L. Rev. 1279, 1325–1326 (1987) (establishing that Title VII's disparate impact theory 'does not allow for challenges to male bias in the structure of business, occupations, or jobs'); Michael Selmi, Was the Disparate Impact Theory a Mistake?, 53 UCLA L. Rev. 701, 738–753 (2006) (arguing that disparate impact theory has only proven useful in a limited universe of testing cases); Kathryn Abrams, Cross-Dressing in the Master's Clothes, 109 Yale L.J. 745, 758 (2000) (reviewing Joan Williams, Unbending Gender: Why Family and Work Conflict and What to Do About It (2000)) (suggesting that employment discrimination law cannot 'actually alter the dominant norms of most workplaces or the kinds of roles that men and women play within them'); see also Tracy E. Higgins & Laura A. Rosenbury, Agency, Equality, and

advocates for greater use of disparate impact theory.[6] Notably, the preceding academic conversation (as well as the pertinent case law) has occurred without much discussion of the current exclusion or the future potential of a disparate impact theory under the ADA.[7] This absence, in turn, reinforces the erroneous notion that the statute's individualized assessment principle militates against group-based theories. It is this lacuna that we address. Taking advantage of the relatively blank slate of writing on group-based disability discrimination, we offer an intrepid vision of the ADA's potential for transforming workplace environments.

This article challenges the exclusion of disability-based employment discrimination claims from group-based theories, and in so doing advocates for applying disparate impact theory to what have heretofore been individualized ADA failure to accommodate claims. Although we acknowledge the difficulty of transferring disparate impact standards to the disability realm, we also believe that a return to earlier notions of group-based rights – in this case expressed through the lens of pandisability theory – argues persuasively for reinvigorating these areas of law. Recurring juridical dialogue on disability discrimination has focused on individualized physical accommodations, as expressed through individual decisions whether to place ramps or to replace computer screens; extending a group-based paradigm to these types of cases would be a positive development. The discussion, however, ought not to stop there. A prevailing but almost unaddressed

---

Antidiscrimination Law, 85 Cornell L. Rev. 1194, 1205–1207 (2000) (noting the decline of disparate impact).

[6] See e.g., Charles A. Sullivan, Re-Reviving Disparate Impact 59–67 (Seton Hall Pub. Law Research Paper No. 9, 2004), available at <http://papers.ssrn.com/abstract id=581503> (commenting on limited ways courts have interpreted disparate impact law, and suggesting a 'more hopeful future' for disparate impact theory); see also Tristin K. Green, Work Culture and Discrimination, 93 Cal. L. Rev. 623, 666 (2005) (advocating the restructuring of disparate impact theory to provide private rights of action based on the realities of work culture); Michelle A. Travis, Recapturing the Transformative Potential of Employment Discrimination Law, 62 Wash. & Lee L. Rev. 3, 92 (2005) (arguing that, with a different interpretation of 'workplace essentialism,' Title VII and ADA disparate impact law could have greater impact).

[7] E.g., Samuel R. Bagenstos, 'Rational Discrimination,' Accommodations, and the Politics of (Disability) Civil Rights, 89 Va. L. Rev. 825, 835 (2003) ('For purposes of this Article, then, my definition of "antidiscrimination law" is limited to prohibitions on intentional discrimination or disparate treatment.').

CHAPTER 13. DISABILITY, DISPARATE IMPACT, AND CLASS ACTIONS

issue in disability integration is the existence of unstated occupational norms and cultural expectations that stymie workplace opportunity for workers with disabilities.[8] Received wisdom asserts that Title VII largely removed the more overtly illegitimate race-and sex-based policies from the modern workplace, and what remains are legitimate, if unfortunate, barriers to disability inclusion. But this conclusion is based on a cramped and disability-free view of what disparate impact can and should do. Disability-related challenges to the modern workplace, as expressed through a return to an earlier paradigm of disparate impact theory and class action law, can help level the playing field and better incorporate the members of other protected groups. Thus, although we present our arguments within the context of ADA actions, these same concepts are relevant to the larger universe of Title VII claims.

The article proceeds as follows. By way of background, 13.2 briefly reviews post-Title VII group-based employment discrimination theories. Focusing first on disparate impact, it describes early challenges to seemingly neutral workplace rules that disproportionately affected members of protected classes. Over this period, panethnicity was used as a proxy for satisfying the requirements of class action certification, particularly the commonality and adequacy of representation conditions. Subsequently, group-based actions, whether viewed through the lens of disparate impact theory or class action procedures, have been curtailed by restrictive interpretations of group identity.

---

[8] To illustrate the difference between facially neutral rules and unwritten cultural norms, consider two of the requirements for being a successful law firm summer associate. The formal, neutral rules described might include research and writing memoranda, observing depositions and trials, and helping to prepare more senior attorneys for oral argument. The first wave of disparate impact litigation ensured these sorts of policies did not have a disproportionate effect on protected groups. An example of an impermissible 'neutral' rule would be a firm that only hired students from law schools that admitted a disproportionately low number of minority students. Classic disparate impact cases did not, however, reach deeper cultural norms that equally govern occupational success. Accordingly, summer associates continue to be judged on their ability to interact with members of the law firm and its clients in a 'professional manner,' to socialize at various events outside the workplace, to provide stimulating conversation (and appear interested) at numerous summer associate lunches, and to be perceived of as 'team players.' Because these sorts of closely assessed job requirements are not formally stated requirements, they have proven harder to reach under Title VII disparate impact law.

EMPLOYMENT CLASS AND COLLECTIVE ACTIONS

Next, 13.3 turns to the different trajectory of ADA employment law. In the ordinary course of disability employment cases, plaintiffs will claim that their employers failed to provide requested reasonable accommodations, and thereby discriminated against them. Although the prejudice asserted derived from the plaintiffs' membership in the disability classification, the case focuses on their particular situations and the specific job alterations requested. This circumstance can be understood as a result of the ADA defining the denial of a reasonable accommodation as one form of prohibited discrimination, as well as its emphasis on individualized assessments. Nevertheless, this approach is neither desirable nor inevitable: the ADA conceptualizes disability-based discrimination as a group-based phenomenon and provides for group-based action.

13.4 advocates for group-based ADA (Title I) employment cases. Pandisability theory presents an analogue to earlier notions of panethnicity and serves as an equally valid heuristic for determining class identity. Class actions have been recognized in both public service (Title II) and public accommodation (Title III) suits, even when those cases sought individualized remedies. The underlying rationale for their certification is that group-based stigma and exclusion militates in favor of collective action as an appropriate judicial response to class-wide harms. This view is consistent with the history underlying the class action device. Accordingly, group-based actions provide the most fruitful means through which to challenge and alter deeply embedded workplace hierarchies and norms. Taking advantage of the absence of disparate impact law under the ADA, the article advocates a return to an earlier paradigm of collection action in the disability field through pandisability theory. Such an adoption provides an exemplar for rethinking the challenges facing Title VII race-and sex-based discrimination.

13.2 TITLE VII GROUP-BASED DISCRIMINATION THEORIES

In the period immediately following Title VII's enactment, courts were receptive to group-based discrimination theories. Racial minorities and women challenged policies and practices that had the effect, if not the intent, of historically excluding them from employment opportunity. By liberally construing disparate impact law and class

CHAPTER 13. DISABILITY, DISPARATE IMPACT, AND CLASS ACTIONS

certification standards, courts condoned and even encouraged these groups to challenge practices that had precluded their occupational participation.

13.2.1 Disparate Impact Theory

The prevailing framework for analyzing employment-based discrimination divides employers' discriminatory actions by motive. If the discriminatory action is alleged to be intentional (whether systemically or against an individual), then the analysis proceeds to look at the effects of 'disparate treatment.'[9] When a prejudicial act is based on seemingly neutral policies that have a disproportionately negative effect upon individuals in protected classes, courts are asked to examine the legitimacy of the policies causing that 'disparate impact.'[10] Both theories permit the use of group-based evidence to avert the exclusion of protected group members; this is especially true for disparate impact claims, in which statistical evidence can create a strong presumption of discrimination even in the absence of actual proof of motive.

The difference between these doctrines can be illustrated by comparing two seminal Supreme Court decisions. In *International Brotherhood of Teamsters v. United States*,[11] the Court found that the plaintiffs had proven their prima facie claims of intentional discrimination with respect to the union's practices regarding the hiring and promotion of African Americans.[12] One fact that was especially probative of intentional discrimination was the absolute lack of African American line

---

[9] *Hazen Paper Co. v. Biggins*, 507 U.S. 604, 609 (1993) (finding a discriminatory motive critical to a claim of disparate treatment).

[10] One litmus test of whether an employer's action manifests into one that is properly remedied through disparate impact analysis is that banning the seemingly neutral rule will have a differential impact upon a protected group. See Owen M. Fiss, A Theory of Fair Employment Laws, 38 U. Chi. L. Rev. 235, 259–262 (1971) (setting forth justifications for a 'blanket ban' on race-based differential wage structures). For an overview of disparate impact's evolution, see generally George Rutherglen, Disparate Impact under Title VII: An Objective Theory of Discrimination, 73 Va. L. Rev. 1297 (1987).

[11] *Int'l Bhd. of Teamsters v. United States*, 431 U.S. 324 (1977).

[12] *Id.* at 336–337. Ultimately, the evidence presented included 'over 40 specific instances of discrimination.' *Id.* at 338.

truck drivers at the time of litigation.[13] The Court found this absence to be the direct result of a policy through which people of color were systematically excluded from employment opportunities left open to white employees.[14] By contrast, *Griggs v. Duke Power Co.*[15] established that an employer may violate Title VII without intentionally discriminating against members of protected groups, even in the pursuit of laudatory policies.[16] In *Griggs*, the employer required a high school education or the passing of certain tests to work in the more desirable sectors of its work force, and funded employees' participation in relevant educational programs.[17] The Court held that as a result of those employment policies disproportionately excluding African Americans from employment opportunities, Duke Power had violated Title VII.[18] Central to the opinion was the ruling that the focus in a disparate impact case is on 'the consequences of employment practices, not simply the motivation.'[19] Because disability-based exclusion arises from subtle forms of exclusion and stigma that fall within the province of disparate impact theory, our focus is on that doctrine.[20]

The *Griggs* interpretation of disparate impact theory is most commonly used in situations in which it is difficult or even impossible to prove motive.[21] Under *Griggs*, plaintiffs could assert that, despite a lack of concrete evidence of discriminatory intention, statistically sustainable circumstantial evidence still pointed to something 'wrong with the

---

[13] *Id.* at 337.

[14] *Id.* Hence, disparate treatment exists in circumstances where an 'employer simply treats some people less favorably than others because of their race, color, religion, sex, or national origin. Proof of discriminatory motive is critical.' *Id.* at 335 n. 15.

[15] *Griggs v. Duke Power Co.*, 401 U.S. 424 (1971).

[16] *Id.* at 432.

[17] *Id.* at 427–432.

[18] *Id.* at 430, 432.

[19] *Id.* at 432.

[20] See *infra* 13.4.1.

[21] It was (further) codified in the Civil Rights Act of 1991. 42 U.S.C. § 2000e-2(k) (2000) ('An unlawful employment practice based on disparate impact is established under this subchapter only if ... a complaining party demonstrates that a respondent uses a particular employment practice that causes a disparate impact on the basis of race, color, religion, sex, or national origin and the respondent fails to demonstrate that the challenged practice is job related for the position in question and consistent with business necessity. ... ').

CHAPTER 13. DISABILITY, DISPARATE IMPACT, AND CLASS ACTIONS

picture' of defendant's employment practices.[22] For example, in *Griggs*, plaintiffs offered evidence that 34% of white males in North Carolina, but only 12% of black males, had completed high school.[23] Although the lower court had found that the employer did not engage in intentional discrimination, the Supreme Court held that these statistics proved a disparate impact, and the high school requirement was held to violate Title VII.[24]

13.2.2 Panethnicity and Class Actions

By its nature, disparate impact theory is group based and provides plaintiffs the means by which to challenge demographic snapshots of their respective employment situations. Stated plainly, plaintiffs allege that due to discriminatory policies or practices, there are no (or proportionately not enough) other employees of the same race or sex as themselves. In *Griggs*, for example, plaintiffs argued that their employer used a high school graduation requirement as a proxy that correlated with race, and in doing so excluded African Americans.[25] Because disparate impact focuses on groups, it was natural that the post-Title VII period saw the theory go hand in hand with another juridical recognition of group identity, the class action device.[26]

Panethnicity was interwoven throughout both disparate impact and class action law during this time frame. Developed by social

---

[22] See e.g., Michael J. Zimmer et al., Cases and Materials on Employment Discrimination 247–251, 366–373 (6th edn 2003) (discussing statistical proof in disparate impact cases); George Rutherglen, Employment Discrimination Law: Visions of Equality in Theory and Doctrine 78–81 (2001) (same for class action disparate impact litigation); see also David Baldus & James W.L. Cole, Statistical Proof of Discrimination (1989).

[23] *Griggs*, 401 U.S. at 430 n. 6.

[24] *Id.* at 428, 435.

[25] *Id.* at 428–429.

[26] See e.g., *Gen. Tel. Co. v. Falcon*, 457 U.S. 147, 157 (1982) ('Racial discrimination is by definition class discrimination.'); *E. Tex. Motor Freight Sys., Inc. v. Rodriguez*, 431 U.S. 395, 405 (1977) ('Suits alleging racial or ethnic discrimination are often by their very nature class suits, involving classwide wrongs.'); see also *Bowe v. Colgate-Palmolive Co.*, 416 F.2d 711, 719 (7th Cir. 1969) ('A suit for violation of Title VII is necessarily a class action as the evil sought to be ended is discrimination on the basis of a class characteristic.').

scientists, panethnicity describes the heuristic processes through which ethnic minority groups that might internally consider themselves heterogeneous are externally perceived by the nongroup majority as homogeneous.[27] Thus, even if the African-American class in *Griggs* was diverse in terms of economic status or other factors, the members formed a cohesive unit for the purpose of antidiscrimination litigation. Because employers historically used race-based proxies to exclude African Americans as a group from the workplace, it was deemed equitable also to allow them to proceed as a community when challenging those practices.[28]

At its core, the class action device allows a group of individuals who have a similar claim as the named plaintiff communally to seek relief. For certification purposes, a putative class must show (amongst other things) that there are questions of law or fact common to the class, that the claims and defenses of the representative parties are typical of the claims or defenses of the class, and that the representative will fairly and adequately protect the interests of the class.[29] These requirements are often referred to, respectively, as commonality, typicality, and adequacy.[30] During the period following Title VII's enactment, courts

---

[27] See generally Yen Le Espiritu, Asian American Panethnicity: Bridging Institutions and Identities (1992) (discussing the construction of pan-Asian ethnicity by accounting for heterogeneities among this population); Jeff Chang, Local Knowledge(s): Notes on Race Relations, Panethnicity and History in Hawaii, 22 Amerasia J. 1 (1996) (describing the effects on self-identification on individuals of overlapping multiethnic origins); Jose Itzigsohn & Carlos Dore-Cabral, Competing Identities? Race, Ethnicity and Panethnicity among Dominicans in the United Status, 15 Soc. Forum 225 (2000) (exploring the intersection of national identity and Hispanic/Latino identity among one group of American immigrants); David Lopez & Yen Le Espiritu, Panethnicity in the United States: A Theoretical Framework, 13 Ethnic & Racial Stud. 198 (1990) (offering thoughts on how to approach a then-relatively new discipline).

[28] For recent work on the internal, and often conflicting diversity within African American civil rights communities, see generally Tomiko Brown-Nagin, Elites, Social Movements, and the Law: The Case of Affirmative Action, 105 Colum. L. Rev. 1436 (2005), and Tomiko Brown-Nagin, Race as Identity Caricature: A Local Legal History Lesson in the Salience of Intra-Racial Conflict, 151 U. Pa. L. Rev. 1913 (2003).

[29] Fed. R. Civ. P. 23(a).

[30] See generally 7A Charles Alan Wright, Arthur R. Miller & Mary Kay Kane, Federal Practice & Procedure § 1763, 1764, 1765, 1771 (3rd edn 2005).

CHAPTER 13. DISABILITY, DISPARATE IMPACT, AND CLASS ACTIONS

adopted a flexible approach to these Rule 23 requirements,[31] routinely certifying 'across-the-board' classes.[32] This meant that courts allowed a plaintiff who was a member of a protected class to represent all members of that class in their various and different employment relationships with a common employer. A Mexican-American worker who had been denied a promotion allegedly on the basis of race, for example, could represent other Mexican Americans who had not been hired. This was viewed as the most practical and efficient way of challenging discrimination, for it allowed a 'broad, rather than...piecemeal, attack upon discriminatory employment practices.'[33] Although the members of the class might be diverse in their relationship to their employer, the class was bound together by the common experience of discrimination.[34]

---

[31] For a discussion of this 'flexibility,' see Melissa Hart, Will Employment Discrimination Class Actions Survive?, 37 Akron L. Rev. 813, 818 (2004). See also Charles Mishkind et al., The Big Risks: Class Actions and Pattern and Practice Cases, 591 Pub. L. Inst. 329, 338 (1998) ('Prior to 1977, employment discrimination lawsuits were routinely certified as class actions based on the rationale that such claims were inherently of a class nature, and presumptively appropriate for class certification.').

[32] See e.g., *Gibson v. Local 40*, Int'l Longshoreman's and Warehouseman's Union, 543 F.2d 1259, 1264 (9th Cir. 1976) (holding that a class may maintain claims of generalized discrimination even though discrimination manifested itself in various ways toward different class members); *Crockett v. Green*, 534 F.2d 715, 718 (7th Cir. 1976) (holding that class action status is particularly appropriate in cases involving group discrimination); *Senter v. Gen. Motors Corp.*, 532 F.2d 511, 524 (6th Cir. 1976) (holding that race discrimination is class discrimination); *Rich v. Martin Marietta Corp.*, 522 F.2d 333, 340 (10th Cir. 1975) (holding that although it may appear as if named plaintiffs have not suffered discrimination, this does not prevent them from representing the class); *Barnett v. W.T. Grant Co.*, 518 F.2d 543, 548 n. 5 (4th Cir. 1975) (holding that even if a named plaintiff's claim is denied, a class action may still be appropriate); *Reed v. Arlington Hotel Co.*, 476 F.2d 721, 723 (8th Cir. 1973) (noting the parallels between Title VII and class actions).

[33] *McLendon v. M. David Lowe Pers. Servs., Inc.*, No. 75-H-1185, 1977 WL 15, at 2 (S.D. Tex. April 29, 1977); see *id.* ('This Court must reject the thesis that a named plaintiff must have been the victim of the entire gamut of ways in which a policy of racial discrimination is manifested by an employer. To hold otherwise would be to burden the Courts with a multiplicity of suits involving piecemeal adjudication of discrimination claims as to each employer. This would be plainly an inefficient method of implementing the policies of Title VII.').

[34] See *Johnson v. Ga. Highway Express*, 417 F.2d 1122, 1124 (5th Cir. 1969) ('While it is true, as the lower court points out, that there are different factual questions with regard to different employees, it is also true that the "Damoclean threat of a racially

Courts also allowed members of one racial minority to represent other racial minorities. For example, in *Sanchez v. Standard Brands, Inc.*,[35] the court held that a Mexican-American plaintiff had standing to challenge employment discrimination on behalf of a class of present and future Mexican-American and African-American employees of the defendant.[36] Similarly, in *Harvey v. International Harvester Co.*,[37] the court held that an African-American plaintiff could represent a class of 'all minority groups' that alleged discrimination.[38] Again, in *Ellis v. Naval Air Rework Facility*,[39] the court held that named plaintiffs who were African American and Mexican American could represent a class of all minority workers.[40] Courts also held that African-American plaintiffs alone could also represent Mexican Americans,[41] people with Spanish surnames,[42] Native Americans,[43] and Asian Americans.[44] In these cases, courts consistently found that cross-minority representation did not defeat adequacy of representation, and that claims made by one minority could be typical of other minorities because the alleged discrimination bound their interests together.[45] This flexible approach

---

discriminatory policy hangs over the racial class [and] is a question of fact common to all members of the class." ' (quoting *Hall v. Werthan Bag Corp.*, 251 F. Supp. 184, 186 (D. Tenn. 1966))).

[35] *Sanchez v. Standard Brands, Inc.*, 431 F.2d 455 (5th Cir. 1970).

[36] *Id.* at 459.

[37] *Harvey v. Int'l Harvester Co.*, 56 F.R.D. 47 (N.D. Cal. 1972).

[38] *Id.* at 48.

[39] *Ellis v. Naval Air Rework Facility*, 404 F. Supp. 391 (N.D. Cal. 1975).

[40] *Id.* at 396–397.

[41] E.g., *Penn v. Stumpf*, 308 F. Supp. 1238–1240 n. 1 (N.D. Cal. 1970); *McLendon v. M. David Lowe Pers. Servs., Inc.*, No. 75-H-1185, 1977 WL 15, at 3 (S.D. Tex. April 29, 1977); *Nat'l Org. of Women v. Bank of Cal.*, No. C-72-441, 1972 WL 246, at 4 (N.D. Cal. December 19, 1972).

[42] *Martinez v. Oakland Scavenger Co.*, 680 F. Supp. 1377, 1396–1397 (N.D. Cal. 1987); see also *Jones v. Milwaukee County*, 68 F.R.D. 638, 640 (E.D. Wis. 1975).

[43] E.g., *Carter v. Gallagher*, 452 F.2d 315, 317 (8th Cir. 1971); see also *Jones v. Milwaukee County*, 68 F.R.D. 638, 640 (E.D. Wis. 1975).

[44] E.g., *Ellis*, 404 F. Supp. at 396–397.

[45] See *McLendon*, 1977 WL 15, at 2–4 ('Although the named plaintiffs in these actions are of Black and Chicano ancestry ... they can adequately represent the claims of a broad spectrum of minority workers. ... '); *Jones*, 68 F.R.D. at 640 ('Black plaintiffs are not precluded from representing a class in a Title VII action which contains persons of other minority racial and ethnic groups.').

CHAPTER 13. DISABILITY, DISPARATE IMPACT, AND CLASS ACTIONS

to class certification countenanced a judicial recognition of the need and desirability of group-driven litigation challenging policies and practices that favored the traditional labor force of white male employees.[46]

Classes that were defined this broadly – in some cases, so broadly that they represented all minorities[47] – were grounded in the idea that a key issue for courts to tap into was the way that the traditional in-group labor force perceives the newly emerging workforce.[48] Whether intentionally or not, this notion was undergirded by the concept of panethnicity. To illustrate, consider the following hypothetical: thirty-four Latina Americans file a racial and sexual discrimination suit under Title VII against Big Impersonal Corporation, claiming illegal employment practices.[49] Of the women comprising the class, thirty are American-born (of whom ten are of Puerto Rican descent, eight are of Mexican origin, six are of Chilean descent, five trace their origins to Spain, and one to Peru), two were born in Cuba, one in Mexico, and one in the Dominican Republic. Twenty of the women are currently

---

[46] In *Penn v. Stumpf*, for example, plaintiff alleged that the Oakland Police Department had discriminated against African Americans, Mexican Americans, and Spanish surnamed people. 308 F. Supp. at 1239. He further argued that the defendant did not take into account the cultural differences of non-Caucasian communities in their testing, interview, and background investigation procedures. The case was allowed to proceed as a class action despite the fact that the named plaintiff was an African American who represented members of two other ethnic groups, and had not progressed beyond the testing phase of the application process (hence, he could not yet have been discriminated against in interviewing and background investigations). *Id.* at 1242, 1239, 1240 & n. 1. The lawsuit thus triggered a broader discussion of how the Oakland Police Department had (albeit unintentionally) created a working environment that catered to and maintained the 'traditional' workforce to the exclusion of new members. *Id.* at 1242.

[47] See e.g., *Carter*, 452 F.2d at 317.

[48] *Martinez v. Oakland Scavenger Co.*, 680 F. Supp. 1377 (N.D. Cal. 1987), provides a clear example. Defendant trash company was started by persons of Italian ancestry, who 'by virtue of hard work and good management' created an expansive and prosperous business. *Id.* at 1381. As the enterprise grew, the original owners needed additional staffing, and 'hired other ethnic minorities at the bottom of the economic ladder, Blacks and Hispanics.' *Id.* These 'new' minorities claimed that defendants were not sharing the higher-level opportunities in the enterprise with them. *Id.* at 1381, 1383–1385.

[49] We return to this hypothetical, *infra* text accompanying notes 178–179, to expand the reasons for suit.

employed as administrative assistants, ten as vice presidents, two are word processors, and two are secretaries. Twenty-four hold university degrees, twenty-two speak Spanish with varying fluency, nineteen have dark complexions, seventeen are from affluent backgrounds, and one is openly lesbian.[50]

Although these individuals are clearly diverse (and because of that diversity, perhaps at odds with one another in other contexts),[51] the fact that they are all 'Latinas' or 'female Hispanics' allows the social majority to treat them as a single group.[52] We argue in section 13.4 that a parallel construction of 'pandisability' is a useful theoretical construct for linking the interests of individuals with diverse disabilities for disparate impact and class action purposes.

13.2.3 Judicial Erosion of Collective Action

Group-based statistical evidence regarding disparate impact, combined with liberal class certification standards, contributed to the post-Title VII era being an exemplar of judicial acceptance of group-based discrimination theories. Courts focused on the socially imposed views

---

[50] See generally W. Christopher Arbery, The Threat of Employment Class Actions Hovers: Companies Need Not Be Always in a Defensive Position on Such Cases, Nat'l L.J., January 13, 2003, at C24 (describing the diversity within a 'typical' race-based class action).

[51] See *supra* n. 27 and accompanying text. Lawrence Friedman offers the following argument in the context of the construct of 'Asian Americans', which applies equally to other groups:

> The people who collectively are called Asian-American certainly did not cohere in any meaningful way in Asia itself. Indeed, some of the groups... roundly hated each other back home. In Asia, there was no pan-Asian sense among Koreans, Japanese, and Chinese; to the contrary, they were historic enemies. Any notion that they had anything in common with Samoans or Cambodians would have struck them as bizarre.

Lawrence Friedman, The Horizontal Society 103 (1999).

[52] For an articulation of diversity within the Latina/o community through a LatCrit perspective, see generally Symposium, Rotating Centers, Expanding Frontiers: LatCrit Theory and Marginal Intersections, 33 U.C. Davis L. Rev. 751 (2000); Symposium, Comparative Latinas/os: Identity, Law and Policy in LatCrit Theory, 53 U. Miami L. Rev. 575 (1999); Symposium, LatCrit Theory: Naming and Launching a New Discourse of Critical Legal Scholarship, 2 Harv. Latino L. Rev. 1 (1997).

CHAPTER 13. DISABILITY, DISPARATE IMPACT, AND CLASS ACTIONS

of minority groups, as reinforced by panethnicity, and allowed this common heuristic to bind groups together for litigation purposes. Over time, however, a fundamental shift has taken place in the way that courts view group-based action. Rather than being attentive to the cultural connections that tie groups together for litigation purposes, courts became focused on intragroup differences, and in particular on the specific relief individuals requested. As remedies became increasingly viewed as more individualized, group-based discrimination theories were cut back.

This change was perhaps most dramatic within disparate impact law. As applied in *Wards Cove Packing Co. v. Atonio*,[53] and later codified in the 1991 Civil Rights Act,[54] a plaintiff must show that a particular employment practice, used by the employer, creates the disparate impact.[55] In this way, Title VII disparate impact law is tethered to specific acts of discrimination, which by and large precludes a discussion of deeper structural relationships – despite the contrary wishes of commentators,[56] as well as some legislators.[57] In *Anderson v. Douglas &*

---

[53] *Wards Cove Packing Co. v. Atonio*, 490 U.S. 642 (1989).

[54] Civil Rights Act of 1991, Pub. L. No. 102-166, 105 Stat. 1071 (1991) (codified at 42 U.S.C. § 2000e-2(k)(1) (2000)).

[55] *Wards Cove*, 490 U.S. at 656; 42 U.S.C. § 2000e-2(k)(1)(A)-(B) (2000). The statute does permit the decision-making process to be analyzed as one employment practice when the plaintiff can prove that 'the elements of [an employer's] decision making process are not capable of separation for analysis.' § 2000e-2(k)(1)(B)(i). Despite this, many commentators dismiss this statutory provision as neither widely used nor effective. See Sullivan, *supra* n. 6, at 54–55 (discussing specific cases where courts struggled to find disparate impact 'in instances in which it is not clear what, if any, employer practice causes a particular bad bottom line'); see also *Stout v. Potter*, 276 F.3d 1118, 1124 (9th Cir. 2002) ('We doubt that the overall screening process should be treated as one employment practice for purposes of disparate impact analysis.'); Bagenstos, *supra* n. 5, at 13 ('That burden has proven difficult for employees to sustain as many decision-making processes can plausibly be separated into constituent elements.').

[56] See Bagenstos, *supra* n. 5, at 13–14 ('These features of disparate impact doctrine make it a poor tool for addressing discrimination that does its work through an accumulation of small, repeated instances of biased perception and evaluation.'); see also Green, *supra* n. 6, at 654–658 (explaining how the disparate impact theory 'falls short' because of the doctrine's difficulties in 'addressing work culture as a source of discrimination').

[57] In 1963, Senator Hubert Humphrey testified that the Civil Rights Act of 1964 should respond to the 'many impersonal institutional processes which nevertheless

Lomason Co.,[58] for example, a class of African Americans contended that the defendant employer discriminated against them in hiring and promotion on the basis of their race.[59] In support of this assertion, plaintiffs pointed to a number of factors including policies requiring individuals to fill out applications in person, failing to post promotion opportunities, lacking written criteria, and giving certain employees temporary upgrades to promotion spots.[60] Citing *Wards Cove*, the court held that plaintiffs could not avail themselves of the disparate impact theory because they 'merely launched a wide-ranging attack on the cumulative effects' of the defendant's policies rather than 'isolating and identifying the specific employment practices' that created specific inequities.[61]

Anderson and other cases like it stand for the proposition that courts will be fairly rigid in policing the requirement that plaintiffs argue an objective, rather than circumstantial, causal connection between a specific employment practice and a specific disparate impact. Claims that subtle, intertwined, and hard-to-detect factors combine to keep minorities from the workforce will preclude use of the disparate impact proof structure. Thus, in *EEOC v. Joe's Stone Crab*,[62] the fact that a restaurant was almost completely devoid of female waiting staff, despite large numbers of women in the relevant labor market, was held inadequate to the task of proving discrimination.[63] Although plaintiffs struggled to point out an official policy or practice that caused these low numbers, the best they could come up with was that defendants maintained an 'old world' atmosphere. The Eleventh Circuit declined to find that this was an 'employment practice' within the province of disparate impact.[64] Courts also have held that mere

---

determine the availability of jobs for nonwhite workers.' William E. Forbath, Civil Rights and Economic Citizenship: Notes on the Past and Future of the Civil Rights and Labor Movements, 2 U. Pa. J. Lab. & Emp. L. 697, 713 (2000) (quoting Senator Hubert Humphrey, testifying in 1963 before the Senate Labor Committee).

[58] *Anderson v. Douglas & Lomason Co.*, 26 F.3d 1277 (5th Cir. 1994).
[59] *Id.* at 1281.
[60] *Id.* at 1282–1283.
[61] *Id.* at 1284.
[62] *EEOC v. Joe's Stone Crab*, 220 F.3d 1263 (11th Cir. 2000).
[63] *Id.* at 1276.
[64] *Id.* at 1278. The court did remand, however, on whether this was sufficient evidence of systemic disparate treatment. *Id.* at 1268. For discussion of the

CHAPTER 13. DISABILITY, DISPARATE IMPACT, AND CLASS ACTIONS

employer 'passivity' in light of disparate circumstances is insufficient to prove discrimination. Instead, the challenged policy or practice must have been 'actively' adopted.[65]

This sea change away from group-based discrimination claims had started even earlier, within the realm of class action law. In General Telephone Co. v. Falcon,[66] the Supreme Court tightened the reins on class certification standards. Criticizing 'across-the-board' classes, the Court held that the general proposition that 'racial discrimination is by definition class discrimination,' though perhaps true, did not mean that an allegation of racial discrimination necessarily satisfied all of Rule 23's requirements.[67] Rather, named class representatives had to demonstrate a greater unanimity of interest with the proposed class. After Falcon, courts have held that plaintiffs who suffered discrimination in hiring may not represent plaintiffs who were discriminated against

---

implications of this case for disparate impact sex discrimination claims, see L. Camille Hebert, The Disparate Impact of Sexual Harassment: Does Motive Matter?, 53 U. Kan. L. Rev. 341, 366–367 (2005). See also Nicole J. DeSario, Reconceptualizing Meritocracy: The Decline of Disparate Impact Discrimination Law, 38 Harv. C.R.-C.L. L. Rev. 479, 505–507 (2003) (stating how the Eleventh Circuit's decision in *Joe's Stone Crab* demonstrates how 'the standards of identification and causation codified in [the Civil Rights Act of 1991] can be insurmountable barriers to establishing a prima facie case'); Christine Jolls, Is There a Glass Ceiling?, 25 Harv. Women's L.J. 1, 13–14 (2002) (discussing *Joe's Stone Crab* and how those circumstances indicate that 'women are prevented by discrimination from attaining positions that are higher level, and pay more, than the ones they have traditionally occupied'); Kimberly A. Yuracko, Private Nurses and Playboy Bunnies: Explaining Permissible Sex Discrimination, 92 Cal. L. Rev. 147, 188–189 (2004) (describing how 'the slippery slope created by permitting employers to make hiring decisions based on sex-specific soft characteristics poses serious group-based equality-of-opportunity dangers').

[65] See e.g., *EEOC v. Chicago Miniature Lamp Works*, 947 F.2d 292, 305 (7th Cir. 1991) (holding that an employer's word of mouth recruiting was a form of 'passive reliance' and not an employer policy for purposes of disparate impact analysis, despite arguments by the EEOC that passive reliance had caused a disparate impact on blacks).

[66] *Gen. Tel. Co. v. Falcon*, 457 U.S. 147 (1982).

[67] *Id.* at 157; see *E. Tex. Motor Freight Sys., Inc. v. Rodriguez*, 431 U.S. 395, 405–406 (1977) ('We are not unaware that suits alleging racial or ethnic discrimination are often by their very nature class suits, involving classwide wrongs. Common questions of law and fact are typically present. But careful attention to the requirements of Fed. Rule Civ Proc. 23 remains nonetheless indispensable.').

in promotion decisions, and vice versa. The doctrinal pleading basis for limiting class representation was that these forms of representation did not rise to the level of typicality or adequacy of representation required by the federal rules.[68]

Although *Falcon* has been criticized for creating a cramped view of group identity,[69] it was not completely revolutionary. Even during the height of judicial acceptance of group-based discrimination theories, a limited number of cases had restricted the ability of internally heterogeneous groups to use the class action device.[70] For example, in *Pagan v. DuBois*[71] a proposed class of Latino inmates challenged a lack of Spanish-speaking prison staff and Latino cultural programs.[72] Denying

---

[68] See *Griffin v. Dugger*, 823 F.2d 1476, 1493 (11th Cir. 1987) (holding that a class could not be certified when one representative complained promotion practices were discriminatory and another alleged the qualification exam was discriminatory); see also *Wagner v. Taylor*, 836 F.2d 578, 595–596 (D.C. Cir. 1987) (holding supervisors are not in same class as non-supervisors because they may have conflicting interests); *Roby v. St. Louis Sw. Ry. Co.*, 775 F.2d 959, 962 (8th Cir. 1985) (holding that employees could not represent a class of individuals affected by the railroad's promotion policies or those who were discharged for violating company rules because the employees' complaint did not derive from either of these circumstances).

[69] See Hart, *supra* n. 31, at 819–820 ('In the years after the Court emphasized the importance of adherence to the requirements of Rule 23, the number of class action suits filed in federal court decreased significantly.'); see also Scotty Shively, Resurgence of the Class Action Lawsuit in Employment Discrimination Cases: New Obstacles Presented by the 1991 Amendments to the Civil Rights Act, 23 U. Ark. Little Rock L. Rev. 925, 935 (2001) (indicating that Falcon ended widespread certification of across-the-board class actions in discrimination lawsuits because 'it was no longer sufficient for one plaintiff, represented by one law firm, to allege across-the-board discrimination'); John A. Tisdale, Deterred Nonapplicants in Title VII Class Actions: Examining the Limits of Equal Employment Opportunity, 64 B.U. L. Rev. 151, 171 (1984) ('The case signals an end to the procedural favoritism often granted Title VII plaintiffs by the federal courts and effectively rejects the across-the-board concept of class certification.').

[70] The court in *Black Grievance Committee v. Philadelphia Electric Co.*, 79 F.R.D. 98 (E.D. Pa. 1978), for instance, held it was 'clear that black plaintiffs possess the same interest and suffer the same injury as only the black class members who experienced the alleged racial discrimination,' but 'do not share the same interest as Spanish-surnamed [workers] who have allegedly suffered discrimination on the basis of national origin,' *id.* at 110.

[71] *Pagan v. DuBois*, 884 F. Supp. 25 (D. Mass. 1995).

[72] *Id.* at 26.

certification, the court reasoned that the designation 'Latino' was 'too general to be useful in formulating the specific judicial remedy sought here,' and also created intraclass conflicts that precluded adequate representation.[73] The court thus attached greater importance to intragroup differences than plaintiffs' allegations that the defendant viewed plaintiffs as a homogenous group of Latinos. As we discuss in 13.4, it is this view of class certification that has carried over to disability discrimination cases, namely, that perceived differences within the group are considered more salient than the common umbrella of alleged discrimination, and, as a consequence, classes are rarely certified.[74]

This conspicuous refusal to accept group claims on the basis of common, though socially imposed, identities has similarly restricted the efficacy of group-based ADA employment discrimination claims. As shown in the next section, rather than focusing on common membership in the disability classification, courts and commentators have dwelt on internal differences within the class, and in particular on what they perceive to be inherently individualized requests for relief. This, in turn, has limited the ability of people with disabilities to challenge workplace barriers that persist in keeping them as a group out of the workforce.

13.3 THE ORDINARY COURSE OF ADA CLAIMS

The early development of ADA Title I has followed a different path than its conceptual predecessor, Title VII. Whereas the period following the Civil Rights Act of 1964 embraced group-based discrimination theories, disability-based employment suits have proceeded almost entirely

---

[73] To quote the court at length:

> Latin-America is a continent comprising many countries consisting of people of many races and ethnic origins. There is a potential conflict within the proposed Latino class between Latinos who are citizens of Brazil, for example, and Latinos who are citizens of the United States ... and between Latinos whose culture derives from Africa and those whose culture derives from Western Europe. ... What Latino culture is to be taught and celebrated?

Id. at 28.

[74] See *infra* 13.3.2.

on an individualized basis.[75] In doing so, antidiscrimination jurisprudence has missed a crucial opportunity for developing ADA principles.

13.3.1 Failure to Accommodate

Cases under Title I of the ADA, and especially plaintiffs' claims for reasonable accommodations, have developed as the antithesis of collective action. The dominant theme of these ADA cases has been an almost exclusive focus on an individual plaintiff's particular circumstances and the specific accommodation that was requested. Yet many of the entrenched barriers keeping people with disabilities out of the workplace are a result of prejudice and neglect (rather than outright animus) that derive from membership in the disability classification. Further, these barriers can affect a wide range of disabilities beyond the specific individual in question.[76]

The ADA defines employment discrimination to include 'not making reasonable accommodations to the known physical or mental limitations of an otherwise qualified individual with a disability' who is a job applicant or current employee.[77] Reasonable accommodations encompass a wide range of adjustments to existing workplace conditions, but are mainly conceptualized as falling into one or another of two categories. The first category requires the alteration or provision of a physical plant.[78] An obvious example is ramping a stair to

---

[75] However, it bears noting that ADA litigation is encumbered by the same selection bias that affects Title VII suits. Because plaintiffs' lawyers typically operate on a contingency fee basis, they prefer discharge cases, especially ones involving well remunerated employees. John J. Donohue III & Peter Siegelman, The Changing Nature of Employment Discrimination Litigation, 43 Stan. L. Rev. 983 (1991) (citing a study that found that 80% of wrongful termination suits in California were filed by workers 'who had been terminated for inadequate performance' and only 20% of workers 'lost their jobs due to exogenous economic factors'). Hence, plaintiffs who seek to bring failure to hire claims under the ADA are relatively unattractive to rational attorneys, as are non-hired Title VII plaintiffs.

[76] See *infra* 13.3.2.

[77] 42 U.S.C. § 12112(b)(5)(A) (2000). Seven other forms of conduct defined as discriminatory are set forth in this provision. We return to the broader, more ecumenical ones, *infra* text accompanying notes 112–116.

[78] 42 U.S.C. § 12111(9)(A) (2000) (requiring an employer to make 'existing facilities used by employees readily accessible to and usable by individuals with disabilities').

CHAPTER 13. DISABILITY, DISPARATE IMPACT, AND CLASS ACTIONS

accommodate the needs of an employee who uses a wheelchair. These types of accommodations involve 'hard' costs, meaning that they invoke readily quantifiable out-of-pocket expenses.[79] Furthermore, their existence becomes quickly known in the workplace; a ramp at the entrance to a store may be welcome but its presence is not unobtrusive. The second type of accommodation involves an alteration of the way in which a job is performed, or the criteria for obtaining that job.[80] Examples of this latter form of accommodation include dispensing a wheelchair-using store employee from having to stack high shelves, or eliminating eye examinations as job criteria for psychologists, some of whom may be visually impaired. These accommodations bring into play 'soft' costs, which are more difficult to quantify.[81] Soft-cost accommodations are harder to discern: there is no reason to know that a coworker is off administering an insulin injection rather than having a bathroom break, or that an employee was not subjected to a Rorschach ink blot test because some persons with cerebral palsy cannot perceive the depth of the diagrams.[82]

Failure-to-accommodate cases typically proceed in a highly atomistic way, with individual claimants requesting what they deem as a reasonable (hard-or soft-cost) accommodation that will enable them to perform the essential functions of a particular job.[83] Should the employer decline the accommodation request as part of the 'interactive process,'[84] the aggrieved workers may file a complaint with the Equal

---

[79] Michael Ashley Stein, Empirical Implications of Title I, 85 Iowa L. Rev. 1671, 1677–1681 (2000).

[80] 42 U.S.C. § 12111(9)(B) (allowing job restructuring or modification, variation in existing methods of administration, and the provision of readers or interpreters).

[81] Stein, *supra* n. 79, at 1677.

[82] See generally Stedman's Medical Dictionary 1301 (27th edn 2000) (listing symptoms of cerebral palsy).

[83] 42 U.S.C. § 12111(8). Statutory protection also extends to disabled workers capable of performing essential job functions without provision of reasonable accommodations, *id.*, but those individuals are beyond the scope of this article.

[84] 29 C.F.R. § 1630.2(o)(3), 1630.9 (2006). One would think that profit-maximizing employers acting in their own self-interest would have already expended resources to figure out the 'real costs,' including positive and negative externalities, of employing disabled workers. That they fail to do so suggests a market failure. See Michael Ashley Stein, Labor Markets, Rationality, and Workers with Disabilities, 21 Berkeley J. Emp. & Lab. L. 314 (2000); see also Sharon Hartman & Pamela M. Robert, The Social Construction of Disability in Organizations: Why Employers Resist

Employment Opportunity Commission (EEOC).[85] In the event that parties cannot resolve their differences, plaintiffs can file suits asserting that the denial of their individual accommodation requests violates the ADA's mandates.[86] If the trial court finds a requested accommodation to be reasonable,[87] then that accommodation is provided, and the specific workplace policy is altered for an individual.[88] Wholly absent from this emblematic account is a discussion of whether other individuals with disabilities might be impacted by the provision of this accommodation.[89] Similarly, these cases do not delve, either

---

Reasonable Accommodation, 25 Work & Occupations 397 (1998) (concluding that although employers frame their resistance to providing accommodations in terms of economics, their real motivation is to maintain hierarchical control of the workplace and the way it is organized).

[85] 42 U.S.C. § 2000(e)(5) (2000); see 29 C.F.R. § 1601.6–1601.8 (2006) (establishing the guidelines for this process). At this point, either the employer or the employee can request mediation of their differences, which the ADA does not require, but strongly advises. 42 U.S.C. § 12212 (2000). In a self-evaluation, the EEOC found the process to be effective. See E. Patrick McDermott et al., An Evaluation of the Equal Employment Opportunity Commission Mediation Program (2000), <www.eeoc.gov/mediate/report/summary.html> (last visited October 15, 2006) (finding 'a high degree of participant satisfaction with the EEOC mediation program').

[86] Other claims beyond failure to accommodate can also be alleged, for instance, disability harassment. See Holland M. Tahvonen, Disability-Based Harassment: Standing and Standards for a 'New' Cause of Action, 44 Wm. & Mary L. Rev. 1489, 1494–1495 (2003) ('Disability harassment as a cause of action is modeled after the Title VII harassment claim.').

[87] Although the reasonable accommodation mandate is fundamental to disability-based employment discrimination, neither the ADA nor interpreting courts have provided much guidance on how to determine the reasonableness of accommodations. For an initial, hopefully useful, economic framework, see generally Michael Ashley Stein, The Law and Economics of Disability Accommodations, 53 Duke L.J. 79 (2003).

[88] For a political science perspective on the hierarchy shift this entails, see Ruth O'Brien, Bodies in Revolt: Gender, Disability, and a Workplace Ethic of Care (2005).

[89] According to Richard Epstein, the prospect of having workers with disabilities employed by the same firm is a positive event; rather than 'handicap ghettoization,' the concentration of workers with disabilities at particular sites increases the likelihood that physical plant or equipment accommodations will see repeated usage. Richard A. Epstein, Forbidden Grounds: The Case Against Employment Discrimination Laws 480–494 (1992). Similarly, J.H. Verkerke argues that employees ideally should be matched with a company capable of duplicating accommodations

CHAPTER 13. DISABILITY, DISPARATE IMPACT, AND CLASS ACTIONS

statistically or anecdotally, into the employer's historical or current patterns of accommodating (or hiring or promoting) people with disabilities in the workplace.[90]

Under this existing model, failure to accommodate claims do not consider the possibility of disparate impact theory. To date, published federal decisions have not specifically determined a single failure to accommodate employment claim under disparate impact analysis.[91] The Supreme Court decision in *Raytheon Co. v. Hernandez*[92] provided a notable exception by acknowledging the broad proposition that 'disparate-impact claims are cognizable under the ADA.'[93] *Raytheon*, however, did not involve workplace accommodation, and the Court did not elaborate its reasoning as to the viability of disparate impact theory in the disability discrimination context.[94] Because *Raytheon* did

---

because an economy of scale would ultimately bring down the accommodation cost. J.H. Verkerke, Is the ADA Efficient?, 50 UCLA L. Rev. 903, 935–937 (2003). An important point that is tangential to this Article bears noting. When advocating in favor of the efficiency of repeated accommodations, Professors Epstein and Verkerke both support, by inference, the notion of directed placements, meaning that they favor specific vocational placements for workers with disabilities who evidence certain skills. To the extent that this policy either limits the development of disabled workers or shunts them into certain careers, we very strongly disagree. However, to the extent that such a policy duplicates some of the gains made in the past through vocational rehabilitation that afforded recipients job support and options, we endorse it.

[90] See Wendy Wilkerson, Judicially Crafted Barriers to Bringing Suit Under the Americans with Disabilities Act, 38 S. Tex. L. Rev. 907, 910–915 (1997).

[91] Some, however, acknowledge the possibility of disparate impact in dicta when the immediate decision is not favorable to the plaintiff. See e.g., *Reichmann v. Cutler-Hammer, Inc.*, 183 F. Supp. 2d 1292, 1296 (D. Kan. 2001) (questioning, tangentially, the application of disparate impact theory to an employment-related medical inquiry).

[92] *Raytheon Co. v. Hernandez*, 540 U.S. 44 (2003).

[93] *Id.* at 53.

[94] *Raytheon* was remanded to the Ninth Circuit to determine whether the defendant had discriminated against Hernandez on the basis of his disability. *Id.* at 55. As a former drug user, Hernandez fell within the ADA's aegis. *Id.* at 50 n. 4. Raytheon asserted that it declined to rehire the rehabilitated Hernandez because he had violated company rules while under the influence of drugs, and hence not (then) disabled. *Id.* at 48–50, 55. Admittedly, Mr. Hernandez, a drug user working for a missile-making defense contractor, *id.* at 46, does not provoke very sympathetic arguments in favor of disparate impact litigation for disabled workers. However, putting to the side Mr. Hernandez's personal circumstances (as well as fears of

not express an opinion one way or the other on disparate impact being applied to failure-to-accommodate claims, it should be viewed as a floor, not a ceiling, to the type of ADA claims that can be brought under disparate impact theory.

Class action litigation is also notably missing from the realm of failure to accommodate cases. Only a handful of disability employment-related class actions have been brought. In this limited pool of reported cases, denials of class certifications vastly outnumber grants of class status. Courts have denied certification to five classes containing individuals with a range of disabilities, and their respective denials were predicated on the notion that the remedies granted, if any, were based on individualized inquiry into disability and the accommodation needed, and thus lacked typicality.[95] Conversely, two classes have been certified which were comprised of individuals with the

---

public injury), the dynamic of the rules he challenged can be extrapolated to individuals with disabilities more generally. See *infra* 13.3.2, 13.4.

[95] See *Dalton v. Subaru-Isuzu Auto., Inc.*, 141 F.3d 667, 680–681 (7th Cir. 1998) (affirming the denial of class certification of employees with various forms of repetitive stress disorder); *Sokol v. New United Motor Mfg., Inc.*, No. C 97-4211 SI, 1999 U.S. Dist. LEXIS 20215, at 3–4, 14–18 (N.D. Cal. September 17, 1999) (denying class certification of individuals with various wrist and shoulder injuries on the ground that two of the four challenged practices were 'inseparable from the interactive process of determining reasonable accommodations'); *Mandichak v. Consol. Rail Corp.*, 94-CV-1071, 1998 U.S. Dist. LEXIS 23005, at 30–31 (W.D. Pa. August 20, 1998) (denying, on the ground of lack of typicality, class certification of diversely disabled employees asserting defendant engaged in a pattern or practice of discrimination in denying workplace accommodations); *Davoll v. Webb*, 160 F.R.D. 142, 146 (D. Colo. 1995) (refusing to certify a class of injured police officers seeking reassignment to light duty because individualized inquiries were needed to determine disability of plaintiffs); *Lintemuth v. Saturn Corp.*, No. 1:93-0211, 1994 U.S. Dist. LEXIS 18601, at 1–15 (M.D. Tenn. August 29, 1994) (magistrate report and recommendation) (eschewing class certification of individuals with carpal tunnel syndrome and/or nerve ailments on the basis that individualizing inquiry necessarily failed the typicality requirement), enforced, No. 1-93-0211, 1994 U.S. Dist. LEXIS 17379 (M.D. Tenn. October 31, 1994); see also *Frank v. United Airlines*, 216 F.3d 845, 856–857 (9th Cir. 2000) (precluding a suit by flight attendants for discrimination based on maximum weight requirements on several grounds, including that plaintiffs failed to demonstrate a causal connection between alleged eating disorders and the contested policy); *Schroedel v. N.Y. Univ. Med. Ctr.*, 885 F. Supp. 594, 597–600 (S.D.N.Y. 1995) (denying certification of class action of hearing impaired people for emergency room

CHAPTER 13. DISABILITY, DISPARATE IMPACT, AND CLASS ACTIONS

same types of disability (hearing and visual impairments).[96] One class composed of two discrete types of disability (diabetes and epilepsy) has been certified,[97] as has one class motion granted for individuals with a variety of disabilities seriously injured in a hog slaughtering plant (including individuals with various workplace injuries that created permanent workplace restrictions).[98] When these suits are certified as class actions it is either the wholesale exclusion of diversely disabled people, or the specific exclusion of a homogeneous group of disabled people, that forms a sufficiently unifying theme to pass Rule 23 muster.[99]

With non-disability discrimination, class action litigation has played a central role in systemic challenges to employment exclusion.[100] This is especially true when actions are brought as part of a program of vigorous public implementation.[101] Public enforcement

---

sign language interpreters on the ground that the named plaintiff failed to demonstrate a likelihood of needing such service in future).

[96] See *Bates v. UPS*, 204 F.R.D. 440, 449 (N.D. Cal. 2001) (certifying a class of employees who ' "use sign language as a primary means of communication due to a hearing loss or limitation" ' (quoting Plaintiff's Motion for Class Certification)); *Wilson v. Pa. State Police Dep't*, No. 94-CV-6547, 1995 U.S. Dist. LEXIS 9981, at 1–12 (E.D. Pa. July 14, 1995) (certifying challenge by individuals with correctable visual impairments under both Title I and the Rehabilitation Act).

[97] See *EEOC v. Nw. Airlines*, 216 F. Supp. 2d 935, 937–938 (D. Minn. 2002) (certifying a class of anti-seizure medicated epileptics and insulin-dependant diabetics who were denied positions as cleaners or equipment service employees).

[98] See *Hendricks-Robinson v. Excel Corp.*, 154 F.3d 685, 687, 700 (7th Cir. 1998) (reporting, and not reversing, the district court's certification of a class of 'former production workers... who were injured on the job and placed on medical layoff after they received permanent medical restrictions that precluded them from performing their regular jobs and any other available production jobs at the plant').

[99] Thus, the court in *Bates* reasoned that the entire class sought 'to remedy policies and practices at UPS that allegedly discriminate illegally against the hearing disabled.' 204 F.R.D. at 447.

[100] On the role that class actions play in employment discrimination as a means and incentive toward changing business practices through combining statistical evidence and proof, see Maimon Schwarzschild, Public Law By Private Bargain: Title VII Consent Decrees and the Fairness of Negotiated Institutional Reform, 1984 Duke L.J. 887, 914–929 (discussing the transformative effect of class action litigation).

[101] See Drew S. Days, III, 'Feedback Loop': The Civil Rights Act of 1964 and Its Progeny, 49 St. Louis U. L.J. 981, 987–988 (2005) (suggesting that forceful and prompt enforcement of Title II of the Civil Rights Act of 1964 was crucial to its success in creating social change; see also U.S. Comm'n on Civil Rights, Federal Civil

authorities like the Department of Justice and the EEOC that extensively litigate employment class action cases under Title VII,[102] however, have not shown a proclivity toward bringing ADA class action suits.[103] The same is true for public interest law firms that have shown themselves willing to use the class action device in disability discrimination cases outside the employment context.[104] Instead,

---

Rights Enforcement Effort 10 (1971) ('Within a few months after enactment, the Department... brought several enforcement actions that tested the constitutionality of the public accommodations law.').

[102] For example, the analysis of one Nobel Prize-winning economist and three of his colleagues indicates that it was protracted governmental enforcement of Title VII that had the greatest effect on narrowing the race-based wage gap in the South. John J. Donohue III & James Heckman, Continuous Versus Episodic Change: The Impact of Civil Rights Policy on the Economic Status of Blacks, 29 J. Econ. Literature 1603, 1605 (1991) ('When all aspects of the Federal attack on Southern discrimination are considered, there is significant alignment the strength of the Federal pressure in the South and the accompanying rise in black economic status there.'); James J. Heckman & Brook S. Payner, Determining the Impact of Federal Antidiscrimination Policy on the Economic Status of Blacks: A Study of South Carolina, 79 Am. Econ. Rev. 138, 173 (1989) ('Government activity... seems to be the most plausible source for this change [in black economic progress].'); see Richard Butler & James J. Heckman, The Government's Impact on the Labor Market Status of Black Americans: A Critical Review, in Equal Rights and Industrial Relations 235, 252 (Leonard J. Hausman et al. eds, 1977).

[103] This is not to belittle either individual employment suits, or actions brought under other provisions of the statute. They are important. However, the commitment to using civil rights statutes to leverage broad social change has been glaringly absent in the context of disability discrimination. For instance, although the EEOC's workload increased dramatically due to the addition of ADA disputes, its budget remained largely unchanged. See Kathryn Moss et al., Unfunded Mandate: An Empirical Study of the Implementation of the Americans with Disabilities Act by the Equal Employment Opportunity Commission, 50 U. Kan. L. Rev. 1, 73 (2001) ('With the enactment of the ADA, the EEOC experienced a 53% increase in yearly charge receipts [from 1990 to 1994].... During this time of a tremendous increase..., the EEOC yearly budget rose less than 10% in real dollar terms.... While the 15% budget increase approved by Congress for the 1999 fiscal year has helped increase staffing and resources, this increase is still not commensurate with the increase in workload the EEOC has experienced in the past decade.' (footnotes omitted)).

[104] See e.g., *Henrietta D. v. Bloomberg*, 331 F.3d 261, 265 (2nd Cir. 2003) (class action challenging accommodations in New York City Social Services); *Barden v. City of Sacramento*, 292 F.3d 1073, 1075 (9th Cir. 2002) (class action challenging inaccessible

CHAPTER 13. DISABILITY, DISPARATE IMPACT, AND CLASS ACTIONS

because courts and commentators hesitate to view individuals with diverse disabilities as having a sufficient community of interest to proceed under a group-based discrimination theory, Title I litigation has focused on the definition of disability or the reasonableness of individual accommodations.[105]

13.3.2 Missed Potential

The use of group-based discrimination theories of disparate impact law and the class action device could have facilitated the entry of people with disabilities into the workplace, much as they previously did on behalf of persons of color and women. Modeled after Title VII, the ADA shares in its desire to eradicate historical and avoidable barriers to workplace participation – the 'built in headwinds' that form the provenance of disparate impact theory.[106] As articulated by Judge Richard Posner in a nondisability disparate impact employment discrimination case: 'The concept of disparate impact was developed for the purpose of identifying situations in which, through inertia or insensitivity, companies were following policies that gratuitously... excluded black or female workers from equal employment opportunities.'[107] Yet, neither judges nor scholars have felt comfortable replacing 'black or female workers' with 'disabled workers.'[108] In consequence, the ADA's first fifteen years may be justly criticized as

---

sidewalks); *Nelson v. Miller*, 170 F.3d 641, 644 (6th Cir. 1999) (class action challenging Michigan voting systems).

[105] See Rutherglen, *supra* n. 22, at 71 & n. 37 (suggesting that the 'most notable example' of a lack of disparate impact class action litigation is the ADA).

[106] See e.g., *DiBiase v. SmithKline Beechum Co.*, 48 F.3d 719, 734 (3rd Cir. 1995) ('The objective of Congress in the enactment of Title VII... was to achieve equality of employment opportunities and remove barriers that have operated in the past. ...' (quoting *Griggs v. Duke Power Co.*, 401 U.S. 424, 429–430 (1971))).

[107] *Finnegan v. Transworld Airways, Inc.*, 967 F.2d 1161, 1164 (7th Cir. 1992).

[108] Cf. Christine Jolls, Antidiscrimination and Accommodation, 115 Harv. L. Rev. 643–644 (2001) ('Observers sharply contrast Title VII... and other older civil rights enactments, which are said to be "real anti-discrimination laws," with the [ADA]... said to be "accommodation" laws. On these observers' view, "antidiscrimination" focuses on "equal" treatment, while "accommodation" focuses on "special" treatment.' (second alteration in original) (footnotes omitted)).

having missed opportunities to challenge barriers excluding workers with disabilities.[109] The shift by courts away from an earlier paradigm of race-and sex-based collective action has exacerbated this failing. This wholesale exclusion of group-based discrimination theories from Title I is myopic, and certainly not inevitable.[110] Despite the interpretive regulations' discussion of individualized assessments,[111] the ADA itself does not foreclose collective action.

As an initial matter, the dearth of failure-to-accommodate claims treated under the Title VII disparate impact framework is puzzling. In addition to prohibiting denials of reasonable accommodation requests, the ADA also proscribes other actions corresponding to those barred by

---

[109] Several studies have documented the inability of the ADA to move people with disabilities in greater numbers into the workforce. The federal government's National Health Information Survey found that when disability is defined as an impairment that imposes limitations on any life activity, the employment rate for working-age people with disabilities declined from 49% in 1990 to 46.6% in 1996. See H. Stephen Kaye, Improved Employment Opportunities for People with Disabilities 9 & fig.1 (2003). Similarly, a 2000 Harris Survey of working-age people with disabilities showed that only 32% of people with disabilities reported being employed, compared with 81% of the general population. Nat'l Org. on Disability, 2000 N.O.D./Harris Survey of Americans with Disabilities 27 (2000). This is not to say that we characterize the overall ADA experience negatively. The jury is still out on how efficacious the statute has been and, perhaps more importantly, on how to measure success. At the same time, much ink has been, and will continue to be spilled on this issue. A balanced, but far from unanimous critique, are the essays in The Americans with Disabilities Act: Empirical Perspectives (Michael Ashley Stein & Samuel Estreicher eds, Kluwer Law International, 2007).

[110] For an intra-Title comparison of ADA litigation, see generally Michael E. Waterstone, The Untold Story of the Rest of the Americans with Disabilities Act, 58 Vand. L. Rev. 1807 (2005).

[111] See 29 C.F.R. pt. 1630 app. (2006) ('The determination of whether an individual is qualified for a particular position must necessarily be made on a case-by-case basis. ... An accommodation must be tailored to match the needs of the disabled individual with the needs of the job's essential functions. This case-by-case approach is essential. ... Neither the ADA nor this part can supply the "correct" answer in advance for each employment decision. ... '); see also id. § 1630.2(j) ('The determination of whether an individual has a disability is not necessarily based on the name or diagnosis of the impairment the person has, but rather on the effect of that impairment on the life of the individual.').

[112] 42 U.S.C. § 12112(b)(5)(A)-(B) (2000); see also id. § 12112(b)(1)–(7) (listing seven varieties of prohibited employment-related activities).

CHAPTER 13. DISABILITY, DISPARATE IMPACT, AND CLASS ACTIONS

Title VII.[112] Specifically, it forbids the use of administrative methods, criteria, and standards that tend to exclude disabled workers in the manner proscribed by disparate impact theories.[113] This confluence is the result of Congress' conscious decision to model the ADA after Title VII.[114] Correspondingly, Title I is as silent on the motivation behind a refusal to provide accommodation as the Civil Rights Act of 1964 is on the level of necessary intent.[115] That failure to accommodate claims were intended to fall somewhere within the panoply of previous civil rights remedies can also be inferred from the inclusion of all ADA remedies among those antidiscrimination provisions amended by the Civil Rights Act of 1991.[116]

---

[113] *Id.* § 12112(b)(3), (6), (7) (banning practices with disproportionate effect). The ADA also makes illegal the conscious exclusion and segregation of disabled workers typical of disparate treatment analysis. *Id.* § 12112(b)(1), (b)(2), (b)(4) (prohibiting overt treatment policies).

[114] See Robert L. Burgdorf Jr., The Americans with Disabilities Act: Analysis and Implications of a Second-Generation Civil Rights Statute, 26 Harv. C.R.-C.L. L. Rev. 413, 464 (1991) (averring that the 'ADA committee reports expressly declare congressional intent that the "futile gesture" doctrine recognized by the courts in actions under Title VII of the Civil Rights Act of 1964 should also apply to actions under this Act.' (footnote omitted)); see also H.R. Rep. No. 101-485(II), at 82 (1990), as reprinted in 1990 U.S.C.C.A.N. 303, 305 ('An agreement was made that people with disabilities should have the same remedies available to all other minorities under Title VII of the Civil Rights Act of 1964.'); S. Rep. No. 100-116, at 42–43 (1989) ('The [ADA] legislation specifies that the remedies and procedures set forth in Sections 706, 707, 709, and 710 of the Civil Rights Act of 1964 shall be available with respect to ... any individual who believes that he or she is being subjected to discrimination on the basis of disability. ... '); Richard K. Scotch, Making Change: The ADA as an Instrument of Social Reform, in Americans with Disabilities: Exploring Implications of the Law for Individuals and Institutions 275, 276 (Leslie Pickering Francis & Anita Silvers eds, 2000) ('Using the Civil Rights Act of 1964 as a legislative template, the ADA seeks to eliminate the marginalization of people with disabilities through established civil rights remedies to discrimination.').

[115] 42 U.S.C. § 12112(b)(5)(A)-(B) (2000). So, too, are the Equal Employment Opportunity Commission's promulgated interpretive guidelines. See 29 C.F.R. § 1630.9(b) (2006) (stating that discrimination occurs when a covered entity 'denies employment opportunities to an otherwise qualified job applicant or employee with a disability based on the need of such covered entity to make reasonable accommodation to such individual's physical or mental impairments').

[116] 42 U.S.C. § 1981a(a) (2000) (incorporating the provisions of both Title VII and the ADA).

Although federal courts have not articulated a reason for not applying disparate impact analysis to ADA failure to accommodate claims, three plausible juridical reasons can be inferred.[117] First, although the handful of judges who have addressed the possibility of applying disparate impact theory to failure to accommodate cases do so tangentially, their oblique references suggest that federal courts view allegations of failure to accommodate as a mutually exclusive and stand-alone alternative to disparate impact claims. For example, while addressing a potential claim, the Seventh Circuit in *Hoffman v. Caterpillar, Inc.*[118] held that once a disabled plaintiff establishes her qualifications to proceed under the ADA, 'she may show discrimination in either of two ways: by presenting evidence of disparate treatment or by showing a failure to accommodate.'[119] The notion that a plaintiff might proceed with a disparate impact theory was not considered by the court as being within the realm of possibility. Similar statements have been made, in dicta, by other courts, thereby lending credence to this supposition.[120] However, neither the ADA's

---

[117] Another plausible (although less appealing) political reason might be judicial hostility to the ADA. To quote one disability rights advocate: 'Many, perhaps most, courts are not enforcing the law, but instead are finding incredibly inventive means of interpreting the ADA to achieve the opposite result that the Act was intended to achieve.' Bonnie Poitras Tucker, The ADA's Revolving Door: Inherent Flaws in the Civil Rights Paradigm, 62 Ohio St. L.J. 335, 338 (2001). Tucker's assertion has been endorsed by a number of scholars. See e.g., Chai R. Feldblum, Definition of Disability Under Federal Anti-Discrimination Law: What Happened? Why? And What Can We Do About It?, 21 Berkeley J. Emp. & Lab. L. 91, 93 (2000) ('How did those of us who helped draft the ADA so completely misread how the courts would apply its definition of disability?'). See generally Linda Hamilton Krieger, Backlash Against the ADA: Interdisciplinary Perspectives and Implications for Social Justice Strategies, 21 Berkeley J. Emp. & Lab. L. 1 (2000).
[118] *Hoffman v. Caterpillar, Inc.*, 256 F.3d 568 (7th Cir. 2001).
[119] *Id.* at 572; cf. *Butlemeyer v. Fort Wayne Cmty. Sch.*, 100 F.3d 1281, 1283 (7th Cir. 1996) ('This is not a disparate treatment claim, but a reasonable accommodation claim, and it must be analyzed differently.').
[120] See e.g., *Henrietta D. v. Bloomberg*, 331 F.3d 261, 275 (2nd Cir. 2003) ('Other courts have explicitly distinguished claims based on failure reasonably to accommodate from those based on disparate impact.'); *Bailey v. Georgia-Pacific Corp.*, 306 F.3d 1162, 1166 (1st Cir. 2002) ('In addition to forbidding disparate treatment of those with disabilities, the ADA makes it unlawful for an employer to fail to provide reasonable accommodations. . . . '); *Wright v. Ill. Dep't of Corr.*, 204 F.3d 727, 730 (7th Cir. 2000)

CHAPTER 13. DISABILITY, DISPARATE IMPACT, AND CLASS ACTIONS

text nor its legislative history support this mutually exclusive perception.[121]

A second, related reason that courts may hesitate to apply disparate impact theory to ADA claims is if they believe Title I to have a relatively less clear statutory basis for disparate impact than Title VII.[122] The 1991 amendments to Title VII, enacted in the aftermath of *Wards Cove*, unequivocally state that the disparate impact proof structure may be applied to all actions brought under its aegis.[123] In contrast, the ADA does not contain as firm a statutory foundation for upholding disparate impact law. But this, too, is unpersuasive. As noted in the previous

---

('There are two types of disability discrimination claims under the ADA: disparate treatment claims and failure to accommodate claims.'); *Garcia-Ayala v. Lederle Parenterals, Inc.*, 212 F.3d 638, 646 n. 9 (1st Cir. 2000) ('The ADA does more than prohibit disparate treatment. It also imposes an affirmative obligation to provide reasonable accommodation to disabled employees.'); *Dunlap v. Ass'n of Bay Area Gov'ts*, 996 F. Supp. 962, 965 (N.D. Cal. 1998) ('A disability discrimination claim may be brought either on the theory that defendant failed to make reasonable accommodations or on a more conventional disparate treatment theory. ... ').

[121] If anything, the legislative history supports the opposite conclusion. See e.g., S. Rep. No. 101-116, 30 (1989) ('Subparagraphs (B) and (C) [of § 102(b)(3) of the ADA] incorporate a disparate impact standard to ensure that the legislative mandate to end discrimination does not ring hollow. This standard is consistent with the interpretation of section 504 [of the Rehabilitation Act] by the U.S. Supreme Court in *Alexander v. Choate*, 469 U.S. 287 (1985).'); see also ADA of 1989: Hearing on S. 933 Before the Comm. on Labor and Human Resources and the Subcomm. on the Handicapped, 101st Cong. 321 (1989) (statement of Arlene Mayerson, Directing Attorney, Disability Rights Education and Defense Fund) ('It is well accepted under Title VII that selection procedures that have a disparate impact on racial minorities and women must be necessary to safe and efficient job performance. The ADA extends that protection to persons with disabilities who, as demonstrated earlier, are often subject to disqualifying physical or mental criteria that bear no relationship to job performance.').

[122] This may not be surprising as the clarity and persuasiveness of legislative history itself differentiates two recent Supreme Court ADA opinions. Compare *Bd. of Trs. of the Univ. of Ala. v. Garrett*, 531 U.S. 356, 368 (2001) (majority of the Court unconvinced of the sufficiency of legislative history of States discriminating in employment), with *Tennessee v. Lane*, 541 U.S. 509, 529–530 (2004) (Court majority won over by legislative evidence of States discriminating in the provision of services).

[123] See 42 U.S.C. § 2000e-2(k)(1)(A) (2000) (providing that 'an unlawful employment practice based on disparate impact is established under this title only if –,' and then continuing by describing disparate impact proof structure).

section, the Supreme Court held in *Raytheon* that disparate impact claims may be brought under the ADA.[124] Although the Court in *Raytheon* had no occasion to consider whether failure to accommodate claims could also be brought under disparate impact theory, there is no statutory reason they should not be. Indeed, in *Raytheon*, the Court held that 'standards, criteria, or methods of administration,' and 'qualification standards, employment tests, or other selection criteria' were cognizable under disparate impact theory, because they were part of Title I's definition of disability.[125] 'Not providing reasonable accommodations' is likewise part of the same statutory definition of disability.[126]

A third reason why courts may not have embraced failure to accommodate as disparate impact cases relates to perceived similarities between the ADA and the Age Discrimination in Employment Act[127] (ADEA).[128] In 2005, in *Smith v. City of Jackson*,[129] the Supreme Court clarified that disparate impact claims can be brought under the ADEA.[130] Before *Smith*, however, courts that had not readily

---

[124] See *supra* text accompanying n. 93.
[125] See *Raytheon Co. v. Hernandez*, 540 U.S. 44, 51 (2003) (quoting 42 U.S.C. § 12112(b)).
[126] 42 U.S.C. § 12112(b)(5)(A) (2000).
[127] 29 U.S.C. § 621–634 (2000).
[128] *Stevens v. Kay Mgmt.*, 907 F. Supp. 169, 171–172 (E.D. Va. 1995) ('When called upon to interpret the ADA, other courts often have looked to the [ADEA]...for guidance. The ADA [and] ADEA...have virtually identical definitions and liability schemes and all are designed with a common purpose: to prohibit discrimination in employment.'). The most extensive treatment of this (now incorrect) analogy in the legal literature is by Samuel Issacharoff. See Samuel Issacharoff, The Difficult Path from Observation to Prescription, 77 N.Y.U. L. Rev. 36, 37 (2002) (concluding that the creation of causes of action for disability and age discrimination required 'significant contortions' of antidiscrimination law); see also Samuel Issacharoff & Erica Worth Harris, Is Age Discrimination Really Age Discrimination?: The ADEA's Unnatural Solution, 72 N.Y.U. L. Rev. 780, 781 (1997) (positing that 'the ADEA statutory scheme misconstrues the antidiscrimination model'); Samuel Issacharoff & Justin Nelson, Discrimination with a Difference: Can Employment Discrimination Law Accommodate the Americans with Disabilities Act?, 79 N.C. L. Rev. 307, 314 (2001) (citing the ADA's reasonable accommodation standard as unique in that it, unlike Title VII, begins its inquiry with 'the claim that different sets of employees who are differently situated').
[129] *Smith v. City of Jackson*, 544 U.S. 228 (2005).
[130] *Id.* at 233–240.

CHAPTER 13. DISABILITY, DISPARATE IMPACT, AND CLASS ACTIONS

recognized disparate impact theory in ADEA cases[131] may have viewed the ADA in the same vein.[132] However, in addition to Supreme Court clarification on both accounts, the argument for applying disparate impact to ADA failure to accommodate claims is even stronger than in the ADEA context. Both the ADA and Title VII were promulgated as a means of eradicating historical barriers to workplace participation, the traditional province of disparate impact theory.[133] The ADEA, in contrast, placed greater emphasis on disparate treatment type of discrimination.[134] Most crucially, the ADEA applies to individuals nearer to the end of their livelihoods than those individuals vulnerable to

---

[131] The basis of this position is *Hazen Paper Co. v. Biggins*, 507 U.S. 604 (1993), wherein the Supreme Court suggested, but did not expressly hold, that disparate impact theory does not apply to the ADEA, see *id.* at 610 ('Disparate treatment... captures the essence of what Congress sought to prohibit in the ADEA.').

[132] According to that argument, age, like disability, reduces individuals' productivity. Consequently, both forms of regulation engender additional costs that employers must bear. When businesses are required to forego discriminatory practices under the ADA, they overlook the same type of lower net-product margin that they do for workers under the ADEA, and thereby redistribute wealth from otherwise profit-maximizing employers to those less economically efficient but protected employees. See *supra* note 128.

[133] See e.g., *DiBiase v. SmithKline Beechum Co.*, 48 F.3d 719, 734 (3rd Cir. 1995) ('The objective of Congress in the enactment of Title VII... was to achieve equality of employment opportunities and remove barriers that have operated in the past. ...' (quoting *Griggs v. Duke Power Co.*, 401 U.S. 424 (1971))); see also 42 U.S.C. § 12101(a)(2)–(5) (2000) (setting forth the legislative findings regarding the historical exclusion of people with disabilities from American society, including the workplace).

[134] See e.g., *Ellis v. United Airlines, Inc.*, 73 F.3d 999, 1008 (10th Cir. 1996) (noting that 'the legislative history of the ADEA suggests it was not enacted to address disparate impact claims'); *Hiatt v. Union Pacific R.R.*, 859 F. Supp. 1416, 1436 (D. Wyo. 1994) ('In *Griggs*, the critical fact was the link between the history of educational discrimination and the use of that discrimination as a means of presently disadvantaging African-Americans. These concerns simply are not present when the alleged disparate impact is based on age.'); Douglas C. Herbert & Lani Schweiker Shelton, A Pragmatic Argument Against Applying the Disparate Impact Doctrine in Age Discrimination Cases, 37 S. Tex. L. Rev. 625, 647 (1996) (noting that the congressional concern 'with eliminating arbitrary barriers to employment' in the Title VII context cannot be extended 'to an history of past discrimination against these particular individuals who were previously younger and possibly the beneficiaries of... age discrimination"' (quoting *Hiatt*, 859 F. Supp. at 1436)).

discrimination over the course of their careers.[135] As a consequence of this different timing, groups of workers covered by Title VII and the ADA are more likely to be adversely affected to the extent that they will not develop their own human capital.[136] In the case of people with disabilities, for whom special welfare legislation has in the past been enacted on the presupposition that they cannot work,[137] the worst-case effect of discouragement from seeking integration in the workplace is that they feel compelled to accept public assistance for sustenance, and are thereby excluded from labor market participation.[138]

---

[135] See 29 U.S.C. § 631(a) (2002) (applying to workers at or over the age of forty).

[136] This is because individuals who are dissuaded by bleak prospects of fully participating in the labor market lower their own expectations, internalize poorer self-worth, and invest less in their own development, for example, in educational or vocational training. This brings about a self-fulfilling prophecy that shunts those individuals toward lower paying, under-demanding positions. See generally Gary S. Becker, Investment in Human Capital: A Theoretical Analysis, 70 J. Pol. Econ. (Supplement) 9, 9 (1962) ('The many ways to invest [in human capital] including schooling... [and] training. ... improve the physical and mental abilities of people and thereby raise real income prospects.'); Ruth Colker, Hypercapitalism: Affirmative Protections for People with Disabilities, Illness and Parenting Responsibilities Under United States Law, 9 Yale J.L. & Feminism 213, 215–216 (1997) ('America's version of capitalism. ... [wrongly] assumes that utility and efficiency for the entrepreneurial class must be the dominant principles. [Other Western countries, however] favor the welfare of the worker out of the conviction that such policies benefit both workers and the economy as a whole.'). This situation also reinforces the notion of people with anomalous biological traits being construed as inauthentic workers. See Vicki Schultz, Life's Work, 100 Colum. L. Rev. 1881, 1898 (2000) ('Courts all too often accept as an excuse for job segregation that women "lack interest" in the higher-paying, more desirable positions held by men. ... Women's work preferences... are seen as fixed by forces that are ontologically and temporally prior to [their] experiences in the world of paid work.').

[137] Michael J. Piore, Beyond Individualism: How Social Demands of the New Identity Groups Challenge American Political and Economic Life 36–44 (1995) ('The goal of employment policy is preeminently individualistic: it is the distribution of jobs and work rewards on the basis of the personal merit of the employee. ... The law was designed to sanction exceptional departures from meritocracy.').

[138] See e.g., U.S. Comm'n on Civil Rights, Accommodating the Spectrum of Individual Abilities 97 (1983) ('The assumption that handicapped people are fundamentally different and inherently restricted in their ability to participate becomes self-fulfilling as handicapped people are excluded from education, employment,

CHAPTER 13. DISABILITY, DISPARATE IMPACT, AND CLASS ACTIONS

Yet even if any of these explanations accurately describes the way in which courts have been reluctant to engage in traditional employment discrimination analyses when disability-related accommodations are at issue, it nonetheless still raises the question of why courts would adopt this approach.[139] Both employment discrimination and disability law literature are nearly silent on the potential for group-based discrimination theories for people with disabilities. There is some limited discussion about the similarities between disparate impact law and reasonable accommodation,[140] but most commentators are otherwise fairly dismissive of the potential of group-based discrimination theories (expressed through disparate impact or class action law) in disability employment discrimination cases.

Although not clearly articulated, the argument against group-based theories seems to be predicated on the notion that race and sex have, as groups, two unifying features that the disabled are missing. First, race and sex are biologically and socially distinct categories,

---

and other aspects of society by these consequences of the handicapped-normal dichotomy.').

[139] Parenthetically, the exclusion of failure to accommodate suits from either prong of the traditional framework might also be a result of courts viewing those claims as equivalent to non-accommodation suits in the religious discrimination context. See generally Laura S. Underkuffler, 'Discrimination' on the Basis of Religion: An Examination of Attempted Value Neutrality in Employment, 30 Wm. & Mary L. Rev. 581 (1989) (exploring the line between religious belief and Title VII religious discrimination in the workplace). Although religion-based protection requires the provision of de minimis (rather than reasonable) accommodations, 42 U.S.C. § 2000(e) (2000), courts have also routinely treated religious non-accommodation claims as falling outside the scope of standard discrimination analysis. See e.g., *Trans World Airlines, Inc. v. Hardison*, 432 U.S. 63, 83 (1977) (finding that an employee's request to observe Sabbath involved an undue hardship for the defendant-employer as it required violating a collective bargaining agreement involving seniority). Whether this reasoning actually motivates courts to reject failure to accommodate claims must remain a matter of conjecture. If judges believe that this parallel exists between disability and religious accommodation claims, they have yet to articulate this position.

[140] See e.g., Mary Crossley, Reasonable Accommodation as Part and Parcel of the Antidiscrimination Project, 35 Rutgers L.J. 861, 911 (2004) ('The fundamental likeness between reasonable accommodation and disparate impact lies in their common goal of eliminating unjustified barriers to equal workplace opportunity and inclusion.'); see also Jolls, *supra* n. 108, at 645 ('Some aspects of antidiscrimination law – in particular its disparate impact branch – are in fact requirements of accommodation.').

whereas the disability classification is comprised of people with many individual variations.[141] Second, racial minorities and women can request classwide relief from discriminatory policies in a 'one-size-fits-all' manner, but that people with disabilities need specific accommodations that vary from individual to individual.[142]

The next section challenges these assumptions. Viewed through the lens of pandisability, we argue that disability is much like race (and to a lesser degree, sex) in being a social construct when used as an exclusionary proxy. The group-based external perception of the disabled, like earlier notions of race and sex, should create a common umbrella for purposes of disparate impact law and class certification. Thus, even if disabled workers request accommodations that are 'individualized' – a concept that itself is overblown when one considers the notion of Universal Design[143] – it is their commonly experienced stigma that should bind the class together for purposes of group-based litigation theories.

13.4 THE ADA AS GROUP-BASED DISCRIMINATION

Section 13.3 demonstrated that group-based discrimination theories have neither been actively pursued nor accepted under Title I. Section 13.4.1 argues for the use of pandisability theory as a heuristic

---

[141] See George Rutherglen, Disparate Impact, Discrimination, and the Essentially Contested Concept of Equality, 74 Fordham L. Rev. 2313, 2319 (2006) ('Few class actions are brought under the employment provisions of the ADA because of the predominance of individual issues, such as the nature and extent of a plaintiff's disability. ... ').

[142] Issacharoff and Nelson come the closest to articulating this point:

> How should courts answer the question whether United Airlines should have to place another co-pilot in each cockpit for every pilot whose vision is worse than 20/100? ... If a pilot is hypertensive, should United be forced to place a doctor in the cockpit in order to give life-sustaining CPR in the case of a heart attack?

Issacharoff & Nelson, *supra* n. 128, at 340–341.

[143] Universal Design is an architectural concept whose goal is to design products that are usable by all people, to the greatest extent possible, without the need for adaptation or special design. Ctr. for Universal Design, N.C. State Univ., Principles of Universal Design, <www.design.ncsu.edu/cud/about ud/about ud.htm> (last visited October 17, 2006).

CHAPTER 13. DISABILITY, DISPARATE IMPACT, AND CLASS ACTIONS

for determining group-based disability employment claims. Next, section 13.4.2 demonstrates the neat convergence of the pandisability model with the class action procedure. Finally, section 13.4.3 shows how group-based disability employment actions, as conceived by pandisability theory and framed by the class action device, can start to challenge deeply entrenched norms that bar disability workplace participation.

13.4.1 Pandisability Theory

Panethnicity has been used as a proxy to treat internally heterogeneous individuals as having a set and unifying identity for the purpose of externally addressing that group's social standing.[144] What makes this norm particularly salient in race discrimination is modern-day recognition that race is an artificial construct.[145] Having evolved from an historical understanding as an inherent biological fact (correlated at one time by the number of African 'drops of blood' a person possessed),[146] race is understood as a contextual[147]

---

[144] See *supra* n. 27 and accompanying text.

[145] A good illustration of this fact is the treatment of race as being capable of encompassing more than one category ('multi-racial') in the most recent census. This represents a significant break with past practice, as it is the first time that individuals may claim multiple racial identities. U.S. Census Bureau, Racial and Ethnic Classifications Used in Census 2000 and Beyond, <www.census.gov/population/www/socdemo/race/racefactcb.html> (last visited October 17, 2006). Scientific evidence also clearly indicates that, from a genetic perspective, race is either a non-existent or an insignificant factor. Noah A. Rosenberg et al., Genetic Structure of Human Populations, 298 Sci. Mag. 2381, 2381 (2002).

[146] F. James Davis, One Nation's Definition 1–15 (1991); Ian F. Haney Lopez, White by Law: The Legal Construction of Race 124–129 (1996); See e.g., *Marre v. Marre*, 168 S.W. 636, 640 (Mo. Ct. App. 1914); *Younger v. Juda*, 111 Mo. 303, 308 (Mo. 1892); *People v. Dean*, 14 Mich. 406, 430 (Mich. 1866).

[147] Ariela Gross' scholarship on the historical use of law in determining race adds further evidence to the notion of race as a social construct. Professor Gross wisely demonstrates how, because the fractions of blood were not determinative, trials in nineteenth century Southern county courts investigated the 'racial "essence" inhering in one's blood' by asking juries to decide whether particular individuals 'performed' white or black. See Ariela J. Gross, Litigating Whiteness: Trials of Racial Determination in the Nineteenth-Century South, 108 Yale L.J. 109, 111 (1998).

and politically contingent category.[148] The Civil Rights Act of 1964 created a similar standard for the less-malleable category of sex[149] by examining socially created gender roles;[150] as a consequence, the Supreme Court has come to evaluate claims of physical difference and equality in light of social convention.[151]

Traditional employment law scholarship draws a bright line between race and sex discrimination, on the one hand, and disability discrimination, on the other. Indeed, the view that disability discrimination is inherently different is so prevalent that one scholar has termed it 'canonical.'[152] According to this received wisdom, discrimination on the basis of race or sex is unjust because these characteristics do not correlate with job performance; conversely, disability is relevant because it is a biological reality that corresponds to lower productivity. In consequence, providing workplace accommodations to the disabled does more than level an uneven playing field, it elevates them to a

---

[148] For recent assertions by two commentators on how race is currently perceived through the lens of behavior rather than biology and so discrimination must be engaged on that level, see Camille Gear Rich, Performing Racial and Ethnic Identity: Discrimination by Proxy and the Future of Title VII, 79 N.Y.U. L. Rev. 1134, 1269 (2005) and Kimberly A. Yuracko, Trait Discrimination as Race Discrimination: An Argument About Assimilation, 74 Geo. Wash. L. Rev. 365, 366 (2006).

[149] 42 U.S.C. 2000e-2(a)(1) (2000). Exceptions from this rule are those few individuals who change their sex. See e.g., Julie A. Greenberg, An Interdisciplinary and Cross-Cultural Analysis of Binary Sex Categories, in Transgender Rights: History, Politics, and Law 212 (Paisley Currah & Shannon Minter eds, 2003).

[150] See generally Kimberly A. Yuracko, Trait Discrimination as Sex Discrimination: An Argument Against Neutrality, 83 Tex. L. Rev. 167 (2004) (arguing that Title VII protects against personal trait discrimination that stems from gender norms and stereotypes that are incongruent with workplace equality).

[151] See e.g., *Miss. Univ. for Women v. Hogan*, 458 U.S. 718, 729 (1982) (observing that sex-based differential treatment was merely a codification of empirically unsubstantiated social convention); *Frontiero v. Richardson*, 411 U.S. 677, 686 (1973) ('And what differentiates sex from such nonsuspect statuses ... and aligns it with the recognized suspect criteria, is that the sex characteristic frequently bears no relation to ability to perform or contribute to society.').

[152] Jolls, *supra* n. 108, at 643 ('Legal requirements that actors take affirmative steps to "accommodate" the special, distinctive needs of particular groups, such as individuals with disabilities ... strike many observers as fundamentally distinct from, broader than, and often less legitimate than legal requirements within the canonical "antidiscrimination" category.').

CHAPTER 13. DISABILITY, DISPARATE IMPACT, AND CLASS ACTIONS

position that is more than equal.[153] As argued previously by one of the coauthors, this is a false dichotomy.[154] It is chiefly predicated on notions regarding disability that parallel now-discredited social conventions that women were physically less capable than men,[155] and that race was a biological absolute.[156]

If these lessons of race and sex as group-based categories have been learned (at least as far as formal legal recognition), society still grapples with the concept of artificial constructs respecting disability. Courts and commentators continue to treat the essential nature of disability as an objectively determinable medical fact[157] that manifests in lower

---

[153] See e.g., Sherwin Rosen, Disability Accommodation and the Labor Market, in Disability and Work: Incentives, Rights, and Opportunities 21 (Carolyn L. Weaver ed., 1991) ('Fundamentally the ADA is not an antidiscrimination law. By forcing employers to pay for work site and other job accommodations that might allow workers with impairing conditions defined by the law to compete on equal terms, it would require firms to treat unequal people equally, thus discriminating in favor of the disabled.').

[154] Michael Ashley Stein, Same Struggle, Different Difference: ADA Accommodations as Antidiscrimination, 153 U. Pa. L. Rev. 579, 581–584 (2004).

[155] In particular, it was asserted that women's reproductive functions evidenced their frailty. Barbara Ehrenreich & Deidre English, For Her Own Good: 150 Years of the Experts' Advice to Women 134 (1979) ('Doctors had established that women are sick, that this sickness is innate, and stems from the very possession of a uterus and ovaries.').

[156] See Stephen Jay Gould, The Mismeasure of Man 30-72 (1981) (describing the use of scientific thought to mold thinking about the intellectual inferiority of blacks); Kenneth L. Karst, Myths of Identity: Individual and Group Portraits of Race and Sexual Orientation, 43 UCLA L. Rev. 263, 270 (1995) (noting that in the past 'science reinforced white supremacy').

[157] Although the ADA is often cast in terms of being a creation of the 'civil rights' model of disability, see Peter Blanck et al., Disability Civil Rights Law & Policy: Cases & Materials 4-4 to -6 (2005), the primary focus of ADA litigation, especially in the employment context, has focused on who is covered under the Act, See e.g., Rutherglen, *supra* n. 22, at 221–223 (surveying principal cases of the last twenty years dealing with the issue of who is covered under the Act). These cases have focused on whether an individual has a physical or mental impairment that substantially limits that individual in one or more major life activities. See 42 U.S.C. § 12102(2) (2000) (requiring that impairment limit a major life activity). The disproportionate emphasis on whether individuals meet this definition actually brings the ADA closer to an earlier (non-civil rights) model of disability, where medical professionals opined whether individuals were truly 'disabled.' See e.g., Blanck et al., *supra*, at 3-4 to -23.

abilities than nondisabled persons.[158] From a group-based litigation perspective, disability is also viewed as being too individualized for claims and interests to be aggregated. In other words, the disability designation is seen to capture too wide a range of human variation to be treated as a coherent community.[159] Much heavy weather is

---

Furthermore, even though the definition of a disability was intended to include society's response to disability, it has generally not been interpreted by courts in this way. See 42 U.S.C. § 12102(2)(C) (2000); Arlene Mayerson, Restoring Regard for the 'Regarded As' Prong: Giving Effect to Congressional Intent, 42 Vill. L. Rev. 587, 587 (1997) (discussing courts' restrictive interpretations of the 'regarded as' definition of the term 'disability').

[158] See Anita Silvers & Michael Ashley Stein, Disability, Equal Protection, and the Supreme Court: Standing at the Crossroads of Progressive and Retrogressive Logic in Constitutional Classification, 35 U. Mich. J.L. Reform 81, 92 (2002) ('Historically, courts have addressed the constitutionality of limiting opportunity for classes delineated in terms of biological differences by considering two related questions. First, does the class members' biological difference relate to ... "reduced ability to cope with and function in the everyday world," ... ? Second, does the class members' reduced ability to cope and function usually place the public in need of special protection?' (quoting *City of Cleburne v. Cleburne Living Ctr., Inc.*, 473 U.S. 432, 442 (1985))); see also Harlan Hahn, Advertising the Acceptably Employable Image: Disability and Capitalism, 15 Pol'y Stud. J. 551, 551–553 (1987) (highlighting the medical orientation and economic understanding used to analyze disabilities).

[159] Disability Studies scholars take issue with this position, averring that disabled people share a common culture. See e.g., Simi Linton, Claiming Disability: Knowledge and Identity 4 (1998) ('We[,] [people with disabilities,] are all bound together, not by [a] list of ... collective symptoms but by the social and political circumstances that have forged us as a group.'); Sharon N. Barnartt, Disability Culture or Disability Consciousness?, 7 J. Disability Pol'y Stud. 1, 2 (1996) ('I suggest that the concept of collective consciousness better describes what is occurring within the disability community ... [which] has implications for policymaking.'); Paul K. Longmore & Lauri Umansky, Introduction: Disability History: From the Margins to the Mainstream, in New Disability History: American Perspectives 1, 4 (Paul K. Longmore & Lauri Umansky eds, 2001) ('There has always been a variety of disability experiences. At the same time, ... experiences of cultural devaluation and socially imposed restriction of personal and collective struggles for self-definition and self-determination[] recur across the various disability groups throughout their particular histories.'); Susan Peters, Is There a Disability Culture? A Syncretisation of Three Possible World Views, 15 Disability & Soc'y 583, 598 (2000) ('The roots of disability cultural identity are the elements of culture contained in the historical/linguistic world-view where we have collectively produced our own cultural

CHAPTER 13. DISABILITY, DISPARATE IMPACT, AND CLASS ACTIONS

made of the heterogeneity of disability with the result that, rather than being viewed as systemically excluded by the environment, disability is held to be the by-product of individual workers not fitting into particular workplace circumstances.[160] Consequently, assertions of disability discrimination have been closeted into a narrow category that examines the reasonableness of a particular accommodation to a single individual rather than questioning the larger issue of whether a hostile workplace environment was constructed that excluded employees with disabilities.

Contrary to this endogenous view, disability studies scholars (much like their critical race predecessors) challenge the disability classification as contingent on biological fact. They argue for a 'social' model of disability in which the physical environment and the attitudes it reflects play a controlling (if not central) role in creating what society terms 'disability.' Factors external to a person's own impairments are therefore determinative of an individual's ability to function in society.[161] This is in sharp contrast to the 'medical' model of

---

meanings, subjectivities and images; e.g. a common language/lexicon that connotes pride and self-love, cohesive social communities.'); Susan Reynolds Whyte, Disability between Discourse and Experience, in Disability and Culture 267, 279 (Susan Reynolds Whyte ed., 1995) ('In practice ... the experience of disability is still embedded in cultural assumptions and social relations, the "local moral worlds," of which even the most committed empathetic humanism must take account.'); cf. Richard K. Scotch & Kay Schriner, Disability as Human Variation: Implications for Policy, 549 Annals Am. Acad. Pol. & Soc. Sci. 148, 154–157 (1997) (asserting that humanity, by definition, is varied with disability merely comprising one manifestation from an idealized norm).

[160] Ruth O'Brien terms this phenomenon the 'whole man' schema and avers that it is influenced by vocational rehabilitation policies. Ruth O'Brien, Crippled Justice: The History of Modern Disability Policy in the Workplace 63–87 (2000).

[161] See e.g., Susan Wendell, The Rejected Body: Feminist Philosophical Reflections on Disability 35 (1996) ('The biological reality of a disability and the social construction of a disability.... are interactive not only in that complex interactions of social factors and our bodies affect health and functioning, but also in that social arrangements can make a biological condition more or less relevant to almost any situation.'); Ron Amundson, Disability, Handicap, and the Environment, 23 J. Soc. Phil. 105, 110 (1992) ('[A] handicap results from the interaction between a disability and an environment.'); Scotch, *supra* n. 114, at 275 ('[A] social model of disability that conceptualizes disability as a social construction that is the result of interaction between physical or mental impairment and the social environment.').

disability that views a disabled person's limitations as naturally (and thus properly, even if unfortunately) excluding her from the mainstream.[162] Several branches of disability studies scholarship grapple with the historical origin of the disability classification,[163] and thus with the source of able-bodied society's negative feelings toward people with disabilities.[164] A few of these commentators identify the source of aversive treatment as animus.[165] To be fair, statutory,[166]

---

[162] See Claire H. Liachowitz, Disability as a Social Construct 11 (1988) ('The medical/pathological paradigm of "disability legislation" effected a shift from physical inferiority to social inferiority by forcing an emphasis on the handicapped individual, and by discouraging acknowledgement of socially created sources of deviance.'); Kenny Fries, Introduction to Staring Back: The Disability Experience From the Inside Out 1, 6–7 (Kenny Fries ed., 1997) ('This view of disability ... puts the blame squarely on the individual.').

[163] See generally Douglas Baynton, Disability and the Justification of Inequality in American History, in New Disability History: American Perspectives, *supra* n. 159, at 33, 33–57; Hanoch Livneh, On the Origins of Negative Attitudes Towards People with Disabilities, 43 Rehabilitation Literature 338 (1982).

[164] For a sociological approach, see Michael Oliver, The Politics of Disablement: A Sociological Approach (1990), R. William English, Correlates of Stigma Toward Physically Disabled Persons, 2 Rehabilitation Res. & Prac. Rev. 1 (1971), Norman Goodman et al., Variant Reactions to Physical Disabilities, 28 Am. Soc. Rev. 429 (1963), Stephen A. Richardson et al., Cultural Uniformity in Reaction to Physical Disabilities, 26 Am. Soc. Rev. 241 (1961).

[165] See e.g., Erving Goffman, Stigma: Notes on the Management of Spoiled Identity 5 (1963) (asserting that stigma manifests when 'we believe the person with a stigma is not quite human'); Jonathan C. Drimmer, Cripples, Overcomers, and Civil Rights: Tracing the Evolution of Federal Legislation and Social Policy For People With Disabilities, 40 UCLA L. Rev. 1341, 1343–1345 (1993) (identifying intolerance and discrimination as part and parcel of the reasons excluding people with disabilities' equal social participation); see also City of Cleburne v. Cleburne Living Ctr., Inc., 473 U.S. 432, 461–462 (1985) (Marshall, J., concurring in part and dissenting in part) ('Fueled by the rising tide of Social Darwinism, the "science" of eugenics, and the extreme xenophobia of those years. . . . [a] regime of state-mandated segregation and degradation soon emerged that in its virulence and bigotry rivaled ... the worst excesses of Jim Crow.').

[166] For example, over the period 1900–1928 more than twenty-five states enacted mandatory sterilization laws for the disabled, often directed at impairments known not to be hereditary such as blindness and epilepsy. See Laurence A. Stith, Sterilization of the Unfit, 32 Law Notes 108 (1928); Amos Reynolds, The Prevention of Pauperism, in Proceedings of the Sixth Annual Conference of Charities Held at

CHAPTER 13. DISABILITY, DISPARATE IMPACT, AND CLASS ACTIONS

anecdotal,[167] and case law[168] evidence does lend selected support to that claim.[169] Nonetheless, the vast majority of these commentators believe that differential treatment is grounded in pity and paternalism.[170] At the same time, nearly all also accord some influence (whether resulting in overt or unconscious differential treatment) to the phenomenon of 'existential anxiety,' which inspires an able-bodied person to think 'there but for the grace of God go I' when encountering a person with a disability.[171] Existential anxiety can lead to both

---

Chicago 210–216 (1879), quoted in Donald K. Pickens, Eugenics and the Progressives 187 (1968) ('The state should prohibit the marriage of all persons who...are suffering from any incurable bodily infirmity or deformity.'). A recent and comprehensive treatment is Edwin Black, War Against the Weak: Eugenics and America's Campaign to Create a Master Race (2003).

[167] Compiled in S. Rep. Nos 101-116 (1989), the more compelling anecdotal evidence included testimony by a wheelchair-using future undersecretary of the Department of Education who was removed from an auction house for being deemed 'disgusting to look at,' and about an academically competitive and nondisruptive child who was barred from attending public school because of a teacher's allegation that his physical appearance 'produced a nauseating effect' upon classmates. *Id.* at 6–7.

[168] See e.g., *Otting v. J.C. Penney Co.*, 223 F.3d 704, 712 (8th Cir. 2000) (ruling that a jury could have reasonably found that the employer had acted maliciously).

[169] A different and interesting approach is provided in Michelle A. Travis, Perceived Disabilities, Social Cognition, and 'Innocent Mistakes,' 55 Vand. L. Rev. 481 (2002). Applying cognitive psychology literature, Professor Travis describes from a psychological perspective how and why members of society, including employers and judges, would consider a nondisabled person as being disabled. *Id.* at 509–542.

[170] See e.g., Alan Gartner & Tom Joe, Images of the Disabled, Disabling Images (1987) (demonstrating how the disabled are characterized as feeble or incapable, and are often objectified); Paul Longmore, Why I Burned My Book and Other Essays on Disability 1131–1148 (2003) (describing images of pity that Hollywood and other mass media disseminate about people with disabilities); Feldblum, *supra* n. 117, at 165 (asserting that the general public's view is that 'disabled people lack value and are to be pitied'). These assertions are substantiated by at least one public opinion poll. See Louis Harris & Assocs., The International Center for the Disabled Survey of Disabled Americans: Bringing Disabled Americans into the Mainstream 13 (1986) (74% of Americans felt pity toward disabled individuals).

[171] The term originates with Harlan Hahn, a political scientist from University of Southern California and one of the founders of the Disability Studies movement, who asserted that repugnance to disabled bodily difference, combined with fear of also attaining such variation in the future, results in a sociological desire to segregate people with disabilities from the mainstream. See e.g., Harlan Hahn, The Politics of

awkward interaction ('people with disabilities make me uncomfortable'[172]) and to pity ('always be nice to blind people'[173]); both instances manifest in a sense of 'otherness' and exclusion that, combined, is unique to the disabled.

Societal perceptions and reactions are crucial to defining disability. Exogenous factors (such as the way mainstream societies create environments), rather than endogenous qualities, are what by and large create the disability classification.[174] Much like people of color, people with disabilities are not inherently dissimilar from one another because of medically ascertainable facts. Rather, the disabled are placed outside the mainstream and constitute a coherent 'other' group that society considers as being apart from the biological norm. Yet, separation and its social consequences are precisely what cause people with disabilities to be alike for group identification purposes. Thus, an individual with cerebral palsy (who has a genius-level IQ) and a person with congenitally missing arms (who happens to be a champion marathon runner) will each be considered different from the mainstream in the negative sense of being less capable (as opposed to being stronger or smarter), and this common prejudicial experience in turn reinforces

---

Physical Differences: Disability and Discrimination, 44 J. Soc. Issues 39, 43–44 (1988) ('Probably the most common threat from disabled individuals is summed up in the concept of existential anxiety: the perceived threat that a disability could interfere with functional capacities deemed necessary to the pursuit of a satisfactory life.').

[172] People with disabilities aver that they can sense when nondisabled people are bent out of shape by their presence, much as gays and lesbians do.

[173] A graphic illustration of this phenomenon (literally) appears in the autobiography of politically incorrect quadriplegic cartoonist John Callahan, as part of a series that he has drawn on 'How to relate to handicapped people.' Among the behavioral don'ts are: (a) acting 'over friendly'; (b) being 'patronizing'; (c) 'directing your questions to the friend of the handicapped person'; (d) 'being over-apologetic'; and (e) 'acting like Leo Buscaglia [a professor at the University of Southern California known for his writings on demonstrating love].' John Callahan, Don't Worry, He Won't Get Far on Foot 189–199 (1989).

[174] A particularly strong version of this assertion is that of feminist and disability rights advocate Susan Wendell, who alleges that 'the entire physical and social organization of life' has been created with the notion in mind that 'everyone was physically strong, as though all bodies were shaped the same, as though everyone could walk, hear, and see well, as though everyone could work and play at a pace that is not compatible with any kind of illness or pain.' Wendell, *supra* n. 161, at 39. Professor Wendell's point, although valid, should not be overstated.

CHAPTER 13. DISABILITY, DISPARATE IMPACT, AND CLASS ACTIONS

their membership in a disability classification. Put another way, disabled persons are identified as 'disabled' and subjected to stigma that derives from membership in an externally created class; in turn, the collective experience of being treated as 'disabled' creates an overall and unifying identity. Disability heuristics create both prejudice and group classification.[175] This is because group identity norms almost by definition equate with negative stereotypes; otherwise, there would not be a need to eliminate civil rights violations that flow from their invocation.[176]

Pandisability theory parallels earlier notions of panethnicity, and demonstrates how disability serves as an equally valuable socially constructed heuristic for determining class identity. A pandisability theory allows us to once more capture the commonality of class interest, as both unwillfully receiving and wishing to eradicate a particular form of group-based stigma and subordination. Just as prejudice and stereotype arise from misperceptions about a category of individuals, so too must litigation be group-based if it is to ameliorate those barriers.

A central predicate to a group-based discrimination proof structure is that people with disabilities have a common-enough group identity to aggregate their interests. This is the case under class action law, in which collective interests must be sufficiently cohesive to meet the typicality, commonality, and adequacy of representation standards. It is equally true under disparate impact doctrine, in which joint interests must be aligned to contrast statistical disparities with the majority group (in this case, workers without disabilities).

---

[175] Several scholars have written on why group membership, as opposed to individual circumstance, is necessary to justify antidiscrimination protection for people with disabilities. See Samuel R. Bagenstos, Subordination, Stigma, and 'Disability,' 86 Va. L. Rev. 397, 422–468 (2000) (arguing that ADA coverage ought to be circumscribed to those individuals whose disability-related stigma subjects them to systematic disadvantage); Mark Kelman, Does Disability Status Matter?, in Americans with Disabilities: Exploring Implications of the Law for Individuals and Institutions, *supra* n. 114, at 91, 96–99 (proposing that norms are best enforced as group, rather than individual, protections because the larger societal benefits stemming from the prevention of market discrimination relate to the incorporation of those groups into the social and economic mainstream).

[176] See generally Anita Silvers, Double Consciousness, Triple Difference: Disability, Race, Gender and the Politics of Recognition, in Disability, Divers-ability and Legal Change 75 (Melinda Jones & Lee Ann Basser Marks eds, 1999).

Shared perceptions provide people with disabilities the commonality of interest necessary to proceed under group-based discrimination theories of class actions and disparate impact proof models.[177] It is to these subjects that we now turn.

13.4.2 The Class Action Device

At the class certification stage, courts have shifted their focus in race-and sex-based employment discrimination cases away from ties that are commonly viewed as socially constructed (as defined by panethnicity) and toward greater intragroup hegemony requirements. One by-product of this increased stringency is that Title I class actions have been viewed with special skepticism when analyzed under Rule 23 criteria. However, it is not inevitable that courts should interpret disability-related collective actions in this manner.

As an initial matter, Title I class actions are fundamentally like their classical Title VII counterparts, despite the putative assumption that the latter request 'one-size-fits-all' remedies, whereas the former necessitate individualized remedies. The notion that race and sex classes each request univocal remedies is overstated. Within these classes, each member may well need a different variation of the generally agreed-upon relief. Returning to the hypothetical, pre-*Falcon* Title VII employment discrimination class action brought against Big Impersonal Corporation[178] some of those women might challenge on disparate impact grounds. Among them might be a challenge to an employer's interviewing policy that emphasizes aggressiveness and thereby excluded their hiring on the basis of sex; others may point to a seniority system that instantiated historic exclusion on the basis of race and precluded their promotion; still others may claim that they were harassed about their cultural and linguistic heritage, and so suffered injuries on the basis of their national origin; and a number may assert that

---

[177] Earlier the article focused on disparate impact first and then on the class action device, due to their chronology within non-disability discrimination cases. It now reverses field and treats the ramifications of class action disability discrimination claims before disparate impact theory. This is because the shared group experience, expressed through class action procedure, should precede and lend structure to the doctrinal application of disparate impact theory.
[178] See *supra* notes 49–50 and accompanying text.

CHAPTER 13. DISABILITY, DISPARATE IMPACT, AND CLASS ACTIONS

their religious observance led to poor performance evaluations and dismissal. Assuming the suit is successful, at least four general policies (hiring, promotion, hostile work environment, and retention) will need to be altered.[179]

More trenchantly, the application of each of those changed policies will be different for each of the class members. In spite of the shared experience of discrimination, which in turn arises from an external view of their shared qualities as Latinas, each of these individuals is unique in terms of her qualifications, qualities, and experiences of discrimination.[180] Along the same lines, the individuality of ADA relief is likewise overstated. Many requests for accommodation dealing with physical accessibility and environmental design, for instance, can be commonly remedied by use of Universal Design principles.

Second, although few class actions have been brought (and fewer still, certified) in Title I cases, collective action is routinely seen in ADA

---

[179] We acknowledge that since the Supreme Court's decision *in General Telephone Co. v. Falcon*, 457 U.S. 147 (1982), it has become more difficult to take an 'across-the-board' approach to challenge employer discrimination (at least in the absence of class representatives who have been directly affected by each employment policy), see *supra* 13.2.3. Even post-Falcon, however, some courts have allowed members of one racial minority to represent another minority. See *Ramirez v. DeCoster*, 203 F.R.D. 30, 32 (D. Me. 2001) (holding that class representatives who were migrant farm workers of exclusively Mexican origin could represent a class of all Hispanics who had worked at the defendant's egg farm); see also *Gulino v. Bd. of Educ. of N.Y.*, 201 F.R.D. 326, 331 (S.D.N.Y. 2001) (holding that a Latina woman of unspecified origin, an African-American woman, and an African-American man could represent a class of all African-American and Latino teachers). Similar cases exist outside of employment law. See *Thompson v. Metro. Life Ins. Co.*, 216 F.R.D. 55, 59 (S.D.N.Y. 2003) (class of non-Caucasian policyholders who alleged racial discrimination in formation, performance, modification, and termination of insurance contracts in violation of § 1981); *Ashe v. Bd. of Elections in N.Y.*, 124 F.R.D. 45, 46 (E.D.N.Y. 1989) (class of all Black and Hispanic citizens alleging racial discrimination in voting procedures).

[180] Parenthetically, given that it is beyond the scope of this article, we also note that the preceding hypothetical does not even account for instances of multiple discrimination, where an individual experiences prejudice because of her membership in more than one vulnerable group. See e.g., Kimberle Williams Crenshaw, Race, Reform, and Retrenchment: Transformation and Legitimation in Antidiscrimination Law, 101 Harv. L. Rev. 1331, 1371 (1988) (describing the cumulative effects of being African American and a woman).

cases involving discrimination in public services (under Title II) and privately owned places of public accommodation (under Title III). Title II classes have been certified for individuals with various mobility or vision disabilities challenging inaccessible sidewalks,[181] and individuals with various disabilities who were eligible under California's Medicaid program and received services at a hospital that was slated for termination.[182] Similarly, Title III class actions seeking to enforce public accommodation accessibility requirements are regularly certified for groups of diversely disabled individuals,[183] even when those classes are defined as encompassing 'all persons in the United States with disabilities' excluded from one medical care facility,[184] or 'all physically handicapped persons who were denied full and equal access' to a ski resort.[185] The uncontroversial acknowledgment of disability group identity as sufficient to justify class actions in nonemployment settings provides a clear example for parallel application in Title I suits.[186]

---

[181] *Barden v. City of Sacramento*, 292 F.3d 1073, 1074–1075 (9th Cir. 2002).

[182] *Rodde v. Bonta*, 357 F.3d 988, 996 (9th Cir. 2004) (including urological and ancillary services, rehabilitation of spinal cord injuries, amputation services, services for chronic liver disease, post-stroke rehabilitation, services for diabetics, and pressure sore management); see also *Armstrong v. Davis*, No. 99-15152, 2000 WL 369622, at 1 (9th Cir. April 5, 2000) (class of all present and future California state prison inmates and parolees with various physical and learning disabilities).

[183] See e.g., *Colo. Cross-Disability Coal. v. Taco Bell Corp.*, 184 F.R.D. 354, 357–363 (D. Colo. 1999) (approving certification of a class comprised of both wheelchair and scooter users); *Bacal v. Se. Pa. Trans. Auth.*, No. 94-6497, 1995 WL 299029, at 9 (E.D. Pa. May 16, 1995) (granting certification for 'all persons eligible for paratransit service' under the ADA).

[184] *Access Now, Inc. v. AHM CGH, Inc.*, No. 98-3004, 2000 U.S. Dist. LEXIS 14788, at 16 (S.D. Fla. July 12, 2000).

[185] *Leiken v. Squaw Valley Ski Corp.*, No. S-93-505, 1994 U.S. Dist. LEXIS 21281, at 10 (E.D. Cal. June 28, 1994).

[186] Clearly, this would be a very different than the typical ADA Title I case, which often focuses at the outset on whether the plaintiff actually meets the definition of disability under the statute. See e.g., *Sutton v. United Airlines*, 527 U.S. 471, 478 (1999) (holding that plaintiffs were not disabled within meaning of statute because in their mitigated states, they were not substantially limited in a major life activity). Nevertheless, there is no salient reason why what can be done in Title II and III cases cannot be done in Title I cases. The ADA's definition of disability, 42 U.S.C. § 12102(2) (2000), is the same for the entire statute.

CHAPTER 13. DISABILITY, DISPARATE IMPACT, AND CLASS ACTIONS

What unifies the classes of disabled persons in these cases? Because the respective classes incorporate individuals with varying modes of disabilities, it cannot be said that the uniting feature is identical biology in the sense that each of the named individuals deviates from the perceived bodily norm in the same way. Instead, it is the confluence of policies, practices and environmental features under the common defendant's control that excludes each of the class members from employment opportunity. Nor is every plaintiff affected in the same way. Uncurbed sidewalks likely affect people with mobility impairments, whereas it is lack of tactile bumps in the same pavements that impact people with visual impairments. Just as nuances in sidewalk construction produce sundry incommodations on assorted categories of disabled people, so too does the relief that each category of individuals will seek. Nevertheless, this class was certified on the ground that the complained-of discrimination (i.e., neglecting to account for ecumenical accessibility when constructing and maintaining sidewalks) sufficiently unified the class and its interests.[187]

To illustrate how this principle could be incorporated into Title I class actions, assume that Snobb Academy, a private elementary school, is hiring teachers. One of the essential job requirements, in addition to proper educational degrees, teaching experience, personal charm, and references, is the ability to safely convey children out of a building during fire alarms (and, especially, in case of a genuine fire). Antonio, whose epilepsy is not readily discernable, applies for a teaching position and is offered a job. After accepting, Antonio reveals to the school his epileptic condition and requests, as a reasonable accommodation, that the strobe lights in the fire alarms (which can initiate epileptic seizures), be replaced with an alternative form of emergency illumination. Snobb Academy refuses on the ground that replacing the lighting will be too expensive, and hence unreasonable. Antonio sues. Assuming that the accommodation did not rise to a level of imposing an undue hardship on the school (and is therefore disposed of through summary judgment),[188] the trial proceeds on the issue of whether

---

[187] *Barden v. City of Sacramento*, 292 F.3d 1073–1075 (9th Cir. 2002).

[188] Common sense would seem to indicate that the issue of reasonableness ought to necessitate just the type of factual inquiry that defeats motions for summary judgment, namely a determination by a jury based upon the set of facts presented by the opposing parties. Thus, granting summary judgment at this stage prevents the type of functional inquiry that appears to be envisioned by the statute. See 42 U.S.C.

641

Antonio's requested accommodation was in fact reasonable. Whoever wins, the resulting verdict reflects the reasonableness of the non-strobe light accommodation. It does not, however, address whether or not Snobb Academy was upholding a workplace norm that adversely impacted other disabled individuals beyond Antonio.

Now consider how Antonio's case might look as a class action. Even under a limited view of the class certification requirements of typicality and adequacy of representation, Antonio should be able to serve as a class representative for other employees (or potential employees) with epilepsy who would be similarly disadvantaged by the strobe light system. But the class represented can be conceived of in an even broader manner, embracing individuals with other disabilities who might be similarly excluded by the strobe light system. People with balance difficulties, brain injuries, and certain visual atypicalities could similarly have been excluded from teaching positions. Thus, any individual with a disability who can identify being excluded from a vocational opportunity at Snobb Academy because of the strobe light alarm could participate in Antonio's class action.

The discrimination here alleged is the maintenance of a workplace feature that rightly serves the interests of teachers and students without disabilities, but which in doing so disserves teachers and students with disabilities. Although Antonio's fellow class members may have different disabilities, they are unified by their communally experienced exclusion and social stigma. For commonality purposes, the common issues of fact are how Snobb Academy did (or did not) perceive the needs of people with disabilities, including what prejudices and mutual stigmas it associated with the disability designation, as well as the effectiveness and reasonableness of the requested accommodations.[189] The common legal issue is whether accommodations appropriate for class members as a whole are required under the ADA.[190]

---

§ 12101 (2000) ('It is the purpose of this chapter ... to provide clear, strong, consistent, enforceable standards addressing discrimination against individuals with disabilities.'). Nonetheless, it is the governing practice. See Ruth Colker, The Americans with Disabilities Act: A Windfall for Defendants, 34 Harv. C.R.-C.L. L. Rev. 99, 101 (1999) ('Courts are abusing the summary judgment device.... [by] refusing to send "normative" factual questions to the jury.').

[189] Fed. R. Civ. P. 23(a)(2).

[190] This tracks the common legal and factual issues in Title VII cases. In *Reeb v. Ohio Department of Rehabilitation*, 203 F.R.D. 315 (S.D. Ohio 2001), a sex discrimination case

CHAPTER 13. DISABILITY, DISPARATE IMPACT, AND CLASS ACTIONS

Equally, this case can also satisfy the elements of typicality and adequacy of representation,[191] which are often analyzed together.[192] In the event that Antonio's requested accommodation benefits other individuals with similar disabilities, there is a complete alignment of requested relief between the class representative and the class, and typicality should be easily met. If, as in the circumstance of the sidewalk case, different class members need dissimilar accommodations to facilitate their entry into Snobb Academy, their shared exclusion should still serve to certify the class.[193] If the requested remedies are too dissimilar, subclasses may be appropriate.[194]

---

where the defendant was alleged to have engaged in a general pattern or practice of discrimination against women by its employment actions that disproportionately harmed female employees, the court held that the requirement of commonality was met because the issue of whether defendant's alleged practices violated Title VII was common to the class, *id.* at 321; see also *Shipes v. Trinity Indus.*, 987 F.2d 311, 316 (5th Cir. 1993) ('Allegations of similar discriminatory employment practices, such as the use of entirely subjective personnel processes that operate to discriminate, satisfy the commonality and typicality requirements of Rule 23(a).'); Alba Conte & Herbert Newberg, Newberg on Class Actions § 3:10, at 283 (4th edn 2002) ('Common issues of actions charging discrimination on the basis of race or sex are the presence of a discriminatory rule or practice and a general policy of discrimination.'). The same is true for ADA non-Title I cases. *Anderson v. Pennsylvania Department of Public Welfare*, 1 F. Supp. 2d 456 (E.D. Pa. 1998), presents a class action challenging a managed care program's compliance with ADA Title II, *id.* at 461–462. The court rejected the defendant's arguments that commonality was not met on the ground that there would be individual fact issues regarding each putative class member's impairment and ability to obtain medical care. *Id.* at 462.

[191] Fed. R. Civ. P. 23(a)(3), (a)(4).

[192] *See Gen. Tel. Co. v. Falcon*, 457 U.S. 147, 157 n. 13 (1982) ('The commonality and typicality requirements of Rule 23(a) tend to merge. Both serve as guideposts for determining whether... the interests of the class members will be fairly and adequately protected in their absence.').

[193] Again, this is a common feature of ADA non-employment law cases. In *Wyatt v. Poundstone*, 169 F.R.D. 155 (M.D. Ala. 1995), a class of residents in state-operated facilities argued that defendants violated Title II of the ADA by not providing sufficient number of community-based placements, *id.* at 158. Defendants argued that the class should be decertified because it was divided between individuals who advocated community placement of residents and those that did not. *Id.* at 160. The court rejected this argument. *Id.* at 162.

[194] See e.g., *Quigley v. Braniff Airways, Inc.*, 85 F.R.D. 74, 84 (N.D. Tex. 1979) (holding, in an employment discrimination action, that conflict over relief between the

EMPLOYMENT CLASS AND COLLECTIVE ACTIONS

When considering what qualities unify groups for purposes of group-based discrimination actions, courts routinely recognize financial interests as sufficient to certify a class. Consider securities fraud cases, which are often brought as class actions and regularly certified, despite the defendant's conduct having affected the class members in different ways.[195] The typicality element of Rule 23 usually is met in these cases even when the named plaintiffs bought numerous categories of stock,[196] or there were differences in overall damage amounts;[197] class members purchased stock in dissimilar manners (for example, at separate times or relying on distinct documents),[198] were diverse types of investors,[199] and varied greatly in the misrepresentation that

---

plaintiff and the class representative could be resolved by subclasses when the proper time arose).

[195] See John C. Coffee, Jr. & Joel Seligman, Securities Regulation: Cases and Materials 1217–1227 (9th edn. 2003) (discussing securities litigation, the frequency of class actions, and how members of the same class may have been affected in different ways). See generally Conte & Newberg, *supra* n. 190, at ch. 7 (discussing class determination generally and citing many securities cases that had been properly certified).

[196] *Endo v. Albertine*, 147 F.R.D. 164, 167–169 (N.D. Ill. 1993) (finding the typicality requirement was met where the named plaintiffs bought only Class A common stock whereas the class members purchased debentures and notes as well as common stock).

[197] See e.g., *Mayer v. Mylod*, 988 F.2d 635, 640 (6th Cir. 1993) (noting that although the named plaintiff made money from the relevant investment while other class members claimed losses, class certification was not necessarily defeated); *Clark v. Cameron-Brown Co.*, 72 F.R.D. 48, 53 (M.D.N.C. 1976) ('[A] difference in damages between [members] ... of the proposed class ... does not affect the proper class formation.').

[198] See e.g., *Spicer v. Chicago Bd. Options Exch., Inc.*, 1990 WL 16983, at 6 (N.D. Ill. January 31, 1990) ('The fact differences relating to the price at which each series traded do not undermine typicality. ... ').

[199] See *In re Mellon Bank S'holder Litig.*, 120 F.R.D. 35, 37 (W.D. Pa. 1988) (holding that the typicality requirement was met even though the shareholder class contained institutional investors who bought stock based on internally developed research); *Backman v. Polaroid Corp.*, No. 79-1031-MC, 1982 U.S. Dist. LEXIS 17640, at 6 (D. Mass. July 16, 1982) ('While the plaintiffs' knowledge and their methods of making trading decisions may differ from those of the class of investors which they seek to represent, those differences do not make plaintiffs atypical or inadequate representatives.'); *Greenfield v. Flying Diamond Oil Corp.*, No. 78 Ci. 3723, 1981 WL 1621, at 6 (S.D.N.Y. March 30, 1981) (finding that the claims of arbitrageurs were not legally different from other shareholders).

CHAPTER 13. DISABILITY, DISPARATE IMPACT, AND CLASS ACTIONS

influenced their purchases.[200] This is because the underlying inquiry for typicality was whether the same alleged unlawful conduct affected both the named plaintiff and the class seeking to be represented.[201] Similarly, variations in the manner in which class members relied on the alleged misrepresentation do not defeat the class certification requirement of adequacy of representation.[202] What is clear is that within securities law, a defendant's conduct does not have to affect every class member in the same way. Instead, the umbrella covering the entire class is the alleged unlawful conduct that has impacted every class member.

Specific requests for monetary relief are, however, a poor proxy for the deeper social dynamics that unify groups of individuals. Rather than a onetime financial loss, it is shared human experience that is far more significant in defining common identity. Securities fraud

---

[200] See e.g., *Priest v. Zayre Corp.*, 118 F.R.D. 552, 555 (D. Mass. 1988) ('The fact that plaintiff's investment decisions were influenced by his own subjective preferences and determined in part by a computer program incorporating a number of factors does not render him atypical.' (footnote omitted)); *Baum v. Centronics Data Computer Corp.*, No. C85-363-L, 1986 WL 15784, at 2 (D.N.H. May 15, 1986) ('Reliance on the advice of others will not defeat typicality if the information from the third parties is based on the alleged misrepresentations that form the basis of plaintiffs' action.').

[201] See Conte & Newberg, *supra* n. 190, §22:24 ('Under this view, the typicality prerequisite may be satisfied though varying fact patterns may underlie individual claims.'); see also *Green v. Wolf Corp.*, 406 F.2d 291, 299 (2nd Cir. 1968) (suggesting that the trial court could find that the typicality requirement was met in a case charging a company with inflating its stock price by issuing false prospectuses, even though the named plaintiffs bought shares relying on a third prospectus, not on the prior two, as the other plaintiffs had done); *Sargent v. Genesco, Inc.*, 75 F.R.D. 79, 83 (M.D. Fla. 1977) (holding that the typicality requirement was met despite the existence of a subclass because all of the plaintiffs' claims 'are premised on the same theories and will survive or fall to the same defenses').

[202] See e.g., *Fox v. Equimark Corp.*, No. 90-1504, 1994 WL 560994, at 5 (W.D. Pa. July 18, 1994) (holding that reliance, by the plaintiffs, on a Wall Street Journal article rather than on defendant's alleged misrepresentation did not render representation inadequate); *Fritesch v. Refco, Inc.*, No. 92 C 6844, 1994 WL 10014, at 7 (N.D. Ill. January 13, 1994) (determining that significant differences in content prospectuses between class representatives and some class members did not render representation inadequate); Priest, 118 F.R.D. at 555 (concluding that the named plaintiff's reliance on factors other than the alleged misrepresentations did not undermine his adequacy as a class representative).

plaintiffs are united only in the sense that they feel collectively aggrieved to the point of seeking financial redress. Beyond the boundaries of the suit, these individuals may not (and need not) share any identity characteristics. For these claimants, the class action procedure defines their joint identity. By contrast, pandisability (and panethnicity) plaintiffs are bound together by their respective experiences of social stigma and subordination. They may coalesce around the focal point of an employer's particular policy or practice for litigation purposes, but their essential identities as people with disabilities (or persons of color) are independent of these claims. The social responses that the group undergoes while mediating society both precede and follow any judicial interaction. Put concretely, disabled people as a whole are subjected to differential treatment and social exclusion throughout their lives because of social constructs created by the able-bodied majority, and identify with one another because of this occurrence. It is this shared life experience that defines both their real world, as well as their legally constructed identities.

Finally, it bears noting that certifying a class of people with diverse disabilities that has been affected by a common set of attitudes and discriminatory behaviors is consistent with the history underlying the class action device. As demonstrated by the scholarship of Stephen Yeazell,[203] the procedure arose as an expedient way to adjudicate the common interests of an already socially constructed group.[204] The earliest forms of collective action that Professor Yeazell documents occurred on behalf of villagers suing individuals or other villages for grievances impacting the village as a whole,[205] and tenants challenging

---

[203] Stephen C. Yeazell, From Medieval Group Litigation to the Modern Class Action (1987); Stephen C. Yeazell, From Group Litigation to Class Action: Part I: The Industrialization of Group Litigation, 27 UCLA L. Rev. 514 (1980) [hereinafter Yeazell, From Group Litigation to Class Action: Part I]; Stephen C. Yeazell, From Group Litigation to Class Action: Part II: Interest, Class, and Representation, 27 UCLA L. Rev. 1067 (1980); Stephen C. Yeazell, Group Litigation and Social Context: Toward a History of the Class Action, 77 Colum. L. Rev. 866 (1977).

[204] See Yeazell, *supra* n. 203, at 40 ('Most medieval group litigation involved groups whose organization antedated the lawsuit itself. ... Unlike some modern collective litigation, medieval group litigation did not overcome the difficulties of organizing a group for collective action. That task had already been done.').

[205] *Id.* at 38–39 (discussing a 1199 case wherein the rector of Barkway 'sued the parishioners of Nuthamstead, a Hertfordshire village, in a suit involving his

CHAPTER 13. DISABILITY, DISPARATE IMPACT, AND CLASS ACTIONS

the amount that the lord of the manor could exact for permitting succession to a tenancy.[206] The socially constructed bonds amongst the villagers and tenants provided the necessary community of interest for the group-based litigation.[207] Indeed, the litigation itself was a fairly insignificant unifying force for the group, given the breadth of their shared communal identity.[208] The idea of a litigation campaign forming the community of interest for the group is of a distinctively more recent vintage. We therefore agree with Professor Yeazell that for 'many modern classes the class members are not a social group but simply those members of society who share some hypothesized interest.'[209]

13.4.3 Challenging Workplace Norms

Just as the class action device is the legal procedure through which to challenge disability-related employment discrimination, disparate impact law provides the theoretical framework for challenging those workplace hierarchies. Classically, disparate impact litigation highlights statistical disparities in an occupational demographic profile that are traceable to an employer's policies or practices.

---

entitlement to certain offerings and theirs to daily services of mass,' and a different case a century later where 'three villagers,' for themselves and for the whole community of the village of Helpingham, 'sued two named persons "and the whole community of the town of Donington"... for the alleged failure of the [defendant] villagers to assist the Helpingham villagers in repairing local dikes').

[206] See Yeazell, From Group Litigation to Class Action: Part I, *supra* n. 203, at 516–518 (noting how this policy applied to all tenants and evolved into 'early group litigation because the custom in question was one theoretically applicable to all tenants holding under similar circumstances').

[207] See Yeazell, *supra* n. 203, at 46–57 (describing both the villagers' common status and the organization of village life as unifying circumstances).

[208] *Id.* at 57 ('To the extent that the issues at stake in such litigation involved incidents of status rather than claims of individual right, group litigation seemed inevitable rather than remarkable.'); *id.* ('Unlike the modern class action, medieval group litigation did not, in itself, alter the relations of power between the group and its adversary.').

[209] *Id.*; see also Yeazell, From Group Litigation to Class Action: Part I, *supra* n. 203, at 516–520 (discussing the move from social entities to litigative units).

Absent direct evidence of a facially discriminatory practice, for example a blanket policy of not considering deaf workers for employment positions,[210] circumstantial evidence forms the basis for a prima facie case of discrimination and shifts the burden to employers of proving that their business practices have a legitimate, nondiscriminatory purpose.[211] In other words, plaintiffs claim that due to the effects of a particular practice of the employer, something is wrong with the overall employment snapshot – people of color apply, but are not hired; women are hired, but not promoted – and frame this discriminatory picture within statistical evidence of relevant labor market demographics.[212] Because disparate impact law is dependent on asserting statistical groupwide disparities ('no/very few people who resemble me/us have been granted employment opportunities by the defendant'), it cannot be theoretically conceived of as atomistic. Even

---

[210] See *Davidson v. Am. Online, Inc.*, 337 F.3d 1179, 1182 (10th Cir. 2003) (holding that the plaintiff established a prima facie case of discrimination when a call center in the Philippines was set up to handle only non-vocal communication and the company did not consider people with deafness for employment).

[211] E.g., *McDonnell Douglas Corp. v. Green*, 411 U.S. 792, 802 (1973) (giving the burden of proof structure for cases involving circumstantial proof, whereby a plaintiff establishes a prima facie case of discrimination, which shifts the burden to the defendant to present a legitimate, nondiscriminatory reason for the challenged employment action, which in turn shifts the burden back to the plaintiff to demonstrate that the defendant's proffered reason is a pretext for discrimination). In *Desert Palace, Inc. v. Costa*, 539 U.S. 90 (2003), the Court clarified that direct evidence of discrimination is not required to shift the burden of proof to the defendant in a mixed-motive discrimination case, i.e., where legitimate and illegitimate reasons motivated the employment action, *id.* at 101–102; see Charles Sullivan, Disparate Impact: Looking Past the Desert Palace Mirage, 47 Wm. & Mary L. Rev. 911 (2005) (arguing that it would be a mistake for Desert Palace to create a renewed emphasis by academics and courts on disparate treatment litigation).

[212] Determining the appropriate baseline demographic is at the heart of this econometric pursuit. Courts have divided over whether plaintiffs ought to focus on actual applicants, the available labor pool within geographic proximity, or national statistics. See e.g., *Int'l Bhd. of Teamsters v. United States*, 431 U.S. 324, 337 (1977) (comparing the proportion of minority workers employed as over-the-road drivers to the proportion of minorities in the national population); *Hazelwood Sch. Dist. v. United States*, 433 U.S. 299, 308 (1977) (using the proportion of blacks in the relevant labor market as a baseline for evaluating a school district's hiring practices); *Dothard v. Rawlinson*, 433 U.S. 321, 347–348 (1977) (White, J., concurring) (noting the importance of the applicant pool data in *Hazelwood, supra*).

CHAPTER 13. DISABILITY, DISPARATE IMPACT, AND CLASS ACTIONS

when brought by a lone claimant,[213] disparate impact cases must be understood in terms of questioning larger structured relationships that affect a broader number of individuals and that in turn challenge those hierarchies.[214]

Consequently, disparate impact theory as applied to failure-to-accommodate cases is necessary to challenge facially neutral policies and practices that have a disproportionately negative effect on people with disabilities. Even commentators who are skeptical of disparate impact litigation have noted its successes in eliminating formal policies that contribute to the unequal exclusion of racial minorities and women.[215] The existing literature and case law, however, has not focused on this most elemental application of disparate impact theory to ADA Title I cases. We therefore turn to this untapped potential.

Employers are unlikely to formally and overtly bar disabled employees, as with the 'no deaf worker' policy described at the beginning of this section.[216] Instead, exclusion is more likely to follow

---

[213] See *Heagney v. Univ. of Wash.*, 642 F.2d 1157, 1163 (9th Cir. 1981) ('Although the disparate impact theory is ordinarily asserted in class actions, an individual claimant may seek relief under such a theory as well.'), overruled on other grounds, *Atonio v. Wards Cove Packing Co.*, 810 F.2d 1477 (9th Cir. 1987).

[214] For a sociological account of this argument, see Mark Gould, Law and Sociology: Some Consequences for the Law of Employment Discrimination Deriving from the Sociological Reconstruction of Economic Theory, 13 Cardozo L. Rev. 1517 (1992).

[215] See Selmi, *supra* n. 5, at 754–755 (noting that disparate impact theory, despite its limitations, has had some successes eliminating discriminatory written tests); see also Tristin K. Green, Discrimination in Workplace Dynamics: Toward a Structural Account of Disparate Treatment Theory, 38 Harv. C.R.-C.L. L. Rev. 91, 137 (2003) ('Disparate impact theory has proven an invaluable tool for reducing employer reliance on job requirements that are unrelated to job performance but that stand in the way of minority progress. Without such a tool, employers would have been free to adopt facially neutral job requirements that maintained the exclusion of blacks and minorities from vast areas of employment.').

[216] Cases involving these more subtle situations often fall within the realm of disparate treatment claims, which are easier to handle. For a discussion of current forms of disparate treatment, see Bagenstos, *supra* n. 7, at 849–850 (arguing that present day disparate treatment often takes the form of either rational statistical discrimination, 'in which employers rationally use protected-class status as a proxy for lower productivity,' or cost-based discrimination, where employers discriminate based on 'the costs [they] believe they will incur in the course of integrating a firm or in managing the conflicts that inevitably arise in a diverse workforce').

the course seen in *Chevron U.S.A. v. Echazabal*,[217] in which Chevron required healthy workers,[218] or the recommended Wal-Mart policy quoted at the beginning of the article that workers be required to engage in job-unrelated 'physical activity' in order to wean away 'unhealthy applicants.'[219] To be fair (and putting to the side for the moment the irrelevance of motive to related legal claims), employers may promulgate these policies in an effort to promote what they view as neutral and cost-effective job descriptions. If questioned, they might justify their actions along the following lines: 'It is too bad that the disabled employees are not as capable and cost-effective (i.e., qualified) as nondisabled ones, but that is both unavoidable and unrelated to any morally incorrect action. We did not construct these facilities, and if we did, we only did so according to established norms. Moreover, the job descriptions and criteria reflect what we have learned from experience as being necessary. We would have been pleased to employ disabled workers,' they might aver. 'It isn't our fault they were unable to meet our criteria.' Nevertheless, the result is unnecessary and systemic exclusion.

Along the same lines, employers might not consider, as an initial matter, that disabled persons ought to equally participate in the employment sector. Much as the circumstances of people of color and women were once ignored in the workplace, employers either create or continue to maintain physical and administrative environments

---

[217] *Chevron U.S.A. v. Echazabal*, 536 U.S. 73 (2002).

[218] *Id.* at 74. Mario Echazabal was denied employment by Chevron because Chevron believed the job would exacerbate his hepatitis. *Id.* at 76. The Court agreed, holding that Title I allows employers to decide whether qualified people with disabilities should be excluded from the workplace based on the employer's conclusion that they create a direct threat of harm solely to themselves. *Id.* at 74. Although the plaintiffs in *Sutton v. United Airlines*, 527 U.S. 471 (1999), twin sisters with myopic vision, were not covered by the ADA's definition of disability, *id.* at 489, the policy at issue – a broad policy excluding pilots with a particular level of uncorrected vision – is another example of the type of policy that could be challenged under disparate impact law, but to date has not been.

[219] See *supra* n. 1 and accompanying text; see also Randy Dotinga, Can Boss Insist on Healthy Habits?, Christian Sci. Monitor, January 11, 2006, at 15 ('In 2006, Weyco employees who refuse to take mandated medical tests and physical examinations will see their monthly health insurance premiums jump by $65. By next year, their annual insurance bills will grow by more than $1,000 if they still fail to follow instructions.').

that exclude those with disabilities. As with historical race-and sex-based exclusion, many embedded policies and practices obstructing the disabled are based on the assumption that, despite their biology, new entrants to the work force should interact with their environment in the same way as traditional groups.[220] Whereas previous restrictions on participation were based on notions that people of color should not intermingle with whites (because of animus), and that women as workers needed limitations that were responsive to their frailties (due to paternalism),[221] historic treatment of people with disabilities lends itself to social incredulity about their workplace participation.[222] Each social convention yields a misperception that the respective workers are 'inauthentic.'[223] Traditional failure to accommodate cases are not structured to reach, in a systemic fashion, this more subtle type of workplace exclusion.[224]

Returning to the Snobb Academy example presented in the previous section, assume that Antonio forgoes pursuing a typical ADA failure to accommodate suit, of the sort that would allege that the Academy's refusal to alter the fire alarm system precluded his employment prospects. Instead, using disparate impact theory Antonio presents statistical evidence of a near-complete absence of people with disabilities at Snobb Academy. Rather than being limited to proving

---

[220] 'As a practical matter, persons with disabilities are far more likely than are blacks or women to regularly face built-in headwinds in the form of performance standards, job structure, or workplace environment.' Crossley, *supra* n. 140, at 918. See generally O'Brien, *supra* n. 160 (detailing instances where disabled workers must either fit into existing norms or be excluded).

[221] This point is discussed in greater detail in Stein, *supra* n. 154, at 608–616.

[222] This is true to the extent that several Supreme Court Justices seem to deny the ADA's role as a civil rights statute. Perhaps the most obvious example is Justice Kennedy's concurrence *in Board of Trustees of the University of Alabama v. Garrett*, 531 U.S. 356, 375 (2001) (Kennedy, J., concurring). Instead of evaluating the circumstances that caused the suit, or referencing the notion of rights, Justice Kennedy characterized the issue as one that invoked a wrestling match between 'our own human instincts' on the one hand, and 'the better angels of our nature' that sympathize for 'those disadvantaged by mental or physical impairments,' on the other. *Id.* at 375–376.

[223] For a discussion of 'inauthentic workers,' see Schultz, *supra* n. 136, at 1919–1928.

[224] Congress recognized this action as 'benign' paternalism. 42 U.S.C. § 12101(a)(5) (2000) (recognizing 'overprotective rules and policies' as a form of discrimination); see also *Chevron U.S.A. v. Echazabal*, 536 U.S. 73, 85 (2002).

the impact of the denial of a specific accommodation, Antonio has made a prima facie case that some official policy or practice has made Snobb Academy an unwelcoming employer for disabled persons.[225] The strobe lights may have caused other individuals with disabilities to be rejected for the same position, or they may have discouraged other disabled persons from applying. Regardless, Antonio's suit (as discussed previously,[226] brought as a class action with him as the class representative) has gained leverage by broadly challenging the dearth of other employees with disabilities. As a group-based, statistically supported disparate impact suit, Antonio can examine the school's history (or lack thereof) of employing teachers and other employees with disabilities.[227] Some may have had visibly identifiable disabilities. Others, like Antonio, may have impairments that are harder to detect. Antonio can also demonstrate that the requested accommodation (changing the existing method of alerting people of an emergency) would also benefit individuals with disabilities who have epilepsy and various brain or vision impairments.[228]

---

[225] See *Watson v. Fort Worth Bank & Trust*, 487 U.S. 977, 986 (1988) (holding that the disparity caused by subjective employment criteria sufficed to establish the plaintiff's prima facie case). Antonio would argue that the Title I claims based on failure to accommodate are doctrinally cognizable under a disparate impact theory, and that nothing in *Raytheon* suggests to the contrary. See *supra* notes 122–124 and accompanying text.

[226] See *supra* notes 189–194 and accompanying text.

[227] See e.g., *NAACP v. Town of E. Haven*, 70 F.3d 219, 225 (2nd Cir. 1995) (directing the district court, on remand, in a disparate impact case, to consider the employer's defense in light of the plaintiff's showing of the 'inexorable zero').

[228] Conceptually, Antonio would argue that the strobe light is an environmental feature that creates two groups – those without disabilities that are not affected by it, and people with disabilities who are adversely affected. But not every person with a disability will be disadvantaged by the strobe light. Deaf employees, for example, might benefit. Doctrinally, then, under existing disparate impact law, Antonio will need to show that the strobe light has deterred a certain subgroup of people with disabilities from employment. Some courts have held this permissible under the ADEA. See *Graffam v. Scott Paper Co.*, 848 F. Supp. 1, 4-5 (D. Me. 1994) ('It is permissible, under the ADEA, for Plaintiffs' [sic] to show that an employer's actions had a disparate impact on a subgroup of individuals within the protected class.'); see also *Klein v. Sec'y of Transp.*, 807 F. Supp. 1517, 1524 (E.D. Wash. 1992) (holding that the plaintiff prevailed after proving that the hiring practices of the FAA 'had a definite disparate impact on qualified applicants over the age of fifty'); *EEOC v.*

CHAPTER 13. DISABILITY, DISPARATE IMPACT, AND CLASS ACTIONS

Working through the hypothetical Snobb Academy case demonstrates how ADA reasonable accommodation theory is more akin to Title VII disparate impact law than most commentators acknowledge.[229] To further demonstrate this point, Christine Jolls offers the following five examples of facially neutral:

(1) no-beard rules that disparately impact African American males whose skin conditions preclude regular shaving;[230]
(2) job selection criteria that tend to exclude women (sometimes for aggression, sometime for passivity)[231] and racial groups (chiefly, standardized ability tests);[232]
(3) English-only rules that adversely effect individuals with alternative national origins;[233]
(4) refusals of non-FMLA pregnancy leave time requests disparately impacting women who elect to bear children;[234] and

---

Borden's, Inc., 551 F. Supp. 1095, 1098–1099 (D. Ariz. 1982) (holding that an employer's 'severance pay policy did have an adverse disparate impact on those employees over fifty-five years of age'). Other courts have held it is not. See *Lowe v. Commack Union Free Sch. Dist.*, 886 F.2d 1364, 1372–1373 (2nd Cir. 1989) (rejecting appellants' use of sub-groups, stating that 'we find no support in the case law or in the ADEA for the approach to disparate impact analysis appellants advocate'); see also *EEOC v. McDonnell Douglas Corp.*, 191 F.3d 948, 950 (8th Cir. 1999) ('The EEOC is thus asking us to expand our recognition of disparate-impact claims under the ADEA to include claims on behalf of subgroups of the protected class. We decline to do so.'). Particularly with the ADA, we believe that the former position is appropriate. Courts have readily acknowledged subgroups of people with disabilities in other contexts, see *supra* note 104, and the limits of statistical analysis will render disparate impact cases impossible to prove where subgroups are too small to obtain statistical results, see Graffam, 848 F. Supp. at 4 n. 6 ('[The] limits of statistical analysis will render disparate impact cases impossible to prove where subgroups are too small to obtain reliable statistical results.').

[229] This overlap was first noted by Christine Jolls. See Jolls, *supra* n. 108.

[230] *Id.* at 653 (citing *Bradley v. Pizzaco of Neb., Inc.*, 939 F.2d 610, 611–612 (8th Cir. 1991)).

[231] *Id.* at 656 (citing *Lanning v. Se. Pa. Trans. Auth.*, 181 F.3d 478, 482–483 (3rd Cir. 1999)).

[232] *Id.* at 657 (citing *Banks v. City of Albany*, 953 F. Supp. 28, 30 (N.D.N.Y. 1997)).

[233] *Id.* at 658 (citing *EEOC v. Synchro-Start Prods.*, Inc., 29 F. Supp. 2d 911–912 (N.D. Ill. 1999)).

[234] *Id.* at 661 (citing *EEOC v. Warshawsky & Co.*, 768 F. Supp. 647, 650 (N.D. Ill. 1991)).

(5) actions effectuating policies on the ground of business necessity that tend to exclude members of protected groups.[235]

Professor Jolls demonstrates that eviscerating disparate impact in each of five 'cases of equivalence' in turn necessitated the provision of an accommodation-type remedy.[236]

Transforming Professor Jolls' non-ADA related accommodation examples to a parallel disability context (something that Jolls herself does not do), these instances could now include, respectively, facially neutral:

(1) rules on the use of physically inaccessible venues when alternative accessible venues are available (such as placing a workstation up a flight of stairs where it is dangerous for someone with a balance disorder);
(2) job selection criteria that tend to exclude people with disabilities, for example the use of physical ability (e.g., asking a quadriplegic bank teller to lift weights) or standardized testing (for instance, written tests that severely dyslexic persons may not be able to perceive);
(3) rules that require the use of specific systems that adversely affect individuals using alternative formats (i.e., visually impaired people who use Braille, computerized readers, or large print);
(4) refusals of leave time or alternative work venue requests (like telecommuting by people with ulcerative bedsores); and
(5) general actions effectuating policies on the ground of business necessity (for example, not allowing a schizophrenic to take a ten-minute respite to refocus his/her attention and eliminate delusional distractions).

Two pertinent themes are common to the foregoing sets of examples. In every situation a court will challenge whether a given work policy was in fact necessary to a particular business; and those employers who are compelled to, will hire or retain workers they previously viewed as less capable.[237] Here, the confluence between the statutes is

---

[235] *Id.* at 665 (*citing Wards Cove Packing Co. v. Atonio*, 490 U.S. 642, 648–649 (1989)).
[236] *Id.* at 652–666.
[237] A third theme, beyond the scope of this Article, is that all employers will be required to bear additional costs when those policies causing disparate impact are abnegated. This is discussed in Stein, *supra* n. 154.

CHAPTER 13. DISABILITY, DISPARATE IMPACT, AND CLASS ACTIONS

clear. Correspondingly, the possible argument that a one-size-fits-all remedy prevails for Title VII, but not Title I, is unconvincing.[238] Returning to some of the preceding examples, a class-based disparate impact challenge to non-shaving rules benefits more than African American men with *pseudofoliliculitis barbea*; it also benefits Sikh, Muslim, and Jewish men who do not shave for religious reasons. Changing interview and promotion modalities protects not only feminine, non-aggressive women, but also passive men. Nor is there a Title VII – Title I divide. Eliminating a spoken English-only rule benefits non-English speakers and deaf persons (who write or can be sign interpreted). Inversely, eliminating irrelevant medical criteria (e.g., regular blood pressure as a criteria for the exciting job of accountant) helps both the disabled and African American men who historically have high blood pressure.

In this way, applying even basic disparate impact theory would enable people with disabilities to challenge the type of 'neutral' workplace policies and practices that Title VII has had success eliminating for women and racial minorities. Admittedly, there is less consensus on whether subtler workplace barriers (referred to as 'structural' barriers or part of 'workplace culture') are susceptible to disparate impact challenges.[239] The scholarship addressing this divide relies heavily on social science research showing the influence of unconscious biases on an increasingly decentralized workplace.[240]

---

[238] See *supra* text accompanying notes 178–179.

[239] See *supra* notes 5–6.

[240] See Jody David Armour, Stereotypes and Prejudice: Helping Legal Decisionmakers Break the Prejudice Habit, 83 Cal. L. Rev. 733, 751–759 (1995) (describing the formation and manifestation of an unconscious social bias concerning race and sex); see also Nilanjana Dasgupta, Implicit Ingroup Favoritism, Outgroup Favoritism, and Their Behavioral Manifestations, 17 Soc. Just. Res. 143, 147 (2004) (detailing how implicit biases against women and minorities remain widespread); Green, *supra* n. 215, at 99–104 (discussing the 'shift in the operation of bias from the blatant to the more subtle and complex'); Linda Hamilton Krieger, The Context of Our Categories: A Cognitive Bias Approach to Discrimination and Equal Employment Opportunity, 47 Stan. L. Rev. 1161, 1186–1217 (1995) (discussing psychological theories of racism and arguing that 'disparate treatment does not necessarily manifest discriminatory notice or intent, but a motive or intent to discriminate must be present to prevent it'); Anne Lawton, The Meritocracy Myth and the Illusion of Equal Opportunity, 85 Minn. L. Rev. 587, 602–612 (2000) (explaining the shift in American society from an overt racism to an unconscious, difficult-to-perceive racism, and concluding that in light of this shift, 'it is a mistake... to then conclude that

To demonstrate the difference in successfully applying disparate impact claims to workplace culture issues, consider the law firm summer associate example discussed earlier in the chapter.[241] A summer associate with a disability who is precluded from participating in law firm lunches, softball games, or dinners at (perhaps inaccessible) partners' houses may be viewed as not being 'a team player.'[242] These occupational norms create an inhospitable job environment for people with disabilities, yet are exactly the types of workplace culture issues Title VII disparate impact law has not had much success in challenging. Similarly, to the extent Antonio is able to demonstrate a specific policy or practice creating statistical disparities in Snobb Academy's hiring and retention history regarding disabled workers, he may be able to achieve some restructuring of the workplace. But, as noted by commentators, the more entrenched issues of the school's culture and unstated workplace norms, symptomatic of deeper attitudes and hidden biases about disability, have proven elusive under existing Title VII disparate impact law in the race and sex context.[243]

Heretofore unaddressed in the literature is the issue of how these more deeply entrenched norms and current workplace realities affect the labor market participation of disabled workers. Technological advances and increasingly horizontal hierarchies are evolving the way that all people, including those with disabilities, work.[244] One

---

discrimination no longer affects the employment opportunities of blacks and women'); Katherine V.W. Stone, The New Psychological Contract: Implications of the Changing Workplace for Labor and Employment Law, 48 UCLA L. Rev. 519, 597–613 (2001) (detailing the changing nature of discrimination in the workplace).

[241] See supra n. 8.

[242] Michelle Travis discusses one such norm, which she terms 'workplace essentialism,' meaning that a 'good job' includes strong preferences for 'full-time work with very long hours or unlimited overtime, rigid work schedules for core work hours, uninterrupted worklife performance' and performance at a central location. Travis, supra n. 6, at 9–10.

[243] See Green, supra n. 6, at 656 (arguing that Title VII's 'particular employment practice' provision limits its ability to target workplace culture); see also Bagenstos, supra n. 5, at 17 (arguing that the same provision limits the ability of disparate impact to restructure workplaces).

[244] See e.g., Letter from Peggy Mastroianni, Assistant Legal Counsel, Equal Employment Opportunity Comm'n (October 27, 2005), available at <www.cupahr.org/publicpolicy/Washington insider/files/BO2986.PDF> (last visited October 19, 2006) (focusing on the potential for ADA discrimination in Internet recruitment and

CHAPTER 13. DISABILITY, DISPARATE IMPACT, AND CLASS ACTIONS

might expect commentators who are chary about disparate impact's potential to eliminate embedded workplace norms in the Title VII context to feel it equally limited when applied to the ADA. Although we take to heart the caveats raised by the nihilists as to Title VII, to move the debate forward we sketch an affirmative vision of what this theory can mean when applied to the ADA. As George Rutherglen notes, disparate impact law has an individualized history within the context of different civil rights statutes.[245] Beyond the basic type of disparate application sketched out in the preceding paragraph, an even greater ambition is to reach more deeply entrenched norms. We turn now to that aspiration.

There are reasons to believe that, even within the parameters of the existing restrictive race-and sex-based disparate impact doctrine, disability-based disparate impact theory stands a better chance at reaching these difficult workplace-norm barriers. The types of accommodations requested in disability cases often relate directly to the way jobs are performed. Accommodations like workplace attendance and schedule modifications,[246] job reassignment,[247] creating a pool of light duty positions,[248] purchasing equipment or modifying existing equipment enabling an employee with a disability to perform essential job functions,[249] and

---

hiring); see also William Erickson, A Review of Selected E-Recruiting Websites: Disability Accessibility Considerations (2002), <http://digitalcommons.ilr.cornell.edu/edicollect/95>. See generally Katherine V.W. Stone, From Widgets to Digits: Employment regulation for the Changing Workplace (2004) (discussing, in particular, the importance of peer review, telecommuting, and the growing prominence of the Internet in workplace recruitment and hiring).

[245] See Rutherglen, *supra* n. 141, at 2314–2323 (exploring the development of disparate impact theory under Title VII, ADEA, Voting Rights Act, and ADA).

[246] See *Amadio v. Ford Motor Co.*, 238 F.3d 919, 927 (7th Cir. 2001) ('We will not say that attendance is an essential function of every employment position. ... ').

[247] See *Smith v. Midland Brake, Inc.*, 180 F.3d 1154, 1174–1175 (10th Cir. 1999) ('The ADA's list of reasonable accommodations specifically refers to "reassignment to a vacant position." ').

[248] See Hendricks-Robinson v. Excel Corp., 154 F.3d 685, 696 (7th Cir. 1998) ('Our case law and the EEOC's interpretation of the ADA have approved of an employer's offer of light-duty assignments as a reasonable accommodation for injured workers.').

[249] See Heather Ritchie & Peter Blanck, The Promise of the Internet for Disability: A Study of Online Services and Web Site Accessibility of Centers for Independent Living Web Sites, 20 Behav. Sci. & L. 5–10 (2003) (noting how new, Internet-based technology has revolutionized the range of available accommodations).

provision of interpreters and job coaches[250] fundamentally impact the pragmatic modalities of job performance. Accordingly, their modification goes directly to issues of workplace culture, defined elsewhere as 'a process of social interaction and impression management, the social creation of a set of practices that signal membership in a group.'[251] Workplace culture lies in the 'rituals of day-to-day conformity.'[252] Disability accommodations (unlike, for example, the high school requirement in *Griggs*[253]) require changes in the daily process of job performance. Over time, these emendations gently guide supervisors and coworkers toward a greater acceptance and understanding of the justice of varying the workplace in a way that existing race-or sex-based policies have not yet captured.[254]

Moreover, statutory factors particular to the ADA may make it even better suited than Title VII to challenge the barriers inherent in the modern workplace through disparate impact theory. Unlike Title VII, Title I requires an interactive dialogue between the employer and the applicant or employee requesting an accommodation.[255] This process creates an initial opportunity for an exchange of information between the employer and employee that does not arise in the race and sex context.[256] More importantly, from a disparate impact standpoint, this dialogue takes away an employer's ability to claim that passivity

---

[250] See *EEOC v. Hertz*, No. 96-72421, 1998 WL 5694, at 2 (E.D. Mich. January 6, 1998) (noting that providing a temporary job coach to assist in job training might be a reasonable accommodation); see also *Miami Univ. v. Ohio Civil Rights Comm'n*, 726 N.E.2d 1032, 1042 (Ohio Ct. App. 1999) (holding that the accommodation of a job coach was reasonable for a plaintiff suffering from mental retardation who did not require job coaching beyond the first week or so in any of her previous jobs).

[251] Green, *supra* n. 6, at 627.

[252] Judith S. McIlwee & J. Gregg Robinson, Women in Engineering: Gender, Power, and Workplace Culture 17 (1992).

[253] *Griggs v. Duke Power Co.*, 401 U.S. 424, 431 (1971).

[254] Michelle Travis sounds a similar optimistic note about the potential for the ADA to change traditional notions of workplace essentialism. See Travis, *supra* n. 6, at 46.

[255] At least one circuit has gone so far as to hold that an employer who does not engage in the interactive process may be precluded from obtaining summary judgment on a failure to accommodate claim. See *Barnett v. U.S. Airways, Inc.*, 228 F.3d 1105, 1112 (9th Cir. 2000) (en banc), vacated on other grounds, 535 U.S. 391, 407 (2002).

[256] The interactive process also provides an opportunity for employers to voluntarily comply with the ADA, whether from concerns of litigation costs or from a desire to increase workplace diversity.

CHAPTER 13. DISABILITY, DISPARATE IMPACT, AND CLASS ACTIONS

(that is, not taking active steps) is not a 'particular employment practice' and therefore outside the purview of Title VII disparate impact law. To commentators' chagrin, this has proven a limiting factor in restructuring structural relationships based on race and gender.[257] Under the ADA, the employer is forced into a choice – to make or not make the accommodation. This choice becomes the employment action that is later challengeable under disparate impact law.[258]

By freeing ourselves of restrictive disparate impact doctrine (particularly the 'particular employment practice' requirement), these types of cases can be even more successful in combating deeper exclusionary workplace norms.[259] If Antonio, for example, was able to proceed under an earlier race- and sex-based disparate impact paradigm, he could use the combination of class action law and disparate impact law to challenge multiple workplace policies – both obvious and hidden – that contribute to an inhospitable working environment for people with disabilities.[260] Antonio could also represent, and show statistical proof, that various communities of people with disabilities

---

[257] See Green, *supra* n. 6, at 654–657 ('Courts have held that an employer's "passive reliance" on relational means of exclusion is not subject to disparate impact attack.' (quoting *EEOC v. Chicago Miniature Lamp Works*, 947 F.2d 292, 298 (7th Cir. 1991))); see also Sullivan, *supra* n. 6, at 55 (' "Passive reliance" on employee action is not an employer policy for purposes of disparate impact analysis.' (quoting *Chicago Miniature Lamp Works*, 947 F.2d at 298)). However, in DeClue *v. Central Illinois Light Co.*, 223 F.3d 434 (7th Cir. 2000), the plaintiff challenged an employer's failure to provide restroom facilities. Although the court failed to find that this constituted sexual harassment, it did suggest that 'insofar as absence of restroom facilities deters women...but not men from seeking or holding a particular type of job...the absence may violate Title VII' under an impact theory. *Id.* at 436. Sullivan, *supra* n. 6, correctly suggests that this could be a particularly broad use of impact theory, *id.* at 55.

[258] See *Council 31, Am. Fed'n of State, County & Mun. Employees v. Ward*, 978 F.2d 373, 377 (7th Cir. 1992) (rejecting the idea that a single decision by an employer is beyond disparate analysis because 'almost any repeated course of conduct can be traced back to a single decision').

[259] Although perhaps aspirational, this is certainly not doctrinally precluded. As discussed earlier, see *supra* notes 215–216 and accompanying text, unlike Title VII, there is a near complete absence of case law explaining and applying disparate impact law to ADA Title I claims.

[260] See e.g., *Martinez v. Oakland Scavenger Co.*, 680 F. Supp. 1377, 1381 (N.D. Cal. 1987) (holding that excluding Blacks and Hispanics from owning company shares allowed

were disadvantaged by this workplace environment.[261] Yet until courts and commentators take the concept of pandisability to heart, these and other benefits of group-based discrimination theories for workers with disabilities will remain unrealized. Also lost will be the potential for disability-related claims that stimulate workplace culture challenges in the broader Title VII context.

13.5 CONCLUSION

Congress' impetus for passing Title VII (and then amending it in 1991) was strikingly similar to that underlying enactment of the ADA's employment provisions. In both cases, Congress recognized the need to eliminate barriers that historically had excluded groups from the workplace. Within the context of race and sex, however, there existed a period wherein the courts were an active partner in realizing Title VII's aspirations. Crucial to this effort were group-based discrimination theories that were supported by disparate impact theory and the class action device. A parallel circumstance has not (yet) existed in regard to the ADA. Indeed, individual claims to accommodate specific impairments in particular jobs have all but eclipsed a coherent theory of disability-related disparate impact law. This absence in turn reinforces the erroneous notion that the statute's individualized assessment principle militates against group-based theories. Taking advantage of the relatively blank slate of writing on group-based disability discrimination, this article offers an alternative and intrepid vision of the ADA's potential for transforming workplace environments.

This article challenged the exclusion of disability-based employment discrimination claims from group-based theories, and in so doing advocated for applying disparate impact theory to what have heretofore been individualized ADA failure to accommodate claims. It demonstrated that there is nothing inherent in the doctrines of disparate impact and class action precluding their use in disability discrimination cases. More importantly, it showed that the theoretical basis for

---

plaintiffs to win on a disparate impact theory); *Penn v. Stumpf*, 308 F. Supp. 1238, 1239–1240 (N.D. Cal. 1970) (challenging, in a class action disparate impact case, an employer's testing, interview, and background investigation procedures which together contributed to white males being favored in the workplace over non-Caucasians).
[261] See *supra* notes 35–45 and accompanying text.

CHAPTER 13. DISABILITY, DISPARATE IMPACT, AND CLASS ACTIONS

aggregating race and sex claims – panethnicity – can and should be imported to disability discrimination employment claims. Pandisability provides a tool to connect the interests of individuals with diverse disabilities. It is the common experience of social exclusion and stigma that binds these groups together in real life. It should do no less for litigation purposes.

CHAPTER 14

Collective and Class Action Issues under the Fair Labor Standards Act and State-Based Wages Statutes

Adam T. Klein,* Nantiya Ruan,** and Sean Farhang***

14.1 LITIGATION ISSUES

14.1.1 Representational Evidence or Sampling

The sufficiency of the evidence in a suit for lost wages under the Fair Labor Standards Act (FLSA) is examined in a burden-shifting framework set out by the Supreme Court in 1964. The Court was concerned that an employer could insulate itself from such suits by failing to maintain employment records that an employee could use to prove she was underpaid. Therefore, the Court ruled that in the absence of adequate employment records, an employee suing for lost wages under the FLSA could 'submit sufficient evidence from which violations of the Act

---

* Adam T. Klein is a partner and chair of the class action practice group of Outten & Golden. He holds a J.D. from Hofstra University. He is a litigation associate with Outten & Golden at the time of this writing.
** Nantiya Ruan is professor of lawyering process at University of Denver, from which she holds a J.D.
*** Sean Farhang is assistant professor of public policy at Goldman School of Public Policy, University of California, Berkeley. He holds a Ph.D. from Columbia University and a J.D. from New York University School of Law.

David Sherwyn and Samuel Estreicher (eds), *Employment Class and Collective Actions*, pp. 663–677.
© 2009, Kluwer Law International BV, Printed in Great Britain.

663

and the amount of an award may be reasonably inferred.'[1] The Supreme Court's oft-cited standard is *Anderson v. Mt. Clemens Pottery Co.*:[2]

> Where the employer's records are inaccurate or inadequate and the employee cannot offer convincing substitutes.... [t]he solution... is not to penalize the employee by denying him any recovery on the ground that he is unable to prove the precise extent of uncompensated work. Such a result would place a premium on an employer's failure to keep proper records in conformity with his statutory duty; it would allow the employer to keep the benefits of an employee's labors without paying due compensation as contemplated by the Fair Labor Standards Act. In such a situation we hold that an employee has carried out his burden if he proves that he has in fact performed work for which he was improperly compensated and if he produces sufficient evidence to show the amount and extent of that work as a matter of just and reasonable inference. The burden then shifts to the employer to come forward with evidence of the precise amount of work performed or with evidence to negative the reasonableness of the inference to be drawn from the employee's evidence. If the employer fails to produce such evidence, the court may then award damages to the employee, even though the result be only approximate.

To meet the burden under *Mt. Clemens*, a class of plaintiffs need not present testimony from each underpaid employee. Instead, the plaintiff class may present the testimony of a representative sample of employees as part of the proof of the prima facie case under the FLSA. The adequacy of the sample information, however, is often challenged in the courts, for example, in *Reich v. Southern New England Telecommunications Corp.*:[3]

> Testimony of representative sample of 2.5% of workers (or 39 of approximately 1,500 employees) was adequate evidence upon which to award

---

[1] *Martin v. Selker Bros., Inc.*, 949 F.2d 1286, 1296–1297 (3rd Cir. 1991).

[2] 328 U.S. 680, 687–688 (1946).

[3] 121 F.3d 58 (2nd Cir. 1997). See also: *Donovan v. New Floridian Hotel, Inc.*, 676 F.2d 468, 472–473 (11th Cir. 1982) (twenty-three employees testified; back wages awarded to 207 employees); *Herman v. Hector I. Nieves Transport, Inc.*, 91 F. Supp. 2d 435 (D. Puerto Rico 2000) (fourteen out of 100 testifying truck drivers provided adequate basis for determining average number of hours worked for testifying and non-testifying drivers); *McLaunhlin v. DialAmerica Mktg., Inc.*, 716 F. Supp. 812, 824–825 (D.N.J. 1989) (testimony of forty-three witnesses, both at trial and by deposition, confirms existence of violations for approximately 350 non-testifying employees); *Donovan v. Kaszvcki & Sons Contractors, Inc.*, 599 F. Supp. 860, 868 (S.D.N.Y.1984)

back wages under the FLSA to entire group of employees because (1) testimony covered each clearly defined category of worker; (2) there was actual consistency among the workers' testimony, both within each category and overall; (3) employer offered no contradictory testimony; (4) abuse arose from admitted policy of employer that was consistently applied; and (5) periods at issue were employees' lunch hours, which were predictable, daily recurring periods of uniform and predetermined duration.

Fenley v. Hinnins:[4]

The Sixth Circuit reversed the district court's refusal to 'extrapolate' an approximation of damages and remanded the action for determination of damages in accordance with the *Mt. Clemens* standard. The circuit court held that the employee workers need not prove their damages with precision.

14.1.2 Administrative Exemption

Workers may qualify as exempt administrative employees for purposes of the FLSA if they meet one of two tests: the Short Test (employees who are paid on a salary basis of USD 250 a week or more whose primary duties relate to managerial or academic office work where discretion and independent judgment is required) and the Long Test (employees who are paid more than USD 155 per week if they meet the primary duty test of the Short Test and meet other specific factors outlined in section 541.2 of the Act). In a growing number of cases, courts have failed to consistently interpret the provisions of the administrative exemption.[5]

Carpenter v. R.M. Shoemaker Co.:[6]

The district court denied the employer's motion for summary judgment on the issue of whether the plaintiff, a former Project Supervisor earning

---

(twenty-nine employees testified by deposition; back wages awarded to over 200 employees).

[4] 19 F.3d 1126 (6th Cir. 1994).

[5] In response, several calls to 'modernize' the exemption have been noted. See 'DOL Would Update FLSA to Allow Comp Time: Calls for Simplifying White-Collar Exemptions,' BNA Wage Hour & Leave Report (July 5, 2002) (reporting on remarks by Asst. Secy. of Employment Standards Victoria Lipnic); Timothy J. Bartl, 'Why the Fair Labor Standards Act Needs to Be Reformed,' BNA Wage Hour & Leave Report (June 21, 2002) (excerpt of monograph urging reform of FLSA and DOL regulations).

The DOL has now proposed regulations. See *infra* at 668 et seq.

[6] 2002 WL 987990, *2 (E.D.Pa. 2002).

$90,000 a year, met the administrative exemption of the FLSA. The court found that 'it [wa]s not plain and unmistakable' that plaintiff's work was directly related to management policies or general business operations. Accordingly, a finding of administrative employee status at the summary judgment stage was inappropriate.

Casas v. Conseco Finance Corp.:[7]

Plaintiffs, a group of nearly 2,900 current and former loan originators for defendant claimed overtime violations. The district court denied the finance company's motion for summary judgment, finding that the plaintiffs lacked the necessary discretion and independent judgment for the administrative exemption given their adherence to the company's guidelines and operating procedures.

But see *Wilshin v. Allstate Ins. Co.*:[8]

The district court granted summary judgment on plaintiff insurance agent's FLSA overtime violation claim. The court found that the defendant insurance company met its burden in proving that plaintiff's work required discretion and independent judgment, satisfying its burden of showing that plaintiff met all of the requirements for the administrative exemption.

14.1.3 Class and Collective Action Certification of Wage-Hour Claims

FLSA claims are often multi-plaintiff cases for an obvious reason – employers who violate the FLSA are usually doing so for many of their employees. Section 216(b) of the FLSA mandates that for collective actions, plaintiffs must 'opt in' to the action by filing a written consent in the court where the action is brought. In contrast, under Rule 23(b)(3) of the Federal Rules of Civil Procedures and analogous state law class action rules, similarly situated employees are automatically part of the class action unless they affirmatively choose to 'opt out.'

---

[7] 2002 WL 507059, *1 (D.Minn. 2002).
[8] 212 F. Supp. 2d 1360, 1379 (M.D.Ga. 2002).

CHAPTER 14. STATE-BASED WAGES STATUTES

14.1.3.1 FLSA Collective Action Certification

Section 216(b) of the FLSA provides that 'an action to recover... liability... may be maintained against any employer... by any one or more employees for and in behalf of himself or themselves and others similarly situated.' There are two conditions for maintaining a collective action. First, the named plaintiffs and the proposed members of the class must be 'similarly situated.' Second, the proposed class members must consent in writing to be bound by the result of the suit, or 'opt-in.'[9]

Scott v. Aetna Serv., Inc.:[10]

> In the first phase of an FLSA collective action inquiry, a court examines the pleadings and affidavits of the proposed class and determines whether the plaintiffs and the proposed class are similarly situated. After discovery is largely complete, the court makes a factual finding on the 'similarly situated' issue, based on the record produced through discovery. The similarly situated standard is considerably less stringent than Rule 23's requirements for the certification of a class. If the court finds that the claimants are 'similarly situated,' the representative action may proceed to trial.

Realite v. Ark Restaurants, Inc.:[11]

> The court certified a FLSA collective action, holding that the basic scheme – to avoid paying overtime and minimum wages – was undertaken at all 15 Ark restaurants with the knowledge and approval of the corporate parent and, thus, satisfied the similarly situated standard.

14.1.3.2 State-Law-Based Class Action Certification

Plaintiffs are increasingly bringing Rule 23 class actions for similar state law claims for wage-hour violations and creating simultaneous 'opt in' classes under the FLSA. States where these hybrid classes have been sanctioned by the court include New York, Illinois, California, Michigan, Washington, Pennsylvania, and North Carolina.

---

[9] See *Sperlinn v. Hoffman-La Roche, Inc.* 118 F.R.D. 392, 399 (D.N. J.), aff'd 862 F.2d 439 (3rd Cir. 1988), aff'd, 493 U.S. 165, 110 S.Ct. 482, 107 L.Ed.2d 480 (1989).
[10] 210 F.R.D 261 (D. Conn. 2002).
[11] 7 F. Supp. 2d 303–304 (S.D.N.Y. 1998).

Ansoumana v. Gristede's Operating Corp.:[12]

Low paid workers provided to retailers by labor agents brought suit claiming violations of the FLSA and New York state minimum wage statute. Workers sought class certification. The district court granted class certification, holding that exercise of supplemental jurisdiction over state minimum wage claims was appropriate.

Beltran-Benitez v. Sea Safari, Ltd.:[13]

The district court denied the employer's Rule 12(b)(6) motion to dismiss plaintiff crab pickers' claims for overtime violations under North Carolina state wage/hour laws and the FLSA. The court exercised supplemental jurisdiction over the factually related state claims under 28 U.S.C. § 1367(c)(4), citing Ansoumana. The court also rejected the employer's argument that the FRCP Rule 23 class allegations were irreconcilable with the 'opt in' provisions of Section 216(b) of the Act, concluding that it could efficiently manage both the federal and state law wage claims in a single action.

Chavez v. IBP, Inc.:[14]

The district court certified a hybrid class of up to 3,900 employees, where 1,100 employees joined the FLSA collective action. The court found that the only major difference between the federal and state causes of action would be the amount of damages due.

De Asencio v. Tyson Foods, Inc.:[15]

The district court granted the plaintiff poultry workers' class certification motion as to claims brought under the Pennsylvania wage-hours state laws. While 504 workers had 'opted in' pursuant to the collective action notice, a class was sought for all 3,400 production workers. The district court found that all the requirements of Rule 23(a) and (b)(3) to certify an 'opt-out' class had been met. The district court rejected the defense arguments that (1) the state law claims should be limited to the 504 workers who 'opted in to the FLSA case, (2) Rule 23 did not apply to the state wage law, (3) Rule 23 was inconsistent or irreconcilable with Section 216(b), and (4) exercise of supplemental jurisdiction was inappropriate (relying in part on *Ansoumana*).

---

[12] 201 F.R.D. 81 (S.D.N.Y. 2001).
[13] 180 F. Supp. 2d 772 (E.D.N.C. 2001).
[14] 2002 WL 31662302, *2 (E.D.Wash. October 28, 2002).
[15] 2002 WL 1635103 (E.D.Pa. July 17, 2002).

CHAPTER 14. STATE-BASED WAGES STATUTES

Sauer v. Snappy Apple Farms, Inc.:[16]

> Plaintiff farm workers brought overtime claims under both the FLSA and the Migrant and Seasonal Agricultural Worker Protection Act ('APWA'),[17] and moved for class certification for APWA overtime claims. Only five claims had been filed under the FLSA 'opt in' procedure, but Plaintiffs estimated a potential class numbering 168 to 173 workers. The court granted the motion for class certification finding sufficient numerosity, and that the plaintiffs had met all the requirements under FRCP 23 (b)(3).

O'Brien v. Encotech Const. Services, Inc.:[18]

> Citing *Ansoumana*, the district court granted plaintiffs' class certification motion 'to concentrate all litigation related to plaintiffs' common set of facts in this forum.'

But see *Thiebes v. Wal-Mart Stores, Inc.*:[19]

> Plaintiffs alleged 'off the clock' overtime violations under both Oregon state law and the FLSA. The district court had previously denied a motion to certify the state claims under Rule 23, but without prejudice to a renewed class motion to be filed after the close of the FLSA 'opt in' period for the collective action approved for all current and former Wal-Mart employees in Oregon. Section 216(b) notices were mailed to approximately 15,000 such employees and an estimated 425 employees had 'opted in' (about 3,000 notices had been returned as undeliverable; the court noted an 'opt in' rate of 2.7%). The court again denied class certification of the state law claims, based on its finding that joinder was not impracticable (as 425 had joined the case) and concerns that a class action would not be superior under Rule 23(b)(3) since state claims could be adjudicated for the 425 persons who had 'opted in.' The court also expressed a concern that a class action would encompass far more workers than those who felt aggrieved.

14.1.4 Seventh Amendment Considerations

Because FLSA collective actions are complex, district courts will often consider whether issues should be severed for trial. Plaintiffs

---

[16] 203 F.R.D. 281 (W.D.Mich. 2001).
[17] 29 U.S.C. 91801 et seq.
[18] 203 F.R.D. 346 (N.D.Ill. 2001).
[19] 2002 WL 479840, 145 Lab.Cas. P 34, 442 (D.Or. January 9, 2002).

argue for bifurcation of the liability and damages issues to simplify the evidence and proofs for the jury.[20] Employer defendants may respond that plaintiffs cannot 'salvage' class certification through bifurcation because of due process considerations. The argument, in its simplest form, is that bifurcation violates the Re-examination Clause of the Seventh Amendment, namely that 'no fact tried by a jury shall be otherwise reexamined in any Court of the United States.' Judge Jack B. Weinstein of the Southern District of New York wrote a well-reasoned opinion denouncing such attempts by defendants.

Simon v. Phillip Morris Inc.:[21]

> In a complex tobacco litigation, Judge Weinstein wrote a minitreatise on severance in complex actions in which he made the following points: (1) the trial judge's broad discretion to sever issues for trial has deep historical roots; (2) the Constitution does not limit this broad discretion to sever issues for trial and is only implicated where a severed issue is presented to a subsequent jury in a confusing or uncertain manner; (3) trial judges enjoy broad powers to employ procedural devices, like special verdicts, to ensure that when issues are severed for separate trial, the respective juries comprehend the proper scope of their inquiry; (4) a recent minority line of limiting cases is inapposite; and (5) bifurcation of punitive damage and general compensatory damage issues comports with Rule 42(b) and Rule 23(c)(4)(A).

Robinson v. Metro-North Commuter R.R. Co.:[22]

> In a footnote, the Second Circuit rejected the argument that bifurcation in determining class certification risks violating the Seventh Amendment. The court disagreed with the argument that given the number of members in the putative class, the district court is likely to try the remedial phase of each class member's claim before a separate jury from the one that considers the liability phase, and that, should this occur, overlapping factual issues would be presented to the liability-phase and remedial-phase juries in violation of the Re-examination Clause.

Specifically, the court held that while trying a bifurcated claim before separate juries does not run afoul of the Seventh Amendment, a 'given

---

[20] See *International Brotherhood of Teamsters v. United States*, 431 U.S. 324 (1977) ('Teamsters bifurcation').
[21] 200 F.R.D. 21 (E.D.N.Y. 2001).
[22] 267 F.3d 147 (2nd Cir. 2001).

CHAPTER 14. STATE-BASED WAGES STATUTES

[factual] issue may not be tried by different, successive juries.' To prevent this, a court should make decisions of:

> sound case management, not [outright] avoidance of the procedure.... First, the court needs to carefully define the roles of the two juries so that the first jury does not decide issues within the prerogative of the second jury. Second, the court must carefully craft the verdict form for the first jury so that the second jury knows what has been decided already. If the first jury makes sufficiently detailed findings, those findings are then akin to instructions for the second jury to follow.

Taylor v. District of Columbia Water & Sewer Authority:[23]

> The district court recognized that the majority of courts find that due process is not violated when a 'hybrid' class certification is granted. Specifically, the court noted that the Re-examination Clause does not prohibit two juries from reviewing the same evidence, only from deciding the same factual issues.[24]

14.2 REGULATORY ISSUES

14.2.1 Introduction

The United States Department of Labor (DOL) has published a proposal to revise its regulations defining exemptions from coverage by the Fair Labor Standards Act's (FLSA) overtime protections. The proposed changes, if adopted after the notice and comment period, are likely to have important repercussions for the FLSA's coverage. Some of the changes to the FLSA regulations would increase coverage of certain low wageworkers, while other proposed changes would

---

[23] 205 F.R.D. 43 (D.D.C. 2002).

[24] See also (holding that the Seventh Amendment does not bar bifurcation): *EEOC v. Dial Corp.*, 156 F. Supp. 2d 926 (N.D.Il1.2001); *Butler v. Home Depot Inc.*, 1996 WL 421436 (N.D.Cal.1996) (noting that 'courts have routinely adopted' bifurcation in disparate treatment class actions); *EEOC. v. McDomell Douglas Corp.*, 960 F. Supp. 203, 205 (E.D.Mo. 1996) (noting that '"pattern-or-practice" claims are routinely bifurcated'). But see (holding that the Seventh Amendment does bar bifurcation): *Allison v. Citgo Petroleum*, 151 F.3d 402 (5th Cir. 1998); *Rink v. Cheminova, Inc.*, 203 F.R.D. 648, 671–672 (M.D.Fla. 2001); *Adler v. Wallace Computer Servs., Inc.*, 202 F.R.D. 666, 673–674 (N.D.Ga. 2001).

apparently exclude some executive, administrative, professional, and outside-sales employees who currently enjoy the right to overtime under the FLSA. Below I review the major elements of the DOL's proposed new regulations.

14.2.2 Minimum Salary Bar Raised

The proposed new regulations would increase the minimum weekly salary threshold to qualify for any of the so-called white-collar exemptions. Under the regulations currently in force, an executive or administrative employee who earns less than USD 155 per week (or USD 8,060 per year) qualifies for automatic FLSA overtime coverage, and the figure is USD 170 per week (or USD 8,840) for professional employees. When an employee's weekly earnings exceed these thresholds, he or she may be lawfully categorized as an exempt executive, administrative, or professional employee if other criteria of exemption are satisfied. The proposed new regulations would raise the minimum salary bar to USD 425 per week (or USD 22,100 per year).[25]

While this would most certainly be a laudable change, it bears emphasis that the change is long overdue and merely adjusts the minimum salary bar upward to partially reflect inflation. The USD 155 per week figure was adopted in 1975 and was not indexed, and thus its upward adjustment to USD 425 per week actually is less than would be necessary to keep up with inflation over the past twenty-eight years according to the cost of living index (which would require increasing the figure to USD 530). Thus, even if this proposed change is adopted, workers will be treated less favorably under the minimum salary bar than they were in 1975.

14.2.3 'Duties' Tests Loosened for White-Collar Exemptions

The DOL's proposed new regulations would also make changes to the duties tests used to determine whether workers are excluded from the FLSA's overtime coverage as executive, administrative,

---

[25] Proposed sections 541.600–541.606.

CHAPTER 14. STATE-BASED WAGES STATUTES

professional, or outside-sales employees. While the Bush Administration's DOL leadership maintains that their purpose in proposing the changes is to 'modernize' and clarify FLSA regulations, it is difficult not to notice that the actual substantive changes appear to consistently militate toward excluding employees now covered by the Act.

Under the existing regulatory regime, two alternative tests are used to evaluate whether an employee is covered by the executive, administrative, or professional exemptions. What is commonly known as the 'short' test is used to determine the exemption status of higher salaried employees and has fewer criteria that must be satisfied. The so-called 'long' test applies to lower salaried employees and contains a larger number of criteria that must be satisfied for exempt status to apply. The DOL's proposed new regulations would replace the 'short' and 'long' tests with single tests for each of the categories of white-collar exemption – administrative, professional, and executive.

14.2.3.1 Administrative Employees

The current administrative exemption applies to employees that have a 'primary duty' of 'performing office or non-manual work related to the management or general business operations of the employer or the employer's customers,' and that exercise 'discretion and independent judgment.' The most important change in the proposed new rule for defining the administrative exemption is replacement of the 'discretion and independent judgment' rule with one that requires the employee to 'hold a position of responsibility.'[26] Two things should be noted about this proposed change. First, it can hardly be claimed that 'position of responsibility' has greater analytical clarity than the concept of 'discretion and independent judgment.' Indeed, given that the 'discretion and independent judgment' standard had considerable judicial elaboration of its meaning behind it, the proposed move to the as yet uninterpreted 'position of responsibility' criterion is more likely to produce confusion than clarity. Second, the 'discretion and independent judgment' criterion is one that had been criticized by the management side not due to lack of clarity, but rather because it exempts large numbers of skilled workers who are highly constrained by written guidelines of conduct. Indeed, in a July 2, 2001 letter to the Office of Management and Budget, the Public

---

[26] Proposed section 541.200.

Policy Association of Human Resources Executives, a management-side advocacy organization, called for the elimination of the 'discretion and independent judgment' rule for precisely this reason.[27]

14.2.3.2 Professional Employees

The proposed regulations also seek to change the duties tests applicable to 'learned professionals.' Under current regulations, this exemption only applies to employees who obtain their knowledge and skills though a 'prolonged and specialized course of academic study.' The proposed new rule would expand the exemption to include employees that have a primary duty of performing office or non-manual work requiring advanced knowledge in a field of science or learning customarily acquired by a college degree, but that can also be acquired by a combination of work experience and technical training, such as in the military, technical school, or community college.[28] This change promises to swell the ranks of the 'learned professional,' again with no increase in clarity, and perhaps at the risk of obscurity.

14.2.3.3 Executive Employees

The proposed test to determine whether an individual is an exempt executive for overtime purposes has three prongs: the employee must:

> (1) have a primary duty of managing the enterprise in which the employee is employed or of a customarily recognized department or subdivision thereof; (2) customarily and regularly direct the work of two or more other employees; and (3) have the authority to hire or fire other employees or have particular weight given to suggestions and recommendations as to the hiring, firing, advancement, promotion or any other change of status of other employees.[29]

This test contains elements of both the current 'long' and 'short' tests for the executive employee exemption. As compared with the current 'long' test, the new rule would eliminate the requirement that exempt employees must regularly exercise discretionary powers, and must

---

[27] <www.lpa.org/memoranda/2001/01-110_FMLA_Comments.pdf.>.
[28] Proposed section 541.301.
[29] Proposed section 541.100.

CHAPTER 14. STATE-BASED WAGES STATUTES

devote a limited percentage of their hours worked to activities that are non-exempt.

14.2.3.4 Outside-Sales People

The proposed revisions to the duties tests for outside-sales employees may be the most far-reaching. Section 13(a)(l) of the FLSA includes an exemption for employees employed as 'outside salesm[e]n.' Under current regulations, outside sales employees must 'customarily and regularly' work away from the employer's offices making sales or pursuing business. In order to be legitimately categorized under this exemption, outside employees may not spend more than 20% of their work week performing duties unrelated to their own outside sales work. Under the proposed regulations, outside sales work would have to be the 'primary duty' of an outside sales employee, and the 20% limitation would be removed.[30] Thus, it appears that under the revised rule many employees who are now non-exempt because more than 20% of their work is unrelated to their outside sales duties would be moved into the exempt category provided that outside sales work is their 'primary duty.'

14.2.4 New USD 65,000 Rule for 'Highly Compensated Employees'

The DOL proposal also introduces an entirely new and expansive basis for exempting employees. It proposes a 'highly compensated employee' exemption for persons earning USD 65,000 per year or more if the employee meets any one of the duties tests.[31] By way of example of how the USD 65,000 rule would be applied, an employee who supervises two workers (one prong of the proposed executive exemption), but has no involvement in hiring or termination decisions, would be exempt.

This rule is particularly troubling. First, it represents an expansion of the very idea of who should be excluded from FLSA overtime coverage. There is no basis in the text of the FLSA or in the DOL's

---

[30] Proposed sections 541.500–541.504.
[31] Proposed section 541.601.

previously implemented regulations for the idea of a salary cap. Rather, in the FLSA Congress chose to specify the white-collar exemptions in terms of job duties (executive, administrative, and professional), and past DOL regulations have been consistent with this understanding. The USD 65,000 salary cap, in combination with only one single-duties criteria, is a significant move away from that understanding.

Further, because the USD 65,000 figure is not indexed, the provision poses a significant danger of exempting increasing numbers of employees, who will be earning a lower and lower real income, due to the effects of inflation over time. Indeed, the minimum salary bar discussed above is an instructive example. It was last changed in 1975, and in the ensuing twenty-eight years its real value, as measured by the consumer price index, has declined by 340%. While this problem has long been recognized, the DOL has been unable or unwilling to act to correct it under a succession of presidential administrations. Conventional wisdom is that the contentiousness that characterizes labor policy has a strong tendency to privilege the status quo. It is easier for the DOL not to act than to get new regulations through. Thus, our experience with the minimum salary bar counsels that enactment of the USD 65,000 provision may have the effect over time of excluding increasing numbers of employees with lower real salaries from overtime protections.

14.2.5 Salary Deductions and the Salary Basis Test

The proposed rules would also eliminate some limitations on salary deductions that currently apply to employees paid on a 'salary basis.' Under existing regulations, the executive, administrative, and professional exemptions require that an employee be paid on a 'salary basis,' which means that the employee must be paid a predetermined salary on a weekly or less frequent basis that 'is not subject to reduction because of variations in the quality or quantity of the work performed.'[32] With a few exceptions, exempt employees must be paid their full salary for any week in which the employee performs any work regardless of the number of days or hours worked. Current regulations allow deductions from exempt workers' salaries based upon violations of safety rules of major significance, and for unpaid

---

[32] Section 541.118.

disciplinary suspensions that last for one week or more. The proposed rules expand these disciplinary deductions by allowing deductions from exempt workers' salaries for disciplinary suspensions of one or more full days for violations of any workplace conduct rules.[33]

14.2.6 Changes in Size of Covered Populations

According to DOL estimates, the increase in the minimum salary bar to application of the white-collar exemptions will move 1.3 million low-wage workers from exempt to non-exempt status, thus entitling them to overtime wages for hours worked over forty per week. With respect to the changes in the duties tests, DOL estimates that 640,000 workers now covered by the FLSA's overtime provisions will become exempt. It must be stressed that this latter estimate is highly speculative. For example, in the case of the criteria for judging whether the administrative exemption applies, it is simply impossible to know how many employees will be affected by the change from the 'discretion and independent judgment' standard to the 'position of responsibility' standard. The consequences of the DOL's proposed systematic expansion of the FLSA's overtime exemptions cannot be firmly predicted, though 640,000 seems a highly conservative estimate.

14.2.7 Conclusion

In aggregate, the DOL's proposed changes to FLSA regulations are unfair to workers. While it is true that the increase in the minimum salary bar for application of the white-collar exemptions will include more low-wage workers under FLSA protections, these changes fail by a significant margin to update the 1975 figures by even the cost of living. Alongside this grudging approach to the minimum salary bar, the proposed regulations to the duties tests work structural changes in the categories of white-collar exemptions that appear calculated to expand the exemptions over the long term. Finally, the USD 65,000 salary cap may lead, in only a few years, to the end of overtime for a vast majority of salaried workers.

---

[33] Proposed section 541.602.

CHAPTER 15

Working with the Equal Employment Opportunity Commission

Wayne N. Outten* and Piper Hoffman**

15.1 INTRODUCTION

Plaintiffs who litigate their cases together with the United States Equal Employment Opportunity Commission (EEOC) gain specific advantages but face particular challenges. This article discusses how to get the EEOC involved in litigating an employment discrimination case, to maximize the benefits to individual plaintiffs and their attorneys, and to avoid the pitfalls.

15.2 THE EEOC'S CASE SELECTION

The EEOC is usually most interested in cases that will have a large impact (i.e., cases that will affect large numbers of employees). But the EEOC also pursues smaller cases where the violations are particularly egregious (e.g., *EEOC v. Tyson Foods, Inc.*),[1] or fit into its enforcement plan. Unlike private plaintiffs' attorneys, the EEOC does not have to consider whether the potential monetary damages of a case are enough to finance the litigation.

---

* Wayne N. Outten is managing partner of Outten & Golden. He holds a J.D. from New York University School of Law.
** Piper Hoffman is a partner at Outten & Golden. She holds a J.D. from Harvard Law School.
[1] CV-05-BE-1704-E (N.D.Ala.).

David Sherwyn and Samuel Estreicher (eds), *Employment Class and Collective Actions*, pp. 679–686.
© 2009, Kluwer Law International BV, Printed in Great Britain.

EMPLOYMENT CLASS AND COLLECTIVE ACTIONS

The EEOC divides incoming charges into three categories: 'C' charges, which it dismisses without investigation; 'B' charges, which may have merit depending on the outcome of the investigation; and 'A' charges, which appear highly likely to result in a finding of 'reasonable cause' and which the EEOC may consider litigating. Some plaintiffs' attorneys have found that when they file a charge that the EEOC categorizes as an 'A,' the EEOC assigns an attorney to the case even before the investigation begins.

The EEOC will prosecute a case only if it finds probable cause on the underlying charge. If a charging party withdraws his/her charge before the EEOC issues a finding, and the EEOC chooses to end its investigation and issue a notice of right to sue, it will not litigate the case. To increase the likelihood that the EEOC will find probable cause, plaintiffs' attorneys should work closely with investigators to help them understand the case and get all the information they need.

A plaintiff's attorney who wants the EEOC to consider prosecuting his/her case should bring the case to the attention of the attorneys in the EEOC office in which he/she filed the charge, and discuss with them the possibility of prosecuting the case jointly. While the EEOC has the authority to intervene in litigation brought by a private plaintiff and used to do so regularly, it now rarely intervenes unilaterally since receiving criticism from both Congress and the plaintiffs' bar for that practice. The EEOC is more likely to litigate in cooperation with a private plaintiff.

The best way to bring a case to the attention of the EEOC attorneys is for the charge to be categorized as an 'A,' so that an attorney is assigned to it. Therefore, plaintiffs' lawyers who want the EEOC to participate in later litigation should strive to file a charge that the EEOC will categorize as an 'A.' Plaintiffs' attorneys who have litigated with the EEOC recommend writing a fulsome charge, with as many powerful facts as possible. A bare-bones charge is not likely to earn an 'A.'

15.3 ADVANTAGES OF LITIGATING WITH THE EEOC

15.3.1 Avoid Rule 23

One of the most significant advantages of litigating a multiple-plaintiff case with the EEOC is freedom from Rule 23 of the Federal Rules of Civil Procedure. Section 706 of Title VII authorizes the EEOC to sue employers for violating Title VII, and section 707 authorizes the agency to bring 'pattern or practice' suits.[2] When the EEOC sues an employer under these provisions, the litigation is not a class action and therefore is not subject to the requirements of Rule 23.[3] This is true whether the EEOC initiates the litigation or intervenes in litigation initiated by an individual plaintiff.[4]

15.3.2 Expand the Scope of the Case

The EEOC has standing to pursue claims even without a plaintiff. A private attorney prosecuting a class action may know that the defendant has discriminatory hiring practices, but be unable to pursue that claim because she cannot locate any rejected applicants. The EEOC, on the other hand, does not need to locate anyone. If it finds evidence during its investigation of discriminatory hiring practices and issues a probable cause finding to that effect, it can prosecute the claim.

15.3.3 Avoid Confidentiality Provisions

Another advantage of litigating with the EEOC is that the agency will not include confidentiality provisions in its consent decrees. This is a welcome change of pace for plaintiffs' lawyers frustrated by employers' ability to cover up continued discrimination with confidentiality agreements.

On the other hand, some plaintiffs' attorneys have found that the EEOC's rejection of confidentiality provisions can hinder settlement. If an employer insists on a confidentiality provision, it is not going to reach a settlement with the EEOC, and therefore it is not going to reach a settlement with a private plaintiff either. In some cases, the employer signs two separate settlement agreements, one with the EEOC that has no confidentiality provision, and one with the individual claimant that does require confidentiality. These parallel

---

[2] 42 U.S.C. §§ 2000e-5, 2000e-6.
[3] See *General Tel. Co. v. EEOC*, 446 U.S. 318, 320 (1980).
[4] See *EEOC v. Dial Corp.*, 156 F. Supp. 2d 926 (N.D. Ill. 2001).

agreements can provide individual plaintiffs who are concerned about their privacy with the best of both worlds: the employer's wrongdoing becomes public, while the individual can keep her settlement confidential.

15.3.4 Increase Credibility

People seem to be more inclined to believe a case has merit if the EEOC is involved than if a private lawyer is prosecuting it alone. For this reason, having the EEOC involved in a case confers significant benefits to plaintiffs' counsel. It enhances the case's credibility with the defendant's customers, shareholders, and others who can pressure the defendant to settle, and with the jury pool.

15.3.5 Invoke Fear of Uncle Sam

In calculating their potential exposure from a lawsuit, defendants may conclude that they are at higher risk from the EEOC than from a private plaintiff, in part because the federal government has the resources to see a case through, even if private plaintiffs and their counsel do not. For that reason (and because the EEOC does not receive attorneys' fees or directly represent individuals), it is harder for defendants to cheaply buy their way out of cases prosecuted by the EEOC. Some plaintiffs' attorneys have found that defendants who refused to discuss settlement before the EEOC joined the litigation changed their minds once the government was involved.

15.3.6 Negotiate Systemic Changes

Some private plaintiffs' attorneys have found that defendants resist discussing structural reform in negotiations with individual plaintiffs. When the EEOC is involved, however, defendants know that without systemic changes, there will be no settlement.

CHAPTER 15. EQUAL EMPLOYMENT OPPORTUNITY COMMISSION

15.3.7 Gain Expertise

The EEOC probably has more experience crafting (and monitoring the implementation of) consent decrees in class actions than all but a few private plaintiffs' attorneys. This can be invaluable in negotiating equitable or injunctive-type measures, such as overhauling an employer's recruiting or promotion policies: the EEOC may have had experience with similar policies at other employers, and has seen what works and what does not.

15.3.8 Increase Media Interest

When a private plaintiff files an employment lawsuit, the media may or may not find it newsworthy. When the EEOC files a lawsuit, it is much more likely to be news. Not all employment litigation can benefit from press coverage, but when the media is part of the litigation strategy, the fact that the federal government is prosecuting a private employer can help gain press coverage. In addition, an EEOC attorney can be the spokesperson for the litigation, shielding the private plaintiff from accusations of publicly bad-mouthing her employer.

15.3.9 Get More Hands at No Cost

Litigating with the EEOC can mean that more attorneys and paralegals are available to work on a case at no additional cost to the private plaintiff or her attorneys. The level of EEOC involvement varies by case and by the attorneys involved: some plaintiffs' attorneys have taken a backseat while the EEOC steered the litigation, some have taken the lead role with the EEOC lending its name and resources, and some have shared the load equally.

15.4 DISADVANTAGES OF LITIGATING WITH THE EEOC

15.4.1 Too Many Chefs in the Kitchen

Litigating with the EEOC can have the same drawbacks as litigating with any other co-counsel: attorneys must share decision-making and other responsibilities, and divide up the workload in a way that promotes efficiency without sacrificing communication. Plaintiffs' attorneys who have litigated with the EEOC recommend reaching explicit agreements early on about who will do what.

15.4.2 Government Bureaucracy

As an agency of the federal government, the EEOC is subject to its share of red tape. One example is the process of obtaining approval for litigation expenses. EEOC attorneys must get many litigation expenses approved, and some (such as deposition transcripts) are more likely to gain approval than others, (such as trial graphics vendors). Private plaintiffs' attorneys who are co-counseling with the EEOC can mitigate the impact of the bureaucracy on their cases by deciding in advance which expenses the EEOC will pay for and which the private plaintiff will pay for.

15.4.3 Culture Clash

Private law firms and government agencies are different environments, with different cultures. For example, the EEOC may be accustomed to allow every attorney and law student involved with a case to attend a court conference, while private attorneys, who must be more cost-conscious, will send only one or two people. Sometimes the differences in culture can create conflicts due to different expectations. Of course, two private law firms can have different cultures as well.

15.4.4 Different Goals and Rewards

While a private attorney represents individual plaintiffs, the EEOC represents the public good. Having different clients creates different priorities and goals. The most obvious is that maximizing the monetary award for the individual plaintiff must be one of the private attorney's primary goals; in a class action, that goal is in tension with the EEOC's goal of maximizing the monetary award for the entire class.

Similarly, the EEOC does not accept attorneys' fees when it prevails in litigation, while private attorneys seek to maximize the amount their clients will receive for attorneys' fees. This can put the EEOC and private counsel at odds. For instance, if an employer has reached an agreement in principle to settle a case for a certain sum, private plaintiff's counsel will have a strong interest in allocating some portion of that sum to attorneys' fees, while the EEOC will have no interest in attorneys' fees and may prefer to allocate the same money to, say, a minority recruitment program.

Plaintiffs' attorneys who have litigated with the EEOC recommend discussing the parties' goals with the EEOC attorneys as soon as they become involved in the litigation, to avoid conflicts later in the process.

15.4.5 Consensus on Settlement

Once a private plaintiff's counsel has joined forces with the EEOC, she will find it very difficult to settle the case on behalf of her client(s) without the EEOC's consent. This is because the EEOC can pursue litigation against an employer even after the employer settles with the individual claimant whose charge forms the basis of the EEOC's case, so the employer has little incentive to settle only with the individual.[5] Because the EEOC and the private plaintiff's goals are different, they may not agree on what constitutes a good settlement.

---

[5] See *EEOC v. Waffle House, Inc.*, 534 U.S. 279 (2002).

15.4.6 Perception of the EEOC

Some private plaintiffs' lawyers have found that defendants believe the EEOC settles cases for less money than they are worth. Such defendants will make very low settlement offers. Their perception of the EEOC's valuation of cases can impede settlement.

15.5 CONCLUSION

Most plaintiffs' lawyers who have litigated with the EEOC have found the agency's participation to be an asset. EEOC attorneys have expertise, resources, and credibility that private lawyers sometimes do not. EEOC attorneys are committed to protecting the civil rights of American workers, and it can be a pleasure to fight side-by-side with them.

CHAPTER 16

Green Tree v. Bazzle in the Supreme Court: 'How to Succeed in Blocking Class Actions in Arbitration without Really Saying So'

Daniel B. Edelman[*,**]

16.1 INTRODUCTION AND SUMMARY

In their treatise on employment law, Estreicher and Harper comment:

> Class actions have been very important to anti-discrimination litigation because they enable individual claimants and advocacy organizations to mount systemic, high-impact challenges to employer decision making. Only class actions enable large numbers of victims of discrimination to obtain relief from the outcome of a single disparate impact or systemic disparate treatment suit.[1]

Will the 'silent treatment' succeed in blocking class actions under predispute agreements for mandatory arbitration in standard-form contracts of adhesion? If the 'silent treatment' fails to block class actions, what then?

---

[*] The article reflects the date May 2003.
[**] Daniel B. Edelman is of counsel to Katz, Marshall, & Banks LLP. He holds a J.D. from Harvard Law School.
[1] S. Estreicher and M. Harper, Cases and Materials on Employment Discrimination and Employment Law (West 2000) at 1087. Few would disagree with this assessment.

David Sherwyn and Samuel Estreicher (eds), *Employment Class and Collective Actions*, pp. 687–711.
© 2009, Kluwer Law International BV, Printed in Great Britain.

EMPLOYMENT CLASS AND COLLECTIVE ACTIONS

In *Green Tree Financial Corp. v. Bazzle*,[2] the Supreme Court is expected to decide the issue it left unresolved twenty years ago in *Southland Corp. v. Keating*:[3] to wit, whether the Federal Arbitration Act[4] (FAA) preempts the application of state class action procedures to arbitrations under agreements which are silent regarding the allowance of class-wide arbitration.[5]

The Supreme Court of South Carolina sustained class-wide arbitration awards against Green Tree totaling approximately USD 20 million for some 3,700 individuals.[6] Construing Green Tree's arbitration agreement as silent regarding class-wide arbitration, it held that South Carolina law authorizes class-wide treatment 'when the arbitration agreement is silent if it would serve efficiency and equity, and would not result in prejudice.'[7] Applying the narrow standard of judicial review afforded by FAA § 10, the South Carolina Court found no basis for setting aside the awards and accordingly sustained them.

If the answer to the question posed by *Bazzle* is 'no'– that the FAA does not preempt class-wide arbitration where the agreement is silent – what then? Employers and other institutions that have not done so already – Green Tree itself added an express ban on class actions

---

[2] No. 02-634 (U.S. Sup. Ct.), cert. granted, 123 S.Ct. 8 17 (January 10, 2003).

[3] 465 U.S. 1, 9 (1984).

[4] 9 U.S.C. 55 1 et seq.

[5] The case was to be argued April 22, 2003. Green Tree was represented in the Supreme Court by Carter Phillips of Sidley, Austin in Washington, D.C. who argued successfully on its behalf in Green Tree Financial Coy. – *Alabama v. Randolph*, 531 U.S. 79 (2000) (whether provision for sharing of costs renders arbitration agreements unenforceable must be determined case-by-case). Professor Cornelia Pillard of the Georgetown University Law Center argued for respondents.

The case drew extensive amicus curiae participation. Amicus curiae briefs were filed in support of Green Tree by the Equal Employment Advisory Council; the Chamber of Commerce of the United States; the American Bankers Association along with other banking and financial services associations; the Washington Legal Foundation; the New England Legal Foundation and Verizon Wireless, Directv, Inc.; and the National Council of Chain Restaurants. Amicus briefs supporting respondents were filed by the Trial Lawyers for Public Justice; the AARP; the Lawyers Committee for Civil Rights under Law and other civil-rights advocacy groups; and Robert Belton along with other law professors.

[6] *Bazzle v. Green Tree Financial Corp.*, 569 S.E.2d 349 (2002).

[7] *Id.* at 360.

CHAPTER 16. GREEN TREE V. BAZZLE IN THE SUPREME COURT

several years ago in 1998 – will be likely to add express bans on class actions to their standard-form agreements.

What role if any will ultimately be allowed for class actions under systems of mandatory arbitration in the standard-form contracts of adhesion increasingly imposed by employers and a broad range of other institutions? If institutional proponents of mandatory arbitration have their way, the answer will be 'none.' The result below in *Bazzle* realizes their worst fears regarding class-wide arbitration – the entry of multimillion dollar awards that are subject to only extremely limited judicial review.

Bazzle comes to the Supreme Court in the wake of important victories for institutional proponents of mandatory arbitration: decisions that have approved the inclusion of all employment claims – state and federal, statutory and common-law – in unilaterally promulgated systems of mandatory arbitration. In *Gilmer v. Interstate/Johnson Lane Corp.*,[8] the Supreme Court held that, so long as it provides a forum in which individuals can effectively vindicate their rights, an arbitration agreement is enforceable under FAA §2 for claims under the Age Discrimination in Employment Act. In *Circuit City Stores, Inc. v. Adams*,[9] the Court took a restrictive view of FAA §1 exemption of employment claims, narrowly limiting the exemption from FAA coverage to employment claims of transportation workers. So whither the possibility of class actions for disputes subject to agreements for mandatory arbitration?[10]

Green Tree contends the FAA preempts the application – in Green Tree's parlance the 'super-imposition' – of state class action procedures where the agreement is silent. Green Tree contends additionally that the South Carolina Court's interpretation of the particular arbitration agreement as silent must be reviewed and overturned under federal law. On the immediate questions before the Court, Green Tree's arguments call for a vast expansion of FAA preemption, federalizing both the rules of procedure for arbitration and the law of contract interpretation for arbitration agreements.

---

[8] 500 U.S. 20 (1991).

[9] 532 U.S. 105 (2001).

[10] Some courts have read Gilmer as establishing that an arbitration agreement may foreclose the right to proceed collectively under the ADEA and other statutes. See e.g., *Johnson v. W. Suburban Bk*, 225 F.3rd 366, 377 (3rd Cir. 2000)(enforcing arbitration agreement notwithstanding that plaintiff sought to pursue class claims under TILA). Notably, the plaintiff in Gilmer did not seek to proceed collectively. The Supreme Court has yet to decide whether an arbitration agreement may legitimately foreclose collective pursuit of statutory claims under ADEA or other statutes.

EMPLOYMENT CLASS AND COLLECTIVE ACTIONS

Green Tree's amici urge the Supreme Court to foreclose class action procedures as incompatible variously with the goals of arbitration and the due process rights of absent parties.[11] In the background lurks the critical question whether the FAA shields express bans on class-wide arbitration from being rejected based on state unconscionability law. While this question is not presented and was not raised below, some of Green Tree's amici urge the Court to use *Bazzle* as an early opportunity to 'dispatch [the] shibboleth' of unconscionability and hold that the FAA forecloses disapproval of class-action bans as unconscionable.[12]

The positions advanced by Green Tree and its amici are part of a broad attempt by corporate and institutional interests to foreclose class actions. The invitation of Green Tree's amici – that the Court hold that the FAA shields express bans on class arbitration from disapproval under state unconscionability – calls for a yet more far-reaching expansion upon the outer limits of FAA preemption.

Acceptance of the contention that class treatment is foreclosed in arbitration would close what has been an essential avenue for vindicating the rights of consumers and employees. *Bazzle* itself represents the paradigm case in which class treatment is appropriate and moreover essential for victims of unlawful practices to secure vindication of their rights. *Bazzle* demonstrates that classwide arbitration can be accomplished without sacrifice of arbitration's advantages of economy and expedition and consistent with the due process rights of absent class members.

16.2 THE DEBATE OVER CLASS ARBITRATION

Bazzle comes to the Supreme Court in the midst of a much broader attack on class actions in arbitration and otherwise. The rationale for allowing arbitrations to proceed as class actions was powerfully stated by the California Supreme Court in *Keating v. Superior Court*:[13]

---

[11] See e.g., Br. of Chamber of Commerce, 10 et seq.; Br. of American Bankers Ass'n et al. 9–16.

[12] See e.g., Chamber of Commerce Br., 5 at n. 2.

[13] 645 P.2d 1192, 1206–1207 (1982), reversed on other grounds in *Southland Corp. v. Keating, supra.*

CHAPTER 16. *GREEN TREE V. BAZZLE* IN THE SUPREME COURT

This court has repeatedly emphasized the importance of the class action device for vindicating rights asserted by large groups of persons. We have observed that the class suit 'both eliminates the possibility of repetitious litigation and provides small claimants with a method of obtaining redress for claims which would otherwise be too small to warrant individual litigation.' ... Denial of a class action in cases where it is appropriate may have the effect of allowing an unscrupulous wrongdoer to 'retain [] the benefits of its wrongful conduct.' ... 'Controversies involving widely used contracts of adhesion present ideal cases for class adjudication; the contracts are uniform, the same principles of interpretation apply to each contract, and all members of the class will share a common interest in the interpretation of an agreement to which each is a party.'

If the right to a class-wide proceeding could be automatically eliminated in relationships governed by adhesion contracts through the inclusion of a provision for arbitration, the potential for undercutting these class action principles and for chilling the effective protection of interests common to a group would be substantial.[14]

As described by Professor Jean Sternlight in an article quoted by the South Carolina Supreme Court,[15] potential defendants in a broad array of industries 'hope they have found a surreptitious way to defeat the feared class action: mandatory binding arbitration.' In the words of Professor Sternlight, 'these companies and their attorneys assert that they may use contracts of adhesion to compel consumers, employees, and others to arbitrate rather than litigate their claims, and to require that such arbitration must proceed on an individual rather than class

---

[14] Since the 1982 decision in Keating, the courts of California and some other states – including most recently the Supreme Court of South Carolina in Bazzle – have applied state class action procedures to arbitration agreements that are silent with respect to authorization of class actions. See ex., *Blue Cross v. Superior Court*, 67 Cal. App. 4th 42, 78 Cal. Rptr. 2d 779 (Cal. App. 1998), cert. denied, 527 U.S. 1003; *Dickler v. Shearson Lehrnan Hutton. Inc.*, 596 A.2d 860 (Pa. Super. Ct. 1991). Other state courts have disagreed, reasoning that applying class action procedures where the agreement is silent impermissibly alters the parties' agreement. See e.g., *Stein v. Geonerco, Inc.*, 17 P.3d 1266 (Wash. Ct. App. 2001); *Med Center Cars, Inc. v. Smith*, 727 So. 2d 9 (Ala. 1998). Cf. *Leonard v. Tenninix Int'l Co.*, 2002 WL 31231048 (Ala. 2002) (silent agreement that had effect of foreclosing class-wide arbitration was unconscionable because it made remedy inaccessible).

[15] 569 S.E.2d at 360 n. 20. Jean R. Sternlight, As Mandatory Binding Arbitration Meets the Class Action, Will the Class Action Survive?, 42 Wm & Mary L. Rev. 1 (October 2000).

basis.' Opposing scholars argue that allowing class proceedings destroys the advantages of arbitration as an expeditious and economical means for dispute resolution.[16]

With increasing frequency, companies are inserting clauses expressly banning class actions, hoping that these clauses will result in court decisions that enforce agreements for mandatory arbitration but simultaneously foreclose class treatment. These companies have won the day in some court decisions.[17] Other decisions – most notably the Ninth Circuit's recent decision in *Ting v. AT&T*[18] – have rejected express bans of class arbitration as unconscionable and allowed plaintiffs to proceed with class claims in a judicial forum.[19]

A split has recently developed among the state courts in California that the Supreme Court of California has recently undertaken to resolve. The California courts since *Keating* have generally allowed class-wide arbitration in cases appropriate for class treatment. A series of decisions by California Courts of Appeals have struck down class-action bans in arbitration agreements and nonarbitration settings as well.[20] In January 2003, another California Court of Appeals disagreed,

---

[16] See e.g., Stephen J. Ware, Paying the Price of Process: Judicial Regulation of Consumer Arbitration Agreements, 2001 J. Disp. Resol. 89 (2001); Edward Wood Dunham, The Arbitration Clause as Class Action Shield, 16 Franchise L.J. 141 (1997); Alan S. Kaplinsky & Mark J. Levin, Excuse Me, But Who's the Predator? Banks Can Use Arbitration Clauses as a Defense, Bus. L. Today, May-June 1998, at 24); J. T. Westermeir, How Arbitration Clauses Can Help Avoid Class Action Damages, 14 Computer L. Strategist, September 1997, at 1. Sternlight, *supra*, n. 2.

[17] See e.g., *Lloyd v. MBNA Am. Bank. N.A.*, 27 Fed. Appx. 82, 84 (3rd Cir. 2002); *Snowden v. Checkpoint Check Cashing*, 290 F.3d 631, 638–639 (4th Cir.), cert. denied, 123 S. Ct. 695 (2002); *Randolph v. Green Tree* Fin. Corn., 244 F.3d 814, 818–819 (11th Cir. 2001). See Br. of Chamber of Commerce at 5, n. 2.

[18] 319 F.3d 1 126 (9th Cir. 2003), aff'g in part. rev'g in part, 182 F.Supp.2d 902 (N.D. Calif.).

[19] See e.g., *Szetela v. Discover Bank*, 97 Cal. App. 4th 1094, 1101–1102 (Cal. Ct. App. 2002), cert. denied, 123 S.Ct. 1258 (2003)(allowing class claims of consumers to proceed in court); *Bailey v. Ameriquest Mortg. Co.*, 2002 WL 10039 1 at *8 (2002)(allowing collective FLSA claims to proceed in court).

[20] See e.g., *Szetela v. Discover Bank, supra*; *Mandel v. Household Bank (Nevada)*, 105 Cal. App. 4th 75 (Cal. Ct. App. 2003)(applying Nevada law), pet. for rev. granted, 03 C.D.O.S. 3080 (April 9, 2003); *America Online. Inc. v. Superior Court*, 90 Cal. App. 4th 1 (Cal. Ct. App. 2001)(contract not containing arbitration clause). In addition to Szetela, the U.S. Supreme Court also recently declined to review a decision of the

CHAPTER 16. GREEN TREE V. BAZZLE IN THE SUPREME COURT

holding that the FAA preempts California's generally applicable law of unconscionability whenever that law would strike down 'the express terms of a validly formed arbitration agreement.'[21]

In the meantime, several federal courts – as recognized by the South Carolina Court in *Bazzle* – have held that FAA §4 precludes a federal court from ordering class arbitration where the agreement is silent.[22] In *Champ v. Siegel Trading Co.*,[23] the Seventh Circuit held that ordering class-wide arbitration, where the agreement is silent, would impermissibly alter the terms of the arbitration agreement in violation of FAA §4.[24] According to the Seventh Circuit, this result followed from holdings of other federal Circuits that district courts lack authority to consolidate arbitration proceedings where the agreement is silent.[25] While concurring, Judge Rovner doubted that 'corporate defendants who draft these agreements...would ever consent...in writing' to class certification and observed that they 'typically have far more to

---

West Virginia Supreme Court that disapproved an express ban on class arbitration as unconscionable. *West Virginia ex rel. Dunlap v. Berger* 567 S.E. 2d 265, 280 (W. Va. 2002), cert. denied sub nom., *Friedman's. Inc. v. West Virginia ex rel. Dunlap*, 123 S.Ct. 695 (2002).

[21] *Discover Bank v. The Superior Court of Los Angeles County*, 105 Cal. App. 4th 326, 330 (Cal. Ct. App. 2003), pet. for rev. granted, 03 C.D.O.S. 3079 (April 9, 2003).

[22] Section 4, which authorizes suits to compel arbitration in *federal* court where jurisdiction is conferred by Title 28, U.S.C., provides:

The court...upon being satisfied that the making of the agreement for arbitration or the failure to comply therewith is not in issue,...shall make an order directing the parties to proceed to arbitration *in accordance with the terms of the agreement*. (Emphasis added).

[23] 55 F.3d 269 (7th Cir. 1995).

[24] See also, *Dominium Austin Partners. LLC v. Emerson*, 248 F.3d 720, 728 (8th Cir. 2001).

[25] *Id.* at 274–275 (e.g., *Govt. of United Kingdom v. Boeing Co.*, 998 F.2d 64, 74 (2nd Cir. 1993). The Seventh Circuit has since disagreed with the decisions it embraced as underpinnings for Champ, holding that a federal court may order consolidation of arbitration proceedings where the arbitration agreement is silent. *Conn. Gen. Life Ins. Co. v. Sun Life Assurance Co.*, 210 F.3d 771, 774 (7th Cir. 2000)(Posner, J.). The Court urged 'practical considerations' including that relitigation of the identical dispute before different arbitration panels is a formula for duplication of effort and a fertile source...of disputes over esoteric issues in the law of res judicata....*Id.* at 775–776. The same 'practical considerations' support the availability of class-wide arbitration in appropriate cases.

gain by forcing unhappy customers to bear the expense of arbitrating individually.'[26]

Proponents of mandatory arbitration who seek to foreclose class-wide arbitration have contended – as Green Tree now contends before the Supreme Court – that class actions are equally foreclosed under agreements that are silent regarding class arbitration as under agreements with express class-action bans.

16.3 THE STATE COURT PROCEEDINGS

The class-wide arbitration awards at issue in *Bazzle* arose from consumer actions by home-loan borrowers in South Carolina complaining of predatory lending practices employed by Green Tree in violation of the South Carolina Consumer Code for many years as a matter of standard procedure.[27] Apart from the availability of class treatment of these claims, there would have been no meaningful prospect for victims of Green Tree's unlawful practices to secure relief or any incentive for Green Tree to change its ways.

The suits were initiated as class actions in trial courts in South Carolina.[28] Green Tree's standard-form agreement provided that '[a]ll disputes, claims or controversies arising from or relating to this contract or the relationships which result from this contract... shall be

---

[26] 55 F.2d at 277.

[27] The plaintiffs claimed that, in all the loan transactions at issue, Green Tree violated the 'Attorney Preference' requirements of the South Carolina Consumer Code, S.C. Code Ann. § 37-010-102. These provisions, enacted in 1982, replaced the state's usury limits with requirements that mortgage lenders ascertain the borrower's choice of legal counsel and insurance agent in matters relating to the transaction prior to the loan closing. Green Tree admittedly maintained a standard practice of not providing the legally-required notice, despite successive non-class adjudications upholding claims by individual consumers. Pet. App. 67a-69a. Absent independent legal advice, consumers remained unaware in many instances that outstanding liens could prevent sale of their property or lead to forfeiture if payments were not promptly made. R. App. 1720, 1722.

[28] *Lackey v. Green Tree*, filed May 28, 1996, claimed that Green Tree systematically violated the Preference Statute in connection with mortgage loans for manufactured-housing secured by South Carolina real estate. *Bazzle v. Green Tree*, filed in March 1997, claimed that Green Tree similarly violated the Preference Statute in home-improvement transactions secured by South Carolina real estate.

CHAPTER 16. *GREEN TREE V. BAZZLE* IN THE SUPREME COURT

resolved by binding arbitration by one arbitrator selected by us with consent of you.'[29] In both cases, the courts resolved the 'gateway' question of arbitrability, ordering the parties to arbitration.

Green Tree's agreement, while reciting that the arbitration provision was entered pursuant to the 'Federal Arbitration Act at 9 U.S.C. section 1', provided: 'This contract will be governed by the law of the State of South Carolina.'[30] The agreement specifically barred jury trials but was otherwise silent regarding procedures for arbitration and made no mention of possible class-wide arbitration. The agreement granted the arbitrator 'all powers provided by the law and the contract,' including specifically 'all legal and equitable remedies, including, but not limited to, monetary damages, declaratory relief, and injunctive relief.'[31]

In both cases, the arbitrator selected by Green Tree – Honorable Thomas J. Ervin, a retired state circuit judge selected by Green Tree – determined that Green Tree's arbitration agreement did not prohibit class treatment and further determined that the claims were appropriate for class treatment under South Carolina law.[32] In both cases, the arbitrator directed that class members be provided with notice and the opportunity to opt out, which some class members exercised. In both cases, the arbitrator determined the merits of the plaintiffs' claims, finding that Green Tree had engaged in egregious violations of the South Carolina Consumer Code, persisting in unlawful lending practices even after being placed on actual notice of their illegality.

In *Lackey*, the arbitrator held an initial hearing to determine whether Green Tree's agreement prevented class arbitration and concluded it did not.[33] The arbitrator conducted a further hearing on class certification, determining that the requirements for class certification under South Carolina law were met and that class certification was

---

[29] Pet. App. 110a.
[30] R. App. 2 162.
[31] Pet. App. 110a.
[32] In *Bazzle*, the trial court initially granted the plaintiffs' motion for class certification prior to taking Green Tree's motion to compel arbitration. R. App. 1350–1358. However, the arbitrator subsequently made an independent determination that Green Tree's arbitration agreement did not prohibit class treatment and that the claims were appropriate for class treatment under South Carolina law.
[33] R. App. 73.

appropriate.[34] The arbitrator approved a notice to class members informing them of their right to opt out which class counsel mailed to each class member.[35] Ten individuals chose to opt out.[36]

After a trial on the merits in March 2000, the arbitrator determined that Green Tree's behavior had been 'willful, wanton, and egregious.'[37] The arbitrator found that Green Tree failed to offer any evidence of compliance with the Preference Statute.[38] The arbitrator awarded USD 5,000 per transaction to each *Lackey* class member.[39]

Referral of the *Bazzle* case to arbitration was delayed for some two years by Green Tree's unsuccessful interlocutory appeal of the trial court's initial order of class certification.[40] Upon the referral, Green Tree requested the arbitrator to dismiss the case or, in the alternative, to decertify the class.[41] The arbitrator denied these requests. The arbitrator's consideration of Green Tree's request for decertification reflects that he exercised his independent powers under the agreement to determine how the case should proceed.

After a hearing on May 31, 2000, the arbitrator issued an award holding that Green Tree violated the Attorney Preference statute and awarding class-wide relief.[42] The arbitrator determined that Green Tree had made no affirmative effort to educate itself regarding

---

[34] R. App. 71–72.
[35] R. App. 17–23.
[36] Pet. App. 91.
[37] Pet. App. 108a.
[38] Pet. App. 67a.
[39] Green Tree moved the state court to vacate the award arguing that its agreement's reference to disputes under 'this contract' barred class arbitration. The trial court disagreed, finding that the agreement's 'all powers' language empowered the arbitrator to determine classwide arbitration. Pet. App. 36a-54a. Green Tree appealed to the South Carolina Supreme Court which consolidated the *Lackey* case with a parallel appeal in *Bazzle*.
[40] Green Tree moved the trial court in January 1998 for reconsideration of the class certification arguing that its arbitration agreement disallowed class-wide arbitration. R. App. 145 1. The trial court denied Green Tree's motion and the South Carolina Court of Appeals and Supreme Court denied interlocutory review. Pet. App. 57a-58a; R. App. 1306. Green Tree then chose Judge Ervin as arbitrator for the *Bazzle* case notwithstanding that he had already certified a class in *Lackey*.
[41] Pet. App. 29; R. App. 1455, 3533–3543.
[42] Pet. App. 55a-81a.

CHAPTER 16. *GREEN TREE V. BAZZLE* IN THE SUPREME COURT

the requirements of the Attorney Preference statute.[43] The arbitrator determined that what began as a 'careless or negligent attitude' became 'willful non-compliance and disregard for South Carolina law.' The arbitrator found: 'After five suits, including [the *Bazzle* suit], having been brought against Green Tree for failing to comply with the preference statute, it still continued to refuse to take any action or to adhere to the statute's requirements'[44]

The arbitrator awarded USD 5,000 to consumers in 1,323 transactions that preceded Green Tree's actual notice of its non-compliance and USD 7,500 to consumers in 576 transactions thereafter, when Green Tree still did nothing to comply.[45]

The trial court confirmed the award.[46] Green Tree appealed to the South Carolina Supreme Court which assumed jurisdiction, consolidating the case with *Lackey*.[47]

16.4 THE SOUTH CAROLINA SUPREME COURT DECISION

The South Carolina Supreme Court sustained the two awards, specifically upholding class treatment of the claims by the arbitrator as consistent with Green Tree's arbitration agreement and South Carolina law.

At the outset, the Court declared that South Carolina law – no less than federal law under the FAA – favors arbitration and, moreover, that South Carolina courts resolve doubts concerning the scope of an arbitration clause in favor of arbitrability.[48] At the same time, it emphasized that South Carolina law resolves ambiguities in contracts against the drafter.[49] It observed that the U.S. Supreme Court applied this rule of construction to the arbitration agreement in *Mastrobuono v. Shearson Lehman Hutton. Inc.*[50] The South Carolina Court looked to its prior

---

[43] Pet. App. 69a.
[44] Pet. App. 67a-69a.
[45] Pet. App. 71a, 80a.
[46] Pet. App. 27a-35a.
[47] Pet. App. 2a.
[48] *Bazzle, supra*, 569 S.E.2d at 358.
[49] *Id.*
[50] 514 U.S. 52 (1995)(ambiguity as to awardability of punitive damages resolved against drafter to permit punitive-damage award). *Id.* at 359.

697

decisions upholding consolidation of arbitrations where the agreement is silent.[51]

Applying South Carolina law regarding the resolution of ambiguities in contracts, the South Carolina Court rejected Green Tree's contention that its agreement prohibited class-wide arbitration. It viewed the language cited by Green Tree as merely creating an ambiguity to be resolved against the drafter under South Carolina law.[52] According to the South Carolina Court, its decision rested on an independent state ground – South Carolina's rule resolving ambiguities against the drafter.[53]

The South Carolina Court rejected the application of *Champ v. Siegel Trading Co.*,[54] and other federal decisions that FAA §4 prohibits a federal court from ordering class-wide arbitration where the arbitration agreement is silent. It observed the issue has not been resolved by the Supreme Court and found it 'debatable' whether FAA §4 applies in state court. The court reasoned:

> If we enforced a mandatory, adhesive arbitration clause, but prohibited class actions in arbitration where the agreement is silent, the drafting party could effectively prevent class actions against it without having to say it was doing so in the agreement.... [P]arties with nominal individual claims, but significant collective claims, would be left with no avenue for relief and the drafting party with no check on its abuses of the law. Further, hearing such claims (involving identical issues against one defendant) individually, in court or before an arbitrator, does not serve the interest of judicial economy.[55]

In the view of the South Carolina Court, the arbitrator's awards command judicial deference and were entitled to be upheld unless shown to be in manifest disregard of the law or derived from fraud, corruption or other misconduct. Finding no such basis for setting them aside, the court sustained the awards.[56]

---

[51] *Id.*
[52] *Id.* at 359.
[53] *Id.* at 360.
[54] *Supra*, at n. 23.
[55] *Bazzle, supra*, at 360–361.
[56] *Id.* at 361. The Court declined to reach Green Tree's contention that class-wide arbitration violated the due process rights of absent class members, the issue not having been raised below. *Id.* at 362.

CHAPTER 16. *GREEN TREE V. BAZZLE* IN THE SUPREME COURT

16.5 DOES THE FAA PREEMPT APPLICATION OF STATE CLASS ACTION PROCEDURES TO A SILENT ARBITRATION AGREEMENT? DOES THE FAA FEDERALIZE INTERPRETATION OF ARBITRATION AGREEMENTS?

Green Tree's position in *Bazzle* calls for a vast expansion of FAA preemption beyond the scope established by Supreme Court decisions to date. Acceptance of Green Tree's position would involve federalization of the rules of procedure governing arbitration proceedings as well as the law of contract interpretation as it pertains to arbitration agreements.

Congress enacted the FAA in 1925 'to reverse the longstanding judicial hostility to arbitration agreements...and to place arbitration agreements upon the same footing as other contracts.'[57] Through the FAA,[58] Congress provided that agreements to arbitrate disputes involving interstate commerce, as a matter of federal law, 'shall be valid, irrevocable, and enforceable, save upon such grounds as exist at law or in equity for the revocation of *any* contract.'[59] To that end, the Supreme Court has held, albeit by narrow majorities, that FAA §§ 1 and 2, the FAA's 'substantive provisions,' apply in state as well as federal courts.[60]

What the Supreme Court held regarding the preemptive effect of the FAA is that the FAA preempts state laws that conflict with enforcement of arbitration agreements in one of two ways. First, the FAA preempts state laws that override agreements to arbitrate so as to reserve a judicial forum for particular categories of disputes.[61] Second, FAA

---

[57] *Gilmer, supra,* 500 U.S. at 24; *Dean Witter Reynolds Inc. v. Byd,* 470 US. 213, 219–220 (1985); *Scherk v. Alberto-Culver Co.,* 417 U.S. 506, 511 (1974); *Prima Paint Corn. v. Flood & Conklin Mfg. Co.,* 388 U.S. 395 (1967).
[58] § 2, 9 U.S.C. § 2.
[59] *Moses H. Cone Memorial Hospital v. Mercury Construction Corp.,* 460 U.S. 1, 24 (1983)(quoting FAA § 2)(emphasis in original).
[60] *Southland Corp. v. Keating, supra,* 465 U.S. at 15. See Resp. Br. at 46, n.25 (describing dissenting views of Justice O'Connor and Chief Justice Rehnquist in *Southland,* supra, and dissenting views of Justices Scalia and Thomas in *Allied-Bruce Terrninix Cos. v. Dobson,* 513 U.S. 265, 284–297 (1995)).
[61] See *Southland Corp. v. Keating, supra,* 465 U.S. at 16 (FAA § 2 preempts provision of California Franchise Investment law interpreted by state courts as requiring a

699

§2 preempts state laws that erect special requirements for arbitration agreements, treating such agreements as suspect or disfavored.[62]

The outer limit of FAA preemption as applicable to the issues in *Bazzle* was delineated in *Volt Information Sciences. Inc. v. Bd. of Trustees. etc.*[63] As in *Bazzle*, the question in *Volt* was whether the FAA preempted application of a state procedural rule, in that case a California statute that authorized state courts to stay arbitration proceedings pending related litigation.[64] Also, as in *Bazzle*, the arbitration agreement contained a choice-of-law provision – in that case specifying that 'the Contract shall be governed by the law of the place where the Project is located.'[65] The Court held:

> Where, as here, the parties have agreed to abide by state rules of arbitration, enforcing those rules according to the terms of the agreement is fully consistent with the goals of the FAA, *even if the result is that arbitration is stayed where the Act would otherwise permit it to go forward.*[66]

Volt bears on the preemption issues in *Bazzle* in three key ways. First, the Court explained that a state law is preempted by the FAA only if it 'actually conflicts with the federal law.'[67] The Court emphasized that the 'FAA contains no express pre-emptive provision nor does it reflect a congressional intent to occupy the entire field of arbitration.'[68]

Second, the Court made plain that the FAA does not federalize the rules of procedure governing arbitration. The Court stated, 'There is no federal policy favoring arbitration under a certain set of procedural rules; the federal policy is simply to ensure the enforceability, according

---

judicial forum for claims thereunder); *Pew v. Thomas*, 482 U.S. 483 (FAA §2 preempts state law requiring judicial forum for wage claims).

[62] *Doctor's Associates. Inc. v. Casarotto*, 517 U.S. 68 1 (1 996)(FAA §2 preempts state statute that imposed special notice requirement on agreements to arbitrate); *Allied-Bruce Terminix Cos. v. Dobson*, 513 U.S. 265 (1995)(FAA §2 preempts state anti-arbitration statute that conditioned enforcement of pre-dispute arbitration agreements on showing that parties contemplated substantial involvement in interstate commerce).

[63] 489 U.S. 468 (1989).

[64] Cal. Civ. Proc. Code Ann. § 1281.2) (West 1982).

[65] *Volt Info. Sciences, supra*, 489 U.S. at 470.

[66] *Id.* at 479. (Emphasis added).

[67] *Id.* at 477.

[68] *Id.* at 477, citing, *Bernhardt v. Polygraphic Co.*, 350 U.S. 198 (1956).

to their terms, of private agreements to arbitrate.'[69] The Court reiterated that it had specifically refrained from holding FAA §§ 3 and 4 – the FAA's 'procedural provisions' – applicable in state courts.[70]

Third, the Court made plain that the FAA does not federalize the interpretation of arbitration agreements, stating: 'the interpretation of private contracts is ordinarily a question of state law.'[71] So long as state law deals with contracts generally and does not construe arbitration agreements 'in a manner different from...nonarbitration agreements,'[72] the interpretation of arbitration agreements remains a question of state law. Green Tree's argument that the South Carolina court misinterpreted its agreement as silent presents a reviewable federal issue only if makes the interpretation of contracts regarding arbitration determinable by federal law.

Green Tree's arguments that the FAA preempts the application of state procedural rules and state-law principles of contract interpretation are irreconcilable with the outer limits of preemption as explained in *Volt*. Green Tree nevertheless claims support in *Volt*'s description of the FAA's primary purpose as 'ensuring that private agreements to arbitrate are enforced according to their terms,'[73] and ensuing decisions including *Mastrobuono v. Shearson Lehman Hutton. Inc.*;[74] *First Options of Chi, Inc. v. Kaplan*;[75] and *Doctor's Assocs. Inc. v. Casarotto*,[76] which similarly speak in terms of enforcing arbitration agreements as written or according to their terms.

In context, these statements reflect merely the repudiation of historical practices of voiding arbitration agreements due to a bias in favor of adjudication.[77] They do not support federalizing the procedural rules governing arbitration nor the interpretation of arbitration agreements. *Volt* made clear that the FAA has no such effect. Green Tree overlooks that the result of enforcing the arbitration agreement 'according to its terms' in *Volt* was to uphold the parties' choice-of-law provision and

---

[69] *Id.* at 476.
[70] *Id.* at 47; *Southland Corp. v. Keating, supra*, 465 U.S. at 16 n. 10.
[71] *Id.* at 474.
[72] *Perry, supra*, 482 U.S. at 492 n. 9,
[73] 489 U.S. at 479.
[74] *Supra*, 514 U.S. at 53–54.
[75] 514 U.S. 938, 947 (1995).
[76] *Supra*, 517 U.S. at 688.
[77] See Resp. Br. 18.

further overlooks that its own agreement includes a parallel choice-of-law provision specifying that South Carolina law would govern. Enforcing Green Tree's agreement 'according to its terms' appears clearly to support the arbitrator's application of South Carolina class action procedures.

The state law upheld in *Volt* – authorizing state courts to stay arbitration pending completion of related litigation and thereby allowing litigation to displace arbitration to a considerable degree – intruded more severely on the goals of the FAA than application of state class-action procedures, allowing a sequence of proceedings directly opposite to that specified by FAA §3. According to Justice Brennan, staying arbitration while the litigation went forward 'means simply that the parties' dispute will be litigated rather than arbitrated,' a result implicating enforcement of the arbitration agreement 'no less than would an interpretation...that erroneously denied the existence of an agreement to arbitrate.'[78] Application of South Carolina class action procedures had no comparable effect.

It appears that the immediate questions in *Bazzle* should be easily resolved, based on prior decisions that limit the FAA's preemptive effect to state laws in actual conflict with the federal law and that make plain that the FAA federalizes neither the procedural rules governing arbitration nor the principles of contract interpretation applicable to arbitration agreements.

16.5.1 Does the FAA Preempt Disapproval of Express Class-Action Bans Based on State Unconscionability Law?

Some of Green Tree's amici urge the Supreme Court to resolve through *Bazzle* the (unposed) question of the permissibility of express bans on class arbitration. For example, the Chamber of Commerce urges that *Bazzle* provides an opportunity for the Court to 'dispatch [the] shibboleth' that contract bans on class actions are unconscionable.[79] The American Bankers Association argues that cases disapproving bans on class actions as unconscionable fail to recognize that the

---

[78] Volt Info. Sciences, *supra*, 489 U.S. 479, 487 (Brennan, J., dissenting).
[79] Br. at 5, n. 2.

CHAPTER 16. GREEN TREE V. BAZZLE IN THE SUPREME COURT

FAA requires enforcement of all arbitration clauses 'in accordance with their terms.'[80] The New England Legal Foundation argues that any state law disapproving a class action ban would violate the FAA for failure to recognize the 'sanctity of contract.'[81]

As a preview of contentions that may be raised in a future case where the issue is properly posed, the arguments advanced by Green Tree's amici appear to call for an even more extreme expansion of FAA preemption law than those made by Green Tree in *Bazzle*. The arguments to foreclose state unconscionability law collide with FAA §2's savings clause that upholds the enforceability of arbitration agreements 'save upon such grounds as exist at law or in equity for the revocation of any contract.' The Supreme Court has previously recognized that unconscionability is such a ground.[82]

16.5.2 Class Action Procedures Are Not Incompatible with Arbitration

Professors Estreicher and Harper are correct in observing that '*only* class actions enable large numbers of victims of discrimination to obtain relief from the outcome of a single disparate impact or systemic disparate treatment suit.'[83] According to the most expansive treatise on employment discrimination, class actions 'have...been implicitly ratified by Congress as an appropriate method of enforcing the requirements of Title VII.'[84]

---

[80] Br. at 6.

[81] Br. at 15, n. 18.

[82] *Casarotto, supra*, 517 U.S. at 687. As noted above, California courts have disapproved class-action bans under California unconscionablity law in arbitration and non-arbitration settings alike.

[83] Emphasis added. See n. 1, *supra*. See *East Texas Motor Freight System, Inc. v. Rodriguez*, 43 1 U.S. 395, 405–406 (1977)('suits alleging racial or ethnic discrimination are often by their very nature class suits, involving classwide wrongs'); *General Telephone Co. v. Falcon*, 457 U.S. 147, 158 (1982)('[w]e cannot disagree with the proposition...that racial discrimination is by definition class discrimination'); *Arnchem, supra*, 52 1 U.S. at 6 14: ('Civil rights cases against parties charged with unlawful, class-based discrimination are prime examples [of class actions allowed by Rule 23(b)(2)1.')

[84] 4 L. Larson, Employment Discrimination, § 81.01 (2002).

703

Professors Wright and Miller have similarly emphasized the essential role of class actions in employment and other cases:

> It now is apparent that the increasing complexity and urbanization of modem American society has tremendously magnified the importance of the class action as a procedural device for resolving disputes affecting numerous people. Nowhere is this more evident than in the context of the increased number of actions involving the federal government, labor unions, business and nonprofit associations, civil rights and consumer groups.[85]

The leading treatise on class actions, *Newberg on Class Actions*, weighs the advantages and disadvantages of class actions respectively for plaintiffs, defendants and the justice system.[86] Professor Newberg observes that class actions offer major advantages for plaintiffs, inter alia, in terms of strengthened litigation posture and that, for the small claimant, 'a class suit represents the only economically available means for judicial relief.'[87] While also recognizing disadvantages, Professor Newberg concludes:

> Class actions are generally more advantageous to plaintiffs because they gain a more powerful adversarial posture than they would have through individual litigation. This stronger litigation posture, when viewed in proper perspective, serves to balance a currently imbalanced adversarial structure, in which large defendants with sufficient economic means are able to enjoy an overwhelming advantage against parties with small individual claims.[88]

Why should large defendants be allowed at will to strip plaintiffs of the advantages of class treatment and to foreclose class actions even for discrimination claims involving a 'single disparate impact' or 'systemic disparate treatment'? The self-serving effort of potential defendants to employ mandatory arbitration systems as a firewall against class actions is surely understandable but it cannot be justified.

An agreement to arbitrate merely substitutes one forum for another.[89] The same considerations that make the availability of class

---

[85] 7A C. Wright & A. Miller, Federal Practice and Procedure § 1751 at 14 (1986).
[86] H. Newberg & A. Conte, Newberg on Class Actions § 5.01 et seq. (1992).
[87] *Id.* §§ 5.02, 5.07, 5.48.
[88] *Id.* § 5.57.
[89] *Gilmer, supra,* 500 U.S. at 26, quoting *Mitsubishi Motors Corn. V. Soler Chrysler-Plymouth. hc.,* 473 U.S. 614, 628 (1985).

CHAPTER 16. GREEN TREE V. BAZZLE IN THE SUPREME COURT

treatment important in court make its availability equally vital in arbitration. Whether in arbitration or in court, there are cases – including employment cases – in which monetary claims are so small that individuals would be unlikely to proceed absent the availability of a class or other collective action.[90] The Lawyers Committee for Civil Rights Under Law ('Lawyers Committee') cites the example of *Bailey v. Ameriquest Mortg. Co.*,[91] an FLSA suit for unpaid overtime.[92] The court found, inter alia that the small size of the individual claims rendered their pursuit impracticable absent the availability of a collective action as afforded by the FLSA.[93]

Where a small number of persons proceed individually and prevail, the combined effect of their efforts may have little influence on the defendants' future behavior.[94] Where more claimants proceed individually, the result may be that the same issues are posed for determination repetitively in successive proceedings.[95]

The observation of Professors Estreicher and Harper regarding the essential role of the class action in cases of 'a single disparate impact or systemic disparate treatment' is true in arbitration just as in court. Class actions particularly offer counsel the incentive to bring essential resources to bear in order to discover and correct across-the-board practices of discrimination. They have been essential to changing the American workplace and to the ongoing process of ridding it of discrimination.

---

[90] The Supreme Court recognizes that this is so. *Deposit Guaranty Nat'l Bank v. Roper*, 445 U.S. 326, 339 (1980) ('Where it is not economically feasible to obtain relief within the traditional framework of a multiplicity of small individual suits for damages, aggrieved persons may be without any effective redress unless they may employ the class-action device.'); *Amchem Products, Inc. v. Windsor*, 521 U.S. 591, 617 (1997) (the policy at the very core of the class action mechanism is to overcome the problem that small recoveries do not provide the incentive for any individual to bring a solo action....)

[91] 2002 WL 100391 at *6 (2002).

[92] Br. 14.

[93] 29 U.S.C. § 216(b).

[94] See *Szetela, supra*, 97 Cal. App. 4th at 1101 (ban on classwide arbitration acts as 'disincentive for [company] to avoid the type of conduct that might lead to class action litigation in the first place.')

[95] *Id.* ('any remedies obtained will only pertain to that single customer without collateral estoppel effect.'); *Conn. General Life Ins., supra*, 210 F.3d at 776.

As explained by the Lawyers Committee, the possibility of a just outcome in cases involving a pattern and practice of discrimination often depends upon the availability of class treatment.[96] A class action affords the discovery needed to prove a pattern and practice of discrimination whereas individual actions typically do not.[97] Based on *Int'l Bhd of Teamsters v. United States*[98] and its progeny, a class action affords unique methods of proof affecting all persons subject to the challenged practice under which each class member enjoys a presumption, once a pattern and practice of discrimination is established, that he was affected by the unlawful practice.[99] A class action permits vindication of the rights of persons who may be unaware that they have been affected by discrimination.[100] Class actions afford opportunities for the broad injunctive relief necessary to end pervasive discrimination; in nonclass actions, courts commonly limit injunctions to granting individual relief to the named plaintiffs.[101]

If class treatment is foreclosed in arbitration and if such treatment is important to prosecution of a claim, claimants must be allowed to litigate their claims in court.[102] *Bazzle* itself reflects the compatibility of class treatment with arbitration in appropriate cases. First, Green Tree and its amici have not disputed – apart from whether Green Tree's agreement allowed class arbitration – that the claims in *Lackey* and *Bazzle* were appropriate for class treatment under South Carolina's established criteria. There was no question that the numerosity requirement was satisfied in that each of the cases comprised a class of close to 2,000 persons. Nor was there serious question as to commonality and

---

[96] Br. 17 et seq.
[97] *Id.*
[98] 431 U.S. 324, 361–362 (1977).
[99] *Id.* at 17 & n. 10.
[100] *Id.*
[101] *Id.* at 18 & n. 13. See *Lowery v. Circuit City Stores. Inc.*, 158 F.3d 742, 766–767 (4th Cir. 1998); vacated and remanded, on other grounds, 527 U.S. 103 1 (1 999), reaff'd, 206 F.3d 43 1, 437 (4th Cir.), cert. denied, 531 U.S. 822 (2000)(disapproving grant of class-wide remedies after class decertified).
[102] See ex., *Bailey v. Ameriquest, supra*, 2002 WL 100391 at *8 (allowing plaintiffs to proceed with collective action in court); *Szetela v. Discover Bank, supra*, 97 Cal. App. 4th at 1101 (allowing class action to proceed in judicial forum); *Leonard v. Terminix Int'l Co.*, 2002 WL 3 123 1048 (Ala. 2002)(same). Cf. *Mandel v. Household Bank (Nevada), supra* (severing unconscionable ban on class treatment and allowing class-wide arbitration to proceed).

typicality. The cases arose under Green Tree's standard-form agreement and stemmed from its standard operating procedure of not providing the notice required by the Attorney Preference statute. Nor was there serious question of the adequacy of representation afforded by the named plaintiffs and their counsel. The fact that some arbitration claims – like some claims not subject to arbitration – will surely be inappropriate for class treatment is not a persuasive reason for foreclosing class treatment of all claims.

Second, the argument advanced by Green Tree and its amici – that individual awards in the magnitude of USD 5,000 and USD 7,500 should have been sufficient to support individual actions – actually demonstrates the need for class treatment even in a case where potential recoveries are comparatively substantial. As pointed out by the arbitrator in *Bazzle*, there had been just five claims against Green Tree in the years since enactment of the Attorney Preference Statute in 1982. Moreover, Green Tree continued its standard unlawful operating practice notwithstanding prior adverse adjudications in non-class actions. The failure of relatively substantial awards to elicit substantial numbers of individual claims or to curb an incorrigible defendant supports the need for class treatment to remain available.

The proceedings in *Lackey* and *Bazzle* likewise dispel the parade of horribles depicted by Green Tree and various of its amici. The record of these cases dispels the notion that class arbitration purports to bind individuals who have not agreed to resolution of their disputes other than through individual arbitration. Individual class members were afforded the opportunity to opt out, which some exercised. Such individuals were free to pursue their claims through individual arbitration as they wished.

The record of these cases equally dispels the notion that a defendant would be exposed to successive claims by individuals who were dissatisfied by the result of the class arbitration. Having been furnished with notice of the class arbitration proceedings, those class members who did not elect to opt out would be no less bound by a class determination in arbitration than by a class determination in a court of law. Notwithstanding the track record of class arbitration in some States – particularly California – Green Tree and its amici cite no case where individuals were held *not* to be bound by a class-wide arbitration determination after being provided with notice and declining an opportunity to opt out.

The record of these cases dispels the supposed conundrum posed by some of Green Tree's amici, particularly the American Bankers Association, to the effect that absent class members cannot be bound by class arbitration consistent with their due process rights unless courts undertake such close supervision of the arbitration process that the arbitrator's role is virtually supplanted and the agreement to resolve disputes by arbitration is rendered a dead letter in violation of FAA §2. Here the state courts compelled arbitration as Green Tree requested. The arbitrator exercised the broad power vested in him by the arbitration agreement to determine that class treatment was legally appropriate and directed that class members be provided with notice and an opportunity to opt out. The arbitrator proceeded, independent of any court, to resolve the claims on their merits. The notion that a court must somehow supplant or subordinate the role of the arbitrator in order to assure due process is illusory.[103]

Involvement of the judiciary in supervising class-wide arbitration as needed to protect the due process rights of absent class members need not supplant nor subordinate the arbitrator's role. Courts routinely become involved with arbitration in enforcing agreements to arbitrate and in deciding whether to enforce or vacate awards once entered. Courts may review the adequacy of class notice and the adequacy of proposed settlements of class claims without infringing upon the role of the arbitrator in determining the merits of the dispute.

Arguments based on expense and expedition are equally dispelled by the record of the *Bazzle* litigation. Green Tree and its amici argue strenuously that allowing class arbitration would undermine arbitration's advantages of quick and expeditious resolution of claims. They fail even to assert that some 3,700 individual claims – had they been initiated – could have been arbitrated on a non-class basis more rapidly

---

[103] The question whether a particular arbitration agreement prohibits or is silent regarding class-wide arbitration and the further question whether particular claims are appropriate for classwide arbitration appear to be procedural questions growing out of the dispute rather than 'gateway' question[s] of arbitrability. *Howsam v. Dean Witter Reynolds. Inc.*, 537 U.S. 79, 84 (2002)('procedural questions, which grow out of the dispute and bear on its final disposition are presumptively not for the judge, but for an arbitrator, to decide'); *Pacificare Health Systems v. Book*, No. 02-215 (April 7, 2003)(Slip Op. at 6, n. 2). Both questions appear to be properly resolved by the arbitrator as occurred in the *Bazzle* case.

CHAPTER 16. *GREEN TREE V. BAZZLE* IN THE SUPREME COURT

and economically than the class disposition in *Lackey* and *Bazzle*. Respondents argue persuasively:

> [Green Tree] does not oppose class arbitration because it believes that there should have been 3,700 individual proceedings instead of one class arbitration. Green Tree and its amici, like other parties with potential exposure to large groups of people, oppose class arbitration in the knowledge that, 'because many claims are not viable if brought individually, plaintiffs will often drop or fail to initiate claims once it is clear that class relief is unavailable.'[104]

Among Green Tree's amici, the National Council of Chain Restaurants and the Equal Employment Advisory Council advance employment-law perspectives. The National Council of Chain Restaurants argues that 'individual resolution of employment disputes fully achieves the goals behind employment-related statutes.'[105] The argument turns a blind eye to the Supreme Court's oft-repeated recognition that employment discrimination is by its nature class discrimination and neither admits nor denies the essential role of class actions in cases involving systemic violations. In such cases, the rights of victims cannot be vindicated and pervasive discrimination curbed without class treatment. The National Council of Chain Restaurants argues that complainants fare better in arbitration then in court.[106] Assuming this to be true, class arbitration should offer parallel advantages over class litigation in a court of law.

The Equal Employment Advisory Council likewise argues that individual arbitration is preferable to litigation from the standpoint of employees; whereas the vast majority of discrimination suits are resolved by summary judgment in court proceedings, individual claimants almost always get a hearing on the merits in arbitration.[107] Again, if this is true, class-wide arbitration should offer parallel advantages for plaintiffs over presentation of disputes to a judicial forum.

Ultimately it is the proponents of mandatory arbitration themselves who show distrust and hostility for arbitration. These proponents of mandatory arbitration know – as reflected by the South Carolina Supreme Court's decision in *Bazzle* – that arbitration decisions

---

[104] Resp. Br. at 50, quoting *Sternlight, supra,* 42 Wm. & Mary L. Rev. at 8.
[105] Br. at 9 et seq.
[106] Br. 7.
[107] Br. 15.

command extraordinary judicial deference and that the grounds for challenging arbitration decisions are extremely narrow.[108]

Prospects are accordingly bleak for securing the vacation of large adverse class awards such as the ones at issue in *Bazzle*.

Concern that the defendant bank could face an unreviewable, multi-million liability in class-wide arbitration is reflected in the recent holding in *Discover Bank v. Superior Court*,[109] that the FAA 'preempts a state court's ability to invalidate on state substantive law grounds the express terms of a validly formed arbitration agreement.' The Court stated:

> *As judicial review of the merits of an arbitrator's decision may not be had under California law*, a multi-million dollar class arbitration award entered on nothing more than mere whim cannot be corrected under California law....
>
> As classwide arbitration in California vastly increases the scope of potential liability and damages that a defendant will face without the ability to seek judicial review of the merits of the arbitrator's decision, *we conclude the decision to strike a classwide arbitration ban from a valid agreement alters substantive, and not just procedural, rights of both parties.*[110]

The attempts by proponents of mandatory arbitration to foreclose disapproval of express class-action bans and the argument in *Bazzle* that FAA §2 forecloses application of state class action procedures – silent agreements both – derive ultimately from the same concern: large class awards entered against the mandatory arbitration proponents will be substantially unreviewable in court.

16.6 CONCLUSION

The immediate question posed in *Bazzle* may yet go undecided. The South Carolina court's professed reliance on an independent state-law ground may cast doubt on the existence of federal jurisdiction, suggesting the possibility that the Supreme Court may yet dismiss the writ of certiorari in *Bazzle* as improvidently granted.

---

[108] See *Major League Baseball Players' Assoc. v. Garvey*, 532 U.S. 504, 509 (2001).
[109] *Supra*, at n. 21.
[110] 105 Cal. App. 4th at 348. (Emphasis added).

CHAPTER 16. *GREEN TREE V. BAZZLE* IN THE SUPREME COURT

Assuming the Supreme Court reaches the question posed, it is likely that the Court's decision will be narrow. To affirm, the Court need only hold that the FAA does not preempt state class action procedures where the agreement is silent. Such a decision could leave decisions such as *Champ*, which rest on FAA §4, standing in federal court.

Alternatively, the Supreme Court could issue a broader decision, holding that applying class procedures where the agreement is silent does not alter the parties' agreement. Such a holding could disapprove Champ's rationale that applying class procedures would violate a federal court's obligation under FAA §4 to enforce the agreement 'in accordance with its terms.'

Either way, a victory for the respondents could be pyrrhic, leading quickly to insertion of 'magic wand' clauses prohibiting arbitration in newly revised arbitration agreements. The question will be whether such clauses are impermissible based on state-law grounds of unconscionability or as incompatible with statutes such as Title VII that depend upon availability of class treatment for claims involving systemic violations. *Ting v. AT&T* may well be the next Supreme Court case involving questions of class-wide arbitration.

Congress recently enacted legislation exempting automobile dealers from enforcement of pre-dispute arbitration agreements in disputes with dealership franchisors.[111] Ultimately legislation may be needed to restore an appropriate balance of the interests in arbitration and proper application of the FAA with interests in proper enforcement of statutory rights and the availability of class treatment in appropriate cases.

---

[111] See § 1028(a)(2), P.L. 107–273, 1 16 Stat. 1836 (November 2, 2002).

CHAPTER 17

Arbitration Agreements, Unconscionability, and Bans on Class Actions: Dueling Magic Wands? The California Experience

Henry D. Lederman*

17.1 INTRODUCTION

Increasingly, employers faced with class action litigation are looking for ways out. The mere filing of a class action complaint in the employment context creates an exposure to the company often well into the seven figures or beyond. Class action cases brought against large employers involve issues ranging from misclassification of employees as exempt, failure to promote due to glass ceilings, sexual and racial harassment, and other forms of employment discrimination.

Discovery in these cases alone on the class issues can run up tens or hundreds of thousands of dollars in legal fees and costs, not to mention opportunity cost caused by redirection of corporate resources to the litigation and away from income producing activity. Speaking as a defense lawyer, without telling too many tales out of school, the reaction to a class action complaint in the executive suites and in-house counsel ranks includes usually shock, some fear, and then resignation to a long drawn out process in which at best the company is spending a small or large fortune vindicating itself, with the risk that an adverse award

---

*Henry D. Lederman acts as counsel to Littler Mendelson. He holds a J.D. from New York University School of Law.

David Sherwyn and Samuel Estreicher (eds), *Employment Class and Collective Actions*, pp. 713–730.
© 2009, Kluwer Law International BV, Printed in Great Britain.

EMPLOYMENT CLASS AND COLLECTIVE ACTIONS

many times that amount awaits if it and its attorneys guessed wrong on their approach. Often, not surprisingly, the word 'blackmail' is heard – along with other less kind descriptions of the new type of case.

17.2 GREEN TREE FINANCIAL CORP. v. BAZZLE

Companies want a way out, and many are turning to arbitration agreements, asking their attorneys to draft 'magic wand' language that will make class actions go 'poof.' Employers do not want to have class actions heard by arbitrators. The danger of that is all too well illustrated in *Green Tree Financial Corp. v. Bazzle*.[1] While not an employment case, the question presented is whether the Federal Arbitration Act (FAA)[2] prohibits class-action procedures from being superimposed onto an arbitration agreement that does not provide for (but also does not forbid) class-action arbitration.

Bazzle involved a retail installment contract containing an arbitration clause that did not refer one way or the other to class-action arbitration. The plaintiff filed an action in a South Carolina state court claiming violation of a South Carolina law requiring notice of right to select counsel or an insurance agent in connection with the type of contract at issue in the case. Green Tree moved to compel arbitration of the plaintiff's individual claims only and to stay court action. The court denied the motion and ordered a class-action arbitration.

At the arbitration, two groups of plaintiffs and classes numbering some 3,799 individuals won an award based on 'penalties,' apparently imposed without any statutory authority, in the amount of USD 20,135,000 and attorneys' fees of USD 6,711,666 (according to defense lawyers, representing a rate of more than USD 900 per hour), with any unclaimed funds going to various charities and schools selected by the arbitrator or the plaintiffs' counsel.

The South Carolina Supreme Court rejected Green Tree's arguments that under the FAA the arbitration agreement, not providing for class actions, could not be held to permit them. Instead, the South Carolina high court adopted an approach long recognized in California that would allow class-wide arbitration even if an arbitration

---

[1] U.S. Sup. Ct. No. 02–634.
[2] 9 U.S.C. §§ 1 et seq.

agreement is silent on the issue. The court also reasoned that class arbitration should be permissible because it would not serve interests of judicial economy to hear the multiple claims individually.[3] Because the South Carolina Supreme Court chose to follow California's approach, it might be useful to survey not only the development of the rules it followed, but also where the California state and federal courts have gone in this evolving area of the law.

17.3 THE CALIFORNIA APPROACH: WHERE THE AGREEMENT IS SILENT

The leading case is *Keating v. Superior Court*,[4] in which the California Supreme Court held that class-wide arbitrations may be ordered even if the arbitration agreement governing the dispute does not provide for – or forbid – such actions. The court's rationale was based broadly on policy grounds, as follows:

- Class actions are an important device for vindicating the rights of large groups of people with small claims;
- Denial of class-action litigation may allow an unscrupulous wrongdoer to retain benefits of its wrongful conduct;
- Controversies involving widely used contracts of adhesion are ideal for class adjudication; and
- Adhesion arbitration contracts should not be used to chill protection of common interests.

The court went on to reason that it was unfair to force hundreds or thousands of litigants to engage in separate proceedings against a party with superior resources. If an arbitration agreement foreclosed class litigation, the court observed, it might be oppressive, defeating the non-drafting parties' expectations. Thus, relying on a mixture of and state federal authority permitting consolidation of arbitration proceedings, the court held that members of the class, even if they are all parties to the same arbitration agreement, can choose either to participate in arbitral class litigation or opt out if they preferred not to do so.[5]

---

[3] The opinion of the South Carolina Supreme Court is published at 569 S.E.2d 349.
[4] 31 Cal. 3d 584 (1982), rev'd on other grounds sub nom., *Southland Corp. v. Keating*, 465 U.S. 1 (1984).
[5] 31 Cal. 3d at 610–612.

The court also pointed out that federal courts in ordering consolidation of arbitration proceedings have relied upon Rule 81(a)(3) of the Federal Rules of Civil Procedure, applying the Federal Rules to certain statutes including the FAA 'only to the extent that matters of procedure are not provided for in those statutes.'[6] The court then analogized consolidation of related proceedings under Fed. R. Civ. P. 42(a) to 'reliance on rule 23, the class-action rule, as a basis for ordering class-wide arbitrations when the interests of justice so require.'[7] Though referring to the FAA, the California Supreme Court did not address the issue of whether the federal law preempted its new judicially made rule.

The United States Supreme Court reversed *Keating* on other grounds.[8] However, the court did not address the question of whether claims brought as a class action could be ordered to arbitration on a class basis because there did not appear to be a federal question it could resolve.[9] The court noted that the appellant had not argued that the FAA preempted state class action procedures, and the California Supreme Court's decision was based on state law.[10]

---

[6] *Id.* at 61.

[7] *Id.* The California Supreme Court devised a hybrid proceeding: 'The court would have to make initial determinations regarding certifications and notice to the class, and if class wide arbitration proceeds it may be called upon to exercise a measure of external supervision in order to safeguard the rights of absent class members to adequate representation and in the event of dismissal or settlement. A good deal of care, and ingenuity, would be required to avoid judicial intrusion upon the merits of the dispute, or upon the conduct of the proceedings themselves and to minimize complexity, costs, or delay.' 31 Cal. 3d at 613.

In dissent, Justice Richardson was pointed in his criticism of the majority's decision: 'In summary, the majority, in the absence of any contractual, statutory, or judicial authority or any demonstrated need, has seen fit to invent a procedure which is hndamentally contrary to the purpose of arbitration and to the public policy encouraging arbitration.' *Id.* at 626.

[8] *Southland Corp. v. Keating, supra,* 465 U.S. 1.

[9] *Id.* at 8–9.

[10] *Id.* 'The California Supreme Court thus ruled that imposing a class-action structure on the arbitration process was permissible. The California Supreme Court devised a hybrid proceeding:

'The court would have to make initial determinations regarding certifications and notice to the class, and if class wide arbitration proceeds it may be called upon to exercise a measure of external supervision in order to safeguard the rights of absent class members to adequate representation and in the event of dismissal or

CHAPTER 17. THE CALIFORNIA EXPERIENCE

The issue of whether the FAA precludes class arbitrations when the arbitration agreement fails to provide for (but does not forbid) the procedure was presented in *Blue Cross of California v. Superior Court*.[11] The Blue Cross court held that class wide arbitration is available under California law (per *Keating*) and is not precluded by the FAA. Accordingly, a class-action arbitration proceeding is not inconsistent with the terms of an arbitration agreement and does not run afoul of the FAA. The court opined:

> [S]tate law authorizes class wide arbitration. In the absence of an express agreement not to proceed to arbitration on a class wide basis, ordering the parties to arbitrate class claims as authorized by state law does not conflict with their contractual agreement.[12]

In *Sanders et al. v. Kinko's, Inc.*,[13] the court of appeal followed *Keating* and *Blue Cross*. Unlike those cases, however, *Sanders* involved an employment dispute arising out of the state wage and hours laws. The trial court dismissed the employer's petition to compel arbitration without prejudice pending resolution by the court of the class-certification issues.

The court of appeal concluded that the FAA did not preempt what it styled 'state procedural law relating to arbitration agreements.'[14] Far from defeating the FAA's objectives, the appellate panel held that the trial court had ordered the parties to present evidence on the number of putative class members who had signed arbitration agreements and whether putative class members who had not signed such agreements could be required to participate in the arbitration of the dispute.[15]

The court concluded its analysis by observing, '[N]othing in the [arbitration] agreement precludes these parties from resolving their

---

settlement. A good deal of care, and ingenuity, would be required to avoid judicial intrusion upon the merits of the dispute, or upon the conduct of the proceedings themselves and to minimize complexity, costs, or delay.' 31 Cal. 3d at 613.

In dissent, Justice Richardson was pointed in his criticism of the majority's decision: 'In summary, the majority, in the absence of any contractual, statutory, or judicial authority or any matter of state law.'

[11] 67 Cal. App. 41h 42 (1998), cert. Denied 527 U.S. 1003 (1999).
[12] *Id.* at 63–54 (Emphasis in the original).
[13] 99 Cal. App. 4th 1 106, 121 Cal. Rptr. 2d 766 (2002).
[14] 121 Cal. Rptr. 2d at 770.
[15] *Id.* at 771.

dispute as part of a classwide arbitration.'[16] It noted: '[C]lasswide arbitration would enhance the benefits of the alternative dispute resolution process by eliminating the need for numerous arbitrations to decide the same issue in individual cases.'[17]

Because of the earlier precedents in *Keating* and *Blue Cross*, the court did not even address the issue now before the United States Supreme Court in *Bazzle,* namely whether under the FAA class action procedures may be superimposed on arbitration agreements not providing for them.

But what of arbitration agreements that expressly ban class actions? In the past year, Discover Bank has been involved in two major cases involving the arbitration agreement applicable to its Discover Card holders. The cases involved the same issue and went in opposite directions.

17.4 WHERE CLASS ACTION ARBITRATIONS ARE EXPRESSLY FORBIDDEN – THE TWO *DISCOVER BANK* CASES

In *Szetela v. Discover Bank*,[18] the Fourth Appellate District of the California Court of Appeal held that a clause in a credit card company's arbitration agreement with its customers that prohibited claims to be brought as representative or class actions was unconscionable and unenforceable.

At first blush, this case would appear to put into question the enforceability of similar arbitration provisions which employers have adopted in an effort to preclude class and representative actions. However, the facts of *Discover Bank* are distinguishable from the usual employment action. Moreover, the *Discover Bank* court did not address the FAA, and the FAA may preempt the result the court reached.

In *Szetela*, the plaintiff brought a class action based on Discover Bank's alleged fraudulent practices that resulted in cardholders being unfairly charged USD 29 over limit fees. Discover Bank moved to

---

[16] *Id.* at 772.
[17] *Id.*
[18] 97 Cal. App. 41h 1094 (2002), rev. denied, cert. Denied _____ U.S. _____ 123 S. Ct. 1258 (2003).

compel arbitration under its arbitration agreement. The trial court granted the motion, but the court of the appeal reversed the trial court.[19]

Discover Bank had promulgated its arbitration policy by including it with customers' bills (a bill stuffer). The agreement provided that if a cardholder did not accept, he or she could notify Discover Bank and his or her account would be closed.

The agreement provided in relevant part:

> Neither you nor we shall be entitled to join or consolidate claims in arbitration by or against other card members with respect to other accounts, or arbitrate any claims as a representative or a member of a class in a private attorney general capacity.[20]

On the writ, the plaintiff argued that the 'no class action' provision was unconscionable. After concluding the agreement was procedurally unconscionable (because it was offered to the weaker party on a 'take it or leave' basis without opportunity for negotiation),[21] the court addressed substantive unconscionability:

> Substantive unconscionability traditionally involves contract terms that are so one-sided as to 'shock the conscience,' or that impose harsh or oppressive terms. The manifest one-sidedness of the no class action provision here is blindingly obvious. [22]

Even though the provision was mutual on its face, the court observed that in practice the no-class-action provision would have no impact on Discover Bank because only consumers bring class actions.[23] The court criticized Discover Bank's apparent motive:

> This provision is clearly meant to prevent customers, such as Szetela and those he seeks to represent, from seeking redress for relatively small amounts of money, such as the USD 29 sought by Szetela. Fully aware

---

[19] The procedural posture of the case was unusual. After the trial court ordered arbitration, the parties arbitrated, the plaintiff prevailed, and then he filed an appeal. Although there is no appealable order, the court of appeal exercised its discretion to treat the appeal as a petition for writ of mandate. The court concluded that without a writ, the issue presented would effectively evade appellate review.
[20] *Id.* at 1096–1097.
[21] *Id.* at 1100.
[22] *Id.*
[23] *Id.* at 1101.

that few customers will go to the time and trouble of suing in small claims court, Discover has instead sought to create for itself virtual immunity from class or representative actions despite their potential merit, while suffering no similar detrrment to its own rights.[24]

The court cited *Strotz v. Dean Witter Reynolds, Inc.*,[25] for the proposition that where an arbitration provision gives an advantage to one party, 'it is not the requirement of arbitration alone which makes the provision unfair but rather the ... manner in which the arbitration is to occur.'[26] However, *Strotz* was referring to cases where, for example, an agreement required disputes in Georgia to be arbitrated in New York or where the arbitrator is presumptively biased. In the *Szetela* case, in contrast, there was nothing inherently biased about the forum; the court just did not think Discover Bank should be able to avoid the procedure of class actions.

The court also considered that the claims of individual cardholders were so small (USD 29) that they were well suited to the class-action procedure. If Discover Bank could avoid class actions, the court reasoned, there would be a 'potential for millions of customers to be overcharged small amounts without an effective method of redress.'[27]

The court relied on the state's legislative policy behind class actions and representative actions:

> While the advantages to Discover are obvious, such a practice contradicts the California Legislature's stated policy of discouraging unfair and unlawful business practices, and of creating a mechanism for a representative to seek relief on behalf of the general public as a privat attorney general.[28] It provides the customer with no benefit whatsoever; to the contrary, it seriously jeopardizes customers' consumer rights by prohibiting any effective means of litigating Discover's business practices. This is not only substantively unconscionable, it violates public policy by granting Discover a 'get out of jail free' card while compromising important consumer rights.[29]

---

[24] *Id.*
[25] 223 Cal. App. 3d 208, 216 n. 7 (1990), rev. denied, cert. denied, 499 U.S. 948 (1991).
[26] 97 Cal. App. at 1101.
[27] *Id.*
[28] See e.g., Cal. Bus. & Prof. Code §§ 17200 et seq.
[29] *Id.*

CHAPTER 17. THE CALIFORNIA EXPERIENCE

The *Szetela* court also held:

> The [no class action] clause violates public policy in another important way. One of the policy reasons for class actions is to promote judicial economy and streamline the litigation process in appropriate cases. To allow litigants to contract away the court's ability to use a procedural mechanism that benefits the court system as a whole is no more appropriate than contracting away the right to bring motions in limine, seek directed verdicts, or use other procedural devices that allow courts to operate in an efficient manner.[30]

On one level, it can reasonably be argued that at least in this last respect that the court was wrong. In arbitration, parties can contract away procedural devices. In *Szetela*, the parties were not agreeing to litigate in state court while contracting away sections of the California Code of Civil Procedure. Instead, they were agreeing to resolve there disputes in a different forum under different rules, which they are free to do.

Indeed, in *General Telephone Co. of the Southwest v. Falcon*,[31] the Supreme Court recognized that far from being a non-waivable substantive right, a class action was 'an exception to the usual rule that litigation is conducted by and on behalf of the individual named parties only.' As stated in *Arriaga v. Cross Country Bank*:[32] 'It is not unreasonable for a party to assume that by agreeing to submit their disputes to an arbitral forum, they might be unable to bring class actions or have other procedural options available in judicial forums.'

The *Szetela* court ordered the trial court to vacate its order compelling arbitration and enter an order striking the provision prohibiting representative or class actions from the arbitration clause. The court did not invalidate the entire arbitration agreement, leaving open the question whether a class or representative action could go forward in court or in arbitration.[33]

In the employment context, a provision in an arbitration agreement prohibiting class and representative actions may still be enforceable in California even if *Szetela* were good law (more on that later). As will be seen, one California state court has so ruled, rejecting *Szetela*

---

[30] *Id.* at 1101–1102.
[31] 457 U.S. 147, 155 (1982).
[32] 163 F. Supp. 2d 1 189, 1 194 (S.D. Cal. 2001).
[33] 97 Cal. App. At 1101.

completely. Another federal court has strongly endorsed *Szetela* and has rejected the California authority finding *Szetela* wrongly decided.

However, before addressing that issue, let us look at the factors that distinguish the consumer claim in *Szetela* from the typical employment claim. These factors may tend to support, or at least do not impair, enforcement of employment arbitration agreements that bar class actions altogether. A typical employment case, in which the liability of the company to each individual may be thousands of dollars with often a prevailing employee being entitled to attorneys' fees as well, is different from a small consumer claim, and thus many of the policy concerns raised in *Szetela* are not present in employment cases.

In *Szetela*, by contrast, the court was concerned that consumers with USD 29 claims would not bother to initiate arbitration proceedings to recover the money on an individual basis. Some courts have noted that class actions are particularly suited to small but numerous consumer claims because the procedure 'both eliminates the possibility of repetition litigation and provides small claimants with a method of obtaining redress for claims which would otherwise be too small to warrant individual litigation.'[34]

Employment claims, on the other hand, are not too small to warrant individual litigation. The potential damages are extensive and attorneys' fees often are available for prevailing plaintiffs in both discrimination[35] and wage and hour claims.[36] Thus, there is obvious incentive to bring such individual claims. The policy concern that claims will go unredressed without the procedure of class actions arguably does not apply in the typical employment dispute.

Moreover, class treatment is not even appropriate in most employment cases. Typical discrimination and harassment cases involve one or a few alleged victims and specific harassers or decision makers in a specific location or departments. Such claims are not well suited to class treatment because factual determinations specific to each alleged victim will predominate. There is no efficiency in joining separate claims simply because the causes of action are similar.

Also, *Szetela* may simply be wrongly decided because the court did not analyze the enforceability of the arbitration agreement under the FAA. The FAA is 'a congressional declaration of a liberal federal policy

---

[34] *Richmond v. Dart Industries, Inc.*, 29 Cal. 3d 462, 469 (1981).
[35] See e.g., 42 U.S.C. 82000e-5(k); Cal. Gov't Code § 12965(b).
[36] 29 U.S.C. § 216(b), and Cal. Labor Code § 8218.5, 1194(a).

CHAPTER 17. THE CALIFORNIA EXPERIENCE

favoring arbitration agreements, notwithstanding any state substantive or procedural policies to the contrary' and preempts any state 'attempts to undercut the enforceability of arbitration agreements.'[37]

In *Szetela*, the court relied solely on state law policies, noting the California Legislature's express policy of discouraging unfair and unlawful business practices and of creating a mechanism for one individual to seek relief on behalf of the general public as a private attorney general. However, the FAA is a substantive federal law requiring that arbitration agreements be enforced and preempting any state laws targeting such agreements for harsher treatment than other contracts.[38] Thus, the FAA may trump state law, such as the policies relied upon by the *Szetela* court.

Contrary to the holdings in *Keating* and *Blue Cross*, where an arbitration agreement is silent as to whether claims can be arbitrated on a class basis, there is a view that under the FAA a party to such an agreement cannot bring covered claims on a class-wide basis. The leading case is *Champ v. Siegel Trading Co., Inc.*,[39] in which the court recognized that such an arbitration agreement effectively precludes the covered parties from bringing a class action, holding, 'The FAA forbids federal judges from ordering class arbitration where the parties' arbitration agreement is silent on the matter.'

The court based its decision on the FAA's requirement 'that district courts enforce arbitration agreements' in accordance with the terms of the agreement.'[40] Because the arbitration agreement in *Champ* did not

---

[37] *Perry v. Thomas*, 482 U.S. 483, 489 (1987) (finding preempted by the FAA Cal. Labor Code section 229, which allowed actions to enforce claims for 'due and unpaid wages claimed by an individual ... without regard to the existence of any private agreement to arbitrate.').

[38] *Perry*, 482 U.S. at 489. The California Supreme Court acknowledged the preemptive effect of the FAA in *Armendariz v. Foundation Health Psychcare Services, Inc.*, 24 Cal. 4th 83, 98 (2000): 'There is, of course, one major difference between the FAA and the CAA [the California Arbitration Act]. The former generally preempts state legislation that would restrict the enforcement of arbitration agreements [citation] while the CAA obviously does not prevent our legislature from selectively prohibiting arbitration in certain areas.'

[39] 55 F. 3d 269, 275 (7th Cir. 1995).

[40] 9 U.S.C. § 4; *Id.* at 274.

provide for class actions, there was no basis for ordering a class-wide arbitration.[41]

As noted earlier, the California Court of Appeal in *Blue Cross of Calfornia v. Superior Court* followed the California Supreme Court's decision in *Keating*. It also explained that the FAA does not preempt all state rules on arbitration, but only those that would frustrate the policy and purpose of the FAA 'to ensure arbitration agreements are enforced according to their terms.'[42] Applying this principle, the court reasoned that allowing class arbitrations as a matter of state procedure could 'further rather than defeat the Act's goal of enforcing agreements to arbitrate' and concluding that the FAA did not bar classwide arbitration.[43] The *Blue Cross* court distinguished *Champ*:

> [U]nder federal law, as articulated in *Champ* and the cases on which the 7th Circuit relied, there is no authority for class wide arbitration. Under those circumstances, the *Champ* court refused to reach such authority into the party's arbitration agreement.[44]

In *Szetela*, the court held that an arbitration agreement could not be enforced according to its terms because to do so it violates state policy and procedure. But even substantive state law cannot undercut the federal policy of enforcing arbitration agreements.[45]

As one federal district court in California explained:

> Determining the California State Legislature's intent as to the arbitrability... is not the end of the analysis.

---

[41] *Id.* See also e.g., *Johnson v. West Suburban Bank*, 225 F. 3d 366 (3rd Cir. 2000), cert. denied 531 U.S. 1145 (2001); *Arriaga v. Cross Country Bank*, 163 F. Supp. 2d at 1195 (neither being employment cases).

[42] 67 Cal. App. 4th at 61.

[43] *Id.* at 62–63. At least one other state court, aside from South Carolina's supreme court, is in accord. In *Dickler v. Shearson Lehman Hutton, Inc.*, 596 A. 2d 860 (Pa. Super. 1991), appeal denied, 532 Pa. 663, 616 A. 2d 984 (1992), a Pennsylvania State Court also recognized that class action procedures could be imposed on an arbitration agreement otherwise silent on the issue.

[44] *Id.* at 63–64.

[45] *Perry v. Thomas*, 482 U.S. at 489 ('a congressional declaration of a liberal federal policy favoring arbitration agreements, notwithstanding any state substantive or procedural policies to the contrary').

CHAPTER 17. THE CALIFORNIA EXPERIENCE

> [S]tatutory claims are not subject to arbitration when Congress itself indicates an intention to the contrary. Because the federal government is supreme in its proper sphere of action, only it may decide when to exempt statutory claims from the FAA. Thus the court still needs to contend with the Supremacy clause of the United States Constitution, which mandates that the FAA trumps state statutory schemes that are contrary to its purposes.[46]

In *Arriaga*, the district court rejected the plaintiffs' contention that the arbitration agreement was unconscionable because it 'denies plaintiffs... the ability to pursue class actions and vindicate small claims.'[47] In doing so, the court recognized 'specific advantages that the arbitration forum affords plaintiff' and noted that such agreements are not always to the defendant's advantage.[48]

Thus, state policy regarding a procedural device should not be the basis for invalidating an arbitration agreement subject to the FAA. As the *Arriaga* court explained:

> State legislatures should not be allowed to do implicitly what the Supreme Court and the FAA do not allow them to do explicitly. If it were enough for a state legislature to declare, through the nature of the remedies it offers in a statute, that it did not wish to have certain claims subjected to arbitration, states would essentially be allowed to undercut the FAA in an area in which Congress is supreme (i.e., Interstate Commerce). It is clear that states cannot insert specific text into their statutes which prohibits parties from waiving their right to vindicate statutory claims in a judicial forum.[49] Therefore, it must be equally invalid for a state to implicitly declare a prohibition on arbitration by fashioning statutory remedies which are inherently inconsistent with the arbitral forum.[50]

With this backdrop, in early 2003 another panel of the California Court of Appeal confronted head on the issue of the FAA and explicit class action bans in arbitration agreements. The company that promulgated the agreement the court reviewed did not change, but the result did. In

---

[46] *Arriaga v. Cross Country Bank*, 163 F. Supp. 2d at 1196.
[47] *Id.* at 1195.
[48] *Id.*
[49] Citing *Perry v. Thomas*, 482 U.S. at 4911.
[50] *Id.* at 1199. The *Szetela* court did not discuss *Arriaga* even though *Arriaga* was issued approximately nine months before the *Szetela* decision.

Discover Bank v. Superior Court,[51] the court scrutinized the same arbitration agreement found unconscionable in *Szetela*. Following *Szetela*, the trial court struck down the class action waiver as substantively unconscionable. After invalidating the waiver, the lower court nonetheless granted Discover Bank's motion to compel arbitration but permitted the plaintiff to attempt to certify a class for arbitration.

Discover Bank sought relief from this order through an extraordinary writ procedure on the ground that the FAA precludes states from forcing parties to arbitrate in a manner contrary to their agreement. The court held:

> that where a valid arbitration agreement governed by the FAA prohibits class wide arbitration, Section 2 of the FAA[52] preempts the state court from applying state substantive law to strike the class action waiver from the agreement.[53]

Accordingly, the Court of Appeal expressly disapproved *Szetela* in granting Discover Bank's motion to compel arbitration on the individual claim alone.

In beginning its analysis of the preemption issue, the court first observed that where an arbitration agreement is governed by the FAA, federal preemption analysis is required to determine whether state policy must bow to the federal act.[54] Only where a state limitation on the formation of a contract applies to 'any contract'[55] may a legislative or judicial rule providing for a revocation of an arbitration agreement apply.[56] Thus, 'a state-law principle that takes its meaning precisely from the fact that a contract to arbitrate is at issue does not comport with [the] requirement of 9 U.S.C. § 2.'[57] More specifically, the court concluded:

> While a state may prohibit the contractual waiver of statutory consumer remedies, including the right to seek relief in a class action, such

---

[51] 105 Cal. App. 4th 326, 129 Cal. Rptr. 2d 393 (2003), pet. for review granted. In an order dated April 9, 2003, California Supreme Court announced it will decide the appeal of this case. Accordingly, this case may no longer be cited as precedent in California State Courts. Cal. Rules of Court 976(d), 977(a).
[52] 9 U.S.C. § 2.
[53] 129 Cal. Rprt. at 396.
[54] *Id.* at 404.
[55] 9 U.S.C. § 2.
[56] *Id.* at 404–405, 408.
[57] *Id.* at 408.

CHAPTER 17. THE CALIFORNIA EXPERIENCE

protections fall by the wayside when the waiver is contained in a validly formed arbitration agreement governed by the FAA.[58]

In distinguishing the court's earlier decision in *Blue Cross* (which followed *Keating*), the *Discover Bank* court observed that 'the critical distinction between this case and *Blue Cross*, however, is that here the agreement contains a class action waiver clause.'[59]

The court further found that whatever unfairness may result to consumers who are barred from class actions by their arbitration agreements, those are balanced by:

> the prejudice to Discover Bank that would be caused by *altering* the parties' agreement.... As class wide arbitration in California vastly increases the scope of potential liability and damages that a defendant will face without the ability to seek judicial review of the merits of the arbitrator's decision, we conclude the decision to strike a class wide arbitration ban from a valid agreement alters substantive, not just procedural, rights of both parties.[60]

Before the most recent *Discover Bank* case was decided, a district court in the Northern District of California rejected an arbitration agreement's ban on class actions. In *Ting v. AT&T*,[61] a magistrate judge held that to do so "violates plaintiffs' right to bring a class action under the CLRA [California's Consumer Legal Remedies Act][62] and is 'contrary to public policy... unenforceable and void.'"[63]

The *Ting* court found many other problems with the arbitration agreement at issue and did not enforce the contract. However, the court indicated that the class action ban alone could have been severed from the agreement.[64]

The *Ting* court, like the *Szetela* court, however, did not address potential FAA preemption and treated the ability to bring a class action as if it were a substantive right under California law rather than simply a procedural mechanism.

---

[58] *Id.*
[59] *Id.* at 409.
[60] *Id.* at 410 (emphasis in original).
[61] 182 F. Supp. 2d 902, 927 (N.D. Cal. 2002).
[62] Cal. Civ. Code §§ 1750 et seq.
[63] Cal. Civ. Code § 1751.
[64] 182 F. Supp. 2d at 935 (arbitration agreement had 'many unlawful or unconscionable clauses. While some, such as the ban on class actions, are easily severable, others... can only be remedied by substantially rewriting the contract.').

That all changed on appeal, however, in *Ting v. AT&T*.[65] There, the court also approached the ban on class actions through the prism of the state law of unconscionability. The court followed the analysis in *Szetela*[66] and found that even though the AT&T agreement forbade class actions both by the customer and the company. 'It is not only difficult to imagine AT&T bringing a class action against its own customers, but AT&T fails to allege that it has ever or would ever do so.'[67]

The court, therefore, not only affirmed the district court's conclusion that the class action ban violated California's unconscionability law but specifically disagreed with the more recent *Discover Bank* case that had rejected the analysis in *Szetela*. The court reasoned: 'We recognize, as does the court in *Discover Bank*, that the FAA preempts state laws of limited applicability, ... but we follow well-settled Supreme Court precedent in rejecting the proposition that unconscionability is one of those laws.'[68]

The court also expressly disapproved the Southern District of California's decision in *Arriaga*, finding that the district court in that case 'ignores the obvious practical implications of the arbitration provision' banning class actions at issue in that case.[69] The court refocused the inquiry from enforcing the language of the agreement to whether the class action ban 'is unduly one-sided.'[70]

The *Ting* court thus expressly found that the FAA permitted it to engage in an unconscionability analysis and, one may argue, waved its own 'magic wand.' Finding that the ban on class actions rendered AT&T's agreement one-sided it found that the agreement lacked 'bilaterality ... a requirement of all California arbitration agreements.'[71]

17.5 THE FUTURE

The California Court of Appeal in the latter *Discover Bank* case may just as well have been referring to the underlying facts in *Bazzle* when it

---

[65] 319 F. 3d 1126 (9th Cir. 2003).
[66] *Id.* at 1150.
[67] *Id.*
[68] *Id.* at 1150 n. 15.
[69] *Id.* at 1150 n. 14.
[70] *Id.*
[71] *Id.* at 1150.

CHAPTER 17. THE CALIFORNIA EXPERIENCE

described the risk that a defendant took in taking a class action before an arbitrator.

If in *Bazzle* the Supreme Court adopts the approach of the same *Keating* decision it had reversed on other grounds some twenty years earlier, employers concerned about the potential for class action litigation would be wise to consider including a written 'magic wand' in an arbitration agreement designed to make class actions go away.

Would this be enforceable? By no means is the California experience predictive. In fact, the California experience, which may be described as potentially involving 'dueling magic wands' (express class action bans versus court findings of unconscionability), is not even predictive of what will occur in California from one case to another!

Ting, refusing to enforce a class action ban when expressed in an arbitration agreement, is inconsistent with the 7th Circuit's decision in *Champ*, which enforced a class action ban when permission to proceed as such was merely absent from an arbitration agreement. The lower California courts in the two *Discover Bank* cases cannot agree, either. The California Supreme Court will address the issue of express class action bans in the latter, but that case involved small individual claims aggregated into a class.

Can arbitration agreements ban employment class actions? *Bazzle* may provide all or part of the answer or none of it at all. *Bazzle* could limit itself to simply deciding whether arbitration agreements silent on the class action issues permit them or not. That issue does not address the unconscionability of an agreement that either expressly or by interpretation forbids class actions entirely.

Arguments on this point that apply to a dispute over a USD 29 over-charge fee on a credit card do not necessarily apply to an employment case. Employment cases typically involve an array of remedies for each individual claimant. If state law concepts such as unconscionability apply, it may be that such express or implied bans on employment class actions will be scrutinized by state and federal courts on a case by case basis and for years to come without there being any clear answer soon.

The FAA, however, precludes judicially created rules hostile to enforcement of arbitration agreements notwithstanding their bases in a state's public policy.[72] While using the generally applicable contract

---

[72] *Mastrobuono v. Shearson Lehman Hutton, Inc.*, 514 U.S. 52, 55, 58 (1995).

729

law principle of 'unconscionability' to strike portions of arbitration agreements or to refuse to enforce them at all, courts must be careful not to apply that principle with greater rigor to an arbitration agreement than it would have to other contracts.[73] Use of such principles to carve up agreements to arbitrate runs the risk of accomplishing 'by indirection' that which is forbidden by the FAA, namely a refusal to enforce an arbitration agreement as written.[74]

---

[73] *Doctor's Associates, Inc. v. Casarotto*, 5 17 U.S. 681, 687 (1996).
[74] *Circuit City Stores v. Adams*, 532 U.S. 105, 122 (2001).

CHAPTER 18

When Is Cost an Unlawful Barrier to Alternative Dispute Resolution? The Ever Green Tree of Mandatory Employment Arbitration*

Michael H. LeRoy** and Peter Feuille***

18.1 INTRODUCTION

> The Agreement thus placed Mr. Shankle between the proverbial rock and a hard place – prohibited use of the judicial forum, where a litigant is not required to pay for a judge's services, and the prohibitive cost substantially limited use of the arbitral forum. Essentially, B-G Maintenance required Mr. Shankle to agree to mandatory arbitration as a term of continued employment, yet failed to provide an accessible forum in which he could resolve his statutory rights. Such a result clearly undermines the remedial and deterrent functions of the federal anti-discrimination laws.
>
> –*Shankle v. B-G Maintenance Management of Colorado, Inc.*[1]

---

*Originally published in 53 UCLA L. Rev. 1353 (2006).
**Michael H. LeRoy is professor, Institute of Labor and Industrial Relations and College of Law, University of Illinois at Urbana-Champaign. He holds a J.D. from the University of North Carolina – Chapel Hill.
***Peter Feuille is director and professor, Institute of Labor and Industrial Relations, University of Illinois at Urbana-Champaign. He holds a Ph.D. from University of California, Berkeley.
[1] 163 F.3d 1230, 1235 (10th Cir. 1999) (citation omitted).

David Sherwyn and Samuel Estreicher (eds), *Employment Class and Collective Actions*, pp. 731–805.
© 2009, Kluwer Law International BV, Printed in Great Britain.

> Contrary to [Ms.] Rosenberg's arguments, arbitration is often far more affordable to plaintiffs and defendants alike than is pursuing a claim in court.
>
> –Rosenberg v. Merrill Lynch, Pierce, Fenner & Smith, Inc.[2]

18.1.1 Statement of Research Question

This chapter explores an important interface between public and private forms of workplace dispute resolution: money. Many firms now require that employees sign agreements to arbitrate, rather than litigate, a dispute arising out of employment. In some cases, these agreements also require employees to pay for part or all the costs of an arbitration. Having no recourse to sue, some employees are denied access to any dispute resolution forum because they cannot pay for arbitration. Courts have begun to scrutinize these barriers only recently.

This current development is rooted in a long history. For over a century, the doctrine of employment-at-will[3] provided workers their main response to perceived wrongs committed by their employers – quitting their jobs.[4] However, from the mid-1960s through the present, fundamental changes in government regulation of employment altered this arrangement. Congress passed sweeping employment discrimination laws.[5] State courts developed common law exceptions to employment-at-will.[6] Today, workers have unprecedented employment

---

[2] 170 F.3d 1, 16 (1st Cir. 1999).
[3] The doctrine was first recognized in Horace G. Wood, A Treatise on the Law of Master and Servant 134, at 272 (1877). Comparing American and English law, Horace Wood wrote that:

> With us the rule is inflexible, that a general or indefinite hiring is prima facie a hiring at will, and if the servant seeks to make it out a yearly hiring, the burden is upon him to establish it by proof.... It is an indefinite hiring and is determinable at the will of either party, and in this respect there is no distinction between domestic and other servants.

Id. (footnote omitted). English law presumed that master and servant were bound to each other for one year, unless varied by contract. Id. 134, at 271.
[4] See Albert O. Hirschman, Exit, Voice and Loyalty 21–29 (1970).
[5] See infra notes 56 and 59.
[6] Early cases include Pugh v. See's Candies, Inc., 171 Cal. Rptr. 917, 925 (Ct. App. 1981), which found an implied oral contract exception to employment-at-will; Petermann v.

CHAPTER 18. MANDATORY EMPLOYMENT ARBITRATION

rights. This expansion mitigated historic patterns of employment discrimination.[7] Progress came at a cost, however, to employers who were found liable for transgressing these rights,[8] and to others who successfully defended themselves in lawsuits.[9]

While the U.S. Congress expanded employment rights by creating new causes of action, it devoted much less attention to the need for courts and judges to adjudicate these claims.[10] As courts grew more

---

Teamsters Local 396, 344 P.2d 25, 27 (Cal. Dist. Ct. App. 1959), which found a public policy exception to employment-at-will; *Toussaint v. Blue Cross and Blue Shield of Michigan*, 292 N.W.2d 880 (Mich. 1980), which found a handbook exception to employment-at-will; and *Monge v. Beebe Rubber Co.*, 316 A.2d 549, 551 (N.H. 1974), which found a covenant of good faith dealing exception to employment-at-will.

[7] In 1960, non-white male wage-earners earned only 59.9% of what their white counterparts earned, while the figure for non-white females was even lower, 50.3%. Mark A. Rothstein & Lance Liebman, Employment Law: Cases and Materials 224 tbl.3 (4th edn 1998) (reporting median annual wage and salary incomes of white and nonwhite persons). By a generation later, these earnings differentials narrowed but remained evident. See U.S. Bureau of Labor Statistics, Employment and Earnings 204 tbl.37 (1997) (reporting that weekly earnings for full-time wage and salary workers in 1996 were USD 580 for white males, USD 412 for African American males, USD 356 for Hispanic males, USD 428 for white females, USD 362 for African American females, and USD 316 for Hispanic females).

[8] See *infra* n. 61.

[9] For a federal judge's analysis of the irrational cost of litigation, see Jon O. Newman, Rethinking Fairness: Perspectives on the Litigation Process, 94 Yale L.J. 1643, 1645 (1985), in which Jon Newman reports that USD 1.56 was spent on litigation expenses for every USD 1.00 awarded to victims of asbestos exposure. A more specific estimate of the cost of employment litigation appears in *Bradford v. Rockwell Semiconductor Systems, Inc.*, 238 F.3d 549, 552 (4th Cir. 2001). "The arbitration of disputes enables parties to avoid the costs associated with pursuing a judicial resolution of their grievances. By one estimate, litigating a typical employment dispute costs at least USD 50,000 and takes two and one-half years to resolve." *Id.* (quoting *Hooters of America, Inc. v. Phillips*, 173 F.3d 933, 936 (4th Cir. 1999)).

[10] See Stephen Reinhardt, Too Few Judges, Too Many Cases, A.B.A.J., January 1993, at 52 ('Simply put, our federal court system is too small for the job.'). But cf. Jon O. Newman, 1,000 Judges – The Limit for an Effective Federal Judiciary, 76 Judicature 187, 188 (1993) (arguing that adding more judges would impair the quality of decision-making by adding mediocre talent to the federal bench). In 1991, there were 828 federal judgeships. *Id.* at 187 & n. 1 This number grew to only 846 by 1998. J. Harvie Wilkinson III, We Don't Need More Federal Judges, Wall St. J., February 9, 1998, at A19. While the number of judgeships has increased marginally,

congested in the 1970s, Chief Justice Warren Burger advocated alternative dispute resolution (ADR) as a remedy.[11]

These historical trends reached a turning point on May 13, 1991, when the U.S. Supreme Court ruled in a landmark decision on employment arbitration in *Gilmer v. Interstate/Johnson Lane Corp.*[12] The Court held that an employee who had been required by his employer to sign an arbitration agreement was precluded from suing on his age discrimination claim. This encouraged privatization of workplace dispute resolution. The Court's recent ruling in *Circuit City Stores, Inc. v. Adams*[13] expanded *Gilmer*.

This is the setting for our empirical research question. As we detail below, employer substitution of arbitration for court adjudication has been controversial. We draw from a sample of 313 federal court decisions in which a party to a mandatory arbitration agreement tried to litigate a legal claim arising from the employment relationship. More specifically, we examine sixty-two cases in which an employee opposed arbitration by arguing that the agreement made this private process too costly. In over 90% of these cases, employees sued under a federal employment discrimination statute.[14] By their view, not only were they were forced to waive their right to a low-cost trial, but they were also required to agree to a private ADR process that imposed prohibitive cost barriers to vindicating their employment rights.

The research we present shows a rapid growth in federal court decisions that compare the costs of workplace dispute resolution in trials and arbitrations.[15] Some courts refuse to enforce arbitration agreements because claimants cannot afford to pay thousands of dollars to arbitrate their claims.[16] Such refusals seem inconsistent with *Gilmer*'s

---

case filings have grown more rapidly. See Administrative Office of the U.S. Courts, Federal Court Management Statistics, Statistics for Filings in Federal District Court, <www.uscourts.gov/cgi-bin/cmsd2000.pl> (showing 281, 681 filings in 1995 and 310, 346 filings in 2000) (last visited September 15, 2002).

[11] See Warren Burger, Isn't There a Better Way?, 68 A.B.A.J. 274, 276–77 (1982); see also Warren Burger, Agenda for 2000 A.D. – A Need for Systematic Anticipation, 70 F.R.D. 83, 93–96 (1976).

[12] 500 U.S. 20 (1991).

[13] 532 U.S. 105 (2001).

[14] See *infra* n. 194 and accompanying text.

[15] See *infra* Tables 1–3.

[16] See *infra* n. 313.

CHAPTER 18. MANDATORY EMPLOYMENT ARBITRATION

message to lower courts that there is a 'liberal federal policy favoring [enforcement of] arbitration agreements.'[17] But most courts reject cost-shifting challenges and enforce mandatory arbitration agreements after comparing the expense of arbitration to litigation.[18] They order arbitration even when an employee has no ability to bargain over the choice of the arbitration service, the arbitrator, or related fees and expenses.

The Supreme Court's recent decision in *Green Tree Financial Corp.-Alabama v. Randolph*[19] shows that allocation of arbitration costs is an important public policy issue. The stakes involved in employment arbitration disputes are no less important than those which arose in the debtor-creditor relationship in *Green Tree*.[20] The strong increase in cost challenges to employment arbitration arrangements suggests that this phenomenon deserves further scrutiny. To the best of our knowledge, this is the first empirical study of federal court decisions in which employees asserted cost challenges to preclude enforcement of mandatory arbitration agreements.

---

[17] Gilmer, 500 U.S. at 25 (quoting *Moses H. Cone Mem'l Hosp. v. Mercury Constr. Corp.*, 460 U.S. 1, 24 (1983)). In reaching this conclusion, the U.S. Supreme Court observed that the U.S. Congress intended the Federal Arbitration Act (FAA) 'to reverse the longstanding judicial hostility to arbitration agreements that had existed at English common law and had been adopted by American courts, and to place arbitration agreements upon the same footing as other contracts.' *Id.*

[18] See *infra* section 18-6(c).

[19] 531 U.S. 79 (2000).

[20] There are notable similarities between the borrower in Green Tree and some employees in the cost-allocation cases we discuss below, such as *Shankle v. G-G Maintenance Management of Colorado, Inc.*, 163 F.3d 1230 (10th Cir. 1999). In both contexts, a large organization with superior bargaining power presented an individual with a contract. When Larketta Randolph arranged financing through a subsidiary of Green Tree Financial Corporation, she was compelled to waive her right to litigate any claim she might have under the federal Truth in Lending Act. See *infra* notes 120–122 and accompanying text. In addition, her contract required her to share the cost of the arbitration forum. See *infra* notes 143–145 and accompanying text. Like Randolph, Matthew Shankle was compelled by a more powerful organization – his employer – to waive his right to sue and submit any dispute to arbitration. See *infra* n. 251 and accompanying text. In another similarity, this waiver involved potential adjudication of federal statutory rights. *Id.* Finally, like Randolph, the agreement over which he had no power to bargain required that he share in the obligation to pay forum fees with the larger organization. See *infra* n. 252 and accompanying text.

18.1.2 Organization of This Article

Section 18.2 provides more detail about the expansion of employment rights. Congress wanted discrimination plaintiffs to have access to federal courts, even if they could not afford a lawyer.[21] Over time, employers found that employment lawsuits were costly.[22] Numerous firms now require their employees to sign pre-dispute arbitration agreements as a condition of new or continued employment, thus substituting arbitration for litigation of employment claims.[23]

The Supreme Court has begun to regulate this aspect of workplace dispute resolution. In *Gilmer*, the Court defended its preclusion of discrimination lawsuits by stating that arbitration is simply a change in dispute resolution forum.[24] We show that some courts sidestep *Gilmer's* strong arbitration signal by interpreting this forum substitution theory to mean that mandatory arbitration cannot cost an employee more than court filing fees.[25] This development is important because some arbitration agreements impose unaffordable forum costs on lower-wage workers.

Section 18.3.1 examines cost elements in employment arbitrations.[26] These include fees for the arbitrator[27] and the arbitration service provider.[28] Attorney's fees, which are usually awarded to prevailing plaintiffs in court, are typically denied or limited in arbitration.[29] But courts are not cost-free alternatives to arbitration. While filing fees are minimal, the civil procedures that courts administer add considerable expense and delay.[30] In addition, only attorneys represent disputants before a court. Thus, representation costs may be higher than in arbitration. Pre-trial disputes over issues of jurisdiction and evidence compound the cost of litigation.[31]

---

[21] See *infra* notes 56–58 and accompanying text.
[22] See *infra* notes 61–62.
[23] See *infra* n. 63.
[24] *Gilmer v. Interstate/Johnson Lane Corp.*, 500 U.S. 20, 28 (1991).
[25] See *infra* section 18-6(b).
[26] See *infra* notes 102–114.
[27] See *infra* notes 93–95.
[28] See *infra* notes 96 and 98.
[29] See *infra* notes 100, 212–219 and accompanying text.
[30] See *infra* notes 103–104.
[31] See *infra* n. 108.

CHAPTER 18. MANDATORY EMPLOYMENT ARBITRATION

Section 18.2.2 focuses on the Supreme Court's regulation of arbitration costs. The Court has consistently viewed arbitration as a cost-saving alternative to litigation. In *Green Tree*, the Court ruled that an arbitration agreement can be enforced against a person who is compelled to sign it, even when it shifts unspecified forum costs to her.[32] We explain *Green Tree*'s facts[33] and majority[34] and dissenting[35] opinions.

Section 18.4.1 presents current research that informs our study. Many commentators criticize mandatory employment arbitration.[36] A current empirical study shows, however, that federal courts rule more often for employers in discrimination lawsuits than for other types of defendants in civil lawsuits.[37] This research implies that arbitration may be more advantageous than previously believed. Also, some studies make a good case for the use of well-designed employment arbitration systems.[38] Relying upon this background, we use section 18.4.2 to describe our criteria for sampling federal court decisions[39] and online research methods.[40]

Section 18.5 presents our empirical findings.[41] Some of these are surprising, given the usual pronouncements made by nearly all federal courts that judicial policy strongly favors enforcement of arbitration agreements. In our sample of sixty-two cost-challenge cases, 77% of trial courts ordered arbitration of an employment dispute, but this figure dropped to 50% in appellate cases. We also observed a split among the circuits. Some courts always or nearly always ordered arbitration,[42] others never or almost never ordered arbitration,[43] and some had mixed results.[44] Our research also measures the current spurt in these cases.[45]

---

[32] See *Green Tree Fin. Corp.-Ala. v. Randolph*, 531 U.S. 79, 79 (2000).
[33] See *infra* notes 120–134.
[34] See *infra* notes 135–150.
[35] See *infra* notes 151–165.
[36] See *infra* notes 166–172.
[37] See *infra* n. 175.
[38] See *infra* notes 173 and 174.
[39] See *infra* notes 181–192.
[40] See *infra* n. 193 and accompanying text.
[41] See *infra* notes 194–211 and accompanying text.
[42] See *infra* notes 201–205.
[43] See *infra* notes 206–208.
[44] See *infra* notes 209–211.
[45] See *infra* last paragraph of section 18.5.

EMPLOYMENT CLASS AND COLLECTIVE ACTIONS

Section 18.6 is a textual analysis of divergent approaches taken by appellate courts in cost-shifting cases. We define forum costs and representation costs.[46] In unusual cases in which employers pay all arbitration costs, we explain how courts view this as evidence of a contract.[47] In section 18.6.2, we examine conflicting approaches taken by appellate courts. In this part we focus on the three courts – the U.S. Courts of Appeals for the D.C.,[48] Tenth,[49] and Eleventh[50] Circuits – that have agreed with employee cost arguments and concomitantly upheld employee access to litigation. Section 18.6.2 discusses courts that reject employee cost challenges: the U.S. Courts of Appeals for the First[51] and Seventh[52] Circuits. Section 18.6.4 discusses a recent tack – a case-by-case approach to cost arguments – taken by the U.S. Courts of Appeals for the Third[53] and Fourth[54] Circuits.

We conclude with consideration of the implications of the growth in cost-shifting cases.[55] These decisions divide into two conflicting streams. First, courts order arbitration for plaintiffs who seem able to afford forum fees, even if these are expensive, but allow lower-wage workers to litigate their claims. Second, judicial decisions are motivated by conflicting cost theories, one of which narrowly compares arbitration forum fees to court filing fees, and a much more expansive conception that compares total arbitration costs to total litigation costs. These differences in analytic doctrines may prompt the Supreme Court to intercede with more clarity about the cost principles set forth in *Gilmer* and *Green Tree*.

18.2 THE GROWTH OF MANDATORY EMPLOYMENT ARBITRATION

Congress was deeply concerned about ensuring access to courts for employment discrimination plaintiffs when it enacted Title VII of the

---

[46] See *infra* notes 212–219.
[47] See *infra* notes 220–227.
[48] See *infra* notes 230–247.
[49] See *infra* notes 248–264.
[50] See *infra* notes 265–281.
[51] See *infra* notes 282–299.
[52] See *infra* notes 300–303.
[53] See *infra* notes 308–309.
[54] See *infra* notes 304–307.
[55] See *infra* notes 310–328.

CHAPTER 18. MANDATORY EMPLOYMENT ARBITRATION

Civil Rights Act of 1964 (Title VII).[56] Concerned about the connection between poverty and discrimination,[57] Congress created a monetary incentive for private attorneys to represent poor plaintiffs. Courts could order law-breaking employers to pay all plaintiff attorney's fees.[58]

---

[56] See S. Rep. No. 88-872, pt. 1, at 11, 24 (1964); H.R. Rep. No. 88-914, pt. 1, at 18 (1963); id., pt. 2, at 1–2. Title VII of the Civil Rights Act of 1964 prohibits discrimination in employment on the basis of 'race, color, religion, sex, or national origin.' 42 U.S.C. 2000e-2 (2000).

[57] See *Newman v. Piggie Park Enters.*, 390 U.S. 400, 401–402 (1968). This brief decision, involving race discrimination in serving restaurant customers under Title II of the 1964 Civil Rights Act, set forth the legal standard for awarding attorney's fees to prevailing plaintiffs under all titles of this landmark legislation:

> When the Civil Rights Act of 1964 was passed, it was evident that enforcement would prove difficult and that the Nation would have to rely in part upon private litigation as a means of securing broad compliance with the law.... If successful plaintiffs were routinely forced to bear their own attorney's fees, few aggrieved parties would be in a position to advance the public interest by invoking the injunctive powers of the federal courts. Congress therefore enacted the provision for counsel fees – not simply to penalize litigants who deliberately advance arguments they know to be untenable but, more broadly, to encourage individuals injured by racial discrimination to seek judicial relief under Title II.

Id. (footnote omitted).

[58] The Civil Rights Act of 1964 accomplished this by providing fee awards to 'prevailing parties' under 42 U.S.C. 2000e-5(k) (2000). To effectuate the purposes of Title VII, a plaintiff 'is the chosen instrument of Congress,' a role underscored by the notion that 'when a district court awards counsel fees to a prevailing plaintiff, it is awarding them against a violator of federal law.' See *Christiansburg Garment Co. v. EEOC*, 434 U.S. 412, 418 (1978). The Supreme Court has stated that Congress provided for attorney's fees to prevailing plaintiffs in order 'to facilitate the bringing of discrimination complaints.' *N.Y. Gaslight Club, Inc. v. Carey*, 447 U.S. 54, 63 (1980). The 'legislative history and purpose of 706(k)' of Title VII was to make 'clear that one of Congress' primary purposes in enacting the section was to "make it easier for a plaintiff of limited means to bring a meritorious suit."' *Id.* (quoting Christiansburg, 434 U.S. at 420) (706(k) of Title VII is codified at 42 U.S.C. 2000e-5(k)).

There are occasions, however, when an employer prevails in a Title VII lawsuit and a court orders the employee to reimburse at least some of the employer's attorney's fees. See e.g., *Spence v. Eastern Airlines, Inc.*, 547 F. Supp. 204, 206 (S.D.N.Y. 1982) (ordering flight attendant who earned USD 20,000 per year to pay USD 1,500 in fees to Eastern Airlines, the prevailing party in a Title VII lawsuit, because her claims

Since then, individual employment rights have grown rapidly on several fronts. Federal laws prohibit other forms of employment discrimination.[59] Disparate impact theory holds employers liable for employment practices that are neutral in form but discriminatory in effect when those actions have no business justification.[60] Pendent state law claims, particularly emotional distress and defamation, afford plaintiffs lucrative damages.[61] Large corporations with long records as equal opportunity employers pay hundreds of millions of dollars to settle class action discrimination lawsuits.[62]

---

were groundless and litigation was continued after it was manifest that it had no factual substance); see also *Harris v. Plastics Mfg.*, 617 F.2d 438, 440 (5th Cir. 1980) (finding no evidence to support plaintiff's claim of race discrimination); *Kaimowitz v. Howard*, 547 F. Supp. 1345, 1351 (E.D. Mich. 1982) (finding 'no basis in fact' for claim of discrimination against ten individual defendants); *Hill v. BASF Wyandotte Corp.*, 547 F. Supp. 348, 354 (E.D. Mich. 1982) (concluding that plaintiff produced no proof of race and sex discrimination claims); Spence, 547 F. Supp. at 205 (concluding that plaintiff's discrimination claim was 'devoid of any evidential support' at trial); *Hughes v. Defender Ass'n of Phila.*, 509 F. Supp. 140, 141 (E.D. Pa. 1981) (determining that there was 'virtually no evidence' to support race discrimination claim); *Dailey v. Dist. 65, UAW*, 505 F. Supp. 1109, 1110 (S.D.N.Y. 1981) (holding that there was 'not a scintilla of evidence' to support discrimination claim); *Keown v. Storti*, 456 F. Supp. 232, 242 (E.D. Pa. 1978).

[59] See e.g., 8 U.S.C. 1324b(a) (2000); 29 U.S.C. 621–634 (2000); 29 U.S.C. 1140 (2000); 42 U.S.C. 12101–12213 (2000).

[60] See *Griggs v. Duke Power Co.*, 401 U.S. 424, 431 (1971) (holding that employment practices that are not justified by business necessity and that cause a 'disparate impact' upon a protected group violates Title VII of the Civil Rights Act of 1964).

[61] See e.g., Susan Hylton, Couple Due $1.2 Million, Tulsa World, January 9, 2001, at 11 (reporting that a jury awarded an employee USD 2.7 million for wrongful discharge and intentional infliction of emotional distress arising out of pregnancy discrimination), available at 2001 WL 6915952; Jury Finds Systems Manager Was Discrimination Target, Nat'l L.J., July 2, 2001, at B7 (reporting that a jury, finding that an employer engaged in unlawful employment discrimination, awarded a manager USD 5 million in damages for emotional distress); Tom Troy, Painter Wins $4M, Nat'l L.J., March 12, 2001, at A5 (reporting that an employee was awarded USD 1 million for past and future mental anguish stemming from racial harassment by a supervisor and coworkers).

[62] See Kathy Bergen & Carol Kleiman, Mitsubishi Will Pay $34 Million, Chi. Trib., June 12, 1998, at 1 (reporting that car-maker agreed to pay USD 34 million to settle class action lawsuit claiming sexual harassment); Jim Fitzgerald, Anti-Bias Efforts, Payments to Blacks OKd, Chi. Sun-Times, November 16, 1996, at 1 (reporting that Texaco

CHAPTER 18. MANDATORY EMPLOYMENT ARBITRATION

For many employers, this regulatory regime has grown to such threatening proportions that they have turned to private forms of dispute resolution – most notably, arbitration.[63] This substitution has stirred controversy, however, because employees are required to agree to arbitrate all legal claims that arise during their employment.[64]

---

agreed to spend USD 176.1 million to settle a two-year-old race discrimination suit); Record $300M Agreement in State Farm Sex-Bias Suit, Newsday, January 20, 1988, at 45 (reporting that the insurance company agreed to pay 1,100 female employees up to USD 300 million to settle a sex discrimination lawsuit); Henry Unger, 17 Coke Class-Action Parties Planning Individual Suits, Atlanta J.-Const., July 7, 2001, at 3F (reporting that a judge approved Coca-Cola's USD 192.5 million settlement of a class action employment discrimination lawsuit), available at 2001 WL 3681156.

[63] See Ken May, Arbitration: Attorney Urges Employers to Adopt Mandatory Programs as Risk-Management, Daily Lab. Rep., May 14, 2001, at A-5, for a report of an employment lawyer's advice that mandatory arbitration helps employers limit damages and eliminate class action lawsuits. The lawyer, David Copus, also noted that the biggest financial risk for employers in termination lawsuits – tort claims in which a single plaintiff can get millions of dollars – is eliminated by arbitration programs that cap damages. Id.

[64] See e.g., *Jones v. Fujitsu Network Communications, Inc.*, 81 F. Supp. 2d 688–690 (N.D. Tex. 1999). In a memo to all employees concerning the company's arbitration policy, the president of Fujitsu explained that 'participation in this program is mandatory for all employees – continuing and new, full time and part time, regular and temporary – and is a condition of employment.' Id. at 692. The policy comprehensively covered most or all causes of action arising out of the employment relationship:

> Any dispute between an employee and [company] arising out of the employee's employment agreement with the Company or its termination, including without limitation any claim of wrongful termination, breach of implied contract, discrimination, unlawful harassment, including sexual harassment, breach of the covenant of good faith and fair dealing, violations of public policy, or any federal or state law, or as to all of the proceeding, any related claims of defamation, or intentional infliction of emotional distress, which are not resolved by the Company and employee through direct discussion or mediation, will be submitted exclusively to final arbitration in accordance with the Company's Arbitration Procedures.

Id. at 691–692; see also *Desiderio v. Nat'l Ass'n of Sec. Dealers, Inc.*, 191 F.3d 198, 200 (2nd Cir. 1999). In Desiderio, Suntrust Bank offered to hire Susan Desiderio on the condition that she sign a pre-dispute arbitration agreement. Id. at 200–201. When she stated she would work only if the mandatory arbitration clause was removed, the National Association of Securities Dealers (NASD) informed Suntrust that

741

Because signing this agreement is regarded as a condition of employment, some employees feel coerced into waiving their rights.[65] Even worse, some employers create arbitration systems that are stacked in their favor. These can be so one-sided that courts find them egregiously unfair.[66]

In the past decade, the Supreme Court has approved the privatization of dispute resolution systems for employment discrimination claims, albeit in close votes and over strident dissents.[67] In *Gilmer*, the Supreme Court ruled that a securities broker's mandatory arbitration

---

she could not work as a registered securities broker. *Id.* Suntrust then revoked its offer of employment. *Id.*

[65] See Katherine Van Wezel Stone, Mandatory Arbitration of Individual Employment Rights: The Yellow Dog Contract of the 1990s, 73 Denv. U. L. Rev. 1017 (1996), in which the author contends that 'many pre-hire arbitral agreements are blatant contracts of adhesion.' *Id.* at 1036. Katherine Van Wezel Stone notes that at 'the moment of hire, employees lack bargaining power and are needful of employment, so they frequently agree to such terms without giving them much thought.' *Id.* Van Wezel Stone concludes that pre-hire arbitration agreements 'discourage workers from asserting statutory rights' and 'operate like the early nineteenth century "yellow dog contracts" – contracts in which employees had to promise not to join a union in order to get a job. Today's "yellow dog contracts" require employees to waive their statutory rights in order to obtain employment.' *Id.* at 1037 (footnote omitted).

[66] See *Hooters of Am., Inc. v. Phillips*, 173 F.3d 933 (4th Cir. 1999). In Hooters of America, the court refused to enforce a Gilmer-type employment arbitration agreement because the dispute resolution system imposed on the complainant by Hooters was 'egregiously unfair.' *Id.* at 938. The court reasoned:

> We hold that the promulgation of so many biased rules – especially the scheme whereby one party to the proceeding so controls the arbitral panel – breaches the contract entered into by the parties. . . . By creating a sham system unworthy even of the name of arbitration, Hooters completely failed in performing its contractual duty.

Id. at 940.

[67] Consider, for example, Justice John Paul Stevens' sharply worded and disparaging criticism of Justice Anthony Kennedy's majority opinion in Circuit City:

> Playing ostrich to the substantial history behind the amendment . . . the Court reasons in a vacuum that 'if all contracts of employment are beyond the scope of the Act under the 2 coverage provision, the separate exemption' in 1 'would be pointless.' But contrary to the Court's suggestion, it is not 'pointless' to adopt a clarifying amendment in order to eliminate opposition to a bill.

CHAPTER 18. MANDATORY EMPLOYMENT ARBITRATION

agreement with his employer precluded him from suing under the Age Discrimination in Employment Act (ADEA).[68] The Supreme Court recently extended *Gilmer* to cover almost all individual employment contracts in *Circuit City*.[69]

In each case, the employer successfully avoided a discrimination lawsuit by enforcing a pre-dispute arbitration agreement. *Gilmer* and *Circuit City* also continued the Supreme Court's modern rejection of judicial hostility to arbitration.[70] Taking advantage of *Gilmer*, employers have designed, imposed, and implemented a variety of arbitration programs.[71] For instance, the American Arbitration Association (AAA)

Circuit City Stores, Inc. v. Adams, 532 U.S. 105, 128 (2001) (Stevens, J., dissenting) (citation omitted). Continuing his verbal assault against the majority opinion, Justice Stevens said, 'When its refusal to look beyond the raw statutory text enables it to disregard countervailing considerations that were expressed by Members of the enacting Congress and that remain valid today, the Court misuses its authority.' *Id.* at 132.

[68] 29 U.S.C. 621–634 (2000).

[69] *Id.* at 109.

[70] Supreme Court cases that approve the use of arbitration include *Allied-Bruce Terminix Cos. v. Dobson*, 513 U.S. 265 (1995); *Rodriguez de Quijas v. Shearson/American Express, Inc.*, 490 U.S. 477 (1989); *Mitsubishi Motors Corp. v. Soler Chrysler-Plymouth, Inc.*, 473 U.S. 614 (1985); *Southland Corp. v. Keating*, 465 U.S. 1 (1984); *Moses H. Cone Mem'l Hosp. v. Mercury Constructions Corp.*, 460 U.S. 1 (1983); *Bernhardt v. Polygraphic Co. of America*, 350 U.S. 198 (1956); *Prima Paint Corp. v. Flood and Conklin Manufacturing Co.*, 388 U.S. 395 (1967); and *Wilko v. Swan*, 346 U.S. 427 (1953).

A history of the jurisdictional rivalry between public courts and private tribunals appears in *United States Asphalt Refining Co. v. Trinidad Lake Petroleum Co.*, 222 F. 1006, 1007 (S.D.N.Y. 1915):

> It has never been denied that the hostility of English-speaking courts to arbitration contracts probably originated (as Lord Campbell said in *Scott v. Avery*, 4 H.L. Cas.811) – 'in the contests of the courts of ancient times for extension of jurisdiction – all of them being opposed to anything that would altogether deprive every one of them of jurisdiction.'
>
> 'A more unworthy genesis cannot be imagined. Since (at the latest) the time of Lord Kenyon, it has been customary to stand rather upon the antiquity of the rule than upon its excellence or reason.'

Id. at 1007 (quoting *Scott v. Avery*, 4 H.L. Cas. 811 (source unavailable)).

[71] See Alternative Dispute Resolution: Most Large Employers Prefer ADR as Alternative to Litigation, Survey Says, Daily Lab. Rep., May 14, 1997, at A-4 (surveying

reports that 'more than 500 employers and five million employees' rely upon the AAA's employment arbitration programs.[72]

In this context, our chapter makes a new contribution to the intense debate about judicial regulation of employment arbitration. Many commentators have concluded that federal courts abdicate their role in ensuring that discrimination claimants are provided a just and fair dispute resolution process.[73] Certainly, employer behavior described in numerous court decisions lend support to this view, and it is true that the Supreme Court sent lower courts two strong signals to leave the arbitration system alone. But our research shows a newly unfolding story. A growing number of federal courts impose minimum standards of procedural fairness on the employment arbitration system. This evolving regulation stems from one or more of judicial perspectives described below.

---

530 Fortune 1000 companies, and finding that 79% of employers use arbitration); see also Mei Bickner et al., Developments in Employment Arbitration, 52 Disp. Resol. J. 8, 10 (reporting a massive increase in the use of arbitration in nonunion workplaces following the Supreme Court's Gilmer decision in 1991). But recently, the pioneering industry for employment arbitration has curtailed the use of mandatory employment arbitration. The Securities and Exchange Commission on June 29, 1998 approved a proposed rule change offered by the NASD that abolishes mandatory NASD arbitration of statutory employment discrimination claims. See Order Granting Approval to Proposed Rule Change Relating to the Arbitration of Employment Discrimination Claims, 63 Fed. Reg. 35,299 (June 29, 1998) (codified at 17 C.F.R. 240) (effective January 1, 1999) [hereinafter Order Granting Approval]. In a separate action, on December 29, 1998, the SEC amended the New York Stock Exchange (NYSE) Rules 347 and 600 'to exclude claims of employment discrimination, including sexual harassment, in violation of a statute from arbitration unless the parties have agreed to arbitrate the claim after it has arisen.' See Order Approving Proposed Rule Change by the New York Stock Exchange, Inc. Relating to Arbitration Rules, SEC Release No. 34-40858, 64 Fed. Reg. 1051 (January 7, 1999), available at 1999 WL 3315.

[72] American Arbitration Association, Proud Past, Bold Future, 2000 Annual Report 28 (2001), available at <www.adr.org/upload/LIVESITE/About/annual reports/annual report 2000.pdf>. The American Arbitration Association (AAA) is one of many alternative dispute resolution (ADR) service providers in this market.

[73] See *infra* notes 166–171.

18.2.1 Some Courts Refuse to Enforce Mandatory Arbitration Agreements that Impose Unfair Procedures on Employees

Although all federal courts are bound by the Supreme Court's broad ruling in *Circuit City* that mandatory arbitration agreements are enforceable under the Federal Arbitration Act (FAA),[74] the Supreme Court did not prohibit them from imposing due process standards in ADR proceedings. In fact, *Gilmer* opened the door to review concerns that the arbitration process unduly burdens a complainant's access to this alternative forum.

This is significant because some judges have encouraged ADR processes to avoid substantial cost barriers in litigating claims.[75] Empirical research supports judges who express concerns about access to their own courts. Employment discrimination plaintiffs have difficulty obtaining counsel.[76] If they succeed in persuading an attorney to represent them in federal court, they face crowded dockets with concomitant delays, and long odds of ever receiving a verdict on the merits of their claims.[77] These access problems are so ingrained that a

---

[74] See *infra* notes 166–171.

[75] See *Bradford v. Rockwell Semiconductor Sys., Inc.*, 238 F.3d 549, 552 (4th Cir. 2001). "The arbitration of disputes enables parties to avoid the costs associated with pursuing a judicial resolution of their grievances. By one estimate, litigating a typical employment dispute costs at least USD 50,000 and takes two and one-half years to resolve." *Id.* (quoting *Hooters of America, Inc. v. Phillips*, 173 F.3d 933, 936 (4th Cir. 1999)). Also, an emerging trend that may promote wider accessibility to low-cost arbitration appears in *Scheehle v. Justices of Supreme Court of State of Arizona*, 257 F.3d 1082 (9th Cir. 2001). The U.S. Court of Appeals for the Ninth Circuit found no violation of the Fifth Amendment Takings Clause in Arizona state and county court arbitration rules that require attorneys to serve as arbitrators in civil cases. *Id.* at 1085. Attorneys are required to hear cases two days a year, with their pay capped at USD 75 per day. *Id.* at 1084.

[76] One survey of attorneys who represent plaintiffs in employment discrimination disputes found that respondents accepted an average of 5% of the cases in which their legal services were requested. William M. Howard, Arbitrating Claims of Employment Discrimination, Disp. Res. J., October-December 1995, at 40, 44.

[77] Statistical measures of this complex problem are reported by Susan K. Gauvey, ADR's Integration in the Federal Court System, Md. B.J., March-April 2001, at 36, 41, in which the author reports that the rate of civil cases that go to trial in federal courts has steadily declined from 8.4% in 1975, to 4.7 % in 1985, to 3.5% in 1995, to 2.3% as of

decade ago Congress amended key employment discrimination laws to foster use of ADR methods, including arbitration.[78]

On the other hand, some judges are skeptical about the basic fairness of employment arbitration. They see 'unconscionable' applications.[79] Judges with this view lost the threshold battle over the

---

June 30, 2000. A study of employment discrimination lawsuits in the federal courts found that the proportion disposed of by trial declined from 8% in 1990 to 5% in 1998. Marika F. X. Litras, Bureau of Justice Statistics Report on Civil Rights, Complaints Filed in U.S. District Courts, Daily Lab. Rep., January 20, 2000, at E-10. This study also found that the median amount of time for processing an employment discrimination case from filing to trial verdict was eighteen months in 1998. *Id.* at E-15.

[78] See Civil Rights Act of 1991, Pub. L. 102–166, 105 Stat. 1071 (amending Title VII of the 1964 Civil Rights Act, 42 U.S.C. 1981-2000h-6); The Americans with Disabilities Act of 1990, Pub. L. 101–336 (codified as amended in scattered sections of 42 U.S.C.). Both laws state: 'Where appropriate... the use of alternative means of dispute resolution, including... arbitration, is encouraged to resolve disputes arising under this chapter.' *Id.* at 1981 n. 12212. Recent examples of ADR initiatives are The Civil Justice Reform Act, 28 U.S.C. 471, 472–482 (2000), which authorizes more ADR programs to be administered by federal courts to alleviate problems with cost and delay, *id.* 471; the Alternative Dispute Resolution Act of 1998, 28 U.S.C. 651–658 (2000); and the Administrative Dispute Resolution Act, enacted in 1990, 5 U.S.C. 571–581, 583 (2000), which authorizes all federal agencies to implement ADR policies for internal disputes, *id.* 571(a).

But the trend of promoting ADR in employment disputes may be subsiding. The Secretary of Labor under President Clinton proposed revised regulations that would forbid ERISA plans to use arbitration clauses. See Amendments to Employee Benefit Plan Claims Procedures Regulation, 65 Fed. Reg. 23,040, 23,041 (April 24, 2000); Employment Retirement Income Security Act of 1974, Rules and Regulations for Administration and Enforcement, Claims Procedure, 63 Fed. Reg. 48,390, 48,405 (September 9, 1998).

[79] See e.g., *Prevot v. Phillips Petroleum Co.*, 133 F. Supp. 2d 937, 940 (S.D. Tex. 2001). In one case, several employees who were injured in an explosion at an oil refinery filed a personal injury lawsuit, but their employer sought to enforce the arbitration agreement that they had signed. *Id.* at 938. Denying part of a motion to compel arbitration, the court noted:

> In this case, there is substantial evidence that the arbitration agreements are unconscionable. The arbitration agreements were written in English. Plaintiffs testify in sworn affidavits presented to the Court that they could not read English at the time that they signed the arbitration agreement. The affidavits

CHAPTER 18. MANDATORY EMPLOYMENT ARBITRATION

enforceability of mandatory employment arbitration agreements under the FAA. However, this clash in the judiciary is still unfolding. This chapter shows that these judges are determining standards for judicially acceptable arbitration practices and procedures.

18.2.2 Some Courts Reject or Revise Mandatory Agreements that Shift Forum Costs to Employees

The Supreme Court's recent promotion of employment arbitration has been part of a broader and sustained trend to encourage disputants to use ADR methods. The Court recently considered an unresolved issue: Is a mandatory arbitration agreement enforceable when it leaves open the question of who bears the cost of this process? While the *Green Tree* Court ruled that a mandatory commercial arbitration agreement is enforceable, the Court also stated that 'it may well be that the existence of large arbitration costs could preclude a litigant... from effectively vindicating her federal statutory rights in the arbitral forum.'[80] This ambiguity has left lower courts to resolve specific issues, for example, under what conditions 'fee splitting can render an arbitration agreement unenforceable where the arbitration fees and costs are so prohibitive as to effectively deny the employee access to the arbitral forum.'[81] Our research shows that a growing number of appellate courts are divided on the cost-barrier issue.[82]

---

also state that the documents were not translated for them and that they did not know the nature of the agreement into which they were entering. According to Plaintiffs, their superiors told them not to worry about it and to quickly sign the documents so they could get back to work.

Id.
[80] *Green Tree Fin. Corp.-Ala. v. Randolph*, 531 U.S. 79, 90 (2000).
[81] *Bradford v. Rockwell Semiconductor Sys., Inc.* 238 F.3d 549, 553–554 (4th Cir. 2001) ('The question, therefore, is whether we should apply a case-by-case basis inquiry in making this determination, or whether we should apply a broad per se rule against all fee-splitting irrespective of the circumstances surrounding each individual's case.').
[82] Compare *infra* section 18.6.2 with section 18.6.3.

18.2.3 Some Courts Reject or Revise Mandatory Agreements because They View the ADR System as Flawed by Comparison to Voluntary Labor Arbitration

Mandatory employment arbitration differs from traditional labor arbitration.[83] Under the mature labor model, unions and employers willingly agree to arbitrate disputes.[84] Both sides have an equal voice in arbitrator selection and choose from a mutually acceptable neutral agency.[85] These referral organizations charge little or no fee to the disputants. Arbitrators on their rosters charged about USD 500–600 per day in the years following *Gilmer*.[86] In short, voluntary labor arbitration

---

[83] These differences are thoroughly considered in *Cole v. Burns International Securities Services*, 105 F.3d 1465, 1473–1479 (D.C. Cir. 1992). Judge Harry T. Edwards stated:

> In order to properly consider the validity of the arbitration agreement in this case, it is crucial to emphasize the distinction between arbitration in the context of collective bargaining and mandatory arbitration of statutory claims outside of the context of a union contract. These are vastly different situations, involving very different considerations.

Id. at 1473.

[84] In the labor-management system, employers have been the party reluctant to agree to arbitration. They have expressed concern that arbitrators favor unions. The views of an experienced management attorney appear in Tracy H. Ferguson, An Appraisal of Arbitration: A Management Viewpoint, 8 Indus. & Lab. Rel. Rev. 79 (1954). 'It is understandable that those who are experts in the field ... would see the problems presented for arbitration in what has been called the "enlightened" view, but which many employers feel is inimical, not alone to their own self-interests, but to ... the general economy.' *Id.* at 81. Nevertheless, only a handful of employers have resisted arbitration clauses in labor contracts, while most have agreed to arbitration procedures. See Characteristics of Major Collective Bargaining Agreements July 1, 1976 (U.S. Bureau of Labor Statistics Bulletin No. 2013, 1979).

[85] The Federal Mediation and Conciliation Service – a government agency – and the American Arbitration Association – a private entity – have been the largest providers of arbitration services for many years. See Peter Feuille & Michael H. LeRoy, Grievance Arbitration Appeals, Arb. J., March 1990, at 35, 41 Table 1 (showing that, for example, in 1987, 4,145 awards and 5,651 awards were issued respectively under the auspices of the FMCS and AAA).

[86] Federal Mediation and Conciliation Service, Forty-Eighth Annual Report, available at <www.fmcs.gov/internet/ (last visited on September 1, 2008). Average arbitrator per diem fees were USD 470.95 in 1991, USD 489.90 in 1992, USD 515.92 in

CHAPTER 18. MANDATORY EMPLOYMENT ARBITRATION

is reasonably priced. Union-represented grievants are not required to pay any direct costs of arbitration, and unions have the same input as employers in the process.

The employment arbitration model differs in several respects. The employer or industry group establishes and maintains the arbitration process,[87] or the employer contracts with a private dispute resolution service.[88] The former has potential for bias. The latter has been criticized for aligning the financial interests of employers with their dispute resolution service providers, because ADR providers would not want the arbitrators they select to impose costly awards on their clients.[89] In addition, the method of selecting arbitrators may tie these neutrals too closely to an industry. Finally, organizations that provide employment arbitration services may impose much higher costs on disputants compared to the labor arbitration model. Sometimes these arbitrators charge several thousand dollars a day.[90] Courts question the fairness

---

1993, USD 540.69 in 1994, and USD 560.10 in 1995. See 'Arbitrator's Per Diem Rate Fees and Expenses Charged Fiscal Years 1991 Through 1995.' The average number of per diem units charged by arbitrators ranged in this period from 3.70 to 3.94. *Id.* Table titled Average Number of Days Charged by Arbitrator for Travel, Hearing and Study Time Based on Closed Arbitration Award Cases Sampled for Fiscal Years 1991 Through 1995. Average total fees were USD 1,975.82 in 1991, USD 2,110.34 in 1992, USD 2,222.38 in 1993, USD 2,351.91 in 1994, and USD 2,458.95 in 1995. *Id.*

[87] See Order Granting Approval, *supra* n. 71, at 1053.

[88] See e.g., *Floss v. Ryan's Family Steak Houses, Inc.*, 211 F.3d 306, 309 (6th Cir. 2000) (involving an employer who selected Employment Dispute Services, Inc. (EDSI) as an arbitration service).

[89] See *id.* at 314 (stating that 'we have concerns with both the fee structure and potential bias of EDSI's arbitral forum').

[90] See e.g., Rick Brundrett, Mediation, Arbitration Keep Cases Out of Court, Knight-Ridder Trib. Bus. News, March 1, 1999, (stating that court-appointed arbitrators in South Carolina charge USD 200 per hour), 1999 WL 13721987; Margaret A. Jacobs, Renting Justice: Retired Judges Seize Rising Role in Settling Disputes in California, Wall St. J., July 26, 1996, at A1 (showing that fees of USD 500 or USD 600 per hour are not uncommon); Ted Rohrlich, Growing Use of Private Judges Raises Questions of Fairness Court, L.A. Times, December 26, 2000, at A1 (reporting that arbitrators charge between USD 275 and USD 600 per hour, thereby denying access to arbitration for poor litigants); see also Reginald Alleyne, Statutory Discrimination Claims: Rights 'Waived' and Lost in the Arbitration Forum, 13 Hofstra Lab. L.J. 381, 410 n. 189 (1996) (noting that an arbitrator charged a USD 9,000 fee in a dispute that resulted in a USD 15,000 award).

of employment arbitration, especially when a complainant cannot afford this ADR method and is required to waive her right to litigate a claim.

18.3 THE ALLOCATION OF COSTS IN ARBITRATION

18.3.1 Elements of Cost in Arbitrating Employment Disputes

Cost-saving is a key benefit of arbitration.[91] This perceived advantage derives from a comparison to litigation.[92] It is important to realize, however, that dispute resolution process costs are bundled in a complex relationship. Thus, a direct comparison to forum costs may be misleading.

For example, fees charged by the arbitrator to the disputants is a major component of ADR costs. Trials have an advantage over arbitrations because litigants do not owe the judge a fee.[93] The average per

---

Some court opinions also reveal the growing expense of arbitration fees. See *Shankle v. B-G Maint. Mgmt. of Colo., Inc.*, 163 F.3d 1230, 1234–1235 (10th Cir. 1999) (finding an arbitration agreement unenforceable under the FAA because it required the employee to pay half of the arbitrator's fees, estimated at USD 1,875-5,000); *LaPrade v. Kidder, Peabody & Co.*, 94 F. Supp. 2d 2, 4 (D.D.C. 2000) (requiring the plaintiff to pay USD 8,376 in arbitration fees); *Davis v. LPK Corp.*, No. C-97-3998, 1998 WL 210262 (N.D. Cal. March 10, 1998) (denying enforcement of an arbitration agreement that would obligate the Title VII plaintiff to pay one-half of the arbitration fee, estimated to be USD 2,000 per day).

[91] See Frank Elkouri, Elkouri & Elkouri: How Arbitration Works 24 (Marlin M. Volz & Edward P. Goggin eds, 5th edn, 1997) (stating that the 'total cost of arbitration can be and often is considerably less than taking the dispute to court').

[92] John S. Murray et al., Processes of Dispute Resolution 504 (2nd edn 1996) ('Any savings in time and in related pre-and post-trial work are likely to be reflected in savings in expense').

[93] The most informative analysis of this appears in *Cole v. Burns International Securities Services*, 105 F.3d 1465, 1484 (D.C. Cir. 1997). This influential court did not provide an estimate of direct court costs in filing a lawsuit, but implied a functional limit in this cost-analysis framework:

> There is no doubt that parties appearing in federal court may be required to assume the cost of filing fees and other administrative expenses, so any reasonable costs of this sort that accompany arbitration are not problematic.

CHAPTER 18. MANDATORY EMPLOYMENT ARBITRATION

diem fee charged by labor arbitrators has risen modestly to about USD 700,[94] compared to USD 2,000 per diem fees for employment arbitrators.[95] So at first blush, individual employment arbitration is not cost-effective compared to courts.

> However, if an employee like Cole is required to pay arbitrators' fees ranging from $500 to $1,000 per day or more, in addition to administrative and attorney's fees, is it likely that he will be able to pursue his statutory claims? We think not.

Id. (citation omitted).

[94] The American Arbitration Association's most recently published estimate is that its average daily fee for a labor arbitrator is USD 700. Kenneth May, Labor Lawyers at ABA Session Debate Role of American Arbitration Association, Daily Lab. Rep., February 15, 1996, at A-12.

[95] Several courts report that employment discrimination disputes arbitrated under the American Arbitration Association rules provide for payment of USD 2,000 per day for arbitrator fees. See e.g., *Solieri v. Ferrovie Dello Stato Spa*, No. 97-Civ.-8844, 1998 WL 419013, at 4 (S.D.N.Y. July 22, 1998).

There is no definitive explanation for the disparity in fees charged by labor arbitrators and employment arbitrators. We also note that some arbitrators serve in both capacities, and therefore charge very different fees that are tied to the distinct markets for these services. One possible explanation is that dispute resolution agencies impose their own fees on arbitrators, which in the case of employment arbitration may be passed on in the form of higher fees to the disputing parties. To illustrate, Judicial Arbitration and Mediation Services, Inc. (JAMS) is a nationally recognized dispute resolution provider that offers employment arbitration, as distinguished from labor arbitration. See JAMS Employment Arbitration Rules and Procedures, at <www.jamsadr.com/rules/rules.asp> (last revised September 2008). A published report indicates that some 'arbitrators...have left or bypassed JAMS...because JAMS generally takes too much of their fees – a whopping 50%.' Kathryn Kranhold, Solo Legal Arbitrators Put Longtime Leader in a Jam, Wall St. J. November 13, 1996, at A2. It is plausible that the much higher fee for employment arbitrators reflects the substantial sum that the arbitrator owes to the referral agency. In contrast, labor arbitrators are presently assessed annual listing fees that range from USD 100–300 by the Federal Mediation and Conciliation Service and the American Arbitration Association. Memorandum from Federal Mediation and Conciliation Service, to Arbitrators on the FMCS Roster (July 2002) (on file with author).

A second explanation is that the higher fees for employment arbitrators originate in the securities industry. One of the criticisms of NASD arbitration is that many arbitrators are industry professionals who have no independent specialization as dispute resolution neutrals. See U.S. Gen. Accounting Office, Health, Education, and Human Servs. Div., Report to the Chairman of the Subcomm. on

This impression is strengthened by the fact that nonprofit organizations such as the American Arbitration Association now charge forum fees. Depending on which AAA procedures are used, these fees are moderate or substantial.[96] In addition, the market for arbitration service providers has grown rapidly and is served primarily by private agencies.[97] Regardless of their nonprofit or for-profit status, they charge whatever fees the market will bear.[98] In sum, the charging of forum fees by service providers further undermines the cost advantage of arbitration.

Mandatory arbitration can result in another cost for complainants: attorney's fees. While a variety of antidiscrimination statutes provide complainants with a remedy for attorney's fees, arbitrators often deny the remedy to complainants.[99] In some cases employees prevail in the award but likely owe more to their attorneys than the sum of their

---

Telecomm. and Fin. Comm. on Energy and Commerce, House of Representatives, 103rd Cong., Employment Discrimination – How Registered Representatives Fare in Discrimination Disputes (GAO Doc. No. GAO/HE HS 94- 17 1994), at 1994 WL 836270 (reporting that only 'about 58 percent of all arbitrators making up the NYSE pool are public arbitrators,' while the balance are 'industry arbitrators' who have significant experience and standing in their financial profession). The per diem fee of USD 2,000 for these arbitrators may reflect the daily compensation for securities professionals who are based in New York City, where this arbitration process is administered.

[96] Compare, Cole, 105 F.3d at 1480 (noting that Rule 35 of the American Arbitration Association's National Rules for the Resolution of Employment Disputes imposes a USD 500 filing fee, to be advanced by the initiating party, and an administrative fee of USD 150 per hearing day), with *Giordano v. Pep Boys – Manny, Moe & Jack, Inc.*, No. Civ. A. 99-1281, 2001 WL 484360, at 6 (E.D. Pa. March 29, 2001) (estimating that plaintiff's 'upfront' costs to AAA would range from USD 600–900 for one-half of the arbitrator's fee, plus filing fees, and 'would function as a barrier to plaintiff's pursuit of arbitration of his claims').

[97] An informative account appears in Johanna Harrington, Comment, To Litigate or Arbitrate? No Matter – The Credit Card Industry Is Deciding for You, 2001 J. Disp. Resol. 101, 106 notes 23–26.

[98] See e.g., *Shankle v. B-G Maint. Mgmt. of Colo., Inc.*, 163 F.3d 1230, 1232 (10th Cir. 1999). In Shankle, the employer imposed a mandatory arbitration agreement that referred disputes to The Judicial Arbiter Group. *Id.* Parties were required to pay USD 250 per each hour of arbitrator time and USD 125 per hour of the arbitrator's travel time. *Id.* The service provider also required parties to pay a USD 6,000 deposit. *Id.*

[99] See e.g., *DeGaetano v. Smith Barney, Inc.*, 983 F. Supp. 459, 460 (S.D.N.Y. 1997).

CHAPTER 18. MANDATORY EMPLOYMENT ARBITRATION

damages, and thus potentially gain nothing from arbitrating – and winning – a meritorious claim.[100]

The cost picture is more complicated, however. Even in the case of ADR services that charge forum fees of several thousands of dollars,[101] arbitrators still may be less expensive than courts. This depends on how arbitration costs are calculated. While courts are virtually cost-free in terms of direct fees, they impose large process costs. Formal rules of civil procedure require legal representation throughout court proceedings, to the point of making litigation costs unacceptably expensive even for large employers.[102] Because many civil trials are preceded by lengthy discovery, this phase can be very expensive.[103] If a plaintiff tries her case, she must be represented by a licensed attorney. This adds to the dispute resolution cost.

By comparison, procedural informality usually makes arbitration less expensive than trial.[104] Labor arbitration provides useful examples,

---

[100] See e.g., *DeGaetano v. Smith Barney, Inc.*, 983 F. Supp. 459, 460 (S.D.N.Y. 1997).

[101] See e.g., *Gardner v. Benefits Communications Corp.*, 175 F.3d 155, 157 (D.C. Cir. 1999) (reporting that a discrimination complainant was charged USD 3,000 in forum fees for arbitration hearings that lasted six days).

[102] See Alternative Dispute Resolution – Employers' Experiences with ADR in the Workplace 50 (GAO doc. No. GAO/GGD 97–157, August 12, 1997), available at 1997 WL 709361 (explaining that one of the surveyed employers who adopted a mandatory arbitration system was motivated to do so after spending over USD 1,000,000 to defend itself in a discrimination suit).

[103] See E. Norman Veasey & Michael P. Dooley, The Role of Corporate Litigation in the Twenty-First Century, 25 Del. J. Corp. L. 131, 150 (2000) ('There are clear cost advantages to arbitration in view of lower discovery costs'); Gerald Walpin, America's Failing Civil Justice System: Can We Learn from Other Countries?, 41 N.Y.L. Sch. L. Rev. 647, 649 (1997) (noting that pretrial discovery is the main component of litigation, accounting for as much as 80% of litigation costs).

[104] See e.g., Mark L. McAlpine, ADR in Large and Complex Cases, 72 Mich. B.J. 1054, 1054 (1993). Mark McAlpine provides this illustration:

> For instance, empowering the arbitrators to summarily rule on dispositive issues, while leading to narrower and more streamlined hearings, may also facilitate the settlement process. This is particularly true where the interpretation of a contract or a ruling on a point of law stands in the way of substantive settlement discussions, or prevents one party from agreeing to arbitration in the first place. In these situations, the party who perceives that there is a chance to obtain a dismissal of all or part of the case may prefer litigation over arbitration. This concern can be addressed by an agreement to arbitrate limited issues or

especially because the employment rights model borrows from it. Attorney representation is not required and is occasionally prohibited by contract.[105] Management is often represented by a lawyer, and the union by a nonlawyer staff representative or elected official.[106] The fact that this arrangement is common suggests that unions do not feel that their interests are compromised by having nonlawyer advocates. This is probably true because arbitration hearings have permissive rules of evidence.[107]

Arbitration has other significant cost advantages. Many employment disputes involve preemption issues. To illustrate, in employee benefits lawsuits, plaintiffs frequently seek relief in state court, where theories of employer liability are broad and lucrative damages are available.[108] The first round in these lawsuits often concerns the

---

> by providing for dispositive motions as a way of resolving the dispute or setting the parameters for later settlement discussions. This also allows threshold issues to be addressed without the cost of preparing for a hearing on all of the issues in dispute, thus blending cost advantages of arbitration with the potential efficiencies of the summary disposition characteristics of litigation.

Id.

[105] See e.g., National Bituminous Coal Wage Agreement of 1993, Art. XXIII, Section (h) (Exclusion of Legal Counsel) (copy on file with authors).

[106] See Elkouri, *supra* n. 91, at 336–337 ('Representatives such as higher union or company officials may be used to present the case at the arbitration stage.').

[107] See Marvin F. Hill, Jr. & Anthony V. Sinicropi, Evidence in Arbitration 50 (1980) ('The rules of evidence are not strictly followed').

[108] See Rothstein & Liebman, *supra* n. 7, at 504, to explain why employers seek to avoid state court benefits-denial lawsuits:

> ERISA preemption defenses, when available, present extraordinary advantages: (1) the complete bar to all state law claims, including 'bad faith' conduct, (2) certain 'deep pocket' defendants, such as the plan sponsor and claims review agents, cannot even be sued under federal law, (3) the participant has no cause of action for delay in processing claims, (4) the participant cannot recover extracontractual compensatory damages or punitive damages, (5) the participant must generally exhaust administrative remedies as a prerequisite to filing suit, (6) the defendants have a statutory right to remove cases to federal court, (7) ERISA bars a jury trial, (8) the courts do not conduct de novo hearings on a participant's [claim] for benefits, and instead uphold the fiduciary's decision unless 'arbitrary or capricious,' and (9) ERISA permits an award of attorney's fees and costs.

Id. (citation omitted).

CHAPTER 18. MANDATORY EMPLOYMENT ARBITRATION

employer's motion to remove to federal court.[109] Naturally, this adds time and cost to the dispute resolution process.[110] Arbitration avoids this encumbrance and likely adds to its cost advantages by allowing disputants to schedule a hearing on the merits sooner than a trial.

Apart from cost-saving features, employment arbitration is potentially advantageous to individual claimants when the rules expressly provide for minimum standards of procedural fairness. Judicial Arbitration and Mediation Services, Inc. (JAMS), a major provider of employment arbitration services, recently revised its policies to ensure that cost is not a barrier.[111] It also adopted a policy to allow arbitrators

---

[109] See e.g., *Kuhl v. Lincoln Nat'l Health Plan of Kan. City*, 999 F.2d 298 (8th Cir. 1993). In Kuhl, a truck driver's widow sued her deceased husband's health insurance plan for medical malpractice when the plan's apparent delay in pre-certifying heart surgery left the employee too debilitated for surgery, thereby hastening his death. *Id.* at 300. The lawsuit, filed in the Circuit Court of Jackson County, Missouri, asserted claims for medical malpractice, emotional distress, tortious interference with the decedent's right to contract for medical care, and breach of contract. *Id.* The employer successfully removed the matter to federal court under ERISA, thus extinguishing the state causes of action. *Id.* at 300–301.

[110] See *id.* at 300–301 (recounting lengthy procedural wrangling). After the Kuhls filed suit, the employer moved for removal, which was followed by the Kuhls' motion for remand to argue that ERISA did not apply. The employer's plan opposed the motion to remand and filed a motion for summary judgment. The Kuhls then moved to amend the judgment and replead their complaint to include a cause of action under ERISA. After filing a second suit in the district court alleging that Lincoln National breached its fiduciary duty under ERISA, the court dismissed the matter, concluding that the state law claims could not be recharacterized as ERISA claims. *Id.*

[111] See Judicial Arbitration and Mediation Services, Inc., JAMS Policy on Employment Arbitration Minimum Standards of Procedural Fairness (2002), at <www.jamsadr.com/rules/consumer_min_std.asp> (revised September 2008). JAMS Policy on Employment Arbitration Minimum Standards on Procedural Fairness provides:

> Standard No. 6: Costs and Location Must Not Preclude Access to Arbitration.
> An employee's access to arbitration must not be precluded by the employee's inability to pay any costs or by the location of the arbitration. The only fee that an employee may be required to pay is JAMS' Case Management Fee.
> Comment: JAMS does not preclude an employee from contributing to administrative and arbitrator fees and expenses. JAMS will not disclose to the arbitrator any information about the fee arrangements with the employer.

Id.

to award attorney's fees to prevailing complainants.[112] AAA procedures provide for the possibility of relieving individuals of most arbitration costs, but only 'in the event of extreme hardship.'[113]

---

[112] *Id.* at Standard No. 1. The appropriate portion provides:

> All remedies that would be available under the applicable law in a court proceeding, including attorneys fees and exemplary damages, must remain available in the arbitration. Post-arbitration remedies, if any, must remain available to an employee.
>
> Comment: This standard does not make any change in the remedies available. Its purpose is to ensure that the remedies available in arbitrations and court proceedings are the same. JAMS does not object if an employer chooses to limit its own post-arbitration remedies.

Id.

[113] See American Arbitration Association, National Rules for Resolution of Employment Disputes, at <www.adr.org/index2.1.jsp?JSPssid=15747&JSPsrc=upload LIVE SITE Rules Procedures National International .... focusArea employment employment rules2.html> (as amended and effective on January 1, 2001). Rule 38, Administrative Fees, states:

> As a not-for-profit organization, the AAA shall prescribe filing and other administrative fees to compensate it for the cost of providing administrative services. The AAA administrative fee schedule in effect at the time the demand for arbitration or submission agreement is received shall be applicable.
>
> The filing fee shall be advanced by the initiating party or parties, subject to final apportionment by the arbitrator in the award.
>
> The AAA may, in the event of extreme hardship on any party, defer or reduce the administrative fees.

Id.

Rule 39 (Expenses) continues:

> Unless otherwise agreed by the parties, the expenses of witnesses for either side shall be borne by the party producing such witnesses. All expenses of the arbitration, including required travel and other expenses of the arbitrator, AAA representatives, and any witness and the costs relating to any proof produced at the direction of the arbitrator, shall be borne equally by the parties, unless they agree otherwise or unless the arbitrator directs otherwise in the award.
>
> The arbitrator's compensation shall be borne equally by the parties unless they agree otherwise, or unless the law provides otherwise.

Id.

CHAPTER 18.   MANDATORY EMPLOYMENT ARBITRATION

In sum, the available evidence supports several conclusions about the comparative costs of arbitration and litigation. First, on a total cost basis, the average employment arbitration process costs less than the average employment discrimination lawsuit.[114] Second, however, employment arbitration is not inexpensive. Its total cost depends on many factors: the arbitrator's hourly rate, the duration of the process, attorney's fees and expenses, and the complexity and scope of the dispute. Under some circumstances, the transaction costs of obtaining an arbitration award may equal or even exceed the cost of a verdict. Third, in cases in which employment arbitration mimics labor arbitration by providing for equal cost-sharing by the disputants, a pseudo-equality results because individuals, unlike labor unions, are less able to bear these costs.

18.3.2   The Supreme Court's Regulation of Arbitration Costs

Congress justified enactment of the FAA in 1925 by stating that arbitration allows disputants to avoid 'the costliness and delays of litigation.'[115] In rulings to uphold arbitration, the Supreme Court has repeatedly invoked this rationale.[116] Congress has also reaffirmed its

---

[114] Most of the cost advantages of arbitration stem from lower billings by attorneys. For example, in a 1994 survey, attorneys who represent employers estimated that their average fee to litigate an employment discrimination lawsuit was USD 96,000, compared to USD 20,000 to defend their clients in an arbitration. See Howard, *supra* n. 76, at 44. This study did not report equivalent dollar cost figures reported by plaintiff lawyers because they customarily work for a contingency fee. *Id.* In arbitration, the disputants must pay forum and arbitrator fees, which can total several thousand dollars, whereas lawsuit filing fees are nominal and judicial services are a public good. However, forum and arbitrator fees do not come close to reaching the amount of attorney's fees in litigation.

[115] S. Rep. No. 68-536, at 3 (1924) (stating that the FAA, by avoiding 'the delay and expense of litigation' would appeal 'to big business and little businesses... corporate interests [and]... individuals'); H.R. Rep. No. 68–96, at 2 (1924) (showing that Congress believed the procedural simplicity of arbitration would 'reduce technicality, delay, and [keep] expense to a minimum and at the same time safeguard[] the rights of the parties').

[116] See e.g., *Allied-Bruce Terminix Cos. v. Dobson*, 513 U.S. 265, 280 (1995) ('Congress, when enacting [the FAA], had the needs of consumers, as well as others, in mind.').

commitment to the cost-saving advantages of arbitration.[117] Many experts agree that arbitration costs less than litigation.[118]

Against this backdrop, the Supreme Court ruled in *Green Tree Financial Corp.-Ala. v. Randolph*[119] on a consumer version of arbitration that can cost more than litigation. To purchase a mobile home, Larketta Randolph arranged financing through a subsidiary of Green Tree Financial Corporation.[120] She signed a retail installment contract that contained an insurance provision to protect the lienholder against the costs of repossession if she defaulted.[121] In addition, the contract also stated that all disputes relating to the contract would be resolved by binding arbitration.[122]

Nevertheless, Randolph sued Green Tree under the federal Truth in Lending Act (TILA).[123] She alleged that the lender did not comply with TILA's requirement to disclose the insurance requirement as a

---

[117] See H.R. Rep. No. 97-542, at 13 (1982). A growing number of arbitrations have been costly and protracted. Still, the following benefits of arbitration are not widely challenged:

> The advantages of arbitration are many: it is usually cheaper and faster than litigation; it can have simpler procedural and evidentiary rules; it normally minimizes hostility and is less disruptive of ongoing and future business dealings among the parties; it is often more flexible in regard to scheduling of times and places of hearings and discovery devices.

Id.

[118] See Stephen B. Goldberg et al., Litigation, Arbitration or Mediation: A Dialogue, 75 A.B.A. J. 70, 72 (1989). Stephen Goldberg explains how the efficiency of arbitration reduces dispute costs compared to litigation:

> My advice on this point would be to provide for only as much discovery as you absolutely need to prepare for trial. This is one of the great advantages of arbitration. If we were to go through normal court discovery in this case, say four or five depositions, plus the five or so days you've told me it should take to try it, that could cost Jones as much as $50,000. That just doesn't make sense in a case with a maximum recovery of $75,000.

Id.

[119] *Green Tree Fin. Corp.-Ala. v. Randolph*, 531 U.S. 79 (2000).
[120] *Id.* at 82.
[121] *Id.*
[122] *Id.* at 82–83.
[123] Truth in Lending Act, 15 U.S.C. 1601–1667f (2000); *Green Tree*, 531 U.S. at 83.

CHAPTER 18. MANDATORY EMPLOYMENT ARBITRATION

finance charge.[124] Later, she amended her complaint to add a claim that Green Tree violated the Equal Credit Opportunity Act by requiring her to arbitrate her statutory causes of action.[125]

Green Tree moved to compel arbitration.[126] The district court granted this motion, and also denied Randolph's motion to certify a class of similarly situated plaintiffs.[127] Randolph requested reconsideration, contending that she could not afford arbitration and would have to forgo her legal claims.[128] After the court denied her request, she appealed.[129]

The court of appeals first decided that the district court's order was final.[130] Thus, the appellate court ruled that it had jurisdiction over Randolph's arbitrability appeal.[131] Analyzing Randolph's claim as it arose under the FAA, the appeals court concluded that the arbitration agreement failed to provide her minimum guarantees to vindicate her rights under TILA.[132] This conclusion rested upon the court's observation that the arbitration agreement was silent about the cost of arbitration (for example, payment of filing fees, arbitrators' costs, and other expenses).[133] Thus, the court held that when 'steep' arbitration costs posed a risk of preventing a party from vindicating a statutory right, the arbitration agreement was unenforceable.[134]

After affirming the appeals court's first ruling that it had jurisdiction over Randolph's claim,[135] the Supreme Court, in a split decision,[136] ruled that 'an arbitration agreement's silence with respect to such

---

[124] Id.
[125] Id.
[126] Id.
[127] Id.
[128] Id. at 83–84.
[129] Id. at 84.
[130] Id.
[131] See id.
[132] Id.
[133] See id.
[134] Id.
[135] See id.
[136] The Court was unanimous in holding that the district court order compelling arbitration was final for purposes of establishing appellate jurisdiction. Id. at 89. However, on the substantive issue of cost as a potential barrier to vindicating statutory rights, the Court split in a 5-4 vote. See id. at 81, 92–97.

759

matters does not render the agreement unenforceable.'[137] The majority cited the FAA's purpose 'to reverse the longstanding judicial hostility to arbitration agreements ... and to place arbitration agreements upon the same footing as other contracts.'[138] They underscored their support for arbitration by rejecting 'generalized attacks on arbitration that rest on "suspicion of arbitration as a method of weakening the protections afforded in the substantive law to would-be complainants." '[139] By their reasoning, 'even claims arising under a statute designed to further important social policies may be arbitrated because "so long as the prospective litigant effectively may vindicate [his or her] statutory cause of action in the arbitral forum," the statute serves its functions.'[140]

Turning to the facts, the majority noted that Randolph and Green Tree agreed to arbitrate all statutory rights related to their contract.[141] The opinion added that Congress did not intend in TILA to preclude a waiver of judicial remedies.[142] As for whether the agreement's silence on costs and fees would make arbitration of her TILA claims prohibitively expensive, the Court stated:

> It may well be that the existence of large arbitration costs could preclude a litigant such as Randolph from effectively vindicating her federal statutory rights in the arbitral forum. But the record does not show that Randolph will bear such costs if she goes to arbitration. Indeed, it contains hardly any information on the matter.[143]

In concluding that she could not afford arbitration, Randolph had estimated the cost of her arbitration.[144] The majority dismissed this

---

[137] *Id.* at 82.
[138] *Id.* at 89 (quoting *Gilmer v. Interstate/Johnson Lane Corp.*, 500 U.S. 20, 24 (1991)).
[139] *Id.* at 89–90 (quoting *Rodriguez de Quijas v. Shearson/American Express, Inc.*, 490 U.S. 477, 481 (1989)).
[140] *Id.* at 90 (quoting *Gilmer*, 500 U.S. at 28) (citation omitted).
[141] *Id.*
[142] See *id.*
[143] *Id.*
[144] *Id.* at 90, 91 n. 6. The agreement did not specify which arbitration provider or arbitrator would resolve their dispute. In her motion for reconsideration before the district court, Randolph therefore assumed that arbitration would occur under auspices of the commercial proceedings administered by the American Arbitration Association. Because the amount in dispute was under USD 10,000, AAA would impose a filing fee of USD 500 for her claim, plus the cost of the arbitrator and administrative fees. Her motion also contained an exhibit showing that a typical

CHAPTER 18. MANDATORY EMPLOYMENT ARBITRATION

calculation, however, as 'unsupported statements [that] provide no basis on which to ascertain the actual costs and fees to which she would be subject in arbitration.'[145]

They returned to an evidentiary matter in arbitration challenges, repeating *Gilmer's* view that 'the party seeking to avoid arbitration bears the burden of establishing that Congress intended to preclude arbitration of the statutory claims at issue.'[146] By analogy, they extended this logic to arbitrability challenges that claim cost as a prohibitive barrier to asserting statutory rights: 'Similarly, we believe that where, as here, a party seeks to invalidate an arbitration agreement on the ground that arbitration would be prohibitively expensive, that party bears the burden of showing the likelihood of incurring such costs.'[147] On this point, the Court concluded that Randolph's proof was too speculative.[148] They also concluded, however, that 'how detailed the showing of prohibitive expense must be before the party seeking arbitration must come forward with contrary evidence is a matter we need not discuss.'[149] Because the U.S. Court of Appeals for the Eleventh Circuit ruled on such indefinite cost information, the *Green Tree* majority reversed the ruling that arbitration would deprive Randolph of an opportunity to pursue her statutory claims.[150]

Justice Ruth Bader Ginsburg limited her dissent to the issue of cost-shifting.[151] She preferred a middle ground between the majority and the Eleventh Circuit. She would not have made a definitive ruling as the majority did,[152] but would instead have vacated the Eleventh Circuit's ruling that the arbitration clause was unenforceable and remanded for more evidence concerning Randolph's access to arbitration.[153]

She believed that the majority placed an unreasonable evidentiary burden on plaintiffs: 'The Court requires a party, situated as Randolph

---

commercial arbitration fee is USD 700 per day. Using these figures, she contended that she could not afford to arbitrate her TILA claim. *Id.*

[145] *Id.* at 91 n. 6.
[146] *Id.* at 92 (citations omitted).
[147] *Id.*
[148] See *id.*
[149] *Id.*
[150] *Id.*
[151] See *id.* at 92–93 (Ginsburg, J., concurring in part and dissenting in part).
[152] See *id.* at 93.
[153] *Id.*

is, either to submit to arbitration without knowing who will pay for the forum or to demonstrate up front that the costs, if imposed on her, will be prohibitive.'[154] She criticized this approach because it overlooked separate inquiries that courts should make in determining whether arbitration can properly substitute for litigation: 'First, is the arbitral forum adequate to adjudicate the claims at issue; second, is that forum accessible to the party resisting arbitration.'[155] The problem is that a party resisting arbitration already bears the burden to prove the inadequacy of the arbitral forum to adjudicate a statutory claim.[156] She reasoned: 'It does not follow like the night the day, however, that the party resisting arbitration should also bear the burden of showing that the arbitral forum would be financially inaccessible to her.'[157]

She emphasized the control that the party imposing arbitration has over the party wanting to sue. The arbitration agreement that Randolph signed was part of a take-it-or-leave-it form contract. This made Randolph's situation different from Robert Gilmer's, even though he, too, was compelled to sign an arbitration agreement. Justice Ginsburg noted that 'who pays' was not an issue in Gilmer's case, because he and others like him were not required under New York Stock Exchange rules to pay for the arbitrator. Relying on an earlier analysis of the securities arbitration system, she observed:

> In *Gilmer*, the Supreme Court endorsed a system of arbitration in which employees are not required to pay for the arbitrator assigned to hear their statutory claims. There is no reason to think that the Court would have approved arbitration in the absence of this arrangement. Indeed, we are unaware of any situation in American jurisprudence in which a

---

[154] See *id*.

[155] *Id*.

[156] See e.g., *Gilmer v. Interstate/Johnson Lane Corp.*, 500 U.S. 20, 20 (1991) (noting that ADEA claims are amenable to arbitration); *Shearson/American Express Inc. v. McMahon*, 482 U.S. 220, 221 (1987) (holding that claims under the Racketeer Influenced and Corrupt Organizations Act (RICO) and Securities Exchange Act are amenable to arbitration). Justice Ruth Bader Ginsburg noted that these decisions hold that 'the party resisting arbitration bears the burden of establishing the inadequacy of the arbitral forum for adjudication of claims of a particular genre.' Green Tree, 531 U.S. at 94 (Ginsburg, J., concurring in part and dissenting in part).

[157] Green Tree, 531 U.S. at 94.

CHAPTER 18. MANDATORY EMPLOYMENT ARBITRATION

beneficiary of a federal statute has been required to pay for the services of the judge assigned to hear her or his case.[158]

In contrast, Randolph's arbitration agreement was too vague to prevent abuse or mischief. It did not specify forum costs or predetermine each party's responsibility for arbitration expenses. Thus, Justice Ginsburg believed that the majority unfairly made Randolph bear the burden of proving that the arbitration system was too expensive for her.[159] Green Tree, as the drafter of the contract, should have been more specific.[160] If the process had been governed by the American Arbitration Association's Consumer Arbitration Rules, Randolph would have known that she owed no filing fee and only USD 125 of the arbitrator's fees.[161] The drafting party would be required to pay all other forum fees and costs.[162]

Justice Ginsburg also thought the majority ruling was unfair to Randolph because Green Tree, 'as a repeat player in the arbitration required by its form contract,... has superior information about the cost to consumers of pursuing arbitration.'[163] She concluded that 'it is hardly clear that Randolph should bear the burden of demonstrating up front the arbitral forum's inaccessibility, or that she should be required to submit to arbitration without knowing how much it will cost her.'[164]

Finally, the dissenting opinion also noted that the majority ruling did not prevent Randolph from returning to court after the arbitration to challenge process costs. But doing so would undermine the advantages of arbitration by creating an additional basis for appealing an arbitration award or ruling: 'Neither certainty nor judicial economy is served by leaving that issue unsettled until the end of the line.'[165]

In sum, the disputed consumer arbitration process in *Green Tree* is pertinent to employment arbitrations. The case arose under the Federal Arbitration Act and involved a mandatory arbitration agreement. Its

---

[158] *Id.* (quoting *Cole v. Burns Int'l Sec. Servs.*, 105 F.3d 1465, 1484 (D.C. Cir. 1997)) (alteration in original).
[159] See *id.* at 96.
[160] See *id.* at 95.
[161] See *id.*
[162] See *id.*
[163] *Id.* at 96.
[164] *Id.*
[165] *Id.* at 97.

763

majority opinion favored drafters of these agreements by allowing vague or silent cost-shifting arrangements to be enforced against a person who claimed inability to pay for arbitration. This decision therefore added to the Supreme Court's strong messages to lower courts to enforce mandatory arbitration agreements. Do lower courts act on these messages or do they distinguish their cases from *Green Tree* and *Gilmer*? The following empirical research offers a preliminary answer.

18.4 RESEARCH LITERATURE AND METHODS

18.4.1 Research Literature

Most of the current research literature criticizes mandatory arbitration. A leading authority compares this form of employment arbitration to antiunion yellow dog contracts from a century ago.[166] Another commentator denounces the expansion of arbitration under the FAA from commercial uses involving evenly matched companies to the employment arena, in which large corporations exert their superior bargaining power over workers.[167] In a related critique, employment arbitration is questioned because its procedures are tailored by one party to serve only its interests.[168] Others express concern that arbitration will arrest the development of public policies that embody employment discrimination law.[169] Mandatory arbitration is also attacked for lacking procedural fairness.[170]

This prescriptive research stream also views employment arbitration as part of a broad extension of corporate power over 'the little guy.'[171] By this view consumers, renters, HMO patients, small

---

[166] See Van Wezel Stone, *supra* n. 65, at 1037.
[167] Margaret M. Harding, The Redefinition of Arbitration by Those with Superior Bargaining Power, 1999 Utah L. Rev. 857, 857–863.
[168] Sarah Rudolph Cole, Managerial Litigants?: The Overlooked Problem of Party Autonomy in Dispute Resolution, 51 Hastings L.J. 1199, 1201 (2000).
[169] Geraldine Szott Moohr, Arbitration and the Goals of Employment Discrimination Law, 56 Wash. & Lee L. Rev. 395, 439 (1999).
[170] Julian J. Moore, N., Arbitral Review (Or Lack Thereof): Examining the Procedural Fairness of Arbitrating Statutory Claims, 100 Colum. L. Rev. 1572, 1593–1597 (2000).
[171] Jean R. Sternlight, Panacea or Corporate Tool?: Debunking the Supreme Court's Preference for Binding Arbitration, 74 Wash. U. L.Q. 637, 638–639 (1996);

CHAPTER 18. MANDATORY EMPLOYMENT ARBITRATION

investors, and employees find a hostile dispute resolution process set between them and more protective courts, even though Congress provides statutory rights to these disadvantaged parties.[172]

There are notable exceptions to this prevailing view. Two authorities summarize the case for mandatory arbitration. Professor Samuel Estreicher contends:

> Arbitration of employment disputes should be encouraged as an alternative, supplementary mechanism – in addition to administrative agencies and courts – for resolving claims arising under public laws as well as contracts. It is an alternative that offers the promise of a less expensive, more expeditious, less draining and divisive process, and yet still effective remedy. Private arbitration will never, and should not, entirely supplant agency or court adjudication. But if properly designed, private arbitration can complement public enforcement and, at the same time, satisfy the public interest objectives of the various statutes governing the employment relationship.[173]

Richard Bales, who studied a positive model of mandatory employment arbitration, struck a similar theme: If designed and implemented carefully, this dispute resolution method produces net gains to all disputants.[174]

Katherine Van Wezel Stone, Rustic Justice: Community and Coercion under the Federal Arbitration Act, 77 N.C. L. Rev. 931, 1025 (1999).

[172] See e.g., Kenneth R. Davis, The Arbitration Claws: Unconscionability in the Securities Industry, 78 B.U. L. Rev. 255, 325 (1998); Stephen J. Ware, Paying the Price of Process: Judicial Regulation of Consumer Arbitration Agreements, 2001 J. Disp. Resol. 89, 91–93.

[173] Samuel Estreicher, Predispute Agreements to Arbitrate Statutory Employment Claims, 72 N.Y.U. L. Rev. 1344, 1349 (1997).

[174] See Richard A. Bales, Compulsory Arbitration: The Grand Experiment in Employment 169 (1997), for an examination of a progressive arbitration system at Brown & Root, a non-union construction company with 30,000 employees. The experience of this firm is noted here because it is the subject of the most comprehensive analysis of a large mandatory arbitration system.

> Compulsory employment arbitration offers tremendous benefits to both employers and employees. It can reduce significantly the costs and time involved in resolving disputes. It also provides a forum for adjudicating grievances to employees currently shut out of the litigation system. Finally, it presents an opportunity for parties to resolve their differences in a way that promotes, rather than discourages, maintaining the employment relationship.
> ....

Then, there is a recent empirical study showing that federal courts often rule against employment discrimination plaintiffs.[175] While its authors do not endorse arbitration, their results imply that a fairly administered and accessible arbitration system could benefit employees with discrimination claims.[176] This study is reinforced by research that shows that only a tiny percentage of discrimination lawsuits ever go to trial,[177] and that the judicial-access problem is largely due to

---

> Employment arbitration is not, however, a panacea for disputes arising in the nonunionized workplace. The dangers of employer abuse require courts to be vigilant in ensuring that arbitration agreements do not become a vehicle for eliminating employees' legal protections. Nonetheless, given the litigation system's current inability to provide any meaningful forum to so many employees who feel they have suffered legal wrongs in the workplace, compulsory arbitration, properly implemented, can be a significant improvement over litigation.

Id.

[175] Results appear in Jess Bravin, U.S. Courts Are Tough on Job-Bias Suits, Wall St. J., July 16, 2001, at A2. After analyzing nine years of federal trial statistics, Professors Stewart J. Schwab and Theodore Eisenberg concluded that federal appeals courts are more hostile to workers who allege job discrimination than they are to almost any other type of plaintiff. See id. Appeals courts reversed victories for plaintiffs in 43.6% of discrimination cases, compared to a plaintiff-win reversal rate of only 32.5% for defendants in all cases who appealed their losses. Id. Moreover, employee job-bias suits were less likely than other types of suits to win at trial. Id. About 30% of the 7,575 job-bias suits that were tried resulted in a win for the employee, compared to a plaintiff win rate of 43% in all 57,878 civil trials. Id. 'The authors concluded that appellate courts have a double standard ... harshly scrutinizing employee victories at trial while gazing benignly' when an employer wins. Id. Their study used data from the Administrative Office of the U.S. Courts, and included lawsuits brought under federal discrimination laws (for example, the ADEA, Title VII of the 1964 Civil Rights Act, and the ADA). Id.

[176] Part of their conclusions can be read as a skeptical reply to employment arbitration critics who prefer to see more access to courts for plaintiffs. Because appellate cases 'typically involve subtle questions of employer intent, where credibility of witnesses is especially important,' it is surprising to see that appellate judges do not defer more often to the factual findings of trial judges and juries. Id.

[177] A study of employment discrimination lawsuits in the federal courts found that the proportion disposed of by trial declined from 8% in 1990 to 5% in 1998. See Litras, supra n. 77. This study also found that the median amount of time for processing an employment discrimination case from filing to trial verdict was eighteen months in 1998. Id.

the very small percentage of cases that plaintiff lawyers accept.[178] Emerging research studies also identify best practices in employment arbitration.[179]

18.4.2 Research Methods

This article does not take sides in the prescriptive debate, but emphasizes instead that mandatory arbitration has a mixture of serious flaws and significant advantages over litigation.[180] As our empirical research shows, employment arbitration processes vary greatly. Categorical condemnations of this ADR method are therefore difficult to support, especially because courts have slow and expensive processes that make trials open to all in theory, but unavailable to many in reality. On the other hand, our research on the cost features of employment arbitration lend some support to critics who claim that this method can be egregiously unfair and one-sided. Our guiding research questions are: What is the aggregate behavior of courts that rule on the enforceability of mandatory employment arbitration agreements when an employee asserts she cannot afford this ADR process? How often do courts enforce these agreements and refer these disputes to arbitration? How often do they deny enforcement and thus allow the possibility of a trial?

To answer these questions, we extensively searched for all reported federal court decisions that dealt with this subject. Our sample was created by applying the following criteria:

- We used only federal court decisions. A large number of state court decisions on this subject were excluded because our focus is only on the federal judiciary.[181]

---

[178] A survey of attorneys who represent plaintiffs in employment discrimination disputes found that respondents accepted 5% of the cases in which their legal services were requested. Howard, *supra* n. 76, at 44.

[179] See Bales, *supra* n. 174, at 103–111.

[180] We are influenced by Harry T. Edwards, Alternative Dispute Resolution: Panacea or Anathema?, 99 Harv. L. Rev. 668, 670–672 (1986).

[181] See e.g., *Armendariz v. Found. Health Psychcare Servs., Inc.*, 99 Cal. Rptr. 2d 745 (2000); *Lee v. Tech. Integration Group*, 82 Cal. Rptr. 2d 387 (Ct. App. 1999); *Spellman v. Sec., Annuities & Ins. Servs., Inc.*, 10 Cal.Rptr.2d 427 (Ct. App. 1992); *Bryant v. American Express Fin. Advisors, Inc.*, 595 N.W.2d 482 (Iowa 1999); *Skewes v. Shearson*

- The sample included only decisions involving pre-dispute arbitration agreements with individual employees.[182] This excluded many employment discrimination claims asserted by union-represented employees, in which the employers contended that these claims should be resolved at arbitration.[183] This approach reflects the Supreme Court's repeated statement that unionized employees may pursue employment claims in arbitration and in court.[184] Because these employees have 'two bites at the apple,' they do not face the same dilemma of nonunion employees who are compelled to arbitrate their claims. For nonunion workers, court is not an option unless a judge rules otherwise.
- For a case to be included, a party to a pre-dispute agreement had to oppose arbitration. If an employee voluntarily proceeded to arbitration, his or her case was not included.[185] There is no way

---

Lehman Bros., 829 P.2d 874 (Kan. 1992); *Freeman v. Minolta Bus. Sys., Inc.*, 699 So. 2d 1182 (La. Ct. App. 1997); *Rushton v. Meijer, Inc.* 570 N.W.2d 271 (Mich. Ct. App. 1997) (on remand); *Johnson v. Piper Jaffray, Inc.*, 515 N.W.2d 752 (Minn. Ct. App. 1994); *Rembert v. Ryan's Family Steak Houses, Inc.*, 596 N.W.2d 208 (Mich. Ct. App. 1999); *Kindred v. Second Judicial Dist. Court ex rel. County of Washoe*, 996 P.2d 903 (Nev. 2000); *Quigley v. KPMG Peat Marwick, LLP*, 749 A.2d 405 (N.J. Super. Ct. App. Div. 2000); *Fletcher v. Kidder, Peabody & Co., Inc.*, 584 N.Y.S.2d 838 (N.Y. App. Div. 1992); *Gunby v. Equitable Life Assurance Soc'y of the United States*, 971 S.W.2d 7 (Tenn. Ct. App. 1997); *Pony Express Courier Corp. v. Morris*, 921 S.W.2d 817 (Tex. Ct. App. 1996).

[182] An unusual case in the sample involved a union-represented employee. In *Nelson v. Cyprus Bagdad Copper Corp.*, 119 F.3d 756, 759 (9th Cir. 1997), a worker who received a kidney transplant claimed that his employer violated his ADA rights. The union did not grieve the matter, believing it should be handled as a lawsuit. The employer sued to compel arbitration, but notably for this Article, the basis for this employer motion was an individual agreement – apart from the collective bargaining agreement – to arbitrate discrimination claims. Thus, Nelson was like a nonunion employee who had signed a mandatory arbitration agreement. This case was therefore included in the sample.

[183] See e.g., *Austin v. Owens-Brockway Glass Container, Inc.*, 78 F.3d 875 (4th Cir. 1996).

[184] See *Wright v. Universal Mar. Serv. Corp.*, 525 U.S. 70, 79–82 (1998); *Lingle v. Norge Div. of Magic Chef, Inc.*, 486 U.S. 399, 409–10 (1988); *Alexander v. Gardner-Denver Co.*, 415 U.S. 36, 47 (1974).

[185] There is another close case in the sample. See *Shankle v. B-G Maint. Mgmt. of Colo., Inc.*, 163 F.3d 1230 (10th Cir. 1999) (stating that the plaintiff voluntarily proceeded to arbitrate his claim, without litigating the mandatory arbitration agreement, until a

CHAPTER 18. MANDATORY EMPLOYMENT ARBITRATION

to compare the percentage of cases involving an employee's initial resistance to arbitration, and cases in which employees submit to arbitration and later challenge the arbitrator's award (that is, ruling). The latter is also an emerging type of challenge to mandatory arbitration.[186]

- Cases that occurred before *Gilmer* were included as long as they involved a pre-dispute mandatory arbitration agreement. To use *Gilmer* as a cutoff would be arbitrary because this was not the first Supreme Court decision to deal with employment arbitration.[187] Two surprises resulted from this open-time parameter. First, mandatory employment arbitration has a longer history than is widely recognized.[188] Also, in a few cases the employee moved to compel arbitration, after the employer tried to bypass mandatory arbitration by suing.[189]
- Cases involving public-sector employment were included, although they were rare. *Boyd v. Town of Hayneville*[190] is an example. In *Boyd*, an African American police chief sued after his governmental employer dismissed him.[191] Like the private-sector employees in the sample, Boyd was compelled to sign a pre-dispute arbitration agreement.[192]

---

high down-payment requirement prompted him to contest the enforceability of this contract).

[186] See *Halligan v. Piper Jaffray, Inc.*, 148 F.3d 197 (2nd Cir. 1998); Michael H. LeRoy & Peter Feuille, Private Justice in the Shadow of Public Courts: The Autonomy of Workplace Arbitration Systems, 17 Ohio St. J. on Disp. Res. 19, 57 (2001), available at <www.ilir.uiuc.edu/faculty/images/privatejustice.pdf>. Cases include *Montes v. Shearson Lehman Bros.*, 128 F.3d 1456 (11th Cir. 1997), and *LaPrade v. Kidder, Peabody & Co.*, 94 F. Supp. 2d 2 (D.D.C. 2000).

[187] See *Bernhardt v. Polygraphic Co. of Am.*, 350 U.S. 198 (1956).

[188] For example, *Dickstein v. DuPont*, 443 F.2d 783 (1st Cir. 1971), was decided twenty years before the Supreme Court ruled in Gilmer.

[189] These cases typically involved an apparently successful stockbroker who accepted employment with a rival firm, prompting the former employer to seek an injunction, notwithstanding the contractual requirement to arbitrate employment disputes. See e.g., *Legg, Mason & Co. v. Mackall & Coe, Inc.*, 351 F. Supp. 1367, 1368–1369 (D.D.C. 1972).

[190] 144 F. Supp. 2d 1272 (M.D. Ala. 2001).

[191] *Id.* at 1274.

[192] *Id.*

EMPLOYMENT CLASS AND COLLECTIVE ACTIONS

The sample was generated by using two case-finding methods in Westlaw's online research service. We began with *Gilmer, Circuit City,* and *Green Tree,* and used the 'Table of Authorities' and 'KeyCite' features to identify previous and subsequent cases associated with these milestone decisions. State Court decisions were excluded. Other decisions were disregarded because the litigants involved a union, or one corporation suing another. Many cases remained and ultimately were rejected because they failed in some way to meet the specified criteria.

As cases were included in the sample, they were listed in a roster.[193] The multitasking ability of computers simplified this research. When a potential new case was identified during online research, it was checked against a growing roster of data-coded cases on a simultaneously running word-processing program. This ensured unduplicated additions to the sample.

Data for seventy-eight variables were extracted from each decision. Although these variables are too numerous to list here, they were grouped by (a) year of decision, (b) type of employment, (c) demographic characteristics of the employee, (d) type of legal claim asserted by the party resisting arbitration, (e) legal argument used to resist arbitration, (f) party (employee or employer) who prevailed in district or circuit court, (g) district or circuit court ruling, and (h) length of time to litigate this arbitrability dispute.

This method produced 313 cases. Sixty-two decisions received a positive code for a legal issue titled 'cost of the dispute resolution process.' While some cases in this subsample involved only a cost issue, most raised other issues as well (for example, whether the agreement was an adhesion contract).

18.5 EMPIRICAL RESULTS: HOW FEDERAL COURTS RULE ON COST-ALLOCATION CHALLENGES TO MANDATORY EMPLOYMENT ARBITRATION

Fifty-nine of the sixty-two cost cases involved a federal statutory claim.[194] Title VII was the most common claim (93%), followed by the

---

[193] See *infra* Appendix I. July 31, 2001, is the cutoff date for this sample.
[194] *Caporale v. National Association of Securities Dealers, Inc.,* No. Civ. A. 90-4070, 1991 WL 281890 (D.N.J. May 10, 1991), involved a breach of contract claim, while

CHAPTER 18. MANDATORY EMPLOYMENT ARBITRATION

ADEA (17%) and the Americans with Disabilities Act (ADA) (16%).[195] Among the 251 cases that did not raise a cost issue, the courts in 226 of the cases ruled either to dismiss or to grant a motion to compel arbitration (the others involved a collateral issue). At the District Court level, 118 of 169 decisions (or 73.3%) ordered arbitration, compared to thirty-seven of fifty-seven decisions (or 64.9%) by appellate courts. These results provide a baseline to compare the results for cost cases.

Cost-challenge cases are organized at the end of this article in Tables 18.1–18.3 in reverse chronological order, beginning with 2001 decisions. In some cases, a circuit court citation appears for district court decisions, because the appellate court discusses the outcome of an unreported district court decision.

Table 18.1 lists decisions in which courts rejected cost challenges and ordered enforcement of arbitration agreements. There are two potentially misleading cases. In *Cole*, the court agreed with the plaintiff that his arbitration agreement imposed a prohibitive cost barrier. The court ordered arbitration of his claim, but revised the contract to require the employer to pay all arbitrator fees and process costs.[196] Thus, *Cole* may be confusing. To classify it properly, it must be grouped with courts that order enforcement of arbitration agreements, even though it set a key precedent for upholding cost challenges to mandatory arbitration. *Rosenberg v. Merrill Lynch, Pierce, Fenner & Smith, Inc.*[197] has the same misleading quality.[198] While analyzing Susan Rosenberg's claim that her arbitration was biased, the U.S. Court of Appeals for the First Circuit rejected her cost contention. Nevertheless, *Rosenberg* denied the employer's motion to enforce an arbitration agreement on other grounds and is therefore listed in Table 18.2.[199]

Campbell v. Cantor, Fitzgerald & Co., 21 F. Supp. 2d 341 (S.D.N.Y. 1998), dealt with a defamation claim. *Dowling v. Anthony Crane International*, No. Civ. 1998/127, 2001 WL 378838 (D.V.I. March 20, 2001), did not specify the underlying employment claim.

[195] These figures were computed by excluding the one case with no statistical information.

[196] *Cole v. Burns Int'l Sec. Servs.*, 105 F.3d 1465, 1486 (D.C. Cir. 1997).

[197] 170 F.3d 1 (1st Cir. 1999).

[198] See *infra* notes 282–299.

[199] See e.g., *Bradford v. Rockwell Semiconductor Sys., Inc.*, 238 F.3d 549, 553 (citing *Rosenberg v. Merrill Lynch, Pierce, Fenner & Smith, Inc.*, 170 F.3d 1, 15–16 (1st Cir. 1999) for the holding: 'refusing to invalidate arbitration scheme simply because of the possibility that the arbitrator would charge the plaintiffs a [high] forum fee').

Table 18.1 shows that thirty-seven district decisions and seven appellate decisions ordered a cost-challenger to arbitrate an employment claim. This compares with eleven district and seven appellate decisions in Table 18.2, in which courts found cost challenges persuasive and denied motions to compel arbitration. The latter effectively cleared the way to litigate these employment claims.

Combining outcomes in Tables 18.1 and 18.2, district courts ordered arbitration in 77.1% (thirty-seven of forty-eight) of cost cases. Among appellate cases, only 50% (seven of fourteen) ordered arbitration.[200] There have been too few decisions after *Green Tree* to reach a definitive conclusion about its effect on employment arbitration (see Table 18.3). We note, however, that in the fourteen cases decided after *Green Tree*, eleven (78.6%) upheld cost-shifting provisions. This rate is very similar to the overall rate for enforcement of these provisions (77.1%).

In addition, some preliminary patterns emerged on a circuit-wide basis (counting appellate and district decisions equally in each circuit). The Second,[201] Third,[202] Fourth,[203] Fifth,[204] and D.C.[205] Circuits favored arbitration over litigation in cases in which cost was asserted as an argument against enforcement of these mandatory agreements. In contrast, the First,[206] Sixth,[207] and Tenth[208] Circuits often denied arbitration in cost-challenge cases. The Seventh,[209] Ninth,[210] and Eleventh[211] Circuits had a less consistent pattern of ordering arbitration.

The results also demonstrate the currency of the cost-shifting issue in employment arbitration. Fifty-two cases reported a date of decision. Twenty-five (48.1%) were decided in 2000 or 2001, while thirteen (25%)

---

[200] Forty-three of the sixty-two cases (69.3%) involved direct cost challenges to arbitration agreements.
[201] Nine of nine (100%) cases resulted in an arbitration order.
[202] Six of six (100%) cases resulted in an arbitration order.
[203] Four of four (100%) cases resulted in an arbitration order.
[204] Seven of nine (77.7%) cases resulted in an arbitration order.
[205] Five of six (83.3%) cases resulted in an arbitration order.
[206] Two of two (100%) cases denied a motion for arbitration.
[207] Two of two (100%) cases denied a motion for arbitration.
[208] Five of seven (71.4%) cases denied a motion for arbitration.
[209] Four of six (66.7%) cases resulted in an arbitration order.
[210] Three of five (60%) cases resulted in an arbitration order.
[211] Four of six (66.7%) cases resulted in an arbitration order.

CHAPTER 18. MANDATORY EMPLOYMENT ARBITRATION

were decided in 1999, and five (9.6%) were decided each year in 1998 and 1997.

18.6 APPELLATE DECISIONS ADOPT DIVERGENT THEORIES: FORUM SUBSTITUTION VERSUS COMPARATIVE COST OF LITIGATION

18.6.1 What Is a Cost Case?

Our sample contained three different types of cost decisions. The most common case involved the cost of the arbitrator's fee or the arbitration service. Other cases involved indirect arbitration costs, for example, denial of attorney's fees that a prevailing plaintiff would be awarded in court. These types are now explained.

– *Forum Costs*: Most decisions ruled directly on the cost issue. A plaintiff complained that forum fees (e.g., payment to the arbitration service, or payment for hearings) or the arbitrator's fee were too costly. Leading examples of forum cost cases are analyzed below.
– *Representation Costs*: In some cases cost was embedded in a web of arguments. For instance, some complainants contended that arbitrators were not required to award attorney's fees to prevailing plaintiffs. In *DeGaetano v. Smith Barney, Inc.*,[212] the court vacated part of an arbitration ruling that denied a complainant's motion for attorney's fees. During an early phase of this sex discrimination arbitration, DeGaetano formally applied for recovery of her attorney's fees.[213] When the arbitration panel awarded her USD 90,355 in damages and interest – an amount equal to one year of pay – they effectively ruled that she was a prevailing plaintiff.[214] Nevertheless, they denied her petition for attorney's fees.[215] This amount was not reported, but had to be substantial because the hearing phase of her arbitration lasted ten days.[216]

---

[212] 983 F. Supp. 459 (S.D.N.Y. 1997).
[213] *Id.* at 461.
[214] *Id.*
[215] *Id.*
[216] *Id.*

773

- Her suit to vacate this part of the award relitigated her initial contention that she should not be compelled to arbitrate her Title VII claim.[217] While the court originally did not accept that argument, it did so after DeGaetano provided specific evidence that she suffered too much of a transaction cost by substituting an arbitral forum for court.[218] The judge ordered reimbursement of DeGaetano's attorney's fees.[219]
- *Cost Allocation as Evidence of a Contract*: In a few cases, cost took on a different but still germane complexion. Access was not the issue. Instead, cost allocation was considered as a form of contract consideration. Employers who offered to pay all direct arbitration costs were found by courts to have supplied enough consideration to transform an ADR policy stated in their handbook into a binding contract.

This occurred in *Kreimer v. Delta Faucet Co.*[220] The employee challenged the validity of her arbitration agreement because it was only a policy in a handbook.[221] After the employer sought to enforce this agreement under the FAA, Sue Kreimer argued that she could not be held to this kind of agreement because it lacked consideration.[222] In rejecting this contention, the court observed: 'Delta Faucet's agreement to pay the expenses and fees of mediation and the entire arbitrator's fee in the

---

[217] *Id.* at 460.
[218] See *id.* at 461. The court reasoned:

> Based on the foregoing authority, the Court finds the governing law in this case to be as follows: contractual clauses purporting to mandate arbitration of statutory claims as a condition of employment are enforceable only to the extent that the arbitration preserves the substantive protections and remedies afforded by the statute; in other words, only if a plaintiff pursuing claims under the statute effectively may vindicate [his or her] statutory cause of action in the arbitral forum.

Id. at 468–469 (alteration in original) (citations omitted).
[219] See *id.* at 470–471.
[220] No. IP99-1507-C, 2000 WL 962817 (S.D. Ind. June 2, 2000).
[221] *Id.* at 1. While Sue Kreimer was employed by Delta Faucet, the company gave every employee a copy of its Corporate Dispute Resolution Policy. This included a detailed explanation of the arbitration process that was being substituted for an employee's right to sue in an employment dispute. *Id.*
[222] *Id.* at 2.

CHAPTER 18. MANDATORY EMPLOYMENT ARBITRATION

event of arbitration, demonstrate a detriment to Delta Faucet that can constitute consideration.'[223]

In contrast, the court in *Dumais v. America Golf Corp.*[224] refused to enforce a waitress's arbitration agreement because it was vague and illusory.[225] The court reasoned: 'The agreement binds Plaintiff to arbitration, but allows AGC free rein to renege. This lopsided arrangement is illusory because it allows AGC to unilaterally modify the terms at any time.'[226] In pertinent part, the arbitration agreement was not enforced because the employer could change the cost-shifting provision at any time to its sole advantage.[227]

18.6.2 Appeals Courts that Accept Cost Arguments: Forum Substitution Theory and Lower-Wage Workers

At the outset of this and the following section, background is provided for the terms 'lower-wage workers' and 'higher-wage employees.' Although there are only a few appellate cases on cost challenges to arbitration, they are divided by an employee's pay. The lower-wage worker cases involved a train station security guard, an airport security guard, and a former janitor who was promoted to crew

---

[223] *Id.* at 3.
[224] 150 F. Supp. 2d 1182 (D.N.M. 2001), aff'd, 299 F.3d 1216 (10th Cir. 2002).
[225] Judge Martha Vazquez reasoned:

> [The court] forum to resolve disputes is a fundamental right that may not be relinquished without consideration. In the case of an arbitration agreement unsupported by consideration, issues surrounding the method of dispute resolution must be clear, unequivocal and apply mutually to both sides before that agreement may be enforced. The alleged arbitration agreement in this case was ambiguous, illusory, not mutual, and unsupported by consideration. For these reasons, the alleged arbitration agreement is unenforceable. Plaintiff should not be compelled to arbitrate her claims brought herein.

Id. at 1194.
[226] *Id.* at 1193.
[227] See *id.* at 1189–1190. The court was presented with an out-of-date set of AAA procedures (dated 1989) that required the filing party to pay a nonrefundable administrative fee of USD 300 and USD 75 for any additional hearing. Thus, the agreement likely failed to reflect the cost of arbitration to Teresita Dumais. *Id.*

supervisor. These decisions invalidated cost-shifting provisions in arbitration agreements. Yet, in higher-wage employee cases – involving a financial consultant and a securities trader – courts upheld cost-shifting contracts.

These terms are imprecise. As the first appellate court to rule on this issue, the *Cole* court adopted this terminology:

> Litigation has become a less-than-ideal method of resolving employees' public law claims.... Employees bringing public law claims in court must endure long waiting periods as governing agencies and the overburdened court system struggle to find time to properly investigate and hear the complaint. Moreover, the average profile of employee litigants... indicates that lower-wage workers may not fare as well as higher-wage professionals in the litigation system; lower-wage workers are less able to afford the time required to pursue a court complaint, and are less likely to receive large monetary relief from juries.[228]

President Clinton's Dunlop Commission, appointed to study alternative forms of workplace dispute resolution, introduced these labels.[229]

18.6.2.1 The U.S. Court of Appeals for the D.C. Circuit: Cole v. Burns International Security Services

The plaintiff was employed as a security guard at Union Station in Washington, D.C. when he was discharged.[230] In 1991, Burns Security required Clinton Cole and other employees to sign a 'Pre-Dispute Resolution Agreement' as a condition of employment.[231] The agreement expressly waived an employee's right to litigate a dispute related to his or her employment, and designated the American Arbitration

---

[228] *Cole v. Burns Int'l Sec. Servs.*, 105 F.3d 1465, 1488 (D.C. Cir. 1997) (quoting Commission on the Future of Worker-Mgmt. Relations, U.S. Dep't of Labor & U.S. Department of Commerce, Report and Recommendations 30 (1994).

[229] The third question that the Commission answered was: '3. What (if anything) should be done to increase the extent to which work-place problems are directly resolved by the parties themselves, rather than [by seeking remedies in] state and federal courts and governmental bodies?' Comm'n on the Future of Worker -Mgmt. Relations, *supra* n. 228, at xvi.

[230] Cole, 105 F.3d at 1469.

[231] *Id.*

CHAPTER 18. MANDATORY EMPLOYMENT ARBITRATION

Association as a service provider. It also stated that Burns would not provide employment unless Cole signed this agreement.[232]

Cole signed the form and remained employed until he was fired in October 1993.[233] He filed a complaint with the Equal Employment Opportunity Commission (EEOC), and in his subsequent lawsuit alleged racial discrimination, harassment, and unlawful retaliation for protecting a co-worker from sexual harassment.[234] In federal district court, his employer moved to compel arbitration of the dispute.[235] The court granted this motion and rejected Cole's numerous arguments to invalidate the arbitration agreement.[236]

The D.C. Circuit rejected Cole's contention that his type of employment was excluded from the FAA[237] before it ruled on his cost argument. Judge Harry T. Edwards's attention was drawn to the AAA's cost-allocation rules that governed Cole's agreement to arbitrate his discrimination claim.[238] These required the parties to share equally in paying arbitrator fees that ranged from USD 500–1000 or more per day.[239]

The court found that this fee allocation system created an unreasonable barrier for Cole. Judge Edwards stated that 'an employee

---

[232] *Id.*
[233] *Id.* at 1469–1470.
[234] *Id.*
[235] *Id.* at 1470.
[236] *Id.*
[237] The court rejected Cole's contention that Section 1 of the FAA excluded his employment. *Id.* He believed that his employment fell within the elastic clause of this section stating 'any other class of workers engaged in foreign or interstate commerce.' *Id.* By his reasoning, this term applied to all workers whose jobs have any effect on commerce. *Id.* The Cole court dismissed this argument, however, because it would ignore the specific inclusion of seamen and railroad workers in the main body of this exclusionary section. *Id.* The court explained that Section 1 'covers only those workers actually involved in the "flow" of commerce, i.e., those workers responsible for the transportation and distribution of goods.' *Id.* at 1472.
[238] See *id.* at 1480. Rule 35 required a filing fee of USD 500 from the initiating party, as well as an administrative fee of USD 150 per hearing day from each party. *Id.* The rule also allowed AAA to 'defer or reduce' this fee 'in the event of extreme hardship on any party.' *Id.* Rule 36 required both parties to share equally in paying the expenses of the arbitration, including travel and other expenses of the arbitrator, AAA representatives, and witnesses. *Id.* Rule 37 bound the parties to agree to pay the arbitrator appropriate compensation for his or her work. *Id.*
[239] *Id.*

cannot be required as a condition of employment to waive access to a neutral forum in which statutory employment discrimination claims may be heard.'[240] He reasoned that these procedural rights must

(1) provide for neutral arbitrators,
(2) allow for more than minimal discovery,
(3) require a written award,
(4) afford all the types of relief that would otherwise be available in court, and
(5) protect employees from unreasonable costs.[241]

All of these conditions were satisfied in Cole's arbitration agreement, except for cost protection. In contrast to Robert Gilmer's arbitration agreement,[242] this contract obligated Cole to submit his statutory claims to arbitration and then required him to pay a substantial part of the arbitrator's fees. Judge Edwards noted that under New York Stock Exchange (NYSE) or National Association of Securities Dealers (NASD) arbitration, employees may be required to pay a filing fee, expenses, or an administrative fee, but these expenses are routinely waived in the event of financial hardship.[243]

This comparison led him to conclude that the Supreme Court would not approve a cost allocation provision that was more expensive than the one approved in *Gilmer*.[244] In a pointed conclusion, he stated: 'Indeed, we are unaware of any situation in American jurisprudence in which a beneficiary of a federal statute has been required to pay for the services of the judge assigned to hear her or his case.'[245] Because *Gilmer* held that 'arbitration is supposed to be a reasonable substitute for a judicial forum,'[246] Congress could not have intended to require employees to arbitrate employment discrimination claims and 'pay for the services of an arbitrator when they would never be required to pay for a judge in court.'[247]

---

[240] *Id.* at 1482.
[241] See *id.*
[242] Judge Edwards observed that 'under NYSE Rules and NASD Rules ... employers pay ... all of the arbitrators' fees.' *Id.* at 1483.
[243] *Id.* at 1483–1484.
[244] See *id.* at 1484.
[245] *Id.*
[246] *Id.*
[247] *Id.* Applying its theory of forum substitution to the facts, the Cole court found that AAA's fees were too costly for the plaintiff. See *id.*

CHAPTER 18. MANDATORY EMPLOYMENT ARBITRATION

18.6.2.2 The U.S. Court of Appeals for the Tenth Circuit: Shankle v. B-G Maintenance Management of Colorado, Inc.

B-G Maintenance employed the plaintiff as a janitor beginning in 1987.[248] In 1995, the company distributed an arbitration agreement to Matthew Shankle and other employees.[249] At first he refused to sign, but ultimately he acquiesced.[250] Under the agreement, employees waived their right to sue for a variety of employment discrimination claims.[251] It also obligated Shankle to 'be responsible for one-half of the arbitrator's fees. . . . If I am unable to pay my share, the company will advance the entirety of the arbitrator's fees; however, I will remain liable for my one-half.'[252]

After the company ended Shankle's employment, he filed a race and age discrimination complaint with the EEOC.[253] When the agency did not sue on his behalf, Shankle and the company referred the dispute to the Judicial Arbiter Group, Inc., as specified by the agreement.[254]

Judicial Arbiter Group wrote to the parties, stating that ' "the arbiter charges $250.00 per each hour of arbiter time and travel time at $125.00 per hour, and where appropriate, $45.00 for each hour of paralegal support time." '[255] Both parties were also directed to pay a USD 6,000 deposit.[256]

Shankle filed a separate charge with the EEOC, this time objecting to his upcoming arbitration. He then canceled the arbitration and sued on his employment discrimination claims. The District Court denied B-G Maintenance's motion to compel arbitration, and the company appealed.[257]

---

[248] *Shankle v. B-G Maintenance Mgmt. of Colorado, Inc.*, 163 F.3d 1230–1231 (10th Cir. 1999).
[249] *Id.* at 1232.
[250] *Id.*
[251] *Id.*
[252] *Id.*
[253] *Id.*
[254] *Id.*
[255] *Id.* (quoting Letter from Judicial Arbiter Group, Inc. to parties).
[256] *Id.*
[257] See *id.*

The appellate court considered only the cost issue.[258] Noting that *Gilmer* stated that an individual does not forgo discrimination rights by submitting that claim to arbitration,[259] the court concluded that the ADR forum must provide an adequate mechanism for furthering public policy goals advanced by the statute.[260] While the Tenth Circuit agreed that a strong national policy favors arbitration, it qualified this view:

> As *Gilmer* emphasized, arbitration of statutory claims works because potential litigants have an adequate forum in which to resolve their statutory claims and because the broader social purposes behind the statute are adhered to. This supposition, falls apart, however, if the terms of an arbitration agreement actually prevent an individual from effectively vindicating his or her statutory rights.[261]

Examining the facts, the Tenth Circuit assumed an average length of time for Shankle's arbitration, and estimated that his share of arbitrator fees would cost between USD 1,875 and USD 5,000.[262] Because (as noted in the introduction)

> Shankle could not afford such a fee...the Agreement thus placed Mr. Shankle between the proverbial rock and a hard place – it prohibited use of the judicial forum, where a litigant is not required to pay for a judge's services, and the prohibitive cost substantially limited use of the arbitral forum.[263]

---

[258] See *id.* at 1233 (stating the issue as whether 'a mandatory arbitration agreement, which is entered into as a condition of continued employment, and which requires an employee to pay a portion of the arbitrator's fees, [is] unenforceable under the Federal Arbitration Act').

[259] *Id.* at 1234 (' "So long as the prospective litigant effectively may vindicate [his or her] statutory cause of action in the arbitral forum, the statute will continue to serve both its remedial and deterrent function." ') (quoting *Gilmer v. Interstate/Johnson Lane Corp.*, 500 U.S. 20, 28 (1991)).

[260] See *id.*

[261] *Id.* (citations omitted).

[262] *Id.* at 1234 n. 5 (stating that the typical employment case averages between fifteen and forty hours of an arbitrator's time).

[263] *Id.* at 1234–1235. B-G Maintenance also argued that the court should enforce the agreement because it allowed fee-shifting for employees unable to pay their share of arbitrator fees. The court disagreed, noting that B-G Maintenance only agreed to advance the employee's share of fees. The employee remained liable for this payment. *Id.* at 1234 n. 4.

Ultimately, the Tenth Circuit concluded that the company required Shankle to agree to mandatory arbitration as a term of continued employment, 'yet failed to provide an accessible forum in which he could resolve his statutory rights. Such a result clearly undermines the remedial and deterrent functions of the federal anti-discrimination laws.'[264]

18.6.2.3 The U.S. Court of Appeals for the Eleventh Circuit: Perez v. Globe Airport Security Services, Inc.

Damiana Perez, a gate security agent at the Miami International Airport, signed a pre-dispute employment arbitration agreement.[265] It had several cost-allocation provisions. Each party agreed 'to pay the costs and attorney's fees to the other party in the event of a breach of this agreement.'[266] The contract also bound Perez to this promise: 'If you refuse to arbitrate after the Company has demanded you do so, and if a court orders arbitration, you agree to pay the Company's legal costs, including attorney's fees, incurred in enforcing this agreement.'[267] The contract added:

> The Company and you agree that, despite any rule providing that any one party must bear the cost of filing and/or the arbitrator's fees, all costs of the American Arbitration Association and all fees imposed by any arbitrator hearing the dispute, will be shared equally between you and the Company.[268]

After Globe discharged Perez, she filed a sex discrimination lawsuit. Globe moved to compel arbitration of her claim. The district court ruled that the fee-sharing provision created an unreasonable cost barrier to Perez's adjudication of Title VII claims. Thus, the district court denied Globe's motion to compel arbitration.

The Eleventh Circuit affirmed this ruling.[269] Globe contended that because Perez failed to show that she would incur prohibitive expenses by pursuing arbitration, her cost challenge was too indefinite under

---

[264] *Id.* at 1235.
[265] *Perez v. Globe Airport Sec. Servs., Inc.*, 253 F.3d 1280, 1282 (11th Cir. 2001).
[266] *Id.*
[267] *Id.*
[268] *Id.*
[269] See *id.* at 1287.

Green Tree.[270] Globe also stated that arbitration would not be prohibitively expensive because the company was willing to forgo use of the American Arbitration Association in favor of less expensive arbitration.[271] The Eleventh Circuit sidestepped these arguments by reasoning that 'this court need not determine whether the evidence of arbitration expense produced by Perez was sufficient to find arbitration prohibitively expensive... [because] the Agreement is illegal and unenforceable for other compelling reasons.'[272]

These reasons still pertained to allocation of arbitration costs. The court noted that even though Perez unambiguously waived her right to sue, the agreement could not limit the arbitrator's authority to award a prevailing plaintiff attorney's fees.[273] In addition, the court found the contract's cost-shifting provision unlawful.[274]

Globe's sloppy or devious drafting of the contract also played a part in the court's decision. The agreement stated that all disputes must be "arbitrated... in accordance with the rules of the American Arbitration Association governing labor arbitration."[275] The court noted that AAA rules governing labor arbitration are separate and distinct from the rules governing employment disputes.[276] Under labor arbitration rules, the parties could agree to 'vary the procedures set forth in these rules.'[277] In contrast, Rule 34(e) for AAA's employment arbitration permits an arbitrator 'to assess fees, expenses, and compensation... in favor of any party,' but does not allow the parties to bargain any limitation on this authority.[278]

Without deciding how this discrepancy occurred, the court rejected Globe's suggestion to sever this provision and enforce the rest of the agreement.[279] Instead, it ruled that the entire agreement

---

[270] See *id.* at 1284.
[271] *Id.* at 1284 n. 2
[272] *Id.* at 1285.
[273] See *id.* at 1285–1286.
[274] See *id.* at 1287. This provision stated, 'Despite any rule providing that any one party must bear the cost of filing and/or the arbitrator's fees, all costs of the American Arbitration Association and all fees imposed by any arbitrator hearing the dispute, will be shared equally between you and the Company.' *Id.* at 1282.
[275] *Id.* at 1286 (alteration in original) (quoting contract language).
[276] *Id.*
[277] *Id.*
[278] *Id.* at 1286 and n. 3.
[279] See *id.* at 1287.

CHAPTER 18. MANDATORY EMPLOYMENT ARBITRATION

was unenforceable.[280] Its reasoning suggested, nonetheless, that the court was suspicious about how Globe interpolated AAA's labor arbitration procedures:

> If an employer could rely on the courts to sever an unlawful provision and compel the employee to arbitrate, the employer would have an incentive to include unlawful provisions in its arbitration agreements. Such provisions could deter an unknowledgeable employee from initiating arbitration, even if they would ultimately not be enforced. It would also add an expensive procedural step to prosecuting a claim; the employee would have to request a court to declare a provision unlawful and sever it before initiating arbitration. Including an unlawful provision would cost the employer little, particularly where, as here, the arbitration agreement provides the employee must bear the employer's court costs and attorney's fees incurred defending the agreement if arbitration is challenged and the employer prevails.[281]

18.6.3 Appeals Courts that Reject Cost Arguments: Comparative Cost of Litigation Theory and Higher-Wage Employees

18.6.3.1 The U.S. Court of Appeals for the First Circuit: Rosenberg v. Merrill Lynch, Pierce, Fenner & Smith, Inc.

Susan Rosenberg sued Merrill Lynch after the company terminated her employment as a financial consultant.[282] Responding to her suit alleging sex and age discrimination, Merrill Lynch moved to compel arbitration of her claims.[283] Rosenberg replied with a series of challenges to the securities industry's use of mandatory arbitration.[284] The district

---

[280] See id.

[281] Id.

[282] Rosenberg v. Merrill Lynch, Pierce, Fenner & Smith, Inc., 170 F.3d 1, 5 (1st Cir. 1999).

[283] Id.

[284] See id. at 5–6, 12, 16. Before the district court, Rosenberg contended that (1) Title VII, as amended by the 1991 Civil Rights Act, prohibits pre-dispute arbitration agreements, id. at 6–7, 9; (2) pre-dispute arbitration agreements to arbitrate ADEA claims are precluded by the Older Workers Benefit Protection Act (OWBPA), id. at 12; (3) the New York Stock Exchange's arbitration system is structurally biased, id. at 6; (4) the securities industry registration form, incorporating the

783

court denied the company's motion on two grounds. It found that the 1991 Civil Rights Act amendments to Title VII precluded enforcement of these employment arbitration agreements.[285] Also, the court believed that the arbitral forum made available to Rosenberg had 'structural bias.'[286]

The First Circuit affirmed the lower court's denial of the company's motion to compel arbitration, but for a different reason.[287] Disagreeing with the district court, it held that an arbitration agreement applied to ADEA and Title VII claims is not precluded by the Older Workers Benefit Protection Act (OWBPA, amending the ADEA),[288] or by the 1991 Civil Rights Act (amending Title VII).[289] The First Circuit also disagreed with the district court's conclusion that the agreement was unenforceable because of structural bias in the securities industry arbitration forum.[290] But in a key ruling the appellate court affirmed the lower court's order because the particular arbitration agreement signed by Rosenberg did not meet a standard set forth in the 1991 Civil Rights Amendment.[291]

---

arbitration agreement, is an adhesion contract, *id.* at 16 (the district court did not rule on this contention); and (5) the arbitration agreement does not meet the standard set forth in the 1991 Civil Rights Act for enforcing arbitration clauses, *id.* at 16–19.

[285] *Id.* at 4, 6.
[286] *Id.*
[287] *Id.*
[288] Older Workers Benefit Protection Act, 29 U.S.C. 621, 623, 626, 630 (2000); see Rosenberg, 170 F.3d at 13.
[289] See *id.* at 11.
[290] See *id.* at 14–16.
[291] See *id.* at 19. On this point, the court observed that the

> arbitration agreement did not by itself 'define the range of claims subject to arbitration, even though Merrill Lynch expressly represented that she would be advised of the rules. It referred only to arbitration of such claims as were required to be arbitrated by the NYSE rules. But those rules were not given to Rosenberg or described to her.

Id. The court continued: 'The question then becomes which party should bear the risk of her ignorance. Given Congress' concern that agreements to arbitrate employment discrimination claims should be enforced only where "appropriate," a concern not expressed in the FAA or at common law, Merrill Lynch should, we believe, bear that risk.' *Id.*

CHAPTER 18. MANDATORY EMPLOYMENT ARBITRATION

For this article's analysis of cost barriers to employment arbitration, the First Circuit's decision is potentially misleading. While addressing Rosenberg's claim that the Merrill Lynch arbitral forum was biased, the court considered whether cost was a prohibitive barrier. It concluded that cost was not a problem, and this part of the decision is isolated and cited by other courts that reach similar conclusions on cost issues.[292]

Our analysis focuses only on the *Rosenberg* court's treatment of cost as a barrier to arbitration. To be clear, on this point the court found that the arbitration system had no legal defect. Rosenberg and *amici briefs* presented two cost arguments to the court. They contended that the New York Stock Exchange's arbitration procedures were inadequate for Title VII claims because arbitrators often refuse to award statutory attorney's fees, and because arbitration panels often require complainants to pay some or all of the forum fees.[293] She noted that these fees can reach USD 3,000 per day and tens of thousands of dollars per case.[294] She reasoned that these costs unlawfully interfered with her right to vindicate her statutory rights.[295]

The court roundly dismissed these arguments. First, it said that just because 'arbitrators may sometimes do undesirable things in individual cases does not mean the arbitral system is structurally inadequate.'[296] The court's point was that NYSE rules do not require arbitrators to order complainants to pay forum fees. Thus, the cost-sharing aspect of Rosenberg's argument failed because 'such outcomes [are not] necessary concomitants of the NYSE arbitral system.'[297] Second, the court reached a preliminary conclusion 'that it does not appear to be the usual situation that a plaintiff is asked to bear forum fees.'[298]

---

[292] See e.g., *Bradford v. Rockwell Semiconductor Sys., Inc.*, 238 F.3d 549, 553 (4th Cir. 2001) (citing Rosenberg in the context of 'refusing to invalidate arbitration scheme simply because of the possibility that the arbitrator would charge the plaintiffs a [high] forum fee').

[293] Rosenberg, 170 F.3d at 15.

[294] *Id.*

[295] *Id.*

[296] *Id.*

[297] *Id.*

[298] *Id.* The record before the court was not extensively developed on this point. Amicus briefs 'in support of Rosenberg cited arbitration decisions in which plaintiffs... [were] required to pay costs.' *Id.* at 15–16. Merrill Lynch disagreed, pointing out that in 'the thirty-three arbitration cases Rosenberg placed in the record, only one plaintiff who prevailed on statutory grounds was denied fees and costs.' *Id.* at 16.

Finally, the court stated that 'contrary to Rosenberg's arguments, arbitration is often far more affordable to plaintiffs and defendants alike than is pursuing a claim in court.'[299]

This last reason amounted to a theoretical justification and was not the product of a factual comparison. Like the *Cole* court, this court measured the affordability of arbitration by comparison to litigation. However, while the *Cole* court only compared arbitration costs to filing fees imposed by a court, the *Rosenberg* court looked at the overall costs of litigation.

18.6.3.2 The U.S. Court of Appeals for the Seventh Circuit: Koveleskie v. SBC Capital Markets, Inc.

After Mary Koveleskie resigned her job as a securities trader, she claimed that she was constructively discharged following a pattern of discrimination. Eventually, she sued under Title VII, the Equal Pay Act,[300] and the New York Human Rights Law[301] for sexual discrimination and harassment, wage discrimination, and retaliation. She also sought to invalidate her mandatory arbitration agreement.

The district refused to compel arbitration of her claims, and SBC appealed. In reversing this ruling, the Seventh Circuit considered a variety of issues, including her two cost-barrier arguments. She claimed that securities industry arbitrators routinely fail to follow Title VII's provision for awarding attorney's fees to prevailing plaintiffs. She also alleged that arbitrators charge plaintiffs expensive forum fees.

The court sidestepped this argument by stating that 'NYSE arbitrators possess discretion to award costs and fees when they decide a dispute.' *Id.* The court also seemed to rely more heavily on interpretive guidance taken from Gilmer and Cole and other authorities. See *id.* (endorsing the view that "the NYSE rules applicable here do not restrict the types of relief an arbitrator may award," and further noting that '"generally, parties to an arbitration are responsible for their personal costs associated with bringing or defending an arbitration action"' (quoting *Gilmer v. Interstate/Johnson Lane Corp.*, 500 U.S. 20, 32 (1991))).

[299] Rosenberg, 170 F.3d at 16 (stating that, although arbitration discovery 'procedures might not be as extensive as in the federal courts, by agreeing to arbitrate, a party "trades the procedures and opportunity for review of the courtroom for the simplicity, informality, and expedition of arbitration"' (quoting *Gilmer*, 500 U.S. at 31)).

[300] N.Y. Lab. Law 194 (McKinney 2002).

[301] N.Y. Exec. Law 290 (McKinney 1996).

Without engaging in its own analysis, the Seventh Circuit rejected these contentions by citing *Rosenberg* and *Cole* at length.[302] A more recent decision, *McCaskill v. SCI Management Corp.*,[303] conflicted with this approach but did not expressly overrule it.

18.6.4 Appeals Courts that Use a Case-by-Case Approach to Cost Arguments

The most recent appellate decisions take an approach that differs from the forum substitution and comparative-cost theories. These two courts adopted a case-by-case methodology for deciding cost-allocation challenges.

18.6.4.1 The U.S. Court of Appeals for the Fourth Circuit: *Bradford v. Rockwell Semiconductor Systems, Inc.*

The *Bradford* court adopted a case-by-case approach to determine whether fee-splitting renders an agreement unenforceable. The court

---

[302] *Kovaleskie v. SBC Capital Mkts., Inc.*, 167 F.3d 361, 364–365 (7th Cir. 1999). The Seventh Circuit quoted from Roseberg extensively: (1) although ' "arbitrators may...do undesirable things in individual cases does not mean that the arbitral system is inadequate,"' (2) '"it does not appear to be the usual situation that a plaintiff is asked to bear forum fees,"' (3) '"if unreasonable fees were to be imposed on a particular employee, the argument that this was inconsistent with the 1991 Civil [Rights] Act could be presented by the employee to the reviewing court,"' (4) '"arbitration is often more affordable to plaintiffs and defendants than litigating a claim in court,"' and (5) '"under NYSE and NASD rules...employers [generally]...pay all of the arbitrators' fees."' *Id.* (quoting Rosenberg, 170 F.3d at 15–16).

[303] 285 F.3d 623 (7th Cir. 2002) (involving an employee's Title VII claim against her employer). McCaskell did not raise the issue of allocation of direct forum costs. However, it involved the related matter of attorney's fees. The arbitration agreement prevented Gloria McCaskill from ever recovering her attorney's fees, even if the arbitrator ruled in her favor. *Id.* at 624. This departed from the litigation model in which the judicial norm is to order employers to pay the attorney's fees of prevailing Title VII plaintiffs. The Seventh Circuit agreed with McCaskill's contention that such an arrangement undermined the deterrent function of Title VII: 'The right to attorney's fees therefore is integral to the purposes of the statute and often is central to the ability of persons to seek redress from violations of Title VII.' *Id.* at 626. Thus, the agreement was held to be unenforceable.

rejected a broad per se rule against all fee-splitting,[304] and stated instead that the 'appropriate inquiry is one that evaluates whether the arbitral forum in a particular case is an adequate and accessible substitute to litigation (i.e., a case-by-case analysis that focuses, among other things, upon the claimant's ability to pay the arbitration fees and costs, the expected cost differential between arbitration and litigation in court, and whether that cost differential is so substantial as to deter the bringing of claims).'[305] The court found that Bradford failed to prove he was unable to pay or that he was deterred from arbitration, because he had initiated arbitration before litigation and proceeded through a full arbitration hearing on the merits of his claim.[306] It also relied upon evidence that, prior to his discharge, he earned a salary of USD 115,000 in addition to yearly bonuses.[307]

18.6.4.2 The U.S. Court of Appeals for the Third Circuit: Blair v. Scott Specialty Gases

A female employee sued her employer for sexual harassment in *Blair*. She claimed financial inability to pay for arbitration, but did not present specific evidence to support her assertion. The Third Circuit rejected her position that 'the mere existence of a fee-splitting provision in an agreement would satisfy the claimant's burden to prove the likelihood of incurring prohibitive costs.'[308] Nevertheless, the court remanded the matter to the district court for further inquiry into Blair's affidavit of her limited financial capacity. The court offered this guidance: 'Limited discovery into the rates charged by the AAA and the approximate length of similar arbitration proceedings should adequately establish the costs of arbitration, and give Blair the opportunity to prove... that resort to arbitration would deny her a forum to vindicate her statutory rights.'[309]

---

[304] *Bradford v. Rockwell Semiconductor Sys., Inc.*, 238 F.3d 549, 556 (4th Cir. 2001).
[305] *Id.*
[306] *Id.* at 558.
[307] *Id.* at 558 n. 6.
[308] *Blair v. Scott Specialty Gases*, 283 F.3d 595, 610 (3rd Cir. 2002).
[309] *Id.*

18.7 CONCLUSIONS

Our research results shed new light on emergent judicial regulation of mandatory employment arbitration. On the academic ledger, most research condemns or seriously questions this dispute resolution method. Considering that employers require this ADR process as a condition of employment, do not engage in any real bargaining, and curtail employee access to courts, these critical views have merit. On the judicial ledger, however, numerous arbitrability decisions intone that 'there is a strong public policy favoring arbitration'[310] to convey the message that courts should approve this ADR method. In short, academic and judicial assessments seem far apart.

But the empirical picture we develop here suggests that these portraits miss a new and intermediate evolutionary step in judicial regulation of employment arbitration. While courts broadly approve this ADR method, they are willing to deny enforcement of contracts that create access barriers for employees. Our research shows that cost allocation is a specific issue that is now fertile for resisting arbitration. Turning to our findings, which we emphasize are preliminary, we answer the following questions:

- What is the significance of the rapid growth of cost-shifting cases? The rapid growth of cost-shifting cases does more than suggest the currency of this issue. It confirms that mandatory employment arbitration is becoming widespread, and more importantly, has great variety. The rapid growth of these cases also shows that the Supreme Court's strong pronouncements in favor of ordering arbitration are not the final word on this subject. Resourceful plaintiffs' lawyers are exploiting *Gilmer*'s isolated observation that arbitration is just a difference in dispute resolution forum,[311] and appear to be arguing that the

---

[310] *McCaskill v. SCI Management Corp.*, No. 00-C-1543, 2000 WL 875396, at 6 (N.D. Ill. June 22, 2000). See e.g., *Alford v. Dean Witter Reynolds, Inc.*, 905 F.2d 104, 105, 107 (5th Cir. 1990); *Prevot v. Phillips Petroleum Co.*, 133 F. Supp. 2d 937, 938 (S.D. Tex. 2001); *Fuller v. Pep Boys – Manny, Moe & Jack of Del., Inc.*, 88 F. Supp. 2d 1158, 1161 (D. Colo. 2000); *Quinn v. EMC Corp.*, 109 F. Supp. 2d 681, 683 (S.D. Tex. 2000); *Cline v. H.E. Butt Grocery Co.*, 79 F. Supp. 2d 730, 732 (S.D. Tex. 1999); *Heller v. MC Fin. Servs., Ltd.*, No. 97-CIV.-5317, 1998 WL 190288, at 2 (S.D.N.Y. Apr. 21, 1998); *Gaylor v. Donald B. MacNeal, Inc.*, No. 95-C-7250, 1996 WL 224566, at 2 (N.D. Ill. May 1, 1996).
[311] *Gilmer v. Interstate/Johnson Lane Corp.*, 500 U.S. 20, 28 (1991).

private arbitration forum should be no more costly for plaintiffs than the public law forum. Our research also shows that this reasoning resonates with a visible minority of courts who perceive *Gilmer* as permitting nothing more than forum substitution, and as a result, are inclined to invalidate cost-sharing provisions or entire employment arbitration agreements.
- What is the significance of the variation in court orders that compel arbitration? Our findings imply that the textual edifice supporting mandatory employment arbitration has noticeable cracks. As the first appellate tribunal to analyze the cost-shifting issue, the *Cole* court doubted that employment arbitration provides the same safeguards as the labor-management model for ordinary workers.[312]

---

[312] See *Cole v. Burns Int'l Sec. Servs.*, 105 F.3d 1465, 1473–1479 (D.C. Cir. 1997). Judge Edwards noted, for example, that 'in the context of collective bargaining arbitration, there are also unique protections for both parties built into the arbitration process that minimize the risk of unfairness or error by the arbitrator.' *Id.* at 1475. He observed that

> because both unions and employers are repeat customers of arbitration and have a hand in selecting the arbitrator to hear their disputes, arbitrators who regularly favor one side or the other will not be hired again. As a result, arbitrators have a strong personal interest in crafting awards that will be respected as fair by both parties regardless of who wins or loses the particular dispute.

Id. He also believed that employment arbitration was more problematic 'because the structural protections inherent in the collective bargaining context are not duplicated in cases involving mandatory arbitration of individual statutory claims.' *Id.* at 1476. He observed that 'unlike the labor case, in which both union and employer are regular participants in the arbitration process, only the employer is a repeat player in cases involving individual statutory claims. As a result, the employer gains some advantage in having superior knowledge with respect to selection of an arbitrator.' *Id.*

Judge Edwards left no doubt that he regarded mandatory arbitration with suspicion: 'Mandatory arbitration agreements in individual employees' contracts often are presented on a take-it-or-leave-it basis; there is no union to negotiate the terms of the arbitration arrangement. Thus, employers are free to structure arbitration in ways that may systematically disadvantage employees.' *Id.* at 1477. He cited a litany of actual and potential problems, including (1) 'there is no organization [like a] union to represent employee interests in developing arbitration procedures,' (2) the employer and its lawyers have a freer hand in drafting arbitration provision, (3) 'some employers may seek to...narrow the legal rights of employees in the

CHAPTER 18. MANDATORY EMPLOYMENT ARBITRATION

Courts are sensitive to the claimant's ability to pay and, by implication, to his or her type of job.[313] When an employee holds a low-paying job, judges are more likely to sever a cost-allocation provision and order arbitration,[314] or void the agreement and deny enforcement of it.[315] Conversely, if a case involves a professional employee, the cost-allocation

---

arbitration clause,' and (4) employers may shield themselves from intrusive discovery and also punitive damages. *Id.* Finally, he specifically worried that 'a company might impose a requirement that the employee pay the fees for an arbitrator's time in order to discourage or prevent employees from bringing a claim.' *Id.*

[313] Courts that have refused to enforce cost-shifting provisions have explicitly based their rulings on evidence that plaintiffs were too poor to afford arbitrator fees. The Cole court stated:

> There is no indication in AAA's rules that an arbitrator's fees may be reduced or waived in cases of financial hardship. These fees would be prohibitively expensive for an employee like Cole, especially after being fired from his job, and it is unacceptable to require Cole to pay arbitrators' fees, because such fees are unlike anything that he would have to pay to pursue his statutory claims in court.

Cole, 105 F.3d at 1484. In *Perez v. Globe Airport Security Services, Inc.*, 253 F.3d 1280 (11th Cir. 2001), the court found: 'Here, the arbitration agreement expressly provides that the parties must share the fees and costs of arbitration equally, and Perez produced evidence of her income and the costs of arbitration before the district court to prove those costs would inhibit her from pursuing her claims.' *Perez v. Globe Airport Sec. Servs., Inc.*, 253 F.3d 1280, 1285 (11th Cir. 2001). The district court in Shankle concluded that 'the agreement's requirement that Shankle assume responsibility for one-half of the arbitrator's fees operates as a disincentive to his submitting a discrimination claim to arbitration. Moreover, Shankle testified that he could not afford the fees.' *Shankle v. B-G Maint. Mgmt. of Colo.*, No. 96-N-2932, 1997 WL 416405, at 4 (D. Colo. Mar. 24, 1997). The appeals court agreed: 'Mr. Shankle could not afford such a fee, and it is unlikely other similarly situated employees could either.' *Shankle v. B-G Maint. Mgmt. of Colo., Inc.*, 163 F.3d 1230, 1234–1235 (10th Cir. 1999). The court also concluded that 'it is unlikely that an employee in Mr. Shankle's position, faced with the mere possibility of being reimbursed for arbitrator fees in the future, would risk advancing those fees in order to access the arbitral forum.' *Id.* at 1234 n. 4. In contrast, no evidence of the plaintiffs' inability to pay for arbitration was introduced in Rosenberg or Koveleskie, the cases involving professional employees. See *Rosenberg v. Merrill Lynch, Pierce, Fenner & Smith, Inc.*, 170 F.3d 1, 15–16 (1st Cir. 1999); *Koveleskie v. SBC Capital Markets, Inc.*, 167 F.3d 361, 366 (7th Cir. 1999).

[314] See e.g., *Cole*, 105 F.3d at 1465.

[315] See e.g., *Perez*, 253 F.3d at 1287.

argument fails.[316] If this trend continues, a two-tiered employment arbitration system may emerge in which higher-wage employees are forced to agree to share the costs of their arbitration, while lower-wage workers are provided arbitrations paid by their employers.

The more pertinent question for courts – and perhaps ultimately, the Supreme Court – is whether our empirical results showing pronounced differences in enforcement rates by judicial circuits represent a split in the law or factual idiosyncrasies in these cases. At this early stage, we cannot say. The two leading appellate decisions that rejected cost arguments involved professional employees. Conversely, in the three leading appellate decisions that responded favorably to employee cost arguments, the plaintiffs were a train station security guard, an airport security agent, and a janitorial supervisor.

There is more to this schism, however, than different fact patterns. Judges take very different approaches in addressing cost arguments. Some recognize that discrimination complainants face very long odds in ever getting to trial.[317] In their judgment, arbitration alleviates a significant problem in the enforcement of employment rights. The contrasting approach makes a direct comparison of forum costs for complainants who are compelled to arbitrate and those who sue. When arbitration forum costs exceed litigation forum costs, these judges distinguish their decisions from *Gilmer*.

This analytical schism may become institutionalized in competing doctrines. Because precedents are in place for this evolution, a future Supreme Court may need to clarify these fundamental differences in ADR perspectives. The differing approaches in cases such as *Cole* and *Rosenberg* re-create the same 5-4 ideological divide that has been visible in the Supreme Court's recent *Circuit City* and *Green Tree* decisions. The slim *Green Tree* majority – consisting of Justices Rehnquist, O'Connor, Scalia, Kennedy, and Thomas – would not permit Larketta Randolph to conjecture about what an arbitration would cost.[318] By dismissing her reasonable pre-hearing cost estimates as 'unsupported statements [that]

---

[316] See *Rosenberg*, 170 F.3d at 16 ('If unreasonable fees were to be imposed on a particular employee, the argument that this was inconsistent with the 1991 CRA could be presented by the employee to the reviewing court. [But] that issue is not presented by this case.' (citation omitted)).

[317] See Howard, *supra* n. 76, at 44.

[318] See *Green Tree Fin. Corp.-Ala. v. Randolph*, 531 U.S. 79, 90 n. 6 (2000); see also *supra* n. 144.

provide no basis on which to ascertain the actual costs and fees to which she would be subject in arbitration,'[319] these Justices endorsed a policy of ordering arbitration and allowing post-hearing appeals based on concrete financial information. The four dissenters – Justices Ginsburg, Stevens, Souter, and Breyer – indignantly responded that 'it is hardly clear that Randolph should bear the burden of demonstrating up front the arbitral forum's inaccessibility, or that she should be required to submit to arbitration without knowing how much it will cost her.'[320]

The cost-shifting issue in cases such as *Cole* and *Rosenberg* is part of the current Court's open ideological dispute over appropriate dispute resolution methods for employment discrimination. Falling just one vote short of a majority, the dissenters struck a discordant note in *Circuit City* when they lambasted their colleagues for 'playing ostrich to the substantial history'[321] behind the FAA and for 'reasoning in a vacuum.'[322] They concluded with this barb:

> A method of statutory interpretation that is deliberately uninformed, and hence unconstrained, may produce a result that is consistent with a court's own views of how things should be, but it may also defeat the very purpose for which a provision was enacted. That is the sad result in this case.[323]

The *Cole* and *Rosenberg* decisions reflect the Justices' internal conflicts. The bitter and frustrated tone in the *Circuit City* dissent implies that four Justices await the opportunity to right some of the wrongs they perceive in mandatory arbitration. Moreover, a January 15, 2002, decision, *EEOC v. Waffle House, Inc.*,[324] created a narrow exception to the pro-arbitration rulings in *Gilmer*, *Circuit City*, and *Green Tree*, but failed to resolve the developing conflict among the circuits concerning cost-shifting. Thus, a future Supreme Court may need to clarify these fundamental differences in ADR perspectives.

On a final note, our empirical investigation prompts new questions about the arbitration profession. If *Cole* continues to be an influential

---

[319] *Green Tree*, 531 U.S. at 91 n. 6.

[320] *Id.* at 96 (Ginsburg, J., concurring in part and dissenting in part).

[321] *Circuit City Stores, Inc. v. Adams*, 532 U.S. 105, 128 (2001) (Stevens, J., dissenting).

[322] *Id.*

[323] *Id.* at 133.

[324] 534 U.S. 279 (2002). This 6–3 decision held that the EEOC is not a party to an individual's mandatory employment arbitration agreement, and therefore is not precluded by such an agreement from suing under any of the statutes that the agency is charged to enforce. See *id.* at 763, 765–766.

decision, will designers of ADR systems respond to the fact that this court used the much lower labor arbitration rate and still found that form of cost-sharing was unlawful? More generally, if a two-tiered cost-sharing system emerges, will expensive arbitration service providers price themselves out of a large segment of the ADR market?[325] If so, this could diminish the supply of arbitrators and arbitration services to handle the burgeoning work load for employment arbitrators. What effect would this have on employee access to arbitration? These questions arise because the findings here show that courts now engage in de facto price regulation of arbitrators and arbitration services.[326]

This leads to a second line of inquiry. Suppose employers address the cost-allocation issue simply by paying all forum costs. That would increase the likelihood that their arbitration agreements would be enforced. Or would it? Some empirical research shows that when employers are repeat players in an arbitration system that they subsidize, while employees are only one-time players, arbitrators are biased in favor of employers.[327] Courts have already expressed disapproval of repeat-player arbitration systems.[328]

---

[325] If employers agreed to pay all arbitration costs, we would answer no.

[326] We emphasize that employers can readily opt out of this regulation by agreeing to pay all arbitration costs, or specifying that employees pay nominal fees as the *Cole* court stated.

[327] See e.g., Lisa B. Bingham, On Repeat Players, Adhesion Contracts, and the Use of Statistics on Judicial Review of Employment Arbitration Awards, 29 McGeorge L. Rev. 223, 254, 258–259 (1998); Sarah Rudolph Cole, A Funny Thing Happened on the Way to the (Alternative) Forum: Reexamining Alexander v. Gardner-Denver in the Wake of Gilmer v. Interstate/Johnson Lane Corp., 1997 BYU L. Rev. 591, 619–624 (discussing the advantages repeat-player employers have when negotiating contracts and later participating in dispute resolution with one-time player employees); Marc Galanter, Why the 'Haves' Come Out Ahead: Speculations on the Limits of Legal Change, 9 Law & Soc'y Rev. 95 (1974) (discussing the systemic advantages of 'repeat players' in the civil justice system over individuals or one-time players); see also *Cole v. Burns Int'l Sec. Servs.*, 105 F.3d 1465, 1485 notes 16–17 (D.C. Cir. 1997) (recognizing the concern that neutrals have a financial interest to favor employers, as repeat players, and that empirical studies demonstrate favoritism based on the party who selects, rather than pays, the neutral).

[328] See for example, *Geiger v. Ryan's Family Steak Houses, Inc.*, 134 F. Supp. 2d 985 (S.D. Ind. 2001), offering this analysis:

> When courts are faced with an arbitration agreement reached in a collective bargaining setting, they know that both employer and union are 'repeat

CHAPTER 18. MANDATORY EMPLOYMENT ARBITRATION

In sum, our research supports two key conclusions. It shows that resistance to mandatory arbitration agreements is an uphill struggle, because courts continue to reject most of these challenges. However, notwithstanding the strong signals sent by *Gilmer* and *Circuit City*, courts are more receptive to these challenges than is generally understood. This tempers the outlook for ADR providers, who could only read *Gilmer*, *Circuit City*, and *Green Tree* as strong market-enhancing precedents. For these arbitrators and organizations, the money tree for their services may not be evergreen.

Table 18.1: Cost-Shifting Challenges to Mandatory Employment Arbitration:

Federal Court Decisions Granting Motions to Arbitrate

Courts of Appeal

LaPrade v. Kidder, Peabody & Co., Inc., 246 F.3d 702 (D.C. Cir. 2001) *
Lyster v. Ryan's Family Steak Houses, Inc., 239 F.3d 943 (8th Cir. 2001) *
Bradford v. Rockwell Semiconductor Sys., Inc., 238 F.3d 549 (4th Cir. 2001) *
Chappel v. Lab. Corp. of Am., 232 F.3d 719 (9th Cir. 2000) *
Williams v. Cigna Fin. Advisors, Inc., 197 F.3d 752 (5th Cir. 1999) *
Koveleskie v. SBC Capital Mkts, Inc., 167 F.3d 361 (7th Cir. 1999) Cole v. Burns International Sec. Servs.*, 105 F.3d 1465 (D.C. Cir. 1997) *

District Courts

Bradford v. Rockwell Semiconductor Sys., Inc., 238 F.3d 549 (4th Cir. 2001) (no district court citation) *
Chappel v. Lab. Corp. of Am., 232 F.3d 719 (9th Cir. 2000) (no district court citation) *

---

players' in the arbitration forum. In clear contrast are cases ... such as the one at bar: while Ryan's is a repeat player (as evidenced in part by the number of cases found in the federal and state courts challenging the validity of arbitration agreements allegedly made with EDSI on behalf of Ryan's), 'any ... plaintiff/employee who signs the [Arbitration Agreement] is not a repeat customer of [EDSI] – there is no equivalent interest on the other side weighing in to balance or provide a check to [EDSI's] incentive to please Ryan's.'

Id. at 994–995 (quoting *Penn. v. Ryan's Family Steak Houses, Inc.*, 95 F. Supp. 2d 940, 946 (N.D. Ind. 2000), aff'd, 269 F.3d 753 (7th Cir. 2001) (alterations in original) (citations omitted)).

EMPLOYMENT CLASS AND COLLECTIVE ACTIONS

Brown v. ITT Consumer Fin. Corp., 211 F.3d 1217 (11th Cir. 2000) (no district court citation) *Williams v. Cigna Fin. Advisors, Inc.*, 197 F.3d 752 (5th Cir. 1999) (no district court citation) *
Nelson v. Cyprus Bagdad Copper Corp., 119 F.3d 756 (9th Cir. 1997) (no district court citation) *Cole v. Burns Int'l Sec. Servs.*, 105 F.3d 1465 (D.C. Cir. 1997) (no district court citation) *
Rajjak v. McFrank & Williams, No. 01-Civ.-0493, 2001 WL 799766 (S.D.N.Y. July 13, 2001) *
Roberson v. Clear Channel Broad., Inc., 144 F. Supp. 2d 1371 (S.D. Fla. 2001) *
Boyd v. Town of Hayneville, 144 F. Supp. 2d 1272 (M.D. Ala. 2001) *
Giordano v. Pep Boys – Manny, Moe & Jack, Inc., No. 99-1281, 2001 WL 484360 (E.D. Pa. March 29, 2001) *
Nur v. K.F.C., USA, Inc., 142 F. Supp. 2d 48 (D.D.C. 2001) *
Dowling v. Anthony Crane Int'l, No. 1998/127, 2001 WL 378838 (D.V.I. March 20, 2001) *
Goodman v. ESPE Am., Inc., No. 00-CV-862, 2001 WL 64749 (E.D. Pa. January 19, 2001) *
Zumpano v. Omnipoint Communications, Inc., No. 00-CV-595, 2001 WL 43781 (E.D. Pa. January 18, 2001) *
Quinn v. EMC Corp., 109 F. Supp. 2d 681 (S.D. Tex. 2000) *
McCaskill v. SCI Mgmt. Corp., No. 00-2839, 2000 WL 875396 (N.D. Ill. June 22, 2000) *
Jenks v. Workman, No. IP 99-C-1389, 2000 WL 962821 (S.D. Ind. June 22, 2000)
Kreimer v. Delta Faucet Co., No. IP 99-C-1507, 2000 WL 962817 (S.D. Ind. June 2, 2000)
Fuller v. Pep Boys – Manny, Moe & Jack of Delaware, Inc., 88 F. Supp. 2d 1158 (D. Colo. 2000)
LaPrade v. Kidder, Peabody & Co., 94 F. Supp. 2d 2 (D.D.C. 2000); see also *LaPrade*, 246 F.3d 702 (D.C. Cir. 2001) *
Blair v. Scott Specialty Gases, No. 00-3865, 2000 WL 1728503 (E.D. Pa. February 6, 2000) *
Moorning-Brown v. Bear, Stearns & Co., No. 99-Civ.-413, 2000 WL 16935 (S.D.N.Y. January 10, 2000) *
Cline v. H.E. Butt Grocery Co., 79 F. Supp. 2d 730 (S.D. Tex. 1999) *
Jones v. Fujitsu Network Communications, Inc., 81 F. Supp. 2d 688 (N.D. Tex. 1999) *
Arakawa v. Japan Network Group, 56 F. Supp. 2d 349 (S.D.N.Y. 1999) *
Hart v. Canadian Imperial Bank of Commerce, 43 F. Supp. 2d 395 (S.D.N.Y. 1999) *Howard v. Anderson*, 36 F. Supp. 2d 183 (S.D.N.Y. 1999) *
EEOC v. World Sav. & Loan Ass'n, Inc., 32 F. Supp. 2d 833 (D. Md. 1999) *
Campbell v. Cantor Fitzgerald & Co., Inc., 21 F. Supp. 2d 341 (S.D.N.Y. 1998) *
Solieri v. Ferrovie Dello Stato Spa, No. 97-Civ.-8844, 1998 WL 419013 (S.D.N.Y. July 23, 1998) *
Martens v. Smith Barney, Inc., 181 F.R.D. 243 (S.D.N.Y. 1998) *
Brooks v. Circuit City Stores, Inc., No. DKC 95-3296, 1997 WL 580364 (D. Md. May 30, 1997); see also *Johnson v. Circuit City Stores, Inc.*, 148 F.3d 373 (4th Cir. 1998)
DeGaetano v. Smith Barney, Inc., 983 F. Supp. 459 (S.D.N.Y. 1997)
McWilliams v. Logicon, Inc., No. 95-2500, 1996 WL 439291 (D. Kan. July 9, 1996); see also *McWilliams*, 143 F.3d 573 (10th Cir. 1998) *

CHAPTER 18.   MANDATORY EMPLOYMENT ARBITRATION

Nazon v. Shearson Lehman Bros., Inc., 832 F. Supp. 1540 (S.D. Fla. 1993) *
Gardner v. Benefits Communications Corp., No. 91-0536, 1991 WL 294564 (D.D.C. December 31, 1991); see also *Gardner*, 175 F.3d 155 (D.C. Cir. 1999) *
Caporale v. Nat'l Ass'n of Sec. Dealers, Inc., No. 90-4074, 1991 WL 281890 (D.N.J. May 10, 1991) *

* Denotes *Forum Cost Case* as discussed in section 18.2(b).2.

Table 18.2: Cost-Shifting Challenges to Mandatory Employment Arbitration

Federal Court Decisions Denying Motions to Arbitrate

Courts of Appeal

Perez v. Globe Airport Sec. Servs., Inc., 253 F.3d 1280 (11th Cir. 2001) *
Floss v. Ryan's Family Steak Houses, Inc., 211 F.3d 306 (6th Cir. 2000)
Rosenberg v. Merrill Lynch, Pierce, Fenner & Smith, Inc., 170 F.3d 1 (1st Cir. 1999) *
Gardner v. Benefits Communications Corp., 175 F.3d 155 (D.C. Cir. 1999) *
Shankle v. B-G Maint. Mgmt. of Colo., Inc., 163 F.3d 1230 (10th Cir. 1999) *
Paladino v. Avnet Computer Techs., Inc., 134 F.3d 1054 (11th Cir. 1998) *
Nelson v. Cyprus Bagdad Copper Corp., 119 F.3d 756 (9th Cir. 1997)

District Courts

Perez v. Globe Airport Sec. Servs., Inc., 253 F.3d 1280 (11th Cir. 2001) (no district court citation) *
Lyster v. Ryan's Family Steak Houses, Inc., 239 F.3d 943 (8th Cir. 2001) (no district court citation)
Floss v. Ryan's Family Steak Houses, Inc., 211 F.3d 306 (6th Cir. 2000) (no district court citation)
Koveleskie v. SBC Capital Mkts., Inc., 167 F.3d 361 (7th Cir. 1999) (no district court citation)
Paladino v. Avnet Computer Techs., Inc., 134 F.3d 1054 (11th Cir. 1998) (no district court citation)
Dumais v. Am. Golf Corp., 150 F. Supp. 2d 1182 (D.N.M. 2001) *
Geiger v. Ryan's Family Steak Houses, Inc., 134 F. Supp. 2d 985 (S.D. Ind. 2001) *
Patterson v. Red Lobster, 81 F. Supp. 2d 681 (S.D. Miss. 1999) *
Davis v. LPK Corp., No. C-97-3988, 1998 WL 210262 (N.D. Cal. March 10, 1998) *Rosenberg v. Merrill Lynch, Pierce, Fenner & Smith, Inc.*, 995 F. Supp. 190 (D. Mass. 1998); see also *Rosenberg*, 170 F.3d 1 (1st Cir. 1999) *Shankle v. B-G Maint. Mgmt. of Colo., Inc.*, No. 96-N-2932, 1997 WL 416405 (D. Colo. March 24, 1997); see also *Shankle*, 163 F.3d 1230 (10th Cir. 1999) *
[hrl 2,r1,r2] [tn1,2][cp7,8]* Denotes Forum Cost Case as Discussed in 18.2.2.

EMPLOYMENT CLASS AND COLLECTIVE ACTIONS

Table 18.3: Federal Court Decisions Ordering and Denying Arbitration in Cost-Shifting Arbitration Cases Decided After *Green Tree*

Decisions Ordering Arbitration

Courts of Appeal

LaPrade v. Kidder, Peabody & Co., Inc., 246 F.3d 702 (D.C. Cir. 2001) *
Bradford v. Rockwell Semiconductor Sys., Inc., 238 F.3d 549 (4th Cir. 2001) *
Lyster v. Ryan's Family Steak Houses, Inc., 239 F.3d 943 (5th Cir. 2001) *

District Courts

Rajjak v. McFrank & Williams, No. 01-CIV-0493, 2001 WL 799766 (S.D.N.Y. July 13, 2001) *
Roberson v. Clear Channel Broad., Inc., 144 F. Supp. 2d 1371 (S.D. Fla. 2001) *
Boyd v. Town of Hayneville, 144 F. Supp. 2d 1272 (M.D. Ala. 2001) *
Giordano v. Pep Boys – Manny, Moe & Jack, Inc., No. 99-1281, 2001 WL 484360 (E.D. Pa. March 29, 2001) *
Nur v. K.F.C., USA, Inc., 142 F. Supp. 2d 48 (D.D.C. 2001) *
Dowling v. Anthony Crane Int'l, No. 1998/127, 2001 WL 378838 (D.V.I. March 20, 2001) *
Goodman v. ESPE Am., Inc., No. 00-CV-862, 2001 WL 64749 (E.D. Pa. January 19, 2001) *
Zumpano v. Omnipoint Communications, Inc., No. 00-CV-595, 2001 WL 43781 (E.D. Pa. January 18, 2001) *

Decisions Denying Arbitration

Courts of Appeal

Perez v. Globe Airport Sec. Servs., Inc., 253 F.3d 1280 (11th Cir. 2001) *

District Courts

Dumais v. Am. Golf Corp., 150 F. Supp. 2d 1182 (D.N.M. 2001) *
Geiger v. Ryan's Family Steak Houses, Inc., 134 F. Supp. 2d 985 (S.D. Ind. 2001) *

* Denotes Forum Cost Case as Discussed in Part VI.A [hrl 2,r1,r2]

CHAPTER 18. MANDATORY EMPLOYMENT ARBITRATION

Appendix 18.1: Federal Decisions Involving Challenges to Mandatory Employment Arbitration

Arce v. Cotton Club of Greenville, Inc., 883 F. Supp. 117 (N.D. Miss. 1995).
Albert v. Nat'l Cash Register Ca., 874 F. Supp. 1328 (S.D. Fla. 1994).
Alford v. Dean Witter Reynolds, Inc., 905 F.2d 104 (5th Cir. 1990).
Arakawa v. Japan Network Group, 56 F. Supp.2d 349 (S.D.N.Y. 1999).
Armijo v. Prudential Ins. Co. of Am., 72 F.3d 793 (10th Cir. 1995).
Aspar v. Pharmacia & Upjohn, Inc., 990 F. Supp. 523 (W.D. Mich. 1997).
Aspero v. Shearson Am. Express, Inc., 768 F.2d 106 (6th Cir. 1985).
Asplundh Tree Expert Co. v. Bates, 71 F.3d 592 (6th Cir. 1995).
Aynes v. Space Guard Prods., Inc., No. IP 99-1299-C, 2000 WL 962826 (S.D. Ind. July 3, 2000).
Barrowclough v. Kidder, Peabody & Co., Inc. 752 F.2d 923 (3d Cir. 1985).
Bauer v. Morton's of Chic., No. 99-C-5996, 2000 WL 149287 (N.D. Ill. February 9, 2000).
Beauchamp v. Great W. Life Assurance Co., 918 F. Supp. 1091 (E.D. Mich. 1996).
Bender v. A.G. Edwards & Sons, Inc., 971 F.2d 698 (11th Cir. 1992).
Benestad v. Interstate/Johnson Land Corp., 946 F.2d 1546 (11th Cir. 1991) (unpublished opinion).
Bernhardt v. Polygraphic Co. of Am., 218 F.2d 948 (2nd Cir. 1955).
Bierdeman v. Shearson Lehman Hutton, Inc., 963 F.2d 378 (9th Cir. 1992) (unpublished opinion).
Bishop v. Smith Barney, Inc., No. 97-CIV-4807, 1998 WL 50210 (S.D.N.Y. February 6, 1998).
Blair v. Scott Specialty Gases, No. 00-3865, 2000 WL 1728503 (E.D. Pa. November 21, 2000).
Borg-Warner Protective Servs. Corp. v. EEOC, 245 F.3d 831 (D.C. Cir. 2001).
Borenstein v. Tucker, 757 F. Supp. 3 (D. Conn. 1991).
Boyd v. Town of Hayneville, 144 F. Supp. 2d 1272 (M.D. Ala. 2001).
Bradford v. KFC Nat'l Mgmt. Co., 5 F. Supp. 2d 1311 (M.D. Ala. 1998)
Bradford v. Rockwell Semiconductor Sys., Inc., 238 F.3d 549 (4th Cir. 2001)
Brown v. ITT Consumer Fin. Corp., 211 F.3d 1217 (11th Cir. 2000).
Brown v. Wheat First Sec., Inc., 257 F.3d 821 (D.C. Cir. 2001).
Buchignani v. Vining-Sparks IBG, 208 F.3d 212 (6th Cir. 2000) (unpublished opinion).
Burns v. N.Y. Life Ins. Co., 202 F.3d 616 (2nd Cir. 2000).
Campbell v. Cantor Fitzgerald & Co., 21 F. Supp. 2d 341 (S.D.N.Y. 1998).
Caporale v. Nat'l Ass'n of Sec. Dealers, Inc., No. 90-4070, 1991 WL 281890 (D.N.J. May 10, 1991).
Carey v. Conn. Gen. Life Ins. Co., 93 F. Supp. 2d 165 (D. Conn. 1999).
Chanchani v. Salomon/Smith Barney, Inc., No. 99-CIV-9219, 2001 WL 204214 (S.D.N.Y. March 1, 2001).
Chappel v. Lab. Corp. of Am., 232 F.3d 719 (9th Cir. 2000).
Cherry v. Wertheim Schroder & Co., Inc., 868 F. Supp. 830 (D.S.C. 1994).

EMPLOYMENT CLASS AND COLLECTIVE ACTIONS

Chisolm v. Kidder, Peabody Asset Mgmt., Inc., 810 F. Supp. 479 (S.D.N.Y. 1992).
Circuit City Stores, Inc. v. Ahmed, 195 F.3d 1131 (9th Cir. 1999).
Cline v. H.E. Butt Grocery Co., 79 F. Supp. 2d 730 (S.D. Tex. 1999).
Cole v. Burns Int'l Sec. Servs., 105 F.3d 1465 (D.C. Cir. 1997).
Cole v. Halliburton Co., No. CIV-00-0862, 2000 WL 1531614 (W.D. Okla. September 6, 2000).
Coudert v. Paine Webber Jackson & Curtis, 705 F.2d 78 (2nd Cir. 1983).
Craft v. Campbell Soup Co., 177 F.3d 1083 (9th Cir. 1999).
Cremin v. Merrill Lynch, Pierce, Fenner & Smith, Inc., 957 F. Supp. 1460 (N.D. Ill. 1997).
Dancu v. Coopers & Lybrand, 972 F.2d 1330 (3d Cir. 1992) (unpublished opinion).
Davis v. LPK Corp., No. C-97-3998, 1998 WL 210262 (N.D. Cal. March 10, 1998).
Desiderio v. Nat'l Ass'n of Sec. Dealers, Inc., 191 F.3d 198 (2nd Cir. 1999).
DeGaetano v. Smith Barney, Inc., 983 F. Supp. 459 (S.D.N.Y. 1997).
Dean Witter Reynolds, Inc., v. Ness, 677 F. Supp. 866 (D.S.C. 1988).
Dickstein v. DuPont, 443 F.2d 783 (1st Cir. 1971).
DiCrisci v. Lyndon Guar. Bank of N.Y., 807 F. Supp. 947 (W.D.N.Y. 1992).
Dowling v. Anthony Crane Int'l, No. 1998/127, 2001 WL 378838 (D.V.I. March 20, 2001).
Downing v. Merrill Lynch, Pierce, Fenner & Smith, Inc., 725 F.2d 192 (2nd Cir. 1984).
Doyle v. Raley's Inc., 158 F.3d 1012 (9th Cir. 1998).
Drayer v. Krasner, 572 F.2d 348 (2d Cir. 1978).
Duffield v. Robertson Stephens & Co., 144 F.3d 1182 (9th Cir. 1998).
Dumais v. Am. Golf Corp., 150 F. Supp. 2d 1182 (D.N.M. 2001).
Durkin v. CIGNA Prop. & Cas. Corp., 942 F. Supp. 481 (D. Kan. 1996).
EEOC v. Frank's Nursery & Crafts, Inc., 177 F.3d 448 (6th Cir. 1999).
EEOC v. Kidder, Peabody & Co., 156 F.3d 298 (2nd Cir. 1998).
EEOC v. Luce, Forward, Hamilton & Scripps, LLP, 122 F. Supp. 2d 1080 (C.D. Cal. 2000).
EEOC v. Waffle House, Inc., 193 F.3d 805 (4th Cir. 1999).
EEOC v. World Sav. & Loan Ass'n, Inc., 32 F. Supp. 2d 833 (D. Md. 1999).
Emeronye v. CACI Int'l, Inc., 141 F. Supp. 2d 82 (D.D.C. 2001).
Etokie v. Carmax Auto Superstores, Inc., 133 F. Supp. 2d 390 (D. Md. 2000).
Farrand v. Lutheran Bhd., 993 F.2d 1253 (7th Cir. 1993).
Feinberg v. Bear, Stearns & Co., No. 90-CIV-5250, 1991 WL 79309 (S.D.N.Y. May 3, 1991).
Feinberg v. Oppenheimer & Co., 658 F. Supp. 892 (S.D.N.Y. 1987).
First Liberty Inv. Group v. Nicholsberg, 145 F.3d 647 (3rd Cir. 1998).
Fleck v. E.F. Hutton Group, Inc., 891 F.2d 1047 (2nd Cir. 1989).
Floss v. Ryan's Family Steak Houses, Inc., 211 F.3d 306 (6th Cir. 2000).
Flynn v. AerChem, Inc., 102 F. Supp. 2d 1055 (S.D. Ind. 2000).
Foley v. Presbyterian Ministers' Fund, No. 90-1053, 1992 WL 63269 (E.D. Pa. March 19, 1992).
Fox v. Merrill Lynch & Co., Inc., 453 F. Supp. 561 (S.D.N.Y. 1978).
Fuller v. Pep Boys – Manny, Moe & Jack of Del. Inc., 88 F. Supp. 2d 1158 (D. Colo. 2000).

CHAPTER 18. MANDATORY EMPLOYMENT ARBITRATION

Gaghich v. Prudential Ins. of Am., No. 96-CV-0464E, 1997 WL 128269 (W.D.N.Y. March 10, 1997).
Gannon v. Circuit City Stores, Inc., 262 F.3d 677 (8th Cir. 2001).
Gardner v. Benefits Communications Corp., 175 F.3d 155 (D.C. Cir. 1999).
Gateson v. Aslk-Bank, N.V., No. 94-CIV-5849, 1995 WL 387720 (S.D.N.Y. June 25, 1995).
Gaylor v. Donald B. MacNeal, Inc., No. 95-C-7250, 1996 WL 224566 (N.D. Ill. May 1, 1996)
Geiger v. Ryan's Family Steak Houses, Inc., 134 F. Supp. 2d 985 (S.D. Ind. 2001).
Gibson v. Neighborhood Health Clinics, Inc., 121 F.3d 1126 (7th Cir. 1997).
Gilmer v. Interstate/Johnson Lane Corp., 895 F.2d 195 (4th Cir. 1990).
Giordano v. Pep Boys – Manny, Moe & Jack, Inc., No. 99-1281, 2001 WL 484360 (E.D. Pa. March 29, 2001).
Golenia v. Bob Baker Toyota, 915 F. Supp. 201 (S.D. Cal. 1996).
Goodman v. ESPE Am., Inc., No. 00-CV-862, 2001 WL 64749 (E.D. Pa. January 19, 2001).
Gonzalez v. Toscorp, Inc., No. 97-Civ.-8158, 1999 WL 595632 (S.D.N.Y. August 5, 1999).
Hall v. Metlife Res., No. 94-CIV-0358, 1995 WL 258061 (S.D.N.Y. May 3, 1995).
Hart v. Canadian Imperial Bank of Commerce, 43 F. Supp. 2d 395 (S.D.N.Y. 1999).
Haviland v. Goldman, Sachs & Co., 947 F.2d 601 (2nd Cir. 1991).
Heller v. MC Fin. Servs., Ltd., No. 97-Civ.-5317, 1998 WL 190288 (S.D.N.Y. April 21, 1998).
Herko v. Metro. Life Ins. Co., 978 F. Supp. 141 (W.D.N.Y. 1997).
Herman v. SBC Warburg Dillon Read, Inc., No. 99-CIV-1593, 1999 WL 688304 (S.D.N.Y. September 3, 1999).
Hoffman v. Aaron Kamhi, Inc., 927 F. Supp. 640 (S.D.N.Y. 1996).
Hooters of Am., Inc., v. Phillips, 173 F.3d 933 (4th Cir. 1999).
Horne v. New England Patriots Football Club, Inc., 489 F. Supp. 465 (D. Mass. 1980).
Howard v. Anderson, 36 F. Supp. 2d 183 (S.D.N.Y. 1999).
Hughes Training Inc. v. Cook, 254 F.3d 588 (5th Cir. 2001).
Hydrick v. Mgmt. Recruiters Int'l, Inc., 738 F. Supp. 1434 (N.D. Ga. 1990).
In re Prudential Ins. Co. of Am. Sales Practice Litig., 133 F.3d 225 (3rd Cir. 1998).
Jenks v. Workman, No. IP 99-C-1389, 2000 WL 962821 (S.D. Ind. June 22, 2000).
Johnson v. Circuit City Stores, Inc., 148 F.3d 373 (4th Cir. 1998).
Johnson v. Hubbard Broad., Inc., 940 F. Supp. 1447 (D. Minn. 1996).
Jones v. Fujitsu Network Communications, Inc., 81 F. Supp. 2d 688 (N.D. Tex. 1999).
Jones v. Wash. Metro. Area Transit Auth., No. 95-2300, 1997 WL 198114 (D.D.C. April 10, 1997).
Kaliden v. Shearson Lehman Hutton, Inc., 789 F. Supp. 179 (W.D. Pa. 1991).
Kidd v. Equitable Life Assurance Soc'y of the United States, 32 F.3d 516 (11th Cir. 1994).
Kinnebrew v. Gulf Ins. Co., No. 3:94-CV-1517, 1994 WL 803508 (N.D. Tex. November 28, 1994).
Koveleskie v. SBC Capital Mkts., Inc., 167 F.3d 361 (7th Cir. 1999).
Kresock v. Bankers Trust Co., 21 F.3d 176 (7th Cir. 1994).
Kreimer v. Delta Faucet Co., No. IP 99-C-1507, 2000 WL 962817 (S.D. Ind. June 2, 2000).

EMPLOYMENT CLASS AND COLLECTIVE ACTIONS

Kropfelder v. Snap-On Tools Corp., 859 F. Supp. 952 (D. Md. 1994).
Kuehner v. Dickinson & Co., 84 F.3d 316 (9th Cir. 1996).
Kummetz v. Tech Mold, Inc., 152 F.3d 1153 (9th Cir. 1998).
Landis v. Finova Capital Corp., No. 00-Civ.-0187, 2000 WL 546985 (S.D.N.Y. May 3, 2000).
Lang v. Burlington N. R.R. Co., 835 F. Supp. 1104 (D. Minn. 1993).
LaPrade v. Kidder, Peabody & Co., 246 F.3d 702 (D.C. Cir. 2001).
Legg, Mason & Co. v. Mackall & Coe, Inc., 351 F. Supp. 1367 (D.D.C. 1972).
Lewis v. Merrill Lynch, Pierce, Fenner & Smith, Inc., 431 F. Supp. 271 (E.D. Pa. 1977).
Litaker v. Lehman Bros. Holdings, Inc., No. 97-Civ.-1607, 1999 WL 619638 (S.D.N.Y. August 16, 1999).
Ludwig v. Equitable Life Assurance Soc'y of the United States, 978 F. Supp. 1379 (D. Kan. 1997).
Lyster v. Ryan's Family Steak Houses, Inc., 239 F.3d 943 (8th Cir. 2001).
McCaskill v. SCI Mgmt. Corp., No. 00-2839, 2000 WL 875396 (N.D. Ill. June 22, 2000).
McDonough v. Equitable Life Assurance Soc'y of U.S., No. 98-Civ.-3921, 1999 WL 731424 (S.D.N.Y. Sept. 20, 1999).
McGill v. Rural/Metro Corp., No. 2:00-CV-192, 2001 WL 484796 (N.D. Miss. February 20, 2001).
McMahon v. RMS Elec., Inc., 618 F. Supp. 189 (S.D.N.Y. 1985).
McWilliams v. Logicon, Inc., 143 F.3d 573 (10th Cir. 1998).
Mago v. Shearson Lehman Hutton, Inc., 956 F.2d 932 (9th Cir. 1992).
Malison v. Prudential-Bache Sec., Inc., 654 F. Supp. 101 (W.D.N.C. 1987).
Manion v. Nagin, 255 F.3d 535 (8th Cir. 2001).
Martens v. Smith Barney, Inc., 181 F.R.D. 243 (S.D.N.Y. 1998).
Mason v. Northwest Airlines, Inc., No. 1:98-CV-1795, 1998 WL 953741 (N.D. Ga. November 23, 1998).
Maye v. Smith Barney Inc., 897 F. Supp. 100 (S.D.N.Y. 1995).
Merrill Lynch, Pierce, Fenner & Smith, Inc. v. DeCaro, 577 F. Supp. 616 (W.D. Mo. 1983).
Merrill Lynch, Pierce, Fenner & Smith, Inc. v. Hovey, 726 F.2d 1286 (8th Cir. 1984).
Merrill Lynch, Pierce, Fenner & Smith, Inc. v. Nixon, 210 F.3d 814 (8th Cir. 2000).
Merrill Lynch, Pierce, Fenner & Smith, Inc. v. Thomson, 574 F. Supp. 1472 (D. Mo. 1983).
Merrill Lynch, Pierce, Fenner & Smith, Inc. v. Thompson, 575 F. Supp. 978 (N.D. Fla. 1983).
Metz v. Merrill Lynch, Pierce, Fenner & Smith, Inc., 39 F.3d 1482 (10th Cir. 1994).
Metzler v. Harris Corp., No. 00-Civ.-5847, 2001 WL 194911 (S.D.N.Y. February 26, 2001).
Meyer v. Starwood Hotels & Resorts Worldwide, Inc., No. 00-Civ.-8339, 2001 WL 396447 (S.D.N.Y. April 18, 2001).
Michalski v. Circuit City Stores, Inc., 177 F.3d 634 (7th Cir. 1999).
Miller v. Pub. Storage Mgmt., Inc., 121 F.3d 215 (5th Cir. 1997).
Moore v. Interacciones Global, Inc., No. 94-Civ.-4789, 1995 WL 33650 (S.D.N.Y. January 27, 1995).

CHAPTER 18. MANDATORY EMPLOYMENT ARBITRATION

Moorning-Brown v. Bear, Stearns & Co., Inc., No. 99-Civ.-4130, 2000 WL 16935 (S.D.N.Y. January 10, 2000).
Morgan v. Smith Barney, Harris Upham & Co., 729 F.2d 1163 (8th Cir. 1984).
Morrison v. Circuit City Stores, Inc., 70 F. Supp. 2d 815 (S.D. Ohio 1999).
Muh v. Newburger, Loeb & Co., Inc., 540 F.2d 970 (9th Cir. 1976).
Nazon v. Shearson Lehman Bros., Inc., 832 F. Supp. 1540 (S.D. Fla. 1993).
Nelson v. Cyprus Bagdad Copper Corp., 119 F.3d 756 (9th Cir. 1997).
Nicholson v. CPC Int'l Inc., 877 F.2d 221 (3rd Cir. 1989).
Nguyen v. City of Cleveland, 138 F. Supp. 2d 938 (N.D. Ohio 2001).
Nur v. K.F.C., USA, Inc., 142 F. Supp. 2d 48 (D.D.C. 2001).
O'Donnell v. First Investors Corp., 872 F. Supp. 1274 (S.D.N.Y. 1995).
Olivares v. Hispanic Broad. Corp., No. CV-00-00354, 2001 WL 477171 (C.D. Cal. April 26, 2001).
Oldroyd v. Elmira Sav. Bank, FSB, 134 F.3d 72 (2nd Cir. 1998).
O'Neel v. Nat'l Ass'n of Sec. Dealers, Inc., 667 F.2d 804 (9th Cir. 1982).
O'Neil v. Hilton Head Hosp., 115 F.3d 272 (4th Cir. 1997).
PaineWebber Inc. v. Faragalli, 61 F.3d 1063 (3rd Cir. 1995).
Paladino v. Avnet Computer Techs., Inc., 134 F.3d 1054 (11th Cir. 1998).
Palmer-Scopetta v. Metro. Life Ins. Co., 37 F. Supp. 2d 1364 (S.D. Fla. 1999).
Patterson v. Red Lobster, 81 F. Supp. 2d 681 (S.D. Miss. 1999).
Patterson v. Tenet Healthcare, Inc., 113 F.3d 832 (8th Cir. 1997).
Paul Revere Variable Annuity Ins. Co v. Kirschhofer, 226 F.3d 15 (1st Cir. 2000).
Paul Revere Variable Annuity Ins. Co v. Zang, 248 F.3d 1 (1st Cir. 2001).
Pearce v. E.F. Hutton Group, Inc., 828 F.2d 826 (D.C. Cir. 1987).
Penn v. Ryan's Family Steak Houses, Inc., 269 F.3d 753 (7th Cir. 2001).
Perez v. Globe Airport Sec. Servs., Inc., 253 F.3d 1280 (11th Cir. 2001).
Phox v. Allied Capital Advisers, Inc., No. 96-2745, 1997 WL 198115 (D.D.C. April 14, 1997).
Pierce v. Shearson Lehman Hutton, Inc., No. C-0722, 1990 WL 60751 (N.D. Ill. April 26, 1990).
Pihl v. Thomson McKinnon Sec., Inc., No. 87-7632, 1988 WL 54036 (E.D. Pa. May 24, 1988).
Pitter v. Prudential Life Ins. Co. of Am., 906 F. Supp. 130 (E.D.N.Y. 1995).
Phillips v. CIGNA Inv., Inc., 27 F. Supp. 2d 345 (D. Conn. 1998).
Porter v. CIGNA, No. 1:96-CV-765, 1997 WL 1068630 (N.D. Ga. March 26, 1997).
Prescott v. N. Lake Christian Sch., No. 01-475, 2001 WL 740506 (E.D. La. June 29, 2001).
Prevot v. Phillips Petroleum Co., 133 F. Supp. 2d 937 (S.D. Tex. 2001).
Prudential Ins. Co. of Am. v. Lai, 42 F.3d 1299 (9th Cir. 1994).
Pruett v. Travelers Ins. Co., 2000 WL 33249826 (E.D. Tenn. October 30, 2000).
Quinn v. EMC Corp., 109 F. Supp. 2d 681 (S.D. Tex. 2000).
Quist v. Empire Funding Corp., No. 98-C-8402, 1999 WL 982953 (N.D. Ill. October 22, 1999).
Raiola v. Union Bank of Switz., LLC, 47 F. Supp. 2d 499 (S.D.N.Y. 1999).

EMPLOYMENT CLASS AND COLLECTIVE ACTIONS

Rajjak v. McFrank & Williams, No. 01-CIV-0493, 2001 WL 799766 (S.D.N.Y. July 13, 2001).
Renteria v. Prudential Ins. Co. of Am., 113 F.3d 1104 (9th Cir. 1997).
Roberson v. Clear Channel Broad., Inc., 144 F. Supp. 2d 1371 (S.D. Fla. 2001).
Roe v. Kidder Peabody & Co., Inc., No. 88-CIV-8507, 1990 WL 52200 (S.D.N.Y. April 19, 1990).
Rojas v. TK Communications, Inc., 87 F.3d 745 (5th Cir. 1996).
Roodveldt v. Merrill Lynch, Pierce, Fenner & Smith, Inc., 585 F. Supp. 770 (E.D. Pa. 1984).
Rosenberg v. Merrill Lynch, Pierce, Fenner & Smith, Inc., 170 F.3d 1 (1st Cir. 1999).
Rudolph v. Alamo Rent A Car, Inc., 952 F. Supp. 311 (E.D. Va. 1997).
Satarino v. A.G. Edwards & Sons, Inc., 941 F. Supp. 609 (N.D. Tex. 1996).
Scher v. Equitable Life Assurance. Soc'y of the United States, 866 F. Supp. 776 (S.D.N.Y. 1994).
Schuetz v. CS First Boston Corp., No. 96-Civ.-5557, 1997 WL 452392 (S.D.N.Y. August 8, 1997).
Scott v. Merrill Lynch, Pierce, Fenner & Smith, Inc. No. 89-Civ.-3749, 1992 WL 245506 (S.D.N.Y. September 14, 1992).
Seus v. John Nuveen & Co., 146 F.3d 175 (3rd Cir. 1998).
Shaw v. Pershing Div. of Donaldson, Lufkin & Jenrette Sec. Corp., 234 F.3d 1274 (7th Cir. 2000) (unpublished opinion).
Shearson Hayden Stone, Inc., v. Liang, 653 F.2d 310 (7th Cir. 1981).
Shankle v. B-G Maint. Mgmt. of Colo., Inc., 163 F.3d 1230 (10th Cir. 1999).
Sheller ex rel. Sheller v. Frank's Nursery & Crafts, Inc., 957 F. Supp. 150 (N.D. Ill. 1997).
Slawsky v. True Form Founds. Corp., No. 91-1822, 1991 WL 98906 (E.D. Pa. June 4, 1991).
Smiga v. Dean Witter Reynolds, Inc., 766 F.2d 698 (2nd Cir. 1985).
Smith v. Lehman Bros., Inc., No. 95-Civ.-10326, 1996 WL 383232 (S.D.N.Y. July 8, 1996).
Snow v. BE&K Constr., Co., 126 F. Supp. 2d 5 (D. Me. 2001).
Solieri v. Ferrovie Dello Stato Spa, No. 97-Civ.-8844, 1998 WL 419013 (S.D.N.Y. July 23, 1998).
Stanley v. Wings Holdings, Inc., No. 3-96-1141, 1997 WL 826175 (D. Minn. September 23, 1997).
Stanton v. Prudential Ins. Co., No. 98-4989, 1999 WL 236603 (E.D. Pa. April 20, 1999).
Steck v. Smith Barney, Harris Upham & Co., Inc., 661 F. Supp. 543 (D.N.J. 1987).
Steele v. L.F. Rothschild & Co., Inc., 864 F.2d 1 (2nd Cir. 1988).
Stewart v. Mitchell Madison Group, No. 98-Civ.-8122, 1999 WL 169688 (S.D.N.Y. March 26, 1999).
Stokes v. Merrill Lynch, Pierce, Fenner & Smith, Inc., 523 F.2d 433 (6th Cir. 1975).
Swenson v. Mgmt. Recruiters Int'l, Inc., 858 F.2d 1304 (8th Cir. 1988).
Tays v. Covenant Life Ins. Co., 964 F.2d 501 (5th Cir. 1992).
Thiele v. Merrill Lynch, Pierce, Fenner & Smith, Inc., 59 F. Supp. 2d 1067 (S.D. Cal. 1999).
Trumbetta v. Metro. Life Ins. Co., No. 94-3275, 1994 WL 481152 (E.D. Pa. September 1, 1994).
Trumbull v. Century Mktg. Corp., 12 F. Supp. 2d 683 (N.D. Ohio 1998).

CHAPTER 18. MANDATORY EMPLOYMENT ARBITRATION

Utley v. Goldman Sachs & Co., 883 F.2d 184 (1st Cir. 1989).
Valdiviezo v. Phelps Dodge Hidalgo Smelter, Inc., 995 F. Supp. 1060 (D. Ariz. 1997).
Venuto v. Ins. Co. of N. Am., No. 98-96, 1998 WL 414723 (E.D. Pa. July 22, 1998).
Walsh v. Goldman, Sachs & Co., No. 89-CIV-8088, 1990 WL 209449 (S.D.N.Y. December 12, 1990).
Webb v. Wellins, No. 98-CV-1113, 1999 WL 31113 (N.D.N.Y. January 21, 1999).
Weston v. ITT-CFC, No. 3:92-CV-2044, 1992 WL 473846 (N.D. Tex. December 3, 1992).
Williams v. Cigna Fin. Advisors, Inc., 197 F.3d 752 (5th Cir. 1999).
Willis v. Dean Witter Reynolds, Inc., 948 F.2d 305 (6th Cir. 1991).
Wojcik v. Aetna Life Ins. & Annuity Co., 901 F. Supp. 1282 (N.D. Ill. 1995).
Wright v. Circuit City Stores, Inc., 82 F. Supp. 2d 1279 (N.D. Ala. 2000).
Zandford v. Prudential-Bache Sec., Inc., 112 F.3d 723 (4th Cir. 1997).
Zolezzi v. Dean Witter Reynolds, Inc., 789 F.2d 1447 (9th Cir. 1986).
Zumpano v. Omnipoint Communications, Inc., NO. 00-CV-595, 2001 WL 43781 (E.D. Pa. January 18, 2001).

CHAPTER 19

Arbitration and the Individuation Critique*

W. Mark C. Weidemaier**

19.1 INTRODUCTION

Skeptics and champions of the use of arbitration for consumer and employment disputes do not agree about much, but each group views arbitration as an individuated dispute resolution process. Many skeptics view arbitration as a tool used by repeat-player businesses to combat the increased influence of the plaintiffs' bar. To a significant extent, that influence derives from lawyers' ability to aggregate claims in both formal and informal ways.[1] Skeptics object that businesses use arbitration to prevent such aggregation, forcing consumer and employee claimants into individualized proceedings where neither they nor their lawyers can counter the advantages enjoyed by more powerful repeat players. I call this the 'individuation critique.' In reply, arbitration proponents defend its fairness as a forum and advance efficiency arguments in its favor, but they do not suggest that arbitration could or should facilitate the aggregation of consumer and employee claims.

This article calls into question skeptics' and proponents' shared conception of arbitration. In section 19.2, I describe the individuation critique, which derives from Professor Marc Galanter's famous

---

* Previously published by 49 Arizona Law Rev. 69 (2007).
** W. Mark C. Weidemaier is Assistant Professor of Law, University of North Carolina at Chapel Hill.
[1] See *infra* text accompanying notes 35–54.

David Sherwyn and Samuel Estreicher (eds), *Employment Class and Collective Actions*, pp. 807–865.
© Arizona Law Review and W.M.C. Weidemaier. Reprinted with permission.

distinction between repeat players (those who routinely encounter the same issue in litigation) and one-shotters (those with only sporadic and unpredictable contact with the legal system).[2] The arbitration debate often focuses on disputes between 'one-shot' consumer or employee claimants and repeat-player businesses as respondents, and that is the type of dispute I am concerned with here.

I view the individuation critique, at least in theory, as one of the more potent objections to the use of pre-dispute arbitration agreements between parties of unequal power.[3] Yet as a description of current arbitration practice, the critique is of uncertain validity. First, the critique takes largely for granted that arbitration agreements routinely include individuating terms, such as terms that prohibit class actions, prevent arbitrators from awarding punitive damages, or require that arbitration results remain confidential. To be sure, such agreements do exist, and they may be particularly common in some industries, but it is not clear that the critique accurately describes consumer and employment arbitration agreements generally.

Second, the critique arguably pays too much attention to arbitration agreements themselves, and too little attention to the institutional context in which arbitration takes place. In particular, arbitration providers like the American Arbitration Association (AAA) and JAMS have adopted 'due process' standards that may significantly improve the 'fairness' of arbitration procedure. If consistently interpreted and enforced (we do not know if they are), these standards may limit the impact of some individuating contract terms. In short, a number of unanswered empirical questions are relevant to the individuation critique, including questions about the contents of arbitration agreements and the role of arbitration providers in shaping arbitration procedure. Systematic analysis of these questions may reveal the critique to be overstated.

Moreover, a full assessment of the individuation critique requires more than an understanding of current arbitration practices. We should also consider arbitration's potential as a forum for aggregate dispute resolution. Relying in part on evidence from the recent, and rather unusual, phenomenon of class arbitration, I argue in section 19.3 that

---

[2] Marc Galanter, Why the 'Haves' Come Out Ahead: Speculations on the Limits of Legal Change, 9 Law & Soc'y Rev. 95 (1974).

[3] A pre-dispute arbitration agreement is a contract that obliges the parties to submit future disputes to binding arbitration.

CHAPTER 19. ARBITRATION AND THE INDIVIDUATION CRITIQUE

arbitration may have significant potential, especially for consumers.[4] I begin by discussing class arbitration.

In class arbitration, an arbitrator selected and paid by the parties, rather than an elected or appointed judge, presides over a class action. The arbitrator decides whether to certify a class, determines the form and manner of notice to class members, resolves all issues of law and fact, and enters an award that may bind many hundreds or thousands of class members. This wholesale privatization of justice is subject only to limited judicial review. A rare occurrence until the Supreme Court's decision in *Green Tree Financial Corp. v. Bazzle*,[5] over 120 class arbitrations are now pending before the AAA.[6]

Both the legal literature and the alternative dispute resolution (ADR) providers involved in administering class arbitrations tend to view these proceedings as little more than a private version of the judicial class action.[7] So narrow a conception fails to take seriously the possibilities of class arbitration. As I will explain, in many cases arbitrators will have the authority to resolve, in collective fashion, large-scale disputes that would have to proceed separately, if at all, in court. I argue that arbitrators should use this authority and that, at least in some circumstances, properly administered class arbitration might be acceptable both to claimants and respondents. I conclude this discussion by arguing that proponents and skeptics of arbitration should each embrace the aggregative possibilities of class arbitration.

Arbitration's potential to facilitate aggregation is not limited to formal methods like class arbitration. Thus, section 19.3 also describes how arbitration might facilitate aggregation of individual consumer claims in informal ways. For example, although arbitrators generally do not create precedent and are not bound by other arbitrators' decisions, evidence from the AAA class arbitrations suggests that they may be strongly influenced by other arbitration awards in similar

---

[4] I use the term 'consumer' to refer to individuals who assert relatively small-value claims, typically not for personal injuries, arising from standardized transactions for credit, services, or goods intended for personal or household use.
[5] 539 U.S. 444 (2003).
[6] Unlike most arbitrations, the AAA class arbitrations are quasi-public. Many of the arbitrators' decisions, and many of the arbitration agreements themselves, are available on the AAA website. Am. Arbitration Ass'n, Class Arbitration Docket, <www.adr.org/sp.asp?id=25562> (last visited January 27, 2007).
[7] See *infra* text accompanying notes 142–143 and n. 153.

cases.[8] Indeed, under the right conditions, arbitrators may produce something akin to informal precedent, and this possibility may encourage plaintiffs' lawyers to invest in creating 'rules' from which multiple claimants can benefit. Section 19.3 goes on to suggest some reforms to ADR provider policies that might encourage specialized, repeat-player lawyers to accept cases destined for arbitration and to make meaningful investments in these disputes. For individual consumers in particular, such a system might prove to be superior to the courts in important respects.

19.2 THE INDIVIDUATION CRITIQUE

As I have explained, the individuation critique derives from Marc Galanter's distinction between repeat players and one-shotters.[9] Forests have gone to the blade discussing Galanter's taxonomy of litigants,[10] so my treatment of it in this section will be brief. I focus primarily on the extent to which repeat players benefit from their ability to aggregate claims.

19.2.1 Automatic Claims Aggregation and the Presumed Repeat-Player Advantage

For a number of reasons, even a formally neutral legal system may favor repeat players, both in individual cases and over the long term.[11] Repeat players can justify significant investments in lobbying and other activities designed to shape the law,[12] and they learn from experience how to structure transactions to their advantage.[13] If a dispute occurs,

---

[8] See *infra* text accompanying notes 197–206.
[9] Galanter, *supra* n. 2. For another important article on repeat players in arbitration, see Carrie Menkel-Meadow, Do the 'Haves' Come Out Ahead in Alternative Judicial Systems?: Repeat Players in ADR, 15 Ohio St. J. on Disp. Resol. 19 (1999), suggesting that repeat players in ADR may duplicate, or enhance, the advantages they enjoy in litigation and calling for research into ADR outcomes and procedures.
[10] For a useful bibliography, see Brian J. Glenn, The Varied and Abundant Progeny, in In Litigation: Do the 'Haves' Still Come Out Ahead? 371, 373–374 (Herbert M. Kritzer & Susan S. Silbey, eds, 2003).
[11] Galanter, *supra* n. 2, at 103–104.
[12] *Id.* at 100.
[13] *Id.* at 98, 109.

CHAPTER 19. ARBITRATION AND THE INDIVIDUATION CRITIQUE

the repeat player may seek to generate a favorable precedent[14] or, conversely, to suppress rule changes that might benefit future adversaries. To that end, a repeat-player defendant might settle weak cases and litigate only those it expects to win.[15] If it does litigate, the defendant may make substantial investments in its defense for a number of reasons. For one thing, it may invest because the result has consequences for future cases.[16] Likewise, the defendant may spend heavily on, say, developing expert witnesses and planning legal strategy, because it can spread these costs, and reap the benefits, over multiple cases.[17] The result is that, in many cases, repeat players will rationally make litigation investments that no individual litigant can hope to match.[18]

---

[14] By 'precedent,' I mean not only published judicial opinions, but also any information of systemic value in similar cases. For example, a defense verdict, or one producing a modest damages award, might temper future plaintiffs' settlement expectations. Conversely, a large award might increase settlement expectations, encourage more lawsuits, or generate an unfavorable reaction from the financial markets.

[15] Galanter, *supra* n. 2, at 101–102; William M. Landes & Richard A. Posner, Adjudication as a Private Good, 8 J. Legal Stud. 235, 273–274 (1979) (noting that, in cases where litigants have asymmetric future stakes, 'a necessary condition for a trial is that the odds favor the party with the greater stake'). As another example, a repeat-player defendant might allow a case to reach a jury without raising a key defense, because it anticipates an adverse ruling and does not wish to generate unfavorable precedent. Cf. Catherine Albiston, The Rule of Law and the Litigation Process: The Paradox of Losing By Winning, 33 Law & Soc'y Rev. 869, 877–885 (1999) (describing various 'rule-making' opportunities in the litigation process, including strategic settlement, dispositive motions at the trial court level, and appeal).

[16] See Galanter, *supra* n. 2, at 100 (noting significance to repeat player of events that will influence outcomes in future cases).

[17] See e.g., David Rosenberg, Mass Tort Class Actions: What Defendants Have and Plaintiffs Don't, 37 Harv. J. on Legis. 393, 399–402 (2000). Note, too, that defense costs are also investments in reputation: by conveying its willingness to fight each claim tooth and nail the defendant may deter future claims or reduce their expected value. See Galanter, *supra* n. 2, at 99; see also Menkel-Meadow, *supra* n. 9, at 27 (noting value to repeat player of cultivating a reputation as a bargainer or litigator).

[18] See e.g., Bruce Hay & David Rosenberg, 'Sweetheart' and 'Blackmail' Settlements in Class Actions: Reality and Remedy, 75 Notre Dame L. Rev. 1377, 1384 (2000); Rosenberg, *supra* n. 17, at 401; William C. Whitford, Structuring Consumer Protection Legislation to Maximize Effectiveness, 1981 Wis. L. Rev. 1018, 1020 (1981). This is not to say that repeat players will always out-invest one-shotters, only that they will often have the ability and incentive to do so.

In part, this reality reflects the fact that defendants automatically aggregate claims presenting common legal and factual questions:

> Faced with numerous actual and potential claims presenting common questions of liability and damages... the defendant always, naturally and necessarily, prepares one defense for all of those claims, litigating from the posture of a *de facto* class action... With class-wide aggregation of the defense interest, the defendant exploits economies of scale to invest far more cost effectively in preparing its side of the case than plaintiffs can in preparing their side.[19]

Substantial litigation investments should pay off by permitting litigants to develop and deploy legal strategies that increase their odds of success. This advantage persists even in the face of positive law that seems to favor a less-resourced adversary.[20] Put baldly, 'adverse legal doctrine defeats only those who believe it can. For nonbelievers, the strategic application of resources can construct outcomes to order, within cultural limits.'[21] Whether or not one accepts that legal indeterminacy permits well-resourced parties to 'construct outcomes to order,' parties who invest more in litigation will likely see superior results, especially across a class of similar cases.[22]

---

[19] Rosenberg, *supra* n. 17, at 393–394. Although Professor Rosenberg focuses on mass torts, he recognizes that his argument applies to many consumer and employment disputes. *Id.* at 393 n. 1. Indeed, a defendant need not be faced with a classic mass tort – in the sense of a fairly cohesive litigation presenting a common set of injuries resulting from exposure to a mass-produced product – in order to aggregate claims. Defendants have similar incentives whenever faced with present or potential future claims involving recurrent factual or legal issues. For a parallel discussion describing the tendency towards informal aggregation in much of American tort law, see Samuel Issacharoff & John Fabian Witt, The Inevitability of Aggregate Settlement: An Institutional Account of American Tort Law, 57 Vand. L. Rev. 1571 (2004).

[20] See Lynn M. LoPucki & Walter O. Weyrauch, A Theory of Legal Strategy, 49 Duke L.J. 1405, 1480–1482 (2000).

[21] *Id.* at 1480–1481.

[22] Repeat-player advantages include expertise, ready access to specialized legal representation, and 'trust and legitimacy' with institutional players like judges and clerks of court. Legal rules are not self-executing, and repeat players can better monitor the officers and agencies charged with their implementation. See Galanter, *supra* n. 2, at 98–99, 103, 109; Menkel-Meadow, *supra* n. 9, at 27–28 & n. 44. In short, 'Repeat players initiate the play, enjoy economies of scale, develop facilitative informal relations, have access to client-specialized legal representation, play the odds in their repetitive engagements, and with regard to the rules of the game, play for

CHAPTER 19. ARBITRATION AND THE INDIVIDUATION CRITIQUE

Galanter's article spawned a vast body of scholarship,[23] including studies searching for evidence of a repeat-player effect. Though the evidence is somewhat mixed, studies generally support the existence of at least a modest advantage for repeat players before trial[24] and appellate[25] courts, in the development of precedent,[26] and, possibly, in arbitration as well.[27]

---

rule-changes as much, or perhaps more than, for immediate gains.' Patricia Ewick & Susan S. Silbey, The Significance of Knowing that the "Haves" Come Out Ahead, in In Litigation: Do the 'Haves' Still Come Out Ahead?, *supra* n. 10, at 273, 273. These advantages may also enhance repeat players' leverage in informal negotiations. E.g., Gary Goodpaster, Lawsuits as Negotiations, Negotiation J., July 1992, at 221, 231–233; see generally Herbert M. Kritzer, Let's Make a Deal: Understanding the Negotiation Process in Ordinary Litigation (1991).

[23] See Glenn, *supra* n. 10.

[24] See e.g., Donald R. Songer, Reginald S. Sheehan & Susan Brodie Haire, Do the 'Haves' Come Out Ahead over Time?: Applying Galanter's Framework to Decisions of the U.S. Courts of Appeals, 1925–1988, in In Litigation: Do the 'Haves' Still Come Out Ahead?, *supra* n. 10, at 85; Craig Wanner, The Public Ordering of Private Relations: Part II: Winning Civil Court Cases, 9 Law & Soc'y Rev. 293, 300–305 (1975); see also Lewis M. Maltby, Private Justice: Employment Arbitration and Civil Rights, 30 Colum. Hum. Rts. L. Rev. 29, 47 (1998) (not testing the repeat-player hypothesis directly, but finding that federal courts granted dispositive, pre-trial motions in 60% of all employment discrimination cases that resulted in a definitive judgment in 1994; employers won 98% of these decisions).

[25] For examples of studies examining appellate decisions for a repeat-player effect, see Songer et al., *supra* n. 24, at 26, and Stanton Wheeler et al., Do the "Haves" Come Out Ahead? Winning and Losing in State Supreme Courts, 1870–1970, 21 Law & Soc'y Rev. 403 (1987).

[26] See Albiston, *supra* n. 15, at 887–896 (reporting study of published judicial opinions under the Family and Medical Leave Act and noting that individual litigants' successes are often not reflected in published judicial opinions); see also Maltby, *supra* n. 24, at 47 (finding that in 1994 employers won 98% of dispositive, pre-trial motions granted by federal courts in employment discrimination cases).

[27] The presence of a repeat-player effect in arbitration is a matter of dispute. See e.g., Lisa B. Bingham, Focus on Arbitration After Gilmer: Employment Arbitration: The Repeat Player Effect, 1 Emp. Rts. & Emp. Pol'y J. 189, 212–215 (1997) [hereinafter Bingham, The Repeat Player Effect] (finding that employees won something in 63% of all employment arbitrations studied, but in only 16% of arbitrations against repeat players; also finding that employees received, on average, a greater percentage of their demand when arbitrating with non-repeat player employers); Lisa B. Bingham, On Repeat Players, Adhesive Contracts, and the Use of Statistics in Judicial Review of Employment Arbitration Awards, 29 McGeorge L. Rev. 223, 238–239

19.2.2 Repeat-Player Lawyers and the Benefits of Aggregation

Something is missing from this picture: lawyers. Lawyers are often repeat players,[28] indeed the only ones involved in many cases.[29] In such cases, any repeat-player advantage may result from 'the repeat play of the large law firm lawyers who represent organizations.'[30] Perhaps plaintiffs' lawyers can confer similar benefits on their one-shotter clients.[31] Indeed, as described most thoroughly by Professor Stephen Yeazell,[32] plaintiffs' firms have gradually restructured

---

(1998) [hereinafter Bingham, On Repeat Players] (finding that employees lose more frequently when arbitrating against a repeat-player employer and when arbitrating before an arbitrator the employer has used before); Elizabeth Hill, Due Process at Low Cost: An Empirical Study of Employment Arbitration Under the Auspices of the American Arbitration Association, 18 Ohio St. J. on Disp. Resol. 777, 817 (2003) (reporting results from thirty-four arbitrations involving repeat-player employers, finding that apparent repeat-player effect could be attributed to the presence of an internal dispute resolution program by which employers screen out and resolve meritorious claims, resulting in weaker claims going to arbitration); David Sherwyn, Samuel Estreicher & Michael Heise, Assessing the Case for Employment Arbitration: A New Path for Empirical Research, 57 Stan. L. Rev. 1557, 1571–1572 (2005) (interpreting Hill and Bingham studies to suggest that 'repeat-player' effect may be attributable to presence of an internal dispute resolution program).

[28] Galanter, *supra* n. 2, at 114. Indeed, it has been argued that lawyers play a more significant role in shaping the law than do repeat-player litigants. See Paul H. Rubin & Martin J. Bailey, The Role of Lawyers in Changing the Law, 23 J. Legal Stud. 807 (1994).

[29] Gillian K. Hadfield, Exploring Economic and Democratic Theories of Civil Litigation: Differences Between Individual and Organizational Litigants in the Disposition of Federal Civil Cases, 57 Stan. L. Rev. 1275, 1319 (2005).

[30] *Ibid.*

[31] Galanter recognized this possibility but doubted that lawyers could offset the fundamental strategic advantage enjoyed by repeat players. Galanter, *supra* n. 2, at 118. Moreover, for lawyers, 'considerations of interest are likely to be fused with ideological commitments: the lawyers' preference for complex and finely-tuned bodies of rules, for adversary proceedings, for individualized case-by-case decision-making.' *Id.* at 119.

[32] Stephen C. Yeazell, Brown, the Civil Rights Movement, and the Silent Litigation Revolution, 57 Vand. L. Rev. 1975, 1991–2003 (2004) [hereinafter Yeazell, The Silent Litigation Revolution]; Stephen C. Yeazell, Re-Financing Civil Litigation, 51 DePaul L. Rev. 183 (2001) [hereinafter Yeazell, Re-Financing].

CHAPTER 19. ARBITRATION AND THE INDIVIDUATION CRITIQUE

themselves – becoming larger, more specialized, and better financed[33] – in ways that potentially offer repeat-player benefits to their clients.[34]

For my purposes, the most noteworthy aspect of this restructuring is the extent to which modern plaintiffs' firms, like other repeat players, aggregate claims. This happens in formal and informal ways. Formal methods include judicial mechanisms for combining multiple claims in a single judicial proceeding, such as joinder, class actions, intervention, and consolidation.[35] Where feasible, these mechanisms allow lawyers more effectively to coordinate and finance large-scale litigation.[36] Firms that undertake such litigation are of necessity specialized, well-financed repeat players.[37]

Moreover, even where formal judicial mechanisms are unavailable, technological and cultural changes have increased the ability and

---

[33] See Richard L. Abel, American Lawyers 122–123, 178–184, 202–207 (1989); Anita Bernstein, The Enterprise of Liability, 39 Val. U. L. Rev. 27, 48–51 (2004); Yeazell, Re-Financing, *supra* n. 32, at 199–200.

[34] Legal services organizations, too, might confer repeat-player benefits on their clients. On the role and repeat-player status of legal services lawyers, and restrictions governing their practice, see generally Richard L. Abel, Law without Politics: Legal Aid Under Advanced Capitalism, 32 UCLA L. Rev. 474 (1985); Kenneth W. Mentor & Richard D. Schwartz, A Tale of Two Offices: Adaptation Strategies of Selected LSC Agencies, 21 Just. Sys. J. 143 (2000). See also David P. McCaffrey, Corporate Resources and Regulatory Pressures: Toward Explaining a Discrepancy, 27 Admin. Sci. Q. 398, 410–413 (1982) (discussing role of public interest groups, including unions, in generating regulatory pressure through litigation).

[35] See Fed. R. Civ. P. 20, 23, 24 & 42. For a general discussion of formal aggregation methods, and their inadequacy to the task of allowing true coordination of related cases, see Howard M. Erichson, Informal Aggregation: Procedural and Ethical Implications of Coordination Among Counsel in Related Lawsuits, 50 Duke L.J. 381, 408–417 (2000).

[36] See Hay & Rosenberg, *supra* n. 18, at 1379–1381; Charles Silver & Lynn A. Baker, Mass Lawsuits and the Aggregate Settlement Rule, 32 Wake Forest L. Rev. 733, 743–744 (1997). On the benefits to plaintiffs of collective representation, through the class action or otherwise, see Howard M. Erichson, Beyond the Class Action: Lawyer Loyalty and Client Autonomy in Non-Class Collective Representation, 2003 U. Chi. Legal F. 519, 543–550, and Hay & Rosenberg, *supra* n. 18, at 1383–1389.

[37] See Yeazell, Re-Financing, *supra* n. 32, at 210–211. Slightly less formal methods of aggregation include federal multi-district litigation, 28 U.S.C. § 1407 (2006), and related state court procedures, e.g., Cal. Civ. Proc. Code § 404 (West 2006), in which related cases are transferred to a single court for coordinated pretrial proceedings.

willingness of plaintiffs' lawyers to pool information and risk, allowing them to match defendants' litigation investments even in the largest cases.[38] For example, plaintiffs' firms may agree to coordinate their efforts in multiple lawsuits, sharing expertise, discovery materials, and strategy,[39] and effectively treating the separate lawsuits as a single litigation.

Each of these aggregation methods is 'formal' to a degree, in that each represents an effort to coordinate litigation in response to the (more or less) contemporaneous filing of many related cases. Yet lawyers aggregate claims in entirely informal ways and in entirely unrelated disputes. As an example, consider a firm that specializes in representing plaintiffs in employment disputes. The law governing lawyers has gradually changed to make it easier for lawyers to market themselves[40] and to share fees in exchange for client referrals.[41] As a result, the firm likely participates in a vibrant referral network in which lawyers routinely refer potential clients to firms with the expertise and resources necessary to litigate the case effectively.[42] Through marketing and referrals, the firm generates an inventory of unrelated cases in its area of specialty. This inventory justifies investment in specialized training[43]

---

[38] See Erichson, *supra* n. 35, at 388–410; Issacharoff & Witt, *supra* n. 19, at 1624.
[39] See Erichson, *supra* n. 35, at 388–389.
[40] See Abel, *supra* n. 33, at 119–122; Yeazell, Re-Financing, *supra* n. 32, at 200–203, 212–213; see also Herbert M. Kritzer, Seven Dogged Myths Concerning Contingency Fees, 80 Wash. U. L.Q. 739, 749–753 (2002) [hereinafter Kritzer, Seven Dogged Myths] (reporting, from study of contingency fee practitioners in Wisconsin, on the relative significance of lawyer referrals, as opposed to direct advertising, in obtaining clients); Herbert M. Kritzer, From Litigators of Ordinary Cases to Litigators of Extraordinary Cases: Stratification of the Plaintiffs' Bar in the Twenty-First Century, 51 DePaul L. Rev. 219, 226 (2001) [hereinafter Kritzer, Extraordinary Cases] (generally describing stratification in plaintiffs' bar and here noting that advertising and modern communications have created markets for legal services 'bounded largely by limitations on legal practice, such as admission to state bars').
[41] See Issacharoff & Witt, *supra* n. 19, at 1622–1623; Yeazell, The Silent Litigation Revolution, *supra* n. 32, at 1996 & n. 89; Yeazell, Re-Financing, *supra* n. 32, at 201.
[42] See Yeazell, Re-Financing, *supra* n. 32, at 205, 212–213; Yeazell, The Silent Litigation Revolution, *supra* n. 32, at 1996. While the work in this area often focuses on personal injury lawyers, there is reason to believe that employment lawyers can be characterized in similar fashion. See *infra* text accompanying notes 52–54.
[43] See generally Yeazell, Re-Financing, *supra* n. 32, at 199–201, 212–214.

CHAPTER 19. ARBITRATION AND THE INDIVIDUATION CRITIQUE

and generates economies of scale,[44] perhaps allowing the firm profitably to represent even clients with relatively low-value claims.[45]

By informally aggregating claims in this manner, the firm may confer repeat-player benefits on its clients.[46] For example, the firm's expertise makes it a credible threat in litigation and permits it to quickly broker favorable settlements.[47] Firm lawyers may seek out and, within ethical constraints,[48] select for litigation cases likely to establish favorable precedent.[49] While the firm may not pass on to its clients the full benefits of its repeat-player status,[50] there are reasons to believe that, on average, 'the plaintiffs' bar is able to offer its clients a more valuable product at a lower cost' than was historically possible.[51] Although

---

[44] See *Id.* at 199.

[45] See Kritzer, Extraordinary Cases, *supra* n. 40, at 228–229 (discussing personal injury practices). I emphasize 'relatively' low-value. It is unlikely that many employment law firms (as in my example) would build a practice around representing clients with very modest claims in court. E.g., William M. Howard, Arbitrating Claims of Employment Discrimination: What Really Does Happen? What Really Should Happen?, 50 Disp. Resol. J., December 1995, at 40, 44. Whether firms might build such practices in arbitration is a separate question.

[46] See Issacharoff & Witt, *supra* n. 19, at 1613–1614; see also Menkel-Meadow, *supra* n. 9, at 30 (noting that developments in the personal injury bar have 'converted the lawyers, if not the clients, into very successful repeat players').

[47] See Issacharoff & Witt, *supra* n. 19, at 1601–1602, 1614–1615; Kritzer, Seven Dogged Myths, *supra* n. 40, at 774–775.

[48] For example, a lawyer could not encourage a client to drop a potentially valid claim simply because the case might generate a precedent unfavorable to other clients. See Galanter, *supra* n. 2, at 117 & n. 52.

[49] This is not to say that lawyers will pursue rules that are optimal for their clients. Lawyers may prefer uncertain rules that are costly to enforce. See *id.* at 119; Rubin & Bailey, *supra* n. 28, at 825. Yet there is likely to be substantial overlap between lawyers' and clients' interests. Moreover, as I mentioned earlier, I use the term 'precedent' to refer to any information of systemic value in future cases. See *supra* n. 14. In this sense, a settlement is precedential; information about the settlement value will inform future settlement decisions in similar cases.

[50] See Menkel-Meadow, *supra* n. 9, at 30.

[51] Yeazell, Re-Financing, *supra* n. 32, at 215–216; see also Richard N. Block & Jack Stieber, The Impact of Attorneys and Arbitrators on Arbitration Awards, 40 Indus. & Lab. Rel. Rev. 543, 553–554 (1987) (describing attorney impact in study of grievance arbitration); Issacharoff & Witt, *supra* n. 19, at 1611–1616 (describing developments in plaintiffs' bar and resulting efficiency benefits – that is, more rapid settlement – for clients).

these developments have been most pronounced in the personal injury and product liability bars,[52] the employment bar has experienced similar changes. Fueled in part by an expansion in the rights and remedies available to aggrieved employees,[53] a sizeable and specialized plaintiffs' employment bar now exists.[54]

19.2.3 Aggregation of Consumer Claims

Consumers, however, have derived limited benefit from this trend towards aggregation.[55] To see why, consider the following example, to which I will return later: A number of consumers buy cars from related dealerships – all subsidiaries of the same parent company – paying an additional fee of less than USD 1,000 for a 'warranty' that promises to pay a specified benefit if the car is stolen. Assume that sales personnel at the various dealerships are alleged to have misrepresented the true cost of the 'warranty,' and that this conduct, if proven, amounts to an unfair trade practice. The 'warranty,' moreover, may be void under state insurance law, and the consumers may be entitled to restitution.[56]

Few of these consumers are likely to obtain specialized legal representation as individuals. One obvious reason for this is the modest

---

[52] See Issacharoff & Witt, *supra* n. 19, at 1610–1614; Menkel-Meadow, *supra* n. 9, at 30; Yeazell, Re-Financing, *supra* n. 32, at 216.

[53] See generally Sherwyn et al., *supra* n. 27, at 76–80.

[54] See e.g., Susan Bisom-Rapp, Bulletproofing the Workplace: Symbol and Substance in Employment Discrimination Law Practice, 26 Fla. St. U. L. Rev. 959, 1019 (1999) (reporting in 1999 that the National Employment Lawyers Association, a national organization of plaintiffs' employment lawyers, had 3,500 members). For information about the prevalence of employment and other class actions drawn from published judicial opinions and media reports, see Deborah H. Hensler et al., Class Action Dilemmas: Pursuing Public Goals for Private Gain 51–61 (2000).

[55] For a general discussion of the barriers to consumer litigation and the need for aggregating devices, see Samuel Issacharoff, Group Litigation of Consumer Claims: Lessons from the U.S. Experience, 34 Tex. Int'l L. J. 135, 142–150 (1999).

[56] These facts are based on two class actions currently pending before the AAA. See Am. Arbitration Ass'n, Class Action Case Docket: *Owens v. Auto. Protection Corp.*, <www.adr.org/sp.asp?id=25825> (last visited January 27, 2007); Am. Arbitration Ass'n, Class Action Case Docket: *Price v. Auto. Protection Corp.*, <www.adr.org/sp.asp?id=25827> (last visited January 27, 2007).

CHAPTER 19. ARBITRATION AND THE INDIVIDUATION CRITIQUE

size of their claims.[57] Even with the prospect of treble damages – authorized by some consumer protection laws – individual claims remain small. The cost and uncertainty involved in collecting any judgment compounds this problem.[58] Moreover, procedural innovations like small claims courts, and statutory inducements like attorney's fees, may not induce lawyers to accept individual consumer cases.[59] Many small claims courts do not allow legal representation at all,[60] and those that do may not offer adequate discovery[61] or a full range of remedies.[62] Nor do small claims courts typically publish their decisions or create precedent;[63] indeed, small claims courts are not always presided over by lawyers.[64] Although many consumer protection statutes

---

[57] See e.g., Jeff Sovern, Toward a Theory of Warranties in Sales of New Homes, 1993 Wis. L. Rev. 13, 85. This problem is not unique to consumer litigants. See *supra* n. 45 (discussing threshold for employment lawyers to accept a case). As a general matter, claimants with modest-size claims are poorly served by the court system. See David M. Trubek et al., The Costs of Ordinary Litigation, 31 UCLA L. Rev. 72, 84 (1983–1984).

[58] This is especially true for unrepresented consumers. See Richard L. Abel, The Contradictions of Informal Justice, in 1 The Politics of Informal Justice 267, 298 (Richard L. Abel ed., 1982).

[59] An ostensible purpose of small claims courts, of course, is to permit individuals to obtain informal, accessible justice without retaining a lawyer at all. But the reality may be somewhat different. See Abel, *supra* n. 58, at 295. ('The notion that these are intended to benefit individuals or tenants is a contemporary post factum legitimation; small claims courts were explicitly established to facilitate debt collection by merchants.').

[60] Mark E. Budnitz, The High Cost of Mandatory Consumer Arbitration, 67 Law & Contemp. Probs., Winter/Spring 2004, at 133, 137–138; James C. Turner & Joyce A. McGee, Small Claims Reform: A Means of Expanding Access to the American Civil Justice System, 5 UDC/DCSL L. Rev. 177, 187 (2000). This may enhance the advantages repeat players already enjoy over one-shotters. See Abel, *supra* n. 58, at 294, 296.

[61] See e.g., *Village of Castleton v. Pillsworth*, 708 N.Y.S.2d 239, 241 (Just. Ct. 2000) (denying request for discovery as inconsistent with expedited nature of small claims actions); Budnitz, *supra* n. 60, at 138.

[62] See Budnitz, *supra* n. 60, at 138; Turner & McGee, *supra* n. 60, at 185–186.

[63] Glenn E. Roper, Eternal Student Loan Liability: Who Can Sue Under 20 U.S.C. §1091A, 20 BYU J. Pub. L. 35, 38 (2005).

[64] See e.g., N.C. Stat. §7A-171.2.

authorize awards of attorney's fees,[65] lawyers may doubt that courts will award enough in fees to justify their investment in the case.[66] For these and other reasons, individual consumers may have limited access to a vibrant and specialized plaintiffs' bar.[67]

Of course, a lawyer might be interested in bringing a class action on behalf of the dispersed consumers. Indeed, that is the primary method of aggregating consumer claims.[68] Although controversial,[69] class actions have undeniable benefits, allowing consumers to assert low-value claims they could not bring as individuals[70] and encouraging the development of a vibrant, well-financed class

---

[65] E.g., Truth in Lending Act, 15 U.S.C. § 1640(a)(3) (2006); Fair Debt Collection Practices Act, 15 U.S.C. § 1692k(a)(3) (2006); see also Debra E. Wax, Annotation, Award of Attorneys' Fees in Actions Under State Deceptive Trade Practice and Consumer Protections Acts, 35 A.L.R.4th 12 (1985) (discussing state consumer protection statutes).

[66] Stewart Macaulay, Lawyers and Consumer Protection Laws, 14 Law & Soc'y Rev. 115, 120–122, 130 (1979); Whitford, *supra* n. 18, at 1030.

[67] E.g., Macaulay, *supra* n. 66, at 122, 130; Laura Nader & Christopher Shugart, Old Solutions for Old Problems, in No Access to Law 57, 58 (Laura Nader ed., 1980).

[68] See Richard M. Alderman, Pre-Dispute Mandatory Arbitration in Consumer Contracts: A Call for Reform, 38 Hous. L. Rev. 1237, 1254–1256 (2001). Public interest lawyers, of course, may also offer specialized representation to some individual consumers. See *supra* n. 34.

[69] For just a sampling of diverse views on the merits and potential abuses of the class action, see Robert G. Bone, Statistical Adjudication: Rights, Justice, and Utility in a World of Process Scarcity, 46 Vand. L. Rev. 561 (1993); Roger C. Cramton, Individualized Justice, Mass Torts, and 'Settlement Class Actions': An Introduction, 80 Cornell L. Rev. 811 (1995); John C. Coffee Jr., Class Wars: The Dilemma of the Mass Tort Class Action, 95 Colum. L. Rev. 1343 (1995); Richard A. Epstein, Class Actions: Aggregation, Amplification, and Distortion, 2003 U. Chi. Legal F. 475; Hay & Rosenberg, *supra* n. 18; Susan P. Koniak, Feasting While the Widow Weeps: *Georgine v. Amchem Products, Inc.*, 80 Cornell L. Rev. 1045 (1995); Richard A. Nagareda, Closure in Damage Class Settlements: The Godfather Guide to Opt-Out Rights, 2003 U. Chi. Legal F. 141; Martin H. Redish, Class Actions and the Democratic Difficulty: Rethinking the Intersection of Private Litigation and Public Goals, 2003 U. Chi. Legal F. 71; David Rosenberg, The Causal Connection in Mass Exposure Cases: A 'Public Law' Vision of the Tort System, 97 Harv. L. Rev. 849 (1984).

[70] See Jean R. Sternlight, As Mandatory Binding Arbitration Meets the Class Action, Will the Class Action Survive?, 42 Wm. & Mary L. Rev. 1, 30 (2000).

CHAPTER 19. ARBITRATION AND THE INDIVIDUATION CRITIQUE

action bar.[71] Yet class certification is far from common. Class actions run counter to a strong individualist streak in American law, which demands respect for the individual litigant's right to control his or her own claim,[72] and which, by and large, requires individualized proof of facts specific to each claimant.[73] Because of the need for such proof, class actions seeking damages may generally be certified only where, among other things, common questions of law or fact predominate over questions affecting only individual class members.[74]

This balancing act leads courts to deny certification to many proposed consumer classes.[75] Recall my example of car buyers who

---

[71] The vibrancy of the consumer class action bar is apparent from the prevalence of consumer class action litigation in state and federal courts and in its prominence in media reports of class actions. See Hensler et al., *supra* n. 54, at 52–53 (reporting that in 1995–1996 consumer cases accounted for around 25% of reported judicial opinions addressing class actions, and also around 25% of reports on class actions in the business and general press).

[72] See e.g., Roger H. Transgrud, Joinder Alternatives in Mass Tort Litigation, 70 Cornell L. Rev. 779, 822 (1985). Given the tendency of legal markets to aggregate claims informally when formal methods are unavailable, one might question whether litigants value the right to 'control' litigation as much as is often supposed. E.g., Erichson, *supra* n. 36, at 543–550; Hay & Rosenberg, *supra* n. 18, at 1380 n. 8; Silver & Baker, *supra* n. 36, at 744; see also Issacharoff & Witt, *supra* n. 19 (describing 'inevitability' of aggregate settlement).

[73] Cf. Bruce L. Hay, Procedural Justice – *Ex Ante v. Ex Post*, 44 UCLA L. Rev. 1803, 1838 (1997) (class actions call for 'less inquiry into the individual circumstances of each case').

[74] I am referring here to class actions under Fed. R. Civ. P. 23(b)(3).

[75] See *Andrews v. AT&T*, 95 F.3d 1014, 1025 (11th Cir. 1996) (reversing class certification in class action filed by customers of long-distance telephone companies; plaintiffs had to prove reliance on alleged misrepresentation, as well as fact and amount of injury, on an individual basis); *Parkhill v. Minn. Mut. Life Ins. Co.*, 188 F.R.D. 332, 343 (D. Minn. 1999) (declining certification in 'vanishing premium' life insurance case due to need for individualized inquiry into whether a misrepresentation was made to, and relied upon by, each plaintiff); *Martin v. Dahlberg, Inc.*, 156 F.R.D. 207, 216–217 (N.D. Cal. 1994) (denying certification because individual issues of reliance on alleged misrepresentations predominated in suit by purchasers of hearing aids against manufacturer and other defendants); *Gross v. Johnson & Johnson-Merck Consumer Pharms. Co.*, 696 A.2d 793, 798 (N.J. Super. Ct. 1997) (denying certification in consumer fraud suit against maker of heartburn medication because of predominance of individual issues concerning whether each consumer saw and relied on alleged misrepresentation). Consumers have had the most success

821

purchase a theft-protection 'warranty' from dealerships operating as subsidiaries of a common parent company.[76] Assume the buyers allege that individual salespersons, acting pursuant to a practice common to all dealerships and encouraged by the parent, misled customers as to key warranty terms. This dispute raises a number of common questions,[77] but also many questions requiring individualized proof in court: Did a salesperson misrepresent a material fact to each buyer? If so, did the buyer justifiably rely on that misrepresentation? To what extent was the buyer injured? Many (probably most) judges would decline to certify a class, reasoning that common questions do not predominate over these 'individual' issues.[78]

For the consumer advocate, at least, this is an unsatisfactory result, one that 'arises from slavish adherence to the fiction that individual members are before the court and hence that the amount of money to be paid by the defendant should be the sum of the individual claims.'[79] Denial of certification, of course, typically means that few if any

---

obtaining class certification where the relevant substantive law dispenses with the need to prove individual reliance and damages, as with the statutory damages provisions of the Truth in Lending Act, U.S.C. § 1640(a)(2) (2006). See generally Christopher L. Peterson, Truth, Understanding, and High-Cost Consumer Credit: The Historical Context of the Truth in Lending Act, 55 Fla. L. Rev. 807, 886–890 (2003) (discussing the expansion and eventual contraction of TILA litigation); Whitford, supra n. 18, at 1030–1031 (noting potential success of TILA in inducing consumer claiming).

[76] Supra text accompanying notes 55–56.

[77] Examples of issues common to the class as a whole, or to appropriate subclasses, might include whether the parent company can be held liable for misrepresentations made by employees of its subsidiaries, and whether state insurance law authorizes a cause of action for rescission. Cf. Order No. 2 (Respondent's Motion to Dismiss) at 12, *Owens v. Auto. Protection Corp.*, No. 30 459 00642 05, 13–17 (May 10, 2006) (Am. Arbitration Ass'n), available at <www.adr.org/si.asp?id=2239> (discussing these issues in the class arbitration from which my example is drawn).

[78] See *supra* n. 75; see also In re Jackson Nat'l Life Ins. Co. Premium Litig., 183 F.R.D. 217, 221 (W.D. Mich. 1998) (holding that plaintiffs failed to satisfy predominance requirement, despite alleging that defendant prepared uniform, misleading sales materials for independent insurance brokers, because of need to determine what materials were presented, and what representations made, by brokers to each plaintiff).

[79] Nader & Shugart, *supra* n. 67, at 93.

CHAPTER 19. ARBITRATION AND THE INDIVIDUATION CRITIQUE

consumers will assert claims at all,[80] and the deterrence objectives of consumer protection laws will go unfulfilled.[81]

19.2.4 The Individuation Critique

19.2.4.1 Does Arbitration Individuate Claiming?

As should be clear from the foregoing discussion, aggregation benefits consumers and employees primarily as claimants[82] Despite difficulties in obtaining certification, many consumer[83] and employment[84] classes have been certified, and employees, at least those with sizeable claims,[85] may also find specialized, effective representation in individual lawsuits.[86] These are significant developments, and they reflect the

---

[80] See Issacharoff, *supra* n. 55, at 147 (noting need for device to aggregate consumer claims); cf. *Carnegie v. Household Int'l, Inc.*, 376 F.3d 656, 661 (7th Cir. 2004) ('[A] class action has to be unwieldy indeed before it can be pronounced an inferior alternative... to no litigation at all.').

[81] See Samuel Issacharoff & Erin F. Delaney, Credit Card Accountability, 73 U. Chi. L. Rev. 157, 168–175 (2006) (noting that arbitration and class action prohibitions may leave credit card industry free to engage in misconduct without challenge); Issacharoff, *supra* n. 55, at 147 ('This problem [of finding a way to aggregate consumer claims] is all the more compelling if the purpose of consumer enforcement is seen to be as much deterrence of misconduct as actual compensation to victims of fraud.').

[82] As defendants ('respondents,' in arbitration), consumers may be even less likely to find a lawyer and, except in rare cases, cannot combine their defense efforts with other claimants. But see *Sears Roebuck & Co. v. Avery*, 593 S.E.2d 424 (N.C. Ct. App. 2004) (credit card holder sued in collections action files class action counterclaim).

[83] E.g., Carnegie, 376 F.3d at 661; *Gordon v. Microsoft Corp.*, No. 00–5994, 2001 WL 366432 (D. Minn. March 30, 2001); *Lopez v. Orlor, Inc.*, 176 F.R.D. 35 (D. Conn. 1997); In re Domestic Air Transp. Antitrust Litig., 137 F.R.D. 677 (N.D. Ga. 1991); *Dix v. Am. Bankers Life Assurance Co.*, 415 N.W.2d 206 (Mich. 1987); *Varacallo v. Mass. Mut. Life Ins. Co.*, 752 A.2d 807 (N.J. Super. Ct. App. Div. 2000).

[84] E.g., *Allen v. Int'l Truck & Engine Corp.*, 358 F.3d 469, 472 (7th Cir. 2004); *Robinson v. Metro-North Commuter R.R.*, 267 F.3d 147, 168–169 (2nd Cir. 2001); *Dukes v. Wal-Mart Stores, Inc.*, 222 F.R.D. 137 (N.D. Cal. 2004); *McReynolds v. Sodexho Marriott Servs., Inc.*, 208 F.R.D. 428 (D.D.C. 2002); *Hendricks-Robinson v. Excel Corp.*, 164 F.R.D. 667 (C.D. Ill. 1996); *Jenson v. Eveleth Taconite Co.*, 139 F.R.D. 657, 665–667 (D. Minn. 1991).

[85] See *supra* n. 45.

[86] See *supra* text accompanying notes 52–54.

increased ability of the plaintiffs' bar to influence the outcome of particular cases and the legal system at large.

The individuation critique sees arbitration as one of a number of tools repeat-player defendants use to combat the increased influence of the plaintiffs' bar.[87] In general terms, the critique posits that businesses will structure the arbitration process in ways that force consumers and employees into individuated proceedings,[88] and that ADR providers,

---

[87] See Alderman, *supra* n. 68, at 1255. ('As consumers have marshaled the resources and expertise to compete with the repeat player in the courts, the repeat player has taken steps to change the forum through the imposition of mandatory arbitration.'). A similar argument might be made about efforts to restrict lawyers' ability to advertise or solicit clients. Cf. Yeazell, The Silent Litigation Revolution, *supra* n. 32, at 1985–1988 (describing how states resisted desegregation efforts by seeking to restrict lawyers' ability to solicit clients and control the strategic direction of litigation). Other possibilities include limits on the fees recoverable by plaintiffs' lawyers and reduced or contingent funding for legal aid, see Thomas F. Burke, Lawyers, Lawsuits, and Legal Rights: The Battle Over Litigation in American Society 27–37 (2002), and many other aspects of the 'tort reform' movement, including public relations efforts to shape public opinion about the legal system, e.g., Stephen Daniels & Joanne Martin, 'The Impact That It Has Had Is Between People's Ears': Tort Reform, Mass Culture, and Plaintiffs' Lawyers, 50 DePaul L. Rev. 453, 461–472 (2000); Michael L. Rustad & Thomas H. Koenig, Taming the Tort Monster: The American Civil Justice System as a Battleground of Social Theory, 68 Brook. L. Rev. 1, 50–52, 65–71, 74–80 (2002). See also John T. Nockleby & Shannon Curreri, 100 Years of Conflict: The Past and Future of Tort Retrenchment, 38 Loy. L.A. L. Rev. 1021 (2005) (characterizing current tort reform movement as a reaction to the expansion of tort rights).

[88] Arbitration skeptics not surprisingly focus on the temptation for repeat-player contract drafters to structure the arbitration process to their advantage. E.g., Jean R. Sternlight, Creeping Mandatory Arbitration: Is It Just?, 57 Stan. L. Rev. 1631, 1649–1652 (2005); Lisa B. Bingham, Control Over Dispute-System Design and Mandatory Commercial Arbitration, 67 Law & Contemp. Probs., Winter/Spring 2004, at 221, 232–239; Richard A. Bales, The Laissez-Faire Arbitration Market and the Need for a Uniform Federal Standard Governing Employment and Consumer Arbitration, 52 U. Kan. L. Rev. 583, 606–608 (2004); Paul D. Carrington, Self-Deregulation, the 'National Policy' of the Supreme Court, 3 Nev. L.J. 259, 285 (2002–2003). That temptation may be enhanced by the Supreme Court's expansive interpretation of the Federal Arbitration Act (FAA), 9 U.S.C. §§ 1–16 (2006), which has restricted states' efforts to regulate the terms of arbitration agreements. See e.g., *Doctor's Assocs., Inc. v. Casarotto*, 517 U.S. 681, 688 (1996) (invalidating state-law 'conspicuous notice'

CHAPTER 19. ARBITRATION AND THE INDIVIDUATION CRITIQUE

in their desire to attract arbitration business,[89] will adopt rules that have a similar effect.

The most obvious way this might happen is by preventing class actions. Especially in the consumer context, arbitration skeptics often assume that businesses use arbitration specifically to prevent class actions,[90] an assumption buttressed by various comments made by consumer finance industry insiders, advocates, and ADR professionals.[91] Indeed, because the class action features so prominently in

---

requirement for arbitration agreements); *Allied-Bruce Terminix Cos., Inc. v. Dobson*, 513 U.S. 265, 277 (1995) (extending the FAA to the limits of Congress' authority under the Commerce Clause); *Mastrobuono v. Shearson Lehman Hutton, Inc.*, 514 U.S. 52, 59 (1995) (noting that unless the parties agreed otherwise, the FAA would preempt a state law rule forbidding arbitral awards of punitive damages); *Perry v. Thomas*, 482 U.S. 483, 492 n. 9 (1987) (describing states' limited authority to regulate arbitration agreements); *Southland Corp. v. Keating*, 465 U.S. 1, 10 (1984) (holding that the FAA established a 'national policy favoring arbitration' applicable in state as well as federal courts).

[89] Cf. Richard C. Reuben, Constitutional Gravity: A Unitary Theory of Alternative Dispute Resolution and Public Civil Justice, 47 UCLA L. Rev. 949, 1063–1064 (2000) (noting incentives for arbitrators to rule in ways that do not offend repeat-player businesses).

[90] E.g., Mark E. Budnitz, Arbitration of Disputes Between Consumers and Financial Institutions: A Serious Threat to Consumer Protection, 10 Ohio St. J. on Disp. Resol. 267, 310, 318, 326–330 (1995); Myriam Gilles, Opting Out of Liability: The Forthcoming, Near-Total Demise of the Modern Class Action, 104 Mich. L. Rev. 373, 396–399 (2005); Jean R. Sternlight & Elizabeth J. Jensen, Using Arbitration to Eliminate Consumer Class Actions: Efficient Business Practice or Unconscionable Abuse?, 67 Law & Contemp. Probs., Winter/Spring 2004, at 75, 75; Sternlight, *supra* n. 70, at 5–12. While contract drafters initially may have assumed that merely including an arbitration agreement in the transaction would prevent class action litigation, that assumption is no longer tenable after *Green Tree Financial Corp. v. Bazzle*, 539 U.S. 444 (2003). Thus, we might expect contracts increasingly to contain express waivers of the right to bring or participate in class proceedings. See Bingham, *supra* n. 88, at 236–237; Gilles, *supra*, at 410.

[91] E.g., Dwight Golann, Consumer Financial Services Litigation: Major Judgments and ADR Responses, 48 Bus. Law. 1141 (1993) (describing class action litigation in California between consumers and financial institutions and the subsequent implementation of arbitration programs); Alan S. Kaplinsky & Mark J. Levin, Drafting and Implementing of a Consumer Loan Arbitration Clause, 51 Consumer Fin. L.Q. Rep. 295, 295 (1997) (opining that consumer financial services companies are pressured to settle lawsuits for reasons having nothing to do with their merits and advocating arbitration

any discussion of consumer litigation—and thus in any discussion of consumer arbitration—debates over consumer arbitration focus primarily on the use of arbitration to eliminate consumer class actions.[92]

But the lack of class actions is only the most obvious example of how arbitration might individuate disputes. Others include arbitrators' failure to develop or follow precedent,[93] issue written, reasoned awards, or award punitive damages, attorney's fees, and injunctive relief.[94] Such individuated arbitration proceedings might not permit the economies of scale needed to justify substantial litigation investments, specialized training, or efforts to develop a case inventory.[95] Contingency-fee lawyers might decline cases destined for arbitration,[96] and those who accepted such cases might be relatively unspecialized, poorly capitalized, and otherwise less effective than their repeat-player peers in the plaintiffs' bar.[97] Indeed, the individuation critique might

---

as a means to prevent such lawsuits, particularly class actions); Lloyd N. Shields, The Role of Mandatory Arbitration for Financial Institutions, 46 Arb. J. 49, 52 (1991) (article by director of AAA stating that 'arbitration may be the financial community's answer to the class-action contingent-fee strike suit'); Letter from Curtis V. Brown, V.P. and General Counsel, National Arbitration Forum, to prospective client (January 14, 1999) (on file with author) (noting that an arbitration clause may eliminate class actions); see also *Complaint, Ross v. Bank of Am., N.A.*, No. 05-CV-07116 (S.D.N.Y. filed August 11, 2005) (on file with author) (alleging major credit card issuers conspired, in violation of antitrust laws, to impose arbitration agreements, in part to avoid class actions).

[92] See *supra* notes 90–91.

[93] See Richard M. Alderman, Consumer Arbitration: The Destruction of the Common Law, 2 J. Am. Arb. 1, 11 (2003):

> (Unlike court opinions, which are published, most decisions of arbitrators are kept secret, often not even accompanied by a written opinion. Even when published and made available to the public, the decision of one arbitrator, or a panel of arbitrators, is in no way binding on any other arbitrator or panel.).

Cf. Abel, *supra* n. 58, at 288–291, 290 ("Conflict can result in prospective aggregation through the declaration or modification of general behavioral norms.").

[94] See Menkel-Meadow, *supra* n. 9, at 37.

[95] See *supra* text accompanying notes 40–45.

[96] Bingham, The Repeat Player Effect, *supra* n. 27, at 198–200.

[97] *Ibid.*

CHAPTER 19. ARBITRATION AND THE INDIVIDUATION CRITIQUE

retain its force even if we thought consumers and employees generally fared well in individual arbitrations.[98] Without formal aggregation

---

[98] At least in the employment context, a growing body of empirical evidence suggests that employees may fare relatively well in arbitration. See e.g., Bingham, The Repeat Player Effect, *supra* n. 27, at 213 (finding 63% employee win-rate in 1993–1994, but only 16% win-rate against 'repeat players'); Theodore Eisenberg & Elizabeth Hill, Arbitration and Litigation of Employment Claims: An Empirical Comparison, 58 Disp. Resol. J., January 2004, at 44, 48–49 (finding that higher-pay employees fare as well or better in arbitration and that lower-pay employees may fare somewhat worse, but noting that apparent superiority of court over arbitration for lower-pay employees may reflect greater likelihood that court plaintiffs are subject only to 'for cause' termination); Hill, *supra* n. 27, at 817 (presenting data suggesting that 'repeat player' effect noted by Bingham may be attributable to the presence of an internal dispute resolution program, which allows employers to screen out and settle meritorious cases before arbitration); Howard, *supra* n. 45 (finding employee win-rate of 28% in court, versus 68% in AAA arbitration and 48% in securities industry arbitration; results do not take into account pre-trial dispositions and may therefore overstate win-rate in court); Maltby, *supra* n. 24, at 47–48 (finding, among other things, that employee claimants receive on average 18% of their demand in arbitration, versus 10.4% in litigation; also noting that 60% of employment cases in federal court are terminated on pretrial motion, with employers winning 98% of those decisions); see also Sherwyn et al., *supra* n. 27, at 1578 (summarizing existing research). But see Michael H. LeRoy, Getting Nothing for Something: When Women Prevail in Employment Arbitration Awards, 16 Stan. L. & Pol'y Rev. 573 (2005) (finding, based on study of employment arbitration awards subjected to judicial review, that employees succeed more often in arbitration than at trial, but recover less, and that women more often received 'split awards,' such as awards denying attorney's fees). A variety of methodological issues make it difficult to draw firm conclusions from this research. E.g., Sherwyn et al., *supra* n. 27, at 1564–1566.

One study of consumer arbitration, conducted by Ernst & Young and funded by the American Bankers Association, suggests that consumers generally fare well as arbitration claimants, although the study makes some debatable assumptions, including that consumers prevailed each time a case was dismissed at the claimant's request. Ernst & Young, Outcomes of Arbitration: An Empirical Study of Consumer Lending Cases (2004) [hereinafter Ernst & Young Study], available at <www.ey.com/global/download.nsf/US/Outcomes_of_Arbitration/$file/OutcomesofArbitrationAnEmpiricalStudy.pdf>. For criticism of this study, see Ctr. for Responsible Lending, Comments on Ernst & Young Arbitration Outcomes Report (February 24, 2005), <www.responsiblelending.org/pdfs/ib025-Ernst_Young_Arbitration_Comments-0205.pdf>.

techniques like the class action, and without repeat-player lawyers, overall claiming rates might remain low,[99] and certain claims – those requiring substantial investments and sophisticated lawyers – might not be brought at all.[100]

While theoretically defensible, these objections to arbitration at present have only modest empirical support.[101] The best available evidence suggests that only a minority of consumer arbitration agreements – albeit a substantial minority – expressly prohibit class actions,[102] although these terms may become more common after *Bazzle*.[103] Employment arbitration agreements may be less likely than

---

[99] See Whitford, *supra* n. 18, at 1030 (noting role of attorneys in informing consumers of rights).

[100] Cf. *id.* at 1030 (noting importance of lawyers in 'informing consumers of their rights in an effort to stimulate legal business').

[101] One can find evidence that some businesses include one-sided terms in arbitration agreements in published judicial opinions ruling on a consumer's or employee's challenge to the agreement's enforceability. See e.g., Bales, *supra* n. 88, at 606–608; Carrington, *supra* n. 88, at 286; David S. Schwartz, Understanding Remedy-Stripping Arbitration Clauses: Validity, Arbitrability, and Preclusion Principles, 38 U.S.F. L. Rev. 49, 56–59 (2003). But focusing on such cases may yield a skewed picture of arbitration agreements generally, as lawyers should be less willing to challenge a scrupulously even-handed arbitration agreement. To my knowledge, Professors Linda Demaine and Deborah Hensler have conducted the most systematic study of consumer arbitration agreements. Linda J. Demaine & Deborah R. Hensler, 'Volunteering' to Arbitrate Through Predispute Arbitration Clauses: The Average Consumer's Experience, 67 Law & Contemp. Probs., Winter/Spring 2004, at 55.

[102] See Demaine & Hensler, *supra* n. 101, at 60, 65 (finding that 30.8% of a sample of consumer arbitration agreements collected in 2001 included contract terms precluding class actions). In conducting research for this paper, I also collected as many of the arbitration agreements at issue in the AAA class arbitrations as I could find. (These agreements are often available on the AAA website; in other cases I downloaded them from PACER.) In total, I collected thirty-two agreements (sixteen consumer and sixteen employment). Of these, five of the sixteen (31%) of the consumer agreements forbid class actions, but none of the sixteen employment agreements contains a similar term. I do not suggest that these results are representative of the broader universe of arbitration agreements. Class action prohibitions in particular may be underrepresented in the sample, as the AAA requires a court order before it will accept for class arbitration a dispute under an agreement that expressly bars class actions. See Am. Arbitration Ass'n, American Arbitration Association Policy on Class Arbitrations (July 14, 2005), <www.adr.org/sp.asp?id=25967>.

[103] Gilles, *supra* n. 90, at 410; Sternlight, *supra* n. 70, at 90–91.

CHAPTER 19. ARBITRATION AND THE INDIVIDUATION CRITIQUE

consumer agreements to prohibit class-wide proceedings.[104] As for other individuating contract terms, such as those restricting arbitration remedies, requiring confidentiality, or preventing arbitrators from issuing written awards, the best available evidence suggests that these terms may be less common than the individuation critique would predict.[105]

While further study may reveal the critique to be an apt description of arbitration contracts in certain industries – the consumer finance industry is an example[106] – the existing evidence suggests that the critique may be somewhat overbroad. There are other reasons why businesses might prefer arbitration to litigation, and it is not obvious that most agreements will contain individuating terms.[107] Furthermore,

---

[104] For example, in a 1995 survey of employment arbitration agreements, the General Accounting Office found that only one of the twenty-six clauses studied limited the remedies available in arbitration. U.S. Gen. Accounting Office, GAO/HEHS-95-150, Employment Discrimination: Most Private Sector Employers Use Alternative Dispute Resolution (1995) [hereinafter 1995 GAO Report]. The 1995 GAO Report did not mention whether any of the agreements forbade class actions, and silence on that point likely indicates that the agreements did not refer to class actions at all. See Mei L. Bickner et al., Developments in Employment Arbitration: Analysis of a New Survey of Employment Arbitration Programs, 52 Disp. Resol. J., January 1997, at 8, 81 (reporting that two-thirds of surveyed employment arbitration plans did not restrict available remedies, although a minority limited damages in some way, and that around one-half of plans specifically permitted punitive damages; no reference to class action prohibitions). Again, in my sample of arbitration agreements drawn from the AAA class arbitrations, none of the employment agreements expressly barred class actions. See *supra* n. 102 (also noting that such terms may be underrepresented in these agreements). For an analysis of arbitration clauses in a sample of franchise agreements, see Christopher R. Drahozal, 'Unfair' Arbitration Clauses, 2001 U. Ill. L. Rev. 695.

[105] See e.g., 1995 GAO Report, *supra* n. 104 (finding in a 1995 survey of employment arbitration agreements that only one of the twenty-six clauses studied limited the remedies available in arbitration); Bickner et al., *supra* n. 104, at 81 (reporting that two-thirds of surveyed employment arbitration plans did not restrict available remedies, although a minority limited damages in some way); Demaine & Hensler, *supra* n. 101, at 69, 71–72 (finding that 13.5% of a sample of consumer agreements collected in 2001 required that some aspect of the arbitration be kept confidential and that 7.7% of the agreements restricted the remedies available in arbitration).

[106] See *supra* n. 91.

[107] Arbitration, for example, likely reduces the cost of resolving disputes, see Stephen J. Ware, Paying the Price of Process: Judicial Regulation of Consumer Arbitration Agreements, 2001 J. Disp. Resol. 89, 90–91, and businesses and employers

as I discuss below, even when an agreement does contain such terms, their impact may be limited. To understand why, we need to examine the institutional context in which many arbitrations occur.

19.2.4.2 The Potential Moderating Effect of ADR Provider Rules

The individuation critique is founded on an explicitly contractualist model of arbitration. The model assigns to the contracting parties themselves primary authority for setting the terms of arbitration and gives correspondingly little weight to the role of extra-contractual forces in shaping arbitration procedure. Of course, consumer and employment contracts tend not to be models of arms' length negotiation. To those skeptical that market forces will produce an acceptable allocation of risk, such contracts are an invitation to overreach for the party with the stronger bargaining position. Put bluntly, the individuation critique posits that arbitration will individuate disputes because that is what

---

may pass some of these savings on in the form of higher wages or lower prices, e.g., Drahozal, *supra* n. 104, at 741; Ware, *supra*, at 90–94. Arbitration may also produce faster results; all else being equal, this is a clear benefit to claimants. Most of the empirical evidence concerning arbitration procedures and results has focused on employment arbitration. In that context, there seems little question that arbitration produces faster results, e.g., Maltby, *supra* n. 24, at 55; Sherwyn et al., *supra* n. 27, at 1572–1573, 1578, 1588–1589, and the same is likely true for consumer arbitration.

Employers in particular may have varied reasons for adopting arbitration programs. Many have long relied on a variety of informal dispute resolution procedures that may reduce the costs associated with disputing: legal expenses, lost management time, increased employee turnover, and reduced employee morale. See Sherwyn et al., *supra* n. 27, at 1579; see also 1995 GAO Report, *supra* n. 104 (finding, in survey of businesses that filed 1992 EEOC reports and had at least 100 employees, that almost 90% used some variety of ADR, though only 9.9% used arbitration (often not mandatory)). For a different perspective on employment arbitration, one focusing on the consequences of permitting private organizations to internalize the disputing process, see Lauren B. Edelman & Mark C. Suchman, When the 'Haves' Hold Court, in In Litigation: Do the 'Haves' Still Come Out Ahead?, *supra* n. 10, at 290. And for a discussion of the risk-management function of arbitration, see Scott Baker, A Risk-Based Approach to Mandatory Arbitration, 83 Or. L. Rev. 861 (2004).

CHAPTER 19. ARBITRATION AND THE INDIVIDUATION CRITIQUE

businesses and employers want, and they will structure their arbitration agreements accordingly.

This explicitly contractualist view of arbitration, however, may oversimplify a far more complex empirical reality – one in which other forces also shape the arbitration process. Here, I will focus on the role played by ADR providers. As I discuss in more detail below, the institutional values and incentives under which providers operate differ in significant ways from those of the businesses who are presumed to dictate the terms of arbitration.[108] For now, the important point is that providers may have a significant impact on arbitration procedure.[109]

For example, the AAA and other providers have adopted 'due process' protocols applicable to consumer and employment cases. These protocols set minimum standards of procedural fairness for arbitrations and have been endorsed by a variety of organizations with an interest in consumer and employment relationships.[110] For illustrative purposes, I will focus primarily on the AAA's Consumer[111] and

---

[108] See *infra* text accompanying notes 225–248.

[109] In a sense, ADR provider rules are not extrinsic to the arbitration agreement. Drafting parties are often aware of these rules, which offer off-the-rack disputing procedures that can be incorporated into the agreement. Yet when provider rules conflict with an express term in the agreement, the provider is typically involved in resolving the conflict, often by insisting that the business waive (or the consumer waive objection to) the offending term. In a sense, the provider's involvement consists of facilitating a second negotiation between the business and the consumer over disputing remedies and procedures. In this negotiation, however, the consumer may be represented by a lawyer.

[110] The employment protocol, for example, was developed by a task force comprised of individuals designated by a number of organizations representing employers, employees, and arbitration providers. Richard A. Bales, The Employment Due Process Protocol at Ten: Twenty Unresolved Issues, and a Focus on Conflicts of Interest, 21 Ohio St. J. on Disp. Resol. 165, 165 (2005). The protocol emphasizes that its principles reflect the views of the designees and not necessarily those of the designating organizations. E.g., Am. Arbitration Ass'n, A Due Process Protocol for Mediation and Arbitration of Statutory Disputes Arising out of the Employment Relationship (1995) [hereinafter Employment Protocol], available <www.adr.org/sp.asp?id=28535>.

[111] See Am. Arbitration Ass'n, Consumer Due Process Protocol (1998) [hereinafter Consumer Protocol], available at <www.adr.org/sp.asp?id=22019>.

Employment[112] protocols, along with its arbitration rules,[113] in the following discussion. Readers should bear in mind that if an arbitration agreement does not substantially and materially comply with the governing protocol, the AAA may decline to administer the arbitration unless the business waives the offending term or revises its agreement to eliminate the term.[114] Other ADR providers have adopted similar rules,[115] though not all are equally favorable from the perspective of consumer advocates.[116]

These rules already limit the ability of businesses to impose certain one-sided arbitration terms. For example, provider rules typically limit

---

[112] See Employment Protocol, *supra* n. 110.

[113] See Am. Arbitration Ass'n, Supplementary Procedures for Consumer-Related Disputes (2005) [hereinafter Consumer Rules], available at <www.adr.org/sp.asp?id=22014>; Am. Arbitration Ass'n, National Rules for the Resolution of Employment Disputes (Including Mediation and Arbitration Rules) (2005) [hereinafter Employment Rules], available at <www.adr.org/sp.asp?id=22075>.

[114] Am. Arbitration Ass'n, Statement of Ethical Principles for the American Arbitration Association, an ADR Provider Organization, <www.adr.org/ sp.asp?id=22036> (last visited January 20, 2007); Am. Arbitration Ass'n, Fair Play: Perspectives from American Arbitration Association on Consumer and Employment Arbitration 33–34 (2003) [hereinafter Fair Play], available <www.adr.org/si.asp?id=1843>. If the business refuses to waive the defect or amend its agreement, the claimant may or may not be entitled to litigate in court. The business might succeed in compelling arbitration before another provider or before another arbitrator. Presumably, however, evidence that the provider views the agreement as inconsistent with minimum standards of fairness would increase the likelihood that a court would invalidate the agreement altogether.

[115] See JAMS, JAMS Policy on Consumer Arbitrations Pursuant to Pre-Dispute Clauses: Minimum Standards of Procedural Fairness (2005) [hereinafter JAMS Consumer Policy], available at <www.jamsadr.com/rules/consumer_ min_std.asp>; JAMS, JAMS Policy on Employment Arbitration: Minimum Standards of Procedural Fairness (2005) [hereinafter JAMS Employment Policy], available at <www.jamsadr.com/rules/employment_Arbitration _min_stds.asp>.

[116] Consumer advocates generally view the National Arbitration Forum's rules as the least favorable. For those rules, see Nat'l Arbitration Forum, Code of Procedure (2006) [hereinafter NAF Code of Procedure], available at <www.arb-forum.com> (follow 'Rules & Forms' hyperlink), and Nat'l Arbitration Forum, Consumer and Employee Arbitration Rights (2006), available at <www.arb-forum.com> (follow 'Rules & Forms' hyperlink).

CHAPTER 19. ARBITRATION AND THE INDIVIDUATION CRITIQUE

the up-front costs of arbitration[117] and may also protect consumers and employees from contract terms requiring them to travel great distances to attend an arbitration hearing.[118] Other rules address more directly some of the potentially individuating aspects of the arbitration process.

19.2.4.2.1 Reasoned versus Summary Awards The lack of a written, reasoned award is potentially one of the more individuating features of arbitration.[119] When present, such awards may influence future arbitrators in similar cases and provide important information to third parties. For instance, in my example of car buyers who purchase an additional theft protection warranty, such an award might facilitate judicial review, alert state regulators to questionable practices, and inform other consumers about dealer practices.

---

[117] For claims that do not exceed USD 75,000, AAA rules limit consumers' and employees' up-front costs to USD 125 or USD 375, depending on the size of the claim. See Consumer Rules, *supra* n. 113, R. C-8. The Employment Rules cap costs for most employees at USD 125, although the employee may agree to pay part of the arbitrator's fee. See Employment Rules, *supra* n. 113, administrative fee schedule. Other ADR providers have adopted similar rules. See JAMS Consumer Policy, *supra* n. 115; JAMS Employment Policy, *supra* n. 115. But see Nat'l Arbitration Forum, Fee Schedule: Fees for Common Claims 3 (2006), available at <www.adrforum.com/users/naf/resources/20060501FeeSchedule2.pdf>. As a general matter, the National Arbitration Forum's fee schedule is the least favorable, and also appears to allow the business to impose a greater fee in the contract. *Ibid*. For a discussion and critique of provider rules generally, see Budnitz, *supra* n. 60, at 136–143.

[118] Am. Arbitration Ass'n, Locale Determinations (2006), available at <www.a-dr.org/sp.asp?id=28629>; see also JAMS Consumer Policy, *supra* n. 115. The AAA, for example, may require the business to 'waive the [contractually required] locale if the locale is not reasonably convenient' for consumers. Am. Arbitration Ass'n, Locale Determinations, *supra*; see also JAMS Consumer Policy, *supra* n. 115, para. 5 (addressing location of consumer arbitration); cf. NAF Code of Procedure, *supra* n. 116, R. 32 (stating that an in-person, participatory hearing is to occur in the federal judicial district where the respondent resides or does business; respondent 'does business where it has minimum contacts with a Consumer [or employee]'). I know of no similar AAA policy expressly protecting employees, but other providers may have more protective policies. See JAMS Employment Policy, *supra* n. 115, Standard No. 6 (location of hearing must not preclude access to arbitration).

[119] A reasoned award is one that explains, even if briefly, the arbitrator's findings and reasoning.

EMPLOYMENT CLASS AND COLLECTIVE ACTIONS

To the extent businesses would prefer that arbitrators avoid written, reasoned awards, provider rules generally do not oblige. Of the three major arbitration providers, two generally require brief written, reasoned awards in both employment and consumer arbitration, and the third entitles parties to receive such an award upon request and payment of a fee.[120] In employment cases, the AAA also makes its awards public, although it redacts the identities of the parties and witnesses.[121] To be sure, businesses might forbid reasoned, written awards in the arbitration agreement itself; it is unclear whether providers like the AAA would view such contract terms as consistent with the due process protocols.[122] It is an open question whether such terms appear with any frequency in consumer and employment arbitration agreements. The scant empirical evidence suggests that they may be relatively rare.[123]

---

[120] See Employment Rules, *supra* n. 113, R. 34; see also Consumer Rules, *supra* n. 113, R. C-7 (only requiring that the award be in writing); Consumer Protocol, *supra* n. 111, Principle 15 (requiring arbitrator, upon timely request of either party, to provide brief written explanation of basis for award); JAMS Employment Policy, *supra* n. 115, Standard No. 8 (providing for 'concise written statement' of reasons for award); JAMS Consumer Policy, *supra* n. 115, para. 10 (same). But see NAF Code of Procedure, *supra* n. 116, R. 37(H) (stating that awards are to be 'summary awards' unless the parties agree otherwise, or unless a party requests findings of fact and conclusions of law and pays a fee).

[121] Employment Rules, *supra* n. 113, R. 34.

[122] Consumer Protocol Principle 15 provides that 'at the timely request of either party, the arbitrator should provide a brief written explanation of the basis for the award.' Consumer Protocol, *supra* n. 111, Principle 15. Likewise, the Employment Protocol provides that 'the arbitrator should issue an opinion and award setting forth a summary of the issues, including the type(s) of dispute(s), the damages and/or other relief requested and awarded, a statement of any other issues resolved, and a statement regarding the disposition of any statutory claim(s).' Employment Protocol, *supra* n. 110, pt. C.5.

[123] One study of consumer arbitration agreements found that only four of fifty-two clauses stated that the arbitrator would not provide a written explanation of their award. See Demaine & Hensler, *supra* n. 101, at 68–69. Likewise, in my review of the consumer and employment agreements at issue in the AAA class arbitrations, none of the twenty-six agreements forbade reasoned, written awards; two of the sixteen consumer and nine of the sixteen employment agreements explicitly called for such awards.

CHAPTER 19. ARBITRATION AND THE INDIVIDUATION CRITIQUE

19.2.4.2.2 Remedies Available in Arbitration Businesses might also include in their agreements terms restricting the remedies available in arbitration. Once again, however, provider rules may limit the impact of these terms. For example, the AAA Consumer and Employment protocols provide that arbitrators should be able to award 'whatever relief would be available in court.'[124] This does not necessarily imply that all contractual limitations on remedies are invalid. One interpretation is that an arbitrator should honor a limitation if a court, applying applicable law, would enforce it in a judicial proceeding.[125] Yet on one occasion, the AAA asserted that an agreement violated the Consumer Protocol by allowing only recovery of direct damages in most cases and barring recovery of punitive and other damages in all cases, without suggesting that its decision depended on whether a court would enforce a similar limitation.[126] This suggests that in some cases AAA policies might offer consumers and employees more protection from one-sided terms than would be available in court.

19.2.4.2.3 Limits on the Right to Bring or Participate in a Class Action There is little evidence concerning how frequently consumer and employment arbitration agreements expressly prohibit class-wide proceedings.[127] Nevertheless, provider rules generally do not disapprove of such terms. The AAA, for example, requires a court order before it will administer a class arbitration if the agreement purports to bar class actions, consolidation, or joinder.[128] This policy is rather

---

[124] See Consumer Protocol, *supra* n. 111, Principle 14; Employment Protocol, *supra* n. 110, pt. C.5; see also JAMS Consumer Policy, *supra* n. 115, para. 3 (stating that remedies that would be available in court must remain available in consumer arbitration); JAMS Employment Policy, *supra* n. 115, Standard No. 1 (same, for employment arbitration). As I indicated earlier, *supra* n. 114, AAA policy is to decline to administer an arbitration if the agreement does not substantially and materially comply with the relevant protocol, unless the business waives the term or amends the agreement.

[125] Cf. NAF Code of Procedure, *supra* n. 116, R. 20D (stating that remedies may not be 'unlawfully restricted' – suggesting lawful restrictions should be enforced).

[126] See Affidavit of Neil B. Currie on Behalf of the American Arbitration Association in Response and Objection to a Subpoena for Documents Issued By Plaintiff, *Ragan v. AT&T Corp.*, No. 02-L-168 (Ill. Cir. Ct. July 15, 2002) (on file with author).

[127] See *supra* n. 102.

[128] See Am. Arbitration Ass'n, American Arbitration Association Policy on Class Arbitrations (July 14, 2005), <www.adr.org/sp.asp?id=25967>. For a rather tendentious

tolerant of class action prohibitions; the implication is that AAA arbitrators may not even consider challenges to the enforceability of such terms.[129] Instead, parties wishing to challenge them must do so in court.[130]

---

summary of the evolution of the JAMS class action policy, see Kelly Thompson Cochran & Eric J. Mogilnicki, Current Issues in Consumer Arbitration, 60 Bus. Law. 785, 793–794 (2005). The National Arbitration Forum ('NAF') rules do not expressly address class arbitration, but the NAF has marketed its services in the past as one way for businesses to avoid class litigation altogether. See Letter from Curtis V. Brown, Vice President and General Counsel, National Arbitration Forum, to prospective client (January 14, 1999) (on file with author) (noting that an arbitration clause may eliminate class actions).

[129] E.g., Letter from Thomas G. Foley Jr. to Karen Fontaine, AAA, 1–2 (December 21, 2004). The letter recounts that, although the arbitration agreement barred class actions, the parties had agreed to let the arbitrator decide whether to allow class arbitration anyway, but that despite this agreement the AAA had declined to accept the case unless the claimants dropped their request for class arbitration or obtained a court order.

[130] Contrast this policy to typical arbitration rules, which permit the arbitrator to decide questions of arbitrability, including questions concerning the existence, scope, or validity of the arbitration clause. E.g., Am. Arbitration Ass'n, Commercial Arbitration Rules and Mediation Procedures R. 7(a) (2005) [hereinafter Commercial Rules], available at <www.adr.org/sp.asp?id=22440>. Just how decision-making authority should be allocated between courts and arbitrators is a matter of some dispute among arbitration scholars. Compare Richard C. Reuben, First Options, Consent to Arbitration, and the Demise of Separability: Restoring Access to Justice for Contracts with Arbitration Provisions, 56 SMU L. Rev. 819, 823–827 (2003) (generally suggesting a more active role for courts in considering challenges to the enforceability of arbitration agreements), with Alan Scott Rau, Everything You Really Need to Know About 'Separability' in Seventeen Simple Propositions, 14 Am. Rev. Int'l Arb. 1 (2003) (generally suggesting a more limited role in which courts decide only questions that legitimately call into question a party's assent to arbitration). Courts, too, have reached conflicting results. Compare *Hawkins v. Aid Ass'n for Lutherans*, 338 F.3d 801, 807 (7th Cir. 2003) (referring to arbitration dispute over enforceability of terms limiting remedies and class actions in arbitration), with *Ting v. AT&T*, 319 F.3d 1126, 1148–1152 (9th Cir. 2003) (considering whether class action ban and other terms rendered arbitration agreement unconscionable). The AAA policy is noteworthy because, whichever decision maker should address these challenges, it is unusual indeed for an ADR provider voluntarily to limit its own decision-making authority.

19.2.4.3 Summary

As we have seen, although arbitration providers are relatively indulgent of contract terms prohibiting class actions, their rules may limit the ability of businesses to impose certain one-sided terms, including some terms that individuate the disputing process. Nevertheless, if aggregation by formal or informal methods is essential to create a level playing field in arbitration, ADR providers do not yet do enough to facilitate this process. For individual consumers, for example, arbitral 'due process' primarily means a neutral decision-maker, limited discovery, and a simplified hearing process.[131] These procedures may be incompatible with cases requiring significant discovery or raising complex issues. Moreover, provider rules do not establish conditions under which an arbitrator's decision may be given precedential effect. This silence is consistent with the view that arbitration is neither 'rule-based' nor 'rule-communicating.'[132] That is, arbitrators need not apply consistent rules in similar cases,[133] nor do they necessarily

---

[131] This often means a 'desk arbitration,' a telephonic hearing, or a streamlined in-person hearing that might last no more than a day. See Consumer Rules, *supra* n. 113, R. C-5 & C-6; Commercial Rules, *supra* n. 130, R. E-8.

[132] Robert A. Baruch Bush, Dispute Resolution Alternatives and the Goals of Civil Justice: Jurisdictional Principles for Process Choice, 1984 Wis. L. Rev. 893, 988–989.

[133] As a general rule, arbitrators need not follow the decisions of other arbitrators, nor apply rules of substantive law: 'The weight of authority permits an arbitrator to "do justice as he sees it" and fashion an award that embodies the individual justice required by a given set of facts.' Edward Brunet, Arbitration and Constitutional Rights, 71 N.C. L. Rev. 81, 85 (1992). The FAA implicitly acknowledges this flexibility by sharply limiting the grounds on which a court may vacate an arbitral award; vacatur is not available for errors of law. See 9 U.S.C. § 10 (2006). And while some courts leave room to vacate awards issued in 'manifest disregard of the law,' or that violate public policy, few awards are vacated on these grounds. See Stephen J. Ware, Default Rules from Mandatory Rules: Privatizing Law Through Arbitration, 83 Minn. L. Rev. 703, 724–725 (1999); see also *George Watts & Son, Inc. v. Tiffany & Co.*, 248 F.3d 577, 580–581 (7th Cir. 2001) (equating arbitrator to parties' agent, who may order any relief parties could agree to themselves; vacatur on 'manifest disregard' or public policy grounds appropriate only where award directs a violation of law). Thus, 'an agreement to arbitrate is, in effect, an agreement to comply with the arbitrator's decision whether or not the arbitrator applies the law.' Ware, *supra*, at 711.

communicate rules to third parties in ways that influence future behavior.[134]

What may be most surprising, however, is the extent to which many provider rules even now do facilitate aggregation. Even outside the class arbitration context, for example, providers may require reasoned, written awards and may refuse to administer arbitrations where the agreement limits the remedies available to consumers or employees.[135] Moreover, providers may sometimes object to one-sided terms, such as terms requiring litigation in a remote forum, even when courts might reach the opposite conclusion.[136] These rules are hard to square with the individuation critique, which presumes that businesses wish to impose an individuated disputing process and that providers will abet them in that goal.

As a description of current arbitration practices, then, the individuation critique is of uncertain validity. Assessing its merit requires answers to a number of empirical questions about the contents of arbitration agreements, the role played by arbitration providers, and the

---

In consumer and employment arbitration, this 'lawless' aspect of arbitration may raise concerns, especially over arbitrators' ability and willingness to apply 'mandatory' public law. E.g., Ware, *supra*, at 727–728 (noting inconsistency of treating legal rules as mandatory in all contexts except arbitration). As an empirical matter, of course, arbitrators may or may not follow substantive law in consumer and employment disputes; there is little evidence on the question. E.g., Patricia A. Greenfield, How Do Arbitrators Treat External Law, 45 Indus. & Lab. Rel. Rev. 683, 694 (1992) (evaluating a sample of labor arbitration awards and concluding that 'few arbitrators consider statutory rights fully and in detail'). If concerns over 'lawlessness' are empirically valid, they may be addressed, at least in part, by provider rules requiring arbitrators to follow the law. E.g., Consumer Protocol, *supra* n. 111, Principle 15(2). Where providers insist on such rules, refusal to apply mandatory substantive law arguably would exceed the arbitrator's power and provide grounds for vacatur. See 9 U.S.C. § 10(a)(4) (2006).

[134] See Baruch Bush, *supra* n. 132, at 989; see also Landes & Posner, *supra* n. 15, at 238–240 (noting reasons why private dispute resolution systems are unlikely to produce rules or precedent). As I note below, there may be conditions under which arbitrators do indeed develop something akin to precedent. See *infra* text accompanying notes 197–213.

[135] See *supra* text accompanying notes 119–126.

[136] E.g., *Carnival Cruise Lines, Inc. v. Shute*, 499 U.S. 585, 596–597 (1991) (upholding forum selection clause requiring residents of Washington State to litigate in Florida).

CHAPTER 19. ARBITRATION AND THE INDIVIDUATION CRITIQUE

participants in consumer and employment arbitrations.[137] For example, to what extent do businesses include individuating terms in their agreements? How effectively and consistently do arbitration providers enforce their due process protocols?[138] How frequently do lawyers represent consumers in arbitration proceedings, and what are the characteristics of those lawyers?[139] Are there conditions under which written, reasoned awards will produce something akin to precedent in arbitration? Without answers to these questions, it is difficult to assess how accurately the individuation critique describes modern consumer and employment arbitration.

Moreover, a full assessment of the individuation critique requires more than an accurate description of current arbitration practices. We must also consider arbitration's potential to facilitate aggregation.

---

[137] Answering these questions requires more than examining the results of arbitration proceedings, though that research is essential as well. See *supra* n. 98 for a description of the existing research on arbitration outcomes, which primarily deals with employment arbitration.

[138] With respect to the AAA, for example, we do not know whether it routinely conducts an adequate, independent review of the governing agreement before accepting a case for arbitration. In theory, specially trained AAA staff review the arbitration agreement at the start of the arbitration, identify any non-conforming terms, and give the business the opportunity to waive the term or revise the agreement. See Fair Play, *supra* n. 114, at 33–34; see also Consumer Rules, *supra* n. 113, R. C-2(a) (requiring claimant to attach agreement to arbitration demand). I know of no data on how effectively this process screens out non-conforming arbitration agreements. Further research, and improved disclosure by providers, is needed to answer this question. See Cal. Dispute Resolution Inst., Consumer and Employment Arbitration in California: A Review of Website Data Posted Pursuant to Section 1281.96 of the Code of Civil Procedure 26–32 (2004) [hereinafter CDRI Review], available at <www.mediate.com/cdri/cdri_print_ Aug_6.pdf> (noting problems with providers' data reporting pursuant to California statute).

[139] There is some, albeit weak, evidence that consumer claimants are finding lawyers in arbitration. California law requires arbitration providers to make public information about certain consumer, employment, and health care arbitrations. See Cal. Civ. Proc. Code § 1281.96 (West Supp. 2006). One recent study of this data found that 79.5% of the consumer-initiated arbitrations were commenced by a lawyer. See CDRI Review, *supra* n. 138, at 20, 26–32 (also noting problems with data reporting). Following California law, however, the study broadly defines 'consumer' to include employment, real estate, insurance, and other disputes, and many of the claims involved amounts (reported in only a minority of arbitrations) large enough to attract a lawyer: USD 90,341 (mean) and USD 19,800 (median). *Id.* at 20.

In the rest of this article, I argue that arbitration may have a great deal of potential. This is especially true for consumers, who except for the class action have little ability to aggregate their claims or to benefit from lawyers' aggregation efforts.[140] The remainder of this paper describes some ways that arbitration might achieve this potential, focusing on consumer disputes. Some of my suggestions are hypothetical and require that we rethink or revise current arbitration practices. But others may already be features of arbitration. Taken together, they suggest a system that, for many consumers, may prove superior to the courts in important respects.

It may seem counterintuitive to argue that arbitration has the potential to be a superior forum for aggregation of consumer claims. After all, how can a system supposedly controlled by more powerful interests be more favorable to consumer litigants? I address this objection in the last section.

19.3 RETHINKING THE ABILITY TO AGGREGATE DISPUTES IN ARBITRATION

19.3.1 Class Arbitration as a Laboratory for Innovation in Formal Aggregation

Although it may turn out to be a short-lived phenomenon,[141] class arbitration is the most obvious example of arbitration's potential to facilitate aggregate dispute resolution. Achieving this potential, however, may require that we re-imagine current class arbitration practices. I do not want to describe the AAA class arbitration rules in detail. Suffice to say that they largely imitate federal class action practice.[142]

---

[140] See *supra* text accompanying notes 55–81.

[141] For example, some businesses may seek to eliminate class-wide proceedings altogether by appending class action prohibitions to their arbitration agreements, or, if courts prove unwilling to enforce such prohibitions, may channel class actions into court. As I discuss below, however, it is also possible that class arbitration is here to stay. See *infra* text accompanying notes 173–188.

[142] For a truncated discussion of that practice in consumer cases, see *supra* text accompanying notes 68–81.

CHAPTER 19. ARBITRATION AND THE INDIVIDUATION CRITIQUE

So do the rules adopted by JAMS, the only other major ADR provider (to my knowledge) with class arbitration rules.[143] Given the variety of unanswered questions raised by class arbitration,[144] perhaps providers can be forgiven for offering a familiar set of procedural rules.[145] Unfortunately, these rules largely fail to engage with the possibilities of class arbitration.

For example, AAA rules parrot the predominance inquiry of Federal Rule of Civil Procedure 23(b)(3), asking whether common questions of law or fact predominate over questions affecting only individual class members.[146] The point of this inquiry is to decide whether class members' claims are sufficiently alike to warrant collective, representative adjudication,[147] or, under another view, whether formal aggregation will promote efficiency without sacrificing fairness.[148] These are necessary questions in any adjudicative context, but there is no reason

---

[143] The JAMS rules are also available on-line. JAMS, JAMS Class Action Procedures <www.jamsadr.com/rules/class_action.asp> (last visited January 27, 2007). For a thorough discussion of provider rules and due process issues raised by class arbitration, see Carole J. Buckner, Due Process in Class Arbitration, 58 Fla. L. Rev. 185 (2006).

[144] For example, what, if any, due process rights do absent class members and defendants have? To what extent and under what conditions will the award bind absent class members? What is the court's role in supervising a class arbitration?

[145] Indeed, the decision to model class arbitration rules on Fed. R. Civ. P. 23 may reflect little more than the AAA's ambivalence. See Russ Bleemer, The Current State of Class Action Arbitration, 22 Alternatives to High Cost Litig. 63, 68–69 (2004) (summarizing comments by William K. Slate II, president and CEO of the AAA, that although the AAA had on occasion administered class arbitration referred by courts, they 'never asked for' the increase in class arbitration occasioned *by Green Tree Financial Corp. v. Bazzle*, 539 U.S. 444 (2003)). It may also merely reflect the tendency of lawyers and courts to favor familiar procedures.

[146] See Am. Arbitration Ass'n, Supplementary Rules for Class Arbitrations R. 4(b) (2003) [hereinafter AAA Class Rules], available at <www.adr.org/sp.asp?id=21936>; JAMS, JAMS Class Action Procedures R. 3(b)(3) (2005), available at <www.jamsadr.com/rules/class_action.asp>.

[147] *Amchem Prods., Inc. v. Windsor*, 521 U.S. 591, 623 (1997).

[148] John Coffee, Jr., Class Action Accountability: Reconciling Exit, Voice, and Loyalty in Representative Litigation, 100 Colum. L. Rev. 370, 401 (2000) (disputing that predominance inquiry asks about class cohesion and locating purposes of requirement in concerns for judicial efficiency).

why they should yield the same answers in arbitration and litigation. Yet that is what the AAA rules seem to suggest.[149] In effect, the AAA class rules encourage arbitrators to view a class arbitration merely as a class action that happens to occur in arbitration.

This is a remarkably impoverished view of class arbitration, one that views arbitration as little more than a private court system and arbitrators as little more than judicial impersonators. But arbitration has potential, in part, precisely because arbitrators are not judges. Subject to constraints imposed by the parties' agreement, arbitrators, unlike judges, have great flexibility to fashion an appropriate remedy[150] and to adopt efficient procedures that are tailored to the parties' dispute.[151] There is no reason why this authority should vanish once the arbitrator contemplates collective dispute resolution procedures. At least in theory, such procedures need bear little resemblance to the class action, and, even under a more limited view, federal class action practice should inform – but rarely dictate – class arbitration practice.

---

[149] For example, in one class arbitration, a panel of arbitrators declined to certify a class of franchisees, operators of retail art galleries, who alleged that franchisor representatives misrepresented the likely profitability of their businesses at a series of meetings. The panel reasoned that 'class action status is generally denied in cases alleging verbal fraud because of the need for individualized proof on key factual issues, including the making of the misrepresentations, materiality, reliance and damages.' Class Determination Award at 6, *Tarek, LLC v. Kincade*, No. 11 Y 114 00578 04 (April 4, 2005) (Am. Arbitration Ass'n), available at <www.adr.org/si.asp?id=1896>.

[150] See *supra* n. 133. Arbitrators may also be constrained by provider rules, of course. For example, the Consumer Rules instruct arbitrators to apply pertinent substantive law. See Consumer Rules, *supra* n. 113, R. C-7(c).

[151] On arbitrators' authority to control arbitration procedure, See e.g., *Keebler Co. v. Truck Drivers, Local 170*, 247 F.3d 8, 11 (1st Cir. 2001); *InterChem Asia 2000 Pte. Ltd. v. Oceana Petrochemicals AG*, 373 F. Supp. 2d 340, 352 (S.D.N.Y. 2005); *M&L Power Servs., Inc. v. Am. Networks Int'l*, 44 F. Supp. 2d 134, 142–144 (D.R.I. 1999). If arbitrators have great flexibility to fashion substantive relief, See e.g., *George Watts & Son, Inc. v. Tiffany & Co.*, 248 F.3d 577, 580–581 (7th Cir. 2001); Ware, *supra n.* 133, at 711, they should have at least as much flexibility to fashion arbitration procedure. If the agreement does not forbid a particular procedure, the arbitrator should, in theory, be free to use it, unless perhaps the process violates some fundamental notion of what is fair in arbitration or permissible as a matter of policy.

CHAPTER 19. ARBITRATION AND THE INDIVIDUATION CRITIQUE

Exactly how arbitrators should approach the decision to certify a class is a complex topic, and one that is tangential to my purposes.[152] But it is one worth exploring.[153] The flexibility and informality of arbitration do not make it unsuitable for class litigation;[154] quite the contrary. These attributes permit arbitrators to implement innovative procedures that courts have been hesitant to accept.[155]

Consider once more my example of car buyers who purchase a theft-protection 'warranty.'[156] I mentioned earlier that class certification was unlikely in court, because, to a judge, questions of misrepresentation, reliance, and damages all require individualized proof.[157] This insistence on individualized proof reflects an almost entirely

---

[152] Also separate issues are the many potential objections to class arbitration, beginning with normative objections to the wholesale privatization of justice. For example, one might argue that juries, not arbitrators, should decide whether the conduct of an employer or business violates the broader community values underlying applicable law. See e.g., Richard A. Bales, Compulsory Employment Arbitration and the EEOC, 27 Pepp. L. Rev. 1, 2 (1999) ('The absence of a jury makes arbitration an inappropriate forum for resolving claims that derive from an employer's violation of external community values.').

[153] Recent scholarship has begun to address the many questions raised by class arbitration, but has not addressed the standards arbitrators should apply to class certification decisions, nor the range of aggregative procedures that might be available in arbitration. Examples of scholarship addressing class arbitration, or the use of arbitration to avoid class actions, include Kristen M. Blankley, Class Actions Behind Closed Doors? How Consumer Claims Can (and Should) be Resolved by Class-Action Arbitration, 20 Ohio St. J. on Disp. Resol. 451 (2005); Buckner, *supra* n. 143; Carole J. Buckner, Toward a Pure Arbitral Paradigm of Classwide Arbitration: Arbitral Power and Federal Preemption, 82 Denv. L. Rev. 301 (2004–2005); Gilles, *supra* n. 90; Sternlight, *supra* n. 70; Jack Wilson, 'No-Class-Action Arbitration Clauses,' State-Law Unconscionability, and the Federal Arbitration Act: A Case for Federal Judicial Restraint and Congressional Action, 23 Quinnipiac L. Rev. 737 (2005).

[154] See Bales, *supra* n. 152, at 2 ('Arbitration's informality makes it an inadequate forum for resolving large, complex, class-based claims.').

[155] In this sense, class arbitration may be more akin to an estimation proceeding in a bankruptcy case involving mass tort claims than to a judicial class action. Bankruptcy judges have exercised substantial discretion in devising efficient methods for estimating the debtor's aggregate liability to a class of individual claimants. See e.g., In re Eagle-Picher Indus., Inc., 189 B.R. 681 (Bankr. S.D. Ohio 1995); In re A.H. Robins Co., 88 B.R. 742 (E.D. Va. 1988).

[156] *Supra* text accompanying notes 55–56.

[157] See *supra* text accompanying notes 75–78.

individuated view of adjudication, one that rejects the use of collective proof even if it is the most efficient method – perhaps even the only economically feasible one – to resolve large numbers of similar disputes. For example, it is unlikely that a judge would agree to estimate that an actionable misrepresentation occurred in 40% of, say, 1,000 transactions, causing an average loss of USD 500, and to devise some formula for allocating the resulting USD 200,000 judgment among class members. At the risk of oversimplifying, the goal of a class action in court is to find out which class members relied to their detriment on a salesperson's misrepresentation and to award to those class members (and no others) the appropriate relief.[158]

An arbitrator, by contrast, might ask the following, different question: Is it consistent with the parties' agreement to resolve this dispute in a collective fashion and, if so, what type of process is fair, efficient, and consistent with the remedial purposes of the relevant substantive law?[159] Answering this question, the arbitrator might decide to hold an initial hearing to resolve common issues,[160] followed by hearings on the merits for a representative sample of car buyers, the results of which would then be extrapolated to the class as a whole. Thus, after finding in favor of 40% of the sample claimants, the arbitrator might award USD 200,000 to the class (again, assuming a class of 1,000 and an average award of USD 500).[161] After fixing the defendant's

---

[158] This goal arguably conflicts with the reality of large-scale litigation – perhaps even with the reality of any routine form of litigation, such as personal injury litigation – in which individual claims are typically resolved by settlement according to essentially actuarial principles. E.g., Issacharoff & Witt, *supra* n. 19, at 1618, 1625–1631.

[159] Because most arbitration agreements will not specify arbitration procedures, much less procedures for collective adjudication, the parties effectively delegate to the arbitrator the authority to devise appropriate dispute resolution procedures, much the same as they have delegated the authority to fashion an appropriate remedy. See *supra* n. 151.

[160] See *supra* n. 77 for examples of common issues.

[161] For arguments in favor of applying similar techniques in court, especially in the mass tort context, see David Rosenberg, Adding a Second Opt-Out to Rule 23(b)(3) Class Actions: Cost Without Benefit, 2003 U. Chi. Legal F. 19, 31–33 [hereinafter Rosenberg, Cost Without Benefit]; David Rosenberg, Decoupling Deterrence and Compensation Functions in Mass Tort Class Actions for Future Loss, 88 Va. L. Rev. 1871, 1892–1897 (2002) [hereinafter Rosenberg, Decoupling]; Laurens Walker & John Monahan, Sampling Damages, 83 Iowa L. Rev. 545 (1998); Laurens Walker & John Monahan, Sampling Liability, 85 Va. L. Rev. 329 (1999).

CHAPTER 19. ARBITRATION AND THE INDIVIDUATION CRITIQUE

aggregate liability, and perhaps discharging it from the case, the arbitrator might devise procedures for allocating funds among class members, might rely on other ADR processes like mediation to allocate funds, or might simply allocate funds pro rata.[162]

The foregoing is only one example modeled on trial plans that have been proposed (though rarely accepted) in judicial proceedings.[163] But the fact that courts use such procedures rarely, if at all, should not be determinative. Many of the constraints that shape class action practice in court do not apply to arbitration: The right to trial by jury in class actions seeking damages is an example.[164] Those that do apply may mean something quite different to an arbitrator than to a judge. So even if there is a right to due process in arbitration,[165] which includes, say,

---

[162] In most consumer cases, it seems unlikely that a pro rata distribution would result in significant numbers of opt-outs, given the relatively modest stakes involved and the expense of individual adjudication. (Though, as I argue, *infra* text accompanying notes 189–224, arbitration may be a more hospitable forum than the courts for resolving individual consumer claims.) One might object that a pro-rata distribution to claimants will overcompensate some and undercompensate others. There are two short answers to this objection. First, an arbitrator could devise simplified procedures for distributing proceeds according to some relevant metric – severity of harm, strength of claim, etc. – without conducting extensive (and expensive) fact-finding. Second, an arbitrator could legitimately conclude that a pro-rata distribution is consistent with the parties' agreement. Arguably, consumers benefit by trading expensive, individualized procedures for simplified procedures that produce higher net proceeds for allocation. Cf. Rosenberg, Decoupling, *supra* n. 161, at 1885–1887 (arguing, in mass tort context, that plaintiffs would prefer, ex ante, a system that distributes proceeds according to severity of loss rather than strength of claim).

[163] Compare *Hilao v. Estate of Marcos*, 103 F.3d 767, 786–787 (9th Cir. 1996) (approving use of sampling to measure damages in suit under Torture Victim Protection Act), with *Cimino v. Raymark Indus.*, 151 F.3d 297, 311 (5th Cir. 1998) (holding that trial plan based on statistical sampling violated state law, due process, and the right to a jury trial).

[164] An arbitration agreement, of course, relinquishes that right. That is why some have suggested that arbitration agreements be judged by a 'knowing, voluntary, and intentional' standard. See Jean R. Sternlight, Mandatory Binding Arbitration and the Demise of the Seventh Amendment Right to a Jury Trial, 16 Ohio St. J. on Disp. Resol. 669, 676 (2001). But see Stephen J. Ware, Arbitration Clauses, Jury-Waiver Clauses, and Other Contractual Waivers of Constitutional Rights, 67 Law & Contemp. Probs., Winter/Spring 2004, at 167, 167–168 (defending use of contract-law standards of assent).

[165] At least in individual arbitrations, most courts hold that there is no right to due process. See Buckner, *supra* n. 143, at 214–216. See generally Sarah Rudolph Cole, Arbitration and State Action, 2005 BYU L. Rev. 7; Richard C. Reuben, Constitutional

the right to obtain essential discovery,[166] no one would suggest that arbitrators follow *Federal Rules of Civil Procedure 26-37*. That is because, although arbitrators may order substantial discovery in appropriate cases, implementing federal discovery practice would compromise arbitration's virtues – informality and efficiency chief among them[167] – without offering a commensurate benefit. There is likewise no reason to compromise these virtues in the class certification decision.

This is not to say that class arbitration should be a free-for-all. Arbitrators should ensure that class representatives and counsel will adequately represent the class, that they have no material conflicts of interest, and that class members have adequate notice and opportunities to participate in the arbitration.[168] Beyond that, arbitration

---

Gravity: A Unitary Theory of Alternative Dispute Resolution and Public Civil Justice, 47 UCLA L. Rev. 949 (2000); Jean R. Sternlight, Rethinking the Constitutionality of the Supreme Court's Preference for Binding Arbitration: A Fresh Assessment of Jury Trial, Separation of Powers, and Due Process Concerns, 72 Tul. L. Rev. 1, 38 (1997).

[166] Cf. *Norman v. Young*, 422 F.2d 470, 474 (10th Cir. 1970) (affirming default judgment granted as sanction for withholding discovery materials and asserting that default judgment protected plaintiff's right to due process).

[167] See Wilson, *supra* n. 153, at 779 (noting these strengths). As should be obvious, I disagree with the view that arbitration's 'relative efficiency, low cost, informality and flexibility, and privacy [] are likely to be substantially diminished or even eliminated in the class action context.' *Ibid*. A class arbitration is surely less efficient, more costly, etc. than one individual arbitration, but that seems the wrong comparison. Compared to a (hypothetical) multitude of individual arbitrations or lawsuits, class arbitration may offer significant efficiency and other advantages. Nor is it obvious that these advantages disappear when we compare class arbitration to class litigation. To be sure, current class arbitration rules sacrifice much of arbitration's potential advantage by slavishly adhering to federal class action practice (and by contemplating a multitude of essentially interlocutory appeals). But these procedures could be refined to make class arbitration a more efficient and flexible process.

[168] Without such protections, it seems unlikely that a class arbitration award would bind absent class members. To the extent *Green Tree Financial Corp. v. Bazzle*, 539 U.S. 444 (2003), implicitly approves class arbitration in at least some cases, see *supra* n. 5, it follows that absent class members can be bound by such proceedings. But it is unclear exactly how they are bound. Does a court order confirming the award bind them if the motion to confirm is filed by the arbitration class representative? Must the court itself certify a class on the common question of whether the award should be confirmed or vacated? Or will subsequent courts and arbitrators simply give preclusive effect to a prior class arbitration award, no matter how (or whether) it is confirmed? For a brief discussion of similar issues in class arbitration, see Kristen

CHAPTER 19. ARBITRATION AND THE INDIVIDUATION CRITIQUE

procedures should be fair to all parties – providing, for defendants, a dispassionate assessment of liability, a reasonably accurate measure of any damages owed to the class as a whole,[169] and a judgment that binds class members. But as long as they honor these restrictions, and any lawfully imposed by the parties' agreement, arbitrators need not mimic judges in deciding whether to certify a class.[170]

The AAA class arbitrations suggest that at least some arbitrators recognize that they have a good deal of procedural flexibility, though perhaps not to the degree I am suggesting.[171] Indeed, both arbitration

---

M. Blankley, Res Judicata and Class Action Arbitration Awards, 4 Mayhew-Hite Rep. on Disp. Resol. & Cts. (2005–2006), <http://moritzlaw.osu.edu/jdr/mayhew-hite/vol4iss1/lead.html>.

[169] E.g., Rosenberg, *supra* n. 161, at 1892–1897 (arguing in mass tort context for separating deterrence and compensation functions, first assessing the defendant's liability and damages in the aggregate, then distributing according to severity of loss).

[170] To some extent, of course, class arbitration rules constrain arbitrators' procedural options. But I do not interpret the current rules to preclude all procedural innovation in class arbitration. Although the rules are modeled on Fed. R. Civ. P. 23, that does not mean that an arbitrator must follow federal case law in deciding, say, whether statistical sampling is both fair and consistent with the parties' agreement. As I have mentioned, many of the principles that inform the case law have limited, or no, relevance to arbitration. See *supra* text accompanying notes 164–167.

[171] As one arbitrator reasoned in certifying a class of physicians challenging an insurer's reimbursement practices:

> If it is found that [the insurer engaged in a scheme to underpay physicians], then how [the scheme] affected various members of the class will have to be dealt with. If all of these contracts were breached, then a remedy will be found. Procedures could be subclasses within this arbitration, separate arbitrations, or some combination thereof... Arbitration is a flexible tool and I am confident that when and if that point is reached, good management will handle the individual claims in a fair and expeditious manner. Since the alternative, denying the class, is essentially to deny these doctors any realistic possibility of redress, I believe that we should go ahead and do the best we can.

Partial Final Class Determination Award of Arbitrator at 11–12, *Sutter v. Oxford Health Plans*, No. 18 193 20593 02 (March 24, 2005) (Am. Arbitration Ass'n), available at <www.adr.org/si.asp?id=1835>. In another, more problematic, example, an arbitrator certified an opt-out class of employees under the Fair Labor Standards Act, which permits only opt-in collective actions. See Class Determination Partial Final Award at 4–10, *Cole v. Long John Silver's Rests.*, No. 11 160 00194 04 (September 19, 2005) (Am. Arbitration Ass'n), available at <www.adr.org/si.asp?id=2011>.

proponents and skeptics, each of whom often take for granted that arbitration will individuate disputes, should acknowledge, even welcome, the potential benefits of class arbitration. Properly administered, class arbitration could preserve many of arbitration's traditional virtues – efficiency, expert decision-making, flexible procedure – while enabling claimants to capture litigation economies and to compete with respondents on relatively even terms.[172]

Of course, arbitrators must honor contractual limits on their authority, which raises an obvious objection: Will not businesses simply revise their agreements expressly to prohibit class proceedings? Arbitration skeptics often assume that such clauses will become common,[173] but this may be unduly pessimistic. To be sure, some businesses, especially in the consumer finance and telecommunications industries, appear to view arbitration as a means to eliminate class litigation, and these businesses may expressly prohibit class actions in their agreements.[174] Except for one study, however, there is little evidence of the frequency with which such prohibitions appear in consumer contracts.[175] As I discuss below in the context of individual arbitration, consumers and consumer advocates ultimately may have significant influence over arbitration procedures[176] and over whether businesses use arbitration agreements in the first place.[177] Over the long-term, whether businesses will routinely seek to contract around the class action remains an open empirical question.

Of course, to the extent arbitration agreements include terms prohibiting class actions, there remains the normative question whether such terms should be enforced. A minority of the reported cases hold that class action prohibitions will be invalid in at least some circumstances.[178] A great deal has been written about the role of the class

---

[172] See *supra* text accompanying notes 35–37.

[173] E.g., Gilles, *supra* I n. 90, at 410; Sternlight, *supra* n. 70, at 90–91.

[174] As I mentioned earlier, *supra* n. 102, of the sixteen consumer arbitration agreements I located from the AAA class arbitrations, five expressly bar class actions. All five of these agreements involve businesses in the consumer finance or telecommunications industries.

[175] See Demaine & Hensler, *supra* n. 101, at 65.

[176] See *infra* text accompanying notes 239–246.

[177] See *infra* n. 246 and accompanying text.

[178] E.g., *Discover Bank v. Superior Court*, 113 P.3d 1100, 1110 (Cal. 2005); *Muhammad v. County Bank*, 912 A.2d 88 (N.J. 2006); *State ex rel. Dunlap v. Berger*, 567 S.E.2d 265,

CHAPTER 19. ARBITRATION AND THE INDIVIDUATION CRITIQUE

action in securing the enforcement of public law, and I will not repeat that discussion here.[179] For my purposes, it is enough to recognize that class action prohibitions can effectively eliminate private rights of action granted by important public laws, and that a principled argument can be made in favor of judicial or legislative intervention to prevent this from happening.

Assuming businesses cannot contract around the class action altogether, of course, they may elect to arbitrate only individual disputes, channeling class actions into court. In fact, some lawyers for businesses engaged in consumer transactions have expressed distaste for class arbitration.[180] This is not surprising; class arbitration is an unfamiliar phenomenon, and current AAA rules do little to make it efficient or cost-effective. But under a more rational set of class arbitration rules, it is at least conceivable that some businesses, like consumers, might benefit from properly-administered class arbitration.

While there are limits to a business' ability to dictate arbitration procedure,[181] it can structure the class arbitration process to eliminate or reduce many of its likely objections to class actions.[182] For example, an arbitration agreement could significantly (and in my view,

---

278–280 (W. Va. 2002); *Luna v. Household Fin. Corp. III*, 236 F. Supp. 2d 1166, 1178–1179 (W.D. Wash. 2002). Arguably, the arbitrator should decide whether to enforce a ban on class proceedings, but that is a topic for a different article. The Supreme Court has yet to decide whether the FAA requires courts to enforce contract terms prohibiting class arbitration. See *Green Tree Fin. Corp. v. Bazzle*, 539 U.S. 444, 455–460 (2003) (Rehnquist, C.J., dissenting) (asserting that FAA requires enforcement of contracts 'according to their terms,' including contract term dissent interpreted to bar class actions).

[179] E.g., Owen M. Fiss, The Political Theory of the Class Action, 53 Wash. & Lee L. Rev. 21 (1996).

[180] See The Current State of Class Action Arbitration, *supra* n. 145, at 67–68 (reporting comment attributed to attorney Alan Kaplinsky – who can fairly be described as a proponent of predispute arbitration agreements – that he advises clients to include terms declaring the entire arbitration agreement void if a court or arbitrator finds the class action prohibition to be unenforceable).

[181] See *infra* text accompanying notes 232–248 (describing how those procedures evolve, in part, in response to other forces).

[182] Contract parties also may tailor judicial procedures, though to a lesser extent. Michael L. Moffitt, Customized Litigation: The Case for Making Civil Procedure Negotiable (Accepted Paper Series, 2007), available at <http://papers.ssrn.com/sol3/ papers.cfm?abstract_id=888221>.

legitimately) reduce the scope of discovery,[183] substantially reducing the cost of arbitration. It could also replace a lay jury with an expert decision-maker,[184] possibly reducing the expected amount of any award,[185] and it could provide a further hedge against large and unpredictable awards by calling for de novo review.[186] Moreover, many of the uncertainties now present in class arbitration will be removed as arbitrators and courts process the disputes now in the system.[187] If the class action does survive, at least some businesses might benefit by choosing tailored class arbitration procedures over the off-the-rack class action procedures in court.[188]

19.3.2 Aggregation in Individual Disputes

Notwithstanding my analysis in the prior section, it is possible that class arbitration will be a short-lived phenomenon.[189] If that is true, many consumers will have to assert claims, if at all, in individual

---

[183] Although arbitrators may order substantial discovery in appropriate cases, the scope of discovery will likely be much more limited in arbitration, whether or not the agreement imposes additional (and enforceable) restrictions. Compare Fed. R. Civ. P. 26(b), with Commercial Rules, *supra* n. 130, R. 21, and Am. Arbitration Ass'n., Commercial Rules and Mediation Procedures (Including Procedures for Large, Complex Commercial Disputes) L3 & L4 (2005), available at <www.adr.org/ sp.asp?id=22440>.
[184] Cf. Graham C. Lilly, The Decline of the American Jury, 72 U. Colo. L. Rev. 53, 66–67 (2001) (noting reasons to doubt jurors' capacity to resolve complex issues in high stakes cases).
[185] *Ibid.*
[186] This review could take place before a panel of arbitrators, see Fair Play, *supra* n. 114, at 21, or, perhaps, in court, e.g., Christopher R. Drahozal, Contracting Around RUAA: Default Rules, Mandatory Rules, and Judicial Review of Arbitral Awards, 3 Pepp. Disp. Resol. L.J. 419, 426–433 (2003).
[187] Ultimately, cost may be the most significant barrier to class arbitration, as arbitrators must be paid for their time. But the arbitration agreement can limit or offset these costs, for example by limiting discovery or by capping the length of the arbitration hearing. Moreover, current provider rules increase the cost of class arbitration by providing for a series of essentially interlocutory appeals. See e.g., AAA Class Rules, *supra* n. 146, R. 3 & 5. These rules should be changed, as they needlessly complicate the process and may significantly increase the expense of class arbitration.
[188] To a degree, of course, parties may of course customize the procedures and remedies that will be available to them in court. But arbitration offers significantly greater opportunities for customization. E.g., Moffitt, *supra* n. 182.
[189] *Supra* n. 173 and accompanying text.

arbitrations. Yet even in individual arbitration, we should not assume that arbitration necessarily will individuate the disputing process. In a number of ways, individual arbitration might facilitate the informal aggregation of consumer claims.

19.3.2.1 Reduced Cost

An obvious and frequently noted potential benefit of arbitration is reduced cost and time of dispute resolution. These potential benefits may not induce repeat-player lawyers to accept consumer arbitration cases, especially if fewer cases are settled in arbitration than in court.[190] To the extent arbitration awards tend to be lower than jury verdicts,[191] lawyers may be less willing to accept cases on a contingency basis,[192] unless they win more frequently in arbitration.[193] Yet repeat-player lawyers are already unlikely to accept large numbers of consumer cases, even those destined for court.[194] If arbitration costs less and yields generally favorable results, it at least raises the possibility that lawyers might build practices around handling large volumes of relatively low-value claims.[195] This would be a clear benefit to consumer claimants.[196]

---

[190] See e.g., Sherwyn et al., *supra* n. 27, at 1575 (noting in employment context that reduced cost and faster disposition may increase lawyers' willingness to take cases, but that reduced defense costs might make settlement less likely).

[191] See *supra* n. 185.

[192] Much, though not all, of the premium lawyers obtain from contingency fee practice may derive from the top 10–20% of case recoveries. See Kritzer, Seven Dogged Myths, *supra* n. 40, at 766–768, 772. To the extent arbitration reduces expected recoveries, lawyers may be less willing to accept arbitration cases. See Bingham, The Repeat Player Effect, *supra* n. 27, at 199–200.

[193] See Sherwyn et al., *supra* n. 27, at 1567–1569 (discussing studies of win-rate in employment arbitration); see also *supra* n. 98 (discussing Ernst & Young Study of consumer arbitration).

[194] See *supra* text accompanying notes 57–67.

[195] See Frederic N. Smalkin & Frederick N.C. Smalkin, The Market for Justice, the 'Litigation Explosion,' and the 'Verdict Bubble': A Closer Look at Vanishing Trials, 2005 Fed. Cts. L. Rev. 8, 40 (2005) ('The speed and low cost ... [of] arbitration ... may work in favor of the plaintiff's attorney who handles a large volume of cases and/or is underwriting costs for an impecunious clientele.').

[196] The frequency with which consumers are represented by lawyers in arbitration and the characteristics of those lawyers (repeat player versus one-shotter), are important areas for further study. See *supra* n. 139.

19.3.2.2 Development of Precedent

It is routine to hear that arbitrators neither follow nor create precedent.[197] There is no doubt some truth to this. But there is also some reason to believe that, over time, arbitrators' decisions may come to form what Professor Richard Reuben has called 'collective arbitral wisdom.'[198] For that to happen, of course, arbitrators may need to issue reasoned awards. Some ADR providers now encourage or require this in consumer and employment cases.[199]

Whether or not these awards become public,[200] they increase the likelihood that information about arbitration results will spread among consumers and their lawyers.[201] In turn, arbitrators will become better informed about how their peers have decided particular issues. As a result, although not bound by prior decisions, arbitrators might develop a consensus about how to interpret particular contract terms or how to view particular business practices. One can imagine, for example, a consistent pattern of awards finding that a particular business

---

[197] See Alderman, *supra* n. 68, at 1242; Baruch Bush, *supra* n. 132, at 988–989; see also Menkel-Meadow, *supra* n. 9, at 37 (noting that lack of reasoned or written opinions may individuate disputing process).

[198] Reuben, *supra* n. 89, at 1085.

[199] The AAA Employment Rules, for example, require arbitrators to state 'the written reasons' for their award, unless the parties agree otherwise, and also make redacted versions of awards available to the public on a cost basis and on the AAA website. Employment Rules, *supra* n. 113, R. 34; see also Consumer Rules, *supra* n. 113, R. C-7 (only requiring that the award be in writing); Consumer Protocol, *supra* n. 111, Principle 15 (requiring arbitrator, upon timely request of either party, to provide brief written explanation of basis for award); JAMS Employment Policy, *supra* n. 115, Standard No. 8 (providing for 'concise written statement' of reasons for award); JAMS Consumer Policy, *supra* n. 115, para. 10 (same). But see NAF Code of Procedure, *supra* n. 116, R. 37(H) (awards to be 'summary awards' unless the parties agree otherwise, or unless a party requests findings of fact and conclusions of law and pays a fee).

[200] Even if not made publicly available by the ADR provider, in many circumstances, the award would become public if the prevailing party sought a court order confirming it. See Reuben, *supra* n. 89, at 1086.

[201] See *id.* at 1085 (noting that spread of information may offset repeat-players' advantage in arbitration); Bingham, The Repeat Player Effect, *supra* n. 27, at 218–219 (noting that repeat-player lawyers might gather information on arbitrators and make other investments in intellectual capital).

CHAPTER 19. ARBITRATION AND THE INDIVIDUATION CRITIQUE

model – say, providing an up-front cash 'rebate' and nominal access to Internet services in exchange for a consumer's agreement to make substantial monthly payments – constitutes consumer lending activity subject to state usury law.[202]

Indeed, the AAA class arbitrations offer an example of how such a consensus might develop. The AAA Class Rules call for a clause construction award, in which the arbitrator determines whether the parties' agreement permits class arbitration.[203] These awards are available to the public, and of course they are of great interest to the lawyers involved in these cases. So far, arbitrators have issued clause construction awards in thirty-one consumer and employment cases, and in all but one they have interpreted the agreement to permit class certification.[204] Now, even judges have limited use for precedent in interpreting actual contract language. Yet while acknowledging they were not bound by other arbitrators' interpretations of other contracts, some arbitrators have discerned, and followed, a 'national pattern of clause

---

[202] See *State ex rel. Cooper v. NCCS Loans, Inc.*, 624 S.E.2d 371, 377 (N.C. App. 2005).
[203] See AAA Class Rules, *supra n.* 146, R. 3.
[204] Perhaps this consistency can be attributed to arbitrators' presumed tendency to issue rulings that favor their continued jurisdiction (and collection of fees). E.g., *Trafalgar Shipping Co. v. Int'l Milling Co.*, 401 F.2d 568, 573–574 (2nd Cir. 1968) (Lumbard, J., dissenting); Robert H. Smit, Separability and Competence-Competence in International Arbitration: Ex Nihilo Nihil Fit? Or Can Something Indeed Come From Nothing?, 13 Am. Rev. Int'l Arb. 19, 27 (2002). But in a number of cases arbitrators who interpreted the agreement to permit class arbitration subsequently denied certification, dismissed the arbitration on the merits, or otherwise ruled contrary to their presumed economic interests. E.g., Class Certification Award of Arbitrator, *Milstein v. Protection One Alarm Servs., Inc.*, No. 11 110 00270 04 (May 12, 2005) (Am. Arbitration Ass'n), available at <www.adr.org/si.asp?id=1876> (denying class certification); Award on Motions (i) for Summary Disposition and (ii) For Posting of Bond at 16–24, *Rhodes College Inc. v. Satz*, No. 11 181 02217 04 (July 5, 2005) (Am. Arbitration Ass'n), available at <www.adr.org/si.asp?id=2133> (granting motion to dismiss); Award on (i) Clause Construction, and (ii) Motion to Dismiss for Lack of Jurisdiction at 8–11, *Warrior Transportation v. FFE Transp. Servs. Inc.*, No. 11 118 00365 05 (August 18, 2005) (Am. Arbitration Ass'n), available at <www.adr.org/si.asp?id=1966> (invalidating entire arbitration agreement – not a consumer or employment case); Partial Final Clause Construction Award, *Budner v. Wellness Int'l Network, Ltd.*, No. 11 181 00828 04 (December 20, 2004) (Am. Arbitration Ass'n), available at <www.adr.org/si.asp?id=1721> (interpreting agreement to require dispute to be brought in court).

construction awards.'[205] Even when they assign little weight to prior clause construction awards, the cases show the arbitrators engaging with those awards much like one trial judge might engage with another's opinion in a similar case.[206] We should not automatically equate class arbitration to the arbitration experiences of individual consumers, nor should we assume that clause construction awards are typical examples of arbitral decision-making. Nonetheless, the class arbitrations suggest that, with an active plaintiffs' bar, reasoned awards, and rapid exchange of information about arbitration results, arbitration may produce a body of law that is essentially 'public' – i.e., a set of publicly available principles that convey information about the arbitration process and guide decision-making in future cases.

In any event, an arbitrator seeking only to maximize fees might think it strategically unwise to prolong class arbitrations. Presumably, these arbitrators derive some (probably most) of their fees from commercial arbitrations between businesses. Class arbitration respondents and their lawyers are likely to be repeat players in these business-to-business disputes and can discipline 'pro-claimant' arbitrators not only by denying them future class arbitration work, but by denying them future work in commercial disputes as well. By contrast, the plaintiffs' class action firms that represent claimants in class arbitrations may appear infrequently in business-to-business disputes. These are all assumptions, of course, but they seem at least plausible.

[205] Clause Construction Award at 14–17, *Awe v. I&M Rail Link, LLC*, No. 11 160 00026 05 (May 4, 2005) (Am. Arbitration Ass'n), available at <www.adr.org/ si.asp?id=1938>; Clause Construction Award at 3 & app., *Grayson v. Rent-A-Center, Inc.*, No. 11 160 01823 04 (August 8, 2005) (Am. Arbitration Ass'n), available at<www.adr.org/si.asp?id=1947> (listing decisions by other arbitrators); see also Clause Construction Award at 2, *Ali v. Morton's of Chicago/Sacramento, Inc.*, No. 11 160 02015 05, (March 22, 2006) (Am. Arbitration Ass'n), available at <www.adr.org/si.asp?id=2177> (referencing the 'vast majority of clause construction awards'); Partial Final Clause Construction Award of Arbitrator at 9–11, *Petsch v. Orkin Exterminating Co.*, No. 11 181 02541 04 (August 31, 2005) (Am. Arbitration Ass'n), available at <www.adr.org/si.asp?id=2153> (discussing award in similar dispute and court's ruling declining to vacate that award).

[206] E.g., Clause Construction Award at 3, *Hearthside v. Qwest Dex, Inc.*, <www.adr.org/si.asp?id=1722> (noting two prior clause construction awards but describing them as 'unhelpful' on the question whether state law relevant to this case, and the parties' agreement, permitted class arbitration); Clause Construction Award at 25–28, *Scher v. Oxford Health Plan, Inc.*, <www.adr.org/si.asp?id=2144> (dissent; noting more than twenty consistent clause construction awards, attempting to distinguish some of them, and finally expressing disagreement with the remainder).

CHAPTER 19. ARBITRATION AND THE INDIVIDUATION CRITIQUE

In fact, arbitrators themselves may have professional values conducive to the development of a 'public' body of law. These values might include a desire to transmit knowledge to future arbitrators, to demystify the process for lawyers who are skeptical of arbitration, or to communicate the nature of the arbitration process to the public or to policymakers. Labor arbitration offers an example of how a private dispute resolution system can create 'public' law in this fashion. Like the *Restatements of the Law*, *The Common Law of the Workplace*, a standard reference in labor arbitration, attempts to distill a large body of 'common law' – in this case the decisions of labor arbitrators – into a set of principles to guide future disputes.[207] Although these principles are not formally binding, arbitrators may hesitate to depart from them in any significant way.[208] Compared to labor arbitration, consumer and employment arbitration are relative newcomers, and it is possible that they will develop similar bodies of 'public' law over time.[209] The AAA's decision to begin publishing its employment awards, even if in redacted form, is a modest step in that direction.[210]

Indeed, there is a sense in which ADR providers already establish precedent, not just informal consensus. As I have explained, the AAA conducts an administrative review of each arbitration agreement prior to accepting a case.[211] If an agreement does not substantially comply with the due process protocol, the business must either waive the

---

[207] The Common Law of the Workplace: The Views of Arbitrators (Theodore J. St. Antoine ed., (2nd edn 1998).

[208] E.g., Clyde W. Summers, Individual Protection Against Unjust Dismissal: Time for a Statute, 62 Va. L. Rev. 481, 501 (1976). According to Summers,

> although arbitrators often cite to no other decisions in their opinion and never consider other cases as binding precedents, they usually are quite aware of the pattern of decisions by other arbitrators and are reluctant to deviate far from that pattern. Results in a discipline case may well depend on the length of the arbitrator's foot, but that leads to relatively small differences, for there are few peg-legs or abominable snowmen among arbitrators, and no one follows in their footsteps.

[209] Cf. Thomas J. Stipanowich, ADR and the 'Vanishing Trial': The Growth and Impact of 'Alternative Dispute Resolution,' 1 J. Empirical Legal Stud. 843, 907 (2004) (noting development of public law attributes in securities arbitration).

[210] See *supra* n. 199.

[211] See *supra* notes 114, 138 and accompanying text.

offending term or amend its agreement.[212] If the process works as designed, the due process rules – such as the rule against restrictions on remedies – effectively act as precedent applicable to all disputes administered by the provider. Perhaps consumer lawyers and advocates should press for a conception of arbitral 'due process' that includes some procedure for multiple claimants to obtain binding rulings on merits issues as well. As I explain below, there is reason to believe provider rules may become more favorable to consumers over time.[213]

19.3.2.3   Facilitating Award Collection

Beyond reducing disputing costs and time and developing precedent, other policies, if implemented by ADR providers, would make arbitration more attractive to consumer claimants and repeat-player lawyers. One simple and effective reform would be for providers to decline to arbitrate disputes when a business has not paid, or sought a court order vacating, awards issued in favor of individual consumers. There is some precedent for such a procedure. The National Association of Securities Dealers has taken steps to reduce the number of unpaid securities arbitration awards issued on behalf of investor claimants.[214] These steps include requiring NASD member broker-dealers to certify

---

[212] See Fair Play, *supra* n. 114, at 33–34. The consequences of AAA's refusal to accept the case are unclear. Possibly, the business could still compel arbitration before another provider, but it might also find itself litigating the case (and all others under the agreement) in court.

[213] See *infra* text accompanying notes 232–248.

[214] In 2001, around 33% of NASD-administered monetary awards issued in favor of investors were not fully paid, down from 64% in 1998, and around 55% of awarded amounts remained unpaid, down from 80% in 1998. Most of the unpaid awards involved brokers who had left the securities industry. U.S. Gen. Accounting Office, GAO-03-162R, Follow-Up Report on Matters Relating to Securities Arbitration 3, 9–10 (2003) [hereinafter 2003 NASD Report]; see also U.S. Gen. Accounting Office, GAO/GGD-00-115, Securities Arbitration: Actions Needed to Address Problem of Unpaid Awards 33–39 (2000) [hereinafter 2000 NASD Report] (discussing data on unpaid awards and NASD procedures); U.S. Gen. Accounting Office, GAO-01-654R, Evaluation of Steps Taken to Address the Problem of Unpaid Arbitration Awards (2001) [hereinafter 2001 NASD Report] (discussing steps taken to monitor award payment).

that they have paid outstanding awards and, in some cases, suspending the license of members who fail to pay.[215]

For individual consumers, such a policy would offer substantial benefits, potentially saving them the delay and expense involved in confirming the award[216] and invoking the judicial execution process,[217] and thereby making consumer arbitration claims far more attractive to lawyers. Nor does it seem outlandish to expect ADR providers to adopt such policies, perhaps modeling them on those implemented by the NASD. Providers have already demonstrated a willingness to decline arbitrations where the agreement does not conform to their standards of fairness.[218] Perhaps a reasonable conception of arbitral 'due process' includes the notion that ADR providers should not lend their services to businesses who refuse to honor their awards.

19.3.2.4 Punitive Damages and Other Remedies

I have already mentioned the AAA's assertion that it will not administer arbitrations under an agreement that prevents consumers from

---

[215] See 2003 NASD Report, *supra* n. 214, at 10. Some have questioned whether these steps adequately address the problem of unpaid securities arbitration awards. Per Jebsen, How to Fix Unpaid Arbitration Awards, 26 Pace L. Rev. 183, 200–205 (2006). Most of the unpaid awards, however, involve broker-dealers who have left the securities industry, filed for bankruptcy, or challenged the award in court. See 2003 NASD Report, *supra* n. 214, at 9–10 & Table 1. Unpaid awards are a problem in any context, but these reasons for non-payment may have little to do with arbitration in general or with NASD rules in particular.

[216] This is a significant point. While there is reason to believe that arbitration is less expensive than litigation for consumers, see *supra* text accompanying notes 190–196, an arbitration award must be confirmed by a court before it becomes a judgment enforceable by judicial process, see 9 U.S.C. § 9 (2006). See also Thomas H. Oehmke, Arbitration Highways to the Courthouse: A Litigator's Roadmap, 86 Am. Jur. Trials 111, § 244 (2006). When comparing the cost (in dollars and time) of arbitration to litigation, then, the proper comparison may be between (1) the cost of arbitration plus the cost of judicial proceedings to confirm the award and (2) the cost of litigating the disputes on the merits.

[217] Unrepresented consumers in particular may struggle to understand and utilize the arcane execution process. See Abel, *supra* n. 58, at 298.

[218] See e.g., *supra* notes 114, 138.

recovering punitive and other damages.[219] That statement was made in an affidavit submitted by an AAA official in opposition to a subpoena seeking discovery of AAA documents.[220] Given that context, the statement may say more about the AAA's desire to avoid discovery than it does about actual AAA policy. As I have said, I know of no data showing how consistently the AAA or other providers enforce their due process protocols.[221] This is an area worthy of further study, although providers will have to make available the necessary data. Yet the AAA's statement is a reasonable interpretation of the Consumer Protocol, and it sets a precedent that may influence, if not control, the analysis of other agreements. It suggests, moreover, that ADR providers can play a role in limiting businesses' efforts to include 'remedy stripping'[222] terms in their arbitration agreements.[223]

19.3.2.5 Summary

A less costly dispute resolution system that shares some aspects of a 'public' legal system, facilitates award collection, and offers some protection from onerous contract terms would offer significant benefits to consumers. Returning once more to my theft-protection warranty example, even if class arbitration were unavailable, it is possible that consumers might find specialized lawyers willing to represent them in individual cases. Seeking to develop favorable rules, those lawyers might make significant litigation investments and seek to build an inventory of cases. The relative ease of collecting awards would further encourage lawyer participation, while making it easier for claimants who wished (or had no choice but) to represent themselves to do so.

---

[219] See *supra* text accompanying n. 126.

[220] See *supra* n. 126.

[221] See *supra* text accompanying n. 138.

[222] Schwartz, *supra* n. 101, at 49.

[223] Other suggested reforms are designed to limit repeat players' potential advantage in arbitration, though not to induce repeat players into arbitration on behalf of consumers and employees. E.g., Margaret M. Harding, The Limits of the Due Process Protocols, 19 Ohio St. J. on Disp. Resol. 369, 452–453 (2004) (suggesting disclosure of relationship between provider and other party, and option to file suit in court if the provider and repeat player have a relationship 'that produces the appearance of partiality').

CHAPTER 19. ARBITRATION AND THE INDIVIDUATION CRITIQUE

Claiming rates might increase, along with settlement rates,[224] further reducing the cost of arbitration on a per-dispute basis. While imperfect, such a system would in many ways represent an improvement over the procedures available to individual consumer litigants in court.

19.3.3 The Effect and Evolution of Provider Rules

The cautiously optimistic view of arbitration underlying my prior discussion raises some obvious objections. For one thing, arbitration is contractual.[225] A business can designate an ADR provider that will enforce its chosen terms, or it can forgo a provider's services and simply require the parties to designate an arbitrator from an acceptable list.[226] For that matter, ADR providers compete fiercely for business.[227] Providers that implement business-friendly terms may have a competitive advantage. If that is true, why should we expect provider rules to become more favorable to consumers, rather than less?

It seems likely, however, that businesses will continue using providers like the AAA. As growing arbitration caseloads suggest,[228] businesses value providers' services, which may include identifying and training potential arbitrators, handling case logistics, and promulgating off-the-rack arbitration procedures.[229] No doubt the market for

---

[224] To the extent arbitration yields predictable results in similar cases – and both precedent and easy award collection increase the likelihood that this will happen – one might expect settlement rates to increase.

[225] See Bales, *supra* n. 88, at 602–604.

[226] See Bingham, *supra* n. 88, at 239–243 (discussing how ADR provider rules can create a more balanced system but noting that drafters can avoid these protections by creating their own arbitration panels or contracting with alternative providers); Harding, *supra* n. 223, at 421–422.

[227] Edward Brunet, Replacing Folklore Arbitration with a Contract Model of Arbitration, 74 Tul. L. Rev. 39, 52 (1999).

[228] E.g., Chris A. Carr & Michael R. Jencks, The Privatization of Business and Commercial Dispute Resolution: A Misguided Policy Decision, 88 Ky. L.J. 183, 199 & n. 43 (2000) (describing increase in AAA and JAMS caseload in 1990s); Deborah R. Hensler, Our Courts, Ourselves: How the Alternative Dispute Resolution Movement is Re-Shaping Our Legal System, 108 Penn. St. L. Rev. 165, 167 & n. 11 (2003) (reporting increase in AAA caseload from 1990–2002).

[229] See Brunet, *supra* n. 227, at 52–53 (also noting that bundling these services may reduce transaction costs). In 'non-administered' arbitration, the parties and the

arbitration services is competitive,[230] and providers that implement unpopular policies risk losing business.[231] So it would be foolish to expect providers to insist on rules that were unacceptable to their customers. But for several reasons providers may implement, and businesses may accept, reasonable arbitration reform.

First, judicial scrutiny limits the extent to which providers can favor their business customers, and in fact may create pressure to increase the level of 'due process' afforded consumers.[232] Providers need courts to view their procedures as fair, and businesses want assurances that courts will respect a provider's rules and enforce awards issued by its arbitrators.[233] Thus, providers may file amicus briefs

---

arbitrator may handle case logistics, and the provider's role, if it has one, may be limited to helping select an arbitrator or ruling on challenges to the arbitrator.

[230] See Reuben, *supra* n. 89, at 1063–1064 (also noting subtle incentives that may cause arbitrators to favor institutional players). In collections cases, in which consumers are respondents, there may be particular cause for concern. Given the modest stakes in many collections cases, few consumer debtors are likely to be represented by repeat-player lawyers, see *supra* n. 82, and this many enhance businesses' ability to shape the arbitration process.

[231] For example, JAMS, a major ADR provider, recently retracted a policy generally viewed as favorable to class arbitration, replacing it with one similar to the AAA's. See Meredith W. Nissen, Class Action Arbitrations, Disp. Resol. Mag., Summer 2005, at 19; Press Release, JAMS, JAMS Reaffirms Commitment to Neutrality Through Withdrawal of Class Action Arbitration Waiver Policy (March 10, 2005) (on file with author); see also *supra* n. 128.

[232] Courts routinely police the fairness of arbitration agreements, most often through state-law unconscionability doctrine, but also when deciding whether to confirm or vacate an arbitration award. See e.g., *Ting v. AT&T*, 319 F.3d 1126, 1152 (9th Cir. 2003) (holding that agreement that, among other things, prevented consumer from bringing class action was unconscionable); *Shankle v. B-G Maint. Mgmt.*, 163 F.3d 1230, 1235 (10th Cir. 1999) (refusing to enforce agreement that required employee to pay half of arbitration expenses); *Cole v. Burns Int'l Sec. Servs.*, 105 F.3d 1465, 1468 (D.C. Cir. 1997) (same, where agreement required employee to pay arbitrator's fee); see also Susan Randall, Judicial Attitudes Toward Arbitration and the Resurgence of Unconscionability, 52 Buff. L. Rev. 185, 222 (2004) (generally describing and critiquing courts' application of unconscionability doctrine to police arbitration agreements).

[233] See Drahozal, *supra* n. 104, at 752, 769–770; Llewellyn Joseph Gibbons, Creating a Market for Justice; A Market Incentive Solution to Regulating the Playing Field: Judicial Deference, Judicial Review, Due Process, and Fair Play in Online Consumer Arbitration, 23 Nw. J. Int'l L. & Bus. 1, 27 (2002).

CHAPTER 19. ARBITRATION AND THE INDIVIDUATION CRITIQUE

defending their procedures,[234] and they may adjust their procedures in response to judicial criticism.[235] These are investments in reputation; to a judge familiar with an ADR provider, designation of that provider in a contract may signal that the agreement should be upheld.[236] This dialogue between courts and providers, moreover, is a two-way street. Provider rules and due process protocols inform courts about best practices in arbitration, and courts may come to view the absence of these practices as a warning sign.[237] Over time, this dialogue may limit contract drafters' efforts to impose procedures that conflict with those 'reputable' providers view as fundamental to a fair arbitration process.[238]

As others have noted, moreover, providers and businesses are subject to a variety of external constraints that, over time, may lead to arbitration reform. Pressure from the plaintiffs' bar, for example,

---

[234] E.g., *Allied-Bruce Terminix Cos., Inc. v. Dobson*, 513 U.S. 265, 280–281 (1995) (noting that AAA had filed an amicus brief); Brief Amicus Curiae of the American Arbitration Ass'n, *Green Tree Financial Corp. v. Randolph*, 531 U.S. 79 (2000) (No. 99-1235), 2000 WL 744161.

[235] See AAA Reduces Arbitration Costs to Be Paid by Employees, 57 Disp. Resol. J., January 2003, at 5 (noting that AAA had reduced cost of arbitration to employees and that change was in response to recent court decisions); Samuel Estreicher & Matt Ballard, Affordable Justice Through Arbitration: A Critique of Public Citizen's Jeremiad on the 'Costs of Arbitration,' 57 Disp. Resol. J., January 2003, at 8, 11–12 (noting provider trend towards reduced cost).

[236] See e.g., *Izzi v. Mesquite Country Club*, 186 Cal. App. 3d 1309, 1318 (Ct. App. 1986) ('The rules of the American Arbitration Association ... are generally regarded to be neutral and fair.'); *Veliz v. Cintas Corp.*, No. C 03-1180 SBA, 2004 WL 2452851, at 15 (N.D. Cal. April 5, 2004) (rejecting challenge to confidentiality requirement under AAA rules: 'The AAA is a reputable arbitration body and the reasons for confidentiality are designed to protect all parties in a dispute'); see also Drahozal, *supra* n. 104, at 752 ('An institution that develops a reputation for unfairness or biased arbitrators risks losing credibility, which courts rely on to recognize and enforce arbitral awards.').

[237] See Harding, *supra* n. 223, at 409 ('At a minimum, the protocols have influenced, to some degree, both the manner in which arbitration agreements are evaluated and the development of the common law regarding the conditions that must be met for a court to compel arbitration.').

[238] Cf. *Hooters of Am., Inc. v. Phillips*, 173 F.3d 933, 939 (4th Cir. 1999) (noting testimony and amicus briefs by ADR providers criticizing as unfair the arbitration process structured by the employer).

may lead ADR providers to reform arbitration procedures.[239] Consumers themselves may create pressure for reform. Businesses and providers that resist needed reform might suffer reputational consequences.[240] As an initial matter, one might think employers more sensitive to reputational concerns than businesses engaged in consumer transactions.[241] Moreover, consumers may have less information about businesses' practices than employees do about the practices of their employers. In the workplace, information about the employer's dispute resolution process may spread easily among employees.[242] By contrast, information may spread less easily among dispersed consumers.[243] Yet new technologies and increased interest among consumers and advocacy groups are facilitating information exchange[244] and enabling campaigns to pressure businesses and arbitration providers.[245] To date, most of these efforts have focused on eliminating pre-dispute arbitration agreements altogether, sometimes

---

[239] E.g., Cynthia Estlund, Rebuilding the Law of the Workplace in an Era of Self-Regulation, 105 Colum. L. Rev. 319, 399 (2005) (noting role of plaintiffs' employment lawyers in shaping arbitration law and practices); Menkel-Meadow, *supra* n. 9, at 41–43 (describing threatened boycott of ADR providers by the employment plaintiffs' bar and creation of resulting employment arbitration due process protocol); David S. Schwartz, Enforcing Small Print to Protect Big Business: Employee and Consumer Rights Claims in an Age of Compelled Arbitration, 1997 Wis. L. Rev. 33, 41 n. 19 (attributing development of employment due process protocol to pressure from plaintiffs' employment bar); Margaret A. Jacobs, Firms With Policies Requiring Arbitration Are Facing Obstacles, Wall St. J., October 16, 1995, at B5 (describing potential boycott of ADR providers).

[240] See Drahozal, *supra* n. 104, at 767–769.

[241] See *Id.* at 768–69.

[242] If the employer hopes to use arbitration and other ADR tools to resolve disputes quickly and with little acrimony – preserving workplace morale and minimizing employee turnover, see Sherwyn et al., *supra* n. 27, at 1579; see also *supra* n. 107 – it will not help to have employees quickly discover that the employer has stacked the deck in its favor.

[243] See Drahozal, *supra* n. 104, at 769.

[244] See *Id.* at 768.

[245] E.g., Give Me Back My Rights!, <www.givemebackmyrights.com> (last visited January 25, 2007); Call Before You Buy, <www.callbeforeyoubuy.com> (last visited January 25, 2007).

CHAPTER 19. ARBITRATION AND THE INDIVIDUATION CRITIQUE

successfully.[246] Consumer groups might have similar success advocating for reforms to existing arbitration practices.

But focusing on the need for consumers to force arbitration reform, or courts to impose it, may overlook a fundamental point about how arbitration procedure evolves. Ultimately, there may be limits to the ability of businesses and other repeat players to control the evolution of arbitration procedure. Instead, to a significant degree those procedures may evolve over time through the combined influence of ADR providers, arbitrators, and lawyers.[247] This process may result in the widespread adoption of a reasonably uniform and fair set of procedures even in transactions between parties of unequal bargaining power.[248]

19.4 CONCLUSION

By aggregating claims in formal and informal ways, one-shot claimants enhance their ability to compete in litigation with their repeat-player adversaries. In what I have called the individuation critique, skeptics assert that arbitration does not permit such aggregation. While arbitration proponents defend arbitration for independent reasons, such as economic efficiency, they do not suggest that arbitration could or should facilitate aggregate dispute resolution. Thus, both sides of the debate view arbitration as an individuated disputing process.

This shared view of arbitration takes too much for granted. As an empirical matter, it is not clear whether the individuation critique

---

[246] For example, in most cases Fannie Mae and Freddie Mac will no longer purchase or securitize mortgage loans that contain pre-dispute arbitration agreements. See Fannie Mae, Announcement 04-06, at 4–5 (2004), available at <www.efanniemae.com/sf/guides/ssg/annltrs/pdf/2004/04-06.pdf>; Freddie Mac, Freddie Mac Promotes Consumer Choice With New Subprime Mortgage Arbitration Policy (December 4, 2003), <www.freddiemac.com/news/archives/afford_housing/2003 consumer_ 120403.html>.

[247] See Laura J. Cooper, The Process of Process: The Historical Development of Procedure in Labor Arbitration, in Arbitration 2005: The Evolving World of Work 99, 119–120 (Charles J. Coleman ed., 2006).

[248] See Id. at 120 (arguing that labor arbitration procedures evolved 'to a point where they are universally accepted as fair by workers, unions, employers and courts, without their having been the product of negotiations between parties of equal bargaining power').

accurately describes current arbitration practices. Perhaps more important, neither side of the arbitration debate gives much thought to arbitration's potential to facilitate aggregate dispute resolution. This is unfortunate, for arbitration has a good deal of potential. In class arbitration, arbitrators have the flexibility to resolve, in fair, efficient, and collective terms, disputes that would have to proceed individually in court. Arbitrators should recognize and use this authority, and courts should respect it. Even in individual cases, arbitration has the potential to facilitate the informal aggregation of disputes. As currently practiced, arbitration may create precedent in a variety of ways and offers consumers and employees some protection from a variety of oppressive terms. Appropriate reforms might strengthen these features of arbitration and offer additional benefits not available in court, such as simplified, low-cost collection of awards.[249]

Both proponents and skeptics have reason to embrace arbitration's aggregative potential, especially but not exclusively in consumer disputes. For proponents, the creation of such a system would further legitimize arbitration, demonstrating its capacity to provide justice on even terms and increasing support for arbitration among consumers, consumer advocates, and plaintiffs' lawyers. Skeptics, too, should recognize the promise of arbitration and advocate for reforms to enhance its aggregative potential. Accomplishing such reforms, however, may require more than a broadside attack on pre-dispute arbitration itself. That such attacks have been staples of consumer

---

[249] See *supra* text accompanying notes 214–218. As I have described, ADR provider rules have gradually become more favorable to consumer and employee claimants. For example, in addition to gradually reducing the cost of arbitration, see Estreicher & Ballard, *supra* n. 235, at 11–12; see also *supra* text accompanying n. 117, ADR providers may now:

(1) require that arbitration agreements be mutually binding, see JAMS Consumer Policy, *supra* n. 115, para. 1; JAMS Employment Policy, *supra* n. 115, Standard No. 7;
(2) require that businesses waive contract terms requiring arbitration in an inconvenient forum, see *supra* n. 118 and accompanying text;
(3) decline arbitrations under agreements that limit the remedies available in arbitration, see *supra* notes 124–126 and accompanying text;
(4) make awards publicly available, see *supra* notes 199–200 and accompanying text; and
(5) require reasoned opinions, see *supra* n. 199.

CHAPTER 19. ARBITRATION AND THE INDIVIDUATION CRITIQUE

advocates and private lawyers is perhaps unsurprising. These actors share a justified suspicion that businesses do not implement arbitration programs as a service to their customers. Objections to consumer arbitration in particular also reflect a concern for the future of the class action. Yet, however justified, these concerns should not lead us to reject pre-dispute arbitration out-of-hand, nor to cease efforts to influence the evolution of arbitration procedure. Potentially, arbitration may prove superior to the courts as a forum for resolving many consumer disputes. Consumers may benefit most if we recognize the possibilities as well as the dangers of arbitration.

CHAPTER 20

Building an Internal Defense Against Class Action Lawsuits: Human Resources Practices Audits

G. Roger King,* Jeffrey D. Winchester,** Lori A. Clary,*** and Kimberly J. Potter****

20.1 INTRODUCTION

The relative ease with which an unhappy employee can transform a single plaintiff lawsuit with limited litigation costs and damages exposure into a putative class action involving dozens, if not hundreds or thousands, of employees represents one of the most significant litigation risks facing today's employers. Employees (and their attorneys) who seek class certification often focus on allegedly unlawful policies or practices that apply throughout the employer's workforce to further their chances of satisfying the requirements for class certification – in particular, the requirements that common legal or factual issues exist and that such common issues predominate over any individual

---

* G. Roger King is a partner in the Labor and Employment Section of Jones Day's Columbus, Ohio office. He holds a J.D. from Cornell Law School.
** Jeffrey D. Winchester is an associate in the Labor and Employment Section of Jones Day. He holds a J.D. from Cornell Law School.
*** Lori A. Clary is an associate in the Labor and Employment Section of Jones Day. She holds a J.D. from The Ohio State University College of Law.
**** Kimberly J. Potter, is an associate in the Labor and Employment Section of Jones Day. She holds a J.D. from Duke Law School.

David Sherwyn and Samuel Estreicher (eds), *Employment Class and Collective Actions*, pp. 867–892.
© 2009, Kluwer Law International BV, Printed in Great Britain.

issues.[1] As a result, employers have a strong incentive to review their policies – in both letter and spirit – and their practices to ensure that they conform to the law and do not provide a basis for class litigation.

To that end, this article will first provide an overview of federal statutory employment claims most often targeted for class treatment, discuss tactics for recognizing potential bases for and avoiding disparate impact class litigation, and outline action steps that employers can take to avoid some of the most common class claims. This article will then discuss internal human resources audits and explore the litigation risks and benefits involved in conducting such an exercise.

20.2 CLASS ACTIONS AND SPECIFIC FEDERAL STATUTORY CLAIMS

There are a number of federal statutes that plaintiffs may rely on in an attempt to pursue class or collective action claims against employers. Outlined below are brief descriptions of the most common federal employment statutes that give rise to class or collective actions.

20.2.1 The Civil Rights Act of 1964, Title VII

Title VII[2] prohibits discrimination in the workplace on the basis of race, color, national origin, religion, or sex. Title VII has also been interpreted by the courts to prohibit harassment based on any of these protected classifications and to prohibit discrimination because of pregnancy. Title VII does not contain its own class action provisions. Potential class lawsuits against an employer under Title VII are governed by Rule 23 and the case law that has developed under this Rule. The number of Title VII class actions filed has risen significantly since the passage of the 1991 Civil Rights Act amendments, which allow Title VII plaintiffs to collect punitive damages and to demand trial by jury.

---

[1] See Fed. R. Civ. P. 23 (a)(2) (requiring that 'there are questions or law or fact common to the class'); Fed. R. Civ. P. 23(b)(3) (requiring that 'the questions of law or fact common to the members of the class predominate over any questions affecting only individual members').

[2] 42 U.S.C. §8 2000e, et seq. (1994).

20.2.2 The Americans with Disabilities Act and the Rehabilitation Act

Both the Americans with Disabilities Act (ADA)[3] and the Rehabilitation Act[4] prohibit workplace discrimination against persons with physical or mental disabilities, and, like cases brought under Title VII, class actions under these statutes are governed by Rule 23. However, certification of class suits under these statutes can be considerably more difficult than certification under other statutes because discrimination claims under these statutes tend to be highly individualized, requiring a case-by-case analysis of the claimant's alleged disability and the reasonable accommodation sought. As a result, it is often difficult for plaintiffs to find a class representative who can adequately 'represent a class of individuals with the same type of disability which affects their ability to perform the duties of a similar position, in a similar manner.'[5]

20.2.3 The Fair Labor Standards Act

The Fair Labor Standards Act (FLSA)[6] requires payment of minimum wage and overtime to employees covered by the Act. The FLSA permits collective actions on behalf of 'similarly situated' employees, but such actions are not controlled by the 'opt out' notice requirements of Rule 23. Instead, section 16(b) of the FLSA requires that notice be provided to putative class members, informing them that they will not be bound by a judgment unless they 'opt in' to the suit.[7] Generally, courts are guided by the elements of Rule 23 in deciding class formation under the FLSA. However, it is well established that plaintiffs need not completely satisfy Rule 23 when section 16(b) applies.

---

[3] 3 42 U.S.C. § 4 12101, et seq. (1994).
[4] 4 29 U.S.C. §§ 701 et seq. (1999).
[5] Barbara Lindeman and Paul Grossman, Employment Discrimination Law 1596. (Paul W. Cane, Jr. ed., ABA Section of Labor and Employment Law 3rd edn 1996) (quoting *Lintemuth v. Saturn Corp.*, 1994 WL 76081 1, at *5 (M.D. Tenn. 1994).
[6] 29 U.S.C. § 5 201 et seq. (1998).
[7] 29 U.S.C. § 216(b); see *Does I thru XXIII v. Advanced Textile Corp.*, 214 F.3d 1058, 1064 (9th Cir. 2000) (citing *Hoffmann-La Roche Inc. v. Sperling*, 493 U.S. 165, 169 (1989)).

In recent years, the plaintiffs' bar has shown increased interest in pursuing FLSA collective action claims. For example, in 2001, FLSA collective actions filed in federal court outnumbered Rule 23 employment class actions.[8]

20.2.4 The Age Discrimination in Employment Act of 1967

The Age Discrimination in Employment Act of 1967 (ADEA)[9] protects persons forty years of age and older from workplace discrimination. Unlike its sister federal antidiscrimination statutes, namely Title VII, the ADA and the Rehabilitation Act, the enforcement provision of the ADEA explicitly incorporate the collective action 'opt in' approach of section 16(b) of the FLSA. As mentioned above, under this approach, only those who affirmatively 'opt in' to the collective action are bound by the ultimate outcome. Those who do not join the collective action remain free to pursue individual actions against the employer, so long as they satisfy the ADEA's procedural prerequisites.

20.2.5 The Equal Pay Act

The Equal Pay Act (EPA)[10] prohibits differentials in employee pay based upon gender. Because the Equal Pay Act is part of the FLSA, class actions under the Equal Pay Act must be brought in accordance with the 'opt in' requirements of section 16(b) of the FLSA, rather than Rule 23. Plaintiffs may choose to bring their class claims under the ins instead of Title VI (which also prohibits gender-based pay discrimination) because the EPA allows for recovery of double back pay as liquidated damages for willful violations. Unlike Title VII, however, the EPA does not allow for non-economic compensatory damages or punitive damages.

---

[8] BNA Employment Policy & Law Daily (March 22, 2002).
[9] 29 U.S.C. §§ 621–634 (1999).
[10] 29 U.S.C. § 206(d) (1998).

CHAPTER 20. HUMAN RESOURCES PRACTICES AUDITS

20.2.6 The Employee Retirement Income Security Act

The Employee Retirement Income Security Act (ERISA), a complex and intricate statute, governs employee benefit and retirement plans.[11] Generally, ERISA class action claims, which are governed by Rule 23, involve nondisclosure, breach of duty, or nonforfeiture with respect to an employee benefit or retirement plan.[12] Because an employer's benefit and retirement plans tend to cover a large number of employees, class actions brought pursuant to ERISA can involve extremely large potential class sizes.

20.3 AVOIDING DISPARATE IMPACT CLASS ACTION LAWSUITS

20.3.1 The Nature and Danger of Disparate Impact Suits

Unlike claims of intentional discrimination or disparate treatment, which allege overt and/or intentional discrimination, claims of 'disparate impact' discrimination stem from allegations that employment practices that are facially neutral nonetheless have an unintentional 'disparate impact,' that is, significant adverse affect, on a protected group.[13] As with intentional discrimination claims, the structure of a disparate impact claim relies upon shifting burdens between the plaintiff and the defendant employer:

> The *Prima Facie* Case: A plaintiff class may establish a *prima facie* case of disparate impact by showing that the challenged practice or selection device resulted in a pattern of hiring, promotion, selection, etc., that had a significant exclusive effect on a protected group.[14] This showing is made

---

[11] 29 U.S.C. §8 1001 et seq. (1999).

[12] 5 James Wm. Moore et al., Moore's Federal Practice §23.23[5][i] (3d Ed. 2002).

[13] See e.g., *Int'l Bhd. of Teamsters v. United States*, 43 1 U.S. 324, 335–336 n. 15 (1977); *Smith v. Xerox Corp.*, 196 F.3d 358, 367–370 (2nd Cir. 1999).

[14] See e.g., *Albemarle Paper Co. v. Moody*, 422 U.S. 405, 425 (1975); *E.E.O.C. v. Joe's Stone Crab, Inc.*, 220 F.3d 1263, 1274 (11th Cir. 2000); *United States v. City of Warren*, 138 F.3d 1083, 1091–1092 (6th Cir. 1998).

through statistical evidence revealing a disparity so great that it cannot reasonably be attributed to chance.[15]

Business Necessity: If impact is established, the burden shifts to the employer to produce evidence that the practice or selection device is 'job-related [for the position in question] and consistent with business necessity.'[16]

Alternatives with Lesser Impact: Even if the employer has established 'business necessity,' the class has the opportunity to rebut the employer's proof by showing that the employer failed to implement an effective alternative practice or selection device that would have had a lesser adverse impact.[17]

For employers, disparate impact claims are dangerous because of their heavy reliance on statistical evidence and lack of a requirement of a showing of intent on the part of the employer to discriminate. Failure to have certain under-represented groups working in a position or positions can leave the employer vulnerable to statistical analyses potentially enabling class representatives to establish a prima facie case.[18] As one court has noted, plaintiffs 'may establish a prima facie case of disparate impact discrimination by proffering statistical evidence which reveals a disparity substantial enough to raise an inference of causation'[19] and that this statistical 'inference' need not have 'a scientific degree of certainty.'[20] Once the class has cleared this hurdle, the employer usually faces the difficult choice between settlement and facing a jury.

The following two statistical analyses, in particular, can establish difficulties for employers faced with disparate impact claims.

---

[15] See e.g., *Hazelwood Sch. Dist. v. United States*, 433 U.S. 299, 307–308 (1977); *E.E.O.C. v. Joint Apprenticeship Cornrn. of Joint Indus. Bd. of Elec. hdus.*, 164 F.3d 89, 95 (2nd Cir. 1998).

[16] *Burlington v. United Air Lines, Inc.*, 186 F.3d 1301, 13 12 (10th Cir. 1999) abrogated on other grounds, *Boyler v. Cordant Technologies, Inc.*, 3 16 F.3d 1137, 1140 (10th Cir. 2003); see also Albemarle, 422 U.S. at 425–428.

[17] See e.g., Albemarle, 422 U.S. at 425–428; *Brunet v. City of Columbus*, 1 F.3d 390, 409–410 (6th Cir. 1993); *Harper v. Bd. of Regents, Ill. State Univ.*, 35 F. Supp. 2d 1118, 1123–124 (C.D. Ill. 1999).

[18] See e.g., Joint Apprenticeship Committee, 164 F.3d at 95.

[19] *Id.*

[20] *Id.*

CHAPTER 20. HUMAN RESOURCES PRACTICES AUDITS

20.3.1.1 The Under-Utilization Analysis

This test involves an analysis of the major job positions of an employer and a statistical analysis to calculate if the protected group at issue is being under-utilized, that is, whether the numbers of minorities or women in a particular job classification is smaller than would be reasonably expected.[21] In making this statistical argument, the plaintiff may rely upon either labor market statistics or, where data related to the racial makeup of the relevant labor market is difficult to obtain, the plaintiff may rely upon demographic figures for the local population.[22] Then a comparison is done between the 'expected' utilization of the group in that occupation and the employer's actual utilization of group members in that occupation.[23]

20.3.1.2 The 80% Benchmark Rule

An often used approach for assessing disparate impact is the 'four-fifths rule' or 80% benchmark rule. The rule was created by the Equal Employment Opportunity Commission (EEOC) and has been widely used by the courts as a 'rule of thumb.'[24] Briefly summarized, the 80% rule states that an employer's selection criterion has an adverse impact, for purposes of plaintiffs' prima facie case, where members of a protected group are selected at a rate less than four-fifths (80%) of that group with the highest rate of selection. For example, if 50% of White employees are promoted to a certain level, but only 30% of African-American employees are promoted to the same level, then the relevant ratio would be 30/50, or 60%, and an adverse impact would thus be demonstrated under the 80% rule.

---

[21] *Williams v. Vukovich*, 720 F.2d 909, 922 (6th Cir. 1983); see also Smith, 196 F.3d at 368 (applying same statistical analysis disparate impact claim based upon reduction in force).
[22] City of Warren, 138 F.3d at 1093.
[23] Joint Apprenticeship Committee, 164 F.3d at 95–96.
[24] See Uniform Guidelines on Employee Selection Procedures, 29 C.F.R. pt. 1607.4 (1978); *Boston Police Superior Officers Fed'n v. City of Boston*, 147 F.3d 13, 21 (1st Cir. 1998); *Bew v. City of Chicago*, 979 F. Supp. 693, 696–697 (N.D. Ill. 1997); *Fickling v. N.Y. State Dep't of Civil Serv.*, 909 F. Supp. 185, 188–189 (S.D.N.Y. 1995).

The assumptions made and data used in the under-utilization analysis outlined above are particularly vulnerable to potential manipulation or misunderstanding. While the employer has the right to challenge any submitted data and offer evidence showing that the calculations are misleading, the employer is still stigmatized by the appearance of impropriety. In a legalistic sense, the burden of proving disparate impact is on the plaintiff, but often, in reality, the employer is the one that will have to prove the statistics offered are inaccurate or misleading.

It may be difficult, particularly for smaller employers, to avoid violating the 80% rule. Even though the Rule is still used by a number of courts as a starting point of analysis, it also has been widely criticized with one circuit court stating:

> [I]f an employer selects 60% of the blacks and 80% of the whites, this likely indicates a real difference in selection procedures if he is choosing 600 blacks out of 1,000 and 800 whites out of 1,000. On the other hand, if he chooses 3 blacks out of 5 applicants and 4 whites out of 5 applicants, [the percentages are the same, and the 80% rule is violated] both common sense and rigorous statistical analysis tell us that it is much more likely that mere chance is the controlling factor.[25]

Unfortunately, a number of courts are reticent to discard the 80% rule, and thus it is a reality with which many employers must deal.[26] Despite the fact that courts may consider the possibility of 'chance' accounting for the observed disparity, employers can ill afford to leave their fate to chance. Employers should routinely evaluate their hiring, promotion, and termination practices for substantial compliance with these rules. Efforts should be made to hire and promote qualified individuals from protected groups. Because class actions are so costly to litigate and devastating to settle or lose, employers need to focus on reasonable, practical opportunities to eliminate the opportunity for one of these lawsuits to develop by closely monitoring their statistics.

---

[25] *Black v. City of Akron*, 83 1 F.2d 13 1, 134 (6th Cir. 1987).
[26] See, e.g., *Langlois v. Abington Hous. Auth.*, 207 F.3d 43, 50 (1st Cir. 2000) ('[W]e have approved use of the four-fifths rule as a pertinent benchmark in the employment context.') (citing Boston Police, 147 F.3d at 21); *Pietras v. Bd. of Fire Cornrn'rs*, 180 F.3d 468, 474 (2nd Cir. 1999) (refusing to abandon the four-fifths rule for disparate impact claims).

20.3.2 Preventing Disparate Impact Suits: How to Uncover Unseen Potential Disparate Impact Liability in an Organization

Because disparate impact claims target facially-neutral hiring practices and requirements, such claims can pose a substantial practical problem in even identifying such practices. Outlined below are examples of hiring and promotion practices that the courts have found to establish a prima facie case of discriminatory disparate impact.

20.3.2.1 *Restriction of Job Advertising to Local Newspapers*

In *United States v. City of Warren*, the municipal government of a predominantly White city in predominantly White Macomb County, Michigan, had for years followed a policy of advertising city employment opportunities only in local county newspapers and not in newspapers distributed in the neighboring city of Detroit, which had a substantial nonwhite work force.[27] The Sixth Circuit Court of Appeals found that the city's 'refusal to publicize jobs outside the racially homogenous county, [created] a *de facto* barrier between employment opportunities and members of a protected class,' especially in light of the fact that the city had employed no black individuals while its advertising policy was in effect, compared to a statistical projection that at least ninety-nine Black employees would have been hired if the city had advertised its job openings to a wider population base.[28]

20.3.2.2 *Requirement that Applicants Meet Certain Minimum Educational Requirements*

In *EEOC v. Joint Apprenticeship Committee of Joint Industry Board of Electrical Industry*, the EEOC successfully argued that an industrial board's requirement of a high school diploma or General Equivalency Diploma (GED) as a prerequisite to admission to its apprenticeship program could support a prima facie claim of disparate impact racial

---

[27] City of Warren, 138 F.3d at 1088.
[28] *Id.* at 1094.

discrimination.[29] The EEOC satisfied its burden of proof by providing the Court with statistical data showing that:

> (1) For counties from which [the Board] received five or more applications, 89.2% of Whites and 68.3% of Blacks between the ages of 18 and 22 possessed a high school diploma or GED, [and] (2) Blacks comprised 18.3% of the potential [local labor force] for [the Board's] apprentice training program but made up [only] 12.2% of actual applicants to the program.[30]

Because both of these discrepancies were statistically significant, the Second Circuit Court of Appeals held that the EEOC had shown that the Board's educational requirement had a racially disparate impact and remanded the case to the district court to determine whether the Board could state a valid business justification for its educational requirement.[31]

20.3.2.3 Reliance upon Subjective Personal or Family Ties as Hiring Criteria

In *Banks v. City of Albany*, an unsuccessful black candidate for the position of firefighter brought a claim of disparate impact racial discrimination against the City of Albany Fire Department, where only 3.1% of the firefighters in the Albany Fire Department were Black, compared to a Black population in the City of Albany of 21.5%.[32] Key to the court's decision was the fact that the Chief of the Fire Department, who had the sole power of determining which candidates would be hired, admitted that he based his hiring decisions on his personal knowledge of candidates and their families. Because this selection process had no demonstrable 'business necessity' and such a selection criteria would tend to perpetuate under-representation of minorities in the fire department, the court held that the plaintiff had made his prima facie case and denied the city's motion for summary judgment.[33]

---

[29] Joint Apprenticeship Committee, 164 F.3d at 95, 98.
[30] *Id.* at 95–96.
[31] *Id.* at 98.
[32] *Bath v. City of Albany*, 953 F. Supp. 28, 35 (N.D. N.Y. 1997).
[33] 33 *Id.* at 35–36.

CHAPTER 20. HUMAN RESOURCES PRACTICES AUDITS

20.3.2.4 Some Tips on Avoiding Disparate Impact Discrimination Claims

In light of recent case law, in order to help prevent exposure to liability for disparate impact claims, employers should:

- carefully consider the likely impact of employment and recruiting policies and procedures on protected groups in the geographical area;
- establish clear, nondiscriminatory standardized hiring and promotion criteria, and take affirmative steps to ensure the standard application of those criteria by employees who conduct interviews and make hiring decisions;
- conduct regular training and reviews of interview and applicant evaluation practices and procedures; and
- apply the statistical analyses used by the courts to their own workplaces, in an effort to identify and eliminate any hiring barriers or 'glass ceilings' that may exist.

20.4 AVOIDING WAGE AND HOUR, SEXUAL HARASSMENT, AND ERISA CLASS ACTION LIABILITY

20.4.1 Wage and Hour Claims under the FLSA

One of the greatest threats posed by wage and hour class actions under the FLSA is that an employer's small error can lead to potential massive liability. For example, an employer might, for a short period of time, fail to pay the proper rate of overtime wages to its non-salaried personnel.[34] Each employee's claim may only total a few hundred dollars in back pay. However, if the company employs a large number of non-salaried personnel, and plaintiffs' counsel is successful in certifying a large class, then the employer may face hundreds of thousands of dollars in liability, in addition to attorneys' fees and costs.[35]

---

[34] See generally, *Klem v. County of Santa Clara*, 208 F.3d 1085 (9th Cir. 2000).

[35] See *Nguyen v. Excel Corp.*, 197 F.3d 200, 202 and n. 1 (5th Cir. 1999) (case in which 2,300 hourly employees sought compensation for alleged unpaid time under FLSA

Wage and hour class actions commonly arise because an employer failed to pay minimum wage, overtime for more than forty hours of work per week, or for miscalculating the proper rate of overtime, as specified in the FLSA.[36] Such claims also arise when an employer has misclassified employees as salaried or 'exempt' under the FLSA, but nonetheless treated them as hourly employees.[37] In addition, an employer who suspects that it has misclassified employees as exempt from the FLSA but does not take immediate action to rectify the situation can be required to pay liquidated damages.[38]

Employers can minimize their exposure to these types of class actions by taking the following steps:

- At the time of hiring, inform employees of their employment status (i.e., salaried exempt or non-salaried non-exempt), review the requirements of the job – including a review of the job description for the position – and detail the terms of their payment, for straight time and overtime, in writing. For example, an employer could require that an employee read and sign such a document and keep the document in the employee's personnel file.
- Where appropriate, install a time clock or other appropriate time keeping procedure and issue a written policy regarding its use. The policy should require non-exempt employees to properly punch in immediately upon arrival and punch out upon departure from work and during all lunch or personal breaks. Discipline for failure to properly use the employer's time keeping mechanism should be administered, particularly since an employee's failure to follow proper timekeeping procedures could leave the employer vulnerable to a class action lawsuit.
- Institute clear and firm policies regarding lunch and break times of non-exempt employees. An employer can be held responsible for unpaid wages or overtime when on a reoccurring basis it

---

against employer); *Brzychnalski v. Unesco, Inc.*, 35 F. Supp. 2d 351, 353 (S.D.N.Y. 1999) (certifying a class of hundreds of asbestos workers bringing FLSA overtime claims even though 'there may be some differences in the calculation of damages' for the individual class members, should they prevail); *Hoffiann v. Sbarro, Inc.*, 982 F. Supp. 249, 252–253 (S.D.N.Y. 1997) (seeking overtime pay for all managers employed by nationwide restaurant chain over a four-year period).

[36] See Brzychnalski, 35 F. Supp. 2d at 352.
[37] See *Heidtman v. County of El Paso*, 171 F.3d 1038, 1042 (5th Cir. 1999).
[38] See *Id.*

utilizes staff during unpaid periods of time. While the occasional few minutes of unpaid work may seem little for the employer to ask, when added up over the span of several years and over a large class of employees, the potential liability can be significant.
- Require employees to review and sign their time cards or time records every week and initial any changes made to their cards or records.
- Implement steps to prevent, to the extent practical, that exempt employees do not perform 'hourly' work.
- Avoid instituting policies docking salaried or exempt employees' pay for disciplinary reasons or for being absent from work in increments of less than a full work day. Such action could create a class of workers who will argue that those actions show they are in practice non-exempt employees and therefore are entitled to hourly wages and overtime.
- Reimburse employees as soon as possible for inadvertent mistaken wage deductions. The law gives the employer a window of opportunity to remedy the situation without encountering liability under the FLSA.[39] The quicker the employer remedies the situation, the less likely it is to find itself facing a class action FLSA suit.

20.4.2 Sexual and Other Workplace Harassment Claims

In light of recent United States Supreme Court rulings, it is imperative that employers follow the Supreme Court's edicts in order to reduce the risk of facing a class action premised upon sexual harassment. Although the Supreme Court has ruled that an employer may in some cases be held strictly liable for supervisor sexual harassment, the Supreme Court has also noted that in certain cases an employer can affirmatively defend itself against a claim of sexual harassment if the employer used reasonable care to prevent harassment and took prompt action to correct the problem.[40] Moreover, the employer may be able to defend itself by showing that the employee(s) initiating any

---

[39] 29 C.F.R. 5 541.1 18(a)(6) (2002).
[40] See generally, *Faragher v. City of Boca Raton*, 524 U.S. 775 (1998); *Burlington Indus., Inc. v. Ellerth*, 524 U.S. 742 (1998).

claim unreasonably failed to take advantage of programs designed to prevent, report, or avoid sexual harassment, or other available options.[41] Although the majority of sexual harassment suits involve one or at most a few plaintiffs alleging individualized harassment, class suits can arise from a pervasive course of sexually harassing conduct affecting a number of people in the workplace.[42]

Thus, in order to prevent a class from forming, employers must take an active role in communicating a zero-tolerance anti-harassment policy, and expeditiously address and resolve each claim of sexual harassment, thereby making it difficult, if not impossible, for plaintiffs to allege the existence of a wide pattern of harassment based upon sex or other protected classifications. Employers can minimize their exposure to class actions premised on sexual and other workplace harassment by taking the following steps:

- Publish a clear anti-discrimination policy forbidding all forms of discrimination and illegal harassment. It is helpful to include in such policies examples of prohibited conduct.
- Institute a comprehensive discrimination or harassment reporting procedure. Be sure that the reporting procedure includes the following features:
  (1) The names and direct-dial phone numbers of persons in the employer's Human Resources or similar department with authority to investigate reports of discrimination. Consider setting up a toll-free number and a mechanism whereby employees can report, anonymously if they choose, discriminatory harassment twenty-four hours a day.
  (2) Clear identification of other management personnel who may be contacted to report harassment. It is important to allow the employee-to report to the company harassment

---

[41] See Faragher, 524 U.S. at 806–808.
[42] See e.g., *Donnelly v. Glickman*, 159 F.3d 405, 408 (9th Cir. 1998). It is also worth noting that the EEOC may bring sexual harassment actions on behalf of a class, without having to satisfy Rule 23's requirement of qualifying as a class representative. See *E.E.O.C. v. Dinuba Med. Clinic*, 222 F.3d 580, 587–588 (9th Cir. 2000). Moreover, each member of the class may be entitled to the individual damages maximum. See *id.* at 588–589.

CHAPTER 20. HUMAN RESOURCES PRACTICES AUDITS

  by direct supervisors who have the power to alter the terms and conditions of the job.
  (3) A clear statement that reports of discrimination will not result in punishment to the person reporting.
- Take measures to ensure that the policy and procedure is, distributed to, and read by, each and every employee. As an added precaution, require employees to sign a form certifying that they have read and understand the policy and that they will abide by it. Keep a signed copy in the employee's personnel file.
- Post copies of the policy and procedure prominently in the workplace, and distribute updates and reminders of the policy periodically to *all* personnel.
- Investigate reports of harassment immediately. During the pendency of an investigation, take precautionary measures to separate the employee claiming harassment from the alleged harasser and protect the complaining employee from possible retaliation by the alleged harasser or other employees.
- Train supervisory personnel thoroughly on their reporting and investigation duties. Be sure that supervisors know that they must not attempt to minimize the seriousness of the complaint by telling the complaining employee that the harasser is 'just that way' or otherwise trivializing the seriousness of sexual harassment.

  Where harassment is found to have occurred:
  (1) Discipline the harasser (including, if appropriate, termination).
  (2) Transfer the harasser to another workplace or shift, where the harasser is unlikely to come into contact with the victim, or
  (3) Offer the victim a transfer to another workplace or shift (do not force the victim to transfer).
  (4) Consider obtaining the victim's signed agreement that the measures taken were an adequate and satisfactory response to the problem, and keep a signed copy of the agreement in the employee's personnel file.

In order to avoid harassment class claims, it is important to understand that the more an employer can do to show a court that it took affirmative steps to prevent harassment, to encourage reports of harassment, and to respond quickly and effectively to harassment, the more likely the court will find that the employer acted in a reasonable manner and is thus not liable for any errant harassment that may have occurred in the workplace.

20.4.3 ERISA Claims

ERISA class actions must be taken seriously, not only because of the threat of substantial damage awards, but because of the complexity and potentially enormous cost of litigating ERISA class claims. Plaintiffs may bring ERISA class actions based upon allegations that an employer's conduct constitutes a 'pattern and practice' of interference with existing or future rights under a benefit plan.[43] Plaintiffs seeking to pursue such claims must show that a pattern or practice of interference exists and this pattern or practice is part of the employer's 'regular and standard operating procedure.'[44] There are a wide variety of claims that plaintiffs can bring under the expansive umbrella of ERISA. A few examples of possible class action claims include:

- unlawful termination of vested health care benefit;[45]
- fraudulent inducement of employees to retire prior to benefit vesting;[46]
- unlawful forfeiture of pension credits;[47] and
- breach of fiduciary duty for failure to adequately advise employees concerning the terms of an employee benefit plan, alteration thereof, or termination of a plan.[48]

---

[43] Employee Benefits Law 540 (Steven J. Sacher et al. eds, ABA Section of Labor and Employment Law 1991).

[44] *Id.* (citation omitted).

[45] See generally, *Int'l Union, United Auto., Aerospace & Agric. Implement Workers of Am. v. Skinner Engine Co.*, 188 F.3d 130 (3rd Cir. 1999) (affirming summary judgment 'dismissal of class of retirees' claims that former employer illegally terminated post-retirement health benefits).

[46] See generally, *McAuley v. Int'l Bus. Mach. Corp.*, 165 F.3d 1038 (6th Cir. 1999).

[47] See generally, *Phillips v. Alaska Hotel & Rest. Employees Pension Fund*, 944 F.2d 509 (9th Cir. 1991).

[48] See generally, *Int'l Union, United Automobile, Aerospace & Agricultural Implement Workers v. Skinner Engine Co.*, 15 F.Supp. 2d 773 (W.D. Pa. 1998). Moreover, the employer is under a duty to truthfully respond to employee questions regarding potential changes to an ERISA plan when the employer is giving 'serious

CHAPTER 20. HUMAN RESOURCES PRACTICES AUDITS

While there is no way of ensuring that an employer will never have to face an ERISA class action, there are certain preventive measures that employers can take to reduce the risk. The following checklist can help employers minimize ERISA class-action exposure:

- State all language pertaining to vesting rights in benefits plans clearly and unambiguously. Courts generally agree that if the vesting language in a plan is clear, those provisions should be enforced.[49] However, if an argument can be made that the language of a plan is ambiguous, such ambiguities are construed against the employer (or its agent) as the plan drafter.
- Plan well in advance for multiple terminations, layoffs, and changes in benefit plans. Employers should determine whether the proposed employment action would have a discriminatory effect on certain employees under the plan. If it can be shown that an employer laid off or terminated a disproportionate percentage of employees that were close to being vested under a benefit plan, the employer may face a class action. Impacted employees may claim that the layoff or termination interfered with their vesting rights under ERISA.[50] Thus, employers should plan any actions affecting employees, taking into account ERISA, as it would under the ADEA and Title VII, and should take steps to ensure that it treats all employees (i.e., vested, nearly vested, far from vesting) equally.
- Be aware of the vesting status of employees who are subject to recall after a layoff. Even if the employer's conduct is not intentionally discriminatory, disproportionately recalling employees less likely to vest could create a class of employees closer to vesting that appear to have been discriminated against.
- Be aware of the pension liability of each work site. Shifting work from a site with high pension liability to one with a low proportion of vested employees, in conjunction with eventual layoffs, may lead to a potential class action.

---

consideration' to such changes. See *Bins v. Exxon Co. U.S.A.*, 220 F.3d 1042, 1048–1049 (9th Cir. 2000) (listing cases).

[49] See *Am. Fed'n of Grain Millers v. Int'l Multifoods Corp.*, 1 16 F.3d 976,980 (2nd Cir. 1997).

[50] See generally, *Amatuzio v. Gandalf Systems Corp.*, 994 F. Supp. 253 (D.N.J. 1998).

883

- Fully disclose all interpretations and material terms of any benefit plan, including summary plan descriptions (and copies of plan documents, if requested), to employees. Failure to adequately do so could lead to class charges of misrepresentation and concealment.
- Ensure that all notices, advisories, or directions given to employees concerning enrollment in, alteration of, or termination of a benefit plan are accurate and timely.

Although the steps outlined above cannot guarantee that an employer will never face class litigation, they can go a long way toward minimizing the risk and enhancing a company's litigation position should it be confronted with class claims.

20.5 HUMAN RESOURCES AUDITS

Preventive steps can only protect a company from litigation if they are universally and uniformly applied throughout the workforce. For this reason; employers may find it helpful from time to time to review their compliance efforts. For ease of reference, this section will refer to any such review as a human resources audit.

At their core, human resources audits examine an organization's personnel policies and practices to ensure compliance with applicable law and to identify and correct areas of non-compliance. In addition, if handled appropriately, such audits can also act as an effective deterrent for deviation from accepted policies and procedures. Human resources audits may be conducted internally, by an outside consulting group, or by counsel. They may be comprehensive or they may focus on discrete human resources functions. Depending on the circumstances, a human resources audit may involve interviews of varying numbers of employees and on-site review of corporate documents such as written policies and procedures, employee handbooks, job descriptions, employee evaluation policies, recruitment materials, employment applications, labor agreements, and employee personnel files. In addition, human resources audits may examine legal, factual, and organizational issues ranging from compliance with posting requirements to adherence to statutory laws against discrimination to harassment training and prevention to employee retention. The work product generated by a human resources audit may include everything from informal recommendations to written audit reports and work papers.

CHAPTER 20. HUMAN RESOURCES PRACTICES AUDITS

Human resources audit results can – for better or worse – come into play in class litigation.[51] For this reason, employers and their counsel must be aware of the factors and legal principles that govern discoverability and admissibility of audit papers in litigation.

The Federal Rules of Evidence define 'relevant evidence' as 'evidence having any tendency to make the existence of any fact that is of consequence to the determination of the action more probable or less probable than it would be without the evidence.'[52] As many class action plaintiffs' attorneys have discovered, one of the most fertile sources for relevant evidence in an employment class action can stem from an employer's internal efforts to identify and correct policies, practices, or circumstances that could lead to liability. In the course of an internal human resources audit, employers often gather all available information, outline the intricacies of the company's organizational structure, and devote significant resources to reviewing just the sort of issues that can give rise to employment litigation. Plaintiffs who obtain access to audit materials that detail potential violations similar to those claimed in a lawsuit may gain a significant tactical advantage. Class action plaintiffs who obtain access to audit materials that outline across-the-board mistakes in the statement or application of an employer's policies may not only gain a tactical advantage as to the merits of the case but may also go a long way toward satisfying the prerequisites for class certification. After all, an employer may find it quite difficult to deny the existence of common factual or legal issues when its own documents identify just such issues and describe their impact and reach on the employee population.

As a result, many employers seek to maintain the confidentiality of their human resources audits through claims of privilege, which, if successful, generally prohibit both discovery by class counsel and admission into evidence.[53] In particular, both the attorney-client privilege and the work-product doctrine may come into play in connection with human resources audits. Further, employers may be able to avail themselves of the self-critical analysis privilege.

---

[51] See e.g., *Stender v. Lucky Stores, Inc.*, 803 F. Supp. 259, 330 (N.D. Cal. 1992) (admitting documentary and testimonial evidence of employer's affirmative action efforts to prove knowledge of disparities and discriminatory attitudes in class action race and sex discrimination suit).
[52] Fed. R. Evid. 401.
[53] Fed. R. Civ. P. 26(b)(l) (generally excluding privileged matters from discovery); Fed. R. Evid. 501, 1 101(c) (addressing rules of privilege).

The attorney-client privilege protects communications between client and attorney 'to encourage full and frank communication between attorneys and their clients.'[54] For the privilege to apply, the attorney generally must be acting as legal counsel to the client – rather than as a business advisor or consultant – when the communication is made.[55] Moreover, 'the privilege extends only to communications and not to facts,' and a client 'may not refuse to disclose any relevant fact within his knowledge merely because he incorporated a statement of such fact into his communication to his attorney.'[56]

The work-product doctrine, which is broader than and different from the attorney-client privilege, protects the right to be 'free from unnecessary intrusion by opposing parties and their counsel' in the course of preparing for litigation.[57] As a result, this doctrine shields from disclosure any 'document prepared in anticipation of litigation by or for the attorney.'[58] This concept is so integral to the legal system that it has been incorporated into the Civil Rules themselves.[59] Work

---

[54] *Upjohn Co. v. United States*, 449 U.S. 383, 389 (1981).

[55] *Cf. Hardy v. New York News, Inc.*, 114 F.R.D. 633, 644 (S.D.N.Y. 1987) (refusing to recognize attorney-client privilege for documents because attorney did not receive them in capacity as legal advisor); Stender, 803 F. Supp. at 330–331 (meetings between attorney and managers not entitled to protection of attorney-client privilege because contract between company and attorney was a consulting agreement that did not identify attorney in his function as an attorney and because meetings were for training purposes rather than for purposes of obtaining or rendering legal advice).

[56] Upjohn Co., 449 U.S. at 395–396 (citation and quotation omitted).

[57] *Hickman v. Taylor*, 329 U.S. 495, 510 (1947).

[58] *Tenn. Laborers Health & Welfare Fund v. Columbia/HCA Healthcare Corp.*, 293 F.3d 289, 304 (6th Cir. 2002) (citation and quotation omitted), petition for cert. filed, 71 U.S.L.W. 3429. (U.S. December 9, 2002) (No. 02-888).

[59] Specifically, Rule 26 provides:

> [A] party may obtain discovery of documents... prepared in anticipation of litigation or for trial by or for another party or by or for that other party's representative... only upon a showing that the party seeking discovery has substantial need of the materials in the preparation of the party's case and that the party is unable without undue hardship to obtain the substantial equivalent of the materials by other means.... [T]he court shall protect against disclosure of the mental impressions, conclusions, opinions, or legal theories of an attorney or other representative of a party concerning the litigation.

Fed. R. Civ. P. 26(b)(3).

CHAPTER 20. HUMAN RESOURCES PRACTICES AUDITS

product may be generated by non-attorneys 'so long as they were working on behalf of the party and preparing the document with the prospect of litigation in mind.'[60]

Courts often divide work product into two categories: fact work-product (information transmitted to the attorney and recorded as conveyed by the client) and opinion work product (including the attorney's mental impressions, judgments and theories).[61] Although fact work product may be discoverable upon 'a showing of substantial need and inability to otherwise obtain [the information] without material hardship,' opinion work product may not be obtained absent waiver of privilege.[62]

Applying these principles, courts have reached mixed results when determining whether internal audit materials are shielded from disclosure by the attorney-client privilege or the work-product doctrine. In *Abdallah v. Coca-Cola Co.*, the employer hired an outside employment law consultant to conduct an internal investigation of the company's compliance with affirmative action requirements.[63] When plaintiffs in a putative class action moved to compel production of the consultant's documents, the court upheld the company's assertion of the work-product doctrine.[64] In so doing, the court found that '[M]ost of the...documents were prepared under the supervision of and at the specific request and direction of company counsel.'[65] The court in *Olen Properties Corp. v. Sheldahl, Inc.* held that internal environmental audits generated by a non-attorney witness were privileged because the witness prepared the documents to gather information to assist counsel in 'evaluating compliance with relevant laws and regulations.'[66] In contrast, *Reich v. Hercules, Inc.* involved a company's claim of privilege in response to a subpoena issued by the Secretary of Labor that requested workplace safety audit reports from 1989–1992.[67] The court rejected the company's privilege claim as to all of the audits except for one. The audit afforded privilege protection was entitled

---

[60] *Joiner v. Hercules, Inc.*, 169 F.R.D. 695, 698 (S.D. Ga. 1996) (citation omitted).
[61] See e.g., Tenn. Laborers, 293 F.3d at 294.
[62] *Id.*; see also Fed. R. Civ. P. 26(b)(3).
[63] 2000 U.S. Dist. LEXIS 21025, at *6–7 (N.D. Ga. January 25, 2000).
[64] *Id.* at *29.
[65] *Id.*
[66] 1994 U.S. Dist. LEXIS 7125, at *2–3 (C.D. Cal. April 12, 1994).
[67] 857 F. Supp. 367, 368–369 (D.N.J. 1994).

'Attorney Directed Kenvil Plant Inspection.'[68] Finally, in *United States v. Chevron U.S.A., Inc.*, the court rejected Chevron's argument that its internal environmental audit was protected by the attorney-client privilege simply because its audit team included an attorney.[69] In so doing, the court noted that the 'communication must be between the client and attorney in his or her capacity as an attorney' and that the 'communication's primary purpose must be to gain or provide legal assistance.'[70] Because Chevron did not indicate that these requirements were met, the privilege did not apply.[71]

In addition to the attorney-client and work-product privileges, in some cases, the so-called self-critical analysis privilege may preclude disclosure or admission of self-critical information. Although this privilege is not well-defined and infrequently invoked, one court generally attributed the following characteristics to this quasi-privilege:

> (1) materials protected have generally been those prepared for mandatory governmental reports; (2) only subjective, evaluative materials have been protected; (3) objective data in those same reports have not been protected; and (4) in sensitivity to plaintiffs' need for such materials, Courts have denied discovery only where the policy favoring exclusion has clearly outweighed plaintiffs' need.[72]

Recognition and application of the self-critical analysis privilege varies widely from court to court.[73] As one court observed 'while the self-critical analysis privilege has been applied by some courts, it has been rejected by many others, and it is neither widely recognized nor firmly established in federal common law.'[74] The same court further

---

[68] *Id.* at 369.
[69] 1989 U.S. Dist. LEXIS 12267, at Ot17-18 (E.D. Pa. October 16, 1989).
[70] *Id.* at *18.
[71] *Id.*
[72] *Whittingham v. Amherst College*, 164 F.R.D. 124, 129 (D. Mass. 1995) (citation omitted).
[73] Compare *Watson v. Carpenter Tech. Corp.*, 1984 U.S. Dist. LEXIS 15645, at *7 (E.D. Pa. June 22, 1984) (affirmative action plan data and internal self-critical analysis was discoverable but self-critical information contained in reports provided to the government was not) with *Hardy v. New York News, Inc.*, 114 F.R.D. 633, 641 (S.D.N.Y. 1987) (refusing to recognize privilege because of plaintiffs' need 'to prove the element of discriminatory intent[] outweighs the interest in fostering candid self-analysis and voluntary compliance with equal employment laws....').
[74] Abdallah, 2000 U.S. Dist. LEXIS 21025, at *18 (citations omitted).

CHAPTER 20. HUMAN RESOURCES PRACTICES AUDITS

observed that '[I]n the context of employment discrimination, the majority of the case law rejects the [self-critical analysis] privilege.'[75]

In light of these general principles, employers can take steps to increase the likelihood that human resources audits will not be turned against them in class litigation. These steps are especially important where the likely outcome of the audit is uncertain or where problems are suspected. In particular, employers contemplating an internal audit may want to consider conducting the audit for the express purpose of obtaining legal advice regarding the lawfulness of their policies and practices. In these instances, counsel (whether in-house counsel or outside counsel) should be substantively involved in all phases of the audit in their capacity as counsel – rather than as an officer of the company, consultant, or business advisor. When non-attorneys perform work in connection with internal human resources audits, those individuals must understand, and any written work product must clearly reflect, that their participation is at the direction of counsel and to aid counsel in rendering legal advice. If an internal audit is performed in response to litigation or anticipated litigation – as may occur when an administrative charge of discrimination or an internal complaint that raises employment-law issues is lodged – all audit activities and materials should reflect this impetus. Where internal audit materials must be provided to governmental agencies – as may be the case with certain equal employment opportunity data – those materials should reflect that their preparation was mandatory and explain why. Because evaluations, mental impressions, and strategic recommendations are generally entitled to greater privilege protection than mere facts, employers may wish to delineate between the facts that form the basis of any audit recommendations or conclusions and the audit recommendations and conclusions themselves. In the event disclosure of audit facts is required, evaluative materials – which can contain frank assessments of potential liabilities and areas for improvement – may still be shielded from disclosure.

In addition to these guidelines for preserving privilege claims over internal human resources audits, employers and their counsel should satisfy themselves before the audit begins that the audit will accurately portray the company's human resources practices and policies and will

---

[75] *Id.* at *20–21 (citations omitted); see also Reich, 857 F. Supp. at 369 (rejecting self-critical analysis privilege in connection with internal workplace safety reports).

best serve the company's business interests. Employers and their counsel should consider the following questions, among others:

- What is the scope of the audit?
- What is the reason for the audit?
- Who will conduct the audit?
- What are the auditors' qualifications?
- What methodology will be used?
- What time period will the audit cover?
- How long will the audit take to complete?
- What information will the audit be based upon?
- Which employees will need to be involved in the audit?
- What time commitment will involved employees need to make?
- Who are the intended recipients of the audit results?

Employers with favorable audit results may be tempted to use those results offensively in class litigation to defeat allegations of class mistreatment. Doing so, however, could result in waiver of any privilege that may have attached to the audit.[76] In addition, because courts are loath to allow parties to use privileges as a sword rather than a shield, waiver as to favorable audit materials may also result in waiver as to all other communications and materials related to the same subject matter:

> When a party reveals part of a privileged communication in order to gain an advantage in litigation, it waives the privilege as to all other communications relating to the same subject matter because 'the privilege of secret consultation is intended only as an incidental means of defense and not as an independent means of attack, and to use it in the latter character is to abandon it in the former.'[77]

As a result, employers who choose to divulge potentially privileged human resources audit materials to rebut class claims must carefully examine other materials that deal with the same subject matter to

---

[76] See e.g., Tenn. Laborers, 293 F.3d at 294 ('As a general rule, the attorney-client privilege is waived by voluntary disclosures of private communications by an individual or corporation to third parties.') (citation and internal quotation omitted).
[77] In re Sealed Case, 676 F.2d 793,818 (D.C. Cir. 1982) (citation omitted); see also In re Grand Jury Proceedings October 12, 1995, 78 F.3d 251, 256 (6th Cir. 1996) (directing district court to compel answers to questions where 'questions involve the same subject matter as those specific points...on which we held the privilege was actually waived').

CHAPTER 20. HUMAN RESOURCES PRACTICES AUDITS

determine whether the benefit of waiving privilege outweighs any potential harm. In addition, because different courts have different views as to what constitutes the same subject matter, employers should take into account the approach their jurisdiction is likely to take.[78]

Although disclosure of privileged human resources audit materials may not make strategic sense, that does not mean that such audits are of no use in employment class action litigation. To the contrary, when faced with a bid for class certification, audit materials can be instrumental in identifying potential evidentiary sources for factors such as variations among departments, localized decision-making, or isolated non-compliance with policies and procedures. This evidence, in turn, may be a valuable tool for rebutting class allegations of practices or policies common to the putative class and defeating class certification.[79]

In sum, human resources audits can be a valuable tool for avoiding litigation – including class claims – and maintaining a satisfied workforce. To obtain the greatest benefit from such audits, however, employers must understand how to create and preserve the confidentiality of the audits, how to gauge the ramifications of revealing audit materials, and how to ensure that internal audits accurately portray the company's strengths and weaknesses.

20.6 CONCLUSION

An unavoidable part of the modem business world is the ever-present threat of being subjected to a class action suit for alleged discrimination or for alleged violation of any number of federal employment laws. While no amount of preventive medicine can completely immunize employers from exposure to suit, employers can

---

[78] See In re Grand Jury Proceedings, 78 F.3d at 255 (noting that 'subject matter can be defined narrowly or broadly').

[79] See In re Am. Med. Sys., Inc., 75 F.3d 1069, 1084–1085 (6th Cir. 1996) (where factual and legal issues differed 'dramatically from individual to individual,' the 'economies of scale achieved by class treatment' were 'more than offset by the individualization of numerous issues relevant only to a particular plaintiff) (quotation omitted); *Rosenberg v. Univ. of Cincinnati*, 654 F. Supp. 774, 778 (S.D. Ohio 1986) ('where employment decisions are subject to nearly complete local or departmental autonomy, the commonality/typicality requirement will not have been met').

nonetheless take steps to ensure that they are in full compliance with all laws and regulations and thereby reduce the risk of class litigation. By understanding the scope and role of internal human resources audits and attendant privilege concepts, moreover, employers can protect themselves from having their own preventive and corrective measures turned against them in a class action. In short, the extent to which employers both understand the mechanisms of class claims and take steps to eliminate the grounds for these claims is predictive of the extent to which employers will avoid being subjected to these burdensome and expensive causes of action.

CHAPTER 21

'Statistical Dueling' with Unconventional Weapons: What Courts Should Know about Experts in Employment Discrimination Class Actions*

William T. Bielby** and Pamela Coukos***

21.1 INTRODUCTION

When statistical evidence is offered in a litigation context, the result can be bad law and bad statistics. Recent high profile, high-stakes employment discrimination class actions bear this out. A series of similar cases litigated over the past several years involve potentially misleading statistical testimony, purporting to show an absence of any pattern of discrimination. Courts in these cases have not always understood the limitations of the statistical evidence before them, or properly weighed its relevance to a ruling on class certification. Because the

---

* Previously published by Emory Law Journal. William T. Bielby & Pamela Coukos, "Statistical Dueling" with Unconventional Weapons: What Courts Should Know About Experts in Employment Discrimination Class Actions, 56 Emory L.J. 1563 (2007).
** William T. Bielby is professor, Department of Sociology, University of Illinois at Chicago. He holds a Ph.D. from University of Wisconsin-Madison and is a Ph.D. candidate in jurisprudence and social policy at University of California, Berkeley.
*** Pamela Coukos is of counsel to Mehri & Skalet. She holds a J.D. from Harvard Law School.

David Sherwyn and Samuel Estreicher (eds), *Employment Class and Collective Actions*, pp. 893–940.
© Emory Law Journal. Reprinted with permission.

decision about whether or not to certify a class is critical to both sides, these errors may generate substantial costs.

In recent cases against large multinationals like UPS,[1] Wal-Mart,[2] and Marriott,[3] plaintiffs have claimed that decentralized and highly discretionary management practices result in systematic gender or racial disparities in pay and promotion. At class certification, plaintiffs have relied in part on statistical analyses of the company's workforce showing companywide inequality. Defendants have responded with statistical presentations of their own, which frequently demonstrate widely varying outcomes for members of protected groups in different geographic areas of the company. These expert submissions usually suggest either that no problems exist, or that any discrimination is isolated and not attributable to institutional-level bias. In adjudicating between these competing visions, courts must referee what the Second Circuit terms 'statistical dueling.'[4]

As we show in this paper, sometimes at least one of the parties is dueling with unconventional weapons. For-profit consulting companies and large defense firms are eagerly marketing unorthodox and unreliable statistical methods to employers anxious about how class actions multiply their potential liability.[5] Of course, plaintiffs can, and sometimes do, submit statistical evidence that is inconsistent with good social science practice and biased in favor of their position. However, a bias in the opposite direction is often built into the statistical approach of experts working for defendants, and courts and litigators have largely ignored this bias. Moreover, while the issue as outlined below will be immediately apparent to social statisticians, it has received little attention from either academic statisticians or consulting experts.

Using simulated data, we show why courts should become more critical of statistical expertise purporting to test for subunit differences, particularly when offered at the class certification phase of the case. Under some circumstances, the statistical approach often used to oppose class certification in employment discrimination litigation is

---

[1] *Abram v. UPS*, 200 F.R.D. 424 (E.D. Wisc. 2001) (declining to certify nationwide class of African-American employees).
[2] *Dukes v. Wal-Mart Stores*, 222 F.R.D. 137 (N.D. Cal. 2004) (certifying nationwide class of female employees). This ruling is currently on appeal to the 9th Circuit.
[3] *McReynolds v. Sodexho Marriott Services, Inc.*, 208 F.R.D. 428 (D.D.C. 2002) (certifying nationwide class of African-American employees).
[4] *Caridad v. Metro North Commuter R.R.*, 191 F.3d 283, 292 (2nd Cir. 1999).
[5] See *infra* text accompanying notes 77–80.

CHAPTER 21. UNCONVENTIONAL WEAPONS

guaranteed to support the defendant's position, regardless of the actual facts of the case. Furthermore, some courts have improperly or unwittingly legitimized the use of this approach, even when it is demonstrably non-probative of the issues before the court. Courts need new ways to think about these problems – approaches that better reflect the relevant legal framework and statistical principles.

The conflicting expert submissions typical of contemporary Title VII class litigation reflect each side's distinct litigation strategy, as framed by the legal requirements for class certification. Rule 23 of the Federal Rules of Civil Procedure requires that courts facing class certification motions determine the existence and extent of common factual and legal issues.[6] The more that individual complaints of discrimination are part and parcel of a challenge to larger common institutional practices, the more appropriate it would be to certify a class. The more idiosyncratic the claims are, the less reasonable class treatment becomes. Thus, when it comes to statistical evidence, plaintiffs and their experts focus on similarities, while defendants and their experts highlight differences. This debate over similarities and differences focuses on two frequently litigated, and interrelated, legal issues. The first is the use of aggregated versus disaggregated analyses, and the second is the potential commonality of subjective practices.

Disputes over aggregation play a central role in a number of recent class action decisions involving multi-facility classes.[7] Where a case challenges company policies or practices across geographically dispersed worksites, be they divisions, regions, or individual retail stores, defendants typically claim that any statistical evidence must account

---

[6] Fed. R. Civ. Proc. 23; *Falcon v. General Tel. & Tel. of the Southwest*, 457 U.S. 147 (1982).

[7] See e.g., *Caridad v. Metro North Commuter R.R.*, 191 F.3d 283 (2nd Cir. 1999); *Anderson v. Boeing*, 222 F.R.D. 521, 536–537 (N.D. Okla. 2004); *Dukes v. Wal-Mart Stores, Inc.*, 222 F.R.D. 137 (N.D. Cal. 2004); *McReynolds v. Sodexho Marriott*, 208 F.R.D. 428 (D.D.C. 2002); *Abram v. UPS*, 200 F.R.D. 424 (E.D. Wisc. 2001). Reviewing reported cases likely understates the prevalence of this defense, as many district court rulings are not published, and this may be particularly true of a procedural ruling such as a class certification motion. Further, the issue may not be discussed in a written ruling, even if it arises it litigation, or the case may settle before a contested battle over class certification. The prominence of this issue at seminars, in practitioner papers, and in informal discussion among the plaintiff and defense attorneys who are most frequently counsel in these types of cases, suggest that it is an increasingly common defense. See *infra* text accompanying notes 69–74.

895

for potential subunit differences. Mainly because of idiosyncrasies in the way case law has evolved, courts place more weight on 'statistical significance' than on the magnitude of disparities between groups. As a result, plaintiffs' statistical experts typically assess disparities with organization-wide data, pooled across geographic subunits. In contrast, defendants' experts take the stance that where the company employs a decentralized management structure, a different employment system exists within each organizational subunit. Therefore statistical estimates of disparities must be computed separately by subunit. These different approaches frequently generate quite different results.

The issue of aggregation becomes heightened in cases involving highly discretionary management practices. Increasingly, plaintiffs alleging systematic discrimination claim that the company-wide mechanism creating bias is discretionary and subjective decision making implemented in the context of a decentralized personnel system with little monitoring and oversight regarding the process and criteria used for making decisions about pay, promotion, and other conditions of employment.[8] While longstanding legal doctrine clearly permits plaintiffs to challenge these mechanisms as a common practice applicable to a class of employees,[9] defendants frequently use the plaintiffs' framing of the problem as a basis to argue against class certification. They maintain that if decision-making is truly discretionary, then by definition there cannot be a common policy or practice causing the alleged bias. Further, they point to statistical evidence of subunit differences, generated through a disaggregated analysis, as support for that position.[10]

Many of the employment discrimination class actions currently being litigated in federal court exemplify what some legal scholars call 'second-generation' employment discrimination.[11] While class action claims brought in the early days of Title VII featured extreme

---

[8] See e.g., *Cooper v. Southern Co.*, 390 F.3d 695 (11th Cir. 2004); Dukes, 222 F.R.D. at 145; *Ingram v. The Coca-Cola Co.*, 200 F.R.D. 685 (N.D. Ga. 2001); McReynolds, 208 F.R.D. at 441; Abram, 200 F.R.D. at 424, Anderson, 222 F.R.D. at 536.

[9] Falcon, 457 U.S. 159 n. 15; *Watson v. Fort Worth Bank and Trust*, 487 U.S. 977 (1988).

[10] See e.g., *Dukes v. Wal-Mart Stores, Inc.*, (Nos. 04-16688 & 04-16720) (9th Cir. November 29, 2004), Principal Brief of Wal-Mart Stores; *Gutierrez, et al v. Johnson & Johnson*, (No. 01-5302), (D.N.J. September 20, 2005), Memorandum in Opposition to Plaintiffs' Motion for Class Certification.

[11] Susan Sturm, Second Generation Employment Discrimination: A Structural Approach, 101 Columbia Law Review 458 (2001).

CHAPTER 21. UNCONVENTIONAL WEAPONS

levels of job segregation and anecdotal evidence of overtly racist and sexist management decisions, their progeny tell a more complex story. Today's major corporate targets typically have at least a token representation of white women and men and women of color at senior levels, avidly describe their good faith steps to combat discrimination within the corporation, and appear to lack significant documented instances of explicit discriminatory animus. Many scholars and advocates supporting both greater and more limited civil rights enforcement openly question whether the existing Title VII legal regime is adequate or appropriate for dealing with these cases.

In this context, one might expect heightened judicial receptivity to arguments that discretionary decision making is not amenable to class treatment, especially when elaborate statistical presentations accompany that argument. In the context of a move to 'second-generation' claims, defendants may be more successfully framing discrimination as individual deviance, rather than as stemming from structural or institutional factors. Thus, while in earlier cases a number of courts have viewed 'excessive subjectivity' as highly suspicious and easily linked to systemic practices,[12] more recent cases seem to treat such practices as neutral until proven otherwise.[13] An argument that a particular highly discretionary negative employment decision is either a reasonable management determination or unrelated to any larger system or

---

[12] See e.g., *Rowe v. General Motors Corp.*, 457 F.2d 348, 359 (5th Cir. 1972):

> (promotion/transfer procedures which depend almost entirely upon the subjective evaluation and favorable recommendation of the immediate foreman are a ready mechanism for discrimination against Blacks);

Pettway v. American Cast Iron Pipe Co., 494 F.2d 211, 231–232 (5th Cir. 1974); *Brown v. Gaston County Dyeing Machine Corp.*, 457 F.2d 1377, 1383 (4th Cir. 1972):

> (the lack of objective guidelines for hiring and promotion and the failure to post notices of job vacancies are badges of discrimination that serve to corroborate, not to rebut, the racial bias pictured by the statistical pattern of the company's work force).

[13] See e.g., *Coleman v. Quaker Oats*, 232 F.3d 1271, 1285 (9th Cir. 2000) ('subjective evaluations are not unlawful per se and "their relevance to proof of a discriminatory intent is weak"'), quoting *Sengupta v. Morrison-Knudsen Co., Inc.*, 804 F.2d 1072, 1975 (9th Cir. 1986); *Denney v. City of Albany*, 247 F.3d 1172, 1186 (11th Cir. 2001) ('an employer's use of subjective factors in making a hiring or promotion decision does not raise a red flag').

pattern of bias may be an easier sell in an environment where second-generation-style class action claims are more common.

Regardless of the reason, in increasing numbers of multi-facility class actions involving less obvious forms of discrimination, courts are reaching radically different conclusions about the relevance of statistical proof of subunit differences to class certification. One set of decisions views these cases as clearly following from prior Title VII class action precedents, and grants little credence to claims that decentralized and discretionary management practices cannot be considered institutional practices.[14] Under this approach, courts give less weight to statistical evidence of subunit differences. Another line of decisions views these kind of cases as well outside traditional class action claims and inconsistent with an efficient group resolution. These decisions generally place great store in a showing of statistical differences from location to location.[15] Thus, disputes over the application of statistical evidence in these cases are deeply intertwined in the larger theoretical and legal debate about decentralized decision making and subtle bias as sources of common 'systemic' injury.

The rapid spread of this strategy, and the typical approaches of each side, reflect the politics of expertise in employment discrimination litigation. This statistical evidence develops in an institutional context in which a relatively small number of players – large law firms, plaintiffs' attorneys, and sophisticated experts – come together repeatedly and enact strategies that become increasingly ritualized over time. Class certification is a critical moment in the life of these cases. If the court certifies the class, a defendant faces vastly increased potential financial liability as compared with an individual case, vulnerability to large-scale injunctive relief, and much higher litigation costs. If the plaintiffs lose at class certification, they will be forced to proceed individually. That may make the case financially unviable, as well as prevent them from adequately addressing any institutional level problems that lead to discrimination. The interests of plaintiffs in bringing forward as much affirmative proof of discrimination as early as possible to bolster their case collides with the interests of defendants in painting a

---

[14] See e.g., *Dukes*, 222 F.R.D. at 157–161; *Caridad*, 191 F.3d at 291–292; *McReynolds*, 208 F.R.D. at 442–443.

[15] See e.g., *Abram*, 200 F.R.D. at 429–31; *Grosz v. Boeing Co.*, 2003 WL 22971025 (C.D. Cal.); *Reid v. Lockheed Martin Aeronautics Co.*, 205 F.R.D. 655, 672–673 (N.D. Ga. 2001).

CHAPTER 21. UNCONVENTIONAL WEAPONS

picture of utterly random and unsystematic outcomes, resulting in the statistical dueling that is creating such challenge for courts to adequately comprehend.

In setting forth this dynamic, the paper begins with the relevant legal and factual framework, presents the statistical simulation, and concludes with some recommendations for courts faced with these dilemmas. The first section sets out the historical evolution of Title VII class action doctrine and some background on the issues that animate much of the current systemic employment discrimination litigation in U.S. federal courts. It also considers the specific question of statistical proof of discrimination in the context of class certification, and the current legal debates over that evidence. The second section presents and explains the statistical simulation that documents why some kinds of statistical results in these cases may be misleading. The conclusion provides some recommendations for how courts can do better – procedural and evidentiary tools that will provide fairness to both sides and that increase the likelihood that courts will reach the correct result when faced with these cases.

As the class action device comes increasingly under fire,[16] and corporate interests raise the specter of frivolous legal claims that detract from efficiency and violate norms of fair play,[17] this seemingly arcane technical dispute over proper statistical modeling takes on much greater urgency. Not only is the typical defense position in these cases statistically unreliable, and in conflict with existing legal doctrine, it also has substantial implications for Title VII enforcement. If implementing decentralized and highly discretionary management practices provides immunity from class action liability, corporations will not hesitate to

---

[16] John C. Coffee, Class Action Accountability: Reconciling Exit, Voice, and Loyalty In Representative Litigation, 100 Columbia Law Review 370 (2000), Richard Epstein, Class Actions: Aggregation, Amplification, and Distortion, 2003 University of Chicago Legal Forum 475 (2003), Myriam Gilles, Opting Out of Liability: The Forthcoming, Near-Total Demise of the Modern Class Action, 104 Michigan Law Review 373 (2005).

[17] Christopher Erath, Disraeli Would Have Loved Employment Discrimination Cases, (2000), Zachary Fasman, The Use and Misuse of Expert Witnesses in Employment Litigation, 729 PLI/Lit 841 (2005), Leslie M. Turner and Paul F. White, The Numbers Game: Statistics Offered to Show Discrimination May Promise More Than They Prove, The Legal Times, vol. 27, (2004).

exploit this regulatory loophole. To the extent that discrimination is less explicit, and is related to a particular set of potentially problematic institutional practices, class remedies become more, rather than less, important. Courts should be aware of the potential for a statistically derived end-run around antidiscrimination law, and ensure that Title VII class actions remain viable enforcement vehicles for twenty-first century discrimination claims.

21.2 STATISTICAL EVIDENCE IN SECOND-GENERATION CLASS ACTIONS

Much contemporary class action litigation under Title VII challenges a particular employment model – decentralized and highly discretionary management practices – as leading to unequal outcomes that violate antidiscrimination law.[18] Many of these cases directly or indirectly invoke 'second generation' theories about the nature of bias in the workplace, and represent a shift from single site classes to classes that span dozens or hundreds of facilities. In this context, disputes over statistical evidence become nested in disputes over the applicability of existing legal doctrine to changing fact patterns. When considering class certification motions in these cases, courts frequently fail to appreciate the limits of statistical evidence to resolving Rule 23 issues.

The doctrinal relationship between statistical evidence of discrimination, and proof of 'commonality' for purposes of class certification, is becoming increasingly incoherent. Courts disagree strongly about whether these cases involve core and relatively straightforward applications of prior case law certifying discrimination class actions – or whether they instead test the limits of the legal concepts of what an appropriate class action is. That tension extends to their view of the statistical evidence submitted at class certification. Courts that place undue weight on the results of potentially unreliable statistical tests may be improperly circumscribing an important component of the Title VII remedial scheme.

---

[18] Melissa Hart, Subjective Decisionmaking and Unconscious Discrimination, 56 Alabama Law Review 741 (2005) at 778; Tristan Green, Targeting Workplace Context: Title VII as a Tool for Institutional Reform, 72 Fordham Law Review 659 (2003) at 683.

21.2.1 The Historical Doctrinal Approach to Discrimination Class Actions

The underlying legal standards applicable to these cases frame the statistical issues in a variety of litigation contexts. Class action discrimination cases proceed in stages – a class certification decision, then a trial or summary adjudication 'on the merits,' and finally a remedial phase. If the class is certified, the merits phase is on behalf of the class; if not, only the individual named plaintiffs try their claims. If the class wins at trial, then usually remedial proceedings are necessary to allocate relief to individual employees. Statistical evidence may be relevant at any phase of the case, but the problems identified in this paper are most significant at the class certification phase.

Discrimination lawsuits seeking class action status frequently rely on both intentional discrimination ('pattern or practice') and disparate impact legal theories. Although the applicable standards and doctrines are distinct, under either approach, proof of liability requires establishing a discriminatory pattern, usually through statistical proof. Under the Supreme Court's framework in *International Brotherhood of Teamsters v. United States*, plaintiffs prove pattern and practice claims using a combination of statistical and anecdotal evidence to show discrimination is the company's 'standard operating procedure.'[19] Disparate impact theory permits a remedy against facially neutral employment practices that nevertheless operate to discriminate, and requires no proof of discriminatory intent.[20] Plaintiffs merely must show that a particular employment practice has a 'significant adverse effect' based on race, gender, or other protected group status.[21] These theories govern the 'merits' phase of the action, and are not the doctrinal basis for class certification. Rule 23 of the Federal Rules of Civil Procedure governs certification of a case as a class action. Rule 23(a) sets out the prerequisites to a class action, including that the class is too numerous to make joinder practicable ('numerosity'); the presence of common

---

[19] 431 U.S. 324, 336 (1977). In Teamsters, the Court reaffirmed that class-wide discrimination cases may rely primarily on statistical proof, especially where anecdotal evidence 'bolsters' the data and serves to bring 'the cold numbers convincingly to life.' *Id.* at 338–339.
[20] Watson, 487 U.S. at 986–987.
[21] *Id.* at 986.

questions of law or fact ('commonality'); that the claims or defenses of the named plaintiff representatives are typical of the claims or defenses of the proposed class ('typicality'); and that the representative plaintiffs will fairly and adequately protect the interests of the class ('adequacy'). In addition, any class action must satisfy at least one provision of Rule 23(b).[22]

Recent disputes over the proper modeling of statistical evidence at the class certification phase generally arise in the context of determining commonality. Although there is no legal requirement that plaintiffs submit statistical evidence at the class certification phase, it has become common practice for plaintiffs to include an expert report with a statistical analysis in support of their motion for class certification. Frequently, plaintiffs seek to present statistical or other evidence of a pattern of decisions pursuant to the policy that are adverse to the class in support of their argument for class treatment. Under the Supreme Court's decision in the *Eisen* case, a court may not resolve disputes going to the 'merits' of the claims when ruling on class certification.[23] This complicates significantly the question of how statistical evidence should influence class certification, because usually these expert reports make claims about the existence and extent of discrimination, seemingly a 'merits' issue. Courts have dealt with this problem in conflicting ways – some have limited their review of the statistical

---

[22] Rule 23(b) sets forth three different circumstances where a class action is appropriate if the factors in 23(a) are satisfied. Rule 23(b)(1) governs situations where there is a risk of inconsistent adjudications or where ruling on an individual case would be dispositive of the interests of other class members not parties to the suit. Claims against a limited fund are one example of a situation that falls under the (b)(1) class. Rule 23(b)(2) applies to cases where the defendant 'has acted or refused to act on grounds generally applicable to the class, thereby making appropriate final injunctive or declaratory relief.' The Advisory Committee Notes to the Rule point out that a civil rights class action is 'illustrative' of the types of actions that would fit under this provision of the rule. Rule 23(b)(3) applies to cases where common questions predominate over individual issues, and a class action is the 'superior' method for the 'fair and efficient adjudication' of the case. This provision covers a variety of actions, where class action treatment is appropriate because of basic and overarching similarities among the individual claims.

[23] At the class certification stage a court is barred from resolving disputed factual issues that go to the merits of the case, *Eisen v. Carlisle & Jacquelin*, 417 U.S. 156, 177 (1974), although in practice this boundary is inconsistently enforced.

evidence,[24] while others ignored the *Eisen* rule and addressed the underlying merits at class certification.[25]

Because these cases also involve decentralized management structures and challenges to discretionary employment practices, how courts treat the statistical evidence also tends to dovetail with the judge's view on the commonality of subjective decision making. Traditionally, legal doctrine has treated a defendant's policy or practice that delegates excessively subjective authority to local decision-makers as a common practice that may present common factual and legal issues. Although some courts have considered only the question of the existence of a common policy or practice of excessive subjectivity,[26] others, particularly more recently, have considered statistical evidence as also relevant to deciding whether or not to certify a class, and to commonality in particular.[27]

In cases alleging bias due to discretionary and subjective decision-making, the allegation usually is that decision-makers have a high degree of discretion. Plaintiffs focus on the absence of sufficient clear, concrete, and relevant criteria for evaluating individuals' skills,

---

[24] Some courts view their review as limited to assessing whether plaintiffs have presented competent, admissible statistical evidence or other evidence that can support a reasonable inference of discrimination. See e.g., *Caridad*, 191 F.3d at 292–293 (statistical evidence); *Staton*, 327 F.3d at 954 (anecdotal evidence); *McReynolds*, 208 F.R.D. at 441 (combination of statistical and anecdotal evidence). In other words, have the plaintiffs created at least a reasonable question as to the existence of class-wide discrimination? Further litigation may ultimately confirm or disprove the inference of class-wide discrimination, a resolution that is left to the merits phase of the case. *Caridad*, 191 F.3d at 293 (statistical showing at class certification sufficient to establish commonality although '[m]ore detailed statistics may be required to sustain Plaintiffs' burden of persuasion').

[25] See e.g., *Cooper*, 390 F.3d at 716–717. These decisions frequently suggest that the presence of subjective decision making creates a need to delve into the merits of the statistical evidence.

[26] *Shipes v. Trinity Industries*, 987 F.2d 311, 316–317 (5th Cir. 1993); *Cox v. American Cast Iron Pipe Co.*, 784 F.2d 1546, 1557 (11th Cir. 1986); *Carpenter v. Stephen F. Austin State Univ.*, 706 F.2d 608, 616 (5th Cir. 1983); see also *Green v. USX Corp.*, 843 F.2d 1511, 1525-1526 (3d Cir. 1988), relevant portion reinstated by *Green v. USX Corp.*, 896 F.2d 801, 807 (3d Cir. 1990) (similar analysis under typicality prong of 23(a)); *Ingram v. The Coca-Cola Company*, 200 F.R.D. 685, 697–698 (N.D. Ga. 2001).

[27] See e.g., *Caridad*, 191 F.3d at 291–293; *Anderson*, 222 F.R.D. at 536–537; *McReynolds*, 208 F.R.D. at 441, 443–444; *Abram*, 200 F.R.D. at 429–431; *Grosz*, 2003 WL 22971025; *Reid*, 205 F.R.D. at 672–673; *Dukes*, 222 F.R.D. at 157–161.

abilities, and interest relevant to a specific job, promotion to a higher-paying position, or other career opportunity. Plaintiffs also typically allege that little exists in the way of organization-wide monitoring and oversight over the process and criteria used to make personnel decisions. It is this discretionary decision-making that is identified as the particular employment practice that results in bias.[28] While a practice of granting wide discretion to lower-level decision-makers might seem to undermine the claim that a specific practice has generated bias, the Supreme Court has ruled otherwise in two separate contexts. The first involves how to assess subjective practices at class certification, while the second involves disparate impact challenges.

In *Falcon v. General Tel. & Tel. of the Southwest*, the Supreme Court recognized that excessive subjectivity can be a common practice applicable to a class.[29] *Falcon*'s oft-cited footnote 15, which deals with 'entirely subjective practices that operate to discriminate,' created an exception to the requirement that each particular employment practice challenged in a class action must have a class representative who was affected by that specific practice. Under footnote 15, an employee can represent a class of applicants and employees where certain circumstances exist. If, under the facts of the case, 'the discrimination manifested itself... in the same general fashion' among distinct employment practices, exact congruence between the practices that affected the class representatives and the practices challenged by the class would not be required.[30]

Falcon observed that an 'entirely subjective decision making process' could be an example of such a common practice, just as a common written test may be.[31] Thus, the Court recognized that excessive subjectivity can be a mechanism for discrimination to 'manifest... itself... in the same general fashion' from decision to decision and can be a concrete employment practice satisfying the commonality requirement like any objective criteria. The Court's subsequent ruling in *Watson v. Fort Worth Bank & Trust*,[32] amplifies this understanding of excessive discretion as an employment practice that can have measurable and consistent effects across a class.

---

[28] William T. Bielby, Minimizing Workplace Gender and Racial Bias, 29 Contemporary Sociology 120 (2000).
[29] 457 U.S. 147, 159 n. 15.
[30] *Ibid*.
[31] *Ibid*.
[32] 487 U.S. 977 (1988).

Although not a class case, the Supreme Court's *Watson* opinion provides an appropriate analytical framework for understanding the commonality issue. In *Watson*, the Supreme Court held that plaintiffs could challenge subjective employment practices using disparate impact theory.[33] This critical doctrinal shift rejected the view that subjective decision-making always constituted distinct and autonomous incidents incapable of systematic analysis. In applying disparate impact theory, the Court recognized that under appropriate circumstances, subjective decision-making constituted an identifiable and measurable practice:

> We are also persuaded that disparate impact analysis is in principle no less applicable to subjective employment criteria than to objective or standardized tests. In either case, a facially neutral practice, adopted without discriminatory intent, may have effects that are indistinguishable from intentionally discriminatory practices.... If an employer's undisciplined system of subjective decision making has precisely the same effects as a system pervaded by impermissible intentional discrimination, it is difficult to see why Title VII's proscription against discriminatory actions should not apply.[34]

One of the most critical concerns facing the justices as they ruled on *Watson* was the hotly debated question of whether one could apply any form of empirical analysis to subjective criteria.[35] By resolving that debate squarely in favor of applying disparate impact analysis, the Court reaffirmed that subjectivity can be a practice amenable to systematic empirical review, not just a series of autonomous decisions.

21.2.2 The Current Conflict over Decentralization and Discretion

In recent class certification rulings, particularly at the District Court level, this seemingly straightforward doctrine has been directly followed at times, and ignored or rejected at others. For some courts, the

---

[33] *Watson*, 487 U.S. at 990–991.

[34] *Watson*, 487 U.S. at 990–991 (emphasis added).

[35] This debate is clear from reviewing amicus briefs filed in that case. See e.g., Brief for Amicus Curiae American Psychological Association, 1987 WL 881423 at 7 & n. 7 (the 'widely held view' that subjective practices are 'less scientific, less reliable, and less facially neutral than their objective counterparts' does not mean they cannot be systematically assessed. 'It is not intrinsic in such devices to be unquantifiable.').

entire assessment of commonality turns on the presence of allegations of subjective decision making.[36] For others, statistical evidence submitted at class certification helps 'bridge the gap' between that allegation and whether an 'aggrieved class exists.'[37] A third set of cases turns *Watson* on its head. Rather than considering excessive subjectivity on par with other discriminatory employment practices, these rulings require a heightened level of proof in cases challenging discretionary decision making, and typically subject the plaintiffs' expert submissions to a heightened level of scrutiny.[38] In these cases, defense evidence of subunit differences appears to carry substantial weight.

For similar reasons, courts considering commonality in cases involving multi-facility classes and decentralized management structures are also coming to different conclusions, especially with respect to aggregated or disaggregated analyses. In many of these cases, plaintiffs, who argue that there is commonality in highly discretionary personnel policy and practice, support that claim with evidence of statistically significant disparities adverse to the class.[39] The defendant, claiming that personnel policy, practice, and implementation differs across decision-making units, precisely *because* of subjective decision-making practices, supports that position with statistics purporting to demonstrate conclusively that disparities are neither consistent nor significant across units. For example, in opposing class certification in *Dukes et al. v. Wal-Mart Stores*, the defendant presented its position succinctly as follows:

> Managers employ distinct criteria in making their individualized decisions. The criteria differ store-by-store, manager-by-manager. Thus, if a discriminatory decision has been made at a particular store, the decision was made by the individual Store Manager. And that fact alone destroys commonality.... Wide differences exist in the *non*discriminatory pay criteria used. Hourly pay therefore cannot be analyzed in the aggregate. The analysis must be store-by-store.[40]

---

[36] For some courts, those kinds of allegations are the basis for finding commonality. See e.g., Ingram, 200 F.R.D. at 697–698; *Beckman v. CBS*, 192 F.R.D. 608 (D. Minn. 2000). For other courts, they are the reason commonality does not exist. See e.g., *Reap v. Continental Casualty*, 199 F.R.D. 536, 544–545 (D.N.J. 2001).

[37] *McReynolds*, 208 F.R.D. at 441; *Dukes*, 222 F.R.D. at 154–158.

[38] *Love v. Johanns*, 224 F.R.D. at 243–244; *Cooper*, 390 F.3d at 715–716.

[39] See e.g., *McReynolds*, 208 F.R.D. at 435.

[40] Defendant Wal-Mart Stores, Inc.'s Opposition to Plaintiffs' Motion for Class Certification, June 12, 2003.

CHAPTER 21. UNCONVENTIONAL WEAPONS

Correspondingly, the company's statistical expert submitted the results of thousands of regression analyses that showed no consistent pattern across geographical subunits.[41]

Many courts are relatively untroubled by the presence of decentralized management schemes and tend to defer examination of the merits of the statistical evidence.[42] Other courts have used evidence of subunit differences to rule that no commonality exists. One example of the latter approach is *Abram v. UPS*, where evidence of subunit differences played a substantial role in the court's decision not to certify the class:

> The parties agree that there is a statistically significant gap in compensation between African-Americans and whites when the data are considered *in the aggregate*. However, closer examination reveals differences that undermine commonality. For example, even the plaintiffs' expert admits that in a majority of districts he could find no statistically significant difference in pay between African-American and white supervisors.... The lack of any *consistent* pattern belies the notion that class members have been affected in common ways by the supposed 'practice' of 'subjective decision making.'[43]

The Court went on to quote the defense expert's explanation that:

> [w]hen pay is analyzed district by district, ... there are almost as many districts of UPS in which African-American supervisors make *more* than white supervisors, as there are districts where they make less.[44]

The opinion draws an explicit connection between the idea of subjective decision making as inherently individualized and the supposed

---

[41] *Dukes*, 222 F.R.D. at 156 (defense performed approximately 7500 separate regressions).

[42] *Staton v. Boeing*, 327 F.3d 938, 954–956 (9th Cir. 2003); *Bates v. UPS*, 204 F.R.D. 440, 446 (N.D. Cal. 2001); *Beckman v. CBS*, 192 F.R.D. 608, 613–614 (D. Minn. 2000); *Orlowski v. Dominick's Finer Foods*, 172 F.R.D. 370, 373, (N.D. Ill. 1997); *Thomas v. Christopher*, 169 F.R.D. 224, 237 (D.D.C. 1996), aff'd in part, rev'd in part on other grounds sub nom. *Thomas v. Albright*, 139 F.3d 227 (D.C. Cir. 1998); *Shores v. Publix Super Mkts., Inc.*, 1996 WL 407850 at *6–*7 (M.D. Fla., March 12, 1996); *Butler v. Home Depot*, 1996 WL 421436 at *1, *3 (N.D. Cal. January 25, 1996); *Morgan v. UPS*, 169 F.R.D. 349, 356 (E.D. Mo. 1996); *Cook v. Billington*, 1992 WL 276936 at *4 (D.D.C. August 14, 1992).

[43] *Abram*, 200 F.R.D. at 431 (emphasis in original).

[44] *Ibid.*

absence of any statistical 'pattern of disparities.' In this case, the disaggregated analysis carried the day, as it has in other similar cases.[45]

Although it is difficult to articulate the precise relevance of statistical evidence to an assessment of commonality, one can at least stake out some theoretical and doctrinal parameters. While courts diverge on how to treat decentralized and discretionary employment practices, the most persuasive and articulate renderings of this test appear to balance competing considerations. Perhaps the truest reading of *Eisen* would exclude all statistical evidence at the class certification phase, but it seems reasonable to favor certification when plaintiffs have made some threshold showing of common injury. However, consistent with maintaining a distinction between class certification and the merits, only some preliminary showing should be required. Establishing precise uniformity of actual class-wide injury in every geographic subunit may be more than plaintiffs must do to win the case outright, let alone certify the class. In any event, the purpose of statistical evidence at class certification is not to show commonality or the lack thereof, but to show that if certified the class could at least muster a prima facie case.

Commonality turns on the existence of common questions of fact or law, and the statistical evidence merely provides a court comfort that all the effort of proceeding to class-wide trial on the merits will not be completely wasted. The decisions in *Abrams* and in other cases that have precluded an aggregated analysis at class certification are therefore inconsistent with the theory of commonality under Rule 23. As we show below, they also may be relying on an unreliable depiction of subunit variation.

21.2.3 Second-Generation Classes and Shifting Fact Patterns

These disputes over the meaning and proper application of statistical evidence in civil rights class actions are connected to a larger dispute over the prevalence and nature of employment discrimination in modern American corporations – a move from 'first' to 'second' generation claims. Shifts in the kinds of cases litigated as class actions have created an opening for statistical dueling over subunit differences.

---

[45] See e.g., *Grosz*, 2003 WL 22971025.

CHAPTER 21. UNCONVENTIONAL WEAPONS

In the face of an unambiguous pronouncement of the Supreme Court that excessive subjectivity is an identifiable and empirically measurable employment practice, some courts nevertheless display marked skepticism that discretionary management practices could be anything but a series of sui generis individual decisions.[46] Both defense bar and scholarly commentary on Title VII class action cases such as *Wal-Mart* challenge the notion that excessive managerial discretion leads to widespread and institutional-level bias, and question the very existence of less overt forms of bias in the workplace.[47] These dynamics have led to an increasingly divergent set of court decisions about class certification in these cases, and opened the door to the increasing frequency of the kind of statistical submission we analyze here.

A quarter-century ago, in *International Brotherhood of Teamsters v. United States*, the Supreme Court considered a classic 'first generation' discrimination case.[48] The defendant company had virtually shut out African-American and Hispanic employees from the more desirable and higher-paying positions – relegating them to jobs that paid less and offered little future. Indeed, the statistical picture of segregation presented in that case was so overwhelming the Court used the phrase 'inexorable zero' – referring to a situation of almost total exclusion.[49]

---

[46] Abram, 200 F.R.D. at 429–431; Cooper, 390 F.3d at 715–716; *Reap v. Continental Casualty*, 199 F.R.D. 536 (D.N.J. 2001).

[47] Richard Epstein, Class Actions: Aggregation, Amplification, and Distortion, 2003 University of Chicago Legal Forum 475 (2003), Christopher Erath, Disraeli Would Have Loved Employment Discrimination Cases, (2000), Zachary Fasman, The Use and Misuse of Expert Witnesses in Employment Litigation, 729 PLI/Lit 841 (2005), Ronald M. Green, Class Actions in Equal Employment Matters, 657 PLI/Lit 303 (2001), Daniel S. Klein, Bridging the Falcon Gap: Do Claims of Subjective Decisionmaking In Employment Discrimination Class Actions Satisfy the Rule 23(A) Commonality and Typicality Requirements?, 25 Review of Litigation 131 (2006), Leslie M. Turner and Paul F. White, The Numbers Game: Statistics Offered to Show Discrimination May Promise More Than They Prove, The Legal Times, vol. 27, (2004), Amy Wax and Philip E. Tetlock, 'We Are All Racists At Heart', Wall Street Journal, (2005), A16.

[48] International Brotherhood *of Teamsters v. United States*, 431 U.S. 324 (1977).

[49] The Supreme Court noted wryly, in rejecting the defense proposition that the government's statistical analysis was inadequate, that:

> fine tuning of the statistics could not have obscured the glaring absence of minority line drivers... the company's inability to rebut the inference of discrimination came not from a misuse of statistics but from 'the inexorable zero.' 431 U.S. at 342 n. 23.

A virtually all-White contingent occupied the coveted line-driver positions, and the handful of Black line drivers had all been hired after the lawsuit.[50]

Individual testimony made clear that this extreme degree of exclusion was no accident but was a direct result of White supervisors making repeated intentionally discriminatory hiring and promotion decisions.[51] For example, one African-American worker seeking a line-driver post was told 'that there would be "a lot of problems on the road ... with different people, Caucasian, *et cetera*"' by a manager, who then stated: '"I don't feel that the company is ready for this right now ... Give us a little time. It will come around, you know."' A personnel officer made an even more blunt comment to an Hispanic applicant, stating 'that he had one strike against him – "You're a Chicano, and as far as we know, there isn't a Chicano driver in the system."'[52] The government, which brought the case against the defendant company and union on behalf of a class, apparently had little trouble convincing the court that its statistics and its stories met the legal test of discrimination as 'standard operating procedure.'[53]

Pattern or practice cases brought today seem to tell a more complicated story than the tale of *Teamsters*. Plaintiffs in these cases typically lack the kind of 'smoking gun' statements or anecdotes frequently found in early Title VII cases.[54] In place of 'the inexorable zero,' plaintiffs and defendants argue over seemingly more ambiguous or disputable race or gender disparities. Today's defendants often successfully defend these lawsuits by trumpeting their antidiscrimination policies, diversity awards, and highly placed minority and female employees, and arguing that any disparities stem from circumstances outside their control.[55]

---

[50] Teamsters, 431 U.S. at 337.

[51] The Court cited 'over forty specific instances of discrimination' in the record. See Teamsters, 431 U.S. at 338.

[52] See Teamsters, 431 U.S. at 338 n. 19.

[53] See Teamsters, 431 U.S. at 336–337.

[54] For example, many of these cases explicitly or implicitly rely on a 'glass ceiling' theory of discrimination, where hard-to-pinpoint barriers nonetheless seem to stall the careers of minority and female employees part way up the ladder. See e.g., Ingram, 200 F.R.D. at 697–698; McReynolds, 208 F.R.D. at 442–444.

[55] Wal-Mart is a textbook example of this approach, where the company pointed to diversity awards, EEO training, and policies in its defense. *Dukes*, 222 F.R.D. at 154.

CHAPTER 21. UNCONVENTIONAL WEAPONS

Many recent court decisions stress the challenge of identifying and proving discrimination, and, in particular, the less obvious nature of contemporary forms of bias. The First Circuit, for example, has observed that 'discrimination tends more and more to operate in subtle ways.'[56] Since the early days of Title VII, inferential proof has become more significant 'since "smoking gun" evidence is "rarely found in today's sophisticated employment world."'[57] Indeed, although the principle that discrimination may be well hidden was established early on, it seems even more likely today that an employer 'is unlikely to leave a well-marked trail' pointing to job bias as the reason for an action, or any 'notation to that effect in the personnel file.'[58]

The views of a federal judge, who recently denied a group of African-American employees the ability to proceed as a class on claims of systemic discrimination, exemplify this view:

> In contrast to the early days of Title VII, it is now more uncommon to find an employer that overtly encourages wholesale discrimination on the basis of race; race discrimination today comes in more subtle forms. It is perhaps more unusual still to find an employer such as a federal defense contractor – required ... to create and implement affirmative action programs, and whose employees are represented by a number of different unions – that can manage to engage in discrimination on a class-wide basis in the face of executive branch oversight and collectively bargained grievance procedures through which issues of discrimination can be brought to light.[59]

Courts tightening legal standards applicable to these cases over time appear guided by a shared social narrative that our nation's workplaces

---

[56] *Fernandes v. Costa Brothers Masonry, Inc.*, 199 F.3d 572, 580 (1st Cir. 1999).

[57] *Thomas v. Eastman Kodak Co.*, 183 F.3d 38, 58 n. 12 (1st Cir. 1999).

[58] *Carlton v. Mystic Transportation, Inc.*, 202 F.3d 129, 135 (2nd Cir. 2000). In *McDonnell-Douglas v. Green*, the Supreme Court set forth the burden-shifting method of proof precisely because discrimination is often lurking in the background without being overt. See also *Bickerstaff v. Vassar College*, 196 F.3d 435, *Iadimarco v. Runyon*, 190 F.3d 151 (3rd Cir. 1999); *Smith v. Borough of Wilkinsburg*, 147 F.3d 272 (3rd Cir. 1998); *Rutherford v. Harris County*, 197 F.3d 173 (5th Cir. 1999); *Scott v. University of Mississippi*, 148 F.3d 493 (5th Cir. 1998); *Robin v. Espo Engineering Corp.*, 200 F.3d 1081 (7th Cir. 2000); *Hasham v. Calif. State Bd. Of Equalization*, 200 F.3d 1035 (7th Cir. 2000).

[59] *Reid v. Lockheed Martin Aeronautics Co.*, 205 F.R.D. 655, 660 (N.D. Ga. 2001).

have, by and large, put the days of overt bias and deliberate segregation behind them, making *Teamsters*-style fact patterns unlikely, and by extension, *Teamsters*-style collective action inappropriate.

Simultaneously, an explosion of legal scholarship grounded in empirical analysis, and largely seeking to expand the universe of actionable discrimination claims, contends that existing legal doctrine fails to account for most kinds of discriminatory harm in today's workplace. These legal scholars draw on a large and widely accepted body of social science research on implicit bias.[60] This work demonstrates the importance of understanding discrimination not just as overt animus, but also as implicit attitudes that may lead to biased decision making.[61] These scholars share the view that changing social conditions have created a disconnect between the doctrine of the past and the problems of the present, but are far less skeptical than some courts that discrimination continues to exist. While a handful of legal scholars have applied this thinking to institutional and organizational behaviors and dynamics,[62] most have focused on interpersonal, 'one-on-one' forms of discriminatory conduct. Almost all conclude that existing law cannot be harmonized with this knowledge and that new legal

---

[60] See e.g., Charles R. Lawrence III The Id, the Ego and Equal Protection: Reckoning with Unconscious Racism, 39 Stanford Law Review 317 (1987); Linda Hamilton Krieger, The Content of Our Categories: A Cognitive Bias Approach to Discrimination and Equal Employment Opportunity, 47 Stanford Law Review 1161 (1995); David Benjamin Oppenheimer, Negligent Discrimination, 141 899 (1993); Rebecca Hanner White, DeMinimus Discrimination, 17 Emory L.J. 1121 (1998); Ann C. McGinley, Viva La Evolucion: Recognizing Unconscious Motive in Title VII, 9 Cornell J.L & Public Policy 415 (2000); Gary Blasi, Advocacy Against the Stereotype: Lessons from Cognitive Social Psychology, 49 UCLA L. Rev. 1241 (2002).

[61] John F. Dovidio and Samuel L. Gaertner, Aversive Racism and Selection Decisions: 1989 and 1999, 11 Psychological Science 319 (2000), Susan Fiske et al, Controlling Other People: The Impact of Power on Stereotyping, 48 American Psychologist 621 (1993), Samuel L. Gaertner and John F. Dovidio, The Subtlety of White Racism, Arousal, and Helping Behavior, 25 Journal of Personality and Social Psychology 691 (1977), Anthony Greenwald and Marzarin Banaji, Implicit Social Cognition: Attitudes, Self-Esteem and Stereotypes, 102 Psychological Review 4 (1995) Barbara F. Reskin, Including Mechanisms in Our Models of Ascriptive Inequality, 68 American Sociological Review 1 (2003).

[62] See e.g., Green, *supra*; Hart, Subjective Decisionmaking, *supra*; Ian Haney-Lopez, Institutional Racism, Judicial Conduct and a New Theory of Racial Discrimination, 109 Yale Law Journal 1717 (2000).

theories must be developed or doctrine changed to accommodate them.[63]

Changes in Title VII class litigation trends mirror this move from first to second generation discrimination. Research increasingly recognizes that bias can infect the workplace through both implicit and explicit means, and expert testimony about implicit bias and stereotyping evidence is findings its way into class action cases.[64] Cases are presenting more complex factual issues and less clear-cut statistical disparities.[65] A change from government to private enforcement also appears to be occurring. This shifting factual ground is perhaps making a defendant's statistical evidence about the absence of any clear pattern of discrimination more plausible.

Following the passage of Title VII of the Civil Rights Act of 1964, banning employment discrimination based on race, gender and certain other classifications, class-wide legal challenges to entrenched racial and gender-based hierarchies and job segregation proliferated. These cases focused on problems in policies and practices, rather than individual claims.[66] Federal judges desegregated entire industries, and held the power to carry out sweeping social and organizational change through the class action device. While similar kinds of pattern or practice claims continued throughout the 1980s and 1990s, their numbers plummeted from the thousands to the dozens,[67] shifting focus from institutional to personal accountability. Originally, the government, through the Department of Justice and the U.S. EEOC, played a visible role in bringing class action lawsuits, but today the private

---

[63] But see Hart, Subjective Decisionmaking, *supra*; Michael Selmi, Subtle Discrimination: A Matter of Perspective Rather than Intent, 34 Columbia Human Rights Law Review 657 (2003).

[64] See e.g., *Dukes*, 222 F.R.D. at 152–153.

[65] Tristan Green, Targeting Workplace Context: Title VII as a Tool for Institutional Reform, 72 Fordham Law Review 659 (2003), Melissa Hart, Skepticism and Expertise: The Supreme Court and the EEOC, 74 Fordham Law Review 1937 (2006), Susan Sturm, Second Generation Employment Discrimination: A Structural Approach, 101 Columbia Law Review 458 (2001).

[66] See e.g., Teamsters, 431 U.S. 324; Rowe, 457 F.2d 348; Pettway, 494 F.2d 211.

[67] Current class action filings for employment discrimination cases are a fraction of their number in the days of the Teamsters ruling, John J. Donohue III and Peter Siegelman, The Changing Nature of Employment Discrimination, 43 Stanford Law Review 983 (1991), while the federal government currently pursues even fewer than its usual handful of systemic cases.

plaintiffs' bar dominates systemic discrimination litigation.[68] Virtually all employment discrimination cases in American courts today proceed largely as competing narratives about deviant individuals – the racist supervisor or the incompetent worker with a frivolous claim – and rarely engage questions of policy or practice.

During the 1990s, a small resurgence in private class actions followed the passage of the Civil Rights Act of 1991, which made damages and jury trials available under Title VII for the first time. It is in these later cases that disputes over aggregation begin to dominate class certification rulings. The passage of the Civil Rights Act of 1991 raised the stakes for both sides. The private bar had greater incentives to develop and bring class action cases, and defendants became more concerned over their potential financial exposure. Private firms obtained some extraordinarily large class action settlements in the 1990s, with headline-making race discrimination lawsuits against Texaco[69] and Coca-Cola,[70] and dramatic gender and race discrimination claims against a series of retail chains, including Shoney's,[71] Lucky Stores,[72] Home Depot,[73] and Publix.[74]

An increase in multi-facility classes is also likely a factor in the increasing disputes over aggregation. The most often-cited class action

---

[68] Title VII grants the Department of Justice and the U.S. EEOC authority to bring pattern or practice cases against public, and private, employers respectively. See 42 U.S.C. 2000e-6. (Prior to 1972, the Department of Justice also had authority to bring pattern or practice claims against private employers.) During the 1980s and 1990s, DOJ filed an average of thirteen cases per year, mostly pattern or practice cases. Doug Huron, No More Enforcers? Legal Times (May 19, 2003). However, under the George W. Bush administration, this relatively low number dropped even further. As of May of 2003, DOJ was averaging about three new filings a year, only one of which was a pattern or practice case. *Ibid.* The EEOC today files less than 2% of all discrimination cases filed in federal court. *EEOC v. Waffle House, Inc.*, 122 S. Ct. 754, 762 n. 7 (2002). Some evidence suggests that government enforcement has never been very significant compared with the work of the private bar, even in the early days of Title VII. Procedure Under Title VII, 84 Harvard Law Review 1195 (1971).
[69] Texaco Settles Race Bias Suit for $176 Million, Los Angeles Times, November 16, 1996.
[70] Henry Unger, Judge OK's Coke Bias Settlement: $192.5 Million Deal Sets New Diversity Goals, Atlanta Journal-Constitution, May 30, 2001 at A1.
[71] *Haynes v. Shoney's, Inc.*, 1992 WL 752127 (N.D. Fla. 1992).
[72] *Stender v. Lucky Stores*, 803 F.Supp. 259 (N.D. Cal. 1992).
[73] *Butler v. Home Depot*, 1996 WL 421436 (N.D. Cal. 1996).
[74] *Shores v. Publix Super Markets*, 1996 WL 407850 (M.D. Fla. 1996).

cases from the early days of Title VII primarily involved race discrimination in single-site manufacturing facilities,[75] and often focused on claims of discrimination in hiring.[76] While these cases frequently involved disputes over statistical evidence, doctrinal issues focused on what variables should be included in the analysis and the proper modeling of applicant pools. Reported cases increasingly deviate from the single-facility model, whether because of shifts in the labor force and the national economy, and increasingly globalized corporations, or because of changes in the behavior of plaintiffs and their lawyers in seeing claims against these companies as presenting potential class issues. These larger, multi-facility companies, and retail chains, raised the prominence of decentralized management.

Finally, an increasingly organized defense bar and consultants marketing to corporate defendants have generated even greater attention to this issue. Expert consulting firms that mainly represent defendants in complex employment litigation actively promote their critiques of plaintiffs' experts' approaches and their own strategies for avoiding an unfavorable ruling on class certification. In particular, they stress their tactics for using particular approaches to modeling statistical evidence to hone an effective class certification defense. One of the largest, National Economic Research Associates, is particularly aggressive in this regard, promoting in-house papers with titles such as 'Common Statistical Fallacies in Pattern-and-Practice Employment Discrimination Cases; A User's Guide for Defense Attorneys,' 'Disraeli Would Have Loved Employment Discrimination Cases,' 'Elvis Told Me It Was Statistically Significant: Keeping Expert Testimony Based on Junk Statistical Science Out of the Courtroom and Responding When It Gets In,' and, most clearly on point, 'Class Dismissed: Using Economic and Statistical Evidence to Defeat Class Certification.'

Among the capabilities in the area of workforce analysis promoted at the NERA website is the following statement of the strategy outlined above:

OUR CAPABILITIES
Liabilities/Class Certification

Our work in these areas involves performing statistical analyses of employment discrimination claims both in a pattern and practice and in

---

[75] Pettway, 494 F.2d 211; Rowe 457 F.2d 348.
[76] See e.g., Teamsters, 431 U.S. 324.

a class certification context.... In a class context, we have participated extensively at the certification phase, performing statistical analyses to determine whether the commonality and typicality prongs of Rule 23 are met and going beyond the broad-brush types of analyses frequently presented to learn whether any alleged disparity pervades the proposed class, is limited to some subgroup, or does not exist at all.[77]

This is, essentially, the kind of 'heterogeneity' defense – promoting a disaggregated analysis to attack the notion of any pattern or any possible finding of 'commonality' that increasingly appears in these kinds of cases.[78]

NERA was one of the first to pursue this approach successfully, and the results they achieved already appear in at least one reported case. In *Abram v. UPS*, the trial judge relied heavily on a NERA statistical expert in criticizing the statistics offered by the plaintiffs, explaining that '[t]he lack of any consistent pattern belies the notion that class members have been affected in common ways by the supposed "practice" of "subjective decision making."' The Court goes on to quote UPS' expert:

> In some of the districts, the advantage to African-Americans is statistically significant and in others the disadvantage is statistically significant, while in most of the districts the difference is insignificant – exactly what would be expected if these differences were unsystematic and random.... The plaintiffs' somewhat tendentious reliance on aggregate data illustrates the perils and misuses of statistical analysis.... In short, the numbers do not

---

[77] NERA paper, available online at <www.nera.com/image/AAG_EmplLabor_3.2005.pdf>. See also <www.nera.com/image/AAG_Class%20Certification_9.2004.pdf> (touting NERA's expertise in providing 'extensive expert testimony on statistical issues related to Rule 23 and whether any statistical claims are artifacts of the statistical model an opposing expert has chosen').

[78] In addition to the frequent mentions of this approach in defense bar papers, the plaintiffs bar is also organizing to counter disaggregated statistical models and promote the more traditional pooled analyses in the context of class certification. See e.g., Jocelyn Larkin and Christine Webber, Challenging Subjective Criteria in Employment Class Actions, available online at <www.impactfund.org/pdfs/Subjective%20Criteria.pdf>. Indeed, that this issue matters appears to be one place where plaintiff and defense counsel can reach agreement. Jocelyn Larkin and Fred Alvarez, Ten Reasons Class Actions Do or Do Not Get Certified, available online at <www.impactfund.org/pdfs/Ten%20Reasons%20Final.pdf>.

reveal a 'pattern or practice' of discrimination (intentional or otherwise) that unites the class.[79]

In sum, when an allegation is brought regarding systematic discrimination due to discretionary and subjective decision making, defendants are able to respond with a ready-made argument about decentralization and organizational heterogeneity, confirmed by a seemingly sophisticated statistical analysis showing that disparities are neither systematic, pervasive, uniform, nor statistically significant. The fact that at least some courts have accepted this approach, coupled with the active promotion by large consulting firms of the 'heterogeneity defense' and accompanying statistical analysis, has guaranteed that this strategy has diffused rapidly. But does the statistical analysis upon which the heterogeneity defense rests really enlighten the court on issues of typicality and commonality? Not necessarily.

21.3 THE MEANING OF STATISTICAL 'PATTERNS': A DEMONSTRATION OF THE STATISTICAL POWER PROBLEM

This 'heterogeneity defense' exploits doctrinal ambiguities in the relevance of statistics to class certification, seeking to generate favorable results for corporate defendants. While courts have taken different views on the propriety of separate subunit analyses, plaintiffs typically argue that courts should disregard defense submissions featuring separate subunit regressions because they lack statistical power – that is, they are unlikely to detect discrimination when it really exists. Usually plaintiffs can only posit the hypothetical implications of defendants' low power analyses. The simulation below provides a clear example of why statistical power really matters, and how an analysis with low statistical power can yield a misleading result.

Using a hypothetical example based on real data, we show how each side's statistical experts would likely approach the typicality and commonality issues central to class certification in a lawsuit alleging discrimination due to discretionary and subjective decision-making. (Please note that the data upon which the example is based were not used in litigating a class certification issue in an actual discrimination case.)

---

[79] Abram, 200 F.R.D at 431.

Using these data, we present regression results using the same kinds models that plaintiffs and defendants in recent similar class actions tend to utilize. As you will see, in some cases the regression results are wildly inconsistent with the real patterns in the underlying data.

21.3.1 *Smith, et al. v. UFS*: A Hypothetical Gender Discrimination Class Action

We will refer to our hypothetical company as Universal Financial Services ('We're Everywhere'). It has 187 offices nationwide and nearly eight thousand financial service agents. The agent workforce is over 86% male, and a lawsuit has been filed by Maggie Smith, a female UFS agent, and several of her colleagues. The *Smith* case alleges that due to a lack of specificity and oversight and a high degree of managerial discretion, the company favors men in assigning agents to accounts. Plaintiffs claim that women receive smaller and less profitable accounts to manage, which reduces how much compensation an agent can earn. The female agents who filed the suit seek to represent a class of nearly 1,100 female agents employed by the company nationwide. Table 21.1 shows the size and gender composition of the UFS offices – composed of 13% women on average. (Some offices are as low as 3.4% women and a few small offices are as high as 50% women.)

Table 21.1: Gender Composition of 'UFS'

Universal Financial Services	
Number of Offices	181
Number of Agents per Office	
Median # Agents	41
Mean # Agents	43.9
Range	2 to 122
IQR (25th–75th percentile)	31 to 54
Office Gender Comp – % Female	
Median % Female	13.0%
Mean % Female	13.8%
Range	3.4% to 50.0%
IQR (25th–75th percentile)	9.5% to 17.8%

We assume that the experts for each side conduct regression analysis to determine whether men and women have relevant differences in compensation. In the typical analyses used in employment discrimination cases, regression techniques calculate the mathematical relationship between belonging to a protected class and an outcome – such as the amount of compensation (the 'dependent' variable).[80] A regression yields an 'estimate' of the 'effect' of the variable of interest, such as race, ethnicity or gender, on that dependent variable, while taking into account ('controlling for') other variables – other factors that also might influence that outcome.[81]

These potential relationships between outcome, membership in a protected class, and potential controls, can be formulated into mathematical equations.[82] An analysis will yield a regression coefficient for each independent variable. That coefficient is a specific number, and is the best 'estimate' of the impact of that independent variable on the dependent variable. In our example, regression analysis will yield a numerical result that represents the salary difference for women as compared to men.[83] Regression also generates a 'standard error' – how

---

[80] For general reference texts on regression analysis, see James H. Stock and Mark W. Watson, Introduction to Econometrics (2003); William H. Greene, Econometric Analysis (4th edn 1999); Eric A. Hanushek and John E. Jackson, Statistical Methods for Social Scientists (1977).

[81] See generally Hanushek & Jackson at 25–28; 35–37. For example, frequently statistical analyses control for what economists term 'human capital' factors such as education and experience. To the extent members of a protected class who have the same qualifications as majority group employees still receive different lower compensation on average, or have different promotion rates, social scientists generally attribute this difference to discrimination. See e.g., Joyce P. Jacobsen, The Economics of Gender 289–317 (2nd edn 1998); William A. Darity, Jr., and Patrick L. Mason, Evidence On Discrimination In Employment: Codes of Color, Codes of Gender, 12 J. Of Econ. Perspectives 63, 67 (1998); Francine D. Blau and Marianne A. Ferber, Discrimination: Empirical Evidence From The United States, 77 American Econ. Review 316 (1987); Orley Ashenfelter, Changes in Labor Market Discrimination over Time, 5 J. Human Resources 403 (1970).

[82] The examples discussed in this section use an 'additive' model, as distinguished from an 'interacted' model. William D. Berry, Understanding Regression Assumptions 3 (1993). Interaction terms are sometimes utilized to generate more refined estimates where an expert believes that the relationship between the dependent and independent variables is more complex.

[83] A sample regression equation might look like this:

$$\text{Salary} = A + B^*\text{Education} - C^*\text{Female} + D^*\text{Experience} + e.$$

much that estimate might vary across different samples of data. With those two pieces of information, one can calculate the 'statistical significance' of the result – how likely it might be to occur by chance.[84]

To understand statistical significance, it is helpful to consider a 'Groundhog Day' analogy[85] – starting over, repeating the process, but getting a slightly different outcome. In other words, if one were to repeat the salary setting process being studied, with the same individuals, one would not get the exact same dollar amounts for each person – a certain amount of random variation would affect the outcome. This is why

---

The letter attached to each variable such as education or experience represents a 'regression coefficient.' Looking at each of the coefficients, one can draw certain conclusions about the relationship – is it positive or negative? How large is the effect? This model proposes to explain salary as a function of an individual's education, experience, and whether or not they are female. Besides these measured factors, the regression model includes a residual factor, 'e.' that represents the impact of unmeasured factors on salary. Using the available data, a regression would generate actual numbers for each regression coefficient B, C, and D, as well as for A, a constant value. It also generates a number for the impact of unmeasured factors, the so-called 'unexplained variance' in a regression model.

Suppose that a linear regression yielded the following results:

Predicted Salary (USD 1000s) = 10 + 2.1*Educ. – 3.4*Female + 1.7*Experience.

This equation shows the 'estimated effect' of each of the variables on the average salary, based on a particular set of data. The regression coefficients in this example represent the average predicted or estimated change in the outcome (in this case salary) when that variable increases by one unit. See e.g., Hanushek & Jackson at 35–37. Thus, each additional year of education increases salary by USD 2,100, everything else being equal, and each additional year of experience for otherwise similarly situated employees is worth an additional USD 1,700. This particular sample equation also uses a binary variable (sometimes called 'dummy variable') to capture the effect of belonging to a protected class on salary. Melissa A. Hardy, Regression with Dummy Variables 7–9; 18–21 (1993).That variable is set to equal one for all women in the dataset, and zero for all men. Thus, the estimated effect of being female on an individual's salary is to decrease it by USD 3,400 according to this hypothetical example.

[84] See generally Daniel L. Rubinfeld, Reference Guide on Multiple Regression, Ann. Reference Manual on Sci. Evid. 179 (2nd edn West 2006).

[85] In the 1993 film Groundhog Day, Bill Murray played a weather reporter forced to repeat a single day over and over until he got it 'right.' Certain things happened exactly the same way each day, but there was also variation each time, an analogy that captures in certain respects the theory of estimation described here.

CHAPTER 21. UNCONVENTIONAL WEAPONS

statisticians refer to the results of an analysis as an 'estimate.' If there is no discrimination present, one would expect that, for example, salaries for females would not be either lower or higher, on average, than those of similarly qualified males – there would be zero difference between them. One might also not expect the difference to be exactly zero in every calculation. A certain amount of random variation might mean that any particular analysis generates some positive or negative differential. (The 'margin of error' reported for an opinion poll reflects a similar concept.)

Statistical significance allows social scientists to draw certain conclusions about whether the difference recorded in an analysis is likely to be a real difference, or simply the result of this kind of random variation. Generally, a test of whether an estimated regression coefficient for an independent variable is 'statistically significant' asks whether it falls more than two standard deviations from zero, a result that would be expected just one time in twenty (5% of the time) when the variable truly has no impact on the dependent variable. When the estimated coefficient falls outside that range it is reasonable to conclude that the true effect differs from zero. Courts, following social science practice, have typically concluded a statistically significant coefficient for a binary variable representing protected class membership reflects discrimination.[86] As explained below, whether one conducts an aggregated or disaggregated analysis may influence whether or not a particular difference is statistically significant.

In a typical case, the experts would likely disagree on the controls to be used in the equation, but for purposes of this analysis we can ignore that complication. In our example, each side agrees that the amount of time spent in the industry affects an agents' productivity, and therefore should be included as a control in the regression analysis. They also agree that any other factors like education that may influence how much an agent earns are unrelated to either gender or to length of service in the industry. Therefore, no other control variables need to be included in the analysis.[87]

---

[86] See e.g., *Hazelwood School Dist. v. United States*, 433 U.S. 299, 311 n. 17 (1977). See generally Ramona L. Paetzold and Steven L. Willborn, The Statistics of Discrimination: Using Statistical Evidence in Discrimination Cases § 4.11 (1999).

[87] Berry at 10–11 (appropriate to exclude variables if they have a weak impact, if data is lacking, or if there is no strong theoretical basis to include them).

In arguing for class certification, plaintiffs seek to show the Court that there have been large, consistent, and statistically significant disparities in compensation favoring men. The plaintiff's expert, Dr. P, offers a regression analysis testing the effect of gender on earnings while taking only years of service into account. That analysis would generate a single regression coefficient that represents the average effect of gender on compensation throughout UFS. These results suggest that there is a large and statistically significant gender gap in compensation of about 13%, consistently, from year-to-year. The first line of Table 21.2 shows the results for each of five years.[88]

Table 21.2: Regression Results of Plaintiffs' Expert

Regression Results	1994	1995	1996	1997	1998
Gender Coef., Controlling Experience	−0.137	−0.141	−0.144	−0.133	−0.123
Gender Coef., Controlling Experience, Office	−0.134	−0.139	−0.142	−0.130	−0.116
Percentage Gender Disparity, Controlling Experience, Office	−12.5%	−13.0%	−13.2%	−12.2%	−11.0%
Number of Offices	7300	7510	7707	7927	7943
Observations	170	180	181	187	181
Gender Coeff. T-Ratio, Controlling Experience	−6.65	−6.83	−7.28	−6.81	−5.98
Gender Coef. T-Ratio Controlling Experience, Office	−6.57	−6.88	−7.30	−6.79	−5.79
R-Square Controlling Experience, Office	0.3136	0.3411	0.3454	0.3720	0.3827

---

[88] Plaintiffs expert would use the following regression specification (where 'Female' is a binary variable and 'experience' is years of service in the industry):

(1) Log Earnings = a + b1*Female + b2*Experience + b3*Experience**2 + e.

Here b1 is the effect of gender on earnings, in this case controlling for length of service. As is common in analyses of compensation, this expert would use the logarithm of earnings, and would include years of service squared.

CHAPTER 21. UNCONVENTIONAL WEAPONS

The defense expert, Dr. D, mercilessly attacks plaintiffs' statistical expert, suggesting that this analysis was performed by someone who is either incompetent or unscrupulous – or possibly both. Dr. D raises two criticisms. The first is the 'fallacy of composition' critique. If women who work at UFS live disproportionately in markets that generate little business, failing to take that into account in a statistical analysis would bias the results. The consequences of working in a low-compensation office might be confounded with gender. The second is the 'decentralization' critique. Dr. D. asserts that decisions about pay are delegated to management in each of the local offices, and as a result the analysis must be done on an office-by-office basis.

Dr. P responds to the criticisms by adding controls for office location.[89] The results, reported in the second line of Table 21.2, show that the gender disparities are indeed smaller after controlling for location,[90] although in this example they remain large, statistically significant, and consistent from year to year.[91] In our hypothetical example, plaintiffs are hopeful that they have met the burden of supplying a statistical analysis sufficient to justify class certification.

Dr. D. is not persuaded. She concedes that including control variables for offices eliminates the possibility of the fallacy of composition, but she insists it fails to address the decentralization critique. She offers an alternative analysis that seems to indicate that certification is not appropriate. According to Dr. D., the 11–13% differences represent an improper averaging across the 181 different offices in each year. Her alternative analysis begins with the same regression equation as Dr. P's

---

[89] The new specification, with a set of binary variables for office location, is as follows:

(2) Log Earnings = a + b1*Female + b2*Experience + b3*Experience**2 + Office Location + e.

[90] For each year, the regression coefficient for Female with controls for office (line 2) is smaller than the corresponding coefficient without those controls (line 1).

[91] When the dependent variable is measured on a logarithmic scale, the coefficients for binary variables correspond approximately but not exactly to percentage disparities. Row three of Table 21.2 translates the regression coefficients in row two into exact estimates of percentage disparities. So, for example, the coefficient for Female for year 1998 of -.116 translates into a gender gap in earnings of 11.0% among men and women comparable with respect to years of experience and office location.

923

original equation, estimating the effect of gender on compensation while controlling for length of service. However, she estimates the effect of gender separately for each of the 181 UFS offices that employ both male and female agents.

She reports 181 gender coefficients for each year. In some offices the disparity favors men, in others it favors women, and in most instances it is not statistically significant.

As defense experts have done in other cases, Dr. D. presents her results graphically. The results for 1998 appear in Figures 21.1 and 21.2. The graphical presentation emphasizes the subunit differences, dramatically demonstrating in Figure 21.1 how the various separate estimates of the effect of gender on earnings vary wildly from office to office. Figure 21.2 arrays the same 181 coefficients from lowest (most negative) to highest (most positive), again illustrating that in most instances the disparities are not significant and in many offices they actually favor women – precisely the finding that the judge found so persuasive in *Abram et al. v. UPS*.[92]

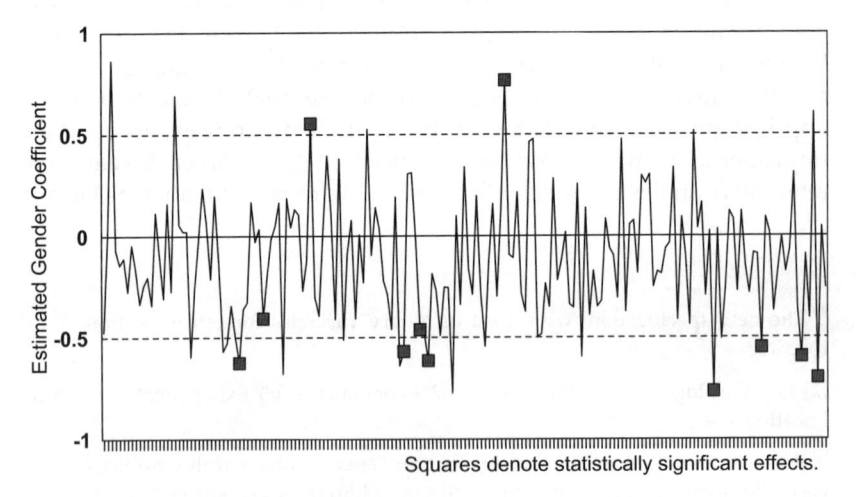

Figure 21.1 Estimated Gender Coefficients

---

[92] See Abram, 200 F.R.D. at 431.

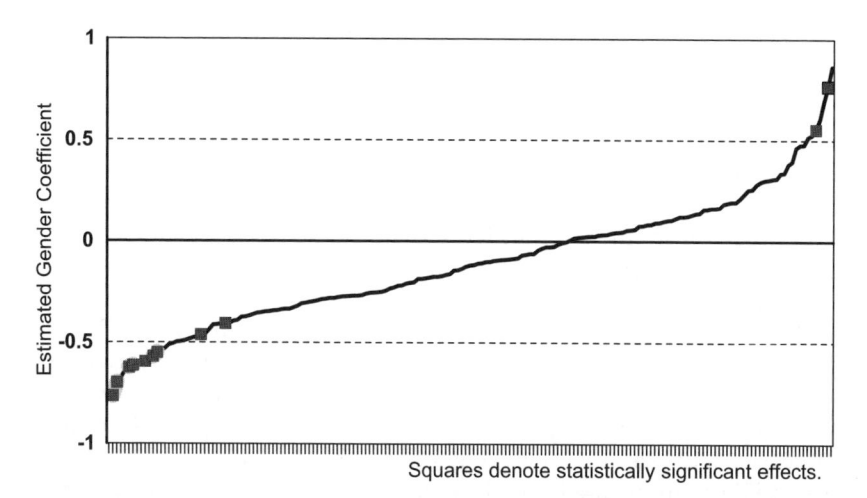

Figure 21.2 Estimated Gender Coefficients Arrayed by Coefficient Value (Most Negative to Least Negative)

Armed with these findings, the defendant presents to the judge a bottom line that seems irrefutable:

- Plaintiffs' achieved their 'statistically significant' disparity purportedly showing a 'pattern and practice' resulting in an 11% gender gap in earnings through *improper aggregation.*
- In fact, in the vast majority of UFS offices there is no significant earnings disparity between men and women, and there is no consistency in the size of those disparities from office to office.

Thus, there is no 'commonality' here and no basis for certifying a class.

In response, plaintiffs argue that by estimating separate regression coefficients for each of 181 offices, Dr. D has dramatically lowered the power of her tests for statistical significance. When studying discrimination, 'power' is the probability of detecting discrimination when it really exists. In other words, a statistical test that lacks power may cause you to wrongly conclude the effect of race or ethnicity on salary is zero. Ramona Paetzold and Steven Willborn explain:

> Power is particularly important for correctly interpreting non-significant results... if there is low power to detect important disparities, then

non-significant results could be due to chance and may not imply there is no discrimination.[93]

In a regression model, several factors affect the power of a statistical test of the hypothesis that the effect of an independent variable is zero. First, power increases with the size of the effect to be detected.[94] In the context of testing for the impact of gender on earnings, this simply means that large disparities, (e.g., a gender gap of 20%) are more likely to show up as 'statistically significant' than small disparities, (e.g., a gender gap of 5%). Second, power increases with overall 'explained variance' of the regression model.[95] This simply means that when unmeasured factors have little impact on earnings, the 'Groundhog Day' effect is smaller than when unmeasured factors have a big impact. Third, and most important, power increases with sample size. A gender gap of a specific magnitude (say 15%) is more likely to show up as statistically significant in a regression analysis based on 1,000 observations than in one based on 100 observations.[96] Aggregation affects the number of observations, and therefore the power of the test.

Some courts have recognized the effect that low statistical power, and a disaggregated analysis of a smaller number of

---

[93] Paetzold & Willborn at § 4.15 (emphasis added).

[94] William T. Bielby and James R. Kluegel, Simultaneous Statistical Inference and Statistical Power in Survey Research Applications of the General Linear Model, 8 American Econ. Review 233, 300 (1977).

[95] Bielby & Kluegel at 300.

[96] Herman Aguinis, Regression Analysis for Categorical Moderators 69–82 (2004); Bielby & Kluegel at 300; also see e.g., Hanushek & Jackson at 54 (increasing the number of observations 'can improve the precision of our estimates (reduce their variance).' Two other factors affect the power of a statistical test of a regression coefficient. First, power decreases to the extent that the factor being tested is highly correlated with other control variables in the regression model. For example, if nearly all men have extensive industry experience and nearly all women have little industry experience, then it is more difficult to precisely disentangle the relative contributions of gender and experience to earnings than when the ratio of men to women is similar at all levels of experience. Second, adding too many control variables relative to the number of observations can also decrease the power of the statistical test, and make the results less precise. Mathematically, adding one extraneous control variable added to the model has the same effect as dropping one observation. (Hanushek & Jackson at 93–94).

CHAPTER 21. UNCONVENTIONAL WEAPONS

observations, can have on the ability to detect discrimination. As Judge Posner explains, it is 'an unacceptable statistical procedure to turn a large sample into a small one by arbitrarily excluding observations.'[97] Some other Title VII cases have addressed statistical power and aggregation, but not in the context presented here of testing for subunit differences.[98]

From the plaintiffs' perspective, the fact that few of the results in our hypothetical example are statistically significant is not surprising in light of the much smaller sample sizes in Dr. D's approach. The pooled data represents a more powerful test, which is more likely to detect discrimination when it occurs. Plaintiffs contend that by controlling for office location, Dr. P addressed any potential relevance of the subunits. However, plaintiffs' analysis as presented here does not provide any information on the extent to which gender disparities differ among subunits, an issue considered in more detail below.

The judge now faces the challenge of adjudicating between these dueling statistical claims within the framework of legal doctrine. Prior case law largely favors plaintiffs, but the defense argument is intuitively appealing. How can there be a class suffering a common injury if the office to office results are all over the map? Though rarely considered explicitly in employment discrimination litigation, these assertions are greatly influenced by statistical power and can actually be tested empirically.

---

[97] *Washington v. Elec. Joint Appren. & Train. Comm.*, 845 F.2d 710, 713 (7th Cir. 1988) (rejecting plaintiff's statistical analysis of a single year in favor of defense analysis pooled across years).

[98] *Eldredge v. Carpenters 46 N. Cal. Counties Joint Appren. & Train. Comm.*, 833 F.2d 1334, 1339 n. 7 (9th Cir. 1987) ('aggregated data presents a more complete and reliable picture'); *Cook v. Boorstein*, 763 F.2d 1462, 1468–1469 (D.C. Cir. 1985) (rejecting defendant's argument to restrict statistical analysis to particular job categories); *Ezell v. Mobile Housing Bd.*, 709 F.2d 1376, 1382 (11th Cir. 1983); *Capaci v. Katz & Bestoff, Inc.*, 711 F.2d 647, 654 (5th Cir. 1983) (rejecting defendant's claim statistical analysis should be fragmented by city and year as 'an unfair and obvious attempt to disaggregate the data to the point where it was difficult to demonstrate statistical significance').

21.3.2 Who's Got the Power: A Simulation Exercise

Suppose that in a parallel universe there was another UFS, one where we know for certain that the exact same gender disparity exists across offices. We assume that some discriminatory mechanism operates the same way in every office. We can assume the disparity corresponds to the same 11% gap Dr. P calculated for the most recent year in her analysis. We can now generate simulated earnings for each individual employed at UFS, using the same data as before, but manipulating it to reflect a consistent 11% gender gap.[99]

Now, with the simulated data, we replicate Dr. P's analysis – the analysis that assumes a uniform gender disparity. We also replicate Dr. D's analysis of the defendant's expert, estimating a separate regression equation for each office – even though we have generated simulated earnings through a process that makes the gender disparity constant from office to office. The results from replicating Dr. P's analysis appear in Table 21.3. Not surprisingly, the estimates from the simulated data (a coefficient of -.108 which is equivalent to a 10.2% gap) conform closely to the simulated gender difference built into the data (a coefficient of -.116 which is equivalent to a 10.9% gap).

---

[99] The following equation is used to generate simulated earnings:

(3) Sim Log Earnings = a -**.116*Female** + b2*Experience + b3*Experience**2 + Office Location + e,

where a, b2, b3, and the coefficients for the office binary variables are also fixed (at values taken from the 1998 regression controlling for experience and office location), and e is generated from a random normal distribution, independently across observations. In other words, for two employees of the same sex in the same office with identical length of service, their simulated earnings will be identical, but for the random component introduced by the disturbance term. If one is a man and the other is a woman with the same experience, their simulated earnings will be identical but for the random component and an 11% penalty subtracted from the woman's earnings.

Table 21.3: Comparing Results Based on Simulated Earnings and Actual Earnings

	Actual	Simulation with b set to -.116
Gender Coef., Controlling Experience, Office	−0.116	−0.108
Percentage Gender Disparity, Controlling Experience, Office	−10.9%	−10.2%
Observations	7941	7941
Number Offices	181	181
Gender Coef. T-Ratio Controlling Experience, Office	−5.76	−5.33
Number of Offices with No Significant Disparity	170	174
Number of Offices with Significant Disparity Favoring Women	2	2
Number of Offices with Significant Disparity Favoring Men	9	5
F-Ratio for Test of Gender by Office Interaction	0.91	0.97
P-Value for Test of Gender by Office Interaction	0.811	0.612

Replicating Dr. D's analysis – a search for differences in the gender gap in earnings – generates much more interesting results. Those results, portrayed in Figures 21.3 and 21.4, are strikingly similar to the original results. Even though the simulated data have a uniform disparity built in, the defendant's expert produces a result that supports her client's litigation position. According to this analysis the disparities favor men in some offices, women in other offices, and in most instances are not significantly different from zero. The statistical picture is at odds with the reality of the data.

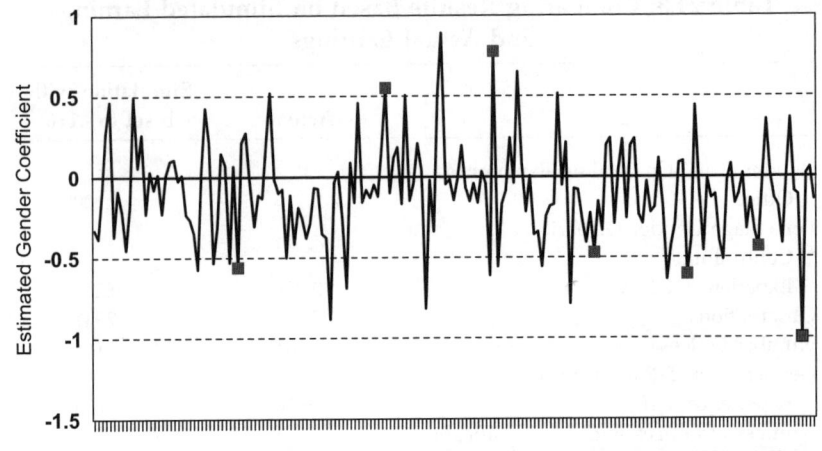

EMPLOYMENT CLASS AND COLLECTIVE ACTIONS

Squares denote statistically significant effects

Figure 21.3 Replicating the Heterogeneity Analysis of the Defendant's Expert with Simulated Data Containing a Uniform Disparity

Squares denote statistically significant effects.

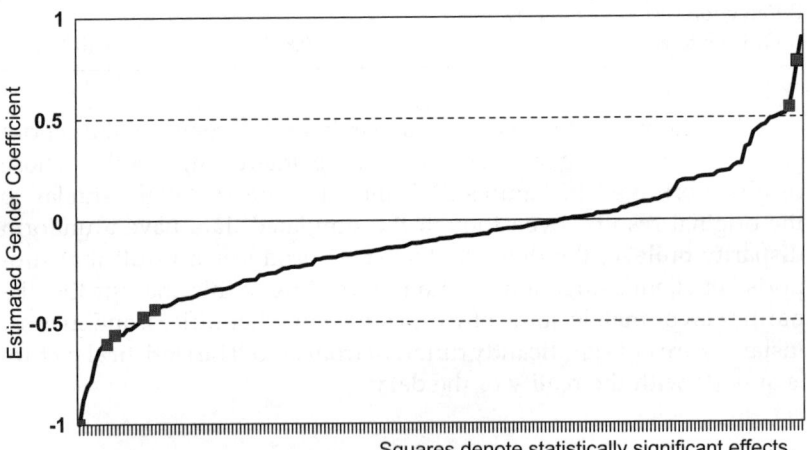

Figure 21.4 Replicating the Heterogeneity Analysis of the Defendant's Expert with Simulated Data Containing a Uniform Disparity (with Estimated Coefficients Displayed from Most Negative to Most Positive)

CHAPTER 21. UNCONVENTIONAL WEAPONS

Armed with these results, the plaintiffs present their argument against disaggregation:

- Defendant's expert achieved the finding of no consistent 'statistically significant' disparity across offices by capitalizing on chance in a way that guaranteed the results even if there is uniform discrimination across organizational units, an example of *improper disaggregation*.
- In fact, while *within* the vast majority of hypothetical UFS offices there is no statistically significant earnings disparities between men and women, this neither proves nor disproves that there is a consistent, uniform disparity by gender.

The results of statistical analysis – seemingly random disparity – fail to line up with the empirical reality – uniform disparity – because of lowered statistical power. By breaking up the dataset into much smaller units, the amount of 'noise,' or random variation, is elevated over any pattern that exists. In this case, any particular individual man or woman might have especially high or low earnings because of factors not measured in the analysis, factors that vary randomly between men and women.[100] Because individual salaries will tend to vary for a host of reasons, looking at smaller groups will tend to diminish evidence that women as a group are harmed more than men.[101]

Think of performing one thousand coin flips. Given such a large sample, the result is likely to be very close to 500 heads and 500 tails. If the result were 600 heads and 400 tails, one would suspect a loaded

---

[100] Indeed, because in this hypothetical the employees work in the financial services industry, and their compensation is determined in part by volatile market forces, the degree of 'noise' in the dataset may be especially high.

[101] This does not mean that the average is deceptive. A woman may be the highest earner in her particular office, but may be paid far lower than a host of equally or lesser-qualified men in other offices. Isolating the comparison to only those in a particular office could unfairly exclude otherwise relevant evidence of gender-based compensation disparities. Conversely, a woman who is penalized because of her gender to the same extent as any other class member could still end up being more highly compensated than the vast majority or men, or even be the highest paid person in the entire company, due to the impact of unmeasured factors. Absent discrimination, her already high salary would have been even higher. Again, this is not an unlikely occurrence in an industry in which earnings are highly volatile due to market factors that have nothing to do with gender or with other measurable determinants of earnings.

coin. Yet each group of ten tosses might be all over the map. Some would be six heads and four tails, but others might include more tails than heads. Looking at the smaller groups might not alert the coin tosser to the underlying problem.

But what happens when the world works the way the defendant maintains? That is, what if there really is considerable heterogeneity in gender disparities across offices, and what if it were truly due to distinctive features of the personnel system in each office?[102] Again, a simulation exercise proves illuminating.[103]

Once more, we generate simulated earnings for a hypothetical UFS where we *know for certain* how disparities vary across offices.[104] This time, however, we generate two sets of simulated earnings reflecting different patterns of heterogeneity. In *Sim 2*, the gender coefficient is set to vary uniformly across offices in the range of -.1158 plus or minus .05. We refer to this as 'continuous heterogeneity': although the disparity is not identical across offices, women face a disadvantage in every office, but a bit more in some offices than in others (a gender gap in earnings ranging from 6% to 15%). In *Sim 3*, the gender disparity is fixed at zero for two-thirds of the offices (gender parity in earnings) and at -.3474 (a gender gap of 29%) at the remaining third of offices. We refer to this as 'radical heterogeneity.' This is clearly a case that raises a plausible question as to whether a common policy or practice is really operating across the company.

The results of the disaggregated heterogeneity analysis conducted by the defendant's expert under different scenarios appear in the bottom three rows of Table 21.4 and in Figure 21.5. No matter what the

---

[102] In establishing causation for purposes of Title VII liability between a particular set of personnel policies and practices and documented disparities, courts do not assume that relationship, and would also look to evidence well beyond these kinds of statistical results to draw a conclusion.

[103] At this point, it is important to keep in mind that the simulation results are shaped not just by the magnitude of the gender disparities, but also by the overall size of the workforce, the size in each office, and the amount of variation due to unmeasured factors, a point we return to below.

[104] This time, the model used to generate simulated earnings is:

(4) Sim Log Earnings = a +b1*Female + b2*Experience + b3*Experience**2 + Office Location + e, where a, b2, b3, and the coefficients for the office binary variables are also fixed (at values taken from the 1998 regression controlling for experience and office location), and e is generated from a random normal distribution, independently across observations.

Table 21.4: Testing for Heterogeneity in Gender Disparities under Alternative Scenarios

	Actual	Sim 1	Sim 2	Sim 3
Type of Hetereogeneity across Offices in Gender Effect				
Uniform Continuous Radical at	−.116	−.066 to −.166	0 or −.37	
Gender Coef., Controlling Experience, Office	−0.116	−0.108	−0.136	−0.121
Percentage Gender Disparity, Controlling Experience, Office	−10.9%	−10.2%	−12.7%	−11.4%
Observations	7941	7941	7941	7941
Number Offices	181	181	181	181
Gender Coef. T-Ratio Controlling Experience, Office	−5.76	−5.33	−6.72	−5.95
Number of Offices with No Significant Disparity	170	174	167	160
Number of Offices with Significant Disparity Favoring Women	2	2	3	6
Number of Offices with Significant Disparity Favoring Men	9	5	11	15
F-Ratio for Test of Gender by Office Interaction	0.91	0.97	1.04	1.48
P-Value for Test of Gender by Office Interaction	0.811	0.612	0.343	<.0001

actual pattern of disparities across offices – uniform (no heterogeneity), continuous, or radical – given the sample sizes in the UFS example the overall pattern of results produced by the defendant's expert are always the same. The always show a pattern of seemingly random results, favoring men in some offices, women in other offices, and no significant disparity in most offices. Indeed, a cynic might argue that the defendant's expert chose to conduct this kind of analysis in order to guarantee a result supporting her client's litigation position, regardless of the underlying facts.

EMPLOYMENT CLASS AND COLLECTIVE ACTIONS

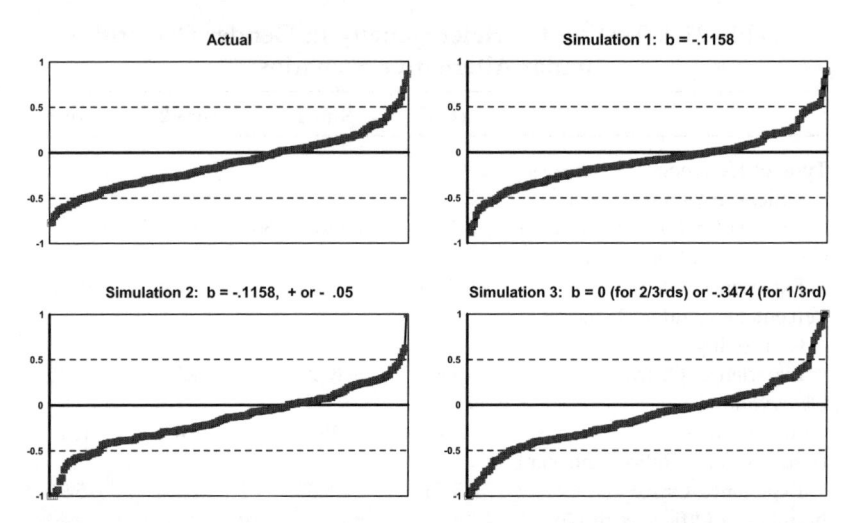

Figure 21.5 Results of a Disaggregated Analysis under Different Patterns of Heterogeneity

In fact, we must ask how large would the disparity have to be before the analysis of the defendant's expert shows any evidence that women face a systematic disadvantage at UFS? The results for that question appear in Table 21.5 and Figure 21.6. Here, we have repeated the *Sim 1* exercise, with simulated compensation data containing a built-in uniform bias towards women, but under six different circumstances, allowing the amount of uniform bias to range from -.05 to -.30 for estimate of the gender difference, (i.e., gender gaps ranging from 5% to about 25%).[105]

---

[105] So, for instance, in the most extreme example with the gender effect set to -.30, data are generated such that for two employees of the same sex in the same office with identical length of service, their simulated earnings will be identical, but for the random component introduced by the disturbance term. However, if one is a man and the other is a woman with the same experience, their simulated earnings will be identical but for the random component and a 25% penalty subtracted from the woman's earnings.

934

Table 21.5: Simulation Results: Detecting Uniform Disparity as a Function of Effect Size

	Actual	0.05	0.1	0.15	0.2	0.25	0.3
Gender Coef., Controlling Experience, Office	−0.116	−0.04	−0.09	−0.14	−0.19	−0.24	−0.29
Percentage Gender Disparity, Controlling Experience, Office	−10.9%	−4.1%	−8.8%	−13.2%	−17.4%	−21.5%	−25.3%
Observations	7941	7941	7941	7941	7941	7941	7941
Number Offices	181	181	181	181	181	181	181
Gender Coef. T-Ratio Controlling Experience, Office	−5.76	−2.07	−4.54	−7.02	−9.5	−11.97	−14.45
Number of Offices with No Significant Disparity	170	175	174	173	169	159	149
Number of Offices with Significant Disparity Favoring Women	2	3	2	1	0	0	0
Number of Offices with Significant Disparity Favoring Men	9	3	5	7	12	22	32

As would be expected, the greater the amount of uniform disparity, the fewer instances when the *estimated* coefficient for a specific office shows a significant disparity favoring women, and once the disparity exceeds -.15, the analysis produces no results that are statistically significant in favor of women. Similarly, the number of offices where the estimated coefficient is significant and favors men increases as the underlying disparity increases, and when the underlying disparity gets as high as -.3, significant disparities are detected in thirty-two of the 181 offices. But as can be seen from Figure 21.6, even in this circumstance, where the underlying gender bias is uniform and substantial, the disaggregated analysis yields a result consistent with the defendant's litigation position: widely ranging disparities sometimes favoring women, other times favoring men, but in the vast majority of instances not statistically significant. Consistent with the case law from *Abram et al. v. UPS* and the arguments set forth in the NERA

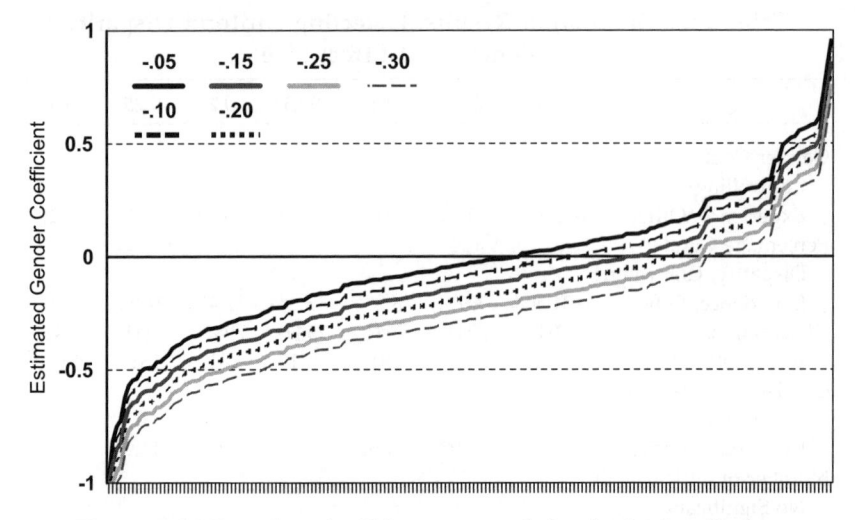

Figure 21.6 Results of a Disaggregated Analysis Applied to Simulated Data Containing Uniform Disparity of Varying Magnitude

publications, the defendant could argue that while there may be problems in a handful of offices, each due to particular circumstances, the practice of decentralized decision making coupled with the statistical evidence convincingly supports a decision to deny class certification.

21.4 CONCLUSION: RECOMMENDATIONS FOR COURTS

This exercise demonstrates that evaluating the nature and character of organization-wide discrimination presents a potentially daunting technical challenge. Further, it implicitly raises a question that is rarely asked regarding statistical evidence used in determining the merits of certifying a class: how much heterogeneity across organizational subunits in the level of disparity between dominant and subordinate groups is sufficient to justify denying class certification?

The technical challenge could be addressed in various ways. A statistical test of interactions between the binary variable for gender and the binary variables for subunits provides a formal test of whether effects are consistent across subunits, an issue we develop fully in a separate paper that also proposes alternative statistical models for measuring heterogeneity in disparities.[106] Again, however, one must be sensitive to the potential impact of statistical power in interpreting the results.[107]

More important, even if one can develop a more reliable statistical method for determining the extent of subunit variation, the legal relevance and broader meaning of those differences remains contested. In the first place, courts must be attentive to the relevant legal and procedural framework. Consideration of this level of factual nuance at the class certification stage of the case is inconsistent with preserving a real boundary between procedural hurdles and merits adjudication. Further, it is clear that even the plaintiffs' burden of proof at trial falls far short of showing consistently equivalent levels of disparity across an entire company.[108] Thus, what variation among subunits might mean in

---

[106] The results of interaction tests for this dataset are reported in the bottom two lines of Tables 21.3 and 21.4. These results test the hypothesis that the regression coefficient for gender (the gender disparity in earnings controlling experience) is the same in every one of the UFS offices. Table 21.3 shows, not surprisingly, that when simulated data are generated with a uniform disparity across offices, the hypothesis that the disparity is the same in every office cannot be rejected (the probability level of .617, and the standard for statistical significance is a probability of less than .05). Table 21.4 shows that for the simulation with continuous heterogeneity the hypothesis of constant disparity still cannot be rejected, (i.e., while the data are generated with a disparity that differs from office to office, that variation across offices is not large enough to generate a statistically significant result). Finally, Table 21.4 shows that when there is radical heterogeneity – no disparity in some offices and a huge disparity in others, the interaction test is indeed statistically significant, rejecting the hypothesis that the gender disparity is the same in every office.

[107] In this example, the interaction test seems reasonably probative of the issues that may be before a court at the liability or remedial stage, since it detects the kind of heterogeneity that is associated with discrimination that is isolated to one part of the organization and is absent elsewhere, and it fails to detect heterogeneity that is associated with discrimination throughout the organization's subunits, but slightly greater in some subunits than in others. However, as with any statistical test, the power of a test for interaction depends on the number of observations and on the relative impact of unmeasured factors. This issue is developed in detail in our other paper.

[108] A pooled analysis clearly suffices to carry the burden for plaintiffs on the merits. See e.g., Teamsters, 431 U.S. at 337. Indeed, a federal district court recently denied summary judgment in a Title VII class case, ruling that aggregated data could be

terms of the legal questions either of Rule 23 commonality, or of a pattern or practice of discrimination, is a critical issue that courts must consider in conjunction with the use of any statistical test in litigation.

Indeed, consideration of this problem raises core questions regarding appropriate class-wide Title VII enforcement. At one extreme, if the *actual* (as opposed to estimated) level of disparity across organizational subunits truly does vary randomly from subunit to subunit, favoring males in some subunits, females in others, and neither group in still others, with no apparent basis in how the organization's policies and practices are designed and implemented, then the statistical basis for certifying a class does not exist. On the other hand, should *any* level of heterogeneity be sufficient to defeat class certification? If a company as a matter of policy establishes a discretionary management regime and fails to ensure equal employment opportunity, and as a result some subunits discriminate just a little and others discriminate a lot, has the company insulated itself from being sued for systematic discrimination?

Put another way, suppose there is a discriminatory mechanism that operates company-wide and creates a uniform level of disparity across subunits, but in addition, there are subunit-specific practices that create additional barriers – and additional disparity – in some units but not others. There is clearly heterogeneity in the organization, yet this is surely a company that practices systematic discrimination of the type that the class action mechanism was meant to address. Further, this kind of individual level variation in harm is akin to the type of problem that Stage II remedial relief is designed to address, suggesting that much of the issue may be best addressed in the context of allocation.[109] At this point, the questions of just how much consistency or variation in

---

sufficient to support a pattern or practice claim. *McReynolds v. Sodexho Marriott Services, Inc.*, 349 F.Supp.2d 1, 15 (D.D.C. 2004).

[109] Typically, these kinds of cases involve post-liability proceedings, either through mini-trials or formula-based distributions, to determine how to calculate and allocate class relief. Even if there is no proven discrimination in certain areas of the company, some individuals in those areas might still be able show harm at the relief phase of the case. It would be unfair to exclude them from the case at the outset under the theory that they are less likely to have been injured because of where they work. If ultimately no injury is shows for those areas or individuals, the defendant will not have to pay their claims. Thus a generous standard for class certification, including all parts of the company subject to a potentially discriminatory policy, regardless of demonstrated consistent impact, would be fair to both sides, and best allocates the risk of error.

CHAPTER 21. UNCONVENTIONAL WEAPONS

the impact of a discriminatory practice is sufficient to establish liability, and the ways that remedies can be most fairly tailored to the areas and individuals who actually suffered harm, remain open.

This hypothetical example represents a real world problem for courts trying to make sense of their responsibilities under Rule 23. Given that today's large corporations frequently span many locations and jurisdictions, the operation of this heterogeneity defense can preclude meaningful class relief. We can expect this issue to continue to confront courts considering class certification motions. To avoid relying on potentially misleading statistical presentations, courts should carefully evaluate the relevance of statistical evidence to class certification issues, consider any such evidence in tandem with other available evidence, and return to the framework of a class-merits distinction.

The simulation above illustrates the limits of relying solely on statistical tests to make determinations about class treatment. Courts should understand how statistical evidence is relevant to the particular questions before them – reserving battles over aggregation to the appropriate phase of the case. In cases where courts are relying on statistical proof of the nature or distribution of workforce disparities to rule on class certification, they are crossing the class-merits divide. Whether a pattern or practice of discrimination exists and whether the policy has an adverse impact, are different questions than whether class-wide evidence will allow an efficient litigation of this issue.

Imagine an alternative scenario – a classic disparate impact problem. Suppose instead of excessive managerial discretion, plaintiffs complained about gender bias in a written test used to differentiate employees for compensation purposes. Even if UFS administered an identical test throughout the company, outcomes would not be uniform. Some women would likely do extremely well on the test, and some men extremely poorly. Varying subunit scores would not show the absence of a uniform policy, nor the absence of discrimination.

Looking at statistical evidence in tandem with other evidence can shed light on how to think about the results. For example, with more complete information about how the company designed and implemented personnel policy, the statistical expert in our UFS case might have had reason to believe that barriers were concentrated in one specific area of the organization, for example, in a specific division where oversight was especially lax and criteria for personnel actions particularly vague. That type of information could guide an appropriate statistical inquiry, at the appropriate point in the litigation.

At the merits phase of litigation, the kind of simulation demonstrated here provides courts with one tool to understand how statistical power may drive the outcomes in the cases they are considering. The analysis above shows that in some circumstances, a disaggregated approach can be guaranteed to support the defendant's litigation position, even when the data upon which it is based comes from a context where members of the protected group face a uniform, consistent, and substantial disadvantage. In *any* organization-wide analysis of group differences on an outcome (whether that outcome is earnings, test scores, performance ratings, promotion rates, or something else), if there is variation within groups that cannot be fully explained my measured factors, disaggregation will necessarily result in variation across subunits in estimates of disparities. The smaller the size of the subunits and the larger the impact of unmeasured factors, the more certain it will be that low statistical power will guarantee that sampling variability – the luck of the draw – results in the appearance of heterogeneity, regardless of whether it in fact exists. In any specific litigation context, whether or not the kind of disaggregated analysis advocated by experts for defendants is at all probative of the issues facing the court can be determined relatively easily by doing the kind of simulation exercise reported here for the hypothetical UPS (which is roughly equivalent to doing a formal analysis of statistical power).

Moreover, undertaking such an exercise forces the parties to the litigation to be clear about the precision of their statistical tests and the kinds of discriminatory patterns their analyses are likely to detect and are likely to miss. In formal terms, it forces them not just to define the null hypothesis, but substantively meaningful alternatives as well. Doing so forces the statistical expert to link her or his analysis more closely to an understanding of the organizational mechanisms presumed to generate (from the plaintiffs' perspective) or minimize (from the defendant's perspective) disparities, at least when the expert has an incentive to devise a more powerful statistical test. These tools can assist the Court in determining what analyses are and are not probative of the issues being decided. They would avoid repeating the error of *the Abram et. al. v. UPS* decision which encourages statistical analyses that have the appearance of scientific rigor but are constructed in a way that guarantees support of one side's litigation position regardless of the facts.

CHAPTER 22

Symposium: Emerging Issues in Class Action Law: Backdoor Federalization

Samuel Issacharoff* and Catherine M. Sharkey**

22.1 INTRODUCTION

Two primary arguments are advanced for the contemporary functional importance of federalist constraints on centralized political power. The first is captured in Justice Brandeis' famous invocation of the states as the laboratories of democracy in which 'a single courageous State' may blaze new paths by trying 'novel social and economic experiments.'[1] The second ties the smaller, decentralized scale of subnational units to a more robust democratic accountability by which 'government is brought closer to the people, and democratic ideals are more fully realized.'[2] Each of these arguments fits well with concerns over the centralization of power inherited from the history of the twentieth century. Federalism, understood in its contemporary role as a vindication of state authority relative to the federal government, stands, as claimed by Judge Easterbrook, as an antidote to the 'central planner,' the figure of mythic economic inefficiencies and staunch

---

* Samuel Issacharoff is Reiss Professor of Constitutional Law, New York University School of Law. He holds a J.D. from Yale Law School.
** Catherine M. Sharkey is an associate professor at New York University School of Law. She holds a J.D. from Yale University Law School.
[1] *New State Ice Co. v. Liebmann*, 285 US 262, 311 (1932) (Brandeis, J., dissenting).
[2] David L. Shapiro, Federalism: A Dialogue 91–92 (1995).

David Sherwyn and Samuel Estreicher (eds), *Employment Class and Collective Actions*, pp. 941–1040.
© 2009, Kluwer Law International BV, Printed in Great Britain.

antidemocratic propensities to totalitarianism.[3] While perhaps these claims saddle the dual sovereignty of federalism with more historic weight than it might bear, the focus on economic heterogeneity and democratic accountability is certainly critical.

This chapter is largely about circumstances in which these two arguments for federalism fail. While Justice Brandeis' aphorism about the states as laboratories of democracy is oft repeated, the tail end of his claim tends to get lost. Brandeis sought to leave open the prospect that 'a single courageous State may, if its citizens choose, serve as a laboratory; and try novel social and economic experiments without risk to the rest of the country.'[4] The question that concerns us is what happens when claims of state sovereignty do pose risks to the rest of the country, when the experiments of democracy within one state's borders have spillover effects that adversely affect citizens of other states.[5] In such circumstances, not only may the benefits of heterogeneity and interstate competition fail, but also the citizens of other states are deprived of the political means of compelling democratic accountability on economic actors shielded by other states' claims of sovereignty.

The novelty of our approach is to think of the battles over federalism as running across two dimensions. The more familiar is the question of which law controls, state or federal. But a second dimension is the battle over which forum should control, state or federal, and which is to be the catalyst for new legal norms. With a two-by-two matrix corresponding to these substantive and procedural dimensions, we aim to underscore aspects of 'horizontal federalism' – namely, policing relations between the states[6] – that have tended to be obscured by the

---

[3] In re Bridgestone/Firestone, Inc., 288 F.3d 1012, 1020 (7th Cir. 2002) (Easterbrook, J.) ('Efficiency is a vital goal of any legal system – but the vision of "efficiency" underlying this class certification is the model of the central planner.').

[4] New State Ice Co., 285 US at 311 (Brandeis, J., dissenting) (emphasis added).

[5] We use the terms 'spillover effects' and 'externalities' interchangeably, though we recognize the different nuances associated with each term. See David G. Post & David R. Johnson, 'Chaos Prevailing on Every Continent': Towards a New Theory of Decentralized Decision-Making in Complex Systems, 73 Chi.-Kent L. Rev. 1055, 1060 n. 12 (1998) ('The notion of a spillover effect is similar to the familiar concept of an "externality." In its most common usage, an "externality" describes a spillover effect that has the additional characteristic that it is not the subject of a market transaction.').

[6] We use the term 'horizontal federalism,' as it has evolved in the literature, to address federalist concerns raised by allocation of authority and relations among

CHAPTER 22. SYMPOSIUM: EMERGING ISSUES IN CLASS ACTION LAW

looming shadow of 'vertical federalism' – namely, the balance of power and division of labor between federal and state sources of authority. By approaching the topic indirectly, focusing primarily on what Richard Fallon terms the 'subconstitutional' domain of preemption and forum selection,[7] we hope to give a broader rendition of the legal response to market pressures toward predictability and uniformity than would emerge from a narrow focus on formal constitutional doctrine.

Our main argument is that the U.S. Supreme Court has, in preemption and forum-allocation cases, attempted to capture the considerable benefits that flow from national regulatory uniformity and to protect an increasingly unified national (and international) commercial market

---

the states. Our concern with state predation on other states is, in some ways, the converse of that raised by Lynn Baker and Ernest Young. See e.g., Lynn A. Baker & Ernest A. Young, Federalism and the Double Standard of Judicial Review, 51 Duke L.J. 75, 111 (2001) (arguing that political safeguards undoubtedly protect the states from some vertical threats, but do nothing to address the horizontal problem of federal 'homogenization' of diverse state policy preferences, which imposes burdens on some states to the benefit of other states); Lynn A. Baker, Should Liberals Fear Federalism?, 70 U. Cin. L. Rev. 433, 434–435 (2002) (arguing that federalism provides 'outlier' or 'minority' states protection from federal homogenization or 'horizontal aggrandizement'). Others have pursued a broader structural understanding of horizontal federalism. See e.g., Scott Fruehwald, The Rehnquist Court and Horizontal Federalism: An Evaluation and a Proposal for Moderate Constitutional Constraints on Horizontal Federalism, 81 Denv. U. L. Rev. 289, 292 (2003) (arguing that 'greater constraints on horizontal federalism should be created in a principled manner based on a neutral reading of the Constitution's structural provisions' – namely, the Due Process, Full Faith and Credit, and Dormant Commerce Clauses); Gillian Metzger, Congress, Interstate Relations, and Article IV, at 3 (November 2, 2005) (unpublished manuscript), available at <www.law.virginia.edu/home2002/pdf/workshops/0506/metzger.pdf> ('Although writing on vertical federalism abounds, the challenges and dilemmas of horizontal federalism are underappreciated in American constitutional scholarship.').

[7] Alternatively, we might characterize the domain of preemption and forum selection as 'second order constitutionalism,' highlighting the role of the U.S. Supreme Court in furthering a certain vision of federal structures through its interpretive decisions that allocate power among institutional actors in these highly technical, fact-specific arenas. On this view, then, preemption and forum-allocation decisions are 'constitutional,' though in a less-obvious manner than, for example, the Eleventh Amendment sovereign immunity cases, which are more-narrowly focused on formal proclamations on the 'first order' interpretations of the Constitution.

from the imposition of externalities by unfriendly state legislation.[8] We highlight the role that such functional principles can play in illuminating the contemporary Court's interpretive method across substantive and procedural areas of the law relating to commercial matters.[9] Rather than standing as an ally of state autonomy against the encroachments of the federal behemoth – the exaggerated but commonplace reading of the Court's highly publicized federalism rulings on the scope of the Eleventh Amendment[10] – the Court appears to

---

[8] While our account focuses on the commercial market in the United States, significant implications can be drawn from the increasing globalization of commercial relations. First, the issues that concern us are at the heart of contemporary debates regarding the formation of new constitutional regimes, as in South Africa, and the development of the European Union. See e.g., S. Afr. Const. 1996 44(2):

> Parliament may intervene, by passing legislation ... with regard to a matter falling within [the following] functional areas ... when it is necessary – (a) to maintain national security; (b) to maintain economic unity; (c) to maintain essential national standards; (d) to establish minimum standards required for the rendering of services; or (e) to prevent unreasonable action taken by a province which is prejudicial to the interests of another province or to the country as a whole. (emphasis added).

Matthias Kumm, Constitutionalizing Subsidiarity in Integrated Markets: The Case of Tobacco Regulation in the European Union, 12 Eur. L.J. 503 (2006). Second, it may well be that, as a functional matter, cross-national competition will replace that of local experimentation and interstate competition – thus significantly reframing, and adding an international dimension to, the regulatory competition and federalism debates in the United States.

[9] We deliberately limit our federalism inquiry to functional accounts of the control of substantive law and the appropriate judicial forum for its enforcement. While a conventional approach in political science or economics, functionalism takes a back seat to legal, doctrinal analysis in federal courts. We leave to one side the debates about the original and textual commitments to different levels of state regulatory independence. Likewise, we make no attempt to intervene in the separation of powers debate surrounding the interplay of domestic political structures – including the Court, Congress, and administrative agencies. Finally, by focusing on federal courts' interpretive methodology, we put to one side political economy stories based upon interest-group politics. By pursuing – somewhat unidimensionally – our functionalist account, we hope to shed new light on this highly ploughed terrain.

[10] A number of critical commentators have argued that the Court's wholehearted embrace of state autonomy in its Eleventh Amendment jurisprudence has had little practical impact on protecting the states from litigation. See e.g., John C. Jeffries, Jr.,

be a willing partner of Congress in providing federal oversight to state interference with the national market.[11]

We can project the Court's work in preemption cases across a spectrum of congressional efforts to exert a federal interest. At one pole are statutes such as the Employee Retirement Income Security Act of 1974 (ERISA)[12] or the Copyright Act,[13] in which field preemption of the substantive law is accompanied by exclusive federal-court jurisdiction. In such cases, the only issue is the boundaries of the field. At the other extreme are Dormant Commerce Clause cases, in which the Court has to define the federal interest in the absence of congressional action. In between are the difficult cases in which the Court assesses Congress' interest in protecting the rational operation of the national market by coordinating state regulation. Products liability cases occupy this middle ground in the federalization process because of the characteristically incomplete manner in which Congress legislates in this area. Typically, Congress acts, in limited product realms, to define standards of liability but leaves to state law the need to provide remedies – an incomplete regulatory regime fraught with the capacity for federal-state conflict.

Within this framework, we address the emergence of partial federalization of commercial areas historically governed by state law. Focusing on the rise of federal preemption of state law, on the expansion of the federal forum through federal question subject matter jurisdiction or the newly minted Class Action Fairness Act of 2005,[14] and on

---

In Praise of the Eleventh Amendment and Section 1983, 84 Va. L. Rev. 47, 49 (1998) ('For all its virtues, Eleventh Amendment scholarship neglects a crucial fact: The Eleventh Amendment almost never matters. More precisely, it matters in ways more indirect and attenuated than is usually acknowledged.'). See generally Henry Paul Monaghan, The Supreme Court, 1995 Term – Comment: The Sovereign Immunity 'Exception,' 110 Harv. L. Rev. 102 (1996).

[11] In addition to courts and Congress, federal regulatory agencies have also been active in the preemption of state law. See Catherine M. Sharkey, Preemption by Preamble: Federal Agencies and the Federalization of Tort Reform, 56 De Paul L. Rev. (forthcoming 2007).

[12] Employee Retirement Income Security Act of 1974 (ERISA), Pub. L. No. 93-406, 88 Stat. 829 (codified in scattered sections of 26 U.S.C. and 29 U.S.C.).

[13] Copyright Act, Pub. L. No. 94-553, 90 Stat. 2541 (1976) (codified as amended at 17 U.S.C.).

[14] Class Action Fairness Act of 2005 (CAFA) (to be codified in scattered sections of 28 U.S.C.).

the constitutional override of matters formally assigned to state law, such as punitive damages, we hope to highlight and explain a quiet federalization of vital areas of law – one far less noticed than the heavily (and perhaps overly) publicized limitations on federal regulation of internal matters of state governance.

Our hope is that by examining contemporary areas of federalization of either the substantive law or the forum we can provide a logic to the less examined, though perhaps more significant, areas in which law has been substantially remolded to meet the demands of the expanded scope of the market. Our account of what we term backdoor federalization, however, is part of a rich historical evolutionary tale. We use the term 'federalization' in the connotation that would ring familiar to the debates of the founding generation, as shorthand for a common national law governing national market activity. We focus on the incompletely realized and under-theorized attempts of federal courts (particularly the Supreme Court) to mediate the tensions between the claimed commitment to the states as sovereign overseers of the quotidian affairs of their citizens and the reality that the lives of citizens are increasingly accountable to broader market commands. Moreover, we identify pressure points where the federal courts may play an especially important role in facilitating transitions to more stable equilibria where the substantive law and forum are aligned.

Our goal in part is to provide another dimension to the federalism debates that embroil constitutional law. When examined as part of the tension between expanding market demands and the original grant of power to the states, the process of federalization, as we term it, extends beyond the narrow reach of state immunity from federal law and reaches more deeply into the domain of preemption, forum allocation, and other manifestations of legal oversight of commerce.

22.2 MATRIX: 'SUBSTANTIVE LAW' BY 'PROCEDURAL FORUM'

We begin with a stylized two-by-two matrix, designed to accentuate our framework of thinking about federalization across two dimensions: substantive law (federal or state) and procedural forum (federal or state). Quadrant IV is the domain of the bulk of private common law – torts and contracts – traditionally within the province of the states; both the substantive state law and the forum align to provide

CHAPTER 22. SYMPOSIUM: EMERGING ISSUES IN CLASS ACTION LAW

command of citizens' primary conduct. This equilibrium is shaken, however, as market conduct expands beyond local command. Specifically, state-imposed rules, such as tort obligations and remedies for their breach, may be orthogonal to the need to coordinate an increasingly national market for goods and services and to police outlier states.

A strong undercurrent of our analysis is that the push toward federal standards and the federal forum flows from the need to coordinate an increasingly national (let alone international) market for goods and services with the inherited presumption of state-level legal oversight. These exigencies galvanize a drive toward federal standards and the federal forum, which can be depicted in our matrix as momentum away from Quadrant IV, toward Quadrant I.

Table 22.1: Drive toward Federal Standards

$		Substantive Law	
		Federal	State
Procedural	Federal	I	II
Forum	State	III	IV

The drive toward Quadrant I – the domain of federal law and forum – is evident in the formal recognition by the Supreme Court of both the broad sweep of federal law (the subject of Part II) and the expansive use of federal jurisdiction to control adjudication of claims (the subject of Part III). National law, presiding over a national market, replaces state law as commander of citizens' primary conduct. And coherence is maintained in the move from Quadrant IV to Quadrant I, where the source of law (federal) is once again aligned with the forum for resolution of the legal dispute (federal).

In many ways, this argument is a familiar one across American constitutional history, reflected in the historic battle between the federalist and antifederalist wings of American political thought. The premise of dual federalism has run up against the demands of a national market time and again. Whether in the initial efforts to secure credit across the fledgling nation,[15] or under the Taft Court's vision of a compelling economic integration,[16] or under the demands of an

---

[15] See *McCulloch v. Maryland*, 17 US (4 Wheat.) 316 (1819).

[16] See e.g., *Lambert v. Yellowley*, 272 US 581, 591–597 (1926) (upholding broad use of commerce power during Prohibition in regulation of physicians prescribing

Internet-driven erasure of state and, increasingly, national lines, efforts to preserve autonomous domains of state regulatory sovereignty repeatedly confront the inexorable logic of the market. Even the contemporary Court, toying with state autonomy at the margins of the Eleventh Amendment, nonetheless retreats to the sweeping nationalism of the New Deal era when California seeks to secede from the federal regulation of marijuana.[17]

22.2.1 Historical Evolution: National Law for a National Market

Quadrant I is inhabited by national legislation, enacted pursuant to Congress' broad Commerce Clause powers, particularly federal regulation with broad preemptive force. Over the last century, the powers of Congress have been greatly expanded, in large part because of a recognition that we live in a world with an increasingly interconnected national commercial market. As markets become more national, the tension arising out of competing sovereign commands threatens private ordering, and the cry for uniformity of regulation becomes more pronounced. Commerce Clause jurisprudence has been animated by a self-conscious desire on the part of the Supreme Court to preserve and protect 'the single, national market still emergent in our own era.'[18]

---

alcohol); see also Robert Post, Federalism in the Taft Court Era: Can It Be 'Revived?', 51 Duke L.J. 1513, 1523–1526 (2002) (describing the effect of World War I's revolutionary expansion of federal power on the Court's approach to federalism).
[17] *Gonzales v. Raich*, 125 S. Ct. 2195, 2198, 2215 (2005).
[18] *United States v. Lopez*, 514 US 549, 568 (1995) (Kennedy, J., concurring):

> The history of the judicial struggle to interpret the Commerce Clause during the transition from the economic system the Founders knew to the single, national market still emergent in our own era counsels great restraint before the Court determines that the Clause is insufficient to support an exercise of national power.

Richard Fallon offers an alternative – though not inconsistent – explanation based on path dependence. See Richard H. Fallon, Jr., The 'Conservative' Paths of the Rehnquist Court's Federalism Decisions, 69 U. Chi. L. Rev. 429, 436 (2002):

> Considerations of path dependence must loom large in any plausible explanation of why the Court has acted with such relative caution in reshaping

CHAPTER 22. SYMPOSIUM: EMERGING ISSUES IN CLASS ACTION LAW

Congress may regulate and protect both the channels of interstate commerce and the instrumentalities, persons, or things in interstate commerce.[19] More controversially, Congress has the power to regulate activities that substantially affect interstate commerce.[20] The main thrust of Commerce Clause jurisprudence – both historically,[21] and

> constitutional doctrines involving Congress's general regulatory powers and its related authority to impose obligations on state and local governments under the Commerce and Spending Clauses.

As numerous commentators have recognized, the same nationalist impulse is equally (if not more) true of the Supreme Court's jurisprudence under the Dormant Commerce Clause, where the Court seeks to protect national markets from discriminatory laws passed by states to impose burdens upon out-of-state goods and shift externalities to neighboring states. See e.g., Shapiro, *supra*, at 74 n. 67 (acknowledging that the Dormant Commerce Clause furthers federalism's values by 'protecting state interests against unfair treatment by other states'); Jenna Bednar & William N. Eskridge, Jr., Steadying the Court's 'Unsteady Path': A Theory of Judicial Enforcement of Federalism, 68 S. Cal. L. Rev. 1447 (1995); Viet D. Dinh, Reassessing the Law of Preemption, 88 Geo. L.J. 2005, 2110 (2000) (characterizing Dormant Commerce Clause jurisprudence as resting upon the 'uniquely federal interest in maintaining national unity and uniformity in interstate economic regulation'); Henry P. Monaghan, Foreword: Constitutional Common Law, 89 Harv. L. Rev. 1, 17 (1975) (asserting that the failure to appreciate the nationalist impulse of the Dormant Commerce Clause cases 'is largely because the sanction of nullity for violation of the free-trade policy is the same as under a Marbury-like invalidation and does not "look like" the affirmative creation of federal regulatory rules').

> In recent years, 'the Court has done more to tighten than to loosen the restrictions that the so-called dormant Commerce Clause imposes on state and local governments.' Fallon, *supra*, at 432. Recently, the Supreme Court reiterated that 'our Constitution "was framed upon the theory that the peoples of the several states must sink or swim together."' *Am. Trucking Ass'n v. Mich. Pub. Serv. Comm'n*, 125 S. Ct. 2419, 2422 (2005) (quoting *Baldwin v. G.A.F. Seelig, Inc.*, 294 US 511, 523 (1935)). A negative command arising from the Commerce Clause prevents states from '"jeopardizing the welfare of the Nation as a whole," by "placing burdens on the flow of commerce across its borders that commerce wholly within those borders would not bear."' *Id.* at 2423 (quoting *Okla. Tax Comm'n v. Jefferson Lines, Inc.*, 514 US 175, 180 (1995)).

[19] *Perez v. United States*, 402 US 146, 150 (1971).
[20] Lopez, 514 US at 558–559.
[21] There is little dispute that the Constitution fundamentally sought to overcome the barriers to economic integration under the Articles of Confederation. Both economic

as embodied in contemporary doctrine – reflects a judicial judgment that Congress should be given broad deference in defining which important matters, like drugs and agriculture, require a uniform nationalist agenda.

We need not be long detained to establish the sweep of the recognized federal interest in national market conduct under current doctrine. The most broad-gauged exposition comes in *Wickard v. Filburn*,[22] a case from the era of the Court's confrontation with the expansive regulatory reach of the New Deal. As we subsequently develop, *Wickard's* broad reading of federal power emerged from the same era as *Erie Railroad Co. v. Tompkins*,[23] the quintessential guarantor of state common law prerogatives. The question posed in *Wickard* was whether the federal Commerce Clause interest in regulating wheat production could reach a farmer's crops grown for private consumption, with no intent to sell that wheat on any market. In upholding the regulation, the Court found that the power to regulate interstate commerce could extend to the protection of the integrity of commercial markets, even from commodities that were not themselves subject to commercial transactions.[24] While *Wickard* could perhaps be characterized as the in extremis version of the Court's retreat from its early attempts to derail the New Deal, the Court has now reaffirmed the broad sweep of *Wickard*, and then some.

---

liberty and innovation under the Articles were thwarted as states often imposed taxes and duties on goods from other states, serving to fragment the economic union of the states and their citizens. The Constitutional Convention was called by the framers to end interstate rivalries under the 'conviction that in order to succeed, the new Union would have to avoid the tendencies toward economic Balkanization that had plagued relations among the Colonies and later among the States under the Articles of Confederation.' *Granholm v. Heald*, 544 US 460, 472 (2005) (quoting *Hughes v. Oklahoma*, 441 US 322, 325–326 (1979)).

[22] 317 US 111 (1942).

[23] 304 US 64 (1938).

[24] The Court upheld the application of the Agricultural Adjustment Act to Filburn, who had exceeded his acreage allotment by roughly twelve acres, even though his wheat was not intended to be sold in the interstate market, never left his farm, and was simply fed to his livestock. Wickard, 317 US at 114. The Court found that, while Filburn's conduct alone might not influence the supply or demand for wheat, the aggregation of all similarly situated people could have an enormous impact. *Id.* at 127–129.

CHAPTER 22. SYMPOSIUM: EMERGING ISSUES IN CLASS ACTION LAW

In *Gonzales v. Raich*,[25] a 2005 medical marijuana case, the issue presented was whether the federal Controlled Substances Act (CSA)[26] could constitutionally be used to prohibit the cultivation and use of marijuana in compliance with California state law.[27] The challenge to the CSA was quite narrow: it asked whether the home cultivation of marijuana that was not intended to be sold and could not be sold, and which was authorized by California's Compassionate Use Act,[28] could nonetheless be subjected to congressional oversight.

Despite its billing as the protector of states' rights, the Court gave almost as expansive an account of federal power under the Commerce Clause as could be imagined. In order to sustain the claimed federal interest, the Court had to find that, as applied, the CSA was a valid exercise of the federal legislative power, notwithstanding the lack of engagement of the home-grown marijuana with any economic markets, intrastate or interstate.[29] A key assumption of the majority's reasoning is that, at least in the case of fungible commodities such as wheat and marijuana, there exists a single, unified economic market. Based on this view of the national market, it was then within the power of Congress to assume authority over all practices that pose a threat to the national market or policies. Thus, the federal power could reach and regulate the entire class of activities – such as production and use of wheat or drugs.

---

[25] 125 S. Ct. 2195 (2005).

[26] Controlled Substances Act (CSA), 21 U.S.C. 801–904 (2000). The main objectives of the CSA were 'to conquer drug abuse and to control legitimate and illegitimate traffic in controlled substances.' *Raich*, 125 S. Ct. at 2203. To effectuate these objectives, the statute provided for a system that allowed drugs to be categorized into five different schedules: Marijuana was categorized by Congress as a Schedule I drug, 'categorized as such because of [its] high potential for abuse, lack of any accepted medical use, and absence of any accepted safety for use in medically supervised treatment.' *Id.* at 2204 (citing 21 U.S.C. 812 (b)(1)).

[27] *Id.* at 2199.

[28] The California Compassionate Use Act of 1996 was designed to ensure that seriously ill residents would be able to obtain marijuana for medical purposes when such treatment was deemed appropriate and recommended by a physician. Cal. Health & Safety Code 11362.5(b)(1)(A) (West 2005).

[29] Justice Stevens wrote for a five-justice majority. Justice Scalia concurred in the judgment on different grounds (the Necessary and Proper Clause), so six Justices voted to reverse the Ninth Circuit Court of Appeals. *Raich*, 125 S. Ct. at 2198, 2215–2216.

Relying heavily upon the 'aggregation principle' of *Wickard*, the Court reasoned:

> In *Wickard*, we had no difficulty concluding that Congress had a rational basis for believing that, when viewed in the aggregate, leaving home-consumed wheat outside the regulatory scheme would have a substantial influence on price and market conditions. Here too, Congress had a rational basis for concluding that leaving home-consumed marijuana outside federal control would similarly affect price and market conditions.[30]

For the majority, once aggregation is accepted, it almost logically follows that Congress must have some power to counteract the individual instances of localized market conduct which, when grouped together, might thwart Congress' overall interstate regulatory purposes.

The *Raich* dissenters inveighed against Congress' clear abrogation of state sovereignty in an area of traditional state concern. Invoking 'one of federalism's chief virtues,' as explicated by Justice Brandeis' dissent in *New State Ice Co. v. Liebmann*,[31] Justice O'Connor extolled 'the role of States as laboratories,' buttressed by 'the States' core police powers [that] have always included the authority to define criminal law and to protect the health, safety, and welfare of their citizens.'[32] The majority's reasoning, the dissent argued, would lead inevitably to a theory of general federal police power – a theory rejected by the framers, as well as by the handful of recent cases limiting the reach of federal power.[33]

---

[30] *Id.* at 2207. Justice Scalia's separate concurrence in *Raich* provides an even broader basis for congressional regulation. Congress's power derives, according to Justice Scalia, not from the Commerce Clause, but instead from the Necessary and Proper Clause:

> The authority to enact laws necessary and proper for the regulation of interstate commerce is not limited to laws governing intrastate activities that substantially affect interstate commerce. Where necessary to make a regulation of interstate commerce effective, Congress may regulate even those intrastate activities that do not themselves substantially affect interstate commerce.

Id. at 2216 (Scalia, J., concurring).
[31] 285 US 262 (1932).
[32] *Raich*, 125 S. Ct. at 2220–2221 (O'Connor, J., dissenting).
[33] See e.g., *id.* at 2236 (Thomas, J., dissenting) ('The Framers understood what the majority does not appear to fully appreciate: There is a danger to concentrating too much, as well as too little, power in the Federal Government.'). The dissent relied unsuccessfully on *United States v. Lopez*, 514 US 549 (1995), for some boundaries on

CHAPTER 22. SYMPOSIUM: EMERGING ISSUES IN CLASS ACTION LAW

What of course unites both the majority and dissent – and what is key for our purposes – is the shared belief in the existence of a unified national economic market for goods and services.[34] Because the existence of a national market was not in dispute, the dissent feared that including intrastate activity not geared to any sales at all would give Congress the power to reach virtually any intrastate conduct it deemed harmful or an obstacle to its regulation. Whatever the strain in *Wickard* in placing domestic wheat production within the scope of interstate commerce, at least there was an interstate wheat market that Congress sought to nurture through its regulation. In *Raich*, by contrast, the question was whether Congress' authority over interstate commerce could override California's experiment with legalizing medically prescribed marijuana that was grown and consumed outside any chain of sale. The Court concluded that Congress' ample powers over commerce could reach any 'fungible commodity for which there is an established, albeit illegal, interstate market.'[35] If anything, *Raich* makes *Wickard* appear tame in restricting its sights to conventional markets whose vitality Congress actually sought to promote.

With *Raich*, the Supreme Court reaffirmed its commitment to broad federal power and a nationalist agenda.[36] *Raich* is the contemporary

---

the Commerce Clause powers, together with *United States v. Morrison*, 529 US 598 (2000), for the authority of the states over matters of traditional state regulation.

Raich, 125 S. Ct. at 2220–2221 (O'Connor, J., dissenting).

[34] Justice Thomas is explicit on this point:

> The majority's rewriting of the Commerce Clause seems to be rooted in the belief that, unless the Commerce Clause covers the entire web of human activity, Congress will be left powerless to regulate the national economy effectively. The interconnectedness of economic activity is not a modern phenomenon unfamiliar to the Framers.

Id. at 2236 (Thomas, J., dissenting) (internal citations omitted).

[35] *Id.* at 2206.

[36] Indeed, for a long unbroken stretch until 1995, 'the Court had not overruled a single case upholding congressional power to regulate commercial activities.' Fallon, *supra*, at 432; see also Bednar & Eskridge, *supra*, at 1451 ('For sixty years (1936 to 1995), the Court deferred to Congress in every Commerce Clause case it decided.'). In *United States v. Lopez*, 514 US 549 (Gun Free Schools Act), and *United States v. Morrison*, 529 US 598 (Violence Against Women Act), the Court struck down federal statutes arguably aimed at intrastate, non-economic activity. We do not engage here the controversial definition of 'economic' for constitutional purposes. For an

embodiment of a broad and sweeping nationalism: In areas affecting commerce in which Congress itself deems it important enough to legislate, the power of the states is displaced notwithstanding how legitimate their own needs and policies may be.[37]

22.2.2 Disequilibrium: Federal Courts' Role in Facilitating Transition

The evolutionary drive toward federalization of law and forum will not, however, always be complete. The trends we analyze in Parts II and III are nonetheless consistent with the general thrust toward an expansive realm of federal law and federal forum. Our stylized two-by-two matrix, then, organizes the subconstitutional doctrines that are our main focus (preemption and forum allocation). In addition to illustrating the main thrust of movement away from Quadrant IV in the direction of Quadrant I, the matrix usefully identifies the fault lines, or pressure points, of this process of federalization. Within Quadrants II and III our focus will be on the ways in which federal courts play a significant role in facilitating transition toward alignment of substantive law and procedural forum – whether fueling the momentum toward Quadrant I, or the return back toward Quadrant IV.

---

insightful criticism of the 'categorization' of federalism as distinctly economic or noneconomic, see Judith Resnik, Categorical Federalism: Jurisdiction, Gender, and the Globe, 111 Yale L.J. 619 (2001).

[37] Consider in this regard Justice Stevens' ringing endorsement of federal power:

> The Supremacy Clause unambiguously provides that if there is any conflict between federal and state law, federal law shall prevail. It is beyond peradventure that federal power over commerce is 'superior to that of the States to provide for the welfare or necessities of their inhabitants,' however legitimate or dire those necessities may be.

Raich, 125 S. Ct. at 2212 (quoting Maryland v. Wirtz, 392 US 183, 196 (1968)). Even more telling, perhaps, is Justice Thomas's dissent last Term in Gonzales v. Oregon, in which he lamented that any attempt to limit congressional power 'in a manner consistent with the principles of federalism and our constitutional structure' was 'water over the dam.' Gonzales v. Oregon, 126 S. Ct. 904, 941 (2006) (Thomas, J., dissenting).

CHAPTER 22. SYMPOSIUM: EMERGING ISSUES IN CLASS ACTION LAW

22.3 PREEMPTION AND FEDERALISM

Over the last half century, the powers of the federal government have expanded through an increasingly muscular reading of the Commerce Clause. With the broadened scope of federal power, the Supreme Court has engaged in the delicate balancing act inherent in a dual-sovereign world, increasingly determining whether state law has been preempted by federal laws, policies, and regulations.[38] Underlying the balance between federal and state power is the critical recognition that 'the extent to which a federal statute displaces (or preempts) state law affects both the substantive legal rules under which we live and the distribution of authority between the states and the federal government.'[39]

Curiously, however, the preemption cases have not played a dominant role in the perennial federalism debates, as if the question of the source of substantive law governing everyday conduct were not the core of the constitutional assignment of authority between the states and the federal government. Instead, these cases have, in large part, ducked under the federalism radar that has commanded such constitutional and scholarly attention over the past quarter century. Perhaps because preemption issues turn largely on the corresponding claims of regulatory oversight, the preemption battles have been largely confined to the realm of statutory interpretation.[40] This view has

---

[38] At least since *McCulloch v. Maryland*, 17 US (4 Wheat.) 316 (1819), and *Gibbons v. Ogden*, 22 US (9 Wheat.) 1 (1824), the Supreme Court has recognized the ability of federal law to trump inconsistent or conflicting state law.

[39] Caleb Nelson, Preemption, 86 Va. L. Rev. 225, 225–226 (2000). That said:

> the powers of the federal government and the powers of the state overlap enormously. Although the Constitution makes a few of the federal government's powers exclusive, the states retain concurrent authority over most of the areas in which the federal government can act.

Id. at 225.

[40] To be sure, the cornerstone of preemption analysis is congressional intent: Did Congress intend to displace state law and, if so, to what extent? See e.g., *Retail Clerks Int'l Ass'n Local 1625 v. Schermerhorn*, 375 US 96, 103 (1963). Generally speaking, the US Supreme Court has recognized that congressional preemption may be either express or implied. A given statute may include a specific provision in which the preemptive effect of the statute is delineated, giving rise to express preemption. Implied preemption is broken down further into two categories: 'field' preemption

prompted Michael Greve (and others) to pronounce that preemption cases are not about federalism at all.[41] In a similar vein, Richard Fallon has challenged commentators to 'link[] the Supreme Court's preemption cases to its federalism agenda.'[42] Scholars who attempt to view

---

and 'conflict' or 'obstacle' preemption. Field preemption exists when the congressional statute is written in such a way that it provides no room for the operation of state law on the subject. See e.g., *Rice v. Santa Fe Elevator Corp.*, 331 US 218, 230 (1947). Conflict preemption is a narrower doctrine, recognizing state law to be preempted when it directly conflicts with existing federal law, or when state regulations interfere with or frustrate the implementation of congressional objectives. See, e.g., *Fla. Lime & Avocado Growers, Inc. v. Paul*, 373 US 132, 142–143 (1963).

[41] Michael S. Greve, Federalism's Frontier, 7 Tex. Rev. L. & Pol. 93, 116–117 (2002). Justice Scalia has expressed 'incredulity' about invocations of federalism in preemption cases. See e.g., *AT&T Corp. v. Iowa Utils. Bd.*, 525 US 366, 379 n. 6 (1999) (terming the invocation of 'States' rights' by Justices Breyer and Thomas, in dissent, 'peculiar' given that, even under their view, federal courts may bring to heel state commissions that are not regulating according to federal policy).

[42] Fallon, *supra*, at 462; see also Thomas W. Merrill, The Making of the Second Rehnquist Court: A Preliminary Analysis, 47 St. Louis U. L.J. 569, 571 (2003) (noting that many sympathetic federalist readings of the Rehnquist Court decisions 'cannot account for the continued willingness of the Court to find state laws preempted by federal regulation'). The puzzle is that the 'Federalism Five' (former Chief Justice Rehnquist, former Justice O'Connor, and Justices Scalia, Kennedy, and Thomas) have been consistently pro-preemption, which is seemingly at odds with their respective disposition toward states rights, at least in the Eleventh Amendment and Commerce Clause areas. See Fallon, *supra*, at 471–472 (noting that the 'pro-federalism justices' found federal preemption in every one of the Court's seven preemption cases during the 1999 and 2000 Terms); Daniel J. Meltzer, The Supreme Court's Judicial Passivity, 2002 Sup. Ct. Rev. 343, 369-370:

> Of eight non-unanimous preemption decisions in the 1999, 2000, and 2001 Terms, Justice Scalia voted to preempt in all eight, the [former] Chief Justice and Justices O'Connor and Kennedy in seven each, and Justice Thomas in six.... Justices Souter, Ginsburg, and Breyer each voted to preempt only twice and Justice Stevens never voted to preempt.

By contrast, in the most comprehensive empirical study of voting lineups in preemption cases – analyzing 105 cases decided by the Rehnquist Court – Michael Greve and Jonathan Klick conclude that 'in contrast to federalism law, we find no clear decisional trend in preemption law. Moreover, we find no firm voting blocs and no swing vote.' Michael S. Greve & Jonathan Klick, Preemption in the Rehnquist Court: A Preliminary Empirical Assessment, 14 Sup. Ct. Econ. Rev. 43, 47 (2006).

CHAPTER 22. SYMPOSIUM: EMERGING ISSUES IN CLASS ACTION LAW

preemption doctrine as somehow providing an important account of the difficulties of the dual-sovereign premises of American constitutionalism tend to be dismissed either with cynicism or derision. The legal realist (or cynic) sees an ideological crusade, waged most recently in the name of substantive conservatism.[43] The traditional defender

---

We may nonetheless make some general observations about the voting patterns of individual Justices. Justice Stevens is the standard-bearer for voting against preemption (consistent with Fallon and Meltzer's more limited samples). Justice Souter has likewise been adamant in the use of a presumption against preemption as a means of protecting the states' traditional regulatory domain. See e.g., *Engine Mfrs. Ass'n v. S. Coast Air Quality Mgmt. Dist.*, 541 US 246, 259 (2004) (Souter, J., dissenting). At the other extreme, Justice Scalia will more readily find for preemption, perhaps because of his 'plain meaning' approach to interpretation and concomitant dislike of 'artificial' presumptions. See e.g., *Cipollone v. Liggett Group, Inc.*, 505 US 504, 548 (1992) (Scalia, J., concurring in part and dissenting in part) (finding all claims preempted and arguing against applying a 'niggardly rule of construction' in what Justice Scalia considered a standard case of statutory construction). Justice Scalia, moreover, has a more nationalist – or perhaps federalist, as opposed to antifederalist – orientation than Justice Thomas, who has in significant cases sided with Justices Stevens or Souter. See e.g., *Geier v. Am. Honda Motor Corp.* 529 US 861, 886 (2000) (Stevens, J., dissenting, joined by Souter, Thomas, and Ginsburg, J.J.); *CSX Transp., Inc. v. Easterwood*, 507 US 658, 679 (1993) (Thomas, J., concurring in part and dissenting in part, joined by Souter, J.) (arguing that none of respondent's claims was preempted and noting that 'respect for the presumptive sanctity of state law should be no less when federal pre-emption occurs by administrative fiat rather than by congressional edict'); see also Antonin Scalia, The Two Faces of Federalism, 6 Harv. J.L. & Pub. Pol'y 19 (1982). Justice Kennedy has likewise departed company from the 'Federalism Five' in several cases, most notably joining Justice Blackmun's dissent in Cipollone, 505 US at 531 (Blackmun J., concurring in part, concurring in the judgment in part, and dissenting in part, joined by Kennedy and Souter, J.J.) (finding none of the claims preempted). Finally, Justice Breyer, consistent with his pragmatic or functionalist approach, often finds that federal statutes preempt state tort law. In addition to his majority decision in Geier – which stands as a testament to the broad scope of conflict preemption – Justice Breyer penned separate concurrences in *Medtronic, Inc. v. Lohr*, 518 US 470, 503 (1996) (Breyer, J., concurring), and *Bates v. Dow Agrosciences*, LLC, 544 US 431, 454 (2005) (Breyer, J., concurring), in which he expressed a willingness to give administrative agencies wide latitude to determine for themselves the preemptive scope of statutes within their purview.

[43] See e.g., Fallon, *supra*, at 474 ('There are a number of doctrinal areas in which the Court is more substantively conservative than it is pro-federalism.'); *id.* at 471 ('Because federal preemption eliminates state regulatory burdens, preemption

957

of federalism (or naysayer) augurs the death of federalism as we know it: 'The whole point of preemption is generally to force national uniformity on a particular issue, stifling state-by-state diversity and experimentation.'[44]

---

rulings have a tendency – welcome to substantive conservatives – to minimize the regulatory requirements to which businesses are subject.'); see also Ruth Colker & Kevin M. Scott, Dissing States?: Invalidation of State Action During the Rehnquist Era, 88 Va. L. Rev. 1301, 1343–1345 (2002) (suggesting division falls along whether underlying state action is 'liberal' or 'conservative'); Frank B. Cross & Emerson H. Tiller, The Three Faces of Federalism: An Empirical Assessment of Supreme Court Federalism Jurisprudence, 73 S. Cal. L. Rev. 741, 756, 767–768 (2000) (concluding, on the basis of a broad empirical study of Supreme Court voting patterns in federalism cases, that the political ideologies of justices play a significant role in explaining outcomes); Jonathan R. Macey, Federal Deference to Local Regulators and the Economic Theory of Regulation: Toward a Public-Choice Explanation of Federalism, 76 Va. L. Rev. 265, 265 (1990) ('Conservatives and liberals alike extol the virtues of state autonomy whenever deference to the states happens to serve their political needs at a particular moment.'); Edward L. Rubin & Malcolm Feeley, Federalism: Some Notes on a National Neurosis, 41 UCLA L. Rev. 903, 948 (1994) ('Claims of federalism are often nothing more than strategies to advance substantive positions.'); David B. Spence & Paula Murray, The Law, Economics, and Politics of Federal Preemption Jurisprudence: A Quantitative Analysis, 87 Cal. L. Rev. 1125, 1194 (1999) (demonstrating a strong trend toward preemption in a statistical analysis of lower federal-court opinions, which 'highlights the irony of the status quo, in which modern preemption jurisprudence, administered by a largely Republican federal judiciary and motivated in part by conservative policy goals and a conservative (Coasean) philosophy of regulation, has facilitated a triumph of interest group politics').

[44] Ernest A. Young, The Rehnquist Court's Two Federalisms, 83 Tex. L. Rev. 1, 130 (2004); see also id. at 131 ('Doctrines limiting federal preemption of state law thus go straight to the heart of the reasons why we care about federalism in the first place.'); Calvin Massey, Federalism and the Rehnquist Court, 53 Hastings L.J. 431, 508 (2002) ('The failure of the Court to apply preemption doctrine sparingly, and with real attention both to Congress's intent and the values of federalism, will in the long run prove disastrous to ... the very real values ... inherent in federalism.').

In an interesting variant of this argument, Roderick Hills would apply a presumption against preemption not only as a useful means of protecting state autonomy, but, more importantly, as a means of encouraging robust debate in the federal legislative process. Roderick M. Hills, Jr., Against Preemption: How Federalism Can Improve the National Legislative Process 2, 15–30 (U. Mich. Law, Pub. Law & Legal Theory Research Paper No. 27, 2003), available at <http://ssrn.com/abstract=412000>.

CHAPTER 22. SYMPOSIUM: EMERGING ISSUES IN CLASS ACTION LAW

Here, we seek to return to a centuries-old concern about the tension between state-based regulation and the commands of a national market. Contrary to the dismissive assertion that the preemption cases are simply a political battleground in the struggle between an overweening federal power and a beleaguered state authority, we advance instead a functionalist account, focusing on interests in promoting national uniformity and protecting against spillover effects.[45] Our aim is not to convince that functional concerns should displace statutory interpretation as a matter of doctrinal development.[46] Instead we seek to provide a positive, analytic framework for understanding the Rehnquist Court's decisions as consistent with a momentum toward

---

[45] We do not claim originality in unearthing these criteria. See e.g., Gary Schwartz, Considering the Proper Federal Role in American Tort Law, 38 Ariz. L. Rev. 917, 922 (1996) [hereinafter Schwartz, American Tort Law] ('The most obvious justifications for federal law that supersedes state law is that state law produces effects that are felt beyond the territorial limits of the states themselves or that there is some significant need for national uniformity in the content of legal rules.'). At the same time, we attempt to link up these considerations – more accentuated in the torts and regulation literature – to the broader federalism debate. Our approach is, in this sense, the mirror image of that adopted by Alan Schwartz. Alan Schwartz, Statutory Interpretation, Capture, and Tort Law: The Regulatory Compliance Defense, 2 Am. L. & Econ. Rev. 1, 2 (2000) [hereinafter Schwartz, Statutory Interpretation] ('The appropriate preemptive reach of national safety laws implicates important issues of statutory interpretation and federalism. Prior studies of what is called the "regulatory compliance defense" slight these broader issues because they take a tort perspective.').

[46] That said, the functionalist approach is not entirely anathema to the way that the Court has self-consciously approached preemption cases. See e.g., Medtronic, 518 US at 486:

> Congress' intent... primarily is discerned from the language of the pre-emption statute and the 'statutory framework' surrounding it. Also relevant, however, is the 'structure and purpose of the statute as a whole,' as revealed not only in the text, but through the reviewing court's reasoned understanding of the way in which Congress intended the statute and its surrounding regulatory scheme to affect business, consumers, and the law.

(internal citations omitted). But see Bates, 544 US at 459 (Thomas, J., concurring) (agreeing with the majority that preemption analysis should not amount to a 'freewheeling judicial inquiry' into the tensions between state and federal objectives, but instead should attempt to discern the original meaning of the preemption provision enacted by Congress).

federalization over the long term.[47] More specifically, we seek to explain the drive toward federalization in numerous areas of the law with reference to two animating principles:

(1) National market exigencies demand uniformity of treatment across the United States in interpreting federal regulations.
(2) States can neither export costs onto their neighbors nor compromise the ability of other states to have a reasonable set of regulations.[48]

The first principle situates federalization within an account of coordination problems in which there is no individual strategy by which a sole actor can achieve socially optimal results. The second principle is a market application of the pollution problem in which individual actors face incentives to engage in harmful behavior because the benefits are localized to them (as with economic gains from coal-burning power plants) while the burdens are externalized to downstream communities.[49]

---

[47] Our interest, in other words, centers on federalism as a standard of policy more than as a formal constitutional doctrine.

[48] These two principles – uniformity of regulation and protection from spillover effects – are intertwined concepts in the sense that one of the primary means of preventing states from externalizing costs of regulation is via implementation of a national regime. See generally Richard Briffault, Taking Home Rule Seriously: The Case of Campaign Finance Reform, 37 Proc. Acad. Pol. Sci. 35, 45 (1989) (arguing in the context of state campaign-finance reform that

> the law of preemption should be viewed as an attempt to reconcile the deep-seated tension between the local diversity that home rule creates and the need, in certain areas, for statewide uniformity. The argument for uniformity ... is strongest when a local law will have considerable effects outside the local boundaries.

[49] The general theoretical framework for the imposition of costs on third parties is found in A.C. Pigou, The Economics of Welfare 134 (Transaction Publishers 2002) (1952), and Charles M. Tiebout, A Pure Theory of Local Expenditures, 64 J. Pol. Econ. 416 (1956). For applications, see Richard L. Revesz, Rehabilitating Interstate Competition: Rethinking the 'Race-to-the-Bottom' Rationale for Federal Environmental Regulation, 67 N.Y.U. L. Rev. 1210, 1222 (1992) ('The presence of interstate externalities is a powerful reason for intervention at the federal level: because some of the benefits of a state's pollution control policies accrue to downwind states, states have an incentive to underregulate.'); Bruce L. Hay, Conflicts of Law and State

CHAPTER 22. SYMPOSIUM: EMERGING ISSUES IN CLASS ACTION LAW

We distinguish two types of preemption, 'vertical' and 'horizontal.' Vertical preemption appears as the more intrusive assertion of a federal interest that, in the extreme, clears the field from all state participation, an analog to the negative Commerce Clause powers that remove all state actors from an area entrusted to federal stewardship. These cases do appear as restrictions on the powers of the states – and rightly so. Perhaps the strongest case for national uniformity is found along the vertical dimension of federalism, mediating the role between the national and state governments in dealing with foreign relations. When what is at stake is a national, integrated scheme for employee benefits, labor law, carrier liability, or arbitration, for example, the vertical dimension to the federalism interest points to the central role of national power in solving the autarchic impulses that doomed the Articles of Confederation and prompted the creation of the modern federal state.

But the preemption cases that interest us the most are the horizontal preemption cases in which the assertion of a federal interest emerges as a necessary default to prevent states from imposing externalities on each other or to overcome the inability to rationalize coordinated national standards for goods and services. Congress frequently regulates activities because state regulation (or lack of regulation) of

---

Competition in the Product Liability System, 80 Geo. L.J. 617, 617 (1992) ('When states can pass laws whose costs are borne by outsiders, self-interested behavior by each makes all worse off.'); Vicki Been, 'Exit' as a Constraint on Land Use Exactions: Rethinking the Unconstitutional Conditions Doctrine, 91 Colum. L. Rev. 473, 509 (1991) (positing the need for coordinated federal regulation 'to avoid underregulation').

'Preemption,' in other words, 'is a way of arresting [states'] perennial quest for a free lunch.' Michael S. Greve, Subprime, but not Half-Bad, AEI Federalist Outlook, September-October 2003, available at <www.aei.org/publications/pubID.19271/pub_detail.asp>. Greve explicates the 'free lunch' metaphor as follows:

> So long as the costs of regulation accrue principally within each regulating state, states should generally be free to do as they please. Overregulated citizens and businesses tend to leave, and that threat will at some point discipline the politicians setting the rules. In contrast, when states impose the costs of their regulatory experiments on citizens in other states, the folks who foot the bill can neither run away nor vote the bums out of office. For that reason, state politicians are extremely creative in exporting the costs of their schemes.

Id.

those activities imposes external costs on neighboring states. Building on this insight, Roderick Hills has noted, 'The whole point of the federal scheme is to suppress state creativity, which might consist only in creatively gaining benefits for their own citizens at the expense of nonresidents.'[50] As Justice Brandeis understood, experimentation – a chief virtue of federalism – may, nonetheless, have nefarious spillover effects upon 'the rest of the country.'[51] The same concession is made by

---

[50] Hills, *supra*, at 3–4. Hills takes this insight in a different direction from ours. His main focus is the way in which state legislation can set the federal lawmaking agenda. He argues for a 'clear statement' rule presumption against preemption on the ground that this will enhance the democratic accountability of Congress. In short, Hills contends that nonfederal politicians have an incentive to externalize the costs of regulatory initiatives on out-of-state interests. This will lead business groups, who have a strong combined interest in uniformity, to lobby Congress for preemptive legislation. Public interest groups will then oppose such legislation, leading to a full debate in the general population. See generally *id*.

Hills challenges Alan Schwartz's contention that courts should adopt, as a default construction of federal regulatory statutes, the view that Congress intended to exculpate from liability firms that comply with regulatory standards, on the ground that it would be easier for Congress to correct such a construction if it is not what was intended. See Schwartz, Statutory Interpretation, *supra*.

[51] *New State Ice Co. v. Liebmann*, 285 US 262, 311 (1932) (Brandeis, J., dissenting). While state experimentation is, in theory, an excellent idea – because it facilitates gradualism, promotes institutional learning, and addresses localized needs and constituencies – in practice:

> such experimentation carries political risks, which are principally from the fact that the governmental experimenters, and the interest groups that hang around them, have huge stakes in exploiting the test population of citizens. Legislative experimentation must therefore be constrained.... The point of [our] constitutional arrangement is to limit what government may do to citizens in the way of experimentation;... to guard against the risk of factious, 'partial' legislation, or what we now call rent seeking.

Michael S. Greve, Laboratories of Democracy: Anatomy of a Metaphor, AEI Federalist Outlook, May 2001, available at <www.aei.org/publications/pubid.12743/pub_detail.asp>. Here, we invoke David Shapiro's argument for a strong national authority, based in part on Madisonian political theory: 'The existence of [an extended republic] is bound to reduce the power of factions seeking government action in order to advance their own interest rather than the broader public good.' Shapiro, *supra*, at 45. While interest groups may be able to capture authorities at the state level where the externalities from state action will be felt beyond the state's

CHAPTER 22. SYMPOSIUM: EMERGING ISSUES IN CLASS ACTION LAW

even the most ardent defendants of the corresponding federalist virtue of interstate regulatory competition in contemporary debates, for example, in corporate and environmental law.[52] By spillover effects, we simply mean state law that, by its operation, shifts costs and favors its own citizens while disproportionately affecting out-of-state interests, or, as the economists would have it, imposes externalities on others. As David Shapiro has noted, state action can create both positive and negative externalities. A negative externality 'arises when action in one state causes disproportionate harm in other states. A positive externality arises when significant benefits from costly action in one state accrue in other states.'[53]

Interstate externality problems associated with diverse state regulations may be solved through interstate compacts or more informal arrangements, or, alternatively, through the promulgation and enactment of codes of uniform laws.[54] Among uniformity's signature advantages:

> Uniform minimum standards may raise the overall standard of ... protection and foreclose the possibility of a race to the bottom while uniform maximum standards may allow the private sector to operate within a predictable and stable environment.[55]

---

boundaries, the range and scope of parties and interests at the federal level will counteract such factious ambition. *Id.*; see also The Federalist No. 10 (James Madison).

[52] See e.g., Roberta Romano, Is Regulatory Competition a Problem or Irrelevant for Corporate Governance?, 21 Oxford Rev. of Econ. Pol'y 212, 226 (2005) ('No participants in that debate [on the theory of charter competition in corporate law] would contend that the federal government has no role in preventing negative externalities from jurisdictional spillovers.'); Richard L. Revesz, Federalism and Interstate Environmental Externalities, 144 U. Pa. L. Rev. 2341, 2414-2415 (1996) (concluding that federal regulation may be necessary to overcome externalities, especially for large-scale and complex environmental problems in which Coasean bargaining is unlikely because uncertainty about pollution's geographic impact bars transactions and because, depending on the source of pollution, the range of affected states will vary).

[53] Shapiro, *supra.* at 44 n. 109.

[54] See *id.* at 132 (recognizing that national uniformity may not always be the preferred solution when regional cooperation is possible); see also Nim Razook, Uniform Private Laws, National Private Laws, National Conference of Commissioners for State Laws Signaling, and Federal Preemption, 38 Am. Bus. L.J. 41, 53–56 (2000).

[55] Paul S. Weiland, Federal and State Preemption of Environmental Law: A Critical Analysis, 24 Harv. Envtl. L. Rev. 237, 276 (2000).

In the absence of 'cooperative' solutions, a solution to solving externality problems is congressional – or judicial – preemption of state laws in favor of a single federal regime.

In the next parts, we assay to give a flavor of how a hidden functional logic may emerge from what Caleb Nelson has called the preemption jurisprudence 'muddle.'[56] By focusing on preemption cases, we inevitably elevate the importance of the layers of subconstitutional decisions, echoing Justice Breyer's dissent in *Egelhoff v. Egelhoff*:[57]

> The true test of federalist principle may lie, not in the occasional effort to trim Congress' commerce power at the edges ... or to protect a state treasury from a private damage action ... but rather in those many statutory cases where courts interpret the mass of technical detail that is the ordinary diet of the law.[58]

We examine a range of preemption cases decided during the Rehnquist Court to show how the Court has read the claims of congressional authority broadly and has correspondingly narrowed the scope for state conduct.[59] While our sample is necessarily partial and cannot account for every data point in which state and federal interests collide, the overall trend is sufficiently compelling to mute the overblown claims of antipathy to regulation. At the outset, moreover, it is important to dampen the rush to political explanations, which may all too readily flow from an overly cabined examination of preemption solely from the vantage point of decided case law.

---

[56] Nelson, *supra*, at 232 ('Most commentators who write about preemption agree on at least one thing: Modern preemption jurisprudence is a muddle.').

[57] 532 US 141, 153 (2001) (Breyer, J., dissenting).

[58] *Id.* at 160–161 (Breyer, J., dissenting) (emphasis added) (citations omitted).

[59] We derived our sample set of thirty-six cases from the universe of cases analyzed by Michael Greve and Jonathan Klick. See Greve & Klick, *supra*. Our sample consists of the thirty-two cases Greve and Klick coded as cases involving the preemption of state tort suits by federal laws and regulations. To these we added *Bates v. Dow Agrosciences*, LLC, 544 US 431 (2005) (which post-dates the Greve and Klick analysis), *United States v. Locke*, 529 US 89 (2000) (which deals with design standards for oil tankers in the foreign-affairs context), and two cases dealing with a variety of state-law regulations likely to give rise to state-law tort suits (but nonetheless not coded as tort by Greve and Klick): *Lorillard Tobacco Co. v. Reilly*, 533 US 525 (2001), and *Gade v. National Solid Wastes Management Ass'n*, 505 US 88 (1992).

CHAPTER 22. SYMPOSIUM: EMERGING ISSUES IN CLASS ACTION LAW

22.3.1 The Systemic Effects of Preemption

When preemption is granted, the effect is to deny a state-law claim either because of its definition of liability or the expansiveness of its remedy. From that, one can draw the conclusion that preemption is simply a tool to disable regulation and give potential tortfeasors a wider berth in which to act. However, it is important to note the cases that do not come into the system. An expansive reading of the federal interest in regulating the national market preempts not only the regulations of states that would impose higher regulatory burdens on interstate actors, but also those that would impose lower burdens as well. In the latter case, however, there will be no trail of litigation because a plaintiff would sue directly on the federal standard and not on the more lax state requirements.[60] The effect would be just as preemptive of state prerogatives, only it would not yield an opinion on preemption. At most there could be a challenge that the federal regulation was not within the scope of Congress' authority under the Commerce Clause, likely a losing proposition after *Raich*.

The systemic bias would result if the effect of preemption was to stifle all state regulation in favor of federal standards that were invariably below that of all the states. In other words, if Occupational Safety and Health Act of 1970 (OSHA)[61] standards were systematically less protective than all nonfederal state safety and health workplace rules, then preemption would have a clear systemic bias.[62] But if the states

---

[60] Because most of the relevant federal statutes do not include an express or implied private right of action, the typical fact pattern involves a plaintiff who relies upon a breach of a federal regulation or statute to make out a prima facie state cause of action. See Restatement (Third) of Torts: Products Liability 4 (1997) ('[A] product's noncompliance with an applicable product safety statute...renders the product defective.'); Restatement (Third) of Torts: Liability for Physical Harm 14 reporter's note cmt. a (Proposed Final Draft 2005) ('The violation of federal statutes and regulations is commonly given negligence per se effect in state tort proceedings.'). Courts differ, however, on the question whether, absent a federal right of action, state tort law may provide an enforcement mechanism for the violation of federal standards. See Sharkey, *supra*. The Court, moreover, has recently shied away from inferring federal implied rights of action. See *id.*

[61] Occupational Safety and Health Act of 1970 (OSHA), 29 U.S.C. 651–678 (2000).

[62] Cf. Spence & Murray, *supra*, at 1160–1161 (noting, in statistical analysis of lower federal-court preemption decisions, a systematic bias toward preemption, but

align across a spectrum of more and less exacting regulations, and if the federal regulations fall somewhere within that spectrum, then the effect of the assertion of a dormant federal interest will be to raise the baseline in some states and lower it in others.[63] However, only cases in which the federal standard is below the most exacting state standard will appear as a preemption challenge in court, leading to the misimpression that federal regulation is invariably a shield and never a sword.[64]

---

explaining it in terms of the propensity for public-sector actors to pursue 'losing' preemption cases for symbolic or political value).

[63] See e.g., Alison D. Morantz, Has Regulatory Devolution Injured American Workers? A Comparison of State and Federal Enforcement of Construction Safety Regulations 4 (Stanford Law Sch. John M. Olin Program in Law & Econ., Working Paper No. 308, January 2007), available at <http://ssrn.com/abstract=755026>, exploring

> the effects of regulatory devolution in the occupational-safety arena by exploiting a unique historical anomaly whereby some state governments have assumed independent responsibility for protective labor regulations otherwise enforced by the Occupational Safety and Health Administration.

[64] Our argument here assumes a heterogeneity of state regulatory responses. Oddly, most of the academic literature assumes races to the bottom in fields like environmental regulation and posits that only federal regulation can rescue the states from their own ineptitude. We join with Richard Revesz's sharp criticisms of that literature. Richard L. Revesz, Federalism and Environmental Regulation: A Public Choice Analysis, 115 Harv. L. Rev. 553, 555–557 (2001) (arguing that the common conception that

> public choice pathologies cause environmental interests to be systematically underrepresented at the state level relative to business interests...[and] that states would 'race to the bottom' by offering industrial sources excessively lax standards is both fundamentally flawed and empirically unsubstantiated); see also Richard L. Revesz, The Race to the Bottom and Federal Environmental Regulation: A Response to Critics, 82 Minn. L. Rev. 535 (1997) [hereinafter Revesz, The Race to the Bottom]; Revesz, supra, at 1233–1244.

On the other hand, much of the academic literature on preemption starts from a diametrically counterposed assumption. In this literature, the commentary assumes a world in which states are no longer engaged in a race to the bottom to attract business investment, but are instead engaged in an equally headlong race to the top of regulatory zeal. Under this view, states are eagerly trying to protect consumer welfare, and preemption emerges as a threat to responsible regulation, scaling back to invariably lower federal standards. See e.g., Fallon, supra, at 471 ('Because

CHAPTER 22. SYMPOSIUM: EMERGING ISSUES IN CLASS ACTION LAW

22.3.2 Federal Regulatory Regimes

22.3.2.1 Vertical Preemption

The quintessential case for vertical uniformity arises in the international context, where the power of the federal government largely occupies the entirety of the field at the expense of any claimed state autonomy. The cases defining field preemption offer the most direct, and readily comprehensible, account of the conflict between federal and state power over the regulation of an entire area of law. Typically these cases turn on an interpretation of the extent of congressional action to determine how completely Congress sought to clear the terrain of impeding state intervention.

Consider, for example, the Ports and Waterways Safety Act (PWSA),[65] which establishes standards for the design and maintenance of ships, the reporting of accidents, and the condition of ships that vessels must meet before entering a U.S. port. The state of Washington enacted its own set of regulations, providing a number of standards that vessels were required to meet in order to enter the state's waters.[66] In *United States v. Locke*,[67] the Court unanimously determined that these state-imposed requirements were preempted by the PWSA.[68]

---

federal preemption eliminates state regulatory burdens, preemption rulings have a tendency – welcome to substantive conservatives – to minimize the regulatory requirements to which businesses are subject.'); S. Candace Hoke, Preemption Pathologies and Civic Republican Values, 71 B.U. L. Rev. 685, 691–692 (1991):

> An ever-larger number of suits are filed with the express objective of invalidating state or local law on a given subject. Business and industry groups have spurred this trend when they have found state regulatory schemes more burdensome, or their enforcement more aggressive, than pertinent federal legislation.

In our view, neither the 'race-to-the-bottom' nor the 'race-to-the-top' account comports with the actual complex world of regulation.

[65] Ports and Waterways Safety Act (PWSA), 33 U.S.C. 1221–1232a (2000).

[66] These requirements included English language proficiency for all crew members, imposition of certain training standards, and accident and navigation watch reporting.

[67] 529 US 89 (2000).

[68] More precisely, the Court held that at least four of the requirements were preempted, and remanded to determine whether any other requirements were also preempted. *Id.* at 112–116.

967

Highlighting the importance of the national interest at stake with respect to regulation of ports and waterways, the Court explained that Washington had enacted 'legislation in an area where the federal interest has been manifest since the beginning of the Republic and is now well established.'[69] Also, the Court explained:

> The state laws now in question bear upon national and international maritime commerce, and in this area there is no beginning assumption that concurrent regulation by the State is a valid exercise of its police power. Rather, we must ask whether the local laws in question are consistent with the federal statutory structure, which has as one of its objectives a uniformity of regulation for maritime commerce.[70]

In passing the federal law, Congress had made clear a desire to allow those tankers that conformed to the PWSA to enter all U.S. ports, instead of having to meet the vagaries of many different state regulations:

> The Supremacy Clause dictates that the federal judgment that a vessel is safe to navigate United States waters prevail over the contrary state judgment. Enforcement of the state requirements would at least frustrate what seems to us to be the evident congressional intention to establish a uniform federal regime controlling the design of oil tankers.[71]

In other words, the federal government had set maximum standards; the states could not supplement them because it would impede the certainty and uniformity that the federal government obviously

---

[69] *Id.* at 99.

[70] *Id.* at 108.

[71] *Id.* at 111 (internal quotation and citation omitted). In short, the scheme envisioned by Washington state represented the very type of state-imposed barriers that the Constitution and the Commerce Clause were designed to prevent. Moreover, the Court made clear that only state rules that impose inconsequential externalities upon ships, operating in a national and international free-trade market, would be allowed to stand under the uniform regime established by the federal government. See *id.* at 112:

> Local rules not pre-empted under ... the PWSA ... do not affect vessel operations outside the jurisdiction, do not require adjustment of systemic aspects of the vessel, and do not impose a substantial burden on the vessel's operation within the local jurisdiction itself.

believed necessary to promote free commercial trade in an area in which federal authority is necessarily exclusive.[72]

Uniformity and subordination of the ability of the states to act is likewise a governing principle in regulating airline-carrier liability. The Warsaw Convention,[73] which limits airline-passenger claims for personal injury damages, is premised upon the recognition (by the nations that ratified the Convention) of the advantage of regulating carrier liability in a uniform manner.[74] In *El Al Israel Airlines, Ltd. v. Tsui Yuan Tseng*,[75] the Court emphasized that allowing state-law claims to be asserted against an airline would undermine this interest in uniformity that the Convention was designed to foster:

> Carriers might be exposed to unlimited liability under diverse legal regimes, but would be prevented, under the treaty, from contracting out of such liability. Passengers injured physically in an emergency landing might be subject to the liability caps of the Convention, while those merely

---

[72] As Locke suggests, the Court has forcefully protected the field of international relations from burdensome state legislation. See also *Am. Ins. Ass'n v. Garamendi*, 539 US 396 (2003) (finding that California's Holocaust Victims Insurance Reporting Act would interfere with the president's ability to speak with one voice for the nation and was thus preempted by certain executive agreements with Germany and Austria); *Crosby v. Nat'l Foreign Trade Council*, 530 US 363, 379–380 (2000) (finding that a Massachusetts law imposing restrictions upon trade with Burma was preempted, on the ground that it interfered with the congressional scheme to have the president control foreign trade policy with Burma, and also because the state law imposed sanctions above and beyond those mandated by Congress).

For criticism of the Supreme Court's use of a broad conception of dormant foreign-affairs preemption power in cases like Garamendi and Crosby, see Jack L. Goldsmith, Federal Courts, Foreign Affairs, and Federalism, 83 Va. L. Rev. 1617 (1997) (arguing that foreign affairs does not constitute an exclusive federal enclave in which federal common law should operate); Jack Goldsmith, Statutory Foreign Affairs Preemption, 2000 Sup. Ct. Rev. 175; Ernest A. Young, Dual Federalism, Concurrent Jurisdiction, and the Foreign Affairs Exceptionalism, 69 Geo. Wash. L. Rev. 139 (2001).

[73] Convention for the Unification of Certain Rules Relating to International Transportation by Air, October 12, 1929, 137 L.N.T.S. 11 [hereinafter Warsaw Convention].

[74] To provide the desired uniformity, Chapter III sets out an array of liability rules applicable to all international air transportation of persons, baggage, and goods. *Id.*

[75] 525 US 155 (1999).

traumatized in the same mishap would be free to sue outside of the Convention for potentially unlimited damages.[76]

A substantial percentage of the Court's regulatory preemption cases involve ERISA, a 'comprehensive statute [passed by Congress in 1974] for the regulation of employee benefit plans' with 'an integrated system of procedures for enforcement.'[77] ERISA's broad preemption, including exclusive jurisdiction in federal courts,[78] is directly linked to the statutory interest in uniformity:

> Section 514(a) [the preemption provision] was intended to ensure that plans and plan sponsors would be subject to a uniform body of benefit law; the goal was to minimize the administrative and financial burden of complying with conflicting directives among States or between States and the Federal Government.[79]

There are inevitably difficult questions of statutory interpretation under ERISA.[80] The statute grants three separate potential sources of

---

[76] *Id.* at 171. Justice Stevens, in dissent, disagreed with the majority's judgment regarding the potential disruption of the uniformity interest:

> It is clear to me that the central purposes of the Convention will not be affected.
> ... The interest in uniformity would not be significantly impaired if the number of cases not preempted, like those involving willful misconduct, was slightly enlarged to encompass those relatively rare cases in which the injury resulted from neither an accident nor a willful wrong.

Id. at 179–180 (Stevens, J., dissenting).

[77] *Aetna Health, Inc. v. Davila*, 542 US 200, 208 (2004). According to Greve and Klick's classification project, of the 105 preemption cases (focusing only on preemption of state statutes) decided by the Rehnquist Court (from 1986–2003), labor and employment cases (in which ERISA predominated) comprised 32, or roughly 1/3 of the total.

[78] 29 U.S.C. 1144(a) (2000) (ERISA provisions 'shall supersede any and all State laws insofar as they may now or hereafter relate to any employee benefit plan'); *id.* 1132(e)(1) ('The district courts of the United States shall have exclusive jurisdiction of civil actions under this title brought by the Secretary or by a participant, beneficiary, fiduciary.').

[79] *Ingersoll-Rand Co. v. McClendon*, 498 US 133, 142 (1990); see also *FMC Corp. v. Holliday*, 498 US 52, 60 (1990) ('To require plan providers to design their programs in an environment of differing state regulations would complicate the administration of nationwide plans.').

[80] As the Court has noted, the complicated preemption and savings clauses 'perhaps are not a model of legislative drafting.' *Metro. Life Ins. Co. v. Massachusetts*, 471 US 724, 739 (1985).

CHAPTER 22. SYMPOSIUM: EMERGING ISSUES IN CLASS ACTION LAW

federal preemptive authority, not all of which are intended to be field clearing in terms of state regulation. Despite the attending difficulties in applying the statute, the Rehnquist Court remained highly protective of the declared federal interest in a common regulatory regime for benefits law.[81] In case after case dealing with the inevitable tension between ERISA and state common law tort and contract obligations, the Court consistently preempted state tort suits that threatened the uniform character of benefit-plan regulation. In *Ingersoll-Rand Co. v. McClendon*,[82] most notably, the Court foreclosed common law wrongful termination claims as inconsistent with ERISA's comprehensive civil enforcement regime:

> Particularly disruptive is the potential for conflict in substantive law. It is foreseeable that state courts, exercising their common law powers, might develop different substantive standards applicable to the same employer conduct, requiring the tailoring of plans and employer conduct to the peculiarities of the law of each jurisdiction. Such an outcome is fundamentally at odds with the goal of uniformity that Congress sought to implement.[83]

Accordingly, any 'state-law cause of action that duplicates, supplements, or supplants the ERISA civil enforcement remedy conflicts with the clear congressional intent to make the ERISA remedy exclusive and is therefore pre-empted.'[84]

---

[81] See *Pilot Life Ins. Co. v. Dedeaux*, 481 US 41, 44 (1987).

[82] 498 US 133.

[83] *Id.* at 142. Similarly, in *Egelhoff v. Egelhoff*, 532 US 141 (2001), the Court found a Washington state statute preempted not only by the express language of ERISA, but also on implied conflict or obstacle preemption grounds because the statute 'interfered with nationally uniform plan administration.' *Id.* at 148. The uniformity goal, the Court explained, would be thwarted 'if plans are subject to different legal obligations in different States.' *Id.*

[84] *Aetna Health, Inc. v. Davila*, 542 US 200, 209 (2004). In *Pilot Life Insurance Co. and Metropolitan Life Insurance Co. v. Taylor*, 481 US 58 (1987), the Court held that tort and breach of contract cases filed by employees or beneficiaries were preempted by the 'exclusive' remedy of ERISA because the claims 'related to' benefits received under the plans. *Id.* at 61, 63.

Pegram v. Herdrich, 530 US 211 (2000), might, however, be read as a narrower application of preemptive scope. The Court held unanimously that Congress did not intend a health maintenance organization (HMO) to be treated as a fiduciary to the extent that it made mixed eligibility decisions acting through its physicians.

In similar fashion, the Labor-Management Relations Act (LMRA)[85] confers jurisdiction upon federal courts to hear suits charging violations of collective-bargaining agreements and 'to fashion a body of federal common law to be used to address disputes arising out of labor contracts.'[86] Given the claimed authority to impose federal common law uniformity on labor regulations, it is not surprising that the Court has consistently held that any state-law claim that might compromise uniformity is preempted.[87] The Court has elaborated upon this nationalist interest in uniformity in the interpretation of labor contract terms:

> The possibility that individual contract terms might have different meanings under state and federal law would inevitably exert a disruptive influence upon both the negotiation and administration of collective agreements.... Once the collective bargain was made, the possibility of conflicting substantive interpretation under competing legal systems would tend to stimulate and prolong disputes as to its interpretation.[88]

The Court seemed concerned that a preemption finding would fundamentally alter the business of HMO groups because it would have meant near-automatic liability for any balancing decision made by a physician. In short, while Pegram was unique in finding nonpreemption, it presented such an extreme choice for the Court that the decision should be read carefully and not taken to mean a retreat from the broad preemptive force of ERISA. Moreover, most recently in Aetna Health, the Court essentially limited the holding of Pegram to a very specific class of cases: those 'where the underlying negligence also plausibly constitutes medical maltreatment by a party who can be deemed to be a treating physician or such a physician's employer.' 542 US at 221 (citing *Cicio v. Does*, 321 F.3d 83, 109 (2nd Cir. 2003) (Calabresi, J., dissenting in part)).

[85] Labor-Management Relations Act, 1947 (LMRA), Ch. 120, 61 Stat. 136 (codified in scattered sections of 29 U.S.C.).

[86] *Allis-Chalmers Corp. v. Lueck*, 471 US 202, 209 (1985).

[87] But see *Hawaiian Airlines, Inc. v. Norris*, 512 US 246 (1994) (holding that the Railway Labor Act did not preempt a claim for wrongful discharge on grounds of retaliation). For an argument that strong preemption has thwarted the development of a more robust labor law as the economy trends from manufacturing to service, see Cynthia L. Estlund, The Ossification of American Labor Law, 102 Colum. L. Rev. 1527 (2002).

[88] *Int'l Brotherhood of Elec. Workers v. Hechler*, 481 US 851, 856 (1987) (internal quotation omitted). In Electrical Workers, the Court held that a union member was precluded from evading the preemptive force of section 301 of the LMRA by casting her claim as a state-law tort action, namely that the union breached its duty of care to provide a safe workplace. *Id.* at 862; see also Allis-Chalmers, 471 US 202;

CHAPTER 22. SYMPOSIUM: EMERGING ISSUES IN CLASS ACTION LAW

Conversely, the Supreme Court has not found preemption where allowing a cause of action would not upend or unduly interfere with the objectives of federal policy. Thus, in *California v. ARC America*

United Steelworkers of Am. v. Rawson, 495 US 362 (1990) (preemption by section 301 cannot be avoided by characterizing union's negligence as state-law tort). But see *Lingle v. Norge Div. of Magic Chef, Inc.*, 486 US 399 (1988) (holding that an employee covered by a collective-bargaining agreement that provided her with a contractual remedy for discharge without just cause could enforce her state-law remedy for retaliatory discharge, because that state-law cause of action was independent of the collective-bargaining agreement); *Caterpillar Inc. v. Williams*, 482 US 386 (1987) (respondents' state-law complaint for breach of individual employment contracts not preempted by section 301, which says nothing about the content or validity of individual employment contracts).

There are numerous examples of other federal statutes whose preemptive force is directly tied to the degree of the national interest in uniformity. A prime example is found in the National Banking Act and the Court's decision in *Beneficial National Bank v. Anderson*, 539 US 1, 10–11 (2003) (recognizing complete preemption doctrine of state-law usury claims and stating that 'uniform rules limiting the liability of national banks and prescribing exclusive remedies for their overcharges are an integral part of a banking system that needed protection from possible unfriendly State legislation') (internal quotation omitted). In addition, in enacting the Federal Arbitration Act (FAA), 'Congress declared a national policy favoring arbitration and withdrew the power of the states to require a judicial forum for the resolution of claims which the contracting parties agreed to resolve by arbitration.' *Perry v. Thomas*, 482 US 483, 484 (1987) (finding that section 2 of the FAA, which mandates enforcement of arbitration agreements, preempts section 229 of the California Labor Code, which provides that actions for the collection of wages may be maintained 'without regard to the existence of any private agreement to arbitrate'); see also *Green Tree Fin. Corp. v. Bazzle*, 539 US 444 (2003) (whether a contract allows class arbitration is a question of contract interpretation that is to be determined by an arbitrator); *Circuit City Stores, Inc. v. Adams*, 532 US 105, 109 (2001) (FAA's section 1 exemption of 'contracts of employment of seamen, railroad employees, or any other class of workers engaged in foreign or interstate commerce' applies only to contracts of transportation workers, and not any worker engaged in interstate commerce); *Mastrobuono v. Shearson Lehman Hutton, Inc.*, 514 US 52 (1995) (FAA ensures that contracting parties' agreement to include punitive damages in the scope of their arbitration agreement will be enforced according to its terms even if a rule of state law would otherwise exclude such claims from arbitration). The FAA therefore is read to further the view that 'Congress intended to foreclose state legislative attempts to undercut the enforceability of arbitration agreements.' *Perry*, 482 US at 489 (internal quotation omitted).

Corp.,[89] the Court held that the judicially created rule[90] limiting recoveries under the Sherman Act[91] to direct purchasers did not preempt express state statutory provisions that gave indirect purchasers a damages cause of action.[92] The Court reasoned that state indirect-purchaser statutes did not undermine the aims of the federal rule to provide some party with an incentive to police anticompetitive behavior, nor would they reduce the likelihood of direct purchasers bringing private federal antitrust actions.

Similar logic prevailed in *English v. General Electric Co.*,[93] where the Court held that federal statutes relating to nuclear power safety should only preempt to the extent that state laws tried to impose their own standards on radiological safety levels.[94] The interpretive key was to fashion uniform emissions rules to provide incubation for a national nuclear power industry meeting predictable safety standards. In this instance, an attempt to preempt customary tort claims concerning employment did not fall within the scope of the federal interest in uniformity of nuclear safety standards. While recognizing that a whistleblower's claim for intentional infliction of emotional distress might have some tangential effect on the operation of nuclear power plants, the Court concluded that 'this effect is neither direct nor substantial enough to place petitioner's claim in the pre-empted field.'[95] We are

---

[89] 490 US 93 (1989).
[90] *Ill. Brick Co. v. Illinois*, 431 US 720 (1977).
[91] Sherman Act, 15 U.S.C. 1–7 (2000).
[92] See ARC Am. Corp., 490 US at 105.
[93] 496 US 72 (1990).
[94] The key issue, according to the Court, was whether the tort claim related to the 'radiological safety aspects involved in the . . . operation of a nuclear [facility].' *Id.* at 82 (internal quotation omitted).
[95] *Id.* at 85. The Court stated:

> We recognize that the claim for intentional infliction of emotional distress at issue here may have some effect on these decisions, because liability for claims like petitioner's will attach additional consequences to retaliatory conduct by employers. As employers find retaliation more costly, they will be forced to deal with complaints by whistle-blowers by other means, including altering radiological safety policies. Nevertheless, we believe that this effect is neither direct nor substantial enough to place petitioner's claim in the pre-empted field.

Id.

CHAPTER 22. SYMPOSIUM: EMERGING ISSUES IN CLASS ACTION LAW

left, then, with a strong sense that the Court simply believed that the connection between the state tort suit and the uniform standards established by the law were simply too far removed: The one, in other words, was unlikely to alter in any meaningful way the obligations imposed by the other.

22.3.2.2 Horizontal Preemption

Whereas vertical preemption aims to achieve federal-state uniformity, the agenda of horizontal preemption is the development of coordinated solutions to matters that cross state lines. Environmental pollution may present the clearest case for a horizontal national solution impelled by significant interstate externalities.[96] The Clean Water Act (CWA),[97] for example, prohibits the discharge of effluents into navigable waters unless the point source has obtained a permit from the Environmental Protection Agency. The Act also allows a state in which the point source is located to impose more stringent discharge limitations than the federal ones, and even to administer its own permit program if certain requirements are met. By contrast, 'affected' states that are subject to pollution originating in source states have only the right to notice and comment before the issuance of a federal or state source permit.[98]

While the CWA establishes federal regulatory authority, the question still remains whether federal regulation preempts potential common law claims arising out of the same events. In *International Paper Co. v. Ouellette*,[99] the Supreme Court held that the CWA preempted a property owner's common law nuisance claim (brought in Vermont state court) for discharges from a New York-based paper

---

[96] See e.g., Weiland, *supra*, at 276 (noting that, absent preemption, interjurisdictional externalities may cause lower levels of government to engage in inefficient behavior); see also Kirsten Engel, State Environmental Standard-Setting: Is There a 'Race' and Is It 'To the Bottom'? 48 Hastings L.J. 271, 285 (1997):

> The interstate spillover rationale is the classic economic efficiency argument that federal intervention is necessary to prevent the environmental, social, and economic losses that accrue when air and water pollution originating in one state are carried by natural forces into other states.

[97] Clean Water Act (CWA), 33 U.S.C. 1251–1387 (2000).
[98] *Int'l Paper Co. v. Ouellette*, 479 US 481, 490 (1987).
[99] 479 US 481.

company into Lake Champlain, which his property abutted on the Vermont side.[100] Unchecked, the common law could as easily alter the regulatory framework as formal participation in the administrative regulatory scheme. The Court was therefore 'convinced that if affected States were allowed to impose separate discharge standards on a single point source, the inevitable result would be a serious interference with the achievement of the full purposes and objectives of Congress.'[101] The assertion of state common law claims would invariably compromise the federal purpose: 'The inevitable result of such suits,' the Court concluded, 'would be that Vermont and other States could do indirectly what they could not do directly – regulate the conduct of out-of-state sources.'[102] Moreover, and most critically, 'a source would be subject to a variety of common-law rules established by the different States along the interstate waterways.'[103]

Worker safety is yet another area that implicates coordination concerns, as evidenced by OSHA. Again, we are not addressing the question whether Congress has the authority to act in the area of occupational safety and health, a rather unchallenging application of the Commerce Clause, but rather the interpretive gloss that the Court places on the sweep of congressional action. Here again we find a strong impulse toward using broad preemption to impose the coordination of national standards. Thus, in *Gade v. National Solid Wastes Management Ass'n*,[104] for example, the Court held that OSHA preempted state regulations dealing with worker safety that had not

---

[100] In the course of its business, International Paper Co. had discharged effluents into the lake through a diffusion pipe that ended shortly before the New York-Vermont border. *Id.* at 484.

[101] *Id.* at 493–494 (internal quotation omitted). Nor – to the dissent's chagrin – was the majority deterred by the broad language of the CWA's explicit savings clause: 'Nothing in this section shall restrict any right which any person (or class of persons) may have under any statute or common law to seek enforcement of any effluent standard or limitation or to seek any other relief.' 33 U.S.C. 1365(e); see also Ouellette, 479 US at 504 (Brennan, J., dissenting) ('The Act's plain language clearly indicates that Congress wanted to leave intact the traditional right of the affected State to apply its own tort law when its residents are injured by an out-of-state polluter.').

[102] Ouellette, 479 US at 495.

[103] *Id.* at 496. The Court continued: 'These nuisance standards often are "vague" and "indeterminate." The application of numerous States' laws would only exacerbate the vagueness and resulting uncertainty.' *Id.*

[104] 505 US 88 (1992).

CHAPTER 22. SYMPOSIUM: EMERGING ISSUES IN CLASS ACTION LAW

been submitted and approved according to the Act. The Court explained:

> To allow a State selectively to 'supplement' certain federal regulations with ostensibly nonconflicting standards would be inconsistent with this federal scheme of establishing uniform federal standards, on the one hand, and encouraging States to assume full responsibility for development and enforcement of their own OSH programs, on the other.[105]

In the Court's view, OSHA called for cooperation between the state and federal authorities: The federal standard provided a benchmark, which the states would then have power to implement or enforce on their own, complementing federal enforcement but not dislodging federal coordination of standards. The Act's objective – namely cooperative federalism – was, however, frustrated by state regulations that imposed substantive obligations that were not authorized under federal law. State requirements that might attempt to tighten or loosen the federal benchmark standard threatened the uniformity with which multi-state employers regulate their workplaces.[106]

22.3.3 Products Liability

The concept of horizontal preemption is best elucidated in areas where the direct federal interest is weakest, such as in the standards governing tort liability for the manufacture of products placed on the national market. Unlike the modern regulatory state, which developed in tandem with the expansion of federal power, 'tort law in America is built on the bedrock of state common law.'[107] Contrary to the federal

---

[105] *Id.* at 103.

[106] Notwithstanding the fact that employee health and safety were areas of traditional state regulation, the Court in *Gade* did not apply any presumption against preemption. Instead, the Court self-consciously adopted a functional approach to the preemption question: 'In assessing the impact of a state law on the federal scheme, we have refused to rely solely on the legislature's professed purpose and have looked as well to the effects of the law.' *Id.* at 105 (emphasis added). The Court's approach prompted a retort from Justice Kennedy (who concurred in the judgment only), chastising the plurality not only for abandoning the presumption against preemption, but also for engaging in a 'freewheeling judicial inquiry into whether [the] state statute is in tension with federal objectives.' *Id.* at 111 (Kennedy, J., concurring).

[107] Robert L. Rabin, Federalism and the Tort System, 50 Rutgers L. Rev. 1, 2 (1997).

regulatory arena (explored in the previous part), here we often find a reluctance of federal courts to interfere by way of preemption in an area of traditional state authority:

> Because of the role of States as separate sovereigns in our federal system, we have long presumed that state laws – particularly those, such as the provision of tort remedies to compensate for personal injuries, that are within the scope of the States' historic police powers – are not to be pre-empted by a federal statute unless it is the clear and manifest purpose of Congress to do so.[108]

Oddly, and perhaps as a residual hangover of *Erie* (to which we shall return in the next part), the Court seems less willing to displace state common law than positive enactments.[109] But when the Court does act

---

[108] *Geier v. Am. Honda Motor Co.*, 529 US 861, 894 (2000) (Stevens, J., dissenting). The Court has seemed to adhere to a 'presumption against preemption,' especially prevalent in situations in which the federal government regulates in areas traditionally within the domain of the states. See e.g., *Rice v. Santa Fe Elevator Corp.*, 331 US 218, 230 (1946) ('We start with the assumption that the historic police powers of the State were not to be superseded by the Federal Act unless that was the clear and manifest purpose of Congress.'). The current viability of the presumption is, however, subject to debate. See e.g., Mary J. Davis, Unmasking the Presumption in Favor of Preemption, 53 S.C. L. Rev. 967 (2002) (claiming that the Court has abandoned the presumption against preemption altogether); Susan Raeker-Jordan, The Pre-emption Presumption that Never Was: Preemption Doctrine Swallows the Rule, 40 Ariz. L. Rev. 1379 (1998). And, in a recent case, *Engine Manufacturers Ass'n v. South Coast Air Quality Management District*, 541 US 246 (2004), Justice Scalia garnered majority support for refusing to apply the presumption – prompting a vehement dissent from Justice Souter.

[109] The Court here has been persuaded that state-law remedies (i.e., damages) are distinct from pure regulatory law. Thus, for example, in *Silkwood v. Kerr-McGee Corp.*, 464 US 238 (1984) – the definitive early case in which the Court tackled the issue of the preemptive effect of federal law upon state tort law – the Court held that Silkwood's claim for punitive damages arising out of radiation injuries from exposure to plutonium was not preempted by the Atomic Energy Act (AEA). Id. at 257–58. This, despite the fact that the previous Term, the Court had held that the AEA preempted state safety regulation of nuclear power plants. See *Pac. Gas & Elec. Co. v. State Energy Res. Conservation & Dev. Comm'n*, 461 US 190 (1983). The majority in Silkwood conceived punitive damages as distinct from pure regulatory law. Moreover, because the AEA did not provide for a private right of action, preemption in the case would have left victims wholly without legal remedy. The dissent ridiculed the majority's reasoning here, arguing that a punitive damages award would,

in the name of creating a common national baseline, it is left to the dissenters to inveigh against 'giving unelected federal judges carte blanche to use federal law as a means of imposing their own ideas of tort reform on the States.'[110] It is here, for example, where Justice Stevens, generally a vote for national authority in the Eleventh Amendment and Commerce Clause contexts,[111] can be found to dissent on the ground that 'this is a case about federalism,' that is, about respect for 'the constitutional role of the States as sovereign entities.'[112]

Not only is tort liability an area traditionally controlled by state law, but the ready sources of potential tort cases – such as the law governing automobiles, landowners, or medical malpractice – generally concern matters that are quite localized in their impact.[113] Seen through the lens of extraterritorial effects, however, the products liability strain of tort law stands as a striking counterexample.[114] It may be possible to

---

in effect, allow a state to enforce a legal standard that was 'more exacting than the federal standard.' Silkwood, 464 US at 265 (Blackmun, J., dissenting).

[110] Geier, 529 US at 894 (Stevens, J., dissenting).

[111] See e.g., Kimel v. Fla. Bd. of Regents, 528 US 62, 92 (2000) (Stevens, J., concurring); Seminole Tribe of Fla. v. Florida, 517 US 44, 76 (1996) (Stevens, J., dissenting) ('This case is about power – the power of the Congress of the United States to create a private federal cause of action against a State, or its Governor, for the violation of a federal right.'); EEOC v. Wyoming, 460 US 226, 244 (1983) (Stevens, J., concurring).

[112] Geier, 529 US at 887 (Stevens, J., dissenting) (quoting, inter alia, Alden v. Maine, 527 US 706, 713 (1999)). Justice Stevens is clearly the justice most concerned with preempting state common law remedies through broad federal preemption. His opinions in Cipollone v. Liggett Group, Inc., 505 US 504 (1992), Medtronic, Inc. v. Lohr, 518 US 470 (1996), and Geier v. American Honda Motor Corp., 529 US 861, 886 (2000) (Stevens, J., dissenting), are the clearest statements of the role of federalism in preemption decisions, and he is the most consistent and outspoken justice in favor of the presumption against preemption. See supra.

[113] See Schwartz, American Tort Law, supra, at 922. A historical exception is tort liability of interstate railroads, and of course the Federal Employer's Liability Act stands in opposition to the longstanding tradition of state common law tort. See generally Gary T. Schwartz, Tort Law and the Economy in Nineteenth Century America: A Reinterpretation, 90 Yale L.J. 1717, 1739 (1981); John Fabian Witt, The Accidental Republic (2004).

[114] See Sherman Joyce, Federal Product Liability Litigation Reform: Recent Developments and Statistics, 19 Seattle U. L. Rev. 421, 427–428 (1996) (advocating federal products liability legislation in light of the fact that the U.S. economy is both national and global, and, according to a U.S. Bureau of the Census report, over 70% of the

hold off property claims as subject to local authority,[115] and to preserve state autonomy in the limited context of state governmental conduct of its own affairs.[116] But in the rich regulatory environment of commercial exchange and the production of goods, a potential federal interest is never too far at bay. Counterarguments pressed in support of 'state sovereignty' and Brandeisian experimentation have been, correspondingly, diminished in the realm of products liability.[117]

---

goods manufactured in one state are shipped and sold out of that state) (citing Bureau of the Census, Commodity Transportation Survey 1–7 (1981)).
Moreover:

> products liability differs from most other fields of tort law in the frequency of diversity cases – and hence the awkward obligation it imposes on federal court judges to marshal their resources not in declaring law in a reasonably authoritative manner, but rather in merely making educated guesses about what results state courts would themselves support.

Schwartz, American Tort Law, *supra*, at 950. Plaintiffs, moreover, may have an additional incentive to engage in forum shopping, especially in mass tort cases, where defendants can be sued in different states. See e.g., Alvin B. Rubin, Mass Torts and Litigation Disasters, 20 Ga. L. Rev. 429, 443 (1986); Comment, In Re Joint Eastern and Southern District Asbestos Litigation: Bankrupt and Backlogged – A Proposal for the Use of Federal Common Law in Mass Tort Class Actions, 58 Brook. L. Rev. 553, 606–607 (1992).

[115] See e.g., *Kelo v. City of New London*, 125 S. Ct. 2655 (2005); see also William A. Fletcher, Property/Takings Talk at Santa Clara Symposium 12 (February 3, 2006) (unpublished manuscript, on file with author)

> Taken together, these decisions [Kelo, 125 S. Ct. 2655; *Lingle v. Chevron U.S.A., Inc.*, 125 S. Ct. 2074 (2005); *San Remo Hotel v. City of San Francisco*, 125 S. Ct. 2491 (2005)] represent a substantial change – entirely in the direction of deferring to the political and legal judgments of the states.;

id. at 13–14 ('With the exception of the Supreme Court's certiorari jurisdiction, the state courts are now the exclusive protectors of private property owners against takings effected by state and local authorities.').

[116] See e.g., *Bd. of Trs. of the Univ. of Ala. v. Garrett*, 531 US 356, 363 (2001); *Kimel v. Fla. Bd. of Regents*, 528 US 62, 72–73 (2000); *Fla. Prepaid Postsecondary Educ. Expense Bd. v. Coll. Sav. Bank*, 527 US 627, 634–635 (1999); *Seminole Tribe of Fla. v. Florida*, 517 US 44, 47 (1996).

[117] For standard arguments in favor of state experimentation in the products realm, see, for example, Betsy J. Grey, The New Federalism Jurisprudence and National Tort Reform, 59 Wash. & Lee L. Rev. 475, 517–518 (2002) (arguing that state

CHAPTER 22.   SYMPOSIUM: EMERGING ISSUES IN CLASS ACTION LAW

22.3.3.1   *The Need for National Regulation*

Because most products are mass produced and mass distributed, without any clear sense of where in the national market they might end up, the need for federal uniformity would seem especially pressing.[118]

---

legislation and common law reflect local interests, and voters play an important role in judicial lawmaking because they can overturn a common law rule by voting to pass a law); Linda S. Mullenix, Mass Tort Litigation and the Dilemma of Federalization, 44 DePaul L. Rev. 755, 768 (1995) (characterizing argument for state sovereignty in defense of differing products standards in fifty states as manifestation of local values and community culture); Rabin, *supra*, at 29 (grounding argument in respect for tradition and sensitivity to local issues); Frances E. Zollors et al., Looking Backward, Looking Forward: Reflections on Twenty Years of Product Liability Reform, 50 Syracuse L. Rev. 1019, 1040–1041 (2000) (extolling role of states as laboratories of democracy in considering products liability reforms); see also Mark C. Weber, Complex Litigation and the State Courts: Constitutional and Practical Advantages of the State Forum Over the Federal Forum in Mass Tort Cases, 21 Hastings Const. L.Q. 215, 238–239 (1994) (arguing that geographic variations influence the kinds of hazards that may arise in the tort or products liability context).
[118] Alan Schwartz makes the case:

> An effective pursuit of optimal product safety often will require national regulation. Uniformity reduces costs because there commonly are economies of scale to production. As a consequence, when firms are required to produce different versions of a product to comply with different state safety standards, each item will be more expensive than it would otherwise have been, and some items may not be produced at all. A single standard thus will often make the best tradeoff between safety and the other benefits that consumers could derive from a product. In addition, increasing the safety or a particular product attribute could make the product less safe as a whole unless other attributes also are modified. This argues for a coordinated form of regulation that the different states could not supply.

Schwartz, Statutory Interpretation, *supra*, at 17; see also Richard B. Stewart, Regulatory Compliance Preclusion of Tort Liability: Limiting the Dual-Track System, 88 Geo. L.J. 2167, 2169 (2000) ('The tort system cannot ensure desirable consistency and coordination in legal requirements, which is especially important for nationally marketed products.').

Richard Revesz would distinguish product standards, 'which regulate[] the environmental consequences of the product itself,' from process standards, which regulate 'the environmental consequences of the industrial process through which the product is produced.' Richard L. Revesz, Federalism and Environmental

Mass production means that goods and services are produced for potential distribution and sale anywhere demand might arise, without a particular purchaser in mind. In the case of the prototypical widget manufactured for a national market, not only is the ultimate buyer unknown, but so is the particular state in which the ultimate sale may occur – except in some actuarial sense by which California may historically have been the market for 30% of national widget sales, for example. This mass production and distribution of products casts a huge cloud of doubt upon the wisdom of individual state courts as the source of liability rules.[119] Given vexing choice of law issues, it is virtually impossible for manufacturers to adjust the price of products they sell in various states to take account of different liability standards.[120] The upshot is that most manufacturers design and market uniform products rather than different products for each state and, correspondingly, design their products to the specifications of the

---

Regulation: Some Lessons for the European Union and the International Community, 83 Va. L. Rev. 1331, 1332 (1997). Revesz argues that the case for uniformity is much stronger for product standards, especially ones that act as both a 'floor' and a 'ceiling,' because 'disparate regulation would break up the national market for the product and be costly in terms of foregone economies of scale.' Revesz, The Race to the Bottom, *supra*, at 544. As he further notes:

> The benefits of uniformity . . . are less compelling in the case of process standards, which govern the environmental consequences of the manner in which goods are produced rather than the consequences of the products themselves. Indeed, unlike the case of dissimilar product standards, there can be a well functioning common market regardless of the process standards governing the manufacture of the products traded in the market.

Id.

[119] There is disagreement as to the extent of variation in products liability law among the states. Compare, e.g., Schwartz, American Tort Law, *supra*, at 929 ('Within products liability . . . the inter-state variations in common law doctrine are both more frequent and more significant than they are in other sectors of the common law of torts.'), with, e.g., Stephen D. Sugarman, Should Congress Engage in Tort Reform?, 1 Mich. L. & Pol'y Rev. 121, 127 (1996) ('State tort laws today are broadly the same in product injury cases,' although there are differences 'around the edges.').

[120] For a discussion of choice of law problems, which increase the complexity, expense, and duration of litigation, and which provide little clear guidance, see generally Samuel Issacharoff, Getting Beyond Kansas, 74 UMKC L. Rev. (forthcoming 2006).

CHAPTER 22. SYMPOSIUM: EMERGING ISSUES IN CLASS ACTION LAW

largest states or to the jurisdiction with the most stringent liability standards, regardless of whether they represent either an efficient solution or the national consensus.[121]

Products liability law raises the specter of spillover effects, whereby a state uses its liability regime to benefit in-state residents with larger compensation payments, or exports the costs of its regulation to out-of-state manufacturers and product consumers in the rest of the nation.[122] Alan Schwartz has termed this the 'cost externalization constraint' on federalism.[123] Competitive forces, in other words, may induce states to adopt policies that run contrary to national

---

[121] See e.g., Schwartz, American Tort Law, *supra*, at 927 ('Manufacturers...must distribute a uniform product on a nationwide basis and cannot modify the price they charge for each product to account for state-law variations in that product's liability exposure.').

[122] Gary Schwartz termed this the 'structural bias problem.' *Id.* at 932; see also Michael W. McConnell, A Choice-of-Law Approach to Products-Liability Reform, in New Directions in Liability Law 90, 97 (Walter Olson ed., 1988) ('States pursue a persistent and one-directional race toward ever-higher plaintiff recoveries, a race whose outcome does not necessarily represent the considered judgment of decision makers in the several states.'); Robert M. Ackerman, Tort Law and Federalism: Whatever Happened to Devolution?, Yale L. & Pol'y Rev. 429, 451 (Symposium Issue, 1996); John S. Baker, Jr., Respecting a State's Tort Law, While Confining its Reach to that State, 1 Seton Hall L. Rev. 698, 704 (2001) ('Congress should respond when the laws of one state, whether it is good or bad, imposes itself on the citizens of other states who have no connection with and who have not invoked the law of that state.'); Harvey S. Perlman, Products Liability Reform in Congress: An Issue of Federalism, 48 Ohio St. L.J. 503, 508 (1987) (arguing that federal legislation should be narrowly directed toward reducing spillover effects – namely where citizens of one state must bear the cost of the policy decisions in another state).

[123] Schwartz, Statutory Interpretation, *supra*, at 21 & n. 26 (specifying as a constraint on the pursuit of local values that 'local regulation will not externalize costs to other states'). Schwartz elaborates further:

> States that require products to be made safer than the federal standard may impose costs on the citizens of other states.... If a large state prefers higher safety standards than smaller states and it is impractical for a national manufacturer to make different versions of the product, then the citizens of smaller states may have to consume more safety than they would like. Similarly, if enough small states prefer more safety than some larger states do, then big state citizens may be bound by the preferences of small state citizens.

Id. at 21.

objectives.[124] Elected state officials could well respond to the political preferences of the voters of any particular state yielding 'intrajurisdictional efficiency' at the expense of the 'interjurisdictional efficiency' concerns of the polity writ large.[125] The end result could be underregulation[126] or overregulation. The basic overregulation argument (traditionally pressed by groups such as the Chamber of Commerce and the National Association of Manufacturers) is that states with little industry of a certain kind impose high liability on out-of-state industry – whether due to pandering to the local trial bar, state courts seeking fees, or local plaintiffs seeking damages.[127] The upshot is that states will

---

[124] See e.g., Michael I. Krauss, Product Liability and Game Theory: One More Trip to the Choice-of-Law Well, 2002 BYU L. Rev. 759, 782–784 (arguing, using prisoners' dilemma approach, that states are better off adopting discriminatory rules to other states no matter what rules other states adopt); William Powers, Jr., Some Pitfalls of Federal Tort Reform Legislation, 38 Ariz. L. Rev. 909, 910 (1996) ('In a classic example of the tragedy of the commons, each state may have a bias in favor of products liability rules that increase recovery.').

[125] The terminology is from Robert P. Inman & Daniel L. Rubinfeld, Making Sense of the Antitrust State-Action Doctrine: Balancing Political Participation and Economic Efficiency in Regulatory Federalism, 75 Tex. L. Rev. 1203, 1234 (1997).

[126] The underregulation argument is that states have an incentive to underregulate in order to pacify an industry that might otherwise leave; hence states do not have incentives to protect their own citizen consumers. The argument for federal standards here is typically an argument for a federal 'floor,' given states' natural inclination to underregulate. Roderick Hills traces the historical origins of the idea of a broad federal power to regulate national markets and elaborates the New Deal argument that market pressure induces states to underregulate. Roderick M. Hills, Jr., Two Concepts of 'The Economic' in Constitutional Law: The Underlying Unity of Due Process and Federalism Jurisprudence 1, 12 (September 8, 2004) (unpublished manuscript), available at <www.law.columbia.edu/faculty/fac_resources/faculty_lunch/fall_2004?exclusive=filemgr.download&file_id=9596&rtcontentdisposition=filename=Hills.pdf>.

[127] See e.g., Richard Neely, The Product Liability Mess (1988) (demonstrating that state judges and legislators shape tort law to favor the interests of resident plaintiffs over nonresident manufacturers); Richard Willard, Comment, 31 Seton Hall L. Rev. 750, 751 (2001) ('Some states.... might use their tort systems to expropriate wealth from, and regulate the conduct of, out-of-state entities. This is a problem the states cannot be expected to resolve individually and thus implicates federalism concerns.'). As general counsel of a manufacturing company, Willard points out the difficulty for manufacturers because they sell in a national market and cannot limit their products to a particular state. Id. This bias against out-of-state defendants has

tend to over-regulate national goods moving in the stream of commerce – and this tendency is exacerbated by lax or uncertain choice of law rules and rules of personal jurisdiction that allow each state to impose its own law and courts on large-scale, out-of-state defendants.

Blankenship v. General Motors Corp., an opinion authored by former West Virginia Supreme Court Justice Richard Neely (a sort of poster child for damaging spillover effects),[128] offers an unusually candid portrayal:

> West Virginia is a small rural state with .66 percent of the population of the United States. Although some members of this Court have reservations about the wisdom of many aspects of tort law, as a court we are utterly powerless to make the overall tort system for cases arising in interstate commerce more rational: Nothing that we do will have any impact whatsoever on the set of economic tradeoffs that occur in the national economy. And, ironically, trying unilaterally to make the American tort system more rational through being uniquely responsible in West Virginia will only punish our residents severely without, in any regard, improving the system for anyone else.[129]

Per Justice Neely, no state has an incentive to disable the recoveries of its citizens so long as there is not a corresponding diminution by other states (the coordination problem) and, besides, the costs are borne elsewhere (the spillover or pollution effect). It is therefore not surprising to see several pivotal preemption cases articulate a need for the

---

some empirical validity. See Eric Helland & Alexander Tabarrok, The Effect of Electoral Institutions on Tort Awards, 4 Am. L. & Econ. Rev. 341, 359 (2002) ('Moving an otherwise average case with an out-of-state defendant from a nonpartisan to a partisan state raises the expected [tort] award by USD 362,988.'); Alexander Tabarrok & Eric Helland, Court Politics: The Political Economy of Tort Awards, 42 J.L. & Econ. 157 (1999). But see Thomas A. Eaton & Susette M. Talarico, Testing Two Assumptions About Federalism and Tort Reform, Yale L. & Pol'y Rev. 371, 377–385 (Symposium Issue, 1996) (finding little evidence, in a study of statutes and court decisions, of a systemic bias against nonresident manufacturers).

[128] Gary Schwartz cautioned against relying too heavily on the Blankenship opinion:

> If one is looking for convincing confirmation of the Neely diagnosis, Blankenship does not suffice. For the Blankenship opinion is coy and self-conscious: plainly Judge Neely was deliberately trying to draw attention to what he saw as an inherent defect in the products liability lawmaking process.

Schwartz, American Tort Law, *supra*, at 934.

[129] Blankenship, 406 S.E.2d at 783.

coordinated power of the federal government to oust state courts of their traditional jurisdiction over common law tort actions. It is also not surprising to see industry groups push for national standards as a way to rationalize potential legal liabilities from their broad market conduct.[130]

22.3.3.2 Horizontal Preemption

Products liability preemption cases occupy a difficult middle ground along a spectrum. At one pole are the areas of law in which Congress has sought to occupy the field, such as ERISA or LMRA. In these areas, the statutes typically announce the exclusive sway of federal law and often provide for exclusive jurisdiction in the federal courts as well. At the other pole stand the Dormant Commerce Clause cases, typified by a judicial determination that Congress' silence as to both substantive law and federal jurisdiction should nonetheless be seen as an exercise in federal power to keep states from regulating in any fashion.[131]

The products liability cases are unlike the vertical preemption cases, in which the Court responds to an assertion of a direct federal interest that claims to occupy the entire field. But they are also unlike the Dormant Commerce Clause cases, in which the Court proclaims the federal interest paramount despite the absence of affirmative action by Congress. The products liability cases lie somewhere between the two poles, typically presenting themselves as part of an incomplete federal regime. Most often the cases deal with the attempt to establish national regulatory objectives that come to govern liability, but with poorly defined remedial schemes.[132] Thus, federal preemption must be

---

[130] See E. Donald Elliott et al., Toward a Theory of Statutory Evolution: The Federalization of Environmental Law, 1 J.L. Econ. & Org. 313, 330, 333–336 (1985).

[131] In Dormant Commerce Clause cases, the Supreme Court has attempted to protect national markets from discriminatory laws passed by states to impose burdens upon out-of-state goods and to shift externalities to neighboring states. In a sense, we seek to extend Bednar & Eskridge's Dormant Commerce Clause analysis. See Bednar & Eskridge, *supra*. We pick up where Bednar and Eskridge left off: 'Should the Supremacy Clause.... be the primary basis for monitoring all sorts of cheating – from shirking ... to externalities and protectionism, which are now regulated primarily under the dormant commerce clause?' *Id.* at 1488.

[132] For an express recognition that common law damages are an integral part of the Court's understanding of legal requirements or prohibitions, see *Cipollone v. Liggett*

CHAPTER 22. SYMPOSIUM: EMERGING ISSUES IN CLASS ACTION LAW

implied against a poorly elaborated regulatory patchwork and force courts in the first instance to resolve difficult questions of statutory interpretation.

We hope to demonstrate that the Supreme Court, in the interpretive space that is created by this patchwork of federal products liability legislation, acts to protect the national market from externalities and spillover effects – albeit in a more tentative, less-comprehensive fashion. While spillover effects would compel a broader swath of preemption in the products liability arena, the Court is no doubt constrained by the absence of comprehensive national legislation and by the absence of a remedial scheme that matches the potential field-clearing sweep of the federal regulatory interest.[133] We are cognizant of the uphill battle we face; any attempt to provide a uniform set of guiding principles to articulate a clear logic and vision in the area of products liability preemption would seem doomed to failure.[134] At the same

---

Group, Inc., 505 US 504, 522 (1992) (relying in turn on William L. Prosser, Handbook of the Law of Torts 4 (4th edn 1971)).

[133] Congress might be looked to as the actor of institutional choice in responding to spillover effects. But, unlike in the contexts we explored *supra* Part II.B (regarding CWA, ERISA, LMRA, OSHA, FAA), Congress has not passed comprehensive federal legislation governing products. Here, the United States stands at odds with the European Community. In 1985, the EC Council of Ministers promulgated a Directive on Products Liability, which governs most of the content of Member States' products liability systems. See Schwartz, American Tort Law, *supra*, at 924. In 1996, the Common Sense Product Liability Legal Reform Act (PLLRA) was proposed as a national solution to respond to the reality that 'rules of law governing product liability actions, damage awards and allocations of liability have evolved inconsistently within and among the states.' See Cynthia C. LeBow, Federalism and Federal Product Liability Reform: A Warning Not Heeded, 64 Tenn. L. Rev. 665, 672 (1997) (quoting 142 Cong. Rec. S2587 (daily edn March 21, 1996); H.R. 956, 104th Cong. 2(a)(8), (10) (1996)). On May 3, 1996, President William Clinton vetoed the bill, charging that it would 'inappropriately intrude[] on state authority.' Neil A. Lewis, President Vetoes Limits on Liability, N.Y. Times, May 3, 1996, at A1, A8, quoted in Schwartz, American Tort Law, *supra*, at 917 (discussing progression of PLLRA through approval in both Houses in Congress).

[134] See e.g., Meltzer, *supra*, at 362–378; Robert L. Rabin, Reassessing Regulatory Compliance, 88 Geo. L.J. 2049, 2058 (2000) ('Preemption analysis by the Court will remain a source of disappointment for those in search of broad constitutional principles regarding the allocation of decisionmaking authority between federal regulatory schemes and state tort law.'). The products liability area, moreover, tends to produce fractured

time, absent such functional criteria, the Court's highly fact-dependent, case-by-case inquiry into congressional purpose and the language employed to effectuate that purpose cannot adequately account for the case outcomes, let alone provide a coherent account of this area of the law.[135]

Consider, for example, *Geier v. American Honda Motor Co.*[136] The Court was asked to decide whether the National Traffic and Motor Vehicle Safety Act of 1966[137] preempted a state common law tort action against a defendant auto manufacturer, which equipped its auto with passive restraints, as required by a regulation promulgated under the Act, but not air bags, which were not required.[138] The Act articulated directly counterposed signals on the extent of the federal interest.[139] Its preemptive clause decreed that 'no State... shall have any authority... to establish... any safety standard... which is not identical to the federal standard.'[140] Yet the accompanying savings clause removed any seeming clarity by directing that 'compliance with any Federal motor vehicle safety standard... does not exempt any person from any liability under common law.'[141]

---

opinions from the Court. See e.g., *Medtronic, Inc. v. Lohr*, 518 US 470 (1996) (plurality opinion); *Cipollone v. Liggett Group, Inc.*, 505 US 504 (1992) (plurality opinion).

[135] As has been emphasized in the relevant literature, 'For a variety of reasons, Congress often does not make its intention known so clearly that one can say with confidence whether it had in mind to statutorily preempt state tort law.' Rabin, *supra*, at 2054.

[136] 529 US 861 (2000).

[137] National Traffic and Motor Vehicle Safety Act of 1966, Pub. L. No. 89-563, 80 Stat. 718 (codified in scattered sections of 15 U.S.C.).

[138] *Geier*, 529 US at 875-876 (discussing the history behind the standard promulgated by the secretary).

[139] As aptly noted by Robert Rabin, 'Once again, Congress demonstrates its capacity for creating ambiguity in the preemption area – in this instance, not by remaining silent about the continuing vitality of state tort law, but by issuing seemingly contradictory commands.' Rabin, *supra*, at 2058–2059.

[140] 15 U.S.C. 1392(d) (1988).

[141] *Id.* 1397(k). Peter Strauss offers an intriguing potential reconciliation: namely that the savings clause might be read narrowly (and weakly) 'as a declaration by Congress that no rights existing when it acted (that is, under the common law as it then was) should be found prejudiced by its action.' Peter L. Strauss, Courts or Tribunals? Federal Courts and the Common Law, 53 Ala. L. Rev. 891, 919 (2002). Strauss reminds us that 'liability for "design defects" was not very well-developed when

CHAPTER 22. SYMPOSIUM: EMERGING ISSUES IN CLASS ACTION LAW

In holding that the regulation (promulgated pursuant to the Act) preempted state common law tort actions premised on the failure to provide state-of-the-art passenger protection, the Court reasoned that, absent preemption, 'state law could impose legal duties that would conflict directly with federal regulatory mandates.'[142] The policy consideration here went beyond a mere ephemeral concern that imposition of tort liability would increase the cost of making cars. The Court was instead concerned that state tort suits themselves would have the perverse effect of limiting the choices available to automobile manufacturers. The regulatory standard itself explicitly invited federal non-uniformity, but a single state's imposition of tort liability would impose a significant spillover effect because of the interstate mobility of cars. Even were manufacturers to limit the distribution of cars to conform sales to the requirements of a particular state, they would remain exposed to suit should an accident ensue after the car had been driven to another state where a different restraint system was required. Because automobile manufacturers cannot restrict the freedom of

---

the savings clause was enacted [in 1966], but liability for manufacturing defects was,' and argues that '[a] member of Congress thinking about the common law liability problem through that lens would not see frequent occasions for actual disabling conflict between common law principles of liability and the federal standards to be developed.' *Id.* at 920. While an admirable attempt to reconcile the seemingly contradictory impulses of Congress, in the end (as Strauss himself recognizes) no traces of its logic can be found in the Court's 2000 opinion – nor, it might be added, in the 1994 amendments to the Act (recodified in scattered sections of 49 U.S.C.). In the end, and as Strauss acknowledges, the Geier majority might best be viewed as performing a type of 'preemptive lawmaking' function as described by Thomas Merrill. Thomas W. Merrill, The Common Law Powers of Federal Courts, 52 U. Chi. L. Rev. 1, 36 (1985):

> Preemptive lawmaking may be invoked when a court, although it can discern no specific intention on the part of the enacting body with respect to the question before it, finds that the adoption of state law as the rule of decision would unduly frustrate or undermine a federal policy as to which there is a specific intention on the part of the enacting body.

[142] *Geier*, 529 US at 871. The majority's decision prompted criticisms that the Court was imposing tort reform in disguise, *id.* at 894 (Stevens, J., dissenting), and had managed, through sleight of hand, to eradicate entirely the presumption against preemption, see e.g., Calvin Massey, 'Joltin' Joe Has Left and Gone Away: The Vanishing Presumption Against Preemption,' 66 Alb. L. Rev. 759, 762 (2003).

movement of end purchasers of their cars, the only way to avoid massive tort liability would be to adopt an airbag-only policy. But, as the Court explained:

> The standard deliberately provided the manufacturer with a range of choices among different passive restraint devices. Those choices would bring about a mix of different devices introduced over time; and ... would thereby lower costs, overcome technical safety problems, encourage technological development, and win widespread consumer acceptance.[143]

In this instance, state law 'would have presented an obstacle to the variety and mix of devices that the federal regulation sought.'[144] And

---

[143] *Geier*, 529 US at 875.

[144] *Id.* at 881. Peter Strauss has commented that 'as neither Congress nor the Secretary had made this judgment, the majority was, necessarily, asserting a law-making authority in the federal courts – corresponding roughly to the law-making authority the courts have exercised in "dormant Commerce Clause" cases excluding various state regulatory measures for conflict with interstate commerce.' Strauss, *supra*, at 906. The solicitor general, nonetheless, argued in *Geier* that the promulgation of Federal Motor Vehicle Safety Standard 208 embodied an affirmative 'policy judgment that safety would best be promoted if manufacturers installed alternative protection systems in their fleets rather than one particular system in every car.' Geier, 529 US at 881 (quoting Brief for the United States as Amicus Curiae Supporting Affirmance at 25, *Geier v. Am. Honda Motor Co.*, 529 US 861 (2000) (No. 98-1811)).

By contrast, the Court rebuffed the preemption argument in *Freightliner Corp. v. Myrick*, 514 US 280 (1995). Like *Geier*, the preemptive effect of a National Highway Traffic Safety Administration regulation was at issue; but, unlike the situation in *Geier*, the agency, while it held hearings, had never formally adopted and reinstated the amended standard at issue (which provided stopping distances and vehicle stability requirements for trucks). The Court held that the Act's preemption clause applied only 'when[] a Federal motor vehicle safety standard ... is in effect'; moreover, the absence of a standard could not itself be considered to constitute regulation, especially where the lack of regulation was due not to an affirmative decision of the agency, but by the ruling of a federal court. *Id.* at 286 (quoting 15 U.S.C. 1392(d) (1994)).

In analogous fashion, in *Sprietsma v. Mercury Marine*, 537 US 51 (2002), the Court held (unanimously) that a state common law tort action seeking damages from the manufacturer of an outboard motor was not preempted either by the enactment of the Federal Boat Safety Act of 1971 or by the decision of the Coast Guard in 1990 not to promulgate a regulation requiring propeller guards on motorboats. Here, too, the interest in securing 'uniformity of boating laws and regulations as among the several States and the Federal Government' would seem paramount.

CHAPTER 22. SYMPOSIUM: EMERGING ISSUES IN CLASS ACTION LAW

it was thus manufacturer choice itself that the Court was protecting from potentially burdensome state liability rules.[145]

The point is confirmed by *Cipollone v. Liggett Group, Inc.*,[146] a watershed decision in which a divided Court signaled a broader approach to preemption and a willingness to set aside state common law in the name of federal objectives. A plurality of the Court held that the Public Health Cigarette Smoking Act of 1969[147] preempted a number of state tort claims that were based on the failure to provide

---

Id. at 57. However, again, unlike in *Geier* and similar to *Freightliner*, here there was no definitive agency regulation – instead, the Court was asked to consider whether the Coast Guard's decision not to regulate propeller guards impliedly preempted any state-law common law liability. *Id.* at 65 ('History teaches us that a Coast Guard decision not to regulate a particular aspect of boating safety is fully consistent with an intent to preserve state regulatory authority pending the adoption of specific federal standards.').

The Court, moreover, was likely heavily swayed by the fact that the solicitor general, joined by counsel for the Coast Guard, took the position that the agency did not view the 1990 refusal to regulate or any subsequent regulatory actions by the Coast Guard as having any preemptive effect. The influence of the position of the solicitor general in cases before the Supreme Court is widely acknowledged. See e.g., Michael S. Greve, The Supreme Court Term that Was and the One that Will Be, AEI Federalist Outlook, July–August 2002, <www.aei.org/publications/pubID.15849/pub_detail.asp> ('The solicitor general participates in every preemption case, and since those cases turn on the interpretation of federal statutes, his views are accorded special weight.'); see also Cross & Tiller, *supra*, at 747 ('When the Solicitor General requests that a case be taken on certiorari, the Court frequently complies. When the Federal government appears as a party before the Court, it has an unusually high rate of success.') (footnote omitted).

[145] Roderick Hills has argued that Geier is wrongly decided because state tort law liability might serve different purposes (e.g., corrective justice) from state regulation, even if it has the same effect. For this reason, in his view, federal law that preempts state regulations should not be read to preempt tort liability. The Supreme Court has wrestled fairly extensively with this purported distinction between state common law and regulatory or statutory regimes. The Court appears uncomfortable with rules that constrict remedies as opposed to liability-determinative rules, a further distinction that is problematic, but at least it does not confuse the source of ultimate regulatory activity for national market conduct. *Bates v. Dow Agrosciences*, LLC, 544 US 431 (2005) highlights this problem.

[146] 505 US 504 (1992).

[147] Public Health Cigarette Smoking Act of 1969, 15 U.S.C. 1340 (2000).

information about the health consequences of cigarette smoking.[148] The issue that divided the Court was whether common law causes of action were 'requirements' (akin to state statutory and administrative regulations) within the meaning of the 1969 statute's express preemption provision.[149] Although this division could be placed within a traditional statutory interpretation framework,[150] the resulting

---

[148] Rose Cipollone, who began smoking in 1942 and died of lung cancer in 1984, brought claims for breach of express warranties, failure to warn, design defects, fraudulent misrepresentation, and conspiracy to defraud. Cipollone, 505 US at 508–509. A plurality of the Court (per Justice Stevens) held that petitioner's claims based upon express warranty and conspiracy were not preempted by the 1969 Act. *Id.* at 525–530. Justice Blackmun (writing for himself, and Justices Kennedy and Souter) concluded that the 1969 Act did not clearly and manifestly exhibit a congressional intent to preempt common law damages actions, and therefore concurred in part that certain of the claims were not preempted. *Id.* at 533–534 (Blackmun, J., dissenting). Justices Scalia and Thomas concurred in part and dissented in part, arguing that all of the claims were preempted by the 1969 Act under ordinary principles of statutory construction. *Id.* at 548–554 (Scalia, J., concurring in the judgment in part and dissenting in part, joined by Thomas, J.).

A majority (again, per Justice Stevens) also held that the previously enacted 1965 Federal Cigarette Labeling and Advertising Act (FCLAA) did not preempt state-law damages actions, but preempted only positive enactments by state and federal rulemaking bodies in the areas of advertising and labeling cigarettes. *Id.* at 518–520.

[149] That provision (section 5(b)) was broader than the 1965 Act because: 'First, the later Act bars not simply "statements" but rather "requirements or prohibitions... imposed under State law." Second, the later Act reaches beyond statements "in the advertising" to obligations "with respect to the advertising or promotion" of cigarettes.' *Id.* at 520.

[150] The plurality decision makes clear that

> when Congress has considered the issue of pre-emption and has included in the enacted legislation a provision explicitly addressing that issue, and when that provision provides a 'reliable indicium of congressional intent with respect to state authority,' there is no need to infer congressional intent to pre-empt state laws from the substantive provisions' of the legislation.

Id. at 517 (quoting *Malone v. White Motor Corp.*, 435 US 497, 505 (1978) and *Cal. Fed. Sav. & Loan Ass'n v. Guelta*, 479 US 272, 282 (1987)). In other words, the Court would employ a variation on expressio unius est exclusion alterius to focus explicitly and exclusively on the express provision included by Congress and would not address implied preemption arguments. For an argument that courts should employ default rules that are ungenerous to Congress in such statutory cases so as to force Congress

CHAPTER 22. SYMPOSIUM: EMERGING ISSUES IN CLASS ACTION LAW

opinions are far from an homage to textualism.[151] Absent some overriding theory of the relation between federal integration and the risk of conflict among state commands, it is difficult to lend any coherence to the Court's approach to implied preemption.

Not surprisingly, we find room for a more functionalist account, much in line with that of the late Gary Schwartz. Schwartz provided a favorable account of the result in *Cipollone* by emphasizing the undesirability of allowing nonuniform rulings from state to state to control the extent of cigarette companies' warning obligations:

> The federal interest in a coherent warning program would be unduly impaired if a jury in Massachusetts could find that the warning should mention addiction while an Oregon jury rules that the warning should include a skull-and-crossbones and a Florida jury concludes that the warning should set forth actual data on the probability of disease.[152]

Thus, the Court found that a state tort claim that was premised upon the notion that the manufacturer 'should have included additional, or more clearly stated, warnings' could not survive.[153] By contrast, the Court let

---

to confront more fully the impact of its decisionmaking, see Einer Elhauge, Preference-Eliciting Statutory Default Rules, 102 Colum. L. Rev. 2162 (2002).

[151] Justice Scalia vigorously dissented in part, arguing that the Court, with its various presumptions against preemption, had done significant damage to the literal wording of the statute. In Justice Scalia's view, both the 1965 and 1969 Acts expressly preempted all of Cipollone's claims. Justice Scalia inveighed against the Court's traditional preemption framework:

> Must express pre-emption provisions really be given their narrowest reasonable construction (as the Court says in Part III), or need they not (as the plurality does in Part V)? Are courts to ignore all doctrines of implied pre-emption whenever the statute at issue contains an express pre-emption provision, as the Court says today, or are they to continue to apply them, as we have in the past? For pre-emption purposes, does 'state law' include legal duties imposed on voluntary acts (as we held last Term in Norfolk & Western R. Co.), or does it not (as the plurality says today)? These and other questions raised by today's decision will fill the lawbooks for years to come. A disposition that raises more questions than it answers does not serve the country well.

Cipollone, 505 US at 555–556 (Scalia, J., dissenting).

[152] See Gary T. Schwartz, Tobacco Liability in the Courts, in Smoking Policy: Law, Politics, and Culture 131, 151 (Robert L. Rabin & Stephen D. Sugarman eds, 1993).

[153] Cipollone, 505 US at 524.

stand a state-law claim for fraudulent misrepresentation on the ground that fraud did little to upend national uniformity: 'Unlike state-law obligations concerning the warning necessary to render a product "reasonably safe," state-law proscriptions on intentional fraud rely only on a single, uniform standard: falsity.'[154] In the wake of *Cipollone*, lower courts have read the fraud exception narrowly and have followed a trend to infer broad preemption of state law.[155]

Nonetheless, the federalization process moves by fits and starts. Most notably, in the 2005 case *Bates v. Dow Agrosciences, LLC*,[156] the Court returned to the preemptive effects of federal labeling requirements, this time under the Federal Insecticide, Fungicide, and Rodenticide Act (FIFRA).[157] This time, and arguably in tension with *Cipollone*, the Court relied on a 'parallel requirements' reading of federal law to hold that FIFRA could coexist with common law claims. The Court concluded that because the common law did not expressly alter the labeling requirements under federal law, but simply added another level of remedial penalties, it did not necessarily do violence to congressional regulation.[158] In other words, states may provide the legal vehicle for

---

[154] *Id.* at 529 (emphasis added).

[155] See e.g., Robert J. Katerberg, Patching the 'Crazy Quilt' of Cipollone: A Divided Court Rethinks Federal Preemption of Products Liability in *Medtronic, Inc. v. Lohr*, 75 N.C. L. Rev. 1440, 1478 n. 260 (1997) (listing post-*Cipollone* cases broadly inferring preemption).

In a more recent preemption case addressing the federal regulation of cigarette marketing, the Court held that cigarette-advertising regulations imposed by Massachusetts were preempted by the FCLAA, which prescribed mandatory health warnings for cigarette packaging and advertising. *Lorillard Tobacco Co. v. Reilly*, 533 US 525, 550 (2001). The clear import of the FCLAA, according to the Court, was to prohibit state cigarette-advertising regulations motivated by concerns about smoking and health. *Id.* at 548. The Court thus held that, because it was clear that Massachusetts had attempted to address the incidence of underage cigarette smoking by regulating advertising, the regulations were preempted. *Id.* at 548–550.

[156] 544 US 431 (2005).

[157] Federal Insecticide, Fungicide, and Rodenticide Act (FIFRA), 7 U.S.C. 136-136y (2000).

[158] Bates, 544 US at 446–449. Here, too, the Court seemed to breathe new life into the presumption against preemption. See *id.* at 449 ('Because the States are independent sovereigns in our federal system, we have long presumed that Congress does not cavalierly pre-empt state causes of action.') (quoting *Medtronic, Inc. v. Lohr*, 518 US 470, 485 (1996) (alteration in original)).

CHAPTER 22. SYMPOSIUM: EMERGING ISSUES IN CLASS ACTION LAW

remedying violations of federal standards, standards from which they are unable to add or subtract. While this does alter the market incentives that attach to business decisions, under the Court's view there is no conflict in the commands that companies are compelled to follow. Here, the Court makes clear that FIFRA retains preemptive force: 'In the main, it pre-empts competing state labeling standards – imagine 50 different labeling regimes prescribing the color, font size, and wording of warnings – that would create significant inefficiencies for manufacturers.'[159]

The distinction between liability and remedies in Bates is conceptually unsatisfying but reflects the tension in areas where the Court wants to promote uniformity in the absence of a complete regulatory framework.[160] The same pressure toward horizontal integration is present in federal oversight over the design of medical devices, an area where the case law likewise does not entirely hold together. Here we are forced to contrast an impulse toward preserving the integrity of the common law in *Medtronic, Inc. v. Lohr*[161] with the more expansive account of the federal interest in *Buckman Co. v. Plaintiffs' Legal Committee*.[162] *Medtronic* held, again by a sharply divided Court, that common law claims concerning the design of medical implements were not preempted by the Medical Device Amendments of 1976 (MDA).[163] The plurality rejected as unpersuasive and implausible Medtronic's

---

[159] *Id.* at 452.

[160] The Court, moreover, was clearly concerned by the fact that most farmers would be left without a remedy if state tort suits for misbranding were entirely preempted. *Id.* at 449:

> The long history of tort litigation against manufacturers of poisonous substances adds force to the basic presumption against pre-emption. If Congress had intended to deprive injured parties of a long available form of compensation, it surely would have expressed that intent more clearly.

Given the contemporary Court's reluctance to infer private rights of action from statutes like FIFRA, the consequence of a preemption decision may be to leave injured plaintiffs entirely bereft of remedies. For an elaboration of the inverse relationship between the comprehensiveness of a federal regulatory scheme and the necessity for private rights of action, see Sharkey, *supra*.

[161] 518 US 470 (1996).

[162] 531 US 341 (2001).

[163] Medical Device Amendments of 1976 (MDA), 21 U.S.C 360–c37 (2000). The case involved negligence and strict liability claims by a plaintiff injured by a pacemaker,

argument that any common law claim altered incentives and imposed additional duties.[164] The case shows the Court's hesitation over the ultimate logic of the national marketplace: the complete displacement of state tort law.[165] The plurality tries to limit the sweep of *Cipollone* by relying on a 'sliding scale' analysis that factors in the breadth of the unwinding of the tort law system: preemption is more likely when the field preempted is narrow and when there is some potential alternative legal remedy available to individuals.[166] By contrast, where a statute

---

which had been approved by the Food and Drug Administration (FDA), as directed by the MDA. Medtronic, 518 US at 470. Section 360k(a) provided:

> No State...may establish or continue in effect with respect to a device intended for human use any requirement (1) which is different from, or in addition to, any requirement applicable under this chapter to the device, and (2) which relates to the safety or effectiveness of the device or to any other matter included in a requirement applicable to the device under this chapter.

21 U.S.C. 360k(a). As is typical, neither the statutory language (nor the legislative history) of the MDA is explicit about barring tort claims. See e.g., Robert S. Adler & Richard A. Mann, Preemption and Medical Devices: The Courts Run Amok, 59 Mo. L. Rev. 895, 923–924 (1994):

> We note that there is no absolutely dispositive language in the MDA regarding preemption and the common law. That is, nowhere in the amendments or in the legislative history of the amendments does Congress indicate that state common law tort claims are preempted or are not preempted.

(footnote omitted).

[164] Moreover, Justice Stevens, writing for the plurality, was concerned that, to accept *Medtronic's* argument would lead to the perverse result that Congress granted complete immunity to an entire industry from suits by users. *Medtronic*, 518 US at 487. As in Silkwood, the plurality was unwilling to infer such an intent on the part of Congress when the language was ambiguous. *Id.*

[165] The plurality frames its argument with its federalism-inspired presumption against preemption: 'Because the States are independent sovereigns in our federal system, we have long presumed that Congress does not cavalierly pre-empt state-law causes of action.' *Id.* at 485.

[166] Justice Stevens created a new sort of balancing test:

> The pre-emptive statute in Cipollone was targeted at a limited set of state requirements – those 'based on smoking and health' – and then only at a limited subset of the possible applications of those requirements – those involving the 'advertising or promotion of any cigarettes the packages of

CHAPTER 22. SYMPOSIUM: EMERGING ISSUES IN CLASS ACTION LAW

covers an entire field, like the design of medical devices, a broad reading will invariably lead to the complete supplanting of the traditional ability of states to provide remedies for their injured citizens. The dissent understood the same tension in federal-state relations, but would have preempted any claim that might potentially alter incentives or impose additional requirements upon entities covered by the statute.[167]

Buckman pushes in the other direction, with the Court showing far greater concern for the potential Balkanization of federal regulatory authority. There, a state common law claim was premised upon allegedly false representations made to the Food and Drug Administration (FDA) in the course of obtaining approval for orthopedic bone screws. The suit claimed that the misrepresentations were the 'but for' cause of the ensuing injuries that plaintiffs sustained from the implantation of these devices.[168] The Court, per then-Chief Justice Rehnquist, did not

---

which are labeled in conformity with the provisions of' the federal statute. In that context, giving the term 'requirement' its widest reasonable meaning did not have nearly the pre-emptive scope nor the effect on potential remedies that Medtronic's broad reading of the term would have in this suit.

Id. at 488 (citation omitted).

[167] Justice O'Connor (writing for herself, then-Chief Justice Rehnquist, and Justices Thomas and Scalia) wrote:

I conclude that 360k(a)'s term 'requirement' encompasses state common-law claims. Because the statutory language does not indicate that a 'requirement' must be 'specific,' either to pre-empt or be pre-empted, I conclude that a state common-law claim is pre-empted if it would impose 'any requirement' 'which is different from, or in addition to,' any requirement applicable to the device under the [Federal Food, Drug, and Cosmetic Act of 1938].

Id. at 514 (O'Connor, J., concurring in part and dissenting in part, joined by Rehnquist, C.J., and Scalia and Thomas, J.J.).

[168] The screws were approved by the FDA as a predicate device, but upon representations that these screws were to be marketed for legs and arms, as opposed to spines. Claiming that the FDA would not have approved the screws had petitioner not made the fraudulent representation, plaintiffs sought damages under state tort law. *Buckman Co. v. Plaintiffs' Legal Comm.*, 531 US 341, 346–347 (2001) (discussing the history of the approval process and the filing of some 2,300 civil actions).

hesitate to preempt based on the functional consequences of allowing such a claim to proceed:

> As a practical matter, complying with the FDA's detailed regulatory regime in the shadow of 50 States' tort regimes will dramatically increase the burdens facing potential applicants.... Would-be applicants may be discouraged from seeking... approval of devices with potentially beneficial off-label uses for fear that such use might expose the manufacturer or its associates... to unpredictable civil liability.[169]

Even within the core of traditional state-law duties, Buckman reaffirms the need for horizontal integration to coordinate the liability standards of goods manufactured for the national market.

22.4 FORUM SELECTION AND FEDERALISM

Federal authority is not simply a matter of control over the formal substantive law, but also over the forum in which the law is elucidated. It is worth recalling that the first great effort to harmonize commercial law in the service of the national market took as its centerpiece the use of federal authority over diversity cases.[170] The target of such reforms was the autarchic division of the markets that stood as a deep inhibition of interstate commerce. As one contemporary rather colorfully expressed the issue:

> Inter-commercial in this united way, our law is essentially defective... where in the North, professing the principles of the English common law, a merchant shall have a contract interpreted in one way in Pennsylvania, another way in New York, and a third way in Boston: and when he

---

[169] Id. at 350. To be sure, the Court was swayed by additional factors:

> Policing fraud against federal agencies is hardly 'a field which the States have traditionally occupied,' such as to warrant a presumption against finding federal pre-emption of a state law cause of action. To the contrary, the relationship between a federal agency and the entity it regulates is inherently federal in character because the relationship originates from, is governed by, and terminates according to federal law.

Id. at 347 (internal citation omitted). Also, the federal statutory scheme empowers the FDA to punish and deter fraud against the Agency. Id. at 349–350.

[170] See generally Henry J. Friendly, The Historic Basis of Diversity Jurisdiction, 41 Harv. L. Rev. 483 (1928).

goes South with it next week, shall find it open to new constructions; – in Florida, by the Partidas of Spain; in Louisiana, by the Code Civil of France, and in Texas and California, by something which is neither and both; half code, half custom... where in fact, law is a science of geography, almost as much as of justice.[171]

The impediments to commerce gave force to the proponents of using a common commercial law as an integral part of the consolidation and expansion of the fledgling American state, what Chief Justice Shaw of the Massachusetts Supreme Court would describe aspirationally as the creation of 'one extended commercial community.'[172] The goal, claimed a bit prematurely as close to an accomplished fact by William Kent in 1838, was to see to it that 'the law of commerce is not confined and local, but, the production of many countries and ages, [and] is in most respects common to them all, and uniform.'[173] As eloquently summarized by Daniel Webster, who would subsequently appear as counsel for Swift in *Swift v. Tyson*:[174] 'Whatever we may think of it now, the Constitution has its immediate origin in the conviction of the necessity for this uniformity, or identity, in commercial regulations.... Unity and identity of commerce among all the States was its seminal principle.'[175] To this day, the Supreme Court has identified the Commerce Clause as emerging from 'the Framers' response to the central problem giving rise to the Constitution itself: the absence of any federal commerce

---

[171] John William Wallace, The Want of Uniformity in the Commercial Law Between the Different States of our Union 28 (Phila., L.R. Bailey 1851).

[172] *Staples v. Franklin Bank*, 42 Mass. (1 Met.) 43, 47 (1840).

[173] William P. LaPiana, Swift v. Tyson and the Brooding Omnipresence in the Sky: An Investigation of the Idea of Law in Antebellum America, 20 Suffolk U. L. Rev. 771, 780–781 (1986) (quoting William Kent, The Rise and Progress of Commercial Law in English Jurisprudence, in Inaugural Address, Delivered by the Professors of Law in the University of the City of New York 45–49 (1838)).

[174] 41 US (16 Pet.) 1 (1842).

[175] Daniel Webster, as quoted in Alfred B. Teton, The Story of Swift v. Tyson, 35 Ill. L. Rev. 519, 538 n. 107 (1940). For historical analysis portraying the constitutional founding as a struggle between creditors and debtors, see generally Merrill Jensen, The Articles of Confederation (1970). In a separate argument before the Court, Webster addressed the link between commerce and diversity jurisdiction: 'It was from a distrust of state tribunals that the provision [diversity jurisdiction] of the Constitution of the United States was introduced.' *Groves v. Slaughter*, 40 US (15 Pet.) 449, 490 (1841).

power under the Articles of Confederation.'[176] We turn now to the role of federal courts as the vehicle of commercial harmonization, most notably in the hands of Justice Story. On this account, federal courts used their powers over diversity cases to provide a more coherent and distinctively American law and to protect against the centripetal pressures of state authority under the sway of localism.

22.4.1 From *Swift* to *Erie*: Federal Power and the Common Law

The role of jurisdiction based on diversity of citizenship in this account is subject to underestimation. From the modern vantage point, it is too easy to invest diversity with a rights gloss, protecting individuals against the passions of local herd-like antipathy.[177] But the concern of the framers was otherwise. It was not the random hostility to a citizen of another jurisdiction that concerned them as much as it was the predictable pattern of hostility to a discrete class of potential parties in state-court litigation: creditors. With the immediate background of Shays' Rebellion and broader concerns that overarching democratic impulses could compromise the integrity of financial markets, not to mention any system of currency,[178] the framers viewed the risk of popular repudiation of commercial obligations as a threat to the economic expansion of the new Republic and a potential source of interstate popular retaliation.[179] Diversity jurisdiction served not so much to

---

[176] *Gonzales v. Raich*, 125 S. Ct. 2195, 2205 (2005).

[177] See e.g., *Burford v. Sun Oil Co.*, 319 US 315, 337 (1943) (Frankfurter, J., dissenting) (using broad rights-oriented language to describe diversity jurisdiction as existing 'to avoid possible unfairness by state courts, state judges and juries, against outsiders'). For academic commentary making the same point, see, for example, Graham C. Lilly, Making Sense of Nonsense: Reforming Supplemental Jurisdiction, 74 Ind. L.J. 181, 190 (1998) ('The principal argument for diversity jurisdiction is the protection of out-of-state litigants from local prejudice.').

[178] See Ron Chernow, Alexander Hamilton 225 (2004) (highlighting the influence on the framers of Shays' Rebellion and the extremist movement in Rhode Island that advocated the abolition of debt and the equal division of wealth).

[179] See Calvin H. Johnson, Righteous Anger at the Wicked States 57 (2005) ('To the extent that creditors were citizens of other states, anti-creditor measures were also considered by the nationalists to be aggressions by one state against its neighboring states.').

protect the unfortunate individual litigant who found himself in unwelcoming environs, but to provide a jurisdictional refuge for the commercial class that, even at the time of the founding, was already spreading its affairs across the new nation.[180] Indeed, the debate over the Judiciary Act of 1801[181] highlighted 'Federalist arguments that expanded federal court jurisdiction was needed to protect commercial interests.'[182] As historian Jackson Turner Main has written: 'The prospect that creditors could sue in the federal courts and recover claims in real was particularly pleasing at a time when the collection of debts was exceptionally difficult and the number of suits in state courts extraordinarily high.'[183]

According to Madison's notes of the Constitutional Convention, the concept of diversity jurisdiction was not much debated in the convention itself; while the wording was left to the Committee of Detail,[184] some version of the clause was an established part of assumed terms of the eventual constitutional compromise.[185] Even the Virginia Plan would have given federal courts jurisdiction over 'cases in which foreigners or citizens of other States applying to such jurisdictions may be interested, or which respect the collection of the National revenue.'[186] In carrying the spirit of the founding to the subsequent debates on

---

[180] See generally Jackson Turner Main, The Antifederalists: Critics of the Constitution 1781–1788 (1961) (explaining the divide over the Constitution 'in terms of a debtor-creditor alignment'); Charles A. Beard, An Economic Interpretation of the Constitution of the United States (1961) (describing the Constitution as springing out of essentially economic interests). In a contemporary discussion of the Constitution in general, Jeremiah Libbey wrote 'it will make them [the States] honest & put it out of their power to cheat every body by tender laws & paper money.' Id. at 341 n. 88.

[181] Judiciary Act of 1801, Ch. 4, 2 Stat. 89.

[182] LaPiana, *supra*, at 795 n. 100.

[183] Main, *supra*, at 164–65.

[184] See generally 1–3 The Records of the Federal Convention of 1787 (Max Farrand ed., 1937); see also Akhil R. Amar, A Neo-Federalist View of Article III: Separating the Two Tiers of Federal Jurisdiction, 65 B.U. L. Rev. 205, 242–245 (1985) (tracing the language of diversity jurisdiction through the drafts of the Committee of Detail).

[185] For a careful account of the historical record on the adoption of diversity jurisdiction and its tie to the protection of national commercial interests, see Debra Lyn Bassett, The Hidden Bias in Diversity Jurisdiction, 81 Wash. U. L.Q. 119, 131–136 (2003).

[186] The Records of the Federal Convention of 1787, *supra* n. 187, at 22.

ratification, Luther Martin argued the centrality of the forum in protecting commerce:

> The injury to commerce, and the oppression to individuals, which may thence arise, need not be enlarged upon. Should a citizen of Virginia, Pennsylvania, or any other of the United States, be indebted to, or have debts due from a citizen of this State, or any other claim be subsisting on one side or the other, in consequence of commercial or other transactions, it is only in the courts of Congress that either can apply for redress.[187]

John Marshall similarly understood that the ability to draw cases into federal court on diversity grounds 'may be necessary with respect to the laws and regulations of commerce, which Congress may make.'[188] As summarized subsequently by Henry Friendly, 'the desire to protect creditors against legislation favorable to debtors was a principal reason for the grant of diversity jurisdiction.'[189] Nor, as Bruce Mann shows in the context of bankruptcy, was this an isolated concern of the framers:

> Credit, like commerce, could not be contained within state boundaries. Full faith and credit helped somewhat, but it could harm out-of-state

---

[187] 3 *id.* at 220–221. On the other side of the aisle, George Mason asked delegates to ponder: 'What effect will this power have between British creditors and the citizens of this State?' George Mason Fears the Power of the Federal Courts: What Will be Left to the States? (June 19, 1788), in 2 The Debate on the Constitution 720, 725 (Bernard Bailyn ed., 1993). It is also relevant that the Anti-Federalist concerns about a state itself being called in front of the federal courts were focused on financial or commercial issues. Hamilton responds to these in The Federalist No. 81, replying that it was without foundation that 'an assignment of the public securities of one State to the citizens of another would enable them to prosecute that State in the federal courts for the amount of those securities.' The Federalist No. 81, at 487 (Alexander Hamilton) (Clinton Rossiter ed., 1961).

[188] John Marshall on the Fairness and Jurisdiction of the Federal Courts (June 20, 1788), in 2 The Debate on the Constitution, *supra*, at 735. Marshall offered as examples the types of cases that could be expected to arise under this clause, such as suits by creditors, issues over trade and product disputes, and disagreements over interest rates. *Id.*

[189] Friendly, *supra*, at 496–497. For other contemporary commentators focusing on the need to protect national creditors from the pro-debtor bias of state interests, see Richard A. Posner, The Federal Courts: Crisis and Reform 141–142 (1985) (arguing that federal-court oversight is essential to protection of commercial interests); Larry Kramer, Diversity Jurisdiction, 1990 BYU L. Rev. 97, 119 (arguing that 'the desire to protect commercial interests from pro-debtor state courts' was key to 'the creation of diversity jurisdiction').

CHAPTER 22. SYMPOSIUM: EMERGING ISSUES IN CLASS ACTION LAW

creditors by imposing on them state bankruptcy discharges that stripped them of their claims without their participation in the process.... Federal 'uniform Laws on the subject of Bankruptcies,' which subjected debtors and creditors to the same rules and procedures regardless of where they lived, would be more in keeping with the interstate nature of commerce and the credit relations on which commerce rested.[190]

The significance of diversity jurisdiction in achieving economic integration came into its own in the first decades of the Republic.[191] For Justice Story, as expressed in the too easily discounted case of *Swift v. Tyson*,[192] access to federal courts resulting from expanding interstate contacts, and hence diversity of citizenship, could counteract the retrograde efforts against economic expansion in two ways. First, the fact of diversity jurisdiction allowed federal courts to stand between commercial creditors and local interests, even if compromised by the right to jury trial. Second, control of the substantive law to be applied in federal court could overcome tendencies toward protectionism and other barriers to the advancement of a national market. *Swift* was entirely consistent with Justice Story's deep attachment to the role of law as cementing the expanding nation and argued that courts must be able to fashion legal principles addressing the distinct needs of the ascendant republic. But *Swift* also resonated with the central intuition behind the establishment of federal courts[193] – which, it must be recalled, were created with only diversity jurisdiction and no independent authority to hear federal claims until after the Civil War.

Perhaps confirming the maxim that 'if you build it, they will come,' federal courts quickly became the forum of choice of creditors,

---

[190] Bruce H. Mann, Republic of Debtors 185–86 (2002).

[191] For a rich account of the intellectual history of the move toward a national common law, and particularly the role of Daniel Webster, James Kent and Joseph Story in the creation of that intellectual tradition, see Daniel J. Hulsebosch, Constituting Empire 274 (2005).

[192] 41 US (16 Pet.) 1 (1842).

[193] Patrick Borchers identifies diversity jurisdiction as rooted in the 'national peace and harmony' clause in the amended Virginia Plan. He argues that the framers recognized that federal courts needed independent substantive rules in order to advance this goal. Patrick J. Borchers, The Origins of Diversity Jurisdiction, the Rise of Legal Positivism, and a Brave New World for Erie and Klaxon, 72 Tex. L. Rev. 79, 90–94 (1993).

particularly after the creation of the circuit courts.[194] *Swift* was itself a fairly unexceptional case for that era in the federal courts. At issue was the enforceability of a type of secured credit in pre-Civil War America, what was known as an 'accommodation loan,' recognized in most states, but not in New York, the site of the litigation. The spread of interstate commerce necessitated some form of uniform rules concerning the enforceability of commercial paper, regardless of the state in which the holder in due course might seek to enforce judgment. In seeking to unburden the new American state from its British and colonial inheritances, Justice Story held that, while federal judges sitting in diversity were obligated to honor state law, 'state law' would be defined to mean only state statutes, but not state common law.[195] Thus, in the absence of express state statutes, federal judges were charged with articulating a 'general common law' to be developed through the federal courts.

For Justice Story, *Swift* reinforced a position he had long expounded, based on an understanding of the common law as

> a system of elementary principles and of general juridical truths, which are continually expanding with the progress of society, and adapting themselves to the gradual changes of trade, and commerce, and the mechanic arts, and the exigencies and usages of the country.[196]

Well prior to *Swift*,[197] in *Van Reimsdyk v. Kane*,[198] he wrote of the inherent limits on the power of state law:

> In controversies between citizens of a state, as to rights derived under that statute, and in controversies respecting territorial interests, in which, by

---

[194] See Wythe Holt, 'The Federal Courts Have Enemies in All Who Fear Their Influence on State Objects': The Failure to Abolish Supreme Court Circuit-Riding in the Judiciary Acts of 1792 and 1793, 36 Buff. L. Rev. 301, 323–324 (1987) ('Out-of-state creditors also began to meet with success in the new federal courts. . . . These trends had begun to become evident by the spring and fall circuits of 1791, and became increasingly prominent through the 1790s.') (citation omitted).

[195] *Swift v. Tyson*, 41 US (16 Pet.) 1, 4–5 (1842).

[196] LaPiana, *supra*, at 774 (quoting J. Story, Codification of the Common Law, in The Miscellaneous Writings of Joseph Story 702 (W. Story ed., 1852)).

[197] See also *Thomas v. Hatch*, 23 F. Cas. 946, 949–951 (C.C.D. Me. 1838) (No. 13, 899); *Robinson v. Commonwealth Ins. Co.*, 20 F. Cas. 1002, 1004 (C.C.D. Mass. 1838) (No. 11, 949).

[198] 28 F. Cas. 1062 (C.C.D. R.I. 1812) (No. 16, 871).

CHAPTER 22. SYMPOSIUM: EMERGING ISSUES IN CLASS ACTION LAW

the laws of nations, the lex rei sitae governs, there can be little doubt, that the regulations of the statute must apply. But in controversies affecting citizens of other states, and in no degree arising from local regulations, as for instance, foreign contracts of a commercial nature, I think that it can hardly be maintained, that the laws of a state, to which they have no reference, however narrow, injudicious and inconvenient they may be, are to be the exclusive guides for judicial decision. Such a construction would defeat nearly all the objects for which the constitution has provided a national court.[199]

Swift, almost unexceptionally,[200] advanced the view that 'questions of commercial law are generally considered, as not justly included in that branch of local law, which the courts of the United Sates are bound to administer, as the State Courts hold it to be.'[201] As Justice Story would later add in *Williams v. Suffolk Insurance Co.*:[202]

Upon commercial questions of a general nature, the courts of the United States possess the same general authority, which belongs to the state tribunals, and are not bound by the local decisions. They are at liberty to consult their own opinions, guided, indeed, by the greatest deference for the acknowledged learning and ability of the state tribunals, but still exercising their own judgment, as to the reasons, on which those decisions are founded.[203]

---

[199] *Id.* at 1065. On appeal to the Supreme Court, John Marshall did not echo Justice Story's assessment, choosing to remand the case to determine the contours of the local law in Batavia, where the contract at issue was written. *Clark's Ex'rs v. Van Reimsdyk*, 13 US (9 Cranch) 164 (1815).

[200] Swift was hardly controversial at the time: It was a unanimous decision garnering support from a Court with a majority of Jacksonian judges. See Tony Freyer, Harmony & Dissonance: The Swift & Erie Cases in American Federalism 2–3 (1981) (noting that even 'Democratic stalwarts... Chief Justice Roger B. Taney and Justice Peter V. Daniel' agreed with the decision 'written by the nationalist Joseph Story'). Justice Story's son did not include Swift in his biography of the justice, though he was detailed in his accounts of Justice Story's other 'great' cases. See William A. Fletcher, The General Common Law and Section 34 of the Judiciary Act of 1789: The Example of Marine Insurance, 97 Harv. L. Rev. 1513, 1514 (1984) (noting that William Story 'does not so much as mention Swift' in the biography).

[201] *Donnell v. Columbian Ins. Co.*, 7 F. Cas. 889, 893 (C.C.D. Mass. 1836) (No. 3987).

[202] 29 F. Cas. 1402 (C.C.D. Mass. 1838) (No. 17,738).

[203] *Id.* at 1405.

The contemporary reaction to *Swift* was unremarkable – especially in light of the overwhelming response the case would later occasion.[204] State courts in Ohio and New York 'seemed persuaded that it would lead to a desirable uniformity in commercial matters.'[205] In fact, 'during *Swift*'s first fifty years there were occasional dissents, but no Justice openly challenged Story's original justification.'[206] Above all, the decision seemed a clarification of the role of the 'general common law' as it applied to commercial transactions unaffected by the particularized concerns of 'local law.'[207] Nor did the decision raise issues about its impact on federal structures.[208]

As *Swift* played itself out, however, and as it began to intersect the decidedly more interventionist jurisprudence of the Supreme Court after the Civil War, it emerged as a symbol of the critical fault line in a system premised on dual sovereignty. The resulting critique of *Swift*, almost as universally accepted as it is likely overly simplistic, follows two tracks. First, Justice Story's efforts at using the common law in aid of nation building ran into the problem of a dual-court system and the risk of divergent bodies of law seeming to control the same daily activities. Federal courts became more enamored of their new common law powers, with Justice Swayne, for example, subsequently proclaiming for the Supreme Court, 'We shall never immolate truth, justice, and the law, because a State tribunal has erected the altar and decreed the

---

[204] See e.g., Grant Gilmore, The Ages of American Law 61 (1977) ('The federalizing – or nationalizing – principle of *Swift v. Tyson* became a headless monster, marked down for destruction by all right-thinking men.').

[205] See Teton, *supra*, at 524 n. 36; see also *Staker v. McDonald*, 6 Hill. 93 (N.Y. 1843); *Treon v. Brown & Fuller*, 14 Ohio 172 (1846); *Carlisle v. Wishart*, 11 Ohio 173 (1842).

[206] William R. Casto, The Erie Doctrine and the Structure of Constitutional Revolutions, 62 Tul. L. Rev. 907, 915 (1988).

[207] This point is carefully worked out by Judge William Fletcher in a review of the application of general common law principles to the necessarily interstate market for marine insurance. See Fletcher, *supra*, at 1517. Fletcher points in particular to Blackstone as upholding commercial transactions governed by 'a great universal law' that was 'regularly and constantly adhered to.' *Id.* at 1518 (quoting William Blackstone, 4 Commentaries 67).

[208] See LaPiana, *supra*, at 814 (noting that Justice Story himself did not see 'the nature of federalism as an important issue'). Indeed, the case passed without mention in law reviews, except for one brief comment that failed even to examine its implications for the federal system. See note, *Swift v. Tyson Exhumed*, 79 Yale L.J. 284, 293 n. 45 (1969).

CHAPTER 22. SYMPOSIUM: EMERGING ISSUES IN CLASS ACTION LAW

sacrifice.'[209] Although wonderfully colorful and more than a touch presumptuous, there was still the problem that state courts remained faithful to the 'altar' of state decisional law and that the needs of 'truth' and 'justice' were a tad difficult to predict ahead of time. As a result, the same case could well be decided differently depending upon the accident of citizenship of the parties. Rather than serve as a unifying agent for the nation, *Swift* threatened arbitrariness, subjecting parties to two different standards of law in their everyday affairs.

The *Black & White Taxicab* case epitomized this problem.[210] Brown & Yellow Taxicab, a Kentucky corporation, had secured an exclusive-dealing contract to provide taxi services at a Kentucky railroad station, thereby preventing its competitor, Black & White Taxicab, another Kentucky corporation, from competing in that market. However, Kentucky courts had refused to enforce exclusive-dealing contracts as contrary to public policy. Federal courts, operating under *Swift*, were not obligated to honor Kentucky state decisional law, and had in fact found exclusive-dealing arrangements lawful and enforceable. Brown & Yellow therefore reincorporated in Tennessee, and then, armed with diversity of citizenship, successfully brought an action against Black & White in federal court. By manipulating its citizenship and taking advantage of federal as opposed to state courts, Brown & Yellow was able to enjoin its rival from interfering with its exclusivity contract, a legal maneuver that was ultimately upheld by the Supreme Court. This sort of manipulation of citizenship to control the legal rules governing the same exact contractual relationship at a Kentucky train station exposed the ultimate vulnerability of *Swift*.

Unpredictability was not the only source of disenchantment with *Swift*. The second ground for *Swift's* demise was that the general common law powers of federal courts had been one of the linchpins of federal intervention to stop regulations of the progressive era, with the most notorious being the use of the labor injunction. In addition, the expansive use of constitutional oversight throughout the Lochner Era had made federal courts a particular enemy of progressive reformers throughout the early part of the twentieth century.[211] The hostility to

---

[209] *Gelpcke v. City of Dubuque*, 68 US (1 Wall.) 175, 206–207 (1863).

[210] *Black & White Taxicab & Transfer Co. v. Brown & Yellow Taxicab & Transfer Co.*, 276 US 518 (1928).

[211] See *Post, supra*, at 1598 n. 295 (tying the Court's attachment to the substantive due process doctrines to its handling of the Black & White Taxicab case).

expansive federal-court power only intensified when the Court struck down the National Industrial Recovery Act[212] and other early pieces of the New Deal. By 1938, however, the Court's resistance to social legislation was beginning to buckle, President Roosevelt's appointees were taking hold, and the Court was prepared to rein in the far reaches of the federal common law, with *Erie* the ultimate result.

The demise of *Swift* and the emergence of *Erie* highlight that forum-allocation questions play a major role in the emergence of legal standards, particularly where the dual sovereignty of American federalism runs up against the need for order and predictability in settling the legal expectations of the citizenry as they go about their day-to-day lives. The facts of *Erie* underscored the systemic inefficiencies of rival state and federal claims upon legal actors. At issue was the level of care owed by a railroad to persons who without permission regularly used an obvious footpath along the rail bed. Under the law of Pennsylvania, the situs of the injury at issue, such pedestrians would be considered trespassers to whom only a limited duty of care attached. But when the case was brought in a New York federal court under diversity jurisdiction, the court decreed that the general common law would treat such persons as invitees to whom a heightened duty was owed. Under the Pennsylvania rule, the railroad would be liable only for known hazards; under the federal approach, the railroad would have to police against potential sources of injury. Regardless of how the policy argument concerning the proper duty is resolved, there is clearly a systemic interest in having a clear standard against which the railroad can measure its anticipated liabilities and invest in the optimal level of care.

The early history of the *Erie* doctrine, as exemplified by Justice Frankfurter's opinion in *York v. Guarantee Trust*,[213] concerned itself primarily with disabling the law-generating capacity of federal courts.[214] *Erie* tried to restore the primacy of state courts in developing common law rules by limiting federal courts to the role of explicating procedural rules, as permitted under the Rules of Decision Act.[215] Justice Frankfurter took this one step further by defining the domain of 'procedure,' as distinct from 'substantive' law, to turn on the impact that the forum

---

[212] National Industrial Recovery Act, Ch. 90, 48 Stat. 195 (1993).
[213] 326 US 99 (1945).
[214] Merrill, *supra*, at 13-19.
[215] Judiciary Act of 1789, Ch. 20, 34 1 Stat. 73, 92.

would have on the conduct of the litigation. Under Justice Frankfurter's 'outcome determinative' standard, federal courts were forbidden to alter how a course would have played out in state court but for the fact of diversity jurisdiction, even down to what were generally thought of as procedural requirements, such as rules for class certification[216] or forms of service.[217]

Sheer animus to the federal courts could not sustain *Erie* through the Warren Court era. By the time of *Hanna v. Plumer*,[218] the inquiry had become more sophisticated and focused on the ambiguity of regulatory control over the day-to-day lives of the citizenry, the problem that emerged directly from the dual-court problem faced after *Swift*. In the commanding concurrence in *Hanna*, Justice Harlan identified the key to the *Erie* problem as the difficulty of ordinary citizens controlling their lives in the face of legal uncertainty.[219] Going back to the *Black & White Taxicab* case, for example, both cab companies had an overriding interest in clear legal rules governing exclusive-dealing contracts so as to be able to make such critical business decisions as whether to invest in new cabs, just as the railroad in *Erie* sought legal standards in order to calculate the proper level of investment in precaution. Consistent with the intellectual ascendance of legal-process approaches at the time,[220] Justice Harlan viewed the primary role of law as an aid to private ordering, a role that privileged settled rules of conduct articulated by the proper rule generators.

Justice Harlan's key insight was that procedural rules, even if outcome determinative after the fact, would not create uncertainty in how citizens conducted their lives. If actual service, not mere filing, were required within the limitations period, or if service had to be made by hand, parties would adjust accordingly in using the legal system to resolve disputes. But such variations in procedural rules for litigation

---

[216] See *Cohen v. Beneficial Indus. Loan Corp.*, 337 US 541 (1949) (requiring plaintiffs in derivative action to post bond pursuant to New Jersey state law, even though suit was filed in federal court).

[217] See *Ragan v. Merchants Transfer & Warehouse Co.*, 337 US 530 (1949) (barring as untimely an action filed in federal court prior to statute of limitations under Fed. R. Civ. P. 3, but inconsistent with Kansas state practice requiring service of process prior to the expiration of the statute of limitations).

[218] 380 US 460 (1965).

[219] *Id.* at 474–475 (Harlan, J., concurring).

[220] See generally Henry M. Hart, Jr. & Albert M. Sacks, The Legal Process (1994).

would not inhibit the ability of parties privately to order their affairs the way that the primary conduct at issue in *Black & White Taxicab* or *Erie* required the ability to identify the clear expositor of legal obligations. Justice Harlan's elegant ex ante approach sought to restore to the state legal systems, including common law courts, the ability to set the terms and conditions of the lives of their citizens in such critical areas as tort, contract, and property.

In limiting the law-generative power of federal courts to the realm of the procedural, however, Justice Harlan may have alleviated the *Erie* common law skirmishes while failing to grasp the impact of the ceaseless assaults upon state autonomy posed by the national market – the core problem that Justice Story and the Federalists had well understood more than a century earlier. Even on its own terms, the resolution of the role of federal courts in generating new legal obligations could not possibly have the significance hoped for in *Erie*, in the dogmatic approaches of York, or even in *Hanna*. As is often noted,[221] *Erie* coexisted uncomfortably with the Court's endorsement of the sweeping expansion of the federal regulatory state in the New Deal period. The same impetus toward market rationalization of federal law that we identified in the preceding discussion of preemption reasserts itself in the domain of forum selection, despite the best efforts of Justice Harlan to cabin hermetically the significance of the choice of forum. Justice Harlan assumed that limiting the source of federal common law innovation in the realms of traditional areas of state law would make clear the source of sovereign authority of those primary areas of life. The expansion of the national market and the corresponding centrality of federal regulatory oversight over traditional areas of state common law powers compromised Justice Harlan's elegant *Hanna* divide between state and federal authority.

22.4.2 The Expanding Federal Interest

Justice Harlan's opinion in *Hanna* provided the best, and perhaps the final, approach at a clean division between the spheres of dual sovereignty, a frequently invoked term in contemporary commentary on the cases exploring the limitation on congressional authority,

---

[221] See e.g., Merrill, *supra*, at 13–19.

primarily under the Eleventh Amendment.[222] Whether invoked at the turn of the twentieth century when dealing with the Taft Court or at the turn of the twenty-first century with regard to the Rehnquist Court, 'dual sovereignty held that the nation and the states were each authorized to control autonomous and distinct domains of social life.'[223] The effectiveness of dual sovereignty depends critically on the ability to maintain the rival sources of authority as truly autonomous and distinct.

As the preemption cases show, however, the assumption of autonomous zones of federal and state authority readily breaks down as soon as we confront an increasingly rapacious national market for goods and services. Going back to *National League of Cities v. Usery*,[224] the emerging Rehnquist Court drew a strong distinction between the ability of Congress to regulate the activities of private actors within the states, and the ability of Congress to regulate the states themselves.[225] That distinction well survives the sovereign immunity cases that have prompted so much commentary,[226] as well as the efforts in *United States v. Lopez*[227] to rein in the use of the Commerce Clause for regulations bearing nonobvious relations to national markets. As Ernest Young aptly notes, the 'attributes of sovereignty' that the recent federalism cases seek to

---

[222] See e.g., *Brzonkala v. Va. Polytechnic Inst. & State Univ.*, 169 F.3d 820, 893 (4th Cir. 1999) (en banc) (Wilkinson, C.J., concurring), aff'd sub nom., *United States v. Morrison*, 529 US 598 (2000). For a historical account of the concept of dual sovereignty in debates about American federalism, see H. Jefferson Powell, The Oldest Question of Constitutional Law, 79 Va. L. Rev. 633, 655–657 (1993).

[223] *Post, supra*, at 1518.

[224] 426 US 833 (1976).

[225] See Young, *supra*, at 25. Although we take issue with Ernest Young's effort to develop a sweeping autonomy model for state regulatory endeavors, he provides a crisp analytic divide for assessing the seemingly contradictory impulses between the more prominent federalism cases involving Eleventh Amendment immunities and the preemption cases, for example. See also Fallon, *supra*, at 482 (similarly arguing that the Rehnquist Court federalism decisions have been most sweeping in the sovereign immunity context).

[226] See e.g., Larry D. Kramer, Foreword: We the Court, 115 Harv. L. Rev. 5, 146-150 (2001) (analyzing *Bd. of Trs. of Univ. of Ala. v. Garrett*, 531 US 356 (2001), and *Kimmel v. Fla. Bd. of Regents*, 528 US 62 (2000), as opinions designed to divest congressional power); Linda Greenhouse, Focus on Federal Power, N.Y. Times, May 24, 1995, at A1.

[227] 514 US 549 (1995).

protect 'conspicuously did not include the right to regulate within the states' own jurisdiction free of federal interference. Rather, sovereignty was limited to the states' right to be free from federal regulation of state institutions themselves.'[228] As we previously noted, following the expansive reading of the Commerce Clause in *Raich*, there is little doubt that Congress has ample powers to reach any traditional area of commercial exchange.

Our concern in this part, however, is not so much with the ample substantive scope of federal power over commerce, but with the jurisdictional effects of the expansive federal regulatory reach. Because the Constitution and 28 USC 1331 grant federal courts the power to hear any case 'arising under' federal law, the expansion of federal regulatory reach gives federal courts the same power to assume primacy over shaping substantive law as was provided by diversity jurisdiction in the days of Justice Story. To a large extent, *Erie* and Justice Frankfurter's subsequent robust reading of the 'outcome determinative test' had much the quality of generals fighting the last war. The history of post-World War II federal jurisdiction is of an ever-increasing amount in controversy for the invocation of 1332,[229] as federal courts look increasingly askance at routine state-law claims coming into the federal system. Rather, the source of increasing federal-court immersion into matters once left to state law and state courts comes directly through the expanding domain of federal law itself, and not through the power to hear diversity cases.

22.4.3 The Federal Ingredient in State Law

As the scale of federal regulation grew, there was a corresponding expansion of the role of federal-court jurisdiction under 1331. The expansion of federal subject matter jurisdiction is most direct in 'the "vast majority" of cases ... covered by Justice Holmes's statement that

---

[228] See Young, *supra*, at 25.

[229] The most recent increase came in 1996 when section 205 of the Federal Courts Improvement Act of 1996, increased the amount in controversy threshold for diversity cases from USD 50,000 to USD 75,000. Pub. L. No. 104–317, 205, 110 Stat. 3847, 3850 (codified as amended at 28 U.S.C. 1332 (2000)). For a history of the increases in diversity jurisdiction requirements, see Jaren Casazza, note, Valuation of Diversity Jurisdiction Claims in the Federal Courts, 104 Colum. L. Rev. 1280, 1283 (2004).

CHAPTER 22. SYMPOSIUM: EMERGING ISSUES IN CLASS ACTION LAW

a "suit arises under the law that creates the cause of action."'[230] Under what is known as the 'Holmes test,' federal question subject matter jurisdiction exists where federal law specifically creates the cause of action. Thus, a plaintiff suing under a federal civil rights statute, or in antitrust or securities law, is claiming recovery directly under the statute that controls the case and the jurisdictional reach is the direct corollary of the expansion of federal regulatory power. Whatever tension there may be in the scope of potential federalization of traditional state prerogatives will likely be played out at the level of the substantive law and not in a dispute over forum allocation.

Once we move beyond the direct creation of federal law commanding the field, however, the inquiry becomes more difficult, as with cases recognizing an implied right of action when Congress has failed to empower federal courts to hear claims that should follow from enabling statutes.[231] Here courts have to be wary of cavalierly expanding federal jurisdiction in such a way that would thwart the operation of state courts. As a result, one key element of the 'settled framework' for the recognition of an implied federal cause of action is whether the subject of the statute is an area traditionally within the province of state courts and state law.[232]

Beyond the question whether a cause of action should be implied where Congress has acted only partially, the true battleground over jurisdictional authority is a third approach distinct from both express and implied federal causes of action: what is termed the 'federal

---

[230] *Merrell Dow Pharms., Inc. v. Thompson*, 478 US 804, 808 (1986) (quoting *Franchise Tax Bd. v. Constr. Laborers Vacation Trust*, 463 US 1, 8–9 (1983) (quoting *Am. Well Works Co. v. Layne & Bowler Co.*, 241 US 257, 260 (1916) (Holmes, J.))).

[231] For example, Title VII of the Civil Rights Act of 1964 covering employment discrimination claims creates an express private right of action. 42 U.S.C. 2000e-5(f) (2000). A corresponding section of the same Act, Title VI, which covers federally funded programs as opposed to employment discrimination, does not. *Id.* 2000d. However, the statutes are designed in similar fashion to achieve similar aims, and without a private right of action, Title VI would fail in its purposes. See *Barnes v. Gorman*, 536 US 181, 185 (2002):

> Although Title VI does not mention a private right of action, our prior decisions have found an implied right of action, e.g., *Cannon v. University of Chicago*, 441 US 677, 703 (1979), and Congress has acknowledged this right in amendments to the statute, leaving it 'beyond dispute that private individuals may sue to enforce' Title VI, *Alexander v. Sandoval*, 532 U.S. 275, 280 (2001).

[232] *Merrell Dow*, 478 US at 810.

1013

ingredient' test for cases arising under federal law. A federal ingredient may emerge in a state-court case pleaded under state law where the state-law claim ultimately turns so indispensably on an interpretation of federal law as to render it, for all intents and purposes, a federal claim.[233] Even in a post-*Erie* world in which state courts are seen primarily as a forum for resolving state-law issues and federal courts for resolving questions of federal law,[234] the absence of a clear boundary between the two sources of law spills over into the jurisdictional domain. So long as the articulation of state law remains the domain of state courts, and corresponding development of federal law rests with federal courts, the gods of the two-by-two matrix smile approvingly. As set forth in our introductory table, we are securely within the first and fourth quadrants in which there is a convergence of the forum and the source of law.

The presence of a federal ingredient introduces a hybrid cause of action in which a claim sounding in state law compels review of federal law as well. Invariably such federal ingredient claims force courts into the uncertain terrain of the second or third quadrants, where federal courts must assume the oversight of state law, or state courts begin to divide up responsibility for the application of federal law. As with all areas of law, the borders are hard to police. The question under the federal ingredient test is whether an interpretation of federal law is so integral to the resolution of a dispute that the state court would be required to interpret federal law in some dispositive fashion.[235]

---

[233] Some courts apparently treat the presence of an important international, or foreign relations, element to a state-law claim as a sufficient 'federal ingredient.' See e.g., *Torres v. S. Peru Copper Corp.*, 113 F.3d 540, 543 (5th Cir. 1997) (asserting jurisdiction over a state tort action brought by hundreds of Peruvian citizens against an American company because of injuries they had allegedly suffered from exposure to toxic gases during copper smelting and refining operations in Peru because '[the] plaintiffs' complaint raises substantial questions of federal common law by implicating important foreign policy concerns'); *Republic of Philippines v. Marcos*, 806 F.2d 344, 354 (2nd Cir. 1986) (suggesting that federal jurisdiction was appropriate 'because of the necessary implications of such an action for United States foreign relations').

[234] For a fuller exposition of this point, see Barry Friedman, Under the Law of Federal Jurisdiction: Allocating Cases Between Federal and State Courts, 104 Colum. L. Rev. 1211 (2004).

[235] Our discussion of the federal ingredient test, up to and including Merrell Dow, in the subsequent three paragraphs, draws from Samuel Issacharoff, Civil Procedure 124–125 (2005).

CHAPTER 22. SYMPOSIUM: EMERGING ISSUES IN CLASS ACTION LAW

Ultimately the definition of the federal ingredient forces courts to define the relative authority of state and federal courts in regard to the importance of the competing state and federal interests. Too broad a definition of the federal ingredient would risk federalizing tort law, as so much of daily market transactions with goods and services that might give rise to a contract or tort claim are in turn covered by some aspect of federal regulatory law. On the other hand, too narrow a definition risks Balkanizing federal regulations by leaving their interpretation to uncoordinated state courts.

In the leading case of *Merrell Dow Pharmaceuticals Inc. v. Thompson*,[236] the Supreme Court confronted directly the expansive potential of federal ingredient jurisdiction. At issue in the sweeping Benedictine litigation was whether the mention of a federal statute on the face of a complaint was a sufficient basis for federal jurisdiction. Although plaintiffs sought to recover for alleged birth defects under Ohio tort law, a critical element of the alleged negligence was premised on the claim that the drug's manufacturer failed to label it adequately under a federal statute, the Federal Food, Drug, and Cosmetic Act (FDCA).[237] According to the complaint, the misbranding of Benedictine in violation of the Act was a proximate cause of the harms suffered that should establish 'negligence per se.'[238]

The Court in *Merrell Dow* split five to four on the definition of the federal ingredient. The narrow majority held that the incorporation of the FDCA as evidence of negligence did not present a sufficient federal ingredient to justify federal question jurisdiction, even if a state court would have to rule on the application of the FDCA to the labeling of Benedictine. By effectively limiting federal jurisdiction to express and implied federal causes of action, the Court created a barrier to the potential federalization of all tort law through the introduction of regulatory violations as an element of the state-law cause of action. For causes of action arising under state law, the Court ultimately reasoned, the primacy of the state interest should direct litigants to state courts.

While the majority could claim to be protecting the integrity of state control of the tort system, the dissent could equally claim to be protecting the integrity of the federal statute from ad hoc interpretation in local state courts around the country. After all, much of the

---

[236] 478 US 804 (1986).
[237] *Id.* at 805–806.
[238] *Id.* at 823 (Brennan, J., dissenting).

justification for subjecting important areas of our economic and social life to federal oversight is the need for uniform regulation of matters such as copyright or bankruptcy or the vast areas that fall under the Commerce Clause. It would be anomalous to enable federal oversight on this basis and then leave the interpretation and implementation to state courts acting more or less autonomously. Bringing federal-law questions to federal court allows oversight by the circuit courts of appeals and allows much greater coordination through the developing law of each circuit that controls subsequent cases. The alternative would be to proceed in more spasmodic fashion through the state courts with the only centralizing and unifying force being the remote possibility of US Supreme Court review of state-court final decisions.

Merrell Dow proved not to be the last word on the federal ingredient test. Recently, in *Grable & Sons Metal Products, Inc. v. Darue Engineering & Manufacturing*,[239] the Court confronted a lurking federal issue in an action to quiet title – about as prototypical a state-court action as one could envision. The difficulty in the case lay in the argument that title had been improperly taken from *Grable* because an earlier tax forfeiture had not provided him with notice as required by the relevant tax statute. *Darue* sought to remove the action on the ground that the ruling would invariably turn on the correct application of federal tax law, something that required both expertise and predictability of treatment that could only be achieved in federal court. In upholding the removal, the Court was careful to consider the sweeping implications for forum alterations that would result were any federal ingredient to suffice for federal subject matter jurisdiction: 'A general rule of exercising federal jurisdiction over state claims resting on federal mislabeling and other statutory violations would thus have heralded a potentially enormous shift of traditionally state cases into federal courts.'[240]

Even so, the Court could not avoid reinvigorating the federal ingredient line of arising under jurisdiction because of the need for forum specialization in the expanding domain of federal law:

> The doctrine [of federal arising under jurisdiction] captures the common-sense notion that a federal court ought to be able to hear claims recognized under state law that nonetheless turn on substantial questions of federal

---

[239] 125 S. Ct. 2363 (2005).
[240] *Id.* at 2370–2371 (distinguishing Merrell Dow).

CHAPTER 22. SYMPOSIUM: EMERGING ISSUES IN CLASS ACTION LAW

law, and thus justify resort to the experience, solicitude, and hope of uniformity that a federal forum offers on federal issues.[241]

Despite the potential sweep of this jurisdictional assertion, the opinion prompted nary a dissent. *Grable* has reinvigorated federal question jurisdiction.[242] Whatever the federalism concerns may have been, they appear secondary to the need to provide an effective forum for claims under national law.

22.5 UNSTABLE HYBRIDS: PARTIAL FEDERALIZATION

This chapter is primarily an analysis of the subconstitutional decisions of the past two decades to show that the Rehnquist Court, despite its federalist billing, has largely been an active promoter of the federalization of large bodies of substantive law and the law governing forum selection. Thus far our project has been an attempt to categorize the impetus to federalization as turning on an effort to align the source of substantive law with the forum. On our account, there is a conceptual integrity to the first and fourth quadrants in which federal and state laws are presented in turn to federal and state judicial fora. However, our model turns not on the notion of an evolved, stable equilibrium, but instead on identifying pressure points (in the second and third quadrants), wherein federal courts can help facilitate transitions toward more stable resting ground, without engaging in wholesale

---

[241] *Id.* at 2367.

[242] Lower courts have begun to adopt a similarly expansive view of Grable. See, e.g., *Nicodemus v. Union Pac. Corp.*, 440 F.3d 1227 (10th Cir. 2006) (reversing course from prior decision governed by Merrell Dow and holding in an unjust enrichment case – requiring interpretation of a federal land grant – that federal jurisdiction was proper under Grable); see also *Broder v. Cablevision Sys. Corp.*, 418 F.3d 187 (2nd Cir. 2005); *McMahon v. Presidential Airways*, 410 F. Supp. 2d 1189 (M.D. Fla. 2006). Most recently, however, in a five-to-four decision, the US Supreme Court has attempted to cabin Grable within a 'special and small category' of cases involving 'a nearly "pure issue of law," one "that could be settled once and for all and therefore would govern numerous tax sale cases."' *Empire HealthChoice Assurance, Inc. v. McVeigh*, No. 05-200, slip op. at 19, 20 (US June 15, 2006) (quoting Richard H. Fallon, Jr., Daniel J. Meltzer & Daniel L. Shapiro, Hart and Wechsler's The Federal Courts and the Federal System 65 (Supp. 2005)).

EMPLOYMENT CLASS AND COLLECTIVE ACTIONS

federalization through federal common law. We have identified the continued pressure that the nationalized market places to move the source of regulatory authority from the fourth quadrant (state-law claims in state court) to the first quadrant (federal-law claims in federal court). Federalization responds to the need to coordinate national market standards, a concern that we can trace back to the framers; and from the need to police against the pollution-like conduct at the state level – actions that externalize costs but concentrate benefits for a particular state at the expense of others. But federal courts may, conversely, intervene in ways that, over time, lead cases to settle back into the comfort of the fourth quadrant.[243]

We now turn away from the quadrants that offer conceptual integrity to those that are most problematic, the second and third quadrants dealing with a mismatch between the source of law and the forum. In this part, we present two examples where our approach yields insights about partial federalization attempts and, more generally, the role of federal courts as facilitators during periods of transition.

22.5.1 The Class Action Fairness Act

The first problem is created by a decision to centralize in federal court cases affecting the national market, but without providing a source of federal law to govern these actions – what serves as Quadrant II in our introductory schematic. The primary effect of the Class Action

---

[243] A contemporary example is provided in the takings context. A historical example (suggested to us by Thomas Merrill) is the Supreme Court's nineteenth-century invocation of the Contract Clause to discipline states that were repudiating their bond obligations. Over time, after repeated federal-court intervention, such cases settled back into stability in Quadrant IV. Although beyond the scope of this article, it is also possible that the expansion of the national commercial market during the period of Swift's ascendancy may have allowed the benefits of homogenized market treatment of transactions to be realized and may have, in turn, laid the foundation for the rapid adoption of the Uniform Commercial Code across the country. This is also suggested to us by Thomas Merrill as an example in which federal-court intervention can further a state interest in coordinated treatment of common problems. The upshot is that the uncertainty of our Quadrants II and III need not lead inevitably to the full federalization of Quadrant I if other means of coordinating state conduct can be found.

CHAPTER 22. SYMPOSIUM: EMERGING ISSUES IN CLASS ACTION LAW

Fairness Act (CAFA)[244] is to expand the scope of federal diversity jurisdiction over class actions bearing on national market conduct, consistent with the tenor of expansive judicial readings of federal question jurisdiction[245] and supplemental jurisdiction[246] to extend similarly the reach of federal courts. By its own terms, Congress in CAFA sought to 'restore the intent of the framers of the United States Constitution by providing for Federal court consideration of interstate cases of national importance under diversity jurisdiction'[247] and to stem 'abuses'[248] that were 'keeping cases of national importance out of Federal court.'[249]

In expanding the scope of diversity jurisdiction, Congress directly tied federal-court review to the national market scope of the alleged improper conduct. CAFA's definition of jurisdiction turns on the multistate scope of the harm and an amount in controversy greater than USD 5 million. As reflected in the senate report, the animating concern was that principles of horizontal federalism needed to be invoked to constrain the ability of one state to impose its desired legal standards on national market conduct:

> The effect of class action abuses in state courts is being exacerbated by the trend toward 'nationwide' class actions, which invite one state court to dictate to 49 others what their laws should be on a particular issue, thereby undermining basic federalism principles.[250]

The congressional response was to open up the federal forum as a bulwark against improper or opportunistic state-court oversight of the national market.

Our inquiry is not directed at the scope of the perceived abuses of class action practice in some notorious captive jurisdictions.[251] Rather,

---

[244] Class Action Fairness Act of 2005, Pub. L. No. 109-2, 119 Stat. 4 (codified in scattered sections of 28 U.S.C.).

[245] See *Grable*, 125 S. Ct. at 2367 (noting expansion of federal question jurisdiction beyond federal causes of action to cases that 'implicate significant federal issues').

[246] See *Exxon Mobil Corp. v. Allapattah Servs., Inc.*, 125 S. Ct. 2611, 2620–2621 (2005) (finding jurisdiction for a single claim 'even if the civil action over which it has jurisdiction comprises fewer claims than were included in the complaint').

[247] Class Action Fairness Act of 2005 2(b)(2), 119 Stat. at 5.

[248] *Id.* 2(a)(4), 119 Stat. at 5.

[249] *Id.* 2(a)(4)(A), 119 Stat. at 5.

[250] S. Rep. No. 109–114, at 24 (2005), as reprinted in 2005 U.S.C.C.A.N. 3, 24.

[251] See e.g., NLJ Roundtable: Class Action Fairness Act, Nat'l L.J., May 16, 2005, at 18 (statement of John Beisner, Partner, O'Melveny & Myers LLP) (suggesting that CAFA was aimed at preventing class action abuses in 'magnet' state courts).

we turn to the broader concern about the need for federal oversight of legal claims that affect the entire national market. National market claims pose the risk that any one state's ability to enforce the judgments of its courts threatens to disable any second state's ability to have corresponding authority over claims affecting the second state's citizens. CAFA responds to this problem by expanding the scope of diversity and removal jurisdiction in federal court.[252] But the act conspicuously eschews any substantive legal oversight at the national level, as with a federal products liability or consumer-protection regime, and instead provides only an alternative forum that is left to struggle with conflicting substantive laws over what is likely to be identical market conduct.

The decision not to reach issues of substantive law was far from inadvertent. The current wedge issue for the viability of many class actions – particularly those like consumer class actions that are not financially viable as individual cases – is oftentimes the manageability for trial of claims that cover multiple jurisdictions.[253] Congress rejected several amendments that would have addressed the manner by which multistate class actions brought into federal court under CAFA should be handled.[254] In the short run, it is difficult to avoid the conclusion that CAFA was designed to offer absolution to potential defendants in what are termed 'negative value' class actions, such as consumer cases, in which the only capacity to bring suit is premised on the ability of an entrepreneurial attorney to organize a class action of suitable dimensions.[255] At least in the short run, removal to federal court is likely to

---

[252] CAFA allows for easier removal of nationwide class actions to federal court by expanding federal jurisdiction for minimal diversity and substituting a class-wide jurisdictional amount of USD 5 million. See Class Action Fairness Act of 2005 4(a)(2), 119 Stat. at 9 (adding new 28 U.S.C. 1332(d)(2)).

[253] See e.g., In re Bridgestone/Firestone, Inc., 288 F.3d 1012 (7th Cir. 2002); In re Rhone-Poulenc Rorer Inc., 51 F.3d 1293 (7th Cir. 1995); see also Richard A. Nagareda, Bootstrapping in Choice of Law After the Class Action Fairness Act, 74 UMKC L. Rev. (forthcoming 2006) (describing centrality of disputes over choice of law issues in certifying nationwide classes).

[254] One rejected amendment, introduced by Senator Dianne Feinstein, would have directed federal courts not to 'deny class certification' simply because 'the law of more than 1 State will be applied.' 151 Cong. Rec. S1215 (daily edn February 9, 2005) (proposed amendment SA4 by Sen. Feinstein). Issacharoff was a primary draftsman for another of the rejected amendments.

[255] See *Amchem Products, Inc. v. Windsor*, 521 US 591, 617 (1997) ('The policy at the very core of the class action mechanism is to overcome the problem that small

prompt endless arguments on the reconcilability of the different legal regimes that might apply had low-value consumer claims been prosecuted individually – an exchange as unrealistic as it is contrary to the animating premise of CAFA: the existence of economic activity of nationwide scope.[256]

The debates over the form that class actions can take under CAFA, and over the burdens that the new federal forum will impose on cases that had previously been the exclusive preserve of state courts, are not our central concern. CAFA changes the conditions for the viability of a large number of class action cases and there invariably will be short-term strategic posturing of the parties as they acclimate to a new legal environment.[257]

Rather, our concern is with the implications of CAFA for federalization. Intriguingly, CAFA takes us back to Justice Story and the attempt to forge national law for the emerging national market nearly two centuries ago. Justice Story understood the centrality of a predictable and uniform body of law to govern interstate commerce, but his efforts foundered on the dual-court problem. So long as both state and federal courts could hear the same claims, depending on the fortuity of the domicile of the parties or of strategic pleading of the diversity requirements (or obstacles thereto), uniformity could not be achieved, as famously demonstrated in the *Black & White Taxicab* case.[258]

CAFA provides a fitting lens through which to view the entire thrust of this article. Judged in retrospect, we can see the root causes of why Justice Story's efforts at rational centralization of law failed. Uniformity required one of two strategies: either preemption of

---

recoveries do not provide the incentive for any individual to bring a solo action prosecuting his or her rights.') (quoting *Mace v. Van Ru Credit Corp.*, 109 F.3d 338, 344 (7th Cir. 1997)).

[256] Also likely, at least in the short run, will be attempts to circumvent CAFA's jurisdictional requirements by some selective filing of single-state class cases. We will leave to the side these sorts of transitional issues that emerge as the plaintiff and defense bars work out their respective strategies for using CAFA.

[257] For a fuller discussion of the impact of CAFA on multistate class actions and the immediate difficulties posed by choice of law questions, see Samuel Issacharoff, Settled Expectations in a World of Unsettled Law, 106 Colum. L. Rev. (forthcoming 2006).

[258] *Black & White Taxicab & Transfer Co. v. Brown & Yellow Taxicab & Transfer Co.*, 276 US 518 (1928).

rivalrous state law, regardless of its source in decisional or statutory law, or concentration of an entire body of cases in federal court. The burden of our argument has been to show that there is an underexplored link between the emergence of predominant federal substantive law overcoming the problems of horizontal coordination among the states, and the correspondingly expanding role of the federal forum in creating a nurturing incubator for that law.

The question then becomes what are federal courts to do with an intermediate legal regime that gives them forum control of 'cases of national importance'[259] without any corresponding invitation to forge the substantive law that governs those cases. Here again, we wish to distinguish the short-term strategies from the longer-term implications of centralizing a body of law in federal courts.

In the initial jockeying under CAFA, the lines of argumentation will presumably follow the inherited minuet from past cases. Opponents of class certification will claim that the overwhelming differences in the substantive laws and the preeminence of choice of law principles, no matter how indeterminate these might be, make aggregation impossible in light of the 'manageability' requirement of Federal Rule of Civil Procedure 23(b)(3).[260] Meanwhile, proponents of class certification will claim either that the differences in substantive law among the states are nonexistent or that they can be handled through patterned jury charges.[261] As summarized by a current draft on the issue of claim aggregation by the American Law Institute:

> advocates of class certification have an incentive to frame legal and factual issues at high levels of generality so as to argue for their commonality,

---

[259] Class Action Fairness Act of 2005, Pub. L. No. 109-2, 2(a)(4)(A), 119 Stat. 4, 5.

[260] For an argument that under *Klaxon Co. v. Stentor Electric Manufacturing Co.*, 313 US 487 (1941), there can be no settled expectation in any stable choice of law regime, see Issacharoff, *supra*. Nonetheless, there is evidence in the legislative history of CAFA that this is exactly what was hoped for: 'Over the past ten years, the federal court system has not produced any final decisions – not even one – applying the law of a single state to all claims in a nationwide or multi-state class action.' See S. Rep. No. 109–14, at 64 (2005), as reprinted in 2005 U.S.C.C.A.N. 3, 59.

[261] This use of patterned jury instructions to isolate all the necessary elements under various state-law regimes is the approach first suggested by the Third Circuit Court of Appeals in re School Asbestos Litigation, 789 F.2d 996, 1010–1011 (3rd Cir. 1986), approvingly cited by the Manual for Complex Litigation (Fourth) 22.317, at 361 n. 1078 (2004).

CHAPTER 22. SYMPOSIUM: EMERGING ISSUES IN CLASS ACTION LAW

whereas opponents of class certification have an incentive to catalogue in microscopic detail each legal or factual variation suggesting the existence of individual questions.[262]

We leave for other commentators and for another time the particulars of how to join cases arising from multiple state laws.

Although CAFA declared its intent to leave *Erie* untouched,[263] once national-market cases are jurisdictionally isolated in federal courts, the need to develop incremental decisional law to address the particular concerns of these cases will be inescapable.[264] And if federal courts are the only courts hearing these cases, then the most relevant source of authority for how to handle similar problems will be the common experience of federal courts in other CAFA cases.[265] The likely effect of CAFA will then be to allow a body of national law to develop that corresponds to the demands of an undifferentiated market in which products are manufactured and sent to consumers across a distributional chain of ever-expanding geographic reach. Despite the entreaties of *Erie*, there is only one term for a body of self-referential decisional law emerging from the federal courts: federalized common law.[266]

---

[262] For further discussion, see Am. Law Inst., Principles of the Law of Aggregate Litigation 2.03, cmt. b (Prelim. Draft No. 3, August 25, 2005). Issacharoff serves as the reporter for this ALI project.

[263] The Senate Report states that 'the Act does not change the application of the Erie Doctrine.' S. Rep. No. 109-14, at 49 (2005), as reprinted in 2005 U.S.C.C.A.N. 3, 46.

[264] Cf. JoEllen Lind, 'Procedural Swift': Complex Litigation Reform, State Tort Law, and Democratic Values, 37 Akron L. Rev. 717, 719 (2004) (suggesting, pre-CAFA, that procedural changes could lead to 'substantially different results than state proceedings').

[265] This is likely to be the case with novel claims for which there is no governing state law. Imagine, for example, an interstate class action involving an internet-based electronic intrusion – an area of indeterminate state law, in a state of flux. Of course, conversely, federal courts might use this as an occasion to deny certification on manageability grounds.

[266] Post-*Erie*, commentators have described 'enclaves' of federal common law – most prominently in admiralty, see US Const. Art. III, 2, and the government contractor defense, see *Boyle v. United Tech. Corp.*, 487 US 500, 504-506 (1988). But, of course, the reach of general common law is not quite so limited. See e.g., Caleb Nelson, The Persistence of General Law, 106 Colum. L. Rev. 503, 505 (2006) ('Our federal system all but requires continuing recourse to rules of general law.'); see also Martha A. Field, Sources of Law: The Scope of Federal Common Law, 99 Harv. L. Rev. 881,

There is, of course, no certainty as to how the law will develop. CAFA could well augur the death knell for all national market class actions if federal courts were to decide that redress in these cases is not to be had.[267] But by creating a centralized forum for all national market class actions, CAFA could very well provide an impetus for the development of a coordinated body of substantive law to address the particular concerns of these cases. Centralized forum law without centralized substantive law is simply not a stable resolution of the concerns giving rise to CAFA.

22.5.2 Punitive Damages

We turn now from Quadrant II, where CAFA resides, to Quadrant III, our second example of partial federalization: the Supreme Court's punitive-damages jurisprudence. Over the past decade, the Supreme Court has been building an increasingly elaborate constitutional edifice around state-law awards of punitive damages.[268] In a series of decisions announcing a due process limit on the amount of punitive damages that the Constitution may be read to tolerate, the Court has largely federalized an area long thought to be a matter solely within the realm of state prerogatives.[269] Undeniably, with its placement of constitutional limitations on punitive damages, the Court 'ventures

---

888 (1986) ('Federal common law is not limited to particular enclaves. Instead, the central issue in all cases is the degree of federal need for a federal rule, and the degree to which that rule would impinge upon state interests.').

[267] See e.g., John C. Coffee, Jr., New World of Class Actions: CAFA, Exxon, and Open Issues, N.Y.L.J., July 21, 2005, at 5 (challenging the 'conventional wisdom about class actions... that [CAFA] will reduce their number, end the certification of nationwide class actions in notorious "magnet" state courts, and largely preclude mass tort class actions').

[268] See *State Farm Mut. Auto. Ins. Co. v. Campbell*, 538 US 408 (2003); *Cooper Indus., Inc. v. Leatherman Tool Group, Inc.*, 532 US 424 (2001); *BMW of N. Am., Inc. v. Gore*, 517 US 559 (1996); *TXO Prod. Corp. v. Alliance Res. Corp.*, 509 US 443 (1993); *Pac. Mut. Life Ins. Co. v. Haslip*, 499 US 1 (1991); *Browning-Ferris Indus. of Vermont, Inc. v. Kelco Disposal, Inc.*, 492 US 257 (1989).

[269] See Catherine M. Sharkey, Punitive Damages as Societal Damages, 113 Yale L.J. 347, 429–432 (2003) (discussing 'federalism-based territorial limitations on punitive damages' imposed by the Supreme Court in *Gore* and *Campbell*).

CHAPTER 22. SYMPOSIUM: EMERGING ISSUES IN CLASS ACTION LAW

into territory traditionally within the States' domain.'[270] Not surprisingly, then, the Court's jurisprudence here has been criticized as usurping state power.[271] Even within the Court, there is strong dissension on federalism grounds; for example, in one scathing retort, Justice Scalia was adamant that 'the Constitution provides no warrant for federalizing yet another aspect of our Nation's legal culture.'[272]

But, as we saw in the preemption cases, federalism objections in the name of state autonomy neglect the horizontal federalism dimension that has been our main concern. Just as in prior areas where there is a substantial federal interest in overcoming the coordination problem among states, here, too, the Court appears sensitive to the impact of local decisions on the national economy and on other states' ability to regulate their affairs. Here again, an insistence upon reserving the traditional function of tort damages to the states would in fact undermine the broader ability of states to regulate locally. The extraterritorial effect of punitive damages awards – not often at the fore of the vociferous debate in this area[273] – is at the heart of our

---

[270] *Gore*, 517 US at 607 (Ginsburg, J., dissenting).

[271] See e.g., Martin H. Redish & Andrew L. Mathews, Why Punitive Damages are Unconstitutional, 53 Emory L.J. 1, 10 (2004) ('A federalized democratic system should not tolerate so blatant a usurpation of state legislative and judicial prerogatives by an unaccountable federal judicial body.').

[272] *Gore*, 517 US at 599 (Scalia, J., dissenting). The dissents of Justices Scalia and Ginsburg, joined, respectively, by Justice Thomas and then-Chief Justice Rehnquist were grounded in federalism concerns. *Id.* at 598 (Scalia, J., dissenting) (finding the Court's holdings in this area 'an unjustified incursion into the province of state governments'); *id.* at 607 (Ginsburg, J., dissenting) ('The Court ... unnecessarily and unwisely ventures into territory traditionally within the States' domain.').

[273] See Michael P. Allen, The Supreme Court, Punitive Damages and State Sovereignty, 13 Geo. Mason L. Rev. 1, 3 (2004) (arguing that the state sovereignty limitation on punitive damages awards is a 'largely ignored aspect of the Supreme Court's developing constitutional jurisprudence relating to punitive damage awards'). But see Paul H. Rubin et al., BMW v. Gore: Mitigating the Punitive Economics of Punitive Damages, 5 Sup. Ct. Econ. Rev. 179, 216 (1997) ('The most interesting issue raised by Gore is the federalism issue: is it appropriate for federal courts to interfere with state court decisions on damages?'); Sharkey, *supra*, at 429–432 (discussing 'vexing issue of extraterritoriality' in Supreme Court punitive damages jurisprudence); *id.* at 350 ('A ... contextualized and nuanced reading of [Campbell] suggests that the Court was primarily concerned with limiting the extraterritorial or out-of-state reach of punitive damages.'). A different approach is suggested by David Shapiro, who

account of the Supreme Court's federalization of the law of punitive damages.[274]

BMW of North America, Inc. v. Gore[275] and *State Farm Mutual Automobile Insurance Co. v. Campbell*[276] – the two cases in which the Supreme Court has reversed state punitive damages judgments – each involved attempts by one state to regulate conduct occurring in another state.[277] In *Gore*, where the Court overturned a USD 2 million punitive damages award in a consumer fraud case involving an undisclosed paint touchup on a BMW (one of roughly 983 such undisclosed reported incidences nationwide), the Court declared that 'one State's power to impose burdens on the interstate market for automobiles is not only subordinate to the federal power over interstate commerce, but is also constrained by the need to respect the interests of other States.'[278]

---

identifies the 'hazards of punitive damage exposure in multiple jurisdictions' as potentially a burden on interstate commerce resulting from 'threatened... overexposure to liability.' Shapiro, *supra*, at 120.

[274] For a contrary account, see Benjamin C. Zipursky, A Theory of Punitive Damages, *84 Tex. L. Rev. 105, 119 (2005)*:

> The Justices were surely aware that [comity and federalism concerns] were only 'hooks' for the proponents of constitutional scrutiny of punitive damages; the larger issue, by far, was whether the Court would strike down the award as excessive, and would hold that – even apart from comity and state sovereignty issues – there are guidelines for constitutional excessiveness that in principle apply to any punitive damages award under any American jurisdiction's tort law.

[275] 517 US 559 (1996).

[276] 538 US 408 (2003).

[277] Rubin et al. provide a persuasive account of the federalism interest at stake. They argue persuasively, relying on Tiebout's 'exit' model, that the pre-BMW cases where the Supreme Court refused to interfere can be viewed as presenting situations where the firms would have more easily been able to exit the awarding jurisdiction. Rubin et al., *supra*, at 212–213. According to the authors, the exit theory holds true for 'goods or services sold within the boundaries of one state, such as trash removal services, medical insurance, and land, all of which were involved in recent cases in which the Court upheld large punitive damages awards.' *Id.* at 216 (discussing *TXO Prod. Corp. v. Alliance Resources Corp.*, 509 US 443 (1993) (land); *Pac. Mut. Life Ins. Co. v. Haslip*, 499 US 1 (1991) (health insurance); *Browning-Ferris Indus. of Vt., Inc. v. Kelco Disposal, Inc.*, 492 US 257 (1989) (disposal services)).

[278] *Gore*, 517 US at 571 (citation omitted). As a general matter, the Court reasoned that 'principles of state sovereignty and comity' required that the imposition of

CHAPTER 22.   SYMPOSIUM: EMERGING ISSUES IN CLASS ACTION LAW

By imposing large punitive damages awards, Alabama appropriates funds from BMW, which BMW recoups not solely from the citizens of Alabama, but from the country as a whole.[279] In this way, Alabama, as a putative Brandeisian laboratory of democracy, imposes harm on the rest of the country.[280] These spillover effects from Alabama's actions, moreover, impede the very autonomy value the dissenters seek to protect with their invocations of federalism.[281]

A similar theme is picked up by the Court in *Campbell* – a case involving a bad faith action against an insurance company that had engaged in various forms of alleged nationwide misconduct:

> A basic principle of federalism is that each State may make its own reasoned judgment about what conduct is permitted or proscribed within its

---

punitive damages 'must be supported by the State's interest in protecting its own consumers and its own economy.' *Id.* at 572.

[279] *Id.* at 572–574. Rubin et al. have proposed that federal regulation of punitive damages is appropriate when two conditions hold: '1. the transaction that yielded the award is part of interstate commerce; and 2. it is impossible for the defendant to charge the citizens of the state with the total value of expected bad judgments.' Rubin et al., *supra*, at 203–204. These two conditions likewise rule out situations where it would be possible to internalize the costs of a state's tort system to affect only its citizens. If the transaction is not part of interstate commerce (i.e., it is a completely local operation), then an increase in prices to offset the punitive damages award will affect only the citizens of the regulating state. This will often be an empirical question. Compare Helland & Tabarrok, *supra*, at 359–361 (discussing effects on out-of-state defendants), with Thomas J. Campbell et al., The Causes and Effects of Liability Reform: Some Empirical Evidence 15 (Nat'l Bureau of Econ. Research, Working Paper No. 4989, 1995), available at <http://papers.nber.org/papers/w4989.v5.pdf> (arguing that the costs of inefficient jury verdicts have primarily local effects).

[280] But see Allen, *supra*, at 38–39 (rejecting the premise that punitive damages based in part on out-of-state conduct amount to extraterritorial regulation, and suggesting instead that 'the approach the Court has taken in the criminal context provides the most analogous paradigm for approaching the use of extraterritorial conduct in the punitive damages context'). The analogy to extraterritoriality in criminal sentencing, however, comes up short with respect to spillover effects. It is difficult to imagine a situation where an aggravating factor used in a criminal sentence in one state would harm the citizens of another.

[281] The effect of the punitive damages award (overturned in *Gore*) would be to privilege Alabama's regulatory decision above the 'patchwork of rules representing the diverse policy judgments of lawmakers in 50 states.' *Gore*, 517 US at 570; see also *id.* at 572 ('By attempting to alter BMW's nationwide policy, Alabama would be infringing on the policy choices of other States.').

borders, and each State alone can determine what measure of punishment, if any, to impose on a defendant who acts within its jurisdiction.[282]

According to the Court, states lack 'a legitimate concern in imposing punitive damages to punish a defendant for unlawful [let alone lawful] acts committed outside of the State's jurisdiction.'[283] For these reasons, the Court chastised the Utah Supreme Court for using the case 'as a platform to expose, and punish, the perceived deficiencies of State Farm's operations throughout the country.'[284]

Consistent with the thrust of our main argument, federalization takes hold of this area of the law at least in part to restrain nefarious spillover effects. But the cost of policing against any given state's encroachment on the autonomy of another has been the increasing removal of authority over punitive damages from the states altogether. The result has been a progressively constricted constitutional collar on state authority in the realm of punitive damages. In this vein, Justice Ginsburg has plaintively criticized the Court for providing 'marching orders' on punitive damages to the states.[285] State courts and legislatures have, to a considerable extent, taken these orders to heart. As a preliminary matter, some state courts have, in line with the Court's

---

[282] *State Farm Mut. Auto. Co. v. Campbell*, 538 US 408, 422 (2003) (citing *Gore*, 517 US at 569). The Ninth Circuit previously elaborated on this same point:

> 'While each State has ample power to protect its own consumers, none may use the punitive damages deterrent as a means of imposing its regulatory policies on the entire Nation.' ... Nevada is free, in the absence of federal legislation to the contrary, to choose a policy that may sacrifice some innovation in favor of safety, and Alaska is free to choose a policy that may sacrifice some safety in favor of innovation.... Neither state is entitled, in our federal republic, to impose its policy on the other.

White v. Ford Motor Co., 312 F.3d 998, 1018 (9th Cir. 2002) (quoting *Gore*, 517 US at 585). But see *Boyd v. Goffoli*, 608 S.E.2d 169, 178–179 (W. Va. 2004) (noting Campbell's approval of *Phillips Petroleum Co. v. Shutts*, 472 US 797 (1985), and holding that 'a State has a legitimate interest in imposing damages to punish a defendant for unlawful acts committed outside of the State's jurisdiction where the State has a significant contact or significant aggregation of contacts to the plaintiffs' claims which arise from the unlawful out-of-state conduct').

[283] Campbell, 538 US at 421.
[284] *Id.* at 42.
[285] *Id.* at 438–439 (Ginsburg, J., dissenting).

CHAPTER 22. SYMPOSIUM: EMERGING ISSUES IN CLASS ACTION LAW

direction in *Cooper Industries, Inc. v. Leatherman Tool Group, Inc.*,[286] replaced their traditional deferential standard of review with de novo review of defendants' state constitution-based or statutory-based claims that a punitive damages award is excessive.[287] Then, in conducting de novo appellate review, notwithstanding the Court's cautious refusal to establish a 'bright-line' test for the ratio between punitive and compensatory damages,[288] many state courts now seem to apply a de facto constitutional cap.[289]

---

[286] 532 US 424 (2001).

[287] In *Cooper Industries, Inc. v. Leatherman Tool Group, Inc.*, the Court held that 'courts of appeals should apply a de novo standard of review when passing on district courts' determinations of the constitutionality of punitive damages awards.' *Id.* at 436. Because Cooper Industries dealt with an excessiveness claim raised under the federal Due Process Clause, it did not address whether the de novo standard of review would apply to the appellate court's review of state-based claims. Numerous state supreme courts have decided, nevertheless, that the Cooper Industries de novo standard applies to state common law claims as well. See, e.g., *Diversified Holdings, L.C. v. Turner*, 63 P.3d 686, 692 (Utah 2002). But see, e.g., *Time Warner Entm't Co. v. Six Flags Over Georgia*, LLC, 563 S.E.2d 178, 181 (Ga. Ct. App. 2002) (holding that state courts may apply the abuse of discretion common law standard for review of factual questions).

[288] *Campbell*, 538 US at 425.

[289] See e.g., *Hudson v. Cook*, 105 S.W.3d 821, 832 (Ark. Ct. App. 2003) (upholding approximate 7 to 1 ratio as within 'the acceptable range... most recently set forth by... Campbell'); *Campbell v. State Farm Mut. Auto. Ins. Co.*, 98 P.3d 409, 418 (Utah 2004) (setting punitive damages at maximum single-digit ratio of 9 to 1 on remand). But see *Simon v. San Paolo U.S. Holding Co.*, 113 P.3d 63, 77 (Cal. 2005) (noting that Campbell's discussion of Gore's single-digit ratio merely establishes a 'type of presumption' that may be exceeded in cases of 'extreme reprehensibility or unusually small, hard-to-detect or hard-to-measure compensatory damages'); *Williams v. Philip Morris Inc.*, 127 P.3d 1165, 1181 (Or. 2006) (upholding USD 79.5 million punitive damage award – where jury awarded USD 800,000 in compensatory damages – reasoning that 'single-digit ratios may mark the boundary in ordinary cases, but the absence of bright-line rules necessarily suggests that the other two guideposts – reprehensibility and comparable sanctions – can provide a basis for overriding the concern that may arise from a double-digit ratio'). The Court granted certiorari in *Williams* and, in the upcoming Term, will take up the issue (raised also in *Simon*) whether highly reprehensible conduct on the part of the defendant 'can "override" the constitutional requirement that punitive damages be reasonably related to the plaintiff's harm' *Philip Morris USA v. Williams*, 126 S. Ct. 2329 (2006).

Beyond following suit in terms of conducting appellate review, states arguably have gone further in terms of incorporating the Court's guideposts for appellate review into their substantive standards for punitive damages.[290] Recent legislative (or committee) modifications of state rules of evidence and pattern jury instructions relating to evidence of out-of-state conduct likewise bear the hallmark of *Gore* and *Campbell*.[291]

---

[290] So, for example, the Court's 'reprehensibility' prong has been incorporated directly into substantive law, with express reliance upon Gore and Campbell. See e.g., Civil Comm. on Cal. Jury Instructions, California Civil Jury Instructions 14.71.2 (2005); Comm. on Pattern Jury Instructions Ass'n of Supreme Court Justices, New York Pattern Jury Instructions – Civil 2:278 (2006) [hereinafter New York Jury Instr.]. Similarly, the 'ratio' prong has been incorporated, at least with respect to requiring a 'reasonable and proportionate' ratio between punitive and compensatory damages. See e.g., Iowa Civil Jury Instructions 210.1 (2005); Md. Inst. for Continuing Prof'l Educ. of Lawyers, Inc., Maryland Civil Pattern Jury Instructions 10:12 (4th edn 2002); New York Jury Instr., *supra*, 3:50; Wash. Supreme Court Comm. on Jury Instructions Prac., Washington Pattern Jury Instructions – Civil 348.02 (5th ed.). The defense bar, not surprisingly, generally applauds (and advocates further) this kind of incorporation of federal procedural standards into state substantive law. See e.g., Andrew L. Frey, No More Blind Man's Bluff on Punitive Damages: A Plea to the Drafters of Pattern Jury Instructions, 29 Litigation 24 (Summer 2003).

Lest one conclude that it follows naturally that states should incorporate the Supreme Court's appellate review guideposts into substantive punitive damages law, see Pennsylvania Suggested Standard Civil Jury Instructions 14.02 (2nd edn 2003) ('The amount you assess as punitive damages need not bear any relationship to the amount you choose to award as compensatory damages.').

[291] For example, Colorado lawmakers, citing Campbell, provide that evidence of dissimilar acts that are independent from acts upon which liability was premised is inadmissible. See John W. Grund et al., Personal Injury Practice – Torts and Insurance 37.30 (West's Colo. Practice Series, 2005); see also Ark. Supreme Court Comm. on Jury Instructions, Arkansas Model Jury Instructions – Civil 2218 (2006) (same); Iowa Civil Jury Instructions on Punitive Damages, Civil Jury Instr. 210.1 (same); New York Jury Instr., *supra*, at 2:278 Special Verdict Form I (directing courts to Campbell for 'a discussion of evidence that may be considered by the jury'). By contrast, in California, the Advisory Committee to the Judicial Council of California's Civil Jury Instructions (CACI) recently decided to refrain from making substantive changes in the CACI punitive damages instructions because California tort law was undergoing rapid developments. Judicial Council of California Civil Jury Instructions 3942 (2006).

State-court judges have likewise felt bound (even absent legislative direction) to incorporate state evidentiary standards from the Supreme Court. See e.g., *Sand*

CHAPTER 22. SYMPOSIUM: EMERGING ISSUES IN CLASS ACTION LAW

To the extent that states have felt obligated to fall in step with the Supreme Court's marching orders,[292] it is not a stretch to suggest that the Court's jurisprudence is in the process of creating a generalized federal common law of punitive damages, with far-reaching potential implications. But, to return to our matrix analysis, it is an unstable equilibrium arrived at in Quadrant III, characterized by an overlay of federal law in cases decided for the most part in state courts. The instability of the partial federalization of punitive damages law manifests itself at present in a power struggle of sorts between federal and state articulation of the purposes of punitive damages and in the seemingly intractable 'multiple punitive damages' problem, which we explore in turn.

With respect to the purposes of punitive damages, a paradox emerges: The Supreme Court has simultaneously proclaimed that

(1) The federal due process inquiry into the excessiveness of a punitive damages award 'appropriately begins with an identification of the state interests that a punitive award is designed to serve.'[293]
(2) The two-fold purposes of punitive damages are to punish and to deter.[294]

Most states appear to be in line here with the Supreme Court; the vast majority of states include punishment and deterrence as the goals of punitive damages, a few even incorporating wholesale the precise language from *Campbell* in their pattern jury instructions.[295] If the state

---

Hill Energy, Inc. v. Smith, 142 S.W.3d 153, 157 (Ky. 2004) (vacating a punitive damages award on the ground that the trial court's jury instructions failed to limit evidence of out-of-state conduct); *Jackson v. State Farm Mut. Auto. Ins. Co.*, 600 S.E.2d 346, 36 (W. Va. 2004) (Davis, J., concurring) ('The ruling in Campbell on the use of a defendant's lawful out-of-state [conduct] is binding on the courts of West Virginia.').

[292] It seems reasonable to assume this is the case. For some of the developments detailed in the foregoing footnotes, we can do better than assume. See e.g., Arkansas Model Jury Instructions, *supra* (noting that the new instruction on evidence of out-of-state conduct was 'necessitated by the Court's explicit mandate in State Farm').

[293] *BMW of N. Am., Inc. v. Gore*, 517 US 559, 568 (1996) (emphasis added).

[294] *Id.*; see Sharkey, *supra*, at 350, 429; see also Allen, *supra*, at 8 n. 24 (noting the 'potentially quite powerful argument that the Court is acting beyond its constitutional role... by itself articulating the "proper" role for punitive damages').

[295] See e.g., New York Jury Instr., *supra*, 2:278 (quoting *Campbell* in articulating purposes of punitive damages).

1031

definition of the purposes of punitive damages coincides with that of the Court, then there is no great conflict between state interests and the constitutional overlay. But what if a state has a different conception of punitive damages?[296] The paradox stems from the fact that *Gore* and *Campbell* have effectuated a substantive rather than merely procedural revision of punitive damages law and have allowed state interests to be realized so long as they are in line with the constitutionally acceptable ends of punishment and deterrence.

A partially federalized punitive damages regime raises a second, deep-seated source of instability that stems from what numerous courts and commentators have termed the 'multiple punishments' conundrum.[297] Repeated awards of punitive damages arising from a defendant's single course of conduct threaten the due process rights of a

---

[296] See Catherine M. Sharkey, Revisiting the Noninsurable Costs of Accidents, 64 Md. L. Rev. 409, 444 (2005) ('In addition to punishment and deterrence rationales, several states embrace compensatory goals.'); *id.* at 447 notes 185-187 (citing cases). What, for example, of the 'bounty' rationale for punitive damages?, see e.g., In re Simon II Litig., 407 F.3d 125, 136 (2nd Cir. 2005) ('In addition to serving the goals of punishment and deterrence, punitive damages have been "justified" as a "bounty" that encourages private lawsuits seeking to assert legal rights.') (quoting *Smith v. Wade*, 461 US 30, 58 (1982) (Rehnquist, J., dissenting)), or the precise relevance of the wealth of the defendant?, see, e.g., *Simon v. San Paolo U.S. Holding Co.* 113 P.3d 63, 79 (Cal. 2005) (declaring that, post-*Campbell*, defendant's financial condition 'remains a legitimate consideration in setting punitive damages' because punitive damages should vindicate the state's legitimate interests in deterring conduct harmful to state residents). See also New York Jury Instr., *supra*, 2:278 (instructing jurors to consider defendant's 'financial condition and the impact your punitive damages award will have on the defendant').

There is considerable ambiguity, moreover, with respect to what the Court means by deterrence. See e.g., Sharkey, *supra*, at 443:

> The general consensus surrounding the standard, articulated purposes of punitive damages – to punish and to deter – in fact masks deep and significant disagreement both in terms of relative emphasis of one goal over the other, as well as the exclusivity of these punitive goals.

See also Mark Geistfeld, Constitutional Tort Reform, 38 Loy. L.A. L. Rev. 1093, 1115 (2005) (arguing that Campbell 'effectively limits the purpose of punitive damages to individual or specific deterrence,' relying on a 'conception of tort liability that is not widely shared').

[297] See Sharkey, *supra*, at 432 ('The multiple punishments problem has confounded jurists and scholars for the better part of the past three decades.').

defendant who faces potentially ruinous sanctions. Such awards likewise contribute to a 'race to the courthouse' mentality that may jeopardize future plaintiffs, especially if a defendant is driven into bankruptcy early in the litigation process.[298] In *Campbell*, the Court identified the multiple-punishment issue as a threat to state sovereignty interests.[299] But the threat of extraterritorial application of punitive damages is only one source of potential excess. There is no way to measure whether the purposes of punishment and deterrence have been realized on a state-by-state basis when the underlying conduct at issue spans the nation, as with a defective pharmaceutical drug sent into the stream of commerce. Moreover, most states do not even provide for consideration of prior punitive damages awards across related cases within the same state, let alone punishment exacted in other jurisdictions.[300] The Court, despite its concern for unconstitutional excess, has never directly addressed whether there is any constitutional limit on the aggregate amount of all punitive damages awards against one defendant for a single course of conduct.[301] While

---

[298] See e.g., In re Exxon Valdez, 229 F.3d 790, 795-796 (9th Cir. 2000) ('Mandatory class actions avoid the unfairness that results when a few plaintiffs – those who win the race to the courthouse – bankrupt a defendant early in the litigation process... [and] also avoid the possible unfairness of punishing a defendant over and over again for the same tortious conduct.').

[299] *State Farm Mut. Auto. Ins. Co. v. Campbell*, 538 US 408, 423 (2003) ('Punishment on these bases creates the possibility of multiple punitive damages awards for the same conduct; for in the usual case nonparties are not bound by the judgment some other plaintiff obtains.'); see also *BMW of N. Am., Inc. v. Gore*, 517 US 559, 593 (1996) (Breyer, J., concurring) ('Larger damages might also "double count" by including in the punitive damages award some of the compensatory, or punitive, damages that subsequent plaintiffs would also recover.').

[300] For a listing of statutory provisions in a few outlier states that do attempt to limit subsequent punitive damages awards for 'the same act or single course of conduct,' see Sharkey, *supra*, at 407 and n. 216; see also Thomas B. Colby, Beyond the Multiple Punishment Problem: Punitive Damages as Punishment for Individual, Private Wrongs, 87 Minn. L. Rev. 583, 628 (2003).

[301] In re Simon II Litig., 407 F.3d 125, 136 (2005):

> Despite the long-recognized possibility that defendants may be subjected to large aggregate sums of punitive damages if large numbers of victims succeed in their individual punitive damages claims... the United States Supreme Court has not addressed whether successive individual or class action punitive awards, each passing constitutional muster under the relevant precedents,

EMPLOYMENT CLASS AND COLLECTIVE ACTIONS

courts and legislatures have proposed various stop-gap measures, it seems clear that, absent a federalized, coordinated solution, the problem will persist. In other words, the partially federalized, Quadrant III solution is inherently incomplete.

22.5.3 Further Implications

Our focus on the instability of Quadrants II and III suggests that hybrids between the source of substantive law and the designated forum may be subject to transitional pressures toward integration of substantive law and forum law.[302] We conclude with an example of a

---

could reach a level beyond which punitive damages may no longer be awarded.

(citing *Roginsky v. Richardson-Merrell, Inc.*, 378 F.2d 832, 839 (2nd Cir. 1967) (Friendly, J.) ('We have the gravest difficulty in perceiving how claims for punitive damages in such a multiplicity of actions throughout the nation can be so administered as to avoid overkill.')). Issacharoff served as counsel in this litigation.

[302] An illuminating example (outside the scope of our Article) may be found in Congress's passage of the Private Securities Litigation Reform Act of 1995 (PSLRA), Pub. L. No. 104-67, 109 Stat. 737 (codified in scattered sections of 15 U.S.C.), followed in quick succession by passage of the Securities Litigation Uniform Standards Act of 1998 (SLUSA), Pub. L. No. 105-353, 112 Stat. 3227 (1998) (codified in scattered sections of 15 U.S.C.). In 1995, Congress passed the PSLRA in order to combat perceived abuses in the use of federal securities law by unscrupulous lawyers. One of the main responses to the enactment of the PSLRA was to push much of the litigation of alleged securities violation into state courts, based on state-law claims. See Joseph A. Grundfest & Michael A. Perino, Securities Litigation Reform: The First Year's Experience, at II (Stanford Law Sch., Release 97.1, 1997), <http://securities.stanford.edu/research/studies/19970227firstyr_firstyr.html>, reprinted in Securities Litigation 1997, at 955, 958 (PLI Corporate Law & Practice Course Handbook Series No. B4-7199, 1997), available at WL 1015 PLI/Corp 955 (finding that approximately 26% of securities class action litigation moved from federal to state court during the year after the passage of the PSLRA); H.R. Rep. No. 105-803, at 14 (1998) (Conf. Rep.) (recognizing a '"substitution effect"' whereby plaintiffs resort to state court to avoid the new, more stringent requirements of federal cases'). Congress reacted relatively quickly to this unexpected phenomenon in 1998 by passing the SLUSA, which preempts state-law class action claims alleging 'a misrepresentation or omission of a material fact in connection with the purchase or sale of a covered security.' 15 U.S.C. 78bb(f)(1)(A) (2000). In Merrill Lynch, Pierce, *Fenner & Smith, Inc. v. Dabit*, 126 S. Ct. 1503 (2006), the Supreme Court adopted a broad

CHAPTER 22. SYMPOSIUM: EMERGING ISSUES IN CLASS ACTION LAW

possible evolutionary direction that would make for a more stable legal regime, one that takes as its starting point the concerns underlying both CAFA and the expanded constitutional realm of punitive damages law. To begin, CAFA represents a dramatic expansion of federal jurisdiction, driven in large part by Congress' recognition of the demands of an integrated national market economy. Instability is introduced, however, by the absence of federal substantive law. By contrast, the Supreme Court has forged a quasi-federal substantive law of punitive damages – leading to the converse instability, namely an absence of federal jurisdictional authority.

Moreover, this instability is likely to persist – even with the Supreme Court's expansion of its partial federalization of punitive damages[303] – given the Court's limited ability to police state-court decision-making in this realm. As Justice Ginsburg has pointed out, 'unlike federal habeas corpus review of state-court convictions under 28 U.S.C. 2254, the Court "works at this business of [checking state courts] alone," unaided by the participation of federal district courts and courts of appeals.'[304] It is indeed rare for the federal constitution to

---

reading of SLUSA's preemptive effect. In so doing, the Court (per Justice Stevens) emphasized the 'magnitude of the federal interest in protecting the integrity and efficient operation of the market for nationally traded securities.' *Id.* at 1509; see also *id.* at 1514 (noting that the prospect of parallel class actions proceeding in state and federal court 'squarely conflicts with the congressional preference for national standards for securities class action lawsuits involving nationally traded securities') (internal quotation omitted).

[303] See *Williams v. Philip Morris Inc.*, 127 P.3d 1165, 1181 (Or. 2006), cert. granted, 126 S. Ct. 2329 (2006). An alternative trajectory (pushing in the direction of Quadrant IV) would be for the Court to continue to police state boundaries for punitive damages, but otherwise refrain from expanding federalization of the substantive law. Moreover:

> lower federal courts may increasingly push the Court toward reconciling its principles of extraterritoriality in the punitive damages and class action spheres. The end result would be a regime in which class actions and punitive damages are equally circumscribed by state lines.

Sharkey, *supra*, at 431–432. As noted above, the disaggregation of class action claims at the state level is still a possibility – though perhaps less likely – in the post-CAFA world.

[304] *Campbell*, 538 US at 431 (Ginsburg, J., dissenting) (quoting *Gore*, 517 US at 613) (alteration in original).

constrain state actors, while leaving implementation solely in the hands of state actors.[305] The dissenters in *Merrell Dow* echoed a parallel sense of doubt that 'this Court's appellate jurisdiction over state-court judgments in cases arising under federal law can be depended upon to correct erroneous state-court decisions and to insure that federal law is interpreted and applied uniformly.'[306]

Even if the core problem of the inability to coordinate the imposition of unified punitive damages were to persist for some time, it is possible to imagine intermediate steps that might tighten the fit between the expanding role of federal substantive law and access to the federal forum.[307] For example, the presence of a claim for punitive damages in the world following *Gore* and *Campbell* necessarily implicates federal issues in terms of the permissible limitations on and objectives of punitive damages. To recognize a federal question sufficient for federal jurisdiction whenever punitive damages are sought would risk a sweeping relocation of much of tort law into the federal courts. But it is also possible to imagine a more limited federal interest that would be created where a colorable demand for punitive damages is combined with a state cause of action based upon a federal regulation. A greater alignment of the federal forum and federal law would be achieved by allowing the combination to suffice for federal question jurisdiction.[308]

---

[305] As Justice Ginsburg references, in the realm of criminal procedure, there is federal habeas review. In other areas, there is a 1983 mechanism for collateral attack. Here, takings challenges are unique, in that they require exhaustion of state procedures before one can bring a 1983 action. There are only a handful of additional examples of constitutional claims that can only be asserted on direct appeal through the state-courts system, such as First Amendment limitations on defamation awards.
[306] *Merrell Dow Pharms. Inc. v. Thompson*, 478 US 804, 827 n. 6 (1986) (Brennan, J., dissenting) ('As any experienced observer of this Court can attest, "Supreme Court review of state courts, limited by docket pressures, narrow review of the facts, the debilitating possibilities of delay, and the necessity of deferring to adequate state grounds of decision, cannot do the whole job."') (quoting D. Currie, Federal Courts 160 (3rd edn 1982)).
[307] Our proposal here focuses on the Supreme Court's ability to interpret the federal interest sufficient to trigger federal jurisdiction. An alternative approach would be for Congress to provide for habeas-type collateral review of state-court punitive damages judgments. This type of legislatively enacted collateral review would likewise effectuate a move from Quadrant III to Quadrant I.
[308] In other words, defendants could remove such cases under 28 U.S.C. 1441(b) (2005).

CHAPTER 22. SYMPOSIUM: EMERGING ISSUES IN CLASS ACTION LAW

This approach would not be a radical expansion of federal law because many state common law cases already begin from a foundation of federal law, most notably when the violation of federal regulatory requirements is asserted as the presumptive basis for common law liability.[309] Such a scheme, in essence, would reconcile *Merrell Dow* and *Grable* with the extraterritoriality insight from *Gore* and *Campbell*. We pick up, then, where we left off in our discussion of *Merrell Dow* and *Grable*. Recall that we asserted that invariably federal ingredient claims – where state-law claims turn indispensably on interpretations of federal law – force courts into the uncertain terrain of Quadrants II or III. But the Court, in *Merrell Dow*, was understandably apprehensive about federalizing the bulk of tort law. In *Grable*, by contrast, the Court did allow for original jurisdiction under 1331 for a claim under state law that incorporated a federal-law standard, because of the centrality of federal tax law in the underlying claim.

We understand the Court's concern that an overly expansive view of the federal interest risks bringing the entirety of the common law into federal court. However, our proposal focuses on two distinct aspects, each of which represents a heightened federal interest and that, taken together, trigger the 'strength of the federal interest' while being attentive to the 'implications of opening the federal forum.'[310] As similarly was the case in our evaluation of preemption, a key consideration is the 'sound division of labor between state and federal courts.'[311] This functional view of the federal interest, represented when both the underlying standard of tort liability is predicated on federal law and the potential for punitive damages threatens to spill across a state's

---

[309] We are concerned specifically with cases in which a claimed violation of a federal regulation or statute is used to make out a prima facie state cause of action. See, e.g., *Lowe v. Gen. Motors Corp.*, 624 F.2d 1373, 1379 (5th Cir. 1980) ('This Court has often held that violation of a Federal law or regulation can be evidence of negligence, and even evidence of negligence per se.').

[310] *Grable & Sons Metal Prods., Inc. v. Darue Eng'g & Mfg.*, 125 S. Ct. 2363, 2369 (2005). The Court in Grable took comfort in the fact that 'it is the rare state quiet title action that involves contested issues of federal law,' such that allowance of federal jurisdiction 'would not materially affect, or threaten to affect, the normal currents of litigation.' *Id.* at 2371. Moreover, the Court subsequently reiterated that 'Grable emphasized that it takes more than a federal element "to open" the "arising under" door.' *Empire HealthChoice Assurance, Inc. v. McVeigh*, No. 05-200, slip. op. at 21 (US June 15, 2006).

[311] Grable, 125 S. Ct. at 2367.

borders, is consistent with the flexible standard employed by the Court in 'exploring the outer reaches of 1331.'[312] It is consistent, moreover, with the thrust of CAFA, which, after all, has granted a federal forum to a significant subsample of cases involving colorable preemption defenses – namely interstate class actions.[313]

All of which leads us back to our functional lens. Whereas the violation of the federal statute in *Merrell Dow* did not, in the Court's mind, 'fundamentally change the state tort nature of the action,'[314] the addition of a claim for punitive damages – with the inherent risk of extraterritorial effects upon other states – may.

22.6 CONCLUSION: THE RISK OF PREDATION

At its core, our article is concerned with how federal substantive law and federal forum law, in tandem, serve to stave off the inherent risk of predation – when one state encroaches upon the decisional autonomy of another. Despite its billing as staunch protector of states' rights, the Rehnquist Court continued down the same path as its forebears, at least within the subconstitutional domains of preemption and forum selection. We are struck by the similarity of the rationales put forward for the preemptive role of federal law to promote horizontal equity among the states and for the need to provide a federal forum for diversity and federal question cases implicating the needs of national market integration. This same theme reemerges in CAFA, with the

---

[312] *Merrell Dow Pharms. Inc. v. Thompson*, 478 US 804, 810 (1986) ('In exploring the outer reaches of 1331, determinations about federal jurisdiction require sensitive judgments about congressional intent, judicial power, and the federal system.'). Or, to quote Justice Brennan, 'a test based upon an ad hoc evaluation of the importance of the federal issue is infinitely malleable: at what point does a federal interest become strong enough to create jurisdiction?' *Id.* at 822 n. 1 (Brennan, J., dissenting).

[313] Under the well-pleaded complaint rule, federal question jurisdiction does not exist to support removal on the basis of a preemption defense. See, e.g., *Pinney v. Nokia, Inc.*, 402 F.3d 430, 448–449 (4th Cir. 2005) (holding preemption defense is not a basis for removal of interstate class action against manufacturers and distributors of wireless telephones, rejecting defendants' argument that state-law claims have a 'sufficient connection' to a federal regulatory scheme to provide a basis for federal jurisdiction). Post-CAFA, cases such as Pinney, however, would be removable to federal court under CAFA given their interstate nature.

[314] *Merrell Dow*, 478 US at 814 n. 12.

CHAPTER 22. SYMPOSIUM: EMERGING ISSUES IN CLASS ACTION LAW

concentration in federal court of class action cases arising from national market conduct, and in the Supreme Court's punitive damages jurisprudence, attuned to the extraterritorial impact of local decisions on the national economy and on other states' ability to regulate their affairs. Adopting a functional lens, our approach here has been to merge the analysis of substantive law with that of forum law in order to illuminate the discernible trend toward federalization, albeit often indirect and partial, in the direction of national law for a national market.

22.7 PREEMPTION CASES IN SAMPLE (CHRONOLOGICAL LISTING)

1. *International Paper Co. v. Ouellette*, 479 US 481 (1987).
2. *Pilot Life Insurance Co. v. Dedeaux*, 481 US 41 (1987).
3. *Metropolitan Life Insurance Co. v. Taylor*, 481 US 58 (1987).
4. *Internationial Brotherhood of Electrical Workers, AFL-CIO v. Hechler*, 481 US 851 (1987).
5. *Caterpillar Inc. v. Williams*, 482 US 386 (1987).
6. *Perry v. Thomas*, 482 US 483 (1987).
7. *Lingle v. Norge Division of Magic Chef, Inc.*, 486 US 399 (1988).
8. *California v. ARC America Corp.*, 490 US 93 (1989).
9. *Adams Fruit Co. v. Barrett*, 494 US 638 (1990).
10. *United Steelworkers of America, AFL-CIO-CLC v. Rawson*, 495 US 362 (1990).
11. *English v. General Electric Co.*, 496 US 72 (1990).
12. *Ingersoll-Rand Co. v. McClendon*, 498 US 133 (1990).
13. *Gade v. National Solid Wastes Management Ass'n*, 505 US 88 (1992).*
14. *Cipollone v. Liggett Group, Inc.*, 505 US 504 (1992).
15. *CSX Transportation, Inc. v. Easterwood*, 507 US 658 (1993).
16. *Hawaiian Airlines, Inc. v. Norris*, 512 US 246 (1994).
17. *American Airlines, Inc. v. Wolens*, 513 US 219 (1995).
18. *Mastrobuono v. Shearson Lehman Hutton*, 514 US 52 (1995).
19. *Freightliner Corp. v. Myrick*, 514 US 280 (1995).
20. *Medtronic, Inc. v. Lohr*, 518 US 470 (1996).
21. *AT&T Co. v. Central Office Telephone, Inc.*, 524 US 214 (1998).
22. *El Al Israel Airlines, Ltd. v. Tsui Yuan Tseng*, 525 US 155 (1999).
23. *Humana Inc. v. Forsyth*, 525 US 299 (1999).

24. *United States v. Locke*, 529 US 89 (2000).*
25. *Norfolk Southern Railway Co. v. Shanklin*, 529 US 344 (2000).
26. *Geier v. American Honda Motor Co.*, 529 US 861 (2000).
27. *Pegram v. Herdrich*, 530 US 211 (2000).
28. *Buckman Co. v. Plaintiffs' Legal Committee*, 531 US 341 (2001).
29. *Circuit City Stores, Inc. v. Adams*, 532 US 105 (2001).
30. *Lorillard Tobacco Co. v. Reilly*, 533 US 525 (2001).*
31. *Sprietsma v. Mercury Marine*, 537 US 51 (2002).
32. *Beneficial National Bank v. Anderson*, 539 US 1 (2003).
33. *American Insurance Ass'n v. Garamendi*, 539 US 396 (2003).
34. *Green Tree Financial Corp. v. Bazzle*, 539 US 444 (2003).
35. *Aetna Health Inc. v. Davila*, 542 US 200 (2004).
36. *Bates v. Dow Agrosciences, LLC*, 544 US 431 (2005).*

CHAPTER 23

From 'Predominance' to 'Resolvability': A New Approach to Regulating Class Actions

Allan Erbsen*

23.1 INTRODUCTION

Despite the critical attention focused on class actions, the debate over how best to reform them has not identified a conceptual flaw at the core of their design. Academic scrutiny of class actions over the past sixty years has usually built upon three overlapping themes: the potential utility and fairness (or disutility and unfairness) of aggregating individual claims as a solution to collective action problems that inhibit enforcement of substantive rights, the extent and significance of agency costs and diminished individual autonomy in representative litigation, and the relative roles that courts, legislators, and administrative agencies should play in redressing widespread injuries. These themes at an abstract level frame the debate over whether class actions are desirable as a matter of public policy, and at a technical level frame arguments for or against the myriad procedural reforms that scholars and legislators have proposed to expand, curtail, or manage class litigation.[1] However, analysis of whether and how to reform class actions

---

* Allan Erbsen is Associate Professor of Law, University of Minnesota Law School. He holds a J.D. from Harvard Law School.
[1] A vast and growing literature analyzes the structure, role, and utility of class actions (as well as other aggregative devices) and proposes an equally vast array of regulatory, remedial, and procedural reforms to federal and state laws governing

David Sherwyn and Samuel Estreicher (eds), *Employment Class and Collective Actions*, pp. 1041–1149.
© 2009, Kluwer Law International BV, Printed in Great Britain.

the prevention and remediation of injuries affecting large groups. Among the many excellent contributions to the field are: Deborah R. Hensler et al., Class Action Dilemmas: Pursuing Public Goals For Private Gain (2000); John C. Coffee, Jr., Class Action Accountability: Reconciling Exit, Voice, and Loyalty in Representative Litigation, 100 Colum. L. Rev. 370 (2000) [hereinafter Coffee, Accountability]; John C. Coffee, Jr., Class Wars: The Dilemma of the Mass Tort Class Action, 95 Colum. L. Rev. 1343 (1995) [hereinafter Coffee, Class Wars]; John C. Coffee, Understanding the Plaintiffs' Attorney: The Implications of Economic Theory for Private Enforcement of Law through Class and Derivative Actions, 86 Colum. L. Rev. 669 (1986) [hereinafter Coffee, Private Enforcement]; Kenneth W. Dam, Class Actions: Efficiency, Compensation, Deterrence, & Conflict of Interest, 4 J. Leg. Stud. 47 (1975); Richard A. Epstein, Class Actions: Aggregation, Amplification, & Distortion, 2003 U. Chi. Leg. F. 475 (2003); Owen M. Fiss, The Political Theory of the Class Action, 53 Wash. & Lee L. Rev. 21 (1996); Samuel Issacharoff, Governance and Legitimacy in the Law of Class Actions, 1999 SUP. CT. Rev. 337; Harry Kalven, Jr. & Maurice Rosenfield, The Contemporary Function of the Class Suit, 8 U. Chi. L. Rev. 684 (1941); Benjamin Kaplan, Continuing Work of the Civil Committee: 1966 Amendments of the Federal Rules of Civil Procedure (I), 81 Harv. L. Rev. 356, 375–400 (1967); Jonathan R. Macey & Geoffrey P. Miller, The Plaintiffs' Attorney's Role in Class Action and Derivative Litigation: Economic Analysis and Recommendations for Reform, 58 U. Chi. L. Rev. 1 (1991); Francis E. McGovern, Class Actions and Social Issue Torts in the Gulf South, 74 Tul. L. Rev. 1655 (2000); Arthur R. Miller, Of Frankenstein Monsters and Shining Knights: Myth, Reality, and the 'Class Action Problem,' 92 Harv. L. Rev. 664 (1979); Geoffrey P. Miller, Class Actions in the Gulf States: Empirical Analysis of a Cultural Stereotype, 74 Tul. L. Rev. 1681 (2000); Richard A. Nagareda, The Preexistence Principle and the Structure of the Class Action, 103 Colum. L. Rev. 149 (2003) [hereinafter Nagareda, Preexistence]; Richard A. Nagareda, Autonomy, Peace, and Put Options in the Mass Tort Class Action, 115 Harv. L. Rev. 747 (2002); George L. Priest, Procedural Versus Substantive Controls of Mass Tort Class Actions, 26 J. Leg. Stud. 521 (1997); Martin H. Redish, Class Actions and the Democratic Difficulty: Rethinking the Intersection of Private Litigation and Public Roles, 2003 U. Chi. Legal F. 71; Judith Resnik et al., Individuals Within the Aggregate: Relationships, Representation & Fees, 71 N.Y.U. L. Rev. 296 (1996); Judith Resnik, From 'Cases' to 'Litigation,' 54 Law & Contemp. Probs. 5, 5–46 (1991); Deborah L. Rhode, Class Conflicts in Class Actions, 34 Stan. L. Rev. 1183 (1982); David Rosenberg, Mandatory-Litigation Class Action: The Only Option for Mass Tort Cases, 115 Harv. L. Rev. 831 (2002) [hereinafter Rosenberg, Mandatory Litigation]; David Rosenberg, The Causal Connection in Mass Exposure Cases: A 'Public Law' Vision of the Tort System, 97 Harv. L. Rev. 849 (1984); Thomas D. Rowe, Jr., Beyond the Class Action Rule: An Inventory of Statutory Possibilities to Improve the Federal Class Action, 71 N.Y.U. L. Rev. 186 (1996); David L. Shapiro, Class Actions: The Class as Party and Client, 73 Notre Dame L. Rev. 913 (1998); Charles Silver, 'We're Scared to Death': Class Certification & Blackmail, 78 N.Y.U. L. Rev. 1357 (2003);

often overlooks a critical theoretical concept that has little direct connection to either the collective action, agency cost, or institutional role strands of class action scholarship. This chapter seeks to correct that theoretical oversight, to explore some of its practical implications, and to demonstrate how rethinking the principles that animate class actions reveals a novel avenue of class action reform.

The pivotal issue in most proposed class actions seeking damages is whether class members' factual and legal circumstances are sufficiently alike to permit resolution of contested claims and defenses collectively rather than through traditional case-by-case adjudication. This issue of 'alikeness' arises because the factual circumstances of multiple plaintiffs seeking to join in a single proceeding are seldom precisely the same. Factual distinctions at various levels of subtlety and materiality usually permeate the legal claims of putative class members, such that their collective claims raise both 'common' and 'individual'[2] questions relevant to proving liability and damages. The answer to common questions (such as whether a product was defectively designed or whether an advertisement was misleading) are identical for every class member, and can often be determined accurately and efficiently in a single proceeding before a single finder of fact. However, the answer to individual questions (such as whether a design defect was the proximate cause of an injury or whether a consumer relied on a misleading representation) can vary from plaintiff to plaintiff and may require time-consuming and costly proceedings to assess the merit and monetary value of each class member's claim.[3]

Charles Silver & Lynn Baker, I Cut, You Choose: The Role of Plaintiffs' Counsel in Allocating Settlement Proceeds, 84 VA. L. Rev. 1465 (1998).

[2] Fed. R. Civ. P. 23(b)(3). Elsewhere in this Article, I use the words 'similar' and 'dissimilar' in lieu of 'common' and 'individual' to illustrate the problems that arise when courts attempt to resolve questions that do not yield identical answers for each class member.

[3] The nature and significance of individual issues is a function of the substantive liability and damage rules applicable to asserted claims and defenses. I assume in this article that most common law and statutory sources of rights that create private remedies will continue to include elements – such as proximate causation – that may require varying proofs depending on particular class members' circumstances. The design of procedural rules should accommodate the individualized elements of substantive laws that the procedures help to enforce. See *infra* Ch. 23.3.2. However, to the extent that the content of substantive law creates undesirable obstacles to the

Common and individual questions pull in opposite directions on the issue of whether a court should certify claims for class action treatment. The prevalence of important common questions suggests that consolidating otherwise disparate claims into a class action would efficiently deploy scarce judicial resources while providing plaintiffs with an opportunity to leverage their own resources against the defendant's inherent economy of scale.[4] In contrast, the presence of salient

---

development of fair and efficient procedures, policymakers can amend substantive rules through appropriate judicial or legislative avenues to better exploit the advantages of available procedures. For example, developments in consumer protection law that permit plaintiffs to prove reliance based on general evidence without offering direct testimony arguably illustrate the evolutionary adaptation of substantive law to a procedural environment that favors common elements over individual elements. Cf. Samuel Issacharoff, The Vexing Problem of Reliance in Consumer Class Actions, 74 Tul. L. Rev. 1633, 1654 (2000) (reviewing developments in the law of reliance and arguing that '[i]n the case of reliance, the certification battles are best understood as ongoing uncertainty over the true state of substantive law'). Similarly, the growing literature considering whether the basic structure of tort law can tolerate relaxation of causation and injury requirements to treat the imposition of risk as an actionable harm is highly relevant to the debate over class actions (although it is usually not framed in those terms) because risk-based claims are easier for large numbers of claimants to prove by common evidence than are claims premised on palpable individual injuries. The question of how the structure of tort constrains the definition of required elements thus has ramifications for which procedural remedies will be available to enforce substantive rights, which in turn determines how effective liability rules are likely to be in vindicating the compensation, deterrence, and insurance objectives of tort law. For a general discussion of risk-based liability theories, see generally Matthew D. Adler, Risk, Death & Harm: The Normative Foundations of Risk Regulation, 87 Minn. L. Rev. 1293, 1436–1442 (2003); Margaret A. Berger, Eliminating General Causation: Notes Toward a New Theory of Justice and Toxic Torts, 97 Colum. L. Rev. 2117 (1997); John C.P. Goldberg & Benjamin C. Zipursky, Unrealized Torts, 88 VA. L. Rev. 1625 (2002); Christopher H. Schroeder, Corrective Justice and Liability for Increasing Risk, 37 UCLA L. Rev. 439 (1990).

[4] Class actions potentially promote social welfare by overcoming collective action problems inherent in the regulation of conduct affecting disorganized groups. Injurers can derive large benefits from imposing comparatively small costs on each member of a risk-bearing population. The injurer's ability to derive a concentrated benefit from imposing diffused costs creates a significant asymmetry of resources and incentives between injurers and victims. The injurer has a strong incentive to continue its conduct and has the resources to defend itself, while no

CHAPTER 23. 'PREDOMINANCE' TO 'RESOLVABILITY'

individual questions suggests that adjudicating a class action would either require numerous hearings on individualized questions of law or fact, or would induce courts to adopt substantive, procedural, or evidentiary shortcuts around such hearings.[5] Extensive hearings may become impractical, while shortcuts around them may become unfair. Courts considering whether to certify proposed class actions thus face a recurring dilemma about how to resolve the tension between common and individual questions that arises when class members present factual circumstances that are similar, but not exactly alike.

The theoretical and practical dimensions of the tension between common and individual questions are strikingly under explored beyond the literature addressing agency costs. The consequences of diversity among class members have been carefully analyzed in the

---

individual victim has a comparably strong incentive or sufficient resources to compel the injurer to stop. When the conduct is complete, the injurer's size and potential exposure provide it with the resources and incentives to avoid being held accountable, while the victims individually often lack the incentives or resources to sustain the effort of investigating potential claims and obtaining a remedy for losses. The traditional single plaintiff versus single defendant model of private dispute resolution thus does not provide a viable means for compensating victims or deterring injurers because victims are unlikely to sue, and if they do sue, injurers are likely to have an advantage in the litigation's war of attrition. The theory underlying the class action is that aggregating victims into a single fictional unit – 'the class' – places incentives and resources into a more equitable balance and neutralizes the defendant's otherwise overwhelming tactical advantage. See e.g., Kalven & Rosenfield, *supra* n. 1, at 686:

Modern society seems increasingly to expose men to such group injuries for which individually they are in a poor position to seek legal redress, either because they do not know enough or because such redress is disproportionately expensive. If each is left to assert his rights alone if and when he can, there will at best be a random and fragmentary enforcement, if there is any at all.

See generally Mancur Olson, Jr., The Logic Of Collective Action: Public Goods And The Theory Of Groups 48 (2nd edn 1971) (analyzing obstacles to the optimal creation of collective goods inherent in the costs of organizing groups and in the variance between marginal costs and marginal benefits to individual group members); Steven Shavell, The Fundamental Divergence Between The Private and the Social Motive to Use the Legal System, 26 J. Leg. Stud. 575 (1997) (noting that victims of wrongs do not fully internalize the benefits of litigation and thus may have insufficient incentives to file socially desirable suits).

[5] See *infra* 23.2.

context of decisions about the propriety of allowing a single agent to represent diverse principles.[6] In contrast, the consequences of diversity for the valuation of aggregated claims – and thus for the effectiveness of aggregative procedures as a tool for implementing substantive rules and remedies – has received comparatively little explicit attention. Politicians, courts, and commentators have focused on controlling when, where, and by whom class actions are filed, managing class actions after they are certified, and policing how they are settled, but have given only minimal scrutiny to the logically antecedent question of how to decide whether a class action is a procedurally viable means of resolving the similar and dissimilar aspects of contested claims and defenses. In particular, rules for assessing the significance of common and individual questions within putative class actions – notably Federal Rule of Civil Procedure 23(b)(3)[7] – have not evolved since their creation in 1966, have received virtually no helpful clarification from the Supreme Court, have bewildered lower courts, and have not attracted substantial scholarly scrutiny.

The lack of critical attention to rules for assessing the similarity of putative class members' claims outside the agency context has allowed a conventional wisdom to evolve that misstates the nature and overlooks the seriousness of the problems that a lack of similarity creates. The consensus view among courts and commentators is that the critical determination in deciding whether to certify claims for class action treatment is whether the factual and legal questions that unite class members are relatively more significant than the questions that divide them.[8] The formal embodiment of this approach is Federal Rule of Civil Procedure 23(b)(3), which asks judges contemplating whether to certify a class action to decide whether 'questions of law or fact common to the members of the class *predominate* over any questions affecting

---

[6] See e.g., Geoffrey P. Miller, Conflicts of Interest in Class Action Litigation: An Inquiry into the Appropriate Standard, 2003 U. Chi. Leg. F. 581; Rhode, *supra* n. 1. This Article does not address issues relating to the construction of principal-agent relationships. Instead, the Article assumes the existence of a representative who can advocate on behalf of the class consistent with due process, and asks when the effect of diversity among putative class members' factual and legal circumstances on the valuation of claims at trial or in a settlement should provide an independent basis for refusing to certify a class action.
[7] For a discussion of Rule 23(b)(3)'s text, purpose, and shortcomings, see *infra* 23.4.
[8] See *infra* notes 128–138, 164 and accompanying text.

CHAPTER 23. 'PREDOMINANCE' TO 'RESOLVABILITY'

only individual members.'[9] The problem with this 'predominance' approach is that the extent of dissimilarity among class members' circumstances turns out to be a much more important indicator of whether claims are suitable for class action treatment than the extent of any similarity. Accordingly, the certification inquiry should not ask whether class members' circumstances are more similar than different, but rather whether their circumstances are sufficiently different to preclude resolving their claims in a single proceeding. Unfortunately, the debate over class action reform does not recognize serious flaws in current certification criteria for assessing the similarity and dissimilarity among class members' circumstances, and thus these criteria remain relatively immune from proposed reforms even though they are the source of many of the problems that reformers are trying to solve. Accordingly, this article seeks to highlight the importance of certification rules that have largely escaped critical scrutiny, to illustrate how these rules hinge on conceptually incoherent criteria and inspire equally confused doctrine, and to explain how reliance on these criteria both inflates and reduces the expected litigation and settlement value of claims processed through class actions. The article then identifies principles from which replacement certification criteria can be drawn, and proposes a new rule for courts to use when deciding if a class action would be an appropriate procedural vehicle for adjudicating the common and individualized elements of contested claims and defenses.[10]

---

[9] Fed. R. Civ. P. 23(b)(3) (emphasis added). For example, in a proposed class action by ratepayers against an electric utility challenging rates exceeding a statutory tariff, the legality of the rate would be a common question, while the amount of any overcharge could vary for each person in the class. Likewise, in a proposed class action by consumers suing a credit card issuer for fraudulent oral misrepresentations, the truthfulness of the issuer's statements in a sales script could be common to the class, but proof of whether a class member heard and relied on the representations in a particular script would depend on each member's individual circumstances. Rule 23(b)(3) would require a court considering a motion to certify a class in these hypothetical cases to decide whether the common questions of rate legality or truthfulness of a telemarketing script 'predominate' over the individual questions of damages or reliance.

[10] My examination of class action principles, rules, and doctrine focuses on Federal Rule of Civil Procedure 23 ('Rule 23'), which governs class certification in federal courts and is the model for most state class action rules. See *infra* notes 119–121 (reviewing state class action rules and noting that predominance is a certification

The article's analysis proceeds in four parts. Section 23.2 establishes the practical importance of dissimilarity among class members' circumstances by explaining how dissimilarity creates subtle distortions in the presentation and assessment of claims and defenses that either inflate or dilute the perceived value of the overall class claim and are a significant source of inaccuracy in class adjudication and settlement.[11] I define and explore three examples of these distortions: 'cherry-picking' (the tendency of aggregate proceedings to generalize from examples that do not fully represent the diversity of individual claims), 'claim fusion' (the process by which claims in the aggregate merge to assume characteristics that no individual claim possesses), and 'ad hoc lawmaking' (the manipulation of substantive rules to assist in resolving or preventing practical difficulties that arise in the course of adjudicating dissimilar questions of fact and law). In addition, section 23.2 explains

---

factor in forty-five of the forty-eight states with rules or statutes permitting class actions). I focus on Rule 23(b)(3), which permits class actions seeking primarily monetary damages, and which has become the most litigated and controversial of the three categories of class actions that Rule 23(b) creates. See Thomas Willging et al., Empirical Study Of Class Actions In Four Federal District Courts: Final Report To The Advisory Committee On Civil Rules 118 (1996). The (b)(3) category has also been the focus of most recent debate over class action reform proposals. See Edward H. Cooper, The (Cloudy) Future of Class Actions, 40 Ariz. L. Rev. 923, 928 (1998). The other two categories of class actions – codified in Rules 23(b)(1) and 23(b)(2) – are generally available when plaintiffs seek primarily injunctive relief or when payment of individual damage claims would risk depleting a common fund and prejudicing litigants whose claims would not be addressed until after the defendant loses the ability to pay them. Neither of these categories relies on the concept of predominance as a criterion for certification. Instead, rules tailored to the unique institutional and policy concerns raised by injunctions (often to enforce civil rights statutes) and common fund distributions have evolved to manage the cases that fall into the (b)(1) and (b)(2) categories. Although this article's analysis tracks the current tripartite structure of Rule 23(b), it would apply even if the rule were rewritten to create a single trans-substantive certification standard because the tension between common and individualized issues that I discuss would affect any effort to parse monetary claims that are suitable for aggregate treatment from those that are unsuitable.

[11] Accuracy is of course not the only value that procedure should promote – others include efficiency, distributive justice, an opportunity to be heard and participate, and the avoidance of invidious bias – but is a useful concept to consider when evaluating the wisdom of a procedural rule. See generally Louis Kaplow, The Value of Accuracy in Adjudication: An Economic Analysis, 23 J. Leg. Stud. 307 (1994).

CHAPTER 23. 'PREDOMINANCE' TO 'RESOLVABILITY'

why the fact that most class actions settle – which is often cited as a reason not to care too deeply about flaws in certification criteria – is actually a reason to reconsider such criteria due to their effect on the outcome of negotiated agreements. Section 23.2 concludes in light of these observations that there is a pressing need to analyze the theoretical and practical coherence of criteria for assessing similarity and dissimilarity among claims in proposed class actions.[12]

Section 23.3 develops three general principles of civil procedure and class actions – 'finality,' 'fidelity,' and 'feasibility'[13] – that should shape the judicial test for assessing similarity and dissimilarity among class member's claims. My goal is to anchor the assessment of individual and common questions more securely in broader principles

---

[12] The certification inquiry (both before the trial court and on interlocutory appeal) on which the Article focuses is generally the judiciary's sole opportunity to assess whether particular claims are suitable for class action treatment. Cases that are not certified are usually dropped or settle, and cases that are certified usually settle before trial, such that there is rarely non-interlocutory appellate review of the certification decision (aside from the relatively unrigorous review of certification criteria that occurs in the context of approving settlements under Fed. R. Civ. P. 23(e)). Cf. *infra* n. 96. The certification decision is therefore the pivotal moment in the life of a putative class action, with the judge acting as a gatekeeper to the procedural benefits of Rule 23. Similarity among claims and defenses is a key that unlocks the gates to class action status, while dissimilarity is a force that slams the gates shut.

[13] For a detailed explanation of each principle, see *infra* text accompanying notes 44–98. Briefly, the 'finality' principle captures the need for class actions to vindicate the dispute resolution and behavior modification goals of civil procedure by eventually resulting in a judgment reflecting the rights and obligations of the parties. The timing and preclusive effect of this judgment may vary from case to case, but at a minimum class actions seeking damages should culminate in a judgment that determines who owes or does not owe what to whom. The 'fidelity' principle addresses the connection between procedural and substantive rules, establishing a constraint on the ability of courts to permit class action procedures to alter analysis of substantive claims and defenses. Certifying classes may have the desirable effect of removing practical obstacles to the fair and efficient determination of the merits of claims and defenses, but certification is not a license for courts to tweak the merits by modifying the content of applicable substantive law. The 'feasibility' principle reflects the tension between aspirations and capacity in the management of complex litigation. Courts often want to accomplish more than they are able to achieve in class actions given constraints of time, talent, and resources, and must therefore think carefully about the feasibility of potentially costly and improvident procedural remedies before embracing them.

that animate civil procedure generally and class actions in particular. The finality, fidelity, and feasibility principles collectively establish guideposts for evaluating how the similar and dissimilar elements of group claims should affect a court's decision about whether to certify a class. The need for a judgment (finality), the need to ensure that each beneficiary of that judgment is entitled to it (fidelity), and the need to resolve individual issues within resource constraints (feasibility) suggest that courts should certify classes featuring some dissimilarity among members' circumstances only if there is a feasible plan for resolving factual and legal disputes regarding each element and defense applicable to each class member's claim and for eventually entering judgment for or against class members for a specified sum of money. The court should either provide an opportunity for the parties to litigate individual claims or defenses, should have a reason to believe that such an opportunity is not necessary under the applicable substantive law, or should have a reason to believe that a settlement can fairly account for dissimilarity without any need for adjudication. The principles leave room for imaginative judicial solutions to complex management problems while providing a check on the permissible scope of experimentation.

Section 23.4 applies the lessons learned from section 23.3 to Rule 23's predominance test, concluding that the concept of predominance and the doctrine that it has spawned are inconsistent with the principles that should guide certification criteria. To prove this point, the section discusses the historical origins of the predominance test, the failure of its drafters to provide any interpretative guidance, the ineffective efforts of the Supreme Court and lower courts to divine its meaning, its inherent conceptual flaws, and the dubious doctrine that courts have developed to apply the predominance rule to recurring fact patterns involving individualized defenses, individualized damages, and choice of law in cases with multi-state contacts.

The basic problem with the predominance test is that it requires elaborate efforts to answer a question that is not worth asking. The answer to the question 'which issues predominate' is neither interesting nor useful, and is not grounded in any relevant principle. The predominance inquiry fixates on the notion that class actions are viable when class members share similar factual circumstances and raise similar legal questions. However, similarity among claims is an unhelpful concept when one thinks about the practical consequences of certifying a class and the procedural principles (such as finality, fidelity, and feasibility) to which class adjudication should conform. A more relevant

CHAPTER 23. 'PREDOMINANCE' TO 'RESOLVABILITY'

concept is *dis*similarity. The existence of some similarity within the class is what makes class actions potentially efficient and appealing, but it is the lack of substantial dissimilarity that makes class actions a fair and procedurally viable means of rendering judgment for or against the class and its members. The predominance concept conflates the similarity and dissimilarity inquiries into a single balancing test, thus obscuring the practical and theoretical importance of dissimilarity standing alone.

The predominance balancing test is an exercise in futility because it relies on a subjective comparison of inherently incomparable factors that is not grounded in a principled assessment of their independent significance. The ensuing weighing process is analogous to asking a starving person to balance the nutritional value of vitamins in his only potential food source against the negative effects of poison in the same food. Any sort of balancing would be pointless. A huge nutritional value would be irrelevant if the poison is fatal, and if the poison is not fatal then any amount of nutrition would justify consumption absent a superior alternative food source. The same analysis applies when deciding whether to certify a class because dissimilarity among class members' claims at a sufficient dose is a fatal poison to class adjudication. When individual questions of law or fact unique to particular class members raise insurmountable obstacles to class adjudication, then the number and importance of common questions is irrelevant. On the other hand, if the proposed class action would be 'superior'[14] to possible alternative forms of litigation even accounting for the efforts needed to cope with difficult – yet manageable – individualized issues, then denying certification based on an arbitrary notion of whether common questions 'predominate' would be gratuitous. Individualized questions of law or fact viewed in isolation thus either should or should not preclude certification in any particular case; their relative 'predominance' with respect to common questions should neither salvage an otherwise uncertifiable class nor derail a class that should otherwise be certified. Certification rules relying on the 'predominance' test thus enshrine a pointless concept that obscures the need to evaluate individual questions of law and fact directly rather than in comparison to common questions.

---

[14] Fed. R. Civ. P. 23(b)(3).

Having rejected the predominance test, I propose in section 23.5 a 'resolvability' test that would reconcile the practical demands of class litigation with theoretical constraints. The new test would permit certification only when the court has a feasible plan to answer all disputed questions of law and fact that must be resolved before entering judgment for or against class members under the law governing each class member's claim and applicable defenses. The test also suggests a framework for considering the propriety of settlements of otherwise uncertifiable classes, although defining the precise limits on such settlements requires developing a normative theory of consent that is beyond the scope of this article.[15] The new resolvability approach to dissimilarity would channel the inherent subjectivity of certification decisions along more clearly defined paths and would realign certification analysis with principled constraints from which the predominance test has drifted. Rules should ideally facilitate the implementation of guiding principles, but the predominance test does the opposite, interposing a meaningless and distracting wedge between principle and practice.

Section 23.5 also notes some of the broader implications of my proposal linked to unraveling the dynamic connection between substantive and procedural constraints on the regulation of behavior that affects large groups. Class actions have become a crutch on which policymakers lean to provide a procedural boost to the efficacy of substantive rules regulating behavior. Replacing the predominance test with a resolvability test would likely make that procedural boost more difficult to obtain, which suggests that policymakers and commentators concerned about deterring corporate wrongdoing and compensating victims should refocus the debate about class actions to consider new approaches to substantive regulation for which class adjudication might be a more suitable enforcement mechanism. In addition, rather than making questionable use of the class action to optimize the remedial power of substantive liability and damage rules, there may be a need to tailor substantive rules to operate more effectively under existing individualized procedures for resolving disputes, or to develop new and more effective aggregative procedures. While procedures must evolve in response to substantive preferences, policymakers must also reconsider substantive preferences in light of limitations on procedure.

---

[15] See *infra* text accompanying notes 196–199.

23.2 THE IMPLICATIONS OF DISSIMILARITY FOR THE LITIGATED AND NEGOTIATED VALUATION OF CLASS MEMBERS' CLAIMS

This section contends that dissimilarity among class members distorts the outcome of class actions through three phenomena – cherry-picking, claim fusion, and ad hoc lawmaking – that current class action scholarship either overlooks or underweights. When class actions are adjudicated to trial, effective advocates can harness these phenomena to exploit dissimilarity among putative class members and thereby alter the probability of a liability finding and the calculation of aggregate damages. Even when parties settle class actions before trial, bargaining occurs in the shadow of the expected trial procedure, and thus a settlement will likely replicate any distortions that dissimilarity would create during formal adjudication.

23.2.1 A Thought Experiment Confirming the Distorting Effect of Dissimilarity

A simple thought experiment confirms the importance of dissimilarity to analysis of certification criteria. Imagine that class actions were available only in cases where the claims of all class members were *exactly* alike in *every* detail and subject to proof through *identical* evidence, and where individuals could prove their membership in the class by purely *objective* submissions, such as the defendant's business records naming the people with whom the defendant interacted.

In these hypothetical circumstances, it is difficult to imagine that class actions would generate substantial controversy or occupy their current position high on political agendas. Class actions featuring such ultra-commonality would present only minor coordination problems, would be only marginally less manageable than any constituent claim standing alone, would be unlikely to confuse juries any more than non-class cases, would have outcomes approximately as predictable as outcomes in ordinary non-class litigation, and would not involve substantial conflicts among class members' interests. The expected outcome of a trial for any one plaintiff picked at random from the homogenous class should not differ from the expected outcome for any other class member. The case presumably would settle after no more than a few sample trials of randomly selected class members' claims that would establish a range of outcomes to serve as the template for a class-wide settlement. The ability to pinpoint a reasonably accurate average claim value would in turn minimize agency costs because the court could monitor settlements with an eye toward the divergence of settlement values from expected litigation outcomes. Settlements would vindicate both the compensation and deterrence objectives of applicable substantive laws because defendants would pay roughly what the merits of claims suggest is warranted, and plaintiffs would receive roughly what they would be entitled to receive (assuming that jury verdicts in sample trials would be roughly accurate). Because all claims would be identical and all class members identifiable, the averaging of sample trial verdicts would not have any distributive consequences beyond the unobjectionable smoothing over of lucky or unlucky high-end or low-end jury awards.[16] Trying a few claims would thus be functionally equivalent to trying them all.[17]

---

[16] Cf. Robert G. Bone, Statistical Adjudication: Rights, Justice, and Utility in a World of Process Scarcity, 46 VAND. L. Rev. 561, 569–570 (1993) ('[W]hen factual issues are identical throughout the class, the class action functions as a trivial form of sampling. The court in effect relies on a sample of one case, that of the representative plaintiff's, to adjudicate liability for the entire class.').

[17] Plaintiffs might object that class proceedings would deprive them of their autonomy, but that objection would wilt if we assume that the economic value of plaintiffs' claims is small relative to the defendant's aggregate stakes in the litigation, such that plaintiffs would likely be unable to litigate at all – let alone autonomously – outside of a class action. In any event, the critique of class actions premised on a plaintiff's right to autonomous control over litigation is questionable given the lack of substantial autonomy that exists even in nominally individualized suits and the costs that an autonomy norm would impose on third parties competing for scarce judicial resources or hoping to benefit from the deterrent effects of collective litigation. See Bruce L. Hay, Procedural Justice – Ex Ante v. Ex Post, 44 UCLA L. Rev. 1803, 1838 (1997) (observing that individuals behind a veil of ignorance might rationally prefer to sacrifice autonomy in favor of efficient and accurate aggregative procedures); Deborah R. Hensler, Resolving Mass Toxic Torts: Myths and Realities, 1989 U. ILL. L. Rev. 89, 92–97 (discussing the obstacles to meaningful participation that plaintiffs face even in traditional non-class suits); Eric D. Green, Advancing Individual Rights Through Group Justice, 30 U.C. Davis L. Rev. 791, 800 (1997) (noting that adjudicative resources are scarce, such that providing autonomy to each litigant has distributional consequences); Rosenberg, Mandatory Litigation, supra n. 1, at 841–843 (noting that litigation autonomy fosters opportunistic personal wealth-maximizing behavior by litigants that undermines the deterrence and

The difference between the thought experiment above and the highly controversial modern class action is that the circumstances of plaintiffs who claim to fit a proposed class definition are rarely exactly alike. Distinctions among class members could include, for example, the degree to which their contact with the defendant was direct or attenuated, the precise nature of the defendant's behavior toward them, the collateral circumstances of their interaction with the defendant, their mental state during their dealings with the defendant, the type and severity of their injuries, the ranking of their remedial preferences, and the nature and strength of the defenses to which they may be subject. If these differences are material – i.e., if the substantive law imposed by the institution with legitimate political authority to create rights and regulate behavior deems the differences potentially outcome-determinative – than procedure should have a mechanism to tailor adjudicated outcomes to the varying circumstances of individual plaintiffs.[18]

Once one moves from an imagined world of complete similarity to the real world of partial dissimilarity, opportunities exist to manipulate the presentation of evidence and legal argument in a manner that highlights favorable or unfavorable aspects of unique individual claims. Judges and jurors trying to assess the merit and value of these distinct claims must then engage in the difficult cognitive task of aggregating their analysis while tracking material variables that differ from claimant to claimant. As the next subsection explains, there is little reason to believe that courts and jurors adjudicating class-wide liability

---

insurance objectives of tort law). But see Lon L. Fuller, The Forms and Limits of Adjudication, 92 Harv. L. Rev. 353, 357, 364 (1978) (defining 'participation' of litigants through the presentation of reasoned argument as a feature distinguishing adjudication from other mechanisms of 'social ordering', such as elections and contracts); Roger H. Trangsrud, Joinder Alternatives in Mass Tort Litigation, 70 Cornell L. Rev. 779, 822 (1985) ('[G]iven the traditional respect afforded an individual tort litigant's right to control the prosecution of a substantial personal injury or wrongful death claim, and that the plaintiff loses much of this individual control when the court certifies a class action, courts should avoid using this joinder device to try these cases.'); Patrick Woolley, Rethinking the Adequacy of Adequate Representation, 75 Tex. L. Rev. 571, 572 (1997) (arguing that due process principles require providing plaintiffs with a right to be heard directly rather than through a representative).
[18] For further development of the normative foundations for the need to integrate substance and procedure, see *infra* section 23.3.2.

and damages questions can accurately account for the full effects of dissimilarity.

23.2.2 Trial Distortions: Cherry-Picking, Claim Fusion and Ad Hoc Lawmaking

The practical problems with certifying class actions despite dissimilarity among claims arise from the natural human instinct to simplify the inherently complex and to create order out of what appears chaotic. These instincts manifest in class actions in the form of procedural shortcuts to squeeze heterogeneous claims into a homogenous mold and thereby avoid the procedural difficulties that dissimilarity would create. The effect is akin to mixing different colors of paint into a large vat: the vibrant reds, greens, and blues will blur into gray. This blurring of constituent parts into an undifferentiated whole may be unobjectionable if one does not care about the color of the final product, but would be a serious problem if one were interested in preserving the palette of original ingredients in the mix. Likewise, aggregating distinct individual claims into a class obscures differences among class members in ways that engender substantive consequences.

The hypothesis that certification of dissimilar claims tends to distort assessment of their merits is grounded in three recurring phenomena of class litigation, which I call 'cherry-picking,' 'claim fusion,' and 'ad hoc lawmaking.' Each of these concepts describes a means by which certification can inflate – and sometimes deflate – the aggregate value of class claims beyond the sum of the values of individual claims.

'Cherry-picking' refers to the fact that plaintiffs' counsel often controls the presentation of plaintiffs' case and can hand-pick the most persuasive individual examples of a defendant's alleged wrongdoing to stand as representatives for the alleged class-wide problem.[19] The 'true' persuasiveness of class members' dissimilar liability claims may lay on a spectrum, but the class can present examples from only the top

---

[19] The extent of plaintiffs' control over witness selection at trial will vary depending on the role that the court plays in managing the presentation of evidence. See Fed. R. Civ. P. 23(d) (vesting broad management powers in district courts presiding over class actions). A defendant contemplating settlement at an early stage of a class action often will not be able to predict the extent of plaintiffs' power to cherry-pick, and must factor that uncertainty into its settlement calculus.

CHAPTER 23. 'PREDOMINANCE' TO 'RESOLVABILITY'

of the spectrum and thus skew the jury's assessment of the merits. For example, in a class action against a credit card issuer for making misleading representations about interest rates, class members may have had varying levels of financial sophistication, may have seen various disclosures that were more or less misleading than others, and may have relied on the misrepresentations to different extents. Yet, a smart class counsel will not make his case through testimony of, say, a doctor who read a relatively benign disclosure on which he did not rely; instead, the star witness is likely to be a very sympathetic and unsophisticated victim of the most egregious example of the defendants' misconduct. The defendant can try to counter the effect of this testimony by spotlighting cases from the bottom of the spectrum, but realistically this is not likely to happen; most defendants want to deny liability, not highlight the fact that sometimes their behavior was less culpable than at other times. The consequence is that plaintiffs' ability to cherry-pick the best examples from among a pool of diverse claims skews the defendants' potential exposure above what a case-by-case merits review would suggest is the appropriate damages figure. Class members with weak claims in essence ride the coattails of class members with stronger claims and benefit from the jury's perception that the defendant's conduct in the aggregate was worse than it may actually have been.

The upward skewing of claim values can apply in reverse if the class representative turns out to be a lemon rather than a cherry. The class in these circumstances would be attempting to prove its claim based on an example drawn from the bottom of the diverse spectrum, which would artificially deflate the jury's assessment of liability and calculation of aggregate damages. The lemon-picking phenomenon thus helps to explain plaintiff-protecting critiques of class actions premised on agency costs by illustrating the potentially adverse effect of dissimilarity among claimants on the selection of a representative.

'Claim fusion' describes the phenomenon that occurs when the claims of the class morph to assume aspects of disparate individual claims, such that the class has a claim that is stronger than the claim of any particular member. The class claim in effect becomes a composite fusing the best components of its dissimilar constituent claims. Building off the example above, suppose that a credit card issuer mails three types of solicitations that are each misleading, but for different reasons. Each class member receives one of these solicitations, but none receive all three. The claims of the class will gain strength from the cumulative effect of the three misrepresentations, which in the jury's mind will likely fuse into one massive misrepresentation despite the fact that no class member received all three solicitations.[20] Even if claimants were divided into three subclasses, each subclass would benefit from the jury's awareness of the defendant's misconduct toward the other subclasses. Moreover, even assuming that only one rather than three types of misrepresentation are at issue, the claim fusion problem could occur with respect to collateral facts surrounding plaintiffs' claims. For example, suppose that one class member called the credit card issuer to complain about unexpectedly high interest rates and testifies as to her perception that she was treated rudely, that another testifies that she was particularly aggrieved because of her low income, and that a third testifies that she suffered substantial stress as a result of her dealings with the defendant. The alleged indifference of the defendant and the alleged stress and poverty of the plaintiffs will infuse the class claim even though most individual class members would not have any basis for alleging any of the grievances of the three testifying plaintiffs. Allowing the jury to know the myriad manifestations of a defendants' misconduct may not seem undesirable, but from the perspective of ensuring accurate judgments the fusion of dissimilar circumstances into a more compelling whole likely skews litigation outcomes above what the merits warrant by making liability findings more probable and inflating damages assessments.[21]

---

[20] Most courts have not recognized the problem of claim fusion, although the Fourth Circuit has noted the practical difficulties that arise when the aggregation of dissimilar claims creates a 'fictional composite' claim that is stronger than its individual components. *Broussard v. Meineke Discount Muffler Shops, Inc.*, 155 F.3d 331, 345 (4th Cir. 1998).

[21] Experiments by psychologists studying juror behavior have not directly addressed the hypothesis that claim fusion and cherry picking exploit cognitive biases and therefore skew claim valuations. However, more general experiments establish that jurors have difficulty compartmentalizing information in complex cases and that the size of a plaintiff population and distinctions among plaintiffs' circumstances can sway assessment of aggregate liability and damages depending on the process by which jurors receive information. See e.g., Irwin A. Horowitz & Kenneth S. Bordens, The Consolidation of Plaintiffs: The Effects of Number of Plaintiffs on Jurors' Liability Decisions, Damage Awards, and Cognitive Processing of Evidence, 85 J. Applied Psychol. 909, 916 (2000); Irwin A. Horowitz & Kenneth S. Bordens, The Effects of Outlier Presence, Plaintiff Population Size, & Aggregation of Plaintiffs on Simulated Civil Jury Decisions, 12 Law & Hum. Behav. 209, 211–213,

CHAPTER 23. 'PREDOMINANCE' TO 'RESOLVABILITY'

The claim fusion problem also applies in reverse as defense fusion. If the defendant has varying defenses to some individual class members' claims, the defenses may fuse to form an artificially strong class-wide defense that skews the value of class members' claims downward. For example, if one of the class representatives in the above credit card hypothetical lied on her application, and another had an independent source of knowledge correcting the omissions in the misleading solicitations, a jury might allow those defenses to blur together and to color their perception of absent class members' claims.[22]

'Ad hoc lawmaking' occurs in class actions when courts attempt to devise substantive and evidentiary shortcuts around management problems that dissimilarity imposes on the resolution of otherwise similar claims. For example, courts will create irrebuttable[23] evidentiary presumptions to avoid having to consider individualized questions of fact on legal elements such as reliance,[24] invent new theories of liability to

---

225–226 (1988); Dennis J. Devine, et al., Jury Decision Making: 45 Years of Empirical Research on Deliberating Groups, 7 Psychol. Pub. Pol'y & L. 622, 671–672, 699 (2001). Further empirical study would be helpful in assessing the cognitive foundation for the claim fusion and cherry picking phenomena in consolidated litigation.

[22] Although this article focuses on claim fusion as a problem affecting the design of class certification standards, another way to conceptualize the problem would consider the standards that should govern the admissibility of evidence in class actions. For example, one area meriting further consideration is whether courts adjudicating class actions should strictly interpret the relevance requirement in Fed R. Evid. 402 to preclude any testimony or evidence at the liability phase of a case that is not relevant to the claims of the entire class. In this manner, courts could prevent parties from introducing evidence about the unique circumstances of particular class members, which in turn would prevent juries from making unwarranted extrapolations that inflate or dilute aggregate claim values.

[23] The inferences must be irrebuttable because if they were rebuttable the individual issues would remain in the case (subject to a flipped burden of proof) and would still present obstacles to adjudicating class actions.

[24] For example, plaintiffs often propose that when liability is premised on a consumer not knowing a certain fact, or relying on a given representation, the court should presume that all class members who acted in a specified manner must have had a certain level of a knowledge or been relying on a misleading statement. See e.g., *Varacallo v. Mass. Mut. Life Ins. Co.*, 752 A.2d 807, 817 (N.J. Super. Ct. App. Div. 2000) (citing cases). Under these proposals, objective evidence (such as the defendant's business records) of how the class member acted, which is generally easy to present in a class action, would substitute for subjective proof of knowledge or

avoid having to consider the circumstances of individual class members,[25] bend the rules of evidence and alter burdens of proof so that contested facts can be resolved on a common rather than individualized basis,[26] manipulate choice of law analysis to minimize the diversity of applicable rules,[27] and try to disentangle claims and defenses so that juries consider aggregate class-wide liability before they consider whether defendants have defenses to individual claims that might reduce the size of their aggregate exposure.[28] Nothing inherent in the class action device distorts substantive or evidentiary rules in

---

reliance, which is generally difficult to present in a class action. See e.g., *Sandwich Chef v. Reliance Nat'l Indem. Ins. Co.*, 319 F.3d 205, 220 (5th Cir. 2003) ('A class cannot be certified when evidence of individual reliance will be necessary.'). Many proposed presumptions depend on analogies to federal securities law, which permits a presumption of reliance in misrepresentation and omission cases based on the specific wording of the applicable statute and the assumption that false or misleading disclosures affect all participants in an efficient market. See e.g., *Basic, Inc. v. Levinson*, 485 U.S. 224, 241–249 (1988); *Affiliated Ute Citizens of Utah v. United States*, 406 U.S. 128, 152–153 (1972). A problem with this analogy is that most consumer markets do not feature the fast and broad transmission of information characteristic of an efficient securities trading regime, so there is no factual basis for presuming that a particular piece of false or misleading information had any effect on any particular consumer. See *Sikes v. Teleline, Inc.*, 281 F.3d 1351, 1362–1363 (11th Cir. 2002) (distinguishing securities and RICO contexts for purposes of applying statutory reliance element).

[25] See e.g., In re Rhone-Poulenc Rorer, Inc., 51 F.3d 1293, 1297, 1300 (7th Cir. 1995) (noting that in attempting to 'streamlin[e]' management of a class action, the district court had merged distinct state law liability standards into an 'Esperanto instruction'); Epstein, *supra* n. 1, at 489–514 (discussing substantive legal developments arising from class actions in the employment, antitrust, and securities fields).

[26] See e.g., *Broussard v. Meineke Discount Muffler Shops, Inc.*, 155 F.3d 331, 343 (4th Cir. 1998) (finding that admission of speculative evidence related to 'average' class member damages impermissibly relieved plaintiffs of their burden of proving actual damages with reasonable precision).

[27] For an overview and critique of how courts attempt to sidestep the inconvenient implications of rigorous choice of law analysis in complex litigation with multi-state contacts, see Larry Kramer, Choice of Law in Complex Litigation, 71 N.Y.U. L. Rev. 547 (1996).

[28] See e.g., *Garner v. Healy*, 184 F.R.D. 598, 602 (N.D. Ill. 1999) (proposing to decide the common question of whether defendants were liable to the class before deciding individualized questions of whether any class member could prove proximate causation); *Wal-Mart Stores, Inc. v. Lopez*, 93 S.W.3d 548, 560–561 (Tex. App. 2002) (noting

CHAPTER 23. 'PREDOMINANCE' TO 'RESOLVABILITY'

this manner, but certification has that practical effect when judges try to manage the dissimilar aspects of class members' claims.[29] These innovations by courts trying to cope with dissimilarity may or may not be legitimate in particular cases, but they collectively help to explain the perception that class actions often produce outcomes that are not consistent with applicable substantive law.[30]

The combined effect of cherry- and lemon-picking, claim and defense fusion, and ad hoc lawmaking is that class actions exploit or obscure dissimilarity rather than resolving it. Plaintiffs' counsel find creative ways to infuse the class claim with the best of its dissimilar aspects, and judges find innovative ways to make any vestiges of dissimilarity disappear from the case. Defendants in turn try to counter these efforts by tarring the class with the least desirable traits of members with the weakest claims. The result of these efforts is that class litigation is a process of forced homogenization; the more heterogeneous claims are to begin with, the greater the effects of homogenizing them.[31]

---

that trial plan had scheduled calculation of class-wide damages prior to presentation of the defendant's individualized defenses to liability).

[29] Some commentators have noted the general practice of courts using the class action as a procedural opportunity to modify substantive rules, but these observations are usually not linked to the problems of dissimilarity that I argue are a primary cause of such substantive modifications. See e.g., Richard L. Marcus, *They Can't Do That, Can They? Tort Reform Via Rule 23*, 80 Cornell L. Rev. 858, 873 (1995) (noting attempts by courts to 'fit... the substantive law into the class action mold').

[30] Ad hoc shortcuts can prejudice both plaintiffs and defendants, although defendants are more likely to suffer prejudice because most shortcuts are designed to facilitate the plaintiffs' preferred manner of proof. Plaintiffs' counsel usually requests the shortcuts, and generally do not do so for the defendant's benefit. However, plaintiffs are not immune from prejudice because their counsel's zeal to ensure certification may lead to shortcuts that circumvent substantive or evidentiary rules that favor some members of the diverse class.

[31] Even apart from the cherry-picking, claim fusion, and ad hoc lawmaking phenomena, problems associated with dissimilarity among claims manifest themselves in other undercurrents of the class action reform debate. For example, debate about conflicts among class members' remedial preferences is usually framed as relating to agency costs inherent within the class action device, but can be re-conceptualized as reflecting a concern about how to balance similarity and dissimilarity among class members' preferences and circumstances when deciding whether to certify a class.

23.2.3 The Distorting Effects of Dissimilarity on Valuation of Class Action Settlements

The problems with dissimilarity discussed in this section arise because of the practical difficulties that individualized questions of law or fact create when a court attempts to litigate a class action. Yet most certified class actions settle,[32] so the practical problems associated with litigating individualized questions rarely arise, or are resolved through the parties' voluntary adoption of expedited claims processing procedures to distribute the proceeds of an agreed settlement. The fact that most class actions settle may suggest that difficulties in managing them should not bar their certification. For example, if a defendant does not plan on litigating the question of liability, then the difficulty that plaintiffs would have in proving liability on a class-wide basis arguably should not bar them from an opportunity to negotiate a fair and efficient settlement of claims that might otherwise go uncompensated.[33] Likewise, the fact that damages would be difficult to prove in jury trials that no party intends to initiate should not be a reason to preclude plaintiffs from proving damages through an alternative dispute resolution mechanism that all parties are willing to accept. However, this Section will show that the distortions that dissimilarity causes in trial outcomes also plague settlement outcomes, such that the near-ubiquity of settlement replicates rather than resolves the problems that the remaining parts of this article seek to correct.

Dissimilarity distorts settlement outcomes in two principal respects. First, dissimilarity among claims prevents judges from effectively monitoring agency slack during settlement, which creates maneuvering room for agents to negotiate low-ball settlements that reward the agents without fully compensating their clients. Second,

---

Likewise, debate over whether class actions create unnecessary burdens for courts can be framed as a disagreement about how courts at the certification stage should balance the similar, easy to manage aspects of proposed class claims against the more difficult to manage dissimilar aspects.

[32] See Nagareda, Preexistence, *supra* n. 1, at 151 ('[C]lass actions today serve as the procedural vehicle not ultimately for adversarial litigation but for dealmaking on a mass basis.').

[33] See Green, *supra* n. 17, at 795 ('Everyone knows the case is not going to be tried, but... appraise the case under the Rule 23 criteria as if it were. That seems to me an Orwellian approach').

CHAPTER 23. 'PREDOMINANCE' TO 'RESOLVABILITY'

settlement bargaining involves an attempt to predict trial outcomes, and thus the value of a negotiated agreement will reflect trial distortions that the parties believe might arise from material dissimilarity among class members.

23.2.3.1 Ineffective Monitoring

A standard critique of class actions is that lawyers who act as agents for the class have financial incentives to negotiate settlements that prioritize their own interests at the expense of class members' interests.[34] One reason that class counsel are able to get away with settling claims for less than their true value is that even well-intentioned potential monitors (such as courts) lack the ability to second-guess settlements because the information needed to determine the expected litigation value of claims is difficult to obtain.[35] Yet one reason why expected

---

[34] For example, class counsel may:
   (1) fear competition for fees from lawyers pursuing rival class actions and therefore engage in reverse auctions with defendants in which they trade diminished client compensation for the certainty of their own reward, see e.g., Coffee, Class Wars, *supra* n. 1, at 1370;
   (2) perceive that the effort necessary to produce a marginal dollar of compensation for clients is not worth the fraction of that dollar that they will see in fees, see e.g., Coffee, Private Enforcement, *supra* n. 1, at 690;
   (3) conclude that the risk of holding out for a better deal for their clients is not worth putting the certainty of their own fee in jeopardy, such that they lose interest in zealously pursuing the case once their fee reaches a satisfactory level, see *Alleghany Corp. v. Kirby*, 333 F.2d 327, 347 ('[A] juicy bird in the hand is worth more than the vision of a much larger one in the bush.'); and
   (4) collude with defendants by accepting a large fee in exchange for agreeing to a settlement that allows the defendant to purchase litigation peace at a low overall cost, see e.g., Coffee, Class Wars, *supra* n. 1, at 1367–1368.

[35] See e.g., Coffee, Accountability, *supra* n. 1, at 376 (noting that a 'distinctive' feature of class actions relative to other contexts in which principals do not directly appoint their representatives is that there is no effective third-party monitoring to minimize agency costs); Macey & Miller, *supra* n. 1, at 46 (noting that settlement hearings ostensibly designed to give courts the information necessary to perform their monitoring function are usually 'pep rallies jointly orchestrated by plaintiffs' counsel and defense counsel').

values are so difficult to calculate is that class members are often differently situated, which increases the number of variables in any calculation of aggregate expected damages.

For example, assume that L equals the probability that an average jury would find the defendant liable to a plaintiff, and that D is the amount of damages that an average jury would award. Now imagine two classes: one class contains one thousand members identical in all respects to representative V, while a second class contains 250 members with circumstances identical to V, 250 with circumstances identical to W, 250 with circumstances identical to Y, and 250 with circumstances identical to Z. The expected aggregate litigation outcome for the more uniform class is 1000 x Lv x Dv. But the expected aggregate litigation outcome for the more fragmented class is (250 x Lv x Dv) + (250 x Lw x Dw) + (250 x Ly x Dy) + (250 x Lz x Dz). The first calculation is obviously much simpler than the second because it requires the court to estimate the value of fewer contested variables. Judicial monitoring of settlements thus becomes more viable when there is relatively little outcome-determinative dissimilarity among class members. The enhanced ability of courts to monitor settlements in homogenous cases should in turn act as at least a partial check on agency costs, assuming that courts are willing to expend the effort necessary to fulfill their monitoring role.[36] Accordingly, there is an often unnoticed – albeit indeterminate – correlation between the extent of dissimilarity among class members' circumstances and a court's ability to monitor and remediate the possible effect of agency costs on settlement values.

23.2.3.2 Tainted Bargaining

Settlements generally cannot produce accurate valuations of dissimilar claims within a class action proceeding because of the distortions that dissimilarity creates in anticipated litigation outcomes. Prevailing models of settlement establish that parties will seek to avoid a prolonged and expensive trial by attempting to anticipate the outcome of litigation and agreeing to accept or pay an amount that approximates

---

[36] For a discussion of why courts lack incentives to monitor class action settlements closely, especially in negative value cases, see Coffee, Class Wars, *supra* n. 1, at 1369–1370.

CHAPTER 23. 'PREDOMINANCE' TO 'RESOLVABILITY'

the expected net gain or loss.[37] Each party will calculate the expected value of claims (which is the probability of success multiplied by the potential reward), adjust for expenses and risk aversion, discount to present value, and thus establish parameters for a potential settlement. The case will then settle if the parties' settlement ranges overlap and if strategic behavior (such as low-ball offers or unrealistically high demands) do not derail negotiations. The settlement value should roughly reflect the relative merit of each side's position, but only if the litigation process whose outcome the parties are trying to predict is an accurate means of resolving disputed claims. For example, a settlement negotiated by experienced lawyers in a typical single-plaintiff versus single-defendant slip-and-fall negligence case in a fair judicial forum will probably closely correlate with the merits of the claim because litigation is presumably a reasonably accurate means of resolving such recurring negligence disputes and the lawyers can draw from prior experience when attempting to predict the suit's outcome. In contrast, if the same two lawyers were told that their clients' dispute would be resolved by a game of chess, the settlement value would bear no relationship to the merit of the claim and would instead reflect the odds associated with the chess game.

For the same reasons that the settlement value of a claim subjected to resolution by chess instead of litigation would not correlate with its merits, the settlement value of a claim that would be resolved through a class action despite distortions – such as cherry-picking, claim fusion, and *ad hoc* lawmaking – created by dissimilarity would also not reflect the merits of the parties' positions. Calculation of expected values would be a function of each party's prediction of who would suffer greater prejudice from the distorted class action trial procedure. The parties would not be attempting to predict the outcome of any rational or known process because no such process exists for the types of claims being discussed, and thus the odds that litigation would produce an accurate outcome that the parties could predict are extremely low. The settlement value of any class action where claims are substantially

---

[37] For a critique of expected value models, see Joseph Grundfest & Peter H. Huang, The Unexpected Value of Litigation (Stanford Law School/Olin Law & Economics Working Paper No. 292) (arguing that claims may settle for more or less than their expected value based on the parties' perception of how each will gather and exploit new information about contested facts and legal theories during multiple stages of litigation).

dissimilar thus relates more to perceptions about which party will suffer greater prejudice from a trial conducted in violation of the principles discussed in section 23.3 than to perceptions about which party has the more meritorious case. An example illustrates the point.

Suppose that a class of insurance policyholders who received lower-than-requested payments for property damage to their homes sue the insurer for systematically underpaying claims. Plaintiffs propose to present as evidence internal corporate memoranda discussing the insurer's claims adjustment techniques, which plaintiffs characterize as a 'common class-wide scheme' to defraud policyholders by providing a level of coverage that is in practice less than what policyholders had expected or paid for. The insurer believes that the challenged general claims practices were used in adjusting half of the one million property damage claims that were resolved during the proposed class period for less than the demanded amount, and that the practices reduced the value of affected claims by an average of USD 500, for a total class-wide loss of USD 250 million, (i.e., 500,000 claims x USD 500 loss). Moreover, the insurer believes that if a court reviewed each of the 500,000 affected claims, there is a 60% chance in each case that the court would conclude that the challenged claims practices were legal under the circumstances. The insurer thus has three individualized 'defenses' to each class members' claim:

(1) that the class member was not one of the insured whose claim was affected by the challenged claims practices;
(2) that the claims practices were legal under the circumstances of the class member's case; and
(3) that the class member is entitled to lower damages than his complaint demands. In the vernacular of plaintiffs' 'common scheme' allegation, the defendant would be using individual counterexamples to refute the existence of the scheme, denying whether the scheme affected any particular person, denying that the scheme was illegal in any particular case, and disputing the extent of damages that the alleged scheme may have caused.

Now imagine the settlement value of the case under each of two proposed procedural mechanisms for litigating it, assuming that the insurer succeeds in convincing the plaintiffs that its calculations discussed above are accurate. For each proposal, assume that the parties are represented by well-financed and competent counsel. Under one proposal, the court would (assuming infinite time and resources) individually examine all one million claims files and assess liability on a file-by-file basis, entering a judgment for or against each class member. The expected value of a judgment in these circumstances would be USD 100 million (the plaintiffs' 40% probability of success multiplied by the USD 250 million potential exposure). The settlement value of the case would therefore begin at USD 100 million and move higher or lower depending on the parties' risk aversion and anticipated litigation costs.

Now suppose that the court decides to permit plaintiffs to litigate as a class action the 'common' question of whether the insurer's claims practices were in general illegal without permitting the insurer to present defenses to individual class members' claims until after the jury rules on the common question, and even then only in a quasi-administrative claims proceeding. The expected value of a judgment would probably change in two ways.

First, the parties may conclude that a trial limited to the abstract question of whether the insurer's general practices were illegal would be more likely than a file-by-file review to result in a finding of liability because the jury would not have a context for assessing the reasonableness of claims decisions in concrete situations and would be influenced by cherry-picking and claims fusion. Moreover, the parties would probably believe that convincing a jury that a large corporate defendant had a propensity to behave poorly is much easier than proving that the defendant behaved poorly in any particular case, especially when the evidence of such a propensity consists of internal corporate documents not linked to a specific context. The prospect of a classwide liability finding (rather than file-by-file liability assessments) may therefore raise the insurer's aggregate expected probability of a loss from 40% to, say, 60%.

Second, the parties would realize that if the insurer loses on the common question of whether its claims practices were in general illegal, then the claims resolution process would be likely to conclude, based on inertia and the truncated scope of alternative dispute resolution procedures, that the previously established illegal claims practice tainted a particular claims file. The parties might therefore conclude that, say, 60% rather than 50% of files would be found to have been tainted, and that the average estimate of damages would be USD 600 rather than USD 500. Settlement values would thus change dramatically. The defendant would face a 40% chance of complete victory (assuming that courts in other jurisdictions grant preclusive effect to the judgment), but a 60% chance of a USD 360 million exposure (600,000 files x USD 600 file). The expected value of a judgment would more than double from USD 100 million to USD 216 million (60% probability of loss x USD 360 million exposure). The starting point for settlement talks would therefore be USD 216 million, and the insurer would likely be more risk averse due to its higher total exposure.[38]

The likely settlement value of the common issues class action would thus be substantially higher than the settlement value of the hypothetical case where a court devoted time and energy to assessing the merits of each individual claim without relying on generalizations based on 'common' evidence and inferences. The settlement value of the class action would not reflect the merits of the case so much as the parties' assessment of how a distorted litigation process would prejudice the defendant by inflating the defendant's probability of losing on common issues, diminishing the defendant's probability of prevailing on defenses, and increasing the defendant's total exposure.

Alternatively, one can imagine a scenario in which the settlement value of the class action would be lower for plaintiffs than if cases were litigated individually. Suppose in the example above that the plaintiffs' 'common' evidence of illegal claims practices is weak, but

---

[38] The supposition that defendants will be risk-averse when threatened with a large damages award may seem counterintuitive in light of conventional models of settlement behavior, which assume that defendants are loss-averse and therefore favor the risk of trial over settlement in the hope of avoiding all liability. See Jeffrey J. Rachlinski, Gains, Losses & the Psychology of Litigation, 70 S. Cal. L. Rev. 113, 123 (1996). However, the cognitive psychology experiments on which these settlement models are founded were not designed to address risk aversion in the context of the large potential losses that are possible in class actions, see Amos Tversky & Daniel Kahneman, Rational Choice and the Framing of Decisions, 59 J. BUS. S251, S258 (1986) (noting that experimental evidence about risk perceptions 'may not apply to ruinous losses'), and to the extent relevant predict that decision makers focus on the magnitude of potential losses while underweighting the low probability of their occurrence, see Amos Tversky & Daniel Kahneman, The Framing of Decisions and the Psychology of Choice, 211 Science 453, 455 (1981). Existing scholarship about risk preferences is therefore consistent with the hypothesis that a corporate defendant faced with a massive potential class action judgment is more likely to avoid risk than to seek it. Cf. Samuel R. Gross & Kent D. Syverud, Getting to No: A Study of Settlement Negotiations & the Selection of Cases for Trial, 90 Mich. L. Rev. 319, 383 (1991) (concluding that the extent of a defendant's risk-aversion may partly depend on the difference between its net worth and its exposure).

that a file-by-file review creates a much stronger inference of wrong doing in the insurer's adjustment of claims. Even assuming that the plaintiffs could present a statistical analysis of selected claims files to support their allegation of class-wide wrongdoing, the parties might conclude that the 'common' claim would be so complicated that the jury might reject it even though a significant percentage of individual claims are meritorious. The expected value of a class action judgment would therefore be lower than the value of a judgment in the hypothetical case where the court reviewed and rendered judgment on each file separately.

Of course, the hypothetical option of adjudicating all one million claims for the small sum of USD 500 does not exist in the real world, so the settlement value of the insurance cases above absent certification of a class is probably USD 0 or nuisance value. The ostensibly neutral point that settlements are problematic when the litigation procedure that motivates them would not accurately value claims is thus in many circumstances a veiled (but no less troubling) way of saying that defendants should escape liability entirely unless somebody invents a more accurate mechanism to hold them accountable for injuries imposed on a large group of somewhat similarly and somewhat dissimilarly situated victims. One could avoid this implication by making the fair and accurate resolution of group claims less difficult by, for example, amending substantive law to jettison hard-to-prove individualized elements, developing streamlined dispute resolution procedures geared toward quickly and accurately resolving large numbers of somewhat similar claims, or rethinking the extent to which society should care if a settlement correlates with the merits of claims.[39] However, as explained in section 23.3, such innovations should be debated and discussed through legitimate democratic channels, and should not be achieved covertly, as they often are now, as an *ad hoc* incident to judicial attempts to squeeze a square peg of dissimilar claims through the round hole of class certification criteria.

I am not arguing here that class action settlements are appropriate only in cases that could be manageably litigated. In some circumstances, the parties might be able to predict how a court would resolve claims if the court had sufficient resources to do the job properly. For example, if the obstacle to certification is that holding a hearing for each of 1 million similarly situated class members would be impossible, a class action settlement might be appropriate if the parties could

---

[39] See *infra* section 23.3.2.

accurately predict the likely outcome of those hearings, perhaps based on statistical analysis of a random sample (assuming that the applicable substantive law permits such sampling).[40] A settlement in these circumstances could embody a fair and accurate assessment of expected values roughly linked to the merits of class members' claims in the aggregate even if a class action trial would not be practicable, although there would still be unresolved questions about how much of an award to distribute to differently situated individual class members.[41] However, where the unwieldy nature of a class action would distort its likely outcome, as in the insurance coverage example above, then its settlement value is likely to incorporate that distortion and unlikely to reflect a socially desirable level of compensation and deterrence. Certification criteria for settlement classes must therefore permit courts to distinguish between class actions that would be manageable but for a lack of resources and class actions where manageability problems would cause the resolution of common questions to distort the valuation of dissimilar individual claims.[42]

---

[40] For discussions of the benefits and limitations of statistical sampling techniques, see Bone, *supra* n. 16, at 568 (noting that a 'critical question' when considering sampling 'is how to distribute fairly a limited number of process opportunities among persons with equal participation rights'); Glen O. Robinson & Kenneth S. Abraham, Collective Justice in Tort Law, 78 Va. L. Rev. 1481, 1490 (1992) (suggesting 'the use of statistical claim profiles, or models, to set baseline appraisals of the value of individual claims'); Rosenberg, Mandatory Litigation, *supra* n. 1, at 853 n. 47 (advocating 'averaging' in the 'sense of disregarding differences in litigation value among claims in order to redistribute claim-related wealth in a manner consistent with tort deterrence and insurance objectives'); Laurens Walker & John Monahan, Sampling Damages, 83 Iowa L. Rev. 545 (1998) (proposing expanded use of established survey methodologies to assess damages).

[41] The existence of class-wide settlements in uncertifiable cases may seem counterintuitive because the lack of manageability would render the plaintiffs' threat of obtaining certification hollow and defendants would have little to fear from refusing to settle. However, defendants may perceive a class action settlement as a favorable alternative to defending against numerous individual claims, and may therefore seek to buy peace on a class-wide basis even though a class action would otherwise be uncertifiable. For an example of such a settlement in the context of asbestos claims, see *Ortiz v. Fibreboard Corp.*, 527 U.S. 815 (1999).

[42] The Supreme Court has partially recognized the need to consider similarity among claims at the certification stage of a proposed settlement class, albeit in a disjointed manner. On the one hand, the Court has held that '[c]onfronted with

CHAPTER 23. 'PREDOMINANCE' TO 'RESOLVABILITY'

Accordingly, underemphasizing dissimilarity among claims on the assumption that class actions will eventually settle without considering whether the action could in theory be fairly litigated injects the unfairness of potential litigation into the terms of settlements. The settlement value of such cases would reflect a reaction to perceived quirks in how an unwieldy class action would be resolved rather than a rational assessment of the case's merits.[43] Assuring that settlements bear a relationship to the merits of claims therefore requires devising certification criteria that account for the potential distorting effect of dissimilarity among class members.

In sum, diversity among the circumstances of individual class members and judicial reactions to that diversity are an often overlooked source of controversial shortcomings in the class action device. Class actions are not inherently incapable of resolving cases accurately, but in practice collectively litigating or settling dissimilar issues can distort the valuation of individual and aggregate claims. Accordingly, a central question for observers concerned about tension between the

---

a request for settlement-only class certification, a district court need not inquire whether the case, if tried, would present intractable management problems...for the proposal is that there be no trial.' *Amchem Prods., Inc. v. Windsor*, 521 U.S. 591, 620 (1997). Yet on the other hand, the Court has held that 'permitting class designation despite the impossibility of litigation' is generally not appropriate because the fair settlement value of the case cannot always be determined without reference to a credible threat of litigation. *Id.* at 621. The gist of the court's seemingly inconsistent reasoning seems to be that manageability is not important if no trial is contemplated, but that the underlying factors that would render the case unmanageable may defeat certification for other reasons. For example, the 'divers[ity]' among claims and defenses that would defeat predominance and inhibit a class-wide trial under Rule 23(b)(3)(D) may likewise render any class-wide representation in settlement negotiations inadequate under Rule 23(a)(4). *Id.* at 622 n. 17. Understood in this manner, the Court's opinion in *Amchem* is consistent with my analysis above suggesting that the propriety of class action settlements is not a function of whether claims could actually be litigated, but rather whether the settlement terms could be tested against the expected outcomes of a predictable and fair adjudicative process.

[43] Such settlements might raise additional problems if the dissimilarity among differently situated claimants leads lawyers representing one group to negotiate a settlement that does not adequately address the needs of other groups. This concern about adequacy of representation has been the primary focus of the Supreme Court's decisions reviewing class action settlements. See e.g., *Amchem*, 521 U.S. at 625–627.

substantive aspirations of regulation and the procedural reality of adjudication should be whether courts have coherent criteria to assess how dissimilarity affects the propriety of certifying a putative class. Section 23.3 seeks to create a principled foundation for such criteria.

23.3 PRINCIPLES THAT SHOULD SHAPE RULES GOVERNING THE EFFECT OF INDIVIDUALIZED ISSUES ON CLASS CERTIFICATION DECISIONS

The previous section demonstrated that dissimilarity among putative class members' circumstances can distort the valuation of claims, raising the question of how certification rules should measure and assess dissimilarity within putative classes. The next three parts of the article seek to answer that question. This part identifies and analyzes three broad principles from which to extract more specific criteria for assessing the significance of individualized issues. Section 23.4 then tests the 'predominance' rule against these criteria and finds the rule conceptually flawed, and section 23.5 proposes a replacement.

The significance of individualized questions in proposed class actions is a matter of degree rather than of absolutes. Different class members often act with different degrees of reasonableness, intent, and knowledge, are injured to different extents, value their losses differently, and have differing goals for the outcome of litigation, but these differences are not necessarily relevant or material in every case. For example, the fact that different purchasers of a computer intended to use it for different purposes would be irrelevant in an antitrust class action against the seller for price-fixing, but would be highly relevant in an implied warranty class action against the seller claiming that the computers were unfit for a particular purpose. Designers of class certification rules must therefore develop criteria capable not only of recognizing the existence of diversity within proposed classes, but also of assessing whether that diversity could materially affect resolution of class members' claims.

Testing whether current rules governing class certification adequately assess and account for diversity among putative class members' circumstances requires identifying a broader set of principles to which such rules should conform. Drawing from general themes of civil procedure, it would be possible to identify at various levels of abstraction hundreds of principles that certification rules would need

CHAPTER 23. 'PREDOMINANCE' TO 'RESOLVABILITY'

to reflect on any number of topics and subtopics from the initial filing of class actions to the final enforcement of class-wide judgments. However, my goal is not to reinvent the class action from scratch. For present purposes, I identify three principles and that set minimum parameters for rules guiding judicial discretion in assessing the similarity and dissimilarity of individual claims in a putative class action. From each principle we can derive preliminary conclusions about how to draft certification rules. We can then combine the three principles to derive more concrete drafting criteria, and then test those criteria against current rules governing class certification.

The three principles, explained in greater detail below, are that:

(1) a certified class action for money damages must eventually result in an enforceable judgment resolving the claims of all class members (the 'finality' principle);
(2) a class member may not receive a judgment in his or her favor unless he or she proves the substantive elements for the applicable cause of action and survives any applicable defenses (the 'fidelity' principle); and
(3) attempts to adjudicate class actions in conformity with principles 1 and 2 must occur within resource and management constraints (the 'feasibility' principle).

Class certification is thus proper only if the court has a plan for eventually reaching an adjudicated or negotiated judgment that reflects the parties' rights under controlling law. These three principles may not seem controversial when phrased at this level of abstraction, but we will see in section 23.4 that current class action rules and doctrine often overlook or contradict these ideals. Alternatively, some of the principles may seem counterintuitive based on conventional wisdom about class actions, but we will see that conventional wisdom has slipped from its theoretical moorings.

23.3.1 The Finality Principle: A Certified Class Action Seeking Damages Should Eventually Result in a Judgment Resolving the Claims of All Class Members

A hallmark of American judicial procedure is that absent a voluntary act by the parties (such as settlement) or dismissal by the court, civil litigation eventually culminates in a final judgment establishing the rights of the litigants with respect to the subject of the suit. If a plaintiff prevails, the judgment requires the defendant to take some action with respect to the plaintiff, such as paying a specified amount of money or refraining from a course of conduct. If a defendant prevails, the doctrines of claim and issue preclusion and the Constitution's Full Faith and Credit Clause generally terminate the plaintiff's ability to litigate against the defendant again about the subject addressed in the judgment.[44] Judgments do not always come quickly, but the judicial system aspires to eventual closure.

The normative foundations of the need for a judgment reflect at least three distinct concerns about civil process – cost, scarcity, and efficiency. First, adjudication is costly to provide and should therefore produce at least some benefit. The principal potential benefits of adjudication in the context of suits for damages are the peaceful resolution of disputes, official determination of culpability (or lack thereof), amelioration of uncertainty about contested rights, payment of compensation (or termination of contingent liabilities), and the modification (or ratification) of contested behavior.[45] These benefits do not fully accrue in cases where the court would be unable to enter a judgment resolving the dispute or ruling on the propriety and consequences of the contested conduct. Indeed, even if the purpose of adjudication is understood in non-instrumental terms – for example, as promoting human dignity by providing a mechanism for the redress of grievances – it is difficult to see how leaving litigants twisting in the wind without an enforceable judgment would promote any plausible value or norm.

---

[44] See e.g., U.S. Const. Art. IV, Ch. 1. Loopholes in the doctrine of claim preclusion permit plaintiffs in some circumstances to file multiple suits challenging different aspects of the same offensive conduct, but finality is still a goal within each separate proceeding with respect to the issues being contested. See *Cooper v. Fed. Reserve Bank*, 467 U.S. 867, 875–881 (1984) (holding that a judgment rejecting class action claims alleging that the defendant engaged in a discriminatory employment practice did not preclude class members from pursuing individual discrimination claims that did not depend on 'pattern or practice' allegations).

[45] Cf. Kenneth E. Scott, Two Models of the Civil Process, 27 Stan. L. Rev. 937 (1975) (reviewing the 'conflict resolution' and 'behavior modification' models of civil procedure). Adjudication may also serve additional purposes when employed as a vehicle for reforming social and political institutions. See Owen M. Fiss, The Forms of Justice, 93 Harv. L. Rev. 1, 2 (1976) ('Adjudication is the social process by which judges give meaning to our public values.').

CHAPTER 23. 'PREDOMINANCE' TO 'RESOLVABILITY'

Second, adjudication is a scarce resource for which demand exceeds supply. A sensible threshold sorting criteria for allocating this resource is to give it only to people who have a chance of becoming better off after adjudication than they were before.[46] A judgment is the embodiment of such potential relief. If there is no realistic possibility that a judgment can be entered for a particular claimant, distributive concerns suggest that the scarce resource of litigation should be given to another claimant who might be able to derive some benefit from it. Finally, from an efficiency perspective, adjudication diverts the parties from more socially productive pursuits, so there is value in eventually terminating litigation in a manner that justifies its existence and that returns the parties to more productive endeavors.[47]

Class actions under Rule 23(b)(3) are no different from ordinary civil suits in their need to result in a judgment. Each class member claims entitlement to a sum of money, and each seeks to walk away from the judicial proceeding enriched by that sum.[48] Defendants have countervailing interests in terminating the case in their favor without paying damages, and in not being sued again by members of the same class raising the same claims.[49] Both sets of parties therefore want the

---

[46] This sorting criteria is evident in federal standing doctrine, which limits the availability of judicial dispute resolution to cases and controversies in which a judgment could redress a plaintiff's injury. See *infra* n. 61.

[47] See Priest, *supra* n. 1, at 543–544 (defining 'finality,' along with 'efficiency' and 'equity,' as a principal goal of tort law because 'there is a value ... to allow[ing] both plaintiffs and defendants to return to increasing social productivity').

[48] In reality, most plaintiffs have no idea of the existence of class actions in which they are potential beneficiaries, and therefore in a formal sense do not seek or expect damages. However, the lawyers who file class actions derive their compensation from the damages awards that they obtain for the class and thus, as proxies for their clients, seek judgments specifying the nature and size of financial entitlements.

[49] The bar against so-called 'one-way intervention' in class actions is a manifestation of defendants' interests in assuring eventual peace: plaintiffs cannot chose to stay on the sidelines of class litigation until the likely outcome is clear, and then intervene only if the result is favorable while avoiding the binding effect of an unfavorable judgment. See *Am. Pipe & Constr. Co. v. Utah*, 414 U.S. 538, 547 (1974):

> A recurrent source of abuse under the former Rule lay in the potential that members of the claimed class could in some situations await developments in the trial or even final judgment on the merits in order to determine whether participation would be favorable to their interests. . . . The 1966 amendments were designed, in part, specifically to mend this perceived defect in the former

arbiter of their dispute – a civil court – to definitively state who owes or does not owe what to whom. Rule 23 recognizes the parties' mutual interest in finality by requiring class actions to culminate in some form of judgment covering all parties to the case,[50] and there is no indication in the Rule – with the exception of a provision for 'issue classes' discussed below[51] – that class actions warrant a departure from the general principle that civil litigation culminates in final judgments specifying the rights and obligations of the parties.[52]

Rule and to assure that members of the class would be identified before trial on the merits and would be bound by all subsequent orders and judgments.

But cf. *Parklane Hosiery Co. v. Shore*, 439 U.S. 322, 332–333 (1979) (endorsing the doctrine of offensive non-mutual collateral estoppel, which is in effect a form of one-way intervention). Potential class members must instead decide whether to participate in the class action before the court resolves the merits so that the defendant is able to bind the entire class to an unfavorable judgment. Without the bar against one-way intervention, defendants would never be certain that even a string of victories in high-stakes class action litigation would prevent an opportunistic plaintiff from eventually getting lucky and subjecting the defendant to the risk of a large class-wide damages award. A defendant faced with the prospect of being unable to achieve peace even by winning multiple trials might therefore be willing to settle cases for far more than their merit warrants simply to limit its potential exposure to windfall verdicts.

[50] See Fed. R. Civ. P. 23(c)(2)(B) & 23(c)(3); *Sosna v. Iowa*, 419 U.S. 393, 399 n. 8 (1975):

The certification of a suit as a class action has important consequences for the unnamed members of the class. If the suit proceeds to judgment on the merits, it is contemplated that the decision will bind all persons who have been found at the time of certification to be members of the class.

The judgment requirement is buried within Rule 23(c)'s provisions governing class action notice rather than in Rule 23(b)'s criteria for certifying classes, and therefore does not factor into certification decisions as frequently as it should (as discussed *infra* in section 23.4).

[51] See *infra* text accompanying notes 58–64.

[52] See generally Fed. R. Civ. P. 68 (governing entry of judgment in federal civil litigation). For an example of a similar context where the Supreme Court has held that class actions do not alter generally applicable procedural principles absent express indication in a statute or rule, see *Coopers & Lybrand v. Livesay*, 437 U.S. 463, 470 (1978):

There are special rules relating to class actions and, to that extent, they are a special kind of litigation. Those rules do not, however, contain any unique

CHAPTER 23. 'PREDOMINANCE' TO 'RESOLVABILITY'

The need for a final judgment specifying the rights of the parties has important implications for how courts should evaluate the significance of similarity and dissimilarity among claims when deciding whether to certify a proposed class action. Similarity among claims facilitates crafting a judgment that specifies the rights of all class members, while dissimilarity may necessitate fact-intensive case-by-case inquiries into the propriety of judgment that would make class litigation difficult, if not impossible.[53] Certification criteria must therefore assist the court in determining which proposed class actions can be litigated to judgment and which cannot, and which can be settled fairly based on the expected value of a final judgment and which cannot.[54]

---

provisions governing appeals. The appealability of any order entered in a class action is determined by the same standards that govern appealability in other types of litigation.

[53] Courts could elect to achieve finality without case-by-case inquiries into the varying circumstances of each individual class member if they decide that the outcome of such inquiries would not be relevant under the applicable substantive liability and damage rules. The temptation to reach such a conclusion can be strong in cases where class certification appears to be the only way to achieve rough justice for groups that lack access to alternative remedies, which explains the ad hoc lawmaking phenomenon described above and illustrates the need for the fidelity principle described below.

[54] Whether a judgment will be preclusive is a separate question from whether it must be final. The drafters of Rule 23 have been hesitant to codify the preclusive effect of class action judgments for fear of violating the Rules Enabling Act by specifying the substantive rights that flow from a procedural rule. See Kaplan, *supra* n. 1, at 393; James Wm. Moore & Marcus Cohn, Federal Class Actions–Jurisdiction and Effect of Judgment, 32 Ill. L. Rev. 555, 556 (1938). The absence of a uniform rule governing preclusion has led to substantial uncertainty in assessing the preclusive effect of class action judgments. See Geoffrey C. Hazard, Jr. et al., An Historical Analysis of the Binding Effect of Class Suits, 146 U. Pa. L. Rev. 1849 (1998) (analyzing the evolving and often inconsistent treatment of preclusion in equity practice and early class action litigation). Preclusion issues have also proven particularly tricky in class actions because unlike traditional suits in which plaintiffs join all transactionally related claims against a defendant into a single action, class actions usually focus on a relatively narrow subset of contestable issues, potentially freeing class members to file additional suits against the defendant on related issues without fear of preclusion. See *supra* n. 44. It is not necessary here to flesh out the extent to which class action judgments must be preclusive. At a minimum, the parties must have a final judgment before they can try to enforce it, attack it, or avoid it. Thus, at a

Three hypothetical examples illustrate how different proposed class actions might be more or less suitable for certification depending on how common and individual questions influence the difficulty of crafting a judgment to resolve all class members' claims. In each example, a significant aspect of the defendant's potential liability to class members is a common question, but aspects of liability and proof of damages vary for each class member. In the first example, resolution of the common question advances class members' quest for a judgment very far, but in the second and third examples resolution of the common question would still leave difficult individual questions for the court to resolve before it could enter a judgment.

Example 1. Suppose that thousands of customers of a local telephone company allege that a surcharge of a few cents for calls to 411 violates a statute setting permissible telephone service rates and seek recovery of the overcharges. Class-wide resolution of the common question of whether the charges were legal would clearly move each class member significantly closer to a final judgment. Further inquiry into each individual case would be necessary to confirm that each class member in fact incurred the alleged overcharge in a particular amount, but merely introducing copies of phone bills should suffice to prove each individual claim to the satisfaction of a fact-finder. The individual issues that remain after resolution of common questions in this example are thus a relatively inconsequential obstacle to rendering a final judgment for each class member.[55]

Example 2. Suppose that thousands of consumers receive an identical written solicitation from a financial planner promising to provide a valuable introductory financial consultation if the consumer makes a 'free' call to a specified ten-digit phone number. The solicitation fails to advise consumers that the specified area code is in the Cayman Islands (which is an international toll call for most U.S. residents despite the absence of an international dialing prefix), and that callers will incur

---

minimum, class certification rules should link the question of certification to the goal of eventually entering a judgment.

[55] Some individual claims might present problems if, for example, the defendant contends that a phone bill submitted into evidence is forged, or that a plaintiff was in arrears on her bill and thus never paid an overcharge. However, a court should presumably be able to cope with these isolated defenses (which would likely depend on the defendant's business records) while still moving the remainder of claims along to a final judgment.

CHAPTER 23. 'PREDOMINANCE' TO 'RESOLVABILITY'

whatever long-distance charges their telephone company normally imposes for such calls. Thousands of consumers have lengthy and helpful conversations with the planning service, but are shocked to receive long-distance telephone charges for the 'free' calls and sue the planner for fraud. Resolution of the common question of whether the solicitation was misleading because it omitted disclosures about long-distance charges or represented the calls as 'free' would help class members to prove liability. However, because a consumer's knowledge of the truth – or failure to exercise reasonable diligence in learning the truth – is usually a defense to a common law or statutory fraud claim,[56] and given the general understanding among most telephone users that dialing strange area codes might result in high telephone bills, the defendant would want an opportunity to explore in each case whether the caller knew that the area code being dialed would incur long-distance charges or took any steps to determine how the call would be billed. Assuming that there is a plausible reason to believe that some class members may have incurred long distance charges voluntarily or negligently, resolution of common liability questions would still leave substantial obstacles to entering a final judgment entitling particular class members to reimbursement of phone charges.[57]

Example 3. Suppose that thousands of purchasers of an automobile contend that the parking brake was defectively designed, causing it to fail when they engaged it, such that the car incurred damage by rolling out of a parking space and striking a blunt object. Answering the

---

[56] See e.g., *Stephenson v. Bell Atl.*, 177 F.R.D. 279, 293–294 (D.N.J. 1997) (refusing to certify statutory fraud class in part because of individual issues of whether plaintiffs 'already knew' allegedly omitted information); *Zekman v. Direct Am. Marketers*, 695 N.E.2d 853, 861 (Ill. 1998) (rejecting statutory fraud claim because plaintiff's knowledge that dialing a '900' number would incur charges precluded him from challenging warnings about such charges); *Agnew v. Great Atl. & Pac. Tea Co.*, 502 S.E.2d 735, 737 (Ga. App. 1998) (Georgia's fraud statute bars claim by plaintiff who already knew information allegedly concealed from him).

[57] Holding the defendant liable for fraud regardless of any idiosyncrasies in what class members knew about the possibility of long distance charges and how diligent they might have been in anticipating such charges may be socially desirable. However, the optimal scope of fraud doctrine and the availability of individualized defenses are questions distinct from whether class certification would be appropriate under existing fraud doctrine. For additional discussion of the relationship between substantive causes of action and procedural mechanisms for obtaining remedies, see *infra* notes 62, 70, 95, and section 23.5.2.

common question of whether the brake was defectively designed would be helpful in resolving each individual class member's claim, sparing them the costly burden of proving a complex scientific point in each of thousands of cases. However, resolving a common question about brake design would still leave class members a long way from establishing entitlement to damages. Each plaintiff would still need to prove that the design defect was the proximate cause of the roll-away (rather than, for example, their failure to properly engage or maintain the brake) and that the damage to the car did not pre-date the accident. Assuming that the defendant elects to put plaintiffs to their proof, resolution of individual claims could require testimony from each of thousands of plaintiffs and examination of each of thousands of brakes. The effort and expense needed to move from resolution of classwide common issues to a final judgment for each class member would thus be substantially greater in Example 3 than in Example 1.

The foregoing examples illustrate that the practical significance of any individual issues remaining as an obstacle to entry of final judgment after resolution of common questions varies from case to case, even when cases appear to involve similar subject matter (such as the dispute over telephone charges in Examples 1 and 2). My point is not to show that certification should always be granted in cases similar to Example 1 and always denied in cases similar to Examples 2 and 3 – more information would be necessary to make that determination. Instead, my point is that a court must be able to understand why the foregoing examples are differently suited to class action status if it is to have any hope of making an appropriate certification decision.

The limitations that the finality principle imposes in damages cases need not entirely frustrate efforts to squeeze specific issues arising in such cases into the class action mold. In theory, courts may be able to fragment damage claims into components, confine certification to only some of these components, and then render a final class action judgment limited to the certified components rather than the ultimate question of who owes or does not owe what to whom. For example, in proposed products liability or securities fraud damages class actions, a court might render a 'judgment' that 'product X is capable of causing disease Y' or 'proxy statement Z is misleading.' Class members who claim to have been aggrieved by X or Z could then attempt to use the judgment offensively in subsequent individualized proceedings against the defendant, either in the same forum or elsewhere. This approach could be useful in cases where rendering a class-wide

CHAPTER 23. 'PREDOMINANCE' TO 'RESOLVABILITY'

judgment on all contested damages questions would be impractical, such that the only alternative to a limited class-wide judgment would be no class-wide judgment at all (and probably no judgment of any kind given the collective action problems that inhibit redress of injuries to large groups). Rendering such a limited judgment could be an efficient use of scarce and costly judicial resources – and therefore consistent with the spirit of the finality principle – if it resolved uncertainty about contested questions and thereby facilitated settlement, or if it materially aided class members in their subsequent individual suits.

Although fragmenting putative class claims may present a safety valve to the demands of the finality principle, the utility of such 'issue classes' in damages cases is questionable – assuming that certification rules even permit them.[58] First, issue classes should be understand as injunction classes rather than as damages classes, and therefore do not directly implicate the concerns addressed in this article. A plea for a court to rule on a discrete factual or legal question is essentially a request for a declaratory judgment rather than a request to adjudicate a claim for damages – the damages component of the case is relevant only to post-class action proceedings rather than to the class action itself. A plaintiff's request to fragment what would otherwise be a 23(b)(3) damages class action into an issues class thus, for practical purposes, seems to transfer the certification inquiry's focus from the 23(b)(3) factors addressed in this section to the 23(b)(2) factors.[59] Second, federal courts may conclude that plaintiffs lack standing to pursue issue classes, either because of prudential constraints on the use of declaratory judgment actions[60] or because the possibility that plaintiffs

---

[58] Federal Rule of Civil Procedure 23(c)(4)(A) provides that 'when appropriate,' 'an action may be brought or maintained as a class action with respect to particular issues.' For competing views about the permissible scope of 'issues' classes, compare Laura J. Hines, Challenging the Issue Class Action End Run, 52 Emory L.J. 709 (2003) (endorsing a relatively narrow view), with Jon Romberg, Half a Loaf is Predominant and Superior to None: Class Certification of Particular Issues Under Rule 23(c)(4)(A), 2002 Utah L. Rev. 249 (endorsing a relatively broad view).

[59] See Fed. R. Civ. P. 23(b)(2) (expressly encompassing requests for injunctive and declaratory relief).

[60] Compare *Calderon v. Ashmus*, 523 U.S. 740, 747 (1998) (holding that Article III precludes adjudication of declaratory judgment actions seeking resolution of 'a collateral legal issue governing certain aspects of [class members'] pending or future suits'), with *Aetna Life Ins. Co. v. Haworth*, 300 U.S. 227 (1937) (holding that Article III

will be unable to exploit an issue-class judgment in subsequent proceedings attenuates the judgment's ability to resolve a concrete case or controversy.[61] Third, issue class actions regarding common liability questions divorced from individualized claims for damages will likely be rare because few lawyers will have an incentive to file them. The lucrative potential payday for class action lawyers arises from securing a damages award, not from obtaining a declaratory judgment that individual class members may – or may not – eventually parlay into damages in future individualized proceedings that the class lawyer would not necessarily control. Fourth, even if a lawyer could obtain a quasi-declaratory ruling on a subset of contested issues, the shift from a class-versus-defendant to an individuals-versus-defendant procedural posture would vitiate the lawyer's settlement leverage and permit defendants to regress to their standard tactic of stonewalling individual cases to deflate settlement values. Indeed, from the defense perspective, such stonewalling would have the added benefit of deterring other plaintiffs' lawyers from attempting similar bifurcated class actions in the future.[62] Fifth, the utility of limiting a class action

---

permits an insurer to seek a declaratory judgment about the validity of an insurance policy in anticipation of future litigation).

[61] See e.g., *United Food & Commercial Workers Union Local 751 v. Brown Group, Inc.*, 517 U.S. 544, 558 (1996) (noting that if class actions and other forms of representative litigation" failed to resolve the claims of the individuals ultimately interested, their disservice to the core Article III requirements would be no secret"); *Lujan v. Defenders of Wildlife*, 504 U.S. 555, 560–561 (1992) (the 'irreducible constitutional minimum' of Article III standing analysis is that a favorable resolution of the plaintiff's claim will 'likely''redress' a concrete injury) (citations omitted); *United States Parole Comm'n v. Geraghty*, 445 U.S. 388, 397 (1980) ('The "personal stake" aspect of mootness doctrine also serves primarily the purpose of assuring that federal courts are presented with disputes they are capable of resolving.'); *Gladstone Realtors v. Vill. of Bellwood*, 441 U.S. 91, 99–100 (1979):

> (Even when a case falls within [Article III's] constitutional boundaries, a plaintiff may still lack standing under the prudential principles by which the judiciary seeks to avoid deciding questions of broad social import where no individual rights would be vindicated.).

[62] There is nothing inherent in the process of allocating damage awards that renders class action litigation impracticable, and thus there is no principled reason why a bifurcated proceeding could not resolve class-wide liability issues and then distribute damages among class members. For example, if the only remedy available under

CHAPTER 23. 'PREDOMINANCE' TO 'RESOLVABILITY'

judgment to common issues is questionable because the rendering court would probably be unable to dictate the preclusive effect of its order in other jurisdictions, creating uncertainty about the order's enforceability and potential inequality of treatment in different fora.[63] In sum, *if* certification rules permit issue classes, and *if* plaintiffs have standing and incentive to file them, and *if* they prevail, there is still a substantial possibility that plaintiffs would face insurmountable practical obstacles to translating their issue-judgment into damages-judgments for all or many class members, which calls into question

---

the applicable substantive law is a USD 100 per person penalty award, then distributing damages to class members would not create any significant procedural challenges after resolution of liability questions (assuming that the identities of class members can be determined objectively). However, most current forms of substantive regulation follow a corrective justice model of remedies in which the court must award damages based on individual class members' proof of entitlement to compensation, which can be time-consuming and costly to establish. I assume for purposes of this article that the entitlement/compensation model of remedies is valid in spite of the constraints that it imposes on the design of efficient adjudication procedures. For an argument that damage allocation criteria should implement principles other than compensation that are easier to prove within the framework of a bifurcated class action trial, see David Rosenberg, Decoupling Deterrence and Compensation Functions in Mass Tort Class Actions for Future Loss, 88 VA. L. Rev. 1871 (2002) (arguing that distribution of damage awards should follow principles of insurance); see also Gary T. Schwartz, Mixed Theories of Tort Law: Affirming Both Deterrence and Corrective Justice, 75 Tex. L. Rev. 1801 (1997) (noting overlooked areas of commonality between deterrence and corrective justice approaches to regulation).

[63] See *Matsushita Elec. Indus. Co. v. Epstein*, 516 U.S. 367, 396 (1996) (Ginsburg, J., concurring in part and dissenting in part), ('A court conducting an action cannot predetermine the res judicata effect of the judgment; that effect can be tested only in a subsequent action.'); *Handschu v. Special Servs. Div.*, 737 F. Supp. 1289, 1307–1308 ('[A] declaration concerning issue preclusion by a court certifying a class action, for intended use in future litigation in another court, is not procedurally viable.'), amended by 838 F. Supp. 81 (S.D.N.Y. 1989); *Kauhane v. Acutron Co.*, 795 P.2d 276, 278 n. 3 (Haw. 1990), (noting 'the fundamental tenet of the doctrine of res judicata that the court issuing the initial judgment lacks the authority to determine the preclusive effect of that judgment'). But cf. Tobias Barrington Wolff, Preclusion in Class Action Litigation, 105 Colum. L. Rev. 717 (2005) (contending that courts have substantial authority to control the preclusive effect of class action judgments).

whether adjudicating the issue-class action would be worth the effort.[64] In any event, for present purposes it is sufficient to observe that the finality principle comes into play whenever a plaintiff seeks to a certify a (b)(3) damages class rather than an issue class, and so it is useful to assess the rules that courts should apply to such requests.

The foregoing discussion suggests a preliminary conclusion that, in combination with conclusions from the sections below, could assist in drafting rules governing certification of classes: courts should certify class actions seeking damages only when the individual questions of law and fact that remain after resolution of common questions can be definitively resolved in a final judgment establishing the rights and responsibilities of the plaintiffs and defendants. This principle leaves room for courts to develop creative adjudication or negotiation mechanisms for resolving individual claims in preparation for a final judgment. There is no single 'correct' way for a court to winnow the scope of a case and to reach conclusions about contested evidence in individual disputes. To the contrary, the large body of scholarship assessing procedural devices for resolving complex factual disputes attests to the variety of paths that courts can take. However, class litigation under Rule 23(b)(3) should eventually culminate in a final judgment informing the plaintiffs and defendants who owes what to whom. If adjudication cannot produce such a judgment, and if a settlement cannot do so fairly[65] (or if the parties are not willing to settle) then the class should either not be certified or should be decertified when the problem becomes apparent. As we will see in section 23.4, current certification rules and doctrine often overlook this principle, resulting in the certification of class actions in circumstances where the court does not have the faintest idea of how the case could be resolved if the parties do not agree to a settlement and insist on litigating the merits.

---

[64] An interesting question for further study is how much of an anticipated benefit should be required to justify the transaction costs of an issue class. Presumably, only a fraction – large or small – of all class members who prevail in an issue class action would be able to parlay that success into a satisfying victory or settlement in subsequent damage proceedings. The anticipated size of this fraction relative to transaction costs may be relevant to deciding if adjudicating the issue class action is worth the court's time and effort.

[65] See *infra* text accompanying notes 88–90.

CHAPTER 23. 'PREDOMINANCE' TO 'RESOLVABILITY'

23.3.2 The Fidelity Principle: A Class Member Should Not Receive a Favorable Judgment Unless He or She Can Prove the Substantive Elements for a Cause of Action and Survive Any Applicable Defenses

This section builds on the previous discussion of finality by exploring how, if at all, class actions alter the manner in which a plaintiff can establish entitlement to a judgment in his or her favor. An underlying assumption of this Section is that substantive laws that regulate behavior and create enforceable entitlements have definable elements and defenses that should constrain how courts resolve contested questions.[66] The section concludes that the procedural context in which a claim is adjudicated should not alter the content of these elements and defenses or the outcome of their application. Class actions should thus feature procedural fidelity to substantive law, meaning that the merit of claims presented in a class action should be assessed using the same

---

[66] Some conceptions of the nature of substantive law would be skeptical of this assumption. For example, instrumentalist (sometimes called realist or reductionist) approaches to tort law often postulate that the compensation and deterrence goals of tort determine the meaning of tort elements in particular cases, such that the content of a rule is partly a function of the context in which it is applied. These visions of tort law suggest that the distinction I draw between procedural fidelity to substantive law and ad hoc lawmaking is illusory because the content of substantive law is in some sense inherently ad hoc. A logical extension of such arguments would be that if class actions can improve the deterrent and compensatory force of tort, then judges in class actions can define 'elements' of torts – such as breach of duty, causation, and injury – to maximize deterrence and compensation without any preconceived notion of how these elements would apply in other procedural contexts. Debating such instrumentalist visions of malleable tort elements is beyond the scope of this article (suffice to say that it is questionable even on instrumentalist terms whether an amorphously defined tort standard provides adequate warning to potential wrongdoers about the likely consequences of their actions, such that actors faced with uncertainty may over- or under-invest in safety). For present purposes, I assume that substantive rules have at least some content capable of transcending procedural context, although this content is flexible and should evolve over time to cope with new regulatory dilemmas. See *infra* section 23.5.2. For a helpful taxonomy and discussion of competing conceptualizations of tort law, see John C.P. Goldberg, Twentieth Century Tort Theory, 91 Geo. L.J. 513 (2003).

substantive rules that would apply if plaintiffs litigated their claims separately.[67]

There are several prerequisites to entry of judgment in ordinary civil litigation where a single plaintiff sues a single defendant. The plaintiff must identify a legally recognized right creating a private remedy, present sufficient evidence to show that the defendant infringed the right, rebut objections that the defendant raises to the significance of that evidence, prove damages, and defeat any affirmative defenses. A plaintiff who cannot carry her burden of proof or overcome defenses cannot obtain a judgment in her favor.[68]

Class actions do not alter the basic proof-and-defense structure of adjudication. A class action merely changes the manner in which class members and defendants present the evidence and argument needed to prove or refute each of their claims or defenses. Instead of each class member presenting her own evidence, a representative plaintiff attempts to prove the claims of all absent class members using evidence common to each of them. Likewise, instead of refuting each class member's claim, the defendant attempts to prevail over the entire class by defeating the claim of the representative plaintiff and attacking the sufficiency of any 'common' evidence of class-wide liability. After resolution of common issues, each party's focus shifts to whatever individualized issues remain. Class actions do not – or should not – change the substantive elements of a claim, relieve class members of their burden of proof, or deprive defendants of their right to raise applicable defenses.[69] Policymakers are, of course, free to mold the content of

---

[67] Section 23.4.4 will discuss how current class action doctrine often overlooks or violates the fidelity principle.

[68] See e.g., Fed. R. Civ. P. 12(b)(6) (allowing dismissal for 'failure to state a claim upon which relief can be granted'); Fed. R. Civ. P. 50 (allowing judgment against a party when 'there is no legally sufficient evidentiary basis for a reasonable jury to find for that party'); Fed. R. Civ. P. 56 (allowing summary judgment when the moving party establishes that there is 'no genuine issue as to any material fact' affecting its entitlement to judgment).

[69] The leading early proponents of class actions did not perceive their proposed procedural innovations as altering the substantive law applicable to claims and defenses. See e.g., Kalven & Rosenfield, *supra* n. 1, at 694 n. 33 ('When the case is conducted as a class suit, regardless of the variety of individual differences, the defendant is never deprived in any way of his right and opportunity to present any defenses arising from any of these individual variations.'). Unfortunately,

CHAPTER 23. 'PREDOMINANCE' TO 'RESOLVABILITY'

substantive regulations to best exploit the procedural benefits of class actions, but nothing within the class action device itself alters the elements and burdens of proof associated with the parties' claims and defenses.[70]

There are several reasons why class actions should not modify the nature of claims and defenses. First, the statutes authorizing courts to promulgate procedural rules governing class actions do not ordinarily allow procedures to modify substantive rights. In the federal system, the Rules Enabling Act forbids the Supreme Court from drafting rules of civil procedure that 'abridge, enlarge or modify any substantive right,'[71] which prevents Rule 23 from altering the nature of the parties'

---

however, these early commentators did not explain how a court should decide when individual variations among claims should preclude certification, and assumed the problem out of existence by speculating that individual variations among class members' claims would likely be 'trivial or irrelevant' and not unduly 'inconvenient.' *Ibid.*

[70] To the extent that some commentators see class actions as a useful tool for permitting novel extensions of substantive law – such as various proposals to impose liability for risk and for altering proof of causation and damages in mass tort cases – the innovation is best understood as an evolution of tort law rather than class action jurisprudence. The practical dispute resolution possibilities that class actions create may provide the inspiration for substantive legal innovation, but the class action device itself ultimately follows where the substantive law leads. See *Deposit Guar. Nat'l Bank v. Roper*, 445 U.S. 326, 332 (1980), ('[T]he right of a litigant to employ Rule 23 is a procedural right only, ancillary to the litigation of substantive claims.'); *United States Parole Comm'n v. Geraghty*, 445 U.S. 388, 423 (1980) (Powell, J., dissenting) ('A motion for class certification, like a motion to join additional parties or to try a case before a jury instead of a judge, seeks only to present a substantive claim in a particular context.'). Cf. Arthur R. Miller, *supra* n. 1, at 674–676 (arguing that the surge of class action litigation in the 1960s and 1970s was a reaction to 'larger social forces' that adopted the class action as a convenient vehicle for implementing, rather than creating, newly recognized substantive rights); Nagareda, Preexistence, *supra* n. 1, at 158 (distinguishing between the structure of procedural mechanisms and their 'external policy goals').

[71] 28 U.S.C. ¶2072(b) (2004). The Rules of Decision Act further constrains the ability of federal courts to modify substantive rules in situations where courts must apply state rather than federal law. See 28 U.S.C. ¶1652 (2004). Federal courts therefore lack authority to create a substantive common law for use as an adjunct to Rule 23 when resolving state law claims. *See Erie R.R. Co. v. Tompkins*, 304 U.S. 64 (1938).

claims or defenses.[72] Many states have their own rules enabling statutes that similarly limit the scope of procedural rules.[73]

Second, even if the Rules Enabling Act did not constrain the permissible scope of procedural rules, there is no indication that rules creating class actions were intended to modify substantive rights or to invalidate otherwise applicable defenses to class members' individual claims. No such intent is evident in the text of Rule 23, in the official notes of its drafters, or in contemporaneous commentaries discussing its origins. Congress or a state legislature could in theory enact a statute allowing certification of a class to alter otherwise applicable substantive laws, but apparently such legislation has not been adopted.

Third, allowing class actions to modify substantive laws as an ad hoc incident to the convenient resolution of a particular case is not consistent with the customary detachment between rule-formulation and rule-application in a democracy, at least with respect to statutory rights and to a lesser extent with respect to common law rights. Substantive conduct-regulating rules and compensation-awarding remedies are usually the product of democratic institutions such as legislatures, administrative agencies subject to democratic oversight, or an established process of common-law rulemaking by courts whose decisions are open to review and debate by political institutions. Regardless of their origin, substantive rules reflect (in theory) a reasoned balancing of their relative social costs and benefits across a range of foreseeable contexts through a process that has some political

---

[72] See e.g., *Ortiz v. Fibreboard Corp.*, 527 U.S. 815, 845 (1999) ('The Rules Enabling Act underscores the need for caution' in interpreting the scope of Rule 23); *Amchem Prods. Inc. v. Windsor*, 521 U.S. 591, 613 (1997) ('Rule 23's requirements must be interpreted in keeping with...the Rules Enabling Act.'); Paul D. Carrington & Derek P. Apanovitch, The Constitutional Limits of Judicial Rulemaking: The Illegitimacy of Mass-Tort Settlements Negotiated Under Federal Rule 23, 39 Ariz. L. Rev. 461, 462 (1997) (arguing that under the Rules Enabling Act, procedural rules 'aim to cause dispositions on the merits, not to redefine those merits').

[73] See e.g., Ala. Code § 12-2-7(4) (2003); Ariz. Rev. Stat. § 12-109(A) (2003); Ark. Const. Amend. 80 § 3; Colo. Rev. Stat. § 13-2-108 (2004); Conn. Gen. Stat. § 51-14(A) (1991); Haw. Rev. Stat. § 602-11 (2005); Idaho Code § 1-213 (2004); Maine Rev. Stat. Ann. Tit. 4 § 8 (2004); Minn. Stat. § 480.051 (2004); Mo. Rev. Stat. § 477.010 (2005); Mont. Code. Ann. § 3-2-701 (2003); Nev. Rev. Stat. § 2.120(2) (2004); N.M. Stat. Ann. § 38-1-1(A) (2005); N.D. Cent. Code § 27-02-10 (2004); Ohio Const.

CHAPTER 23. 'PREDOMINANCE' TO 'RESOLVABILITY'

legitimacy. If the content of substantive law is altered to accommodate complexities raised by the procedural device that the plaintiff chooses to use in filing her claim – for example, by creatively interpreting a statute or regulation to apply differently in class actions than one might expect based on its application in non-class cases – then courts in effect would be rebalancing the social costs and benefits of a particular rule on an ad hoc basis. This rebalancing would occur without the oversight and political legitimacy that normally accompanies a decision about the nature of a substantive rule and without the detachment that one would expect to see between the formulation of a rule and its application to a particular circumstance.[74]

The ad hoc lawmaking problem is less acute, although still serious, when a court accommodates the complexities of a class action by modifying a common law rule rather than a statute or regulation. Unlike legislative statutes or executive regulations, common law rules are judicial creations and therefore prone to judicially-imposed changes that adapt rules to new demands. There is no reason why a class action cannot be a catalyst for the reform of the common law any more or

---

Art. Iv, § 5(B) (2004); Or. Rev. Stat. § 1.735(1) (2004); Pa. Const. Art. 5, § 10(C); Tenn. Code. Ann. § 16-3-403 (2004); Tex. Gov't Code Ann. § 22.004(A) (2005); Vt. Stat. Ann. Tit. 12, § 1 (2004); Wyo. Stat. Ann. § 5-2-115(b) (2004) ('[procedural rules] shall neither abridge, enlarge nor modify the substantive rights of any person'). Class actions in some states are creations of statute rather than administratively promulgated rules and therefore could, in theory, alter substantive rights, although none of the state class action statutes indicate such an intent. See e.g., Ga. Code Ann. § 9-11-23 (2004); 735 Ill. Comp. Stat. 5/2-801 et seq. (2005); Kan. Stat. Ann. § 60-223 (2005); La. Code Civ. Proc. Ann. Art. 591 et seq. (West 2005); Neb. Rev. Stat. § 25-319 (2004); Okla. Stat. Tit. 12, § 2023 (2004); S.D. Codified Laws §§ 15-6-23 et seq. (2003); Wis. Stat. § 803.08 (2004).

[74] Ad hoc lawmaking of this type could in theory have democratic legitimacy if Congress authorized it by delegating substantive rulemaking power to the judiciary as an incident to judicial authority to craft procedural rules, but the Rules Enabling Act expressly disclaims any such delegation. See *supra* notes 71–73 and accompanying text. The constitutionality of such a delegation of legislative power to the judicial branch would be hotly contested. See generally Eric A. Posner & Adrian Vermeule, Interring the Nondelegation Doctrine, 69 U. Chi. L. Rev. 1621 (2002) (assessing the debate over the nondelegation doctrine's constitutional origins). For a discussion of the practical consequences of legislative delegation of rulemaking power to courts, see Catherine T. Struve, The Paradox of Delegation, Interpreting the Federal Rules of Civil Procedure, 150 U. Pa. L. Rev. 1099 (2002).

less than the myriad other facts that have transformed common law rules over the centuries.[75] Nevertheless, there is something discomforting about changing common law liability or damage rules as an afterthought to a procedural dilemma in a particular case, rather than with full consideration of the costs and benefits of modifying the rule in all of the procedural contexts in which the rule might be litigated.[76] The discomfort grows when one considers that many successful class actions can have unintended consequences on matters that involve a delicate balance between competing policy interests. For example, a large damage award based on the side effects of a drug or vaccine might prematurely pull the product off the market to the disadvantage of people who need it. Likewise, a successful class-wide challenge to insurance claims adjustment practices can have the effect of raising premiums and pricing consumers out of the insurance market. Facilitating claims against drug manufacturers and insurance companies for the massive levels of damages that class actions can deliver is thus not as clearly desirable as it might seem when viewed in the narrow context of a particular class action filed by aggrieved victims, rather than in a more self-consciously detached lawmaking context designed to weigh competing social interests in the abstract without regard for the facts of particular cases or the emotional pressure of dealing with a large class of injured claimants.[77] Allowing courts to bend substantive rules to the procedural needs of particular cases is thus inconsistent with the normal process of rulemaking and prone to prioritize the welfare of

---

[75] Cf. *Phillips Petroleum Co. v. Shutts*, 472 U.S. 797, 824 (1985) (Stevens, J., concurring in part and dissenting in part) (observing that state courts had 'developed general common-law principles to accommodate the novel facts of this litigation').

[76] The concern over democratic legitimacy would be even greater if there were reason to suspect that the interests of diverse class members were not fully represented in the litigation process. See Christopher J. Peters, Adjudication as Representation, 97 Colum. L. Rev. 312 (1997) (developing a model of democratic legitimacy for judicial outcomes premised on interest representation).

[77] The tension between private and public perspectives on risk management is particularly acute in an emerging category of class actions known as 'social issue' or 'social policy' suits, in which plaintiffs seek remedies against actors whose profits arise from activities that cause negative social externalities, such as tobacco companies, gun manufacturers, and health maintenance organizations (HMOs). For a general discussion of this trend, see Deborah R. Hensler, Revisiting the Monster: New Myths and Realities of Class Action and Other Large Scale Litigation, 11 Duke J. Comp. & Int'lL. 179, 206–212 (2001); McGovern, *supra* n. 1, at 1656 n. 1.

CHAPTER 23. 'PREDOMINANCE' TO 'RESOLVABILITY'

litigants over broader social welfare with undesirable distributive consequences.[78]

Fourth, a corollary to the previous argument is that allowing courts to depart from substantive rules to facilitate the resolution of particular claims raises questions about democratic transparency and accountability. Lawmakers – whether elected or subject to the oversight of elected officials – should be accountable for the rules that they create. If the content of these rules varies depending on the procedural context of particular cases, then the public will have greater difficulty assessing the rules that their representatives have created or supervised because the content of rules would be fluid; sometimes the rules would mean one thing, and sometimes they would mean something else.[79] Class actions thus create a troubling opportunity for lawmakers and courts to dodge accountability by permitting the implementation of substantive rules in a manner distinct from their apparent and advertised meaning.[80]

Finally, allowing certification of a class to alter the substantive law applicable to claims and defenses arguably raises due process concerns

---

[78] Cf. Nagareda, Preexistence, *supra* n. 1, at 204 (arguing that the 'central planning' inherent in reform of broadly applicable substantive laws should occur through political institutions rather than self-appointed class representatives).

[79] Accountability and transparency problems arising from ad hoc lawmaking affect the judicial branch as well as the legislative branch because procrustean distortion of substantive rules to accommodate novel procedural circumstances enables judges to cloak substantive innovations with a procedural gloss. The significance of a judicial opinion endorsing a particular substantive theory thus will often not be apparent to readers who lack a detailed familiarity with the facts of the case and the applicable law. This lack of transparency reduces the extent to which the court can be held accountable for its decision. For a general discussion of the importance of transparency in judicial opinions, see David L. Shapiro, In Defense of Judicial Candor, 100 Harv. L. Rev. 731 (1987); Suzanna Sherry, The Unmaking of a Precedent, 2003 SUP. CT. Rev. 231, 255–256.

[80] This article approaches the problem of democratic accountability within aggregative litigation as a function of the ad hoc nature of substantive rulemaking when conducted as an incident to facilitating application of a particular procedural device to particular facts. An alternative approach would be to conceptualize the accountability problem as arising from the displacement of traditional compensatory models of litigation with a bounty hunter model that alters the remedial focus of substantive laws. For an argument developing this latter view, see Redish, *supra* n. 1, at 107–129.

by inhibiting defendants' ability to raise defenses that would be valid if plaintiffs pursued their claims individually rather than as a class. There is nothing inherently wrong with denying a defendant the defenses of its choice. For example, defendants in federal securities fraud cases would prefer to argue that particular purchasers of an overpriced security did not rely on the defendant's misrepresentations and thus have no claim for damages, but the fraud-on-the-market rule makes the question of reliance irrelevant.[81] Likewise, defendants in employment discrimination cases would prefer to avoid being held liable for violating Title VII of the Civil Rights Act[82] if they did not intend to discriminate, but their lack of intent can be irrelevant if their actions have a disparate impact on a protected minority group.[83] Neither the fraud-on-the-market theory nor the disparate impact doctrine violate procedural due process – even though they deprive defendants of their preferred means of defending themselves from allegations of wrongdoing – because defendants must adjust to generally applicable laws and tailor their defenses to the elements of claims. However, suppose that the fraud-on-the-market and disparate impact theories did not generally exist, but were invented by courts solely to facilitate the efficient resolution of class actions. An individual securities purchaser who wished to sue an issuer for misrepresentation would have to prove reliance, but a member of a class of purchasers would not. Likewise, an individual job applicant protesting hiring criteria would have to prove a discriminatory intent, but a member of a class of job applicants would not. Due process concerns in these circumstances would appear much more significant. The defendant would have a statutory right under the applicable substantive law to raise a defense to individual claims, but would lose that right depending on the procedural mechanism chosen by plaintiffs for adjudication. A defendant might find itself unable to conform its conduct to rules that vary with the procedural context of a claim, thus rendering it liable to groups for conduct that is not illegal with respect to any individual member of the group. The case law and scholarship in this area are undeveloped, but there is a plausible reason to believe that using the class action device to deny a defendant its otherwise applicable right to raise

---

[81] See *supra* n. 24.

[82] 42 U.S.C. §§ 2000e et seq. (2005).

[83] See e.g., *Albemarle Paper Co. v. Moody*, 422 U.S. 405, 422–423 (1975); *Griggs v. Duke Power Co.*, 401 U.S. 424, 431 (1971).

CHAPTER 23. 'PREDOMINANCE' TO 'RESOLVABILITY'

defenses to individual claims, or to relieve class members of their obligation to prove otherwise required elements of their individual claims, would violate the defendant's rights to procedural due process.[84] At a minimum, the scope of defendants' procedural due process rights in the class action context warrants additional scholarship.

In short, class certification should not transform an individual class member's losing claim into a winning claim, except in the sense that it may level the procedural playing field by giving class members access to better counsel and more resources with which to develop and pursue their claims.[85] The merit of each class member's claim – and the applicable elements and defenses – should remain the same whether or not the claim is certified for class treatment. A class member who would deservedly lose his case in a traditional suit against the defendant for want of sufficient proof or ability to overcome defenses – even if represented by adequate counsel with adequate resources – should also lose in a class action. The same principle applies in reverse. A defendant who would be unable to overcome a suit by any one class member should not be able to manipulate the class action device into a victory (or a low-ball settlement) over all class members. Rules governing class actions thus must provide some mechanism for ensuring that the beneficiaries of a judgment are in fact entitled to that benefit, and likewise that the persons whose rights a judgment prejudices deserve to suffer such prejudice.

A concrete example illustrates the foregoing abstract point by positing four claims that remain constant despite changes in the

---

[84] See e.g., *Lindsey v. Normet*, 405 U.S. 56, 66 (1972) ('Due process requires that there be an opportunity to present every available defense.'); *Newton v. Merrill Lynch, Pierce, Fenner & Smith, Inc.*, 259 F.3d 154, 192 (3rd Cir. 2001) (vacating certification in part because 'defendants have the right to raise individual defenses against each class member'); *Western Elec. Co. v. Stern*, 544 F.2d 1196, 1199 (3rd Cir. 1976) (denying defendants a right to 'present a full defense on the issues would violate due process'); *Southwestern Ref. Co. v. Bernal*, 22 S.W.3d 425, 437 (Tex. 2000) (noting in the context of class action litigation that 'basic to the right to a fair trial – indeed, basic to the very essence of the adversarial process – is that each party have the opportunity to adequately and vigorously present any material claims and defenses').

[85] Certification may arguably have a more transformative effect on claims for injunctions against public actors by creating a class that is an entity with rights and characteristics distinct from its individual members. For a theory of how group rights in institutional reform litigation may differ from the sum of constituent individual rights, see Fiss, *supra* n. 45, at 19.

procedural mechanism through which they are brought. The change in procedural context cannot alter the merit of the claims and should not alter the outcome of the suit. If the outcomes nevertheless differ from one context to another – despite equivalent juries, judges, lawyers, and available resources – then procedural rules are not being properly formulated or applied.

Assume that four consumers – W, X, Y, and Z – each purchase the same model of Acme waffle iron from the same authorized retailer on the same day. Each plugs the waffle iron into an electrical outlet, precipitating an immediate explosion. Evidence suggests that a manufacturing defect that randomly effects some, but not all, Acme waffle irons could cause such an explosion. W, X, Y, and Z each file separate suits against Acme for property damage caused by the allegedly defective exploding waffle irons. As explained above, W, X, Y, and Z can prevail only if each can prove all the elements of their claims: for example, that Acme breached a duty of care to purchasers by negligently manufacturing the waffle iron, and that this breach proximately caused injury in a specified amount. Acme would have an opportunity to challenge plaintiff's proof by evidence, argument, and cross-examination. Assuming that W, X, Y, and Z survived these challenges, Acme would also have an opportunity to raise affirmative defenses.

Assume that at each trial, each plaintiff testifies about how he or she was injured, and Acme's counsel vigorously cross-examines them. Acme also conducts discovery into the circumstances of each claim and incorporates what it learns into its defenses.

The trials result in the following outcomes. W wins because her testimony persuasively shows that she followed the waffle iron's instructions, acted with great care, suffered extensive damages that could have been caused only by a manufacturing defect, and Acme's lawyers could not find any persuasive defenses. X loses because cross-examination reveals that he ignored Acme's explicit instructions to plug the iron into a grounded outlet, and only when the iron was dry. X instead plugged the iron into a jury-rigged outlet overloaded with extension cords after having washed the iron's circuitry with a damp cloth. The jury concludes that the cause of his injuries was his own negligence and that there was no evidence that any manufacturing defect affected the particular iron that he purchased. Y loses because discovery of repair invoices for his kitchen reveals that all of the claimed damage was caused by a cooking mishap that pre-dated his purchase of the iron. Z loses because Acme is able to show that a series

CHAPTER 23. 'PREDOMINANCE' TO 'RESOLVABILITY'

of pre-suit letters between Z and Acme in which Z requested and Acme paid limited compensation constituted an accord and satisfaction and waiver of all legal claims. In sum: W proves all elements and survives all defenses, X and Y fail to prove their claims, and Z loses on an affirmative defense.

Now assume the exact same facts, but that W, X, Y, and Z all have the same lawyer and elect to bring their claims in a single action under Federal Rule of Civil Procedure 20 or 42(a) or similar state joinder and consolidation rules. The results of their individual claims should clearly be the same (assuming equivalent lawyering, judges, and juries): W should still win, and X, Y, and Z should still lose. Nothing inherent in the joinder of the four individual consumers' cases should affect the cases' merit. Assuming that the judge and jury properly do their jobs, X, Y, and Z cannot ride W's coattails to victory.

Now assume that instead of a joined action under Rule 20 or a consolidated action under Rule 42(a), W files a class action under Rule 23 for damages on behalf of all Acme waffle iron purchasers claiming to have suffered property damage caused by defective waffle irons during the relevant time period. X, Y, and Z (and hundreds of others) meet the class definition. Instead of appearing in court (as in the prior examples) X, Y, and Z are anonymous class members who attempt to have their claims proven by W – the named plaintiff who acts as their representative. Assuming that W tells her compelling story and prevails on her individual claim, X, Y, and Z should not be entitled to judgment in their favor as well. W is merely a representative for X, Y, and Z. Her existence cannot change the strength of their personal claims, nor can W's invulnerability to Acme's defenses immunize X, Y, and Z. If Acme is able to make a showing that the outcome of X, Y, and Z's cases might differ from W's based on the unique circumstances of their individual claims, then some mechanism must exist to allow Acme to present that information to the finder of fact before entry of judgment in X, Y, and Z's favor. If such a mechanism does not exist, then it would be inappropriate to allow X, Y, and Z to ride on W's coattails despite their own claims' lack of merit. Similarly, if one assumes that X is the named class representative instead of W, it would be inappropriate to extinguish W's meritorious claim based on X's failure of proof.

The waffle iron hypothetical thus confirms the abstract principle discussed above: class certification should not entitle a class member to a judgment to which that person would not be entitled if required to litigate on her own rather than as part of a class. Certification might as a practical matter improve a class member's chances of prevailing by giving her access to a better lawyer who presents better arguments and has the resources to locate better evidence than the class member would have found if required to litigate on her own, but certification should not alter the merits of her claim.

There is a difference between allowing the resources that certification brings to polish a diamond hidden in the rough and allowing the pressure that certification brings to create a diamond from coal. For example, if certification provides Z with access to a skilled lawyer who can defeat Acme's accord and satisfaction claim, then certification has served a useful purpose by helping to neutralize the defendant's often overpowering resource advantage.[86] But if certification creates a situation where the court simply ignores Acme's otherwise dispositive accord and satisfaction defense and allows Z to prevail, then certification has achieved an impermissible purpose by manufacturing a whole (the class) whose claims exceed the sum of its parts (individual class members).[87]

The fidelity principle remains an important constraint on certification even when the parties are willing to settle in lieu of trial. A negotiated settlement is nominally a voluntary agreement that waives recourse to procedural alternatives. Settlements thus in theory should not raise any concerns about fidelity to substantive law because the contractual law that the parties negotiate displaces whatever principles

---

[86] Cf. Benjamin Kaplan, A Prefatory Note, 10 B.C. Indus. & Com. L. Rev. 497, 500 (1969) ('[I]nsofar as class actions will enhance the forensic opportunities of hitherto powerless groups, they will tend to probe the terrae incognitae of substantive law.').

[87] Some commentators perceive a certified class as a legal 'entity' whose interests are distinct from the interests of its individual members. See e.g., Shapiro, *supra* n. 1, at 919. This may be a helpful way to conceptualize classes when confronting issues related to defining the 'parties' to a class action for purposes of assessing the adequacy of representation and the binding effect of judgments. However, for the reasons explained in the main text, the claims of the class 'entity' do not have special merit merely because a class raises them. The merit of class claims is a function of the merit of individual claims, although that merit might be easier to discern or to prove when individuals aggregate their resources. Of course, one could rewrite substantive law to create rights and remedies tailored specifically for 'entity' litigants rather than individual litigants, see *id.* at 941–942, but that is a change that should arise from politically legitimate sources external to the class action rather than as a result of ad hoc procedural convenience, see *supra* text accompanying notes 74–80.

of law might have governed if the parties had instead elected to risk a trial. However, if a settlement occurs solely because one or more parties fears the outcome of a trial that would be conducted in violation of the fidelity principle, the contractual law that the settlement creates might not be voluntary in any meaningful sense, and the negotiated contractual law would be no more legitimate than the ad hoc law whose threatened application motivated the settlement.[88] The prospect of settlement in the shadow of a certification order that would violate the fidelity principle thus adds an extra complication to class action doctrine, requiring courts to develop a theory of consent to operate in tandem with the fidelity principle so that courts can decide when fidelity-related obstacles to trial also bar certification aimed at encouraging a settlement. Developing such a theory of consent would be beyond the scope of this article, and would require addressing several emerging fields where the consent norms underlying contract law overlap and potentially conflict with the due process norms underlying civil adjudication.[89] For present purposes, it is sufficient to note that aggregate settlements of dissimilar claims do not avoid the fidelity constraint on certification so much as shift its emphasis from the legitimacy of the substantive law that would apply at trial to the legitimacy of the contractual law that would be created by negotiation in the shadow of trial.[90]

---

[88] Cf. *infra* section 23.3.3 (discussing the distortions in settlement value that occur when parties attempt to resolve class actions encompassing individual claims of varying merit).

[89] For a discussion of 'privatization of public processes' through contractual opt-outs to otherwise binding state-created procedures and its implications for analysis of civil adjudication, see Judith Resnik, Procedure as Contract, 80 Notre Dame L. Rev. 593, 623 (2005). See also Myriam Gilles, Opting Out of Liability: The Forthcoming Near-Total Demise of the Modern Class Action, Mich. L. Rev. (forthcoming 2005) (discussing the enforceability of contractual waivers of amenability to aggregative litigation). Cf. Marcus, *supra* n. 29, at 881 ('Rule 23 may provide the glue that allows the parties to arrange tort reform by consent,' but only if the consent is 'meaningful.'); Nagareda, Preexistence, *supra* n. 1, at 158 ('The power to alter rights in a manner that individuals may not avoid generally rests with democratic institutions, not class counsel and courts by way of a judgment approving a class settlement.').

[90] An entirely different problem arises when all parties affirmatively want to settle a dispute, and seek class certification as a vehicle for giving their agreement maximum effect. In these circumstances, the settlement is truly voluntary (assuming that the agents representing the class are in fact implementing class members' preferences), and the parties do not care how a trial would be conducted because the

The discussion in this section thus suggests a second preliminary conclusion to help shape the drafting of certification criteria in cases involving claims with some degree of similarity and some degree of dissimilarity where the parties have no ex ante agreement to settle. A class should not be certified unless either:

(1) proof of the named plaintiff's individual claim would also prove the claims of the absent class members based on the similarity between the representative and absentees, such that there is no need to inquire separately into the merit of each individual class member's claims; *or*
(2) there is an appropriate litigation or negotiation mechanism for resolving individual questions unique to particular class members at some point between resolution of common questions and entry of judgment.

Either way, the procedural device of certification should not circumvent resolution of individual issues that would be salient under applicable substantive law if each class member's claim were tried separately. Potentially outcome-determinative issues unique to individual class members' claims thus either preclude certification or must be accommodated in a manner consistent with applicable substantive laws (or norms governing the scope of permissible consent in settlements) before entry of judgment.[91]

---

point of certification is merely to ratify a negotiated agreement (indeed, in some cases the agreement may pre-date the court's involvement in the case). Fidelity theory has no role in these circumstances, although there may be other reasons to question the propriety of certifying a 'settlement class.' See generally Linda S. Mullenix, Taking Adequacy Seriously: The Inadequate Assessment of Adequacy in Litigation and Settlement Classes, 57 Vand. L. Rev. 1687 (2004).

[91] An interesting question for future scholarship and empirical study concerns the extent to which the individual issues that defendants identify as obstacles to certification are as a practical matter relevant to the outcome of disputes. A clever defendant can almost always identify a theoretically relevant factual or legal variation among claims that could be resolved only through burdensome individualized procedures, but these variations are not always significant. For example, a defendant might insist on its right to cross-examine every class member in a fraud case in order to determine if the class member had some specialized knowledge that defeated his claim to have been misled, but it is difficult to predict whether such a protracted inquiry would reveal any material information. The defendant will claim that it cannot know what class members will say unless it interrogates

CHAPTER 23. 'PREDOMINANCE' TO 'RESOLVABILITY'

23.3.3 The Feasibility Principle: Attempts to Adjudicate Class Actions Should Occur within Resource and Management Constraints

Class actions often inspire in lawyers the same boundless enthusiasm and confidence that candy stores inspire in children. A child in a candy store has remarkable confidence in his ability to consume an inordinate quantity of enticing deserts, and an unflappable desire to empirically test any limitations on his eating capacity that an adult might have the temerity to suggest. Lawyers and judges are often similarly smitten with the alluring potential of class actions to compensate victims and deter wrongdoers, and tend to overestimate their ability to cope with the burdens that class actions impose. Certification criteria must recognize this certify-now, ask-questions-later impulse that class actions inspire by grounding certification decisions in a realistic assessment of how a case can be litigated.

The burdens of class litigation are particularly acute when cases involve both common and individualized questions of fact and law and the court respects the finality and fidelity principles. A court with infinite time and resources may have the theoretical ability to resolve common questions in a consolidated proceeding, and then to review the individual circumstances of each class member's claim to resolve disputes about any remaining elements and defenses.[92] But if review of

---

them, and the plaintiff will oppose such examinations absent proof that they will be productive. Courts must somehow decide how likely the individual issue is to affect the case before concluding whether the issue is relevant to the certification decision. A ruling on the defendant's right to pursue individual defenses by cross-examining class members has the potential either to deny plaintiffs the opportunity to obtain the benefits of class litigation based on speculation about a dubious defense, or to deny the defendant the opportunity to raise what might be a meritorious defense simply because doing so would be inconvenient. There is presently no data or scholarship to help courts make that judgment call. Plaintiffs' advocates speculate that defendants routinely rely on 'hypothetical' defenses, while defense advocates insist that most ostensibly 'common' class claims actually rest on individualized inquiries, but it is unclear which side has the stronger argument. The truth is probably somewhere in between advocates' extreme positions. Empirical study devoted specifically to this question could therefore help to improve decision making on a recurring question in class actions.

[92] The practical ability of a court to resolve a complex dispute is often a function of the level of generality at which lawmakers define the applicable liability rule and the

individual questions requires a mini-trial on thousands or millions of claims, doing so may be practically impossible; the case would outlive its participants.[93] Thus, regardless of whether certifying a class action would in some sense be desirable, there cannot be a class action if the resources and time are not available.[94] Desire should not obscure reality.[95]

A corollary to the point that courts have finite resources that in practice limit their ability to adjudicate class actions featuring substantial dissimilarity among claimants is that courts need to have a realistic sense of what they can accomplish before they certify classes. Decertification is always an available remedy for an improvident certification, but there are substantial costs to relying on that remedy rather than making the certification decision correctly in the first instance.

---

extent to which lawmakers resolve policy questions at the rulemaking stage rather than delegating these questions to courts for case-by-case consideration. See James A. Henderson, Jr., Process Constraints in Tort, 67 Cornell L. Rev. 901, 916 (1982). The feasibility principle is thus not merely procedural in nature because it helps to illuminate shortcomings in the drafting of substantive rules that inhibit the effective integration of substantive rights with procedural remedies.

[93] See e.g., *Galloway v. Am. Brands, Inc.*, 81 F.R.D. 580, 585–586 (E.D.N.C. 1978) (estimating that adjudicating putative class members' individualized damage claims would 'consume well-over 100 years'). In reality, century-long litigation is unlikely because the parties presumably would settle to avoid the expense of trial. However, distortions that dissimilarity would create in the anticipated trial process would affect the value of any settlements. See *supra* section 23.2.3.

[94] Whether judicial resources are 'available' is partly a function of a court's discretion because judges must decide how much of their time to allocate to each case on their docket. Courts applying the feasibility principle in circumstances where adjudicating a class action could be possible if sufficient resources were diverted from other cases will therefore face difficult questions about how to weigh the competing demands of multiple claimants for scarce judicial time.

[95] The frustration that arises when the desire to certify a class confronts the reality that certification is impossible may motivate policymakers to tailor substantive law more closely to the resources that are available for enforcing it. For example, common law legal rules requiring proof of causation in toxic tort cases or reliance in fraud cases create management burdens that often preclude certification of class actions asserting tort or fraud claims, and thus limit the effectiveness of private law deterrents to corporate misconduct. Some commentators have therefore proposed altering common law causes of action to eliminate these elements. See *supra* n. 3. Whether these proposals are desirable is a question of substantive tort policy, not a question of procedural class action policy.

CHAPTER 23. 'PREDOMINANCE' TO 'RESOLVABILITY'

Certification creates immediate settlement pressures and induces substantial investment in the case by the parties and the court. Certification also creates momentum that courts may be unwilling to halt. Thus, while courts have discretion to second-guess themselves by decertifying classes, they seldom have an opportunity to do so and are in practice reluctant to do so.[96] Well-reasoned plans for managing class actions are therefore necessary before certification rather than after so that the powerful and potentially irreparable consequences of certification are not unleashed absent some confidence that the case can in fact be tried as a class action[97] or fairly settled consistent with the fidelity principle. Courts have ample flexibility to be imaginative when confronting management problems raised by individual questions of fact and law, but must recognize the fine line between healthy creativity and blind overconfidence.

An implication of this observation is that certification criteria should require courts to assess at the time of a certification decision whether class adjudication would be feasible in light of dissimilar questions of fact and law. The concept of 'feasibility' is intentionally vague to give courts flexibility in approaching the task of managing complex claims. Factors for determining whether a management plan is feasible could include:

(1) the time necessary to implement the plan;
(2) the ability of the parties to adduce the evidence necessary to resolve disputed questions;
(3) the extent to which the plan relies on questionable predictions or assumptions about how various stages of the litigation are likely to proceed;
(4) the cost of resolving claims relative to available resources;

---

[96] See e.g., Robert G. Bone & David S. Evans, Class Certification and the Substantive Merits, 51 Duke L.J. 1251, 1301 & notes 188–89 (2002):

(When a trial judge believes that settlement is likely with certification, Chi has little incentive to decertify the class. Accordingly, defendants have little incentive to file motions to decertify, with the result that there should be few such motions and a high settlement rate – predictions consistent with the available data.) (citing Willging et al., *supra* n. 10, at 175 tbl. 32).

[97] Cf. Manual for Complex Litigation (Third) §30.11 (1995) (discouraging 'conditional' certification orders used to 'defer' final certification decisions because of their '[u]ndesirable' practical consequences).

(5) the consistency of the plan with applicable constraints on procedure, such as constitutional or statutory requirements for a jury trial; and
(6) the likelihood that certification would facilitate a voluntary settlement (as opposed to a settlement negotiated in fear of a trial conducted in violation of the principles discussed in this part) that would obviate an extensive use of judicial resources.

These factors should be sufficiently flexible to ensure that courts are not forced to adjudicate class actions according to a cookie-cutter ideal of complex litigation procedures, sufficiently attuned to the settlement pressures that certification can create to ensure that the parties are free either to settle or not to settle depending on their desire to buy peace, and sufficiently firm to ensure that courts have a realistic plan for extricating themselves from a class action before they leap into it.[98]

23.3.4 Synthesis of the Three Principles

The finality, fidelity, and feasibility principles discussed above suggest several criteria that can be used to test existing rules governing class certification and to formulate new rules. The principles are particularly helpful in guiding courts confronting proposed class actions where the answers to disputed questions may not be the same for each class member. Combining the need for a judgment (principle 1), with the need to ensure that each beneficiary of that judgment is entitled to it (principle 2), and with the need for a management plan for resolving individual issues within resource constraints (principle 3) helps to frame the potential significance of similar and dissimilar questions that the parties will ask the court to resolve. The three principles suggest

---

[98] Conventional wisdom has until recently posited that the Supreme Court's decision in *Eisen v. Carlisle & Jacquelin*, 417 U.S. 156 (1974), limits the power of judges to incorporate practical considerations such as feasibility into their certification analysis for fear of prematurely assessing the merits of class members' claims. However, recent scholarship and the modern trend of judicial decisions establish that courts may consider how a claim would be tried before deciding whether to certify it, even if such nominally procedural analysis requires addressing some of the substantive aspects of contested claims and defenses. For a general discussion of pre-certification 'merits' analysis, see Geoffrey P. Miller, Review of the Merits in Class Action Certification, 33 Hofstra L. Rev. 51 (2004).

CHAPTER 23. 'PREDOMINANCE' TO 'RESOLVABILITY'

that when a plaintiff asks a court to certify her as a representative of absent class members seeking damages, the court may do so only if it has a feasible plan for resolving factual and legal disputes regarding each element and defense applicable to each class member's claim and for eventually entering judgment for or against each class member. There must either be an opportunity for the parties to litigate individual claims or defenses, or a reason to believe that such an opportunity is not necessary to reach a judgment that accurately values class members' claims. The existence of individualized issues of fact and law unique to the circumstances of particular class members thus does not *necessarily* preclude certification if the court has a plan for coping with individual factual and legal inquiries. In *practice*, however, certification will not be possible when there is no manageable way of reaching a final judgment that resolves all factual and legal disputes relevant to each class member's entitlement to relief under applicable substantive law, and when one or more parties is unwilling to settle voluntarily.

As we will see in the next section, the predominance test at the heart of Rule 23(b)(3) does not link the certification inquiry to either the finality or fidelity principles, and is only loosely connected to the feasibility principle. Despite the large stakes riding on certification decisions, the rule on which courts currently base such decisions does not formally account for any of the factors that this section demonstrates are essential to properly deploying the class action device.

23.4 INCONSISTENCIES BETWEEN CLASS CERTIFICATION PRINCIPLES AND EXISTING CLASS CERTIFICATION RULES AND DOCTRINE

This section assesses how well existing certification criteria conform to the principles discussed in section 23.3. The unfortunate answer is that a wide gap separates principle and practice on the critical issue of how courts should assess similarity and dissimilarity among claims when deciding whether to certify proposed damages classes. The predominance test at the heart of Rule 23(b)(3) strives to balance the competing pull of similar and dissimilar elements within proposed class actions, but is inherently incapable of assisting courts in making principled certification decisions.

Section 23.4.1 explores the historical origins and role of the predominance rule, revealing that it was created from thin air in 1966 with virtually no explanation or guidance to courts. Section B analyzes the practical and conceptual defects of the predominance rule, explaining that it is inscrutably vague, not grounded in any principled or practical assessment of whether dissimilarity among claims creates a significant obstacle to certification, and premised on a balancing test that does not serve any useful purpose. Section C then reviews the typicality and manageability components of Rule 23 and concludes that they are not capable of supplementing the predominance test in addressing whether dissimilarity among class members' claims should preclude certification. Section D examines doctrine that courts have created to help apply the predominance test to recurring fact patterns, concluding that this doctrine shares the conceptual flaws of the predominance test that spawned it and provides an additional reason for replacing the concept of predominance with a more practical and principled alternative.

23.4.1 The Origins and Role of the Predominance Test

The predominance test was the culmination of a gradual evolution in class action rules from the broad and unstructured generalities of early equity practice toward more formal constraints on judicial discretion.[99] The architects of the 1966 *Federal Rules of Civil Procedure* had an intuition that evaluating the significance of similar and dissimilar aspects of proposed class claims would be important and crafted the predominance test to codify that intuition. Yet the drafters never explained the meaning of their innovative new predominance standard, leaving courts and commentators to drift between competing visions of how goals of fairness and efficiency affected the significance of similarity and dissimilarity among claims and defenses.

Early federal rules governing class actions did not contain any criteria for evaluating the effect of dissimilar individualized issues on a court's decision about whether to permit a representative to litigate claims on behalf of an absent class. The first federal class action rule –

---

[99] For a discussion of the origins of nineteenth-century equity practice regarding group and representative litigation, see Stephen C. Yeazell, From Medieval Group Litigation To The Modern Class Action 213–220 (1987); Hazard, *supra* n. 54, at 1858–1923; Robert G. Bone, Personal and Impersonal Litigative Forms: Reconceiving the History of Adjudicative Representation, 70 B.U. L. Rev. 213, 262–287 (1990).

CHAPTER 23. 'PREDOMINANCE' TO 'RESOLVABILITY'

Equity Rule 48, adopted in 1842 – focused on numerosity and the impracticability of joinder rather than similarity or dissimilarity among class members' substantive claims.[100] Rule 48 did not even mention commonality as a relevant factor, although the Supreme Court in 1853 read a commonality requirement into the rule.[101] In 1912, the Supreme Court renumbered Rule 48 as Rule 38 and rewrote it to include an explicit commonality requirement, although there was still no corresponding limitation on class litigation linked to the existence of individualized questions.[102] Equity Rule 38 survived until 1938, when law and equity procedures merged into the new Federal Rules of Civil Procedure. The new rules addressed class actions in Rule 23, which permitted certification of three categories of classes. Only the so-called 'spurious'[103] category of class actions explicitly required 'a

---

[100] Rule 48 stated:

> Where the parties on either side are very numerous, and cannot, without manifest inconvenience and oppressive delays in the suit, be brought before it, the Court in its discretion may dispense with making all of them parties, and may proceed in the suit, having sufficient parties before it to represent all the adverse interest of the plaintiffs and the defendants in the suit properly before it. But, in such cases, the decree shall be without prejudice to the rights and claims of all the absent parties.

42 U.S. (1 How.) 1v, 1vi (1842).

[101] See *Smith v. Swormstedt*, 57 U.S. (16 How.) 288, 302 (1853) (class suit must pursue 'an object common' to all class members).

[102] Rule 38 stated that: 'When the question is one of common or general interest to many persons constituting a class so numerous as to make it impracticable to bring them all before the court, one or more may sue or defend for the whole.' Order Promulgating Rules of Practice for the Courts of Equity of the United States, 226 U.S. 629, 659 (1912). The procedural codes of most states roughly tracked the language of Rule 38. See William Wirt Blume, The 'Common Questions' Principle in the Code Provision for Representative Suits, 30 MICH. L. Rev. 878, 878 n. 4 (1932) (reviewing code language and precedent from law and equity courts).

[103] The 1938 version of Rule 23 created three categories of class actions – 'true,' 'hybrid,' and 'spurious' – based on the nature of the asserted substantive right. See James Wm. Moore, Federal Rules of Civil Procedure: Some Problems Raised By The Preliminary Draft, 25 Geo. L.J. 551, 571–576 (1937) (proposing and explaining the new class action rule). Commonality was not an explicit element of either the true or hybrid class action, although as a practical matter such actions were possible only when class members shared a substantial common interest. See *ibid*. For a summary of the practical and theoretical problems that plagued litigation under

common question of law or fact,' but it did not require any formal consideration of individualized questions.

The emphasis of early class action rules on commonality among claims without any corresponding focus on individuality was likely an artifact of the partial evolution of class actions from joinder principles and equity practice. The central inquiry in joinder cases usually involves identifying a single common issue, status, or right uniting otherwise distinct claims or claimants. The possibility that claims might be too distinct to litigate in a joined proceeding is a subsidiary question related to whether practical concerns warrant severance. In contrast, equity practice offered judges substantial flexibility in bifurcating resolution of common and individual questions to an extent not present in common law damages cases requiring trial by jury.[104] Early class action formulations apparently adapted joinder's fixation on commonality without developing a counterpart to the doctrine of severance, and extended equity's flexible treatment of concurrent common and individual questions into a modern context in which law and equity had merged and bifurcation was substantially more difficult. Class action rules thus evolved to focus on common issues that united class claims without formal consideration of individualized issues that divided class claims.

Emphasis on commonality at the expense of individuality persisted until the substantial redrafting of Rule 23 in 1966.[105] The 1966 revisions invented the concept of 'predominance' to capture the importance of individual issues to a court's decision about whether to certify a class action seeking damages. The amended Rule 23(b)(3) permitted courts to certify a class only upon a finding that 'questions of law or fact common to the members of the class predominate over any

---

the 1938 version of Rule 23, see Joseph J. Simeone, Procedural Problems of Class Suits, 60 Mich. L. Rev. 905 (1962).

[104] See Zechariah Chafee, Jr., Bills of Peace with Multiple Parties, 45 Harv. L. Rev. 1297, 1300–1302 (1932) (contrasting the power of law and equity courts in complex litigation).

[105] The 1946 revisions to the Federal Rules of Civil Procedure added a note to Rule 23 discussing the effect of *Erie R.R. Co. v. Tompkins*, 304 U.S. 64 (1938), on shareholder derivative litigation, but did not amend the text of the rule or address questions about similarity and dissimilarity among class members' claims. See Advisory Committee On Rules For Civil Procedure, Report Of Proposed Amendments To Rules Of Civil Procedure For District Courts Of The United States 24–29 (1946).

CHAPTER 23. 'PREDOMINANCE' TO 'RESOLVABILITY'

questions affecting only individual members.'[106] The federal class action rule thus for the first time explicitly recognized that courts must consider both common and individual questions when deciding whether class certification is procedurally appropriate for particular substantive claims.

The 1966 amendments did not define 'predominate.' The drafters' official notes and unofficial working papers likewise neither explain what the predominance concept was intended to mean nor identify its origin.[107] The notes suggest that courts should not certify classes when individual questions of fact or law are 'material' or 'significant,'[108] but do not offer any criteria for assessing materiality or significance or for

---

[106] Fed. R. Civ. P. 23(b)(3).

[107] The predominance test was developed without explanation at some point between November 1960 and March 1963. Compare Reporter's Memorandum on Proposed Amendments (Sub-Memorandum V at 4) (1960) (noting need to replace the 1938 version of Rule 23 but not proposing specific language), with Reporter's Memorandum on Proposed Amendments at EE-2 (Preliminary Draft, March 15, 1963) (including the predominance test amongst proposed reforms to Rule 23). The explanatory memorandum accompanying the March 1963 draft did not explain the predominance test, which apparently was not considered controversial and may have appeared in earlier drafts (of which there is no record in the Advisory Committee's publicly available files). See Memorandum from Benjamin Kaplan & Albert Sacks to Advisory Committee on Civil Rules at 3-4 (March 18, 1963). A contentious meeting of the advisory committee in late 1963 briefly alluded to the predominance test as being important, but did not explain what it was intended to mean and focused almost exclusively on other aspects of the proposed amendments to Rule 23. See Transcript of Advisory Committee on Civil Rules meeting on class actions (October 31–November 2, 1963). The notes to the 1964 preliminary draft of Rule 23 also omit any explanation of the origin or meaning of the predominance concept. See Committee On Rules of Practice and Procedure, Preliminary Draft of Proposed Amendments to Rules of Civil Procedure (1964), reprinted in 34 F.R.D. 325, 387–395. Although this is pure speculation, the origin of the predominance concept may trace to an influential article by Zechariah Chafee, who proposed that one critical consideration for determining whether equity courts should resolve multiple related suits in a single forum was the 'relative magnitude of the common questions and the independent questions.' Chafee, *supra* n. 104, at 1327. Chafee offered only minimal guidance about how to conduct this balancing inquiry, see Zechariah Chafee, Jr., Some Problems Of Equity 282–283 (1950), although he did suggest caution in extending the availability of representative suits beyond historical precedents featuring a high degree of commonality among claims, see *id.* at 215, 224.

[108] Fed. R. Civ. P. 23(b)(3) advisory committee's note (1966).

comparing the materiality and significance of individual questions with the materiality and significance of common questions. Contemporaneous commentary about the 1966 amendments also does not illuminate the meaning of predominance despite the innovative nature of the concept and its central position in the new Rule 23(b)(3).[109]

Although the drafters did not define 'predominate,' they did provide four factors to help courts apply the predominance test. Yet these factors did nothing to clarify the relationship between common and individualized questions in class litigation. The first sentence of Rule 23(b)(3) creates two tests: predominance ('questions of law or fact common to the members of the class [must] predominate over any questions affecting only individual members') and superiority ('a class action [must be] superior to other available methods for the fair and efficient adjudication of the controversy').[110] The second sentence then lists four 'matters pertinent' to 'these findings,' with 'these findings' presumably referring to both the predominance and superiority inquiries identified in the prior sentence.[111]

The four listed factors in substance address only the question of superiority and have little relevance to assessing predominance.

---

[109] See e.g., Kaplan, *supra* n. 1, at 390 (devoting one sentence to the predominance test in the course of a twenty-five page discussion of the new Rule 23: 'a class action loses attractiveness as the individual questions are seen to have such scope or variety as to overload the action'); Kaplan, *supra* n. 86, at 498 (describing the predominance inquiry as establishing the 'tough' task of 'sensing' 'important themes' that run 'pervasively through the entire litigation'); Charles Donelan, Prerequisites to a Class Action Under New Rule 23, 10 B.C. Indus. & Com. L. Rev. 527, 533 (1969) (noting that the predominance inquiry is 'more difficult' than the commonality inquiry but not elaborating on how to conduct it); Sherman L. Cohn, The New Federal Rules of Civil Procedure, 54 Geo. L.J. 1204, 1216 (1966) (describing the (b)(3) category as 'pragmatic' but not defining the predominance inquiry); Marvin E. Frankel, Some Preliminary Observations Concerning Civil Rule 23, 43 F.R.D. 39, 43 (1967) (noting that (b)(3) actions will involve both common and individual questions but not explaining how the predominance test should balance them); Charles W. Joiner, The New Civil Rules: A Substantial Improvement, 40 F.R.D. 359, 367 (1966) (describing 'great and important' important innovations in Rule 23 without discussing predominance).
[110] Fed R. Civ. P. 23(b)(3).
[111] *Ibid.*; see also *Amchem Prods. Inc. v. Windsor*, 521 U.S. 591, 615 (1997) (linking the four factors to both predominance and superiority); *Eisen v. Carlisle & Jacquelin*, 417 U.S. 156, 164 (1974) (same).

CHAPTER 23. 'PREDOMINANCE' TO 'RESOLVABILITY'

The first factor is 'the interest of members of the class in individually controlling the prosecution or defense of separate actions.'[112] This factor clearly bears on whether a class action is 'superior' to alternatives, but does not provide practical guidance for assessing the relative predominance of common and individual questions of fact and law. The factor's emphasis on plaintiffs' 'interests' seems to link the question of predominance to whether a knowledgeable plaintiff would prefer class adjudication to available alternatives, yet a plaintiff might prefer litigating alone merely because he values autonomy without disputing that a case involves substantial common questions, or he might favor free-riding as an absent class member without disputing that the case involves substantial individualized questions. A plaintiff's 'interests' in controlling litigation therefore do not seem to have any bearing on whether common or individualized questions 'predominate.' The second factor is 'the extent and nature of any litigation concerning the controversy already commenced by or against members of the class.'[113] This factor instructs a court to incorporate empirical information about the conduct of related suits into its assessment of predominance (which the court presumably would have done anyway without being told), but fails to explain how. The factor seems to focus on the question of superiority by linking the availability of a class action to an assessment of the adequacy of alternative remedies, and does not add any insight into how a court should decide when a common question 'predominates' over an individual question.[114] The third factor is 'the desirability or undesirability of concentrating the litigation of the claims in the particular forum.'[115] This factor is obviously relevant to the superiority inquiry, but is circular when read in context of the predominance inquiry. Concentrating predominant common questions in a single forum is presumably desirable, while concentrating predominant individualized questions in a single forum is presumably undesirable, but that observation does not explain how a court is

---

[112] Fed R. Civ. P. 23(b)(3)(A).
[113] Fed R. Civ. P. 23(b)(3)(B).
[114] This factor has added importance when the related suits are pending in state court because the Anti-Injunction Act limits the ability of federal courts to enjoin state proceedings, see 28 U.S.C. § 2283 (2005), and thus a federal court could conclude under Rule 23(b)(3)(B) that the pendency of related state court actions may pose coordination problems that would diminish the utility of a federal class action.
[115] Fed R. Civ. P. 23(b)(3)(C).

supposed to know which questions predominate in which circumstances. Finally, the fourth factor is 'the difficulties likely to be encountered in the management of a class action.'[116] This factor potentially offers limited assistance in applying the predominance test, and I therefore discuss it in section 24.4.3 below. Thus, with the possible exception of the manageability factor, the four 'matters pertinent' in Rule 23(b)(3) do not add any content to the otherwise undefined concept of predominance.

The rest of Rule 23 likewise fails to clarify or supplement the predominance inquiry. Aside from the predominance test, the only certification criteria that directly bears on the evaluation of individualized questions is the requirement in Rule 23(a)(3) that 'the claims or defenses of the representative parties [be] typical of the claims or defenses of the class.' The typicality inquiry, coupled with the Rule 23(b)(3)(D) manageability factor, supplements the predominance inquiry but, as shown below in section 24.4.3, does not mitigate any of the deficiencies in the predominance concept. The typicality and manageability tests provide some clues about how individual issues should influence the (b)(3) certification calculus, but the determination of whether individual issues are significant rests primarily on whether a court believes that they 'predominate' over common issues. The predominance test is for this reason the most hotly litigated of the (b)(3) certification factors and the one on which certification usually hinges.[117]

The 1966 version of Rule 23(b) remains operative today and for the foreseeable future. There are no pending legislative or administrative proposals to modify the Rule's criteria for certifying class actions. Substantial amendments to Rule 23 became effective on December 1, 2003, but none of the amendments addressed the 23(a) or 23(b) certification factors. Congress likewise recently adopted various class action reforms, but has focused on the scope of diversity jurisdiction and the fairness of settlements rather than on questions of similarity and dissimilarity among class members' claims.[118] Rule 23(b)(3) is therefore

---

[116] Fed R. Civ. P. 23(b)(3)(D); see also *Eisen v. Carlisle & Jacquelin*, 417 U.S. 156, 164 (1974) ('Commonly referred to as "manageability," this consideration encompasses the whole range of practical problems that may render the class action format inappropriate for a particular suit.').
[117] See *supra* n. 10.
[118] See Class Action Fairness Act, Pub. L. No. 109-2, § 3-4, 119 Stat. 4 (2005).

CHAPTER 23. 'PREDOMINANCE' TO 'RESOLVABILITY'

likely to remain frozen in its 1966 state unless commentators begin to question it and propose alternatives.

The conceptual problems in federal Rule 23 also undermine state class action rules. Predominance is a certification factor in forty-five of the forty-eight states with rules or statutes permitting class actions;[119] forty states essentially copy the predominance test from Rule 23,[120] and in five others the state rule is a close variant of the federal rule.[121]

---

[119] Mississippi and Virginia do not have rules or statutes authorizing class actions. California, Nebraska, and South Carolina permit class actions but do not require or suggest that courts consider predominance. See Cal. Civ. Pro. Code § 382 (2005):

> ([W]hen the question is one of a common or general interest, of many persons, or when the parties are numerous, and it is impracticable to bring them all before the court, one or more may sue or defend for the benefit of all.); Neb. Rev. Stat. § 25-319 (2004) (same); S.C. R. Civ. Pro. 23 (multifactor certification test).

But see Cal. CIV. Code § 1781(b)(2) (West 2005) (requiring predominance in consumer class actions under Cal. CIV. Code § 1780).

[120] Thirty-nine states have rules or statutes requiring courts to consider predominance, and one state has added a predominance requirement through case law. See Ala. R. Civ. Pro. 23(B)(3); Alaska R. Civ. Pro. 23(B)(3); Ariz. R. Civ. Pro. 23(B)(3); Ark. R. Civ. Pro. 23(B); Colo. R. Civ. Pro. 23(B)(3); Conn. Super. Ct. R. § 9-8; Del. R. Civ. Pro. 23(B)(3); Fla. R. Civ. Pro. 1.220(B)(3); Ga. Code Ann. § 9-11-23(B)(3) (2003); Haw. R. Civ. Pro. 23(B)(3); Idaho R. Civ. Pro. 23(B)(3); 735 Ill. Comp. Stat. 5/2-801(2) (2005); Ind. R. Trial Pro. 23(B)(3); Kan. Stat. Ann. § 60-223(B)(3) (2005); Ky. R. Civ. Pro. 23.02(C); La. Code Civ. Proc. Ann. Art. 591(B)(3) (West 2005); Me. R. Civ. Pro. 23(B)(3); Md. R. Civ. Pro. 2-231(B)(3); Mass. R. Civ. P. 23(B); Mich. Ct. R. 3.501(A)(1)(B); Minn. R. Civ. Pro. 23.02(C); Mo. R. Civ. Pro. 52.08(B)(3); Mont. R. Civ. Pro. 23(B)(3); Nev. R. Civ. Pro. 23(B)(3); N.H. Super. Ct. R. 27-A(A)(2); N.J. R. Ct. 4:32-1(B)(3); N.M. R. Civ. Pro. 1-023(C)(3); N.Y. CPLR § 901(A)(2) (Mckinney 2005); Ohio R. Civ. Pro. 23(B)(3); Okla. Stat. Tit. 12, § 2023(B)(3) (West 2005); R.I. Sup. Ct. R. Civ. Pro. 23(B)(3); S.D. Codified Laws § 15-6-23(B)(3) (Michie 2003); Tenn. R. Civ. Pro. 23.02(3); Tex. R. Civ. Pro. 42(B)(4); Utah R. Civ. Pro. 23(B)(3); Vt. R. Civ. Pro. 23(B)(3); Wash. Sup. Ct. Civ. R. 23(B)(3); West Va. R. Civ. Pro. 23(B)(3); Wy. R. Civ. Pro. 23(b)(3); *Crow v. Citicorp Acceptance Co.*, 354 S.E.2d 459, 464 (N.C. 1987):

> ([A] 'class' exists under [North Carolina] Rule 23 when the named and unnamed members each have an interest in either the same issue of law or of fact, and that issue predominates over issues affecting only individual class members.).

[121] Predominance is a discretionary rather than required certification factor in five states. See Iowa CT. R. 1.263(e); N.D. R. Civ. Pro. 23(c)(1)(E); Or. R. Civ. P. 32(B)(3);

The 'typicality' and 'manageability' factors discussed below have similarly seeped from Rule 23 into state law: typicality is a factor in forty-one states,[122] and manageability is a factor in thirty-eight states.[123]

The lack of attention to predominance and related concepts amidst the sound and fury of the debate over class action reform – which one commentator has analogized to a 'holy war'[124] – is startling. One would have thought that the steadily increasing discussion of class actions since the last major rules amendment in 1966 would have included constant attention to and reevaluation of the basic principles that justify converting ordinary claims into class actions, and in particular to the method for assessing dissimilarity among class members' claims. Yet that scrutiny has not occurred. To the contrary, the advisory committee that reviews proposed amendments to the federal class action rule recently reached the seemingly inconsistent conclusions that:

(1) the authors of the 1966 class action amendments 'had little conception' of how the rule would operate in practice and recognized that it would 'require re-examination after a period of experience,' but

(2) 'questions surrounding certification standards were not ripe for rulemaking' thirty-five years later.[125]

PA. R. Civ. Pro. 1708(a)(1); *Derzon v. Appleton Papers, Inc.*, No. 96-CV-3678, 1998 WL 1031504, at *3 (Wisc. Cir. Ct. July 7, 1998) (noting that the 'predominance' test 'finds an echo' in and 'reflects a similar purpose' as state class action statute).

[122] Of the forty-five states cited *supra* in notes 120 and 121 that have adopted a predominance rule, Illinois, Iowa, North Carolina, North Dakota, and Wisconsin have not adopted a typicality requirement. In contrast, South Carolina requires typicality but not predominance. See S.C. R. Civ. Pro. 23(a)(3).

[123] At least thirty-eight of the forty-five states that have adopted a predominance rule have also adapted a manageability rule; the exceptions are Arkansas, Connecticut, Illinois, Massachusetts, New Hampshire, North Carolina, and Wisconsin. See *supra* n. 120. Kansas has adopted a manageability test by implication rather than explicitly. See KAN. Stat. ANN. § 60-223(b)(3)(C) (noting that court should consider 'procedural measures which may be needed' in litigating the class action).

[124] Miller, *supra* n. 70, at 664.

[125] Report of the Civil Rules Advisory Committee to the Judicial Conference Standing Committee on Rules of Practice and Procedure 24-25 (rev. July 31, 2001), reprinted in 201 F.R.D. 586, 588–589. In fairness to the committee, amendments to rules as controversial as Rule 23 are extremely difficult to adopt. The minutes of advisory committee meetings during the 1990s reflect intermittent concern about

CHAPTER 23. 'PREDOMINANCE' TO 'RESOLVABILITY'

The amendments to Rule 23 that took effect in December 2003 track this conclusion by focusing on post-certification management rather on than on pre-certification concepts such as predominance.[126] The predominance concept thus remains far more under theorized and overlooked then its importance would suggest.

23.4.2 Defects in the Predominance Concept

The predominance inquiry in Rule 23(b)(3) commits courts to answering a meaningless question, and then offers them no guidance for doing so. At the outset, the test is needlessly vague because it fails to communicate why the relationship between common and individual questions is conceptually and practically important, and fails to identify principles that might guide courts in assessing the relationship. Aside from being vague, the predominance test is also incoherent because the balancing process it envisions seeks to compare two incomparable values. The answer to the question of whether common or individual issues predominate in a particular case is meaningless because the practical implications of individual issues can defeat certification regardless of how individual issues relate in the abstract to common issues, and regardless of the efficiencies that might arise from resolving common issues in a single proceeding. Learning how an individual question relates to a common question on some indeterminate balancing scale does not reveal any useful information about the significance of the individual question and cannot assist in determining whether a court should certify a proposed class.

An initial problem with the concept of predominance is that it is has no generally accepted meaning, leading to substantial confusion and inconsistency in judicial efforts to apply it. A consequence of the

---

predominance and related concepts, but there was no consensus on how to proceed and apparently the discussion did not lead to any concrete proposals. See Civil Rules Advisory Committee Minutes (February 16–17, 1995) (observing that '[Rule] b(3) has no workable definition of predominance'); Civil Rules Advisory Committee Minutes (March 20–21, 1997) (briefly discussing whether Rule 23(b)(3) should be amended to include a 'common proof' or 'common evidence' requirement); Civil Rules Advisory Committee Minutes (May 1–2, 1997) (same).

[126] See e.g., Fed. R. Civ. P. 23(e) (new provisions governing review of settlements); Fed. R. Civ. P. 23(h) (new provision governing fee awards in class actions).

drafters' decision not to define 'predominate' in the text or notes to the 1966 amendments to Rule 23 is that commentators were left to divine the concept's meaning and purpose without any substantial guideposts. The effect of the lack of guidance is evident in the leading civil procedure and class action treatises, which offer differing conceptions of how courts should assess common and individual issues when deciding whether to certify a class.[127] The lack of any consensus among commentators spills over to judicial opinions attempting to apply the predominance test. Despite the critical importance of predominance analysis in deciding whether to certify (b)(3) classes, courts apply the test in a myriad of vague and distinct formulations, finding predominance when common issues of liability are 'central,'[128] 'significant,'[129] or 'overriding,'[130] or when there is a 'common nucleus of operative fact,'[131] or when 'resolution of one issue or a small group of them,' even if not 'conclusive,' will 'so advance the litigation that they may be fairly said to predominate,'[132] or when common liability questions are the 'dominant core'[133] or 'most important'[134] aspect of a case, or when common questions will require 'most of the efforts of the litigants and the court'[135] or will 'outweigh'[136] individual questions, or when proving common questions would require 'the same quantum of

---

[127] See e.g., 2 Alba Conte & Herbert B. Newberg, Newberg On Class Actions §§ 4:21, 4:25 (4th edn 2004) (stating that the predominance and superiority factors 'blend' and describing at length the standards that courts should not use in assessing predominance without identifying a standard that should be used); 5 James Wm. Moore et al., Moore's Federal Practice § 23.44 (3rd edn) (noting that the predominance inquiry is 'pragmatic' rather than 'precise'); 7A Charles Alan Wright et al., Federal Practice & Procedure § 1778 (3rd edn 2005) (reviewing several distinct judicial approaches to predominance without endorsing any particular test).

[128] See e.g., *Radmanovich v. Combined Ins. Co.*, 216 F.R.D. 424, 435 (N.D. Ill. 2003).

[129] See e.g., *Jenkins v. Raymark Indus., Inc.*, 782 F.2d 468, 472 (5th Cir. 1986).

[130] See e.g., In re *Workers' Comp.*, 130 F.R.D. 99, 109 (D. Minn. 1990).

[131] See e.g., *Clark v. Bonded Adjustment Co.*, 204 F.R.D. 662, 666 (E.D. Wash. 2002) (citation omitted).

[132] See e.g., In re *Sch. Asbestos Litig.*, 789 F.2d 996, 1010 (3rd Cir. 1986).

[133] See e.g., In re *Energy Sys. Equip. Leasing Securities Litig.*, 642 F. Supp. 718, 752 (E.D.N.Y. 1986).

[134] See e.g., *Chiang v. Veneman*, 213 F.R.D. 256, 263 (D.V.I. 2003).

[135] See e.g., *Southwestern Ref. Co. v. Bernal*, 22 S.W.3d 425, 434 (Tex. 2000) (citations omitted).

[136] See e.g., In re *West Virginia Rezulin Litig.*, 585 S.E.2d 52, 71 (W. Va. 2003).

CHAPTER 23. 'PREDOMINANCE' TO 'RESOLVABILITY'

evidence' even if the size of the class were expanded or contracted,[137] or when issues subject to 'generalized proof' are 'more substantial' than issues subject to individualized proof.[138] Alternatively, courts sidestep the definitional problem by ignoring it and jumping directly into predominance analysis without articulating a guiding standard.[139] The *Manual for Complex Litigation* likewise fails to fill the definitional void left by Rule 23 and does not demystify the predominance test. Indeed, the Manual's thirty-seven-page discussion of class actions does not discuss the predominance standard at all, and instead fosters confusion by suggesting that class definitions can encompass 'diverse interests' without explaining how courts should assess the permissible scope of diversity.[140]

The Supreme Court could have helped ease confusion by clarifying the meaning of the predominance rule (which the Court itself promulgated),[141] but instead amplified interpretative uncertainty by blurring the distinct elements of Rule 23 into a single vague test while simultaneously condemning the subjectivity in certification analysis that the Court's own doctrine creates. The Court's opinion in *Amchem Products, Inc. v. Windsor*[142] exemplifies the problem. The Court held in *Amchem* that the Rule 23(a)(2) commonality test blurs into the Rule 23(a)(3) typicality test,[143] that the typicality test blurs into the Rule 23(a)(4)

---

[137] See e.g., *Klay v. Humana, Inc.*, 382 F.3d 1241, 1255 (11th Cir. 2004).

[138] See e.g., *Moore v. Painewebber, Inc.*, 306 F.3d 1247, 1252 (2nd Cir. 2002).

[139] See e.g., *Castano v. Am. Tobacco Co.*, 84 F.3d 734, 744 (5th Cir. 1996) (criticizing the district court's 'incomplete and inadequate predominance inquiry' without identifying a framework to guide appellate review).

[140] Manual for Complex Litigation, *supra* n. 97, § 30.15.

[141] The Rules Enabling Act, 28 U.S.C. § 2072(b) (2005), delegates to the Supreme Court responsibility for promulgating rules of civil procedure subject to a potential congressional veto. The Supreme Court in turn delegates responsibility for proposing rules to the Judicial Conference of the United States Standing Committee on Practice and Procedure, which further delegates responsibility to an Advisory Committee on Civil Rules.

[142] 521 U.S. 591 (1997).

[143] *Id.* at 626 n. 20 (citing *Gen. Tel. Co. v. Falcon*, 457 U.S. 147, 157 n. 13 (1982):

The commonality and typicality requirements of Rule 23(a) tend to merge. Both serve as guideposts for determining whether under the particular circumstances maintenance of a class action is economical and whether the named plaintiff's claim and the class claims are so interrelated that the interests of the class members

adequacy test,[144] and that the adequacy test blurs into the Rule 23(b)(3) predominance test.[145] These observations led the Court to collapse the commonality, typicality, adequacy, and predominance inquiries into a search for 'unity'[146] and 'cohesion'[147] within the proposed class. Yet the Court did not develop any standards that might help judges to evaluate the relative significance of unity and disunity (or similarity and dissimilarity) among claims and defenses. The Court achieved this reduction of Rule 23 into a 'unity and cohesion' test while simultaneously repudiating the tendency of district courts to reduce certification analysis to a 'gestalt' and 'chancellor's foot' assessment of fairness.[148] Yet the Court's own focus on 'unity' embodies precisely the sort of impressionistic analysis that the Court purports to have rejected. The Court then added that the predominance inquiry is 'demanding,'[149] but did not articulate any criteria – such as the criteria in section 23.3 above – that judges could use in implementing the 'demanding' quest for 'unity.' The Court in *Amchem* thus had the proper intuition – that dissimilarity is important – but reacted to that intuition with insufficient focus and clarity. Indeed, the *Amchem* opinion is a step backward in the nearly forty-year effort of judges and commentators to understand the meaning of predominance because it layers an additional set of inscrutable concepts – unity and cohesion – on to an already inscrutable rule.

The Court's few other class action decisions are no more helpful than *Amchem* on the question of predominance. In fact, a striking aspect of the Court's burgeoning class action jurisprudence is that the Court

---

will be fairly and adequately protected in their absence. Those requirements therefore also tend to merge with the adequacy-of-representation requirement.
[144] *Ibid.*
[145] *Id.* at 621 (noting relationship of Rule 23(b) to the question of whether 'absent members can fairly be bound by decisions of class representatives'); *id.* at 623 ('The Rule 23(b)(3) predominance inquiry tests whether proposed classes are sufficiently cohesive to warrant adjudication by representation.').
[146] *Id.* at 621 (The 'dominant concern' of Rules 23(a) and 23(b) is 'whether a proposed class has sufficient unity.').
[147] *Id.* at 623.
[148] *Id.* at 621.
[149] *Id.* at 624; see also *Zahn v. Int'l Paper Co.*, 414 U.S. 291, 306–307 (1973) (Brennan, J., dissenting) (stating that the predominance test provides 'ample assurances' that claims are not 'unrelated').

CHAPTER 23. 'PREDOMINANCE' TO 'RESOLVABILITY'

assiduously avoids reviewing certification criteria – except as these criteria relate to conflicts of interest among class members, which is an issue that seems to preoccupy the Court[150] – focusing instead on

---

[150] See *Ortiz v. Fibreboard Corp.*, 527 U.S. 815, 852–859 (1999) (reversing approval of class action settlement of asbestos claims ostensibly because the trial court failed to properly apply certification standards governing suits against limited funds, but also because of perceived conflicts of interest among class counsel, class members with present damages, and class members likely to accrue damages in the future); *Amchem Prods., Inc. v. Windsor*, 521 U.S. 591, 626 (1997) ('In significant respects, the interests of those within the single class are not aligned.'); *E. Texas Motor Freight Sys., Inc. v. Rodriguez*, 431 U.S. 395, 405 (1977) (holding that 'the named plaintiffs' failure to protect the interests of class members by moving for certification' and demand for a remedy in 'conflict' with the preferences of class members rendered them inadequate class representatives); *Sosna v. Iowa*, 419 U.S. 393, 403 n. 13 (1975) (finding that the class representative was adequate but noting that '[t]here are frequently cases in which it appears that the particular class a party seeks to represent does not have sufficient homogeneity of interests to warrant certification'); *Hansberry v. Lee*, 311 U.S. 32, 45 (1940):

> ([S]election of representatives for purposes of litigation, whose substantial interests are not necessarily or even probably the same as those whom they are deemed to represent, does not afford that protection to absent parties which due process requires.)

Smith v. Swormstedt, 57 U.S. (16 How.) 288, 303 (1853):

> (In all cases where . . . a few are permitted to sue and defend on behalf of the many, by representation, care must be taken that persons are brought on the record fairly representing the interest or right involved, so that it may be fully and honestly tried.)

See also *Matsushita Elec. Indus. Co. v. Epstein*, 516 U.S. 367, 399 (1996) (Ginsburg, J., concurring in part and dissenting in part) (noting 'the centrality of the procedural due process protection of adequate representation in class action lawsuits'). See *Ortiz v. Fibreboard Corp.*, 527 U.S. 815, 852–859 (1999) (reversing approval of class action settlement of asbestos claims ostensibly because the trial court failed to properly apply certification standards governing suits against limited funds, but also because of perceived conflicts of interest among class counsel, class members with present damages, and class members likely to accrue damages in the future); *Amchem Prods., Inc. v. Windsor*, 521 U.S. 591, 626 (1997) ('In significant respects, the interests of those within the single class are not aligned.'); *E. Texas Motor Freight Sys., Inc. v. Rodriguez*, 431 U.S. 395, 405 (1977) (holding that 'the named plaintiffs' failure to protect the interests of class members by moving for certification' and demand for a remedy in 'conflict' with the preferences of class members rendered

other areas of class action doctrine such as standing and mootness,[151]

---

them inadequate class representatives); *Sosna v. Iowa*, 419 U.S. 393, 403 n. 13 (1975) (finding that the class representative was adequate but noting that '[t]here are frequently cases in which it appears that the particular class a party seeks to represent does not have sufficient homogeneity of interests to warrant certification'); *Hansberry v. Lee*, 311 U.S. 32, 45 (1940):

> ([S]election of representatives for purposes of litigation, whose substantial interests are not necessarily or even probably the same as those whom they are deemed to represent, does not afford that protection to absent parties which due process requires.)

Smith v. Swormstedt, 57 U.S. (16 How.) 288, 303 (1853):

> (In all cases where ... a few are permitted to sue and defend on behalf of the many, by representation, care must be taken that persons are brought on the record fairly representing the interest or right involved, so that it may be fully and honestly tried.)

See also *Matsushita Elec. Indus. Co. v. Epstein*, 516 U.S. 367, 399 (1996) (Ginsburg, J., concurring in part and dissenting in part) (noting 'the centrality of the procedural due process protection of adequate representation in class action lawsuits').

[151] See *Gratz v. Bollinger*, 539 U.S. 244, 261–268 (2003) (rejecting standing and adequacy challenges to named plaintiff in class action opposing affirmative action in undergraduate admissions); *County of Riverside v. McLaughlin*, 500 U.S. 44, 51 (1991) (reaffirming Gerstein, *infra*); *United States Parole Comm'n v. Geraghty*, 445 U.S. 388, 404 (1980) ('an action brought on behalf of a class does not become moot upon expiration of the named plaintiff's substantive claim, even though class certification has been denied;' mootness instead depends on how certification issues are resolved on appeal); *Deposit Guar. Nat'l Bank v. Roper*, 445 U.S. 326, 340 (1980) ('[E]ntry of judgment in favor of named plaintiffs over their objections did not moot their private case or controversy' or prevent them from appealing the denial of class certification); *Kremens v. Bartley*, 431 U.S. 119, 134–135 (1977) (holding that when a change in substantive law moots the claims of the class representative and a substantial number of class members, courts should defer ruling on the merits of remaining claims within the 'fragmented' class pending reconsideration of whether the class meets the Rule 23(a) certification criteria); *Simon v. E. Ky. Welfare Rights Org.*, 426 U.S. 26, 40 n. 20 (1976):

> (That a suit may be a class action, however, adds nothing to the question of standing, for even named plaintiffs who represent a class 'must allege and Chi that they personally have been injured, not that injury has been suffered by other, unidentified members of the class to which they belong and which they purport to represent' (quoting *Warth v. Seldin*, 422 U.S. 490, 502 (1975)))

CHAPTER 23. 'PREDOMINANCE' TO 'RESOLVABILITY'

diversity jurisdiction,[152] tolling of statutes of limitations,[153] personal jurisdiction and choice of law,[154] the preclusive effect of class action

---

Franks v. Bowman Transp. Co., 424 U.S. 747, 755 (1976) ('Given a properly certified class action ... mootness turns on whether, in the specific circumstances of the given case at the time it is before this Court, an adversary relationship' exists to ensure a sharp presentation of issues); *Gerstein v. Pugh*, 420 U.S. 103, 110–111 & n. 11 (1975) (holding that certification of a class action after the representatives' claims have become moot does not render the class claims moot when the nature of the claim is inherently transitory); *Sosna*, 419 U.S. at 399–403 (holding that resolution of the named plaintiffs' claim after certification of a class does not moot the claims of class members); *Schlesinger v. Reservists Comm. to Stop the War*, 418 U.S. 208, 216 (1974) ('To have standing to sue as a class representative it is essential that a plaintiff must be a part of that class, that is, he must possess the same interest and suffer the same injury shared by all members of the class he represents'); *O'Shea v. Littleton*, 414 U.S. 488, 494 (1974) ('[I]f none of the named plaintiffs purporting to represent a class establishes the requisite of a case or controversy with the defendants, none may seek relief on behalf of himself or any other member of the class.'); *Hall v. Beals*, 396 U.S. 45, 48–49 (1969) (holding that a plaintiff cannot revive claims that were moot when filed by denominating the suit as a class action on behalf of members with live claims).

[152] See *Zahn*, 414 U.S. at 301 ('Each plaintiff in a Rule 23(b)(3) class action must satisfy the jurisdictional amount, and any plaintiff who does not must be dismissed from the case.'); *Snyder v. Harris*, 394 U.S. 332, 336–337 (1969) (holding that the claims of individual class members cannot be aggregated to satisfy the jurisdictional amount in controversy requirement). The Court is currently reconsidering the questions deciding in Zahn in *Exxon Mobil Corp. v. Allapattah Servs., Inc.*, Docket 04-70.

[153] See *Chardon v. Soto*, 462 U.S. 650, 661–662 (1983) (holding that federal law requires at a minimum that the filing of a class action suspends the limitations period on absent class members' claims, but that state law can supplement federal tolling by permitting renewal of the limitations period after denial of certification); *Crown, Cork & Seal Co. v. Parker*, 462 U.S. 345, 350 (1983) ('The filing of a class action tolls the statute of limitations "as to all asserted members of the class," not just as to interveners.') (internal citation omitted); *Am. Pipe & Constr. Co. v. Utah*, 414 U.S. 538, 554 (1974) ('[T]he commencement of a class action suspends the applicable statute of limitations as to all asserted members of the class who would have been parties had the suit been permitted to continue as a class action.').

[154] See *Phillips Petroleum Co. v. Shutts*, 472 U.S. 797, 811–812 (1985):

> ([A] forum state may exercise jurisdiction over the claim of an absent class-action plaintiff, even though that plaintiff may not possess the minimum contacts with the forum which would support personal jurisdiction over a defendant,

judgments,[155] the formality of certification analysis,[156] the form and cost of notice,[157] the appealability of orders relating to certification and resolution of class claims,[158] and miscellaneous questions with

---

if it provides 'minimal procedural due process protection'); *id.* at 821:

> ([W]hile a State may ... assume jurisdiction over the claims of plaintiffs whose principal contacts are with other States, it may not use this assumption of jurisdiction as an added weight in the scale when considering the permissible constitutional limits on choice of substantive law).

[155] See Matsushita Elec. Indus. Co., 516 U.S. at 380–386 (holding that state court class action settlement releasing claims exclusively within the jurisdiction of federal courts precludes class members from re-litigating the federal claims in federal court); *Martin v. Wilks*, 490 U.S. 755, 761–769 (1989) (holding that consent decree resolving class action claims does not preclude non-members of the class from challenging class-wide remedies); *Cooper v. Fed. Reserve Bank*, 467 U.S. 867, 876–881 (1984) (holding that a judgment rejecting class action claims alleging that a defendant engaged in a pattern or practice of employment discrimination does not preclude individual class members from pursuing discrimination claims unique to their individual circumstances); *Supreme Tribe of Ben Hur v. Cauble*, 255 U.S. 356, 367 (1921) ('If the federal courts are to have the jurisdiction in class suits to which they are obviously entitled, the decree when rendered must bind all of the class properly represented.').

[156] See *Gen. Tel. Co. v. Falcon*, 457 U.S. 147, 161 (1982) (certification requires a 'specific presentation' and 'rigorous analysis' of Rule 23 factors); *Pasadena City Bd. of Educ. v. Spangler*, 427 U.S. 424, 430 (1976) (holding that fact that all parties 'treated' the case as a class action does not make the case a class action absent certification under Rule 23); *Baxter v. Palmigiano*, 425 U.S. 308, 312 n. 1 (1976) ('Without such certification and identification of the class [under Rule 23], the action is not properly a class action' even if informally 'treated' as such); *Bd. of Sch. Comm'rs v. Jacobs*, 420 U.S. 128, 129–130 (1975) (finding that class was not properly certified where district court failed to follow procedures in Rule 23(c)).

[157] See *Oppenheimer Fund, Inc. v. Sanders*, 437 U.S. 340, 350, 356 (1978):

> ([W]here a defendant can perform one of the tasks necessary to send notice, such as identification, more efficiently than the representative plaintiff, the district court has discretion to order him to perform the task "but" ordinarily there is no warrant for shifting the cost of the representative plaintiff's performance of these tasks to the defendant.);

Eisen v. Carlisle & Jacquelin, 417 U.S. 156, 177–179 (1974) (holding that plaintiffs must bear the cost of sending individual notice to identifiable class members).

[158] See *Devlin v. Scardelletti*, 536 U.S. 1, 14 (2002) (holding that absent class members who object in the district court to the fairness of a settlement may appeal from an

CHAPTER 23. 'PREDOMINANCE' TO 'RESOLVABILITY'

no connection to predominance.[159] One would have expected that the thousands of class actions litigated in federal court would have generated at least a few grants of *certiorari* to guide lower courts in applying the predominance test, but such review has not occurred,[160] and 'predominate' continues to lack an authoritative judicial gloss.

---

order approving the settlement without first intervening as a named party); *Deposit Guar. Nat'l Bank v. Roper*, 445 U.S. 326, 336 (1980) ('[T]he denial of class certification [is] an example of a procedural ruling, collateral to the merits of a litigation, that is appealable after the entry of final judgment.'); *Coopers & Lybrand v. Livesay*, 437 U.S. 463, 469–477 (1978) (holding that certification orders are not appealable under the collateral order or 'death knell' doctrines); Oppenheimer Fund, 437 U.S. at 347 n. 8 (an 'order allocating the expense of identification [of class members for purposes of notice is] appealable under the collateral-order doctrine'); *United Airlines, Inc. v. McDonald*, 432 U.S. 385, 394–395 (1977) (holding that when the district court denies class certification, an absent member may wait until after entry of judgment on the named plaintiffs' individual claims before filing a motion to intervene for the purpose of appealing the district court's denial of class certification).

[159] See e.g., *Green Tree Fin. Corp. v. Bazzle*, 539 U.S. 444, 453–454 (2003) (plurality opinion) (analyzing applicability of contractual arbitration clause to class action claims); *Gulf Oil Co. v. Bernard*, 452 U.S. 89, 104 (1981):

> (We recognize the possibility of abuses in class-action litigation, and agree with petitioners that such abuses may implicate communications with potential class members. But the mere possibility of abuses does not justify routine adoption of a communications ban that interferes with the formation of a class or the prosecution of a class action in accordance with the Rules.) (footnote omitted);

Evans v. Jeff D., 475 U.S. 717, 726 (1986):

> (Rule 23(e) wisely requires court approval of the terms of any settlement of a class action, but the power to approve or reject a settlement negotiated by the parties before trial does not authorize the court to require the parties to accept a settlement to which they have not agreed);

Boeing Co. v. Gemert, 444 U.S. 472, 480–482 (1980) (permitting class counsel to claim attorney fees from the common damages fund created for class members).

[160] See e.g., *Roper*, 445 U.S. at 329 n. 2, 331 (denying petition for writ of certiorari on question of whether certification was consistent with Rule 23s predominance test, granting writ on question of whether the representative plaintiffs' claims were moot, and remanding to the district court after finding that claims were live without addressing the merits of the court of appeals' predominance analysis); *Exxon Mobil Corp. v. Allapattah Servs., Inc.*, Docket 04-70 (granting certiorari on question related to scope of diversity jurisdiction in class actions, but denying certiorari on a question related to application of Rule 23's predominance test).

Aside from being vague, the predominance test is not grounded in any principle that could guide courts in applying it to the facts of particular cases. Even if 'predominate' had a precise and authoritatively determined meaning, courts would still need to know *why* common issues and individual issues are important in order to know in any particular case which predominates over the others.[161] For example, if the animating principle of predominance is a need to promote efficient resolution of disputes, then courts might be relatively more willing to tolerate individual variations among claims as the price of achieving rough justice in complex cases. Alternatively, if the predominance concept is intended to provide the defendant with a fair opportunity to defend itself, then courts would be relatively less impressed with the volume of common questions and more interested in the practical effect of individual issues on accurate adjudication of class claims and defenses. However, rather than link the predominance inquiry to a broader purpose, Rule 23(b)(3) does not specify any purpose. The Advisory Committee notes to the Rule try to fill this vacuum by linking the predominance inquiry to both fairness and efficiency, but fail to explain how judges should reconcile these often conflicting goals.[162] Predominance analysis was thus predestined to stumble aimlessly between competing ends without doing justice to either.

The predominance inquiry is further flawed because it is not linked to any practical assessment of how individual questions of fact or law would affect a class action trial. As explained in section 23.3, issues of law or fact unique to individual class members are significant because they may pose obstacles to entering a class-wide judgment (finality), to adjudicating claims and defenses under the appropriate substantive law (fidelity), and to developing a realistic plan for managing litigation within resource constrains (feasibility). Aside from the unhelpful 'matters pertinent' discussed above (and below in Section C), the

---

[161] Cf. Robert A. Bone, Rule 23 Redux: Empowering the Federal Class Action, 14 Rev. LITIG. 79, 97 (1994) (noting the need for procedural rules to contain 'general norms' for guiding judicial discretion).

[162] See Fed. R. Civ. P. 23(b)(3) advisory committee's note (1966):

> (Subdivision (b)(3) encompasses those cases in which a class action would achieve economies of time, effort, and expense, and promote uniformity of decision as to persons similarly situated, without sacrificing procedural fairness or bringing about other undesirable results.).

CHAPTER 23. 'PREDOMINANCE' TO 'RESOLVABILITY'

predominance test does not explicitly recognize the foregoing concerns – or *any* concerns – that might justify denying certification when individualized issues are salient. As a result, the strong policy arguments in favor of class actions when a case raises important common questions often overshadow relatively amorphous concerns about individualized inquiries and lead courts to certify classes without any realistic sense of how to cope with the dissimilarities among class claims. The problem is then magnified because no other aspect of Rule 23 picks up where predominance leaves off by explaining how to handle individual issues within the context of a certified class action.[163] The predominance test read in conjunction with the rest of Rule 23 thus has the twin effects of encouraging courts to discount the significance of individual issues before certification and then to ignore individual issues after certification.

The predominance concept would remain fatally flawed even if all of the foregoing defects could be repaired because the concept's premise is incoherent. If the meaning of predominance were clarified with an authoritative interpretation grounded in principle and linked to practical guidance, the test would still require courts to balance the inherently unbalanceable. Commentators and courts do not attach

---

[163] Rule 23(c)(4)(B) ostensibly addresses the problem of dissimilarity among class members by permitting the court to divide a class into subclasses. However, relying on subclasses is an ineffective alternative to replacing the predominance test. First, Rule 23 does not offer any criteria for assessing the permissible degree of dissimilarity within a subclass, and thus Rule 23(c)(4)(B) replicates the defect in Rule 23(b)(3). Second, subclassing accommodates variances among homogenous groups of class members, but does not explain how to handle issues that require review of individual class members' circumstances. For example, subclasses would be useful in a product-liability class action if the only contested issue were whether versions of the product produced in different years shared the same defect. In that case, the court could establish a subclass for purchasers of each year's version, substituting several homogenous subclasses for the otherwise heterogeneous original class. In contrast, if the only contested issue were damages, and if proof of the existence or amount of damages depended on evidence unique to each class member, then subclasses would not fill the void left by the failure of the predominance test to account for significant dissimilarity among claims and defenses. Finally, presenting the facts of multiple distinct subclasses to a single jury may mitigate, but would not eliminate, the cherry-picking and claim fusion problems that arise from jurors' cognitive inability to parse individualized issues in complex litigation. See generally sources cited *supra* n. 21.

much inherent meaning to the word 'predominate' in Rule 23(b)(3), but generally agree that the word connotes a comparative assessment and thus requires judges to balance the significance of common and individual questions when deciding whether to certify a class.[164] Balancing common and individual questions is a pointless exercise that confuses the reasons that class actions are attractive in general with the reasons that class actions are viable in particular cases. Class actions are attractive mechanisms for resolving disputes because the existence of a common question uniting otherwise disparate claims can create an economy of scale that overcomes collective action problems, mitigates the defendant's resource advantages, and permits efficient resolution of the issues common to class members. But as explained in section 23.3, class actions are viable only when the individual issues that accompany common issues are also amenable to resolution within the class action framework. The existence of common questions is thus a necessary but not a sufficient condition for certifying a class, while the existence of individualized issues beyond some threshold is a sufficient reason to deny certification. Certification standards should therefore focus on determining whether individual issues exceed a threshold level of significance – and on defining what that threshold might be – rather than on comparing common and individual questions in a gestalt balancing process. The predominance test thus systematically understates the importance of individual questions by trying to balance them against common questions instead of evaluating them independently.

In addition to understating the importance of individual questions, the predominance test also overstates the importance of common questions. The predominance test, in theory, permits courts to deny certification in cases where individual issues can be resolved within the parameters discussed in section 23.3, but nevertheless 'predominate' over comparatively less significant common questions. Yet other provisions of

---

[164] See e.g., 5 James Wm. Moore et al., Moore's Federal Practice ¶23.44 (3rd edn 1999) (predominance inquiry 'focuses on the number and significance of common questions, as compared to individual issues'); Hines, *supra* n. 58, at 760 (stating that the predominance inquiry requires a determination of whether 'class members' claims are more dissimilar than alike'). But see Romberg, *supra* n. 58, at 287–288 (suggesting that the predominance inquiry does not involve an assessment of whether common issues 'outweigh' individual issues and instead requires courts to determine as a 'threshold' matter whether adjudicating the proposed common questions would produce a 'meaningful benefit').

CHAPTER 23. 'PREDOMINANCE' TO 'RESOLVABILITY'

Rule 23 address this situation more directly than the predominance test, and if those provisions would permit certification there is no apparent reason why a predominance analysis would add any useful information to the certification calculus. For example, suppose that a court concludes that a proposed class action would allow 'numerous' class members represented by an 'adequate' and 'typical' plaintiff to litigate a 'common' question of fact in a manner that is 'superior' to available alternatives. Further suppose that the court identifies significant questions of law and fact unique to individual class members' claims, but develops a feasible and substantively acceptable method to cope with these individual questions within the context of a class action. In such a case there would be no reason to care whether common questions 'predominate.' Whatever issues in some abstract sense 'predominate,' the class action would still be potentially useful and would be consistent with the principles discussed in section 23.3. The predominance test is thus pointless in cases where individual issues are insufficient to defeat certification of their own force and common issues are sufficient to satisfy the Rule 23(a)(2) commonality test and the Rule 23(b)(3) superiority test.[165] In contrast, the predominance test is moot when common questions are insufficient to render class actions 'superior' to alternatives. Either way, in circumstances where individualized issues do not impose sufficient obstacles to render certification impracticable, the predominance test does not accomplish anything useful that the commonality and superiority tests do not already accomplish more directly.[166]

The predominance test thus fails to achieve its apparently intended purpose. The drafters of the 1966 amendments to Rule 23 recognized that claims brought as putative (b)(3) class actions would often entail both common and individualized elements, and that courts would need a mechanism to determine when claims were sufficiently similar or too dissimilar to warrant certification for class treatment. The mechanism

---

[165] One could argue that common questions by definition predominate when individual questions are manageable and class adjudication is superior, but that would confirm that the predominance test does not add anything to Rule 23(b)(3)'s superiority and manageability tests.

[166] Predominance could arguably be a factor in determining superiority, but is best excised from the class action vernacular for the reasons noted in the text: it is vague, unprincipled, and impractical. (The superiority test is also vague, unprincipled, and impractical, but that is an issue for another article, and in any event would not justify introducing additional imprecision by linking superiority to predominance.).

that the drafters developed was the predominance test, but that test is too vague, too unprincipled, too impractical, and too linked to a pointless balancing inquiry to provide any meaningful guidance to courts. As we see in Section C, no other provision in Rule 23 can pick up the slack left by the conceptual implosion of the predominance test.

23.4.3 The Failure of Additional Rule 23 Certification Criteria to Cure Defects in the Predominance Standard

The predominance test is the only element of Rule 23's certification criteria that explicitly refers to the significance of individual issues. The typicality[167] and manageability[168] inquiries indirectly address dissimilarity among class members' claims, but neither is an effective substitute or supplement for predominance.

23.4.3.1 *Typicality*

Typicality is a concept that sounds sensible but means little.[169] The typicality inquiry apparently codifies the unobjectionable sentiment that the representative of a class supposedly pursuing a common claim should not himself pursue an atypical claim, apparently because the 1966 drafters felt that such atypicality would drive a wedge between the goals and interests of the agent and his principals.[170] Yet

---

[167] Fed. R. Civ. P. 23(a)(3).

[168] Fed. R. Civ. P. 23(b)(3)(D).

[169] See e.g., Jack H. Friedenthal et al., Civil Procedure § 16.2 (2nd edn 1993) ('It is not entirely clear what the rule makers intended to achieve with this requirement.'); Issacharoff, *supra* n. 1, at 354 (noting 'amorphous' nature of the rule).

[170] See Kaplan, *supra* n. 1, at 387 n. 120 ('[The typicality requirement] emphasizes that the representatives ought to be squarely aligned in interest with the represented group.'). The Supreme Court has thoroughly muddled the meaning of the typicality test to the point where it no longer appears to have any unique content. See *Gen. Tel. Co. v. Falcon*, 457 U.S. 147, 157 n. 13 (1982):

> The commonality and typicality requirements of Rule 23(a) tend to merge. Both serve as guideposts for determining whether under the particular circumstances maintenance of a class action is economical and whether the named

CHAPTER 23. 'PREDOMINANCE' TO 'RESOLVABILITY'

Rule 23's requirement that class representatives be 'adequate' more effectively captures this desire to link the interests of class representatives and class members by grounding the linkage in relatively well-developed principles of due process rather than in comparatively undefined notions of what is 'typical.' If a class representative will adequately represent class members consistent with due process, then it is difficult to see why somebody concerned with agency costs should care that the representative is atypical, especially given the consensus among commentators that a class representative is merely a figurehead in class litigation and thus not worth substantial judicial scrutiny.[171] Likewise, if the class representative is so inadequate that allowing him to act as an agent for absent class members would violate due process, then his typicality would not be a consolation.

The typicality requirement at best promotes in a limited fashion the class action's goal of efficiency by ensuring that litigation focuses directly on the core common issues in a case without the distraction of atypical satellite issues. Analysis of typicality can thus be understood as an effort to control the potential sprawl of class actions by limiting the range of issues for the court to address. From this perspective, already complicated class litigation should not be needlessly broadened to include claims by class members that the named representative does not raise, or claims by the named representative that the class does not raise.[172] This practical aspect of the typicality test may also serve as a prudential adjunct to the general principle of Article III standing that 'a plaintiff who has been subject to injurious conduct of one kind' does not 'possess by virtue of that injury the necessary stake in litigating conduct of another kind, although similar, to which he has not been subject.'[173] Nowhere in this vision of typicality, however, is there any

---

plaintiff's claim and the class claims are so interrelated that the interests of the class members will be fairly and adequately protected in their absence. Those requirements therefore also tend to merge with the adequacy-of-representation requirement.

[171] See e.g., Coffee, Accountability, *supra* n. 1, at 406 ('Commentators have generally agreed that the representative in a class action is more a figurehead than an actual decisionmaker.').

[172] Cf. *Gen. Tel. Co. v. EEOC*, 446 U.S. 318, 330 (1980) ('The typicality requirement is said to limit the class claims to those fairly encompassed by the named plaintiff's claims.').

[173] *Blum v. Yaretsky*, 457 U.S. 991, 999 (1982).

suggestion that monitoring the relationship between the claims of the representative and the claims of the class is an effective means of determining whether class claims are sufficiently similar to justify certification. To the contrary, the typicality inquiry is ill-suited to assess dissimilarity among class members' claims and thus cannot fix the deficiencies of the predominance test.

The flaw in the typicality test when considered in light of defects in the predominance test is that the typicality inquiry compares class representatives to absent class members without comparing absent class members to each other. Typicality analysis therefore tolerates substantial variation among class members' circumstances and cannot fill the void that a more effective version of the predominance test would occupy. Moreover, the typicality and predominance factors in practice speak past each other. The remedy when a class representative is atypical is often to find a new class representative, but not to change the class definition. The initial atypical representative thus remains a member of the class. One would expect that the atypical claimant's continued membership in the class would raise a red flag about predominance; after all, if individual questions of law or fact unique to the proposed class representative are so salient as to render claims encompassed by the class definition atypical, then perhaps these individual questions likewise 'predominate' and render class claims too dissimilar for class action treatment.[174] Yet courts and commentators have not drawn this seemingly clear connection between the typicality and predominance inquiries because the connection appears nowhere in the text of Rule 23, which does not link the inquiry into a representative's typicality with the broader question of dissimilarity among the claims of absent class members. The Rule 23(a) typicality factor thus cannot overcome the defects in the Rule 23(b) predominance factor.

---

[174] The fact that a proposed class representative is atypical should be particularly troubling to courts because lawyers who finance and initiate class action litigation usually hand-pick the representative. If lawyers are unable to find a representative whose circumstances typify those on whose behalf the lawyers want to litigate, a court should be concerned about whether there is a properly defined class encompassing sufficiently similar claims.

CHAPTER 23. 'PREDOMINANCE' TO 'RESOLVABILITY'

23.4.3.2 Manageability

The manageability inquiry in Rule 23(b)(3)(D) holds some promise for helping to grapple with questions of similarity and dissimilarity, but ultimately is not sufficient in its present form. Individual questions of fact or law unique to particular class members pose obstacles to the efficient management of a class action, and thus assessment of the manageability of a class action could be an opportune time to consider the significance of dissimilarity. However, two problems undermine the appeal of using 23(b)(3)(D) manageability analysis to patch holes in the predominance inquiry. First, amongst the mischief that individual questions of law or fact create when embedded in class actions are attempts at 'management' that violate substantive law or due process, such as attempts to presume individual facts out of existence or efforts to defer individual issues to post-judgment claims proceedings without allowing a complete presentation of defenses.[175] Using the manageability inquiry to control the extent of dissimilarity among class claims is thus analogous to asking the fox to guard the henhouse. Absent some principled guidance for determining whether a management device is substantively acceptable – which Rule 23 currently does not provide – analysis of manageability is as likely to create problems as it is to prevent them. Second, the manageability inquiry is tied to the superiority inquiry as well as the predominance inquiry. The comparative nature of the superiority inquiry replicates the balancing approach of the predominance test and thus tends to share the defects of the predominance test in evaluating the independent significance of individual questions of law or fact. The superiority inquiry also presupposes that a class action is one of several 'available methods for the fair and efficient adjudication of the controversy.'[176] Analysis of superiority thus presumes that a class *could* be certified and asks whether it *should* be as a matter of judicial discretion. The questions about dissimilarity that I address in this section relate to the antecedent question of whether a class action is even 'available' in particular circumstances, and thus the superiority rule and its attendant manageability inquiry are not a relevant source of guidance. Accordingly, a modified form of manageability inquiry (as I propose in section 23.5) might help solve or

---

[175] See *supra* notes 24 and 28.
[176] Fed. R. Civ. P. 23(b)(3).

prevent problems related to dissimilarity among claims in proposed class actions, but the present incarnation of the manageability test as a vague adjunct to both the predominance and superiority factors in Rule 23(b)(3)(D) cannot overcome the defects of the predominance test.

23.4.4 Doctrinal Consequences of Judicial Reliance on Predominance

The analysis in this article has so far sought to identify intrinsic defects in the predominance rule related to its inscrutability and to the incoherence of the balancing inquiry at its conceptual core. This section seeks to confirm the prior theoretical analysis by reviewing practical applications of the predominance test to determine if the test's conceptual flaws have infused the doctrine that courts have developed to ensure procedural consistency when handling recurring fact patterns in Rule 23(b)(3) litigation. Not surprisingly, predominance doctrine reflects – and in fact amplifies – the conceptual flaws in the underlying rule that the doctrine seeks to implement. In particular, doctrine addressing three critical and recurring issues highlight the need to integrate more principled and practical guidelines into the Rule 23(b)(3) certification inquiry. These three issues involve the implications for certification of individualized evidence of damages, individualized defenses to liability, and conflicts among applicable state laws.

23.4.4.1 *Doctrine De-emphasizing Individualized Damages*

The analysis in section 23.3 establishes that questions related to proving and calculating individual class members' damages could raise significant obstacles to the principled resolution of class claims. If the applicable substantive law (the fidelity principle) links a class member's entitlement to judgment (the finality principle) to proof of loss in a reasonably precise amount, then practical resource constraints (the feasibility principle) may preclude the court from adjudicating contested damages claims as a class action, especially as the size of the class – and thus the number of damages calculations – grows into the thousands or millions. The problem would be even more acute if there is a contested question of comparative fault, in which case the amount of individual damages would be a function of individual liability, which would complicate or preclude efforts to streamline class litigation by litigating liability issues as if they were common to the entire class.[177] The existence of individualized evidence relevant to proving and calculating damages is thus a factor that courts should consider before deciding whether to certify a class.

The doctrine that courts have developed to assess the propriety of certifying common questions despite the need for individualized damages calculations highlights the flaws at the heart of the predominance balancing concept. The general rule in most jurisdictions is that individualized damages do not defeat certification if questions of liability otherwise predominate.[178] This doctrine is usually stated as a self-evident truth, yet the doctrine suffers from what should be an obvious flaw: it circularly assumes its own conclusion. The question being asked is, in effect, 'do individualized damages questions predominate' and the answer being given is, in effect, 'not when liability questions predominate.' Lost in the shuffle is any attention to how the court should

---

[177] See Nagareda, Preexistence, *supra* n. 1, at 239–241 (noting that analysis of damages in class actions governed by comparative fault principles requires revisiting evidence from the liability phase of litigation).

[178] See e.g., *Klay v. Humana, Inc.*, 382 F.3d 1241, 1260 (11th Cir. 2004) ('It is primarily when there are significant individualized questions going to liability that the need for individualized assessments of damages is enough to preclude 23(b)(3) certification'); *Smilow v. Southwestern Bell Mobile Sys., Inc.*, 323 F.3d 32, 40 (1st Cir. 2003) ('Where, as here, common questions predominate regarding liability, then courts generally find the predominance requirement to be satisfied even if individual damages issues remain'); In re Visa Check/MasterMoney Antitrust Litig., 280 F.3d 124, 139 (2nd Cir. 2001) (citing numerous cases); *State ex rel. Am. Family Mut. Ins. Co. v. Clark*, 106 S.W.3d 483, 488 (Mo. 2003) (en banc) (holding that '[t]he need for inquiry as to individual damages does not preclude a finding of predominance,' finding the liability question to be 'common,' and not addressing the practical significance of individualized damages questions); In re Bell Atl. Corp. Sec. Litig., 1995 WL 733381, at *6 (E.D.Pa. December 11, 1995) ('To determine whether common questions predominate, the court's inquiry is directed primarily towards the issue of liability; individual questions of damages will not preclude class certification.'). Courts will sometimes deny certification when damages questions are highly individualized even if liability issues present common questions. See e.g., *Bell Atl. Corp. v. AT&T Corp.*, 339 F.3d 294, 306 (5th Cir. 2003) (holding that although '[e]ven wide disparity among class members as to the amount of damages suffered does not necessarily mean that class certification is inappropriate,' on the facts of the particular case a need for 'individualized damages inquiries' predominated over common liability questions).

determine which set of questions in fact predominates – the finding that liability questions predominate over damages questions is assumed rather than proven on the facts of particular cases. This circularity is at first glance surprising, but is alluring within the stilted context of the predominance balancing calculus. As discussed above, the conceptual flaw in the predominance rule is that it invites a gestalt balancing of common and individual questions without independent consideration of how individual questions may in practice undermine the principled resolution of class members' claims. Doctrine attempting to assess the significance of individualized damages calculations manifests this flaw in the predominance balancing test because the doctrine reflects a normative conclusion that, on balance, common liability questions are relatively more significant – along some unspecified metric – than individual damages questions.[179] This general conclusion about the propriety of certification would be impossible to reach if the certification inquiry required independent assessment of how dissimilarity among damages calculations would influence resolution of class members' claims, but becomes conceivable if the 'predominance' of common liability questions is considered in the abstract and without recourse to the guiding principles discussed in section 23.3.

The under emphasis on individualized damages calculations in current doctrine does not mean that individualized damages should always be fatal to certification. For example, certification notwithstanding the need to determine individual damages may be justified when proof of individual damages is either:

(1) a mechanical process easily accomplished through the defendant's business records (as in many cases challenging false billings) or through other accessible records (as in most securities fraud cases);[180] or

---

[179] An example of this phenomenon is *In re American Honda Motor Co., Inc.* Dealer Relations Litigation, in which the court lumped together individualized issues of 'causation, injury-in-fact, and extent of damages' and found that common issues of liability predominated because of their relative 'complexity.' 979 F. Supp. 365, 366 n. 1 & 367 (D. Md. 1997). The court apparently did not consider whether individual damages questions, even if *relatively* 'more mundane' than common liability questions, *id.* at 367, were nevertheless *sufficiently* complex to defeat certification.

[180] Although securities fraud suits are often cited as the paradigm case for class certification, recent analysis demonstrates that the paradigm is less solid than

CHAPTER 23. 'PREDOMINANCE' TO 'RESOLVABILITY'

(2) not necessary before entry of judgment because the applicable substantive law permits assessment of lump-sum damages followed by a claims proceeding to allocate the award (as in some equity cases where disgorgement is a proper remedy for unjust enrichment).

However, proof of individual damages before the trier of fact is not always mechanical or avoidable in complex multiparty litigation – there may be clever means of doing it efficiently, but one cannot simply assume that such means are available or desirable. Doctrine applying the predominance balancing test to focus on common liability questions without independent consideration of individual damages questions thus fails to respect the finality, fidelity, and feasibility principles discussed in section 23.3.

23.4.4.2 Doctrine Under-Weighting Individualized Defenses

The analytic flaw that infects doctrine about the propriety of certifying dissimilar damages claims is also evident in doctrine about the significance of individualized defenses. Courts routinely state that the possibility that a defendant will have unique defenses to individual claims is generally not a basis for denying certification.[181] This doctrine leaves

---

commonly believed. See Kermit Roosevelt III, Defeating Class Certification in Securities Fraud Actions, 22 Rev. LITIG. 405 (2003).

[181] See e.g., *Waste Mgmt. Holdings, Inc., v. Mowbray*, 208 F.3d 288, 296 n. 4 (1st Cir. 2000) (rejecting a more stringent emphasis on variation among defenses as inconsistent with 'the essence of the predominance inquiry'); *Lender's Title Co. v. Chandler*, No. 04-41, 2004 WL 1354265 (Ark. June 17, 2004):

> ([T]he mere fact that individual issues and defenses may be raised regarding the recovery of individual members cannot defeat class certification where there are common questions concerning the defendant's alleged wrongdoing that must be resolved for all class members.);

Haywood v. Superior Bank FSB, 614 N.E.2d 461, 464 (Ill. App. Ct. 1993):

> ([T]he existence of individual issues, individual defenses of individual damages, multiple theories of recovery, or even the inability of some class members to obtain relief because of a particular individual factor will not, standing alone, defeat a class certification if the common questions of fact or law are otherwise predominant.).

room for exceptions when the breadth and complexity of individualized defenses pose a clear practical obstacle to aggregate adjudication,[182] but nevertheless tends to permit certification notwithstanding the presence of dissimilar defenses that raise problems under the finality, fidelity, and feasibility principles.

The intense focus on commonality at the certification stage arises from the balancing test inherent in the concept of predominance, reflecting a value judgment that the most important question in a class action is the defendant's general liability to the class, and that this question is so important that it outweighs – i.e., predominates over – collateral questions unique to individual class members. The doctrine likewise reflects a belief that the predominance inquiry is inextricably linked to the procedural goal of efficiency, to the point where courts are reluctant to allow the prospect of individualized inquiries to derail consolidated review of more immediately pressing common questions.

The notion that individualized defenses are categorically less significant than common questions of liability is dubious even if one assumes that predominance is a coherent certification standard, but is fatally flawed when one rethinks the viability of the predominance test in light of the principles discussed in section 23.3. First, with the exception of affirmative defenses (such as laches and waiver), most 'defenses' are merely the mirror image of arguments necessary to prove liability. For example, the defense in a fraud case that the defendant did not induce the plaintiff to take any action is the equivalent of arguing that the plaintiff has not carried her burden of proving reliance. Likewise, the defense in a product liability case that a particular item was safe and precipitated an injury only due to misuse is the equivalent of saying that the plaintiff has not carried her burden of proving causation. The doctrinal assumption that 'liability' and 'defenses' are somehow distinct is therefore suspect, particularly when the defendant

---

[182] See e.g., *O'Connor v. Boeing N. Am, Inc.*, 197 F.R.D. 404, 414 (C.D. Cal. 2000) (finding that 'individualized, fact-intensive' questions about statute of limitations defenses predominated over common liability questions). Cf. *Barnes v. Am. Tobacco Co.*, 161 F.3d 127, 147 n. 25 (3rd Cir. 1998) (affirming decertification of class and noting that '[w]e acknowledge that the existence of affirmative defenses as to some class members may not by itself enough warrant the denial of certification... But we note that the defenses are only one of many matters raising individual issues in this case.') (internal citations omitted).

CHAPTER 23. 'PREDOMINANCE' TO 'RESOLVABILITY'

proposes to disprove allegations of a common class-wide course of conduct with individual counterexamples – in other words, by attempting to disprove aggregate liability by stating defenses to individual claims.

Second, doctrine allowing certification notwithstanding salient individualized defenses violates all three principles discussed in section 23.3. The doctrine permits a certification decision without substantial consideration of how defenses might affect the court's ability to reach a judgment (finality), without any assessment of how defenses affect the plaintiffs' ability to prove liability consistent with the substantive law underlying the claim (fidelity), and without any concrete plan for managing the case after resolution of common liability questions (feasibility). The doctrine flourishes only because the predominance concept hinges on a balancing test, which in turn permits courts to define the *relative* importance of common questions and individualized defenses without considering that the practical difficulty of litigating individualized defenses might preclude certification regardless of whether resolving common questions would otherwise be desirable. Judicial underemphasis of defenses is thus a manifestation of the predominance test's failure to assess the significance of dissimilarity among claims independently from the fairness and efficiency considerations that generally favor aggregate resolution of common questions. The practical consequence of this conceptual failure is that courts routinely run the risk either that a certified action will grind to a halt before judgment when defenses raise insurmountable management obstacles, which would render the entire litigation a waste of time and money;[183] that unwieldy defenses confronted late in litigation will instigate questionable ad hoc lawmaking to accommodate them;[184]

---

[183] A striking example of a class action collapsing under the weight of deferred individualized issues occurred in the twenty-five-year saga of litigation arising from the 1971 prison riots in Attica, New York. The district court held a trial on common liability questions, only to realize after several years of fruitless management efforts that the remaining individualized defense and damage questions raised intractable management problems that ultimately led the Second Circuit to hold, '[w]ith the benefit of hindsight,' that certification had not produced any 'benefit' to the class. *Blyden v. Mancusi*, 186 F.3d 252, 269–271 (2nd Cir. 1999). Foresight is presumably preferable to hindsight in structuring complex and time-consuming litigation, which further supports the need for a class action rule that focuses substantial attention on dissimilarity before certification.

[184] See *supra* text accompanying notes 23–30.

or that the dissimilarities among defenses will distort settlement outcomes.[185] Accordingly, the doctrinal treatment of individualized defenses under the predominance balancing analysis is less rigorous than the finality, fidelity, and feasibility principles would recommend.

23.4.4.3 Doctrine Postponing Conflict of Laws Analysis

The phenomenon of allowing a balancing test to discount otherwise serious individualized questions is also evident in doctrine holding that courts need not consider potential conflicts of law during the predominance inquiry. Many class actions involve plaintiffs from multiple states challenging conduct that occurred in their home states or that originated in an array of intermediary states. If the laws of states with significant contacts to the dispute materially differ, then the court must conduct a conflict of law analysis to select the applicable law for each contested issue, consistent with constitutional[186] and common

---

[185] In practice, most certified class actions settle, rendering the question of defenses moot. However, settlement does not solve the distortion problem – it merely displaces it to a new context. See *infra* section 23.2.3 (analyzing how dissimilarity distorts the valuation of claims for settlement).

[186] The Due Process and Full Faith and Credit Clauses, and possibly the Dormant Commerce Clause, preclude states from applying forum law to the claims of class members with whom the forum has no relevant connection. See U.S. Const. Amend. XIV, § 1; *id.* at Art. IV, § 1; *id.* at Art. I, § 8. For example, if a New York resident files a nationwide class action against a Delaware company in New York state court for fraudulent representations issued from the company's Delaware headquarters, New York law might apply to the claims of class members from New York, but cannot apply to the claims of class members from, say, Alaska. Plaintiffs might argue that Delaware law should apply to the claims of all class members regardless of domicile because the tortious contract arose in Delaware, but the viability of that argument would depend on the content of the applicable choice of law rule; some choice of law rules would favor applying the laws of each of the fifty states where injury occurred, and some might favor applying the law of the one state where injury-causing conduct originated. Cf. Friedrich K. Juenger, Mass Disasters and the Conflict of Laws, 1989 U. ILL. L. Rev. 105, 110–121 (summarizing the myriad methodologies for resolving conflict of laws in complex litigation with multi-state contacts). For analysis of the applicable constitutional questions, see *BMW v. Gore*, 517 U.S. 559, 572–573 (1996) (state lacks power 'to punish [a defendant] for conduct that was lawful where it occurred and that had no impact on [the state] or its residents'); *Healy v. Beer Inst.*, 491 U.S. 324, 336–337 (1989) (states cannot 'control

CHAPTER 23. 'PREDOMINANCE' TO 'RESOLVABILITY'

law[187] constraints. Substantial management problems arise when the outcome of the choice of the law calculus requires applying the varying laws of multiple states to class members' claims. For example, each substantive motion would require as many as fifty distinct rulings, the court would need to instruct the jury about the law in each of as many as fifty states, and the court would need to advise the jury about the limited admissibility of evidence that is relevant to claims in some states but not others. Even if the laws of the fifty states cluster into only a few distinct formulations on each issue, the practical burden of identifying, analyzing, and ruling on each cluster for each claim would be daunting.[188]

Courts in many jurisdictions prefer to avoid conflicts analysis by holding that certification is permissible when there is an important common question of disputed fact, regardless of whether the implications of that fact would vary under the applicable laws of different

---

conduct beyond the boundaries of the State' and regulate 'commercial activity occurring wholly outside' their borders); *Phillips Petroleum Co. v. Shutts*, 472 U.S. 797, 822 (1985) (state ' "may not abrogate the rights of parties beyond its borders having no relation to anything done or to be done within them." ' (quoting *Home Ins. Co. v. Dick*, 281 U.S. 397, 410 (1930))); *Brown-Forman Distillers Corp. v. New York State Liquor Auth.*, 476 U.S. 573, 582–583 (1986) (rejecting state's attempt to 'project its legislation' into other states); *Allstate Ins. Co. v. Hague*, 449 U.S. 302, 308 (1981) (plurality opinion) (Due Process and Full Faith and Credit Clauses forbid a state from applying its law to a transaction absent 'significant contact or significant aggregation of contacts, creating state interests, with the parties and the occurrence or transaction'); *Aetna Life Ins. Co. v. Dunken*, 266 U.S. 389, 399 (1924) (stating that a Texas statute cannot govern a Tennessee insurance policy); *New York Life Ins. Co. v. Head*, 234 U.S. 149, 161 (1914):

> ([I]t would be impossible to permit the statutes of [a State] to operate beyond the jurisdiction of that State ... without throwing down the constitutional barriers by which all the States are restricted within the orbits of their lawful authority and upon the preservation of which the Government under the Constitution depends.)

Bonaparte v. Tax Court, 104 U.S. 592, 594 (1881) ('No State can legislate except with reference to its own jurisdiction.').

[187] See generally Restatement (Second) Conflict Of Laws (1971).

[188] See e.g., *Georgine v. Amchem Prods.*, 83 F.3d 610, 627 (3rd Cir. 1996) ('[B]ecause we must apply an individualized choice of law analysis ... the proliferation of disparate factual and legal issues is compounded exponentially'), aff'd, 521 U.S. 591 (1997).

1137

EMPLOYMENT CLASS AND COLLECTIVE ACTIONS

states.[189] Although there is a contrary trend emerging in federal appellate courts,[190] numerous state courts (who may soon no longer face this question)[191] and federal district courts cling to the notion that

---

[189] See e.g., *Singer v. AT&T Corp.*, 185 F.R.D. 681, 691 (S.D. Fla. 1998) ('It is well-established that consideration of choice of law issues at the class certification stage is generally premature. Many courts find that it is inappropriate to decide choice of law issues incident to a motion for class certification.'); In re *Kirschner Med. Corp. Sec. Litig.*, 139 F.R.D. 74, 84 (D. Md. 1991) ('[M]any courts have found it inappropriate to decide choice of law issues incident to a motion for class certification.'); In re Crazy Eddie Sec. Litig., 135 F.R.D. 39, 41 (E.D.N.Y. 1991) ('Along with other district courts in this circuit, this court declines to decide choice of law issues on a class certification motion.'); *Peterson v. Dougherty Dawkins, Inc.*, 583 N.W.2d 626, 630 (N.D. 1998) ('[C]ourts often decline to decide choice of law issues when determining whether to certify a class action.'); *Lobo Exploration Co. v. Amoco Prod. Co.*, 991 P.2d 1048, 1051–1052 (Okla. Civ. App. 1999) (affirming certification order that 'declined to decide choice of law issues incident to a motion for class certification'). But see *Dragon v. Vanguard Indus.*, 89 P.3d 908, 916–918 (Kan. 2004) (holding that plaintiffs bear the burden of submitting a conflict of laws analysis sufficient to justify certification).

[190] See e.g., *Zinser v. Accufix Research Inst.*, 253 F.3d 1180, 1189 (9th Cir. 2001) ('Because [plaintiff] seeks certification of a nationwide class for which the law of forty-eight states potentially applies, Chi bears the burden of demonstrating "a suitable and realistic plan for trial of the class claims"' as '[u]nderstanding which law will apply before making a predominance determination is important when there are variations in applicable state law.'); In re LifeUSA Holding, 242 F.3d 136, 147 (3rd Cir. 2001) (faulting district court that 'failed to consider how individualized choice of law analysis of the forty-eight different jurisdictions would impact on Rule 23's predominance requirement'); In re Am. Med. Sys., 75 F.3d 1069, 1085 (6th Cir. 1996) (faulting district court that 'failed to consider how the law of negligence differs from jurisdiction to jurisdiction' before certifying nationwide state law class, and holding that the plaintiffs bore the 'burden' on this issue); *Castano v. Am. Tobacco Co.*, 84 F.3d 734, 741 (5th Cir. 1996) (district courts have a 'duty' to 'consider variations in state law when a class action involves multiple jurisdictions' and the 'requirement that a court know which law will apply before making a predominance determination is especially important when there may be differences in state law'); *Walsh v. Ford Motor Co.*, 807 F.2d 1000, 1016–1017 (D.C. Cir. 1986) (declining to accept, 'on faith,' plaintiffs' 'assertion' that state laws are uniform and instead making a 'considered' judgment about choice of law questions based on 'extensive analysis of state law variances' before certifying class).

[191] A new federal statute allowing removal to federal court of class actions involving plaintiffs from multiple states will probably limit the opportunity of state courts to

choice of law is not relevant to the certification inquiry when there is a 'predominant' common question of fact.[192]

The failure of courts to conduct a rigorous conflict of laws analysis before certifying a class violates the finality, fidelity, and feasibility principles. A court cannot know whether it has the capacity to try claims (feasibility) consistent with substantive law (fidelity) if it does not know which substantive laws apply and the extent of any variations that the trier of fact would need to consider in rendering a judgment (finality). Certification under such conditions of uncertainty amounts to a blind guess about whether a class action would be viable. A certification standard that focused more directly on the finality, fidelity, and feasibility principles therefore would not permit a court to certify a class without first carefully considering which states' laws applied, how those laws conflicted, and whether the conflicts would render class adjudication impracticable.

Doctrine permitting courts to defer consideration of damages, defenses, and choice of law until after the decision to certify a class thus helps to underscore the flaws in the predominance test. The predominance inquiry is not grounded in any determination about how individualized questions affect a court's ability to litigate claims to a final judgment pursuant to a feasible plan and consistent with substantive law, and thus many courts have developed doctrine that is likewise not grounded in such determinations. The result is that certification decisions overlook factors – such as the need to litigate individualized defenses or damages and to resolve or account for conflicts of law – that a certification standard should consider before determining whether a class action is a procedurally appropriate mechanism for resolving a particular dispute. The misplaced emphasis of predominance doctrine on similarity among claims at the expense of attention to dissimilarity is thus another reason to rethink the viability of the underlying predominance concept.

---

rule on complex choice of law questions in class actions. See Class Action Fairness Act, Pub. L. No. 109-2, §4, 119 Stat. 4 (2005).

[192] See *supra* n. 189.

23.5 PROPOSED REVISION TO RULE (23)(B)(3) AND IMPLICATIONS

The conceptual and practical flaws in the predominance test raise the question of what should replace it.[193] This section proposes a new 'resolvability' test that would focus on whether a class action is an appropriate means of resolving disputed claims that involve both common and individualized elements. The proposal incorporates the principles discussed in section 23.3 in an effort to avoid the practical problems discussed in section 23.2 and section 23.4. After presenting my proposal for replacing the predominance test, I discuss some of its practical and normative implications and suggest how these implications might inspire further scholarship about the dynamic overlap between substantive regulation of mass risks and procedural reform of group litigation.

23.5.1 The 'Resolvability' Test

The principles discussed in section 23.3 provide a foundation for formulating a replacement to the predominance test. Instead of focusing on the gestalt relationship between common and individual

---

[193] The predominance concept is so vague that in theory there is no need to replace it; courts and commentators could simply interpret it to more closely track the finality, fidelity, and feasibility principles discussed in section 23.3. A common question would thus 'predominate' over an individual question only if the court has a feasible plan for entering a judgment on both common and individual questions consistent with applicable substantive law. However, trying to fix the predominance concept rather than abandoning it would be a second-best solution. The test would still be vague and susceptible to drifting from any newly-imposed gloss, and would still rest on an inapposite notion of balancing inherent in the meaning of the word 'predominate.' Reinterpretation (or a more principled refinement of existing interpretations) of the predominance test would at best be an interim solution pending revision of the Rule, but is not a substitute for writing a more coherent certification standard to manage the increasingly high-stakes process of group litigation. Notably, the 1966 drafters of Rule 23 (who wrote the predominance test, as well as most of the rest of the current rule) did not intend for their work to be permanently etched in stone, and recognized that further refinements might be necessary with the benefit of accumulated experience. See *supra* text accompanying note 125.

CHAPTER 23. 'PREDOMINANCE' TO 'RESOLVABILITY'

questions, a new certification standard can more directly implement broader principles that address the need for:

(1) final judgments establishing the rights and responsibilities of the parties,
(2) fidelity to substantive law, and
(3) feasible plans for managing class actions within resource constraints.

A new rule should be sufficiently broad to encompass the diverse array of potential class actions, sufficiently narrow to guide the development of additional layers of doctrine geared toward specific recurring problems, and sufficiently flexible to permit class-wide settlements in appropriate circumstances.

My proposal would eliminate the predominance concept by rewriting the first clause of Rule 23(b)(3), which currently states that certification is permissible when the court finds that 'questions of law or fact common to members of the class predominate over any questions affecting only individual members.'[194] The amended Rule 23(b)(3) (and similar state rules) would permit certification when the court finds that:

> The court has a feasible plan to answer all disputed questions of law and fact that must be resolved before entering judgment for or against class members under the law governing each class member's claim and applicable defenses.[195]

Given the inexorable desire of lawyers to create shorthand monikers for certification concepts – such as 'typicality' and 'adequacy' – the new test could be called 'resolvability.'

The new resolvability test would combine with the existing Rule 23(b)(3) superiority and 23(a)(2) commonality tests to require a four-step analysis of how similarity and dissimilarity among putative class members' claims should affect certification. First, the court would have to determine if there is a question of law or fact common to all class members that if answered would materially facilitate entry of judgment

---

[194] Fed. R. Civ. P. 23(b)(3). The proposal would require action either by the Supreme Court under the Rules Enabling Act process, see *supra* n. 141, or by Congress, and then parallel action by state courts or legislatures.

[195] The rest of the current rule would then continue as a new sentence: 'The court must also find that a class action is superior...'.

for or against the class. Second, assuming that such a common question exists, the court would have to determine if any questions of law or fact specific to individual class members could affect the propriety of entering judgment for or against them. Third, assuming that material individualized questions exist, the court would have to determine if it could feasibly resolve the individual questions consistent with applicable substantive law governing claims and defenses before entering judgment. Finally, assuming that there is a feasible way to resolve individualized issues, the court would have to decide if doing so within a class action would be superior to using available alternative remedies. Class actions seeking damages under Rule 23(b)(3) would thus be permissible only if they were a superior method of feasibly adjudicating both the similar and dissimilar aspects of class members' claims to judgment under the substantive law governing claims and defenses.[196]

Settlements of otherwise uncertifiable classes would still be possible even under the new certification rubric, but careful scrutiny of the negotiation process and the terms of the agreement would be necessary to determine if the settlement is consistent with the principles underlying the resolvability test. As explained in section 23.2.3, negotiated resolutions of class actions featuring excessive dissimilarity among claims incorporate the potential prejudicial effects of trial into the terms of settlements, and thus courts considering certification motions cannot assume that a future settlement will cure the defects of an improvident certification decision. This observation, coupled with

---

[196] The resolvability test is unlikely to create problems related to the timing of certification decisions that are not already present under the predominance test. If a case is sufficiently complicated that an early resolvability decision is not possible – see Fed. R. Civ. P. 23(c)(1)(A) (requiring courts to address certification 'at an early practicable time') – then it is difficult to imagine how a meaningful predominance analysis could be possible under the same circumstances. Indeed, the resolvability test is an improvement over the predominance test because its greater specificity will help to guide courts in deciding what information they need to know and in structuring pre-trial proceedings to permit acquisition of that knowledge in preparation for the certification decision. Although courts at the beginning of a case – before substantial discovery – cannot always know exactly which factual and legal questions will be salient at the end of a case, limited discovery coupled with the parties' analysis of what each hopes to prove and disprove should be sufficient in most cases to permit courts to make reasonably informed certification decisions.

CHAPTER 23. 'PREDOMINANCE' TO 'RESOLVABILITY'

the analysis in 23.3, suggests that class action settlements generally fall into one of three categories, each raising different levels of concern:

(1) when a class action can be certified for trial consistent with the resolvability test, it can be fairly settled (assuming that class members are represented adequately);
(2) when a class action cannot be certified for trial consistent with the resolvability test, but both parties would prefer a group settlement to individualized litigation, then a settlement *might* be permissible even though the resolvability test is not satisfied, depending on myriad considerations addressed in the literature on 'settlement classes';[197] but
(3) when a class action cannot be certified for trial consistent with the resolvability test, and a party would prefer the absence of a class action to a negotiated class-wide agreement, then any settlement negotiated by that party in the shadow of a certification order raises questions – beyond the scope of this part – about due process, voluntariness, and the normative role that consent should play in dispute resolution.[198] The resolvability test thus does not conclusively answer the question of when courts should encourage or approve settlements, but does provide a new framework for considering the question and for rethinking Rule 23's requirement that class action settlements be 'fair, reasonable, and adequate.'[199]

The revised version of Rule 23(b)(3) would track the principles discussed in section 23.3 and avoid the problems with the predominance test discussed in section 23.4. Instead of relegating analysis of dissimilarity to the vague and conceptually hollow predominance balancing test, a revised rule would ground certification analysis directly in broader principles that should animate the class action device. Rather than silently hoping that courts apply class action rules consistently with broader principles, the new rule would require courts to do so by incorporating these principles directly into the text of the rule. The principles regarding final judgments, fidelity to substantive law, and feasible management within resource constraints discussed in section 23.3 would no longer be mere aspirations of class action jurisprudence, and instead would factor directly into day-to-day decision making. The dubious doctrines that predominance has spawned – such as the notions that

---

[197] See *supra* n. 90.
[198] See *supra* n. 89 and accompanying text.
[199] Fed. R. Civ. P. 23(e)(1)(C).

consideration of defenses, damages, and choice of law are irrelevant at the certification stage – would fade away because they are facially inconsistent with the concept of resolvability.[200]

The proposed resolvability test would also mitigate the problems of cherry-picking, claim fusion, and ad hoc lawmaking discussed in section 23.2. All three problems arise when courts permit certification to obscure the differences among dissimilar aspects of claims and defenses, such that the trier of fact perceives commonality in circumstances where there is really individuality. A revised certification standard that spotlights dissimilarity will make individualized issues much less prevalent in certified class actions and much more prominent in the cases in which they remain. Adherence to the fidelity principle should reduce instances of ad hoc lawmaking, and adherence to the finality and feasibility principles should ensure that procedural mechanisms exist to highlight the dissimilar aspects of class members' claims so that claim fusion and cherry-picking become harder to attempt and easier to detect.[201]

---

[200] Plaintiffs might attempt to evade revisions to Rule 23(b)(3) by trying to squeeze (b)(3) classes into the (b)(1) or (b)(2) molds, but doctrine exists to prevent such circumvention of the (b)(3) requirements. See e.g., *Ortiz v. Fibreboard Corp.*, 527 U.S. 815, 834–848 (1999) (reviewing limits on (b)(1) class actions); *Allison v. Citgo Petroleum Corp.*, 151 F.3d 402, 410–418 (5th Cir. 1998) (reviewing limits on (b)(2) class actions).

[201] The resolvability test's focus on dissimilarity may also have the added benefit of creating incentives for plaintiffs' lawyers to structure class definitions in a manner that minimizes the likelihood that class members with strong claims will subsidize members with weaker claims. Plaintiffs' lawyers currently have an incentive to define proposed classes as broadly as possible to encompass the maximum number of fee-generating damages recipients. If we assume that lawyers initially focus on claims with the highest value, we can surmise that as the class definition grows broader, the new entrants will have claims with progressively less merit and value, in effect diluting the value of the initial members' claims. Amending Rule 23(b)(3) creates an opportunity to reverse incentives regarding the breadth of class definitions. A rational plaintiffs' lawyer must balance the marginal potential gain from expanding the class definition against the catastrophic loss that would ensue if a court concludes that the class definition is too broad and therefore refuses to certify any class or *sua sponte* defines a much narrower class. The lawyer will assess the risk of expanding the class definition in light of how the court is likely to react, which in turn is a function of the procedural standard governing judicial review of class definitions. Thus, if the resolvability standard would be less receptive than the

CHAPTER 23. 'PREDOMINANCE' TO 'RESOLVABILITY'

Eliminating the predominance test would not eliminate subjectivity from certification decisions, but would help to redirect subjective analysis along more relevant lines and facilitate development of doctrine to guide decision making. Both the predominance and resolvability tests entail subjective elements, but the predominance test is so conceptually hollow that it has not generated coherent doctrine to help structure judicial discretion. In contrast, the subjective inquiries arising from the proposed resolvability test are linked to practical and theoretical guideposts that should permit courts to develop a helpful body of precedent to guide certification analysis. The primary areas of subjectivity under the proposed rule involve:

(1) determining what is and is not 'feasible' for a court to accomplish in a class action;
(2) identifying creative and yet acceptable mechanisms to 'resolve' claims in a class proceeding; and
(3) deciding when a defense is sufficiently likely to be 'applicable,' or when a question is sufficiently 'disputed,' to raise a potential obstacle to certification.

These questions will recur in numerous contexts but will raise similar practical problems that should over time generate a body of precedent to provide relatively concrete guidance to courts struggling with certification decisions.[202]

---

predominance standard to broadly defined classes that encompass substantial dissimilarity, then lawyers will likely try to frame their proposed classes more narrowly (unless they are risk-takers, in which case they might still frame classes broadly with the hope of being able to submit a narrower class definition if the court rejects the broad definition). Assuming that a narrow class has a higher proportion of members with meritorious claims, then the resolvability test would help to ensure that marginal claimants with comparatively low-value claims do not dilute the distribution of an aggregate award. Plaintiffs with low-value claims could of course still file their own separate class actions, but the settlement value of their claims would presumably be relatively low.

[202] For example, plaintiffs and defendants will often dispute whether the myriad individual defenses that the defendant insists must be litigated are likely to meaningfully alter the outcome of any particular class member's claim or are simply hypothetical musings designed to throw a wrench into the certification machinery. See *supra* n. 91. As this dispute recurs, courts will develop standards for parsing credible defenses that should be adjudicated from dubious defenses thrust into the case solely for tactical purposes. The ensuing doctrine would not be unduly novel, as

1145

Jettisoning the concept of predominance in favor of a more nuanced focus on the ability of class litigation to resolve both common and individualized aspects of claims and defenses should therefore better align the principle and practice of class litigation. A new procedural rule will not end the debate over the desirability of class actions as remedies for group injuries, but could help reorient that debate by eliminating the distracting practical and conceptual problems that the predominance inquiry creates.

23.5.2 Avenues for Further Scholarship

The resolvability test – and in particular its emphasis on fidelity to substantive law – is likely to reduce the frequency of class actions absent countervailing changes to the substantive rules that class actions enforce. The primary reason that some cases will not be amenable to certification is that traditional tort law and many statutory causes of action incorporate a compensation model of entitlements that hinges on proof of individualized questions of fact and law, such that plaintiffs are entitled to judgment in their favor only if they can prove elements of a claim that are tied to each person's unique circumstances.[203] Defendants presumably will latch on to individualized issues involved in

---

many federal courts already engage in similar pre-certification analysis of substantive issues that are likely to arise in the course of class litigation. See *Gen. Tel. Co. v. Falcon*, 457 U.S. 147, 160 (1982) ('[S]ometimes it may be necessary for the court to probe behind the pleadings before coming to rest on the certification question.'); *E. Texas Motor Freight Sys., Inc. v. Rodriguez*, 431 U.S. 395, 406 n. 12 (1977):

> (Where no class has been certified, however, and the class claims remain to be tried, the decision whether the named plaintiffs should represent a class is appropriately made on the full record, including the facts developed at the trial of plaintiffs' individual claims.).

Similar kinds of questions about tactical pleading also arise in diversity cases when courts must determine if a non-diverse party is properly part of a case or has been 'fraudulently joined' solely to defeat federal jurisdiction. See e.g., *Marshall v. Manville Sales Corp.*, 6 F.3d 229, 232–233 (4th Cir. 1993).

[203] Compare n. 3 *supra* (discussing common law and statutory causation and reliance elements that hinder certification), with n. 24 *supra* (discussing how federal statutes regulating securities permit inferences of causation and reliance that facilitate certification).

CHAPTER 23. 'PREDOMINANCE' TO 'RESOLVABILITY'

proving entitlement to judgment as a basis for defeating certification. Thus, while the predominance test tolerates comparatively heavy emphasis on common elements of class members' claims, the resolvability test would attach heightened significance to individualized aspects of claims and defenses that materially affect the propriety of entering judgment for or against individual claimants, which would tend to justify fewer proposed class actions.

The practical consequences of the resolvability test raise three interrelated questions for future scholarship that highlight the indeterminate boundaries between substantive and procedural considerations in group litigation. The first question posits a need to develop procedures responsive to substantive objectives, the second question posits that achieving substantive objectives may require tailoring liability and damages rules to available procedures, and the third question posits that the criteria for measuring the quality of a procedure requires a value judgment linked to the aspirations of the substantive laws that the procedure must implement. All three questions address the regulatory vacuum that decreased availability of the class action would create while illuminating the dynamic interplay of substantive and procedural considerations in the regulation of mass risks.

First, if class actions will be less available to compensate victims of legal wrongs, procedural architects must develop alternative compensation mechanisms to overcome the collective action problems that often make civil litigation impracticable in cases involving large numbers of somewhat similar and somewhat dissimilar injuries. Class actions are not the only means of aggregating claims, and thus any procedural reform that makes class actions more difficult to sustain without removing claimants' underlying preference to aggregate requires investigating alternatives to class litigation.[204] Second, courts

---

[204] Cf. Samuel Issacharoff & John Fabian Witt, The Inevitability of Aggregate Settlement: An Institutional Account of American Tort Law, 57 Vand. L. Rev. 1571, 1573 (2004) (noting that even without class actions, tort claims have 'persistently resolved themselves into what are essentially bureaucratized, aggregate settlement structures'); Howard M. Erichson, Mississippi Class Actions and the Inevitability of Aggregate Litigation, Miss. C. L. Rev. (forthcoming 2005) ('[A] prohibition on class actions channels mass disputes into other modes of formal and informal aggregate dispute resolution.'). Even when individualized claim processing is preferable to aggregation, some procedures are relatively more amenable to high volumes of claims than others. For example, Congress has created compensation systems that

and legislators should consider the extent to which substantive remedies favoring compensation over deterrence are worth their cost in procedural flexibility. By stressing the practical consequences of dissimilarity among otherwise common class claims, this section highlights how substantive laws that fixate on individual entitlements to damages rather than the scope of the defendant's wrongful behavior complicate and potentially preclude aggregative litigation.[205] If the price of focusing on individual entitlements is that those entitlements become more difficult to vindicate in class actions, then it is worth thinking about whether the focus of statutory and common law rights should transform to facilitate group litigation and the deterrent pressures that such litigation creates.[206]

Finally, a corollary to the preceding point about the relative importance of compensation and deterrence is that this chapter's emphasis on dissimilarity among claims highlights an open question about the distributive implications and relative desirability of over- and under-deterrence, and over- and under-compensation. A consequence of aggregating dissimilar claims is that the trial and settlement distortions discussed in section 23.2 may cause defendants to pay higher or lower damages than the applicable substantive law requires. Likewise, the allocation of damage awards among class members may be imperfect, such that some will receive more than they deserve under the applicable substantive law, and some will receive less. Aggregation of dissimilar claims can thus over- or under-deter, and both over- and under-compensate. Yet not aggregating claims creates analogous harms. The collective action problems that arise absent aggregation may prevent victims of a wrong from obtaining a remedy,[207] and

---

depend on administrative rather than judicial adjudication, such as programs linked to black lung disease, see 30 U.S.C. §§ 901 et seq, the side effects of vaccines, see 42 U.S.C. §§ 300aa et seq., and the September 11 terrorist attacks, see Air Transportation Safety and System Stabilization Act, Pub. L. No. 107-42, 115 Stat. 230 (2001).

[205] See *supra* n. 3 (citing examples of substantive reforms that facilitate aggregate litigation).

[206] Assessments of procedural innovations are inextricably intertwined with preferences regarding the laws that procedures enforce. See e.g., Jack B. Weinstein, Some Reflections on the 'Abusiveness' of Class Actions, 58 F.R.D. 299, 299–300 (1973) ('Whether we characterize any revised [class action] practice as an 'abuse' or a 'reform' depends largely on our evaluation of policies underlying the type of litigation likely to be affected.').

[207] See *supra* n. 4 and accompanying text.

even when adjudication is feasible plaintiffs will have varying chances of success depending on their ability to bear the burdens of litigating alone, the quality of their counsel, and the idiosyncrasies of the judge and jury. Alternatively, individual nuisance suits on weak claims might extract larger settlements than would be possible if the defendant could lower its transaction costs by fighting all related claims in the same proceeding. Thus, the absence of aggregation creates the potential for over- or under-deterrence and both over- and under-compensation. Among the normative questions that arise from this analysis are whether over-deterrence is preferable to under-deterrence, whether over-compensation is preferable to under-compensation, and whether either preference depends on if the procedural cause of the over and under problem is a rule fostering access to adjudication or a rule foreclosing it. The answers to these questions will influence the design of substantive regulations and procedural rules by helping to prioritize the relative importance of access to adjudication, accurate resolution of aggregate claims, and accurate resolution of individual claims. Highlighting the procedural consequences of aggregating dissimilar claims thus helps to illuminate a broader set of problems affecting deterrence and remediation of large-scale injuries.

Refining certification criteria to grapple more directly with dissimilarity among claims would thus have both substantive and procedural consequences, necessitating further creative efforts at substantive and procedural innovation. There is a connection between when class actions are available, what class actions can accomplish, and how much compensation and deterrence substantive laws can achieve. Adjusting one link in the chain requires rethinking the others.

In sum, it is time to excise 'predominance' from the vernacular of class action discourse and replace it with a more practical 'resolvability' approach that recognizes the problems of cherry-picking, claim fusion, and ad hoc lawmaking and respects the principles of finality, fidelity, and feasibility.